W9-BRB-653

Principles of
Managerial Finance
GLOBAL EDITION

The Prentice Hall Series in Finance

Adelman/Marks
Entrepreneurial Finance

Andersen
Global Derivatives: A Strategic Risk Management Perspective

Bekaert/Hodrick
International Financial Management

Berk/DeMarzo
Corporate Finance*

Berk/DeMarzo
Corporate Finance: The Core*

Berk/DeMarzo/Harford
Fundamentals of Corporate Finance*

Boakes
Reading and Understanding the Financial Times

Brooks
Financial Management: Core Concepts*

Copeland/Weston/Shastri
Financial Theory and Corporate Policy

Dorfman/Cather
Introduction to Risk Management and Insurance

Eiteman/Stonehill/Moffett
Multinational Business Finance

Fabozzi
Bond Markets: Analysis and Strategies

Fabozzi/Modigliani
Capital Markets: Institutions and Instruments

Fabozzi/Modigliani/Jones/Ferri
Foundations of Financial Markets and Institutions

Finkler
Financial Management for Public, Health, and Not-for-Profit Organizations

Frasca
Personal Finance

Gitman/Joehnk/Smart
Fundamentals of Investing*

Gitman/Zutter
Principles of Managerial Finance*

Gitman/Zutter
Principles of Managerial Finance— Brief Edition*

Goldsmith
Consumer Economics: Issues and Behaviors

Haugen
The Inefficient Stock Market: What Pays Off and Why

Haugen
The New Finance: Overreaction, Complexity, and Uniqueness

Holden
Excel Modeling and Estimation in Corporate Finance

Holden
Excel Modeling and Estimation in Investments

Hughes/MacDonald
International Banking: Text and Cases

Hull
Fundamentals of Futures and Options Markets

Hull
Options, Futures, and Other Derivatives

Hull
Risk Management and Financial Institutions

Keown
Personal Finance: Turning Money into Wealth*

Keown/Martin/Petty
Foundations of Finance: The Logic and Practice of Financial Management*

Kim/Nofsinger
Corporate Governance

Madura
Personal Finance*

Marthinsen
Risk Takers: Uses and Abuses of Financial Derivatives

McDonald
Derivatives Markets

McDonald
Fundamentals of Derivatives Markets

Mishkin/Eakins
Financial Markets and Institutions

Moffett/Stonehill/Eiteman
Fundamentals of Multinational Finance

Nofsinger
Psychology of Investing

Ormiston/Fraser
Understanding Financial Statements

Pennacchi
Theory of Asset Pricing

Rejda
Principles of Risk Management and Insurance

Seiler
Performing Financial Studies: A Methodological Cookbook

Shapiro
Capital Budgeting and Investment Analysis

Sharpe/Alexander/Bailey
Investments

Solnik/McLeavey
Global Investments

Stretcher/Michael
Cases in Financial Management

Titman/Keown/Martin
Financial Management: Principles and Applications*

Titman/Martin
Valuation: The Art and Science of Corporate Investment Decisions

Van Horne
Financial Management and Policy

Van Horne/Wachowicz
Fundamentals of Financial Management

Weston/Mitchel/Mulherin
Takeovers, Restructuring, and Corporate Governance

Principles of
Managerial Finance

GLOBAL EDITION

Thirteenth Edition

Lawrence J. Gitman
San Diego State University

Chad J. Zutter
University of Pittsburgh

Boston   Columbus   Indianapolis   New York   San Francisco   Upper Saddle River
Amsterdam   Cape Town   Dubai   London   Madrid   Milan   Munich   Paris   Montreal   Toronto
Delhi   Mexico City   Sao Paulo   Sydney   Hong Kong   Seoul   Singapore   Taipei   Tokyo

Editor in Chief: Donna Battista
Acquisitions Editor: Tessa O'Brien
Senior International Acquisitions Editor: Laura Dent
Editorial Assistant: Kerri McQueen
International Editorial Assistant: Emily Jones
Editorial Project Manager: Melissa Pellerano
Managing Editor: Nancy Fenton
Senior Production Project Manager: Nancy Freihofer
Supplements Editor: Alison Eudsen

International Marketing Manager: Dean Erasmus
Marketing Assistant: Ian Gould
Media Producer: Nicole Sackin
MyFinanceLab Content Lead: Miguel Leonarte
Senior Manufacturing Buyer: Carol Melville
Cover Designer: Jodi Notowitz
Cover Image: © Kok Mun Hoo – Fotolia.com
Image Permission Coordinator: Rachel Youdelman
Interior Design, Project Coordination: Nesbitt Graphics, Inc.

Pearson Education Limited
Edinburgh Gate
Harlow
Essex CM20 2JE
England

and Associated Companies throughout the world

Visit us on the World Wide Web at:
www.pearsoned.co.uk

© Pearson Education Limited 2012

The rights of Lawrence J. Gitman and Chad J. Zutter to be identified as authors of this work have been asserted by them in accordance with the Copyright, Designs and Patents Act 1988.

Authorised adaptation from the United States edition, entitled Principles of Managerial Finance, ISBN 978-0-13-611946-3 by Lawrence J. Gitman and Chad J. Zutter, published by Pearson Education, publishing as Prentice Hall © 2012.

All rights reserved. No part of this publication may be reproduced, stored in a retrieval system, or transmitted in any form or by any means, electronic, mechanical, photocopying, recording or otherwise, without either the prior written permission of the publisher or a licence permitting restricted copying in the United Kingdom issued by the Copyright Licensing Agency Ltd, Saffron House, 6–10 Kirby Street, London EC1N 8TS.

All trademarks used herein are the property of their respective owners. The use of any trademark in this text does not vest in the author or publisher any trademark ownership rights in such trademarks, nor does the use of such trademarks imply any affiliation with or endorsement of this book by such owners.

Credits and acknowledgments borrowed from other sources and reproduced, with permission, in this textbook appear on the appropriate page within the text.

ISBN 13: 978-0-273-75428-2
ISBN 10: 0-273-75428-9

British Library Cataloguing-in-Publication Data
A catalogue record for this book is available from the British Library
10 9 8 7 6 5 4 3
15 14 13 12

Typeset in 10/12 Sabon by Nesbitt Graphics, Inc.
Printed and bound by Courier Kendallville.

*Dedicated to the memory
of my mother, Dr. Edith Gitman,
who instilled in me the importance
of education and hard work.*
LJG

*Dedicated to my wonderful wife,
Heidi Zutter, who unconditionally
supports my every endeavor.*
CJZ

Our Proven Teaching and Learning System

Users of *Principles of Managerial Finance* have praised the effectiveness of the book's Teaching and Learning System, which they hail as one of its hallmarks. The system, driven by a set of carefully developed learning goals, has been retained and polished in this thirteenth edition. The "walkthrough" on the pages that follow illustrates and describes the key elements of the Teaching and Learning System. We encourage both students and instructors to acquaint themselves at the start of the semester with the many useful features the book offers.

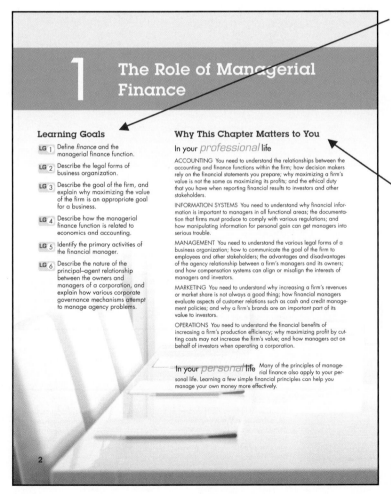

1 The Role of Managerial Finance

Learning Goals

LG 1 Define *finance* and the managerial finance function.

LG 2 Describe the legal forms of business organization.

LG 3 Describe the goal of the firm, and explain why maximizing the value of the firm is an appropriate goal for a business.

LG 4 Describe how the managerial finance function is related to economics and accounting.

LG 5 Identify the primary activities of the financial manager.

LG 6 Describe the nature of the principal–agent relationship between the owners and managers of a corporation, and explain how various corporate governance mechanisms attempt to manage agency problems.

Why This Chapter Matters to You

In your *professional* life

ACCOUNTING You need to understand the relationships between the accounting and finance functions within the firm; how decision makers rely on the financial statements you prepare; why maximizing a firm's value is not the same as maximizing its profits; and the ethical duty that you have when reporting financial results to investors and other stakeholders.

INFORMATION SYSTEMS You need to understand why financial information is important to managers in all functional areas; the documentation that firms must produce to comply with various regulations; and how manipulating information for personal gain can get managers into serious trouble.

MANAGEMENT You need to understand the various legal forms of a business organization; how to communicate the goal of the firm to employees and other stakeholders; the advantages and disadvantages of the agency relationship between a firm's managers and its owners; and how compensation systems can align or misalign the interests of managers and investors.

MARKETING You need to understand why increasing a firm's revenues or market share is not always a good thing; how financial managers evaluate aspects of customer relations such as cash and credit management policies; and why a firm's brands are an important part of its value to investors.

OPERATIONS You need to understand the financial benefits of increasing a firm's production efficiency; why maximizing profit by cutting costs may not increase the firm's value; and how managers act on behalf of investors when operating a corporation.

In your *personal* life Many of the principles of managerial finance also apply to your personal life. Learning a few simple financial principles can help you manage your own money more effectively.

2

Six **Learning Goals** at the start of the chapter highlight the most important concepts and techniques in the chapter. Students are reminded to think about the learning goals while working through the chapter by strategically placed **learning goal icons**.

Every chapter opens with a feature, titled **Why This Chapter Matters to You**, that helps motivate student interest by highlighting both professional and personal benefits from achieving the chapter learning goals.

Its first part, **In Your Professional Life**, discusses the intersection of the finance topics covered in the chapter with the concerns of other major business disciplines. It encourages students majoring in accounting, information systems, management, marketing, and operations to appreciate how financial acumen will help them achieve their professional goals.

The second part, **In Your Personal Life**, identifies topics in the chapter that will have particular application to personal finance. This feature also helps students appreciate the tasks performed in a business setting by pointing out that the tasks are not necessarily different from those that are relevant in their personal lives.

Each chapter begins with a short **opening vignette** that describes a recent real-company event related to the chapter topic. These stories raise interest in the chapter by demonstrating its relevance in the business world.

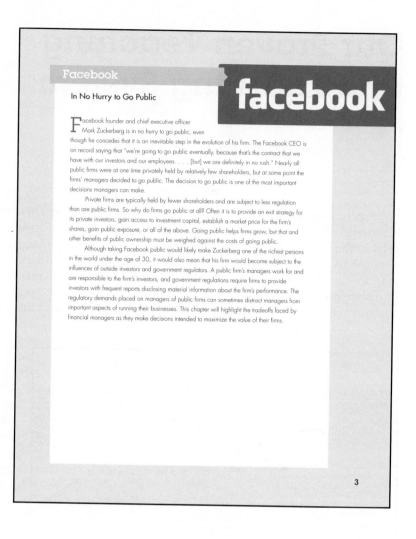

Learning goal icons tie chapter content to the learning goals and appear next to related text sections and again in the chapter-end summary, end-of-chapter homework materials, and supplements such as the *Study Guide, Test Item File,* and MyFinanceLab.

LG 1   LG 2   **1.1 Finance and Business**

The field of finance is broad and dynamic. Finance influences everything that firms do, from hiring personnel to building factories to launching new advertising campaigns. Because there are important financial dimensions to almost any aspect of business, there are many financially oriented career opportunities for those who understand the basic principles of finance described in this textbook. Even if you do not see yourself pursuing a career in finance, you'll find that an understanding of a few key ideas in finance will help make you a smarter consumer and a wiser investor with your own money.

For help in study and review, boldfaced **key terms** and their definitions appear in the margin where they are first introduced. These terms are also boldfaced in the book's index and appear in the end-of-book glossary.

corporation
An entity created by law.

stockholders
The owners of a corporation, whose ownership, or *equity,* takes the form of either common stock or preferred stock.

Corporations

A **corporation** is an entity created by law. A corporation has the legal powers of an individual in that it can sue and be sued, make and be party to contracts, and acquire property in its own name. Although only about 20 percent of all U.S. businesses are incorporated, the largest businesses nearly always are; corporations account for nearly 90 percent of total business revenues. Although corporations engage in all types of businesses, manufacturing firms account for the largest portion of corporate business receipts and net profits. Table 1.1 lists the key strengths and weaknesses of corporations.

Matter of fact

Problems with P/E Valuation

The P/E multiple approach is a fast and easy way to estimate a stock's value. However, P/E ratios vary widely over time. In 1980, the average stock had a P/E ratio below 9, but by the year 2000, the ratio had risen above 40. Therefore, analysts using the P/E approach in the 1980s would have come up with much lower estimates of value than analysts using the model 20 years later. In other words, when using this approach to estimate stock values, the estimate will depend more on whether stock market valuations generally are high or low rather than on whether the particular company is doing well or not.

Matter of Fact boxes provide interesting empirical facts that add background and depth to the material covered in the chapter.

In more depth

To read about *Deriving the Constant-Growth Model*, go to www.myfinancelab.com

myfinancelab

$$P_0 = \frac{D_0 \times (1 + g)^1}{(1 + r_s)^1} + \frac{D_0 \times (1 + g)^2}{(1 + r_s)^2} + \cdots + \frac{D_0 \times (1 + g)^\infty}{(1 + r_s)^\infty} \qquad (7.3)$$

If we simplify Equation 7.3, it can be rewritten as:

In More Depth boxes point students to additional material, available on MyFinanceLab, intended to further highlight a particular topic for students who want to explore a topic in greater detail.

Example 6.3 ▶ The nominal interest rates on a number of classes of long-term securities in May 2010 were as follows:

Security	Nominal interest rate
U.S. Treasury bonds (average)	3.30%
Corporate bonds (by risk ratings):	
High quality (Aaa–Aa)	3.95
Medium quality (A–Baa)	4.98
Speculative (Ba–C)	8.97

Because the U.S. Treasury bond would represent the risk-free, long-term security, we can calculate the risk premium of the other securities by subtracting the risk-free rate, 3.30%, from each nominal rate (yield):

Security	Risk premium
Corporate bonds (by ratings):	
High quality (Aaa–Aa)	3.95% − 3.30% = 0.65%
Medium quality (A–Baa)	4.98 − 3.30 = 1.68
Speculative (Ba–C)	8.97 − 3.30 = 5.67

Examples are an important component of the book's learning system. Numbered and clearly set off from the text, they provide an immediate and concrete demonstration of how to apply financial concepts, tools, and techniques.

Some Examples demonstrate time-value-of-money techniques. These examples often show the use of time lines, equations, financial calculators, and spreadsheets (with cell formulas).

Personal Finance Example 5.7 ▶ Fran Abrams wishes to determine how much money she will have at the end of 5 years if she chooses annuity A, the ordinary annuity. She will deposit $1,000 annually, at the *end of each* of the next 5 years, into a savings account paying 7% annual interest. This situation is depicted on the following time line:

Time line for future value of an ordinary annuity ($1,000 end-of-year deposit, earning 7%, at the end of 5 years)

$1,310.80
1,225.04
1,144.90
1,070.00
1,000.00
$5,750.74 **Future Value**

$1,000 $1,000 $1,000 $1,000 $1,000

Personal Finance Examples demonstrate how students can apply managerial finance concepts, tools, and techniques to their personal financial decisions.

The Equation for Present Value

The present value of a future amount can be found mathematically by solving Equation 5.4 for *PV*. In other words, the present value, *PV*, of some future amount, FV_n, to be received *n* periods from now, assuming an interest rate (or opportunity cost) of *r*, is calculated as follows:

$$PV = \frac{FV_n}{(1 + r)^n} \qquad (5.7)$$

Note the similarity between this general equation for present value and the equation in the preceding example (Equation 5.6). Let's use this equation in an example.

Key equations appear in green boxes throughout the text to help readers identify the most important mathematical relationships. The variables used in these equations are, for convenience, printed on the final pages of the book.

Review Questions appear at the end of each major text section. These questions challenge readers to stop and test their understanding of key concepts, tools, techniques, and practices before moving on to the next section.

→ **REVIEW QUESTIONS**

5–14 What effect does compounding interest more frequently than annually have on (**a**) future value and (**b**) the *effective annual rate (EAR)*? Why?

5–15 How does the future value of a deposit subject to continuous compounding compare to the value obtained by annual compounding?

5–16 Differentiate between a *nominal annual rate* and an *effective annual rate (EAR)*. Define *annual percentage rate (APR)* and *annual percentage yield (APY)*.

In Practice boxes offer insights into important topics in managerial finance through the experiences of real companies, both large and small. There are three categories of In Practice boxes:

Focus on Ethics boxes in every chapter help readers understand and appreciate important ethical issues and problems related to managerial finance.

Focus on Practice boxes take a corporate focus that relates a business event or situation to a specific financial concept or technique.

Global Focus boxes look specifically at the managerial finance experiences of international companies.

All three types of In Practice boxes end with one or more *critical thinking questions* to help readers broaden the lesson from the content of the box.

---

focus on **ETHICS**

If It Seems Too Good to Be True Then It Probably Is

in practice For many years, investors around the world clamored to invest with Bernard Madoff. Those fortunate enough to invest with "Bernie" might not have understood his secret trading system, but they were happy with the double-digit returns that they earned. Madoff was well connected, having been the chairman of the board of directors of

fraud. Madoff's hedge fund, Ascot Partners, turned out to be a giant Ponzi scheme.

Over the years, suspicions were raised about Madoff. Madoff generated high returns year after year, seemingly with very little risk. Madoff credited his complex trading strategy for his investment performance, but other investors employed similar strate-

Madoff's arrest indicated that investors' accounts contained over $64 billion, in aggregate. Many investors pursued claims based on the balance reported in these statements. However, a recent court ruling permits claims up to the difference between the amount an investor deposited with Madoff and the amount they withdrew. The judge also ruled that investors who managed to with-

---

focus on **PRACTICE**

Limits on Payback Analysis

in practice In tough economic times, the standard for a payback period is often reduced. Chief information officers (CIOs) are apt to reject projects with payback periods of more than 2 years. "We start with payback period," says Ron Fijalkowski, CIO at Strategic Distribution, Inc., in Bensalem, Pennsylvania. "For sure, if the payback period is over 36 months, it's not going to get approved. But our rule of thumb is we'd like to see 24 months. And if it's close to 12, it's probably a no-brainer."

While easy to compute and easy to understand, the payback periods simplicity brings with it some drawbacks. "Payback gives you an answer that tells you a bit about the beginning stage of a project, but it doesn't tell you much about the full lifetime of the project," says Chris Gardner, a cofounder of

in Barrington, Illinois. "The simplicity of computing payback may encourage sloppiness, especially the failure to include all costs associated with an investment, such as training, maintenance, and hardware upgrade costs," says Douglas Emond, senior vice president and chief technology officer at Eastern Bank in Lynn, Massachusetts. For example, he says, "you may be bringing in a hot new technology, but uh-oh, after implementation you realize that you need a dot-net guru in-house, and you don't have one."

But the payback method's emphasis on the short term has a special appeal for IT managers. "That's because the history of IT projects that take longer than 3 years is disastrous," says Gardner. Indeed, Ian Campbell, chief research officer at Nucleus Research, Inc., in Wellesley, Massachusetts, says payback period is an absolutely essen-

even more important than discounted cash flow (NPV and IRR)—because it spotlights the risks inherent in lengthy IT projects. "It should be a hard and fast rule to never take an IT project with a payback period greater than 3 years, unless it's an infrastructure project you can't do without," Campbell says.

Whatever the weaknesses of the payback period method of evaluating capital projects, the simplicity of the method does allow it to be used in conjunction with other, more sophisticated measures. It can be used to screen potential projects and winnow them down to the few that merit more careful scrutiny with, for example, net present value (NPV).

▶ *In your view, if the payback period method is used in conjunction with the NPV method, should it be used before or after the NPV evaluation?*

GLOBAL focus

An International Flavor to Risk Reduction

in practice Earlier in this chapter (see Table 8.3 on page 318), we learned that from 1900 through 2009 the U.S. stock market produced an average annual nominal return of 9.3 percent, but that return was associated with a relatively high standard deviation: 20.4 percent per year. Could U.S. investors have done better by diversifying globally? The answer is a qualified yes. Elroy Dimson, Paul Marsh, and Mike

Staunton calculated the historical returns on a portfolio that included U.S. stocks as well as stocks from 18 other countries. This diversified portfolio produced returns that were not quite as high as the U.S. average, just 8.6 percent per year. However, the globally diversified portfolio was also less volatile, with an annual standard deviation of 17.8 percent. Dividing the standard deviation by the annual return produces a coefficient of variation for the globally

diversified portfolio of 2.07, slightly lower than the 2.10 coefficient of variation reported for U.S. stocks in Table 8.5.

▶ *International mutual funds do not include any domestic assets whereas global mutual funds include both foreign and domestic assets. How might this difference affect their correlation with U.S. equity mutual funds?*

Source: Elroy Dimson, Paul Marsh, and Mike Staunton, *Triumph of the Optimists: 101 Years of Global Investment Returns* (Princeton University Press, 2002).

Summary

FOCUS ON VALUE

Time value of money is an important tool that financial managers and other market participants use to assess the effects of proposed actions. Because firms have long lives and some decisions affect their long-term cash flows, the effective application of time-value-of-money techniques is extremely important. These techniques enable financial managers to evaluate cash flows occurring at different times so as to combine, compare, and evaluate them and link them to the firm's **overall goal of share price maximization.** It will become clear in Chapters 6 and 7 that the application of time value techniques is a key part of the value determination process needed to make intelligent value-creating decisions.

REVIEW OF LEARNING GOALS

LG 1 **Discuss the role of time value in finance, the use of computational tools, and the basic patterns of cash flow.** Financial managers and investors use time-value-of-money techniques when assessing the value of expected cash flow streams. Alternatives can be assessed by either compounding to find future value or discounting to find present value. Financial managers rely primarily on present value techniques. Financial calculators, electronic spreadsheets, and financial tables can streamline the application of time value techniques. The cash flow of a firm can be described by its pattern—single amount, annuity, or mixed stream.

The end-of-chapter **Summary** consists of two sections. The first section, **Focus on Value**, explains how the chapter's content relates to the firm's goal of maximizing owner wealth. The feature helps reinforce understanding of the link between the financial manager's actions and share value.

The second part of the Summary, the **Review of Learning Goals**, restates each learning goal and summarizes the key material that was presented to support mastery of the goal. This review provides students with an opportunity to reconcile what they have learned with the learning goal and to confirm their understanding before moving forward.

Opener-in-Review

In the chapter opener you learned that it costs Eli Lilly close to $1 billion to bring a new drug to market, and by the time all of the R&D and clinical trials are completed, Lilly may have fewer than 10 years left to sell the drug under patent protection.

Assume that the $1 billion cost of bringing a new drug to market is spread out evenly over 10 years, and then 10 years remain for Lilly to recover their investment. How much cash would a new drug have to generate in the last 10 years to justify the $1 billion spent in the first 10 years? Assume that Lilly uses a required rate of return of 10%.

Self-Test Problems   (Solutions in Appendix)

LG 2 **LG 5** **ST5–1** **Future values for various compounding frequencies** Delia Martin has $10,000 that she can deposit in any of three savings accounts for a 3-year period. Bank A compounds interest on an annual basis, bank B compounds interest twice each year, and bank C compounds interest each quarter. All three banks have a stated annual interest rate of 4%.
  a. What amount would Ms. Martin have at the end of the third year, leaving all interest paid on deposit, in each bank?
  b. What *effective annual rate* (EAR) would she earn in each of the banks?
  c. On the basis of your findings in parts **a** and **b**, which bank should Ms. Martin deal with? Why?
  d. If a fourth bank (bank D), also with a 4% stated interest rate, compounds interest continuously, how much would Ms. Martin have at the end of the third year? Does this alternative change your recommendation in part **c**? Explain why or why not.

An **Opener-in-Review** question at the end of each chapter revisits the opening vignette and asks students to apply a lesson from the chapter to that business situation.

Self-Test Problems, keyed to the learning goals, give readers an opportunity to strengthen their understanding of topics by doing a sample problem. For reinforcement, solutions to the Self-Test Problems appear in the appendix at the back of the book.

Warm-Up Exercises   All problems are available in myfinancelab.

LG 2 **E5–1** Assume a firm makes a $2,500 deposit into its money market account. If this account is currently paying 0.7% (yes, that's right, less than 1%!), what will the account balance be after 1 year?

LG 2 **LG 5** **E5–2** If Bob and Judy combine their savings of $1,260 and $975, respectively, and deposit this amount into an account that pays 2% annual interest, compounded monthly, what will the account balance be after 4 years?

Warm-Up Exercises follow the Self-Test Problems. These short, numerical exercises give students practice in applying tools and techniques presented in the chapter.

Problems

All problems are available in **myfinancelab**.

LG 1 **P5-1** **Using a time line** The financial manager at Starbuck Industries is considering an investment that requires an initial outlay of $25,000 and is expected to result in cash inflows of $3,000 at the end of year 1, $6,000 at the end of years 2 and 3, $10,000 at the end of year 4, $8,000 at the end of year 5, and $7,000 at the end of year 6.
    a. Draw and label a time line depicting the cash flows associated with Starbuck Industries' proposed investment.
    b. Use arrows to demonstrate, on the time line in part **a**, how compounding to find future value can be used to measure all cash flows at the end of year 6.

LG 5 **P4-19** **Integrative—Pro forma statements** Red Queen Restaurants wishes to prepare financial plans. Use the financial statements on page 155 and the other information provided below to prepare the financial plans.

Personal Finance Problem

LG 2 **P5-7** **Time value** You can deposit $10,000 into an account paying 9% annual interest either today or exactly 10 years from today. How much better off will you be at the end of 40 years if you decide to make the initial deposit today rather than 10 years from today?

LG 6 **P5-62** **ETHICS PROBLEM** A manager at a "Check Into Cash" business (see *Focus on Ethics* box on page 187) defends his business practice as simply "charging what the market will bear." "After all," says the manager, "we don't force people to come in the door." How would you respond to this ethical defense of the payday-advance business?

Comprehensive **Problems**, keyed to the learning goals, are longer and more complex than the Warm-Up Exercises. In this section, instructors will find multiple problems that address the important concepts, tools, and techniques in the chapter.

A short descriptor identifies the essential concept or technique of the problem. Problems labeled as **Integrative** tie together related topics.

Personal Finance Problems specifically relate to personal finance situations and Personal Finance Examples in each chapter. These problems will help students see how they can apply the tools and techniques of managerial finance in managing their own finances.

The last item in the chapter Problems is an **Ethics Problem**. The ethics problem gives students another opportunity to think about and apply ethics principles to managerial financial situations.

All exercises and problems are available in MyFinanceLab.

Spreadsheet Exercise

You are interested in purchasing the common stock of Azure Corporation. The firm recently paid a dividend of $3 per share. It expects its earnings—and hence its dividends—to grow at a rate of 7% for the foreseeable future. Currently, similar-risk stocks have required returns of 10%.

Every chapter includes a **Spreadsheet Exercise**. This exercise gives students an opportunity to use Excel® software to create one or more spreadsheets with which to analyze a financial problem. The spreadsheet to be created often is modeled on a table or Excel screenshot located in the chapter. Students can access working versions of the Excel screenshots in MyFinanceLab.

Integrative Case 1

Merit Enterprise Corp.

Sara Lehn, chief financial officer of Merit Enterprise Corp., was reviewing her presentation one last time before her upcoming meeting with the board of directors. Merit's business had been brisk for the last two years, and the company's CEO was pushing for a dramatic expansion of Merit's production capacity. Executing the CEO's plans would require $4 billion in capital in addition to $2 billion in excess cash that the firm had built up. Sara's immediate task was to brief the board on options for raising the needed $4 billion.

Unlike most companies its size, Merit had maintained its status as a private company, financing its growth by reinvesting profits and, when necessary, borrowing from banks. Whether Merit could follow that same strategy to raise the $4 billion necessary to expand at the pace envisioned by the firm's CEO was uncertain, though it seemed unlikely to Sara. She had identified two options for the board to consider:

An **Integrative Case** at the end of each part of the book challenges students to use what they have learned over the course of several chapters.

Additional chapter resources, such as Chapter Cases, Group Exercises, Critical Thinking Problems, and numerous online resources, intended to provide further means for student learning and assessment are available in MyFinanceLab at www.myfinancelab.com.

Brief Contents

Contents

Part 1 ▶ Introduction to Managerial Finance   1

11
Capital Budgeting Cash Flows
page 426

ExxonMobil—Maintaining Its Project Inventory page 427

14
Payout Policy
page 559

Global Investment House—
The Payback Time page 560

Part 7 ▶ **Short-Term Financial Decisions** 597

Part 8 ▶ **Special Topics in Managerial Finance** 675

About the Authors

Lawrence J. Gitman is an emeritus professor of finance at San Diego State University. Dr. Gitman has published more than 50 articles in scholarly journals as well as textbooks covering undergraduate- and graduate-level corporate finance, investments, personal finance, and introduction to business. Dr. Gitman is past president of the Academy of Financial Services, the San Diego Chapter of the Financial Executives Institute, the Midwest Finance Association, and the FMA National Honor Society. Dr. Gitman served as Vice-President of Financial Education of the Financial Management Association, as a director of the San Diego MIT Enterprise Forum, and on the CFP® Board of Standards. He received his B.S.I.M. from Purdue University, his M.B.A. from the University of Dayton, and his Ph.D. from the University of Cincinnati. He and his wife have two children and live in La Jolla, California, where he is an avid bicyclist, having twice competed in the coast-to-coast Race Across America.

Chad J. Zutter is an associate professor of finance at the University of Pittsburgh. Dr. Zutter recently won the Jensen Prize for the best paper published in the *Journal of Financial Economics* and has also won a best paper award from the *Journal of Corporate Finance*. His research has a practical, applied focus and has been the subject of feature stories in, among other prominent outlets, *The Economist* and *CFO Magazine*. His papers have been cited in arguments before the U.S. Supreme Court and in consultation with companies such as Google and Intel. Dr. Zutter has also won teaching awards at Indiana University and the University of Pittsburgh. He received his B.B.A. from the University of Texas at Arlington and his Ph.D. from Indiana University. He and his wife have four children and live in Pittsburgh, Pennsylvania. Prior to his career in academics, Dr. Zutter was a submariner in the U.S. Navy.

Preface

The desire to write *Principles of Managerial Finance* came from the experience of teaching the introductory managerial finance course. Those who have taught the introductory course many times can appreciate the difficulties that some students have absorbing and applying financial concepts. Students want a book that speaks to them in plain English and a book that ties concepts to reality. These students want more than just description—they also want demonstration of concepts, tools, and techniques. This book is written with the needs of students in mind, and it effectively delivers the resources that students need to succeed in the introductory finance course.

Courses and students have changed since the first edition of this book, but the goals of the text have not changed. The conversational tone and wide use of examples set off in the text still characterize *Principles of Managerial Finance*. Building on those strengths, 13 editions, numerous translations, and well over half a million U.S. users, *Principles* has evolved based on feedback from both instructors and students, from adopters, nonadopters, and practitioners.

In this edition, Chad Zutter of the University of Pittsburgh joins the author team. A recent recipient of the Jensen Prize for the best paper published in the *Journal of Financial Economics*, Chad brings a fresh perspective to *Principles*. Larry and Chad have worked together to incorporate contemporary thinking and pedagogy with the classic topics that Gitman users have come to expect.

NEW TO THE THIRTEENTH EDITION

As we made plans to publish the thirteenth edition, we carefully assessed market feedback about content changes that would better meet the needs of instructors teaching the course.

The chapter sequence is similar to the prior edition, but there are some noteworthy changes. The thirteenth edition contains 19 chapters divided into eight parts. Each part is introduced by a brief overview, which is intended to give students an advance sense for the collective value of the chapters included in the part.

In Part 1, a new Chapter 2 expands coverage of financial markets and institutions, with particular emphasis on the recent financial crisis and recession. This chapter not only explores the root causes and consequences of the financial crisis, but it also discusses the changing regulatory landscape within which financial institutions and markets function.

Part 2 contains three chapters in the same order in which they appeared in the twelfth edition. These chapters focus on basic financial skills such as financial statement analysis, cash flow analysis, and time-value-of-money calculations.

Part 3 focuses on bond and stock valuation. We moved these two chapters forward in this edition, just ahead of the risk and return chapter, to provide students with exposure to basic material on bonds and stocks that is easier to grasp than some of the more theoretical concepts in the next part.

Part 4 contains the risk and return chapter as well as the chapter on the cost of capital, which we have moved forward to lead into Part 5 on capital budgeting. We also moved up the chapter on the cost of capital so that it follows directly on the heels of the risk and return material. We believe that this makes the subsequent discussion of capital budgeting topics more meaningful because students will already have an idea of where a project "hurdle rate" comes from.

Part 5 contains three chapters on various capital budgeting topics. A change from the last edition here is that we present capital budgeting methods before the chapter on capital budgeting cash flows.

Parts 6, 7, and 8 contain the same seven chapters in the same order that appeared in the latter part of the twelfth edition. These chapters cover topics such as capital structure, payout policy, working capital management, derivatives, mergers, and international finance. Details about the revisions made to these chapters appear below.

Although the text content is sequential, instructors can assign almost any chapter as a self-contained unit, enabling instructors to customize the text to various teaching strategies and course lengths.

A number of new topics have been added at appropriate places, and new features appear in each chapter. The Matter of Fact feature provides additional detail and interesting empirical facts that help students understand the practical implications of financial concepts. For students who want to explore particular topics more deeply on their own, the In More Depth feature, available on MyFinanceLab, offers a guide for further study. In addition, as the detailed list shows, the chapter-opening vignettes and In Practice boxes have been replaced or heavily revised: For example, three-quarters of the chapter-opening vignettes are new, focusing on companies such as Facebook, Abercrombie & Fitch, and Air Asia that have student appeal, and more than half of the Focus on Ethics boxes are new. Also new to this edition are Opener-in-Review questions, which appear at the end of each chapter.

The following chapter-by-chapter list details several of the notable content changes in the thirteenth edition.

Chapter 1   **The Role of Managerial Finance**
- Revised opening vignette discusses Facebook's possible IPO.
- New Focus on Practice box discusses professional certifications in finance.
- New Matter of Fact feature provides statistics on the number of businesses and the revenues they generate by legal form of organization.
- Sections on financial markets and business taxes have been moved to a new, expanded Chapter 2.
- Coverage of the difference between cash flow and profit as part of the discussion surrounding the goal of the firm has been revised.
- New Focus on Ethics box highlights the ethical issues that Google faced during its expansion to China.
- Coverage of agency issues has been substantially revised, and a new Matter of Fact feature provides data on the link between pay and performance for several prominent firms.

Chapter 2   **The Financial Market Environment**
- This new chapter focuses on financial markets and institutions as well as the recent financial crisis.
- New opening vignette traces JP Morgan's performance during the crisis.

- New section provides coverage of commercial banks, investment banks, and the shadow banking system.
- New Focus on Ethics box is related to the Martha Stewart insider trading scandal.
- New section has been added on causes and consequences of financial crisis.
- Coverage of regulatory issues has been updated.

Chapter 3 Financial Statements and Ratio Analysis

- New opening vignette has been added (financial results, Abercrombie & Fitch).
- New Global Focus box covers International Financial Reporting Standards (IFRS).
- New Focus on Ethics box describes ethical issues related to corporate earnings reports.
- New table shows values of key ratios for several prominent firms and the related industry averages. Five related Matter of Fact features explain why certain ratio values vary systematically across industries.

Chapter 4 Cash Flow and Financial Planning

- New opening vignette highlights Apple's huge cash hoard.
- New Matter of Fact box illustrates where Apple's cash flow comes from.
- New Focus on Practice box dissects a recent earnings report by Cisco Systems to explore the firm's underlying cash generation.
- Discussion of alternative cash flow measures has been revised.
- New In More Depth feature (on MyFinanceLab) discusses the value of using regression analysis to estimate fixed costs.

Chapter 5 Time Value of Money

- New In More Depth feature (on MyFinanceLab) shows how the firm Royalty Pharma makes lump-sum payments to acquire royalty streams from other firms.
- References to financial tables and interest rate factors have been eliminated.
- Coverage of calculations using Excel has been expanded.
- New Matter of Fact feature describes a Kansas truck driver's choice to take a lump-sum payment rather than an annuity due after winning the lottery.
- The Focus on Ethics box on subprime loans has been revised.

Chapter 6 Interest Rates and Bond Valuation

- New opening vignette discusses the arrival of Renminbi-Denominated International Bonds.
- New Matter of Fact feature highlights a 2008 U.S. Treasury auction in which bill returns briefly turned negative.
- Discussion of factors that influence interest rates, particularly inflation, has been substantially revised.
- New In More Depth feature (on MyFinanceLab) points students to an animation on the Web that illustrates historical yield curve behavior.
- Major revisions have been made to coverage of the term structure of interest rates.
- Focus on Ethics box on the performance of rating agencies during the financial crisis has been revised.

Chapter 7   **Stock Valuation**
- New opening vignette has been added about Air Asia, an airline whose business model hinges upon low fare air travel.
- New In More Depth feature (on MyFinanceLab) discusses the U.S. bankruptcy process.
- New Matter of Fact box describes how assets are divided in bankruptcy.
- New In More Depth feature (on MyFinanceLab) discusses the hierarchy of the efficient market hypothesis.
- New In More Depth feature (on MyFinanceLab) illustrates the derivation of the constant-growth model.
- New Matter of Fact box describes how P/E ratios fluctuate over time.

Chapter 8   **Risk and Return**
- New opening vignette has been added about a mutual fund that ranked near the bottom and then at the top of all mutual funds in consecutive years.
- New Focus on Ethics box features Bernie Madoff.
- New numerical examples have data drawn from the real world.
- Historical returns on U.S. stocks, bonds, and bills have been updated.
- Discussion of investor risk preferences has been substantially revised.
- New Matter of Fact feature discusses Nicholas Taleb's *Black Swan*.
- New Matter of Fact box compares historical returns on large stocks versus small stocks.
- New Global Focus box features data on international diversification.

Chapter 9   **The Cost of Capital**
- New opening vignette focuses on General Electric.
- New Focus on Ethics box deals with Merck's handling of Vioxx.
- New In More Depth feature (on MyFinanceLab) discusses changes in the weighted average cost of capital.
- New Matter of Fact box presents a more comprehensive cost of retained earnings.
- New Focus on Practice feature focuses on WACC's susceptibility to the 2008 financial crisis and the 2009 great recession.
- New integrative case for Part 4 has been added.

Chapter 10   **Capital Budgeting Techniques**
- New opening vignette has been added about Treats—Waffles and More, a dessert shop in Egypt, which was opened with the help of capital budgeting techniques.
- New In More Depth feature (on MyFinanceLab) discusses the Accounting Rate of Return method.
- Substantially revised opening section discusses the capital budgeting process.
- Coverage of profitability index approach has been expanded.
- Coverage of economic value added has been expanded.
- New Matter of Fact box provides evidence on the extent to which firms use different capital budgeting methods.

Chapter 11   **Capital Budgeting Cash Flows**
- Opening vignette (project costs at ExxonMobil) has been updated.
- New Matter of Fact box provides statistics on foreign direct investment in the Middle East.

- Global Focus box (foreign direct investment in China) has been updated.
- Focus on Ethics box (accuracy of cash flow estimates) has been updated.
- Two new Integrative Problems have been added.

Chapter 12 Risk and Refinements in Capital Budgeting

- New opening vignette discusses BP oil spill.
- New In More Depth feature (on MyFinanceLab) directs students to a Crystal Ball simulation of a mining investment on the Internet.
- New Matter of Fact box provides evidence on the frequency with which firms make adjustments to their investment analysis to account for currency risk.
- New Focus on Ethics box discusses the implications of the BP oil spill on the firm's cost of capital.

Chapter 13 Leverage and Capital Structure

- New opening vignette discuss the value created by Genzyme when it added debt to its capital structure in response to a proxy fight with Carl Icahn.
- Substantially revised opening section discusses the nature and risks of leverage.
- Revised Focus on Practice box calculates Adobe's operating leverage.
- New Focus on Ethics box discusses Lehman Brothers' use of off–balance sheet transactions to understate its leverage.
- New Matter of Fact box offers data on the use of financial leverage by firms in different countries.
- New In More Depth feature (on MyFinanceLab) explains why capital structure does not affect firm value in perfect markets.
- Major revisions have been made to the discussion of the pecking order and signaling theories of capital structure.

Chapter 14 Payout Policy

- New chapter title reflects broader focus on payout policy, including share repurchases as opposed to a narrow focus on dividends.
- New opening vignette about Global Investment House, an investment company in Kuwait.
- New opening section discusses long-term trends in earnings, dividends, and repurchases.
- New Matter of Fact box describes Procter & Gamble's long dividend history.
- New figure shows relative frequency of firms increasing and decreasing dividends over time.
- New examples have real-world data.
- Extensive new discussion of share repurchase programs and procedures has been added.
- New discussion covers effects of dividend and share repurchase decisions on firm value.
- New In More Depth feature (on MyFinanceLab) explains the conditions under which dividend policy has no impact on firm value.
- Extensive revisions have been made to discussions of alternative dividend theories and a brief introduction to the new catering theory of dividends has been added.

Chapter 15   **Working Capital and Current Assets Management**
- New opening vignette focuses on working capital at Hing Yiap.
- New figure shows the yearly median working capital values for all U.S.-listed manufacturing companies.
- Updated example for calculating the cash conversion cycle uses real data for IBM.
- Updated Focus on Practice box discusses Walmart's use of RFID.
- New In More Depth feature (on MyFinanceLab) discusses accounts receivable financing.
- New Matter of Fact box cites finding from a survey of CFOs regarding the value they place on working capital management.

Chapter 16   **Current Liabilities Management**
- Updated opening vignette covers reducing accounts payable expenses at Memorial Sloan-Kettering.
- Revised in-chapter examples use real data for Hewlett-Packard.
- Focus on Practice box (commercial paper) has been updated.
- New Focus on Ethics box discusses the accounting fraud case against Diebold Inc.
- Two new Matter of Fact boxes have been added, one on lending limits and the other on quasi-factoring.
- Several In More Depth features (on MyFinanceLab) have been added, including one that discusses floating inventory liens.

Chapter 17   **Hybrid and Derivative Securities**
- New opening vignette discusses airlines sale-leaseback transactions.
- New Matter of Fact feature provides recent data on the size of the convertibles market.
- Major revisions to options coverage include a Matter of Fact box that describes the decline in trading volume during the financial crisis and another one outlining some popular options trading strategies.
- Updated Focus on Ethics box discusses the options backdating scandal.

Chapter 18   **Mergers, LBOs, Divestitures, and Business Failure**
- New opening vignette on creating value by going private has been added.
- New In More Depth (on MyFinanceLab) discusses prioritizing claims in liquidation.
- Global Focus box (News Corp acquisitions) has been updated.
- New Focus on Ethics box discusses Gulf Bank and the "too big to fail" policy.
- New Matter of Fact box provides statistics on the ten largest U.S. bankruptcies.

Chapter 19   **International Managerial Finance**
- Opening vignette (GE's business in China) has been updated.
- Two new Matter of Fact boxes have been added, one on diversifying operations and the other on adjusting discount rates.
- Global Focus box (overseas assignments) has been updated.
- New Focus on Ethics box discusses Chiquita's policy of paying protection money in Colombia.

THE THIRTEENTH EDITION

Like the previous editions, the thirteenth edition incorporates a proven learning system, which integrates pedagogy with concepts and practical applications. It concentrates on the knowledge that is needed to make keen financial decisions in an increasingly competitive business environment. The strong pedagogy and generous use of examples—including personal finance examples—make the text an easily accessible resource for in-class learning or out-of-class learning, such as online courses and self-study programs.

ORGANIZATION

The text's organization conceptually links the firm's actions and its value, as determined in the financial market. Each major decision area is presented in terms of both risk and return factors and their potential impact on owners' wealth. A Focus on Value element at the end of each chapter helps reinforce the student's understanding of the link between the financial manager's actions and the firm's share value.

In organizing each chapter, we have adhered to a managerial decision-making perspective, relating decisions to the firm's overall goal of wealth maximization. Once a particular concept has been developed, its application is illustrated by an example—a hallmark feature of this book. These examples demonstrate, and solidify in the student's thought, financial decision-making considerations and their consequences.

INTERNATIONAL CONSIDERATIONS

We live in a world where international considerations cannot be divorced from the study of business in general and finance in particular. As in prior editions, discussions of international dimensions of chapter topics are integrated throughout the book. International material is integrated into learning goals and end-of-chapter materials. In addition, for those who want to spend more time addressing the topic, a separate chapter on international managerial finance concludes the book.

PERSONAL FINANCE LINKAGES

The thirteenth edition contains several features designed to help students see the value of applying financial principles and techniques in their personal lives. At the start of each chapter, the feature titled *Why This Chapter Matters to You* helps motivate student interest by discussing how the topic of the chapter relates to the concerns of other major business disciplines and to personal finance. Within the chapter, Personal Finance Examples explicitly link the concepts, tools, and techniques of each chapter to personal finance applications. Throughout the homework material, the book provides numerous personal finance problems. The purpose of these personal finance materials is to demonstrate to students the usefulness of managerial finance knowledge in both business and personal financial dealings.

ETHICAL ISSUES

The need for ethics in business remains as important as ever. Students need to understand the ethical issues that financial managers face as they attempt to maximize shareholder value and to solve business problems. Thus, every chapter includes an In Practice box that focuses on current ethical issues.

HOMEWORK OPPORTUNITIES

Of course, practice is essential for students' learning of managerial finance concepts, tools, and techniques. To meet that need, the book offers a rich and varied menu of homework assignments: short, numerical Warm-Up Exercises; a comprehensive set of Problems, including more than one problem for each important concept or technique and personal finance problems; an Ethics Problem for each chapter; a Spreadsheet Exercise; and, at the end of each part of the book, an Integrative Case. In addition, the end-of-chapter problems are available in algorithmic form in 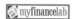. These materials (see pages xi through xii for detailed descriptions) offer students solid learning opportunities, and they offer instructors opportunities to expand and enrich the classroom environment.

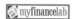 ### MyFinanceLab

This fully integrated online homework system gives students the hands-on practice and tutorial help they need to learn finance efficiently. There are ample opportunities for online practice and assessment that is automatically graded in MyFinanceLab (www.myfinancelab.com).

Chapter Cases with automatically graded assessment are also provided in MyFinanceLab. These cases have students apply the concepts they have learned to a more complex and realistic situation. These cases help strengthen practical application of financial tools and techniques.

MyFinanceLab also has **Group Exercises** where students can work together in the context of an ongoing company. Each group creates a company and follows it through the various managerial finance topics and business activities presented in the textbook.

MyFinanceLab provides **Critical Thinking Problems**, which require students to apply the various finance concepts and managerial techniques presented in the textbook. These are rigorous problems that are designed to test a student's ability to understand the financial management situation, apply the necessary managerial finance concepts, and find the value-maximizing solution.

An online glossary, digital flashcards, financial calculator tutorials, videos, Spreadsheet Use examples from the text in Excel, and numerous other premium resources are available in MyFinanceLab.

From classroom to boardroom, the thirteenth edition of *Principles of Managerial Finance* can help users get to where they want to be. We believe that it is the best edition yet—more relevant, more accurate, and more effective than ever. We hope you agree that *Principles of Managerial Finance*, Thirteenth Edition, is the most effective introductory managerial finance text for your students.

Lawrence J. Gitman
La Jolla, California

Chad J. Zutter
Pittsburgh, Pennsylvania

Supplements to the Thirteenth Edition

The *Principles of Managerial Finance* Teaching and Learning System includes a variety of useful supplements for teachers and for students.

TEACHING TOOLS FOR INSTRUCTORS

The key teaching tools available to instructors are the *Instructor's Manual*, testing materials, and *PowerPoint Lecture Presentations*.

Instructor's Manual *Revised by Thomas Krueger, Texas A&M University-Kingsville and accuracy-checked by Gordon Stringer, University of Colorado, Colorado Springs.* This comprehensive resource pulls together the teaching tools so that instructors can use the textbook easily and effectively in the classroom. Each chapter provides an overview of key topics and detailed answers and solutions to all review questions, Opener-in-Review questions, Warm-Up Exercises, end-of-chapter problems, and chapter cases, plus suggested answers to all critical thinking questions in chapter boxes, Ethics Problems, and Group Exercises. At the end of the manual are practice quizzes and solutions. The complete *Instructor's Manual*, including Spreadsheet Exercises, is available online at www.pearsonglobaleditions.com/gitman.

Test Item File *Revised by Shannon Donovan, Bridgewater State University.* Thoroughly revised to accommodate changes in the text, the *Test Item File* consists of a mix of true/false, multiple-choice, and essay questions. Each test question includes identifiers for type of question, skill tested by learning goal, and key topic tested plus, where appropriate, the formula(s) or equation(s) used in deriving the answer.

The *Test Item File* is also available in *Test Generator Software (TestGen)* for either Windows or Macintosh. The *Test Item File* and *TestGen* are available online at www.pearsonglobaleditions.com/gitman.

PowerPoint Lecture Presentation *Revised by Thomas Boulton, Miami University.* This presentation combines lecture notes with all of the art from the textbook. The PowerPoint Lecture Presentation is available online at www.pearsonglobaleditions.com/gitman.

LEARNING TOOLS FOR STUDENTS

Beyond the book itself, students have access to valuable resources, such as MyFinanceLab and the *Study Guide,* that if taken advantage of can help ensure their success.

MyFinanceLab MyFinanceLab opens the door to a powerful Web-based diagnostic testing and tutorial system designed specifically for the Gitman/Zutter, *Principles of Managerial Finance* textbooks. With MyFinanceLab, instructors can create, edit, and assign online homework and test and track all student work in the online gradebook. MyFinanceLab allows students to take practice tests correlated to the textbook and receive a customized study plan based on the test results.

Most end-of-chapter problems are available in MyFinanceLab, and because the problems have algorithmically generated values, no student will have the same homework as another; there is an unlimited opportunity for practice and testing. Students get the help they need, when they need it, from the robust tutorial options, including "View an Example" and "Help Me Solve This," which breaks the problem into its steps and links to the relevant textbook page.

This fully integrated online homework system gives students the hands-on practice and tutorial help they need to learn finance efficiently. There are ample opportunities for online practice and assessment that is automatically graded in MyFinanceLab (www.myfinancelab.com).

Advanced reporting features in MyFinanceLab also allow you to easily report on AACSB accreditation and assessment in just a few clicks.

Chapter Cases with automatically graded assessment are also provided in MyFinanceLab. These cases have students apply the concepts they have learned to a more complex and realistic situation. These cases help strengthen practical application of financial tools and techniques.

MyFinanceLab also has Group Exercises where students can work together in the context of an ongoing company. Each group creates a company and follows it through the various managerial finance topics and business activities presented in the textbook.

MyFinanceLab provides Critical Thinking Problems, which require students to apply the various finance concepts and managerial techniques presented in the textbook. These are rigorous problems that are designed to test a student's ability to understand the financial management situation, apply the necessary managerial finance concepts, and find the value-maximizing solution.

An online glossary, digital flashcards, financial calculator tutorials, videos, and numerous other premium resources are available in MyFinanceLab.

Students can use MyFinanceLab with no instructor intervention. However, to take advantage of the full capabilities of MyFinanceLab, including assigning homework and tracking student progress in the automated gradebook, instructors will want to set up their class. To view a demo of MyFinanceLab or to request instructor access go to www.myfinancelab.com.

Study Guide   *Revised by Shannon Donovan, Bridgewater State University.* The *Study Guide* is an integral component of the *Principles of Managerial Finance* Teaching and Learning System. It offers many tools for studying finance. Each chapter contains the following features: chapter summary enumerated by learning goals; topical chapter outline, also broken down by learning goals for quick review; sample problem solutions; study tips and a full sample exam with the answers at the end of the chapter. A financial dictionary of key terms is located at the end of the *Study Guide*, along with an appendix with tips on using financial calculators.

Acknowledgments

TO OUR COLLEAGUES, FRIENDS, AND FAMILY

Prentice Hall sought the advice of a great many excellent reviewers, all of whom influenced the revisions of this book. The following individuals provided extremely thoughtful and useful comments for the preparation of the thirteenth edition:

Johnny C. Chan, *Western Kentucky University*
Kent Cofoid, *Seminole Community College*
Shannon Donovan, *Bridgewater State University*
Suk Hun Lee, *Loyola University Chicago*
Hao Lin, *California State University–Sacramento*
Larry Lynch, *Roanoke College*
Alvin Nishimoto, *Hawaii Pacific University*
William Sawatski, *Southwestern College*
Steven R. Scheff, *Florida Gulf Coast University*
Michael Schellenger, *University of Wisconsin, Oshkosh*
Gordon M. Stringer, *University of Colorado–Colorado Springs*
Barry Uze, *University of Southwestern Louisiana*
Sam Veraldi, *Duke University*
John Zietlow, *Malone University*

Our special thanks go to the following individuals who analyzed the manuscript in previous editions:

Saul W. Adelman
M. Fall Ainina
Gary A. Anderson
Ronald F. Anderson
James M. Andre
Gene L. Andrusco
Antonio Apap
David A. Arbeit
Allen Arkins
Saul H. Auslander
Peter W. Bacon
Richard E. Ball
Thomas Bankston
Alexander Barges
Charles Barngrover
Michael Becker
Omar Benkato
Scott Besley
Douglas S. Bible
Charles W. Blackwell
Russell L. Block
Calvin M. Boardman
Paul Bolster
Robert J. Bondi

Jeffrey A. Born
Jerry D. Boswell
Denis O. Boudreaux
Kenneth J. Boudreaux
Wayne Boyet
Ron Braswell
Christopher Brown
William Brunsen
Samuel B. Bulmash
Francis E. Canda
Omer Carey
Patrick A. Casabona
Robert Chatfield
K. C. Chen
Roger G. Clarke
Terrence M. Clauretie
Mark Cockalingam
Boyd D. Collier
Thomas Cook
Maurice P. Corrigan
Mike Cudd
Donnie L. Daniel
Prabir Datta
Joel J. Dauten

Lee E. Davis
Irv DeGraw
Richard F. DeMong
Peter A. DeVito
James P. D'Mello
R. Gordon Dippel
Carleton Donchess
Thomas W. Donohue
Vincent R. Driscoll
Betty A. Driver
Lorna Dotts
David R. Durst
Dwayne O. Eberhardt
Ronald L. Ehresman
Ted Ellis
F. Barney English
Greg Filbeck
Ross A. Flaherty
Rich Fortin
Timothy J. Gallagher
George W. Gallinger
Sharon Garrison
Gerald D. Gay
Deborah Giarusso

R. H. Gilmer
Anthony J. Giovino
Michael Giuliano
Philip W. Glasgo
Jeffrey W. Glazer
Joel Gold
Ron B. Goldfarb
Dennis W. Goodwin
David A. Gordon
J. Charles Granicz
C. Ramon Griffin
Reynolds Griffith
Arthur Guarino
Lewell F. Gunter
Melvin W. Harju
John E. Harper
Phil Harrington
George F. Harris
George T. Harris
John D. Harris
Mary Hartman
R. Stevenson Hawkey
Roger G. Hehman
Harvey Heinowitz
Glenn Henderson
Russell H. Hereth
Kathleen T. Hevert
J. Lawrence Hexter
Douglas A. Hibbert
Roger P. Hill
Linda C. Hittle
James Hoban
Hugh A. Hobson
Keith Howe
Kenneth M. Huggins
Jerry G. Hunt
Mahmood Islam
James F. Jackson
Stanley Jacobs
Dale W. Janowsky
Jeannette R. Jesinger
Nalina Jeypalan
Timothy E. Johnson
Roger Juchau
Ashok K. Kapoor
Daniel J. Kaufman Jr.
Joseph K. Kiely
Terrance E. Kingston
Raj K. Kohli
Thomas M. Krueger
Lawrence Kryzanowski
Harry R. Kuniansky
Richard E. La Near
William R. Lane

James Larsen
Rick LeCompte
B. E. Lee
Scott Lee
Michael A. Lenarcic
A. Joseph Lerro
Thomas J. Liesz
Alan Lines
Christopher K. Ma
James C. Ma
Dilip B. Madan
Judy Maese
James Mallet
Inayat Mangla
Bala Maniam
Timothy A. Manuel
Brian Maris
Daniel S. Marrone
William H. Marsh
John F. Marshall
Linda J. Martin
Stanley A. Martin
Charles E. Maxwell
Timothy Hoyt McCaughey
Lee McClain
Jay Meiselman
Vincent A. Mercurio
Joseph Messina
John B. Mitchell
Daniel F. Mohan
Charles Mohundro
Gene P. Morris
Edward A. Moses
Tarun K. Mukherjee
William T. Murphy
Randy Myers
Lance Nail
Donald A. Nast
Vivian F. Nazar
G. Newbould
Charles Ngassam
Gary Noreiko
Dennis T. Officer
Kathleen J. Oldfather
Kathleen F. Oppenheimer
Richard M. Osborne
Jerome S. Osteryoung
Prasad Padmanabahn
Roger R. Palmer
Don B. Panton
John Park
Ronda S. Paul
Bruce C. Payne
Gerald W. Perritt

Gladys E. Perry
Stanley Piascik
Gregory Pierce
Mary L. Piotrowski
D. Anthony Plath
Jerry B. Poe
Gerald A. Pogue
Suzanne Polley
Ronald S. Pretekin
Fran Quinn
Rich Ravichandran
David Rayone
Walter J. Reinhart
Jack H. Reubens
Benedicte Reyes
William B. Riley Jr.
Ron Rizzuto
Gayle A. Russell
Patricia A. Ryan
Murray Sabrin
Kanwal S. Sachedeva
R. Daniel Sadlier
Hadi Salavitabar
Gary Sanger
Mukunthan
    Santhanakrishnan
William L. Sartoris
Michael Schinski
Tom Schmidt
Carl J. Schwendiman
Carl Schweser
Jim Scott
John W. Settle
Richard A. Shick
A. M. Sibley
Sandeep Singh
Surendra S. Singhvi
Stacy Sirmans
Barry D. Smith
Gerald Smolen
Ira Smolowitz
Jean Snavely
Joseph V. Stanford
John A. Stocker
Lester B. Strickler
Elizabeth Strock
Donald H. Stuhlman
Sankar Sundarrajan
Philip R. Swensen
S. Tabriztchi
John C. Talbott
Gary Tallman
Harry Tamule
Richard W. Taylor

Rolf K. Tedefalk
Richard Teweles
Kenneth J. Thygerson
Robert D. Tollen
Emery A. Trahan
Pieter A. Vandenberg
Nikhil P. Varaiya
Oscar Varela
Kenneth J. Venuto
James A. Verbrugge
Ronald P. Volpe
John M. Wachowicz Jr.

Faye (Hefei) Wang
William H. Weber III
Herbert Weinraub
Jonathan B. Welch
Grant J. Wells
Larry R. White
Peter Wichert
C. Don Wiggins
Howard A. Williams
Richard E. Williams
Glenn A. Wilt Jr.
Bernard J. Winger

Tony R. Wingler
I. R. Woods
John C. Woods
Robert J. Wright
Richard H. Yanow
Seung J. Yoon
Charles W. Young
Philip J. Young
Joe W. Zeman
J. Kenton Zumwalt
Tom Zwirlein

A special thanks goes to Thomas J. Boulton of Miami University for his work on the Focus on Ethics boxes and to Alan Wolk of the University of Georgia for accuracy checking the quantitative content in the textbook. We are pleased by and proud of all their efforts.

No textbook would be complete, let alone usable, if not for the accompanying instructor and student supplements. We are grateful to the following individuals for their work creating, revising, and accuracy checking all of the valuable instructor and student resources that support the use of *Principles:* Thomas Krueger of Texas A&M University–Kingsville for updating the *Instructor's Manual*, Gordon Stringer of University of Colorado–Colorado Springs for accuracy checking the *Instructor's Manual*, Thomas J. Boulton of Miami University for revising the *PowerPoint Lecture Presentation*, and Shannon Donovan of Bridgewater State University for revising the *Test Item File* and the *Study Guide*.

A hearty round of applause also goes to the publishing team assembled by Prentice Hall—including Donna Battista, Tessa O'Brien, Kerri McQueen, Melissa Pellerano, Nancy Freihofer, Alison Eusden, Nicole Sackin, Miguel Leonarte, and others who worked on the book—for the inspiration and the perspiration that define teamwork. Also, special thanks to the formidable Prentice Hall sales force in finance, whose ongoing efforts keep the business fun!

Finally, and most important, many thanks to our families for patiently providing support, understanding, and good humor throughout the revision process. To them we will be forever grateful.

Lawrence J. Gitman
La Jolla, California

Chad J. Zutter
Pittsburgh, Pennsylvania

Pearson gratefully acknowledges and thanks the following people for their work on the Global Edition:

International Contributors

Rashid Ameer, University Technology MARA

Rola El Kabbani, The German University in Cairo

Hassan Ahmad El Sady, Gulf University for Science and Technology

Dr. Joyce Nga Koe Hwee, Sunway University College

Christian Kalhoefer, The German University in Cairo

Sara Shenouda, The German University in Cairo

International Reviewers

Ye Bai, The University of Nottingham

Patricia Buijs, The Hague University

Wassim Dbouk, The American University of Beruit

Stephen Everhart, The American University in Cairo

Janine Krüger, Nelson Mandela Metropolitan University

Alex Mackay, Robert Gordon University

Ghulam Sorwar, The University of Nottingham

To the Student

Because you have a good many options for getting your assigned reading materials we appreciate your choosing this textbook as the best means for learning in your managerial finance course. You should not be disappointed. In writing this edition, we have been mindful of students and careful to maintain a student focus.

The learning system in this book has been used by many of your predecessors in the course and has been proven effective. It integrates various learning tools with the concepts, tools, techniques, and practical applications you will need to learn about managerial finance. We have worked hard to present in a clear and interesting way the information you will need. This book is loaded with features designed to motivate your study of finance and to help you learn the course material. Go to pages vii–xii ("Our Proven Teaching and Learning System") for an overview and walkthrough of those features. Notice that the book includes Personal Finance Examples (and related end-of-chapter problems) that show how to apply managerial finance concepts and tools to your personal financial life.

About some of the specific features: First, pay attention to the learning goals, which will help you focus on what material you need to learn, where you can find it in the chapter, and whether you've mastered it by the end of the chapter.

Second, avoid the temptation to rush past the Review Questions at the end of each major text section. Pausing briefly to test your understanding of the section content will help you cement your understanding. Give yourself an honest assessment. If some details are fuzzy, go back (even briefly) and review anything that still seems unclear.

Third, look for (or make) opportunities to talk with classmates or friends about what you are reading and learning in the course. Talking about the concepts and techniques of finance demonstrates how much you've learned, uncovers things you haven't yet understood fully, and gives you valuable practice for class and (eventually) the business world. While you're talking, don't neglect to discuss the issues raised in the Focus on Ethics boxes, which look at some of the opportunities to do right (or not) that business people face.

MyFinanceLab opens the door to a powerful Web-based diagnostic testing and tutorial system designed for this text. MyFinanceLab allows you to take practice exams correlated to the textbook and receive a customized study plan based on your results. The assignment Problems in MyFinanceLab, based on the even-numbered end-of-chapter Problems in the book, have algorithmically generated values. Thus, the numbers in your homework will differ from those of your classmates, and there is an unlimited opportunity for practice and testing. You can get the help you need, when you need it, from the robust tutorial options, including "View an Example" and "Help Me Solve This," which breaks the problem into steps and links to the relevant textbook page.

Given today's rapidly changing technology, who knows what might be available next? We are striving to keep pace with your needs and interests, and would like to hear your ideas for improving the teaching and learning of finance.

We wish you all the best in this course and in your academic and professional careers.

Lawrence J. Gitman
La Jolla, California

Chad J. Zutter
Pittsburgh, Pennsylvania

Part 1 Introduction to Managerial Finance

Part 1 of *Principles of Managerial Finance* discusses the role that financial managers play in businesses and the financial market environment in which firms operate. We argue that the goal of managers should be to maximize the value of the firm and by doing so maximize the wealth of its owners. Financial managers act on behalf of the firm's owners by making operating and investment decisions whose benefits exceed their costs. These decisions create wealth for shareholders. Maximizing shareholder wealth is important because firms operate in a highly competitive financial market environment that offers shareholders many alternatives for investing their funds. To raise the financial resources necessary to fund the firm's ongoing operations and future investment opportunities, managers have to deliver value to the firm's investors. Without smart financial managers and access to financial markets, firms are unlikely to survive, let alone achieve the long-term goal of maximizing the value of the firm.

1 The Role of Managerial Finance

Learning Goals

LG 1 Define *finance* and the managerial finance function.

LG 2 Describe the legal forms of business organization.

LG 3 Describe the goal of the firm, and explain why maximizing the value of the firm is an appropriate goal for a business.

LG 4 Describe how the managerial finance function is related to economics and accounting.

LG 5 Identify the primary activities of the financial manager.

LG 6 Describe the nature of the principal–agent relationship between the owners and managers of a corporation, and explain how various corporate governance mechanisms attempt to manage agency problems.

Why This Chapter Matters to You

In your *professional* life

ACCOUNTING You need to understand the relationships between the accounting and finance functions within the firm; how decision makers rely on the financial statements you prepare; why maximizing a firm's value is not the same as maximizing its profits; and the ethical duty that you have when reporting financial results to investors and other stakeholders.

INFORMATION SYSTEMS You need to understand why financial information is important to managers in all functional areas; the documentation that firms must produce to comply with various regulations; and how manipulating information for personal gain can get managers into serious trouble.

MANAGEMENT You need to understand the various legal forms of a business organization; how to communicate the goal of the firm to employees and other stakeholders; the advantages and disadvantages of the agency relationship between a firm's managers and its owners; and how compensation systems can align or misalign the interests of managers and investors.

MARKETING You need to understand why increasing a firm's revenues or market share is not always a good thing; how financial managers evaluate aspects of customer relations such as cash and credit management policies; and why a firm's brands are an important part of its value to investors.

OPERATIONS You need to understand the financial benefits of increasing a firm's production efficiency; why maximizing profit by cutting costs may not increase the firm's value; and how managers act on behalf of investors when operating a corporation.

In your *personal* life

Many of the principles of managerial finance also apply to your personal life. Learning a few simple financial principles can help you manage your own money more effectively.

In No Hurry to Go Public

Facebook founder and chief executive officer Mark Zuckerberg is in no hurry to go public, even though he concedes that it is an inevitable step in the evolution of his firm. The Facebook CEO is on record saying that "we're going to go public eventually, because that's the contract that we have with our investors and our employees. . . . [but] we are definitely in no rush." Nearly all public firms were at one time privately held by relatively few shareholders, but at some point the firms' managers decided to go public. The decision to go public is one of the most important decisions managers can make.

Private firms are typically held by fewer shareholders and are subject to less regulation than are public firms. So why do firms go public at all? Often it is to provide an exit strategy for its private investors, gain access to investment capital, establish a market price for the firm's shares, gain public exposure, or all of the above. Going public helps firms grow, but that and other benefits of public ownership must be weighed against the costs of going public.

Although taking Facebook public would likely make Zuckerberg one of the richest persons in the world under the age of 30, it would also mean that his firm would become subject to the influences of outside investors and government regulators. A public firm's managers work for and are responsible to the firm's investors, and government regulations require firms to provide investors with frequent reports disclosing material information about the firm's performance. The regulatory demands placed on managers of public firms can sometimes distract managers from important aspects of running their businesses. This chapter will highlight the tradeoffs faced by financial managers as they make decisions intended to maximize the value of their firms.

LG 1 LG 2 **1.1 Finance and Business**

The field of finance is broad and dynamic. Finance influences everything that firms do, from hiring personnel to building factories to launching new advertising campaigns. Because there are important financial dimensions to almost any aspect of business, there are many financially oriented career opportunities for those who understand the basic principles of finance described in this textbook. Even if you do not see yourself pursuing a career in finance, you'll find that an understanding of a few key ideas in finance will help make you a smarter consumer and a wiser investor with your own money.

WHAT IS FINANCE?

finance
The science and art of managing money.

Finance can be defined as the science and art of managing money. At the personal level, finance is concerned with individuals' decisions about how much of their earnings they spend, how much they save, and how they invest their savings. In a business context, finance involves the same types of decisions: how firms raise money from investors, how firms invest money in an attempt to earn a profit, and how they decide whether to reinvest profits in the business or distribute them back to investors. The keys to good financial decisions are much the same for businesses and individuals, which is why most students will benefit from an understanding of finance regardless of the career path they plan to follow. Learning the techniques of good financial analysis will not only help you make better financial decisions as a consumer, but it will also help you understand the financial consequences of the important business decisions you will face no matter what career path you follow.

CAREER OPPORTUNITIES IN FINANCE

Careers in finance typically fall into one of two broad categories: (1) financial services and (2) managerial finance. Workers in both areas rely on a common analytical "tool kit," but the types of problems to which that tool kit is applied vary a great deal from one career path to the other.

financial services
The area of finance concerned with the design and delivery of advice and financial products to individuals, businesses, and governments.

Financial Services

Financial services is the area of finance concerned with the design and delivery of advice and financial products to individuals, businesses, and governments. It involves a variety of interesting career opportunities within the areas of banking, personal financial planning, investments, real estate, and insurance.

managerial finance
Concerns the duties of the *financial manager* in a business.

Managerial Finance

Managerial finance is concerned with the duties of the *financial manager* working in a business. **Financial managers** administer the financial affairs of all types of businesses—private and public, large and small, profit seeking and not for profit. They perform such varied tasks as developing a financial plan or budget, extending credit to customers, evaluating proposed large expenditures, and raising money to fund the firm's operations. In recent years, a number of factors have increased the importance and complexity of the financial manager's duties. These factors include the recent global financial crisis and subsequent responses

financial manager
Actively manages the financial affairs of all types of businesses, whether private or public, large or small, profit seeking or not for profit.

by regulators, increased competition, and technological change. For example, globalization has led U.S. corporations to increase their transactions in other countries, and foreign corporations have done likewise in the United States. These changes increase demand for financial experts who can manage cash flows in different currencies and protect against the risks that arise from international transactions. These changes increase the finance function's complexity, but they also create opportunities for a more rewarding career. The increasing complexity of the financial manager's duties has increased the popularity of a variety of professional certification programs outlined in the *Focus on Practice* box below. Financial managers today actively develop and implement corporate strategies aimed at helping the firm grow and improving its competitive position. As a result, many corporate presidents and chief executive officers (CEOs) rose to the top of their organizations by first demonstrating excellence in the finance function.

LEGAL FORMS OF BUSINESS ORGANIZATION

One of the most basic decisions that all businesses confront is how to choose a legal form of organization. This decision has very important financial implications because how a business is organized legally influences the risks that the

focus on PRACTICE

Professional Certifications in Finance

in practice To be successful in finance and just about any other field, you need to continue your education beyond your undergraduate degree. For some people that means getting an MBA, but there are many other ways to advance your education and enhance your credentials without getting a graduate degree. In finance, there are a variety of professional certification programs that are widely recognized in the field.

Chartered Financial Analyst (CFA)—Offered by the CFA Institute, the CFA program is a graduate-level course of study focused primarily on the investments side of finance. To earn the CFA Charter, students must pass a series of three exams, usually over a 3-year period, and have 48 months of professional experience. Although this program appeals primarily to those who work in the investments field, the skills developed in the CFA program are useful in a variety of corporate finance jobs as well.

Certified Treasury Professional (CTP)—The CTP program requires students to pass a single exam that is focused on the knowledge and skills needed for those working in a corporate treasury department. The program emphasizes topics such as liquidity and working capital management, payment transfer systems, capital structure, managing relationships with financial service providers, and monitoring and controlling financial risks.

Certified Financial Planner (CFP)—To obtain CFP status, students must pass a 10-hour exam covering a wide range of topics related to personal financial planning. The CFP program also requires 3 years of full-time relevant experience. The program focuses primarily on skills relevant for advising individuals in developing their personal financial plans.

American Academy of Financial Management (AAFM)—The AAFM administers a host of certification programs for financial professionals

in a wide range of fields. Their certifications include the Chartered Portfolio Manager, Chartered Asset Manager, Certified Risk Analyst, Certified Cost Accountant, Certified Credit Analyst, and many other programs. See the AAFM website for complete details on all of the AAFM educational programs.

Professional Certifications in Accounting—Most professionals in the field of managerial finance need to know a great deal about accounting to succeed in their jobs. Professional certifications in accounting include the Certified Public Accountant (CPA), Certified Management Accountant (CMA), Certified Internal Auditor (CIA), and many other programs.

▶ *Why do employers value having employees with professional certifications?*

firm's owners must bear, how the firm can raise money, and how the firm's profits will be taxed. The three most common legal forms of business organization are the *sole proprietorship*, the *partnership*, and the *corporation*. More businesses are organized as sole proprietorships than any other legal form. However, the largest businesses are almost always organized as corporations. Even so, each type of organization has its advantages and disadvantages.

Sole Proprietorships

sole proprietorship
A business owned by one person and operated for his or her own profit.

A **sole proprietorship** is a business owned by one person who operates it for his or her own profit. About 73 percent of all businesses are sole proprietorships. The typical sole proprietorship is small, such as a bike shop, personal trainer, or plumber. The majority of sole proprietorships operate in the wholesale, retail, service, and construction industries.

Typically, the owner (proprietor), along with a few employees, operates the proprietorship. The proprietor raises capital from personal resources or by borrowing, and he or she is responsible for all business decisions. As a result, this form of organization appeals to entrepreneurs who enjoy working independently.

unlimited liability
The condition of a sole proprietorship (or general partnership), giving creditors the right to make claims against the owner's personal assets to recover debts owed by the business.

A major drawback to the sole proprietorship is **unlimited liability,** which means that liabilities of the business are the entrepreneur's responsibility, and creditors can make claims against the entrepreneur's personal assets if the business fails to pay its debts. The key strengths and weaknesses of sole proprietorships are summarized in Table 1.1.

Partnerships

partnership
A business owned by two or more people and operated for profit.

A **partnership** consists of two or more owners doing business together for profit. Partnerships account for about 7 percent of all businesses, and they are typically larger than sole proprietorships. Partnerships are common in the finance, insurance, and real estate industries. Public accounting and law partnerships often have large numbers of partners.

articles of partnership
The written contract used to formally establish a business partnership.

Most partnerships are established by a written contract known as **articles of partnership.** In a *general* (or *regular*) *partnership,* all partners have unlimited liability, and each partner is legally liable for *all* of the debts of the partnership. Table 1.1 summarizes the strengths and weaknesses of partnerships.

Matter of fact

BizStats.com Total Receipts by Type of U.S. Firm

Although there are vastly more sole proprietorships than there are partnerships and corporations combined, they generate the lowest level of receipts. In total, sole proprietorships generated more than $969 billion in receipts, but this number hardly compares to the more than $17 trillion in receipts generated by corporations.

BizStats.com Total Receipts by Type of U.S. Firm			
	Sole proprietorships	Partnerships	Corporations
Number of firms (millions)	17.6	1.8	4.8
Percentage of all firms	73%	7%	20%
Total receipts ($ billions)	969	1,142	17,324
Percentage of all receipts	5%	6%	89%

TABLE 1.1	**Strengths and Weaknesses of the Common Legal Forms of Business Organization**		
	Sole proprietorship	Partnership	Corporation
Strengths	• Owner receives all profits (and sustains all losses) • Low organizational costs • Income included and taxed on proprietor's personal tax return • Independence • Secrecy • Ease of dissolution	• Can raise more funds than sole proprietorships • Borrowing power enhanced by more owners • More available brain power and managerial skill • Income included and taxed on partner's personal tax return	• Owners have *limited liability*, which guarantees that they cannot lose more than they invested • Can achieve large size via sale of ownership (stock) • Ownership (stock) is readily transferable • Long life of firm • Can hire professional managers • Has better access to financing
Weaknesses	• Owner has *unlimited liability*—total wealth can be taken to satisfy debts • Limited fund-raising power tends to inhibit growth • Proprietor must be jack-of-all-trades • Difficult to give employees long-run career opportunities • Lacks continuity when proprietor dies	• Owners have *unlimited liability* and may have to cover debts of other partners • Partnership is dissolved when a partner dies • Difficult to liquidate or transfer partnership	• Taxes generally higher because corporate income is taxed, and dividends paid to owners are also taxed at a maximum 15% rate • More expensive to organize than other business forms • Subject to greater government regulation • Lacks secrecy because regulations require firms to disclose financial results

corporation
An entity created by law.

stockholders
The owners of a corporation, whose ownership, or *equity*, takes the form of either common stock or preferred stock.

limited liability
A legal provision that limits stockholders' liability for a corporation's debt to the amount they initially invested in the firm by purchasing stock.

common stock
The purest and most basic form of corporate ownership.

Corporations

A **corporation** is an entity created by law. A corporation has the legal powers of an individual in that it can sue and be sued, make and be party to contracts, and acquire property in its own name. Although only about 20 percent of all U.S. businesses are incorporated, the largest businesses nearly always are; corporations account for nearly 90 percent of total business revenues. Although corporations engage in all types of businesses, manufacturing firms account for the largest portion of corporate business receipts and net profits. Table 1.1 lists the key strengths and weaknesses of corporations.

The owners of a corporation are its **stockholders,** whose ownership, or *equity,* takes the form of either common stock or preferred stock. Unlike the owners of sole proprietorships or partnerships, stockholders of a corporation enjoy **limited liability,** meaning that they are not personally liable for the firm's debts. Their losses are limited to the amount they invested in the firm when they purchased shares of stock. In Chapter 7 you will learn more about common and preferred stock, but for now it is enough to say that **common stock** is the purest and most basic form of corporate ownership. Stockholders expect to earn a

dividends
Periodic distributions of cash to the stockholders of a firm.

return by receiving **dividends**—periodic distributions of cash—or by realizing gains through increases in share price. Because the money to pay dividends generally comes from the profits that a firm earns, stockholders are sometimes referred to as *residual claimants,* meaning that stockholders are paid last—after employees, suppliers, tax authorities, and lenders receive what they are owed. If the firm does not generate enough cash to pay everyone else, there is nothing available for stockholders.

As noted in the upper portion of Figure 1.1, control of the corporation functions a little like a democracy. The stockholders (owners) vote periodically to elect members of the *board of directors* and to decide other issues such as amending the corporate charter. The **board of directors** is typically responsible for approving strategic goals and plans, setting general policy, guiding corporate affairs, and approving major expenditures. Most importantly, the board decides when to hire or fire top managers and establishes compensation packages for the most senior executives. The board consists of "inside" directors, such as key corporate executives, and "outside" or "independent" directors, such as executives from other companies, major shareholders, and national or community leaders. Outside directors for major corporations receive compensation in the form of cash, stock, and stock options. This compensation often totals $100,000 per year or more.

board of directors
Group elected by the firm's stockholders and typically responsible for approving strategic goals and plans, setting general policy, guiding corporate affairs, and approving major expenditures.

FIGURE 1.1

Corporate Organization
The general organization of a corporation and the finance function (which is shown in yellow)

president or chief executive officer (CEO)
Corporate official responsible for managing the firm's day-to-day operations and carrying out the policies established by the board of directors.

limited partnership (LP)

S corporation (S corp)

limited liability company (LLC)

limited liability partnership (LLP)
See "In More Depth" feature.

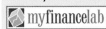

In more depth

To read about *Other Limited Liability Organizations*, go to www.myfinancelab.com

myfinancelab

The **president or chief executive officer (CEO)** is responsible for managing day-to-day operations and carrying out the policies established by the board of directors. The CEO reports periodically to the firm's directors.

It is important to note the division between owners and managers in a large corporation, as shown by the dashed horizontal line in Figure 1.1. This separation and some of the issues surrounding it will be addressed in the discussion of *the agency issue* later in this chapter.

Other Limited Liability Organizations

A number of other organizational forms provide owners with limited liability. The most popular are **limited partnership (LP)**, **S corporation (S corp)**, **limited liability company (LLC)**, and **limited liability partnership (LLP)**. Each represents a specialized form or blending of the characteristics of the organizational forms described previously. What they have in common is that their owners enjoy limited liability, and they typically have fewer than 100 owners.

WHY STUDY MANAGERIAL FINANCE?

An understanding of the concepts, techniques, and practices presented throughout this text will fully acquaint you with the financial manager's activities and decisions. Because the consequences of most business decisions are measured in financial terms, the financial manager plays a key operational role. People in all areas of responsibility—accounting, information systems, management, marketing, operations, and so forth—need a basic awareness of finance so they will understand how to quantify the consequences of their actions.

OK, so you're not planning to major in finance! You still will need to understand how financial managers think to improve your chance of success in your chosen business career. Managers in the firm, regardless of their job descriptions, usually have to provide financial justification for the resources they need to do their job. Whether you are hiring new workers, negotiating an advertising budget, or upgrading the technology used in a manufacturing process, understanding the financial aspects of your actions will help you gain the resources you need to be successful. The "Why This Chapter Matters to You" section that appears on each chapter opening page should help you understand the importance of each chapter in both your professional and personal life.

As you study this text, you will learn about the career opportunities in managerial finance, which are briefly described in Table 1.2 on page 10. Although this text focuses on publicly held profit-seeking firms, the principles presented here are equally applicable to private and not-for-profit organizations. The decision-making principles developed in this text can also be applied to personal financial decisions. We hope that this first exposure to the exciting field of finance will provide the foundation and initiative for further study and possibly even a future career.

→ **REVIEW QUESTIONS**

1–1 What is *finance*? Explain how this field affects all of the activities in which businesses engage.

1–2 What is the *financial services* area of finance? Describe the field of *managerial finance*.

TABLE 1.2	Career Opportunities in Managerial Finance
Position	**Description**
Financial analyst	Prepares the firm's financial plans and budgets. Other duties include financial forecasting, performing financial comparisons, and working closely with accounting.
Capital expenditures manager	Evaluates and recommends proposed long-term investments. May be involved in the financial aspects of implementing approved investments.
Project finance manager	Arranges financing for approved long-term investments. Coordinates consultants, investment bankers, and legal counsel.
Cash manager	Maintains and controls the firm's daily cash balances. Frequently manages the firm's cash collection and disbursement activities and short-term investments and coordinates short-term borrowing and banking relationships.
Credit analyst/manager	Administers the firm's credit policy by evaluating credit applications, extending credit, and monitoring and collecting accounts receivable.
Pension fund manager	Oversees or manages the assets and liabilities of the employees' pension fund.
Foreign exchange manager	Manages specific foreign operations and the firm's exposure to fluctuations in exchange rates.

1–3 Which legal form of business organization is most common? Which form is dominant in terms of business revenues?

1–4 Describe the roles and the basic relationships among the major parties in a corporation—stockholders, board of directors, and managers. How are corporate owners rewarded for the risks they take?

1–5 Briefly name and describe some organizational forms other than corporations that provide owners with limited liability.

1–6 Why is the study of managerial finance important to your professional life regardless of the specific area of responsibility you may have within the business firm? Why is it important to your personal life?

LG 3 **1.2 Goal of the Firm**

What goal should managers pursue? There is no shortage of possible answers to this question. Some might argue that managers should focus entirely on satisfying customers. Progress toward this goal could be measured by the market share attained by each of the firm's products. Others suggest that managers must first inspire and motivate employees; in that case, employee turnover might be the key success metric to watch. Clearly the goal that managers select will affect many of the decisions that they make, so choosing an objective is a critical determinant of how businesses operate.

MAXIMIZE SHAREHOLDER WEALTH

Finance teaches that managers' primary goal should be to maximize the wealth of the firm's owners—the stockholders. The simplest and best measure of stockholder wealth is the firm's share price, so most textbooks (ours included) instruct

To succeed in a company make the customers happy and employee so everyone can win.

managers to take actions that increase the firm's share price. A common misconception is that when firms strive to make their shareholders happy, they do so at the expense of other constituencies such as customers, employees, or suppliers. This line of thinking ignores the fact that in most cases, to enrich shareholders, managers must first satisfy the demands of these other interest groups. Recall that dividends that stockholders receive ultimately come from the firm's profits. It is unlikely that a firm whose customers are unhappy with its products, whose employees are looking for jobs at other firms, or whose suppliers are reluctant to ship raw materials will make shareholders rich because such a firm will likely be less profitable in the long run than one that better manages its relations with these stakeholder groups.

Therefore, we argue that the goal of the firm, and also of managers, should be *to maximize the wealth of the owners for whom it is being operated,* or equivalently, to maximize the stock price. This goal translates into a straightforward decision rule for managers—*only take actions that are expected to increase the share price.* Although that goal sounds simple, implementing it is not always easy. To determine whether a particular course of action will increase or decrease a firm's share price, managers have to assess what return (that is, cash inflows net of cash outflows) the action will bring and how risky that return might be. Figure 1.2 depicts this process. In fact, we can say that *the key variables that managers must consider when making business decisions are return (cash flows) and risk.*

MAXIMIZE PROFIT?

It might seem intuitive that maximizing a firm's share price is equivalent to maximizing its profits, but that is not always correct.

earnings per share (EPS)
The amount earned during the period on behalf of each outstanding share of common stock, calculated by dividing the period's total earnings available for the firm's common stockholders by the number of shares of common stock outstanding.

Corporations commonly measure profits in terms of **earnings per share (EPS)**, which represent the amount earned during the period on behalf of each outstanding share of common stock. EPS are calculated by dividing the period's total earnings available for the firm's common stockholders by the number of shares of common stock outstanding.

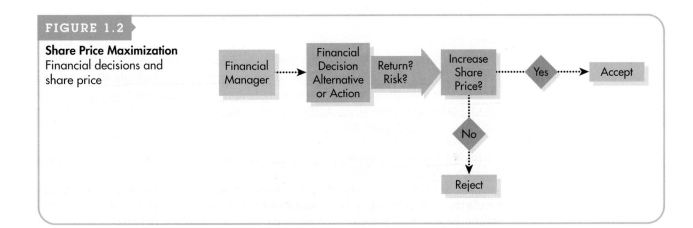

FIGURE 1.2

Share Price Maximization
Financial decisions and share price

Example 1.1 ▶ Nick Dukakis, the financial manager of Neptune Manufacturing, a producer of marine engine components, is choosing between two investments, Rotor and Valve. The following table shows the EPS that each investment is expected to have over its 3-year life.

Investment	Earnings per share (EPS)			
	Year 1	Year 2	Year 3	Total for years 1, 2, and 3
Rotor	$1.40	$1.00	$0.40	$2.80
Valve	0.60	1.00	1.40	3.00

In terms of the profit maximization goal, Valve would be preferred over Rotor because it results in higher total earnings per share over the 3-year period ($3.00 EPS compared with $2.80 EPS).

But does profit maximization lead to the highest possible share price? For at least three reasons the answer is often no. First, timing is important. An investment that provides a lower profit in the short run may be preferable to one that earns a higher profit in the long run. Second, profits and cash flows are not identical. The profit that a firm reports is simply an estimate of how it is doing, an estimate that is influenced by many different accounting choices that firms make when assembling their financial reports. Cash flow is a more straightforward measure of the money flowing into and out of the company. Companies have to pay their bills with cash, not earnings, so cash flow is what matters most to financial managers. Third, risk matters a great deal. A firm that earns a low but reliable profit might be more valuable than another firm with profits that fluctuate a great deal (and therefore can be very high or very low at different times).

① Timing

Because the firm can earn a return on funds it receives, *the receipt of funds sooner rather than later is preferred.* In our example, in spite of the fact that the total earnings from Rotor are smaller than those from Valve, Rotor provides much greater earnings per share in the first year. The larger returns in year 1 could be reinvested to provide greater future earnings.

② Cash Flows

Profits do *not* necessarily result in cash flows available to the stockholders. There is no guarantee that the board of directors will increase dividends when profits increase. In addition, the accounting assumptions and techniques that a firm adopts can sometimes allow a firm to show a positive profit even when its cash outflows exceed its cash inflows.

Furthermore, higher earnings do not necessarily translate into a higher stock price. Only when earnings increases are accompanied by increased future cash flows is a higher stock price expected. For example, a firm with a high-quality product sold in a very competitive market could increase its earnings by significantly reducing its equipment maintenance expenditures. The firm's expenses would be reduced, thereby increasing its profits. But if the reduced maintenance results in lower product quality, the firm may impair its competitive position, and its stock price could drop as many well-informed investors sell the stock in anticipation of lower future cash flows. In this case, the earnings increase was accompanied by lower future cash flows and therefore a lower stock price.

③ Risk

risk
The chance that actual outcomes may differ from those expected.

Profit maximization also fails to account for **risk**—the chance that actual outcomes may differ from those expected. A basic premise in managerial finance is that a trade-off exists between return (cash flow) and risk. *Return and risk are, in fact, the key determinants of share price, which represents the wealth of the owners in the firm.*

Cash flow and risk affect share price differently: Holding risk fixed, higher cash flow is generally associated with a higher share price. In contrast, holding cash flow fixed, higher risk tends to result in a lower share price because the stockholders do not like risk. For example, Apple's CEO, Steve Jobs, took a leave of absence to battle a serious health issue, and the firm's stock suffered as a result. This occurred not because of any near-term cash flow reduction but in response to the firm's increased risk—there's a chance that the firm's lack of near-term leadership could result in reduced future cash flows. Simply put, the increased risk reduced the firm's share price. In general, stockholders are **risk averse**—that is, they must be compensated for bearing risk. In other words, investors expect to earn higher returns on riskier investments, and they will accept lower returns on relatively safe investments. The key point, which will be fully developed in Chapter 5, is that differences in risk can significantly affect the value of different investments.

risk averse
Requiring compensation to bear risk.

WHAT ABOUT STAKEHOLDERS?

stakeholders
Groups such as employees, customers, suppliers, creditors, owners, and others who have a direct economic link to the firm.

Although maximization of shareholder wealth is the primary goal, many firms broaden their focus to include the interests of *stakeholders* as well as shareholders. **Stakeholders** are groups such as employees, customers, suppliers, creditors, owners, and others who have a direct economic link to the firm. A firm with a *stakeholder focus* consciously avoids actions that would prove detrimental to stakeholders. The goal is not to maximize stakeholder well-being but to preserve it.

The stakeholder view does not alter the goal of maximizing shareholder wealth. Such a view is often considered part of the firm's "social responsibility." It is expected to provide long-run benefit to shareholders by maintaining positive relationships with stakeholders. Such relationships should minimize stakeholder turnover, conflicts, and litigation. Clearly, the firm can better achieve its goal of shareholder wealth maximization by fostering cooperation with its other stakeholders, rather than conflict with them.

THE ROLE OF BUSINESS ETHICS

business ethics
Standards of conduct or moral judgment that apply to persons engaged in commerce.

Business ethics are the standards of conduct or moral judgment that apply to persons engaged in commerce. Violations of these standards in finance involve a variety of actions: "creative accounting," earnings management, misleading financial forecasts, insider trading, fraud, excessive executive compensation, options backdating, bribery, and kickbacks. The financial press has reported many such violations in recent years, involving such well-known companies as

Apple and Bank of America. As a result, the financial community is developing and enforcing ethical standards. The goal of these ethical standards is to motivate business and market participants to adhere to both the letter and the spirit of laws and regulations concerned with business and professional practice. Most business leaders believe businesses actually strengthen their competitive positions by maintaining high ethical standards.

Considering Ethics

Robert A. Cooke, a noted ethicist, suggests that the following questions be used to assess the ethical viability of a proposed action.[1]

1. Is the action arbitrary or capricious? Does it unfairly single out an individual or group?
2. Does the action violate the moral or legal rights of any individual or group?
3. Does the action conform to accepted moral standards?
4. Are there alternative courses of action that are less likely to cause actual or potential harm?

Clearly, considering such questions before taking an action can help to ensure its ethical viability.

Today, many firms are addressing the issue of ethics by establishing corporate ethics policies. The *Focus on Ethics* box provides an example of ethics policies at Google. A major impetus toward the development of ethics policies has been the Sarbanes-Oxley Act of 2002. Frequently, employees are required to sign a formal pledge to uphold the firm's ethics policies. Such policies typically apply to employee actions in dealing with all corporate stakeholders, including the public.

Ethics and Share Price

An effective ethics program can enhance corporate value by producing a number of positive benefits. It can reduce potential litigation and judgment costs, maintain a positive corporate image, build shareholder confidence, and gain the loyalty, commitment, and respect of the firm's stakeholders. Such actions, by maintaining and enhancing cash flow and reducing perceived risk, can positively affect the firm's share price. *Ethical behavior is therefore viewed as necessary for achieving the firm's goal of owner wealth maximization.*

→ REVIEW QUESTIONS

1–7 What is the goal of the firm and, therefore, of all managers and employees? Discuss how one measures achievement of this goal.

1–8 For what three basic reasons is profit maximization inconsistent with wealth maximization?

---

1. Robert A. Cooke, "Business Ethics: A Perspective," in *Arthur Andersen Cases on Business Ethics* (Chicago: Arthur Andersen, September 1991), pp. 2 and 5.

focus on ETHICS

Will Google Live Up to Its Motto?

in practice   Google offers an interesting case study on value maximization and corporate ethics. In 2004, Google's founders provided "An Owner's Manual" for shareholders, which stated that "Google is not a conventional company" and that the company's ultimate goal "is to develop services that significantly improve the lives of as many people as possible." The founders stressed that it was not enough for Google to run a successful business but that they want to use the company to make the world a better place. The "Owner's Manual" also unveiled Google's corporate motto, "Don't Be Evil." The motto is intended to convey Google's willingness to do the right thing even when doing so requires the firm to sacrifice in the short run. Google's approach does not appear to be limiting its ability to maximize value—the company's share price increased from $100 to approximately $500 in 6 years.

Google's business goal is "instantly delivering relevant information on any topic" to the world. However, when the company launched its search engine in China in early 2006, it agreed to the Chinese government's request to censor search results. Some observers felt that the opportunity to gain access to the vast Chinese market led Google to compromise its principles.

In January 2010, Google announced that the Gmail accounts of Chinese human-rights activists and a number of technology, financial, and defense companies had been hacked. The company threatened to pull out of China unless an agreement on uncensored search results could be reached. Two months later, Google began routing Chinese web searches to their uncensored servers in Hong Kong, a move that was cheered by activists and human-rights groups, but criticized by the Chinese government. In the short term, Google's shareholders suffered.

During the first quarter of 2010, Google's share price declined by 8.5 percent, compared to an increase of 45.2 percent for Google's main rival in China, Baidu.com.

Google's founders seemed to anticipate the current situation in the firm's "Owner's Manual." According to the firm, "If opportunities arise that might cause us to sacrifice short-term results but are in the best long-term interest of our shareholders, we will take those opportunities. We have the fortitude to do this. We would request that our shareholders take the long-term view." It remains to be seen whether Google's short-term sacrifice will benefit shareholders in the long run.

▶ *Is the goal of maximization of shareholder wealth necessarily ethical or unethical?*

▶ *How can Google justify its actions in the short run to its long-run investors?*

*Source: 2004 Founders' IPO Letter, **http://investor.google.com/corporate/2004/ipo-founders-letter.html***

1–9 What is *risk?* Why must risk as well as return be considered by the financial manager who is evaluating a decision alternative or action?

1–10 Describe the role of corporate ethics policies and guidelines, and discuss the relationship that is believed to exist between ethics and share price.

LG 4 LG 5   **1.3** Managerial Finance Function

People in all areas of responsibility within the firm must interact with finance personnel and procedures to get their jobs done. For financial personnel to make useful forecasts and decisions, they must be willing and able to talk to individuals in other areas of the firm. For example, when considering a new product, the financial manager needs to obtain sales forecasts, pricing guidelines, and advertising and promotion budget estimates from marketing personnel. The managerial finance function can be broadly described by considering its role within the organization, its relationship to economics and accounting, and the primary activities of the financial manager.

ORGANIZATION OF THE FINANCE FUNCTION

The size and importance of the managerial finance function depend on the size of the firm. In small firms, the finance function is generally performed by the accounting department. As a firm grows, the finance function typically evolves into a separate department linked directly to the company president or CEO through the chief financial officer (CFO). The lower portion of the organizational chart in Figure 1.1 on page 8 shows the structure of the finance function in a typical medium- to large-size firm.

Reporting to the CFO are the treasurer and the controller. The **treasurer** (the chief financial manager) typically manages the firm's cash, investing surplus funds when available and securing outside financing when needed. The treasurer also oversees a firm's pension plans and manages critical risks related to movements in foreign currency values, interest rates, and commodity prices. The **controller** (the chief accountant) typically handles the accounting activities, such as corporate accounting, tax management, financial accounting, and cost accounting. The treasurer's focus tends to be more external, whereas the controller's focus is more internal.

If international sales or purchases are important to a firm, it may well employ one or more finance professionals whose job is to monitor and manage the firm's exposure to loss from currency fluctuations. A trained financial manager can "hedge," or protect against such a loss, at a reasonable cost by using a variety of financial instruments. These **foreign exchange managers** typically report to the firm's treasurer.

RELATIONSHIP TO ECONOMICS

The field of finance is closely related to economics. Financial managers must understand the economic framework and be alert to the consequences of varying levels of economic activity and changes in economic policy. They must also be able to use economic theories as guidelines for efficient business operation. Examples include supply-and-demand analysis, profit-maximizing strategies, and price theory. The primary economic principle used in managerial finance is **marginal cost–benefit analysis,** the principle that financial decisions should be made and actions taken only when the added benefits exceed the added costs. Nearly all financial decisions ultimately come down to an assessment of their marginal benefits and marginal costs.

treasurer
The firm's chief financial manager, who manages the firm's cash, oversees its pension plans, and manages key risks.

controller
The firm's chief accountant, who is responsible for the firm's accounting activities, such as corporate accounting, tax management, financial accounting, and cost accounting.

foreign exchange manager
The manager responsible for managing and monitoring the firm's exposure to loss from currency fluctuations.

marginal cost–benefit analysis
Economic principle that states that financial decisions should be made and actions taken only when the added benefits exceed the added costs.

Example 1.2 ▶ Jamie Teng is a financial manager for Nord Department Stores, a large chain of upscale department stores operating primarily in the western United States. She is currently trying to decide whether to replace one of the firm's computer servers with a new, more sophisticated one that would both speed processing and handle a larger volume of transactions. The new computer would require a cash outlay of $8,000, and the old computer could be sold to net $2,000. The total benefits from the new server (measured in today's dollars) would be $10,000. The benefits over a similar time period from the old computer (measured in today's dollars) would be $3,000. Applying marginal cost–benefit analysis, Jamie organizes the data as follows:

Benefits with new computer	$10,000
Less: Benefits with old computer	3,000
(1) Marginal (added) benefits	$ 7,000
Cost of new computer	$ 8,000
Less: Proceeds from sale of old computer	2,000
(2) Marginal (added) costs	$ 6,000
Net benefit [(1) − (2)]	$ 1,000

Because the marginal (added) benefits of $7,000 exceed the marginal (added) costs of $6,000, Jamie recommends that the firm purchase the new computer to replace the old one. The firm will experience a net benefit of $1,000 as a result of this action.

RELATIONSHIP TO ACCOUNTING

The firm's finance and accounting activities are closely related and generally overlap. In small firms accountants often carry out the finance function, and in large firms financial analysts often help compile accounting information. However, there are two basic differences between finance and accounting; one is related to the emphasis on cash flows and the other to decision making.

Emphasis on Cash Flows

The accountant's primary function is to develop and report data for measuring the performance of the firm, assess its financial position, comply with and file reports required by securities regulators, and file and pay taxes. Using generally accepted accounting principles, the accountant prepares financial statements that recognize revenue at the time of sale (whether payment has been received or not) and recognize expenses when they are incurred. This approach is referred to as the **accrual basis.**

The financial manager, on the other hand, places primary emphasis on *cash flows,* the intake and outgo of cash. He or she maintains the firm's solvency by planning the cash flows necessary to satisfy its obligations and to acquire assets needed to achieve the firm's goals. The financial manager uses this **cash basis** to recognize the revenues and expenses only with respect to actual inflows and outflows of cash. Whether a firm earns a profit or experiences a loss, *it must have a sufficient flow of cash to meet its obligations as they come due.*

accrual basis
In preparation of financial statements, recognizes revenue at the time of sale and recognizes expenses when they are incurred.

cash basis
Recognizes revenues and expenses only with respect to actual inflows and outflows of cash.

Example 1.3 ▶ Nassau Corporation, a small yacht dealer, sold one yacht for $100,000 in the calendar year just ended. Nassau originally purchased the yacht for $80,000. Although the firm paid in full for the yacht during the year, at year-end it has yet to collect the $100,000 from the customer. The accounting view and the financial view of the firm's performance during the year are given by the following income and cash flow statements, respectively.

Accounting view (accrual basis)		Financial view (cash basis)	
Nassau Corporation income statement for the year ended 12/31		**Nassau Corporation cash flow statement for the year ended 12/31**	
Sales revenue	$100,000	Cash inflow	$ 0
Less: Costs	80,000	Less: Cash outflow	80,000
Net profit	$ 20,000	Net cash flow	($80,000)

In an accounting sense, Nassau Corporation is profitable, but in terms of actual cash flow it is a financial failure. Its lack of cash flow resulted from the uncollected accounts receivable of $100,000. Without adequate cash inflows to meet its obligations, the firm will not survive, regardless of its level of profits.

As the example shows, accrual accounting data do not fully describe the circumstances of a firm. Thus the financial manager must look beyond financial statements to obtain insight into existing or developing problems. Of course, accountants are well aware of the importance of cash flows, and financial managers use and understand accrual-based financial statements. Nevertheless, the financial manager, by concentrating on cash flows, should be able to avoid insolvency and achieve the firm's financial goals.

Personal Finance Example 1.4 ▶ Individuals do not use accrual concepts. Rather, they rely solely on cash flows to measure their financial outcomes. Generally, individuals plan, monitor, and assess their financial activities using cash flows over a given period, typically a month or a year. Ann Bach projects her cash flows during October 2012 as follows:

	Amount	
Item	**Inflow**	**Outflow**
Net pay received	$4,400	
Rent		$1,200
Car payment		450
Utilities		300
Groceries		800
Clothes		750
Dining out		650
Gasoline		260
Interest income	220	
Misc. expense		425
Totals	$4,620	$4,835

Ann subtracts her total outflows of $4,835 from her total inflows of $4,620 and finds that her *net cash flow* for October will be –$215. To cover the $215 shortfall, Ann will have to either borrow $215 (putting it on a credit card is a form of borrowing) or withdraw $215 from her savings. Or she may decide to reduce her outflows in areas of discretionary spending—for example, clothing purchases, dining out, or areas that make up the $425 of miscellaneous expense.

Decision Making

The second major difference between finance and accounting has to do with decision making. Accountants devote most of their attention to the *collection and presentation of financial data*. Financial managers evaluate the accounting statements, develop additional data, and *make decisions* on the basis of their assessment of the associated returns and risks. Of course, this does not mean that accountants never make decisions or that financial managers never gather data but rather that the primary focuses of accounting and finance are distinctly different.

PRIMARY ACTIVITIES OF THE FINANCIAL MANAGER

In addition to ongoing involvement in financial analysis and planning, the financial manager's primary activities are making investment and financing decisions. Investment decisions determine what types of assets the firm holds. Financing decisions determine how the firm raises money to pay for the assets in which it invests. One way to visualize the difference between a firm's investment and financing decisions is to refer to the balance sheet shown in Figure 1.3. Investment decisions generally refer to the items that appear on the left-hand side of the balance sheet, and financing decisions relate to the items on the right-hand side. Keep in mind, though, that financial managers make these decisions based on their impact on the value of the firm, not on the accounting principles used to construct a balance sheet.

→ REVIEW QUESTIONS

1–11 In what financial activities does a corporate treasurer engage?

1–12 What is the primary economic principle used in managerial finance?

1–13 What are the major differences between accounting and finance with respect to emphasis on cash flows and decision making?

1–14 What are the two primary activities of the financial manager that are related to the firm's balance sheet?

FIGURE 1.3

Financial Activities
Primary activities of the financial manager

Making Investment Decisions

Balance Sheet

| Current Assets | Current Liabilities |
| Fixed Assets | Long-Term Funds |

Making Financing Decisions

LG 6 | 1.4 Governance and Agency

As noted earlier, the majority of owners of a corporation are normally distinct from its managers. Nevertheless, managers are entrusted to only take actions or make decisions that are in the best interests of the firm's owners, its shareholders. In most cases, if managers fail to act on the behalf of the shareholders, they will also fail to achieve the goal of maximizing shareholder wealth. To help ensure that managers act in ways that are consistent with the interests of shareholders and mindful of obligations to other stakeholders, firms aim to establish sound corporate governance practices.

CORPORATE GOVERNANCE

corporate governance
The rules, processes, and laws by which companies are operated, controlled, and regulated.

Corporate governance refers to the rules, processes, and laws by which companies are operated, controlled, and regulated. It defines the rights and responsibilities of the corporate participants such as the shareholders, board of directors, officers and managers, and other stakeholders, as well as the rules and procedures for making corporate decisions. A well-defined corporate governance structure is intended to benefit all corporate stakeholders by ensuring that the firm is run in a lawful and ethical fashion, in accordance with best practices, and subject to all corporate regulations.

A firm's corporate governance is influenced by both internal factors such as the shareholders, board of directors, and officers as well as external forces such as clients, creditors, suppliers, competitors, and government regulations. The corporate organization, depicted in Figure 1.1 on page 8, helps to shape a firm's corporate governance structure. In particular, the stockholders elect a board of directors, who in turn hire officers or managers to operate the firm in a manner consistent with the goals, plans, and policies established and monitored by the board on behalf of the shareholders.

Individual versus Institutional Investors

individual investors
Investors who own relatively small quantities of shares so as to meet personal investment goals.

To better understand the role that shareholders play in shaping a firm's corporate governance, it is helpful to differentiate between the two broad classes of owners—individuals and institutions. Generally, **individual investors** own relatively small quantities of shares and as a result do not typically have sufficient means to directly influence a firm's corporate governance. In order to influence the firm, individual investors often find it necessary to act as a group by voting collectively on corporate matters. The most important corporate matter individual investors vote on is the election of the firm's board of directors. The corporate board's first responsibility is to the shareholders. The board not only sets policies that specify ethical practices and provide for the protection of stakeholder interests, but it also monitors managerial decision making on behalf of investors.

institutional investors
Investment professionals, such as banks, insurance companies, mutual funds, and pension funds, that are paid to manage and hold large quantities of securities on behalf of others.

Although they also benefit from the presence of the board of directors, institutional investors have advantages over individual investors when it comes to influencing the corporate governance of a firm. **Institutional investors** are investment professionals that are paid to manage and hold large quantities of securities on behalf of individuals, businesses, and governments. Institutional investors include banks, insurance companies, mutual funds, and pension funds. Unlike individual investors, institutional investors often monitor and directly influence a firm's corporate governance by exerting pressure on management to perform or communicating their concerns to the firm's board. These large investors can also threaten to exercise their voting rights or liquidate their holdings if the board does not respond positively to their concerns. Because individual and institutional investors share the same goal, individual investors benefit from the shareholder activism of institutional investors.

Government Regulation

Unlike the impact that clients, creditors, suppliers, or competitors can have on a particular firm's corporate governance, government regulation generally shapes the corporate governance of all firms. During the past decade, corporate governance has received increased attention due to several high-profile corporate scandals involving abuse of corporate power and, in some cases, alleged criminal activity by corporate officers. The misdeeds derived from two main types of issues: (1) false disclosures in financial reporting and other material information releases and (2) undisclosed conflicts of interest between corporations and their analysts, auditors, and attorneys and between corporate directors, officers, and shareholders. Asserting that an integral part of an effective corporate governance regime is provisions for civil or criminal prosecution of individuals who conduct unethical or illegal acts in the name of the firm, in July 2002 the U.S. Congress passed the **Sarbanes-Oxley Act of 2002** (commonly called **SOX**).

Sarbanes-Oxley is intended to eliminate many of the disclosure and conflict of interest problems that can arise when corporate managers are not held personally accountable for their firm's financial decisions and disclosures. SOX accomplished the following: established an oversight board to monitor the accounting industry; tightened audit regulations and controls; toughened penalties against executives who commit corporate fraud; strengthened accounting disclosure requirements and ethical guidelines for corporate officers; established corporate board structure and membership guidelines; established guidelines with regard to analyst conflicts of interest; mandated instant disclosure of stock sales by corporate executives; and increased securities regulation authority and budgets for auditors and investigators.

Sarbanes-Oxley Act of 2002 (SOX)
An act aimed at eliminating corporate disclosure and conflict of interest problems. Contains provisions about corporate financial disclosures and the relationships among corporations, analysts, auditors, attorneys, directors, officers, and shareholders.

THE AGENCY ISSUE

We know that the duty of the financial manager is to maximize the wealth of the firm's owners. Shareholders give managers decision-making authority over the firm; thus managers can be viewed as the *agents* of the firm's shareholders. Technically, any manager who owns less than 100 percent of the firm is an agent acting on behalf of other owners. This separation of owners and managers is shown by the dashed horizontal line in Figure 1.1 on page 8, and it is representative of the classic **principal–agent relationship,** where the shareholders are the principals. In general, a contract is used to specify the terms of a principal–agent relationship. This arrangement works well when the agent makes decisions that are in the principal's best interest but doesn't work well when the interests of the principal and agent differ.

principal–agent relationship
An arrangement in which an agent acts on the behalf of a principal. For example, shareholders of a company (principals) elect management (agents) to act on their behalf.

In theory, most financial managers would agree with the goal of shareholder wealth maximization. In reality, however, managers are also concerned with their personal wealth, job security, and fringe benefits. Such concerns may cause managers to make decisions that are not consistent with shareholder wealth maximization. For example, financial managers may be reluctant or unwilling to take more than moderate risk if they perceive that taking too much risk might jeopardize their job or reduce their personal wealth.

In more depth

To read about *Agency Problems*, go to www.myfinancelab.com

agency problems
Problems that arise when managers place personal goals ahead of the goals of shareholders.

agency costs
Costs arising from agency problems that are borne by shareholders and represent a loss of shareholder wealth.

incentive plans
Management compensation plans that tie management compensation to share price; one example involves the granting of *stock options*.

stock options
Options extended by the firm that allow management to benefit from increases in stock prices over time.

performance plans
Plans that tie management compensation to measures such as EPS or growth in EPS. *Performance shares* and/or *cash bonuses* are used as compensation under these plans.

performance shares
Shares of stock given to management for meeting stated performance goals.

cash bonuses
Cash paid to management for achieving certain performance goals.

The Agency Problem

An important theme of corporate governance is to ensure the accountability of managers in an organization through mechanisms that try to reduce or eliminate the principal–agent problem; however, when these mechanisms fail agency problems arise. **Agency problems** arise when managers deviate from the goal of maximization of shareholder wealth by placing their personal goals ahead of the goals of shareholders. These problems in turn give rise to agency costs. **Agency costs** are costs borne by shareholders due to the presence or avoidance of agency problems, and in either case represent a loss of shareholder wealth. For example, shareholders incur agency costs when managers fail to make the best investment decision or when managers have to be monitored to ensure that the best investment decision is made, because either situation is likely to result in a lower stock price.

Management Compensation Plans

In addition to the roles played by corporate boards, institutional investors, and government regulations, corporate governance can be strengthened by ensuring that managers' interests are aligned with those of shareholders. A common approach is to *structure management compensation* to correspond with firm performance. In addition to combating agency problems, the resulting performance-based compensation packages allow firms to compete for and hire the best managers available. The two key types of managerial compensation plans are incentive plans and performance plans.

Incentive plans tie management compensation to share price. One incentive plan grants **stock options** to management. If the firm's stock price rises over time, managers will be rewarded by being able to purchase stock at the market price in effect at the time of the grant and then to resell the shares at the prevailing higher market price.

Many firms also offer **performance plans** that tie management compensation to performance measures such as earnings per share (EPS) or growth in EPS. Compensation under these plans is often in the form of performance shares or cash bonuses. **Performance shares** are shares of stock given to management as a result of meeting the stated performance goals, whereas **cash bonuses** are cash payments tied to the achievement of certain performance goals.

The execution of many compensation plans has been closely scrutinized in light of the past decade's corporate scandals and financial woes. Both individual and institutional stockholders, as well as the Securities and Exchange Commission (SEC) and other government entities, continue to publicly question the appropriateness of the multimillion-dollar compensation packages that many corporate executives receive. The total compensation in 2009 for the chief executive officers of the 500 biggest U.S. companies is considerable. For example, the three highest-paid CEOs in 2009 were (1) H. Lawrence Culp Jr. of Danaher Corp., who earned $141.36 million; (2) Lawrence J. Ellison of Oracle Corp., who earned $130.23 million; and (3) Aubrey K. McClendon of Chesapeake Energy Corp., who earned

Matter of fact

Forbes.com CEO Performance versus Pay

A quick check of the most recent Forbes.com reporting of CEO performance versus pay for the top 500 U.S. companies reveals that the highest-paid CEOs are not necessarily the best-performing CEOs. In fact, the total compensation of the top three performing CEOs is less than 4 percent of the total compensation for the top-paid CEOs, all of whom have performances ranked 82nd or worse.

Forbes.com CEO Performance vs. Pay				
Efficiency ranking	Chief executive officer	Company	Compensation	Compensation rank
1st	Jeffery H. Boyd	Priceline.com	$7.49 mil.	135th
2nd	Jeffrey P. Bezos	Amazon.com	$1.28 mil.	463rd
3rd	Leonard Bell	Alexion Pharmaceuticals	$4.26 mil.	286th
90th	H. Lawrence Culp Jr.	Danaher Corp.	$141.36 mil.	1st
82nd	Lawrence J. Ellison	Oracle Corp.	$130.23 mil.	2nd
163rd	Aubrey K. McClendon	Chesapeake Energy Corp.	$114.29 mil.	3rd

$114.29 million. Tenth on the same list is Jen-Hsun Huang of NVIDIA Corp., who earned $31.40 million.

Most studies have failed to find a strong relationship between the performance that companies achieve and the compensation that CEOs receive. During the past few years, publicity surrounding these large compensation packages (without corresponding performance) has driven down executive compensation. Contributing to this publicity is the SEC requirement that publicly traded companies disclose to shareholders and others the amount of compensation to their CEO, CFO, three other highest-paid executives, and directors; the method used to determine it; and a narrative discussion regarding the underlying compensation policies. At the same time, new compensation plans that better link managers' performance to their compensation are being developed and implemented. As evidence of this trend, consider that the average total compensation for the top three CEOs in 2009 was down slightly more than 69 percent from the average for the top three CEOs in 2006. The average in 2006 was $421.13 million versus an average of $128.63 million in 2009.

The Threat of Takeover

When a firm's internal corporate governance structure is unable to keep agency problems in check, it is likely that rival managers will try to gain control of the firm. Because agency problems represent a misuse of the firm's resources and impose agency costs on the firm's shareholders, the firm's stock is generally depressed, making the firm an attractive takeover target. The *threat of takeover* by another firm that believes it can enhance the troubled firm's value by restructuring its management, operations, and financing can provide a strong source of external corporate governance. The constant threat of a takeover tends to motivate management to act in the best interests of the firm's owners.

Unconstrained, managers may have other goals in addition to share price maximization, but much of the evidence suggests that share price maximization—the focus of this book—is the primary goal of most firms.

→ REVIEW QUESTIONS

1–15 What is *corporate governance?* How has the Sarbanes-Oxley Act of 2002 affected it? Explain.

1–16 Define *agency problems,* and describe how they give rise to *agency costs.* Explain how a firm's *corporate governance structure* can help avoid agency problems.

1–17 How can the firm *structure management compensation* to minimize agency problems? What is the current view with regard to the execution of many compensation plans?

1–18 How do market forces—both shareholder activism and the threat of takeover—act to prevent or minimize the *agency problem?* What role do *institutional investors* play in shareholder activism?

Summary

FOCUS ON VALUE

Chapter 1 established the primary goal of the firm—**to maximize the wealth of the owners for whom the firm is being operated.** For public companies, value at any time is reflected in the stock price. Therefore, management should act only on those opportunities that are expected to create value for owners by increasing the stock price. Doing this requires management to consider the returns (magnitude and timing of cash flows), the risk of each proposed action, and their combined effect on value.

REVIEW OF LEARNING GOALS

LG 1   Define *finance* **and the managerial finance function.** Finance is the science and art of managing money. It affects virtually all aspects of business. Managerial finance is concerned with the duties of the *financial manager* working in a business. Financial managers administer the financial affairs of all types of businesses—private and public, large and small, profit seeking and not for profit. They perform such varied tasks as developing a financial plan or budget, extending credit to customers, evaluating proposed large expenditures, and raising money to fund the firm's operations.

LG 2   **Describe the legal forms of business organization.** The legal forms of business organization are the sole proprietorship, the partnership, and the corporation. The corporation is dominant in terms of business receipts, and its owners are its common and preferred stockholders. Stockholders expect to earn a return by receiving dividends or by realizing gains through increases in share price.

LG 3 Describe the goal of the firm, and explain why maximizing the value of the firm is an appropriate goal for a business. The goal of the firm is to maximize its value and therefore the wealth of its shareholders. Maximizing the value of the firm means running the business in the interest of those who own it—the shareholders. Because shareholders are paid after other stakeholders, it is generally necessary to satisfy the interests of other stakeholders to enrich shareholders.

LG 4 Describe how the managerial finance function is related to economics and accounting. All areas of responsibility within a firm interact with finance personnel and procedures. The financial manager must understand the economic environment and rely heavily on the economic principle of marginal cost–benefit analysis to make financial decisions. Financial managers use accounting but concentrate on cash flows and decision making.

LG 5 Identify the primary activities of the financial manager. The primary activities of the financial manager, in addition to ongoing involvement in financial analysis and planning, are making investment decisions and making financing decisions.

LG 6 Describe the nature of the principal–agent relationship between the owners and managers of a corporation, and explain how various corporate governance mechanisms attempt to manage agency problems. This separation of owners and managers of the typical firm is representative of the classic principal–agent relationship, where the shareholders are the principals and managers are the agents. This arrangement works well when the agent makes decisions that are in the principal's best interest but can lead to agency problems when the interests of the principal and agent differ. A firm's corporate governance structure is intended to help ensure that managers act in the best interests of the firm's shareholders, and other stakeholders, and it is usually influenced by both internal and external factors.

Opener-in-Review

In the chapter opener you read about Facebook and its founder's reluctance to go public. If Zuckerberg is expected to remain the CEO of Facebook after the IPO, why would he be worried about going public?

Self-Test Problem (Solution in Appendix)

LG 4 **ST1–1** **Emphasis on Cash Flows** Worldwide Rugs is a rug importer located in the United States that resells its import products to local retailers. Last year Worldwide Rugs imported $2.5 million worth of rugs from around the world, all of which were paid for prior to shipping. On receipt of the rugs, the importer immediately resold them to local retailers for $3 million. To allow its retail clients time to resell the rugs, Worldwide Rugs sells to retailers on credit. Prior to the end of its business year, Worldwide Rugs collected 85% of its outstanding accounts receivable.

a. What is the accounting profit that Worldwide Rugs generated for the year?

b. Did Worldwide Rugs have a successful year from an accounting perspective?

c. What is the financial cash flow that Worldwide Rugs generated for the year?

d. Did Worldwide Rugs have a successful year from a financial perspective?

e. If the current pattern persists, what is your expectation for the future success of Worldwide Rugs?

Warm-Up Exercises   All problems are available in ⟨myfinancelab⟩.

LG 2   E1–1   Ann and Jack have been partners for several years. Their firm, A & J Tax Preparation, has been very successful, as the pair agree on most business-related questions. One disagreement, however, concerns the legal form of their business. Ann has tried for the past 2 years to get Jack to agree to incorporate. She believes that there is no downside to incorporating and sees only benefits. Jack strongly disagrees; he thinks that the business should remain a partnership forever.

First, take Ann's side, and explain the positive side to incorporating the business. Next, take Jack's side, and state the advantages to remaining a partnership. Lastly, what information would you want if you were asked to make the decision for Ann and Jack?

LG 4   E1–2   The end-of-year parties at Yearling, Inc., are known for their extravagance. Management provides the best food and entertainment to thank the employees for their hard work. During the planning for this year's bash, a disagreement broke out between the treasurer's staff and the controller's staff. The treasurer's staff contended that the firm was running low on cash and might have trouble paying its bills over the coming months; they requested that cuts be made to the budget for the party. The controller's staff felt that any cuts were unwarranted as the firm continued to be very profitable.

Can both sides be right? Explain your answer.

LG 5   E1–3   You have been made treasurer for a day at AIMCO, Inc. AIMCO develops technology for video conferencing. A manager of the satellite division has asked you to authorize a capital expenditure in the amount of $10,000. The manager states that this expenditure is necessary to continue a long-running project designed to use satellites to allow video conferencing anywhere on the planet. The manager admits that the satellite concept has been surpassed by recent technological advances in telephony, but he feels that AIMCO should continue the project. His reasoning is based on the fact that $2.5 million has already been spent over the past 15 years on this project. Although the project has little chance to be viable, the manager believes it would be a shame to waste the money and time already spent.

Use *marginal cost–benefit analysis* to make your decision regarding whether you should authorize the $10,000 expenditure to continue the project.

LG 6 **E1–4** Recently, some branches of Donut Shop, Inc., have dropped the practice of allowing employees to accept tips. Customers who once said, "Keep the change," now have to get used to waiting for their nickels. Management even instituted a policy of requiring that the change be thrown out if a customer drives off without it. As a frequent customer who gets coffee and doughnuts for the office, you notice that the lines are longer and that more mistakes are being made in your order.

Explain why tips could be viewed as similar to stock options and why the delays and incorrect orders could represent a case of *agency costs*. If tips are gone forever, how could Donut Shop reduce these agency costs?

Problems

All problems are available in [myfinancelab].

LG 2 **P1–1** **Liability comparisons** Merideth Harper has invested $25,000 in Southwest Development Company. The firm has recently declared bankruptcy and has $60,000 in unpaid debts. Explain the nature of payments, if any, by Ms. Harper in each of the following situations.
a. Southwest Development Company is a *sole proprietorship* owned by Ms. Harper.
b. Southwest Development Company is a 50–50 *partnership* of Ms. Harper and Christopher Black.
c. Southwest Development Company is a *corporation*.

LG 4 **P1–2** **Accrual income versus cash flow for a period** Thomas Book Sales, Inc., supplies textbooks to college and university bookstores. The books are shipped with a proviso that they must be paid for within 30 days but can be returned for a full refund credit within 90 days. In 2009, Thomas shipped and billed book titles totaling $760,000. Collections, net of return credits, during the year totaled $690,000. The company spent $300,000 acquiring the books that it shipped.
a. Using accrual accounting and the preceding values, show the firm's net profit for the past year.
b. Using cash accounting and the preceding values, show the firm's net cash flow for the past year.
c. Which of these statements is more useful to the financial manager? Why?

Personal Finance Problem

LG 4 **P1–3** **Cash flows** It is typical for Jane to plan, monitor, and assess her financial position using cash flows over a given period, typically a month. Jane has a savings account, and her bank loans money at 6% per year while it offers short-term investment rates of 5%. Jane's cash flows during August were as follows:

Item	Cash inflow	Cash outflow
Clothes		$1,000
Interest received	$ 450	
Dining out		500
Groceries		800
Salary	4,500	
Auto payment		355
Utilities		280
Mortgage		1,200
Gas		222

a. Determine Jane's total cash inflows and cash outflows.

b. Determine the *net cash flow* for the month of August.

c. If there is a shortage, what are a few options open to Jane?

d. If there is a surplus, what would be a prudent strategy for her to follow?

LG 3   **LG 5**   **P1–4**   **Marginal cost–benefit analysis and the goal of the firm**   Ken Allen, capital budgeting analyst for Bally Gears, Inc., has been asked to evaluate a proposal. The manager of the automotive division believes that replacing the robotics used on the heavy truck gear line will produce total benefits of $560,000 (in today's dollars) over the next 5 years. The existing robotics would produce benefits of $400,000 (also in today's dollars) over that same time period. An initial cash investment of $220,000 would be required to install the new equipment. The manager estimates that the existing robotics can be sold for $70,000. Show how Ken will apply *marginal cost–benefit analysis* techniques to determine the following:

a. The marginal (added) benefits of the proposed new robotics.

b. The marginal (added) cost of the proposed new robotics.

c. The net benefit of the proposed new robotics.

d. What should Ken Allen recommend that the company do? Why?

e. What factors besides the costs and benefits should be considered before the final decision is made?

LG 6   **P1–5**   **Identifying agency problems, costs, and resolutions**   Explain why each of the following situations is an agency problem and what costs to the firm might result from it. Suggest how the problem might be dealt with short of firing the individual(s) involved.

a. The front desk receptionist routinely takes an extra 20 minutes of lunch time to run personal errands.

b. Division managers are padding cost estimates so as to show short-term efficiency gains when the costs come in lower than the estimates.

c. The firm's chief executive officer has had secret talks with a competitor about the possibility of a merger in which she would become the CEO of the combined firms.

d. A branch manager lays off experienced full-time employees and staffs customer service positions with part-time or temporary workers to lower employment costs and raise this year's branch profit. The manager's bonus is based on profitability.

LG 3   **P1–6**   **ETHICS PROBLEM**   What does it mean to say that managers should maximize shareholder wealth "subject to ethical constraints"? What ethical considerations might enter into decisions that result in cash flow and stock price effects that are less than they might otherwise have been?

Spreadsheet Exercise

Assume that Monsanto Corporation is considering the renovation and/or replacement of some of its older and outdated carpet-manufacturing equipment. Its objective is to improve the efficiency of operations in terms of both speed and reduction in the number of defects. The company's finance department has compiled pertinent data that will allow it to conduct a *marginal cost–benefit analysis* for the proposed equipment replacement.

The cash outlay for new equipment would be approximately $600,000. The net book value of the old equipment and its potential net selling price add up to $250,000. The total benefits from the new equipment (measured in today's dollars) would be $900,000. The benefits of the old equipment over a similar period of time (measured in today's dollars) would be $300,000.

TO DO

Create a spreadsheet to conduct a *marginal cost–benefit analysis* for Monsanto Corporation, and determine the following:

a. The marginal (added) benefits of the proposed new equipment.
b. The marginal (added) cost of the proposed new equipment.
c. The net benefit of the proposed new equipment.
d. What would you recommend that the firm do? Why?

 Visit www.myfinancelab.com for **Chapter Case: *Assessing the Goal of Sports Products, Inc.,*** Group Exercises, and numerous online resources.

2 The Financial Market Environment

Learning Goals

LG 1 Understand the role that financial institutions play in managerial finance.

LG 2 Contrast the functions of financial institutions and financial markets.

LG 3 Describe the differences between the capital markets and the money markets.

LG 4 Explain the root causes of the 2008 financial crisis and recession.

LG 5 Understand the major regulations and regulatory bodies that affect financial institutions and markets.

LG 6 Discuss business taxes and their importance in financial decisions.

Why This Chapter Matters to You

In your *professional* life

ACCOUNTING You need to understand how business income is taxed and the difference between average and marginal tax rates.

INFORMATION SYSTEMS You need to understand how information flows between the firm and financial markets.

MANAGEMENT You need to understand why healthy financial institutions are an integral part of a healthy economy and how a crisis in the financial sector can spread and affect almost any type of business.

MARKETING You need to understand why it is important for firms to communicate about their operating results with external investors and how regulations constrain the types of communication that occur.

OPERATIONS You need to understand why external financing is, for most firms, an essential aspect of ongoing operations.

In your *personal* life
Making financial transactions will be a regular occurrence throughout your entire life. These transactions may be as simple as depositing your paycheck in a bank or as complex as deciding how to allocate the money you save for retirement among different investment options. Many of these transactions have important tax consequences, which vary over time and from one type of transaction to another. The content in this chapter will help you make better decisions when you engage in any of these transactions.

JPMorgan Chase & Co.

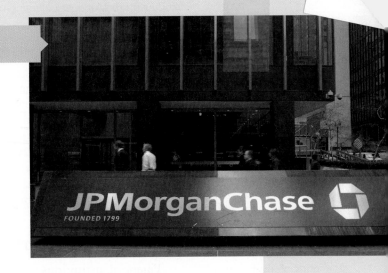

Cut to the Chase

Since the recession of the early 1990s, business had been booming for JPMorgan Chase, one of the leading investment banking firms on Wall Street. After hitting a low of roughly $2 per share in October 1990, Chase stock went on a tear, rising at a rate of about 21 percent per year and hitting the $50 range by April 2007. The bank's investors enjoyed increasing dividend payments along with the rising stock price. JPMorgan Chase increased its dividend payout from $0.0833 per share in December 1990 to $0.38 per share in July 2007, an increase of more than 350 percent.

Trouble was brewing, however. In the summer of 2007, data began to emerge that prices of single-family homes were falling in many U.S. cities and homeowners were starting to default on their mortgages. Rumors swirled that JPMorgan and other banks held large investments in securities tied to residential mortgages. On September 15, 2008, the venerable investment banking firm, Lehman Brothers, filed for bankruptcy, and JPMorgan shares fell 10 percent in a single day. Bad news about the economy and the financial sector continued through the fall, and Chase's stock hit a low point on November 21 near $20, losing more than half its value in roughly 18 months.

All of this prompted JPMorgan management to make two difficult decisions. The first was to accept a $25 billion "investment" (some referred to it as a bailout) from the U.S. Treasury on October 28, 2008. The second was to cut its quarterly dividend by almost 87 percent, from $0.38 to $0.05 per share. These decisions, combined with a slowly improving economy, helped JPMorgan survive the 2008 financial crisis and the subsequent recession. By the summer of 2009, JPMorgan Chase repaid the $25 billion (with interest) that it had received from the government, and the bank's stock had recovered most of the value that it had lost.

LG 1   LG 2   LG 3 **2.1** **Financial Institutions and Markets**

Most successful firms have ongoing needs for funds. They can obtain funds from external sources in three ways. The first source is through a *financial institution* that accepts savings and transfers them to those that need funds. A second source is through *financial markets,* organized forums in which the suppliers and demanders of various types of funds can make transactions. A third source is through *private placement*. Because of the unstructured nature of private placements, here we focus primarily on the role of financial institutions and financial markets in facilitating business financing.

FINANCIAL INSTITUTIONS

financial institution
An intermediary that channels the savings of individuals, businesses, and governments into loans or investments.

Financial institutions serve as intermediaries by channeling the savings of individuals, businesses, and governments into loans or investments. Many financial institutions directly or indirectly pay savers interest on deposited funds; others provide services for a fee (for example, checking accounts for which customers pay service charges). Some financial institutions accept customers' savings deposits and lend this money to other customers or to firms; others invest customers' savings in earning assets such as real estate or stocks and bonds; and some do both. Financial institutions are required by the government to operate within established regulatory guidelines.

Key Customers of Financial Institutions

For financial institutions, the key suppliers of funds and the key demanders of funds are individuals, businesses, and governments. The savings that individual consumers place in financial institutions provide these institutions with a large portion of their funds. Individuals not only supply funds to financial institutions but also demand funds from them in the form of loans. However, individuals as a group are the *net suppliers* for financial institutions: They save more money than they borrow.

Business firms also deposit some of their funds in financial institutions, primarily in checking accounts with various commercial banks. Like individuals, firms borrow funds from these institutions, but firms are *net demanders* of funds: They borrow more money than they save.

Governments maintain deposits of temporarily idle funds, certain tax payments, and Social Security payments in commercial banks. They do not borrow funds *directly* from financial institutions, although by selling their debt securities to various institutions, governments indirectly borrow from them. The government, like business firms, is typically a *net demander* of funds: It typically borrows more than it saves. We've all heard about the federal budget deficit.

Major Financial Institutions

The major financial institutions in the U.S. economy are commercial banks, savings and loans, credit unions, savings banks, insurance companies, mutual funds, and pension funds. These institutions attract funds from individuals, businesses, and governments, combine them, and make loans available to individuals and businesses.

COMMERCIAL BANKS, INVESTMENT BANKS, AND THE SHADOW BANKING SYSTEM

commercial banks
Institutions that provide savers with a secure place to invest their funds and that offer loans to individual and business borrowers.

Commercial banks are among the most important financial institutions in the economy because they provide savers with a secure place to invest funds and they offer both individuals and companies loans to finance investments, such as the purchase of a new home or the expansion of a business. **Investment banks** are institutions that (1) assist companies in raising capital, (2) advise firms on major transactions such as mergers or financial restructurings, and (3) engage in trading and market making activities.

investment banks
Institutions that assist companies in raising capital, advise firms on major transactions such as mergers or financial restructurings, and engage in trading and market making activities.

The traditional business model of a commercial bank—taking in and paying interest on deposits and investing or lending those funds back out at higher interest rates—works to the extent that depositors believe that their investments are secure. Since the 1930s, the U.S. government has given some assurance to depositors that their money is safe by providing deposit insurance (currently up to $250,000 per depositor). Deposit insurance was put in place in response to the banking runs or panics that were part of the Great Depression. The same act of Congress that introduced deposit insurance, the **Glass-Steagall Act,** also created a separation between commercial banks and investment banks, meaning that an institution engaged in taking in deposits could not also engage in the somewhat riskier activities of securities underwriting and trading.

Glass-Steagall Act
An act of Congress in 1933 that created the federal deposit insurance program and separated the activities of commercial and investment banks.

Commercial and investment banks remained essentially separate for more than 50 years, but in the late 1990s Glass-Steagall was repealed. Companies that had formerly engaged only in the traditional activities of a commercial bank began competing with investment banks for underwriting and other services. In addition, the 1990s witnessed tremendous growth in what has come to be known as the shadow banking system. The **shadow banking system** describes a group of institutions that engage in lending activities, much like traditional banks, but these institutions do not accept deposits and are therefore not subject to the same regulations as traditional banks.[1] For example, an institution such as a pension fund might have excess cash to invest, and a large corporation might need short-term financing to cover seasonal cash flow needs. A business like Lehman Brothers acted as an intermediary between these two parties, helping to facilitate a loan, and thereby became part of the shadow banking system. In March 2010, Treasury Secretary Timothy Geithner noted that at its peak the shadow banking system financed roughly $8 trillion in assets and was roughly as large as the traditional banking system.

shadow banking system
A group of institutions that engage in lending activities, much like traditional banks, but do not accept deposits and therefore are not subject to the same regulations as traditional banks.

Matter of fact

Consolidation in the U.S. Banking Industry

The U.S. banking industry has been going through a long period of consolidation. According to the FDIC, the number of commercial banks in the United States declined from 11,463 in 1992 to 8,012 at the end of 2009, a decline of 30 percent. The decline is concentrated among small community banks, which larger institutions have been acquiring at a rapid pace.

---

1. The Dodd-Frank Wall Street Reform and Consumer Protection Act was passed in 2010 in response to the financial crisis and recession of 2008–2009. This legislation will likely have a dramatic impact on the regulation of both traditional and shadow banking institutions, but it is too early to tell exactly what the new law's effects will be. In the wake of the law's passage, many commentators suggested that the law did not exercise enough oversight of the shadow banking system to prevent a financial meltdown similar to the one that motivated the law's enactment.

FINANCIAL MARKETS

financial markets
Forums in which suppliers of funds and demanders of funds can transact business directly.

Financial markets are forums in which suppliers of funds and demanders of funds can transact business directly. Whereas the loans made by financial institutions are granted without the direct knowledge of the suppliers of funds (savers), suppliers in the financial markets know where their funds are being lent or invested. The two key financial markets are the money market and the capital market. Transactions in short-term debt instruments, or marketable securities, take place in the *money market*. Long-term securities—bonds and stocks—are traded in the *capital market*.

private placement
The sale of a new security directly to an investor or group of investors.

To raise money, firms can use either private placements or public offerings. A **private placement** involves the sale of a new security directly to an investor or group of investors, such as an insurance company or pension fund. Most firms, however, raise money through a **public offering** of securities, which is the sale of either bonds or stocks to the general public.

public offering
The sale of either bonds or stocks to the general public.

When a company or government entity sells stocks or bonds to investors and receives cash in return, it is said to have sold securities in the **primary market**. After the primary market transaction occurs, any further trading in the security does not involve the issuer directly, and the issuer receives no additional money from these subsequent transactions. Once the securities begin to trade between investors, they become part of the **secondary market**. On large stock exchanges, billions of shares may trade between buyers and sellers on a single day, and these are all secondary market transactions. Money flows from the investors buying stocks to the investors selling them, and the company whose stock is being traded is largely unaffected by the transactions. The primary market is the one in which "new" securities are sold. The secondary market can be viewed as a "preowned" securities market.

primary market
Financial market in which securities are initially issued; the only market in which the issuer is directly involved in the transaction.

secondary market
Financial market in which preowned securities (those that are not new issues) are traded.

THE RELATIONSHIP BETWEEN INSTITUTIONS AND MARKETS

Financial institutions actively participate in the financial markets as both suppliers and demanders of funds. Figure 2.1 depicts the general flow of funds through and between financial institutions and financial markets as well as the

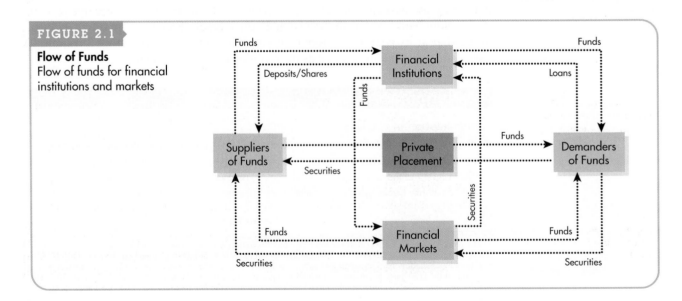

FIGURE 2.1

Flow of Funds
Flow of funds for financial institutions and markets

mechanics of private placement transactions. Domestic or foreign individuals, businesses, and governments may supply and demand funds. We next briefly discuss the money market, including its international equivalent—the *Eurocurrency market.* We then end this section with a discussion of the capital market, which is of key importance to the firm.

THE MONEY MARKET

money market
A financial relationship created between suppliers and demanders of *short-term funds.*

The **money market** is created by a financial relationship between suppliers and demanders of *short-term funds* (funds with maturities of one year or less). The money market exists because some individuals, businesses, governments, and financial institutions have temporarily idle funds that they wish to invest in a relatively safe, interest-bearing asset. At the same time, other individuals, businesses, governments, and financial institutions find themselves in need of seasonal or temporary financing. The money market brings together these suppliers and demanders of short-term funds.

marketable securities
Short-term debt instruments, such as U.S. Treasury bills, commercial paper, and negotiable certificates of deposit issued by government, business, and financial institutions, respectively.

Most money market transactions are made in **marketable securities**—short-term debt instruments, such as U.S. Treasury bills, commercial paper, and negotiable certificates of deposit issued by government, business, and financial institutions, respectively. Investors generally consider marketable securities to be among the least risky investments available. Marketable securities are described in Chapter 15.

Eurocurrency market
International equivalent of the domestic money market.

The international equivalent of the domestic money market is called the **Eurocurrency market.** This is a market for short-term bank deposits denominated in U.S. dollars or other major currencies. Eurocurrency deposits arise when a corporation or individual makes a bank deposit in a currency other than the local currency of the country where the bank is located. If, for example, a multinational corporation were to deposit U.S. dollars in a London bank, this would create a Eurodollar deposit (a dollar deposit at a bank in Europe). Nearly all Eurodollar deposits are *time deposits.* This means that the bank would promise to repay the deposit, with interest, at a fixed date in the future—say, in 6 months. During the interim, the bank is free to lend this dollar deposit to creditworthy corporate or government borrowers. If the bank cannot find a borrower on its own, it may lend the deposit to another international bank.

THE CAPITAL MARKET

capital market
A market that enables suppliers and demanders of *long-term funds* to make transactions.

The **capital market** is a market that enables suppliers and demanders of *long-term funds* to make transactions. Included are securities issues of business and government. The backbone of the capital market is formed by the broker and dealer markets that provide a forum for bond and stock transactions. International capital markets also exist.

Key Securities Traded: Bonds and Stocks

The key capital market securities are *bonds* (long-term debt) and both *common stock* and *preferred stock* (equity, or ownership).

bond
Long-term debt instrument used by business and government to raise large sums of money, generally from a diverse group of lenders.

Bonds are long-term debt instruments used by business and government to raise large sums of money, generally from a diverse group of lenders. *Corporate bonds* typically pay interest *semiannually* (every 6 months) at a stated *coupon interest rate.* They have an initial *maturity* of from 10 to 30 years, and a *par,* or *face, value* of $1,000 that must be repaid at maturity. Bonds are described in detail in Chapter 7.

Example 2.1 ▶

Lakeview Industries, a major microprocessor manufacturer, has issued a 9% coupon interest rate, 20-year bond with a $1,000 par value that pays interest semiannually. Investors who buy this bond receive the contractual right to $90 annual interest (9% coupon interest rate × $1,000 par value) distributed as $45 at the end of each 6 months (1/2 × $90) for 20 years, plus the $1,000 par value at the end of year 20.

As noted earlier, shares of *common stock* are units of ownership, or equity, in a corporation. Common stockholders earn a return by receiving dividends—periodic distributions of cash—or by realizing increases in share price. **Preferred stock** is a special form of ownership that has features of both a bond and common stock. Preferred stockholders are promised a fixed periodic dividend that must be paid prior to payment of any dividends to common stockholders. In other words, preferred stock has "preference" over common stock. Preferred stock and common stock are described in detail in Chapter 8. See the *Focus on Practice* box for the story of one legendary stock price and the equally legendary man who brought it about.

Broker Markets and Dealer Markets

By far the vast majority of trades made by individual investors take place in the secondary market. When you look at the secondary market *on the basis of how securities are traded,* you will find you can essentially divide the market into two segments: broker markets and dealer markets.

The key difference between broker and dealer markets is a technical point dealing with the way trades are executed. That is, when a trade occurs in a **broker market,** the two sides to the transaction, the buyer and the seller, are brought together and the trade takes place at that point: Party A sells his or her securities directly to the buyer, Party B. In a sense, with the help of a *broker,* the securities effectively change hands on the floor of the exchange. The broker market consists of national and regional **securities exchanges,** which are organizations that provide a marketplace in which firms can raise funds through the sale of new securities and purchasers can resell securities.

In contrast, when trades are made in a **dealer market,** the buyer and the seller are never brought together directly. Instead, **market makers** execute the buy/sell orders. Market makers are *securities dealers* who "make markets" by offering to buy or sell certain securities at stated prices. Essentially, two separate trades are made: Party A sells his or her securities (in, say, Dell) to a dealer, and Party B buys his or her securities (in Dell) from another, or possibly even the same, dealer. Thus, there is always a dealer (*market maker*) on one side of a dealer–market transaction. The dealer market is made up of both the **Nasdaq market,** an all-electronic trading platform used to execute securities trades, and the **over-the-counter (OTC) market,** where smaller, unlisted securities are traded.

Broker Markets   If you are like most people, when you think of the "stock market" the first name to come to mind is the New York Stock Exchange, known currently as the NYSE Euronext after a series of mergers that expanded the

---

preferred stock
A special form of ownership having a fixed periodic dividend that must be paid prior to payment of any dividends to common stockholders.

broker market
The securities exchanges on which the two sides of a transaction, the buyer and seller, are brought together to trade securities.

securities exchanges
Organizations that provide the marketplace in which firms can raise funds through the sale of new securities and purchasers can resell securities.

dealer market
The market in which the buyer and seller are not brought together directly but instead have their orders executed by securities dealers that "make markets" in the given security.

market makers
Securities dealers who "make markets" by offering to buy or sell certain securities at stated prices.

Nasdaq market
An all-electronic trading platform used to execute securities trades.

over-the-counter (OTC) market
Market where smaller, unlisted securities are traded.

focus on PRACTICE

Berkshire Hathaway—Can Buffett Be Replaced?

in practice In early 1980, investors could buy one share of Berkshire Hathaway Class A common stock (stock symbol: BRKA) for $285. That may have seemed expensive at the time, but by September 2010 the price of just one share had climbed to $125,000. The wizard behind such phenomenal growth in shareholder value is the chairman of Berkshire Hathaway, Warren Buffett, nicknamed the Oracle of Omaha.

With his partner, Vice-Chairman Charlie Munger, Buffett runs a large conglomerate of dozens of subsidiaries with 222,000 employees and more than $112 billion in annual revenues. He makes it look easy. In his words, "I've taken the easy route, just sitting back and working through great managers who run their own shows. My only tasks are to cheer them on, sculpt and harden our corporate culture, and make major capital-allocation decisions. Our managers have returned this trust by working hard and effectively."[a]

Buffett's style of corporate leadership seems rather laid back, but behind that "aw-shucks" manner is one of the best analytical minds in business. He believes in aligning managerial incentives with performance. Berkshire employs many different incentive arrangements, with their terms depending on such elements as the economic potential or capital intensity of a CEO's business. Whatever the compensation arrangement, Buffett tries to keep it both simple and fair. Buffett himself receives an annual salary of $100,000—not much in this age of supersized CEO compensation packages. Listed for many years among the world's wealthiest people, Buffett has donated most of his Berkshire stock to the Bill and Melinda Gates Foundation.

Berkshire's annual report is a must-read for many investors due to the popularity of Buffett's annual letter to shareholders with his homespun take on such topics as investing, corporate governance, and corporate leadership.

Shareholder meetings in Omaha, Nebraska, have turned into cultlike gatherings, with thousands traveling to listen to Buffett answer questions from shareholders. One question that has been firmly answered is the question of Mr. Buffett's ability to create shareholder value.

The next question that needs to be answered is whether Berkshire Hathaway can successfully replace Buffett (age 80) and Munger (age 86). In October 2010, Berkshire hired hedge fund manager Todd Combs to handle a significant portion of the firm's investments. Berkshire shareholders hope that Buffett's special wisdom applies as well to identifying new managerial talent as it does to making strategic investment decisions.

▶ *The share price of BRKA has never been split. Why might the company refuse to split its shares to make them more affordable to average investors?*

[a]Berkshire Hathaway, Inc., "Letter to Shareholders of Berkshire Hathaway, Inc.," *2006 Annual Report*, p. 4.

exchange's global reach. In point of fact, the NYSE Euronext is the dominant broker market. The American Stock Exchange (AMEX), which is another *national exchange,* and several so-called *regional exchanges* are also broker markets. These exchanges account for about 60 percent of *the total dollar volume* of all shares traded in the U.S. stock market. In broker markets all the trading takes place on centralized trading floors.

Most exchanges are modeled after the New York Stock Exchange. For a firm's securities to be listed for trading on a stock exchange, a firm must file an application for listing and meet a number of requirements. For example, to be eligible for listing on the NYSE, a firm must have at least 400 stockholders owning 100 or more shares; a minimum of 1.1 million shares of publicly held stock outstanding; pretax earnings of at least $10 million over the previous 3 years, with at least $2 million in the previous 2 years; and a minimum market value of public shares of $100 million. Clearly, only large, widely held firms are candidates for NYSE listing.

Once placed, an order to buy or sell on the NYSE can be executed in minutes, thanks to sophisticated telecommunication devices. New Internet-based brokerage systems enable investors to place their buy and sell orders electronically.

Information on publicly traded securities is reported in various media, both print, such as the *Wall Street Journal,* and electronic, such as MSN Money (www.moneycentral.msn.com).

Dealer Markets   One of the key features of the *dealer market* is that it has no centralized trading floors. Instead, it is made up of a large number of *market makers* who are linked together via a mass-telecommunications network.

Each market maker is actually a securities dealer who makes a market in one or more securities by offering to buy or sell them at stated bid/ask prices. The **bid price** and **ask price** represent, respectively, the highest price offered to purchase a given security and the lowest price at which the security is offered for sale. In effect, an investor pays the ask price when buying securities and receives the bid price when selling them.

As described earlier, the dealer market is made up of both the *Nasdaq market* and the *over-the-counter (OTC) market,* which together account for about 40 percent of all shares traded in the U.S. market—with the Nasdaq accounting for the overwhelming majority of those trades. (As an aside, the *primary market* is also a dealer market because all new issues are sold to the investing public by securities dealers, acting on behalf of the investment banker.)

The largest dealer market consists of a select group of stocks that are listed and traded on the *National Association of Securities Dealers Automated Quotation System,* typically referred to as *Nasdaq.* Founded in 1971, Nasdaq had its origins in the OTC market but is today considered *a totally separate entity that's no longer a part of the OTC market.* In fact, in 2006 Nasdaq was formally recognized by the SEC as a "listed exchange," essentially giving it the same stature and prestige as the NYSE.

International Capital Markets

Although U.S. capital markets are by far the world's largest, there are important debt and equity markets outside the United States. In the **Eurobond market,** corporations and governments typically issue bonds denominated in dollars and sell them to investors located outside the United States. A U.S. corporation might, for example, issue dollar-denominated bonds that would be purchased by investors in Belgium, Germany, or Switzerland. Through the Eurobond market, issuing firms and governments can tap a much larger pool of investors than would be generally available in the local market.

bid price
The highest price offered to purchase a security.

ask price
The lowest price at which a security is offered for sale.

Eurobond market
The market in which corporations and governments typically issue bonds denominated in dollars and sell them to investors located outside the United States.

Matter of fact

NYSE Euronext is the World's Largest Stock Exchange

According to the World Federation of Exchanges, the largest stock market in the world, as measured by the total market value of securities listed on that market, is the NYSE Euronext, with listed securities worth more than $11.8 trillion in the United States and $2.9 trillion in Europe. Next largest is the London Stock Exchange, with securities valued at £1.7 trillion, which is equivalent to $2.8 trillion given the exchange rate between pounds and dollars prevailing at the end of 2009.

foreign bond
A bond that is issued by a foreign corporation or government and is denominated in the investor's home currency and sold in the investor's home market.

international equity market
A market that allows corporations to sell blocks of shares to investors in a number of different countries simultaneously.

efficient market
A market that allocates funds to their most productive uses as a result of competition among wealth-maximizing investors and that determines and publicizes prices that are believed to be close to their true value.

The *foreign bond market* is an international market for long-term debt securities. A **foreign bond** is a bond issued by a foreign corporation or government that is denominated in the investor's home currency and sold in the investor's home market. A bond issued by a U.S. company that is denominated in Swiss francs and sold in Switzerland is a foreign bond. Although the foreign bond market is smaller than the Eurobond market, many issuers have found it to be an attractive way of tapping debt markets around the world.

Finally, the **international equity market** allows corporations to sell blocks of shares to investors in a number of different countries simultaneously. This market enables corporations to raise far larger amounts of capital than they could in any single market. International equity sales have been indispensable to governments that have sold state-owned companies to private investors.

The Role of Capital Markets

From a firm's perspective, the role of a capital market is to be a liquid market where firms can interact with investors to obtain valuable external financing resources. From investors' perspectives, the role of a capital market is to be an **efficient market** that allocates funds to their most productive uses. This is especially true for securities that are actively traded in broker or dealer markets, where the competition among wealth-maximizing investors determines and publicizes prices that are believed to be close to their true value.

The price of an individual security is determined by the interaction between buyers and sellers in the market. If the market is efficient, the price of a stock is an unbiased estimate of its true value, and changes in the price reflect new information that investors learn about and act on. For example, suppose a certain stock currently trades at $40 per share. If this company announces that sales of a new product have been higher than expected, investors will raise their estimate of what the stock is truly worth. At $40, the stock is a relative bargain, so there will temporarily be more buyers than sellers wanting to trade the stock, and its price will have to rise to restore equilibrium in the market. The more efficient the market is, the more rapidly this whole process works. In theory, even information known only to insiders may become incorporated in stock prices as the *Focus on Ethics* box on page 40 explains.

Not everyone agrees that prices in financial markets are as efficient as described in the preceding paragraph. Advocates of *behavioral finance,* an emerging field that blends ideas from finance and psychology, argue that stock prices and prices of other securities can deviate from their true values for extended periods. These people point to episodes such as the huge run-up and subsequent collapse of the prices of Internet stocks in the late 1990s and the failure of markets to accurately assess the risk of mortgage-backed securities in the more recent financial crisis as examples of the principle that stock prices sometimes can be wildly inaccurate measures of value.

Just how efficient are the prices in financial markets? That is a question that will be debated for a long time. It is clear that prices do move in response to new information, and for most investors and corporate managers the best advice is probably to be cautious when betting against the market. Identifying securities that the market has over- or undervalued is extremely difficult, and very few people have demonstrated an ability to bet against the market correctly for an extended time.

In more depth

To read about
The Efficient Markets Hypothesis, go to
www.myfinancelab.com

focus on ETHICS

The Ethics of Insider Trading

in practice On December 27, 2001, Martha Stewart sold nearly 4,000 shares in ImClone Systems stock. The following day, the Food and Drug Administration delivered some bad news regarding ImClone's cancer drug, Erbitux, and ImClone's stock price dropped substantially. It appeared that Martha Stewart had picked the right time to sell.

Martha Stewart was not the only ImClone shareholder who was selling. The company's founder, Sam Waksal, also tried to sell his stock (brokers refused to execute the sales), as did his daughter. The U.S. Securities and Exchange Commission and the Federal Bureau of Investigation were soon looking into the transactions. Sam Waksal ultimately received an 87-month prison sentence and $3 million in fines for insider trading and tax evasion. Martha Stewart was convicted of conspiracy, obstruction, and making false statements to federal investigators and served 5 months in jail, 5 months of home confinement, and 2 years of probation and paid a $30,000 fine. In addition, she was forced to resign as chairman and CEO of the company she had founded, Martha Stewart Living Omnimedia. On the day of her conviction, the company's shares lost 23 percent of their value.

Laws prohibiting insider trading were established in the United States in the 1930s. These laws are designed to ensure that all investors have access to relevant information on the same terms. However, many market participants believe that insider trading should be permitted. Their argument is rooted in the efficient-market hypothesis (EMH). According to the EMH, stock prices fully reflect all publicly available information. Of course, a significant amount of information about every company is not publicly available. Thus, stock prices may not accurately reflect all that is known about a company.

Those who argue for allowing insider trading believe that market prices influence the allocation of resources among companies. Firms with higher stock prices find it easier to raise capital, for example. Therefore, it is important that market prices reflect as much information as possible. Advocates of allowing insider trading argue that investors would quickly convert inside information into publicly available information if insider trading were permitted. If, for example, Sam Waksal had been permitted to sell his stock after learning of the FDA's decision, market participants might view his actions and come to the judgment that ImClone's prospects had dimmed. Of course, the other necessary condition is that outsiders can observe the stock market transactions of insiders.

Interestingly, Eugene Fama, who is viewed by many as the father of the efficient-market hypothesis, does not believe that insider trading should be permitted.[a] Fama believes that allowing insider trading creates a moral hazard problem. For example, if insiders are allowed to trade on proprietary information, they may have the incentive to hold back information for their personal gain.

▶ *If efficiency is the goal of financial markets, is allowing or disallowing insider trading more unethical?*

▶ *Does allowing insider trading create an ethical dilemma for insiders?*

[a] www.dimensional.com/famafrench/2010/04/qa-is-insider-trading-beneficial.html

→ REVIEW QUESTIONS

2–1 Who are the key participants in the transactions of financial institutions? Who are *net suppliers*, and who are *net demanders*?

2–2 What role do *financial markets* play in our economy? What are *primary* and *secondary* markets? What relationship exists between financial institutions and financial markets?

2–3 What is the *money market*? What is the *Eurocurrency market*?

2–4 What is the *capital market*? What are the primary securities traded in it?

2–5 What are *broker markets*? What are *dealer markets*? How do they differ?

2–6 Briefly describe the international capital markets, particularly the *Eurobond market* and the *international equity market*.

2–7 What are *efficient markets*? What determines the price of an individual security in such a market?

2.2 The Financial Crisis

In the summer and fall of 2008, the U.S. financial system, and financial systems around the world, appeared to be on the verge of collapse. Troubles in the financial sector spread to other industries, and a severe global recession ensued. In this section, we outline some of the main causes and consequences of that crisis.

FINANCIAL INSTITUTIONS AND REAL ESTATE FINANCE

In the classic film *It's a Wonderful Life*, the central character is George Bailey, who runs a financial institution called the Bailey Building and Loan Association. In a key scene in that movie, a bank run is about to occur and depositors demand that George return the money that they invested in the Building and Loan. George pleads with one man to keep his funds at the bank, saying:

> You're thinking of this place all wrong, as if I have the money back in a safe. The money's not here. Your money is in Joe's house. That's right next to yours—and then the Kennedy house, and Mrs. Maklin's house, and a hundred others. You're lending them the money to build, and then they're going to pay it back to you as best they can. What are you going to do, foreclose on them?

This scene offers a relatively realistic portrayal of the role that financial institutions played in allocating credit for investments in residential real estate for many years. Local banks took deposits and made loans to local borrowers. However, since the 1970s, a process called securitization has changed the way that mortgage finance works. **Securitization** refers to the process of pooling mortgages or other types of loans and then selling claims or securities against that pool in a secondary market. These securities, called **mortgage-backed securities,** can be purchased by individual investors, pension funds, mutual funds, or virtually any other investor. As homeowners repay their loans, those payments eventually make their way into the hands of investors who hold the mortgage-backed securities. Therefore, a primary risk associated with mortgage-backed securities is that homeowners may not be able to, or may choose not to, repay their loans. Banks today still lend money to individuals who want to build or purchase new homes, but they typically bundle those loans together and sell them to organizations that securitize them and pass them on to investors all over the world.

securitization
The process of pooling mortgages or other types of loans and then selling claims or securities against that pool in the secondary market.

mortgage-backed securities
Securities that represent claims on the cash flows generated by a pool of mortgages.

FALLING HOME PRICES AND DELINQUENT MORTGAGES

Prior to the 2008 financial crisis, most investors viewed mortgage-backed securities as relatively safe investments. Figure 2.2 on page 42 illustrates one of the main reasons for this view. The figure shows the behavior of the Standard & Poor's Case-Shiller Index, a barometer of home prices in ten major U.S. cities, in each month from January 1987 to February 2010. Historically, declines in the index were relatively infrequent, and between July 1995 and April 2006 the index rose continuously without posting even a single monthly decline. When house prices are rising, the gap between what a borrower owes on a home and what the home is worth widens. Lenders will allow borrowers who have difficulty making payments on their mortgages to tap this built-up home equity to refinance their loans and lower their payments. Therefore, rising home prices helped keep mortgage default rates low from the mid-1990s through 2006. Investing in real estate and mortgage-backed securities seemed to involve very little risk during this period.

FIGURE 2.2

Housing Values
Standard & Poor's Case-Shiller Home Price Index, January 1987 through February 2010

In part because real estate investments appeared to be relatively safe, lenders began relaxing their standards for borrowers. This led to tremendous growth in a category of loans called subprime mortgages. Subprime mortgages are mortgage loans made to borrowers with lower incomes and poorer credit histories as compared to "prime" borrowers. Often, loans granted to subprime borrowers have adjustable, rather than fixed, interest rates. This makes subprime borrowers particularly vulnerable if interest rates rise, and many of these borrowers (and lenders) assumed that rising home prices would allow borrowers to refinance their loans if they had difficulties making payments. Partly through the growth of subprime mortgages, banks and other financial institutions gradually increased their investments in real estate loans. In the year 2000, real estate loans accounted for less than 40 percent of the total loan portfolios of large banks. By 2007, real estate loans grew to more than half of all loans made by large banks, and the fraction of these loans in the subprime category increased as well.

Unfortunately, as Figure 2.2 shows, home prices fell almost without interruption from May 2006 through May 2009. Over that three-year period, home prices fell on average by more than 30 percent. Not surprisingly, when homeowners had difficulty making their mortgage payments, refinancing was no longer an option, and delinquency rates and foreclosures began to climb. By 2009, nearly 25 percent of subprime borrowers were behind schedule on their mortgage payments. Some borrowers, recognizing that the value of their homes was far less than the amount they owed on their mortgages, simply walked away from their homes and let lenders repossess them.

CRISIS OF CONFIDENCE IN BANKS

With delinquency rates rising, the value of mortgage-backed securities began to fall, and so too did the fortunes of financial institutions that had invested heavily in real estate assets. In March 2008, the Federal Reserve provided financing for the acquisition (that is, the rescue) of Bear Stearns by JPMorgan Chase. Later that year, Lehman Brothers filed for bankruptcy. Throughout 2008 and 2009, the Federal Reserve, the Bush administration, and finally the Obama administration took unprecedented steps to try to shore up the banking sector and stimulate the economy, but these measures could not completely avert the crisis.

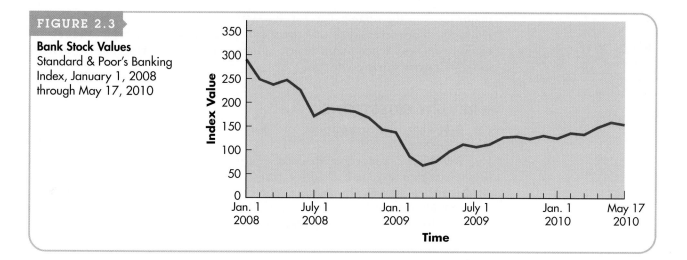

FIGURE 2.3

Bank Stock Values
Standard & Poor's Banking
Index, January 1, 2008
through May 17, 2010

Figure 2.3 shows the behavior of the Standard & Poor's Banking Index, an index that tracks bank stocks. Bank stocks fell 81 percent between January 2008 and March 2009, and the number of bank failures skyrocketed. According to the Federal Deposit Insurance Corporation (FDIC), only three banks failed in 2007. In 2008 that number rose by a factor of eight to 25 failed banks, and the number increased nearly six times to 140 failures in 2009. While the economy began to recover in 2010, bank failures continued at a rapid pace, with 139 institutions failing in the first 10 months of that year.

SPILLOVER EFFECTS AND THE GREAT RECESSION

As banks came under intense financial pressure in 2008, they began to tighten their lending standards and dramatically reduced the quantity of loans they made. In the aftermath of the Lehman Brothers bankruptcy, lending in the money market contracted very sharply. Corporations who had relied on the money market as a source of short-term funding found that they could no longer raise money in this market or could do so only at extraordinarily high rates.

As a consequence, businesses began to hoard cash and cut back on expenditures, and economic activity contracted. Gross domestic product (GDP) declined in five out of six quarters starting in the first quarter of 2008, and the economy shed more than 8 million jobs in 2008–2009 as the unemployment rate reached 10 percent. Congress passed an $862 billion stimulus package to try to revive the economy, and the Federal Reserve pushed short-term interest rates close to 0 percent. By late 2009 and early 2010, there were signs that a gradual economic recovery had begun, but the job market remained stagnant, and most forecasts called for anemic economic growth.

Perhaps the most important lesson from this episode is how important financial institutions are to a modern economy. By some measures, the 2008–2009 recession was the worst experienced in the United States since the Great Depression. Indeed, there many parallels between those two economic contractions. Both were preceded by a period of rapid economic growth, rising stock prices, and movements by banks into new lines of business, and both involved a major crisis in the financial sector. Recessions associated with a banking crisis tend to be more severe than other recessions because so many businesses rely on credit to operate. When financial institutions contract borrowing, activity in most other industries slows down too.

→ REVIEW QUESTIONS

2–8 What is securitization, and how does it facilitate investment in real estate assets?

2–9 What is a mortgage-backed security? What is the basic risk associated with mortgage-backed securities?

2–10 How do rising home prices contribute to low mortgage delinquencies?

2–11 Why do falling home prices create an incentive for homeowners to default on their mortgages even if they can afford to make the monthly payments?

2–12 Why does a crisis in the financial sector spill over into other industries?

LG 5   2.3   Regulation of Financial Institutions and Markets

The previous section discussed just how vulnerable modern economies are when financial institutions are in a state of crisis. Partly to avoid these types of problems, governments typically regulate financial institutions and markets as much or more than almost any other sector in the economy. This section provides an overview of the financial regulatory landscape in the United States.

REGULATIONS GOVERNING FINANCIAL INSTITUTIONS

Federal Deposit Insurance Corporation (FDIC)
An agency created by the Glass-Steagall Act that provides insurance for deposits at banks and monitors banks to ensure their safety and soundness.

As mentioned in the previous section, Congress passed the Glass-Steagall Act in 1933 during the depths of the Great Depression. The early 1930s witnessed a series of banking panics that caused almost one-third of the nation's banks to fail. Troubles within the banking sector and other factors contributed to the worst economic contraction in U.S. history, in which industrial production fell by more than 50 percent, the unemployment rate peaked at almost 25 percent, and stock prices dropped roughly 86 percent. The Glass-Steagall Act attempted to calm the public's fears about the banking industry by establishing the **Federal Deposit Insurance Corporation (FDIC)**, which provided deposit insurance, effectively guaranteeing that individuals would not lose their money if they held it in a bank that failed. The FDIC was also charged with examining banks on a regular basis to ensure that they were "safe and sound." The Glass-Steagall Act also prohibited institutions that took deposits from engaging in activities such as securities underwriting and trading, thereby effectively separating commercial banks from investment banks.

Over time, U.S. financial institutions faced competitive pressures from both domestic and foreign businesses that engaged in facilitating loans or making loans directly. Because these competitors either did not accept deposits or were located outside the United States, they were not subject to the same regulations as domestic banks. As a result, domestic banks began to lose market share in their core businesses. Pressure mounted to repeal the Glass-Steagall Act to enable U.S. banks to compete more effectively, and in 1999 Congress enacted and President Clinton signed the **Gramm-Leach-Bliley Act,** which allows commercial banks, investment banks, and insurance companies to consolidate and compete for business in a wider range of activities.

Gramm-Leach-Bliley Act
An act that allows business combinations (that is, mergers) between commercial banks, investment banks, and insurance companies, and thus permits these institutions to compete in markets that prior regulations prohibited them from entering.

In the aftermath of the recent financial crisis and recession, Congress passed the Dodd-Frank Wall Street Reform and Consumer Protection Act in July 2010. In print, the new law runs for hundreds of pages and calls for the creation of several new agencies including the Financial Stability Oversight Council, the Office of Financial Research, and the Bureau of Consumer Financial Protection. The act also realigns the duties of several existing agencies and requires existing and new agencies to report to Congress regularly. As this book was going to press, the various agencies affected or created by the new law were writing rules specifying how the new law's provisions would be implemented, so exactly how the new legislation will affect financial institutions and markets remains unclear.

REGULATIONS GOVERNING FINANCIAL MARKETS

Securities Act of 1933
An act that regulates the sale of securities to the public via the primary market.

Two other pieces of legislation were passed during the Great Depression that had an enormous impact on the regulation of financial markets. The **Securities Act of 1933** imposed new regulations governing the sale of new securities. That is, the 1933 act was intended to regulate activity in the primary market in which securities are initially issued to the public. The act was designed to insure that the sellers of new securities provided extensive disclosures to the potential buyers of those securities.

Securities Exchange Act of 1934
An act that regulates the trading of securities such as stocks and bonds in the secondary market.

Securities and Exchange Commission (SEC)
The primary government agency responsible for enforcing federal securities laws.

The **Securities Exchange Act of 1934** regulates the secondary trading of securities such as stocks and bonds. The Securities Exchange Act of 1934 also created the **Securities and Exchange Commission (SEC),** which is the primary agency responsible for enforcing federal securities laws. In addition to the one-time disclosures required of security issuers by the Securities Act of 1933, the Securities Exchange Act of 1934 requires ongoing disclosure by companies whose securities trade in secondary markets. Companies must make a 10-Q filing every quarter and a 10-K filing annually. The 10-Q and 10-K forms contain detailed information about the financial performance of the firm during the relevant period. Today, these forms are available online through the SEC's website known as EDGAR (Electronic Data Gathering, Analysis, and Retrieval). The 1934 act also imposes limits on the extent to which corporate "insiders," such as senior managers, can trade in their firm's securities.

→ REVIEW QUESTIONS

2–13 Why do you think so many pieces of important legislation related to financial markets and institutions were passed during the Great Depression?

2–14 What different aspects of financial markets do the Securities Act of 1933 and the Securities Exchange Act of 1934 regulate?

2.4 Business Taxes

Taxes are a fact of life, and businesses, like individuals, must pay taxes on income. The income of sole proprietorships and partnerships is taxed as the income of the individual owners; corporate income is subject to corporate taxes.

Regardless of their legal form, all businesses can earn two types of income, ordinary and capital gains. Under current law, these two types of income are treated differently in the taxation of individuals; they are not treated differently for entities subject to corporate taxes. However, frequent amendments are made to the tax code, particularly as economic conditions change and when party control of the legislative and executive branches of government shifts.

ORDINARY INCOME

ordinary income
Income earned through the sale of a firm's goods or services.

The **ordinary income** of a corporation is income earned through the sale of goods or services. Ordinary income in 2010 was taxed subject to the rates depicted in the corporate tax rate schedule in Table 2.1.

> **Example 2.2** ▶   Webster Manufacturing, Inc., a small manufacturer of kitchen knives, has before-tax earnings of $250,000. The tax on these earnings can be found by using the tax rate schedule in Table 2.1:
>
> $$\text{Total taxes due} = \$22,250 + [0.39 \times (\$250,000 - \$100,000)]$$
> $$= \$22,250 + (0.39 \times \$150,000)$$
> $$= \$22,250 + \$58,500 = \underline{\$80,750}$$

From a financial point of view, it is important to understand the difference between average and marginal tax rates, the treatment of interest and dividend income, and the effects of tax deductibility.

Marginal versus Average Tax Rates

marginal tax rate
The rate at which *additional income* is taxed.

The **marginal tax rate** represents the rate at which *the next dollar of income* is taxed. In the current corporate tax structure, the marginal tax rate is 15 percent

TABLE 2.1 ▶ **Corporate Tax Rate Schedule**

Range of taxable income			Tax calculation					
			Base tax	+	(Marginal rate	×	amount over base bracket)	
$ 0	to	$ 50,000	$ 0	+	(15%	×	amount over	$ 0)
50,000	to	75,000	7,500	+	(25	×	amount over	50,000)
75,000	to	100,000	13,750	+	(34	×	amount over	75,000)
100,000	to	335,000	22,250	+	(39	×	amount over	100,000)
335,000	to	10,000,000	113,900	+	(34	×	amount over	335,000)
10,000,000	to	15,000,000	3,400,000	+	(35	×	amount over	10,000,000)
15,000,000	to	18,333,333	5,150,000	+	(38	×	amount over	15,000,000)
Over 18,333,333			6,416,667	+	(35	×	amount over	18,333,333)

if the firm earns less than $50,000. If a firm earns more than $50,000 but less than $75,000, the marginal tax rate is 25 percent. As a firm's income rises, the marginal tax rate that it faces changes as shown in Table 2.1. In the example above, if Webster Manufacturing's earnings increase to $250,001, the last $1 in income would be taxed at the marginal rate of 39 percent.

average tax rate
A firm's taxes divided by its taxable income.

The **average tax rate** paid on the firm's ordinary income can be calculated by dividing its taxes by its taxable income. For most firms, the average tax rate does not equal the marginal tax rate because tax rates change with income levels. In the example above, Webster Manufacturing's marginal tax rate is 39 percent, but its average tax rate is 32.3 percent ($80,750 ÷ $250,000). For very large corporations with earnings in the hundreds of millions or even billions of dollars, the average tax rate is very close to the 35 percent marginal rate in the top bracket because most of the firm's income is taxed at that rate.

In most of the business decisions that managers make, *it's the marginal tax rate that really matters*. To keep matters simple, the examples in this text will use a *flat 40 percent tax rate*. That means that *both the average tax rate and the marginal tax rate equal 40 percent*.

Interest and Dividend Income

double taxation
Situation that occurs when after-tax corporate earnings are distributed as cash dividends to stockholders, who then must pay personal taxes on the dividend amount.

In the process of determining taxable income, any *interest received* by the corporation is included as ordinary income. Dividends, on the other hand, are treated differently. This different treatment moderates the effect of **double taxation**, which occurs when the already once-taxed earnings of a corporation are distributed as cash dividends to stockholders, who must pay taxes on dividends up to a maximum rate of 15 percent. Dividends that the firm receives on common and preferred stock held in other corporations are subject to a 70 percent exclusion for tax purposes.[2] The dividend exclusion in effect eliminates most of the potential tax liability from the dividends received by the second and any subsequent corporations.

Tax-Deductible Expenses

In calculating their taxes, corporations are allowed to deduct operating expenses, as well as interest expense. The tax deductibility of these expenses reduces their after-tax cost. The following example illustrates the benefit of tax deductibility.

Example 2.3 ▶

Two companies, Debt Co. and No-Debt Co., both expect in the coming year to have earnings before interest and taxes of $200,000. During the year, Debt Co. will have to pay $30,000 in interest. No-Debt Co. has no debt and therefore will

---

2. The 70 percent exclusion applies if the firm receiving dividends owns less than 20 percent of the shares of the firm paying the dividends. The exclusion is 80 percent if the corporation owns between 20 percent and 80 percent of the stock in the corporation paying it dividends; 100 percent of the dividends received are excluded if it owns more than 80 percent of the corporation paying it dividends. For convenience, we are assuming here that the ownership interest in the dividend-paying corporation is less than 20 percent.

have no interest expense. Calculation of the earnings after taxes for these two firms is as follows:

	Debt Co.	No-Debt Co.
Earnings before interest and taxes	$200,000	$200,000
Less: Interest expense	30,000	0
Earnings before taxes	$170,000	$200,000
Less: Taxes (40%)	68,000	80,000
Earnings after taxes	$102,000	$120,000
Difference in earnings after taxes		$18,000

Debt Co. had $30,000 more interest expense than No-Debt Co., but Debt Co.'s earnings after taxes are only $18,000 less than those of No-Debt Co. This difference is attributable to the fact that Debt Co.'s $30,000 interest expense deduction provided a tax savings of $12,000 ($68,000 for Debt Co. versus $80,000 for No-Debt Co.). This amount can be calculated directly by multiplying the tax rate by the amount of interest expense ($0.40 \times \$30,000 = \$12,000$). Similarly, the $18,000 *after-tax cost* of the interest expense can be calculated directly by multiplying 1 minus the tax rate by the amount of interest expense [$(1 - 0.40) \times \$30,000 = \$18,000$].

The tax deductibility of expenses reduces their actual (after-tax) cost to the firm as long as the firm is profitable. If a firm experiences a net loss in a given year, its tax liability is already zero. Even in this case, losses in one year can be used to offset taxes paid on profits in prior years, and in some cases losses can be "carried forward" to offset income and lower taxes in subsequent years. Note that both for accounting and tax purposes *interest is a tax-deductible expense, whereas dividends are not.* Because dividends are not tax deductible, their after-tax cost is equal to the amount of the dividend. Thus a $30,000 cash dividend has an after-tax cost of $30,000.

CAPITAL GAINS

capital gain
The amount by which the sale price of an asset exceeds the asset's purchase price.

If a firm sells a capital asset (such as stock held as an investment) for more than it paid for the asset, the difference between the sale price and purchase price is called a **capital gain.** For corporations, capital gains are added to ordinary corporate income and taxed at the regular corporate rates.

Example 2.4 ▶

Ross Company, a manufacturer of pharmaceuticals, has pretax operating earnings of $500,000 and has just sold for $150,000 an asset that was purchased 2 years ago for $125,000. Because the asset was sold for more than its initial purchase price, there is a capital gain of $25,000 ($150,000 sale price − $125,000 initial purchase price). The corporation's taxable income will total $525,000 ($500,000 ordinary income plus $25,000 capital gain). Multiplying their taxable income by 40% produces Ross Company's tax liability of $210,000.

→ **REVIEW QUESTIONS**

2–15 Describe the tax treatment of *ordinary income* and that of *capital gains*. What is the difference between the *average tax rate* and the *marginal tax rate?*

2–16 How does the tax treatment of dividend income by the corporation moderate the effects of *double taxation?*

2–17 What benefit results from the tax deductibility of certain corporate expenses?

Summary

THE ROLE OF FINANCIAL INSTITUTIONS AND MARKETS

Chapter 2 described why financial institutions and markets are an integral part of managerial finance. Companies cannot get started or survive without raising capital, and financial institutions and markets give firms access to the money they need to grow. As we have seen in recent years, however, financial markets can be quite turbulent, and when large financial institutions get into trouble, access to capital is reduced and firms throughout the economy suffer as a result. Taxes are an important part of this story as well because the rules governing how business income is taxed shape the incentives of firms to make new investments.

REVIEW OF LEARNING GOALS

LG 1 **Understand the role that financial institutions play in managerial finance.** Financial institutions bring net suppliers of funds and net demanders together to help translate the savings of individuals, businesses, and governments into loans and other types of investments. The net suppliers of funds are generally individuals or households who save more money than they borrow. Businesses and governments are generally net demanders of funds, meaning that they borrow more money than they save.

LG 2 **Contrast the functions of financial institutions and financial markets.** Both financial institutions and financial markets help businesses raise the money that they need to fund new investments for growth. Financial institutions collect the savings of individuals and channel those funds to borrowers such as businesses and governments. Financial markets provide a forum in which savers and borrowers can transact business directly. Businesses and governments issue debt and equity securities directly to the public in the primary market. Subsequent trading of these securities between investors occurs in the secondary market.

LG 3 **Describe the differences between the capital markets and the money markets.** In the money market, savers who want a temporary place to deposit funds where they can earn interest interact with borrowers who have a short-term need for funds. Marketable securities including Treasury bills, commercial paper, and other instruments are the primary securities traded in the money market. The Eurocurrency market is the international equivalent of the domestic money market.

In contrast, the capital market is the forum in which savers and borrowers interact on a long-term basis. Firms issue either debt (bonds) or equity (stock) securities in the capital market. Once issued, these securities trade on secondary markets that are either broker markets or dealer markets. An important function of the capital market is to determine the underlying value of the securities issued by businesses. In an efficient market, the price of a security is an unbiased estimate of its true value.

LG 4   **Explain the root causes of the 2008 financial crisis and recession.** The financial crisis was caused by several factors related to investments in real estate. Financial institutions lowered their standards for lending to prospective homeowners, and institutions also invested heavily in mortgage-backed securities. When home prices fell and mortgage delinquencies rose, the value of the mortgage-backed securities held by banks plummeted, causing some banks to fail and many others to restrict the flow of credit to business. That in turn contributed to a severe recession in the United States and abroad.

LG 5   **Understand the major regulations and regulatory bodies that affect financial institutions and markets.** The Glass-Steagall Act created the FDIC and imposed a separation between commercial and investment banks. The act was designed to limit the risks that banks could take and to protect depositors. More recently, the Gramm-Leach-Bliley Act essentially repealed the elements of Glass-Steagall pertaining to the separation of commercial and investment banks. After the recent financial crisis, much debate has occurred regarding the proper regulation of large financial institutions.

The Securities Act of 1933 and the Securities Exchange Act of 1934 are the major pieces of legislation shaping the regulation of financial markets. The 1933 act focuses on regulating the sale of securities in the primary market, whereas the 1934 act deals with regulations governing transactions in the secondary market. The 1934 act also created the Securities and Exchange Commission, the primary body responsible for enforcing federal securities laws.

LG 6   **Discuss business taxes and their importance in financial decisions.** Corporate income is subject to corporate taxes. Corporate tax rates apply to both ordinary income (after deduction of allowable expenses) and capital gains. The average tax rate paid by a corporation ranges from 15 to 35 percent. Corporate taxpayers can reduce their taxes through certain provisions in the tax code: dividend income exclusions and tax-deductible expenses. A capital gain occurs when an asset is sold for more than its initial purchase price; gains are added to ordinary corporate income and taxed at regular corporate tax rates. (For convenience, we assume a 40 percent marginal tax rate in this book.)

Opener-in-Review

In the chapter opener you read about JPMorgan's tumultuous ride through the 2008 financial crisis, and in the chapter itself you learned about capital market efficiency. What role do you think market efficiency (or inefficiency) played in the 10 percent fall of JPMorgan's share price in a single day?

Self-Test Problem (Solution in Appendix)

LG 6 **ST2–1** **Corporate taxes** Montgomery Enterprises, Inc., had operating earnings of $280,000 for the year just ended. During the year the firm sold stock that it held in another company for $180,000, which was $30,000 above its original purchase price of $150,000, paid 1 year earlier.

    a. What is the amount, if any, of capital gains realized during the year?

    b. How much total taxable income did the firm earn during the year?

    c. Use the corporate tax rate schedule given in Table 2.1 to calculate the firm's total taxes due.

    d. Calculate both the *average tax rate* and the *marginal tax rate* on the basis of your findings.

Warm-Up Exercises All problems are available in myfinancelab.

LG 1 **E2–1** What does it mean to say that individuals as a group are net suppliers of funds for financial institutions? What do you think the consequences might be in financial markets if individuals consumed more of their incomes and thereby reduced the supply of funds available to financial institutions?

LG 2 **E2–2** You are the chief financial officer (CFO) of Gaga Enterprises, an edgy fashion design firm. Your firm needs $10 million to expand production. How do you think the process of raising this money will vary if you raise it with the help of a financial institution versus raising it directly in the financial markets?

LG 3 **E2–3** For what kinds of needs do you a think firm would issue securities in the money market versus the capital market?

LG 4 **E2–4** Your broker calls to offer you the investment opportunity of a lifetime, the chance to invest in mortgage-backed securities. The broker explains that these securities are entitled to the principal and interest payments received from a pool of residential mortgages. List some of the questions you would ask your broker to assess the risk of this investment opportunity.

LG 6 **E2–5** Reston, Inc., has asked your corporation, Pruro, Inc., for financial assistance. As a long-time customer of Reston, your firm has decided to give that assistance. The question you are debating is whether Pruro should take Reston stock with a 5% annual dividend or a promissory note paying 5% annual interest.

    Assuming payment is guaranteed and the dollar amounts for annual interest and dividend income are identical, which option will result in greater after-tax income for the first year?

Problems All problems are available in myfinancelab.

LG 6 **P2–1** **Corporate taxes** Tantor Supply, Inc., is a small corporation acting as the exclusive distributor of a major line of sporting goods. During 2010 the firm earned $92,500 before taxes.

    a. Calculate the firm's tax liability using the corporate tax rate schedule given in Table 2.1.

    b. How much are Tantor Supply's 2010 after-tax earnings?

c. What was the firm's *average tax rate*, based on your findings in part **a?**

d. What is the firm's *marginal tax rate*, based on your findings in part **a?**

LG 6   P2–2   **Average corporate tax rates**   Using the corporate tax rate schedule given in Table 2.1, perform the following:

a. Calculate the tax liability, after-tax earnings, and average tax rates for the following levels of corporate earnings before taxes: $10,000; $80,000; $300,000; $500,000; $1.5 million; $10 million; and $20 million.

b. Plot the *average tax rates* (measured on the *y* axis) against the pretax income levels (measured on the *x* axis). What generalization can be made concerning the relationship between these variables?

LG 6   P2–3   **Marginal corporate tax rates**   Using the corporate tax rate schedule given in Table 2.1, perform the following:

a. Find the marginal tax rate for the following levels of corporate earnings before taxes: $15,000; $60,000; $90,000; $200,000; $400,000; $1 million; and $20 million.

b. Plot the *marginal tax rates* (measured on the *y* axis) against the pretax income levels (measured on the *x* axis). Explain the relationship between these variables.

LG 6   P2–4   **Interest versus dividend income**   During the year just ended, Shering Distributors, Inc., had pretax earnings from operations of $490,000. In addition, during the year it received $20,000 in income from interest on bonds it held in Zig Manufacturing and received $20,000 in income from dividends on its 5% common stock holding in Tank Industries, Inc. Shering is in the 40% tax bracket and is eligible for a 70% dividend exclusion on its Tank Industries stock.

a. Calculate the firm's tax on its operating earnings only.

b. Find the tax and the after-tax amount attributable to the interest income from Zig Manufacturing bonds.

c. Find the tax and the after-tax amount attributable to the dividend income from the Tank Industries, Inc., common stock.

d. Compare, contrast, and discuss the after-tax amounts resulting from the interest income and dividend income calculated in parts **b** and **c.**

e. What is the firm's total tax liability for the year?

LG 6   P2–5   **Interest versus dividend expense**   Michaels Corporation expects earnings before interest and taxes to be $40,000 for the current period. Assuming an ordinary tax rate of 40%, compute the firm's earnings after taxes and earnings available for common stockholders (earnings after taxes and preferred stock dividends, if any) under the following conditions:

a. The firm pays $10,000 in interest.

b. The firm pays $10,000 in preferred stock dividends.

LG 6   P2–6   **Capital gains taxes**   Perkins Manufacturing is considering the sale of two nondepreciable assets, X and Y. Asset X was purchased for $2,000 and will be sold today for $2,250. Asset Y was purchased for $30,000 and will be sold today for $35,000. The firm is subject to a 40% tax rate on capital gains.

a. Calculate the amount of capital gain, if any, realized on each of the assets.

b. Calculate the tax on the sale of each asset.

LG 6   P2–7   **Capital gains taxes**   The following table contains purchase and sale prices for the nondepreciable capital assets of a major corporation. The firm paid taxes of 40% on capital gains.

Asset	Purchase price	Sale price
A	$ 3,000	$ 3,400
B	12,000	12,000
C	62,000	80,000
D	41,000	45,000
E	16,500	18,000

   a. Determine the amount of capital gain realized on each of the five assets.
   b. Calculate the amount of tax paid on each of the assets.

LG 5   **P2–8**   **ETHICS PROBLEM**   The Securities Exchange Act of 1934 limits, but does not prohibit, corporate insiders from trading in their own firm's shares. What ethical issues might arise when a corporate insider wants to buy or sell shares in the firm where he or she works?

Spreadsheet Exercise

Hemingway Corporation is considering expanding its operations to boost its income, but before making a final decision they have asked you to calculate the corporate tax consequences of their decision. Currently Hemingway generates before-tax yearly income of $200,000 and has no debt outstanding. Expanding operations would allow Hemingway to increase before-tax yearly income to $350,000. Hemingway can use either cash reserves or debt to finance its expansion. If Hemingway uses debt, it will have yearly interest expense of $70,000.

TO DO

Create a spreadsheet to conduct a *tax analysis* for Hemingway Corporation and determine the following:

   a. What is Hemingway's current annual corporate tax liability?
   b. What is Hemingway's current average tax rate?
   c. If Hemingway finances its expansion using cash reserves, what will be its new corporate tax liability and average tax rate?
   d. If Hemingway finances its expansion using debt, what will be its new corporate tax liability and average tax rate?
   e. What would you recommend that the firm do? Why?

 Visit **www.myfinancelab.com** for **Chapter Case: *The Pros and Cons of Being Publicly Listed,*** Group Exercises, and numerous online resources.

Integrative Case 1

Merit Enterprise Corp.

Sara Lehn, chief financial officer of Merit Enterprise Corp., was reviewing her presentation one last time before her upcoming meeting with the board of directors. Merit's business had been brisk for the last two years, and the company's CEO was pushing for a dramatic expansion of Merit's production capacity. Executing the CEO's plans would require $4 billion in capital in addition to $2 billion in excess cash that the firm had built up. Sara's immediate task was to brief the board on options for raising the needed $4 billion.

Unlike most companies its size, Merit had maintained its status as a private company, financing its growth by reinvesting profits and, when necessary, borrowing from banks. Whether Merit could follow that same strategy to raise the $4 billion necessary to expand at the pace envisioned by the firm's CEO was uncertain, though it seemed unlikely to Sara. She had identified two options for the board to consider:

Option 1: Merit could approach JPMorgan Chase, a bank that had served Merit well for many years with seasonal credit lines as well as medium-term loans. Lehn believed that JPMorgan was unlikely to make a $4 billion loan to Merit on its own, but it could probably gather a group of banks together to make a loan of this magnitude. However, the banks would undoubtedly demand that Merit limit further borrowing and provide JPMorgan with periodic financial disclosures so that they could monitor Merit's financial condition as it expanded its operations.

Option 2: Merit could convert to public ownership, issuing stock to the public in the primary market. With Merit's excellent financial performance in recent years, Sara thought that its stock could command a high price in the market and that many investors would want to participate in any stock offering that Merit conducted.

Becoming a public company would also allow Merit, for the first time, to offer employees compensation in the form of stock or stock options, thereby creating stronger incentives for employees to help the firm succeed. On the other hand, Sara knew that public companies faced extensive disclosure requirements and other regulations that Merit had never had to confront as a private firm. Furthermore, with stock trading in the secondary market, who knew what kind of individuals or institutions might wind up holding a large chunk of Merit stock?

TO DO

a. Discuss the pros and cons of option 1, and prioritize your thoughts. What are the most positive aspects of this option, and what are the biggest drawbacks?
b. Do the same for option 2.
c. Which option do you think Sara should recommend to the board and why?

Part 2 ▶ Financial Tools

Chapters in This Part

Financial Statements and Ratio Analysis
Cash Flow and Financial Planning
Time Value of Money

INTEGRATIVE CASE 2 Track Software, Inc.

In Part 2 you will learn about some of the basic analytical tools that financial managers use almost every day. Chapter 3 reviews the main financial statements that are the primary means by which firms communicate with investors, analysts, and the rest of the business community. Chapter 3 also illustrates some simple tools that managers use to analyze the information contained in financial statements to identify and diagnose financial problems.

Firms create financial statements using the accrual principles of accounting, but in finance it is cash flow that really matters. Chapter 4 shows how to use financial statements to determine how much cash flow a firm is generating and how it is spending that cash flow. Chapter 4 also explains how firms develop short-term and long-term financial plans.

Managers have to decide whether the up-front costs of investments are justified by the subsequent cash that those investments are likely to produce. Chapter 5 illustrates techniques that firms use to evaluate these sorts of trade-offs.

3 Financial Statements and Ratio Analysis

Learning Goals

LG 1 Review the contents of the stockholders' report and the procedures for consolidating international financial statements.

LG 2 Understand who uses financial ratios and how.

LG 3 Use ratios to analyze a firm's liquidity and activity.

LG 4 Discuss the relationship between debt and financial leverage and the ratios used to analyze a firm's debt.

LG 5 Use ratios to analyze a firm's profitability and its market value.

LG 6 Use a summary of financial ratios and the DuPont system of analysis to perform a complete ratio analysis.

Why This Chapter Matters to You

In your *professional* life

ACCOUNTING You need to understand the stockholders' report and preparation of the four key financial statements; how firms consolidate international financial statements; and how to calculate and interpret financial ratios for decision making.

INFORMATION SYSTEMS You need to understand what data are included in the firm's financial statements to design systems that will supply such data to those who prepare the statements and to those in the firm who use the data for ratio calculations.

MANAGEMENT You need to understand what parties are interested in the stockholders' report and why; how the financial statements will be analyzed by those both inside and outside the firm to assess various aspects of performance; the caution that should be exercised in using financial ratio analysis; and how the financial statements affect the value of the firm.

MARKETING You need to understand the effects your decisions will have on the financial statements, particularly the income statement and the statement of cash flows, and how analysis of ratios, especially those involving sales figures, will affect the firm's decisions about levels of inventory, credit policies, and pricing decisions.

OPERATIONS You need to understand how the costs of operations are reflected in the firm's financial statements and how analysis of ratios, particularly those involving assets, cost of goods sold, or inventory, may affect requests for new equipment or facilities.

In your *personal* life
A routine step in personal financial planning is to prepare and analyze personal financial statements, so that you can monitor progress toward your financial goals. Also, you need to understand and analyze corporate financial statements to build and monitor your investment portfolio.

Abercrombie & Fitch

The Value of Casual Luxury

A May 15, 2010, post on an investment website, Motley Fool, provided a valuation analysis for clothing retailer Abercrombie & Fitch. Abercrombie's stock price had been trending down for several weeks, and given that recent months had only just seen the end of one of the worst recessions in two generations, Motley Fool analysts did not expect the firm's financial condition to be particularly impressive. However, they noted that Abercrombie's current ratio was a healthy 2.79, and its quick ratio was also strong at 1.79. Furthermore, analysts noted that Abercrombie's receivables collection period had quickened to 43 days in the prior year, and they concluded their report with a relatively positive outlook for the stock.

Just a few days later, Abercrombie & Fitch announced that it would scale back planned overseas store openings, the markets where it had been enjoying the most rapid growth. In addition, the company reported that its gross profit margin declined in the most recent quarter. Markets responded to this information by sending Abercrombie stock down 7 percent on that day.

Valuing the shares of a company is a difficult task. Analysts try to simplify that task by drawing data from financial reports produced by the company and calculating a variety of financial ratios using those data. These ratios help analysts answer questions such as, Does the firm have enough liquidity to pay the bills that will come due in the short term? and, How effectively does the firm collect cash from its customers? In this chapter, you will learn about the main financial statements that analysts rely on for this type of analysis, and you will see how information from those statements can be used to assess the overall performance of a company.

LG 1 **3.1 The Stockholders' Report**

generally accepted accounting principles (GAAP)
The practice and procedure guidelines used to prepare and maintain financial records and reports; authorized by the *Financial Accounting Standards Board (FASB)*.

Financial Accounting Standards Board (FASB)
The accounting profession's rule-setting body, which authorizes *generally accepted accounting principles (GAAP)*.

Public Company Accounting Oversight Board (PCAOB)
A not-for-profit corporation established by the *Sarbanes-Oxley Act of 2002* to protect the interests of investors and further the public interest in the preparation of informative, fair, and independent audit reports.

Every corporation has many and varied uses for the standardized records and reports of its financial activities. Periodically, reports must be prepared for regulators, creditors (lenders), owners, and management. The guidelines used to prepare and maintain financial records and reports are known as **generally accepted accounting principles (GAAP).** These accounting practices and procedures are authorized by the accounting profession's rule-setting body, the **Financial Accounting Standards Board (FASB).**

In addition, the *Sarbanes-Oxley Act of 2002*, enacted in an effort to eliminate the many disclosure and conflict-of-interest problems of corporations, established the **Public Company Accounting Oversight Board (PCAOB),** a not-for-profit corporation that oversees auditors of public corporations. The PCAOB is charged with protecting the interests of investors and furthering the public interest in the preparation of informative, fair, and independent audit reports. The expectation is that it will instill confidence in investors with regard to the accuracy of the audited financial statements of public companies.

Publicly owned corporations with more than $5 million in assets and 500 or more stockholders are required by the Securities and Exchange Commission (SEC)—the federal regulatory body that governs the sale and listing of securities—to provide their stockholders with an annual **stockholders' report.** The stockholders' report summarizes and documents the firm's financial activities during the past year. It begins with a letter to the stockholders from the firm's president and/or chairman of the board.

THE LETTER TO STOCKHOLDERS

The **letter to stockholders** is the primary communication from management. It describes the events that are considered to have had the greatest effect on the firm

GLOBAL focus

More Countries Adopt International Financial Reporting Standards

in practice In the United States, public companies are required to report financial results using GAAP. However, accounting standards vary around the world, and that makes comparing the financial results of firms located in different countries quite challenging. In recent years, many countries have adopted a system of accounting principles known as International Financial Reporting Standards (IFRS), which are established by an independent standards-setting body known as the International Accounting Standards

Board (IASB). These standards are designed with the goal of making financial statements everywhere understandable, reliable, comparable, and accurate. More than 80 countries now require listed firms to comply with IFRS, and dozens more permit or require firms to follow IFRS to some degree.

Why hasn't the United States followed the global trend of IFRS adoption? Some argue that GAAP is still the "gold standard," and a movement to IFRS would lower the overall quality of financial reporting made by U.S. firms.

It is true that IFRS generally requires less detail than GAAP. Even so, the Securities and Exchange Commission has expressed its view that U.S. investors will benefit as GAAP and IFRS converge though there is no expectation that firms in the United States will be required to switch to IFRS in the near future.

▶ *What costs and benefits might be associated with a switch to IFRS in the United States?*

stockholders' report
Annual report that publicly owned corporations must provide to stockholders; it summarizes and documents the firm's financial activities during the past year.

letter to stockholders
Typically, the first element of the annual stockholders' report and the primary communication from management.

income statement
Provides a financial summary of the firm's operating results during a specified period.

during the year. It also typically discusses management philosophy, corporate governance issues, strategies, and actions, as well as plans for the coming year.

THE FOUR KEY FINANCIAL STATEMENTS

The four key financial statements required by the SEC for reporting to shareholders are (1) the income statement, (2) the balance sheet, (3) the statement of stockholders' equity, and (4) the statement of cash flows. The financial statements from the 2012 stockholders' report of Bartlett Company, a manufacturer of metal fasteners, are presented and briefly discussed in this section. Most likely, you have studied these four financial statements in an accounting course, so the purpose of looking at them here is to refresh your memory of the basics, rather than provide an exhaustive review.

Income Statement

The **income statement** provides a financial summary of the firm's operating results during a specified period. Most common are income statements covering a 1-year period ending at a specified date, ordinarily December 31 of the calendar year.

focus on ETHICS

Taking Earnings Reports at Face Value

in practice Near the end of each quarter, Wall Street's much anticipated "earnings season" arrives. During earnings season, many companies unveil their quarterly performance. Interest is high, as media outlets rush to report the latest announcements, analysts slice and dice the numbers, and investors buy and sell based on the news. The most anticipated performance metric for most companies is earnings per share (EPS), which is typically compared to the estimates of the analysts that cover a firm. Firms that beat analyst estimates often see their share prices jump, while those that miss estimates, by even a small amount, tend to suffer price declines.

Many investors are aware of the pitfalls of judging firms based on reported earnings. Specifically, the complexity of financial reports makes it easy for managers to mislead investors. Sometimes, the methods used to mislead investors are within the rules,

albeit not the spirit, of acceptable accounting practices. Other times, firms break the rules to make their numbers. The practice of manipulating earnings to mislead investors is known as earnings management.

Some firms are notorious for consistently beating analysts' estimates. For example, for one 10-year period (1995–2004), General Electric Co. (GE) beat Wall Street earnings estimates every quarter, often by only a penny or two per share. However, in 2009, the U.S. Securities and Exchange Commission (SEC) fined GE $50 million for improper accounting practices, including recording sales that had not yet occurred. When GE went back to correct the problems identified by the SEC, they found that net earnings between 2001 and 2007 were a total of $280 million lower than originally reported.

In one of his famous letters to the shareholders of Berskshire Hathaway,

Warren Buffett offers three bits of advice regarding financial reporting.[a] First, he warns that weak visible accounting practices are typically a sign of bigger problems. Second, he suggests that, when you can't understand management, the reason is probably that management doesn't want you to understand them. Third, he warns that investors should be suspicious of projections because earnings and growth do not typically progress in an orderly fashion. Finally, Buffett notes that "Managers that always promise to 'make the numbers' will at some point be tempted to *make up* the numbers."

▶ *Why might financial managers be tempted to manage earnings?*

▶ *Is it unethical for managers to manage earnings if they disclose their activities to investors?*

[a]www.berkshirehathaway.com/letters/2002pdf.pdf

Many large firms, however, operate on a 12-month financial cycle, or *fiscal year,* that ends at a time other than December 31. In addition, monthly income statements are typically prepared for use by management, and quarterly statements must be made available to the stockholders of publicly owned corporations.

Table 3.1 presents Bartlett Company's income statements for the years ended December 31, 2012 and 2011. The 2012 statement begins with *sales revenue*—the total dollar amount of sales during the period—from which the *cost of goods sold* is deducted. The resulting *gross profit* of $986,000 represents the amount remaining to satisfy operating, financial, and tax costs. Next, *operating expenses,* which include selling expense, general and administrative expense, lease expense, and depreciation expense, are deducted from gross profits. The resulting *operating profits* of $418,000 represent the profits earned from producing and selling products; this amount does not consider financial and tax costs. (Operating profit is often called *earnings before interest and taxes,* or *EBIT.*) Next, the financial cost—*interest expense*—is subtracted from operating profits

TABLE 3.1 > Bartlett Company Income Statements ($000)		
	For the years ended December 31	
	2012	**2011**
Sales revenue	$3,074	$2,567
Less: Cost of goods sold	2,088	1,711
Gross profits	$ 986	$ 856
Less: Operating expenses		
Selling expense	$ 100	$ 108
General and administrative expenses	194	187
Lease expense[a]	35	35
Depreciation expense	239	223
Total operating expense	$ 568	$ 553
Operating profits	$ 418	$ 303
Less: Interest expense	93	91
Net profits before taxes	$ 325	$ 212
Less: Taxes	94	64
Net profits after taxes	$ 231	$ 148
Less: Preferred stock dividends	10	10
Earnings available for common stockholders	$ 221	$ 138
Earnings per share (EPS)[b]	$2.90	$1.81
Dividend per share (DPS)[c]	$1.29	$0.75

[a]Lease expense is shown here as a separate item rather than being included as part of interest expense, as specified by the FASB for financial reporting purposes. The approach used here is consistent with tax reporting rather than financial reporting procedures.

[b]Calculated by dividing the earnings available for common stockholders by the number of shares of common stock outstanding—76,262 in 2012 and 76,244 in 2011. Earnings per share in 2012: $221,000 ÷ 76,262 = $2.90; in 2011: $138,000 ÷ 76,244 = $1.81.

[c]Calculated by dividing the dollar amount of dividends paid to common stockholders by the number of shares of common stock outstanding. Dividends per share in 2012: $98,000 ÷ 76,262 = $1.29; in 2011: $57,183 ÷ 76,244 = $0.75.

to find *net profits* (or *earnings*) *before taxes*. After subtracting $93,000 in 2012 interest, Bartlett Company had $325,000 of net profits before taxes.

Next, taxes are calculated at the appropriate tax rates and deducted to determine *net profits* (or *earnings*) *after taxes*. Bartlett Company's net profits after taxes for 2012 were $231,000. Any preferred stock dividends must be subtracted from net profits after taxes to arrive at *earnings available for common stockholders*. This is the amount earned by the firm on behalf of the common stockholders during the period.

Dividing earnings available for common stockholders by the number of shares of common stock outstanding results in *earnings per share (EPS)*. EPS represent the number of dollars earned during the period on behalf of each outstanding share of common stock. In 2012, Bartlett Company earned $221,000 for its common stockholders, which represents $2.90 for each outstanding share. The actual cash **dividend per share (DPS)**, which is the dollar amount of cash distributed during the period on behalf of each outstanding share of common stock, paid in 2012 was $1.29.

dividend per share (DPS)
The dollar amount of cash distributed during the period on behalf of each outstanding share of common stock.

Personal Finance Example 3.1 ▶ Jan and Jon Smith, a mid-30s married couple with no children, prepared a personal income and expense statement, which is similar to a corporate income statement. A condensed version of their income and expense statement follows.

Jan and Jon Smith's Income and Expense Statement for the Year Ended December 31, 2012	
Income	
Salaries	$72,725
Interest received	195
Dividends received	120
(1) Total income	$73,040
Expenses	
Mortgage payments	$16,864
Auto loan payments	2,520
Utilities	2,470
Home repairs and maintenance	1,050
Food	5,825
Car expense	2,265
Health care and insurance	1,505
Clothes, shoes, accessories	1,700
Insurance	1,380
Taxes	16,430
Appliance and furniture payments	1,250
Recreation and entertainment	4,630
Tuition and books for Jan	1,400
Personal care and other items	2,415
(2) Total expenses	$61,704
(3) Cash surplus (or deficit) [(1) − (2)]	$11,336

During the year, the Smiths had total income of $73,040 and total expenses of $61,704, which left them with a cash surplus of $11,336. They can use the surplus to increase their savings and investments.

Balance Sheet

balance sheet
Summary statement of the firm's financial position at a given point in time.

The **balance sheet** presents a summary statement of the firm's financial position at a given time. The statement balances the firm's *assets* (what it owns) against its financing, which can be either *debt* (what it owes) or *equity* (what was provided by owners). Bartlett Company's balance sheets as of December 31 of 2012 and 2011 are presented in Table 3.2. They show a variety of asset, liability (debt), and equity accounts.

current assets
Short-term assets, expected to be converted into cash within 1 year or less.

current liabilities
Short-term liabilities, expected to be paid within 1 year or less.

An important distinction is made between short-term and long-term assets and liabilities. The **current assets** and **current liabilities** are *short-term* assets and liabilities. This means that they are expected to be converted into cash (current assets) or paid (current liabilities) within 1 year or less. All other assets and liabilities, along with stockholders' equity, which is assumed to have an infinite life, are considered *long-term,* or *fixed,* because they are expected to remain on the firm's books for more than 1 year.

As is customary, the assets are listed from the most liquid—*cash*—down to the least liquid. *Marketable securities* are very liquid short-term investments, such as U.S. Treasury bills or certificates of deposit, held by the firm. Because they are highly liquid, marketable securities are viewed as a form of cash ("near cash"). *Accounts receivable* represent the total monies owed the firm by its customers on credit sales. *Inventories* include raw materials, work in process (partially finished goods), and finished goods held by the firm. The entry for *gross fixed assets* is the original cost of all fixed (long-term) assets owned by the firm.[1] *Net fixed assets* represent the difference between gross fixed assets and *accumulated depreciation*—the total expense recorded for the depreciation of fixed assets. The net value of fixed assets is called their *book value.*

long-term debt
Debt for which payment is not due in the current year.

Like assets, the liabilities and equity accounts are listed from short-term to long-term. Current liabilities include *accounts payable,* amounts owed for credit purchases by the firm; *notes payable,* outstanding short-term loans, typically from commercial banks; and *accruals,* amounts owed for services for which a bill may not or will not be received. Examples of accruals include taxes due the government and wages due employees. **Long-term debt** represents debt for which payment is not due in the current year. *Stockholders' equity* represents the owners' claims on the firm. The *preferred stock* entry shows the historical proceeds from the sale of preferred stock ($200,000 for Bartlett Company).

paid-in capital in excess of par
The amount of proceeds in excess of the par value received from the original sale of common stock.

Next, the amount paid by the original purchasers of common stock is shown by two entries, common stock and paid-in capital in excess of par on common stock. The *common stock* entry is the *par value* of common stock. **Paid-in capital in excess of par** represents the amount of proceeds in excess of the par value received from the original sale of common stock. The sum of the common stock and paid-in capital accounts divided by the number of shares outstanding represents the original price per share received by the firm on a single issue of common stock.

---

1. For convenience the term *fixed assets* is used throughout this text to refer to what, in a strict accounting sense, is captioned "property, plant, and equipment." This simplification of terminology permits certain financial concepts to be more easily developed.

TABLE 3.2	Bartlett Company Balance Sheets ($000)	

	December 31	
Assets	**2012**	**2011**
Cash	$ 363	$ 288
Marketable securities	68	51
Accounts receivable	503	365
Inventories	289	300
Total current assets	$1,223	$1,004
Land and buildings	$2,072	$1,903
Machinery and equipment	1,866	1,693
Furniture and fixtures	358	316
Vehicles	275	314
Other (includes financial leases)	98	96
Total gross fixed assets (at cost)[a]	$4,669	$4,322
Less: Accumulated depreciation	2,295	2,056
Net fixed assets	$2,374	$2,266
Total assets	$3,597	$3,270
Liabilities and Stockholders' Equity		
Accounts payable	$ 382	$ 270
Notes payable	79	99
Accruals	159	114
Total current liabilities	$ 620	$ 483
Long-term debt (includes financial leases)[b]	1,023	967
Total liabilities	$1,643	$1,450
Preferred stock—cumulative 5%, $100 par, 2,000 shares authorized and issued[c]	$ 200	$ 200
Common stock—$2.50 par, 100,000 shares authorized, shares issued and outstanding in 2012: 76,262; in 2011: 76,244	191	190
Paid-in capital in excess of par on common stock	428	418
Retained earnings	1,135	1,012
Total stockholders' equity	$1,954	$1,820
Total liabilities and stockholders' equity	$3,597	$3,270

[a]In 2012, the firm has a 6-year financial lease requiring annual beginning-of-year payments of $35,000. Four years of the lease have yet to run.

[b]Annual principal repayments on a portion of the firm's total outstanding debt amount to $71,000.

[c]The annual preferred stock dividend would be $5 per share (5% × $100 par), or a total of $10,000 annually ($5 per share × 2,000 shares).

retained earnings
The cumulative total of all earnings, net of dividends, that have been retained and reinvested in the firm since its inception.

Bartlett Company therefore received about $8.12 per share [($191,000 par + $428,000 paid-in capital in excess of par) ÷ 76,262 shares] from the sale of its common stock.

Finally, **retained earnings** represent the cumulative total of all earnings, net of dividends, that have been retained and reinvested in the firm since its inception. It is important to recognize that retained earnings are not cash but rather have been utilized to finance the firm's assets.

Bartlett Company's balance sheets in Table 3.2 show that the firm's total assets increased from $3,270,000 in 2011 to $3,597,000 in 2012. The $327,000 increase was due primarily to the $219,000 increase in current assets. The asset increase, in turn, appears to have been financed primarily by an increase of $193,000 in total liabilities. Better insight into these changes can be derived from the statement of cash flows, which we will discuss shortly.

Personal Finance Example 3.2 ▶ The following personal balance sheet for Jan and Jon Smith—the couple introduced earlier, who are married, in their mid-30s, and have no children—is similar to a corporate balance sheet.

Jan and Jon Smith's Balance Sheet: December 31, 2012			
Assets		**Liabilities and Net Worth**	
Cash on hand	$ 90	Credit card balances	$ 665
Checking accounts	575	Utility bills	120
Savings accounts	760	Medical bills	75
Money market funds	800	Other current liabilities	45
Total liquid assets	$ 2,225	Total current liabilities	$ 905
Stocks and bonds	$ 2,250	Real estate mortgage	$ 92,000
Mutual funds	1,500	Auto loans	4,250
Retirement funds, IRA	2,000	Education loan	3,800
Total investments	$ 5,750	Personal loan	4,000
Real estate	$120,000	Furniture loan	800
Cars	14,000	Total long-term liabilities	$104,850
Household furnishings	3,700	Total liabilities	$105,755
Jewelry and artwork	1,500	Net worth (N/W)	41,420
Total personal property	$139,200	Total liabilities	
Total assets	$147,175	and net worth	$147,175

statement of stockholders' equity
Shows all equity account transactions that occurred during a given year.

statement of retained earnings
Reconciles the net income earned during a given year, and any cash dividends paid, with the change in retained earnings between the start and the end of that year. An abbreviated form of the *statement of stockholders' equity.*

The Smiths have total assets of $147,175 and total liabilities of $105,755. Personal net worth (N/W) is a "plug figure"—the difference between total assets and total liabilities—which in the case of Jan and Jon Smith is $41,420.

Statement of Retained Earnings

The *statement of retained earnings* is an abbreviated form of the statement of stockholders' equity. Unlike the **statement of stockholders' equity**, which shows all equity account transactions that occurred during a given year, the **statement of retained earnings** reconciles the net income earned during a given year, and any

TABLE 3.3	Bartlett Company Statement of Retained Earnings ($000) for the Year Ended December 31, 2012
Retained earnings balance (January 1, 2012)	$1,012
Plus: Net profits after taxes (for 2012)	231
Less: Cash dividends (paid during 2012)	
Preferred stock	10
Common stock	98
Total dividends paid	$ 108
Retained earnings balance (December 31, 2012)	$1,135

cash dividends paid, with the change in retained earnings between the start and the end of that year. Table 3.3 presents this statement for Bartlett Company for the year ended December 31, 2012. The statement shows that the company began the year with $1,012,000 in retained earnings and had net profits after taxes of $231,000, from which it paid a total of $108,000 in dividends, resulting in year-end retained earnings of $1,135,000. Thus the net increase for Bartlett Company was $123,000 ($231,000 net profits after taxes minus $108,000 in dividends) during 2012.

Statement of Cash Flows

statement of cash flows
Provides a summary of the firm's operating, investment, and financing cash flows and reconciles them with changes in its cash and marketable securities during the period.

The **statement of cash flows** is a summary of the cash flows over the period of concern. The statement provides insight into the firm's operating, investment, and financing cash flows and reconciles them with changes in its cash and marketable securities during the period. Bartlett Company's statement of cash flows for the year ended December 31, 2012, is presented in Table 3.4 (see page 66). Further insight into this statement is included in the discussion of cash flow in Chapter 4.

NOTES TO THE FINANCIAL STATEMENTS

notes to the financial statements
Explanatory notes keyed to relevant accounts in the statements; they provide detailed information on the accounting policies, procedures, calculations, and transactions underlying entries in the financial statements.

Included with published financial statements are explanatory notes keyed to the relevant accounts in the statements. These **notes to the financial statements** provide detailed information on the accounting policies, procedures, calculations, and transactions underlying entries in the financial statements. Common issues addressed by these notes include revenue recognition, income taxes, breakdowns of fixed asset accounts, debt and lease terms, and contingencies. Since passage of Sarbanes-Oxley, notes to the financial statements have also included some details about compliance with that law. Professional securities analysts use the data in the statements and notes to develop estimates of the value of securities that the firm issues, and these estimates influence the actions of investors and therefore the firm's share value.

CONSOLIDATING INTERNATIONAL FINANCIAL STATEMENTS

So far, we've discussed financial statements involving only one currency, the U.S. dollar. The issue of how to consolidate a company's foreign and domestic financial statements has bedeviled the accounting profession for many years.

TABLE 3.4	Bartlett Company Statement of Cash Flows ($000) for the Year Ended December 31, 2012

Cash Flow from Operating Activities	
Net profits after taxes	$231
Depreciation	239
Increase in accounts receivable	(138)[a]
Decrease in inventories	11
Increase in accounts payable	112
Increase in accruals	45
Cash provided by operating activities	$500
Cash Flow from Investment Activities	
Increase in gross fixed assets	(347)
Change in equity investments in other firms	0
Cash provided by investment activities	($347)
Cash Flow from Financing Activities	
Decrease in notes payable	(20)
Increase in long-term debts	56
Changes in stockholders' equity[b]	11
Dividends paid	(108)
Cash provided by financing activities	($ 61)
Net increase in cash and marketable securities	$ 92

[a]As is customary, parentheses are used to denote a negative number, which in this case is a cash outflow.

[b]Retained earnings are excluded here because their change is actually reflected in the combination of the "net profits after taxes" and "dividends paid" entries.

Financial Accounting Standards Board (FASB) Standard No. 52
Mandates that U.S.–based companies translate their foreign-currency-denominated assets and liabilities into dollars, for consolidation with the parent company's financial statements. This is done by using the *current rate (translation) method.*

current rate (translation) method
Technique used by U.S.–based companies to translate their foreign-currency-denominated assets and liabilities into dollars, for consolidation with the parent company's financial statements, using the year-end (current) exchange rate.

The current policy is described in **Financial Accounting Standards Board (FASB) Standard No. 52,** which mandates that U.S.–based companies translate their foreign-currency-denominated assets and liabilities into dollars, for consolidation with the parent company's financial statements. This is done by using a technique called the **current rate (translation) method,** under which all of a U.S. parent company's foreign-currency-denominated assets and liabilities are converted into dollar values using the exchange rate prevailing at the fiscal year ending date (the current rate). Income statement items are treated similarly. Equity accounts, on the other hand, are translated into dollars by using the exchange rate that prevailed when the parent's equity investment was made (the historical rate). Retained earnings are adjusted to reflect each year's operating profits or losses.

→ REVIEW QUESTIONS

3–1 What roles do GAAP, the FASB, and the PCAOB play in the financial reporting activities of public companies?

3–2 Describe the purpose of each of the four major financial statements.

3–3 Why are the notes to the financial statements important securities analysts?

3–4 How is the *current rate (translation) method* used to con foreign and domestic financial statements?

3.2 Using Financial Ratios

The information contained in the four basic financial statements is of major significance to a variety of interested parties who regularly need to have relative measures of the company's performance. *Relative* is the key word here, because the analysis of financial statements is based on the use of *ratios or relative values*. **Ratio analysis** involves methods of calculating and interpreting financial ratios to analyze and monitor the firm's performance. The basic inputs to ratio analysis are the firm's income statement and balance sheet.

ratio analysis
Involves methods of calculating and interpreting financial ratios to analyze and monitor the firm's performance.

INTERESTED PARTIES

Ratio analysis of a firm's financial statements is of interest to shareholders, creditors, and the firm's own management. Both current and prospective shareholders are interested in the firm's current and future level of risk and return, which directly affect share price. The firm's creditors are interested primarily in the short-term liquidity of the company and its ability to make interest and principal payments. A secondary concern of creditors is the firm's profitability; they want assurance that the business is healthy. Management, like stockholders, is concerned with all aspects of the firm's financial situation, and it attempts to produce financial ratios that will be considered favorable by both owners and creditors. In addition, management uses ratios to monitor the firm's performance from period to period.

TYPES OF RATIO COMPARISONS

Ratio analysis is not merely the calculation of a given ratio. More important is the *interpretation* of the ratio value. A meaningful basis for comparison is needed to answer such questions as "Is it too high or too low?" and "Is it good or bad?" Two types of ratio comparisons can be made, cross-sectional and time-series.

cross-sectional analysis
Comparison of different firms' financial ratios at the same point in time; involves comparing the firm's ratios to those of other firms in its industry or to industry averages.

benchmarking
A type of *cross-sectional analysis* in which the firm's ratio values are compared to those of a key competitor or group of competitors that it wishes to emulate.

Cross-Sectional Analysis

Cross-sectional analysis involves the comparison of different firms' financial ratios at the same point in time. Analysts are often interested in how well a firm has performed in relation to other firms in its industry. Frequently, a firm will compare its ratio values to those of a key competitor or group of competitors that it wishes to emulate. This type of cross-sectional analysis, called **benchmarking**, has become very popular.

Comparison to industry averages is also popular. These figures can be found in the *Almanac of Business and Industrial Financial Ratios*, *Dun & Bradstreet's Industry Norms and Key Business Ratios*, *RMA Annual Statement Studies*, *Value Line*, and industry sources. It is also possible to derive financial ratios for yourself using financial information reported in financial databases, such as Compustat. Table 3.5 illustrates a brief cross-sectional ratio analysis by comparing several

TABLE 3.5 Financial Ratios for Select Firms and Their Industry Median Values[a]

	Current ratio	Quick ratio	Inventory turnover	Average collection period (days)	Total asset turnover	Debt ratio	Net profit margin (%)	Return on total assets (%)	Return on Common Equity (%)
Dell	1.3	1.2	40.5	58.9	1.6	0.8	2.7	4.3	25.4
Hewlett-Packard	1.2	1.1	13.8	80.6	1.0	0.6	6.7	6.7	18.9
Computers	2.5	2.1	5.8	61.3	0.9	0.4	−3.1	−2.2	−2.6
Home Depot	1.3	0.4	4.3	5.3	1.6	0.5	4.0	6.5	13.7
Lowe's	1.3	0.2	3.7	0.0	1.4	0.4	3.7	5.4	9.3
Building Materials	2.8	0.8	3.7	5.3	1.6	0.3	4.0	6.5	13.7
Kroger	1.0	0.3	12.0	4.3	3.3	0.8	0.1	0.3	1.4
Whole Foods Market	1.3	1.0	25.6	7.0	3.6	0.4	2.3	8.0	14.5
Grocery Stores	1.3	0.7	11.1	7.5	2.4	0.6	2.1	3.1	9.8
Sears	1.3	0.3	3.7	5.4	1.8	0.6	0.5	0.9	2.6
Wal-Mart	0.9	0.3	9.0	3.7	2.4	0.6	3.5	8.4	20.3
Merchandise Stores	1.7	0.6	4.1	3.7	2.3	0.5	1.5	4.9	10.8

[a]The data used to calculate these ratios are drawn from the Compustat North American database.

ratios as of early 2010 for two select firms to each other and the median value for their particular industry.

Analysts have to be very careful when drawing conclusions from ratio comparisons. It's tempting to assume that if one ratio for a particular firm is above the industry norm, this is a sign that the firm is performing well, at least along the dimension measured by that ratio. However, ratios may be above or below the industry norm for both positive and negative reasons, and it is necessary to determine why a firm's performance differs from its industry peers. *Thus, ratio analysis on its own is probably most useful in highlighting areas for further investigation.*

Example 3.3 ▶ In early 2013, Mary Boyle, the chief financial analyst at Caldwell Manufacturing, a producer of heat exchangers, gathered data on the firm's financial performance during 2012, the year just ended. She calculated a variety of ratios and obtained industry averages. She was especially interested in inventory turnover, which reflects the speed with which the firm moves its inventory from raw materials through production into finished goods and to the customer as a completed sale. Generally, higher values of this ratio are preferred, because they indicate a quicker turnover of inventory and more efficient inventory management. Caldwell Manufacturing's calculated inventory turnover for 2012 and the industry average inventory turnover were as follows:

	Inventory Turnover, 2012
Caldwell Manufacturing	14.8
Industry average	9.7

Mary's initial reaction to these data was that the firm had managed its inventory significantly *better than* the average firm in the industry. The turnover was nearly 53% faster than the industry average. On reflection, however, she realized that a very high inventory turnover could be a sign that the firm is not holding enough inventories. The consequence of low inventory could be excessive stockouts (insufficient inventory to meet customer needs). Discussions with people in the manufacturing and marketing departments did, in fact, uncover such a problem: Inventories during the year were extremely low, the result of numerous production delays that hindered the firm's ability to meet demand and resulted in disgruntled customers and lost sales. A ratio that initially appeared to reflect extremely efficient inventory management was actually the symptom of a major problem.

Time-Series Analysis

time-series analysis
Evaluation of the firm's financial performance over time using financial ratio analysis.

Time-series analysis evaluates performance over time. Comparison of current to past performance, using ratios, enables analysts to assess the firm's progress. Developing trends can be seen by using multiyear comparisons. Any significant year-to-year changes may be symptomatic of a problem, especially if the same trend is not an industry-wide phenomenon.

Combined Analysis

The most informative approach to ratio analysis combines cross-sectional and time-series analyses. A combined view makes it possible to assess the trend in the behavior of the ratio in relation to the trend for the industry. Figure 3.1 depicts this type of approach using the average collection period ratio of Bartlett Company, over the years 2009–2012. This ratio reflects the average amount of time (in days) it takes the firm to collect bills, and lower values of this ratio generally are preferred. The figure quickly discloses that (1) Bartlett's effectiveness in collecting its receivables is poor in comparison to the industry, and (2) Bartlett's trend is toward longer collection periods. Clearly, Bartlett needs to shorten its collection period.

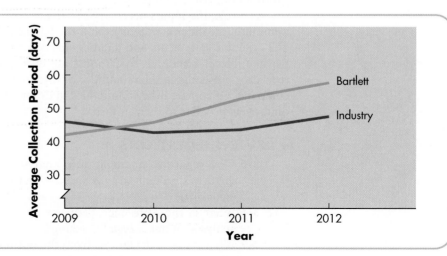

FIGURE 3.1

Combined Analysis
Combined cross-sectional and time-series view of Bartlett Company's average collection period, 2009–2012

In more depth

To read about *Perils of Ratio Analysis*, go to www.myfinancelab.com

 myfinancelab

CAUTIONS ABOUT USING RATIO ANALYSIS

Before discussing specific ratios, we should consider the following cautions about their use:

1. Ratios that reveal large deviations from the norm merely indicate *the possibility* of a problem. Additional analysis is typically needed to determine whether there is a problem and to isolate the *causes* of the problem.

2. A single ratio does not generally provide sufficient information from which to judge the *overall* performance of the firm. However, if an analysis is concerned only with certain *specific* aspects of a firm's financial position, one or two ratios may suffice.

3. The ratios being compared should be calculated using financial statements dated at the same point in time during the year. If they are not, the effects of *seasonality* may produce erroneous conclusions and decisions.

4. It is preferable to use *audited financial statements* for ratio analysis. If they have not been audited, the data in them may not reflect the firm's true financial condition.

5. The financial data being compared should have been developed in the same way. The use of differing accounting treatments—especially relative to inventory and depreciation—can distort the results of ratio comparisons, regardless of whether cross-sectional or time-series analysis is used.

6. Results can be distorted by *inflation,* which can cause the book values of inventory and depreciable assets to differ greatly from their replacement values. Additionally, inventory costs and depreciation write-offs can differ from their true values, thereby distorting profits. Without adjustment, inflation tends to cause older firms (older assets) to appear more efficient and profitable than newer firms (newer assets). Clearly, in using ratios, you must be careful when comparing older to newer firms or a firm to itself over a long period of time.

CATEGORIES OF FINANCIAL RATIOS

Financial ratios can be divided for convenience into five basic categories: liquidity, activity, debt, profitability, and market ratios. Liquidity, activity, and debt ratios primarily measure risk. Profitability ratios measure return. Market ratios capture both risk and return.

As a rule, the inputs necessary for an effective financial analysis include, at a minimum, the income statement and the balance sheet. We will use the 2012 and 2011 income statements and balance sheets for Bartlett Company, presented earlier in Tables 3.1 and 3.2, to demonstrate ratio calculations. Note, however, that the ratios presented in the remainder of this chapter can be applied to almost any company. Of course, many companies in different industries use ratios that focus on aspects peculiar to their industry.

→ **REVIEW QUESTIONS**

3–5 With regard to financial ratio analysis, how do the viewpoints held by the firm's present and prospective shareholders, creditors, and management differ?

3–6 What is the difference between *cross-sectional* and *time-series* ratio analysis? What is *benchmarking?*

3–7 What types of deviations from the norm should the analyst pay primary attention to when performing cross-sectional ratio analysis? Why?

3–8 Why is it preferable to compare ratios calculated using financial statements that are dated at the same point in time during the year?

LG 3 ## 3.3 Liquidity Ratios

liquidity
A firm's ability to satisfy its short-term obligations *as they come due.*

The **liquidity** of a firm is measured by its ability to satisfy its short-term obligations *as they come due.* Liquidity refers to the solvency of the firm's *overall* financial position—the ease with which it can pay its bills. Because a common precursor to financial distress and bankruptcy is low or declining liquidity, these ratios can provide early signs of cash flow problems and impending business failure. Clearly it is desirable that a firm is able to pay its bills, so having enough liquidity for day-to-day operations is important. However, liquid assets, like cash held at banks and marketable securities, do not earn a particularly high rate of return, so shareholders will not want a firm to *overinvest* in liquidity. Firms have to balance the need for safety that liquidity provides against the low returns that liquid assets generate for investors. The two basic measures of liquidity are the current ratio and the quick (acid-test) ratio.

CURRENT RATIO

current ratio
A measure of liquidity calculated by dividing the firm's current assets by its current liabilities.

The **current ratio,** one of the most commonly cited financial ratios, measures the firm's ability to meet its short-term obligations. It is expressed as follows:

$$\text{Current ratio} = \text{Current assets} \div \text{Current liabilities}$$

The current ratio for Bartlett Company in 2012 is

$$\$1,223,000 \div \$620,000 = 1.97$$

A higher current ratio indicates a greater degree of liquidity. How much liquidity a firm needs depends on a variety of factors, including the firm's size, its access to short-term financing sources like bank credit lines, and the volatility of its business. For example, a grocery store whose revenues are relatively predictable may not need as much liquidity as a manufacturing firm who faces sudden and unexpected shifts in demand for its products. The more predictable a firm's cash flows, the lower the acceptable current ratio. Because Bartlett Company is in a business with a relatively predictable annual cash flow, its current ratio of 1.97 should be quite acceptable.

Matter of fact

Determinants of Liquidity Needs

Glance back at the first column of data in Table 3.5 that shows the current ratio for a variety of companies and industries. Notice that the industry with the highest current ratio (that is, most liquidity) is building materials, a business that is notoriously sensitive to business cycle swings. The current ratio for that industry is 2.8, indicating that the typical firm in that business has almost three times as much in current assets as in current liabilities. Two of the largest competitors in that industry, The Home Depot and Lowe's, operate with a current ratio of 1.3, less than half the industry average. Does this mean that these firms have a liquidity problem? Not necessarily. Large enterprises generally have well-established relationships with banks that can provide lines of credit and other short-term loan products in the event that the firm has a need for liquidity. Smaller firms may not have the same access to credit, and therefore they tend to operate with more liquidity.

Personal Finance Example 3.4 ▶   Individuals, like corporations, can use financial ratios to analyze and monitor their performance. Typically, personal finance ratios are calculated using the personal income and expense statement and personal balance sheet for the period of concern. Here we use these statements, presented in the preceding personal finance examples, to demonstrate calculation of Jan and Jon Smith's liquidity ratio for calendar year 2012.

The personal *liquidity ratio* is calculated by dividing total liquid assets by total current debt. It indicates the percent of annual debt obligations that an individual can meet using current liquid assets. The Smiths' total liquid assets were $2,225. Their total current debts are $21,539 (total current liabilities of $905 + mortgage payments of $16,864 + auto loan payments of $2,520 + appliance and furniture payments of $1,250). Substituting these values into the ratio formula, we get:

$$\text{Liquidity ratio} = \frac{\text{Total liquid assets}}{\text{Total current debts}} = \frac{\$2,225}{\$21,539} = 0.1033, \text{ or } 10.3\%$$

That ratio indicates that the Smiths can cover only about 10% of their existing 1-year debt obligations with their current liquid assets. Clearly, the Smiths plan to meet these debt obligations from their income, but this ratio suggests that their liquid funds do not provide a large cushion. One of their goals should probably be to build up a larger fund of liquid assets to meet unexpected expenses.

QUICK (ACID-TEST) RATIO

quick (acid-test) ratio
A measure of liquidity calculated by dividing the firm's current assets minus inventory by its current liabilities.

The **quick (acid-test) ratio** is similar to the current ratio except that it excludes inventory, which is generally the least liquid current asset. The generally low liquidity of inventory results from two primary factors: (1) Many types of inventory cannot be easily sold because they are partially completed items, special-purpose items, and the like; and (2) inventory is typically sold on credit, which means that it becomes an account receivable before being converted into cash. An additional problem with inventory as a liquid asset is that the times when companies face the most dire need for liquidity, when business is bad, are precisely the times when it is most difficult to convert inventory into cash by selling it. The quick ratio is calculated as follows:

$$\text{Quick ratio} = \frac{\text{Current assets} - \text{Inventory}}{\text{Current liabilities}}$$

The quick ratio for Bartlett Company in 2012 is

$$\frac{\$1,223,000 - \$289,000}{\$620,000} = \frac{\$934,000}{\$620,000} = 1.51$$

As with the current ratio, the quick ratio level that a firm should strive to achieve depends largely on the nature of the business in which it operates. The quick ratio provides a better measure of overall liquidity only when a firm's inventory cannot be easily converted into cash. If inventory is liquid, the current ratio is a preferred measure of overall liquidity.

> ## Matter of fact
>
> ### The Importance of Inventories
>
> Turn again to Table 3.5 and examine the columns listing current and quick ratios for different firms and industries. Notice that Dell has a current ratio of 1.3, and so do The Home Depot and Lowe's. However, although the quick ratios for The Home Depot and Lowe's are dramatically lower than their current ratios, for Dell the current and quick ratios have nearly the same value. Why? For many years, Dell operated on a "built-to-order" business model that required them to hold very little inventory. In contrast, all it takes is a trip to your local Home Depot or Lowe's store to see that the business model in this industry requires a massive investment in inventory, which implies that the quick ratio will be much less than the current ratio for building materials firms.

→ REVIEW QUESTIONS

3–9 Under what circumstances would the current ratio be the preferred measure of overall firm liquidity? Under what circumstances would the quick ratio be preferred?

3–10 In Table 3.5, most of the specific firms listed have current ratios that fall below the industry average. Why? The exception to this general pattern is Whole Foods Market, which competes at the very high end of the retail grocery market. Why might Whole Foods Market operate with greater-than-average liquidity?

LG 3   3.4 Activity Ratios

activity ratios
Measure the speed with which various accounts are converted into sales or cash—inflows or outflows.

Activity ratios measure the speed with which various accounts are converted into sales or cash—inflows or outflows. In a sense, activity ratios measure how efficiently a firm operates along a variety of dimensions such as inventory management, disbursements, and collections. A number of ratios are available for measuring the activity of the most important current accounts, which include inventory, accounts receivable, and accounts payable. The efficiency with which total assets are used can also be assessed.

INVENTORY TURNOVER

inventory turnover
Measures the activity, or liquidity, of a firm's inventory.

Inventory turnover commonly measures the activity, or liquidity, of a firm's inventory. It is calculated as follows:

$$\text{Inventory turnover} = \text{Cost of goods sold} \div \text{Inventory}$$

Applying this relationship to Bartlett Company in 2012 yields

$$\$2,088,000 \div \$289,000 = 7.2$$

The resulting turnover is meaningful only when it is compared with that of other firms in the same industry or to the firm's past inventory turnover. An inventory turnover of 20 would not be unusual for a grocery store, whose goods are highly perishable and must be sold quickly, whereas an aircraft manufacturer might turn its inventory just four times per year.

average age of inventory
Average number of days' sales in inventory.

Another inventory activity ratio measures how many days of inventory the firm has on hand. Inventory turnover can be easily converted into an **average age of inventory** by dividing it into 365. For Bartlett Company, the average age of inventory in 2012 is 50.7 days (365 ÷ 7.2). This value can also be viewed as the average number of days' sales in inventory.

AVERAGE COLLECTION PERIOD

average collection period
The average amount of time needed to collect accounts receivable.

The **average collection period,** or average age of accounts receivable, is useful in evaluating credit and collection policies. It is arrived at by dividing the average daily sales into the accounts receivable balance:[2]

$$\text{Average collection period} = \frac{\text{Accounts receivable}}{\text{Average sales per day}}$$
$$= \frac{\text{Accounts receivable}}{\dfrac{\text{Annual sales}}{365}}$$

The average collection period for Bartlett Company in 2012 is

$$\frac{\$503,000}{\dfrac{\$3,074,000}{365}} = \frac{\$503,000}{\$8,422} = 59.7 \text{ days}$$

On the average, it takes the firm 59.7 days to collect an account receivable.

The average collection period is meaningful only in relation to the firm's credit terms. If Bartlett Company extends 30-day credit terms to customers, an average collection period of 59.7 days may indicate a poorly managed credit or collection department, or both. It is also possible that the lengthened collection period resulted from an intentional relaxation of credit-term enforcement in response to competitive pressures. If the firm had extended 60-day credit terms, the 59.7-day average collection period would be quite acceptable. Clearly, additional information is needed to evaluate the effectiveness of the firm's credit and collection policies.

Matter of fact

Who Gets Credit?

Notice in Table 3.5 the vast differences across industries in the average collection periods. Companies in the building materials, grocery, and merchandise store industries collect in just a few days, whereas firms in the computer industry take roughly two months to collect on their sales. The difference is primarily due to the fact that these industries serve very different customers. Grocery and retail stores serve individuals who pay cash or use credit cards (which to the store are essentially the same as cash). Computer manufacturers sell to retail chains, businesses, and other large organizations that negotiate agreements that allow them to pay for the computers they order well after the sale is made.

2. The formula as presented assumes, for simplicity, that all sales are made on a credit basis. If this is not the case, *average credit sales per day* should be substituted for average sales per day.

AVERAGE PAYMENT PERIOD

average payment period
The average amount of time
needed to pay accounts
payable.

The **average payment period,** or average age of accounts payable, is calculated in the same manner as the average collection period:

$$\text{Average payment period} = \frac{\text{Accounts payable}}{\text{Average purchases per day}}$$

$$= \frac{\text{Accounts payable}}{\dfrac{\text{Annual purchases}}{365}}$$

The difficulty in calculating this ratio stems from the need to find annual purchases,[3] a value not available in published financial statements. Ordinarily, purchases are estimated as a given percentage of cost of goods sold. If we assume that Bartlett Company's purchases equaled 70 percent of its cost of goods sold in 2012, its average payment period is

$$\frac{\$382,000}{\dfrac{0.70 \times \$2,088,000}{365}} = \frac{\$382,000}{\$4,004} = 95.4 \text{ days}$$

This figure is meaningful only in relation to the average credit terms extended to the firm. If Bartlett Company's suppliers have extended, on average, 30-day credit terms, an analyst would give Bartlett a low credit rating because it was taking too long to pay its bills. Prospective lenders and suppliers of trade credit are interested in the average payment period because it provides insight into the firm's bill-paying patterns.

TOTAL ASSET TURNOVER

total asset turnover
Indicates the efficiency with
which the firm uses its assets to
generate sales.

The **total asset turnover** indicates the efficiency with which the firm uses its assets to generate sales. Total asset turnover is calculated as follows:

$$\text{Total asset turnover} = \text{Sales} \div \text{Total assets}$$

The value of Bartlett Company's total asset turnover in 2012 is

$$\$3,074,000 \div \$3,597,000 = 0.85$$

This means the company turns over its assets 0.85 times per year.

Generally, the higher a firm's total asset turnover, the more efficiently its assets have been used. This measure is probably of greatest interest to management because it indicates whether the firm's operations have been financially efficient.

Matter of fact

Sell It Fast

Observe in Table 3.5 that the grocery business turns over assets faster than any of the other industries listed. That makes sense because inventory is among the most valuable assets held by these firms, and grocery stores have to sell baked goods, dairy products, and produce quickly or throw them away when they spoil. It's true that some items in a grocery store have a shelf life longer than anyone really wants to know (think Twinkies), but on average a grocery store has to replace its entire inventory in just a few days or weeks, and that contributes to the rapid turnover of the firm's total assets.

---

3. Technically, annual *credit* purchases—rather than annual purchases—should be used in calculating this ratio. For simplicity, this refinement is ignored here.

→ **REVIEW QUESTION**

3–11 To assess the firm's average collection period and average payment period ratios, what additional information is needed, and why?

LG 4   **3.5** Debt Ratios

The *debt position* of a firm indicates the amount of other people's money being used to generate profits. In general, the financial analyst is most concerned with long-term debts because these commit the firm to a stream of contractual payments over the long run. The more debt a firm has, the greater its risk of being unable to meet its contractual debt payments. Because creditors' claims must be satisfied before the earnings can be distributed to shareholders, current and prospective shareholders pay close attention to the firm's ability to repay debts. Lenders are also concerned about the firm's indebtedness.

In general, the more debt a firm uses in relation to its total assets, the greater its *financial leverage*. **Financial leverage** is the magnification of risk and return through the use of fixed-cost financing, such as debt and preferred stock. The more fixed-cost debt a firm uses, the greater will be its expected risk and return.

financial leverage
The magnification of risk and return through the use of fixed-cost financing, such as debt and preferred stock.

Example 3.5 ▶

Patty Akers is in the process of incorporating her new business. After much analysis she determined that an initial investment of $50,000—$20,000 in current assets and $30,000 in fixed assets—is necessary. These funds can be obtained in either of two ways. The first is the *no-debt plan,* under which she would invest the full $50,000 without borrowing. The other alternative, the *debt plan,* involves investing $25,000 and borrowing the balance of $25,000 at 12% annual interest.

Patty expects $30,000 in sales, $18,000 in operating expenses, and a 40% tax rate. Projected balance sheets and income statements associated with the two plans are summarized in Table 3.6. The no-debt plan results in after-tax profits of $7,200, which represent a 14.4% rate of return on Patty's $50,000 investment. The debt plan results in $5,400 of after-tax profits, which represent a 21.6% rate of return on Patty's investment of $25,000. The debt plan provides Patty with a higher rate of return, but the risk of this plan is also greater, because the annual $3,000 of interest must be paid whether Patty's business is profitable or not.

The example demonstrates that *with increased debt comes greater risk as well as higher potential return.* Therefore, the greater the financial leverage, the greater the potential risk and return. A detailed discussion of the impact of debt on the firm's risk, return, and value is included in Chapter 12. Here, we emphasize the use of financial debt ratios to assess externally a firm's debt position.

There are two general types of debt measures: measures of the degree of indebtedness and measures of the ability to service debts. The **degree of indebtedness** measures the amount of debt relative to other significant balance sheet amounts. A popular measure of the degree of indebtedness is the debt ratio.

The second type of debt measure, the **ability to service debts**, reflects a firm's ability to make the payments required on a scheduled basis over the life of a debt.

degree of indebtedness
Measures the amount of debt relative to other significant balance sheet amounts.

ability to service debts
The ability of a firm to make the payments required on a scheduled basis over the life of a debt.

TABLE 3.6	Financial Statements Associated with Patty's Alternatives	

Balance Sheets	No-debt plan	Debt plan
Current assets	$20,000	$20,000
Fixed assets	30,000	30,000
Total assets	$50,000	$50,000
Debt (12% interest)	$ 0	$25,000
(1) Equity	50,000	25,000
Total liabilities and equity	$50,000	$50,000

Income Statements		
Sales	$30,000	$30,000
Less: Operating expenses	18,000	18,000
Operating profits	$12,000	$12,000
Less: Interest expense	0	$0.12 \times \$25,000 =$ 3,000
Net profits before taxes	$12,000	$ 9,000
Less: Taxes (rate = 40%)	4,800	3,600
(2) Net profits after taxes	$ 7,200	$ 5,400
Return on equity [(2) ÷ (1)]	$\frac{\$7,200}{\$50,000} = $ 14.4%	$\frac{\$5,400}{\$25,000} = $ 21.6%

coverage ratios
Ratios that measure the firm's ability to pay certain fixed charges.

The term *to service debts* simply means to pay debts on time. The firm's ability to pay certain fixed charges is measured using **coverage ratios.** Typically, higher coverage ratios are preferred (especially by the firm's lenders), but a very high ratio might indicate that the firm's management is too conservative and might be able to earn higher returns by borrowing more. In general, the lower the firm's coverage ratios, the less certain it is to be able to pay fixed obligations. If a firm is unable to pay these obligations, its creditors may seek immediate repayment, which in most instances would force a firm into bankruptcy. Two popular coverage ratios are the times interest earned ratio and the fixed-payment coverage ratio.

DEBT RATIO

debt ratio
Measures the proportion of total assets financed by the firm's creditors.

The **debt ratio** measures the proportion of total assets financed by the firm's creditors. The higher this ratio, the greater the amount of other people's money being used to generate profits. The ratio is calculated as follows:

$$\text{Debt ratio} = \text{Total liabilities} \div \text{Total assets}$$

The debt ratio for Bartlett Company in 2012 is

$$\$1,643,000 \div \$3,597,000 = 0.457 = 45.7\%$$

This value indicates that the company has financed close to half of its assets with debt. The higher this ratio, the greater the firm's degree of indebtedness and the more financial leverage it has.

TIMES INTEREST EARNED RATIO

times interest earned ratio
Measures the firm's ability to make contractual interest payments; sometimes called the *interest coverage ratio.*

The **times interest earned ratio,** sometimes called the *interest coverage ratio,* measures the firm's ability to make contractual interest payments. The higher its value, the better able the firm is to fulfill its interest obligations. The times interest earned ratio is calculated as follows:

$$\text{Times interest earned ratio} = \text{Earnings before interest and taxes} \div \text{taxes}$$

The figure for *earnings before interest and taxes (EBIT)* is the same as that for *operating profits* shown in the income statement. Applying this ratio to Bartlett Company yields the following 2012 value:

$$\text{Time interest earned ratio} = \$418,000 \div \$93,000 = 4.5$$

The times interest earned ratio for Bartlett Company seems acceptable. A value of at least 3.0—and preferably closer to 5.0—is often suggested. The firm's earnings before interest and taxes could shrink by as much as 78 percent $[(4.5 - 1.0) \div 4.5]$, and the firm would still be able to pay the $93,000 in interest it owes. Thus it has a large margin of safety.

FIXED-PAYMENT COVERAGE RATIO

fixed-payment coverage ratio
Measures the firm's ability to meet all fixed-payment obligations.

The **fixed-payment coverage ratio** measures the firm's ability to meet all fixed-payment obligations, such as loan interest and principal, lease payments, and preferred stock dividends. As is true of the times interest earned ratio, the higher this value the better. The formula for the fixed-payment coverage ratio is

$$\frac{\text{Fixed-payment coverage ratio}}{} = \frac{\text{Earnings before interest and taxes} + \text{Lease payments}}{\text{Interest} + \text{Lease payments} + \{(\text{Principal payments} + \text{Preferred stock dividends}) \times [1/(1 - T)]\}}$$

where T is the corporate tax rate applicable to the firm's income. The term $1/(1 - T)$ is included to adjust the after-tax principal and preferred stock dividend payments back to a before-tax equivalent that is consistent with the before-tax values of all other terms. Applying the formula to Bartlett Company's 2012 data yields

$$\frac{\text{Fixed-payment coverage ratio}}{} = \frac{\$418,000 + \$35,000}{\$93,000 + \$35,000 + \{(\$71,000 + \$10,000) \times [1/(1 - 0.29)]\}}$$

$$= \frac{\$453,000}{\$242,000} = 1.9$$

Because the earnings available are nearly twice as large as its fixed-payment obligations, the firm appears safely able to meet the latter.

Like the times interest earned ratio, the fixed-payment coverage ratio measures risk. The lower the ratio, the greater the risk to both lenders and owners, and the greater the ratio, the lower the risk. This ratio allows interested parties to assess the firm's ability to meet additional fixed-payment obligations without being driven into bankruptcy.

→ REVIEW QUESTIONS

3–12 What is *financial leverage?*

3–13 What ratio measures the firm's *degree of indebtedness?* What ratios assess the firm's *ability to service debts?*

LG 5   ## 3.6 Profitability Ratios

There are many measures of profitability. As a group, these measures enable analysts to evaluate the firm's profits with respect to a given level of sales, a certain level of assets, or the owners' investment. Without profits, a firm could not attract outside capital. Owners, creditors, and management pay close attention to boosting profits because of the great importance the market places on earnings.

COMMON-SIZE INCOME STATEMENTS

common-size income statement
An income statement in which each item is expressed as a percentage of sales.

A useful tool for evaluating profitability in relation to sales is the **common-size income statement.** Each item on this statement is expressed as a percentage of sales. Common-size income statements are especially useful in comparing performance across years because it is easy to see if certain categories of expenses are trending up or down as a percentage of the total volume of business that the company transacts. Three frequently cited ratios of profitability that come directly from the common-size income statement are (1) the gross profit margin, (2) the operating profit margin, and (3) the net profit margin.

Common-size income statements for 2012 and 2011 for Bartlett Company are presented and evaluated in Table 3.7 on page 80. These statements reveal that the firm's cost of goods sold increased from 66.7 percent of sales in 2011 to 67.9 percent in 2012, resulting in a worsening gross profit margin. However, thanks to a decrease in total operating expenses, the firm's net profit margin rose from 5.4 percent of sales in 2011 to 7.2 percent in 2012. The decrease in expenses more than compensated for the increase in the cost of goods sold. A decrease in the firm's 2012 interest expense (3.0 percent of sales versus 3.5 percent in 2011) added to the increase in 2012 profits.

GROSS PROFIT MARGIN

gross profit margin
Measures the percentage of each sales dollar remaining after the firm has paid for its goods.

The **gross profit margin** measures the percentage of each sales dollar remaining after the firm has paid for its goods. The higher the gross profit margin, the better (that is, the lower the relative cost of merchandise sold). The gross profit margin is calculated as follows:

$$\text{Gross profit margin} = \frac{\text{Sales} - \text{Cost of goods sold}}{\text{Sales}} = \frac{\text{Gross profits}}{\text{Sales}}$$

Bartlett Company's gross profit margin for 2012 is

$$\frac{\$3,074,000 - \$2,088,000}{\$3,074,000} = \frac{\$986,000}{\$3,074,000} = 32.1\%$$

This value is labeled (1) on the common-size income statement in Table 3.7.

TABLE 3.7	Bartlett Company Common-Size Income Statements		
	For the Years Ended December 31		Evaluation[a] 2011–2012
	2012	2011	
Sales revenue	100.0%	100.0%	Same
Less: Cost of goods sold	67.9	66.7	Worse
(1) Gross profit margin	32.1%	33.3%	Worse
Less: Operating expenses			
Selling expense	3.3%	4.2%	Better
General and administrative expenses	6.8	6.7	Better
Lease expense	1.1	1.3	Better
Depreciation expense	7.3	9.3	Better
Total operating expense	18.5%	21.5%	Better
(2) Operating profit margin	13.6%	11.8%	Better
Less: Interest expense	3.0	3.5	Better
Net profits before taxes	10.6%	8.3%	Better
Less: Taxes	3.1	2.5	Worse[b]
Net profits after taxes	7.5%	5.8%	Better
Less: Preferred stock dividends	0.3	0.4	Better
(3) Net profit margin	7.2%	5.4%	Better

[a]Subjective assessments based on data provided.

[b]Taxes as a percentage of sales increased noticeably between 2011 and 2012 because of differing costs and expenses, whereas the average tax rates (taxes ÷ net profits before taxes) for 2011 and 2012 remained about the same—30% and 29%, respectively.

OPERATING PROFIT MARGIN

operating profit margin
Measures the percentage of each sales dollar remaining after all costs and expenses *other than* interest, taxes, and preferred stock dividends are deducted; the "pure profits" earned on each sales dollar.

The **operating profit margin** measures the percentage of each sales dollar remaining after all costs and expenses *other than* interest, taxes, and preferred stock dividends are deducted. It represents the "pure profits" earned on each sales dollar. Operating profits are "pure" because they measure only the profits earned on operations and ignore interest, taxes, and preferred stock dividends. A high operating profit margin is preferred. The operating profit margin is calculated as follows:

$$\text{Operating profit margin} = \text{Operating profits} \div \text{Sales}$$

Bartlett Company's operating profit margin for 2012 is

$$\$418,000 \div \$3,074,000 = 13.6\%$$

$$\frac{\$418,000}{\$3,074,000} = 13.6\%$$

net profit margin
Measures the percentage of each sales dollar remaining after all costs and expenses, *including* interest, taxes, and preferred stock dividends, have been deducted.

This value is labeled (2) on the common-size income statement in Table 3.7.

NET PROFIT MARGIN

The **net profit margin** measures the percentage of each sales dollar remaining after all costs and expenses, *including* interest, taxes, and preferred stock dividends, have been deducted. The higher the firm's net profit margin, the better. The net profit margin is calculated as follows:

Net profit margin = Earnings available for common stockholders ÷ Sales

Bartlett Company's net profit margin for 2012 is:

$$\$221,000 \div \$3,074,000 = 0.072 = 7.2\%$$

$$\frac{\$221,000}{\$3,074,000} = 7.2\%$$

This value is labeled (3) on the common-size income statement in Table 3.7.

The net profit margin is a commonly cited measure of the firm's success with respect to earnings on sales. "Good" net profit margins differ considerably across industries. A net profit margin of 1 percent or less would not be unusual for a grocery store, whereas a net profit margin of 10 percent would be low for a retail jewelry store.

EARNINGS PER SHARE (EPS)

The firm's *earnings per share (EPS)* is generally of interest to present or prospective stockholders and management. As we noted earlier, EPS represents the number of dollars earned during the period on behalf of each outstanding share of common stock. Earnings per share is calculated as follows:

$$\text{Earnings per share} = \frac{\text{Earnings available for common stockholders}}{\text{Number of shares of common stock outstanding}}$$

Bartlett Company's earnings per share in 2012 is

$$\$221,000 \div 76,262 = \$2.90$$

This figure represents the dollar amount earned *on behalf of* each outstanding share of common stock. The dollar amount of cash *actually distributed* to each shareholder is the *dividend per share (DPS)*, which, as noted in Bartlett Company's income statement (Table 3.1), rose to $1.29 in 2012 from $0.75 in 2011. EPS is closely watched by the investing public and is considered an important indicator of corporate success.

RETURN ON TOTAL ASSETS (ROA)

return on total assets (ROA)
Measures the overall effectiveness of management in generating profits with its available assets; also called the *return on investment (ROI)*.

The **return on total assets (ROA)**, often called the *return on investment (ROI)*, measures the overall effectiveness of management in generating profits with its available assets. The higher the firm's return on total assets the better. The return on total assets is calculated as follows:

ROA = Earnings available for common stockholders ÷ Total assets

Bartlett Company's return on total assets in 2012 is

$$\frac{\$221,000}{\$3,597,000} = 6.1\%$$

$$\$221,000 \div \$3,597,000 = 0.061 = 6.1\%$$

This value indicates that the company earned 6.1 cents on each dollar of asset investment.

RETURN ON COMMON EQUITY (ROE)

return on common equity (ROE)
Measures the return earned on the common stockholders' investment in the firm.

The **return on common equity (ROE)** measures the return earned on the common stockholders' investment in the firm. Generally, the owners are better off the higher is this return. Return on common equity is calculated as follows:

ROE = Earnings available for common stockholders ÷ Common stock equity

This ratio for Bartlett Company in 2012 is

$$\$221,000 \div \$1,754,000 = 0.126 = 12.6\%$$

$$\frac{\$221,000}{\$1,754,000} = 12.6\%$$

Note that the value for common stock equity ($1,754,000) was found by subtracting the $200,000 of preferred stock equity from the total stockholders' equity of $1,954,000 (see Bartlett Company's 2012 balance sheet in Table 3.2). The calculated ROE of 12.6 percent indicates that during 2012 Bartlett earned 12.6 cents on each dollar of common stock equity.

→ **REVIEW QUESTIONS**

3–14 What three ratios of profitability are found on a *common-size income statement?*

3–15 What would explain a firm's having a high gross profit margin and a low net profit margin?

3–16 Which measure of profitability is probably of greatest interest to the investing public? Why?

LG 5   **3.7 Market Ratios**

market ratios
Relate a firm's market value, as measured by its current share price, to certain accounting values.

Market ratios relate the firm's market value, as measured by its current share price, to certain accounting values. These ratios give insight into how investors in the marketplace feel the firm is doing in terms of risk and return. They tend to reflect, on a relative basis, the common stockholders' assessment of all aspects of the firm's past and expected future performance. Here we consider two widely quoted market ratios, one that focuses on earnings and another that considers book value.

PRICE/EARNINGS (P/E) RATIO

price/earnings (P/E) ratio
Measures the amount that investors are willing to pay for each dollar of a firm's earnings; the higher the P/E ratio, the greater the investor confidence.

The **price/earnings (P/E) ratio** is commonly used to assess the owners' appraisal of share value. The P/E ratio measures the amount that investors are willing to pay for each dollar of a firm's earnings. The level of this ratio indicates the degree of confidence that investors have in the firm's future performance. The higher the P/E ratio, the greater the investor confidence. The P/E ratio is calculated as follows:

P/E ratio = Market price per share of common stock ÷ Earnings per share

If Bartlett Company's common stock at the end of 2012 was selling at $32.25, using the EPS of $2.90, the P/E ratio at year-end 2012 is

$$\$32.25 \div \$2.90 = 11.1$$

This figure indicates that investors were paying $11.10 for each $1.00 of earnings. The P/E ratio is most informative when applied in cross-sectional analysis using an industry average P/E ratio or the P/E ratio of a benchmark firm.

MARKET/BOOK (M/B) RATIO

market/book (M/B) ratio
Provides an assessment of
how investors view the firm's
performance. Firms expected
to earn high returns relative to
their risk typically sell at higher
M/B multiples.

The **market/book (M/B) ratio** provides an assessment of how investors view the firm's performance. It relates the market value of the firm's shares to their book—strict accounting—value. To calculate the firm's M/B ratio, we first need to find the *book value per share of common stock:*

$$\text{Book value per share of common stock} = \frac{\text{Common stock equity}}{\text{Number of shares of common stock outstanding}}$$

Substituting the appropriate values for Bartlett Company from its 2012 balance sheet, we get

$$\text{Book value per share of common stock} = \frac{\$1,754,000}{76,262} = \$23.00$$

The formula for the market/book ratio is

$$\text{Market/book (M/B) ratio} = \frac{\text{Market price per share of common stock}}{\text{Book value per share of common stock}}$$

Substituting Bartlett Company's end of 2012 common stock price of $32.25 and its $23.00 book value per share of common stock (calculated above) into the M/B ratio formula, we get

$$\$32.25 \div \$23.00 = 1.40$$

This M/B ratio means that investors are currently paying $1.40 for each $1.00 of book value of Bartlett Company's stock.

The stocks of firms that are expected to perform well—improve profits, increase their market share, or launch successful products—typically sell at higher M/B ratios than the stocks of firms with less attractive outlooks. Simply stated, firms expected to earn high returns relative to their risk typically sell at higher M/B multiples. Clearly, Bartlett's future prospects are being viewed favorably by investors, who are willing to pay more than their book value for the firm's shares. Like P/E ratios, M/B ratios are typically assessed cross-sectionally to get a feel for the firm's return and risk compared to peer firms.

→ **REVIEW QUESTION**

3–17 How do the *price/earnings (P/E) ratio* and the *market/book (M/B) ratio* provide a feel for the firm's return and risk?

LG 6   ## 3.8 A Complete Ratio Analysis

Analysts frequently wish to take an overall look at the firm's financial performance and status. Here we consider two popular approaches to a complete ratio analysis: (1) summarizing all ratios and (2) the DuPont system of analysis. The summary analysis approach tends to view *all aspects* of the firm's financial activities to isolate key areas of responsibility. The DuPont system acts as a search technique aimed at finding the *key areas* responsible for the firm's financial condition.

SUMMARIZING ALL RATIOS

We can use Bartlett Company's ratios to perform a complete ratio analysis using both cross-sectional and time-series analysis approaches. The 2012 ratio values calculated earlier and the ratio values calculated for 2010 and 2011 for Bartlett Company, along with the industry average ratios for 2012, are summarized in Table 3.8 (see pages 86 and 87), which also shows the formula used to calculate each ratio. Using these data, we can discuss the five key aspects of Bartlett's performance—liquidity, activity, debt, profitability, and market.

Liquidity

The overall liquidity of the firm seems to exhibit a reasonably stable trend, having been maintained at a level that is relatively consistent with the industry average in 2012. The firm's liquidity seems to be good.

Activity

Bartlett Company's inventory appears to be in good shape. Its inventory management seems to have improved, and in 2012 it performed at a level above that of the industry. The firm may be experiencing some problems with accounts receivable. The average collection period seems to have crept up above that of the industry. Bartlett also appears to be slow in paying its bills; it pays nearly 30 days slower than the industry average. This could adversely affect the firm's credit standing. Although overall liquidity appears to be good, the management of receivables and payables should be examined. Bartlett's total asset turnover reflects a decline in the efficiency of total asset utilization between 2010 and 2011. Although in 2012 it rose to a level considerably above the industry average, it appears that the pre-2011 level of efficiency has not yet been achieved.

Debt

Bartlett Company's indebtedness increased over the 2010–2012 period and is currently above the industry average. Although this increase in the debt ratio could be cause for alarm, the firm's ability to meet interest and fixed-payment obligations improved, from 2011 to 2012, to a level that outperforms the industry. The firm's increased indebtedness in 2011 apparently caused deterioration in its ability to pay debt adequately. However, Bartlett has evidently improved its income in 2012 so that it is able to meet its interest and fixed-payment obligations at a level consistent with the average in the industry. In summary, it appears that although 2011 was an off year, the company's improved ability to pay debts in 2012 compensates for its increased degree of indebtedness.

Profitability

Bartlett's profitability relative to sales in 2012 was better than the average company in the industry, although it did not match the firm's 2010 performance. Although the *gross* profit margin was better in 2011 and 2012 than in 2010, higher levels of operating and interest expenses in 2011 and 2012 appear to have caused the 2012 *net* profit margin to fall below that of 2010. However, Bartlett Company's 2012 net profit margin is quite favorable when compared to the industry average.

The firm's earnings per share, return on total assets, and return on common equity behaved much as its net profit margin did over the 2010–2012 period. Bartlett appears to have experienced either a sizable drop in sales between 2010 and 2011 or a rapid expansion in assets during that period. The exceptionally high 2012 level of return on common equity suggests that the firm is performing quite well. The firm's above-average returns—net profit margin, EPS, ROA, and ROE—may be attributable to the fact that it is more risky than average. A look at market ratios is helpful in assessing risk.

Market

Investors have greater confidence in the firm in 2012 than in the prior 2 years, as reflected in the price/earnings (P/E) ratio of 11.1. However, this ratio is below the industry average. The P/E ratio suggests that the firm's risk has declined but remains above that of the average firm in its industry. The firm's market/book (M/B) ratio has increased over the 2010–2012 period, and in 2012 it exceeds the industry average. This implies that investors are optimistic about the firm's future performance. The P/E and M/B ratios reflect the firm's increased profitability over the 2010–2012 period: Investors expect to earn high future returns as compensation for the firm's above-average risk.

In summary, the firm appears to be growing and has recently undergone an expansion in assets, financed primarily through the use of debt. The 2011–2012 period seems to reflect a phase of adjustment and recovery from the rapid growth in assets. Bartlett's sales, profits, and other performance factors seem to be growing with the increase in the size of the operation. In addition, the market response to these accomplishments appears to have been positive. In short, the firm seems to have done well in 2012.

DUPONT SYSTEM OF ANALYSIS

DuPont system of analysis
System used to dissect the firm's financial statements and to assess its financial condition.

The **DuPont system of analysis** is used to dissect the firm's financial statements and to assess its financial condition. It merges the income statement and balance sheet into two summary measures of profitability, return on total assets (ROA) and return on common equity (ROE). Figure 3.2 (see page 88) depicts the basic DuPont system with Bartlett Company's 2012 monetary and ratio values. The upper portion of the chart summarizes the income statement activities; the lower portion summarizes the balance sheet activities.

DuPont Formula

The DuPont system first brings together the *net profit margin,* which measures the firm's profitability on sales, with its *total asset turnover,* which indicates how

TABLE 3.8 Summary of Bartlett Company Ratios (2010–2012, Including 2012 Industry Averages)

Ratio	Formula	Year 2010[a]	Year 2011[b]	Year 2012[b]	Industry Average 2012[c]	Evaluation[d] Cross-Sectional 2012	Evaluation[d] Time-Series 2010–2012	Evaluation[d] Overall
Liquidity								
Current ratio	$\dfrac{\text{Current assets}}{\text{Current liabilities}}$	2.04	2.08	1.97	2.05	OK	OK	OK
Quick (acid-test) ratio	$\dfrac{\text{Current assets} - \text{Inventory}}{\text{Current liabilities}}$	1.32	1.46	1.51	1.43	OK	Good	Good
Activity								
Inventory turnover	$\dfrac{\text{Cost of goods sold}}{\text{Inventory}}$	5.1	5.7	7.2	6.6	Good	Good	Good
Average collection period	$\dfrac{\text{Accounts receivable}}{\text{Average sales per day}}$	43.9 days	51.2 days	59.7 days	44.3 days	Poor	Poor	Poor
Average payment period	$\dfrac{\text{Accounts payable}}{\text{Average purchases per day}}$	75.8 days	81.2 days	95.4 days	66.5 days	Poor	Poor	Poor
Total assets turnover	$\dfrac{\text{Sales}}{\text{Total assets}}$	0.94	0.79	0.85	0.75	OK	OK	OK
Debt								
Debt ratio	$\dfrac{\text{Total liabilities}}{\text{Total assets}}$	36.8%	44.3%	45.7%	40.0%	OK	OK	OK
Times interest earned ratio	$\dfrac{\text{Earnings before interest and taxes}}{\text{Interest}}$	5.6	3.3	4.5	4.3	Good	OK	OK
Fixed-payment coverage ratio	$\dfrac{\text{Earnings before interest and taxes} + \text{Lease payments}}{\text{Int.} + \text{Lease pay.} + \{(\text{Prin.} + \text{Pref. div.}) \times [1/(1 - T)]\}}$	2.4	1.4	1.9	1.5	Good	OK	Good
Profitability								
Gross profit margin	$\dfrac{\text{Gross profits}}{\text{Sales}}$	31.4%	33.3%	32.1%	30.0%	OK	OK	OK
Operating profit margin	$\dfrac{\text{Operating profits}}{\text{Sales}}$	14.6%	11.8%	13.6%	11.0%	Good	OK	Good
Net profit margin	$\dfrac{\text{Earnings available for common stockholders}}{\text{Sales}}$	8.2%	5.4%	7.2%	6.2%	Good	OK	Good

Ratio	Formula	Year 2010[a]	Year 2011[b]	Year 2012[b]	Industry Average 2012[c]	Evaluation[d] Cross-Sectional 2012	Evaluation[d] Time-Series 2010–2012	Overall
Profitability (cont.)								
Earnings per share (EPS)	$\dfrac{\text{Earnings available for common stockholders}}{\text{Number of shares of common stock outstanding}}$	$3.26	$1.81	$2.90	$2.26	Good	OK	Good
Return on total assets (ROA)	$\dfrac{\text{Earnings available for common stockholders}}{\text{Total assets}}$	7.8%	4.2%	6.1%	4.6%	Good	OK	Good
Return on common equity (ROE)	$\dfrac{\text{Earnings available for common stockholders}}{\text{Common stock equity}}$	13.7%	8.5%	12.6%	8.5%	Good	OK	Good
Market								
Price/earnings (P/E) ratio	$\dfrac{\text{Market price per share of common stock}}{\text{Earnings per share}}$	10.5	10.0[e]	11.1	12.5	OK	OK	OK
Market/book (M/B) ratio	$\dfrac{\text{Market price per share of common stock}}{\text{Book value per share of common stock}}$	1.25	0.85[e]	1.40	1.30	OK	OK	OK

[a]Calculated from data not included in this chapter.
[b]Calculated by using the financial statements presented in Tables 3.1 and 3.2.
[c]Obtained from sources not included in this chapter.
[d]Subjective assessments based on data provided.
[e]The market price per share at the end of 2011 was $18.06.

FIGURE 3.2

DuPont System of Analysis
The DuPont system of analysis with application to Bartlett Company (2012)

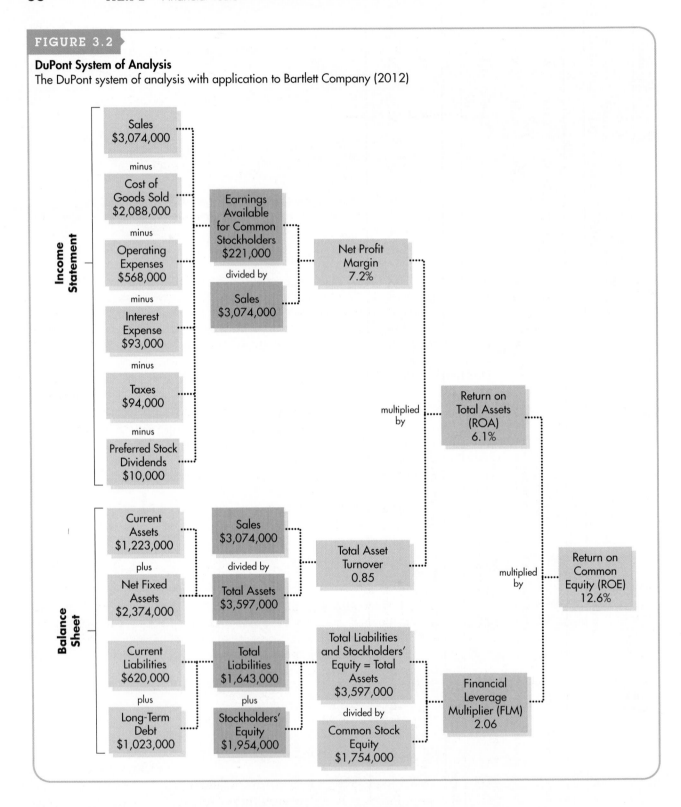

DuPont formula
Multiplies the firm's *net profit margin* by its *total asset turnover* to calculate the firm's *return on total assets (ROA)*.

Matter of fact

Dissecting ROA

Return to Table 3.5, and examine the total asset turnover figures for Dell and The Home Depot. Both firms turn their assets 1.6 times per year. Now look at the return on assets column. Dell's ROA is 4.3 percent, but The Home Depot's is significantly higher at 6.5 percent. If the two firms are equal in terms of the efficiency with which they manage their assets (that is, equal asset turns), why is The Home Depot more profitable relative to assets? The answer lies in the DuPont formula. Notice that Home Depot's net profit margin is 4.0 percent compared to Dell's 2.7 percent. That drives the superior ROA figures for The Home Depot.

efficiently the firm has used its assets to generate sales. In the **DuPont formula,** the product of these two ratios results in the *return on total assets (ROA):*

$$ROA = \text{Net profit margin} \times \text{Total asset turnover}$$

Substituting the appropriate formulas into the equation and simplifying results in the formula given earlier,

$$ROA = \frac{\text{Earnings available for common stockholders}}{\text{Sales}} \times \frac{\text{Sales}}{\text{Total assets}} = \frac{\text{Earnings available for common stockholders}}{\text{Total assets}}$$

When the 2012 values of the net profit margin and total asset turnover for Bartlett Company, calculated earlier, are substituted into the DuPont formula, the result is

$$ROA = 7.2\% \times 0.85 = 6.1\%$$

This value is the same as that calculated directly in an earlier section (page 81). The DuPont formula enables the firm to break down its return into profit-on-sales and efficiency-of-asset-use components. Typically, a firm with a low net profit margin has a high total asset turnover, which results in a reasonably good return on total assets. Often, the opposite situation exists.

Modified DuPont Formula

The second step in the DuPont system employs the **modified DuPont formula.** This formula relates the firm's *return on total assets (ROA)* to its *return on common equity (ROE)*. The latter is calculated by multiplying the return on total assets (ROA) by the **financial leverage multiplier (FLM),** which is the ratio of total assets to common stock equity:

$$ROE = ROA \times FLM$$

modified DuPont formula
Relates the firm's *return on total assets (ROA)* to its *return on common equity (ROE)* using the *financial leverage multiplier (FLM)*.

financial leverage multiplier (FLM)
The ratio of the firm's total assets to its common stock equity.

Substituting the appropriate formulas into the equation and simplifying results in the formula given earlier,

$$ROE = \frac{\text{Earnings available for common stockholders}}{\text{Total assets}} \times \frac{\text{Total assets}}{\text{Common stock equity}} = \frac{\text{Earnings available for common stockholders}}{\text{Common stock equity}}$$

Use of the financial leverage multiplier (FLM) to convert the ROA into the ROE reflects the impact of financial leverage on owners' return. Substituting the values for Bartlett Company's ROA of 6.1 percent, calculated earlier, and Bartlett's FLM of 2.06 ($3,597,000 total assets ÷ $1,754,000 common stock equity) into the modified DuPont formula yields

$$ROE = 6.1\% \times 2.06 = 12.6\%$$

The 12.6 percent ROE calculated by using the modified DuPont formula is the same as that calculated directly (page 82).

Applying the DuPont System

The advantage of the DuPont system is that it allows the firm to break its return on equity into a profit-on-sales component (net profit margin), an efficiency-of-asset-use component (total asset turnover), and a use-of-financial-leverage component (financial leverage multiplier). The total return to owners therefore can be analyzed in these important dimensions.

The use of the DuPont system of analysis as a diagnostic tool is best explained using Figure 3.2. Beginning with the rightmost value—the ROE—the financial analyst moves to the left, dissecting and analyzing the inputs to the formula to isolate the probable cause of the resulting above-average (or below-average) value.

Example 3.6 ▶

For the sake of demonstration, let's ignore all industry average data in Table 3.8 and assume that Bartlett's ROE of 12.6% is actually below the industry average. Moving to the left in Figure 3.2, we would examine the inputs to the ROE—the ROA and the FLM—relative to the industry averages. Let's assume that the FLM is in line with the industry average, but the ROA is below the industry average. Moving farther to the left, we examine the two inputs to the ROA—the net profit margin and total asset turnover. Assume that the net profit margin is in line with the industry average, but the total asset turnover is below the industry average. Moving still farther to the left, we find that whereas the firm's sales are consistent with the industry value, Bartlett's total assets have grown significantly during the past year. Looking farther to the left, we would review the firm's activity ratios for current assets. Let's say that whereas the firm's inventory turnover is in line with the industry average, its average collection period is well above the industry average.

We can readily trace the possible problem back to its cause: Bartlett's low ROE is primarily the consequence of slow collections of accounts receivable, which resulted in high levels of receivables and therefore high levels of total assets. The high total assets slowed Bartlett's total asset turnover, driving down its ROA, which then drove down its ROE. By using the DuPont system of analysis to dissect Bartlett's overall returns as measured by its ROE, we found that slow collections of receivables caused the below-industry-average ROE. Clearly, the firm needs to better manage its credit operations.

→ REVIEW QUESTIONS

3–18 Financial ratio analysis is often divided into five areas: *liquidity, activity, debt, profitability,* and *market* ratios. Differentiate each of these areas of analysis from the others. Which is of the greatest concern to creditors?

3–19 Describe how you would use a large number of ratios to perform a complete ratio analysis of the firm.

3–20 What three areas of analysis are combined in the *modified DuPont formula?* Explain how the *DuPont system of analysis* is used to dissect the firm's results and isolate their causes.

Summary

FOCUS ON VALUE

Financial managers review and analyze the firm's financial statements periodically, both to uncover developing problems and to assess the firm's progress toward achieving its goals. These actions are aimed at **preserving and creating value for the firm's owners.** Financial ratios enable financial managers to monitor the pulse of the firm and its progress toward its strategic goals. Although financial statements and financial ratios rely on accrual concepts, they can provide useful insights into important aspects of risk and return (cash flow) that affect share price.

REVIEW OF LEARNING GOALS

LG 1 **Review the contents of the stockholders' report and the procedures for consolidating international financial statements.** The annual stockholders' report, which publicly owned corporations must provide to stockholders, documents the firm's financial activities of the past year. It includes the letter to stockholders and various subjective and factual information. It also contains four key financial statements: the income statement, the balance sheet, the statement of stockholders' equity (or its abbreviated form, the statement of retained earnings), and the statement of cash flows. Notes describing the technical aspects of the financial statements follow. Financial statements of companies that have operations whose cash flows are denominated in one or more foreign currencies must be translated into dollars in accordance with *FASB Standard No. 52.*

LG 2 **Understand who uses financial ratios and how.** Ratio analysis enables stockholders, lenders, and the firm's managers to evaluate the firm's financial performance. It can be performed on a cross-sectional or a time-series basis. Benchmarking is a popular type of cross-sectional analysis. Users of ratios should understand the cautions that apply to their use.

LG 3 **Use ratios to analyze a firm's liquidity and activity.** Liquidity, or the ability of the firm to pay its bills as they come due, can be measured by the current ratio and the quick (acid-test) ratio. Activity ratios measure the speed with which accounts are converted into sales or cash—inflows or outflows. The activity of inventory can be measured by its turnover: that of accounts receivable by the average collection period and that of accounts payable by the average payment period. Total asset turnover measures the efficiency with which the firm uses its assets to generate sales.

LG 4 **Discuss the relationship between debt and financial leverage and the ratios used to analyze a firm's debt.** The more debt a firm uses, the greater its financial leverage, which magnifies both risk and return. Financial debt ratios measure both the degree of indebtedness and the ability to service debts. A common measure of indebtedness is the debt ratio. The ability to pay fixed charges can be measured by times interest earned and fixed-payment coverage ratios.

LG 5 **Use ratios to analyze a firm's profitability and its market value.** The common-size income statement, which shows each item as a percentage of sales, can be used to determine gross profit margin, operating profit margin, and net profit margin. Other measures of profitability include earnings per share, return on total assets, and return on common equity. Market ratios include the price/earnings ratio and the market/book ratio.

LG 6 **Use a summary of financial ratios and the DuPont system of analysis to perform a complete ratio analysis.** A summary of all ratios can be used to perform a complete ratio analysis using cross-sectional and time-series analysis. The

DuPont system of analysis is a diagnostic tool used to find the key areas responsible for the firm's financial performance. It enables the firm to break the return on common equity into three components: profit on sales, efficiency of asset use, and use of financial leverage.

Opener-in-Review

In the chapter opener you read about how financial analysts gave Abercrombie's stock a relatively positive outlook based on a current ratio of 2.79, a quick ratio of 1.79, and a receivables collection period of 43 days. Based on what you learned in this chapter, do you agree with the analysts' assessment? Explain why or why not.

Self-Test Problems (Solutions in Appendix)

LG 3 LG 4 LG 5 ST3–1   Ratio formulas and interpretations   Without referring to the text, indicate for each of the following ratios the formula for calculating it and the kinds of problems, if any, the firm may have if that ratio is too high relative to the industry average. What if the ratio is too low relative to the industry average? Create a table similar to the one that follows and fill in the empty blocks.

Ratio	Too High	Too Low
Current ratio =		
Inventory turnover =		
Times interest earned =	╳	
Gross profit margin =		
Return on total assets =	╳	
Price/earnings (P/E) ratio =		

LG 3 LG 4 LG 5 ST3–2   Balance sheet completion using ratios   Complete the 2012 balance sheet for O'Keefe Industries using the information that follows it.

O'Keefe Industries Balance Sheet December 31, 2012			
Assets		**Liabilities and Stockholders' Equity**	
Cash	$32,720	Accounts payable	$120,000
Marketable securities	25,000	Notes payable	_____
Accounts receivable	_____	Accruals	20,000
Inventories	_____	Total current liabilities	
Total current assets	_____	Long-term debt	_____
Net fixed assets	_____	Stockholders' equity	$600,000
Total assets	$_____	Total liabilities and stockholders' equity	$_____

The following financial data for 2012 are also available:
1. Sales totaled $1,800,000.
2. The gross profit margin was 25%.
3. Inventory turnover was 6.0.
4. There are 365 days in the year.
5. The average collection period was 40 days.
6. The current ratio was 1.60.
7. The total asset turnover ratio was 1.20.
8. The debt ratio was 60%.

Warm-Up Exercises

All problems are available in myfinancelab.

LG 1 **E3–1** You are a summer intern at the office of a local tax preparer. To test your basic knowledge of financial statements, your manager, who graduated from your alma mater 2 years ago, gives you the following list of accounts and asks you to prepare a simple income statement using those accounts.

Accounts	($000,000)
Depreciation	25
General and administrative expenses	22
Sales	345
Sales expenses	18
Cost of goods sold	255
Lease expense	4
Interest expense	3

a. Arrange the accounts into a well-labeled income statement. Make sure you label and solve for gross profit, operating profit, and net profit before taxes.
b. Using a 35% tax rate, calculate taxes paid and net profit after taxes.
c. Assuming a dividend of $1.10 per share with 4.25 million shares outstanding, calculate EPS and additions to retained earnings.

LG 1 **E3–2** Explain why the income statement can also be called a "profit-and-loss statement." What exactly does the word *balance* mean in the title of the balance sheet? Why do we balance the two halves?

LG 1 **E3–3** Cooper Industries, Inc., began 2012 with retained earnings of $25.32 million. During the year it paid four quarterly dividends of $0.35 per share to 2.75 million common stockholders. Preferred stockholders, holding 500,000 shares, were paid two semiannual dividends of $0.75 per share. The firm had a net profit after taxes of $5.15 million. Prepare the statement of retained earnings for the year ended December 31, 2012.

LG 3 **E3–4** Bluestone Metals, Inc., is a metal fabrication firm that manufactures prefabricated metal parts for customers in a variety of industries. The firm's motto is "If you need it, we can make it." The CEO of Bluestone recently held a board meeting during which he extolled the virtues of the corporation. The company, he stated confidently, had the capability to build any product and could do so using a lean manufacturing model. The firm would soon be profitable, claimed the CEO, because the company used state-of-the-art technology to build a variety of products while keeping inventory levels low. As a business press reporter, you have calculated some ratios to analyze the financial health of the firm. Bluestone's current ratios and quick ratios for the past 6 years are shown in the table below:

	2007	2008	2009	2010	2011	2012
Current ratio	1.2	1.4	1.3	1.6	1.8	2.2
Quick ratio	1.1	1.3	1.2	0.8	0.6	0.4

What do you think of the CEO's claim that the firm is lean and soon to be profitable? (*Hint:* Is there a possible warning sign in the relationship between the two ratios?)

LG 5 **E3–5** If we know that a firm has a net profit margin of 4.5%, total asset turnover of 0.72, and a financial leverage multiplier of 1.43, what is its ROE? What is the advantage to using the DuPont system to calculate ROE over the direct calculation of earnings available for common stockholders divided by common stock equity?

Problems All problems are available in myfinancelab .

LG 1 **P3–1** **Reviewing basic financial statements** The income statement for the year ended December 31, 2012, the balance sheets for December 31, 2012 and 2011, and the statement of retained earnings for the year ended December 31, 2012, for Technica, Inc., are given below and on the following page. Briefly discuss the form and informational content of each of these statements.

Technica, Inc. Income Statement for the Year Ended December 31, 2012	
Sales revenue	$600,000
Less: Cost of goods sold	460,000
Gross profits	$140,000
Less: Operating expenses	
General and administrative expenses	$ 30,000
Depreciation expense	30,000
Total operating expense	$ 60,000
Operating profits	$ 80,000
Less: Interest expense	10,000
Net profits before taxes	$ 70,000
Less: Taxes	27,100
Earnings available for common stockholders	$ 42,900
Earnings per share (EPS)	$2.15

Technica, Inc. Balance Sheets		
	December 31	
Assets	2012	2011
Cash	$ 15,000	$ 16,000
Marketable securities	7,200	8,000
Accounts receivable	34,100	42,200
Inventories	82,000	50,000
Total current assets	$138,300	$116,200
Land and buildings	$150,000	$150,000
Machinery and equipment	200,000	190,000
Furniture and fixtures	54,000	50,000
Other	11,000	10,000
Total gross fixed assets	$415,000	$400,000
Less: Accumulated depreciation	145,000	115,000
Net fixed assets	$270,000	$285,000
Total assets	$408,000	$401,200
Liabilities and Stockholders' Equity		
Accounts payable	$ 57,000	$ 49,000
Notes payable	13,000	16,000
Accruals	5,000	6,000
Total current liabilities	$ 75,000	$ 71,000
Long-term debt	$150,000	$160,000
Common stock equity (shares outstanding: 19,500 in 2012 and 20,000 in 2011)	$110,200	$120,000
Retained earnings	73,100	50,200
Total stockholders' equity	$183,300	$170,200
Total liabilities and stockholders' equity	$408,300	$401,200

Technica, Inc. Statement of Retained Earnings for the Year Ended December 31, 2012	
Retained earnings balance (January 1, 2012)	$50,200
Plus: Net profits after taxes (for 2012)	42,900
Less: Cash dividends (paid during 2012)	20,000
Retained earnings balance (December 31, 2012)	$73,100

LG 1 **P3–2** **Financial statement account identification** Mark each of the accounts listed in the following table as follows:

  a. In column (1), indicate in which statement—income statement (IS) or balance sheet (BS)—the account belongs.

  b. In column (2), indicate whether the account is a current asset (CA), current liability (CL), expense (E), fixed asset (FA), long-term debt (LTD), revenue (R), or stockholders' equity (SE).

Account name	(1) Statement	(2) Type of account
Accounts payable	_____	_____
Accounts receivable	_____	_____
Accruals	_____	_____
Accumulated depreciation	_____	_____
Administrative expense	_____	_____
Buildings	_____	_____
Cash	_____	_____
Common stock (at par)	_____	_____
Cost of goods sold	_____	_____
Depreciation	_____	_____
Equipment	_____	_____
General expense	_____	_____
Interest expense	_____	_____
Inventories	_____	_____
Land	_____	_____
Long-term debts	_____	_____
Machinery	_____	_____
Marketable securities	_____	_____
Notes payable	_____	_____
Operating expense	_____	_____
Paid-in capital in excess of par	_____	_____
Preferred stock	_____	_____
Preferred stock dividends	_____	_____
Retained earnings	_____	_____
Sales revenue	_____	_____
Selling expense	_____	_____
Taxes	_____	_____
Vehicles	_____	_____

LG 1   **P3–3   Income statement preparation**   On December 31, 2012, Cathy Chen, a self-employed certified public accountant (CPA), completed her first full year in business. During the year, she billed $360,000 for her accounting services. She had two employees, a bookkeeper and a clerical assistant. In addition to her *monthly* salary of $8,000, Ms. Chen paid *annual* salaries of $48,000 and $36,000 to the book-keeper and the clerical assistant, respectively. Employment taxes and benefit costs for Ms. Chen and her employees totaled $34,600 for the year. Expenses for office supplies, including postage, totaled $10,400 for the year. In addition, Ms. Chen spent $17,000 during the year on tax-deductible travel and entertainment associated with client visits and new business development. Lease payments for the office space rented (a tax-deductible expense) were $2,700 *per month*. Depreciation expense on the office furniture and fixtures was $15,600 for the year. During the year, Ms. Chen paid interest of $15,000 on the $120,000 borrowed to start the business. She paid an average tax rate of 30% during 2012.

a. Prepare an income statement for Cathy Chen, CPA, for the year ended December 31, 2012.

b. Evaluate her 2012 financial performance.

Personal Finance Problem

LG 1 **P3–4** **Income statement preparation** Adam and Arin Adams have collected their personal income and expense information and have asked you to put together an income and expense statement for the year ended December 31, 2012. The following information is received from the Adams family.

Adam's salary	$45,000	Utilities	$ 3,200
Arin's salary	30,000	Groceries	2,200
Interest received	500	Medical	1,500
Dividends received	150	Property taxes	1,659
Auto insurance	600	Income tax, Social Security	13,000
Home insurance	750	Clothes and accessories	2,000
Auto loan payment	3,300	Gas and auto repair	2,100
Mortgage payment	14,000	Entertainment	2,000

a. Create a personal *income and expense statement* for the period ended December 31, 2012. It should be similar to a corporate income statement.
b. Did the Adams family have a cash surplus or cash deficit?
c. If the result is a surplus, how can the Adams family use that surplus?

LG 1 **P3–5** **Calculation of EPS and retained earnings** Philagem, Inc., ended 2012 with a net profit *before* taxes of $218,000. The company is subject to a 40% tax rate and must pay $32,000 in preferred stock dividends before distributing any earnings on the 85,000 shares of common stock currently outstanding.
a. Calculate Philagem's 2012 earnings per share (EPS).
b. If the firm paid common stock dividends of $0.80 per share, how many dollars would go to retained earnings?

LG 1 **P3–6** **Balance sheet preparation** Use the *appropriate items* from the following list to prepare in good form Owen Davis Company's balance sheet at December 31, 2012.

Item	Value ($000) at December 31, 2012	Item	Value ($000) at December 31, 2012
Accounts payable	$ 220	Inventories	$ 375
Accounts receivable	450	Land	100
Accruals	55	Long-term debts	420
Accumulated depreciation	265	Machinery	420
Buildings	225	Marketable securities	75
Cash	215	Notes payable	475
Common stock (at par)	90	Paid-in capital in excess	
Cost of goods sold	2,500	of par	360
Depreciation expense	45	Preferred stock	100
Equipment	140	Retained earnings	210
Furniture and fixtures	170	Sales revenue	3,600
General expense	320	Vehicles	25

LG 1   P3–7   Balance sheet preparation   Adam and Arin Adams have collected their personal asset and liability information and have asked you to put together a balance sheet as of December 31, 2012. The following information is received from the Adams family.

Cash	$ 300	Retirement funds, IRA	$ 2,000
Checking	3,000	2011 Sebring	15,000
Savings	1,200	2010 Jeep	8,000
IBM stock	2,000	Money market funds	1,200
Auto loan	8,000	Jewelry and artwork	3,000
Mortgage	100,000	Net worth	76,500
Medical bills payable	250	Household furnishings	4,200
Utility bills payable	150	Credit card balance	2,000
Real estate	150,000	Personal loan	3,000

a. Create a personal balance sheet as of December 31, 2012. It should be similar to a corporate balance sheet.
b. What must the total assets of the Adams family be equal to by December 31, 2012?
c. What was their *net working capital (NWC)* for the year? (*Hint:* NWC is the difference between total liquid assets and total current liabilities.)

LG 1   P3–8   Impact of net income on a firm's balance sheet   Conrad Air, Inc., reported net income of $1,365,000 for the year ended December 31, 2013. Show how Conrad's balance sheet would change from 2012 to 2013 depending on how Conrad "spent" those earnings as described in the scenarios that appear below.

Conrad Air, Inc. Balance Sheet as of December 31, 2012			
Assets		**Liabilities and Stockholders' Equity**	
Cash	$ 120,000	Accounts payable	$ 70,000
Marketable securities	35,000	Short-term notes	55,000
Accounts receivable	45,000	Current liabilities	$ 125,000
Inventories	130,000	Long-term debt	2,700,000
Current assets	$ 330,000	Total liabilities	$2,825,000
Equipment	$2,970,000	Common stock	$ 500,000
Buildings	1,600,000	Retained earnings	1,575,000
Fixed assets	$4,570,000	Stockholders' equity	$2,075,000
Total assets	$4,900,000	Total liabilities and equity	$4,900,000

a. Conrad paid no dividends during the year and invested the funds in marketable securities.
b. Conrad paid dividends totaling $500,000 and used the balance of the net income to retire (pay off) long-term debt.
c. Conrad paid dividends totaling $500,000 and invested the balance of the net income in building a new hangar.
d. Conrad paid out all $1,365,000 as dividends to its stockholders.

LG 1 **P3–9** **Initial sale price of common stock** Beck Corporation has one issue of preferred stock and one issue of common stock outstanding. Given Beck's stockholders' equity account that follows, determine the original price per share at which the firm sold its single issue of common stock.

Stockholders' Equity ($000)	
Preferred stock	$ 125
Common stock ($0.75 par, 300,000 shares outstanding)	225
Paid-in capital in excess of par on common stock	2,625
Retained earnings	900
Total stockholders' equity	$3,875

LG 1 **P3–10** **Statement of retained earnings** Hayes Enterprises began 2012 with a retained earnings balance of $928,000. During 2012, the firm earned $377,000 after taxes. From this amount, preferred stockholders were paid $47,000 in dividends. At year-end 2012, the firm's retained earnings totaled $1,048,000. The firm had 140,000 shares of common stock outstanding during 2012.

a. Prepare a statement of retained earnings for the year ended December 31, 2012, for Hayes Enterprises. (*Note:* Be sure to calculate and include the amount of cash dividends paid in 2012.)

b. Calculate the firm's 2012 earnings per share (EPS).

c. How large a per-share cash dividend did the firm pay on common stock during 2012?

LG 1 **P3–11** **Changes in stockholders' equity** Listed are the equity sections of balance sheets for years 2011 and 2012 as reported by Mountain Air Ski Resorts, Inc. The overall value of stockholders' equity has risen from $2,000,000 to $7,500,000. Use the statements to discover how and why this happened.

Mountain Air Ski Resorts, Inc. Balance Sheets (partial)		
Stockholders' equity	2011	2012
Common stock ($1.00 par)		
Authorized—5,000,000 shares		
Outstanding—1,500,000 shares 2012		$1,500,000
— 500,000 shares 2011	$ 500,000	
Paid-in capital in excess of par	500,000	4,500,000
Retained earnings	1,000,000	1,500,000
Total stockholders' equity	$2,000,000	$7,500,000

The company paid total dividends of $200,000 during fiscal 2012.

a. What was Mountain Air's net income for fiscal 2012?

b. How many new shares did the corporation issue and sell during the year?

c. At what average price per share did the new stock sold during 2012 sell?

d. At what price per share did Mountain Air's original 500,000 shares sell?

LG 2   **LG** 3   **P3–12**   **Ratio comparisons**   Robert Arias recently inherited a stock portfolio from his uncle. Wishing to learn more about the companies in which he is now invested, Robert performs a ratio analysis on each one and decides to compare them to each other. Some of his ratios are listed below.

LG 4   **LG** 5

Ratio	Island Electric Utility	Burger Heaven	Fink Software	Roland Motors
Current ratio	1.10	1.3	6.8	4.5
Quick ratio	0.90	0.82	5.2	3.7
Debt ratio	0.68	0.46	0.0	0.35
Net profit margin	6.2%	14.3%	28.5%	8.4%

Assuming that his uncle was a wise investor who assembled the portfolio with care, Robert finds the wide differences in these ratios confusing. Help him out.

a. What problems might Robert encounter in comparing these companies to one another on the basis of their ratios?
b. Why might the current and quick ratios for the electric utility and the fast-food stock be so much lower than the same ratios for the other companies?
c. Why might it be all right for the electric utility to carry a large amount of debt, but not the software company?
d. Why wouldn't investors invest all of their money in software companies instead of in less profitable companies? (Focus on risk and return.)

LG 3   **P3–13**   **Liquidity management**   Bauman Company's total current assets, total current liabilities, and inventory for each of the past 4 years follow:

Item	2009	2010	2011	2012
Total current assets	$16,950	$21,900	$22,500	$27,000
Total current liabilities	9,000	12,600	12,600	17,400
Inventory	6,000	6,900	6,900	7,200

a. Calculate the firm's current and quick ratios for each year. Compare the resulting time series for these measures of liquidity.
b. Comment on the firm's liquidity over the 2009–2010 period.
c. If you were told that Bauman Company's inventory turnover for each year in the 2009–2012 period and the industry averages were as follows, would this information support or conflict with your evaluation in part **b**? Why?

Inventory turnover	2009	2010	2011	2012
Bauman Company	6.3	6.8	7.0	6.4
Industry average	10.6	11.2	10.8	11.0

Personal Finance Problem

LG 3 **P3–14** **Liquidity ratio**   Josh Smith has compiled some of his personal financial data in order to determine his liquidity position. The data are as follows.

Account	Amount
Cash	$3,200
Marketable securities	1,000
Checking account	800
Credit card payables	1,200
Short-term notes payable	900

a. Calculate Josh's *liquidity ratio.*
b. Several of Josh's friends have told him that they have liquidity ratios of about 1.8. How would you analyze Josh's liquidity relative to his friends?

LG 3 **P3–15** **Inventory management**   Wilkins Manufacturing has annual sales of $4 million and a gross profit margin of 40%. Its *end-of-quarter inventories* are

Quarter	Inventory
1	$ 400,000
2	800,000
3	1,200,000
4	200,000

a. Find the average quarterly inventory and use it to calculate the firm's inventory turnover and the average age of inventory.
b. Assuming that the company is in an industry with an average inventory turnover of 2.0, how would you evaluate the activity of Wilkins' inventory?

LG 3 **P3–16** **Accounts receivable management**   An evaluation of the books of Blair Supply, which follows, gives the end-of-year accounts receivable balance, which is believed to consist of amounts originating in the months indicated. The company had annual sales of $2.4 million. The firm extends 30-day credit terms.

Month of origin	Amounts receivable
July	$ 3,875
August	2,000
September	34,025
October	15,100
November	52,000
December	193,000
Year-end accounts receivable	$300,000

a. Use the year-end total to evaluate the firm's collection system.
b. If 70% of the firm's sales occur between July and December, would this affect the validity of your conclusion in part **a**? Explain.

LG 3   **P3–17**   **Interpreting liquidity and activity ratios**   The new owners of Bluegrass Natural Foods, Inc., have hired you to help them diagnose and cure problems that the company has had in maintaining adequate liquidity. As a first step, you perform a liquidity analysis. You then do an analysis of the company's short-term activity ratios. Your calculations and appropriate industry norms are listed.

Ratio	Bluegrass	Industry norm
Current ratio	4.5	4.0
Quick ratio	2.0	3.1
Inventory turnover	6.0	10.4
Average collection period	73 days	52 days
Average payment period	31 days	40 days

a. What recommendations relative to the amount and the handling of inventory could you make to the new owners?

b. What recommendations relative to the amount and the handling of accounts receivable could you make to the new owners?

c. What recommendations relative to the amount and the handling of accounts payable could you make to the new owners?

d. What results, overall, would you hope your recommendations would achieve? Why might your recommendations not be effective?

LG 4   **P3–18**   **Debt analysis**   Springfield Bank is evaluating Creek Enterprises, which has requested a $4,000,000 loan, to assess the firm's financial leverage and financial risk. On the basis of the debt ratios for Creek, along with the industry averages (see top of page 103) and Creek's recent financial statements (following), evaluate and recommend appropriate action on the loan request.

Creek Enterprises Income Statement for the Year Ended December 31, 2012	
Sales revenue	$30,000,000
Less: Cost of goods sold	21,000,000
Gross profits	$ 9,000,000
Less: Operating expenses	
Selling expense	$ 3,000,000
General and administrative expenses	1,800,000
Lease expense	200,000
Depreciation expense	1,000,000
Total operating expense	$ 6,000,000
Operating profits	$ 3,000,000
Less: Interest expense	1,000,000
Net profits before taxes	$ 2,000,000
Less: Taxes (rate = 40%)	800,000
Net profits after taxes	$ 1,200,000
Less: Preferred stock dividends	100,000
Earnings available for common stockholders	$ 1,100,000

Creek Enterprises Balance Sheet December 31, 2012			
Assets		**Liabilities and Stockholders' Equity**	
Cash	$ 1,000,000	Accounts payable	$ 8,000,000
Marketable securities	3,000,000	Notes payable	8,000,000
Accounts receivable	12,000,000	Accruals	500,000
Inventories	7,500,000	Total current liabilities	$16,500,000
Total current assets	$23,500,000	Long-term debt (includes financial leases)[b]	$20,000,000
Land and buildings	$11,000,000		
Machinery and equipment	20,500,000	Preferred stock (25,000 shares, $4 dividend)	$ 2,500,000
Furniture and fixtures	8,000,000		
Gross fixed assets (at cost)[a]	$39,500,000	Common stock (1 million shares at $5 par)	5,000,000
Less: Accumulated depreciation	13,000,000		
Net fixed assets	$26,500,000	Paid-in capital in excess of par value	4,000,000
Total assets	$50,000,000	Retained earnings	2,000,000
		Total stockholders' equity	$13,500,000
		Total liabilities and stockholders' equity	$50,000,000

Industry averages	
Debt ratio	0.51
Times interest earned ratio	7.30
Fixed-payment coverage ratio	1.85

[a]The firm has a 4-year financial lease requiring annual beginning-of-year payments of $200,000. Three years of the lease have yet to run.
[b]Required annual principal payments are $800,000.

LG 5   P3–19   Common-size statement analysis   A common-size income statement for Creek Enterprises' 2011 operations follows. Using the firm's 2012 income statement presented in Problem 3–18, develop the 2012 common-size income statement and compare it to the 2011 statement. Which areas require further analysis and investigation?

Creek Enterprises Common-Size Income Statement for the Year Ended December 31, 2011	
Sales revenue ($35,000,000)	100.0%
Less: Cost of goods sold	65.9
Gross profits	34.1%
Less: Operating expenses	
Selling expense	12.7%
General and administrative expenses	6.3
Lease expense	0.6
Depreciation expense	3.6
Total operating expense	23.2
Operating profits	10.9%
Less: Interest expense	1.5
Net profits before taxes	9.4%
Less: Taxes (rate = 40%)	3.8
Net profits after taxes	5.6%
Less: Preferred stock dividends	0.1
Earnings available for common stockholders	5.5%

LG 4 **LG 5** **P3–20** **The relationship between financial leverage and profitability** Pelican Paper, Inc., and Timberland Forest, Inc., are rivals in the manufacture of craft papers. Some financial statement values for each company follow. Use them in a ratio analysis that compares the firms' financial leverage and profitability.

Item	Pelican Paper, Inc.	Timberland Forest, Inc.
Total assets	$10,000,000	$10,000,000
Total equity (all common)	9,000,000	5,000,000
Total debt	1,000,000	5,000,000
Annual interest	100,000	500,000
Total sales	25,000,000	25,000,000
EBIT	6,250,000	6,250,000
Earnings available for common stockholders	3,690,000	3,450,00

a. Calculate the following debt and coverage ratios for the two companies. Discuss their financial risk and ability to cover the costs in relation to each other.
   (1) Debt ratio
   (2) Times interest earned ratio
b. Calculate the following profitability ratios for the two companies. Discuss their profitability relative to each other.
   (1) Operating profit margin
   (2) Net profit margin
   (3) Return on total assets
   (4) Return on common equity
c. In what way has the larger debt of Timberland Forest made it more profitable than Pelican Paper? What are the risks that Timberland's investors undertake when they choose to purchase its stock instead of Pelican's?

LG 6 **P3–21** **Ratio proficiency** McDougal Printing, Inc., had sales totaling $40,000,000 in fiscal year 2012. Some ratios for the company are listed below. Use this information to determine the dollar values of various income statement and balance sheet accounts as requested.

McDougal Printing, Inc. Year Ended December 31, 2012	
Sales	$40,000,000
Gross profit margin	80%
Operating profit margin	35%
Net profit margin	8%
Return on total assets	16%
Return on common equity	20%
Total asset turnover	2
Average collection period	62.2 days

Calculate values for the following:
a. Gross profits
b. Cost of goods sold
c. Operating profits
d. Operating expenses
e. Earnings available for common stockholders
f. Total assets
g. Total common stock equity
h. Accounts receivable

LG 6 **P3–22** **Cross-sectional ratio analysis** Use the financial statements below and on page 106 for Fox Manufacturing Company for the year ended December 31, 2012, along with the industry average ratios below, to:
a. Prepare and interpret a complete ratio analysis of the firm's 2012 operations.
b. Summarize your findings and make recommendations.

Fox Manufacturing Company Income Statement for the Year Ended December 31, 2012	
Sales revenue	$600,000
Less: Cost of goods sold	460,000
Gross profits	$140,000
Less: Operating expenses	
General and administrative expenses	$30,000
Depreciation expense	30,000
Total operating expense	60,000
Operating profits	$ 80,000
Less: Interest expense	10,000
Net profits before taxes	$ 70,000
Less: Taxes	27,100
Net profits after taxes (earnings available for common stockholders)	$ 42,900
Earnings per share (EPS)	$2.15

Ratio	Industry average, 2012
Current ratio	2.35
Quick ratio	0.87
Inventory turnover[a]	4.55
Average collection period[a]	35.8 days
Total asset turnover	1.09
Debt ratio	0.300
Times interest earned ratio	12.3
Gross profit margin	0.202
Operating profit margin	0.135
Net profit margin	0.091
Return on total assets (ROA)	0.099
Return on common equity (ROE)	0.167
Earnings per share (EPS)	$3.10

[a]Based on a 365-day year and on end-of-year figures.

Fox Manufacturing Company Balance Sheet December 31, 2012	
Assets	
Cash	$ 15,000
Marketable securities	7,200
Accounts receivable	34,100
Inventories	82,000
Total current assets	$138,300
Net fixed assets	270,000
Total assets	$408,300
Liabilities and Stockholders' Equity	
Accounts payable	$ 57,000
Notes payable	13,000
Accruals	5,000
Total current liabilities	$ 75,000
Long-term debt	$150,000
Common stock equity (20,000 shares outstanding)	$110,200
Retained earnings	73,100
Total stockholders' equity	$183,300
Total liabilities and stockholders' equity	$408,300

LG 6 **P3–23** **Financial statement analysis** The financial statements of Zach Industries for the year ended December 31, 2012, follow.

Zach Industries Income Statement for the Year Ended December 31, 2012	
Sales revenue	$160,000
Less: Cost of goods sold	106,000
Gross profits	$ 54,000
Less: Operating expenses	
Selling expense	$ 16,000
General and administrative expenses	10,000
Lease expense	1,000
Depreciation expense	10,000
Total operating expense	$ 37,000
Operating profits	$ 17,000
Less: Interest expense	6,100
Net profits before taxes	$ 10,900
Less: Taxes	4,360
Net profits after taxes	$ 6,540

Zach Industries Balance Sheet December 31, 2012	
Assets	
Cash	$ 500
Marketable securities	1,000
Accounts receivable	25,000
Inventories	45,500
Total current assets	$ 72,000
Land	$ 26,000
Buildings and equipment	90,000
Less: Accumulated depreciation	38,000
Net fixed assets	$ 78,000
Total assets	$150,000
Liabilities and Stockholders' Equity	
Accounts payable	$ 22,000
Notes payable	47,000
Total current liabilities	$ 69,000
Long-term debt	22,950
Common stock[a]	31,500
Retained earnings	26,550
Total liabilities and stockholders' equity	$150,000

[a]The firm's 3,000 outstanding shares of common stock closed 2012 at a price of $25 per share.

a. Use the preceding financial statements to complete the following table. Assume the industry averages given in the table are applicable for both 2011 and 2012.

Ratio	Industry average	Actual 2011	Actual 2012
Current ratio	1.80	1.84	_____
Quick ratio	0.70	0.78	_____
Inventory turnover[a]	2.50	2.59	_____
Average collection period[a]	37.5 days	36.5 days	_____
Debt ratio	65%	67%	_____
Times interest earned ratio	3.8	4.0	_____
Gross profit margin	38%	40%	_____
Net profit margin	3.5%	3.6%	_____
Return on total assets	4.0%	4.0%	_____
Return on common equity	9.5%	8.0%	_____
Market/book ratio	1.1	1.2	_____

[a]Based on a 365-day year and on end-of-year figures.

b. Analyze Zach Industries' financial condition as it is related to (1) liquidity, (2) activity, (3) debt, (4) profitability, and (5) market. Summarize the company's overall financial condition.

LG 6 **P3–24** **Integrative—Complete ratio analysis** Given the following financial statements (following and on page 109), historical ratios, and industry averages, calculate Sterling Company's financial ratios for the most recent year. (Assume a 365-day year.)

Sterling Company Income Statement for the Year Ended December 31, 2012	
Sales revenue	$10,000,000
Less: Cost of goods sold	7,500,000
Gross profits	$ 2,500,000
Less: Operating expenses	
Selling expense	$300,000
General and administrative expenses	650,000
Lease expense	50,000
Depreciation expense	200,000
Total operating expense	$ 1,200,000
Operating profits	$ 1,300,000
Less: Interest expense	200,000
Net profits before taxes	$ 1,100,000
Less: Taxes (rate = 40%)	440,000
Net profits after taxes	$ 660,000
Less: Preferred stock dividends	50,000
Earnings available for common stockholders	$ 610,000
Earnings per share (EPS)	$3.05

Sterling Company Balance Sheet December 31, 2012			
Assets		**Liabilities and Stockholders' Equity**	
Cash	$ 200,000	Accounts payable[b]	$ 900,000
Marketable securities	50,000	Notes payable	200,000
Accounts receivable	800,000	Accruals	100,000
Inventories	950,000	Total current liabilities	$ 1,200,000
Total current assets	$ 2,000,000	Long-term debt (includes	
Gross fixed assets (at cost)[a]	$12,000,000	financial leases)[c]	$ 3,000,000
Less: Accumulated depreciation	3,000,000	Preferred stock (25,000 shares,	
Net fixed assets	$ 9,000,000	$2 dividend)	$ 1,000,000
Other assets	1,000,000	Common stock (200,000	
Total assets	$12,000,000	shares at $3 par)[d]	600,000
		Paid-in capital in excess of	
		par value	5,200,000
		Retained earnings	1,000,000
		Total stockholders' equity	$ 7,800,000
		Total liabilities and	
		stockholders' equity	$12,000,000

[a]The firm has an 8-year financial lease requiring annual beginning-of-year payments of $50,000. Five years of the lease have yet to run.
[b]Annual credit purchases of $6,200,000 were made during the year.
[c]The annual principal payment on the long-term debt is $100,000.
[d]On December 31, 2012, the firm's common stock closed at $39.50 per share.

Analyze its overall financial situation from both a cross-sectional and a time-series viewpoint. Break your analysis into evaluations of the firm's liquidity, activity, debt, profitability, and market.

Historical and Industry Average Ratios for Sterling Company			
Ratio	Actual 2010	Actual 2011	Industry average, 2012
Current ratio	1.40	1.55	1.85
Quick ratio	1.00	0.92	1.05
Inventory turnover	9.52	9.21	8.60
Average collection period	45.6 days	36.9 days	35.5 days
Average payment period	59.3 days	61.6 days	46.4 days
Total asset turnover	0.74	0.80	0.74
Debt ratio	0.20	0.20	0.30
Times interest earned ratio	8.2	7.3	8.0
Fixed-payment coverage ratio	4.5	4.2	4.2
Gross profit margin	0.30	0.27	0.25
Operating profit margin	0.12	0.12	0.10
Net profit margin	0.062	0.062	0.053
Return on total assets (ROA)	0.045	0.050	0.040
Return on common equity (ROE)	0.061	0.067	0.066
Earnings per share (EPS)	$1.75	$2.20	$1.50
Price/earnings (P/E) ratio	12.0	10.5	11.2
Market/book (M/B) ratio	1.20	1.05	1.10

LG 6 **P3–25** **DuPont system of analysis**   Use the following ratio information for Johnson International and the industry averages for Johnson's line of business to:
a. Construct the DuPont system of analysis for both Johnson and the industry.
b. Evaluate Johnson (and the industry) over the 3-year period.
c. Indicate in which areas Johnson requires further analysis. Why?

Johnson	2010	2011	2012
Financial leverage multiplier	1.75	1.75	1.85
Net profit margin	0.059	0.058	0.049
Total asset turnover	2.11	2.18	2.34
Industry Averages			
Financial leverage multiplier	1.67	1.69	1.64
Net profit margin	0.054	0.047	0.041
Total asset turnover	2.05	2.13	2.15

LG 6 **P3–26** **Complete ratio analysis, recognizing significant differences**   Home Health, Inc., has come to Jane Ross for a yearly financial checkup. As a first step, Jane has prepared a complete set of ratios for fiscal years 2011 and 2012. She will use them to look for significant changes in the company's situation from one year to the next.

Home Health, Inc. Financial Ratios		
Ratio	2011	2012
Current ratio	3.25	3.00
Quick ratio	2.50	2.20
Inventory turnover	12.80	10.30
Average collection period	42.6 days	31.4 days
Total asset turnover	1.40	2.00
Debt ratio	0.45	0.62
Times interest earned ratio	4.00	3.85
Gross profit margin	68%	65%
Operating profit margin	14%	16%
Net profit margin	8.3%	8.1%
Return on total assets	11.6%	16.2%
Return on common equity	21.1%	42.6%
Price/earnings ratio	10.7	9.8
Market/book ratio	1.40	1.25

a. To focus on the degree of change, calculate the year-to-year proportional change by subtracting the year 2011 ratio from the year 2012 ratio, then dividing the difference by the year 2011 ratio. Multiply the result by 100. Preserve the positive or negative sign. The result is the percentage change in the ratio from 2011 to 2012. Calculate the proportional change for the ratios shown here.

b. For any ratio that shows a year-to-year difference of 10% or more, state whether the difference is in the company's favor or not.

c. For the most significant changes (25% or more), look at the other ratios and cite at least one other change that may have contributed to the change in the ratio that you are discussing.

LG 1   **P3–27   ETHICS PROBLEM**   Do some reading in periodicals and/or on the Internet to find out more about the Sarbanes-Oxley Act's provisions for companies. Select one of those provisions, and indicate why you think financial statements will be more trustworthy if company financial executives implement this provision of SOX.

Spreadsheet Exercise

The income statement and balance sheet are the basic reports that a firm constructs for use by management and for distribution to stockholders, regulatory bodies, and the general public. They are the primary sources of historical financial information about the firm. Dayton Products, Inc., is a moderate-sized manufacturer. The company's management has asked you to perform a detailed financial statement analysis of the firm.

The income statements for the years ending December 31, 2012 and 2011, respectively, are presented in the table below. (*Note:* Purchases of inventory during 2012 amounted to $109,865.)

Annual Income Statements (Values in millions)		
	For the year ended	
	December 31, 2012	December 31, 2011
Sales	$178,909	$187,510
Cost of goods sold	?	111,631
Selling, general, and administrative expenses	12,356	12,900
Other tax expense	33,572	33,377
Depreciation and amortization	12,103	7,944
Other income (add to EBIT to arrive at EBT)	3,147	3,323
Interest expense	398	293
Income tax rate (average)	35.324%	37.945%
Dividends paid per share	$1.47	$0.91
Basic EPS from total operations	$1.71	$2.25

You also have the following balance sheet information as of December 31, 2012 and 2011, respectively.

Annual Balance Sheets (Values in millions)		
	December 31, 2012	December, 31, 2011
Cash and equivalents	$ 7,229	$ 6,547
Receivables	21,163	19,549
Inventories	8,068	7,904
Other current assets	1,831	1,681
Property, plant, and equipment, gross	204,960	187,519
Accumulated depreciation and depletion	110,020	97,917
Other noncurrent assets	19,413	17,891
Accounts payable	13,792	22,862
Short-term debt payable	4,093	3,703
Other current liabilities	15,290	3,549
Long-term debt payable	6,655	7,099
Deferred income taxes	16,484	16,359
Other noncurrent liabilities	21,733	16,441
Retained earnings	74,597	73,161
Total common shares outstanding	6.7 billion	6.8 billion

TO DO

a. Create a spreadsheet similar to Table 3.1 to model the following:
   (1) A multiple-step comparative income statement for Dayton, Inc., for the periods ending December 31, 2012 and 2011. You must calculate the cost of goods sold for the year 2012.
   (2) A common-size income statement for Dayton, Inc., covering the years 2012 and 2011.

b. Create a spreadsheet similar to Table 3.2 to model the following:
   (1) A detailed, comparative balance sheet for Dayton, Inc., for the years ended December 31, 2012 and 2011.
   (2) A common-size balance sheet for Dayton, Inc., covering the years 2012 and 2011.

c. Create a spreadsheet similar to Table 3.8 to perform the following analysis:
   (1) Create a table that reflects both 2012 and 2011 operating ratios for Dayton, Inc., segmented into (a) liquidity, (b) activity, (c) debt, (d) profitability, and (e) market. Assume that the current market price for the stock is $90.
   (2) Compare the 2012 ratios to the 2011 ratios. Indicate whether the results "outperformed the prior year" or "underperformed relative to the prior year."

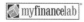 Visit **www.myfinancelab.com** for **Chapter Case: *Assessing Martin Manufacturing's Current Financial Position,*** Group Exercises, and numerous online resources.

4 Cash Flow and Financial Planning

Learning Goals

LG 1 Understand tax depreciation procedures and the effect of depreciation on the firm's cash flows.

LG 2 Discuss the firm's statement of cash flows, operating cash flow, and free cash flow.

LG 3 Understand the financial planning process, including long-term (strategic) financial plans and short-term (operating) financial plans.

LG 4 Discuss the cash-planning process and the preparation, evaluation, and use of the cash budget.

LG 5 Explain the simplified procedures used to prepare and evaluate the pro forma income statement and the pro forma balance sheet.

LG 6 Evaluate the simplified approaches to pro forma financial statement preparation and the common uses of pro forma statements.

Why This Chapter Matters to You

In your *professional* life

ACCOUNTING You need to understand how depreciation is used for both tax and financial reporting purposes; how to develop the statement of cash flows; the primary focus on cash flows, rather than accruals, in financial decision making; and how pro forma financial statements are used within the firm.

INFORMATION SYSTEMS You need to understand the data that must be kept to record depreciation for tax and financial reporting; the information needed for strategic and operating plans; and what data are needed as inputs for preparing cash plans and profit plans.

MANAGEMENT You need to understand the difference between strategic and operating plans, and the role of each; the importance of focusing on the firm's cash flows; and how use of pro forma statements can head off trouble for the firm.

MARKETING You need to understand the central role that marketing plays in formulating the firm's long-term strategic plans, and the importance of the sales forecast as the key input for both cash planning and profit planning.

OPERATIONS You need to understand how depreciation affects the value of the firm's plant assets; how the results of operations are captured in the statement of cash flows; that operations provide key inputs into the firm's short-term financial plans; and the distinction between fixed and variable operating costs.

In your *personal* life
Individuals, like corporations, should focus on cash flow when planning and monitoring finances. You should establish short- and long-term financial goals (destinations) and develop personal financial plans (road maps) that will guide their achievement. Cash flows and financial plans are as important for individuals as for corporations.

Investors Want Apple to Take a Bite Out of Its Cash Hoard

Many people would be surprised to learn that U.S. firms emerged from the worst recession in at least two decades with more cash on their balance sheets than they had before the downturn hit. Non-financial firms in the S&P 500 stock index ended 2009 with $832 billion in cash and short-term marketable securities on hand, an increase of more than 25 percent from 2008 and the highest figure on record. Among the firms with the largest cash hoards were the titans of high technology—Microsoft ($39.7 billion), Cisco Systems ($39.1 billion), Google ($26.5 billion), Oracle ($17.5 billion), and Intel ($16.3 billion).

At the top of this list was Apple Inc., with $41.7 billion in cash in early 2010, equivalent to roughly one-fifth of the firm's total market value (or $40 of the $200 share price). Is holding that much cash a good thing? Investors buy Apple shares because they believe that the company will continue to produce great high-tech gadgets and generate high returns as a result, but the money that Apple held in cash earned no more than 1 percent in 2010. Thus, some investors complained that Apple should distribute a chunk of its cash via a large dividend or share repurchase program.

Steve Jobs, Apple's CEO, responded that distributing cash would not have a lasting impact on the firm's value. Instead, he argued that billions in cash could be used to do "big, bold things," and he worried, "Who knows what's around the next corner?" The latter statement may be the most revealing for Apple and the other high-tech firms. Having survived a recession in which cash was hard to come by, many executives appeared to be taking a very conservative posture and holding on to as much cash as they could—just in case.

LG 1   LG 2   **4.1 Analyzing the Firm's Cash Flow**

An old saying in finance is "Cash is king." Cash flow, the lifeblood of the firm, is the primary ingredient in any financial valuation model. Whether an analyst wants to put a value on an investment that a firm is considering or the objective is to value the firm itself, estimating cash flow is central to the valuation process. This chapter explains where the cash flow numbers used in valuations come from.

DEPRECIATION

depreciation
A portion of the costs of fixed assets charged against annual revenues over time.

For tax and financial reporting purposes, businesses generally cannot deduct as an expense the full cost of an asset that will be in use for several years. Instead, each year firms are required to charge a portion of the costs of fixed assets against revenues. This allocation of historical cost over time is called **depreciation.** Depreciation deductions, like any other business expenses, reduce the income that a firm reports on its income statement and therefore reduce the taxes that the firm must pay. However, depreciation deductions are not associated with any cash outlay. That is, when a firm deducts depreciation expense, it is allocating a portion of an asset's original cost (that the firm has already paid for) as a charge against that year's income. The net effect is that *depreciation deductions increase a firm's cash flow because they reduce a firm's tax bill.*

For tax purposes, the depreciation of business assets is regulated by the Internal Revenue Code. Because the objectives of financial reporting sometimes differ from those of tax legislation, firms often use different depreciation methods for financial reporting than those required for tax purposes. Keeping two different sets of records for these two purposes is legal in the United States.

modified accelerated cost recovery system (MACRS)
System used to determine the depreciation of assets for tax purposes.

Depreciation for tax purposes is determined by using the **modified accelerated cost recovery system (MACRS);** a variety of depreciation methods are available for financial reporting purposes. All depreciation methods require you to know an asset's depreciable value and its depreciable life.

Depreciable Value of an Asset

Under the basic MACRS procedures, the depreciable value of an asset (the amount to be depreciated) is its *full* cost, including outlays for installation. Even if the asset is expected to have some salvage value at the end of its useful life, the firm can still take depreciation deductions equal to the asset's full initial cost.

Example 4.1 ▶

Baker Corporation acquired a new machine at a cost of $38,000, with installation costs of $2,000. When the machine is retired from service, Baker expects to sell it for scrap metal and receive $1,000. Regardless of its expected salvage value, the depreciable value of the machine is $40,000: $38,000 cost + $2,000 installation cost.

depreciable life
Time period over which an asset is depreciated.

Depreciable Life of an Asset

The time period over which an asset is depreciated is called its **depreciable life.** The shorter the depreciable life, the larger the annual depreciation deductions

TABLE 4.1	First Four Property Classes under MACRS

Property class (recovery period)	Definition
3 years	Research equipment and certain special tools
5 years	Computers, printers, copiers, duplicating equipment, cars, light-duty trucks, qualified technological equipment, and similar assets
7 years	Office furniture, fixtures, most manufacturing equipment, railroad track, and single-purpose agricultural and horticultural structures
10 years	Equipment used in petroleum refining or in the manufacture of tobacco products and certain food products

will be, and the larger will be the tax savings associated with those deductions, all other things being equal. Accordingly, firms generally would like to depreciate their assets as rapidly as possible. However, the firm must abide by certain Internal Revenue Service (IRS) requirements for determining depreciable life. These MACRS standards, which apply to both new and used assets, require the taxpayer to use as an asset's depreciable life the appropriate MACRS **recovery period.** There are six MACRS recovery periods—3, 5, 7, 10, 15, and 20 years—excluding real estate. It is customary to refer to the property classes as 3-, 5-, 7-, 10-, 15-, and 20-year property. The first four property classes—those routinely used by business—are defined in Table 4.1.

recovery period
The appropriate depreciable life of a particular asset as determined by MACRS.

DEPRECIATION METHODS

For *financial reporting purposes,* companies can use a variety of depreciation methods (straight-line, double-declining balance, and sum-of-the-years'-digits). For *tax purposes,* assets in the first four MACRS property classes are depreciated by the double-declining balance method, using a half-year convention (meaning that a half-year's depreciation is taken in the year the asset is purchased) and switching to straight-line when advantageous. The *approximate percentages* (rounded to the nearest whole percent) written off each year for the first four property classes are shown in Table 4.2. Rather than using the percentages in the table, the firm can either use straight-line depreciation over the asset's recovery period with the half-year convention or use the alternative depreciation system. For purposes of this text, we will use the MACRS depreciation percentages because they generally provide for the fastest write-off and therefore the best cash flow effects for the profitable firm.

Because MACRS requires use of the half-year convention, assets are assumed to be acquired in the middle of the year; therefore, only one-half of the first year's depreciation is recovered in the first year. As a result, the final half-year of depreciation is recovered in the year immediately following the asset's stated recovery period. In Table 4.2, the depreciation percentages for an n-year class asset are given for $n + 1$ years. For example, a 5-year asset is depreciated over 6 recovery years. The application of the tax depreciation percentages given in Table 4.2 can be demonstrated by a simple example.

TABLE 4.2	Rounded Depreciation Percentages by Recovery Year Using MACRS for First Four Property Classes

	Percentage by recovery year[a]			
Recovery year	3 years	5 years	7 years	10 years
1	33%	20%	14%	10%
2	45	32	25	18
3	15	19	18	14
4	7	12	12	12
5		12	9	9
6		5	9	8
7			9	7
8			4	6
9				6
10				6
11	—	—	—	4
Totals	100%	100%	100%	100%

[a]These percentages have been rounded to the nearest whole percent to simplify calculations while retaining realism. To calculate the *actual* depreciation for tax purposes, be sure to apply the actual unrounded percentages or directly apply double-declining balance depreciation using the half-year convention.

Example 4.2 ▶ Baker Corporation acquired, for an installed cost of $40,000, a machine having a recovery period of 5 years. Using the applicable percentages from Table 4.2, Baker calculates the depreciation in each year as follows:

Year	Cost (1)	Percentages (from Table 4.2) (2)	Depreciation [(1) × (2)] (3)
1	$40,000	20%	$ 8,000
2	40,000	32	12,800
3	40,000	19	7,600
4	40,000	12	4,800
5	40,000	12	4,800
6	40,000	5	2,000
Totals		100%	$40,000

Column 3 shows that the full cost of the asset is written off over 6 recovery years.

Because financial managers focus primarily on cash flows, *only tax depreciation methods will be used throughout this textbook.*

DEVELOPING THE STATEMENT OF CASH FLOWS

The *statement of cash flows,* introduced in Chapter 3, summarizes the firm's cash flow over a given period. Keep in mind that analysts typically lump cash and

operating flows
Cash flows directly related to sale and production of the firm's products and services.

investment flows
Cash flows associated with purchase and sale of both fixed assets and equity investments in other firms.

financing flows
Cash flows that result from debt and equity financing transactions; include incurrence and repayment of debt, cash inflow from the sale of stock, and cash outflows to repurchase stock or pay cash dividends.

Matter of fact

Apple's Cash Flows

In its 2009 annual report, Apple reported over $10 billion in cash from its operating activities. In the same year, Apple used $17.4 billion in cash to invest in marketable securities and other investments. By comparison, its financing cash flows were negligible, resulting in a cash inflow of about $663 million, mostly from stock issued to employees as part of Apple's compensation plans.

marketable securities together when assessing the firm's liquidity because both cash and marketable securities represent a reservoir of liquidity. That reservoir is *increased by cash inflows* and *decreased by cash outflows*.

Also note that the firm's cash flows fall into three categories: (1) operating flows, (2) investment flows, and (3) financing flows. The **operating flows** are cash inflows and outflows directly related to the sale and production of the firm's products and services. **Investment flows** are cash flows associated with the purchase and sale of both fixed assets and equity investments in other firms. Clearly, purchase transactions would result in cash outflows, whereas sales transactions would generate cash inflows. The **financing flows** result from debt and equity financing transactions. Incurring either short-term or long-term debt would result in a corresponding cash inflow; repaying debt would result in an outflow. Similarly, the sale of the company's stock would result in a cash inflow; the repurchase of stock or payment of cash dividends would result in an outflow.

Classifying Inflows and Outflows of Cash

The statement of cash flows, in effect, summarizes the inflows and outflows of cash during a given period. Table 4.3 classifies the basic inflows (sources) and outflows (uses) of cash. For example, if a firm's accounts payable balance increased by $1,000 during the year, the change would be an *inflow of cash*. The change would be an *outflow of cash* if the firm's inventory increased by $2,500.

A few additional points can be made with respect to the classification scheme in Table 4.3:

1. A *decrease* in an asset, such as the firm's cash balance, is an *inflow of cash*. Why? Because cash that has been tied up in the asset is released and can be used for some other purpose, such as repaying a loan. On the other hand, an *increase* in the firm's cash balance is an *outflow of cash* because additional cash is being tied up in the firm's cash balance.

   The classification of decreases and increases in a firm's cash balance is difficult for many to grasp. To clarify, imagine that you store all your cash in a bucket. Your cash balance is represented by the amount of cash in the bucket. When you need cash, you withdraw it from the bucket, which *decreases your cash balance and provides an inflow* of cash to you. Conversely, when you have excess cash, you deposit it in the bucket, which *increases your cash balance and represents an outflow* of cash from you. Focus on the movement of funds *in and out of your pocket*: Clearly, a decrease in cash (from the bucket) is an inflow (to your pocket); an increase in cash (in the bucket) is an outflow (from your pocket).

TABLE 4.3	**Inflows and Outflows of Cash**
Inflows (sources)	**Outflows (uses)**
Decrease in any asset	Increase in any asset
Increase in any liability	Decrease in any liability
Net profits after taxes	Net loss
Depreciation and other noncash charges	Dividends paid
Sale of stock	Repurchase or retirement of stock

noncash charge
An expense that is deducted on the income statement but does not involve the actual outlay of cash during the period; includes depreciation, amortization, and depletion.

2. Depreciation (like amortization and depletion) is a **noncash charge**—an expense that is deducted on the income statement but does not involve an actual outlay of cash. Therefore, when measuring the amount of cash flow generated by a firm, we have to add depreciation back to net income or we will understate the cash that the firm has truly generated. For this reason, depreciation appears as a source of cash in Table 4.3.

3. Because depreciation is treated as a separate cash inflow, only *gross* rather than *net* changes in fixed assets appear on the statement of cash flows. The change in net fixed assets is equal to the change in gross fixed assets minus the depreciation charge. Therefore, if we treated depreciation as a cash inflow as well as the reduction in net (rather than gross) fixed assets, we would be double counting depreciation.

4. Direct entries of changes in retained earnings are not included on the statement of cash flows. Instead, entries for items that affect retained earnings appear as net profits or losses after taxes and dividends paid.

Preparing the Statement of Cash Flows

The statement of cash flows uses data from the income statement, along with the beginning- and end-of-period balance sheets. The income statement for the year ended December 31, 2012, and the December 31 balance sheets for 2011 and 2012 for Baker Corporation are given in Tables 4.4 and 4.5 (see page 120), respectively. The statement of cash flows for the year ended December 31, 2012, for Baker Corporation is presented in Table 4.6 (see page 121). Note that all cash inflows as well as net profits after taxes and depreciation are treated as positive values.

TABLE 4.4	Baker Corporation 2012 Income Statement ($000)
Sales revenue	$1,700
Less: Cost of goods sold	1,000
Gross profits	$ 700
Less: Operating expenses	
Selling, general, and administrative expense	$ 230
Depreciation expense	100
Total operating expense	$ 330
Earnings before interest and taxes (EBIT)	$ 370
Less: Interest expense	70
Net profits before taxes	$ 300
Less: Taxes (rate = 40%)	120
Net profits after taxes	$ 180
Less: Preferred stock dividends	10
Earnings available for common stockholders	$ 170
Earnings per share (EPS)[a]	$1.70

[a]Calculated by dividing the earnings available for common stockholders by the number of shares of common stock outstanding ($170,000 ÷ 100,000 shares = $1.70 per share).

TABLE 4.5 **Baker Corporation Balance Sheets ($000)**

	December 31	
Assets	2012	2011
Cash and marketable securities	$1,000	$ 500
Accounts receivable	400	500
Inventories	600	900
Total current assets	$2,000	$1,900
Land and buildings	$1,200	$1,050
Machinery and equipment, furniture and fixtures, vehicles, and other	1,300	1,150
Total gross fixed assets (at cost)	$2,500	$2,200
Less: Accumulated depreciation	1,300	1,200
Net fixed assets	$1,200	$1,000
Total assets	$3,200	$2,900
Liabilities and Stockholders' Equity		
Accounts payable	$ 700	$ 500
Notes payable	600	700
Accruals	100	200
Total current liabilities	$1,400	$1,400
Long-term debt	600	400
Total liabilities	$2,000	$1,800
Preferred stock	$ 100	$ 100
Common stock—$1.20 par, 100,000 shares outstanding in 2012 and 2011	120	120
Paid-in capital in excess of par on common stock	380	380
Retained earnings	600	500
Total stockholders' equity	$1,200	$1,100
Total liabilities and stockholders' equity	$3,200	$2,900

All cash outflows, any losses, and dividends paid are treated as negative values. The items in each category—operating, investment, and financing—are totaled, and the three totals are added to get the "Net increase (decrease) in cash and marketable securities" for the period. As a check, this value should reconcile with the actual change in cash and marketable securities for the year, which is obtained from the beginning- and end-of-period balance sheets.

Interpreting the Statement

The statement of cash flows allows the financial manager and other interested parties to analyze the firm's cash flow. The manager should pay special attention both to the major categories of cash flow and to the individual items of cash inflow and outflow, to assess whether any developments have occurred that are contrary to the company's financial policies. In addition, the statement can be used to evaluate progress toward projected goals or to isolate inefficiencies. The

TABLE 4.6	Baker Corporation Statement of Cash Flows ($000) for the Year Ended December 31, 2012	
Cash Flow from Operating Activities		
Net profits after taxes		$180
Depreciation		100
Decrease in accounts receivable		100
Decrease in inventories		300
Increase in accounts payable		200
Decrease in accruals		(100)[a]
Cash provided by operating activities		$780
Cash Flow from Investment Activities		
Increase in gross fixed assets		($300)
Changes in equity investments in other firms		0
Cash provided by investment activities		($300)
Cash Flow from Financing Activities		
Decrease in notes payable		($100)
Increase in long-term debts		200
Changes in stockholders' equity[b]		0
Dividends paid		(80)
Cash provided by financing activities		$ 20
Net increase in cash and marketable securities		$500

[a]As is customary, parentheses are used to denote a negative number, which in this case is a cash outflow.

[b]Retained earnings are excluded here, because their change is actually reflected in the combination of the "Net profits after taxes" and "Dividends paid" entries.

financial manager also can prepare a statement of cash flows developed from projected financial statements to determine whether planned actions are desirable in view of the resulting cash flows.

operating cash flow (OCF)
The cash flow a firm generates from its normal operations; calculated as *net operating profits after taxes (NOPAT)* plus depreciation.

Operating Cash Flow   A firm's **operating cash flow** (OCF) is the cash flow it generates from its normal operations—producing and selling its output of goods or services. A variety of definitions of OCF can be found in the financial literature. The definition introduced here excludes the impact of interest on cash flow. We exclude those effects because we want a measure that captures the cash flow generated by the firm's operations, not by how those operations are financed and taxed. The first step is to calculate **net operating profits after taxes (NOPAT)**, which represent the firm's earnings before interest and after taxes. Letting T equal the applicable corporate tax rate, NOPAT is calculated as follows:

net operating profits after taxes (NOPAT)
A firm's earnings before interest and after taxes, $EBIT \times (1 - T)$.

$$NOPAT = EBIT \times (1 - T) \tag{4.1}$$

To convert NOPAT to operating cash flow (OCF), we merely add back depreciation:

$$OCF = NOPAT + Depreciation \tag{4.2}$$

We can substitute the expression for NOPAT from Equation 4.1 into Equation 4.2 to get a single equation for OCF:

$$OCF = [EBIT \times (1 - T)] + Depreciation \tag{4.3}$$

Example 4.3 ▶

Substituting the values for Baker Corporation from its income statement (Table 4.4) into Equation 4.3, we get

$$OCF = [\$370 \times (1.00 - 0.40)] + \$100 = \$222 + \$100 = \$322$$

During 2012, Baker Corporation generated $322,000 of cash flow from producing and selling its output. Therefore, we can conclude that Baker's operations are generating positive cash flows.

FREE CASH FLOW

free cash flow (FCF)
The amount of cash flow available to investors (creditors and owners) after the firm has met all operating needs and paid for investments in net fixed assets and net current assets.

The firm's **free cash flow (FCF)** represents the cash available to investors—the providers of debt (creditors) and equity (owners)—after the firm has met all operating needs and paid for net investments in fixed assets and current assets. Free cash flow can be defined as follows:

$$\begin{aligned} FCF = OCF &- \text{Net fixed asset investment (NFAI)} \\ &- \text{Net current asset investment (NCAI)} \end{aligned} \tag{4.4}$$

The *net fixed asset investment (NFAI)* is the *net investment* that the firm makes in fixed assets and refers to purchases minus sales of fixed assets. You can calculate the NFAI using Equation 4.5.

$$NFAI = \text{Change in net fixed assets} + Depreciation \tag{4.5}$$

The NFAI is also equal to the change in gross fixed assets from one year to the next.

Example 4.4 ▶

Using the Baker Corporation's balance sheets in Table 4.5, we see that its change in net fixed assets between 2011 and 2012 was +$200 ($1,200 in 2012 − $1,000 in 2011). Substituting this value and the $100 of depreciation for 2012 into Equation 4.5, we get Baker's net fixed asset investment (NFAI) for 2012:

$$NFAI = \$200 + \$100 = \$300$$

Baker Corporation therefore invested a net $300,000 in fixed assets during 2012. This amount would, of course, represent a cash outflow to acquire fixed assets during 2012.

Looking at Equation 4.5, we can see that if net fixed assets decline by an amount exceeding the depreciation for the period, the NFAI would be negative. A negative NFAI represents a net cash *inflow* attributable to the fact that the firm sold more assets than it acquired during the year.

The *net current asset investment (NCAI)* represents the net investment made by the firm in its current (operating) assets. "Net" refers to the difference between current assets and the sum of accounts payable and accruals. Notes payable are not included in the NCAI calculation because they represent a negotiated creditor claim on the firm's free cash flow. Equation 4.6 shows the NCAI calculation:

$$\text{NCAI} = \text{Change in current assets} - \text{Change in (accounts payable} + \text{accruals)}$$

(4.6)

Example 4.5 ▶   Looking at the Baker Corporation's balance sheets for 2011 and 2012 in Table 4.5, we see that the change in current assets between 2011 and 2012 is +$100 ($2,000 in 2012 − $1,900 in 2011). The difference between Baker's accounts payable plus accruals of $800 in 2012 ($700 in accounts payable + $100 in accruals) and of $700 in 2011 ($500 in accounts payable + $200 in accruals) is +$100 ($800 in 2012 − $700 in 2011). Substituting into Equation 4.6 the change in current assets and the change in the sum of accounts payable plus accruals for Baker Corporation, we get its 2012 NCAI:

$$\text{NCAI} = \$100 - \$100 = \$0$$

This means that during 2012 Baker Corporation made no investment ($0) in its current assets net of accounts payable and accruals.

Now we can substitute Baker Corporation's 2012 operating cash flow (OCF) of $322, its net fixed asset investment (NFAI) of $300, and its net current asset investment (NCAI) of $0 into Equation 4.4 to find its free cash flow (FCF):

$$\text{FCF} = \$322 - \$300 - \$0 = \$22$$

We can see that during 2012 Baker generated $22,000 of free cash flow, which it can use to pay its investors—creditors (payment of interest) and owners (payment of dividends). Thus, the firm generated adequate cash flow to cover all of its operating costs and investments and had free cash flow available to pay investors. However, Baker's interest expense in 2012 was $70,000, so the firm is not generating enough FCF to provide a sufficient return to its investors.

Clearly, cash flow is the lifeblood of the firm. The *Focus on Practice* box discusses Cisco System's free cash flow.

focus on PRACTICE

Free Cash Flow at Cisco Systems

in practice   On May 13, 2010, Cisco Systems issued what at first glance appeared to be a favorable earnings report, saying that they had achieved earnings per share of $0.42 for the most recent quarter, ahead of the expectations of Wall Street experts who had projected EPS of $0.39. Oddly, though, Cisco stock began to fall after the earnings announcement.

In subsequent analysis, one analyst observed that of the three cents by which Cisco beat the street's forecast, one cent could be attributed to the fact that the quarter was 14 weeks rather than the more typical 13 weeks. Another penny was attributable to unusual tax gains, and the third was classified with the somewhat vague label, "other income." Other analysts were even more skeptical. One noted that Cisco's free cash flow in the prior three quarters had been $6.24 billion, but $5.55 billion of that had been spent to buy shares to offset dilution from the stock options that Cisco granted its employees. The analyst complained, "Cisco is being run for the benefit of its employees and not its public shareholders."

▶ *Free cash flow is often considered a more reliable measure of a company's income than reported earnings. What are some possible ways that corporate accountants might be able to change their earnings to portray a more favorable earnings statement?*

Source: "Update Cisco Systems (CSCO)," May 13, 2010, http://jubakpicks.com; Eric Savitz, "Cisco Shares Off Despite Strong FYQ3; Focus on Q4 Guidance," May 13, 2010, http://blogs.barrons.com.

In the next section, we consider various aspects of financial planning for cash flow and profit.

→ REVIEW QUESTIONS

4–1 Briefly describe the first four *modified accelerated cost recovery system (MACRS)* property classes and recovery periods. Explain how the depreciation percentages are determined by using the MACRS recovery periods.

4–2 Describe the overall cash flow through the firm in terms of operating flows, investments flows, and financing flows.

4–3 Explain why a decrease in cash is classified as a *cash inflow (source)* and why an increase in cash is classified as a *cash outflow (use)* in preparing the statement of cash flows.

4–4 Why is depreciation (as well as amortization and depletion) considered a *noncash charge*?

4–5 Describe the general format of the statement of cash flows. How are cash inflows differentiated from cash outflows on this statement?

4–6 Why do we exclude interest expense and taxes from operating cash flow?

4–7 From a strict financial perspective, define and differentiate between a firm's *operating cash flow (OCF)* and its *free cash flow (FCF)*.

LG 3   4.2 The Financial Planning Process

Financial planning is an important aspect of the firm's operations because it provides road maps for guiding, coordinating, and controlling the firm's actions to achieve its objectives. Two key aspects of the financial planning process are *cash planning* and *profit planning*. Cash planning involves preparation of the firm's cash budget. Profit planning involves preparation of pro forma statements. Both the cash budget and the pro forma statements are useful for internal financial planning. They also are routinely required by existing and prospective lenders.

financial planning process
Planning that begins with long-term, or *strategic,* financial plans that in turn guide the formulation of short-term, or *operating,* plans and budgets.

The **financial planning process** begins with long-term, or *strategic,* financial plans. These, in turn, guide the formulation of short-term, or *operating,* plans and budgets. Generally, the short-term plans and budgets implement the firm's long-term strategic objectives. Although the remainder of this chapter places primary emphasis on short-term financial plans and budgets, a few preliminary comments on long-term financial plans are in order.

LONG-TERM (STRATEGIC) FINANCIAL PLANS

long-term (strategic) financial plans
Plans that lay out a company's planned financial actions and the anticipated impact of those actions over periods ranging from 2 to 10 years.

Long-term (strategic) financial plans lay out a company's planned financial actions and the anticipated impact of those actions over periods ranging from 2 to 10 years. Five-year strategic plans, which are revised as significant new information becomes available, are common. Generally, firms that are subject to high degrees of operating uncertainty, relatively short production cycles, or both, tend to use shorter planning horizons.

Long-term financial plans are part of an integrated strategy that, along with production and marketing plans, guides the firm toward strategic goals. Those long-term plans consider proposed outlays for fixed assets, research and development activities, marketing and product development actions, capital structure, and major sources of financing. Also included would be termination of existing projects, product lines, or lines of business; repayment or retirement of outstanding debts; and any planned acquisitions. Such plans tend to be supported by a series of annual budgets. The *Focus on Ethics* box shows how one CEO dramatically reshaped his company's operating structure, although it later cost him his job.

SHORT-TERM (OPERATING) FINANCIAL PLANS

short-term (operating) financial plans
Specify short-term financial actions and the anticipated impact of those actions.

Short-term (operating) financial plans specify short-term financial actions and the anticipated impact of those actions. These plans most often cover a 1- to 2-year period. Key inputs include the sales forecast and various forms of operating and financial data. Key outputs include a number of operating budgets, the cash budget, and pro forma financial statements. The entire short-term financial planning process is outlined in Figure 4.1 on page 126. Here we focus solely on cash and profit planning from the financial manager's perspective.

---

focus on ETHICS

How Much Is a CEO Worth?

in practice When Jack Welch retired as chairman and CEO of General Electric in 2000, Robert L. Nardelli was part of a lengthy and well-publicized succession planning saga; he eventually lost the job to Jeff Immelt. Nardelli was quickly hired by The Home Depot, one of several companies competing for his services, who offered generous incentives for him to come on board.

Using the "Six Sigma" management strategy from GE, Nardelli dramatically overhauled The Home Depot and replaced its freewheeling entrepreneurial culture. He changed the decentralized management structure by eliminating and consolidating division executives. He also installed processes and streamlined operations, most notably implementing a computerized automated inventory system and centralizing supply orders at the Atlanta headquarters. Nardelli was credited with doubling the sales of the chain and

improving its competitive position. Revenue increased from $45.7 billion in 2000 to $81.5 billion in 2005, while profit rose from $2.6 billion to $5.8 billion.

However, the company's stagnating share price; Nardelli's results-driven management style, which turned off both employees and customers; and his compensation package eventually earned the ire of investors. Despite having received the solid support of The Home Depot's board of directors, Nardelli abruptly resigned on January 3, 2007. He was not destined for poverty, as his severance package had been negotiated years earlier when he joined The Home Depot. The total severance package amounted to $210 million, including $55.3 million of life insurance coverage, reimbursement of $1.3 million of Nardelli's personal taxes related to the life insurance, $50,000 to cover his legal fees, $33.8 million in cash due July 3,

2007, an additional $18 million over 4 years for abiding by the terms of the deal, and the balance of the package from accelerated vesting of stock options. In addition, Nardelli and his family would receive health care benefits from the company for the next 3 years.

The mammoth payoff for Nardelli's departure caused uproar among many shareholder activists because The Home Depot's stock fell 8 percent during his 6-year tenure. Clearly, the mantra of shareholder activists today is, "Ask not what you can do for your company, ask what your company can do for shareholders." The spotlight will no longer be only on what a CEO does, but also on how much the CEO is paid.

▶ *Do you think shareholder activists would have been as upset with Nardelli's severance package had The Home Depot's stock performed much better under his leadership?*

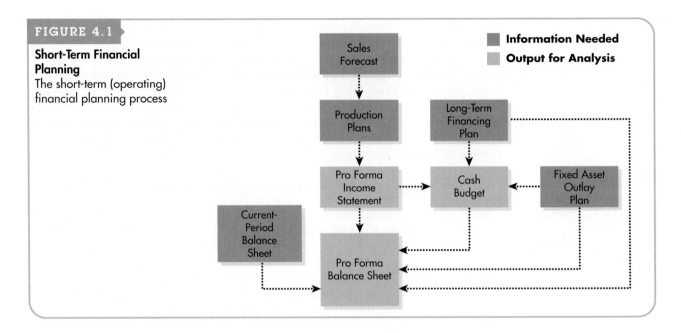

FIGURE 4.1

Short-Term Financial Planning
The short-term (operating) financial planning process

Short-term financial planning begins with the sales forecast. From it, companies develop production plans that take into account lead (preparation) times and include estimates of the required raw materials. Using the production plans, the firm can estimate direct labor requirements, factory overhead outlays, and operating expenses. Once these estimates have been made, the firm can prepare a pro forma income statement and cash budget. With these basic inputs, the firm can finally develop a pro forma balance sheet.

Personal Finance Example 4.6 ▶ The first step in personal financial planning requires you to define your goals. Whereas in a corporation, the goal is to maximize owner wealth (that is, share price), individuals typically have a number of major goals.

Generally personal goals can be short-term (1 year), intermediate-term (2 to 5 years), or long-term (6 or more years). The short- and intermediate-term goals support the long-term goals. Clearly, types of long-term personal goals depend on the individual's or family's age, and goals will continue to change with one's life situation.

You should set your personal financial goals carefully and realistically. Each goal should be clearly defined and have a priority, time frame, and cost estimate. For example, a college senior's intermediate-term goal in 2012 might include earning a master's degree at a cost of $40,000 by 2014, and his or her long-term goal might be to buy a condominium at a cost of $125,000 by 2016.

Throughout the remainder of this chapter, we will concentrate on the key outputs of the short-term financial planning process: the cash budget, the pro forma income statement, and the pro forma balance sheet.

→ REVIEW QUESTIONS

4–8 What is the *financial planning process?* Contrast *long-term (strategic) financial plans* and *short-term (operating) financial plans*.

4–9 Which three statements result as part of the short-term (operating) financial planning process?

LG 4 ## 4.3 Cash Planning: Cash Budgets

cash budget (cash forecast)
A statement of the firm's planned inflows and outflows of cash that is used to estimate its short-term cash requirements.

The **cash budget,** or **cash forecast,** is a statement of the firm's planned inflows and outflows of cash. It is used by the firm to estimate its short-term cash requirements, with particular attention being paid to planning for surplus cash and for cash shortages.

Typically, the cash budget is designed to cover a 1-year period, divided into smaller time intervals. The number and type of intervals depend on the nature of the business. The more seasonal and uncertain a firm's cash flows, the greater the number of intervals. Because many firms are confronted with a seasonal cash flow pattern, the cash budget is quite often presented on a *monthly basis*. Firms with stable patterns of cash flow may use quarterly or annual time intervals.

THE SALES FORECAST

sales forecast
The prediction of the firm's sales over a given period, based on external and/or internal data; used as the key input to the short-term financial planning process.

The key input to the short-term financial planning process is the firm's **sales forecast.** This prediction of the firm's sales over a given period is ordinarily prepared by the marketing department. On the basis of the sales forecast, the financial manager estimates the monthly cash flows that will result from projected sales and from outlays related to production, inventory, and sales. The manager also determines the level of fixed assets required and the amount of financing, if any, needed to support the forecast level of sales and production. In practice, obtaining good data is the most difficult aspect of forecasting. The sales forecast may be based on an analysis of external data, internal data, or a combination of the two.

external forecast
A sales forecast based on the relationships observed between the firm's sales and certain key external economic indicators.

An **external forecast** is based on the relationships observed between the firm's sales and certain key external economic indicators such as the gross domestic product (GDP), new housing starts, consumer confidence, and disposable personal income. Forecasts containing these indicators are readily available.

internal forecast
A sales forecast based on a buildup, or consensus, of sales forecasts through the firm's own sales channels.

Internal forecasts are based on a consensus of sales forecasts through the firm's own sales channels. Typically, the firm's salespeople in the field are asked to estimate how many units of each type of product they expect to sell in the coming year. These forecasts are collected and totaled by the sales manager, who may adjust the figures using knowledge of specific markets or of the salesperson's forecasting ability. Finally, adjustments may be made for additional internal factors, such as production capabilities.

Firms generally use a combination of external and internal forecast data to make the final sales forecast. The internal data provide insight into sales expectations, and the external data provide a means of adjusting these expectations to take into account general economic factors. The nature of the firm's product also often affects the mix and types of forecasting methods used.

TABLE 4.7	The General Format of the Cash Budget					
	Jan.	Feb.	. . .	Nov.	Dec.	
Cash receipts	$XXX	$XXG		$XXM	$XXT	
Less: Cash disbursements	XXA	XXH	. . .	XXN	XXU	
Net cash flow	$XXB	$XXI		$XXO	$XXV	
Add: Beginning cash	XXC	XXD	XXJ	XXP	XXQ	
Ending cash	$XXD	$XXJ		$XXQ	$XXW	
Less: Minimum cash balance	XXE	XXK	. . .	XXR	XXY	
Required total financing		$XXL		$XXS		
Excess cash balance	$XXF				$XXZ	

PREPARING THE CASH BUDGET

The general format of the cash budget is presented in Table 4.7. We will discuss each of its components individually.

Cash Receipts

cash receipts
All of a firm's inflows of cash during a given financial period.

Cash receipts include all of a firm's inflows of cash during a given financial period. The most common components of cash receipts are cash sales, collections of accounts receivable, and other cash receipts.

Example 4.7 ▶

Coulson Industries, a defense contractor, is developing a cash budget for October, November, and December. Coulson's sales in August and September were $100,000 and $200,000, respectively. Sales of $400,000, $300,000, and $200,000 have been forecast for October, November, and December, respectively. Historically, 20% of the firm's sales have been for cash, 50% have generated accounts receivable collected after 1 month, and the remaining 30% have generated accounts receivable collected after 2 months. Bad-debt expenses (uncollectible accounts) have been negligible. In December, the firm will receive a $30,000 dividend from stock in a subsidiary. The schedule of expected cash receipts for the company is presented in Table 4.8. It contains the following items:

    Forecast sales   This initial entry is *merely informational*. It is provided as an aid in calculating other sales-related items.

    Cash sales   The cash sales shown for each month represent 20% of the total sales forecast for that month.

    Collections of A/R   These entries represent the collection of accounts receivable (A/R) resulting from sales in earlier months.

    Lagged 1 month   These figures represent sales made in the preceding month that generated accounts receivable collected in the current month. Because 50% of the current month's sales are collected 1 month later, the collections of A/R with a 1-month lag shown for September represent 50% of the sales in August, collections for October represent 50% of September sales, and so on.

TABLE 4.8	A Schedule of Projected Cash Receipts for Coulson Industries ($000)				
Sales forecast	Aug. $100	Sept. $200	Oct. $400	Nov. $300	Dec. $200
Cash sales (0.20)	$20	$40	$ 80	$ 60	$ 40
Collections of A/R:					
Lagged 1 month (0.50)		50	100	200	150
Lagged 2 months (0.30)			30	60	120
Other cash receipts					30
Total cash receipts	$20	$90	$210	$320	$340

Lagged 2 months These figures represent sales made 2 months earlier that generated accounts receivable collected in the current month. Because 30% of sales are collected 2 months later, the collections with a 2-month lag shown for October represent 30% of the sales in August, and so on.

Other cash receipts These are cash receipts expected from sources other than sales. Interest received, dividends received, proceeds from the sale of equipment, stock and bond sale proceeds, and lease receipts may show up here. For Coulson Industries, the only other cash receipt is the $30,000 dividend due in December.

Total cash receipts This figure represents the total of all the cash receipts listed for each month. For Coulson Industries, we are concerned only with October, November, and December, as shown in Table 4.8.

Cash Disbursements

cash disbursements
All outlays of cash by the firm during a given financial period.

Cash disbursements include all outlays of cash by the firm during a given financial period. The most common cash disbursements are

Cash purchases	Fixed-asset outlays
Payments of accounts payable	Interest payments
Rent (and lease) payments	Cash dividend payments
Wages and salaries	Principal payments (loans)
Tax payments	Repurchases or retirements of stock

It is important to recognize that *depreciation and other noncash charges are NOT included in the cash budget,* because they merely represent a scheduled write-off of an earlier cash outflow. The impact of depreciation, as we noted earlier, is reflected in the reduced cash outflow for tax payments.

Example 4.8 ▶ Coulson Industries has gathered the following data needed for the preparation of a cash disbursements schedule for October, November, and December.

Purchases The firm's purchases represent 70% of sales. Of this amount, 10% is paid in cash, 70% is paid in the month immediately following the month of purchase, and the remaining 20% is paid 2 months following the month of purchase.

Rent payments Rent of $5,000 will be paid each month.

Wages and salaries Fixed salaries for the year are $96,000, or $8,000 per month. In addition, wages are estimated as 10% of monthly sales.

Tax payments Taxes of $25,000 must be paid in December.

Fixed-asset outlays New machinery costing $130,000 will be purchased and paid for in November.

Interest payments An interest payment of $10,000 is due in December.

Cash dividend payments Cash dividends of $20,000 will be paid in October.

Principal payments (loans) A $20,000 principal payment is due in December.

Repurchases or retirements of stock No repurchase or retirement of stock is expected between October and December.

The firm's cash disbursements schedule, using the preceding data, is shown in Table 4.9. Some items in the table are explained in greater detail below.

Purchases This entry is *merely informational*. The figures represent 70% of the forecast sales for each month. They have been included to facilitate calculation of the cash purchases and related payments.

Cash purchases The cash purchases for each month represent 10% of the month's purchases.

Payments of A/P These entries represent the payment of accounts payable (A/P) resulting from purchases in earlier months.

Lagged 1 month These figures represent purchases made in the preceding month that are paid for in the current month. Because 70% of the firm's purchases are paid for 1 month later, the payments with a 1-month lag shown for September represent 70% of the August purchases, payments for October represent 70% of September purchases, and so on.

TABLE 4.9	A Schedule of Projected Cash Disbursements for Coulson Industries ($000)				
	Aug.	Sept.	Oct.	Nov.	Dec.
Purchases (0.70 × sales)	$70	$140	$280	$210	$140
Cash purchases (0.10)	$7	$14	$ 28	$ 21	$ 14
Payments of A/P:					
Lagged 1 month (0.70)		49	98	196	147
Lagged 2 months (0.20)			14	28	56
Rent payments			5	5	5
Wages and salaries			48	38	28
Tax payments					25
Fixed-asset outlays				130	
Interest payments					10
Cash dividend payments			20		
Principal payments	—	—	—	—	20
Total cash disbursements	$7	$63	$213	$418	$305

net cash flow
The mathematical difference between the firm's cash receipts and its cash disbursements in each period.

ending cash
The sum of the firm's beginning cash and its net cash flow for the period.

required total financing
Amount of funds needed by the firm if the ending cash for the period is less than the desired minimum cash balance; typically represented by notes payable.

excess cash balance
The (excess) amount available for investment by the firm if the period's ending cash is greater than the desired minimum cash balance; assumed to be invested in marketable securities.

Lagged 2 months These figures represent purchases made 2 months earlier that are paid for in the current month. Because 20% of the firm's purchases are paid for 2 months later, the payments with a 2-month lag for October represent 20% of the August purchases, and so on.

Wages and salaries These amounts were obtained by adding $8,000 to 10% of the *sales* in each month. The $8,000 represents the salary component; the rest represents wages.

The remaining items on the cash disbursements schedule are self-explanatory.

Net Cash Flow, Ending Cash, Financing, and Excess Cash

Look back at the general-format cash budget in Table 4.7 on page 128. We have inputs for the first two entries, and we now continue calculating the firm's cash needs. The firm's **net cash flow** is found by subtracting the cash disbursements from cash receipts in each period. Then we add beginning cash to the firm's net cash flow to determine the **ending cash** for each period.

Finally, we subtract the desired minimum cash balance from ending cash to find the **required total financing** or the **excess cash balance**. If the ending cash is less than the minimum cash balance, *financing* is required. Such financing is typically viewed as short-term and is therefore represented by notes payable. If the ending cash is greater than the minimum cash balance, *excess cash* exists. Any excess cash is assumed to be invested in a liquid, short-term, interest-paying vehicle—that is, in marketable securities.

Example 4.9 ▶ Table 4.10 presents Coulson Industries' cash budget. The company wishes to maintain, as a reserve for unexpected needs, a minimum cash balance of $25,000. For Coulson Industries to maintain its required $25,000 ending cash balance, it will need total borrowing of $76,000 in November and $41,000 in December. In October the firm will have an excess cash balance of $22,000, which can be held

TABLE 4.10 ▷ A Cash Budget for Coulson Industries ($000)

	Oct.	Nov.	Dec.
Total cash receipts[a]	$210	$320	$340
Less: Total cash disbursements[b]	213	418	305
Net cash flow	($ 3)	($ 98)	$ 35
Add: Beginning cash	50	47	(51)
Ending cash	$ 47 ↗	($ 51) ↗	($ 16)
Less: Minimum cash balance	25	25	25
Required total financing (notes payable)[c]		$ 76	$ 41
Excess cash balance (marketable securities)[d]	$ 22		

[a]From Table 4.8.

[b]From Table 4.9.

[c]Values are placed in this line when the ending cash is less than the desired minimum cash balance. These amounts are typically financed short-term and therefore are represented by notes payable.

[d]Values are placed in this line when the ending cash is greater than the desired minimum cash balance. These amounts are typically assumed to be invested short-term and therefore are represented by marketable securities.

in an interest-earning marketable security. The required total financing figures in the cash budget refer to *how much will be owed at the end of the month;* they do *not* represent the monthly changes in borrowing.

The monthly changes in borrowing and in excess cash can be found by further analyzing the cash budget. In October the $50,000 beginning cash, which becomes $47,000 after the $3,000 net cash outflow, results in a $22,000 excess cash balance once the $25,000 minimum cash is deducted. In November the $76,000 of required total financing resulted from the $98,000 net cash outflow less the $22,000 of excess cash from October. The $41,000 of required total financing in December resulted from reducing November's $76,000 of required total financing by the $35,000 of net cash inflow during December. Summarizing, the *financial activities for each month* would be as follows:

October: **Invest the $22,000** excess cash balance in marketable securities.

November: Liquidate the $22,000 of marketable securities and **borrow $76,000** (notes payable).

December: **Repay $35,000** of notes payable to leave $41,000 of outstanding required total financing.

EVALUATING THE CASH BUDGET

The cash budget indicates whether a cash shortage or surplus is expected in each of the months covered by the forecast. Each month's figure is based on the internally imposed requirement of a minimum cash balance and *represents the total balance at the end of the month.*

At the end of each of the 3 months, Coulson expects the following balances in cash, marketable securities, and notes payable:

	End-of-month balance ($000)		
Account	Oct.	Nov.	Dec.
Cash	$25	$25	$25
Marketable securities	22	0	0
Notes payable	0	76	41

Note that the firm is assumed first to liquidate its marketable securities to meet deficits and then to borrow with notes payable if additional financing is needed. As a result, it will not have marketable securities and notes payable on its books at the same time. Because it may be necessary to borrow up to $76,000 for the 3-month period, the financial manager should be certain that some arrangement is made to ensure the availability of these funds.

Personal Finance Example 4.10 ▶ Because individuals receive only a finite amount of income (cash inflow) during a given period, they need to prepare budgets to make sure they can cover their expenses (cash outflows) during the period. The *personal budget* is a short-term financial planning report that helps individuals or families achieve short-term financial goals. Personal budgets typically cover a 1-year period, broken into months.

A condensed version of a personal budget for the first quarter (3 months) is shown below.

	Jan.	Feb.	Mar.
Income			
Take-home pay	$4,775	$4,775	$4,775
Investment income			90
(1) Total income	$4,775	$4,775	$4,865
Expenses			
(2) Total expenses	$4,026	$5,291	$7,396
Cash surplus or deficit [(1) − (2)]	$ 749	($ 516)	($2,531)
Cumulative cash surplus or deficit	$ 749	$ 233	($2,298)

The personal budget shows a cash surplus of $749 in January followed by monthly deficits in February and March of $516 and $2,531, resulting in a cumulative deficit of $2,298 through March. Clearly, to cover the deficit, some action—such as increasing income, reducing expenses, drawing down savings, or borrowing—will be necessary to bring the budget into balance. Borrowing by using credit can offset a deficit in the short term but can lead to financial trouble if done repeatedly.

COPING WITH UNCERTAINTY IN THE CASH BUDGET

Aside from careful estimation of cash budget inputs, there are two ways of coping with uncertainty in the cash budget. One is to prepare several cash budgets—based on pessimistic, most likely, and optimistic forecasts. From this range of cash flows, the financial manager can determine the amount of financing necessary to cover the most adverse situation. The use of several cash budgets, based on differing scenarios, also should give the financial manager a sense of the riskiness of the various alternatives. This *scenario analysis*, or "what if" approach, is often used to analyze cash flows under a variety of circumstances. Clearly, the use of electronic spreadsheets simplifies the process of performing scenario analysis.

Example 4.11 ▶   Table 4.11 presents the summary of Coulson Industries' cash budget prepared for each month using pessimistic, most likely, and optimistic estimates of total cash receipts and disbursements. The most likely estimate is based on the expected outcomes presented earlier.

During October, Coulson will, at worst, need a maximum of $15,000 of financing and, at best, will have a $62,000 excess cash balance. During November, its financing requirement will be between $0 and $185,000, or it could experience an excess cash balance of $5,000. The December projections show maximum borrowing of $190,000 with a possible excess cash balance of $107,000. By considering the extreme values in the pessimistic and optimistic

TABLE 4.11 A Scenario Analysis of Coulson Industries' Cash Budget ($000)

| | October | | | November | | | December | | |
	Pessi-mistic	Most likely	Opti-mistic	Pessi-mistic	Most likely	Opti-mistic	Pessi-mistic	Most likely	Opti-mistic
Total cash receipts	$160	$210	$285	$210	$320	$410	$275	$340	$422
Less: Total cash disbursements	200	213	248	380	418	467	280	305	320
Net cash flow	($ 40)	($ 3)	$ 37	($170)	($ 98)	($ 57)	($ 5)	$ 35	$102
Add: Beginning cash	50	50	50	10	47	87	(160)	(51)	30
Ending cash	$ 10	$ 47	$ 87	($160)	($ 51)	$ 30	($165)	($ 16)	$132
Less: Minimum cash balance	25	25	25	25	25	25	25	25	25
Required total financing	$ 15			$185	$ 76		$190	$ 41	
Excess cash balance		$ 22	$ 62			$ 5			$107

outcomes, Coulson Industries should be better able to plan its cash requirements. For the 3-month period, the peak borrowing requirement under the worst circumstances would be $190,000, which happens to be considerably greater than the most likely estimate of $76,000 for this period.

A second and much more sophisticated way of coping with uncertainty in the cash budget is *simulation* (discussed in Chapter 12). By simulating the occurrence of sales and other uncertain events, the firm can develop a probability distribution of its ending cash flows for each month. The financial decision maker can then use the probability distribution to determine the amount of financing needed to protect the firm adequately against a cash shortage.

CASH FLOW WITHIN THE MONTH

Because the cash budget shows cash flows only on a total monthly basis, the information provided by the cash budget is not necessarily adequate for ensuring solvency. A firm must look more closely at its pattern of daily cash receipts and cash disbursements to ensure that adequate cash is available for paying bills as they come due.

The synchronization of cash flows in the cash budget at month-end does not ensure that the firm will be able to meet its daily cash requirements. Because a firm's cash flows are generally quite variable when viewed on a daily basis, effective cash planning requires a look *beyond* the cash budget. The financial manager must therefore plan and monitor cash flow more frequently than on a monthly basis. The greater the variability of cash flows from day to day, the greater the amount of attention required.

→ **REVIEW QUESTIONS**

4–10 What is the purpose of the *cash budget?* What role does the sales forecast play in its preparation?

4–11 Briefly describe the basic format of the cash budget.

4–12 How can the two "bottom lines" of the cash budget be used to determine the firm's short-term borrowing and investment requirements?

4–13 What is the cause of uncertainty in the cash budget, and what two techniques can be used to cope with this uncertainty?

LG 5 | **4.4 Profit Planning: Pro Forma Statements**

pro forma statements
Projected, or forecast, income statements and balance sheets.

Whereas cash planning focuses on forecasting cash flows, *profit planning* relies on accrual concepts to project the firm's profit and overall financial position. Shareholders, creditors, and the firm's management pay close attention to the **pro forma statements** which are projected income statements and balance sheets. The basic steps in the short-term financial planning process were shown in the flow diagram of Figure 4.1. The approaches for estimating the pro forma statements are all based on the belief that the financial relationships reflected in the firm's past financial statements will not change in the coming period. The commonly used simplified approaches are presented in subsequent discussions.

Two inputs are required for preparing pro forma statements: (1) financial statements for the preceding year and (2) the sales forecast for the coming year. A variety of assumptions must also be made. The company that we will use to illustrate the simplified approaches to pro forma preparation is Vectra Manufacturing, which manufactures and sells one product. It has two basic product models, X and Y, which are produced by the same process but require different amounts of raw material and labor.

PRECEDING YEAR'S FINANCIAL STATEMENTS

The income statement for the firm's 2012 operations is given in Table 4.12 on page 136. It indicates that Vectra had sales of $100,000, total cost of goods sold of $80,000, net profits before taxes of $9,000, and net profits after taxes of $7,650. The firm paid $4,000 in cash dividends, leaving $3,650 to be transferred to retained earnings. The firm's balance sheet for 2012 is given in Table 4.13 on page 136.

SALES FORECAST

Just as for the cash budget, the key input for pro forma statements is the sales forecast. Vectra Manufacturing's sales forecast for the coming year (2013), based on both external and internal data, is presented in Table 4.14 on page 136. The unit sale prices of the products reflect an increase from $20 to $25 for model X and from $40 to $50 for model Y. These increases are necessary to cover anticipated increases in costs.

→ **REVIEW QUESTION**

4–14 What is the purpose of *pro forma statements?* What inputs are required for preparing them using the simplified approaches?

TABLE 4.12	Vectra Manufacturing's Income Statement for the Year Ended December 31, 2012

Sales revenue		
Model X (1,000 units at $20/unit)		$ 20,000
Model Y (2,000 units at $40/unit)		80,000
Total sales		$100,000
Less: Cost of goods sold		
Labor		$ 28,500
Material A		8,000
Material B		5,500
Overhead		38,000
Total cost of goods sold		$ 80,000
Gross profits		$ 20,000
Less: Operating expenses		10,000
Operating profits		$ 10,000
Less: Interest expense		1,000
Net profits before taxes		$ 9,000
Less: Taxes (0.15 × $9,000)		1,350
Net profits after taxes		$ 7,650
Less: Common stock dividends		4,000
To retained earnings		$ 3,650

TABLE 4.13	Vectra Manufacturing's Balance Sheet, December 31, 2012

Assets		Liabilities and Stockholders' Equity	
Cash	$ 6,000	Accounts payable	$ 7,000
Marketable securities	4,000	Taxes payable	300
Accounts receivable	13,000	Notes payable	8,300
Inventories	16,000	Other current liabilities	3,400
Total current assets	$39,000	Total current liabilities	$19,000
Net fixed assets	51,000	Long-term debt	18,000
Total assets	$90,000	Total liabilities	$37,000
		Common stock	30,000
		Retained earnings	23,000
		Total liabilities and stockholders' equity	$90,000

TABLE 4.14	2013 Sales Forecast for Vectra Manufacturing

Unit sales		Dollar sales	
Model X	1,500	Model X ($25/unit)	$ 37,500
Model Y	1,950	Model Y ($50/unit)	97,500
		Total	$135,000

LG 5 ## 4.5 Preparing the Pro Forma Income Statement

percent-of-sales method
A simple method for developing the pro forma income statement; it forecasts sales and then expresses the various income statement items as percentages of projected sales.

A simple method for developing a pro forma income statement is the **percent-of-sales method.** It forecasts sales and then expresses the various income statement items as percentages of projected sales. The percentages used are likely to be the percentages of sales for those items in the previous year. By using dollar values taken from Vectra's 2012 income statement (Table 4.12), we find that these percentages are

$$\frac{\text{Cost of goods sold}}{\text{Sales}} = \frac{\$80,000}{\$100,000} = 80.0\%$$

$$\frac{\text{Operating expenses}}{\text{Sales}} = \frac{\$10,000}{\$100,000} = 10.0\%$$

$$\frac{\text{Interest expense}}{\text{Sales}} = \frac{\$1,000}{\$100,000} = 1.0\%$$

Applying these percentages to the firm's forecast sales of $135,000 (developed in Table 4.14), we get the 2013 pro forma income statement shown in Table 4.15. We have assumed that Vectra will pay $4,000 in common stock dividends, so the expected contribution to retained earnings is $6,327. This represents a considerable increase over $3,650 in the preceding year (see Table 4.12).

CONSIDERING TYPES OF COSTS AND EXPENSES

The technique that is used to prepare the pro forma income statement in Table 4.15 assumes that all the firm's costs and expenses are *variable*. That is, for a given percentage increase in sales, the same percentage increase in cost of goods sold, operating expenses, and interest expense would result. For example, as Vectra's sales increased by 35 percent, we assumed that its costs of goods sold also increased by 35 percent. On the basis of this assumption, the firm's net profits before taxes also increased by 35 percent.

TABLE 4.15	A Pro Forma Income Statement, Using the Percent-of-Sales Method, for Vectra Manufacturing for the Year Ended December 31, 2013
Sales revenue	$135,000
Less: Cost of goods sold (0.80)	108,000
Gross profits	$ 27,000
Less: Operating expenses (0.10)	13,500
Operating profits	$ 13,500
Less: Interest expense (0.01)	1,350
Net profits before taxes	$ 12,150
Less: Taxes (0.15 × $12,150)	1,823
Net profits after taxes	$ 10,327
Less: Common stock dividends	4,000
To retained earnings	$ 6,327

In more depth

To read about *What Costs Are Fixed?* go to www.myfinancelab.com

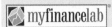

Because this approach assumes that all costs are variable, it may understate the increase in profits that will occur when sales increase if some of the firm's costs are fixed. Similarly, if sales decline, the percentage-of-sales method may overstate profits if some costs are fixed and do not fall when revenues decline. Therefore, a pro forma income statement constructed using the percentage-of-sales method generally *tends to understate profits when sales are increasing and overstate profits when sales are decreasing*. The best way to adjust for the presence of fixed costs when preparing a pro forma income statement is to break the firm's historical costs and expenses into *fixed* and *variable* components. The potential returns as well as risks resulting from use of fixed (operating and financial) costs to create "leverage" are discussed in Chapter 13. The key point to recognize here is that fixed costs make a firm's profits more variable than its revenues. That is, when both profits and sales are rising, profits tend to increase at a faster rate, but when profits and sales are in decline, the percentage drop in profits is often greater than the rate of decline in sales.

Example 4.12 ▶ Vectra Manufacturing's 2012 actual and 2013 pro forma income statements, broken into fixed and variable cost and expense components, follow:

Vectra Manufacturing Income Statements		
	2012 Actual	2013 Pro forma
Sales revenue	$100,000	$135,000
Less: Cost of goods sold		
Fixed cost	40,000	40,000
Variable cost (0.40 × sales)	40,000	54,000
Gross profits	$ 20,000	$ 41,000
Less: Operating expenses		
Fixed expense	$ 5,000	$ 5,000
Variable expense (0.05 × sales)	5,000	6,750
Operating profits	$ 10,000	$ 29,250
Less: Interest expense (all fixed)	1,000	1,000
Net profits before taxes	$ 9,000	$ 28,250
Less: Taxes (0.15 × net profits before taxes)	1,350	4,238
Net profits after taxes	$ 7,650	$ 24,012

Breaking Vectra's costs and expenses into fixed and variable components provides a more accurate projection of its pro forma profit. By assuming that *all* costs are variable (as shown in Table 4.15), we find that projected net profits before taxes would continue to equal 9% of sales (in 2012, $9,000 net profits before taxes ÷ $100,000 sales). Therefore, the 2013 net profits before taxes would have been $12,150 (0.09 × $135,000 projected sales) instead of the $28,250 obtained by using the firm's fixed-cost–variable-cost breakdown.

Clearly, when using a simplified approach to prepare a pro forma income statement, we should break down costs and expenses into fixed and variable components.

→ **REVIEW QUESTIONS**

4–15 How is the *percent-of-sales method* used to prepare pro forma income statements?

4–16 Why does the presence of fixed costs cause the percent-of-sales method of pro forma income statement preparation to fail? What is a better method?

LG 5 ██ **4.6** **Preparing the Pro Forma Balance Sheet**

judgmental approach
A simplified approach for preparing the pro forma balance sheet under which the firm estimates the values of certain balance sheet accounts and uses its external financing as a balancing, or "plug," figure.

A number of simplified approaches are available for preparing the pro forma balance sheet. One involves estimating all balance sheet accounts as a strict percentage of sales. A better and more popular approach is the **judgmental approach,** under which the firm estimates the values of certain balance sheet accounts and uses its external financing as a balancing, or "plug," figure. The judgmental approach represents an improved version of the percent-of-sales approach to pro forma balance sheet preparation. Because the judgmental approach requires only slightly more information and should yield better estimates than the somewhat naive percent-of-sales approach, it is presented here.

To apply the judgmental approach to prepare Vectra Manufacturing's 2013 pro forma balance sheet, a number of assumptions must be made about levels of various balance sheet accounts:

1. A minimum cash balance of $6,000 is desired.
2. Marketable securities will remain unchanged from their current level of $4,000.
3. Accounts receivable on average represent about 45 days of sales (about 1/8 of a year). Because Vectra's annual sales are projected to be $135,000, accounts receivable should average $16,875 (1/8 × $135,000).
4. The ending inventory should remain at a level of about $16,000, of which 25 percent (approximately $4,000) should be raw materials and the remaining 75 percent (approximately $12,000) should consist of finished goods.
5. A new machine costing $20,000 will be purchased. Total depreciation for the year is $8,000. Adding the $20,000 acquisition to the existing net fixed assets of $51,000 and subtracting the depreciation of $8,000 yields net fixed assets of $63,000.
6. Purchases will represent approximately 30 percent of annual sales, which in this case is approximately $40,500 (0.30 × $135,000). The firm estimates that it can take 73 days on average to satisfy its accounts payable. Thus accounts payable should equal one-fifth (73 days ÷ 365 days) of the firm's purchases, or $8,100 (1/5 × $40,500).
7. Taxes payable will equal one-fourth of the current year's tax liability, which equals $455 (one-fourth of the tax liability of $1,823 shown in the pro forma income statement in Table 4.15).
8. Notes payable will remain unchanged from their current level of $8,300.
9. No change in other current liabilities is expected. They remain at the level of the previous year: $3,400.

10. The firm's long-term debt and its common stock will remain unchanged at $18,000 and $30,000, respectively; no issues, retirements, or repurchases of bonds or stocks are planned.

11. Retained earnings will increase from the beginning level of $23,000 (from the balance sheet dated December 31, 2012, in Table 4.13) to $29,327. The increase of $6,327 represents the amount of retained earnings calculated in the year-end 2013 pro forma income statement in Table 4.15.

external financing required ("plug" figure)
Under the judgmental approach for developing a pro forma balance sheet, the amount of external financing needed to bring the statement into balance. It can be either a positive or a negative value.

A 2013 pro forma balance sheet for Vectra Manufacturing based on these assumptions is presented in Table 4.16. A **"plug"** figure—called the **external financing required**—of $8,293 is needed to bring the statement into balance. This means that the firm will have to obtain about $8,300 of additional external financing to support the increased sales level of $135,000 for 2013.

A *positive* value for "external financing required," like that shown in Table 4.16, means that, based on its plans, the firm will not generate enough internal financing to support its forecast growth in assets. To support the forecast level of operation, the firm must raise funds externally by using debt and/or equity financing or by reducing dividends. Once the form of financing is determined, the pro forma balance sheet is modified to replace "external financing required" with the planned increases in the debt and/or equity accounts.

A *negative* value for "external financing required" indicates that, based on its plans, the firm will generate more financing internally than it needs to support its forecast growth in assets. In this case, funds are available for use in repaying debt, repurchasing stock, or increasing dividends. Once the specific actions are determined, "external financing required" is replaced in the pro forma balance sheet with the planned reductions in the debt and/or equity accounts. Obviously, besides

TABLE 4.16 A Pro Forma Balance Sheet, Using the Judgmental Approach, for Vectra Manufacturing (December 31, 2013)

Assets			Liabilities and Stockholders' Equity	
Cash		$ 6,000	Accounts payable	$ 8,100
Marketable securities		4,000	Taxes payable	455
Accounts receivable		16,875	Notes payable	8,300
Inventories			Other current liabilities	3,400
Raw materials	$ 4,000		Total current liabilities	$ 20,255
Finished goods	12,000		Long-term debt	18,000
Total inventory		16,000	Total liabilities	$ 38,255
Total current assets		$ 42,875	Common stock	30,000
Net fixed assets		63,000	Retained earnings	29,327
Total assets		$105,875	Total	$ 97,582
			External financing required[a]	8,293
			Total liabilities and stockholders' equity	$105,875

[a]The amount of external financing needed to force the firm's balance sheet to balance. Because of the nature of the judgmental approach, the balance sheet is not expected to balance without some type of adjustment.

being used to prepare the pro forma balance sheet, the judgmental approach is frequently used specifically to estimate the firm's financing requirements.

→ **REVIEW QUESTIONS**

   4–17 Describe the *judgmental approach* for simplified preparation of the pro forma balance sheet.

   4–18 What is the significance of the "plug" figure, *external financing required?* Differentiate between strategies associated with positive values and with negative values for external financing required.

LG 6 **4.7 Evaluation of Pro Forma Statements**

It is difficult to forecast the many variables involved in preparing pro forma statements. As a result, investors, lenders, and managers frequently use the techniques presented in this chapter to make rough estimates of pro forma financial statements. Yet, it is important to recognize the basic weaknesses of these simplified approaches. The weaknesses lie in two assumptions: (1) that the firm's past financial condition is an accurate indicator of its future; and (2) that certain variables (such as cash, accounts receivable, and inventories) can be forced to take on certain "desired" values. These assumptions cannot be justified solely on the basis of their ability to simplify the calculations involved. However, despite their weaknesses, the simplified approaches to pro forma statement preparation are likely to remain popular because of their relative simplicity. The widespread use of spreadsheets certainly helps to streamline the financial planning process.

However pro forma statements are prepared, analysts must understand how to use them to make financial decisions. Both financial managers and lenders can use pro forma statements to analyze the firm's inflows and outflows of cash, as well as its liquidity, activity, debt, profitability, and market value. Various ratios can be calculated from the pro forma income statement and balance sheet to evaluate performance. Cash inflows and outflows can be evaluated by preparing a pro forma statement of cash flows. After analyzing the pro forma statements, the financial manager can take steps to adjust planned operations to achieve short-term financial goals. For example, if projected profits on the pro forma income statement are too low, a variety of pricing and/or cost-cutting actions might be initiated. If the projected level of accounts receivable on the pro forma balance sheet is too high, changes in credit or collection policy may be called for. Pro forma statements are therefore of great importance in solidifying the firm's financial plans for the coming year.

→ **REVIEW QUESTIONS**

   4–19 What are the two basic weaknesses of the simplified approaches to preparing pro forma statements?

   4–20 What is the financial manager's objective in evaluating pro forma statements?

Summary

FOCUS ON VALUE

Cash flow, the lifeblood of the firm, is a key determinant of the value of the firm. The financial manager must plan and manage the firm's cash flow. The goal is to ensure the firm's solvency and to generate positive cash flow for the firm's owners. Both the magnitude and the risk of the cash flows generated on behalf of the owners determine the firm's value.

To carry out the responsibility **to create value for owners,** the financial manager uses tools such as cash budgets and pro forma financial statements as part of the process of generating positive cash flow. Good financial plans should result in large free cash flows. Clearly, the financial manager must deliberately and carefully plan and manage the firm's cash flows to achieve the firm's goal of maximizing share price.

REVIEW OF LEARNING GOALS

LG 1 **Understand tax depreciation procedures and the effect of depreciation on the firm's cash flows.** Depreciation is an important factor affecting a firm's cash flow. An asset's depreciable value and depreciable life are determined by using the MACRS standards in the federal tax code. MACRS groups assets (excluding real estate) into six property classes based on length of recovery period.

LG 2 **Discuss the firm's statement of cash flows, operating cash flow, and free cash flow.** The statement of cash flows is divided into operating, investment, and financing flows. It reconciles changes in the firm's cash flows with changes in cash and marketable securities for the period. Interpreting the statement of cash flows involves both the major categories of cash flow and the individual items of cash inflow and outflow. From a strict financial point of view, a firm's operating cash flow is defined to exclude interest. Of greater importance is a firm's free cash flow, which is the amount of cash flow available to creditors and owners.

LG 3 **Understand the financial planning process, including long-term (strategic) financial plans and short-term (operating) financial plans.** The two key aspects of the financial planning process are cash planning and profit planning. Cash planning involves the cash budget or cash forecast. Profit planning relies on the pro forma income statement and balance sheet. Long-term (strategic) financial plans act as a guide for preparing short-term (operating) financial plans. Long-term plans tend to cover periods ranging from 2 to 10 years; short-term plans most often cover a 1- to 2-year period.

LG 4 **Discuss the cash-planning process and the preparation, evaluation, and use of the cash budget.** The cash-planning process uses the cash budget, based on a sales forecast, to estimate short-term cash surpluses and shortages. The cash budget is typically prepared for a 1-year period divided into months. It nets cash receipts and disbursements for each period to calculate net cash flow.

Ending cash is estimated by adding beginning cash to the net cash flow. By subtracting the desired minimum cash balance from the ending cash, the firm can determine required total financing or the excess cash balance. To cope with uncertainty in the cash budget, scenario analysis or simulation can be used. A firm must also consider its pattern of daily cash receipts and cash disbursements.

LG 5 **Explain the simplified procedures used to prepare and evaluate the pro forma income statement and the pro forma balance sheet.** A pro forma income statement can be developed by calculating past percentage relationships between certain cost and expense items and the firm's sales and then applying these percentages to forecasts. Because this approach implies that all costs and expenses are variable, it tends to understate profits when sales are increasing and to overstate profits when sales are decreasing. This problem can be avoided by breaking down costs and expenses into fixed and variable components. In this case, the fixed components remain unchanged from the most recent year, and the variable costs and expenses are forecast on a percent-of-sales basis.

Under the judgmental approach, the values of certain balance sheet accounts are estimated and the firm's external financing is used as a balancing, or "plug," figure. A positive value for "external financing required" means that the firm will not generate enough internal financing to support its forecast growth in assets and will have to raise funds externally or reduce dividends. A negative value for "external financing required" indicates that the firm will generate more financing internally than it needs to support its forecast growth in assets and funds will be available for use in repaying debt, repurchasing stock, or increasing dividends.

LG 6 **Evaluate the simplified approaches to pro forma financial statement preparation and the common uses of pro forma statements.** Simplified approaches for preparing pro forma statements assume that the firm's past financial condition is an accurate indicator of the future. Pro forma statements are commonly used to forecast and analyze the firm's level of profitability and overall financial performance so that adjustments can be made to planned operations to achieve short-term financial goals.

Opener-in-Review

The chapter opener mentions that in 2010, Apple's stock sold for approximately $200. Apple had just over $40 billion in cash on its balance sheet and just fewer than 1 billion shares outstanding, so each Apple share represented a claim on $40 of Apple's cash. Suppose that when Apple invests in the resources necessary to create new technology products, it expects to earn a 20% rate of return. Suppose also that when it invests its cash, Apple earns just 1%. Given this, what rate of return should investors expect if they pay $200 to acquire one share of Apple?

Self-Test Problems   (Solutions in Appendix)

LG 1 **LG 2** **ST4–1** **Depreciation and cash flow**   A firm expects to have earnings before interest and taxes (EBIT) of $160,000 in each of the next 6 years. It pays annual interest of $15,000. The firm is considering the purchase of an asset that costs $140,000, requires $10,000 in installation cost, and has a recovery period of 5 years. It will be the firm's only asset, and the asset's depreciation is already reflected in its EBIT estimates.

a. Calculate the annual depreciation for the asset purchase using the MACRS depreciation percentages in Table 4.2 on page 117.

b. Calculate the firm's operating cash flows for each of the 6 years, using Equation 4.3. Assume that the firm is subject to a 40% tax rate on all the profit that it earns.

c. Suppose the firm's net fixed assets, current assets, accounts payable, and accruals had the following values at the start and end of the final year (year 6). Calculate the firm's free cash flow (FCF) for that year.

Account	Year 6 start	Year 6 end
Net fixed assets	$ 7,500	$ 0
Current assets	90,000	110,000
Accounts payable	40,000	45,000
Accruals	8,000	7,000

d. Compare and discuss the significance of each value calculated in parts **b** and **c**.

LG 4 **LG 5** **ST4–2** **Cash budget and pro forma balance sheet inputs**   Jane McDonald, a financial analyst for Carroll Company, has prepared the following sales and cash disbursement estimates for the period February–June of the current year.

Month	Sales	Cash disbursements
February	$500	$400
March	600	300
April	400	600
May	200	500
June	200	200

McDonald notes that historically, 30% of sales have been for cash. Of *credit sales*, 70% are collected 1 month after the sale, and the remaining 30% are collected 2 months after the sale. The firm wishes to maintain a minimum ending balance in its cash account of $25. Balances above this amount would be invested in short-term government securities (marketable securities), whereas any deficits would be financed through short-term bank borrowing (notes payable). The beginning cash balance at April 1 is $115.

a. Prepare cash budgets for April, May, and June.

b. How much financing, if any, at a maximum would Carroll Company require to meet its obligations during this 3-month period?

c. A pro forma balance sheet dated at the end of June is to be prepared from the information presented. Give the size of each of the following: cash, notes payable, marketable securities, and accounts receivable.

LG 5 **ST4–3** **Pro forma income statement**   Euro Designs, Inc., expects sales during 2013 to rise from the 2012 level of $3.5 million to $3.9 million. Because of a scheduled large loan payment, the interest expense in 2013 is expected to drop to $325,000. The firm plans to increase its cash dividend payments during 2013 to $320,000. The company's year-end 2012 income statement follows.

Euro Designs, Inc. Income Statement for the Year Ended December 31, 2012	
Sales revenue	$3,500,000
Less: Cost of goods sold	1,925,000
Gross profits	$1,575,000
Less: Operating expenses	420,000
Operating profits	$1,155,000
Less: Interest expense	400,000
Net profits before taxes	$ 755,000
Less: Taxes (rate = 40%)	302,000
Net profits after taxes	$ 453,000
Less: Cash dividends	250,000
To retained earnings	$ 203,000

a. Use the *percent-of-sales method* to prepare a 2013 pro forma income statement for Euro Designs, Inc.

b. Explain why the statement may underestimate the company's actual 2013 pro forma income.

Warm-Up Exercises

All problems are available in myfinancelab .

LG 1 **E4–1** The installed cost of a new computerized controller was $65,000. Calculate the depreciation schedule by year assuming a recovery period of 5 years and using the appropriate MACRS depreciation percentages given in Table 4.2 on page 117.

LG 2 **E4–2** Classify the following changes in each of the accounts as either an *inflow* or an *outflow* of cash. During the year (a) marketable securities increased, (b) land and buildings decreased, (c) accounts payable increased, (d) vehicles decreased, (e) accounts receivable increased, and (f) dividends were paid.

LG 2 **E4–3** Determine the *operating cash flow (OCF)* for Kleczka, Inc., based on the following data. (All values are in thousands of dollars.) During the year the firm had sales of $2,500, cost of goods sold totaled $1,800, operating expenses totaled $300, and depreciation expenses were $200. The firm is in the 35% tax bracket.

LG 2 **E4–4** During the year, Xero, Inc., experienced an increase in net fixed assets of $300,000 and had depreciation of $200,000. It also experienced an increase in current assets of $150,000 and an increase in accounts payable and accruals of $75,000. If operating cash flow (OCF) for the year was $700,000, calculate the firm's *free cash flow (FCF)* for the year.

LG 5 **E4–5** Rimier Corp. forecasts sales of $650,000 for 2013. Assume the firm has fixed costs of $250,000 and variable costs amounting to 35% of sales. Operating expenses are estimated to include fixed costs of $28,000 and a variable portion equal to 7.5% of sales. Interest expenses for the coming year are estimated to be $20,000. Estimate Rimier's net profits before taxes for 2013.

Problems

All problems are available in myfinancelab .

LG 1 **P4–1** **Depreciation** On March 20, 2012, Norton Systems acquired two new assets. Asset A was research equipment costing $17,000 and having a 3-year recovery period. Asset B was duplicating equipment having an installed cost of $45,000 and a 5-year recovery period. Using the MACRS depreciation percentages in Table 4.2 on page 117, prepare a depreciation schedule for each of these assets.

LG 1 **P4–2** **Depreciation** In early 2012, Sosa Enterprises purchased a new machine for $10,000 to make cork stoppers for wine bottles. The machine has a 3-year recovery period and is expected to have a salvage value of $2,000. Develop a depreciation schedule for this asset using the MACRS depreciation percentages in Table 4.2.

LG 1 LG 2 **P4–3** **MACRS depreciation expense and accounting cash flow** Pavlovich Instruments, Inc., a maker of precision telescopes, expects to report pretax income of $430,000 this year. The company's financial manager is considering the timing of a purchase of new computerized lens grinders. The grinders will have an installed cost of $80,000 and a cost recovery period of 5 years. They will be depreciated using the MACRS schedule.
a. If the firm purchases the grinders before year-end, what depreciation expense will it be able to claim this year? (Use Table 4.2 on page 117.)
b. If the firm reduces its reported income by the amount of the depreciation expense calculated in part **a**, what tax savings will result?

LG 1 LG 2 **P4–4** **Depreciation and accounting cash flow** A firm in the third year of depreciating its only asset, which originally cost $180,000 and has a 5-year MACRS recovery period, has gathered the following data relative to the current year's operations:

Accruals	$ 15,000
Current assets	120,000
Interest expense	15,000
Sales revenue	400,000
Inventory	70,000
Total costs before depreciation, interest, and taxes	290,000
Tax rate on ordinary income	40%

a. Use the *relevant data* to determine the operating cash flow (see Equation 4.2) for the current year.
b. Explain the impact that depreciation, as well as any other noncash charges, has on a firm's cash flows.

LG 2   **P4–5**   **Classifying inflows and outflows of cash**   Classify each of the following items as an inflow (I) or an outflow (O) of cash, or as neither (N).

Item	Change ($)	Item	Change ($)
Cash	+100	Accounts receivable	−700
Accounts payable	−1,000	Net profits	+600
Notes payable	+500	Depreciation	+100
Long-term debt	−2,000	Repurchase of stock	+600
Inventory	+200	Cash dividends	+800
Fixed assets	+400	Sale of stock	+1,000

LG 2   **P4–6**   **Finding operating and free cash flows**   Consider the balance sheets and selected data from the income statement of Keith Corporation that appear below and on the next page.

Keith Corporation Balance Sheets		
	December 31	
Assets	**2012**	**2011**
Cash	$ 1,500	$ 1,000
Marketable securities	1,800	1,200
Accounts receivable	2,000	1,800
Inventories	2,900	2,800
Total current assets	$ 8,200	$ 6,800
Gross fixed assets	$29,500	$28,100
Less: Accumulated depreciation	14,700	13,100
Net fixed assets	$14,800	$15,000
Total assets	$23,000	$21,800
Liabilities and Stockholders' Equity		
Accounts payable	$ 1,600	$ 1,500
Notes payable	2,800	2,200
Accruals	200	300
Total current liabilities	$ 4,600	$ 4,000
Long-term debt	5,000	5,000
Total liabilities	$ 9,600	$ 9,000
Common stock	$10,000	$10,000
Retained earnings	3,400	2,800
Total stockholders' equity	$13,400	$12,800
Total liabilities and stockholders' equity	$23,000	$21,800

Keith Corporation Income Statement Data (2012)	
Depreciation expense	$1,600
Earnings before interest and taxes (EBIT)	2,700
Interest expense	367
Net profits after taxes	1,400
Tax rate	40%

a. Calculate the firm's *net operating profit after taxes (NOPAT)* for the year ended December 31, 2012, using Equation 4.1.

b. Calculate the firm's *operating cash flow (OCF)* for the year ended December 31, 2012, using Equation 4.3.

c. Calculate the firm's *free cash flow (FCF)* for the year ended December 31, 2012, using Equation 4.5.

d. Interpret, compare, and contrast your cash flow estimates in parts **b** and **c**.

LG 4   **P4–7**   **Cash receipts**   A firm has actual sales of $65,000 in April and $60,000 in May. It expects sales of $70,000 in June and $100,000 in July and in August. Assuming that sales are the only source of cash inflows and that half of them are for cash and the remainder are collected evenly over the following 2 months, what are the firm's expected cash receipts for June, July, and August?

LG 4   **P4–8**   **Cash disbursements schedule**   Maris Brothers, Inc., needs a cash disbursement schedule for the months of April, May, and June. Use the format of Table 4.9 (on page 130) and the following information in its preparation.

Sales: February = $500,000; March = $500,000; April = $560,000; May = $610,000; June = $650,000; July = $650,000

Purchases: Purchases are calculated as 60% of the next month's sales, 10% of purchases are made in cash, 50% of purchases are paid for 1 month after purchase, and the remaining 40% of purchases are paid for 2 months after purchase.

Rent: The firm pays rent of $8,000 per month.

Wages and salaries: Base wage and salary costs are fixed at $6,000 per month plus a variable cost of 7% of the current month's sales.

Taxes: A tax payment of $54,500 is due in June.

Fixed asset outlays: New equipment costing $75,000 will be bought and paid for in April.

Interest payments: An interest payment of $30,000 is due in June.

Cash dividends: Dividends of $12,500 will be paid in April.

Principal repayments and retirements: No principal repayments or retirements are due during these months.

LG 4   **P4–9**   **Cash budget—Basic**   Grenoble Enterprises had sales of $50,000 in March and $60,000 in April. Forecast sales for May, June, and July are $70,000, $80,000, and $100,000, respectively. The firm has a cash balance of $5,000 on May 1 and wishes to maintain a minimum cash balance of $5,000. Given the following data, prepare and interpret a cash budget for the months of May, June, and July.

(1) The firm makes 20% of sales for cash, 60% are collected in the next month, and the remaining 20% are collected in the second month following sale.

(2) The firm receives other income of $2,000 per month.

(3) The firm's actual or expected purchases, all made for cash, are $50,000, $70,000, and $80,000 for the months of May through July, respectively.

(4) Rent is $3,000 per month.

(5) Wages and salaries are 10% of the previous month's sales.

(6) Cash dividends of $3,000 will be paid in June.

(7) Payment of principal and interest of $4,000 is due in June.

(8) A cash purchase of equipment costing $6,000 is scheduled in July.

(9) Taxes of $6,000 are due in June.

Personal Finance Problem

LG 4   **P4–10**   **Preparation of cash budget**   Sam and Suzy Sizeman need to prepare a cash budget for the last quarter of 2013 to make sure they can cover their expenditures during the period. Sam and Suzy have been preparing budgets for the past several years and have been able to establish specific percentages for most of their cash outflows. These percentages are based on their take-home pay (that is, monthly utilities normally run 5% of monthly take-home pay). The information in the following table can be used to create their fourth-quarter budget for 2013.

Income	
Monthly take-home pay	$4,900
Expenses	
Housing	30%
Utilities	5%
Food	10%
Transportation	7%
Medical/dental	.5%
Clothing for October and November	3%
Clothing for December	$440
Property taxes (November only)	11.5%
Appliances	1%
Personal care	2%
Entertainment for October and November	6%
Entertainment for December	$1,500
Savings	7.5%
Other	5%
Excess cash	4.5%

a. Prepare a quarterly cash budget for Sam and Suzy covering the months October through December 2013.

b. Are there individual months that incur a deficit?

c. What is the cumulative cash surplus or deficit by the end of December 2013?

LG 4   **P4–11**   **Cash budget—Advanced**   The actual sales and purchases for Xenocore, Inc., for September and October 2012, along with its forecast sales and purchases for the period November 2012 through April 2013, follow.

The firm makes 20% of all sales for cash and collects on 40% of its sales in each of the 2 months following the sale. Other cash inflows are expected to be $12,000 in September and April, $15,000 in January and March, and $27,000 in February. The firm pays cash for 10% of its purchases. It pays for 50% of its purchases in the following month and for 40% of its purchases 2 months later.

Year	Month	Sales	Purchases
2012	September	$210,000	$120,000
2012	October	250,000	150,000
2012	November	170,000	140,000
2012	December	160,000	100,000
2013	January	140,000	80,000
2013	February	180,000	110,000
2013	March	200,000	100,000
2013	April	250,000	90,000

Wages and salaries amount to 20% of the preceding month's sales. Rent of $20,000 per month must be paid. Interest payments of $10,000 are due in January and April. A principal payment of $30,000 is also due in April. The firm expects to pay cash dividends of $20,000 in January and April. Taxes of $80,000 are due in April. The firm also intends to make a $25,000 cash purchase of fixed assets in December.

a. Assuming that the firm has a cash balance of $22,000 at the beginning of November, determine the end-of-month cash balances for each month, November through April.

b. Assuming that the firm wishes to maintain a $15,000 minimum cash balance, determine the required total financing or excess cash balance for each month, November through April.

c. If the firm were requesting a line of credit to cover needed financing for the period November to April, how large would this line have to be? Explain your answer.

LG 4   **P4–12**   **Cash flow concepts**   The following represent financial transactions that Johnsfield & Co. will be undertaking in the next planning period. For each transaction, check the statement or statements that will be affected immediately.

	Statement		
Transaction	Cash budget	Pro forma income statement	Pro forma balance sheet
Cash sale			
Credit sale			
Accounts receivable are collected			
Asset with 5-year life is purchased			
Depreciation is taken			
Amortization of goodwill is taken			
Sale of common stock			
Retirement of outstanding bonds			
Fire insurance premium is paid for the next 3 years			

LG 4   **P4–13**   **Cash budget—Scenario analysis**   Trotter Enterprises, Inc., has gathered the following data to plan for its cash requirements and short-term investment opportunities for October, November, and December. All amounts are shown in thousands of dollars.

	October			November			December		
	Pessi-mistic	Most likely	Opti-mistic	Pessi-mistic	Most likely	Opti-mistic	Pessi-mistic	Most likely	Opti-mistic
Total cash receipts	$260	$342	$462	$200	$287	$366	$191	$294	$353
Total cash disbursements	285	326	421	203	261	313	287	332	315

    a. Prepare a *scenario analysis* of Trotter's cash budget using –$20,000 as the beginning cash balance for October and a minimum required cash balance of $18,000.

    b. Use the analysis prepared in part **a** to predict Trotter's financing needs and investment opportunities over the months of October, November, and December. Discuss how knowledge of the timing and amounts involved can aid the planning process.

LG 4   **P4–14**   **Multiple cash budgets—Scenario analysis**   Brownstein, Inc., expects sales of $100,000 during each of the next 3 months. It will make monthly purchases of $60,000 during this time. Wages and salaries are $10,000 per month plus 5% of sales. Brownstein expects to make a tax payment of $20,000 in the next month and a $15,000 purchase of fixed assets in the second month and to receive $8,000 in cash from the sale of an asset in the third month. All sales and purchases are for cash. Beginning cash and the minimum cash balance are assumed to be zero.

    a. Construct a cash budget for the next 3 months.

    b. Brownstein is unsure of the sales levels, but all other figures are certain. If the most pessimistic sales figure is $80,000 per month and the most optimistic is $120,000 per month, what are the monthly minimum and maximum ending cash balances that the firm can expect for each of the 1-month periods?

    c. Briefly discuss how the financial manager can use the data in parts **a** and **b** to plan for financing needs.

LG 5   **P4–15**   **Pro forma income statement**   The marketing department of Metroline Manufacturing estimates that its sales in 2013 will be $1.5 million. Interest expense is expected to remain unchanged at $35,000, and the firm plans to pay $70,000 in cash dividends during 2013. Metroline Manufacturing's income statement for the year ended December 31, 2012, is given on page 152, along with a breakdown of the firm's cost of goods sold and operating expenses into their fixed and variable components.

    a. Use the *percent-of-sales method* to prepare a pro forma income statement for the year ended December 31, 2013.

    b. Use *fixed and variable cost data* to develop a pro forma income statement for the year ended December 31, 2013.

    c. Compare and contrast the statements developed in parts **a** and **b**. Which statement probably provides the better estimate of 2013 income? Explain why.

Metroline Manufacturing Income Statement for the Year Ended December 31, 2012	
Sales revenue	$1,400,000
Less: Cost of goods sold	910,000
Gross profits	$ 490,000
Less: Operating expenses	120,000
Operating profits	$ 370,000
Less: Interest expense	35,000
Net profits before taxes	$ 335,000
Less: Taxes (rate = 40%)	134,000
Net profits after taxes	$ 201,000
Less: Cash dividends	66,000
To retained earnings	$ 135,000

Metroline Manufacturing Breakdown of Costs and Expenses into Fixed and Variable Components for the Year Ended December 31, 2012	
Cost of goods sold	
Fixed cost	$210,000
Variable cost	700,000
Total costs	$910,000
Operating expenses	
Fixed expenses	$ 36,000
Variable expenses	84,000
Total expenses	$120,000

LG 5   **P4–16**   **Pro forma income statement—Scenario analysis**   Allen Products, Inc., wants to do a *scenario analysis* for the coming year. The pessimistic prediction for sales is $900,000; the most likely amount of sales is $1,125,000; and the optimistic prediction is $1,280,000. Allen's income statement for the most recent year follows.

Allen Products, Inc. Income Statement for the Year Ended December 31, 2012	
Sales revenue	$937,500
Less: Cost of goods sold	421,875
Gross profits	$515,625
Less: Operating expenses	234,375
Operating profits	$281,250
Less: Interest expense	30,000
Net profits before taxes	$251,250
Less: Taxes (rate = 25%)	62,813
Net profits after taxes	$188,437

a. Use the *percent-of-sales method,* the income statement for December 31, 2012, and the sales revenue estimates to develop pessimistic, most likely, and optimistic pro forma income statements for the coming year.

b. Explain how the percent-of-sales method could result in an overstatement of profits for the pessimistic case and an understatement of profits for the most likely and optimistic cases.

c. Restate the pro forma income statements prepared in part **a** to incorporate the following assumptions about the 2012 costs:

$250,000 of the cost of goods sold is fixed; the rest is variable.
$180,000 of the operating expenses is fixed; the rest is variable.
All of the interest expense is fixed.

d. Compare your findings in part **c** to your findings in part **a**. Do your observations confirm your explanation in part **b**?

LG 5 **P4–17** **Pro forma balance sheet—Basic** Leonard Industries wishes to prepare a pro forma balance sheet for December 31, 2013. The firm expects 2013 sales to total $3,000,000. The following information has been gathered.

(1) A minimum cash balance of $50,000 is desired.

(2) Marketable securities are expected to remain unchanged.

(3) Accounts receivable represent 10% of sales.

(4) Inventories represent 12% of sales.

(5) A new machine costing $90,000 will be acquired during 2013. Total depreciation for the year will be $32,000.

(6) Accounts payable represent 14% of sales.

(7) Accruals, other current liabilities, long-term debt, and common stock are expected to remain unchanged.

(8) The firm's net profit margin is 4%, and it expects to pay out $70,000 in cash dividends during 2013.

(9) The December 31, 2012, balance sheet follows.

Leonard Industries Balance Sheet December 31, 2012			
Assets		**Liabilities and Stockholders' Equity**	
Cash	$ 45,000	Accounts payable	$ 395,000
Marketable securities	15,000	Accruals	60,000
Accounts receivable	255,000	Other current liabilities	30,000
Inventories	340,000	Total current liabilities	$ 485,000
Total current assets	$ 655,000	Long-term debt	350,000
Net fixed assets	600,000	Total liabilities	$ 835,000
Total assets	$1,255,000	Common stock	200,000
		Retained earnings	220,000
		Total liabilities and stockholders' equity	$1,255,000

a. Use the *judgmental approach* to prepare a pro forma balance sheet dated December 31, 2013, for Leonard Industries.

b. How much, if any, additional financing will Leonard Industries require in 2013? Discuss.

c. Could Leonard Industries adjust its planned 2013 dividend to avoid the situation described in part **b?** Explain how.

LG 5 **P4–18** **Pro forma balance sheet** Peabody & Peabody has 2012 sales of $10 million. It wishes to analyze expected performance and financing needs for 2014—2 years ahead. Given the following information, respond to parts **a** and **b**.

(1) The percents of sales for items that vary directly with sales are as follows:

Accounts receivable, 12%
Inventory, 18%
Accounts payable, 14%
Net profit margin, 3%

(2) Marketable securities and other current liabilities are expected to remain unchanged.

(3) A minimum cash balance of $480,000 is desired.

(4) A new machine costing $650,000 will be acquired in 2013, and equipment costing $850,000 will be purchased in 2014. Total depreciation in 2013 is forecast as $290,000, and in 2014 $390,000 of depreciation will be taken.

(5) Accruals are expected to rise to $500,000 by the end of 2014.

(6) No sale or retirement of long-term debt is expected.

(7) No sale or repurchase of common stock is expected.

(8) The dividend payout of 50% of net profits is expected to continue.

(9) Sales are expected to be $11 million in 2013 and $12 million in 2014.

(10) The December 31, 2012, balance sheet follows.

Peabody & Peabody Balance Sheet December 31, 2012 ($000)			
Assets		**Liabilities and Stockholders' Equity**	
Cash	$ 400	Accounts payable	$1,400
Marketable securities	200	Accruals	400
Accounts receivable	1,200	Other current liabilities	80
Inventories	1,800	Total current liabilities	$1,880
Total current assets	$3,600	Long-term debt	2,000
Net fixed assets	4,000	Total liabilities	$3,880
Total assets	$7,600	Common equity	3,720
		Total liabilities and stockholders' equity	$7,600

a. Prepare a pro forma balance sheet dated December 31, 2014.

b. Discuss the financing changes suggested by the statement prepared in part **a.**

LG 5   **P4–19**   **Integrative—Pro forma statements**   Red Queen Restaurants wishes to prepare financial plans. Use the financial statements on page 155 and the other information provided below to prepare the financial plans.

The following financial data are also available:

(1) The firm has estimated that its sales for 2013 will be $900,000.

(2) The firm expects to pay $35,000 in cash dividends in 2013.

(3) The firm wishes to maintain a minimum cash balance of $30,000.

(4) Accounts receivable represent approximately 18% of annual sales.

(5) The firm's ending inventory will change directly with changes in sales in 2013.

(6) A new machine costing $42,000 will be purchased in 2013. Total depreciation for 2013 will be $17,000.

(7) Accounts payable will change directly in response to changes in sales in 2013.

(8) Taxes payable will equal one-fourth of the tax liability on the pro forma income statement.

(9) Marketable securities, other current liabilities, long-term debt, and common stock will remain unchanged.

a. Prepare a pro forma income statement for the year ended December 31, 2013, using the *percent-of-sales method.*

b. Prepare a pro forma balance sheet dated December 31, 2013, using the *judgmental approach.*

c. Analyze these statements, and discuss the resulting *external financing required.*

**Red Queen Restaurants Income Statement
for the Year Ended December 31, 2012**

Sales revenue	$800,000
Less: Cost of goods sold	600,000
Gross profits	$200,000
Less: Operating expenses	100,000
Net profits before taxes	$100,000
Less: Taxes (rate = 40%)	40,000
Net profits after taxes	$ 60,000
Less: Cash dividends	20,000
To retained earnings	$ 40,000

Red Queen Restaurants Balance Sheet December 31, 2012

Assets		Liabilities and Stockholders' Equity	
Cash	$ 32,000	Accounts payable	$100,000
Marketable securities	18,000	Taxes payable	20,000
Accounts receivable	150,000	Other current liabilities	5,000
Inventories	100,000	Total current liabilities	$125,000
Total current assets	$300,000	Long-term debt	200,000
Net fixed assets	350,000	Total liabilities	$325,000
Total assets	$650,000	Common stock	150,000
		Retained earnings	175,000
		Total liabilities and stockholders' equity	$650,000

LG 5 **P4–20** **Integrative—Pro forma statements** Provincial Imports, Inc., has assembled past (2012) financial statements (income statement below and balance sheet on page 156) and financial projections for use in preparing financial plans for the coming year (2013).

**Provincial Imports, Inc. Income Statement
for the Year Ended December 31, 2012**

Sales revenue	$5,000,000
Less: Cost of goods sold	2,750,000
Gross profits	$2,250,000
Less: Operating expenses	850,000
Operating profits	$1,400,000
Less: Interest expense	200,000
Net profits before taxes	$1,200,000
Less: Taxes (rate = 40%)	480,000
Net profits after taxes	$ 720,000
Less: Cash dividends	288,000
To retained earnings	$ 432,000

Information related to financial projections for the year 2013:

Provincial Imports, Inc. Balance Sheet December 31, 2012			
Assets		**Liabilities and Stockholders' Equity**	
Cash	$ 200,000	Accounts payable	$ 700,000
Marketable securities	225,000	Taxes payable	95,000
Accounts receivable	625,000	Notes payable	200,000
Inventories	500,000	Other current liabilities	5,000
Total current assets	$1,550,000	Total current liabilities	$1,000,000
Net fixed assets	1,400,000	Long-term debt	500,000
Total assets	$2,950,000	Total liabilities	$1,500,000
		Common stock	75,000
		Retained earnings	1,375,000
		Total liabilities and equity	$2,950,000

(1) Projected sales are $6,000,000.
(2) Cost of goods sold in 2012 includes $1,000,000 in fixed costs.
(3) Operating expense in 2012 includes $250,000 in fixed costs.
(4) Interest expense will remain unchanged.
(5) The firm will pay cash dividends amounting to 40% of net profits after taxes.
(6) Cash and inventories will double.
(7) Marketable securities, notes payable, long-term debt, and common stock will remain unchanged.
(8) Accounts receivable, accounts payable, and other current liabilities will change in direct response to the change in sales.
(9) A new computer system costing $356,000 will be purchased during the year. Total depreciation expense for the year will be $110,000.
(10) The tax rate will remain at 40%.

a. Prepare a pro forma income statement for the year ended December 31, 2013, using the *fixed cost data* given to improve the accuracy of the *percent-of-sales method*.
b. Prepare a pro forma balance sheet as of December 31, 2013, using the information given and the *judgmental approach*. Include a reconciliation of the retained earnings account.
c. Analyze these statements, and discuss the resulting *external financing required*.

LG 3   **P4–21   ETHICS PROBLEM**   The SEC is trying to get companies to notify the investment community more quickly when a "material change" will affect their forthcoming financial results. In what sense might a financial manager be seen as "more ethical" if he or she follows this directive and issues a press release indicating that sales will not be as high as previously anticipated?

Spreadsheet Exercise

You have been assigned the task of putting together a statement for the ACME Company that shows its expected inflows and outflows of cash over the months of July 2013 through December 2013.

You have been given the following data for ACME Company:

(1) Expected gross sales for May through December, respectively, are $300,000, $290,000, $425,000, $500,000, $600,000, $625,000, $650,000, and $700,000.

(2) 12% of the sales in any given month are collected during that month. However, the firm has a credit policy of 3/10 net 30, so factor a 3% discount into the current month's sales collection.

(3) 75% of the sales in any given month are collected during the following month after the sale.

(4) 13% of the sales in any given month are collected during the second month following the sale.

(5) The expected purchases of raw materials in any given month are based on 60% of the expected sales during the following month.

(6) The firm pays 100% of its current month's raw materials purchases in the following month.

(7) Wages and salaries are paid on a monthly basis and are based on 6% of the current month's expected sales.

(8) Monthly lease payments are 2% of the current month's expected sales.

(9) The monthly advertising expense amounts to 3% of sales.

(10) R&D expenditures are expected to be allocated to August, September, and October at the rate of 12% of sales in those months.

(11) During December a prepayment of insurance for the following year will be made in the amount of $24,000.

(12) During the months of July through December, the firm expects to have miscellaneous expenditures of $15,000, $20,000, $25,000, $30,000, $35,000, and $40,000, respectively.

(13) Taxes will be paid in September in the amount of $40,000 and in December in the amount of $45,000.

(14) The beginning cash balance in July is $15,000.

(15) The target cash balance is $15,000.

TO DO

a. Prepare a cash budget for July 2013 through December 2013 by creating a combined spreadsheet that incorporates spreadsheets similar to those in Tables 4.8, 4.9, and 4.10. Divide your spreadsheet into three sections:
   (1) Total cash receipts
   (2) Total cash disbursements
   (3) Cash budget covering the period of July through December

   The cash budget should reflect the following:
   (1) Beginning and ending monthly cash balances
   (2) The required total financing in each month required
   (3) The excess cash balance in each month with excess

b. Based on your analysis, briefly describe the outlook for this company over the next 6 months. Discuss its specific obligations and the funds available to meet them. What could the firm do in the case of a cash deficit? (Where could it get the money?) What should the firm do if it has a cash surplus?

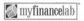 Visit www.myfinancelab.com for **Chapter Case: *Preparing Martin Manufacturing's 2013 Pro Forma Financial Statements,*** Group Exercises, and numerous online resources.

5 Time Value of Money

Learning Goals

LG 1 Discuss the role of time value in finance, the use of computational tools, and the basic patterns of cash flow.

LG 2 Understand the concepts of future value and present value, their calculation for single amounts, and the relationship between them.

LG 3 Find the future value and the present value of both an ordinary annuity and an annuity due, and find the present value of a perpetuity.

LG 4 Calculate both the future value and the present value of a mixed stream of cash flows.

LG 5 Understand the effect that compounding interest more frequently than annually has on future value and on the effective annual rate of interest.

LG 6 Describe the procedures involved in (1) determining deposits needed to accumulate a future sum, (2) loan amortization, (3) finding interest or growth rates, and (4) finding an unknown number of periods.

Why This Chapter Matters to You

In your *professional* life

ACCOUNTING You need to understand time-value-of-money calculations to account for certain transactions such as loan amortization, lease payments, and bond interest rates.

INFORMATION SYSTEMS You need to understand time-value-of-money calculations to design systems that accurately measure and value the firm's cash flows.

MANAGEMENT You need to understand time-value-of-money calculations so that you can manage cash receipts and disbursements in a way that will enable the firm to receive the greatest value from its cash flows.

MARKETING You need to understand time value of money because funding for new programs and products must be justified financially using time-value-of-money techniques.

OPERATIONS You need to understand time value of money because the value of investments in new equipment, in new processes, and in inventory will be affected by the time value of money.

In your *personal* life
Time-value-of-money techniques are widely used in personal financial planning. You can use them to calculate the value of savings at given future dates and to estimate the amount you need now to accumulate a given amount at a future date. You also can apply them to value lump-sum amounts or streams of periodic cash flows and to the interest rate or amount of time needed to achieve a given financial goal.

Eli Lilly and Company

Riding the Pipeline

Companies spend money on new investments if they believe that those investments will later generate enough cash flow to justify the up-front cost. For pharmaceutical companies like Eli Lilly, the average length of time from the discovery of a new drug until delivery to a patient is 10 to 15 years. After R&D produces a promising lead, a drug is still a long way from being ready for human testing. Researchers must probe further to determine what dosage will be required and at what level it might be toxic to the patient. They also must explore practical issues such as whether Lilly will be able to manufacture the compound on a large scale. The clinical trials themselves can take years.

To help recoup its investment, a drug manufacturer can get a 20-year patent that grants the company exclusive rights to the new drug. However, with the lengthy research and approval process, companies may have fewer than 10 years to sell the drug while the patent is in force. Once patent protection expires, generic drug manufacturers enter the market with low-priced alternatives to the name-brand drug.

For Eli Lilly, the cost of bringing a new drug to market runs from $800 million to $1.2 billion. To keep its drug pipeline full, Eli Lilly plows some 20 percent of sales back into the R&D programs on which its future depends. With large cash expenditures occurring years before any cash return, the time value of money is an important factor in calculating the economic viability of a new drug. In this chapter, you will learn how to determine the present value of future cash flows and other time-value-of-money calculations.

LG 1 **5.1 The Role of Time Value in Finance**

The *time value of money* refers to the observation that it is better to receive money sooner than later. Money that you have in hand today can be invested to earn a positive rate of return, producing more money tomorrow. For that reason, a dollar today is worth more than a dollar in the future. In business, managers constantly face trade-offs in situations where actions that require outflows of cash today may produce inflows of cash later. Because the cash that comes in the future is worth less than the cash that firms spend up front, managers need a set of tools to help them compare cash inflows and outflows that occur at different times. This chapter introduces you to those tools.

In more depth

To read about *The Royalty Treatment*, go to www.myfinancelab.com

FUTURE VALUE VERSUS PRESENT VALUE

Suppose a firm has an opportunity to spend $15,000 today on some investment that will produce $17,000 spread out over the next five years as follows:

Year 1	$3,000
Year 2	$5,000
Year 3	$4,000
Year 4	$3,000
Year 5	$2,000

Is this a wise investment? It might seem that the obvious answer is yes because the firm spends $15,000 and receives $17,000. Remember, though, that the value of the dollars the firm receives in the future is less than the value of the dollars that they spend today. Therefore, it is not clear whether the $17,000 inflows are enough to justify the initial investment.

Time-value-of-money analysis helps managers answer questions like these. The basic idea is that managers need a way to compare cash today versus cash in the future. There are two ways of doing this. One way is to ask the question, What amount of money in the future is equivalent to $15,000 today? In other words, what is the *future value* of $15,000? The other approach asks, What amount today is equivalent to $17,000 paid out over the next 5 years as outlined above? In other words, what is the *present value* of the stream of cash flows coming in the next 5 years?

A **time line** depicts the cash flows associated with a given investment. It is a horizontal line on which time zero appears at the leftmost end and future periods are marked from left to right. A time line illustrating our hypothetical investment problem appears in Figure 5.1. The cash flows occurring at time zero (today) and

time line
A horizontal line on which time zero appears at the leftmost end and future periods are marked from left to right; can be used to depict investment cash flows.

FIGURE 5.1

Time Line
Time line depicting an investment's cash flows

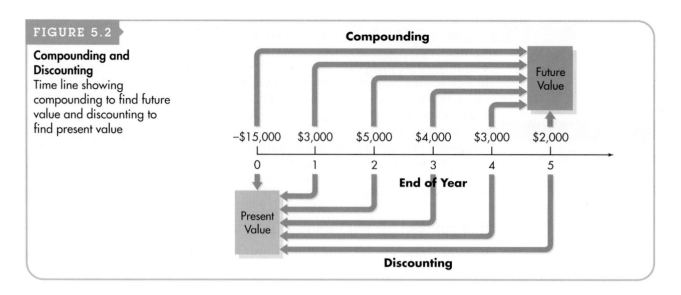

FIGURE 5.2

Compounding and Discounting
Time line showing compounding to find future value and discounting to find present value

at the end of each subsequent year are above the line; the negative values represent *cash outflows* ($15,000 invested today at time zero), and the positive values represent *cash inflows* ($3,000 inflow in 1 year, $5,000 inflow in 2 years, and so on).

To make the right investment decision, managers need to compare the cash flows depicted in Figure 5.1 at a single point in time. Typically, that point is either the end or the beginning of the investment's life. The future value technique uses *compounding* to find the *future value* of each cash flow at the end of the investment's life and then sums these values to find the investment's future value. This approach is depicted above the time line in Figure 5.2. The figure shows that the future value of each cash flow is measured at the end of the investment's 5-year life. Alternatively, the present value technique uses *discounting* to find the *present value* of each cash flow at time zero and then sums these values to find the investment's value today. Application of this approach is depicted below the time line in Figure 5.2. In practice, when making investment decisions, *managers usually adopt the present value approach*.

COMPUTATIONAL TOOLS

Finding present and future values can involve time-consuming calculations. Although you should understand the concepts and mathematics underlying these calculations, financial calculators and spreadsheets streamline the application of time value techniques.

Financial Calculators

Financial calculators include numerous preprogrammed financial routines. Learning how to use these routines can make present and future values calculations a breeze.

We focus primarily on the keys pictured in Figure 5.3. We typically use four of the first five keys shown in the left column, along with the compute (**CPT**) key. One of the four keys represents the unknown value being calculated. The keystrokes on

FIGURE 5.3

Calculator Keys
Important financial keys on
the typical calculator

N — Number of periods
I — Interest rate per period
PV — Present value
PMT — Amount of payment (used only for annuities)
FV — Future value
CPT — Compute key used to initiate financial calculation
once all values are input

some of the more sophisticated calculators are menu-driven: After you select the appropriate routine, the calculator prompts you to input each value. Regardless, any calculator with the basic future and present value functions can simplify time-value-of-money calculations. The keystrokes for financial calculators are explained in the reference guides that accompany them.

Once you understand the basic underlying concepts, you probably will want to use a calculator to streamline calculations. With a little practice, you can increase both the speed and the accuracy of your financial computations. Remember that *conceptual understanding of the material is the objective.* An ability to solve problems with the aid of a calculator does not necessarily reflect such an understanding, so don't just settle for answers. Work with the material until you are sure you also understand the concepts.

Electronic Spreadsheets

Like financial calculators, electronic spreadsheets have built-in routines that simplify time value calculations. We provide in the text a number of spreadsheet solutions that identify the cell entries for calculating time values. The value for each variable is entered in a cell in the spreadsheet, and the calculation is programmed using an equation that links the individual cells. Changing any of the input variables automatically changes the solution as a result of the equation linking the cells.

BASIC PATTERNS OF CASH FLOW

The cash flow—both inflows and outflows—of a firm can be described by its general pattern. It can be defined as a single amount, an annuity, or a mixed stream.

Single amount: A lump-sum amount either currently held or expected at some future date. Examples include $1,000 today and $650 to be received at the end of 10 years.

Annuity: A level periodic stream of cash flow. For our purposes, we'll work primarily with *annual* cash flows. Examples include either paying out or receiving $800 at the end of each of the next 7 years.

Mixed stream: A stream of cash flow that is *not* an annuity; a stream of unequal periodic cash flows that reflect no particular pattern. Examples include the following two cash flow streams A and B.

	Mixed cash flow stream	
End of year	A	B
1	$ 100	−$ 50
2	800	100
3	1,200	80
4	1,200	− 60
5	1,400	
6	300	

Note that neither cash flow stream has equal, periodic cash flows and that A is a 6-year mixed stream and B is a 4-year mixed stream.

In the next three sections of this chapter, we develop the concepts and techniques for finding future and present values of single amounts, annuities, and mixed streams, respectively. Detailed demonstrations of these cash flow patterns are included.

→ **REVIEW QUESTIONS**

5–1 What is the difference between *future value* and *present value?* Which approach is generally preferred by financial managers? Why?

5–2 Define and differentiate among the three basic patterns of cash flow: (1) a single amount, (2) an annuity, and (3) a mixed stream.

LG 2 **5.2 Single Amounts**

Imagine that at age 25 you began investing $2,000 per year in an investment that earns 5 percent interest. At the end of 40 years, at age 65, you would have invested a total of $80,000 (40 years × $2,000 per year). How much would you have accumulated at the end of the fortieth year? $100,000? $150,000? $200,000? No, your $80,000 would have grown to $242,000! Why? Because the time value of money allowed your investments to generate returns that built on each other over the 40 years.

FUTURE VALUE OF A SINGLE AMOUNT

The most basic future value and present value concepts and computations concern single amounts, either present or future amounts. We begin by considering problems that involve finding the future value of cash that is on hand immediately. Then we will use the underlying concepts to solve problems that determine the value today of cash that will be received or paid in the future.

future value
The value at a given future date of an amount placed on deposit today and earning interest at a specified rate. Found by applying *compound interest* over a specified period of time.

We often need to find the value at some future date of a given amount of money placed on deposit today. For example, if you deposit $500 today into an account that pays 5 percent annual interest, how much would you have in the account in 10 years? **Future value** is the value at a given future date of an amount placed on deposit today and earning interest at a specified rate. The future value depends on the rate of interest earned and the length of time the money is left on deposit. Here we explore the future value of a single amount.

The Concept of Future Value

compound interest
Interest that is earned on a given deposit and has become part of the *principal* at the end of a specified period.

principal
The amount of money on which interest is paid.

We speak of **compound interest** to indicate that the amount of interest earned on a given deposit has become part of the *principal* at the end of a specified period. The term **principal** refers to the amount of money on which the interest is paid. Annual compounding is the most common type.

The *future value* of a present amount is found by applying *compound interest* over a specified period of time. Savings institutions advertise compound interest returns at a rate of *x* percent, or *x* percent interest, compounded annually, semi-annually, quarterly, monthly, weekly, daily, or even continuously. The concept of future value with annual compounding can be illustrated by a simple example.

Personal Finance Example 5.1 ▶ If Fred Moreno places $100 in a savings account paying 8% interest compounded annually, at the end of 1 year he will have $108 in the account—the initial principal of $100 plus 8% ($8) in interest. The future value at the end of the first year is calculated by using Equation 5.1:

$$\text{Future value at end of year 1} = \$100 \times (1 + 0.08) = \$108 \qquad (5.1)$$

If Fred were to leave this money in the account for another year, he would be paid interest at the rate of 8% on the new principal of $108. At the end of this second year there would be $116.64 in the account. This amount would represent the principal at the beginning of year 2 ($108) plus 8% of the $108 ($8.64) in interest. The future value at the end of the second year is calculated by using Equation 5.2:

$$\text{Future value at end of year 2} = \$108 \times (1 + 0.08)$$
$$= \$116.64 \qquad (5.2)$$

Substituting the expression between the equals signs in Equation 5.1 for the $108 figure in Equation 5.2 gives us Equation 5.3:

$$\text{Future value at end of year 2} = \$100 \times (1 + 0.08) \times (1 + 0.08)$$
$$= \$100 \times (1 + 0.08)^2 \qquad (5.3)$$
$$= \$116.64$$

The equations in the preceding example lead to a more general formula for calculating future value.

The Equation for Future Value

The basic relationship in Equation 5.3 can be generalized to find the future value after any number of periods. We use the following notation for the various inputs:

FV_n = future value at the end of period n

PV = initial principal, or present value

$\quad r$ = annual rate of interest paid. (Note: On financial calculators, **I** is typically used to represent this rate.)

$\quad n$ = number of periods (typically years) that the money is left on deposit

The general equation for the future value at the end of period n is

$$FV_n = PV \times (1 + r)^n \qquad (5.4)$$

A simple example will illustrate how to apply Equation 5.4.

Personal Finance Example 5.2 ▶ Jane Farber places $800 in a savings account paying 6% interest compounded annually. She wants to know how much money will be in the account at the end of 5 years. Substituting $PV = \$800$, $r = 0.06$, and $n = 5$ into Equation 5.4 gives the amount at the end of year 5:

$$FV_5 = \$800 \times (1 + 0.06)^5 = \$800 \times (1.33823) = \$1,070.58$$

This analysis can be depicted on a time line as follows:

Time line for future value of a single amount ($800 initial principal, earning 6%, at the end of 5 years)

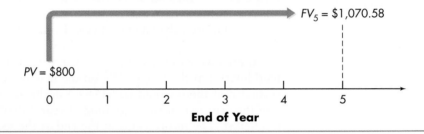

In more depth

To read about *The Rule of 72*, go to www.myfinancelab.com

myfinancelab

Solving the equation in the preceding example involves raising 1.06 to the fifth power. Using a financial calculator or electronic spreadsheet greatly simplifies the calculation.

Personal Finance Example 5.3 ▶ In Personal Finance Example 5.2, Jane Farber placed $800 in her savings account at 6% interest compounded annually and wishes to find out how much will be in the account at the end of 5 years.

Input	Function
800	PV
5	N
6	I
	CPT
	FV

Solution
1,070.58

Calculator Use[1]   The financial calculator can be used to calculate the future value directly. First punch in $800 and depress **PV**; next punch in 5 and depress **N**; then punch in 6 and depress **I** (which is equivalent to "r" in our notation); finally, to calculate the future value, depress **CPT** and then **FV**. The future value of $1,070.58 should appear on the calculator display as shown at the left. On many calculators, this value will be preceded by a minus sign (–1,070.58). *If a minus sign appears on your calculator, ignore it here as well as in all other*

---

1. Many calculators allow the user to set the number of payments per year. Most of these calculators are preset for monthly payments—12 payments per year. Because we work primarily with annual payments—one payment per year—it is important to *be sure that your calculator is set for one payment per year*. And although most calculators are preset to recognize that all payments occur at the end of the period, it is important to *make sure that your calculator is correctly set on the END mode*. To avoid including previous data in current calculations, *always clear all registers of your calculator before inputting values and making each computation*. The known values *can be punched into the calculator in any order*; the order specified in this as well as other demonstrations of calculator use included in this text merely reflects convenience and personal preference.

"Calculator Use" illustrations in this text.[2] (*Note:* In future examples of calculator use, we will use only a display similar to that shown on page 166. If you need a reminder of the procedures involved, go back and review this paragraph.)

Spreadsheet Use Excel offers a mathematical function that makes the calculation of future values easy. The format of that function is FV(rate,nper,pmt,pv, type). The terms inside the parentheses are inputs that Excel requires to calculate the future value. The terms *rate* and *nper* refer to the interest rate and the number of time periods respectively. The term *pv* represents the lump sum (or present value) that you are investing today. For now, we will ignore the other two inputs, *pmt* and *type,* and enter a value of zero. The future value of the single amount also can be calculated as shown on the following Excel spreadsheet.

	A	B
1	FUTURE VALUE OF A SINGLE AMOUNT	
2	Present value	$800
3	Interest rate, pct per year compounded annually	6%
4	Number of years	5
5	Future value	$1,070.58
Entry in Cell B5 is =FV(B3,B4,0,−B2,0) The minus sign appears before B2 because the present value is an outflow (i.e., a deposit made by Jane Farber).		

Changing any of the values in cells B2, B3, or B4 automatically changes the result shown in cell B5 because the formula in that cell links back to the others. As with the calculator, Excel reports cash inflows as positive numbers and cash outflows as negative numbers. In the example here, we have entered the $800 present value as a negative number, which causes Excel to report the future value as a positive number. Logically, Excel treats the $800 present value as a cash outflow, as if you are paying for the investment you are making, and it treats the future value as a cash inflow when you reap the benefits of your investment 5 years later.

A Graphical View of Future Value

Remember that we measure future value at the *end* of the given period. Figure 5.4 (see page 168) illustrates how the future value depends on the interest rate and the number of periods that money is invested. The figure shows that (1) the higher the interest rate, the higher the future value, and (2) the longer the period of time, the higher the future value. Note that for an interest rate of 0 percent, the future value always equals the present value ($1.00). But for any interest rate greater than zero, the future value is greater than the present value of $1.00.

---

2. The calculator differentiates inflows from outflows by preceding the outflows with a negative sign. For example, in the problem just demonstrated, the $800 present value (PV), because it was keyed as a positive number, is considered an inflow. Therefore, the calculated future value (FV) of −1,070.58 is preceded by a minus sign to show that it is the resulting outflow. Had the $800 present value been keyed in as a negative number (−800), the future value of $1,070.58 would have been displayed as a positive number (1,070.58). Simply stated, *the cash flows—present value (PV) and future value (FV)—will have opposite signs.*

FIGURE 5.4

Future Value Relationship
Interest rates, time periods, and future value of one dollar

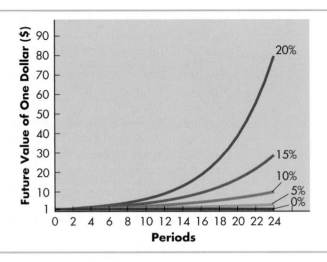

PRESENT VALUE OF A SINGLE AMOUNT

It is often useful to determine the value today of a future amount of money. For example, how much would I have to deposit today into an account paying 7 percent annual interest to accumulate $3,000 at the end of 5 years? **Present value** is the current dollar value of a future amount—the amount of money that would have to be invested today at a given interest rate over a specified period to equal the future amount. Like future value, the present value depends largely on the interest rate and the point in time at which the amount is to be received. This section explores the present value of a single amount.

present value
The current dollar value of a future amount—the amount of money that would have to be invested today at a given interest rate over a specified period to equal the future amount.

The Concept of Present Value

The process of finding present values is often referred to as **discounting cash flows.** It is concerned with answering the following question: If I can earn r percent on my money, what is the most I would be willing to pay now for an opportunity to receive FV_n dollars n periods from today?

This process is actually the inverse of compounding interest. Instead of finding the future value of present dollars invested at a given rate, discounting determines the present value of a future amount, assuming an opportunity to earn a certain return on the money. This annual rate of return is variously referred to as the *discount rate, required return, cost of capital,* and *opportunity cost.* These terms will be used interchangeably in this text.

discounting cash flows
The process of finding present values; the inverse of compounding interest.

Personal Finance Example 5.4 ▶ Paul Shorter has an opportunity to receive $300 one year from now. If he can earn 6% on his investments in the normal course of events, what is the most he should pay now for this opportunity? To answer this question, Paul must determine how many dollars he would have to invest at 6% today to have $300 one year from now. Letting PV equal this unknown amount and using the same notation as in the future value discussion, we have

$$PV \times (1 + 0.06) = \$300 \tag{5.5}$$

Solving Equation 5.5 for *PV* gives us Equation 5.6:

$$PV = \frac{\$300}{(1 + 0.06)}$$
$$= \$283.02 \tag{5.6}$$

The value today ("present value") of $300 received one year from today, given an interest rate of 6%, is $283.02. That is, investing $283.02 today at 6% would result in $300 at the end of one year.

The Equation for Present Value

The present value of a future amount can be found mathematically by solving Equation 5.4 for *PV*. In other words, the present value, *PV*, of some future amount, FV_n, to be received *n* periods from now, assuming an interest rate (or opportunity cost) of *r*, is calculated as follows:

$$PV = \frac{FV_n}{(1 + r)^n} \tag{5.7}$$

Note the similarity between this general equation for present value and the equation in the preceding example (Equation 5.6). Let's use this equation in an example.

Personal Finance Example 5.5 ▶ Pam Valenti wishes to find the present value of $1,700 that she will receive 8 years from now. Pam's opportunity cost is 8%. Substituting $FV_8 = \$1,700$, $n = 8$, and $r = 0.08$ into Equation 5.7 yields Equation 5.8:

$$PV = \frac{\$1,700}{(1 \times 0.08)^8} = \frac{\$1,700}{1.85093} = \$918.46 \tag{5.8}$$

The following time line shows this analysis.

Time line for present value of a single amount ($1,700 future amount, discounted at 8%, from the end of 8 years)

Calculator Use Using the calculator's financial functions and the inputs shown at the left, you should find the present value to be $918.46.

Spreadsheet Use The format of Excel's present value function is very similar to the future value function covered earlier. The appropriate syntax is PV(rate,nper, pmt,fv,type). The input list inside the parentheses is the same as in Excel's future value function with one exception. The present value function contains the term *fv*, which represents the future lump sum payment (or receipt) whose present value you are trying to calculate. The present value of the single future amount also can be calculated as shown on the following Excel spreadsheet.

	A	B
1	PRESENT VALUE OF A SINGLE AMOUNT	
2	Future value	$1,700
3	Interest rate, pct per year compounded annually	8%
4	Number of years	8
5	Present value	$918.46
	Entry in Cell B5 is =–PV(B3,B4,0,B2) The minus sign appears before PV to change the present value to a positive amount.	

A Graphical View of Present Value

Remember that present value calculations assume that the future values are measured at the *end* of the given period. The relationships among the factors in a present value calculation are illustrated in Figure 5.5. The figure clearly shows that, everything else being equal, (1) the higher the discount rate, the lower the present value, and (2) the longer the period of time, the lower the present value. Also note that given a discount rate of 0 percent, the present value always equals the future value ($1.00). But for any discount rate greater than zero, the present value is less than the future value of $1.00.

→ REVIEW QUESTIONS

5–3 How is the *compounding process* related to the payment of interest on savings? What is the general equation for future value?

5–4 What effect would a *decrease* in the interest rate have on the future value of a deposit? What effect would an *increase* in the holding period have on future value?

5–5 What is meant by "the present value of a future amount"? What is the general equation for present value?

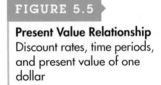

FIGURE 5.5

Present Value Relationship
Discount rates, time periods, and present value of one dollar

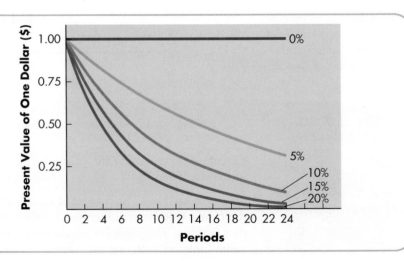

5–6 What effect does *increasing* the required return have on the present value of a future amount? Why?

5–7 How are present value and future value calculations related?

LG 3 **5.3** Annuities

annuity
A stream of equal periodic cash flows over a specified time period. These cash flows can be *inflows* of returns earned on investments or *outflows* of funds invested to earn future returns.

ordinary annuity
An annuity for which the cash flow occurs at the *end* of each period.

annuity due
An annuity for which the cash flow occurs at the *beginning* of each period.

How much would you pay today, given that you can earn 7 percent on low-risk investments, to receive a guaranteed $3,000 at the end of *each* of the next 20 years? How much will you have at the end of 5 years if your employer withholds and invests $1,000 of your bonus at the end of *each* of the next 5 years, guaranteeing you a 9 percent annual rate of return? To answer these questions, you need to understand the application of the time value of money to *annuities*.

An **annuity** is a stream of equal periodic cash flows, over a specified time period. These cash flows are usually annual but can occur at other intervals, such as monthly rent or car payments. The cash flows in an annuity can be *inflows* (the $3,000 received at the end of each of the next 20 years) or *outflows* (the $1,000 invested at the end of each of the next 5 years).

TYPES OF ANNUITIES

There are two basic types of annuities. For an **ordinary annuity,** the cash flow occurs at the *end* of each period. For an **annuity due,** the cash flow occurs at the *beginning* of each period.

Personal Finance Example 5.6 ▶ Fran Abrams is evaluating two annuities. Both are 5-year, $1,000 annuities; annuity A is an ordinary annuity and annuity B is an annuity due. To better understand the difference between these annuities, she has listed their cash flows in Table 5.1. Note that the amount of each annuity totals $5,000. The two annuities differ only in the timing of their cash flows: The cash flows are received sooner with the annuity due than with the ordinary annuity.

TABLE 5.1	Comparison of Ordinary Annuity and Annuity Due Cash Flows ($1,000, 5 Years)	
	Annual cash flows	
Year	Annuity A (*ordinary*)	Annuity B (*annuity due*)
0	$ 0	$1,000
1	1,000	1,000
2	1,000	1,000
3	1,000	1,000
4	1,000	1,000
5	1,000	0
Totals	$5,000	$5,000

Although the cash flows of both annuities in Table 5.1 total $5,000, the annuity due would have a higher future value than the ordinary annuity because each of its five annual cash flows can earn interest for 1 year more than each of the ordinary annuity's cash flows. In general, as will be demonstrated later in this chapter, *the value (present or future) of an annuity due is always greater than the value of an otherwise identical ordinary annuity.*

Because ordinary annuities are more frequently used in finance, *unless otherwise specified, the term* annuity *is intended throughout this book to refer to ordinary annuities.*

FINDING THE FUTURE VALUE OF AN ORDINARY ANNUITY

One way to find the future value of an ordinary annuity is to calculate the future value of each of the individual cash flows and then add up those figures. Fortunately, there are several shortcuts to get to the answer. You can calculate the future value of an ordinary annuity that pays an annual cash flow equal to *CF* by using Equation 5.9:

$$FV_n = CF \times \left\{ \frac{[(1 + r)^n - 1]}{r} \right\} \tag{5.9}$$

As before, in this equation *r* represents the interest rate, and *n* represents the number of payments in the annuity (or equivalently, the number of years over which the annuity is spread). The calculations required to find the future value of an ordinary annuity are illustrated in the following example.

Personal Finance Example 5.7 ▶ Fran Abrams wishes to determine how much money she will have at the end of 5 years if she chooses annuity A, the ordinary annuity. She will deposit $1,000 annually, at the *end of each* of the next 5 years, into a savings account paying 7% annual interest. This situation is depicted on the following time line:

Time line for future value of an ordinary annuity ($1,000 end-of-year deposit, earning 7%, at the end of 5 years)

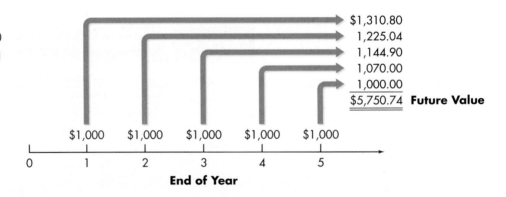

As the figure shows, at the end of year 5, Fran will have $5,750.74 in her account. Note that because the deposits are made at the end of the year the first deposit will earn interest for 4 years, the second for 3 years, and so on. Plugging the relevant values into Equation 5.9 we have

$$FV_5 = \$1{,}000 \times \left\{ \frac{[(1 + 0.07)^5 - 1]}{0.07} \right\} = \$5{,}750.74 \qquad (5.10)$$

Input	Function
1000	PMT
5	N
7	I
	CPT
	FV

Solution
5,750.74

Calculator Use Using the calculator inputs shown at the left, you can confirm that the future value of the ordinary annuity equals $5,750.74.

Spreadsheet Use To calculate the future value of an annuity in Excel, we will use the same future value function that we used to calculate the future value of a lump sum, but we will add two new input values. Recall that the future value function's syntax is FV(rate,nper,pmt,pv,type). We have already explained the terms *rate*, *nper*, and *pv* in this function. The term *pmt* refers to the annual payment that the annuity offers. The term *type* is an input that lets Excel know whether the annuity being valued is an ordinary annuity (in which case the input value for *type* is 0 or omitted) or an annuity due (in which case the correct input value for *type* is 1). In this particular problem, the input value for *pv* is 0 or omitted because there is no up-front money received. The only cash flows are those that are part of the annuity stream. The future value of the ordinary annuity can be calculated as shown on the following Excel spreadsheet.

	A	B
1	FUTURE VALUE OF AN ORDINARY ANNUITY	
2	Annual payment	$1,000
3	Annual rate of interest, compounded annually	7%
4	Number of years	5
5	Future value of an ordinary annuity	$5,750.74
	Entry in Cell B5 is =FV(B3,B4,−B2) The minus sign appears before B2 because the annual payment is a cash outflow.	

FINDING THE PRESENT VALUE OF AN ORDINARY ANNUITY

Quite often in finance, there is a need to find the present value of a *stream* of cash flows to be received in future periods. An annuity is, of course, a stream of equal periodic cash flows. The method for finding the present value of an ordinary annuity is similar to the method just discussed. One approach would be to calculate the present value of each cash flow in the annuity and then add up those present values. Alternatively, the algebraic shortcut for finding the present value of an ordinary annuity that makes an annual payment of *CF* for *n* years looks like this:

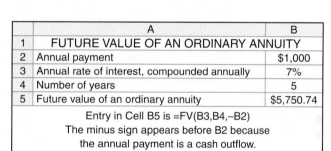

$$PV_n = \left(\frac{CF}{r} \right) \times \left[1 - \frac{1}{(1 + r)^n} \right] \qquad (5.11)$$

Of course the simplest approach is to solve problems like these with a financial calculator or spreadsheet program.

Example 5.8 ▶

Braden Company, a small producer of plastic toys, wants to determine the most it should pay to purchase a particular ordinary annuity. The annuity consists of cash flows of $700 at the end of each year for 5 years. The firm requires the annuity to provide a minimum return of 8%. This situation is depicted on the following time line:

Time line for present value of an ordinary annuity ($700 end-of-year cash flows, discounted at 8%, over 5 years)

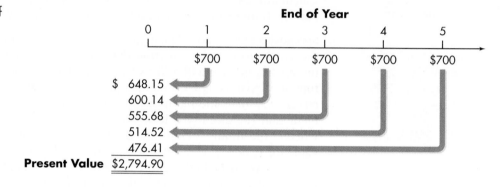

Table 5.2 shows one way to find the present value of the annuity—simply calculate the present values of all the cash payments using the present value equation (Equation 5.7 on page 169) and sum them. This procedure yields a present value of $2,794.90. Calculators and spreadsheets offer streamlined methods for arriving at this figure.

Calculator Use   Using the calculator's inputs shown at the left, you will find the present value of the ordinary annuity to be $2,794.90.

Spreadsheet Use   The present value of the ordinary annuity also can be calculated as shown on the Excel spreadsheet on the next page.

Input	Function
700	PMT
5	N
8	I
	CPT
	PV

Solution
2,794.90

TABLE 5.2	Long Method for Finding the Present Value of an Ordinary Annuity

Year (n)	Cash flow	Present value calculation	Present value
1	$700	$\dfrac{700}{(1 + 0.08)^1} =$	$ 648.15
2	700	$\dfrac{700}{(1 + 0.08)^2} =$	600.14
3	700	$\dfrac{700}{(1 + 0.08)^3} =$	555.68
4	700	$\dfrac{700}{(1 + 0.08)^4} =$	514.52
5	700	$\dfrac{700}{(1 + 0.08)^5} =$	476.41
		Present value of annuity	$2,794.90

	A	B
1	PRESENT VALUE OF AN ORDINARY ANNUITY	
2	Annual payment	$700
3	Annual rate of interest, compounded annually	8%
4	Number of years	5
5	Present value of an ordinary annuity	$2,794.90
	Entry in Cell B5 is =PV(B3,B4,−B2) The minus sign appears before B2 because the annual payment is a cash outflow.	

FINDING THE FUTURE VALUE OF AN ANNUITY DUE

We now turn our attention to annuities due. Remember that the cash flows of an annuity due occur at the *start of the period*. In other words, if we are dealing with annual payments, each payment in an annuity due comes one year earlier than it would in an ordinary annuity. This in turn means that each payment can earn an extra year's worth of interest, which is why the future value of an annuity due exceeds the future value of an otherwise identical ordinary annuity.

The algebraic shortcut for the future value of an annuity due that makes annual payments of *CF* for *n* years is

$$FV_n = CF \times \left\{ \frac{[(1 + r)^n - 1]}{r} \right\} \times (1 + r) \tag{5.12}$$

Compare this to Equation 5.9 on page 172, which shows how to calculate the future value of an ordinary annuity. The two equations are nearly identical, but Equation 5.12 has an added term, $(1 + r)$, at the end. In other words, the value obtained from Equation 5.12 will be $(1 + r)$ times greater than the value in Equation 5.9 if the other inputs (*CF* and *n*) are the same, and that makes sense because all the payments in the annuity due earn one more year's worth of interest compared to the ordinary annuity.

Personal Finance Example 5.9 ▶ Recall from an earlier example, illustrated in Table 5.1 on page 171, that Fran Abrams wanted to choose between an ordinary annuity and an annuity due, both offering similar terms except for the timing of cash flows. We calculated the future value of the ordinary annuity in Example 5.7. We now will calculate the future value of the annuity due.

Calculator Use Before using your calculator to find the future value of an annuity due, depending on the specific calculator, you must either switch it to BEGIN mode or use the DUE key. Then, using the inputs shown at the left, you will find the future value of the annuity due to be $6,153.29. (*Note:* Because we nearly always assume end-of-period cash flows, *be sure to switch your calculator back to END mode when you have completed your annuity-due calculations.*)

Spreadsheet Use The future value of the annuity due also can be calculated as shown on the following Excel spreadsheet. Remember that for an annuity due the *type* input value must be set to 1, and we must also specify the *pv* input value as 0 since the inputs are in an ordered series.

Note: Switch calculator to BEGIN mode.

Input	Function
1000	PMT
5	N
7	I
	CPT
	FV

Solution
6,153.29

	A	B
1	FUTURE VALUE OF AN ANNUITY DUE	
2	Annual payment	$1,000
3	Annual rate of interest, compounded annually	7%
4	Number of years	5
5	Future value of an annuity due	$6,153.29
	Entry in Cell B5 is =FV(B3,B4,−B2,0,1) The minus sign appears before B2 because the annual payment is a cash outflow.	

Comparison of an Annuity Due with an Ordinary Annuity Future Value

The future value of an annuity due is *always greater* than the future value of an otherwise identical ordinary annuity. We can see this by comparing the future values at the end of year 5 of Fran Abrams's two annuities:

Ordinary annuity = $5,750.74   versus   Annuity due = $6,153.29

Because the cash flow of the annuity due occurs at the beginning of the period rather than at the end (that is, each payment comes one year sooner in the annuity due), its future value is greater. How much greater? It is interesting to calculate the percentage difference between the value of the annuity and the value of the annuity due:

($6,153.29 − $5,750.74) ÷ $5,750.74 = 0.07 = 7%

Recall that the interest rate in this example is 7 percent. It is no coincidence that the annuity due is 7 percent more valuable than the annuity. An extra year's interest on each of the annuity due's payments make the annuity due 7 percent more valuable than the annuity.

FINDING THE PRESENT VALUE OF AN ANNUITY DUE

We can also find the present value of an annuity due. This calculation can be easily performed by adjusting the ordinary annuity calculation. Because the cash flows of an annuity due occur at the beginning rather than the end of the period, to find their present value, each annuity due cash flow is discounted back one less year than for an ordinary annuity. The algebraic formula for the present value of an annuity due looks like this:

$$PV_n = \left(\frac{CF}{r}\right) \times \left[1 - \frac{1}{(1+r)^n}\right] \times (1+r) \qquad (5.13)$$

Notice the similarity between this equation and Equation 5.11 on page 173. The two equations are identical except that Equation 5.13 has an extra term at the end, $(1 + r)$. The reason for this extra term is the same as in the case when we calculated the future value of the annuity due. In the annuity due, each payment arrives one year earlier (compared to the annuity), so each payment is worth a little more—one year's interest more.

Example 5.10 ▶

In Example 5.8 of Braden Company, we found the present value of Braden's $700, 5-year ordinary annuity discounted at 8% to be $2,794.90. If we now assume that Braden's $700 annual cash flow occurs at the *start* of each year and is thereby an annuity due, we can calculate its present value using a calculator or a spreadsheet.

Calculator Use   Before using your calculator to find the present value of an annuity due, depending on the specifics of your calculator, you must either switch it to BEGIN mode or use the DUE key. Then, using the inputs shown at the left, you will find the present value of the annuity due to be $3,018.49 (*Note:* Because we nearly always assume end-of-period cash flows, *be sure to switch your calculator back to END mode when you have completed your annuity-due calculations.*)

Spreadsheet Use   The present value of the annuity due also can be calculated as shown on the following Excel spreadsheet.

Note: Switch calculator to BEGIN mode.

Input	Function
700	PMT
5	N
8	I
	CPT
	PV

Solution
3,018.49

	A	B
1	PRESENT VALUE OF AN ANNUITY DUE	
2	Annual payment	$700
3	Annual rate of interest, compounded annually	8%
4	Number of years	5
5	Present value of an annuity due	$3,018.49
	Entry in Cell B5 is =PV(B3,B4,−B2,0,1) The minus sign appears before B2 because the annual payment is a cash outflow.	

Comparison of an Annuity Due with an Ordinary Annuity Present Value

The present value of an annuity due is always greater than the present value of an otherwise identical ordinary annuity. We can see this by comparing the present values of the Braden Company's two annuities:

Ordinary annuity = $2,794.90   versus   Annuity due = $3,018.49

Because the cash flow of the annuity due occurs at the beginning of the period rather than at the end, its present value is greater. If we calculate the percentage difference in the values of these two annuities, we will find that the annuity due is 8 percent more valuable than the annuity:

$$(\$3,018.49 - \$2,794.90) \div \$2,794.90 = 0.08 = 8\%$$

Matter of fact

Getting Your (Annuity) Due

Kansas truck driver Donald Damon got the surprise of his life when he learned he held the winning ticket for the Powerball lottery drawing held November 11, 2009. The advertised lottery jackpot was $96.6 million. Damon could have chosen to collect his prize in 30 annual payments of $3,220,000 (30 × $3.22 million = $96.6 million), but instead he elected to accept a lump sum payment of $48,367,329.08, roughly half the stated jackpot total.

FINDING THE PRESENT VALUE OF A PERPETUITY

perpetuity
An annuity with an infinite life, providing continual annual cash flow.

A **perpetuity** is an annuity with an infinite life—in other words, an annuity that never stops providing its holder with a cash flow at the end of each year (for example, the right to receive $500 at the end of each year forever).

It is sometimes necessary to find the present value of a perpetuity. Fortunately, the calculation for the present value of a perpetuity is one of the easiest in all of finance. If a perpetuity pays an annual cash flow of CF, starting one year from now, the present value of the cash flow stream is

$$PV = CF \div r \tag{5.14}$$

Personal Finance Example 5.11 ▶ Ross Clark wishes to endow a chair in finance at his alma mater. The university indicated that it requires $200,000 per year to support the chair, and the endowment would earn 10% per year. To determine the amount Ross must give the university to fund the chair, we must determine the present value of a $200,000 perpetuity discounted at 10%. Using equation 5.14, we can determine that the present value of a perpetuity paying $200,000 per year is $2 million when the interest rate is 10%:

$$PV = \$200,000 \div 0.10 = \$2,000,000$$

In other words, to generate $200,000 every year for an indefinite period requires $2,000,000 today if Ross Clark's alma mater can earn 10% on its investments. If the university earns 10% interest annually on the $2,000,000, it can withdraw $200,000 per year indefinitely.

→ **REVIEW QUESTIONS**

5–8 What is the difference between an *ordinary annuity* and an *annuity due?* Which is more valuable? Why?

5–9 What are the most efficient ways to calculate the present value of an ordinary annuity?

5–10 How can the formula for the future value of an annuity be modified to find the future value of an annuity due?

5–11 How can the formula for the present value of an ordinary annuity be modified to find the present value of an annuity due?

5–12 What is a *perpetuity?* Why is the present value of a perpetuity equal to the annual cash payment divided by the interest rate?

LG 4 ## 5.4 Mixed Streams

mixed stream
A stream of unequal periodic cash flows that reflect no particular pattern.

Two basic types of cash flow streams are possible, the annuity and the mixed stream. Whereas an *annuity* is a pattern of equal periodic cash flows, a **mixed stream** is a stream of unequal periodic cash flows that reflect no particular pattern. Financial managers frequently need to evaluate opportunities that are expected to provide mixed streams of cash flows. Here we consider both the future value and the present value of mixed streams.

FUTURE VALUE OF A MIXED STREAM

Determining the future value of a mixed stream of cash flows is straightforward. We determine the future value of each cash flow at the specified future date and then add all the individual future values to find the total future value.

Example 5.12 ▶   Shrell Industries, a cabinet manufacturer, expects to receive the following mixed stream of cash flows over the next 5 years from one of its small customers.

End of year	Cash flow
1	$11,500
2	14,000
3	12,900
4	16,000
5	18,000

If Shrell expects to earn 8% on its investments, how much will it accumulate by the end of year 5 if it immediately invests these cash flows when they are received? This situation is depicted on the following time line:

Time line for future value of a mixed stream (end-of-year cash flows, compounded at 8% to the end of year 5)

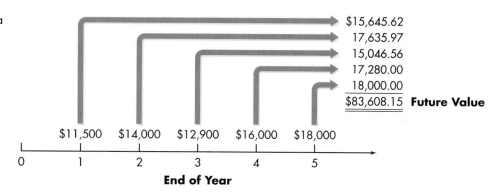

Calculator Use   You can use your calculator to find the future value of each individual cash flow, as demonstrated earlier (on page 167), and then sum the future values to get the future value of the stream. Unfortunately, unless you can program your calculator, most calculators lack a function that would allow you to input *all of the cash flows,* specify the interest rate, and directly calculate the future value of the entire cash flow stream. Had you used your calculator to find the individual cash flow future values and then summed them, the future value of Shrell Industries' cash flow stream at the end of year 5 would have been $83,608.15.

Spreadsheet Use   A relatively simple way to use Excel to calculate the future value of a mixed stream is to use the Excel future value (FV) function discussed on page 167 combined with the net present value (NPV) function (which will be discussed on page 181). The trick is to use the NPV function to first find the present value of the mixed stream and then find the future of this present value amount. The following Excel spreadsheet illustrates this approach:

	A	B
1	FUTURE VALUE OF A MIXED STREAM	
2	Interest rate, pct/year	8%
3	Year	Year-End Cash Flow
4	1	$11,500
5	2	$14,000
6	3	$12,900
7	4	$16,000
8	5	$18,000
9	Future value	$83,608.15

Entry in Cell B9 is
=−FV(B2,A8,0,NPV(B2,B4:B8)).
The minus sign appears before FV to convert
the future value to a positive amount.

PRESENT VALUE OF A MIXED STREAM

Finding the present value of a mixed stream of cash flows is similar to finding the future value of a mixed stream. We determine the present value of each future amount and then add all the individual present values together to find the total present value.

Example 5.13 ▶   Frey Company, a shoe manufacturer, has been offered an opportunity to receive the following mixed stream of cash flows over the next 5 years:

End of year	Cash flow
1	$400
2	800
3	500
4	400
5	300

If the firm must earn at least 9% on its investments, what is the most it should pay for this opportunity? This situation is depicted on the following time line:

Time line for present value of a mixed stream (end-of-year cash flows, discounted at 9% over the corresponding number of years)

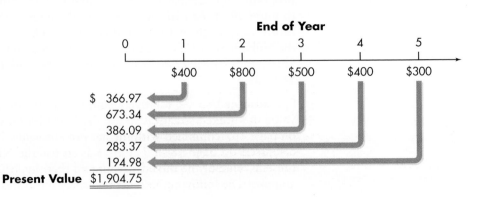

Calculator Use You can use a calculator to find the present value of each individual cash flow, as demonstrated earlier (on page 169), and then sum the present values, to get the present value of the stream. However, most financial calculators have a function that allows you to punch in *all cash flows,* specify the discount rate, and then directly calculate the present value of the entire cash flow stream. The present value of Frey Company's cash flow stream found using a calculator is $1,904.75.

Spreadsheet Use To calculate the present value of a mixed stream in Excel, we will make use of a new function. The syntax of that function is NPV(rate,value1, value2,value3, . . .). The *rate* argument is the interest rate, and *value1, value2,value3,* . . . represent the stream of cash flows. The NPV function assumes that the first payment in the stream arrives one year in the future, and all subsequent payments arrive at one-year intervals. The present value of the mixed stream of future cash flows can be calculated as shown on the following Excel spreadsheet:

	A	B
1	PRESENT VALUE OF A MIXED STREAM OF CASH FLOWS	
2	Interest rate, pct/year	9%
3	Year	Year-End Cash Flow
4	1	$400
5	2	$800
6	3	$500
7	4	$400
8	5	$300
9	Present value	$1,904.75
	Entry in Cell B9 is =NPV(B2,B4:B8).	

→ **REVIEW QUESTION**

5–13 How is the future value of a mixed stream of cash flows calculated? How is the present value of a mixed stream of cash flows calculated?

LG 5 **5.5 Compounding Interest More Frequently Than Annually**

Interest is often compounded more frequently than once a year. Savings institutions compound interest semiannually, quarterly, monthly, weekly, daily, or even continuously. This section discusses various issues and techniques related to these more frequent compounding intervals.

SEMIANNUAL COMPOUNDING

semiannual compounding
Compounding of interest over two periods within the year.

Semiannual compounding of interest involves two compounding periods within the year. Instead of the stated interest rate being paid once a year, one-half of the stated interest rate is paid twice a year.

TABLE 5.3	Future Value from Investing $100 at 8% Interest Compounded Semiannually over 24 Months (2 Years)		
Period	Beginning principal	Future value calculation	Future value at end of period
6 months	$100.00	$100.00 \times (1 + 0.04) =$	$104.00
12 months	104.00	$104.00 \times (1 + 0.04) =$	108.16
18 months	108.16	$108.16 \times (1 + 0.04) =$	112.49
24 months	112.49	$112.49 \times (1 + 0.04) =$	116.99

Personal Finance Example 5.14 ▶ Fred Moreno has decided to invest $100 in a savings account paying 8% interest *compounded semiannually*. If he leaves his money in the account for 24 months (2 years), he will be paid 4% interest compounded over four periods, each of which is 6 months long. Table 5.3 shows that at the end of 12 months (1 year) with 8% semiannual compounding, Fred will have $108.16; at the end of 24 months (2 years), he will have $116.99.

QUARTERLY COMPOUNDING

quarterly compounding
Compounding of interest over four periods within the year.

Quarterly compounding of interest involves four compounding periods within the year. One-fourth of the stated interest rate is paid four times a year.

Personal Finance Example 5.15 ▶ Fred Moreno has found an institution that will pay him 8% interest *compounded quarterly*. If he leaves his money in this account for 24 months (2 years), he will be paid 2% interest compounded over eight periods, each of which is 3 months long. Table 5.4 shows the amount Fred will have at the end of each period. At the end of 12 months (1 year), with 8% quarterly compounding, Fred will have $108.24; at the end of 24 months (2 years), he will have $117.17.

TABLE 5.4	Future Value from Investing $100 at 8% Interest Compounded Quarterly over 24 Months (2 Years)		
Period	Beginning principal	Future value calculation	Future value at end of period
3 months	$100.00	$100.00 \times (1 + 0.02) =$	$102.00
6 months	102.00	$102.00 \times (1 + 0.02) =$	104.04
9 months	104.04	$104.04 \times (1 + 0.02) =$	106.12
12 months	106.12	$106.12 \times (1 + 0.02) =$	108.24
15 months	108.24	$108.24 \times (1 + 0.02) =$	110.41
18 months	110.41	$110.41 \times (1 + 0.02) =$	112.62
21 months	112.62	$112.62 \times (1 + 0.02) =$	114.87
24 months	114.87	$114.87 \times (1 + 0.02) =$	117.17

TABLE 5.5	Future Value at the End of Years 1 and 2 from Investing $100 at 8% Interest, Given Various Compounding Periods		
		Compounding period	
End of year	Annual	Semiannual	Quarterly
1	$108.00	$108.16	$108.24
2	116.64	116.99	117.17

Table 5.5 compares values for Fred Moreno's $100 at the end of years 1 and 2 given annual, semiannual, and quarterly compounding periods at the 8 percent rate. The table shows that *the more frequently interest is compounded, the greater the amount of money accumulated.* This is true for *any interest rate* for *any period of time.*

A GENERAL EQUATION FOR COMPOUNDING MORE FREQUENTLY THAN ANNUALLY

The future value formula (Equation 5.4) can be rewritten for use when compounding takes place more frequently. If *m* equals the number of times per year interest is compounded, the formula for the future value of a lump sum becomes

$$FV_n = PV \times \left(1 + \frac{r}{m}\right)^{m \times n} \tag{5.15}$$

If *m* = 1, Equation 5.15 reduces to Equation 5.4. Thus, if interest compounds annually, Equation 5.15 will provide the same result as Equation 5.4. The general use of Equation 5.15 can be illustrated with a simple example.

Personal Finance Example 5.16 ▶ The preceding examples calculated the amount that Fred Moreno would have at the end of 2 years if he deposited $100 at 8% interest compounded semiannually and compounded quarterly. For semiannual compounding, *m* would equal 2 in Equation 5.15; for quarterly compounding, *m* would equal 4. Substituting the appropriate values for semiannual and quarterly compounding into Equation 5.14, we find that

1. *For semiannual compounding:*

$$FV_2 = \$100 \times \left(1 + \frac{0.08}{2}\right)^{2 \times 2} = \$100 \times (1 + 0.04)^4 = \$116.99$$

2. *For quarterly compounding:*

$$FV_2 = \$100 \times \left(1 + \frac{0.08}{4}\right)^{4 \times 2} = \$100 \times (1 + 0.02)^8 = \$117.17$$

These results agree with the values for FV_2 in Tables 5.5 and 5.6.

If the interest were compounded monthly, weekly, or daily, *m* would equal 12, 52, or 365, respectively.

USING COMPUTATIONAL TOOLS FOR COMPOUNDING MORE FREQUENTLY THAN ANNUALLY

As before, we can simplify the process of doing the calculations by using a calculator or spreadsheet program.

Personal Finance Example 5.17 ▶ Fred Moreno wished to find the future value of $100 invested at 8% interest compounded both semiannually and quarterly for 2 years.

Calculator Use   If the calculator were used for the semiannual compounding calculation, the number of periods would be 4 and the interest rate would be 4%. The future value of $116.99 will appear on the calculator display as shown at the top left.

For the quarterly compounding case, the number of periods would be 8 and the interest rate would be 2%. The future value of $117.17 will appear on the calculator display as shown in the second display at the left.

Spreadsheet Use   The future value of the single amount with semiannual and quarterly compounding also can be calculated as shown on the following Excel spreadsheet:

	A	B
1	FUTURE VALUE OF A SINGLE AMOUNT WITH SEMIANNUAL AND QUARTERLY COMPOUNDING	
2	Present value	$100
3	Interest rate, pct per year compounded semiannually	8%
4	Number of years	2
5	Future value with semiannual compounding	$116.99
6	Present value	$100
7	Interest rate, pct per year compounded quarterly	8%
8	Number of years	2
9	Future value with quarterly compounding	$117.17
	Entry in Cell B5 is =FV(B3/2,B4*2,0,−B2,0). Entry in Cell B9 is =FV(B7/4,B8*4,0,−B2,0). The minus sign appears before B2 because the present value is a cash outflow (i.e., a deposit made by Fred Moreno).	

CONTINUOUS COMPOUNDING

continuous compounding
Compounding of interest an infinite number of times per year at intervals of microseconds.

In the extreme case, interest can be compounded continuously. **Continuous compounding** involves compounding over every nanosecond—the smallest time period imaginable. In this case, m in Equation 5.15 would approach infinity. Through the use of calculus, we know that as m approaches infinity, Equation 5.15 converges to

$$FV_n = (PV) \times (e^{r \times n})$$ (5.16)

where e is the exponential function,[3] which has a value of approximately 2.7183.

---

3. Most calculators have the exponential function, typically noted by e^x, built into them. The use of this key is especially helpful in calculating future value when interest is compounded continuously.

Personal Finance Example 5.18 ▶ To find the value at the end of 2 years ($n = 2$) of Fred Moreno's $100 deposit ($PV = \$100$) in an account paying 8% annual interest ($r = 0.08$) compounded continuously, we can substitute into Equation 5.16:

$$FV_2 \text{ (continuous compounding)} = \$100 \times e^{0.08 \times 2}$$
$$= \$100 \times 2.7183^{0.16}$$
$$= \$100 \times 1.1735 = \$117.35$$

Input	Function
0.16	2nd
	eˣ
1.1735	
100	×
	=

Solution
117.35

Calculator Use To find this value using the calculator, you need first to find the value of $e^{0.16}$ by punching in 0.16 and then pressing **2nd** and then eˣ to get 1.1735. Next multiply this value by $100 to get the future value of $117.35 as shown at the left. (*Note:* On some calculators, you may not have to press **2nd** before pressing eˣ.)

Spreadsheet Use The future value of the single amount with continuous compounding of Fred's deposit also can be calculated as shown on the following Excel spreadsheet:

	A	B
1	FUTURE VALUE OF A SINGLE AMOUNT WITH CONTINUOUS COMPOUNDING	
2	Present value	$100
3	Annual rate of interest, compounded continuously	8%
4	Number of years	2
5	Future value with continuous compounding	$117.35
	Entry in Cell B5 is =B2*EXP(B3*B4).	

The future value with continuous compounding therefore equals $117.35. As expected, the continuously compounded value is larger than the future value of interest compounded semiannually ($116.99) or quarterly ($117.17). In fact, continuous compounding produces a greater future value than any other compounding frequency.

NOMINAL AND EFFECTIVE ANNUAL RATES OF INTEREST

Both businesses and investors need to make objective comparisons of loan costs or investment returns over different compounding periods. To put interest rates on a common basis, so as to allow comparison, we distinguish between nominal and effective annual rates. The **nominal**, or **stated**, **annual rate** is the contractual annual rate of interest charged by a lender or promised by a borrower. The **effective**, or **true**, **annual rate (EAR)** is the annual rate of interest actually paid or earned. The effective annual rate reflects the effects of compounding frequency, whereas the nominal annual rate does not.

Using the notation introduced earlier, we can calculate the effective annual rate, *EAR*, by substituting values for the nominal annual rate, *r*, and the compounding frequency, *m*, into Equation 5.17:

nominal (stated) annual rate
Contractual annual rate of interest charged by a lender or promised by a borrower.

effective (true) annual rate (EAR)
The annual rate of interest actually paid or earned.

$$EAR = \left(1 + \frac{r}{m}\right)^m - 1 \tag{5.17}$$

We can apply this equation using data from preceding examples.

Personal Finance Example 5.19 ▶ Fred Moreno wishes to find the effective annual rate associated with an 8% nominal annual rate ($r = 0.08$) when interest is compounded (1) annually ($m = 1$); (2) semiannually ($m = 2$); and (3) quarterly ($m = 4$). Substituting these values into Equation 5.17, we get

1. *For annual compounding:*

$$EAR = \left(1 + \frac{0.08}{1}\right)^1 - 1 = (1 + 0.08)^1 - 1 = 1 + 0.08 - 1 = 0.08 = 8\%$$

2. *For semiannual compounding:*

$$EAR = \left(1 + \frac{0.08}{2}\right)^2 - 1 = (1 + 0.04)^2 - 1 = 1.0816 - 1 = 0.0816 = 8.16\%$$

3. *For quarterly compounding:*

$$EAR = \left(1 + \frac{0.08}{4}\right)^4 - 1 = (1 + 0.02)^4 - 1 = 1.0824 - 1 = 0.0824 = 8.24\%$$

These values demonstrate two important points: The first is that nominal and effective annual rates are equivalent for annual compounding. The second is that the effective annual rate increases with increasing compounding frequency, up to a limit that occurs with *continuous compounding*.[4]

annual percentage rate (APR)
The *nominal annual rate* of interest, found by multiplying the periodic rate by the number of periods in one year, that must be disclosed to consumers on credit cards and loans as a result of "truth-in-lending laws."

annual percentage yield (APY)
The *effective annual rate* of interest that must be disclosed to consumers by banks on their savings products as a result of "truth-in-savings laws."

For an EAR example related to the "payday loan" business, with discussion of the ethical issues involved, see the *Focus on Ethics* box.

At the consumer level, "truth-in-lending laws" require disclosure on credit card and loan agreements of the **annual percentage rate (APR)**. The APR is the *nominal annual rate* found by multiplying the periodic rate by the number of periods in one year. For example, a bank credit card that charges 1.5 percent per month (the periodic rate) would have an APR of 18 percent (1.5% per month × 12 months per year).

"Truth-in-savings laws," on the other hand, require banks to quote the **annual percentage yield (APY)** on their savings products. The APY is the *effective annual rate* a savings product pays. For example, a savings account that pays 0.5 percent per month would have an APY of 6.17 percent $[(1.005)^{12} - 1]$.

---

4. The effective annual rate for this extreme case can be found by using the following equation:

$$EAR \text{ (continuous compounding)} = e^r - 1 \qquad (5.17a)$$

For the 8% nominal annual rate ($r = 0.08$), substitution into Equation 5.24a results in an effective annual rate of

$$e^{0.08} - 1 = 1.0833 - 1 = 0.0833 = 8.33\%$$

in the case of continuous compounding. This is the highest effective annual rate attainable with an 8% nominal rate.

focus on ETHICS

How Fair Is "Check Into Cash"?

in practice In 1993, the first Check Into Cash location opened in Cleveland, Tennessee. Today there are more than 1,100 Check Into Cash centers among an estimated 22,000 payday-advance lenders in the United States. There is no doubt about the demand for such organizations, but the debate continues on the "fairness" of payday-advance loans.

A payday loan is a small, unsecured, short-term loan ranging from $100 to $1,000 (depending on the state) offered by a payday lender such as Check Into Cash. A payday loan can solve temporary cash-flow problems without bouncing a check or incurring late-payment penalties. To receive a payday advance, borrowers simply write a personal post-dated check for the amount they wish to borrow, plus the payday loan fee. Check Into Cash holds their checks until payday when the loans are either paid off in person or the check is presented to the borrowers' bank for payment.

Although payday-advance borrowers usually pay a flat fee in lieu of interest, it is the size of the fee in relation to the amount borrowed that is particularly aggravating to opponents of the payday-advance industry. A typical fee is $15 for every $100 borrowed. Payday advance companies that belong to the Community Financial Services Association of America (CFSA), an organization dedicated to promoting responsible regulation of the industry, limit their member companies to a maximum of four rollovers of the original amount borrowed. Thus, a borrower who rolled over an initial $100 loan for the maximum of four times would accumulate a total of $75 in fees all within a 10-week period. On an annualized basis, the fees would amount to a whopping 391 percent.

An annual rate of 391 percent is a huge cost in relation to interest charged on home equity loans, personal loans, and even credit cards. However, advocates of the payday-advance industry make the following arguments: Most payday loan recipients do so either because funds are unavailable through conventional loans or because the payday loan averts a penalty or bank fee which is, in itself, onerous. According to Check Into Cash, the cost for $100 of overdraft protection is $26.90, a credit card late fee on $100 is $37,

and the late/disconnect fee on a $100 utility bill is $46.16. Bankrate.com reports that nonsufficient funds (NSF) fees average $26.90 per occurrence.

A payday advance could be useful, for example, if you have six outstanding checks at the time you are notified that the first check has been returned for insufficient funds and you have been charged an NSF fee of $26. A payday advance could potentially avert subsequent charges of $26 per check for each of the remaining five checks and allow you time to rearrange your finances. When used judiciously, a payday advance can be a viable option to meet a short-term cash flow problem despite its high cost. Used unwisely, or by someone who continuously relies on a payday loan to try to make ends meet, payday advances can seriously harm one's personal finances.

▶ *The 391 percent mentioned above is an annual nominal rate [15% × (365 ÷ 14)]. Should the 2-week rate (15 percent) be compounded to calculate the effective annual interest rate?*

Quoting loan interest rates at their lower nominal annual rate (the APR) and savings interest rates at the higher effective annual rate (the APY) offers two advantages: It tends to standardize disclosure to consumers, and it enables financial institutions to quote the most attractive interest rates: low loan rates and high savings rates.

→ REVIEW QUESTIONS

5–14 What effect does compounding interest more frequently than annually have on (**a**) future value and (**b**) the *effective annual rate (EAR)*? Why?

5–15 How does the future value of a deposit subject to continuous compounding compare to the value obtained by annual compounding?

5–16 Differentiate between a *nominal annual rate* and an *effective annual rate (EAR)*. Define *annual percentage rate (APR)* and *annual percentage yield (APY)*.

LG 6 **5.6** Special Applications of Time Value

Future value and present value techniques have a number of important applications in finance. We'll study four of them in this section: (1) determining deposits needed to accumulate a future sum, (2) loan amortization, (3) finding interest or growth rates, and (4) finding an unknown number of periods.

DETERMINING DEPOSITS NEEDED TO ACCUMULATE A FUTURE SUM

Suppose you want to buy a house 5 years from now, and you estimate that an initial down payment of $30,000 will be required at that time. To accumulate the $30,000, you will wish to make equal annual end-of-year deposits into an account paying annual interest of 6 percent. The solution to this problem is closely related to the process of finding the future value of an annuity. You must determine what size annuity will result in a single amount equal to $30,000 at the end of year 5.

Earlier in the chapter, Equation 5.9 was provided for the future value of an ordinary annuity that made a payment, *CF*, each year. In the current problem, we know the future value we want to achieve, $30,000, but we want to solve for the annual cash payment that we'd have to save to achieve that goal. Solving Equation 5.9 for *CF* gives the following:

$$CF = FV_n \div \left\{ \frac{[(1 + r)^n - 1]}{r} \right\} \qquad (5.18)$$

As a practical matter, to solve problems like this one, analysts nearly always use a calculator or Excel as demonstrated in the following example.

Personal Finance Example 5.20 ▶   As just stated, you want to determine the equal annual end-of-year deposits required to accumulate $30,000 at the end of 5 years, given an interest rate of 6%.

Calculator Use   Using the calculator inputs shown at the left, you will find the annual deposit amount to be $5,321.89. Thus, if $5,321.89 is deposited at the end of each year for 5 years at 6% interest, there will be $30,000 in the account at the end of 5 years.

Spreadsheet Use   In Excel, solving for the annual cash flow that helps you reach the $30,000 means using the payment function. Its syntax is PMT(rate,nper,pv, fv,type). All of the inputs in this function have been discussed previously. The following Excel spreadsheet illustrates how to use this function to find the annual payment required to save $30,000.

Input	Function
30000	FV
5	N
6	I
	CPT
	PMT

Solution
5,321.89

	A	B
1	ANNUAL DEPOSITS NEEDED TO ACCUMULATE A FUTURE SUM	
2	Future value	$30,000
3	Number of years	5
4	Annual rate of interest	6%
5	Annual deposit	$5,321.89

Entry in Cell B5 is =−PMT(B4,B3,0,B2).
The minus sign appears before PMT because the annual deposits are cash outflows.

LOAN AMORTIZATION

loan amortization
The determination of the equal periodic loan payments necessary to provide a lender with a specified interest return and to repay the loan principal over a specified period.

loan amortization schedule
A schedule of equal payments to repay a loan. It shows the allocation of each loan payment to interest and principal.

The term **loan amortization** refers to the determination of equal periodic loan payments. These payments provide a lender with a specified interest return and repay the loan principal over a specified period. The loan amortization process involves finding the future payments, over the term of the loan, whose present value at the loan interest rate equals the amount of initial principal borrowed. Lenders use a **loan amortization schedule** to determine these payment amounts and the allocation of each payment to interest and principal. In the case of home mortgages, these tables are used to find the equal *monthly* payments necessary to *amortize,* or pay off, the mortgage at a specified interest rate over a 15- to 30-year period.

Amortizing a loan actually involves creating an annuity out of a present amount. For example, say you borrow $6,000 at 10 percent and agree to make equal annual end-of-year payments over 4 years. To find the size of the payments, the lender determines the amount of a 4-year annuity discounted at 10 percent that has a present value of $6,000. This process is actually the inverse of finding the present value of an annuity.

Earlier in the chapter, Equation 5.11 demonstrated how to find the present value of an ordinary annuity given information about the number of time periods, the interest rate, and the annuity's periodic payment. We can rearrange that equation to solve for the payment, our objective in this problem:

$$CF = (PV \times r) \div \left[1 - \frac{1}{(1 + r)^n} \right] \qquad (5.19)$$

Personal Finance Example 5.21 ▶ As just stated, you want to determine the equal annual end-of-year payments necessary to amortize fully a $6,000, 10% loan over 4 years.

Input	Function
6000	PV
4	N
10	I
	CPT
	PMT

Solution
1,892.82

Calculator Use Using the calculator inputs shown at the left, you will find the annual payment amount to be $1,892.82. Thus, to repay the interest and principal on a $6,000, 10%, 4-year loan, equal annual end-of-year payments of $1,892.82 are necessary.

The allocation of each loan payment to interest and principal can be seen in columns 3 and 4 of the *loan amortization schedule* in Table 5.6 on page 190. The portion of each payment that represents interest (column 3) declines over the repayment period, and the portion going to principal repayment (column 4) increases. This pattern is typical of amortized loans; as the principal is reduced, the interest component declines, leaving a larger portion of each subsequent loan payment to repay principal.

Spreadsheet Use The annual payment to repay the loan also can be calculated as shown on the first Excel spreadsheet shown on page 190. The amortization schedule, shown in Table 5.6, allocating each loan payment to interest and principal can be calculated precisely as shown on the second spreadsheet on page 190.

TABLE 5.6	Loan Amortization Schedule ($6,000 Principal, 10% Interest, 4-Year Repayment Period)

			Payments		
End of-year	Beginning-of-year principal (1)	Loan payment (2)	Interest [0.10 × (1)] (3)	Principal [(2) − (3)] (4)	End-of-year principal [(1) − (4)] (5)
1	$6,000.00	$1,892.82	$600.00	$1,292.82	$4,707.18
2	4,707.18	1,892.82	470.72	1,422.10	3,285.08
3	3,285.08	1,892.82	328.51	1,564.31	1,721.77
4	1,720.77	1,892.82	172.08	1,720.74	—[a]

[a]Because of rounding, a slight difference ($0.03) exists between the beginning-of-year-4 principal (in column 1) and the year-4 principal payment (in column 4).

	A	B
1	ANNUAL PAYMENT TO REPAY A LOAN	
2	Loan principal (present value)	$6,000
3	Annual rate of interest	10%
4	Number of years	4
5	Annual payment	$1,892.82

Entry in Cell B5 is =−PMT(B3,B4,B2).
The minus sign appears before PMT because
the annual payments are cash outflows.

	A	B	C	D	E
1			LOAN AMORTIZATION SCHEDULE		
2		Data: Loan principal		$6,000	
3		Annual rate of interest		10%	
4		Number of years		4	
5		Annual Payments			
6	Year	Total	To Interest	To Principal	Year-End Principal
7	0				$6,000.00
8	1	$1,892.82	$600.00	$1,292.82	4,707.18
9	2	$1,892.82	$470.72	$1,422.11	3,285.07
10	3	$1,892.82	$328.51	$1,564.32	1,720.75
11	4	$1,892.82	$172.07	$1,720.75	0.00

Key Cell Entries
Cell B8: =−PMT(D3,D4,D2), copy to B9:B11
Cell C8: =−CUMIPMT(D3,D4,D2,A8,A8,0), copy to C9:C11
Cell D8: =−CUMPRINC(D3,D4,D2,A8,A8,0), copy to D9:D11
Cell E8: =E7−D8, copy to E9:E11
The minus signs appear before the entries in Cells B8, C8, and D8
because these are cash outflows.

To attract buyers who could not immediately afford 15- to 30-year mortgages of equal annual payments, lenders offered mortgages whose interest rates adjusted at certain points. The *Focus on Practice* box discusses how such mortgages have worked out for some "subprime" borrowers.

focus on PRACTICE

New Century Brings Trouble for Subprime Mortgages

in practice As the housing market began to boom at the end of the twentieth century and into the early twenty-first, the market share of subprime mortgages climbed from near 0 percent in 1997 to about 20 percent of mortgage originations in 2006. Several factors combined to fuel the rapid growth of lending to borrowers with tarnished credit, including a low interest rate environment, loose underwriting standards, and innovations in mortgage financing such as "affordability programs" to increase rates of homeownership among lower-income borrowers.

Particularly attractive to new home buyers was the hybrid adjustable rate mortgage (ARM), which featured a low introductory interest rate that reset upward after a preset period of time. Interest rates began a steady upward trend beginning in late 2004. In 2006, some $300 billion worth of adjustable ARMs were reset to higher rates. In a market with rising home values, a borrower has the option to refinance the mortgage, using some of the equity created by the home's increasing value to reduce the mortgage payment. But after 2006, home prices started a 3-year slide, so refinancing was not an option for many subprime borrowers. Instead, borrowers in trouble could try to convince their lenders to allow a "short sale," in which the borrower sells the home for whatever the market will bear, and the lender agrees to accept the proceeds from that sale as settlement for the mortgage debt. For lenders and borrowers alike, foreclosure is the last, worst option.

▶ *As a reaction to problems in the subprime area, lenders tightened lending standards. What effect do you think this had on the housing market?*

FINDING INTEREST OR GROWTH RATES

It is often necessary to calculate the compound annual interest or *growth rate* (that is, the annual rate of change in values) of a series of cash flows. Examples include finding the interest rate on a loan, the rate of growth in sales, and the rate of growth in earnings. In doing this, we again make use of Equation 5.4. In this case, we want to solve for the interest rate (or growth rate) representing the increase in value of some investment between two time periods. Solving Equation 5.4 for r we have

$$r = \left(\frac{FV_n}{PV}\right)^{1/n} - 1 \tag{5.20}$$

The simplest situation is one in which an investment's value has increased over time, and you want to know the annual rate of growth (that is, interest) that is represented by the increase in the investment.

Personal Finance Example 5.22 ▶ Ray Noble purchased an investment four years ago for $1,250. Now it is worth $1,520. What compound annual rate of return has Ray earned on this investment? Plugging the appropriate values into Equation 5.20, we have

$$r = (\$1,520 \div \$1,250)^{(1/4)} - 1 = 0.0501 = 5.01\% \text{ per year}$$

Calculator Use Using the calculator to find the interest or growth rate, we treat the earliest value as a present value, PV, and the latest value as a future value, FV_n. (*Note:* Most calculators require *either* the PV or the FV value to be input as a negative number to calculate an unknown interest or growth rate. That approach is used here.) Using the inputs shown at the left, you will find the interest or growth rate to be 5.01%.

Input	Function
1250	PV
−1520	FV
4	N
	CPT
	I

Solution
5.01

Spreadsheet Use The interest or growth rate for the series of cash flows also can be calculated as shown on the following Excel spreadsheet:

	A	B
1	INTEREST OR GROWTH RATE– SERIES OF CASH FLOWS	
2	Year	Cash Flow
3	2008	$1,250
4	2012	$1,520
5	Annual growth rate	5.01%
	Entry in Cell B5 is =RATE(A4–A3,0,–B3,B4,0). The expression A4–A3 in the entry calculates the number of years of growth. The minus sign appears before B3 because the investment in 2008 is treated as a cash outflow.	

Another type of interest-rate problem involves finding the interest rate associated with an *annuity,* or equal-payment loan.

Personal Finance Example 5.23 ▶ Jan Jacobs can borrow $2,000 to be repaid in equal annual end-of-year amounts of $514.14 for the next 5 years. She wants to find the interest rate on this loan.

Input	Function
514.14	PMT
−2000	PV
5	N
	CPT
	I

Solution
9.00

Calculator Use (*Note:* Most calculators require *either* the *PMT* or the *PV* value to be input as a negative number to calculate an unknown interest rate on an equal-payment loan. That approach is used here.) Using the inputs shown at the left, you will find the interest rate to be 9.00%.

Spreadsheet Use The interest or growth rate for the annuity also can be calculated as shown on the following Excel spreadsheet:

	A	B
1	INTEREST OR GROWTH RATE– ANNUITY	
2	Present value (loan principal)	$2,000
3	Number of years	5
4	Annual payments	$514.14
5	Annual interest rate	9.00%
	Entry in Cell B5 is =RATE(B3,B4,–B2). The minus sign appears before B2 because the loan principal is treated as a cash outflow.	

FINDING AN UNKNOWN NUMBER OF PERIODS

Sometimes it is necessary to calculate the number of time periods needed to generate a given amount of cash flow from an initial amount. Here we briefly consider this calculation for both single amounts and annuities. This simplest case is when a person wishes to determine the number of periods, n, it will take for an initial deposit, PV, to grow to a specified future amount, FV_n, given a stated interest rate, r.

Personal Finance Example 5.24 ▶ Ann Bates wishes to determine the number of years it will take for her initial $1,000 deposit, earning 8% annual interest, to grow to equal $2,500. Simply stated, at an 8% annual rate of interest, how many years, *n,* will it take for Ann's $1,000, *PV,* to grow to $2,500, *FV$_n$*?

Calculator Use Using the calculator, we treat the initial value as the present value, *PV,* and the latest value as the future value, *FV$_n$.* (*Note:* Most calculators require *either* the *PV* or the *FV* value to be input as a negative number to calculate an unknown number of periods. That approach is used here.) Using the inputs shown at the left, we find the number of periods to be 11.91 years.

Spreadsheet Use The number of years for the present value to grow to a specified future value can be calculated as shown on the following Excel spreadsheet:

	A	B
1	YEARS FOR A PRESENT VALUE TO GROW TO A SPECIFIED FUTURE VALUE	
2	Present value (deposit)	$1,000
3	Annual rate of interest, compounded annually	8%
4	Future value	$2,500
5	Number of years	11.91
	Entry in Cell B5 is =NPER(B3,0,B2,−B4). The minus sign appears before B4 because the future value is treated as a cash outflow.	

Another type of number-of-periods problem involves finding the number of periods associated with an *annuity.* Occasionally we wish to find the unknown life, *n,* of an annuity that is intended to achieve a specific objective, such as repaying a loan of a given amount.

Personal Finance Example 5.25 ▶ Bill Smart can borrow $25,000 at an 11% annual interest rate; equal, annual, end-of-year payments of $4,800 are required. He wishes to determine how long it will take to fully repay the loan. In other words, he wishes to determine how many years, *n,* it will take to repay the $25,000, 11% loan, *PV$_n$,* if the payments of $4,800 are made at the end of each year.

Calculator Use (*Note:* Most calculators require *either* the *PV* or the *PMT* value to be input as a negative number to calculate an unknown number of periods. That approach is used here.) Using the inputs shown at the left, you will find the number of periods to be 8.15 years. This means that after making 8 payments of $4,800, Bill will still have a small outstanding balance.

Spreadsheet Use The number of years to pay off the loan also can be calculated as shown on the following Excel spreadsheet:

	A	B
1	YEARS TO PAY OFF A LOAN	
2	Annual payment	$4,800
3	Annual rate of interest, compounded annually	11%
4	Present value (loan principal)	$25,000
5	Number of years to pay off the loan	8.15
	Entry in Cell B5 is =NPER(B3,−B2,B4). The minus sign appears before B2 because the payments are treated as cash outflows.	

→ **REVIEW QUESTIONS**

5–17 How can you determine the size of the equal, annual, end-of-period deposits necessary to accumulate a certain future sum at the end of a specified future period at a given annual interest rate?

5–18 Describe the procedure used to amortize a loan into a series of equal periodic payments.

5–19 How can you determine the unknown number of periods when you know the present and future values—single amount or annuity—and the applicable rate of interest?

Summary

FOCUS ON VALUE

Time value of money is an important tool that financial managers and other market participants use to assess the effects of proposed actions. Because firms have long lives and some decisions affect their long-term cash flows, the effective application of time-value-of-money techniques is extremely important. These techniques enable financial managers to evaluate cash flows occurring at different times so as to combine, compare, and evaluate them and link them to the firm's **overall goal of share price maximization.** It will become clear in Chapters 6 and 7 that the application of time value techniques is a key part of the value determination process needed to make intelligent value-creating decisions.

REVIEW OF LEARNING GOALS

LG 1   Discuss the role of time value in finance, the use of computational tools, and the basic patterns of cash flow. Financial managers and investors use time-value-of-money techniques when assessing the value of expected cash flow streams. Alternatives can be assessed by either compounding to find future value or discounting to find present value. Financial managers rely primarily on present value techniques. Financial calculators, electronic spreadsheets, and financial tables can streamline the application of time value techniques. The cash flow of a firm can be described by its pattern—single amount, annuity, or mixed stream.

LG 2   Understand the concepts of future value and present value, their calculation for single amounts, and the relationship between them. Future value (FV) relies on compound interest to measure future amounts. The initial principal or deposit in one period, along with the interest earned on it, becomes the beginning principal of the following period.

The present value (PV) of a future amount is the amount of money today that is equivalent to the given future amount, considering the return that can be earned. Present value is the inverse of future value.

LG 3   Find the future value and the present value of both an ordinary annuity and an annuity due, and find the present value of a perpetuity. An annuity is a pattern of equal periodic cash flows. For an ordinary annuity, the cash flows occur at the end of the period. For an annuity due, cash flows occur at the beginning of the period.

The future or present value of an ordinary annuity can be found by using algebraic equations, a financial calculator, or a spreadsheet program. The value of an annuity due is always *r*% greater than the value of an identical annuity. The present value of a perpetuity—an infinite-lived annuity—equals the annual cash payment divided by the discount rate.

LG 4   **Calculate both the future value and the present value of a mixed stream of cash flows.** A mixed stream of cash flows is a stream of unequal periodic cash flows that reflect no particular pattern. The future value of a mixed stream of cash flows is the sum of the future values of each individual cash flow. Similarly, the present value of a mixed stream of cash flows is the sum of the present values of the individual cash flows.

LG 5   **Understand the effect that compounding interest more frequently than annually has on future value and on the effective annual rate of interest.** Interest can be compounded at intervals ranging from annually to daily and even continuously. The more often interest is compounded, the larger the future amount that will be accumulated, and the higher the effective, or true, annual rate (EAR).

The annual percentage rate (APR)—a nominal annual rate—is quoted on credit cards and loans. The annual percentage yield (APY)—an effective annual rate—is quoted on savings products.

LG 6   **Describe the procedures involved in (1) determining deposits needed to accumulate a future sum, (2) loan amortization, (3) finding interest or growth rates, and (4) finding an unknown number of periods.** (1) The periodic deposit to accumulate a given future sum can be found by solving the equation for the future value of an annuity for the annual payment. (2) A loan can be amortized into equal periodic payments by solving the equation for the present value of an annuity for the periodic payment. (3) Interest or growth rates can be estimated by finding the unknown interest rate in the equation for the present value of a single amount or an annuity. (4) The number of periods can be estimated by finding the unknown number of periods in the equation for the present value of a single amount or an annuity.

Opener-in-Review

In the chapter opener you learned that it costs Eli Lilly close to $1 billion to bring a new drug to market, and by the time all of the R&D and clinical trials are completed, Lilly may have fewer than 10 years left to sell the drug under patent protection.

Assume that the $1 billion cost of bringing a new drug to market is spread out evenly over 10 years, and then 10 years remain for Lilly to recover their investment. How much cash would a new drug have to generate in the last 10 years to justify the $1 billion spent in the first 10 years? Assume that Lilly uses a required rate of return of 10%.

Self-Test Problems   (Solutions in Appendix)

LG 2   LG 5   ST5–1   Future values for various compounding frequencies   Delia Martin has $10,000 that she can deposit in any of three savings accounts for a 3-year period. Bank A compounds interest on an annual basis, bank B compounds interest twice each year, and bank C compounds interest each quarter. All three banks have a stated annual interest rate of 4%.

a. What amount would Ms. Martin have at the end of the third year, leaving all interest paid on deposit, in each bank?

b. What *effective annual rate* (*EAR*) would she earn in each of the banks?

c. On the basis of your findings in parts **a** and **b**, which bank should Ms. Martin deal with? Why?

d. If a fourth bank (bank D), also with a 4% stated interest rate, compounds interest continuously, how much would Ms. Martin have at the end of the third year? Does this alternative change your recommendation in part **c**? Explain why or why not.

LG 3   ST5–2   Future values of annuities   Ramesh Abdul wishes to choose the better of two equally costly cash flow streams: annuity X and annuity Y. X is an *annuity due* with a cash inflow of $9,000 for each of 6 years. Y is an *ordinary annuity* with a cash inflow of $10,000 for each of 6 years. Assume that Ramesh can earn 15% on his investments.

a. On a purely subjective basis, which annuity do you think is more attractive? Why?

b. Find the future value at the end of year 6 for both annuities.

c. Use your finding in part **b** to indicate which annuity is more attractive. Why? Compare your finding to your subjective response in part **a**.

LG 2   LG 3   LG 4   ST5–3   Present values of single amounts and streams   You have a choice of accepting either of two 5-year cash flow streams or single amounts. One cash flow stream is an ordinary annuity, and the other is a mixed stream. You may accept alternative A or B—either as a cash flow stream or as a single amount. Given the cash flow stream and single amounts associated with each (see the following table), and assuming a 9% opportunity cost, which alternative (A or B) and in which form (cash flow stream or single amount) would you prefer?

	Cash flow stream	
End of year	Alternative A	Alternative B
1	$700	$1,100
2	700	900
3	700	700
4	700	500
5	700	300
	Single amount	
At time zero	$2,825	$2,800

LG 6 **ST5–4** **Deposits needed to accumulate a future sum** Judi Janson wishes to accumulate $8,000 by the end of 5 years by making equal, annual, end-of-year deposits over the next 5 years. If Judi can earn 7% on her investments, how much must she deposit at the *end of each year* to meet this goal?

Warm-Up Exercises

All problems are available in myfinancelab.

LG 2 **E5–1** Assume a firm makes a $2,500 deposit into its money market account. If this account is currently paying 0.7% (yes, that's right, less than 1%!), what will the account balance be after 1 year?

LG 2 **LG 5** **E5–2** If Bob and Judy combine their savings of $1,260 and $975, respectively, and deposit this amount into an account that pays 2% annual interest, compounded monthly, what will the account balance be after 4 years?

LG 3 **E5–3** Gabrielle just won $2.5 million in the state lottery. She is given the option of receiving a total of $1.3 million now, or she can elect to be paid $100,000 at the end of each of the next 25 years. If Gabrielle can earn 5% annually on her investments, from a strict economic point of view which option should she take?

LG 4 **E5–4** Your firm has the option of making an investment in new software that will cost $130,000 today and is estimated to provide the savings shown in the following table over its 5-year life:

Year	Savings estimate
1	$35,000
2	50,000
3	45,000
4	25,000
5	15,000

Should the firm make this investment if it requires a minimum annual return of 9% on all investments?

LG 5 **E5–5** Joseph is a friend of yours. He has plenty of money but little financial sense. He received a gift of $12,000 for his recent graduation and is looking for a bank in which to deposit the funds. Partners' Savings Bank offers an account with an annual interest rate of 3% compounded semiannually, while Selwyn's offers an account with a 2.75% annual interest rate compounded continuously. Calculate the value of the two accounts at the end of one year, and recommend to Joseph which account he should choose.

LG 6 **E5–6** Jack and Jill have just had their first child. If college is expected to cost $150,000 per year in 18 years, how much should the couple begin depositing annually at the end of each year to accumulate enough funds to pay the first year's tuition at the beginning of the 19th year? Assume that they can earn a 6% annual rate of return on their investment.

Problems

All problems are available in ⬛myfinancelab .

LG 1 **P5–1** **Using a time line** The financial manager at Starbuck Industries is considering an investment that requires an initial outlay of $25,000 and is expected to result in cash inflows of $3,000 at the end of year 1, $6,000 at the end of years 2 and 3, $10,000 at the end of year 4, $8,000 at the end of year 5, and $7,000 at the end of year 6.

a. Draw and label a time line depicting the cash flows associated with Starbuck Industries' proposed investment.

b. Use arrows to demonstrate, on the time line in part **a,** how compounding to find future value can be used to measure all cash flows at the end of year 6.

c. Use arrows to demonstrate, on the time line in part **b,** how discounting to find present value can be used to measure all cash flows at time zero.

d. Which of the approaches—*future value* or *present value*—do financial managers rely on most often for decision making? Why?

LG 2 **P5–2** **Future value calculation** *Without referring to the preprogrammed function on your financial calculator,* use the basic formula for future value along with the given interest rate, *r,* and the number of periods, *n,* to calculate the future value of $1 in each of the cases shown in the following table.

Case	Interest rate, *r*	Number of periods, *n*
A	12%	2
B	6	3
C	9	2
D	3	4

LG 1 **P5–3** **Future value** You have $100 to invest. If you can earn 12% interest, about how long does it take for your $100 investment to grow to $200? Suppose the interest rate is just half that, at 6%. At half the interest rate, does it take twice as long to double your money? Why or why not? How long does it take?

LG 2 **P5–4** **Future values** For each of the cases shown in the following table, calculate the future value of the single cash flow deposited today at the end of the deposit period if the interest is compounded annually at the rate specified.

Case	Single cash flow	Interest rate	Deposit period (years)
A	$ 200	5%	20
B	4,500	8	7
C	10,000	9	10
D	25,000	10	12
E	37,000	11	5
F	40,000	12	9

Personal Finance Problem

LG 2   **P5–5**   **Time value**   You have $1,500 to invest today at 7% interest compounded annually.

a. Find how much you will have accumulated in the account at the end of
(1) 3 years, (2) 6 years, and (3) 9 years.

b. Use your findings in part **a** to calculate the amount of interest earned in (1) the
first 3 years (years 1 to 3), (2) the second 3 years (years 4 to 6), and (3) the third
3 years (years 7 to 9).

c. Compare and contrast your findings in part **b**. Explain why the amount of
interest earned increases in each succeeding 3-year period.

Personal Finance Problem

LG 2   **P5–6**   **Time value**   As part of your financial planning, you wish to purchase a new car
exactly 5 years from today. The car you wish to purchase costs $14,000 today, and
your research indicates that its price will increase by 2% to 4% per year over the
next 5 years.

a. Estimate the price of the car at the end of 5 years if inflation is (1) 2% per year
and (2) 4% per year.

b. How much more expensive will the car be if the rate of inflation is 4% rather
than 2%?

c. Estimate the price of the car if inflation is 2% for the next 2 years and 4% for
3 years after that.

Personal Finance Problem

LG 2   **P5–7**   **Time value**   You can deposit $10,000 into an account paying 9% annual interest
either today or exactly 10 years from today. How much better off will you be at the
end of 40 years if you decide to make the initial deposit today rather than 10 years
from today?

Personal Finance Problem

LG 2   **P5–8**   **Time value**   Misty needs to have $15,000 at the end of 5 years to fulfill her goal of
purchasing a small sailboat. She is willing to invest a lump sum today and leave the
money untouched for 5 years until it grows to $15,000, but she wonders what sort
of investment return she will need to earn to reach her goal. Use your calculator or
spreadsheet to figure out the approximate annually compounded rate of return
needed in each of these cases:

a. Misty can invest $10,200 today.

b. Misty can invest $8,150 today.

c. Misty can invest $7,150 today.

Personal Finance Problem

LG 2   **P5–9**   **Single-payment loan repayment**   A person borrows $200 to be repaid in 8 years
with 14% annually compounded interest. The loan may be repaid at the end of any
earlier year with no prepayment penalty.

a. What amount will be due if the loan is repaid at the end of year 1?

b. What is the repayment at the end of year 4?

c. What amount is due at the end of the eighth year?

LG 2   **P5–10**   **Present value calculation**   *Without referring to the preprogrammed function on
your financial calculator*, use the basic formula for present value, along with the
given opportunity cost, *r*, and the number of periods, *n*, to calculate the present
value of $1 in each of the cases shown in the following table.

Case	Opportunity cost, r	Number of periods, n
A	2%	4
B	10	2
C	5	3
D	13	2

LG 2   **P5–11**   **Present values**   For each of the cases shown in the following table, calculate the present value of the cash flow, discounting at the rate given and assuming that the cash flow is received at the end of the period noted.

Case	Single cash flow	Discount rate	End of period (years)
A	$ 7,000	12%	4
B	28,000	8	20
C	10,000	14	12
D	150,000	11	6
E	45,000	20	8

LG 2   **P5–12**   **Present value concept**   Answer each of the following questions.
   a. What single investment made today, earning 12% annual interest, will be worth $6,000 at the end of 6 years?
   b. What is the present value of $6,000 to be received at the end of 6 years if the discount rate is 12%?
   c. What is the most you would pay today for a promise to repay you $6,000 at the end of 6 years if your opportunity cost is 12%?
   d. Compare, contrast, and discuss your findings in parts **a** through **c**.

Personal Finance Problem

LG 2   **P5–13**   **Time value**   Jim Nance has been offered an investment that will pay him $500 three years from today.
   a. If his opportunity cost is 7% compounded annually, what value should he place on this opportunity today?
   b. What is the most he should pay to purchase this payment today?
   c. If Jim can purchase this investment for less than the amount calculated in part **a**, what does that imply about the rate of return that he will earn on the investment?

LG 2   **P5–14**   **Time value**   An Iowa state savings bond can be converted to $100 at maturity 6 years from purchase. If the state bonds are to be competitive with U.S. savings bonds, which pay 8% annual interest (compounded annually), at what price must the state sell its bonds? Assume no cash payments on savings bonds prior to redemption.

Personal Finance Problem

LG 2   **P5–15**   **Time value and discount rates**   You just won a lottery that promises to pay you $1,000,000 exactly 10 years from today. Because the $1,000,000 payment is guaranteed by the state in which you live, opportunities exist to sell the claim today for an immediate single cash payment.

a. What is the least you will sell your claim for if you can earn the following rates of return on similar-risk investments during the 10-year period?
   (1) 6%
   (2) 9%
   (3) 12%
b. Rework part **a** under the assumption that the $1,000,000 payment will be received in 15 rather than 10 years.
c. On the basis of your findings in parts **a** and **b,** discuss the effect of both the size of the rate of return and the time until receipt of payment on the present value of a future sum.

Personal Finance Problem

LG 2   **P5–16**   **Time value comparisons of single amounts**   In exchange for a $20,000 payment today, a well-known company will allow you to choose *one* of the alternatives shown in the following table. Your opportunity cost is 11%.

Alternative	Single amount
A	$28,500 at end of 3 years
B	$54,000 at end of 9 years
C	$160,000 at end of 20 years

a. Find the value today of each alternative.
b. Are all the alternatives acceptable—that is, worth $20,000 today?
c. Which alternative, if any, will you take?

Personal Finance Problem

LG 2   **P5–17**   **Cash flow investment decision**   Tom Alexander has an opportunity to purchase any of the investments shown in the following table. The purchase price, the amount of the single cash inflow, and its year of receipt are given for each investment. Which purchase recommendations would you make, assuming that Tom can earn 10% on his investments?

Investment	Price	Single cash inflow	Year of receipt
A	$18,000	$30,000	5
B	600	3,000	20
C	3,500	10,000	10
D	1,000	15,000	40

LG 2   **P5–18**   **Calculating deposit needed**   You put $10,000 in an account earning 5%. After 3 years, you make another deposit into the same account. Four years later (that is, 7 years after your original $10,000 deposit), the account balance is $20,000. What was the amount of the deposit at the end of year 3?

LG 3   **P5–19**   **Future value of an annuity**   For each case in the accompanying table, answer the questions that follow.

Case	Amount of annuity	Interest rate	Deposit period (years)
A	$ 2,500	8%	10
B	500	12	6
C	30,000	20	5
D	11,500	9	8
E	6,000	14	30

a. Calculate the future value of the annuity assuming that it is
   (1) An ordinary annuity.
   (2) An annuity due.
b. Compare your findings in parts a(1) and a(2). All else being identical, which type of annuity—ordinary or annuity due—is preferable? Explain why.

LG 3   **P5-20**   **Present value of an annuity**   Consider the following cases.

Case	Amount of annuity	Interest rate	Period (years)
A	$ 12,000	7%	3
B	55,000	12	15
C	700	20	9
D	140,000	5	7
E	22,500	10	5

a. Calculate the present value of the annuity assuming that it is
   (1) An ordinary annuity.
   (2) An annuity due.
b. Compare your findings in parts a(1) and a(2). All else being identical, which type of annuity—ordinary or annuity due—is preferable? Explain why.

Personal Finance Problem

LG 3   **P5-21**   **Time value—Annuities**   Marian Kirk wishes to select the better of two 10-year annuities, C and D. Annuity C is an *ordinary annuity* of $2,500 per year for 10 years. Annuity D is an *annuity due* of $2,200 per year for 10 years.
a. Find the *future value* of both annuities at the end of year 10, assuming that Marian can earn (1) 10% annual interest and (2) 20% annual interest.
b. Use your findings in part a to indicate which annuity has the greater future value at the end of year 10 for both the (1) 10% and (2) 20% interest rates.
c. Find the *present value* of both annuities, assuming that Marian can earn (1) 10% annual interest and (2) 20% annual interest.
d. Use your findings in part c to indicate which annuity has the greater present value for both (1) 10% and (2) 20% interest rates.
e. Briefly compare, contrast, and explain any differences between your findings using the 10% and 20% interest rates in parts b and d.

Personal Finance Problem

LG 3 **P5–22** **Retirement planning** Hal Thomas, a 25-year-old college graduate, wishes to retire at age 65. To supplement other sources of retirement income, he can deposit $2,000 each year into a tax-deferred individual retirement arrangement (IRA). The IRA will earn a 10% return over the next 40 years.

a. If Hal makes annual end-of-year $2,000 deposits into the IRA, how much will he have accumulated by the end of his sixty-fifth year?

b. If Hal decides to wait until age 35 to begin making annual end-of-year $2,000 deposits into the IRA, how much will he have accumulated by the end of his sixty-fifth year?

c. Using your findings in parts **a** and **b**, discuss the impact of delaying making deposits into the IRA for 10 years (age 25 to age 35) on the amount accumulated by the end of Hal's sixty-fifth year.

d. Rework parts **a**, **b**, and **c**, assuming that Hal makes all deposits at the beginning, rather than the end, of each year. Discuss the effect of beginning-of-year deposits on the future value accumulated by the end of Hal's sixty-fifth year.

Personal Finance Problem

LG 3 **P5–23** **Value of a retirement annuity** An insurance agent is trying to sell you an immediate-retirement annuity, which for a single amount paid today will provide you with $12,000 at the end of each year for the next 25 years. You currently earn 9% on low-risk investments comparable to the retirement annuity. Ignoring taxes, what is the most you would pay for this annuity?

Personal Finance Problem

LG 2 **LG 3** **P5–24** **Funding your retirement** You plan to retire in exactly 20 years. Your goal is to create a fund that will allow you to receive $20,000 at the end of each year for the 30 years between retirement and death (a psychic told you would die exactly 30 years after you retire). You know that you will be able to earn 11% per year during the 30-year retirement period.

a. How large a fund will you need *when you retire* in 20 years to provide the 30-year, $20,000 retirement annuity?

b. How much will you need *today* as a single amount to provide the fund calculated in part **a** if you earn only 9% per year during the 20 years preceding retirement?

c. What effect would an increase in the rate you can earn both during and prior to retirement have on the values found in parts **a** and **b**? Explain.

d. Now assume that you will earn 10% from now through the end of your retirement. You want to make 20 end-of-year deposits into your retirement account that will fund the 30-year stream of $20,000 annual annuity payments. How large do your annual deposits have to be?

Personal Finance Problem

LG 2 **LG 3** **P5–25** **Value of an annuity versus a single amount** Assume that you just won the state lottery. Your prize can be taken either in the form of $40,000 at the end of each of the next 25 years (that is, $1,000,000 over 25 years) or as a single amount of $500,000 paid immediately.

a. If you expect to be able to earn 5% annually on your investments over the next 25 years, ignoring taxes and other considerations, which alternative should you take? Why?

      b. Would your decision in part **a** change if you could earn 7% rather than 5% on your investments over the next 25 years? Why?

      c. On a strictly economic basis, at approximately what earnings rate would you be indifferent between the two plans?

LG 3   **P5–26**   **Perpetuities**   Consider the data in the following table.

Perpetuity	Annual amount	Discount rate
A	$ 20,000	8%
B	100,000	10
C	3,000	6
D	60,000	5

Determine the present value of each perpetuity.

Personal Finance Problem

LG 3   **P5–27**   **Creating an endowment**   On completion of her introductory finance course, Marla Lee was so pleased with the amount of useful and interesting knowledge she gained that she convinced her parents, who were wealthy alumni of the university she was attending, to create an endowment. The endowment is to allow three needy students to take the introductory finance course each year in perpetuity. The guaranteed annual cost of tuition and books for the course is $600 per student. The endowment will be created by making a single payment to the university. The university expects to earn exactly 6% per year on these funds.

      a. How large an initial single payment must Marla's parents make to the university to fund the endowment?

      b. What amount would be needed to fund the endowment if the university could earn 9% rather than 6% per year on the funds?

LG 4   **P5–28**   **Value of a mixed stream**   For each of the mixed streams of cash flows shown in the following table, determine the future value at the end of the final year if deposits are made into an account paying annual interest of 12%, assuming that no withdrawals are made during the period and that the deposits are made:

      a. At the *end* of each year.

      b. At the *beginning* of each year.

	Cash flow stream		
Year	A	B	C
1	$ 900	$30,000	$1,200
2	1,000	25,000	1,200
3	1,200	20,000	1,000
4		10,000	1,900
5		5,000	

Personal Finance Problem

LG 4   **P5–29**   **Value of a single amount versus a mixed stream**   Gina Vitale has just contracted to sell a small parcel of land that she inherited a few years ago. The buyer is willing to pay $24,000 at the closing of the transaction or will pay the amounts shown in the following table at the *beginning* of each of the next 5 years. Because Gina doesn't really need the money today, she plans to let it accumulate in an account that earns 7% annual interest. Given her desire to buy a house at the end of 5 years after closing on the sale of the lot, she decides to choose the payment alternative— $24,000 single amount or the mixed stream of payments in the following table— that provides the higher future value at the end of 5 years. Which alternative will she choose?

Mixed stream	
Beginning of year	Cash flow
1	$ 2,000
2	4,000
3	6,000
4	8,000
5	10,000

LG 4   **P5–30**   **Value of mixed streams**   Find the present value of the streams of cash flows shown in the following table. Assume that the firm's opportunity cost is 12%.

A		B		C	
Year	Cash flow	Year	Cash flow	Year	Cash flow
1	−$2,000	1	$10,000	1–5	$10,000/yr
2	3,000	2–5	5,000/yr	6–10	8,000/yr
3	4,000	6	7,000		
4	6,000				
5	8,000				

LG 4   **P5–31**   **Present value—Mixed streams**   Consider the mixed streams of cash flows shown in the following table.

	Cash flow stream	
Year	A	B
1	$ 50,000	$ 10,000
2	40,000	20,000
3	30,000	30,000
4	20,000	40,000
5	10,000	50,000
Totals	$150,000	$150,000

a. Find the present value of each stream using a 15% discount rate.
b. Compare the calculated present values and discuss them in light of the fact that the undiscounted cash flows total $150,000 in each case.

LG 1   **LG 4**   **P5–32**   **Value of a mixed stream**   Harte Systems, Inc., a maker of electronic surveillance equipment, is considering selling to a well-known hardware chain the rights to market its home security system. The proposed deal calls for the hardware chain to pay Harte $30,000 and $25,000 at the end of years 1 and 2 and to make annual year-end payments of $15,000 in years 3 through 9. A final payment to Harte of $10,000 would be due at the end of year 10.
a. Lay out the cash flows involved in the offer on a time line.
b. If Harte applies a required rate of return of 12% to them, what is the present value of this series of payments?
c. A second company has offered Harte an immediate one-time payment of $100,000 for the rights to market the home security system. Which offer should Harte accept?

Personal Finance Problem

LG 4   **P5–33**   **Funding budget shortfalls**   As part of your personal budgeting process, you have determined that in each of the next 5 years you will have budget shortfalls. In other words, you will need the amounts shown in the following table at the end of the given year to balance your budget—that is, to make inflows equal outflows. You expect to be able to earn 8% on your investments during the next 5 years and wish to fund the budget shortfalls over the next 5 years with a single amount.

End of year	Budget shortfall
1	$ 5,000
2	4,000
3	6,000
4	10,000
5	3,000

a. How large must the single deposit today into an account paying 8% annual interest be to provide for full coverage of the anticipated budget shortfalls?
b. What effect would an increase in your earnings rate have on the amount calculated in part **a?** Explain.

LG 4   **P5–34**   **Relationship between future value and present value—Mixed stream**   Using the information in the accompanying table, answer the questions that follow.

Year (t)	Cash flow
1	$ 800
2	900
3	1,000
4	1,500
5	2,000

a. Determine the *present value* of the mixed stream of cash flows using a 5% discount rate.
b. How much would you be willing to pay for an opportunity to buy this stream, assuming that you can at best earn 5% on your investments?
c. What effect, if any, would a 7% rather than a 5% opportunity cost have on your analysis? (Explain verbally.)

LG 4 **P5–35** **Relationship between future value and present value—Mixed stream** The table below shows a mixed cash flow stream, except that the cash flow for year 3 is missing.

Year 1	$10,000
Year 2	5,000
Year 3	
Year 4	20,000
Year 5	3,000

Suppose that somehow you know that the present value of the entire stream is $32,911.03, and the discount rate is 4%. What is the amount of the missing cash flow in year 3?

LG 5 **P5–36** **Changing compounding frequency** Using annual, semiannual, and quarterly compounding periods for each of the following, (1) calculate the future value if $5,000 is deposited initially, and (2) determine the *effective annual rate (EAR)*.
a. At 12% annual interest for 5 years.
b. At 16% annual interest for 6 years.
c. At 20% annual interest for 10 years.

LG 5 **P5–37** **Compounding frequency, time value, and effective annual rates** For each of the cases in the following table:
a. Calculate the future value at the end of the specified deposit period.
b. Determine the *effective annual rate, EAR.*
c. Compare the nominal annual rate, r, to the effective annual rate, EAR. What relationship exists between compounding frequency and the nominal and effective annual rates?

Case	Amount of initial deposit	Nominal annual rate, r	Compounding frequency, m (times/year)	Deposit period (years)
A	$ 2,500	6%	2	5
B	50,000	12	6	3
C	1,000	5	1	10
D	20,000	16	4	6

LG 5   **P5–38**   **Continuous compounding**   For each of the cases in the following table, find the future value at the end of the deposit period, assuming that interest is compounded continuously at the given nominal annual rate.

Case	Amount of initial deposit	Nominal annual rate, r	Deposit period (years), n
A	$1,000	9%	2
B	600	10	10
C	4,000	8	7
D	2,500	12	4

Personal Finance Problem

LG 5   **P5–39**   **Compounding frequency and time value**   You plan to invest $2,000 in an individual retirement arrangement (IRA) today at a *nominal annual rate* of 8%, which is expected to apply to all future years.

  a. How much will you have in the account at the end of 10 years if interest is compounded (1) annually, (2) semiannually, (3) daily (assume a 365-day year), and (4) continuously?
  b. What is the *effective annual rate, EAR,* for each compounding period in part **a?**
  c. How much greater will your IRA balance be at the end of 10 years if interest is compounded continuously rather than annually?
  d. How does the compounding frequency affect the future value and effective annual rate for a given deposit? Explain in terms of your findings in parts **a** through **c.**

Personal Finance Problem

LG 5   **P5–40**   **Comparing compounding periods**   René Levin wishes to determine the future value at the end of 2 years of a $15,000 deposit made today into an account paying a nominal annual rate of 12%.

  a. Find the future value of René's deposit, assuming that interest is compounded (1) annually, (2) quarterly, (3) monthly, and (4) continuously.
  b. Compare your findings in part **a,** and use them to demonstrate the relationship between compounding frequency and future value.
  c. What is the maximum future value obtainable given the $15,000 deposit, the 2-year time period, and the 12% nominal annual rate? Use your findings in part **a** to explain.

Personal Finance Problem

LG 3   **LG 5**   **P5–41**   **Annuities and compounding**   Janet Boyle intends to deposit $300 per year in a credit union for the next 10 years, and the credit union pays an annual interest rate of 8%.

  a. Determine the future value that Janet will have at the end of 10 years, given that end-of-period deposits are made and no interest is withdrawn, if
  (1) $300 is deposited annually and the credit union pays interest annually.
  (2) $150 is deposited semiannually and the credit union pays interest semiannually.
  (3) $75 is deposited quarterly and the credit union pays interest quarterly.
  b. Use your finding in part **a** to discuss the effect of more frequent deposits and compounding of interest on the future value of an annuity.

LG 6   **P5–42**   **Deposits to accumulate future sums**   For each of the cases shown in the following table, determine the amount of the equal, annual, end-of-year deposits necessary to accumulate the given sum at the end of the specified period, assuming the stated annual interest rate.

Case	Sum to be accumulated	Accumulation period (years)	Interest rate
A	$ 5,000	3	12%
B	100,000	20	7
C	30,000	8	10
D	15,000	12	8

Personal Finance Problem

LG 6   **P5–43**   **Creating a retirement fund**   To supplement your planned retirement in exactly 42 years, you estimate that you need to accumulate $220,000 by the end of 42 years from today. You plan to make equal, annual, end-of-year deposits into an account paying 8% annual interest.

   a. How large must the annual deposits be to create the $220,000 fund by the end of 42 years?

   b. If you can afford to deposit only $600 per year into the account, how much will you have accumulated by the end of the forty-second year?

Personal Finance Problem

LG 6   **P5–44**   **Accumulating a growing future sum**   A retirement home at Deer Trail Estates now costs $185,000. Inflation is expected to cause this price to increase at 6% per year over the 20 years before C. L. Donovan retires. How large an equal, annual, end-of-year deposit must be made each year into an account paying an annual interest rate of 10% for Donovan to have the cash needed to purchase a home at retirement?

Personal Finance Problem

LG 3   **LG** 6   **P5–45**   **Deposits to create a perpetuity**   You have decided to endow your favorite university with a scholarship. It is expected to cost $6,000 per year to attend the university into perpetuity. You expect to give the university the endowment in 10 years and will accumulate it by making equal annual (end-of-year) deposits into an account. The rate of interest is expected to be 10% for all future time periods.

   a. How large must the endowment be?

   b. How much must you deposit at the end of each of the next 10 years to accumulate the required amount?

Personal Finance Problem

LG 2   **LG** 3   **P5–46**   **Inflation, time value, and annual deposits**   While vacationing in Florida, John
LG 6   Kelley saw the vacation home of his dreams. It was listed with a sale price of $200,000. The only catch is that John is 40 years old and plans to continue working until he is 65. Still, he believes that prices generally increase at the overall rate of inflation. John believes that he can earn 9% annually after taxes on his investments. He is willing to invest a fixed amount at the end of each of the next 25 years to fund the cash purchase of such a house (one that can be purchased today for $200,000) when he retires.

a. Inflation is expected to average 5% per year for the next 25 years. What will John's dream house cost when he retires?

b. How much must John invest at the *end* of each of the next 25 years to have the cash purchase price of the house when he retires?

c. If John invests at the *beginning* instead of at the end of each of the next 25 years, how much must he invest each year?

LG 6   **P5–47**   **Loan payment**   Determine the equal, annual, end-of-year payment required each year over the life of the loans shown in the following table to repay them fully during the stated term of the loan.

Loan	Principal	Interest rate	Term of loan (years)
A	$12,000	8%	3
B	60,000	12	10
C	75,000	10	30
D	4,000	15	5

Personal Finance Problem

LG 6   **P5–48**   **Loan amortization schedule**   Joan Messineo borrowed $15,000 at a 14% annual rate of interest to be repaid over 3 years. The loan is amortized into three equal, annual, end-of-year payments.

a. Calculate the annual, end-of-year loan payment.

b. Prepare a loan amortization schedule showing the interest and principal breakdown of each of the three loan payments.

c. Explain why the interest portion of each payment declines with the passage of time.

LG 6   **P5–49**   **Loan interest deductions**   Liz Rogers just closed a $10,000 business loan that is to be repaid in three equal, annual, end-of-year payments. The interest rate on the loan is 13%. As part of her firm's detailed financial planning, Liz wishes to determine the annual interest deduction attributable to the loan. (Because it is a business loan, the interest portion of each loan payment is tax-deductible to the business.)

a. Determine the firm's annual loan payment.

b. Prepare an amortization schedule for the loan.

c. How much interest expense will Liz's firm have in *each* of the next 3 years as a result of this loan?

Personal Finance Problem

LG 6   **P5–50**   **Monthly loan payments**   Tim Smith is shopping for a used car. He has found one priced at $4,500. The dealer has told Tim that if he can come up with a down payment of $500, the dealer will finance the balance of the price at a 12% annual rate over 2 years (24 months).

a. Assuming that Tim accepts the dealer's offer, what will his *monthly* (end-of-month) payment amount be?

b. Use a financial calculator or spreadsheet to help you figure out what Tim's *monthly* payment would be if the dealer were willing to finance the balance of the car price at a 9% annual rate.

LG 6   **P5–51**   **Growth rates**   You are given the series of cash flows shown in the following table.

	Cash flows		
Year	A	B	C
1	$500	$1,500	$2,500
2	560	1,550	2,600
3	640	1,610	2,650
4	720	1,680	2,650
5	800	1,760	2,800
6		1,850	2,850
7		1,950	2,900
8		2,060	
9		2,170	
10		2,280	

a. Calculate the compound annual growth rate between the first and last payment in each stream.

b. If year-1 values represent initial deposits in a savings account paying annual interest, what is the annual rate of interest earned on each account?

c. Compare and discuss the growth rate and interest rate found in parts **a** and **b**, respectively.

Personal Finance Problem

LG 6   **P5–52**   **Rate of return**   Rishi Singh has $1,500 to invest. His investment counselor suggests an investment that pays no stated interest but will return $2,000 at the end of 3 years.

a. What annual rate of return will Rishi earn with this investment?

b. Rishi is considering another investment, of equal risk, that earns an annual return of 8%. Which investment should he make, and why?

Personal Finance Problem

LG 6   **P5–53**   **Rate of return and investment choice**   Clare Jaccard has $5,000 to invest. Because she is only 25 years old, she is not concerned about the length of the investment's life. What she is sensitive to is the rate of return she will earn on the investment. With the help of her financial advisor, Clare has isolated four equally risky investments, each providing a single amount at the end of its life, as shown in the following table. All of the investments require an initial $5,000 payment.

Investment	Single amount	Investment life (years)
A	$ 8,400	6
B	15,900	15
C	7,600	4
D	13,000	10

a. Calculate, to the nearest 1%, the rate of return on each of the four investments available to Clare.

b. Which investment would you recommend to Clare, given her goal of maximizing the rate of return?

LG 6   **P5–54**   **Rate of return—Annuity**   What is the rate of return on an investment of $10,606 if the company will receive $2,000 each year for the next 10 years?

Personal Finance Problem

LG 6   **P5–55**   **Choosing the best annuity**   Raina Herzig wishes to choose the best of four immediate-retirement annuities available to her. In each case, in exchange for paying a single premium today, she will receive equal, annual, end-of-year cash benefits for a specified number of years. She considers the annuities to be equally risky and is not concerned about their differing lives. Her decision will be based solely on the rate of return she will earn on each annuity. The key terms of the four annuities are shown in the following table.

Annuity	Premium paid today	Annual benefit	Life (years)
A	$30,000	$3,100	20
B	25,000	3,900	10
C	40,000	4,200	15
D	35,000	4,000	12

a. Calculate to the nearest 1% the rate of return on each of the four annuities Raina is considering.
b. Given Raina's stated decision criterion, which annuity would you recommend?

Personal Finance Problem

LG 6   **P5–56**   **Interest rate for an annuity**   Anna Waldheim was seriously injured in an industrial accident. She sued the responsible parties and was awarded a judgment of $2,000,000. Today, she and her attorney are attending a settlement conference with the defendants. The defendants have made an initial offer of $156,000 per year for 25 years. Anna plans to counteroffer at $255,000 per year for 25 years. Both the offer and the counteroffer have a present value of $2,000,000, the amount of the judgment. Both assume payments at the end of each year.
a. What interest rate assumption have the defendants used in their offer (rounded to the nearest whole percent)?
b. What interest rate assumption have Anna and her lawyer used in their counteroffer (rounded to the nearest whole percent)?
c. Anna is willing to settle for an annuity that carries an interest rate assumption of 9%. What annual payment would be acceptable to her?

Personal Finance Problem

LG 6   **P5–57**   **Loan rates of interest**   John Flemming has been shopping for a loan to finance the purchase of a used car. He has found three possibilities that seem attractive and wishes to select the one with the lowest interest rate. The information available with respect to each of the three $5,000 loans is shown in the following table.

Loan	Principal	Annual payment	Term (years)
A	$5,000	$1,352.81	5
B	5,000	1,543.21	4
C	5,000	2,010.45	3

   a. Determine the interest rate associated with each of the loans.

   b. Which loan should John take?

LG 6 **P5–58** **Number of years to equal future amount** For each of the following cases, determine the number of years it will take for the initial deposit to grow to equal the future amount at the given interest rate.

Case	Initial deposit	Future amount	Interest rate
A	$ 300	$ 1,000	7%
B	12,000	15,000	5
C	9,000	20,000	10
D	100	500	9
E	7,500	30,000	15

Personal Finance Problem

LG 6 **P5–59** **Time to accumulate a given sum** Manuel Rios wishes to determine how long it will take an initial deposit of $10,000 to double.

   a. If Manuel earns 10% annual interest on the deposit, how long will it take for him to double his money?

   b. How long will it take if he earns only 7% annual interest?

   c. How long will it take if he can earn 12% annual interest?

   d. Reviewing your findings in parts **a, b,** and **c,** indicate what relationship exists between the interest rate and the amount of time it will take Manuel to double his money.

LG 6 **P5–60** **Number of years to provide a given return** In each of the following cases, determine the number of years that the given annual *end-of-year* cash flow must continue to provide the given rate of return on the given initial amount.

Case	Initial amount	Annual cash flow	Rate of return
A	$ 1,000	$ 250	11%
B	150,000	30,000	15
C	80,000	10,000	10
D	600	275	9
E	17,000	3,500	6

Personal Finance Problem

LG 6 **P5–61** **Time to repay installment loan** Mia Salto wishes to determine how long it will take to repay a loan with initial proceeds of $14,000 where annual *end-of-year* installment payments of $2,450 are required.

   a. If Mia can borrow at a 12% annual rate of interest, how long will it take for her to repay the loan fully?

   b. How long will it take if she can borrow at a 9% annual rate?

   c. How long will it take if she has to pay 15% annual interest?

   d. Reviewing your answers in parts **a, b,** and **c,** describe the general relationship between the interest rate and the amount of time it will take Mia to repay the loan fully.

LG 6 **P5–62** **ETHICS PROBLEM** A manager at a "Check Into Cash" business (see *Focus on Ethics* box on page 187) defends his business practice as simply "charging what the market will bear." "After all," says the manager, "we don't force people to come in the door." How would you respond to this ethical defense of the payday-advance business?

Spreadsheet Exercise

At the end of 2012, Uma Corporation was considering undertaking a major long-term project in an effort to remain competitive in its industry. The production and sales departments determined the potential annual cash flow savings that could accrue to the firm if it acts soon. Specifically, they estimate that a mixed stream of future cash flow savings will occur at the end of the years 2013 through 2018. The years 2019 through 2023 will see consecutive and equal cash flow savings at the end of each year. The firm estimates that its discount rate over the first 6 years will be 7%. The expected discount rate over the years 2019 through 2023 will be 11%.

The project managers will find the project acceptable if it results in present cash flow savings of at least $860,000. The following cash flow savings data are supplied to the finance department for analysis.

End of year	Cash flow savings
2013	$110,000
2014	120,000
2015	130,000
2016	150,000
2017	160,000
2018	150,000
2019	90,000
2020	90,000
2021	90,000
2022	90,000
2023	90,000

TO DO

Create spreadsheets similar to Table 5.2, and then answer the following questions:

a. Determine the value (at the beginning of 2013) of the future cash flow savings expected to be generated by this project.
b. Based solely on the one criterion set by management, should the firm undertake this specific project? Explain.
c. What is the "interest rate risk," and how might it influence the recommendation made in part **b**? Explain.

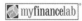 Visit **www.myfinancelab.com** for **Chapter Case: *Funding Jill Moran's Retirement Annuity,*** Group Exercises, and numerous online resources.

Track Software, Inc.

Seven years ago, after 15 years in public accounting, Stanley Booker, CPA, resigned his position as manager of cost systems for Davis, Cohen, and O'Brien Public Accountants and started Track Software, Inc. In the 2 years preceding his departure from Davis, Cohen, and O'Brien, Stanley had spent nights and weekends developing a sophisticated cost-accounting software program that became Track's initial product offering. As the firm grew, Stanley planned to develop and expand the software product offerings—all of which would be related to streamlining the accounting processes of medium- to large-sized manufacturers.

Although Track experienced losses during its first 2 years of operation—2006 and 2007—its profit has increased steadily from 2008 to the present (2012). The firm's profit history, including dividend payments and contributions to retained earnings, is summarized in Table 1.

Stanley started the firm with a $100,000 investment—his savings of $50,000 as equity and a $50,000 long-term loan from the bank. He had hoped to maintain his initial 100 percent ownership in the corporation, but after experiencing a $50,000 loss during the first year of operation (2006), he sold 60 percent of the stock to a group of investors to obtain needed funds. Since then, no other stock transactions have taken place. Although he owns only 40 percent of the firm, Stanley actively manages all aspects of its activities; the other stockholders are not active in management of the firm. The firm's stock was valued at $4.50 per share in 2011 and at $5.28 per share in 2012.

TABLE 1

	Track Software, Inc. Profit, Dividends, and Retained Earnings, 2006–2012		
Year	Net profits after taxes (1)	Dividends paid (2)	Contribution to retained earnings [(1) − (2)] (3)
2006	($50,000)	$ 0	($50,000)
2007	(20,000)	0	(20,000)
2008	15,000	0	15,000
2009	35,000	0	35,000
2010	40,000	1,000	39,000
2011	43,000	3,000	40,000
2012	48,000	5,000	43,000

Stanley has just prepared the firm's 2012 income statement, balance sheet, and statement of retained earnings, shown in Tables 2, 3, and 4, along with the 2011 balance sheet. In addition, he has compiled the 2011 ratio values and industry average ratio values for 2012, which are applicable to both 2011 and 2012 and are summarized in Table 5 (on page 218). He is quite pleased to have achieved record earnings of $48,000 in 2012, but he is concerned about the firm's cash flows. Specifically, he is finding it more and more difficult to pay the firm's bills in a timely manner and generate cash flows to investors—both creditors and owners. To gain insight into these cash flow problems, Stanley is planning to determine the firm's 2012 operating cash flow (OCF) and free cash flow (FCF).

Stanley is further frustrated by the firm's inability to afford to hire a software developer to complete development of a cost estimation package that is believed to have "blockbuster" sales potential. Stanley began development of this package 2 years ago, but the firm's growing complexity has forced him to devote more of his time to administrative duties, thereby halting the development of this product. Stanley's reluctance to fill this position stems from his concern that the added $80,000 per year in salary and benefits for the position would certainly lower the firm's earnings per share (EPS) over the next couple of years. Although the project's success is in no way guaranteed, Stanley believes that if the money were spent to hire the software developer, the firm's sales and earnings would significantly rise once the 2- to 3-year development, production, and marketing process was completed.

With all of these concerns in mind, Stanley set out to review the various data to develop strategies that would help to ensure a bright future for Track Software. Stanley believed that as part of this process, a thorough ratio analysis of the firm's 2012 results would provide important additional insights.

TABLE 2

Track Software, Inc. Income Statement ($000) for the Year Ended December 31, 2012		
Sales revenue		$1,550
Less: Cost of goods sold		$1,030
Gross profits		$ 520
Less: Operating expenses		
Selling expense	$ 150	
General and administrative expenses	270	
Depreciation expense	11	
Total operating expense		431
Operating profits (EBIT)		$ 89
Less: Interest expense		29
Net profits before taxes		$ 60
Less: Taxes (20%)		12
Net profits after taxes		$ 48

TABLE 3

Track Software, Inc. Balance Sheet ($000)

Assets	December 31 2012	December 31 2011
Cash	$ 12	$ 31
Marketable securities	66	82
Accounts receivable	152	104
Inventories	191	145
Total current assets	$421	$362
Gross fixed assets	$195	$180
Less: Accumulated depreciation	63	52
Net fixed assets	$132	$128
Total assets	$553	$490
Liabilities and Stockholders' Equity		
Accounts payable	$136	$126
Notes payable	200	190
Accruals	27	25
Total current liabilities	$363	$341
Long-term debt	$ 38	$ 40
Total liabilities	$401	$381
Common stock (50,000 shares outstanding at $0.40 par value)	$ 20	$ 20
Paid-in capital in excess of par	30	30
Retained earnings	102	59
Total stockholders' equity	$152	$109
Total liabilities and stockholders' equity	$553	$490

TABLE 4

Track Software, Inc. Statement of Retained Earnings ($000) for the Year Ended December 31, 2012

Retained earnings balance (January 1, 2012)	$ 59
Plus: Net profits after taxes (for 2012)	48
Less: Cash dividends on common stock (paid during 2012)	5
Retained earnings balance (December 31, 2012)	$102

TABLE 5

Ratio	Actual 2011	Industry average 2012
Current ratio	1.06	1.82
Quick ratio	0.63	1.10
Inventory turnover	10.40	12.45
Average collection period	29.6 days	20.2 days
Total asset turnover	2.66	3.92
Debt ratio	0.78	0.55
Times interest earned ratio	3.0	5.6
Gross profit margin	32.1%	42.3%
Operating profit margin	5.5%	12.4%
Net profit margin	3.0%	4.0%
Return on total assets (ROA)	8.0%	15.6%
Return on common equity (ROE)	36.4%	34.7%
Price/earnings (P/E) ratio	5.2	7.1
Market/book (M/B) ratio	2.1	2.2

TO DO

a. (1) On what financial goal does Stanley seem to be focusing? Is it the correct goal? Why or why not?

   (2) Could a potential *agency problem* exist in this firm? Explain.

b. Calculate the firm's earnings per share (EPS) for each year, recognizing that the number of shares of common stock outstanding has remained *unchanged* since the firm's inception. Comment on the EPS performance in view of your response in part **a**.

c. Use the financial data presented to determine Track's *operating cash flow (OCF)* and *free cash flow (FCF)* in 2012. Evaluate your findings in light of Track's current cash flow difficulties.

d. Analyze the firm's financial condition in 2012 as it relates to (1) liquidity, (2) activity, (3) debt, (4) profitability, and (5) market, using the financial statements provided in Tables 2 and 3 and the ratio data included in Table 5. Be sure to *evaluate* the firm on both a cross-sectional and a time-series basis.

e. What recommendation would you make to Stanley regarding hiring a new software developer? Relate your recommendation here to your responses in part **a**.

f. Track Software paid $5,000 in dividends in 2012. Suppose an investor approached Stanley about buying 100% of his firm. If this investor believed that by owning the company he could extract $5,000 per year in cash from the company in perpetuity, what do you think the investor would be willing to pay for the firm if the required return on this investment is 10%?

g. Suppose that you believed that the FCF generated by Track Software in 2012 could continue forever. You are willing to buy the company in order to receive this perpetual stream of free cash flow. What are you willing to pay if you require a 10% return on your investment?

Part 3 > Valuation of Securities

In Part 2, you learned how to use time-value-of-money tools to compare cash flows at different times. In the next two chapters you'll put those tools to practice valuing the two most common types of securities—bonds and stocks.

Chapter 6 introduces you to the world of interest rates and bonds. Though bonds are considered to be among the safest investments available, they are not without risk. The primary risk that bond investors face is the risk that market interest rates will fluctuate. Those fluctuations cause bond prices to move, and those movements affect the returns that bond investors earn. Chapter 6 explains why interest rates vary from one bond to another and the factors that cause interest rates to move.

Chapter 7 focuses on stock valuation. Chapter 7 explains the characteristics of stock that distinguish it from debt and the chapter describes how companies issue stock to investors. You'll have another chance to practice time-value-of-money techniques as the chapter illustrates how to value stocks by discounting either (1) the dividends that stockholders receive or (2) the free cash flows that the firm generates over time.

Interest Rates and Bond Valuation

Learning Goals

LG 1 Describe interest rate fundamentals, the term structure of interest rates, and risk premiums.

LG 2 Review the legal aspects of bond financing and bond cost.

LG 3 Discuss the general features, yields, prices, ratings, popular types, and international issues of corporate bonds.

LG 4 Understand the key inputs and basic model used in the bond valuation process.

LG 5 Apply the basic valuation model to bonds, and describe the impact of required return and time to maturity on bond values.

LG 6 Explain yield to maturity (YTM), its calculation, and the procedure used to value bonds that pay interest semiannually.

Why This Chapter Matters to You

In your *professional* life

ACCOUNTING You need to understand interest rates and the various types of bonds to be able to account properly for amortization of bond premiums and discounts and for bond issues and retirements.

INFORMATION SYSTEMS You need to understand the data that is necessary to track bond valuations and bond amortization schedules.

MANAGEMENT You need to understand the behavior of interest rates and how they affect the types of funds the firm can raise and the timing and cost of bond issues and retirements.

MARKETING You need to understand how the interest rate level and the firm's ability to issue bonds may affect the availability of financing for marketing research projects and new-product development.

OPERATIONS You need to understand how the interest rate level may affect the firm's ability to raise funds to maintain and grow the firm's production capacity.

In your *personal* life

Interest rates have a direct impact on personal financial planning. Movements in interest rates occur frequently and affect the returns from and values of savings and investments. The rate of interest you are charged on credit cards and loans can have a profound effect on your personal finances. Understanding the basics of interest rates is important to your personal financial success.

Asian Development Bank

Renminbi-Denominated International Bonds Are Finally Out

On October 19, 2010, the Asian Development Bank (ADB) finally priced the first international bond denominated in renminbi yuan (RMB). A 10-year bullet maturity bond had been available since 2007, but this could only be sold in Hong Kong, therefore restricting foreign investors from either issuing or investing in these bonds. However, as part of a much bigger plan to increase the international role of the currency and lessen China's dependence on the U.S. dollar, Beijing liberalized the market. Accordingly, international bonds denominated in Chinese currency are now tradable, allowing foreign market participants to use them as a source of funding or as an investment destination.

As an investment tool, the ADB renminbi bond proved to be quite attractive. Once the bond was announced, it received strong investor demand and was more than doubly oversubscribed. Therefore, the size of the issue by ADB increased from RMB 1 billion to RMB 1.2 billion. Additionally, the bond received an AAA rating due to its high credit quality.

Foreign corporations with ongoing business in China took this as an opportunity to raise capital in renminbi to facilitate their operations. The issuing of renminbi bonds has therefore provided a source of funding in Chinese currency. Two multinational U.S. corporations have already started to use the currency. McDonald's was the first foreign corporation to issue renminbi bonds in the form of a 3-year bond with a 3 percent coupon due in September 2013. A total of RMB 200 million was raised, and the offer was oversubscribed and sold directly to institutional investors. The second corporation to issue these bonds, having 30 years of ongoing operations in China, was Caterpillar, the U.S. manufacturer of earth-moving equipment. Caterpillar issued a 2-year RMB 1 billion bond with a 2 percent coupon in Hong Kong.

Due to the tight policies followed on the mainland, the renminbi international bond market is still in its infant stage. So far, the only maturities available are of 2 to 3 years. However, higher maturities of up to 10 to 20 years might be needed to match other project cash flows. The international Chinese corporate bond market therefore may take some time and face some obstacles in its development, but successful growth can already be seen.

6.1 Interest Rates and Required Returns

As noted in Chapter 2, financial institutions and markets create the mechanism through which funds flow between savers (funds suppliers) and borrowers (funds demanders). All else being equal, savers would like to earn as much interest as possible, and borrowers would like to pay as little as possible. The interest rate prevailing in the market at any given time reflects the equilibrium between savers and borrowers.

INTEREST RATE FUNDAMENTALS

The *interest rate* or *required return* represents the cost of money. It is the compensation that a supplier of funds expects and a demander of funds must pay. Usually the term **interest rate** is applied to debt instruments such as bank loans or bonds, and the term **required return** is applied to equity investments, such as common stock, that give the investor an ownership stake in the issuer. In fact, the meaning of these two terms is quite similar because, in both cases, the supplier is compensated for providing funds to the demander.

A variety of factors can influence the equilibrium interest rate. One factor is **inflation**, a rising trend in the prices of most goods and services. Typically, savers demand higher returns (that is, higher interest rates) when inflation is high because they want their investments to more than keep pace with rising prices. A second factor influencing interest rates is risk. When people perceive that a particular investment is riskier, they will expect a higher return on that investment as compensation for bearing the risk. A third factor that can affect the interest rate is a **liquidity preference** among investors. The term *liquidity preference* refers to the general tendency of investors to prefer short-term securities (that is, securities that are more liquid). If, all other things being equal, investors would prefer to buy short-term rather than long-term securities, interest rates on short-term instruments such as Treasury bills will be lower than rates on longer-term securities. Investors will hold these securities, despite the relatively low return that they offer, because they meet investors' preferences for liquidity.

interest rate
Usually applied to debt instruments such as bank loans or bonds; the compensation paid by the borrower of funds to the lender; from the borrower's point of view, the cost of borrowing funds.

required return
Usually applied to equity instruments such as common stock; the cost of funds obtained by selling an ownership interest.

inflation
A rising trend in the prices of most goods and services.

liquidity preference
A general tendency for investors to prefer short-term (that is, more liquid) securities.

Matter of fact

Fear Turns T-Bill Rates Negative

Near the height of the financial crisis in December 2008, interest rates on Treasury bills briefly turned negative, meaning that investors paid more to the Treasury than the Treasury promised to pay back. Why would anyone put their money into an investment that they *know* will lose money? Remember that 2008 saw the demise of Lehman Brothers, and fears that other commercial banks and investments banks might fail were rampant. Evidently, some investors were willing to pay the U.S. Treasury to keep their money safe for a short time.

---

real rate of interest
The rate that creates equilibrium between the supply of savings and the demand for investment funds in a perfect world, without inflation, where suppliers and demanders of funds have no liquidity preferences and there is no risk.

The Real Rate of Interest

Imagine a *perfect world* in which there is no inflation, in which investors have no liquidity preferences, and in which there is no risk. In this world, there would be one cost of money—the **real rate of interest**. The real rate of interest creates equilibrium

FIGURE 6.1

Supply–Demand Relationship
Supply of savings and demand for investment funds

Funds Supplied/Demanded

between the supply of savings and the demand for funds. It represents the most basic cost of money. Historically, the real rate of interest in the United States has averaged about 1 percent per year, but that figure does fluctuate over time. This supply–demand relationship is shown in Figure 6.1 by the supply function (labeled S_0) and the demand function (labeled D). An equilibrium between the supply of funds and the demand for funds ($S_0 = D$) occurs at a rate of interest r_0^*, the real rate of interest.

Clearly, the real rate of interest changes with changing economic conditions, tastes, and preferences. To combat a recession, the Board of Governors of the Federal Reserve System might initiate actions to increase the supply of credit in the economy, causing the supply function in Figure 6.1 to shift to, say, S_1. This could result in a lower real rate of interest, r_1^*, at equilibrium ($S_1 = D$). With a lower cost of money, firms might find that investments that were previously unattractive are now worth undertaking, and as firms hire more workers and spend more on plant and equipment, the economy begins to expand again.

Nominal or Actual Rate of Interest (Return)

nominal rate of interest
The actual rate of interest charged by the supplier of funds and paid by the demander.

The **nominal rate of interest** is the actual rate of interest charged by the supplier of funds and paid by the demander. *Throughout this book, interest rates and required rates of return are nominal rates unless otherwise noted.* The nominal rate of interest differs from the real rate of interest, r^*, as a result of two factors, inflation and risk. When people save money and invest it, they are sacrificing consumption today (that is, they are spending less than they could) in return for higher future consumption. When investors expect inflation to occur, they believe that the price of consuming goods and services will be higher in the future than in the present. Therefore, they will be reluctant to sacrifice today's consumption unless the return they can earn on the money they save (or invest) will be high enough to allow them to purchase the goods and services they desire at a higher future price. That is, *investors will demand a higher nominal rate of return if they expect inflation.* This higher rate of return is called the expected inflation premium (*IP*).

Similarly, investors generally demand higher rates of return on risky investments as compared to safe ones. Otherwise, there is little incentive for investors to bear the additional risk. Therefore, *investors will demand a higher nominal rate of return on risky investments*. This additional rate of return is called the risk premium (*RP*). Therefore, the nominal rate of interest for security 1, r_1, is given in Equation 6.1:

$$r_1 = \underbrace{r^* + IP}_{\substack{\text{risk-free} \\ \text{rate, } R_F}} + \underbrace{RP_1}_{\substack{\text{risk} \\ \text{premium}}} \tag{6.1}$$

As the horizontal braces below the equation indicate, the nominal rate, r_1, can be viewed as having two basic components: a risk-free rate of return, R_F, and a risk premium, RP_1:

$$r_1 = R_F + RP_1 \tag{6.2}$$

For the moment, ignore the risk premium, RP_1, and focus exclusively on the risk-free rate. Equation 6.1 says that the risk-free rate can be represented as

$$R_F = r^* + IP \tag{6.3}$$

The risk-free rate (as shown in Equation 6.3) embodies the real rate of interest plus the expected inflation premium. The inflation premium is driven by investors' expectations about inflation—the more inflation they expect, the higher will be the inflation premium and the higher will be the nominal interest rate.

Three-month *U.S. Treasury bills* (*T-bills*) are short-term IOUs issued by the U.S. Treasury, and they are widely regarded as the safest investments in the world. They are as close as we can get in the real world to a risk-free investment. To estimate the real rate of interest, analysts typically try to determine what rate of inflation investors expect over the coming 3 months. Next, *they subtract the expected inflation rate from the nominal rate on the 3-month T-bill to arrive at the underlying real rate of interest*. For the risk-free asset in Equation 6.3, the real rate of interest, r^*, would equal $R_F - IP$. A simple personal finance example can demonstrate the practical distinction between nominal and real rates of interest.

Personal Finance Example 6.1 ▶ Marilyn Carbo has $10 that she can spend on candy costing $0.25 per piece. She could buy 40 pieces of candy ($10.00 ÷ $0.25) today. The nominal rate of interest on a 1-year deposit is currently 7%, and the expected rate of inflation over the coming year is 4%. Instead of buying the 40 pieces of candy today, Marilyn could invest the $10. After one year she would have $10.70 because she would have earned 7% interest—an additional $0.70 (0.07 × $10.00)—on her $10 deposit. During that year, inflation would have increased the cost of the candy by 4%—an additional $0.01 (0.04 × $0.25)—to $0.26 per piece. As a result, at the end of the 1-year period Marilyn would be able to buy about 41.2 pieces of candy ($10.70 ÷ $0.26), or roughly 3% more (41.2 ÷ 40.0 = 1.03). The 3% increase in Marilyn's buying power represents her real rate of return. The nominal rate of return on her investment (7%), is partly eroded by inflation (4%), so her real return during the year is the difference between the nominal rate and the inflation rate (7% − 4% = 3%).

focus on PRACTICE

Bond's Valuation and Interest Rate Risk

in practice The value of bonds, as fixed income security, is negatively related to changes in the nominal interest rate. One component of interest rate under the control of the government is real interest rate, which is determined by the Federal Reserve or the central bank of the respective country. The other component of interest rate is determined by the market prices and measured through the Consumer Price Index (inflation). Over time, the real interest rate does not fluctuate sharply, but inflation usually does, resulting in a higher or lower nominal interest rate.

Saving and Loans Bank (S&LB) is a governmental social bank located in Kuwait with paid-up capital of $8,850 million and more than $12,500 million in outstanding loans. Recently, the S&LB finalized an in-depth plan to securitize the $12,500 million in outstanding loans. Backed by the full faith of the

Kuwaiti government the bank plans to issue bonds against the outstanding loans. The treasury bonds will be free of default risk but not free of inflation or reinvestment risk. Based on a regional market's survey, the maturity will range between 5, 7, and 10 years.

To avoid the negative effect of inflation on the bond value, S&LB plans to index the bonds to inflation or to an equity index. If issued bonds are indexed to inflation, the periodic coupon will be equal to the inflation level plus 150 to 200 basis points. If they are equity indexed, the coupon rate will be equal to the equity index minus 100 to 150 basis points. Another proposed method of indexing these bonds is to adjust their par value to the inflation or equity index. Therefore, the issued bonds will not be viewed as fixed income securities but treated as floating income securities.

To avoid the reinvestment risk, it was planned to issue bonds as deeply discounted bonds with a zero coupon rate. The investors of the treasury bonds will have to hold them until maturity to get the maximum benefits. This, in turn, will reduce the liquidity of the bonds in the secondary market, resulting in lower market value. The idea was to sell each issue to one major institutional investor who could strip the issue by selling securities with different maturities to increase the liquidity of the issues.

▶ *Which method do you think is the best to adjust bond income and interest rate from the issuer and bond holder points of view?*

▶ *Is it better to issue deeply discounted bonds to the public or to sell the issue to a major financial institution, which in turn can strip them?*

deflation
A general trend of falling prices.

The premium for *expected inflation* in Equation 6.3 represents the average rate of *inflation* expected over the life of an investment. It is *not* the rate of inflation experienced over the immediate past, although investors' inflation expectations are undoubtedly influenced by the rate of inflation that has occurred in the recent past. Even so, the inflation premium reflects the expected rate of inflation. The expected inflation premium changes over time in response to many factors, such as changes in monetary and fiscal policies, currency movements, and international political events. For a discussion of the effect of inflation on Kuwaiti bonds, see the nearby *Focus on Practice* box.

Figure 6.2 (see page 226) illustrates the annual movement of the rate of inflation and the risk-free rate of return from 1961 through 2009. During this period the two rates tended to move in a similar fashion. Note that T-bill rates were slightly above the inflation rate most of the time, meaning that T-bills generally offered a small positive real return. Between 1978 and the early 1980s, inflation and interest rates were quite high, peaking at over 13 percent in 1980–1981. Since then, rates have gradually declined. To combat a severe recession, the Federal Reserve pushed interest rates down to almost 0% in 2009, and for the first time in decades, the rate of inflation turned slightly negative (that is, there was slight deflation that year).

FIGURE 6.2

Impact of Inflation
Relationship between annual rate of inflation and 3-month U.S. Treasury bill average annual returns, 1961–2009

[a] Average annual rate of return on 3-month U.S. Treasury bills.
[b] Annual pecentage change in the consumer price index.

Sources: Data from selected *Federal Reserve Bulletins* and *U.S. Department of Labor Bureau of Labor Statistics.*

TERM STRUCTURE OF INTEREST RATES

term structure of interest rates
The relationship between the maturity and rate of return for bonds with similar levels of risk.

yield curve
A graphic depiction of the term structure of interest rates.

The **term structure of interest rates** is the relationship between the maturity and rate of return for bonds with similar levels of risk. A graph of this relationship is called the **yield curve.** A quick glance at the yield curve tells analysts how rates vary between short-, medium-, and long-term bonds, but it may also provide information on where interest rates and the economy in general are headed in the future. Usually, when analysts examine the term structure of interest rates, they focus on Treasury securities because these are generally considered to be free of default risk.

Yield Curves

yield to maturity (YTM)
Compound annual rate of return earned on a debt security purchased on a given day and held to maturity.

A bond's **yield to maturity (YTM)** (discussed later in this chapter) represents the compound annual rate of return that an investor earns on the bond assuming that the bond makes all promised payments and the investor holds the bond to maturity. In a yield curve, the yield to maturity is plotted on the vertical axis and time to maturity is plotted on the horizontal axis. Figure 6.3 shows three yield curves for U.S. Treasury securities: one at May 22, 1981, a second at September 29, 1989, and a third at May 28, 2010.

Observe that both the position and the shape of the yield curves change over time. The yield curve of May 22, 1981, indicates that short-term interest rates at that time were above longer-term rates. For reasons that a glance at the figure makes obvious, this curve is described as *downward-sloping.* Interest rates in May 1981 were also quite high by historical standards, so the overall level of the yield curve is high. Historically, a downward-sloping yield curve, which is often called an **inverted yield curve,** occurs infrequently and is often a sign that the economy is weakening. Most recessions in the United States have been preceded by an inverted yield curve.

inverted yield curve
A *downward-sloping* yield curve indicates that short-term interest rates are generally higher than long-term interest rates.

normal yield curve
An *upward-sloping* yield curve indicates that long-term interest rates are generally higher than short-term interest rates.

Usually, short-term interest rates are lower than long-term interest rates, as they were on May 28, 2010. That is, the **normal yield curve** is *upward-sloping.* Notice that the May 2010 yield curve lies entirely beneath the other two curves

FIGURE 6.3

Treasury Yield Curves
Yield curves for U.S.
Treasury securities: May
22, 1981; September 29,
1989; and May 28, 2010

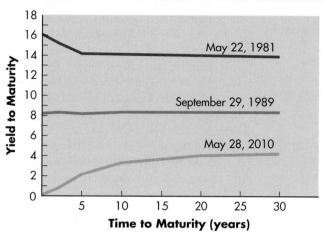

Sources: Data from U.S. Department of the Treasury, Office of Domestic Finance, Office of Debt Management.

flat yield curve
A yield curve that indicates that interest rates do not vary much at different maturities.

shown in Figure 6.3. In other words, interest rates in May 2010 were unusually low, largely because at that time the economy was just beginning to recover from a deep recession and inflation was very low. Sometimes, a **flat yield curve,** similar to that of September 29, 1989, exists. A flat yield curve simply means that rates do not vary much at different maturities.

The shape of the yield curve may affect the firm's financing decisions. A financial manager who faces a downward-sloping yield curve may be tempted to rely more heavily on cheaper, long-term financing. However, a risk in following this strategy is that interest rates may fall in the future, so long-term rates that seem cheap today may be relatively expensive tomorrow. Likewise, when the yield curve is upward-sloping, the manager may feel that it is wise to use cheaper, short-term financing. Relying on short-term financing has its own risks. Firms that borrow on a short-term basis may see their costs rise if interest rates go up. Even more serious is the risk that a firm may not be able to refinance a short-term loan when it comes due. A variety of factors influence the choice of loan maturity, but the shape of the yield curve is something that managers must consider when making decisions about borrowing short-term versus long-term.

In more depth

To read about *Yield Curve Animation,* go to www.myfinancelab.com

 myfinancelab®

Theories of Term Structure

Three theories are frequently cited to explain the general shape of the yield curve: the expectations theory, the liquidity preference theory, and the market segmentation theory.

Expectations Theory   One theory of the term structure of interest rates, the **expectations theory,** suggests that the yield curve reflects investor expectations about future interest rates. According to this theory, when investors expect short-term interest rates to rise in the future (perhaps because investors believe that inflation will rise in the future), today's long-term rates will be higher than current short-term rates, and the yield curve will be upward sloping. The opposite is

expectations theory
The theory that the yield curve reflects investor expectations about future interest rates; an expectation of rising interest rates results in an upward-sloping yield curve, and an expectation of declining rates results in a downward-sloping yield curve.

true when investors expect declining short-term rates—today's short-term rates will be higher than current long-term rates, and the yield curve will be inverted.

To understand the expectations theory, consider this example. Suppose that the yield curve is flat. The rate on a 1-year Treasury note is 4 percent, and so is the rate on a 2-year Treasury note. Now, consider an investor who has money to place into a low-risk investment for 2 years. The investor has two options. First, he could purchase the 2-year Treasury note and receive a total of 8 percent (ignoring compounding) in 2 years. Second, he could invest in the 1-year Treasury earning 4 percent, and then when that security matures, he could reinvest in another 1-year Treasury note. If the investor wants to maximize his expected return, the decision between the first and second options above depends on whether he expects interest rates to rise, fall, or remain unchanged during the next year.

If the investor believes that interest rates will rise, that means next year's return on a 1-year Treasury note will be greater than 4 percent (that is, greater than the 1-year Treasury rate right now). Let's say the investor believes that the interest rate on a 1-year note next year will be 5 percent. If the investor expects rising rates, then his expected return is higher if he follows the second option, buying a 1-year Treasury note now (paying 4 percent) and reinvesting in a new security that pays 5 percent next year. Over 2 years, the investor would expect to earn about 9 percent (ignoring compounding) in interest, compared to just 8 percent earned by holding the 2-year bond.

If the current 1-year rate is 4 percent and investors generally expect that rate to go up to 5 percent next year, what would the 2-year Treasury note rate have to be right now to remain competitive? The answer is 4.5 percent. An investor who buys this security and holds it for 2 years would earn about 9 percent interest (again, ignoring compounding), the same as the expected return from investing in two consecutive 1-year bonds. In other words, *if investors expect interest rates to rise, the 2-year rate today must be higher than the 1-year rate today, and that in turn means that the yield curve must have an upward slope.*

Example 6.2 ▶

Suppose that a 5-year Treasury note currently offers a 3% annual return. Investors believe that interest rates are going to decline, and 5 years from now, they expect the rate on a 5-year Treasury note to be 2.5%. According to the expectations theory, what is the return that a 10-year Treasury note has to offer today? What does this imply about the slope of the yield curve?

Consider an investor who purchases a 5-year note today and plans to reinvest in another 5-year note in the future. Over the 10-year investment horizon, this investor expects to earn about 27.5%, ignoring compounding (that's 3% per year for the first 5 years and 2.5% per year for the next 5 years). To compete with that return, a 10-year bond today could offer 2.75% per year. That is, a bond that pays 2.75% for each of the next 10 years produces the same 27.5% total return that the series of two 5-year notes is expected to produce. Therefore, the 5-year rate today is 3% and the 10-year rate today is 2.75%, and the yield curve is downward sloping.

---

liquidity preference theory Theory suggesting that long-term rates are generally higher than short-term rates (hence, the yield curve is upward sloping) because investors perceive short-term investments to be more liquid and less risky than long-term investments. Borrowers must offer higher rates on long-term bonds to entice investors away from their preferred short-term securities.

Liquidity Preference Theory   Most of the time, yield curves are upward sloping. According to the expectations theory, this means that investors expect interest rates to rise. An alternative explanation for the typical upward slope of the yield curve is the **liquidity preference theory**. This theory holds that, all else being equal, investors generally prefer to buy short-term securities, while issuers prefer to sell long-term securities. For investors, short-term securities are attractive because they are highly liquid and their prices are not particularly volatile.[1] Hence, investors will accept somewhat lower rates on short-term bonds because they are less risky than long-term bonds. Conversely, when firms or governments want to lock in their borrowing costs for a long period of time by selling long-term bonds, those bonds have to offer higher rates to entice investors away from the short-term securities that they prefer. Borrowers are willing to pay somewhat higher rates because long-term debt allows them to eliminate or reduce the risk of not being able to refinance short-term debts when they come due. Borrowing on a long-term basis also reduces uncertainty about future borrowing costs.

market segmentation theory
Theory suggesting that the market for loans is segmented on the basis of maturity and that the supply of and demand for loans within each segment determine its prevailing interest rate; the slope of the yield curve is determined by the general relationship between the prevailing rates in each market segment.

Market Segmentation Theory The **market segmentation theory** suggests that the market for loans is totally segmented on the basis of maturity and that the supply of and demand for loans within each segment determine its prevailing interest rate. In other words, the equilibrium between suppliers and demanders of short-term funds, such as seasonal business loans, would determine prevailing short-term interest rates, and the equilibrium between suppliers and demanders of long-term funds, such as real estate loans, would determine prevailing long-term interest rates. The slope of the yield curve would be determined by the general relationship between the prevailing rates in each market segment. Simply stated, an upward-sloping yield curve indicates greater borrowing demand relative to the supply of funds in the long-term segment of the debt market relative to the short-term segment.

All three term structure theories have merit. From them we can conclude that at any time the slope of the yield curve is affected by (1) interest rate expectations, (2) liquidity preferences, and (3) the comparative equilibrium of supply and demand in the short- and long-term market segments. Upward-sloping yield curves result from expectations of rising interest rates, lender preferences for shorter-maturity loans, and greater supply of short-term loans than of long-term loans relative to demand. The opposite conditions would result in a downward-sloping yield curve. At any time, the interaction of these three forces determines the prevailing slope of the yield curve.

RISK PREMIUMS: ISSUER AND ISSUE CHARACTERISTICS

So far we have considered only risk-free U.S. Treasury securities. We now reintroduce the risk premium and assess it in view of risky non-Treasury issues. Recall Equation 6.1:

$$r_1 = \underbrace{r^* + IP}_{\substack{\text{risk-free} \\ \text{rate, } R_F}} + \underbrace{RP_1}_{\substack{\text{risk} \\ \text{premium}}}$$

In words, the nominal rate of interest for security 1 (r_1) is equal to the risk-free rate, consisting of the real rate of interest (r^*) plus the inflation expectation

---

1. Later in this chapter we demonstrate that debt instruments with longer maturities are more sensitive to changing market interest rates. For a given change in market rates, the price or value of longer-term debts will be more significantly changed (up or down) than the price or value of debts with shorter maturities.

premium (*IP*), plus the risk premium (*RP*$_1$). The *risk premium* varies with specific issuer and issue characteristics.

Example 6.3 ▶

The nominal interest rates on a number of classes of long-term securities in May 2010 were as follows:

Security	Nominal interest rate
U.S. Treasury bonds (average)	3.30%
Corporate bonds (by risk ratings):	
High quality (Aaa–Aa)	3.95
Medium quality (A–Baa)	4.98
Speculative (Ba–C)	8.97

Because the U.S. Treasury bond would represent the risk-free, long-term security, we can calculate the risk premium of the other securities by subtracting the risk-free rate, 3.30%, from each nominal rate (yield):

Security	Risk premium
Corporate bonds (by ratings):	
High quality (Aaa–Aa)	3.95% − 3.30% = 0.65%
Medium quality (A–Baa)	4.98 − 3.30 = 1.68
Speculative (Ba–C)	8.97 − 3.30 = 5.67

These risk premiums reflect differing issuer and issue risks. The lower-rated (speculative) corporate issues have a far higher risk premium than that of the higher-rated corporate issues (high quality and medium quality), and that risk premium is the compensation that investors demand for bearing the higher default risk of lower quality bonds.

The risk premium consists of a number of issuer- and issue-related components, including business risk, financial risk, interest rate risk, liquidity risk, and tax risk, as well as the purely debt-specific risks—default risk, maturity risk, and contractual provision risk, briefly defined in Table 6.1. In general, the highest risk premiums and therefore the highest returns result from securities issued by firms with a high risk of default and from long-term maturities that have unfavorable contractual provisions.

→ REVIEW QUESTIONS

6–1 What is the *real rate of interest*? Differentiate it from the *nominal rate of interest* for the risk-free asset, a 3-month U.S. Treasury bill.

6–2 What is the *term structure of interest rates*, and how is it related to the *yield curve*?

TABLE 6.1	Debt-Specific Issuer- and Issue-Related Risk Premium Components
Component	**Description**
Default risk	The possibility that the issuer of debt will not pay the contractual interest or principal as scheduled. The greater the uncertainty as to the borrower's ability to meet these payments, the greater the risk premium. High bond ratings reflect low default risk, and low bond ratings reflect high default risk.
Maturity risk	The fact that the longer the maturity, the more the value of a security will change in response to a given change in interest rates. If interest rates on otherwise similar-risk securities suddenly rise as a result of a change in the money supply, the prices of long-term bonds will decline by more than the prices of short-term bonds, and vice versa.[a]
Contractual provision risk	Conditions that are often included in a debt agreement or a stock issue. Some of these reduce risk, whereas others may increase risk. For example, a provision allowing a bond issuer to retire its bonds prior to their maturity under favorable terms increases the bond's risk.

[a]A detailed discussion of the effects of interest rates on the price or value of bonds and other fixed-income securities is presented later in this chapter.

6–3 For a given class of similar-risk securities, what does each of the following yield curves reflect about interest rates: (**a**) downward-sloping; (**b**) upward-sloping; and (**c**) flat? What is the "normal" shape of the yield curve?

6–4 Briefly describe the following theories of the general shape of the yield curve: (**a**) expectations theory; (**b**) liquidity preference theory; and (**c**) market segmentation theory.

6–5 List and briefly describe the potential issuer- and issue-related risk components that are embodied in the risk premium. Which are the purely debt-specific risks?

LG 2   LG 3   **6.2 Corporate Bonds**

corporate bond
A long-term debt instrument indicating that a corporation has borrowed a certain amount of money and promises to repay it in the future under clearly defined terms.

A **corporate bond** is a long-term debt instrument indicating that a corporation has borrowed a certain amount of money and promises to repay it in the future under clearly defined terms. Most bonds are issued with maturities of 10 to 30 years and with a par value, or face value, of $1,000. The **coupon interest rate** on a bond represents the percentage of the bond's par value that will be paid annually, typically in two equal semiannual payments, as interest. The bondholders, who are the lenders, are promised the semiannual interest payments and, at maturity, repayment of the principal amount.

LEGAL ASPECTS OF CORPORATE BONDS

Certain legal arrangements are required to protect purchasers of bonds. Bondholders are protected primarily through the indenture and the trustee.

Bond Indenture

A **bond indenture** is a legal document that specifies both the rights of the bondholders and the duties of the issuing corporation. Included in the indenture are descriptions of the amount and timing of all interest and principal payments, various standard and restrictive provisions, and, frequently, sinking-fund requirements and security interest provisions. The borrower commonly must (1) *maintain satisfactory accounting records* in accordance with generally accepted accounting principles (GAAP); (2) periodically *supply audited financial statements;* (3) *pay taxes and other liabilities when due;* and (4) *maintain all facilities in good working order.*

Standard Provisions   The **standard debt provisions** in the bond indenture specify certain record-keeping and general business practices that the bond issuer must follow.

Restrictive Provisions   Bond indentures also normally include certain **restrictive covenants,** which place operating and financial constraints on the borrower. These provisions help protect the bondholder against increases in borrower risk. Without them, the borrower could increase the firm's risk but not have to pay increased interest to compensate for the increased risk.

The most common restrictive covenants do the following:

1. Require a *minimum level of liquidity,* to ensure against loan default.
2. *Prohibit the sale of accounts receivable* to generate cash. Selling receivables could cause a long-run cash shortage if proceeds were used to meet current obligations.
3. Impose *fixed-asset restrictions.* The borrower must maintain a specified level of fixed assets to guarantee its ability to repay the bonds.
4. *Constrain subsequent borrowing.* Additional long-term debt may be prohibited, or additional borrowing may be *subordinated* to the original loan. **Subordination** means that subsequent creditors agree to wait until all claims of the *senior debt* are satisfied.
5. *Limit the firm's annual cash dividend payments* to a specified percentage or amount.

Other restrictive covenants are sometimes included in bond indentures.

The violation of any standard or restrictive provision by the borrower gives the bondholders the right to demand immediate repayment of the debt. Generally, bondholders evaluate any violation to determine whether it jeopardizes the loan. They may then decide to demand immediate repayment, continue the loan, or alter the terms of the bond indenture.

Sinking-Fund Requirements   Another common restrictive provision is a **sinking-fund requirement.** Its objective is to provide for the systematic retirement of bonds prior to their maturity. To carry out this requirement, the corporation makes semiannual or annual payments that are used to retire bonds by purchasing them in the marketplace.

---

coupon interest rate
The percentage of a bond's par value that will be paid annually, typically in two equal semiannual payments, as interest.

bond indenture
A legal document that specifies both the rights of the bondholders and the duties of the issuing corporation.

standard debt provisions
Provisions in a *bond indenture* specifying certain record-keeping and general business practices that the bond issuer must follow; normally, they do not place a burden on a financially sound business.

restrictive covenants
Provisions in a *bond indenture* that place operating and financial constraints on the borrower.

subordination
In a bond indenture, the stipulation that subsequent creditors agree to wait until all claims of the *senior debt* are satisfied.

sinking-fund requirement
A restrictive provision often included in a bond indenture, providing for the systematic retirement of bonds prior to their maturity.

Security Interest The bond indenture identifies any collateral pledged against the bond and specifies how it is to be maintained. The protection of bond collateral is crucial to guarantee the safety of a bond issue.

Trustee

trustee
A paid individual, corporation, or commercial bank trust department that acts as the third party to a *bond indenture* and can take specified actions on behalf of the bondholders if the terms of the indenture are violated.

A **trustee** is a third party to a *bond indenture.* The trustee can be an individual, a corporation, or (most often) a commercial bank trust department. The trustee is paid to act as a "watchdog" on behalf of the bondholders and can take specified actions on behalf of the bondholders if the terms of the indenture are violated.

COST OF BONDS TO THE ISSUER

The cost of bond financing is generally greater than the issuer would have to pay for short-term borrowing. The major factors that affect the cost, which is the rate of interest paid by the bond issuer, are the bond's maturity, the size of the offering, the issuer's risk, and the basic cost of money.

Impact of Bond Maturity

Generally, as we noted earlier, long-term debt pays higher interest rates than short-term debt. In a practical sense, the longer the maturity of a bond, the less accuracy there is in predicting future interest rates, and therefore the greater the bondholders' risk of giving up an opportunity to lend money at a higher rate. In addition, the longer the term, the greater the chance that the issuer might default.

Impact of Offering Size

The size of the bond offering also affects the interest cost of borrowing but in an inverse manner: Bond flotation and administration costs per dollar borrowed are likely to decrease with increasing offering size. On the other hand, the risk to the bondholders may increase, because larger offerings result in greater risk of default.

Impact of Issuer's Risk

The greater the issuer's *default risk,* the higher the interest rate. Some of this risk can be reduced through inclusion of appropriate restrictive provisions in the bond indenture. Clearly, bondholders must be compensated with higher returns for taking greater risk. Frequently, bond buyers rely on bond ratings (discussed later) to determine the issuer's overall risk.

Impact of the Cost of Money

The cost of money in the capital market is the basis for determining a bond's coupon interest rate. Generally, the rate on U.S. Treasury securities of equal maturity is used as the lowest-risk cost of money. To that basic rate is added a *risk premium* (as described earlier in this chapter) that reflects the factors mentioned above (maturity, offering size, and issuer's risk).

GENERAL FEATURES OF A BOND ISSUE

Three features sometimes included in a corporate bond issue are a conversion feature, a call feature, and stock purchase warrants. These features provide the issuer or the purchaser with certain opportunities for replacing or retiring the bond or supplementing it with some type of equity issue.

conversion feature
A feature of *convertible bonds* that allows bondholders to change each bond into a stated number of shares of common stock.

call feature
A feature included in nearly all corporate bond issues that gives the issuer the opportunity to repurchase bonds at a stated *call price* prior to maturity.

call price
The stated price at which a bond may be repurchased, by use of a *call feature,* prior to maturity.

call premium
The amount by which a bond's *call price* exceeds its par value.

stock purchase warrants
Instruments that give their holders the right to purchase a certain number of shares of the issuer's common stock at a specified price over a certain period of time.

current yield
A measure of a bond's cash return for the year; calculated by dividing the bond's annual interest payment by its current price.

Convertible bonds offer a **conversion feature** that allows bondholders to change each bond into a stated number of shares of common stock. Bondholders convert their bonds into stock only when the market price of the stock is such that conversion will provide a profit for the bondholder. Inclusion of the conversion feature by the issuer lowers the interest cost and provides for automatic conversion of the bonds to stock if future stock prices appreciate noticeably.

The **call feature** is included in nearly all corporate bond issues. It gives the issuer the opportunity to repurchase bonds prior to maturity. The **call price** is the stated price at which bonds may be repurchased prior to maturity. Sometimes the call feature can be exercised only during a certain period. As a rule, the call price exceeds the par value of a bond by an amount equal to 1 year's interest. For example, a $1,000 bond with a 10 percent coupon interest rate would be callable for around $1,100 [$1,000 + (10% × $1,000)]. The amount by which the call price exceeds the bond's par value is commonly referred to as the **call premium.** This premium compensates bondholders for having the bond called away from them; to the issuer, it is the cost of calling the bonds.

The call feature enables an issuer to call an outstanding bond when interest rates fall and issue a new bond at a lower interest rate. When interest rates rise, the call privilege will not be exercised, except possibly to meet *sinking-fund requirements.* Of course, to sell a callable bond in the first place, the issuer must pay a higher interest rate than on noncallable bonds of equal risk, to compensate bondholders for the risk of having the bonds called away from them.

Bonds occasionally have stock purchase warrants attached as "sweeteners" to make them more attractive to prospective buyers. **Stock purchase warrants** are instruments that give their holders the right to purchase a certain number of shares of the issuer's common stock at a specified price over a certain period of time. Their inclusion typically enables the issuer to pay a slightly lower coupon interest rate than would otherwise be required.

BOND YIELDS

The *yield,* or rate of return, on a bond is frequently used to assess a bond's performance over a given period of time, typically 1 year. Because there are a number of ways to measure a bond's yield, it is important to understand popular yield measures. The three most widely cited bond yields are (1) *current yield,* (2) *yield to maturity (YTM),* and (3) *yield to call (YTC).* Each of these yields provides a unique measure of the return on a bond.

The simplest yield measure is the **current yield,** the annual interest payment divided by the current price. For example, a $1,000 par value bond with an 8 percent coupon interest rate that currently sells for $970 would have a current yield of 8.25% [(0.08 × $1,000) ÷ $970]. This measure indicates the cash return for the year from the bond. However, because current yield ignores any change in bond value, it does not measure the total return. As we'll see later in this chapter, both the yield to maturity and the yield to call measure the total return.

BOND PRICES

Because most corporate bonds are purchased and held by institutional investors, such as banks, insurance companies, and mutual funds, rather than individual investors, bond trading and price data are not readily available to individuals. Table 6.2 includes some assumed current data on the bonds of five companies, noted A through E. Looking at the data for Company C's bond, which is highlighted

TABLE 6.2	Data on Selected Bonds			
Company	**Coupon**	**Maturity**	**Price**	**Yield (YTM)**
Company A	6.125%	Nov. 15, 2011	105.336	4.788%
Company B	6.000	Oct. 31, 2036	94.007	6.454
Company C	7.200	Jan. 15, 2014	103.143	6.606
Company D	5.150	Jan. 15, 2017	95.140	5.814
Company E	5.850	Jan. 14, 2012	100.876	5.631

in the table, we see that the bond has a coupon interest rate of 7.200 percent and a maturity date of January 15, 2017. These data identify a specific bond issued by Company C. (The company could have more than a single bond issue outstanding.) The price represents the final price at which the bond traded on the current day.

Although most corporate bonds are issued with a *par*, or *face*, *value* of $1,000, *all bonds are quoted as a percentage of par.* A $1,000-par-value bond quoted at 94.007 is priced at $940.07 (94.007% × $1,000). Corporate bonds are quoted in dollars and cents. Thus, Company C's price of 103.143 for the day was $1,031.43—that is, 103.143% × $1,000.

The final column of Table 6.2 represents the bond's *yield to maturity (YTM)*, which is the compound annual rate of return that would be earned on the bond if it were purchased and held to maturity. (YTM is discussed in detail later in this chapter.)

BOND RATINGS

Independent agencies such as Moody's, Fitch, and Standard & Poor's assess the riskiness of publicly traded bond issues. These agencies derive their ratings by using financial ratio and cash flow analyses to assess the likely payment of bond interest and principal. Table 6.3 summarizes these ratings. For

TABLE 6.3	Moody's and Standard & Poor's Bond Ratings[a]			
Moody's	**Interpretation**	**Standard & Poor's**	**Interpretation**	
Aaa	Prime quality	AAA	Investment grade	
Aa	High grade	AA		
A	Upper medium grade	A		
Baa	Medium grade	BBB		
Ba	Lower medium grade	BB	Speculative	
	or speculative	B		
B	Speculative			
Caa	From very speculative	CCC		
Ca	to near or in default	CC		
C	Lowest grade	C	Income bond	
		D	In default	

[a]Some ratings may be modified to show relative standing within a major rating category; for example, Moody's uses numerical modifiers (1, 2, 3), whereas Standard & Poor's uses plus (+) and minus (−) signs.

Sources: Moody's Investors Service, Inc., and Standard & Poor's Corporation.

focus on ETHICS

Can We Trust the Bond Raters?

in practice   Moody's Investors Service, Standard & Poor's, and Fitch Ratings play a crucial role in the financial markets. These credit-rating agencies evaluate and attach ratings to credit instruments (for example, bonds). Historically, bonds that received higher ratings were almost always repaid, while lower-rated, more speculative "junk" bonds experienced much higher default rates. The agencies' ratings have a direct impact on firms' cost of raising external capital and investors' appraisals of fixed-income investments.

Recently, the credit-rating agencies have been criticized for their role in the subprime crisis. The agencies attached ratings to complex securities that did not reflect the true risk of the underlying investments. For example, securities backed by mortgages issued to borrowers with bad credit and no documented income often received investment-grade ratings that implied almost zero probability of default. However, when home prices began to decline in 2006, securities backed by risky mortgages did default, including many that had been rated investment grade.

It is not entirely clear why the rating agencies assigned such high ratings to these securities. Did the agencies believe that complex financial engineering could create investment-grade securities out of risky mortgage loans? Did the agencies understand the securities they were rating? Were they unduly influenced by the security issuers, who also happened to pay for the ratings? Apparently, some within the rating agencies were suspicious. In a December, 2006 e-mail exchange between colleagues at Standard & Poor's, one individual proclaimed, "Let's hope we are all wealthy and retired by the time this house of cards falters."[a]

▶ *What ethical issues may arise because the companies that issue bonds pay the rating agencies to rate their bonds?*

[a]http://oversight.house.gov/images/stories/Hearings/Committee_on_Oversight/E-mail_from_Belinda_Ghetti_to_Nicole_Billick_et_al._December_16_2006.pdf

discussion of ethical issues related to the bond-rating agencies, see the *Focus on Ethics* box.

Normally an inverse relationship exists between the quality of a bond and the rate of return that it must provide bondholders: High-quality (high-rated) bonds provide lower returns than lower-quality (low-rated) bonds. This reflects the lender's risk–return trade-off. When considering bond financing, the financial manager must be concerned with the expected ratings of the bond issue, because these ratings affect salability and cost.

COMMON TYPES OF BONDS

debentures
subordinated debentures
income bonds
mortgage bonds
collateral trust bonds
equipment trust certificates
See Table 6.4.

zero- (or low-) coupon bonds
junk bonds
floating-rate bonds
extendible notes
putable bonds
See Table 6.5 on page 238.

Bonds can be classified in a variety of ways. Here we break them into traditional bonds (the basic types that have been around for years) and contemporary bonds (newer, more innovative types). The traditional types of bonds are summarized in terms of their key characteristics and priority of lender's claim in Table 6.4. Note that the first three types—**debentures, subordinated debentures,** and **income bonds**—are unsecured, whereas the last three—**mortgage bonds, collateral trust bonds,** and **equipment trust certificates**—are secured.

Table 6.5 (see page 238) describes the key characteristics of five contemporary types of bonds: **zero- (or low-) coupon bonds, junk bonds, floating-rate bonds, extendible notes,** and **putable bonds.** These bonds can be either unsecured or secured. Changing capital market conditions and investor preferences have spurred further innovations in bond financing in recent years and will probably continue to do so.

TABLE 6.4	Characteristics and Priority of Lender's Claim of Traditional Types of Bonds	
Bond type	Characteristics	Priority of lender's claim
Unsecured bonds		
Debentures	Unsecured bonds that only creditworthy firms can issue. Convertible bonds are normally debentures.	Claims are the same as those of any general creditor. May have other unsecured bonds subordinated to them.
Subordinated debentures	Claims are not satisfied until those of the creditors holding certain (senior) debts have been fully satisfied.	Claim is that of a general creditor but not as good as a senior debt claim.
Income bonds	Payment of interest is required only when earnings are available. Commonly issued in reorganization of a failing firm.	Claim is that of a general creditor. Are not in default when interest payments are missed, because they are contingent only on earnings being available.
Secured Bonds		
Mortgage bonds	Secured by real estate or buildings.	Claim is on proceeds from sale of mortgaged assets; if not fully satisfied, the lender becomes a general creditor. The *first-mortgage* claim must be fully satisfied before distribution of proceeds to *second-mortgage* holders, and so on. A number of mortgages can be issued against the same collateral.
Collateral trust bonds	Secured by stock and (or) bonds that are owned by the issuer. Collateral value is generally 25% to 35% greater than bond value.	Claim is on proceeds from stock and (or) bond collateral; if not fully satisfied, the lender becomes a general creditor.
Equipment trust certificates	Used to finance "rolling stock"—airplanes, trucks, boats, railroad cars. A trustee buys the asset with funds raised through the sale of trust certificates and then leases it to the firm; after making the final scheduled lease payment, the firm receives title to the asset. A type of leasing.	Claim is on proceeds from the sale of the asset; if proceeds do not satisfy outstanding debt, trust certificate lenders become general creditors.

INTERNATIONAL BOND ISSUES

Eurobond
A bond issued by an international borrower and sold to investors in countries with currencies other than the currency in which the bond is denominated.

Companies and governments borrow internationally by issuing bonds in two principal financial markets: the Eurobond market and the foreign bond market. Both give borrowers the opportunity to obtain large amounts of long-term debt financing quickly, in the currency of their choice and with flexible repayment terms.

A **Eurobond** is issued by an international borrower and sold to investors in countries with currencies other than the currency in which the bond is denominated. An example is a dollar-denominated bond issued by a U.S. corporation and sold to Belgian investors. From the founding of the Eurobond market in the 1960s until the mid-1980s, "blue chip" U.S. corporations were the largest single class of Eurobond issuers. Some of these companies were able to borrow in this market at interest rates below those the U.S. government paid on Treasury bonds. As the market matured, issuers became able to choose the currency in which they borrowed, and European and Japanese borrowers rose to prominence. In more recent years, the Eurobond market has become much more balanced in terms of the mix of borrowers, total issue volume, and currency of denomination.

TABLE 6.5	Characteristics of Contemporary Types of Bonds
Bond type	**Characteristics**[a]
Zero- (or low-) coupon bonds	Issued with no (zero) or a very low coupon (stated interest) rate and sold at a large discount from par. A significant portion (or all) of the investor's return comes from gain in value (that is, par value minus purchase price). Generally callable at par value. Because the issuer can annually deduct the current year's interest accrual without having to pay the interest until the bond matures (or is called), its cash flow each year is increased by the amount of the tax shield provided by the interest deduction.
Junk bonds	Debt rated Ba or lower by Moody's or BB or lower by Standard & Poor's. Commonly used by rapidly growing firms to obtain growth capital, most often as a way to finance mergers and takeovers. High-risk bonds with high yields—often yielding 2% to 3% more than the best-quality corporate debt.
Floating-rate bonds	Stated interest rate is adjusted periodically within stated limits in response to changes in specified money market or capital market rates. Popular when future inflation and interest rates are uncertain. Tend to sell at close to par because of the automatic adjustment to changing market conditions. Some issues provide for annual redemption at par at the option of the bondholder.
Extendible notes	Short maturities, typically 1 to 5 years, that can be renewed for a similar period at the option of holders. Similar to a floating-rate bond. An issue might be a series of 3-year renewable notes over a period of 15 years; every 3 years, the notes could be extended for another 3 years, at a new rate competitive with market interest rates at the time of renewal.
Putable bonds	Bonds that can be redeemed at par (typically, $1,000) at the option of their holder either at specific dates after the date of issue and every 1 to 5 years thereafter or when and if the firm takes specified actions, such as being acquired, acquiring another company, or issuing a large amount of additional debt. In return for its conferring the right to "put the bond" at specified times or when the firm takes certain actions, the bond's yield is lower than that of a nonputable bond.

[a]The claims of lenders (that is, bondholders) against issuers of each of these types of bonds vary, depending on the bonds' other features. Each of these bonds can be unsecured or secured.

foreign bond
A bond that is issued by a foreign corporation or government and is denominated in the investor's home currency and sold in the investor's home market.

In contrast, a **foreign bond** is issued by a foreign corporation or government and is denominated in the investor's home currency and sold in the investor's home market. A Swiss-franc–denominated bond issued in Switzerland by a U.S. company is an example of a foreign bond. The three largest foreign-bond markets are Japan, Switzerland, and the United States.

→ **REVIEW QUESTIONS**

6–6 What are typical maturities, denominations, and interest payments of a corporate bond? What mechanisms protect bondholders?

6–7 Differentiate between *standard debt provisions* and *restrictive covenants* included in a bond indenture. What are the consequences if a bond issuer violates any of these covenants?

6–8 How is the cost of bond financing typically related to the cost of short-term borrowing? In addition to a bond's maturity, what other major factors affect its cost to the issuer?

6–9 What is a *conversion feature*? A *call feature*? What are *stock purchase warrants*?

6–10 What is the *current yield* for a bond? How are bond prices quoted? How are bonds rated, and why?

6–11 Compare the basic characteristics of *Eurobonds* and *foreign bonds*.

LG 4   6.3 Valuation Fundamentals

valuation
The process that links risk and return to determine the worth of an asset.

Valuation is the process that links risk and return to determine the worth of an asset. It is a relatively simple process that can be applied to *expected* streams of benefits from bonds, stocks, income properties, oil wells, and so on. To determine an asset's worth at a given point in time, a financial manager uses the time-value-of-money techniques presented in Chapter 5 and the concepts of risk and return that we will develop in Chapter 8.

KEY INPUTS

There are three key inputs to the valuation process: (1) cash flows (returns), (2) timing, and (3) a measure of risk, which determines the required return. Each is described below.

Cash Flows (Returns)

The value of any asset depends on the cash flow(s) it is *expected* to provide over the ownership period. To have value, an asset does not have to provide an annual cash flow; it can provide an intermittent cash flow or even a single cash flow over the period.

Personal Finance Example 6.4 ▶ Celia Sargent wishes to estimate the value of three assets she is considering investing in: common stock in Michaels Enterprises, an interest in an oil well, and an original painting by a well-known artist. Her cash flow estimates for each are as follows:

Stock in Michaels Enterprises *Expect* to receive cash dividends of $300 per year indefinitely.

Oil well *Expect* to receive cash flow of $2,000 at the end of year 1, $4,000 at the end of year 2, and $10,000 at the end of year 4, when the well is to be sold.

Original painting *Expect* to be able to sell the painting in 5 years for $85,000.

With these cash flow estimates, Celia has taken the first step toward placing a value on each of the assets.

Timing

In addition to making cash flow estimates, we must know the timing of the cash flows.[2] For example, Celia expects the cash flows of $2,000, $4,000, and $10,000 for the oil well to occur at the ends of years 1, 2, and 4, respectively. The combination of the cash flow and its timing fully defines the return expected from the asset.

---

2. Although cash flows can occur at any time during a year, for computational convenience as well as custom, we will assume they occur at the *end of the year* unless otherwise noted.

Risk and Required Return

The level of risk associated with a given cash flow can significantly affect its value. In general, the greater the risk of (or the less certain) a cash flow, the lower its value. Greater risk can be incorporated into a valuation analysis by using a higher required return or discount rate. The higher the risk, the greater the required return, and the lower the risk, the less the required return.

Personal Finance Example 6.5 ▶ Let's return to Celia Sargent's task of placing a value on the original painting and consider two scenarios.

Scenario 1—Certainty A major art gallery has contracted to buy the painting for $85,000 at the end of 5 years. Because this is considered a certain situation, Celia views this asset as "money in the bank." She thus would use the prevailing risk-free rate of 3% as the required return when calculating the value of the painting.

Scenario 2—High risk The values of original paintings by this artist have fluctuated widely over the past 10 years. Although Celia expects to be able to sell the painting for $85,000, she realizes that its sale price in 5 years could range between $30,000 and $140,000. Because of the high uncertainty surrounding the painting's value, Celia believes that a 15% required return is appropriate.

These two estimates of the appropriate required return illustrate how this rate captures risk. The often subjective nature of such estimates is also evident.

BASIC VALUATION MODEL

Simply stated, the value of any asset is *the present value of all future cash flows it is expected to provide over the relevant time period.* The time period can be any length, even infinity. The value of an asset is therefore determined by discounting the expected cash flows back to their present value, using the required return commensurate with the asset's risk as the appropriate discount rate. Using the present value techniques explained in Chapter 5, we can express the value of any asset at time zero, V_0, as

$$V_0 = \frac{CF_1}{(1 + r)^1} + \frac{CF_2}{(1 + r)^2} + \cdots + \frac{CF_n}{(1 + r)^n} \tag{6.4}$$

where

$$V_0 = \text{value of the asset at time zero}$$
$$CF_t = \text{cash flow } expected \text{ at the end of year } t$$
$$r = \text{appropriate required return (discount rate)}$$
$$n = \text{relevant time period}$$

We can use Equation 6.4 to determine the value of any asset.

Personal Finance Example 6.6 ▶ Celia Sargent uses Equation 6.4 to calculate the value of each asset. She values Michaels Enterprises stock using Equation 5.14 on page 178, which says that the present value of a perpetuity equals the annual payment divided by the required return. In the case of Michaels stock, the annual cash flow is $300, and Celia decides that a 12% discount rate is appropriate for this investment. Therefore, her estimate of the value of Michaels Enterprises stock is

$$\$300 \div 0.12 = \$2,500$$

Next, Celia values the oil well investment, which she believes is the most risky of the three investments. Using a 20% required return, Celia estimates the oil well's value to be

$$\frac{\$2,000}{(1 + 0.20)^1} + \frac{\$4,000}{(1 + 0.20)^2} + \frac{\$10,000}{(1 + 0.20)^4} = \$9,266.98$$

Finally, Celia estimates the value of the painting by discounting the expected $85,000 lump sum payment in 5 years at 15%:

$$\$85,000 \div (1 + 0.15)^5 = \$42,260.02$$

Note that, regardless of the pattern of the expected cash flow from an asset, the basic valuation equation can be used to determine its value.

→ **REVIEW QUESTIONS**

6–12 Why is it important for financial managers to understand the valuation process?

6–13 What are the three key inputs to the valuation process?

6–14 Does the valuation process apply only to assets that provide an annual cash flow? Explain.

6–15 Define and specify the general equation for the value of any asset, V_0.

LG 5 LG 6 ## 6.4 Bond Valuation

The basic valuation equation can be customized for use in valuing specific securities: bonds, common stock, and preferred stock. We describe bond valuation in this chapter, and valuation of common stock and preferred stock in Chapter 7.

BOND FUNDAMENTALS

As noted earlier in this chapter, *bonds* are long-term debt instruments used by business and government to raise large sums of money, typically from a diverse group of lenders. Most corporate bonds pay interest *semiannually* (every 6 months) at a stated *coupon interest rate*, have an initial *maturity* of 10 to 30 years, and have a *par value*, or *face value*, of $1,000 that must be repaid at maturity.

Example 6.7 ▶ Mills Company, a large defense contractor, on January 1, 2013, issued a 10% coupon interest rate, 10-year bond with a $1,000 par value that pays interest annually. Investors who buy this bond receive the contractual right to two cash flows: (1) $100 annual interest (10% coupon interest rate × $1,000 par value) distributed at the end of each year and (2) the $1,000 par value at the end of the tenth year.

We will use data for Mills's bond issue to look at basic bond valuation.

BASIC BOND VALUATION

The value of a bond is the present value of the payments its issuer is contractually obligated to make, from the current time until it matures. The basic model for the value, B_0, of a bond is given by Equation 6.5:

$$B_0 = I \times \left[\sum_{t=1}^{n} \frac{1}{(1 + r_d)^t} \right] + M \times \left[\frac{1}{(1 + r_d)^n} \right] \qquad (6.5)$$

where

$$
\begin{aligned}
B_0 &= \text{value of the bond at time zero} \\
I &= \textit{annual} \text{ interest paid in dollars} \\
n &= \text{number of years to maturity} \\
M &= \text{par value in dollars} \\
r_d &= \text{required return on the bond}
\end{aligned}
$$

We can calculate bond value by using Equation 6.5 and a financial calculator or by using a spreadsheet.

Personal Finance Example 6.8 ▶ Tim Sanchez wishes to determine the current value of the Mills Company bond. *Assuming that interest on the Mills Company bond issue is paid annually* and that the required return is equal to the bond's coupon interest rate, $I = \$100$, $r_d = 10\%$, $M = \$1,000$, and $n = 10$ years.

The computations involved in finding the bond value are depicted graphically on the following time line.

Time line for bond valuation (Mills Company's 10% coupon interest rate, 10-year maturity, $1,000 par, January 1, 2013, issue date, paying annual interest, and required return of 10%)

Calculator Use   Using the Mills Company's inputs shown at the left, you should find the bond value to be exactly $1,000. Note that *the calculated bond value is equal to its par value; this will always be the case when the required return is equal to the coupon interest rate.*[3]

Spreadsheet Use   The value of the Mills Company bond also can be calculated as shown in the following Excel spreadsheet.

	A	B
1	BOND VALUE, ANNUAL INTEREST, REQUIRED RETURN = COUPON INTEREST RATE	
2	Annual interest payment	$100
3	Coupon interest rate	10%
4	Number of years to maturity	10
5	Par value	$1,000
6	Bond value	$1,000.00
	Entry in Cell B6 is	
	=PV(B3,B4,B2,B5,0)	
	Note that Excel will return a negative $1000	
	as the price that must be paid to acquire this bond.	

BOND VALUE BEHAVIOR

In practice, the value of a bond in the marketplace is rarely equal to its par value. In the bond data (see Table 6.2 on page 235), you can see that the prices of bonds often differ from their par values of 100 (100 percent of par, or $1,000). Some bonds are valued below par (current price below 100), and others are valued above par (current price above 100). A variety of forces in the economy, as well as the passage of time, tend to affect value. Although these external forces are in no way controlled by bond issuers or investors, it is useful to understand the impact that required return and time to maturity have on bond value.

Required Returns and Bond Values

Whenever the required return on a bond differs from the bond's coupon interest rate, the bond's value will differ from its par value. The required return is likely to differ from the coupon interest rate because either (1) economic conditions have changed, causing a shift in the basic cost of long-term funds; or (2) the firm's risk has changed. Increases in the basic cost of long-term funds or in risk will raise the required return; decreases in the cost of funds or in risk will lower the required return.

---

3. Note that because bonds pay interest in arrears, the prices at which they are quoted and traded reflect their value *plus* any accrued interest. For example, a $1,000 par value, 10% coupon bond paying interest semiannually and having a calculated value of $900 would pay interest of $50 at the end of each 6-month period. If it is now 3 months since the beginning of the interest period, three-sixths of the $50 interest, or $25 (that is, 3/6 × $50), would be accrued. The bond would therefore be quoted at $925—its $900 value plus the $25 in accrued interest. For convenience, *throughout this book, bond values will always be assumed to be calculated at the beginning of the interest period*, thereby avoiding the need to consider accrued interest.

discount
The amount by which a bond sells at a value that is less than its par value.

premium
The amount by which a bond sells at a value that is greater than its par value.

Regardless of the exact cause, what is important is the relationship between the required return and the coupon interest rate: When the required return is greater than the coupon interest rate, the bond value, B_0, will be less than its par value, M. In this case, the bond is said to sell at a **discount**, which will equal $M - B_0$. When the required return falls below the coupon interest rate, the bond value will be greater than par. In this situation, the bond is said to sell at a **premium**, which will equal $B_0 - M$.

Example 6.9 ▶

The preceding example showed that when the required return equaled the coupon interest rate, the bond's value equaled its $1,000 par value. If for the same bond the required return were to rise to 12% or fall to 8%, its value in each case could be found using Equation 6.5 or as follows.

Calculator Use   Using the inputs shown at the left for the two different required returns, you will find the value of the bond to be below or above par. At a 12% required return, the bond would sell at a *discount* of $113.00 ($1,000 par value − $887.00 value). At the 8% required return, the bond would sell for a *premium* of $134.20 ($1,134.20 value − $1,000 par value). The results of these calculations for Mills Company's bond values are summarized in Table 6.6 and graphically depicted in Figure 6.4. The inverse relationship between bond value and required return is clearly shown in the figure.

Spreadsheet Use   The values for the Mills Company bond at required returns of 12% and 8% also can be calculated as shown in the following Excel spreadsheet. Once this spreadsheet has been configured you can compare bond values for any two required returns by simply changing the input values.

	A	B	C
1	BOND VALUE, ANNUAL INTEREST, REQUIRED RETURN NOT EQUAL TO COUPON INTEREST RATE		
2	Annual interest payment	$100	$100
3	Coupon interest rate	10%	10%
4	Annual required return	12%	8%
5	Number of years to maturity	10	10
6	Par value	$1,000	$1,000
7	Bond value	$887.00	$1,134.20

Entry in Cell B7 is =PV(B4,B5,B2,B6,0)
Note that the bond trades at a discount (i.e., below par) because the bond's coupon rate is below investors' required return.

Entry in Cell C7 is =PV(C4,C5,C2,C6,0)
Note that the bond trades at a premium because the bond's coupon rate is above investors' required return.

TABLE 6.6	Bond Values for Various Required Returns (Mills Company's 10% Coupon Interest Rate, 10-Year Maturity, $1,000 Par, January 1, 2013, Issue Date, Paying Annual Interest)		
Required return, r_d	Bond value, B_0		Status
12%	$ 887.00		Discount
10	1,000.00		Par value
8	1,134.20		Premium

FIGURE 6.4

Bond Values and Required Returns
Bond values and required returns (Mills Company's 10% coupon interest rate, 10-year maturity, $1,000 par, January 1, 2013, issue date, paying annual interest)

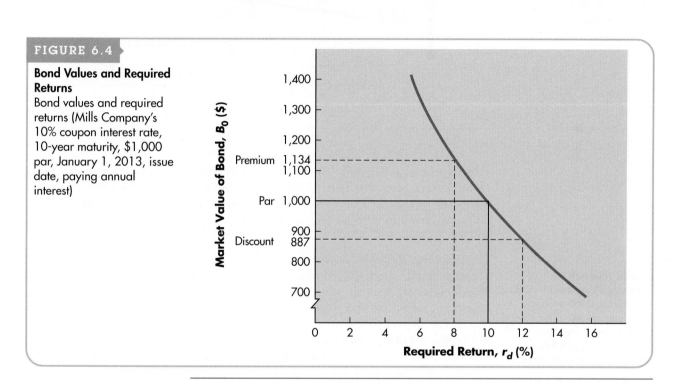

Time to Maturity and Bond Values

Whenever the required return is different from the coupon interest rate, the amount of time to maturity affects bond value. An additional factor is whether required returns are constant or change over the life of the bond.

Constant Required Returns When the required return is different from the coupon interest rate and is *constant until maturity,* the value of the bond will approach its par value as the passage of time moves the bond's value closer to maturity. (Of course, when the required return *equals* the coupon interest rate, the bond's value will remain at par until it matures.)

Example 6.10 ▶ Figure 6.5 depicts the behavior of the bond values calculated earlier and presented in Table 6.6 for Mills Company's 10% coupon interest rate bond paying annual interest and having 10 years to maturity. Each of the three required

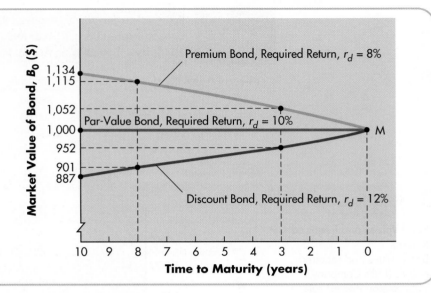

FIGURE 6.5

Time to Maturity and Bond Values
Relationship among time to maturity, required returns, and bond values (Mills Company's 10% coupon interest rate, 10-year maturity, $1,000 par, January 1, 2013, issue date, paying annual interest)

returns—12%, 10%, and 8%—is assumed to remain constant over the 10 years to the bond's maturity. The bond's value at both 12% and 8% approaches and ultimately equals the bond's $1,000 par value at its maturity, as the discount (at 12%) or premium (at 8%) declines with the passage of time.

Changing Required Returns The chance that interest rates will change and thereby change the required return and bond value is called **interest rate risk.**[4] Bondholders are typically more concerned with rising interest rates because a rise in interest rates, and therefore in the required return, causes a decrease in bond value. The shorter the amount of time until a bond's maturity, the less responsive is its market value to a given change in the required return. In other words, *short maturities have less interest rate risk than long maturities when all other features (coupon interest rate, par value, and interest payment frequency) are the same.* This is because of the mathematics of time value; the present values of short-term cash flows change far less than the present values of longer-term cash flows in response to a given change in the discount rate (required return).

interest rate risk
The chance that interest rates will change and thereby change the required return and bond value. Rising rates, which result in decreasing bond values, are of greatest concern.

Example 6.11 ▶

The effect of changing required returns on bonds with differing maturities can be illustrated by using Mills Company's bond and Figure 6.5. If the required return rises from 10% to 12% when the bond has 8 years to maturity (see the dashed line at 8 years), the bond's value decreases from $1,000 to $901—a 9.9% decrease. If the same change in required return had occurred with only 3 years to

---

4. A more robust measure of a bond's response to interest rate changes is *duration*. Duration measures the sensitivity of a bond's prices to changing interest rates. It incorporates both the interest rate (coupon rate) and the time to maturity into a single statistic. Duration is simply a weighted average of the maturity of the present values of all the contractual cash flows yet to be paid by the bond. Duration is stated in years, so a bond with a 5-year duration will decrease in value by 5 percent if interest rates rise by 1 percent or will increase in value by 5 percent if interest rates fall by 1 percent.

maturity (see the dashed line at 3 years), the bond's value would have dropped to just $952—only a 4.8% decrease. Similar types of responses can be seen for the change in bond value associated with decreases in required returns. The shorter the time to maturity, the less the impact on bond value caused by a given change in the required return.

YIELD TO MATURITY (YTM)

When investors evaluate bonds, they commonly consider yield to maturity (YTM). This is the compound annual rate of return earned on a debt security purchased on a given day and held to maturity. (The measure assumes, of course, that the issuer makes all scheduled interest and principal payments as promised.)[5] The yield to maturity on a bond with a current price equal to its par value (that is, $B_0 = M$) will always equal the coupon interest rate. When the bond value differs from par, the yield to maturity will differ from the coupon interest rate.

Assuming that interest is paid annually, the yield to maturity on a bond can be found by solving Equation 6.5 for r_d. In other words, the current value, the annual interest, the par value, and the number of years to maturity are known, and the required return must be found. The required return is the bond's yield to maturity. The YTM can be found by using a financial calculator, by using an Excel spreadsheet, or by trial and error. The calculator provides accurate YTM values with minimum effort.

Personal Finance Example 6.12 ▶ Earl Washington wishes to find the YTM on Mills Company's bond. The bond currently sells for $1,080, has a 10% coupon interest rate and $1,000 par value, pays interest annually, and has 10 years to maturity.

Input	Function
10	N
−1080	PV
100	PMT
1000	FV
	CPT
	I

Solution
8.766

Calculator Use Most calculators require *either* the present value (B_0 in this case) or the future values (I and M in this case) to be input as negative numbers to calculate yield to maturity. That approach is employed here. Using the inputs shown at the left, you should find the YTM to be 8.766%.

Spreadsheet Use The yield to maturity of Mills Company's bond also can be calculated as shown in the following Excel spreadsheet. First, enter all the bond's cash flows. Notice that you begin with the bond's price as an outflow (a negative number). In other words, an investor has to pay the price up front to receive the cash flows over the next 10 years. Next, use Excel's *internal rate of return* function. This function calculates the discount rate that makes the present value of a series of cash flows equal to zero. In this case, when the present value of all cash flows is zero, the present value of the inflows (interest and principal) equals the present value of the outflows (the bond's initial price). In other words, the internal rate of return function is giving us the bond's YTM, the discount rate that equates the bond's price to the present value of its cash flows.

---

5. Many bonds have a *call feature*, which means they may not reach maturity if the issuer, after a specified time period, calls them back. Because the call feature typically cannot be exercised until a specific future date, investors often calculate the *yield to call (YTC)*. The yield to call represents the rate of return that investors earn if they buy a callable bond at a specific price and hold it until it is called back and they receive the *call price*, which would be set above the bond's par value. Here our focus is solely on the more general measure of yield to maturity.

	A	B
1	YIELD TO MATURITY, ANNUAL INTEREST	
2	Year	Cash Flow
3	0	($1,080)
4	1	$100
5	2	$100
6	3	$100
7	4	$100
8	5	$100
9	6	$100
10	7	$100
11	8	$100
12	9	$100
13	10	$1,100
14	YTM	8.766%
Entry in Cell B14 is =IRR(B3:B13)		

SEMIANNUAL INTEREST AND BOND VALUES

The procedure used to value bonds paying interest semiannually is similar to that shown in Chapter 5 for compounding interest more frequently than annually, except that here we need to find present value instead of future value. It involves

1. Converting annual interest, I, to semiannual interest by dividing I by 2.
2. Converting the number of years to maturity, n, to the number of 6-month periods to maturity by multiplying n by 2.
3. Converting the required stated (rather than effective)[6] annual return for similar-risk bonds that also pay semiannual interest from an annual rate, r_d, to a semiannual rate by dividing r_d by 2.

Substituting these three changes into Equation 6.5 yields

$$B_0 = \frac{I}{2} \times \left[\sum_{t=1}^{2n} \frac{1}{\left(1 + \frac{r_d}{2}\right)^t} \right] + M \times \left[\frac{1}{\left(1 + \frac{r_d}{2}\right)^{2n}} \right] \qquad (6.6)$$

---

6. As we noted in Chapter 5, the effective annual rate of interest, *EAR*, for stated interest rate r, when interest is paid semiannually ($m = 2$), can be found by using Equation 5.17:

$$EAR = \left(1 + \frac{r}{2}\right)^2 - 1$$

For example, a bond with a 12% required stated annual return, r_d, that pays semiannual interest would have an effective annual rate of

$$EAR = \left(1 + \frac{0.12}{2}\right)^2 - 1 = (1.06)^2 - 1 = 1.1236 - 1 = 0.1236 = 12.36\%$$

Because most bonds pay semiannual interest at semiannual rates equal to 50 percent of the stated annual rate, their effective annual rates are generally higher than their stated annual rates.

Example 6.13 ▶   Assuming that the Mills Company bond pays interest semiannually and that the required stated annual return, r_d, is 12% for similar-risk bonds that also pay semiannual interest, substituting these values into Equation 6.6 yields

$$B_0 = \frac{\$100}{2} \times \left[\sum_{t=1}^{20} \frac{1}{\left(1 + \frac{0.12}{2}\right)^t} \right] + \$1,000 \times \left[\frac{1}{\left(1 + \frac{0.12}{2}\right)^{20}} \right] = \$885.30$$

Input	Function
20	N
6	I
50	PMT
1000	FV
	CPT
	PV

Solution
885.30

Calculator Use   In using a calculator to find bond value when interest is paid semiannually, we must double the number of periods and divide both the required stated annual return and the annual interest by 2. For the Mills Company bond, we would use 20 periods (2 × 10 years), a required return of 6% (12% ÷ 2), and an interest payment of $50 ($100 ÷ 2). Using these inputs, you should find the bond value with semiannual interest to be $885.30, as shown at the left.

Spreadsheet Use   The value of the Mills Company bond paying semiannual interest at a required return of 12% also can be calculated as shown in the following Excel spreadsheet.

	A	B
1	BOND VALUE, SEMIANNUAL INTEREST	
2	Semiannual interest payment	$50
3	Semiannual required return	6%
4	Number of periods to maturity	20
5	Par value	$1,000
6	Bond value	$885.30
	Entry in Cell B6 is =PV(B3,B4,B2,B5,0) Note that Excel will produce a negative value for the bond's price	

Comparing this result with the $887.00 value found earlier for annual compounding, we can see that the bond's value is lower when semiannual interest is paid. *This will always occur when the bond sells at a discount.* For bonds selling at a premium, the opposite will occur: The value with semiannual interest will be greater than with annual interest.

→ REVIEW QUESTIONS

6–16 What basic procedure is used to value a bond that pays annual interest? Semiannual interest?

6–17 What relationship between the required return and the coupon interest rate will cause a bond to sell at a *discount?* At a *premium?* At its *par value?*

6–18 If the required return on a bond differs from its coupon interest rate, describe the behavior of the bond value over time as the bond moves toward maturity.

6–19 As a risk-averse investor, would you prefer bonds with short or long periods until maturity? Why?

6–20 What is a bond's *yield to maturity* (*YTM*)? Briefly describe the use of a financial calculator and the use of an Excel spreadsheet for finding YTM.

Summary

FOCUS ON VALUE

Interest rates and required returns embody the real cost of money, inflationary expectations, and issuer and issue risk. They reflect the level of return required by market participants as compensation for the risk perceived in a specific security or asset investment. Because these returns are affected by economic expectations, they vary as a function of time, typically rising for longer-term maturities. The yield curve reflects such market expectations at any point in time.

The value of an asset can be found by calculating the present value of its expected cash flows, using the required return as the discount rate. Bonds are the easiest financial assets to value; both the amounts and the timing of their cash flows are contractual and, therefore, known with certainty (at least for high-grade bonds). The financial manager needs to understand how to apply valuation techniques to bonds, stocks, and tangible assets (as we will demonstrate in the following chapters) to make decisions that are consistent with the firm's **share price maximization goal.**

REVIEW OF LEARNING GOALS

LG 1 Describe interest rate fundamentals, the term structure of interest rates, and risk premiums. The flow of funds between savers and borrowers is regulated by the interest rate or required return. In a perfect, inflation-free, certain world there would be one cost of money—the real rate of interest. The nominal or actual interest rate is the sum of the risk-free rate and a risk premium reflecting issuer and issue characteristics. The risk-free rate is the real rate of interest plus an inflation premium.

For any class of similar-risk bonds, the term structure of interest rates reflects the relationship between the interest rate or rate of return and the time to maturity. Yield curves can be downward sloping (inverted), upward sloping (normal), or flat. The expectations theory, liquidity preference theory, and market segmentation theory are cited to explain the shape of the yield curve. Risk premiums for non-Treasury debt issues result from business risk, financial risk, interest rate risk, liquidity risk, tax risk, default risk, maturity risk, and contractual provision risk.

LG 2 Review the legal aspects of bond financing and bond cost. Corporate bonds are long-term debt instruments indicating that a corporation has borrowed an amount that it promises to repay in the future under clearly defined terms. Most bonds are issued with maturities of 10 to 30 years and a par value of $1,000. The bond indenture, enforced by a trustee, states all conditions of the bond issue. It contains both standard debt provisions and restrictive covenants, which may include a sinking-fund requirement and/or a security interest. The cost of a bond to an issuer depends on its maturity, offering size, and issuer risk and on the basic cost of money.

LG 3 **Discuss the general features, yields, prices, ratings, popular types, and international issues of corporate bonds.** A bond issue may include a conversion feature, a call feature, or stock purchase warrants. The yield, or rate of return, on a bond can be measured by its current yield, yield to maturity (YTM), or yield to call (YTC). Bond prices are typically reported along with their coupon, maturity date, and yield to maturity (YTM). Bond ratings by independent agencies indicate the risk of a bond issue. Various types of traditional and contemporary bonds are available. Eurobonds and foreign bonds enable established creditworthy companies and governments to borrow large amounts internationally.

LG 4 **Understand the key inputs and basic model used in the valuation process.** Key inputs to the valuation process include cash flows (returns), timing, and risk and the required return. The value of any asset is equal to the present value of all future cash flows it is *expected* to provide over the relevant time period.

LG 5 **Apply the basic valuation model to bonds, and describe the impact of required return and time to maturity on bond values.** The value of a bond is the present value of its interest payments plus the present value of its par value. The discount rate used to determine bond value is the required return, which may differ from the bond's coupon interest rate. A bond can sell at a discount, at par, or at a premium, depending on whether the required return is greater than, equal to, or less than its coupon interest rate. The amount of time to maturity affects bond values. The value of a bond will approach its par value as the bond moves closer to maturity. The chance that interest rates will change and thereby change the required return and bond value is called interest rate risk. The shorter the amount of time until a bond's maturity, the less responsive is its market value to a given change in the required return.

LG 6 **Explain yield to maturity (YTM), its calculation, and the procedure used to value bonds that pay interest semiannually.** Yield to maturity is the rate of return investors earn if they buy a bond at a specific price and hold it until maturity. YTM can be calculated by using a financial calculator or by using an Excel spreadsheet. Bonds that pay interest semiannually are valued by using the same procedure used to value bonds paying annual interest, except that the interest payments are one-half of the annual interest payments, the number of periods is twice the number of years to maturity, and the required return is one-half of the stated annual required return on similar-risk bonds.

Opener-in-Review

In the chapter opener you learned that China has issued its first renminbi-denominated bonds which can be sold in Hong Kong. This provided an opportunity to both investors and corporations to either use the bonds as a high quality investment tool or as a financing source in renminbi currency. The avail-ability of these bonds differed in both their maturities and coupon rate.

a. Both McDonald's and Caterpillar issued renminbi bonds but they did this with different coupon rates. What are the reasons behind these differences?

b. Currently, China is raising the interest rates to reduce the amount of liquidity available in the market, thus reducing the increased inflation rate. What is the expected effect on the yield curve and how would that affect the value of the bonds?

c. Suppose that McDonald's announced a loss for the year 2010, and therefore a decrease in its rating from an AAA Bond to BBB Bond. What effect will this have on the cost of financing?

Self-Test Problems   (Solutions in Appendix)

LG 5 **LG 6** **ST6–1** **Bond valuation**   Lahey Industries has outstanding a $1,000 par-value bond with an 8% coupon interest rate. The bond has 12 years remaining to its maturity date.

a. If interest is paid *annually*, find the value of the bond when the required return is (1) 7%, (2) 8%, and (3) 10%.

b. Indicate for each case in part **a** whether the bond is selling at a discount, at a pre-mium, or at its par value.

c. Using the 10% required return, find the bond's value when interest is paid *semi-annually.*

LG 3 **LG 6** **ST6–2** **Bond yields**   Elliot Enterprises' bonds currently sell for $1,150, have an 11% coupon interest rate and a $1,000 par value, pay interest *annually,* and have 18 years to maturity.

a. Calculate the bonds' *current yield.*

b. Calculate the bonds' *yield to maturity (YTM).*

c. Compare the YTM calculated in part **b** to the bonds' coupon interest rate and current yield (calculated in part **a**). Use a comparison of the bonds' current price and par value to explain these differences.

Warm-Up Exercises   All problems are available in myfinancelab .

LG 1 **E6–1**   The risk-free rate on T-bills recently was 1.23%. If the real rate of interest is estimated to be 0.80%, what was the expected level of inflation?

LG 1 **E6–2**   The yields for Treasuries with differing maturities on a recent day were as shown in the table on page 253.

a. Use the information to plot a *yield curve* for this date.

b. If the expectations hypothesis is true, approximately what rate of return do investors expect a 5-year Treasury note to pay 5 years from now?

Maturity	Yield
3 months	1.41%
6 months	1.71
2 years	2.68
3 years	3.01
5 years	3.70
10 years	4.51
30 years	5.25

    c. If the expectations hypothesis is true, approximately (ignoring compounding) what rate of return do investors expect a 1-year Treasury security to pay starting 2 years from now?

    d. Is it possible that even though the yield curve slopes up in this problem, investors do not expect rising interest rates? Explain.

LG 1   **E6–3** The yields for Treasuries with differing maturities, including an estimate of the real rate of interest, on a recent day were as shown in the following table:

Maturity	Yield	Real rate of interest
3 months	1.41%	0.80%
6 months	1.71	0.80
2 years	2.68	0.80
3 years	3.01	0.80
5 years	3.70	0.80
10 years	4.51	0.80
30 years	5.25	0.80

Use the information in the preceding table to calculate the *inflation expectation* for each maturity.

LG 1   **E6–4** Recently, the annual inflation rate measured by the Consumer Price Index (CPI) was forecast to be 3.3%. How could a T-bill have had a negative real rate of return over the same period? How could it have had a zero real rate of return? What minimum rate of return must the T-bill have earned to meet your requirement of a 2% real rate of return?

LG 1   **E6–5** Calculate the *risk premium* for each of the following rating classes of long-term securities, assuming that the yield to maturity (YTM) for comparable Treasuries is 4.51%.

Rating class	Nominal interest rate
AAA	5.12%
BBB	5.78
B	7.82

LG 4   **E6–6**   You have two assets and must calculate their values today based on their different payment streams and appropriate required returns. Asset 1 has a required return of 15% and will produce a stream of $500 at the end of each year indefinitely. Asset 2 has a required return of 10% and will produce an end-of-year cash flow of $1,200 in the first year, $1,500 in the second year, and $850 in its third and final year.

LG 5   **E6–7**   A bond with 5 years to maturity and a coupon rate of 6% has a par, or face, value of $20,000. Interest is paid annually. If you required a return of 8% on this bond, what is the value of this bond to you?

LG 5   **E6–8**   Assume a 5-year Treasury bond has a coupon rate of 4.5%.
  a. Give examples of required rates of return that would make the bond sell at a discount, at a premium, and at par.
  b. If this bond's par value is $10,000, calculate the differing values for this bond given the required rates you chose in part **a.**

Problems

All problems are available in ⬛myfinancelab .

LG 1   **P6–1**   **Interest rate fundamentals: The real rate of return**   Carl Foster, a trainee at an investment banking firm, is trying to get an idea of what real rate of return investors are expecting in today's marketplace. He has looked up the rate paid on 3-month U.S. Treasury bills and found it to be 5.5%. He has decided to use the rate of change in the Consumer Price Index as a proxy for the inflationary expectations of investors. That annualized rate now stands at 3%. On the basis of the information that Carl has collected, what estimate can he make of the *real rate of return?*

LG 1   **P6–2**   **Real rate of interest**   To estimate the real rate of interest, the economics division of Mountain Banks—a major bank holding company—has gathered the data summarized in the following table. Because there is a high likelihood that new tax legislation will be passed in the near future, current data as well as data reflecting the probable impact of passage of the legislation on the demand for funds are also

	Currently		With passage of tax legislation
Amount of funds supplied/demanded ($ billion)	Interest rate required by funds suppliers	Interest rate required by funds demanders	Interest rate required by funds demanders
$ 1	2%	7%	9%
5	3	6	8
10	4	4	7
20	6	3	6
50	7	2	4
100	9	1	3

included in the table. (*Note:* The proposed legislation will not affect the supply schedule of funds. Assume a perfect world in which inflation is expected to be zero, funds suppliers and demanders have no liquidity preference, and all outcomes are certain.)

a. Draw the supply curve and the demand curve for funds using the current data. (*Note:* Unlike the functions in Figure 6.1 on page 223, the functions here will not appear as straight lines.)

b. Using your graph, label and note the *real rate of interest* using the current data.

c. Add to the graph drawn in part **a** the new demand curve expected in the event that the proposed tax legislation is passed.

d. What is the new real rate of interest? Compare and analyze this finding in light of your analysis in part **b**.

Personal Finance Problem

LG 1 **P6–3** **Real and nominal rates of interest**   Zane Perelli currently has $100 that he can spend today on polo shirts costing $25 each. Alternatively, he could invest the $100 in a risk-free U.S. Treasury security that is expected to earn a 9% nominal rate of interest. The consensus forecast of leading economists is a 5% rate of inflation over the coming year.

a. How many polo shirts can Zane purchase today?

b. How much money will Zane have at the end of 1 year if he forgoes purchasing the polo shirts today?

c. How much would you expect the polo shirts to cost at the end of 1 year in light of the expected inflation?

d. Use your findings in parts **b** and **c** to determine how many polo shirts (fractions are OK) Zane can purchase at the end of 1 year. In percentage terms, how many more or fewer polo shirts can Zane buy at the end of 1 year?

e. What is Zane's *real rate of return* over the year? How is it related to the percentage change in Zane's buying power found in part **d**? Explain.

LG 1 **P6–4** **Yield curve**   A firm wishing to evaluate interest rate behavior has gathered yield data on five U.S. Treasury securities, each having a different maturity and all measured at the same point in time. The summarized data follow.

U.S. Treasury security	Time to maturity	Yield
A	1 year	12.6%
B	10 years	11.2
C	6 months	13.0
D	20 years	11.0
E	5 years	11.4

a. Draw the yield curve associated with these data.

b. Describe the resulting yield curve in part **a**, and explain the general expectations embodied in it.

LG 1 **P6–5** **Nominal interest rates and yield curves**   A recent study of inflationary expectations has revealed that the consensus among economic forecasters yields the following average annual rates of inflation expected over the periods noted. (*Note:* Assume that the risk that future interest rate movements will affect longer maturities more than shorter maturities is zero; that is, there is no *maturity risk*.)

Period	Average annual rate of inflation
3 months	5%
2 years	6
5 years	8
10 years	8.5
20 years	9

a. If the real rate of interest is currently 2.5%, find the *nominal rate of interest* on each of the following U.S. Treasury issues: 20-year bond, 3-month bill, 2-year note, and 5-year bond.

b. If the real rate of interest suddenly dropped to 2% without any change in inflationary expectations, what effect, if any, would this have on your answers in part **a?** Explain.

c. Using your findings in part **a,** draw a yield curve for U.S. Treasury securities. Describe the general shape and expectations reflected by the curve.

d. What would a follower of the *liquidity preference theory* say about how the preferences of lenders and borrowers tend to affect the shape of the yield curve drawn in part **c?** Illustrate that effect by placing on your graph a dotted line that approximates the yield curve without the effect of liquidity preference.

e. What would a follower of the *market segmentation theory* say about the supply and demand for long-term loans versus the supply and demand for short-term loans given the yield curve constructed for part **c** of this problem?

LG 1   **P6–6**   **Nominal and real rates and yield curves**   A firm wishing to evaluate interest rate behavior has gathered data on the nominal rate of interest and on inflationary expectations for five U.S. Treasury securities, each having a different maturity and each measured at a different point in time during the year just ended. (*Note:* Assume that the risk that future interest rate movements will affect longer maturities more than shorter maturities is zero; that is, there is no *maturity risk*.) These data are summarized in the following table.

U.S. Treasury security	Point in time	Maturity	Nominal rate of interest	Inflationary expectation
A	Jan. 7	2 years	12.6%	9.5%
B	Mar. 12	10 years	11.2	8.2
C	May 30	6 months	13.0	10.0
D	Aug. 15	20 years	11.0	8.1
E	Dec. 30	5 years	11.4	8.3

   a. Using the preceding data, find the *real rate of interest* at each point in time.
   b. Describe the behavior of the real rate of interest over the year. What forces might be responsible for such behavior?
   c. Draw the yield curve associated with these data, assuming that the nominal rates were measured at the same point in time.
   d. Describe the resulting yield curve in part **c**, and explain the general expectations embodied in it.

LG 1   P6–7   Term structure of interest rates   The following yield data for a number of highest-quality corporate bonds existed at each of the three points in time noted.

	Yield		
Time to maturity (years)	5 years ago	2 years ago	Today
1	9.1%	14.6%	9.3%
3	9.2	12.8	9.8
5	9.3	12.2	10.9
10	9.5	10.9	12.6
15	9.4	10.7	12.7
20	9.3	10.5	12.9
30	9.4	10.5	13.5

   a. On the same set of axes, draw the yield curve at each of the three given times.
   b. Label each curve in part **a** with its general shape (downward-sloping, upward-sloping, flat).
   c. Describe the general interest rate expectation existing at each of the three times.
   d. Examine the data from 5 years ago. According to the expectations theory, what approximate return did investors expect a 5-year bond to pay as of today?

LG 1   P6–8   Risk-free rate and risk premiums   The real rate of interest is currently 3%; the inflation expectation and risk premiums for a number of securities follow.

Security	Inflation expectation Premium	Risk premium
A	6%	3%
B	9	2
C	8	2
D	5	4
E	11	1

   a. Find the *risk-free rate of interest*, R_F, that is applicable to each security.
   b. Although not noted, what factor must be the cause of the differing risk-free rates found in part **a**?
   c. Find the *nominal rate of interest* for each security.

LG 1   **P6–9**   **Risk premiums**   Eleanor Burns is attempting to find the nominal rate of interest for each of two securities—A and B—issued by different firms at the same point in time. She has gathered the following data:

Characteristic	Security A	Security B
Time to maturity	3 years	15 years
Inflation expectation premium	9.0%	7.0%
Risk premium for:		
Liquidity risk	1.0%	1.0%
Default risk	1.0%	2.0%
Maturity risk	0.5%	1.5%
Other risk	0.5%	1.5%

    a. If the real rate of interest is currently 2%, find the *risk-free rate of interest* applicable to each security.

    b. Find the total risk premium attributable to each security's issuer and issue characteristics.

    c. Calculate the *nominal rate of interest* for each security. Compare and discuss your findings.

LG 2   **P6–10**   **Bond interest payments before and after taxes**   Charter Corp. has issued 2,500 debentures with a total principal value of $2,500,000. The bonds have a coupon interest rate of 7%.

    a. What dollar amount of interest per bond can an investor expect to receive each year from Charter?

    b. What is Charter's total interest expense per year associated with this bond issue?

    c. Assuming that Charter is in a 35% corporate tax bracket, what is the company's net after-tax interest cost associated with this bond issue?

LG 4   **P6–11**   **Bond prices and yields**   Assume that the Financial Management Corporation's $1,000-par-value bond had a 5.700% coupon, matured on May 15, 2020, had a current price quote of 97.708, and had a yield to maturity (YTM) of 6.034%. Given this information, answer the following questions:

    a. What was the dollar price of the bond?

    b. What is the bond's *current yield?*

    c. Is the bond selling at par, at a discount, or at a premium? Why?

    d. Compare the bond's current yield calculated in part **b** to its YTM and explain why they differ.

Personal Finance Problem

LG 4   **P6–12**   **Valuation fundamentals**   Imagine that you are trying to evaluate the economics of purchasing an automobile. You expect the car to provide annual after-tax cash benefits of $1,200 at the end of each year and assume that you can sell the car for after-tax proceeds of $5,000 at the end of the planned 5-year ownership period. All funds for purchasing the car will be drawn from your savings, which are currently earning 6% after taxes.

    a. Identify the cash flows, their timing, and the required return applicable to valuing the car.

    b. What is the maximum price you would be willing to pay to acquire the car? Explain.

LG 4 **P6–13 Valuation of assets** Using the information provided in the following table, find the value of each asset.

Asset	Cash flow End of year	Cash flow Amount	Appropriate required return
A	1	$ 5,000	18%
	2	5,000	
	3	5,000	
B	1 through ∞	$ 300	15%
C	1	$ 0	16%
	2	0	
	3	0	
	4	0	
	5	35,000	
D	1 through 5	$ 1,500	12%
	6	8,500	
E	1	$ 2,000	14%
	2	3,000	
	3	5,000	
	4	7,000	
	5	4,000	
	6	1,000	

Personal Finance Problem

LG 4 **P6–14 Asset valuation and risk** Laura Drake wishes to estimate the value of an asset expected to provide cash inflows of $3,000 per year at the end of years 1 through 4 and $15,000 at the end of year 5. Her research indicates that she must earn 10% on low-risk assets, 15% on average-risk assets, and 22% on high-risk assets.
  a. Determine what is the most Laura should pay for the asset if it is classified as (1) low-risk, (2) average-risk, and (3) high-risk.
  b. Suppose Laura is unable to assess the risk of the asset and wants to be certain she's making a good deal. On the basis of your findings in part **a**, what is the most she should pay? Why?
  c. All else being the same, what effect does increasing risk have on the value of an asset? Explain in light of your findings in part **a**.

LG 5 **P6–15 Basic bond valuation** Complex Systems has an outstanding issue of $1,000-par-value bonds with a 12% coupon interest rate. The issue pays interest *annually* and has 16 years remaining to its maturity date.
  a. If bonds of similar risk are currently earning a 10% rate of return, how much should the Complex Systems bond sell for today?
  b. Describe the *two* possible reasons why the rate on similar-risk bonds is below the coupon interest rate on the Complex Systems bond.
  c. If the required return were at 12% instead of 10%, what would the current value of Complex Systems' bond be? Contrast this finding with your findings in part **a** and discuss.

LG 5 **P6–16** **Bond valuation—Annual interest**   Calculate the value of each of the bonds shown in the following table, all of which pay interest *annually*.

Bond	Par value	Coupon interest rate	Years to maturity	Required return
A	$1,000	14%	20	12%
B	1,000	8	16	8
C	100	10	8	13
D	500	16	13	18
E	1,000	12	10	10

LG 5 **P6–17** **Bond value and changing required returns**   Midland Utilities has outstanding a bond issue that will mature to its $1,000 par value in 12 years. The bond has a coupon interest rate of 11% and pays interest *annually*.
   a. Find the value of the bond if the required return is (1) 11%, (2) 15%, and (3) 8%.
   b. Plot your findings in part **a** on a set of "required return (*x* axis)–market value of bond (*y* axis)" axes.
   c. Use your findings in parts **a** and **b** to discuss the relationship between the coupon interest rate on a bond and the required return and the market value of the bond relative to its par value.
   d. What *two* possible reasons could cause the required return to differ from the coupon interest rate?

LG 5 **P6–18** **Bond value and time—Constant required returns**   Pecos Manufacturing has just issued a 15-year, 12% coupon interest rate, $1,000-par bond that pays interest *annually*. The required return is currently 14%, and the company is certain it will remain at 14% until the bond matures in 15 years.
   a. Assuming that the required return does remain at 14% until maturity, find the value of the bond with (1) 15 years, (2) 12 years, (3) 9 years, (4) 6 years, (5) 3 years, and (6) 1 year to maturity.
   b. Plot your findings on a set of "time to maturity (*x* axis)–market value of bond (*y* axis)" axes constructed similarly to Figure 6.5 on page 246.
   c. All else remaining the same, when the required return differs from the coupon interest rate and is assumed to be constant to maturity, what happens to the bond value as time moves toward maturity? Explain in light of the graph in part **b**.

Personal Finance Problem

LG 5 **P6–19** **Bond value and time—Changing required returns**   Lynn Parsons is considering investing in either of two outstanding bonds. The bonds both have $1,000 par values and 11% coupon interest rates and pay *annual* interest. Bond A has exactly 5 years to maturity, and bond B has 15 years to maturity.
   a. Calculate the value of bond A if the required return is (1) 8%, (2) 11%, and (3) 14%.
   b. Calculate the value of bond B if the required return is (1) 8%, (2) 11%, and (3) 14%.

c. From your findings in parts **a** and **b,** complete the following table, and discuss the relationship between time to maturity and changing required returns.

Required return	Value of bond A	Value of bond B
8%	?	?
11	?	?
14	?	?

d. If Lynn wanted to minimize *interest rate risk,* which bond should she purchase? Why?

LG 6   P6–20   Yield to maturity   The relationship between a bond's yield to maturity and coupon interest rate can be used to predict its pricing level. For each of the bonds listed, state whether the price of the bond will be at a premium to par, at par, or at a discount to par.

Bond	Coupon interest rate	Yield to maturity	Price
A	6%	10%	_____
B	8	8	_____
C	9	7	_____
D	7	9	_____
E	12	10	_____

LG 6   P6–21   Yield to maturity   The Salem Company bond currently sells for $955, has a 12% coupon interest rate and a $1,000 par value, pays interest *annually,* and has 15 years to maturity.

a. Calculate the *yield to maturity (YTM)* on this bond.

b. Explain the relationship that exists between the coupon interest rate and yield to maturity and the par value and market value of a bond.

LG 6   P6–22   Yield to maturity   Each of the bonds shown in the following table pays interest *annually.*

Bond	Par value	Coupon interest rate	Years to maturity	Current value
A	$1,000	9%	8	$ 820
B	1,000	12	16	1,000
C	500	12	12	560
D	1,000	15	10	1,120
E	1,000	5	3	900

a. Calculate the *yield to maturity (YTM)* for each bond.

b. What relationship exists between the coupon interest rate and yield to maturity and the par value and market value of a bond? Explain.

Personal Finance Problem

LG 2   **LG 5**   **P6–23**   **Bond valuation and yield to maturity**   Mark Goldsmith's broker has shown him
LG 6   two bonds. Each has a maturity of 5 years, a par value of $1,000, and a yield to
maturity of 12%. Bond A has a coupon interest rate of 6% paid annually. Bond B
has a coupon interest rate of 14% paid annually.

a. Calculate the selling price for each of the bonds.
b. Mark has $20,000 to invest. Judging on the basis of the price of the bonds, how
   many of either one could Mark purchase if he were to choose it over the other?
   (Mark cannot really purchase a fraction of a bond, but for purposes of this question, pretend that he can.)
c. Calculate the yearly interest income of each bond on the basis of its coupon rate
   and the number of bonds that Mark could buy with his $20,000.
d. Assume that Mark will reinvest the interest payments as they are paid (at the end
   of each year) and that his rate of return on the reinvestment is only 10%. For
   each bond, calculate the value of the principal payment plus the value of Mark's
   reinvestment account at the end of the 5 years.
e. Why are the two values calculated in part **d** different? If Mark were worried that
   he would earn less than the 12% yield to maturity on the reinvested interest payments, which of these two bonds would be a better choice?

LG 6   **P6–24**   **Bond valuation—Semiannual interest**   Find the value of a bond maturing in
6 years, with a $1,000 par value and a coupon interest rate of 10% (5% paid semi-
annually) if the required return on similar-risk bonds is 14% annual interest
(7% paid semiannually).

LG 6   **P6–25**   **Bond valuation—Semiannual interest**   Calculate the value of each of the bonds
shown in the following table, all of which pay interest *semiannually.*

Bond	Par value	Coupon interest rate	Years to maturity	Required stated annual return
A	$1,000	10%	12	8%
B	1,000	12	20	12
C	500	12	5	14
D	1,000	14	10	10
E	100	6	4	14

LG 6   **P6–26**   **Bond valuation—Quarterly interest**   Calculate the value of a $5,000-par-value
bond paying quarterly interest at an annual coupon interest rate of 10% and having
10 years until maturity if the required return on similar-risk bonds is currently a
12% annual rate paid *quarterly.*

LG 1   **P6–27**   **ETHICS PROBLEM**   Bond rating agencies have invested significant sums of money
in an effort to determine which quantitative and nonquantitative factors best predict
bond defaults. Furthermore, some of the raters invest time and money to meet privately with corporate personnel to get nonpublic information that is used in
assigning the issue's bond rating. To recoup those costs, some bond rating agencies
have tied their ratings to the purchase of additional services. Do you believe that this
is an acceptable practice? Defend your position.

Spreadsheet Exercise

CSM Corporation has a bond issue outstanding at the end of 2012. The bond has 15 years remaining to maturity and carries a coupon interest rate of 6%. Interest on the bond is compounded on a semiannual basis. The par value of the CSM bond is $1,000 and it is currently selling for $874.42.

TO DO

Create a spreadsheet similar to the Excel spreadsheet examples located in the chapter for yield to maturity and semiannual interest to model the following:

a. Create a spreadsheet similar to the Excel spreadsheet examples located in the chapter to solve for the yield to maturity.
b. Create a spreadsheet similar to the Excel spreadsheet examples located in the chapter to solve for the price of the bond if the yield to maturity is 2% higher.
c. Create a spreadsheet similar to the Excel spreadsheet examples located in the chapter to solve for the price of the bond if the yield to maturity is 2% lower.
d. What can you summarize about the relationship between the price of the bond, the par value, the yield to maturity, and the coupon rate?

 Visit **www.myfinancelab.com** for **Chapter Case: *Evaluating Annie Hegg's Proposed Investment in Atilier Industries Bonds,*** Group Exercises, and other numerous resources.

7 Stock Valuation

Learning Goals

LG 1 Differentiate between debt and equity.

LG 2 Discuss the features of both common and preferred stock.

LG 3 Describe the process of issuing common stock, including venture capital, going public, and the investment banker.

LG 4 Understand the concept of market efficiency and basic stock valuation using zero-growth, constant-growth, and variable-growth models.

LG 5 Discuss the free cash flow valuation model and the book value, liquidation value, and price/earnings (P/E) multiple approaches.

LG 6 Explain the relationships among financial decisions, return, risk, and the firm's value.

Why This Chapter Matters to You

In your *professional* life

ACCOUNTING You need to understand the difference between debt and equity in terms of tax treatment; the ownership claims of capital providers, including venture capitalists and stockholders; and the differences between book value per share and other market-based valuations.

INFORMATION SYSTEMS You need to understand the procedures used to issue common stock, the information needed to value stock, how to collect and process the necessary information from each functional area, and how to disseminate information to investors.

MANAGEMENT You need to understand the difference between debt and equity capital, the rights and claims of stockholders, the process of issuing common stock, and the effects each functional area has on the value of the firm's stock.

MARKETING You need to understand that the firm's ideas for products and services will greatly affect investors' beliefs regarding the likely success of the firm's projects; projects that are viewed as more likely to succeed are also viewed as more valuable and therefore lead to a higher stock value.

OPERATIONS You need to understand that the evaluations of venture capitalists and other would-be investors will in part depend on the efficiency of the firm's operations; more cost-efficient operations lead to better growth prospects and, therefore, higher stock valuations.

In your *personal* life

At some point, you are likely to hold stocks as an asset in your retirement program. You may want to estimate a stock's value. If the stock is selling below its estimated value, you may buy the stock; if its market price is above its value, you may sell it. Some individuals rely on financial advisors to make such buy or sell recommendations. Regardless of how you approach investment decisions, it will be helpful for you to understand how stocks are valued.

Air Asia

Jewel in the Skies?

Air Asia (AASIA), which initially owned two old planes and serviced five local destinations, has grown over eight years into a company with a fleet of 90 planes flying to over 60 destinations with 3,500 flights a week. Air Asia X ("AASIAX"), a subsidiary, is also operating long-haul flights to London, Mumbai, China, India, and Taiwan with Paris in the 2011 pipeline. AASIA was listed on Bursa Malaysia in 2004 at an initial price of RM 2.66.

The business model of AASIA hinges on delivering no-frills, low-fare air travel to Malaysians. It focuses on value and achieves this through a high rate of aircraft utilization, online reservations, and streamlining maintenance costs via a single airline fleet. Operating from the Low Cost Carrier Terminal, Sepang, Air Asia has redefined Malaysian leisure choices, and its affiliations with the Manchester United football team have boosted its mileage.

In responding to the flourishing demand for air travel among middle-class Asians, AASIA has challenged the services provided by Malaysian Airline System Bhd and regional budget carriers such as Tiger Air and JetStar. AASIA has also pioneered the world's first budget carrier alliance with JetStar, which is estimated to reduce costs by AUD300 million annually.

Since the listing on Bursa Malaysia, AASIA has chartered phenomenal growth in sales of almost 800 percent. However, the return on assets has been declining with the lowest of 4 percent (in 2009) attributed to Influenza A (H1N1), volatile oil prices, and intense regional competition. In October 2010, AASIA had surpassed Malaysian Airline System in terms of market capitalization at RM 7.6 billion. The return on shareholders' equity has, however, been fairly stable. With 100 aircraft, AASIA forecasted 30 million passengers in 2010. AASIAX is planning an initial public offering in 2011.

AASIA's success is attributed to its animated CEO, whose wit and "walkabout" leadership has contributed to prestigious global accolades. The question remains as to whether the intense competition, aggressive RM0 promotions, high leverage, and oil prices will erode profit margins. Pressure by shareholders for dividends may also drain funds for growth.

For now, AASIA is riding high in its customers' eyes. "Now everybody can fly," and the rest is history.

Sources: "Sabah Rises Further in Malaysia Tourism Thanks to Air Connections," *Global Travel Industry News* (August 9, 2010), retrieved on November 24, 2010, from http://www.eturbonews.com/17788/sabah-rises-further-malaysia-tourism-thanks-air-connection; H. Y. Leong, "Air Asia X plans IPO next year," *The Star Online* (2010), retrieved on November 25, 2010, from http://biz.thestar.com.my/news/story.asp?file=/2010/6/9/business/6427192&sec=business; B. K. Sidhu, "Air Asia-Jet Star in World's First Budget Airline Tie-up," *The Star Online* (2010), retrieved on November 25, 2010, from http://biz.thestar.com.my/news/story.asp?file=/2010/1/7/business/5423049&sec=business; D. Yap, "AirAsia Overtakes MAS in Market Capitalization," *The Star Online* (2010), retrieved on November 25, 2010, from http://biz.thestar.com.my/news/story.asp?file=/2010/10/22/business/7276227&sec=business.

LG ① ## 7.1 Differences between Debt and Equity

debt
Includes all borrowing incurred by a firm, including bonds, and is repaid according to a fixed schedule of payments.

equity
Funds provided by the firm's owners (investors or stockholders) that are repaid subject to the firm's performance.

Although debt and equity capital are both sources of external financing used by firms, they are very different in several important respects. Most importantly, debt financing is obtained from creditors, and equity financing is obtained from investors who then become part owners of the firm. Creditors (lenders or debtholders) have a legal right to be repaid, whereas investors have only an expectation of being repaid. **Debt** includes all borrowing incurred by a firm, including bonds, and is repaid according to a fixed schedule of payments. **Equity** consists of funds provided by the firm's owners (investors or stockholders) and is repaid subject to the firm's performance. A firm can obtain equity either *internally*, by retaining earnings rather than paying them out as dividends to its stockholders, or *externally*, by selling common or preferred stock. The key differences between debt and equity capital are summarized in Table 7.1 and discussed in the following pages.

VOICE IN MANAGEMENT

Unlike creditors, holders of equity (stockholders) are owners of the firm. Stockholders generally have voting rights that permit them to select the firm's directors and vote on special issues. In contrast, debtholders do not receive voting privileges but instead rely on the firm's contractual obligations to them to be their voice.

CLAIMS ON INCOME AND ASSETS

Equityholders' claims on income and assets are secondary to the claims of creditors. Their *claims on income* cannot be paid until the claims of all creditors, including both interest and scheduled principal payments, have been satisfied. After satisfying creditor's claims, the firm's board of directors decides whether to distribute dividends to the owners.

> ### Matter of fact
>
> **How Are Assets Divided in Bankruptcy?**
>
> According to the U.S. Securities and Exchange Commission, in bankruptcy assets are divided up as follows:
>
> 1. **Secured creditors:** Secured bank loans or secured bonds are paid first.
> 2. **Unsecured creditors:** Unsecured bank loans or unsecured bonds, suppliers, or customers have the next claim.
> 3. **Equityholders:** Equityholders or the owners of the company have the last claim on assets, and they may not receive anything if the secured and unsecured creditors' claims are not fully repaid.

In more depth

To read about *The Bankruptcy Process*, go to www.myfinancelab.com

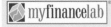

Equityholders' *claims on assets* also are secondary to the claims of creditors. If the firm fails, its assets are sold, and the proceeds are distributed in this order: secured creditors, unsecured creditors, and equityholders. Because equityholders are the last to receive any distribution of assets, they expect greater returns from their investment in the firm's stock than the returns creditors require on the firm's

TABLE 7.1	Key Differences between Debt and Equity		
		Type of capital	
Characteristic		Debt	Equity
Voice in management[a]		No	Yes
Claims on income and assets		Senior to equity	Subordinate to debt
Maturity		Stated	None
Tax treatment		Interest deduction	No deduction

[a]Debtholders do not have voting rights, but instead they rely on the firm's contractual obligations to them to be their voice.

borrowings. The higher rate of return expected by equityholders leads to a higher cost of equity financing relative to the cost of debt financing for the firm.

MATURITY

Unlike debt, equity is a *permanent form* of financing for the firm. It does not "mature," so repayment is not required. Because equity is liquidated only during bankruptcy proceedings, stockholders must recognize that, although a ready market may exist for their shares, the price that can be realized may fluctuate. This fluctuation of the market price of equity makes the overall returns to a firm's stockholders even more risky.

TAX TREATMENT

Interest payments to debtholders are treated as tax-deductible expenses by the issuing firm, whereas dividend payments to a firm's stockholders are not tax deductible. The tax deductibility of interest lowers the corporation's cost of debt financing, further causing it to be lower than the cost of equity financing.

→ REVIEW QUESTION

7–1 What are the key differences between *debt* and *equity?*

LG 2   LG 3   **7.2 Common and Preferred Stock**

A firm can obtain equity capital by selling either common or preferred stock. All corporations initially issue common stock to raise equity capital. Some of these firms later issue either additional common stock or preferred stock to raise more equity capital. Although both common and preferred stock are forms of equity capital, preferred stock has some similarities to debt that significantly differentiate it from common stock. Here we first consider the features of both common and preferred stock and then describe the process of issuing common stock, including the use of venture capital.

privately owned (stock)
The common stock of a firm is owned by private investors; this stock is not publicly traded.

publicly owned (stock)
The common stock of a firm is owned by public investors; this stock is publicly traded.

closely owned (stock)
The common stock of a firm is owned by an individual or a small group of investors (such as a family); these are usually privately owned companies.

widely owned (stock)
The common stock of a firm is owned by many unrelated individual or institutional investors.

par-value common stock
An arbitrary value established for legal purposes in the firm's corporate charter and which can be used to find the total number of shares outstanding by dividing it into the book value of common stock.

preemptive right
Allows common stockholders to maintain their proportionate ownership in the corporation when new shares are issued, thus protecting them from dilution of their ownership.

dilution of ownership
A reduction in each previous shareholder's fractional ownership resulting from the issuance of additional shares of common stock.

dilution of earnings
A reduction in each previous shareholder's fractional claim on the firm's earnings resulting from the issuance of additional shares of common stock.

rights
Financial instruments that allow stockholders to purchase additional shares at a price below the market price, in direct proportion to their number of owned shares.

COMMON STOCK

The true owners of a corporate business are the common stockholders. Common stockholders are sometimes referred to as *residual owners* because they receive what is left—the residual—after all other claims on the firm's income and assets have been satisfied. They are assured of only one thing: that they cannot lose any more than they have invested in the firm. As a result of this generally uncertain position, common stockholders expect to be compensated with adequate dividends and, ultimately, capital gains.

Ownership

The common stock of a firm can be **privately owned** by private investors or **publicly owned** by public investors. Private companies are often **closely owned** by an individual investor or a small group of private investors (such as a family). Public companies are **widely owned** by many unrelated individual or institutional investors. The shares of privately owned firms, which are typically small corporations, are generally not traded; if the shares are traded, the transactions are among private investors and often require the firm's consent. Large corporations, which are emphasized in the following discussions, are publicly owned, and their shares are generally actively traded in the broker or dealer markets described in Chapter 2.

Par Value

The market value of common stock is completely unrelated to its par value. The **par value** of common stock is an arbitrary value established for legal purposes in the firm's corporate charter and is generally set quite low, often an amount of $1 or less. Recall that when a firm sells new shares of common stock, the par value of the shares sold is recorded in the capital section of the balance sheet as part of common stock. One benefit of this recording is that at any time the total number of shares of common stock outstanding can be found by dividing the book value of common stock by the par value.

Setting a low par value is advantageous in states where certain corporate taxes are based on the par value of stock. A low par value is also beneficial in states that have laws against selling stock at a discount to par. For example, a company whose common stock has a par value of $20 per share would be unable to issue stock if investors are unwilling to pay more than $16 per share.

Preemptive Rights

The **preemptive right** allows common stockholders to maintain their *proportionate* ownership in the corporation when new shares are issued, thus protecting them from dilution of their ownership. A **dilution of ownership** is a reduction in each previous shareholder's fractional ownership resulting from the issuance of additional shares of common stock. Preemptive rights allow preexisting shareholders to maintain their preissuance voting control and protects them against the dilution of earnings. Preexisting shareholders experience a **dilution of earnings** when their claim on the firm's earnings is *diminished* as a result of new shares being issued.

In a *rights offering,* the firm grants **rights** to its shareholders. These financial instruments allow stockholders to purchase additional shares at a price below the market price, in direct proportion to their number of owned shares. In these

authorized shares
Shares of common stock that a firm's corporate charter allows it to issue.

outstanding shares
Issued shares of common stock held by investors, including both private and public investors.

treasury stock
Issued shares of common stock held by the firm; often these shares have been repurchased by the firm.

issued shares
Shares of common stock that have been put into circulation; the sum of *outstanding shares* and *treasury stock*.

situations, *rights* are an important financing tool without which shareholders would run the risk of losing their proportionate control of the corporation. From the firm's viewpoint, the use of rights offerings to raise new equity capital may be less costly than a public offering of stock.

Authorized, Outstanding, and Issued Shares

A firm's corporate charter indicates how many **authorized shares** it can issue. The firm cannot sell more shares than the charter authorizes without obtaining approval through a shareholder vote. To avoid later having to amend the charter, firms generally attempt to authorize more shares than they initially plan to issue.

Authorized shares become **outstanding shares** when they are issued or sold to investors. If the *firm* repurchases any of its outstanding shares, these shares are recorded as **treasury stock** and are no longer considered to be outstanding shares. **Issued shares** are the shares of common stock that have been put into circulation; they represent the sum of *outstanding shares* and *treasury stock*.

Example 7.1 ▶

Golden Enterprises, a producer of medical pumps, has the following stockholders' equity account on December 31:

Stockholders' Equity

Common stock—$0.80 par value:

Authorized 35,000,000 shares; issued 15,000,000 shares	$ 12,000,000
Paid-in capital in excess of par	63,000,000
Retained earnings	31,000,000
	$106,000,000
Less: Cost of treasury stock (1,000,000 shares)	4,000,000
Total stockholders' equity	$102,000,000

How many shares of additional common stock can Golden sell without gaining approval from its shareholders? The firm has 35 million authorized shares, 15 million issued shares, and 1 million shares of treasury stock. Thus 14 million shares are outstanding (15 million issued shares minus 1 million shares of treasury stock), and Golden can issue 21 million additional shares (35 million authorized shares minus 14 million outstanding shares) without seeking shareholder approval. This total includes the treasury shares currently held, which the firm can reissue to the public without obtaining shareholder approval.

Voting Rights

Generally, each share of common stock entitles its holder to one vote in the election of directors and on special issues. Votes are generally assignable and may be cast at the annual stockholders' meeting.

Because most small stockholders do not attend the annual meeting to vote, they may sign a **proxy statement** transferring their votes to another party. The solicitation of proxies from shareholders is closely controlled by the Securities and Exchange Commission to ensure that proxies are not being solicited on the

proxy statement
A statement transferring the votes of a stockholder to another party.

proxy battle
The attempt by a nonmanagement group to gain control of the management of a firm by soliciting a sufficient number of proxy votes.

supervoting shares
Stock that carries with it multiple votes per share rather than the single vote per share typically given on regular shares of common stock.

nonvoting common stock
Common stock that carries no voting rights; issued when the firm wishes to raise capital through the sale of common stock but does not want to give up its voting control.

basis of false or misleading information. Existing management generally receives the stockholders' proxies because it is able to solicit them at company expense.

Occasionally, when the firm is widely owned, outsiders may wage a **proxy battle** to unseat the existing management and gain control of the firm. To win a corporate election, votes from a majority of the shares voted are required. However, the odds of an outside group winning a proxy battle are generally slim.

In recent years, many firms have issued two or more classes of common stock with unequal voting rights. A firm can use different classes of stock as a defense against a *hostile takeover* in which an outside group, without management support, tries to gain voting control of the firm by buying its shares in the marketplace. **Supervoting shares**, which have multiple votes per share, allow "insiders" to maintain control against an outside group whose shares have only one vote each. At other times, a class of **nonvoting common stock** is issued when the firm wishes to raise capital through the sale of common stock but does not want to give up its voting control.

When different classes of common stock are issued on the basis of unequal voting rights, class A common typically—but not universally—has one vote per share, and class B common has supervoting rights. In most cases, the multiple share classes are equal with respect to all other aspects of ownership, although there are some exceptions to this general rule. In particular, there is usually no difference in the distribution of earnings (dividends) and assets. Treasury stock, which is held within the corporation, generally *does not* have voting rights, *does not* earn dividends, and *does not* have a claim on assets in liquidation.

Dividends

The payment of dividends to the firm's shareholders is at the discretion of the company's board of directors. Most corporations that pay dividends pay them quarterly. Dividends may be paid in cash, stock, or merchandise. Cash dividends are the most common, merchandise dividends the least.

Common stockholders are not promised a dividend, but they come to expect certain payments on the basis of the historical dividend pattern of the firm. Before firms pay dividends to common stockholders, they must pay any past due dividends owed to preferred stockholders. The firm's ability to pay dividends can be affected by restrictive debt covenants designed to ensure that the firm can repay its creditors.

Since passage of the *Jobs and Growth Tax Relief Reconciliation Act of 2003*, many firms now pay larger dividends to shareholders, who are subject to a maximum tax rate of 15 percent on dividends rather than the maximum tax rate of 39 percent in effect prior to passage of the act. Because of the importance of the dividend decision to the growth and valuation of the firm, dividends are discussed in greater detail in Chapter 14.

International Stock Issues

Although the international market for common stock is not as large as the international market for bonds, cross-border issuance and trading of common stock have increased dramatically in the past 30 years.

Some corporations *issue stock in foreign markets*. For example, the stock of General Electric trades in Frankfurt, London, Paris, and Tokyo; the stocks of Time Warner and Microsoft trade in Frankfurt and London; and the stock of McDonald's trades in Frankfurt, London, and Paris. The Frankfurt, London, and Tokyo markets are the most popular. Issuing stock internationally broadens the ownership base and helps a company to integrate into the local business environment. Having locally traded stock can facilitate corporate acquisitions because shares can be used as an acceptable method of payment.

American depositary shares (ADSs)
Dollar-denominated receipts for the stocks of foreign companies that are held by a U.S. financial institution overseas.

Foreign corporations have also discovered the benefits of trading their stock in the United States. The disclosure and reporting requirements mandated by the U.S. Securities and Exchange Commission have historically discouraged all but the largest foreign firms from directly listing their shares on the New York Stock Exchange or the American Stock Exchange.

American depositary receipts (ADRs)
Securities, backed by *American depositary shares (ADSs)*, that permit U.S. investors to hold shares of non-U.S. companies and trade them in U.S. markets.

As an alternative, most foreign companies choose to tap the U.S. market through **American depositary shares (ADSs)**. These are dollar-denominated receipts for the stocks of foreign companies that are held by a U.S. financial institution overseas. They serve as backing for **American depositary receipts (ADRs)**, which are securities that permit U.S. investors to hold shares of non-U.S. companies and trade them in U.S. markets. Because ADRs are issued, in dollars, to U.S. investors, they are subject to U.S. securities laws. At the same time, they give investors the opportunity to diversify their portfolios internationally.

PREFERRED STOCK

Preferred stock gives its holders certain privileges that make them senior to common stockholders. Preferred stockholders are promised a fixed periodic dividend, which is stated either as a percentage or as a dollar amount. How the dividend is specified depends on whether the preferred stock has a *par value*. **Par-value preferred stock** has a stated face value, and its annual dividend is specified as a percentage of this value. **No-par preferred stock** has no stated face value, but its annual dividend is stated in dollars. Preferred stock is most often issued by public utilities, by acquiring firms in merger transactions, and by firms that are experiencing losses and need additional financing.

par-value preferred stock
Preferred stock with a stated face value that is used with the specified dividend percentage to determine the annual dollar dividend.

no-par preferred stock
Preferred stock with no stated face value but with a stated annual dollar dividend.

Basic Rights of Preferred Stockholders

The basic rights of preferred stockholders are somewhat stronger than the rights of common stockholders. Preferred stock is often considered *quasi-debt* because, much like interest on debt, it specifies a fixed periodic payment (dividend). Preferred stock is unlike debt in that it has no maturity date. Because they have a fixed claim on the firm's income that takes precedence over the claim of common stockholders, preferred stockholders are exposed to less risk.

Preferred stockholders are also given *preference over common stockholders in the liquidation of assets* in a legally bankrupt firm, although they must "stand in line" behind creditors. The amount of the claim of preferred stockholders in liquidation is normally equal to the par or stated value of the preferred stock. Preferred stockholders are *not normally given a voting right*, although preferred stockholders are sometimes allowed to elect one member of the board of directors.

Features of Preferred Stock

A preferred stock issue generally includes a number of features, which, along with the stock's par value, the amount of dividend payments, the dividend payment dates, and any restrictive covenants, are specified in an agreement similar to a *bond indenture*.

cumulative (preferred stock)
Preferred stock for which all passed (unpaid) dividends in arrears, along with the current dividend, must be paid before dividends can be paid to common stockholders.

noncumulative (preferred stock)
Preferred stock for which passed (unpaid) dividends do not accumulate.

callable feature (preferred stock)
A feature of *callable preferred stock* that allows the issuer to retire the shares within a certain period of time and at a specified price.

conversion feature (preferred stock)
A feature of *convertible preferred stock* that allows holders to change each share into a stated number of shares of common stock.

Restrictive Covenants   The restrictive covenants in a preferred stock issue focus on ensuring the firm's continued existence and regular payment of the dividend. These covenants include provisions about passing dividends, the sale of senior securities, mergers, sales of assets, minimum liquidity requirements, and repurchases of common stock. The violation of preferred stock covenants usually permits preferred stockholders either to obtain representation on the firm's board of directors or to force the retirement of their stock at or above its par or stated value.

Cumulation   Most preferred stock is **cumulative** with respect to any dividends passed. That is, all dividends in arrears, along with the current dividend, must be paid before dividends can be paid to common stockholders. If preferred stock is **noncumulative,** passed (unpaid) dividends do not accumulate. In this case, only the current dividend must be paid before dividends can be paid to common stockholders. Because the common stockholders can receive dividends only after the dividend claims of preferred stockholders have been satisfied, it is in the firm's best interest to pay preferred dividends when they are due.

Other Features   Preferred stock can be *callable* or *convertible*. Preferred stock with a **callable feature** allows the issuer to retire outstanding shares within a certain period of time at a specified price. The call price is normally set above the initial issuance price, but it may decrease as time passes. Making preferred stock callable provides the issuer with a way to bring the fixed-payment commitment of the preferred issue to an end if conditions make it desirable to do so.

Preferred stock with a **conversion feature** allows *holders* to change each share into a stated number of shares of common stock, usually anytime after a predetermined date. The conversion ratio can be fixed, or the number of shares of common stock that the preferred stock can be exchanged for changes through time according to a predetermined formula.

ISSUING COMMON STOCK

Because of the high risk associated with a business startup, a firm's initial financing typically comes from its founders in the form of a common stock investment. Until the founders have made an equity investment, it is highly unlikely that others will contribute either equity or debt capital. Early-stage investors in the firm's equity, as well as lenders who provide debt capital, want to be assured that they are taking no more risk than the founders. In addition, they want confirmation that the founders are confident enough in their vision for the firm that they are willing to risk their own money.

Typically, the initial nonfounder financing for business startups with attractive growth prospects comes from private equity investors. Then, as the firm establishes the viability of its product or service offering and begins to generate revenues, cash flow, and profits, it will often "go public" by issuing shares of common stock to a much broader group of investors.

Before we consider the initial *public* sale of equity, let's discuss some of the key aspects of early-stage equity financing in firms that have attractive growth prospects.

venture capital
Privately raised external equity capital used to fund early-stage firms with attractive growth prospects.

Venture Capital

The initial external equity financing privately raised by firms, typically early-stage firms with attractive growth prospects, is called **venture capital.** Those who

venture capitalists (VCs)
Providers of venture capital; typically, formal businesses that maintain strong oversight over the firms they invest in and that have clearly defined exit strategies.

angel capitalists (angels)
Wealthy individual investors who do not operate as a business but invest in promising early-stage companies in exchange for a portion of the firm's equity.

provide venture capital are known as **venture capitalists (VCs)**. They typically are formal business entities that maintain strong oversight over the firms they invest in and that have clearly defined exit strategies. Less visible early-stage investors called **angel capitalists** (or **angels**) tend to be investors who do not actually operate as a business; they are often wealthy individual investors who are willing to invest in promising early-stage companies in exchange for a portion of the firm's equity. Although angels play a major role in early-stage equity financing, we will focus on VCs because of their more formal structure and greater public visibility.

Organization and Investment Stages Venture capital investors tend to be organized in one of four basic ways, as described in Table 7.2. The *VC limited partnership* is by far the dominant structure. These funds have as their sole objective to earn high returns, rather than to obtain access to the companies in order to sell or buy other products or services.

VCs can invest in early-stage companies, later-stage companies, or buyouts and acquisitions. Generally, about 40 to 50 percent of VC investments are devoted to early-stage companies (for startup funding and expansion) and a similar percentage to later-stage companies (for marketing, production expansion, and preparation for public offering); the remaining 5 to 10 percent are devoted to the buyout or acquisition of other companies. Generally, VCs look for compound annual rates of return ranging from 20 to 50 percent or more, depending on both the development stage and the attributes of each company. Earlier-stage investments tend to demand higher returns than later-stage investments because of the higher risk associated with the earlier stages of a firm's growth.

Deal Structure and Pricing Regardless of the development stage, venture capital investments are made under a legal contract that clearly allocates responsibilities and ownership interests between existing owners (founders) and the VC fund or limited partnership. The terms of the agreement will depend on numerous

TABLE 7.2 > Organization of Venture Capital Investors	
Organization	**Description**
Small business investment companies (SBICs)	Corporations chartered by the federal government that can borrow at attractive rates from the U.S. Treasury and use the funds to make venture capital investments in private companies.
Financial VC funds	Subsidiaries of financial institutions, particularly banks, set up to help young firms grow and, it is hoped, become major customers of the institution.
Corporate VC funds	Firms, sometimes subsidiaries, established by nonfinancial firms, typically to gain access to new technologies that the corporation can access to further its own growth.
VC limited partnerships	Limited partnerships organized by professional VC firms, which serve as the general partner and organize, invest, and manage the partnership using the limited partners' funds; the professional VCs ultimately liquidate the partnership and distribute the proceeds to all partners.

factors related to the founders; the business structure, stage of development, and outlook; and other market and timing issues. The specific financial terms will, of course, depend on the value of the enterprise, the amount of funding, and the perceived risk. To control the VC's risk, various covenants are included in the agreement, and the actual funding may be pegged to the achievement of *measurable milestones*. The VC will negotiate numerous other provisions into the contract, both to ensure the firm's success and to control its risk exposure. The contract will have an explicit exit strategy for the VC that may be tied both to measurable milestones and to time.

The amount of equity to which the VC is entitled will, of course, depend on the value of the firm, the terms of the contract, the exit terms, and the minimum compound annual rate of return required by the VC on its investment. Although each VC investment is unique and no standard contract exists, the transaction will be structured to provide the VC with a high rate of return that is consistent with the typically high risk of such transactions. The exit strategy of most VC investments is to take the firm public through an initial public offering.

Going Public

When a firm wishes to sell its stock in the primary market, it has three alternatives. It can make (1) a *public offering,* in which it offers its shares for sale to the general public; (2) a *rights offering,* in which new shares are sold to existing stockholders; or (3) a *private placement,* in which the firm sells new securities directly to an investor or group of investors. Here we focus on public offerings, particularly the **initial public offering (IPO)**, which is the first public sale of a firm's stock. IPOs are typically made by small, rapidly growing companies that either require additional capital to continue expanding or have met a milestone for going public that was established in a contract signed earlier in order to obtain VC funding.

To go public, the firm must first obtain the approval of its current shareholders, the investors who own its privately issued stock. Next, the company's auditors and lawyers must certify that all documents for the company are legitimate. The company then finds an investment bank willing to *underwrite* the offering. This underwriter is responsible for promoting the stock and facilitating the sale of the company's IPO shares. The underwriter often brings in other investment banking firms as participants. We'll discuss the role of the investment banker in more detail in the next section.

The company files a registration statement with the SEC. One portion of the registration statement is called the **prospectus.** It describes the key aspects of the issue, the issuer, and its management and financial position. During the waiting period between the statement's filing and its approval, prospective investors can receive a preliminary prospectus. This preliminary version is called a **red herring,** because a notice printed in red on the front cover indicates the tentative nature of the offer. The cover of the preliminary prospectus describing the 2010 stock issue of Convio, Inc., is shown in Figure 7.1. Note the red herring printed across the top of the page.

After the SEC approves the registration statement, the investment community can begin analyzing the company's prospects. However, from the time it files until at least one month after the IPO is complete, the company must observe a *quiet period,* during which there are restrictions on what company officials may say

initial public offering (IPO)
The first public sale of a firm's stock.

prospectus
A portion of a security registration statement that describes the key aspects of the issue, the issuer, and its management and financial position.

red herring
A preliminary prospectus made available to prospective investors during the waiting period between the registration statement's filing with the SEC and its approval.

FIGURE 7.1

Cover of a Preliminary Prospectus for a Stock Issue
Some of the key factors related to the 2010 common stock issue by Convio, Inc., are summarized on the cover of the preliminary prospectus. The disclaimer printed in red across the top of the page is what gives the preliminary prospectus its "red herring" name.

The information in this preliminary prospectus is not complete and may be changed. These securities may not be sold until the registration statement filed with the Securities and Exchange Commission is effective. This preliminary prospectus is not an offer to sell nor does it seek an offer to buy these securities in any jurisdiction where the offer or sale is not permitted.

SUBJECT TO COMPLETION. DATED APRIL 23, 2010.

IPO PRELIMINARY PROSPECTUS

5,132,728 Shares
Common Stock
$ per share

Convio, Inc. is selling 3,636,364 shares of our common stock and the selling stockholders identified in this prospectus are selling additional 1,496,364 shares. We will not receive any of the proceeds from the sale of the shares being sold by the selling stockholders. We have granted the underwriters a 30-day option to purchase up to an additional 769,909 shares from us to cover over-allotments, if any.

This is an initial public offering of our common stock. We currently expect the initial public offering price to be between $10.00 and $12.00 per share. We have applied for the listing of our common stock on the NASDAQ Global Market under the symbol "CNVO."

INVESTING IN OUR COMMON STOCK INVOLVES RISKS. SEE "RISK FACTORS" BEGINNING ON PAGE 10

	Per Share		Total
Initial public offering price	$	$	
Underwriting discount	$	$	
Proceeds, before expenses, to Convio	$	$	
Proceeds, before expenses, to the selling stockholders	$	$	

Neither the Securities and Exchange Commission nor any state securities commission has approved or disapproved of these securities or passed upon the accuracy or adequacy of this prospectus. Any representation to the contrary is a criminal offense.

Thomas Weisel Partners LLC   **Piper Jaffray**

William Blair & Company

JMP Securities

Pacific Crest Securities

The date of this prospectus is   , 2010.

Source: SEC filing Form S-1/A, Convio, Inc., filed April 26, 2010, p. 4.

about the company. The purpose of the quiet period is to make sure that all potential investors have access to the same information about the company—the information presented in the preliminary prospectus—and not to any unpublished data that might give them an unfair advantage.

The investment bankers and company executives promote the company's stock offering through a *road show,* a series of presentations to potential investors around the country and sometimes overseas. In addition to providing investors with information about the new issue, road show sessions help the investment bankers gauge the demand for the offering and set an expected pricing range. After the underwriter sets terms and prices the issue, the SEC must approve the offering.

The Investment Banker's Role

Most public offerings are made with the assistance of an **investment banker.** The investment banker is a financial intermediary (such as Morgan Stanley or Goldman Sachs) that specializes in selling new security issues and advising firms with regard to major financial transactions. The main activity of the investment banker is **underwriting.** This process involves purchasing the security issue from the issuing corporation at an agreed-on price and bearing the risk of reselling it to the public at a profit. The investment banker also provides the issuer with advice about pricing and other important aspects of the issue.

investment banker
Financial intermediary that specializes in selling new security issues and advising firms with regard to major financial transactions.

underwriting
The role of the *investment banker* in bearing the risk of reselling, at a profit, the securities purchased from an issuing corporation at an agreed-on price.

FIGURE 7.2

The Selling Process for a Large Security Issue
The investment banker hired by the issuing corporation may form an underwriting syndicate. The underwriting syndicate buys the entire security issue from the issuing corporation at an agreed-on price. The underwriters then have the opportunity (and bear the risk) of reselling the issue to the public at a profit. Both the originating investment banker and the other syndicate members put together a selling group to sell the issue on a commission basis to investors.

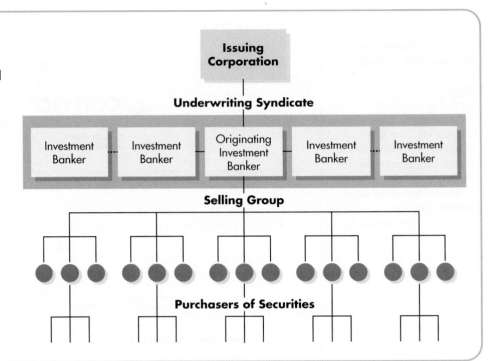

underwriting syndicate
A group of other bankers formed by an investment banker to share the financial risk associated with *underwriting* new securities.

selling group
A large number of brokerage firms that join the originating investment banker(s); each accepts responsibility for selling a certain portion of a new security issue on a commission basis.

In the case of very large security issues, the investment banker brings in other bankers as partners to form an **underwriting syndicate.** The syndicate shares the financial risk associated with buying the entire issue from the issuer and reselling the new securities to the public. The originating investment banker and the syndicate members put together a **selling group,** normally made up of themselves and a large number of brokerage firms. Each member of the selling group accepts the responsibility for selling a certain portion of the issue and is paid a commission on the securities it sells. The selling process for a large security issue is depicted in Figure 7.2.

Compensation for underwriting and selling services typically comes in the form of a discount on the sale price of the securities. For example, an investment banker may pay the issuing firm $24 per share for stock that will be sold for $26 per share. The investment banker may then sell the shares to members of the selling group for $25.25 per share. In this case, the original investment banker earns $1.25 per share ($25.25 sale price minus $24 purchase price). The members of the selling group earn 75 cents for each share they sell ($26 sale price minus $25.25 purchase price). Although some primary security offerings are directly placed by the issuer, the majority of new issues are sold through public offering via the mechanism just described.

→ **REVIEW QUESTIONS**

7–2 What risks do common stockholders take that other suppliers of capital do not?

7–3 How does a *rights offering* protect a firm's stockholders against the *dilution of ownership?*

7–4 Explain the relationships among authorized shares, outstanding shares, treasury stock, and issued shares.

7–5 What are the advantages to both U.S.-based and foreign corporations of issuing stock outside their home markets? What are *American depositary receipts (ADRs)?* What are *American depositary shares (ADSs)?*

7–6 What claims do preferred stockholders have with respect to distribution of earnings (dividends) and assets?

7–7 Explain the *cumulative feature* of preferred stock. What is the purpose of a *call feature* in a preferred stock issue?

7–8 What is the difference between a *venture capitalist (VC)* and an *angel capitalist (angel)?*

7–9 What are the four ways that VCs are most commonly organized? How are their deals structured and priced?

7–10 What general procedures must a private firm follow to go public via an *initial public offering (IPO)?*

7–11 What role does an *investment banker* play in a public offering? Describe an underwriting syndicate.

LG 4 LG 5 ## 7.3 Common Stock Valuation

Common stockholders expect to be rewarded through periodic cash dividends and an increasing share value. Some of these investors decide which stocks to buy and sell based on a plan to maintain a broadly diversified portfolio. Other investors have a more speculative motive for trading. They try to spot companies whose shares are *undervalued*—meaning that the true value of the shares is greater than the current market price. These investors buy shares that they believe to be undervalued and sell shares that they think are *overvalued* (that is, the market price is greater than the true value). Regardless of one's motive for trading, understanding how to value common stocks is an important part of the investment process. Stock valuation is also an important tool for financial managers—how can they work to maximize the stock price without understanding the factors that determine the value of the stock? In this section, we will describe specific stock valuation techniques. First, we will consider the relationship between market efficiency and stock valuation.

MARKET EFFICIENCY

Economically rational buyers and sellers use their assessment of an asset's risk and return to determine its value. To a buyer, the asset's value represents the maximum purchase price, and to a seller it represents the minimum sale price. In competitive markets with many active participants, such as the New York Stock Exchange, the interactions of many buyers and sellers result in an equilibrium price—the *market value*—for each security. This price reflects the collective actions that buyers and sellers take on the basis of all available information. Buyers and sellers digest new information quickly as it becomes available and, through their purchase and sale activities, create a new market equilibrium price. Because the flow of new information is almost constant, stock prices fluctuate, continuously moving toward a new equilibrium that reflects the most recent information available. This general concept is known as *market efficiency*.

efficient-market hypothesis (EMH)
Theory describing the behavior of an assumed "perfect" market in which (1) securities are in equilibrium, (2) security prices fully reflect all available information and react swiftly to new information, and (3), because stocks are fully and fairly priced, investors need not waste time looking for mispriced securities.

In more depth

To read about *The Hierarchy of the Efficient-Market Hypothesis*, go to www.myfinancelab.com

behavioral finance
A growing body of research that focuses on investor behavior and its impact on investment decisions and stock prices. Advocates are commonly referred to as "behaviorists."

THE EFFICIENT-MARKET HYPOTHESIS

As noted in Chapter 2, active broker and dealer markets, such as the New York Stock Exchange and the Nasdaq market, are *efficient*—they are made up of many rational investors who react quickly and objectively to new information. The **efficient-market hypothesis (EMH)**, which is the basic theory describing the behavior of such a "perfect" market, specifically states that

1. Securities are typically in equilibrium, which means that they are fairly priced and that their expected returns equal their required returns.
2. At any point in time, security prices fully reflect all information available about the firm and its securities, and these prices react swiftly to new information.
3. Because stocks are fully and fairly priced, investors need not waste their time trying to find mispriced (undervalued or overvalued) securities.

Not all market participants are believers in the efficient-market hypothesis. Some feel that it is worthwhile to search for undervalued or overvalued securities and to trade them to profit from market inefficiencies. Others argue that it is mere luck that would allow market participants to anticipate new information correctly and as a result earn *abnormal returns*—that is, actual returns greater than average market returns. They believe it is unlikely that market participants can *over the long run* earn abnormal returns. Contrary to this belief, some well-known investors such as Warren Buffett and Bill Gross *have* over the long run consistently earned abnormal returns on their portfolios. It is unclear whether their success is the result of their superior ability to anticipate new information or of some form of market inefficiency.

The Behavioral Finance Challenge

Although considerable evidence supports the concept of market efficiency, a growing body of academic evidence has begun to cast doubt on the validity of this notion. The research documents various *anomalies*—outcomes that are inconsistent with efficient markets—in stock returns. A number of academics and practitioners have also recognized that emotions and other subjective factors play a role in investment decisions.

This focus on investor behavior has resulted in a significant body of research, collectively referred to as **behavioral finance**. Advocates of behavioral finance are commonly referred to as "behaviorists." Daniel Kahneman was awarded the 2002 Nobel Prize in economics for his work in behavioral finance, specifically for integrating insights from psychology and economics. Ongoing research into the psychological factors that can affect investor behavior and the resulting effects on stock prices will likely result in growing acceptance of behavioral finance. The *Focus on Practice* box further explains some of the findings of behavioral finance.

While challenges to the efficient market hypothesis, such as those presented by advocates of behavioral finance, are interesting and worthy of study, in this text we generally take the position that markets are efficient. This means that the terms *expected return* and *required return* will be used interchangeably because they should be equal in an efficient market. In other words, we will operate under the assumption that a stock's market price at any point in time is the best estimate of its value. We're now ready to look closely at the mechanics of common stock valuation.

focus on PRACTICE

Understanding Human Behavior Helps Us Understand Investor Behavior

in practice Market anomalies are patterns inconsistent with the efficient market hypothesis. Behavioral finance has a number of theories to help explain how human emotions influence people in their investment decision-making processes.

Regret theory deals with the emotional reaction people experience after realizing they have made an error in judgment. When deciding whether to sell a stock, investors become emotionally affected by the price at which they purchased the stock. A sale at a loss would confirm that the investor miscalculated the value of the stock when it was purchased. The correct approach when considering whether to sell a stock is, "Would I buy this stock today if it were already liquidated?" If the answer is "no," it is time to sell. Regret theory also holds true for investors who passed up buying a stock that now is selling at a much higher price. Again, the correct approach is to value the stock today without regard to its prior value.

Herding is another market behavior affecting investor decisions. Some investors rationalize their decision to buy certain stocks with "everyone else is doing it." Investors may feel less embarrassment about losing money on a popular stock than about losing money on an unknown or unpopular stock.

People have a tendency to place particular events into *mental accounts*, and the difference between these compartments sometimes influences behavior more than the events themselves. Researchers have asked people the following question: "Would you purchase a $20 ticket at the local theater if you realize after you get there that you have lost a $20 bill?" Roughly 88 percent of people would do so. Under another scenario, people were asked whether they would buy a second $20 ticket if they arrived at the theater and realized that they had left at home a ticket purchased in advance for $20. Only 40 percent of respondents would buy another. In both scenarios the person is out $40, but mental accounting leads to a different outcome. In investing, compartmentalization is best illustrated by the hesitation to sell an investment that once had monstrous gains and now has a modest gain. During bull markets, people get accustomed to paper gains. When a market correction deflates investors' net worth, they are hesitant to sell, causing them to wait for the return of that gain.

Other investor behaviors are prospect theory and anchoring. According to *prospect theory*, people express a different degree of emotion toward gains than losses. Individuals are stressed more by prospective losses than they are buoyed by the prospect of equal gains. *Anchoring* is the tendency of investors to place more value on recent information. People tend to give too much credence to recent market opinions and events and mistakenly extrapolate recent trends that differ from historical, long-term averages and probabilities. Anchoring is a partial explanation for the longevity of some bull markets.

Most stock-valuation techniques require that all relevant information be available to properly determine a stock's value and potential for future gain. Behavioral finance may explain the connection between valuation and an investor's actions based on that valuation.

▶ *Theories of behavioral finance can apply to other areas of human behavior in addition to investing. Think of a situation in which you may have demonstrated one of these behaviors. Share your situation with a classmate.*

BASIC COMMON STOCK VALUATION EQUATION

Like the value of a bond, which we discussed in Chapter 6, *the value of a share of common stock is equal to the present value of all future cash flows (dividends) that it is expected to provide.* Although a stockholder can earn capital gains by selling stock at a price above that originally paid, what the buyer really pays for is the right to all future dividends. What about stocks that do not currently pay dividends? Such stocks have a value attributable to a future dividend stream or to the proceeds from the sale of the company. Therefore, *from a valuation viewpoint, future dividends are relevant.*

The basic valuation model for common stock is given in Equation 7.1:

$$P_0 = \frac{D_1}{(1 + r_s)^1} + \frac{D_2}{(1 + r_s)^2} + \cdots + \frac{D_\infty}{(1 + r_s)^\infty} \tag{7.1}$$

where

$$P_0 = \text{value today of common stock}$$
$$D_t = \text{per-share dividend } expected \text{ at the end of year } t$$
$$r_s = \text{required return on common stock}$$

The equation can be simplified somewhat by redefining each year's dividend, D_t, in terms of anticipated growth. We will consider three models here: zero growth, constant growth, and variable growth.

Zero-Growth Model

zero-growth model
An approach to dividend valuation that assumes a constant, nongrowing dividend stream.

The simplest approach to dividend valuation, the **zero-growth model,** assumes a constant, nongrowing dividend stream. In terms of the notation already introduced,

$$D_1 = D_2 = \cdots = D_\infty$$

When we let D_1 represent the amount of the annual dividend, Equation 7.1 under zero growth reduces to

$$P_0 = D_1 \times \sum_{t=1}^{\infty} \frac{1}{(1 + r_s)^t} = D_1 \times \frac{1}{r_s} = \frac{D_1}{r_s} \tag{7.2}$$

The equation shows that with zero growth, the value of a share of stock would equal the present value of a perpetuity of D_1 dollars discounted at a rate r_s. (Perpetuities were introduced in Chapter 5; see Equation 5.14 and the related discussion.)

Personal Finance Example 7.2 ▶   Chuck Swimmer estimates that the dividend of Denham Company, an established textile producer, is expected to remain constant at $3 per share indefinitely. If his required return on its stock is 15%, the stock's value is $20 ($3 ÷ 0.15) per share.

Preferred Stock Valuation   Because preferred stock typically provides its holders with a fixed annual dividend over its assumed infinite life, *Equation 7.2 can be used to find the value of preferred stock.* The value of preferred stock can be estimated by substituting the stated dividend on the preferred stock for D_1 and the required return for r_s in Equation 7.2. For example, a preferred stock paying a $5 stated annual dividend and having a required return of 13 percent would have a value of $38.46 ($5 ÷ 0.13) per share.

Constant-Growth Model

constant-growth model
A widely cited dividend valuation approach that assumes that dividends will grow at a constant rate, but a rate that is less than the required return.

The most widely cited dividend valuation approach, the **constant-growth model,** assumes that dividends will grow at a constant rate, but a rate that is less than the required return. (The assumption that the constant rate of growth, g, is less than the required return, r_s, is a necessary mathematical condition for deriving this model.[1]) By letting D_0 represent the most recent dividend, we can rewrite Equation 7.1 as follows:

In more depth

To read about *Deriving the Constant-Growth Model*, go to www.myfinancelab.com

$$P_0 = \frac{D_0 \times (1 + g)^1}{(1 + r_s)^1} + \frac{D_0 \times (1 + g)^2}{(1 + r_s)^2} + \cdots + \frac{D_0 \times (1 + g)^\infty}{(1 + r_s)^\infty} \quad (7.3)$$

If we simplify Equation 7.3, it can be rewritten as:

$$P_0 = \frac{D_1}{r_s - g} \quad (7.4)$$

Gordon growth model
A common name for the *constant-growth model* that is widely cited in dividend valuation.

The constant-growth model in Equation 7.4 is commonly called the **Gordon growth model.** An example will show how it works.

Example 7.3 ▶ Lamar Company, a small cosmetics company, from 2007 through 2012 paid the following per-share dividends:

Year	Dividend per share
2012	$1.40
2011	1.29
2010	1.20
2009	1.12
2008	1.05
2007	1.00

We assume that the historical annual growth rate of dividends is an accurate estimate of the future constant annual rate of dividend growth, g. To find the historical annual growth rate of dividends, we must solve the following for g:

$$D_{2012} = D_{2007} \times (1 + g)^5$$

$$\frac{D_{2007}}{D_{2012}} = \frac{1}{(1 + g)^5}$$

$$\frac{\$1.00}{\$1.40} = \frac{1}{(1 + g)^5}$$

---

1. Another assumption of the constant-growth model as presented is that earnings and dividends grow at the same rate. This assumption is true only in cases in which a firm pays out a fixed percentage of its earnings each year (has a fixed payout ratio). In the case of a declining industry, a negative growth rate ($g < 0\%$) might exist. In such a case, the constant-growth model, as well as the variable-growth model presented in the next section, remains fully applicable to the valuation process.

Input	Function
1.00	PV
−1.40	FV
5	N
	CPT
	I

Solution
6.96

Using a financial calculator or a spreadsheet, we find that the historical annual growth rate of Lamar Company dividends equals 7%.[2] The company estimates that its dividend in 2013, D_1, will equal $1.50 (about 7% more than the last dividend). The required return, r_s, is 15%. By substituting these values into Equation 7.4, we find the value of the stock to be

$$P_0 = \frac{\$1.50}{0.15 - 0.07} = \frac{\$1.50}{0.08} = \underline{\$18.75} \text{ per share}$$

Assuming that the values of D_1, r_s, and g are accurately estimated, Lamar Company's stock value is $18.75 per share.

Variable-Growth Model

variable-growth model
A dividend valuation approach that allows for a change in the dividend growth rate.

The zero- and constant-growth common stock models do not allow for any shift in expected growth rates. Because future growth rates might shift up or down because of changing business conditions, it is useful to consider a **variable-growth model** that allows for a change in the dividend growth rate.[3] We will assume that a single shift in growth rates occurs at the end of year N, and we will use g_1 to represent the initial growth rate and g_2 for the growth rate after the shift. To determine the value of a share of stock in the case of variable growth, we use a four-step procedure:

Step 1 Find the value of the cash dividends at the end of *each year*, D_t, during the initial growth period, years 1 through N. This step may require adjusting the most recent dividend, D_0, using the initial growth rate, g_1, to calculate the dividend amount for each year. Therefore, for the first N years,

$$D_t = D_0 \times (1 + g_1)^t$$

Step 2 Find the present value of the dividends expected during the initial growth period. Using the notation presented earlier, we can give this value as

$$\sum_{t=1}^{N} \frac{D_0 \times (1 + g_1)^t}{(1 + r_s)^t} = \sum_{t=1}^{N} \frac{D_t}{(1 + r_s)^t}$$

Step 3 Find the value of the stock *at the end of the initial growth period*, $P_N = (D_{N+1})/(r_s - g_2)$, which is the present value of all dividends expected from year N + 1 to infinity, assuming a constant dividend growth rate, g_2. This value is found by applying the constant-growth model (Equation 7.4) to the dividends expected from year N + 1 to infinity.

---

2. A financial calculator can be used. (*Note:* Most calculators require *either* the PV or FV value to be input as a negative number to calculate an unknown interest or growth rate. That approach is used here.) Using the inputs shown at the left, you should find the growth rate to be 6.96%, which we round to 7%.

An electronic spreadsheet could also be used to make this computation. Given space considerations, we have forgone that computational aid here.

3. More than one change in the growth rate can be incorporated into the model, but to simplify the discussion we will consider only a single growth-rate change. The number of variable-growth valuation models is technically unlimited, but concern over all possible shifts in growth is unlikely to yield much more accuracy than a simpler model.

The present value of P_N would represent the value *today* of all dividends that are expected to be received from year $N + 1$ to infinity. This value can be represented by

$$\frac{1}{(1 + r_s)^N} \times \frac{D_{N+1}}{r_s - g_2}$$

Step 4 Add the present value components found in Steps 2 and 3 to find the value of the stock, P_0, given in Equation 7.5:

$$P_0 = \underbrace{\sum_{t=1}^{N} \frac{D_0 \times (1 + g_1)^t}{(1 + r_s)^t}}_{\substack{\textit{Present value of} \\ \textit{dividends} \\ \textit{during initial} \\ \textit{growth period}}} + \underbrace{\left[\frac{1}{(1 + r_s)^N} \times \frac{D_{N+1}}{r_s - g_2} \right]}_{\substack{\textit{Present value of} \\ \textit{price of stock} \\ \textit{at end of initial} \\ \textit{growth period}}} \qquad (7.5)$$

The following example illustrates the application of these steps to a variable-growth situation with only one change in growth rate.

Personal Finance Example 7.4 ▶ Victoria Robb is considering purchasing the common stock of Warren Industries, a rapidly growing boat manufacturer. She finds that the firm's most recent (2012) annual dividend payment was $1.50 per share. Victoria estimates that these dividends will increase at a 10% annual rate, g_1, over the next 3 years (2013, 2014, and 2015) because of the introduction of a hot new boat. At the end of the 3 years (the end of 2015), she expects the firm's mature product line to result in a slowing of the dividend growth rate to 5% per year, g_2, for the foreseeable future. Victoria's required return, r_s, is 15%. To estimate the current (end-of-2012) value of Warren's common stock, $P_0 = P_{2012}$, she applies the four-step procedure to these data.

Step 1 The value of the cash dividends in each of the next 3 years is calculated in columns 1, 2, and 3 of Table 7.3. The 2013, 2014, and 2015 dividends are $1.65, $1.82, and $2.00, respectively.

TABLE 7.3 | Calculation of Present Value of Warren Industries Dividends (2013–2015)

t	End of year	$D_0 = D_{2012}$ (1)	$(1 + g_1)^t$ (2)	D_t [(1) × (2)] (3)	$(1 + r_s)^t$ (4)	Present value of dividends [(3) ÷ (4)] (5)
1	2013	$1.50	1.100	$1.65	1.150	$1.43
2	2014	1.50	1.210	1.82	1.323	1.37
3	2015	1.50	1.331	2.00	1.521	1.32

$$\text{Sum of present value of dividends} = \sum_{t=1}^{3} \frac{D_0 \times (1 + g_1)^t}{(1 + r_s)^t} = \$4.12$$

Step 2 The present value of the three dividends expected during the 2013–2015 initial growth period is calculated in columns 3, 4, and 5 of Table 7.3. The sum of the present values of the three dividends is $4.12.

Step 3 The value of the stock at the end of the initial growth period ($N = 2015$) can be found by first calculating $D_{N+1} = D_{2016}$:

$$D_{2016} = D_{2015} \times (1 + 0.05) = \$2.00 \times (1.05) = \$2.10$$

By using $D_{2016} = \$2.10$, a 15% required return, and a 5% dividend growth rate, the value of the stock at the end of 2015 is calculated as follows:

$$P_{2015} = \frac{D_{2016}}{r_s - g_2} = \frac{\$2.10}{0.15 - 0.05} = \frac{\$2.10}{0.10} = \$21.00$$

Finally, in Step 3, the share value of $21 at the end of 2015 must be converted into a present (end-of-2012) value. Using the 15% required return, we get

$$\frac{P_{2015}}{(1 + r_s)^3} = \frac{\$21}{(1 + 0.15)^3} = \$13.81$$

Step 4 Adding the present value of the initial dividend stream (found in Step 2) to the present value of the stock at the end of the initial growth period (found in Step 3) as specified in Equation 7.5, the current (end-of-2012) value of Warren Industries stock is:

$$P_{2012} = \$4.12 + \$13.81 = \underline{\$17.93} \text{ per share}$$

Victoria's calculations indicate that the stock is currently worth $17.93 per share.

FREE CASH FLOW VALUATION MODEL

As an alternative to the dividend valuation models presented earlier in this chapter, a firm's value can be estimated by using its projected *free cash flows* (*FCFs*). This approach is appealing when one is valuing firms that have no dividend history or are startups or when one is valuing an operating unit or division of a larger public company. Although dividend valuation models are widely used and accepted, in these situations it is preferable to use a more general free cash flow valuation model.

free cash flow valuation model
A model that determines the value of an entire company as the present value of its expected *free cash flows* discounted at the firm's *weighted average cost of capital,* which is its expected average future cost of funds over the long run.

The **free cash flow valuation model** is based on the same basic premise as dividend valuation models: The value of a share of common stock is the present value of all future cash flows it is expected to provide over an infinite time horizon. However, in the free cash flow valuation model, instead of valuing the firm's expected dividends, we value the firm's expected *free cash flows*, defined in Equation 4.4 (on page 122). They represent the amount of cash flow available to investors—the providers of debt (creditors) and equity (owners)—after all other obligations have been met.

The free cash flow valuation model estimates the value of the entire company by finding the present value of its expected free cash flows discounted at its *weighted average cost of capital,* which is its expected average future cost of funds (we'll say more about this in Chapter 9), as specified in Equation 7.6:

$$V_C = \frac{FCF_1}{(1 + r_a)^1} + \frac{FCF_2}{(1 + r_a)^2} + \cdots + \frac{FCF_\infty}{(1 + r_a)^\infty} \tag{7.6}$$

where

$$V_C = \text{value of the entire company}$$
$$FCF_t = \text{free cash flow } \textit{expected} \text{ at the end of year } t$$
$$r_a = \text{the firm's weighted average cost of capital}$$

Note the similarity between Equations 7.6 and 7.1, the general stock valuation equation.

Because the value of the entire company, V_C, is the market value of the entire enterprise (that is, of all assets), to find common stock value, V_S, we must subtract the market value of all of the firm's debt, V_D, and the market value of preferred stock, V_P, from V_C:

$$V_S = V_C - V_D - V_P \tag{7.7}$$

Because it is difficult to forecast a firm's free cash flow, specific annual cash flows are typically forecast for only about 5 years, beyond which a constant growth rate is assumed. Here we assume that the first 5 years of free cash flows are explicitly forecast and that a constant rate of free cash flow growth occurs beyond the end of year 5 to infinity. This model is methodologically similar to the variable-growth model presented earlier. Its application is best demonstrated with an example.

Example 7.5 ▶

Dewhurst, Inc., wishes to determine the value of its stock by using the free cash flow valuation model. To apply the model, the firm's CFO developed the data given in Table 7.4. Application of the model can be performed in four steps.

Step 1 Calculate the present value of the free cash flow occurring from the end of 2018 to infinity, measured at the beginning of 2018 (that is, at the end of 2017). Because a constant rate of growth in FCF is forecast beyond 2017, we can use the constant-growth dividend valuation model

TABLE 7.4 ▶ Dewhurst, Inc.'s, Data for the Free Cash Flow Valuation Model

Year (t)	Free cash flow (FCF_t)	Other data
2013	$400,000	Growth rate of FCF, beyond 2017 to infinity, $g_{FCF} = 3\%$
2014	450,000	Weighted average cost of capital, $r_a = 9\%$
2015	520,000	Market value of all debt, $V_D = \$3,100,000$
2016	560,000	Market value of preferred stock, $V_P = \$800,000$
2017	600,000	Number of shares of common stock outstanding = 300,000

(Equation 7.4) to calculate the value of the free cash flows from the end of 2018 to infinity:

$$\text{Value of } FCF_{2018 \to \infty} = \frac{FCF_{2018}}{r_a - g_{FCF}}$$

$$= \frac{\$600{,}000 \times (1 + 0.03)}{0.09 - 0.03}$$

$$= \frac{\$618{,}000}{0.06} = \$10{,}300{,}000$$

Note that to calculate the FCF in 2018, we had to increase the 2017 FCF value of $600,000 by the 3% FCF growth rate, g_{FCF}.

Step 2 Add the present value of the FCF from 2018 to infinity, which is measured at the end of 2017, to the 2017 FCF value to get the total FCF in 2017.

$$\text{Total } FCF_{2017} = \$600{,}000 + \$10{,}300{,}000 = \$10{,}900{,}000$$

Step 3 Find the sum of the present values of the FCFs for 2013 through 2017 to determine the value of the entire company, V_C. This calculation is shown in Table 7.5.

TABLE 7.5	Calculation of the Value of the Entire Company for Dewhurst, Inc.		
Year (t)	FCF_t (1)	$(1 + r_a)^t$ (2)	Present value of FCF_t [(1) ÷ (2)] (3)
2013	$ 400,000	1.090	$ 366,972
2014	450,000	1.188	378,788
2015	520,000	1.295	401,544
2016	560,000	1.412	396,601
2017	10,900,000[a]	1.539	7,082,521
		Value of entire company, V_C =	$8,626,426[b]

[a]This amount is the sum of the FCF_{2017} of $600,000 from Table 7.4 and the $10,300,000 value of the $FCF_{2018 \to \infty}$ calculated in Step 1.

[b]This value of the entire company is based on the rounded values that appear in the table. The precise value found without rounding is $8,628,234.

Step 4 Calculate the value of the common stock using Equation 7.7. Substituting into Equation 7.7 the value of the entire company, V_C, calculated in Step 3, and the market values of debt, V_D, and preferred stock, V_P, given in Table 7.4, yields the value of the common stock, V_S:

$$V_S = \$8{,}626{,}426 - \$3{,}100{,}000 - \$800{,}000 = \underline{\$4{,}726{,}426}$$

The value of Dewhurst's common stock is therefore estimated to be $4,726,426. By dividing this total by the 300,000 shares of common stock that the firm has outstanding, we get a common stock value of *$15.76 per share* ($4,726,426 ÷ 300,000).

It should now be clear that the free cash flow valuation model is consistent with the dividend valuation models presented earlier. The appeal of this approach is its focus on the free cash flow estimates rather than on forecasted dividends, which are far more difficult to estimate given that they are paid at the discretion of the firm's board. The more general nature of the free cash flow model is responsible for its growing popularity, particularly with CFOs and other financial managers.

OTHER APPROACHES TO COMMON STOCK VALUATION

Many other approaches to common stock valuation exist. The more popular approaches include book value, liquidation value, and some type of price/earnings multiple.

book value per share
The amount per share of common stock that would be received if all of the firm's assets were *sold for their exact book (accounting) value* and the proceeds remaining after paying all liabilities (including preferred stock) were divided among the common stockholders.

Book Value

Book value per share is simply the amount per share of common stock that would be received if all of the firm's assets were *sold for their exact book (accounting) value* and the proceeds remaining after paying all liabilities (including preferred stock) were divided among the common stockholders. This method lacks sophistication and can be criticized on the basis of its reliance on historical balance sheet data. It ignores the firm's expected earnings potential and generally lacks any true relationship to the firm's value in the marketplace. Let us look at an example.

Example 7.6 ▶ At year-end 2012, Lamar Company's balance sheet shows total assets of $6 million, total liabilities (including preferred stock) of $4.5 million, and 100,000 shares of common stock outstanding. Its book value per share therefore would be

$$\frac{\$6,000,000 - \$4,500,000}{100,000 \text{ shares}} = \underline{\$15} \text{ per share}$$

Because this value assumes that assets could be sold for their book value, it may not represent the minimum price at which shares are valued in the marketplace. As a matter of fact, although most stocks sell above book value, it is not unusual to find stocks selling below book value when investors believe either that assets are overvalued or that the firm's liabilities are understated.

---

liquidation value per share
The *actual amount* per share of common stock that would be received if all of the firm's assets were *sold for their market value,* liabilities (including preferred stock) were paid, and any remaining money were divided among the common stockholders.

Liquidation Value

Liquidation value per share is the *actual amount* per share of common stock that would be received if all of the firm's assets were *sold for their market value,* liabilities (including preferred stock) were paid, and any remaining money were divided among the common stockholders. This measure is more realistic than book value—because it is based on the current market value of the firm's assets—but it still fails to consider the earning power of those assets. An example will illustrate.

Example 7.7 ▶ Lamar Company found on investigation that it could obtain only $5.25 million if it sold its assets today. The firm's liquidation value per share therefore would be

$$\frac{\$5,250,000 - \$4,500,000}{100,000 \text{ shares}} = \underline{\$7.50} \text{ per share}$$

Ignoring liquidation expenses, this amount would be the firm's minimum value.

Price/Earnings (P/E) Multiples

price/earnings multiple approach
A popular technique used to estimate the firm's share value; calculated by multiplying the firm's expected earnings per share (EPS) by the average price/earnings (P/E) ratio for the industry.

The *price/earnings (P/E) ratio*, introduced in Chapter 3, reflects the amount investors are willing to pay for each dollar of earnings. The average P/E ratio in a particular industry can be used as a guide to a firm's value—if it is assumed that investors value the earnings of that firm in the same way they do the "average" firm in the industry. The **price/earnings multiple approach** is a popular technique used to estimate the firm's share value; it is calculated by multiplying the firm's expected earnings per share (EPS) by the average price/earnings (P/E) ratio for the industry. The average P/E ratio for the industry can be obtained from a source such as *Standard & Poor's Industrial Ratios*.

The P/E ratio valuation technique is a simple method of determining a stock's value and can be quickly calculated after firms make earnings announcements, which accounts for its popularity. Naturally, this has increased the demand for more frequent announcements or "guidance" regarding future earnings. Some firms feel that pre-earnings guidance creates additional costs and can lead to ethical issues, as discussed in the *Focus on Ethics* box below.

focus on ETHICS

Psst—Have You Heard Any Good Quarterly Earnings Forecasts Lately?

in practice Corporate managers have long complained about the pressure to focus on the short term, and now business groups are coming to their defense. "The focus on the short term is a huge problem," says William Donaldson, former chairman of the Securities and Exchange Commission. "With all of the attention paid to quarterly performance, managers are taking their eyes off long-term strategic goals."

Donaldson, the U.S. Chamber of Commerce, and others believe that the best way to focus companies toward long-term goals is to do away with the practice of giving quarterly earnings guidance. In March 2007 the CFA Centre for Financial Market Integrity and the Business Roundtable Institute for Corporate Ethics proposed a template for quarterly earnings reports that would, in their view, obviate the need for earnings guidance.

Meanwhile, many companies are hesitant to give up issuing quarterly

guidance. The practice of issuing earnings forecasts began in the early 1980s, a few years after the SEC's decision to allow companies to include forward-looking projections, provided they were accompanied by appropriate cautionary language. The result was what former SEC chairman Arthur Levitt once called a "game of winks and nods." Companies used earnings guidance to lower analysts' estimates; when the actual numbers came in higher, their stock prices jumped. The practice reached a fever pitch during the late 1990s when companies that missed the consensus earnings estimate, even by just a penny, saw their stock prices tumble.

One of the first companies to stop issuing earnings guidance was Gillette, in 2001. Others that abandoned quarterly guidance were Coca-Cola, Intel, and McDonald's. It became a trend. By 2005, just 61 percent of companies were offering quarterly projections to the public; according to the National

Investor Relations Institute, the number declined to 52 percent in 2006.

Not everyone agrees with eliminating quarterly guidance. A survey conducted by New York University's Stern School of Business finance professor Baruch Lev, along with University of Florida professors Joel Houston and Jennifer Tucker, showed that companies that ended quarterly guidance reaped almost no benefit from doing so. Their study found no evidence that guidance stoppers increased capital investments or research and development. So when should companies give up earnings guidance? According to Lev, they should do so only when they are not very good at predicting their earnings. "If you are not better than others at forecasting, then don't bother," he says.

▶ *What temptations might managers face if they have provided earnings guidance to investors and later find it difficult to meet the expectations that they helped create?*

The use of P/E multiples is especially helpful in valuing firms that are not publicly traded, but analysts use this approach for public companies too. In any case, the price/earnings multiple approach is considered superior to the use of book or liquidation values because it considers *expected* earnings. An example will demonstrate the use of price/earnings multiples.

Personal Finance Example 7.8 ▶   Ann Perrier plans to use the price/earnings multiple approach to estimate the value of Lamar Company's stock, which she currently holds in her retirement account. She estimates that Lamar Company will earn $2.60 per share next year (2013). This expectation is based on an analysis of the firm's historical earnings trend and of expected economic and industry conditions. She finds the price/earnings (P/E) ratio for firms in the same industry to average 7. Multiplying Lamar's expected earnings per share (EPS) of $2.60 by this ratio gives her a value for the firm's shares of $18.20, assuming that investors will continue to value the average firm at 7 times its earnings.

So how much is Lamar Company's stock really worth? That's a trick question because there's no one right answer. It is important to recognize that the answer depends on the assumptions made and the techniques used. Professional securities analysts typically use a variety of models and techniques to value stocks. For example, an analyst might use the constant-growth model, liquidation value, and a price/earnings (P/E) multiple to estimate the worth of a given stock. If the analyst feels comfortable with his or her estimates, the stock would be valued at no more than the largest estimate. Of course, should the firm's estimated liquidation value per share exceed its "going concern" value per share, estimated by using one of the valuation models (zero-, constant-, or variable-growth or free cash flow) or the P/E multiple approach, the firm would be viewed as being "worth more dead than alive." In such an event, the firm would lack sufficient earning power to justify its existence and should probably be liquidated.

Matter of fact

Problems with P/E Valuation

The P/E multiple approach is a fast and easy way to estimate a stock's value. However, P/E ratios vary widely over time. In 1980, the average stock had a P/E ratio below 9, but by the year 2000, the ratio had risen above 40. Therefore, analysts using the P/E approach in the 1980s would have come up with much lower estimates of value than analysts using the model 20 years later. In other words, when using this approach to estimate stock values, the estimate will depend more on whether stock market valuations generally are high or low rather than on whether the particular company is doing well or not.

→ REVIEW QUESTIONS

7–12 Describe the events that occur in an *efficient market* in response to new information that causes the expected return to exceed the required return. What happens to the market value?

7–13 What does the *efficient-market hypothesis (EMH)* say about (**a**) securities prices, (**b**) their reaction to new information, and (**c**) investor opportunities to profit? What is the *behavioral finance* challenge to this hypothesis?

7–14 Describe, compare, and contrast the following common stock dividend valuation models: (**a**) zero-growth, (**b**) constant-growth, and (**c**) variable-growth.

7–15 Describe the *free cash flow valuation model* and explain how it differs from the dividend valuation models. What is the appeal of this model?

7–16 Explain each of the three other approaches to common stock valuation: (**a**) book value, (**b**) liquidation value, and (**c**) price/earnings (P/E) multiples. Which of these is considered the best?

LG 6   7.4 Decision Making and Common Stock Value

Valuation equations measure the stock value at a point in time based on expected return and risk. Any decisions of the financial manager that affect these variables can cause the value of the firm to change. Figure 7.3 depicts the relationship among financial decisions, return, risk, and stock value.

CHANGES IN EXPECTED DIVIDENDS

Assuming that economic conditions remain stable, any management action that would cause current and prospective stockholders to raise their dividend expectations should increase the firm's value. In Equation 7.4, we can see that P_0 will increase for any increase in D_1 or g. Any action of the financial manager that will increase the level of expected dividends without changing risk (the required return) should be undertaken, because it will positively affect owners' wealth.

Example 7.9 ▶   Using the constant-growth model in an earlier example (on pages 281 and 282), we found Lamar Company to have a share value of $18.75. On the following day, the firm announced a major technological breakthrough that would revolutionize its industry. Current and prospective stockholders would not be expected to adjust their required return of 15%, but they would expect that future dividends will increase. Specifically, they expect that although the dividend next year, D_1, will remain at $1.50, the expected rate of growth thereafter will increase from 7% to 9%. If we substitute $D_1 = \$1.50$, $r_s = 0.15$, and $g = 0.09$ into Equation 7.4, the resulting share value is $25 $[\$1.50 \div (0.15 - 0.09)]$. The increased value therefore resulted from the higher expected future dividends reflected in the increase in the growth rate.

FIGURE 7.3

Decision Making and Stock Value
Financial decisions, return, risk, and stock value

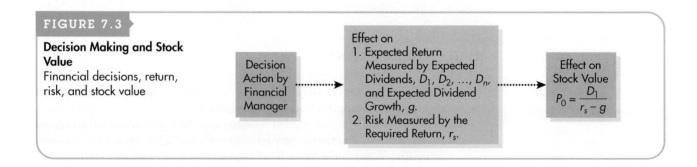

CHANGES IN RISK

Although the required return, r_s, is the focus of Chapters 8 and 9, at this point we can consider its fundamental components. Any measure of required return consists of two components, a risk-free rate and a risk premium. We expressed this relationship as Equation 6.1 in the previous chapter, which we repeat here in terms of r_s:

$$r_s = \underbrace{r^* + IP}_{\substack{\text{risk-free} \\ \text{rate, } R_F}} + \underbrace{RP_s}_{\substack{\text{risk} \\ \text{premium}}}$$

In the next chapter you will learn that the real challenge in finding the required return is determining the appropriate risk premium. In Chapters 8 and 9 we will discuss how investors and managers can estimate the risk premium for any particular asset. For now, recognize that r_s represents the minimum return that the firm's stock must provide to shareholders to compensate them for bearing the risk of holding the firm's equity.

Any action taken by the financial manager that increases the risk shareholders must bear will also increase the risk premium required by shareholders, and hence the required return. Additionally, the required return can be affected by changes in the risk free rate—even if the risk premium remains constant. For example, if the risk-free rate increases due to a shift in government policy, then the required return goes up too. In Equation 7.1, we can see that an increase in the required return, r_s, will reduce share value, P_0, and a decrease in the required return will increase share value. Thus, any action of the financial manager that increases risk contributes to a reduction in value, and any action that decreases risk contributes to an increase in value.

Example 7.10 ▶ Assume that Lamar Company's 15% required return resulted from a risk-free rate of 9% and a risk premium of 6%. With this return, the firm's share value was calculated in an earlier example (on pages 280 and 281) to be $18.75.

Now imagine that the financial manager makes a decision that, without changing expected dividends, causes the firm's risk premium to increase to 7%. Assuming that *the risk-free rate remains at 9%, the new required return on Lamar stock will be 16% (9% + 7%)*, substituting $D_1 = \$1.50$, $r_s = 0.16$, and $g = 0.07$ into the valuation equation (Equation 7.3), results in a new share value of $16.67 [$1.50 ÷ (0.16 − 0.07)]. As expected, raising the required return, without any corresponding increase in expected dividends, causes the firm's stock value to decline. Clearly, the financial manager's action was not in the owners' best interest.

COMBINED EFFECT

A financial decision rarely affects dividends and risk independently; most decisions affect both factors often in the same direction. As firms take on more risk, their shareholders expect to see higher dividends. The net effect on value depends on the relative size of the changes in these two variables.

Example 7.11 ►   If we assume that the two changes illustrated for Lamar Company in the preceding examples occur simultaneously, the key variable values would be $D_1 = \$1.50$, $r_s = 0.16$, and $g = 0.09$. Substituting into the valuation model, we obtain a share price of $21.43 [$1.50 ÷ (0.16 − 0.09)]. The net result of the decision, which increased dividend growth (g, from 7% to 9%) as well as required return (r_s, from 15% to 16%), is positive. The share price increased from $18.75 to $21.43. Even with the combined effects, the decision appears to be in the best interest of the firm's owners because it increases their wealth.

→ **REVIEW QUESTIONS**

7–17 Explain the linkages among financial decisions, return, risk, and stock value.

7–18 Assuming that all other variables remain unchanged, what impact would *each* of the following have on stock price? (**a**) The firm's risk premium increases. (**b**) The firm's required return decreases. (**c**) The dividend expected next year decreases. (**d**) The rate of growth in dividends is expected to increase.

Summary

FOCUS ON VALUE

The price of each share of a firm's common stock is the value of each ownership interest. Although common stockholders typically have voting rights, which indirectly give them a say in management, their most significant right is their claim on the residual cash flows of the firm. This claim is subordinate to those of vendors, employees, customers, lenders, the government (for taxes), and preferred stockholders. The value of the common stockholders' claim is embodied in the future cash flows they are entitled to receive. The present value of those expected cash flows is the firm's share value.

To determine this present value, forecast cash flows are discounted at a rate that reflects their risk. Riskier cash flows are discounted at higher rates, resulting in lower present values than less risky expected cash flows, which are discounted at lower rates. The value of the firm's common stock is therefore driven by its expected cash flows (returns) and risk (certainty of the expected cash flows).

In pursuing the firm's goal of **maximizing the stock price**, the financial manager must carefully consider the balance of return and risk associated with each proposal and must undertake only those actions that create value for owners. By focusing on value creation and by managing and monitoring the firm's cash flows and risk, the financial manager should be able to achieve the firm's goal of share price maximization.

REVIEW OF LEARNING GOALS

LG 1   **Differentiate between debt and equity.** Holders of equity capital (common and preferred stock) are owners of the firm. Typically, only common stockholders have a voice in management. Equityholders' claims on income and assets are secondary to creditors' claims, there is no maturity date, and dividends paid to stockholders are not tax deductible.

LG 2   **Discuss the features of both common and preferred stock.** The common stock of a firm can be privately owned, closely owned, or publicly owned. It can be sold with or without a par value. Preemptive rights allow common stockholders to avoid dilution of ownership when new shares are issued. Not all shares authorized in the corporate charter are outstanding. If a firm has treasury stock, it will have issued more shares than are outstanding. Some firms have two or more classes of common stock that differ mainly in having unequal voting rights. Proxies transfer voting rights from one party to another. The decision to pay dividends to common stockholders is made by the firm's board of directors. Firms can issue stock in foreign markets. The stock of many foreign corporations is traded in U.S. markets in the form of American depositary receipts (ADRs), which are backed by American depositary shares (ADSs).

Preferred stockholders have preference over common stockholders with respect to the distribution of earnings and assets. They do not normally have voting privileges. Preferred stock issues may have certain restrictive covenants, cumulative dividends, a call feature, and a conversion feature.

LG 3   **Describe the process of issuing common stock, including venture capital, going public, and the investment banker.** The initial nonfounder financing for business startups with attractive growth prospects typically comes from private equity investors. These investors can be either angel capitalists or venture capitalists (VCs). VCs usually invest in both early-stage and later-stage companies that they hope to take public so as to cash out their investments.

The first public issue of a firm's stock is called an initial public offering (IPO). The company selects an investment banker to advise it and to sell the securities. The lead investment banker may form a selling syndicate with other investment bankers. The IPO process includes getting SEC approval, promoting the offering to investors, and pricing the issue.

LG 4   **Understand the concept of market efficiency and basic stock valuation using zero-growth, constant-growth, and variable-growth models.** Market efficiency assumes that the quick reactions of rational investors to new information cause the market value of common stock to adjust upward or downward quickly. The efficient-market hypothesis (EMH) suggests that securities are fairly priced, that they reflect fully all publicly available information, and that investors should therefore not waste time trying to find and capitalize on mispriced securities. Behavioral finance advocates challenge this hypothesis by arguing that emotion and other factors play a role in investment decisions.

The value of a share of stock is the present value of all future dividends it is expected to provide over an infinite time horizon. Three dividend growth models—zero-growth, constant-growth, and variable-growth—can be considered in common stock valuation. The most widely cited model is the constant-growth model.

LG 5   **Discuss the free cash flow valuation model and the book value, liquidation value, and price/earnings (P/E) multiple approaches.** The free cash flow valuation model values firms that have no dividend history, startups, or an operating unit or division of a larger public company. The model finds the value of the entire company by discounting the firm's expected free cash flow at its weighted average cost of capital. The common stock value is found by subtracting the market values of the firm's debt and preferred stock from the value of the entire company.

Book value per share is the amount per share of common stock that would be received if all of the firm's assets were *sold for their exact book (accounting) value* and the proceeds remaining after paying all liabilities (including preferred stock) were divided among the common stockholders. Liquidation value per share is the *actual amount* per share of common stock that would be received if all of the firm's assets were *sold for their market value,* liabilities (including preferred stock) were paid, and the remaining money were divided among the common stockholders. The price/earnings (P/E) multiple approach estimates stock value by multiplying the firm's expected earnings per share (EPS) by the average price/earnings (P/E) ratio for the industry.

LG 6   **Explain the relationships among financial decisions, return, risk, and the firm's value.** In a stable economy, any action of the financial manager that increases the level of expected dividends without changing risk should increase share value; any action that reduces the level of expected dividends without changing risk should reduce share value. Similarly, any action that increases risk (required return) will reduce share value; any action that reduces risk will increase share value. An assessment of the combined effect of return and risk on stock value must be part of the financial decision-making process.

Opener-in-Review

Air Asia Group currently trades at RM 2.63 (closing as of November 30, 2010). Assuming that the return on equity remains at 19 percent and market capitalization is RM 7.6 billion, what would be the expected RM annual return for 2010? Assume also that the expected sales growth in 2009 and beyond is 10 percent. The sales for 2009 are RM 3,133 million. If the net profit margin remains at its 2009 level of 16 percent of sales, from the perspective of a financial analyst, what would you recommend to potential investors? What other factors may influence your decision?

Self-Test Problems   (Solutions in Appendix)

LG 4   **ST7–1**   **Common stock valuation**   Perry Motors' common stock just paid its annual dividend of $1.80 per share. The required return on the common stock is 12%. Estimate the value of the common stock under each of the following assumptions about the dividend:

   a. Dividends are expected to grow at an annual rate of 0% to infinity.

   b. Dividends are expected to grow at a constant annual rate of 5% to infinity.

   c. Dividends are expected to grow at an annual rate of 5% for each of the next 3 years, followed by a constant annual growth rate of 4% in years 4 to infinity.

LG 5   **ST7–2   Free cash flow valuation**   Erwin Footwear wishes to assess the value of its Active Shoe Division. This division has debt with a market value of $12,500,000 and no preferred stock. Its weighted average cost of capital is 10%. The Active Shoe Division's estimated free cash flow each year from 2013 through 2016 is given in the following table. Beyond 2016 to infinity, the firm expects its free cash flow to grow at 4% annually.

Year (t)	Free cash flow (FCF_t)
2013	$ 800,000
2014	1,200,000
2015	1,400,000
2016	1,500,000

a. Use the *free cash flow valuation model* to estimate the value of Erwin's entire Active Shoe Division.

b. Use your finding in part **a** along with the data provided above to find this division's common stock value.

c. If the Active Shoe Division as a public company will have 500,000 shares outstanding, use your finding in part **b** to calculate its value per share.

Warm-Up Exercises

All problems are available in ⟨myfinancelab⟩.

LG 1   **E7–1**   A balance sheet balances assets with their sources of debt and equity financing. If a corporation has assets equal to $5.2 million and a debt ratio of 75.0%, how much debt does the corporation have on its books?

LG 2   **E7–2**   Angina, Inc., has 5 million shares outstanding. The firm is considering issuing an additional 1 million shares. After selling these shares at their $20 per share offering price and netting 95% of the sale proceeds, the firm is obligated by an earlier agreement to sell an additional 250,000 shares at 90% of the offering price. In total, how much cash will the firm net from these stock sales?

LG 2   **E7–3**   Figurate Industries has 750,000 shares of cumulative preferred stock outstanding. It has passed the last three quarterly dividends of $2.50 per share and now (at the end of the current quarter) wishes to distribute a total of $12 million to its shareholders. If Figurate has 3 million shares of common stock outstanding, how large a per-share common stock dividend will it be able to pay?

LG 3   **E7–4**   Today the common stock of Gresham Technology closed at $24.60 per share, down $0.35 from yesterday. If the company has 4.6 million shares outstanding and annual earnings of $11.2 million, what is its P/E ratio today? What was its P/E ratio yesterday?

LG 4   **E7–5**   Stacker Weight Loss currently pays an annual year-end dividend of $1.20 per share. It plans to increase this dividend by 5% next year and maintain it at the new level for the foreseeable future. If the required return on this firm's stock is 8%, what is the value of Stacker's stock?

LG 6   **E7–6**   Brash Corporation initiated a new corporate strategy that fixes its annual dividend at $2.25 per share forever. If the risk-free rate is 4.5% and the risk premium on Brash's stock is 10.8%, what is the value of Brash's stock?

Problems

All problems are available in ⬢ myfinancelab .

LG 2   **P7–1**   **Authorized and available shares**   Aspin Corporation's charter authorizes issuance of 2,000,000 shares of common stock. Currently, 1,400,000 shares are outstanding, and 100,000 shares are being held as treasury stock. The firm wishes to raise $48,000,000 for a plant expansion. Discussions with its investment bankers indicate that the sale of new common stock will net the firm $60 per share.
a. What is the maximum number of new shares of common stock that the firm can sell without receiving further authorization from shareholders?
b. Judging on the basis of the data given and your finding in part **a,** will the firm be able to raise the needed funds without receiving further authorization?
c. What must the firm do to obtain authorization to issue more than the number of shares found in part **a?**

LG 2   **P7–2**   **Preferred dividends**   Slater Lamp Manufacturing has an outstanding issue of preferred stock with an $80 par value and an 11% annual dividend.
a. What is the annual dollar dividend? If it is paid quarterly, how much will be paid each quarter?
b. If the preferred stock is *noncumulative* and the board of directors has passed the preferred dividend for the last 3 quarters, how much must be paid to preferred stockholders in the current quarter before dividends are paid to common stockholders?
c. If the preferred stock is *cumulative* and the board of directors has passed the preferred dividend for the last 3 quarters, how much must be paid to preferred stockholders in the current quarter before dividends are paid to common stockholders?

LG 2   **P7–3**   **Preferred dividends**   In each case in the following table, how many dollars of preferred dividends per share must be paid to preferred stockholders in the current period before common stock dividends are paid?

Case	Type	Par value	Dividend per share per period	Periods of dividends passed
A	Cumulative	$ 80	$ 5	2
B	Noncumulative	110	8%	3
C	Noncumulative	100	$11	1
D	Cumulative	60	8.5%	4
E	Cumulative	90	9%	0

LG 2   **P7–4**   **Convertible preferred stock**   Valerian Corp. convertible preferred stock has a fixed conversion ratio of 5 common shares per 1 share of preferred stock. The preferred stock pays a dividend of $10.00 per share per year. The common stock currently sells for $20.00 per share and pays a dividend of $1.00 per share per year.

a. Judging on the basis of the conversion ratio and the price of the common shares, what is the current conversion value of each preferred share?

b. If the preferred shares are selling at $96.00 each, should an investor convert the preferred shares to common shares?

c. What factors might cause an investor not to convert from preferred to common stock?

Personal Finance Problem

LG 4 **P7–5 Common stock valuation—Zero growth** Scotto Manufacturing is a mature firm in the machine tool component industry. The firm's most recent common stock dividend was $2.40 per share. Because of its maturity as well as its stable sales and earnings, the firm's management feels that dividends will remain at the current level for the foreseeable future.

a. If the required return is 12%, what will be the value of Scotto's common stock?

b. If the firm's risk as perceived by market participants suddenly increases, causing the required return to rise to 20%, what will be the common stock value?

c. Judging on the basis of your findings in parts **a** and **b**, what impact does risk have on value? Explain.

Personal Finance Problem

LG 4 **P7–6 Common stock value—Zero growth** Kelsey Drums, Inc., is a well-established supplier of fine percussion instruments to orchestras all over the United States. The company's class A common stock has paid a dividend of $5.00 per share per year for the last 15 years. Management expects to continue to pay at that amount for the foreseeable future. Sally Talbot purchased 100 shares of Kelsey class A common 10 years ago at a time when the required rate of return for the stock was 16%. She wants to sell her shares today. The current required rate of return for the stock is 12%. How much capital gain or loss will Sally have on her shares?

LG 4 **P7–7 Preferred stock valuation** Jones Design wishes to estimate the value of its outstanding preferred stock. The preferred issue has an $80 par value and pays an annual dividend of $6.40 per share. Similar-risk preferred stocks are currently earning a 9.3% annual rate of return.

a. What is the market value of the outstanding preferred stock?

b. If an investor purchases the preferred stock at the value calculated in part **a,** how much does she gain or lose per share if she sells the stock when the required return on similar-risk preferred stocks has risen to 10.5%? Explain.

LG 4 **P7–8 Common stock value—Constant growth** Use the constant-growth model (Gordon growth model) to find the value of each firm shown in the following table.

Firm	Dividend expected next year	Dividend growth rate	Required return
A	$1.20	8%	13%
B	4.00	5	15
C	0.65	10	14
D	6.00	8	9
E	2.25	8	20

LG 4   **P7–9**   **Common stock value—Constant growth**   McCracken Roofing, Inc., common stock paid a dividend of $1.20 per share last year. The company expects earnings and dividends to grow at a rate of 5% per year for the foreseeable future.

a. What required rate of return for this stock would result in a price per share of $28?

b. If McCracken expects both earnings and dividends to grow at an annual rate of 10%, what required rate of return would result in a price per share of $28?

Personal Finance Problem

LG 4   **P7–10**   **Common stock value—Constant growth**   Elk County Telephone has paid the dividends shown in the following table over the past 6 years.

Year	Dividend per share
2012	$2.87
2011	2.76
2010	2.60
2009	2.46
2008	2.37
2007	2.25

The firm's dividend per share next year is expected to be $3.02.

a. If you can earn 13% on similar-risk investments, what is the most you would be willing to pay per share?

b. If you can earn only 10% on similar-risk investments, what is the most you would be willing to pay per share?

c. Compare and contrast your findings in parts **a** and **b**, and discuss the impact of changing risk on share value.

LG 4   **P7–11**   **Common stock value—Variable growth**   Newman Manufacturing is considering a cash purchase of the stock of Grips Tool. During the year just completed, Grips earned $4.25 per share and paid cash dividends of $2.55 per share ($D_0 = \$2.55$). Grips' earnings and dividends are expected to grow at 25% per year for the next 3 years, after which they are expected to grow at 10% per year to infinity. What is the maximum price per share that Newman should pay for Grips if it has a required return of 15% on investments with risk characteristics similar to those of Grips?

Personal Finance Problem

LG 4   **P7–12**   **Common stock value—Variable growth**   Home Place Hotels, Inc., is entering into a 3-year remodeling and expansion project. The construction will have a limiting effect on earnings during that time, but when it is complete, it should allow the company to enjoy much improved growth in earnings and dividends. Last year, the company paid a dividend of $3.40. It expects zero growth in the next year. In years 2 and 3, 5% growth is expected, and in year 4, 15% growth. In year 5 and thereafter, growth should be a constant 10% per year. What is the maximum price per share that an investor who requires a return of 14% should pay for Home Place Hotels common stock?

LG 4   **P7–13**   **Common stock value—Variable growth**   Lawrence Industries' most recent annual dividend was $1.80 per share ($D_0 = \$1.80$), and the firm's required return is 11%. Find the market value of Lawrence's shares when:

a. Dividends are expected to grow at 8% annually for 3 years, followed by a 5% constant annual growth rate in years 4 to infinity.

b. Dividends are expected to grow at 8% annually for 3 years, followed by a 0% constant annual growth rate in years 4 to infinity.

c. Dividends are expected to grow at 8% annually for 3 years, followed by a 10% constant annual growth rate in years 4 to infinity.

Personal Finance Problem

LG 4   **P7–14**   **Common stock value—All growth models**   You are evaluating the potential purchase of a small business currently generating $42,500 of after-tax cash flow ($D_0 = \$42,500$). On the basis of a review of similar-risk investment opportunities, you must earn an 18% rate of return on the proposed purchase. Because you are relatively uncertain about future cash flows, you decide to estimate the firm's value using several possible assumptions about the growth rate of cash flows.

a. What is the firm's value if cash flows are expected to grow at an annual rate of 0% from now to infinity?

b. What is the firm's value if cash flows are expected to grow at a constant annual rate of 7% from now to infinity?

c. What is the firm's value if cash flows are expected to grow at an annual rate of 12% for the first 2 years, followed by a constant annual rate of 7% from year 3 to infinity?

LG 5   **P7–15**   **Free cash flow valuation**   Nabor Industries is considering going public but is unsure of a fair offering price for the company. Before hiring an investment banker to assist in making the public offering, managers at Nabor have decided to make their own estimate of the firm's common stock value. The firm's CFO has gathered data for performing the valuation using the free cash flow valuation model.

The firm's weighted average cost of capital is 11%, and it has $1,500,000 of debt at market value and $400,000 of preferred stock at its assumed market value. The estimated free cash flows over the next 5 years, 2013 through 2017, are given below. Beyond 2017 to infinity, the firm expects its free cash flow to grow by 3% annually.

Year (t)	Free cash flow (FCF_t)
2013	$200,000
2014	250,000
2015	310,000
2016	350,000
2017	390,000

a. Estimate the value of Nabor Industries' entire company by using the *free cash flow valuation model*.

b. Use your finding in part **a**, along with the data provided above, to find Nabor Industries' common stock value.

c. If the firm plans to issue 200,000 shares of common stock, what is its estimated value per share?

Personal Finance Problem

LG 5   **P7–16**   **Using the free cash flow valuation model to price an IPO**   Assume that you have an opportunity to buy the stock of CoolTech, Inc., an IPO being offered for $12.50 per share. Although you are very much interested in owning the company, you are concerned about whether it is fairly priced. To determine the value of the shares, you have decided to apply the free cash flow valuation model to the firm's financial data that you've developed from a variety of data sources. The key values you have compiled are summarized in the following table.

Free cash flow		
Year (t)	FCF_t	Other data
2013	$ 700,000	Growth rate of FCF, beyond 2013 to infinity = 2%
2014	800,000	Weighted average cost of capital = 8%
2015	950,000	Market value of all debt = $2,700,000
2016	1,100,000	Market value of preferred stock = $1,000,000
		Number of shares of common stock outstanding = 1,100,000

a. Use the *free cash flow valuation model* to estimate CoolTech's common stock value per share.
b. Judging on the basis of your finding in part **a** and the stock's offering price, should you buy the stock?
c. On further analysis, you find that the growth rate in FCF beyond 2016 will be 3% rather than 2%. What effect would this finding have on your responses in parts **a** and **b**?

LG 5   **P7–17**   **Book and liquidation value**   The balance sheet for Gallinas Industries is as follows.

Gallinas Industries Balance Sheet December 31			
Assets		**Liabilities and Stockholders' Equity**	
Cash	$ 40,000	Accounts payable	$100,000
Marketable securities	60,000	Notes payable	30,000
Accounts receivable	120,000	Accrued wages	30,000
Inventories	160,000	Total current liabilities	$160,000
Total current assets	$380,000	Long-term debt	$180,000
Land and buildings (net)	$150,000	Preferred stock	$ 80,000
Machinery and equipment	250,000	Common stock (10,000 shares)	260,000
Total fixed assets (net)	$400,000	Retained earnings	100,000
Total assets	$780,000	Total liabilities and stockholders' equity	$780,000

Additional information with respect to the firm is available:
(1) Preferred stock can be liquidated at book value.
(2) Accounts receivable and inventories can be liquidated at 90% of book value.
(3) The firm has 10,000 shares of common stock outstanding.
(4) All interest and dividends are currently paid up.

(5) Land and buildings can be liquidated at 130% of book value.

(6) Machinery and equipment can be liquidated at 70% of book value.

(7) Cash and marketable securities can be liquidated at book value.

Given this information, answer the following:

a. What is Gallinas Industries' *book value per share?*

b. What is its *liquidation value per share?*

c. Compare, contrast, and discuss the values found in parts **a** and **b**.

LG 5 **P7–18** **Valuation with price/earnings multiples** For each of the firms shown in the following table, use the data given to estimate its common stock value employing price/earnings (P/E) multiples.

Firm	Expected EPS	Price/earnings multiple
A	$3.00	6.2
B	4.50	10.0
C	1.80	12.6
D	2.40	8.9
E	5.10	15.0

LG 6 **P7–19** **Management action and stock value** REH Corporation's most recent dividend was $3 per share, its expected annual rate of dividend growth is 5%, and the required return is now 15%. A variety of proposals are being considered by management to redirect the firm's activities. Determine the impact on share price for each of the following proposed actions, and indicate the best alternative.

a. Do nothing, which will leave the key financial variables unchanged.

b. Invest in a new machine that will increase the dividend growth rate to 6% and lower the required return to 14%.

c. Eliminate an unprofitable product line, which will increase the dividend growth rate to 7% and raise the required return to 17%.

d. Merge with another firm, which will reduce the growth rate to 4% and raise the required return to 16%.

e. Acquire a subsidiary operation from another manufacturer. The acquisition should increase the dividend growth rate to 8% and increase the required return to 17%.

LG 4 **LG 6** **P7–20** **Integrative—Risk and Valuation** Given the following information for the stock of Foster Company, calculate the risk premium on its common stock.

Current price per share of common	$50.00
Expected dividend per share next year	$ 3.00
Constant annual dividend growth rate	9%
Risk-free rate of return	7%

LG 4 **LG 6** **P7–21** **Integrative—Risk and valuation** Giant Enterprises' stock has a required return of 14.8%. The company, which plans to pay a dividend of $2.60 per share in the coming year, anticipates that its future dividends will increase at an annual rate

consistent with that experienced over the 2006–2012 period, when the following dividends were paid:

Year	Dividend per share
2012	$2.45
2011	2.28
2010	2.10
2009	1.95
2008	1.82
2007	1.80
2006	1.73

   a. If the risk-free rate is 10%, what is the risk premium on Giant's stock?

   b. Using the constant-growth model, estimate the value of Giant's stock.

   c. Explain what effect, if any, a decrease in the risk premium would have on the value of Giant's stock.

LG 4   **LG 6**   **P7–22**   **Integrative—Risk and Valuation**   Hamlin Steel Company wishes to determine the value of Craft Foundry, a firm that it is considering acquiring for cash. Hamlin wishes to determine the applicable discount rate to use as an input to the constant-growth valuation model. Craft's stock is not publicly traded. After studying the required returns of firms similar to Craft that are publicly traded, Hamlin believes that an appropriate risk premium on Craft stock is about 5%. The risk-free rate is currently 9%. Craft's dividend per share for each of the past 6 years is shown in the following table.

Year	Dividend per share
2012	$3.44
2011	3.28
2010	3.15
2009	2.90
2008	2.75
2007	2.45

   a. Given that Craft is expected to pay a dividend of $3.68 next year, determine the maximum cash price that Hamlin should pay for each share of Craft.

   b. Describe the effect on the resulting value of Craft of:

      (1) A decrease in its dividend growth rate of 2% from that exhibited over the 2007–2012 period.

      (2) A decrease in its risk premium to 4%.

LG 4   **P7–23**   **ETHICS PROBLEM**   Melissa is trying to value Generic Utility, Inc.'s, stock, which is clearly not growing at all. Generic declared and paid a $5 dividend last year. The required rate of return for utility stocks is 11%, but Melissa is unsure about the financial reporting integrity of Generic's finance team. She decides to add an extra

1% "credibility" risk premium to the required return as part of her valuation analysis.

a. What is the value of Generic's stock, assuming that the financials are trustworthy?

b. What is the value of Generic's stock, assuming that Melissa includes the extra 1% "credibility" risk premium?

c. What is the difference between the values found in parts **a** and **b,** and how might one interpret that difference?

Spreadsheet Exercise

You are interested in purchasing the common stock of Azure Corporation. The firm recently paid a dividend of $3 per share. It expects its earnings—and hence its dividends—to grow at a rate of 7% for the foreseeable future. Currently, similar-risk stocks have required returns of 10%.

TO DO

a. Given the data above, calculate the present value of this security. Use the constant-growth model (Equation 7.4) to find the stock value.

b. One year later, your broker offers to sell you additional shares of Azure at $73. The most recent dividend paid was $3.21, and the expected growth rate for earnings remains at 7%. If you determine that the appropriate risk premium is 6.74% and you observe that the risk-free rate, R_F, is currently 5.25%, what is the firm's current required return, r_{Azure}?

c. Applying Equation 7.4, determine the value of the stock using the new dividend and required return from part **b.**

d. Given your calculation in part **c,** would you buy the additional shares from your broker at $73 per share? Explain.

e. Given your calculation in part **c,** would you sell your old shares for $73? Explain.

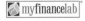 Visit **www.myfinancelab.com** for **Chapter Case: *Assessing the Impact of Suarez Manufacturing's Proposed Risky Investment on Its Stock Value,*** Group Exercises, and numerous online resources.

Integrative Case 3

Encore International

In the world of trendsetting fashion, instinct and marketing savvy are prerequisites to success. Jordan Ellis had both. During 2012, his international casual-wear company, Encore, rocketed to $300 million in sales after 10 years in business. His fashion line covered the young woman from head to toe with hats, sweaters, dresses, blouses, skirts, pants, sweatshirts, socks, and shoes. In Manhattan, there was an Encore shop every five or six blocks, each featuring a different color. Some shops showed the entire line in mauve, and others featured it in canary yellow.

Encore had made it. The company's historical growth was so spectacular that no one could have predicted it. However, securities analysts speculated that Encore could not keep up the pace. They warned that competition is fierce in the fashion industry and that the firm might encounter little or no growth in the future. They estimated that stockholders also should expect no growth in future dividends.

Contrary to the conservative securities analysts, Jordan Ellis felt that the company could maintain a constant annual growth rate in dividends per share of 6% in the future, or possibly 8% for the next 2 years and 6% thereafter. Ellis based his estimates on an established long-term expansion plan into European and Latin American markets. Venturing into these markets was expected to cause the risk of the firm, as measured by the risk premium on its stock, to increase immediately from 8.8% to 10%. Currently, the risk-free rate is 6%.

In preparing the long-term financial plan, Encore's chief financial officer has assigned a junior financial analyst, Marc Scott, to evaluate the firm's current stock price. He has asked Marc to consider the conservative predictions of the securities analysts and the aggressive predictions of the company founder, Jordan Ellis.

Marc has compiled these 2012 financial data to aid his analysis:

Data item	2012 value
Earnings per share (EPS)	$6.25
Price per share of common stock	$40.00
Book value of common stock equity	$60,000,000
Total common shares outstanding	2,500,000
Common stock dividend per share	$4.00

TO DO

a. What is the firm's current book value per share?

b. What is the firm's current P/E ratio?

c. (1) What is the current required return for Encore stock?

    (2) What will be the new required return for Encore stock assuming that they expand into European and Latin American markets as planned?

d. If the securities analysts are correct and there is no growth in future dividends, what will be the value per share of the Encore stock? (*Note:* Use the new required return on the company's stock here.)

e. (1) If Jordan Ellis's predictions are correct, what will be the value per share of Encore stock if the firm maintains a constant annual 6% growth rate in future dividends? (*Note:* Continue to use the new required return here.)

   (2) If Jordan Ellis's predictions are correct, what will be the value per share of Encore stock if the firm maintains a constant annual 8% growth rate in dividends per share over the next 2 years and 6% thereafter?

f. Compare the current (2012) price of the stock and the stock values found in parts **a, d,** and **e.** Discuss why these values may differ. Which valuation method do you believe most clearly represents the true value of the Encore stock?

Risk and the Required Rate of Return

Most people intuitively understand the principle that risk and return are linked. After all, as the old saying goes, "Nothing ventured, nothing gained." In the next two chapters, we'll explore how investors and financial managers quantify the notion of risk and how they determine how much additional return is appropriate compensation for taking extra risk.

Chapter 8 lays the groundwork, defining the terms *risk* and *return* and explaining why investors think about risk in different ways depending on whether they want to understand the risk of a specific investment or the risk of a broad portfolio of investments. Perhaps the most famous and widely applied theory in all of finance, the Capital Asset Pricing Model (or CAPM), is introduced here. The CAPM tells investors and managers alike what return they should expect given the risk of the asset they want to invest in.

Chapter 9 applies these lessons in a managerial finance setting. Firms raise money from two broad sources, owners and lenders. Owners provide equity financing, and lenders provide debt. To maximize the value of the firm, managers have to satisfy both groups, and doing so means earning returns high enough to meet investors' expectations. Chapter 9's focus is on the cost of capital or, more precisely, the weighted average cost of capital (WACC). The WACC tells managers exactly what kind of return their investments in plant and equipment, advertising, and human resources have to earn if the firm is to satisfy its investors. Essentially, the WACC is a hurdle rate, the minimum acceptable return that a firm should earn on any investment that it makes.

8 Risk and Return

Learning Goals

LG 1 Understand the meaning and fundamentals of risk, return, and risk preferences.

LG 2 Describe procedures for assessing and measuring the risk of a single asset.

LG 3 Discuss the measurement of return and standard deviation for a portfolio and the concept of correlation.

LG 4 Understand the risk and return characteristics of a portfolio in terms of correlation and diversification and the impact of international assets on a portfolio.

LG 5 Review the two types of risk and the derivation and role of beta in measuring the relevant risk of both a security and a portfolio.

LG 6 Explain the capital asset pricing model (CAPM), its relationship to the security market line (SML), and the major forces causing shifts in the SML.

Why This Chapter Matters to You

In your *professional* life

ACCOUNTING You need to understand the relationship between risk and return because of the effect that riskier projects will have on the firm's financial statements.

INFORMATION SYSTEMS You need to understand how to do scenario and correlation analyses to build decision packages that help management analyze the risk and return of various business opportunities.

MANAGEMENT You need to understand the relationship between risk and return and how to measure that relationship to evaluate data that come from finance personnel and translate those data into decisions that increase the value of the firm.

MARKETING You need to understand that although higher-risk projects may produce higher returns, they may not be the best choice for the firm if they produce erratic financial results and fail to maximize firm value.

OPERATIONS You need to understand why investments in plant, equipment, and systems need to be evaluated in light of their impact on the firm's risk and return, which together will affect the firm's value.

In your *personal* life
The tradeoff between risk and return enters into numerous personal financial decisions. You will use risk and return concepts when you invest your savings, buy real estate, finance major purchases, purchase insurance, invest in securities, and implement retirement plans. Although risk and return are difficult to measure precisely, you can get a feel for them and make decisions based on the trade-offs between risk and return in light of your personal disposition toward risk.

Mutual Funds

Fund's Returns Not Even Close to Average

For most investors, 2008 was a miserable year. In the United States the Standard & Poor's 500 stock index, a barometer of the overall market, fell 37.2 percent. Returns were even worse in many other countries. The Morgan Stanley Europe, Australasia, and Far East (EAFE) Index dropped 45 percent, wiping out the previous five years worth of gains. For Deryck Noble-Nesbitt, manager of the Close Special Situations Fund in the United Kingdom, 2008 was close to a career-ending catastrophe. The Close Fund, which invests in small companies, lost nearly 60 percent of its value that year and ranked in the bottom 2 percent of all funds in its category. That performance followed a loss of nearly 5 percent in 2007, so the Close Fund was on a two-year losing streak going into 2009.

What a difference a year makes. In 2009, the Close Fund earned a return of 247 percent and ranked first among all funds specializing in small stocks. An investor who put £1,000 in the fund at the beginning of 2007 would have had roughly £1,411 by December 31, 2009, far ahead of what investors in most other funds would have earned over the same period. However, the first five months of 2010 were unkind to the Close Fund as it experienced another 5 percent loss, once again falling in the bottom 3 percent of all funds in the small stock category.

The experience of the Close Special Situations Fund illustrates two key points. First, investments with high returns tend to be associated with high risk. Small stocks as a category, and the recent performance of the Close Fund, clearly demonstrate that principle. In fact, investors ought to be suspicious of investment opportunities that appear to offer high returns without also having high risk. (See the *Focus on Ethics* box on page 310.) Second, predicting how any particular fund or investment will perform in any given period is difficult. In three consecutive years, the Close Fund ranked near the bottom, at the very top, and then near the bottom again of its peer group. Together, these two points suggest that investors must be very mindful of risk and should diversify their investments. This chapter explains how to put that advice into action.

LG 1   # 8.1 Risk and Return Fundamentals

In most important business decisions there are two key financial considerations: risk and return. Each financial decision presents certain risk and return characteristics, and the combination of these characteristics can increase or decrease a firm's share price. Analysts use different methods to quantify risk, depending on whether they are looking at a single asset or a **portfolio**—a collection, or group, of assets. We will look at both, beginning with the risk of a single asset. First, though, it is important to introduce some fundamental ideas about risk, return, and risk preferences.

portfolio
A collection, or group, of assets.

RISK DEFINED

In the most basic sense, **risk** is a measure of the uncertainty surrounding the return that an investment will earn. Investments whose returns are more uncertain are generally viewed as being riskier. More formally, the term *risk* is used interchangeably with *uncertainty* to refer to the *variability of returns associated with a given asset*. A $1,000 government bond that guarantees its holder $5 interest after 30 days has no risk, because there is no variability associated with the return. A $1,000 investment in a firm's common stock, the value of which over the same 30 days may move up or down a great deal, is very risky because of the high variability of its return.

risk
A measure of the uncertainty surrounding the return that an investment will earn or, more formally, the *variability of returns associated with a given asset.*

---

focus on ETHICS

If It Seems Too Good to Be True Then It Probably Is

in practice For many years, investors around the world clamored to invest with Bernard Madoff. Those fortunate enough to invest with "Bernie" might not have understood his secret trading system, but they were happy with the double-digit returns that they earned. Madoff was well connected, having been the chairman of the board of directors of the NASDAQ Stock Market and a founding member of the International Securities Clearing Corporation. His credentials seemed to be impeccable.

However, as the old saying goes, if something sounds too good to be true, it probably is. Madoff's investors learned this lesson the hard way when, on December 11, 2008, the U.S. Securities and Exchange Commission (SEC) charged Madoff with securities

fraud. Madoff's hedge fund, Ascot Partners, turned out to be a giant Ponzi scheme.

Over the years, suspicions were raised about Madoff. Madoff generated high returns year after year, seemingly with very little risk. Madoff credited his complex trading strategy for his investment performance, but other investors employed similar strategies with much different results than Madoff reported. Harry Markopolos went as far as to submit a report to the SEC three years prior to Madoff's arrest titled "The World's Largest Hedge Fund Is a Fraud" that detailed his concerns.[a]

On June 29, 2009, Madoff was sentenced to 150 years in prison. Madoff's investors are still working to recover what they can. Fraudulent account statements sent just prior to

Madoff's arrest indicated that investors' accounts contained over $64 billion, in aggregate. Many investors pursued claims based on the balance reported in these statements. However, a recent court ruling permits claims up to the difference between the amount an investor deposited with Madoff and the amount they withdrew. The judge also ruled that investors who managed to withdraw at least their initial investment before the fraud was uncovered are not eligible to recover additional funds. Total out-of-pocket cash losses as a result of Madoff's fraud were recently estimated at slightly over $20 billion.

▶ *What are some hazards of allowing investors to pursue claims based on their most recent account statements?*

[a]www.sec.gov/news/studies/2009/oig-509/exhibit-0293.pdf

RETURN DEFINED

total rate of return
The total gain or loss experienced on an investment over a given period of time; calculated by dividing the asset's cash distributions during the period, plus change in value, by its beginning-of-period investment value.

Obviously, if we are going to assess risk on the basis of variability of return, we need to be certain we know what *return* is and how to measure it. The **total rate of return** is the total gain or loss experienced on an investment over a given period. Mathematically, an investment's total return is the sum of any cash distributions (for example, dividends or interest payments) plus the change in the investment's value, divided by the beginning-of-period value. The expression for calculating the total rate of return earned on any asset over period t, r_t, is commonly defined as

$$r_t = \frac{C_t + P_t - P_{t-1}}{P_{t-1}} \tag{8.1}$$

where

r_t = actual, expected, or required rate of return during period t

C_t = cash (flow) received from the asset investment in the time period $t - 1$ to t

P_t = price (value) of asset at time t

P_{t-1} = price (value) of asset at time $t - 1$

The return, r_t, reflects the combined effect of cash flow, C_t, and changes in value, $P_t - P_{t-1}$, over the period.[1]

Equation 8.1 is used to determine the rate of return over a time period as short as 1 day or as long as 10 years or more. However, in most cases, t is 1 year, and r therefore represents an annual rate of return.

Example 8.1 ▶

Robin wishes to determine the return on two stocks that she owned during 2009, Apple Inc. and Wal-Mart. At the beginning of the year, Apple stock traded for $90.75 per share, and Wal-Mart was valued at $55.33. During the year, Apple paid no dividends, but Wal-Mart shareholders received dividends of $1.09 per share. At the end of the year, Apple stock was worth $210.73 and Wal-Mart sold for $52.84. Substituting into Equation 8.1, we can calculate the annual rate of return, r, for each stock.

Apple: ($0 + $210.73 − $90.75) ÷ $90.75 = 132.2%

Wal-Mart: ($1.09 + $52.84 − $55.33) ÷ $55.33 = −2.5%

Robin made money on Apple and lost money on Wal-Mart in 2009, but notice that her losses on Wal-Mart would have been greater had it not been for the dividends that she received on her Wal-Mart shares. When calculating the total rate of return, it is important to take into account the effects of both cash disbursements and changes in the price of the investment during the year.

---

1. This expression does not imply that an investor necessarily buys the asset at time $t - 1$ and sells it at time t. Rather, it represents the increase (or decrease) in wealth that the investor has experienced during the period by holding a particular investment. If the investor sells the asset at time t, we say that the investor has *realized* the return on the investment. If the investor continues to hold the investment, we say that the return is *unrealized*.

TABLE 8.1 Historical Returns on Selected Investments (1900–2009)		
Investment	Average nominal return	Average real return
Treasury bills	3.9%	0.9%
Treasury bonds	5.0	1.9
Common stocks	9.3	6.2

Source: Elroy Dimson, Paul Marsh, and Mike Staunton, *Triumph of the Optimists: 101 Years of Global Investment Returns* (Princeton, NJ: Princeton University Press, 2002).

Investment returns vary both over time and between different types of investments. By averaging historical returns over a long period of time, we can focus on the differences in returns that different kinds of investments tend to generate. Table 8.1 shows both the nominal and real average annual rates of return from 1900 to 2009 for three different types of investments: Treasury bills, Treasury bonds, and common stocks. Although bills and bonds are both issued by the U.S. government and are therefore viewed as relatively safe investments, bills have maturities of 1 year or less, while bonds have maturities ranging up to 30 years. Consequently, the interest rate risk associated with Treasury bonds is much higher than with bills. Over the last 109 years, bills earned the lowest returns, just 3.9 percent per year on average in nominal returns and only 0.9 percent annually in real terms. The latter number means that average Treasury bill returns barely exceeded the average rate of inflation. Bond returns were higher, 5.0 percent in nominal terms and 1.9 percent in real terms. Clearly, though, stocks outshined the other types of investments, earning average annual nominal returns of 9.3 percent and average real returns of 6.2 percent.

In light of these statistics, you might wonder, "Why would anyone invest in bonds or bills if the returns on stocks are so much higher?" The answer, as you will soon see, is that stocks are much riskier than either bonds or bills and that risk leads some investors to prefer the safer, albeit lower, returns on Treasury securities.

RISK PREFERENCES

Different people react to risk in different ways. Economists use three categories to describe how investors respond to risk. The first category, *and the one that describes the behavior of most people most of the time*, is called risk aversion. A person who is a **risk-averse** investor prefers less risky over more risky investments, holding the rate of return fixed. A risk-averse investor who believes that two different investments have the same expected return will choose the investment whose returns are more certain. Stated another way, when choosing between two investments, *a risk-averse investor will not make the riskier investment unless it offers a higher expected return to compensate the investor for bearing the additional risk.*

A second attitude toward risk is called risk neutrality. An investor who is **risk neutral** chooses investments based solely on their expected returns, disregarding the risks. When choosing between two investments, *a risk-neutral investor will always choose the investment with the higher expected return regardless of its risk.*

In more depth

To read about *Inflation and Returns*, go to www.myfinancelab.com

myfinancelab

risk averse
The attitude toward risk in which investors would require an increased return as compensation for an increase in risk.

risk neutral
The attitude toward risk in which investors choose the investment with the higher return regardless of its risk.

risk seeking
The attitude toward risk in which investors prefer investments with greater risk even if they have lower expected returns.

Finally, a **risk-seeking** investor is one who prefers investments with higher risk and may even sacrifice some expected return when choosing a riskier investment. By design, the average person who buys a lottery ticket or gambles in a casino loses money. After all, state governments and casinos make money off of these endeavors, so individuals lose on average. This implies that the expected return on these activities is negative. Yet people do buy lottery tickets and visit casinos, and in doing so they exhibit risk-seeking behavior.

→ REVIEW QUESTIONS

8–1 What is *risk* in the context of financial decision making?

8–2 Define *return,* and describe how to find the rate of return on an investment.

8–3 Compare the following risk preferences: (**a**) risk averse, (**b**) risk neutral, and (**c**) risk seeking. Which is most common among financial managers?

LG 2   8.2 Risk of a Single Asset

In this section we refine our understanding of risk. Surprisingly, the concept of risk changes when the focus shifts from the risk of a single asset held in isolation to the risk of a portfolio of assets. Here, we examine different statistical methods to quantify risk, and next we apply those methods to portfolios.

RISK ASSESSMENT

The notion that risk is somehow connected to uncertainty is intuitive. The more uncertain you are about how an investment will perform, the riskier that investment seems. Scenario analysis provides a simple way to quantify that intuition, and probability distributions offer an even more sophisticated way to analyze the risk of an investment.

scenario analysis
An approach for assessing risk that uses several possible alternative outcomes (scenarios) to obtain a sense of the variability among returns.

range
A measure of an asset's risk, which is found by subtracting the return associated with the pessimistic (worst) outcome from the return associated with the optimistic (best) outcome.

Scenario Analysis

Scenario analysis uses several possible alternative outcomes (scenarios) to obtain a sense of the variability of returns.[2] One common method involves considering pessimistic (worst), most likely (expected), and optimistic (best) outcomes and the returns associated with them for a given asset. In this one measure of an investment's risk is the range of possible outcomes. The **range** is found by subtracting the return associated with the pessimistic outcome from the return associated with the optimistic outcome. The greater the range, the more variability, or risk, the asset is said to have.

Example 8.2 ▶

Norman Company, a manufacturer of custom golf equipment, wants to choose the better of two investments, A and B. Each requires an initial outlay of $10,000, and each has a *most likely* annual rate of return of 15%. Management has estimated

---

2. The term *scenario analysis* is intentionally used in a general rather than a technically correct fashion here to simplify this discussion. A more technical and precise definition and discussion of this technique and of *sensitivity analysis* are presented in Chapter 12.

TABLE 8.2	Assets A and B	
	Asset A	**Asset B**
Initial investment	$10,000	$10,000
Annual rate of return		
Pessimistic	13%	7%
Most likely	15%	15%
Optimistic	17%	23%
Range	4%	16%

returns associated with each investment's *pessimistic* and *optimistic* outcomes. The three estimates for each asset, along with its range, are given in Table 8.2. Asset A appears to be less risky than asset B; its range of 4% (17% minus 13%) is less than the range of 16% (23% minus 7%) for asset B. The risk-averse decision maker would prefer asset A over asset B, because A offers the same most likely return as B (15%) with lower risk (smaller range).

It's not unusual for financial managers to think about the best and worst possible outcomes when they are in the early stages of analyzing a new investment project. No matter how great the intuitive appeal of this approach, looking at the range of outcomes that an investment might produce is a very unsophisticated way of measuring its risk. More sophisticated methods require some basic statistical tools.

Probability Distributions

probability
The *chance* that a given outcome will occur.

Probability distributions provide a more quantitative insight into an asset's risk. The **probability** of a given outcome is its *chance* of occurring. An outcome with an 80 percent probability of occurrence would be expected to occur 8 out of 10 times. An outcome with a probability of 100 percent is certain to occur. Outcomes with a probability of zero will never occur.

Matter of fact

Beware of the Black Swan

Is it ever possible to know for sure that a particular outcome can never happen, that the chance of it occurring is 0 percent? In the 2007 best seller, *The Black Swan: The Impact of the Highly Improbable*, Nassim Nicholas Taleb argues that seemingly improbable or even impossible events are more likely to occur than most people believe, especially in the area of finance. The book's title refers to the fact that for many years, people believed that all swans were white until a black variety was discovered in Australia. Taleb reportedly earned a large fortune during the 2007–2008 financial crisis by betting that financial markets would plummet.

Example 8.3 ▶

Norman Company's past estimates indicate that the probabilities of the pessimistic, most likely, and optimistic outcomes are 25%, 50%, and 25%, respectively. Note that the sum of these probabilities must equal 100%; that is, they must be based on all the alternatives considered.

FIGURE 8.1

Bar Charts
Bar charts for asset A's and asset B's returns

probability distribution
A model that relates probabilities to the associated outcomes.

bar chart
The simplest type of probability distribution; shows only a limited number of outcomes and associated probabilities for a given event.

continuous probability distribution
A probability distribution showing all the possible outcomes and associated probabilities for a given event.

A **probability distribution** is a model that relates probabilities to the associated outcomes. The simplest type of probability distribution is the **bar chart**. The bar charts for Norman Company's assets A and B are shown in Figure 8.1. Although both assets have the same average return, the range of return is much greater, or more dispersed, for asset B than for asset A—16 percent versus 4 percent.

Most investments have more than two or three possible outcomes. In fact, the number of possible outcomes in most cases is practically infinite. If we knew all the possible outcomes and associated probabilities, we could develop a **continuous probability distribution.** This type of distribution can be thought of as a bar chart for a very large number of outcomes. Figure 8.2 presents continuous probability distributions for assets C and D. Note that although the two assets have the same average return (15 percent), the distribution of returns for asset D has much greater *dispersion* than the distribution for asset C. Apparently, asset D is more risky than asset C.

RISK MEASUREMENT

In addition to considering the *range* of returns that an investment might produce, the risk of an asset can be measured quantitatively by using statistics. The most common statistical measure used to describe an investment's risk is its standard deviation.

FIGURE 8.2

Continuous Probability Distributions
Continuous probability distributions for asset C's and asset D's returns

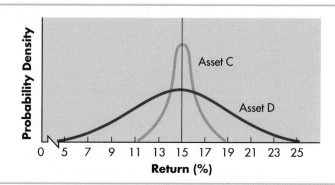

standard deviation (σ_r)
The most common statistical indicator of an asset's risk; it measures the dispersion around the *expected value*.

expected value of a return ($\bar{r}$)
The average return that an investment is expected to produce over time.

Standard Deviation

The **standard deviation, σ_r,** measures the dispersion of an investment's return around the *expected return*. The **expected return, $\bar{r}$,** is the average return that an investment is expected to produce over time. For an investment that has j different possible returns, the expected return is calculated as follows:[3]

$$\bar{r} = \sum_{j=1}^{n} r_j \times Pr_j \qquad (8.2)$$

where

r_j = return for the jth outcome
Pr_j = probability of occurrence of the jth outcome
n = number of outcomes considered

Example 8.4 ▶ The expected values of returns for Norman Company's assets A and B are presented in Table 8.3. Column 1 gives the Pr_j's and column 2 gives the r_j's. In each case n equals 3. The expected value for each asset's return is 15%.

TABLE 8.3	Expected Values of Returns for Assets A and B		
Possible outcomes	Probability (1)	Returns (2)	Weighted value [(1) × (2)] (3)
Asset A			
Pessimistic	0.25	13%	3.25%
Most likely	0.50	15	7.50
Optimistic	0.25	17	4.25
Total	1.00		Expected return 15.00%
Asset B			
Pessimistic	0.25	7%	1.75%
Most likely	0.50	15	7.50
Optimistic	0.25	23	5.75
Total	1.00		Expected return 15.00%

---

3. The formula for finding the expected value of return, $\bar{r}$, when all of the outcomes, r_j, are known *and* their related probabilities are equal, is a simple arithmetic average:

$$\bar{r} = \frac{\sum_{j=1}^{n} r_j}{n} \qquad (8.2a)$$

where n is the number of observations.

The expression for the *standard deviation of returns, σ_r*, is[4]

$$\sigma_r = \sqrt{\sum_{j=1}^{n}(r_j - \bar{r})^2 \times Pr_j} \tag{8.3}$$

In general, the higher the standard deviation, the greater the risk.

Example 8.5 ▶ Table 8.4 presents the standard deviations for Norman Company's assets A and B, based on the earlier data. The standard deviation for asset A is 1.41%, and the standard deviation for asset B is 5.66%. The higher risk of asset B is clearly reflected in its higher standard deviation.

TABLE 8.4 **The Calculation of the Standard Deviation of the Returns for Assets A and B[a]**

j	r_j	$\bar{r}$	$r_j - \bar{r}$	$(r_j - \bar{r})^2$	Pr_j	$(r_j - \bar{r})^2 \times Pr_j$
Asset A						
1	13%	15%	−2%	4%	.25	1%
2	15	15	0	0	.50	0
3	17	15	2	4	.25	1

$$\sum_{j=1}^{3}(r_j - \bar{r})^2 \times Pr_j = 2\%$$

$$\sigma_{r_A} = \sqrt{\sum_{j=1}^{3}(r_j - \bar{r})^2 \times Pr_j} = \sqrt{2\%} = \underline{1.41\%}$$

j	r_j	$\bar{r}$	$r_j - \bar{r}$	$(r_j - \bar{r})^2$	Pr_j	$(r_j - \bar{r})^2 \times Pr_j$
Asset B						
1	7%	15%	−8%	64%	.25	16%
2	15	15	0	0	.50	0
3	23	15	8	64	.25	16

$$\sum_{j=1}^{3}(r_j - \bar{r})^2 \times Pr_j = 32\%$$

$$\sigma_{r_B} = \sqrt{\sum_{j=1}^{3}(r_j - \bar{r})^2 \times Pr_j} = \sqrt{32\%} = \underline{5.66\%}$$

[a]Calculations in this table are made in percentage form rather than decimal form—for example, 13% rather than 0.13. As a result, some of the intermediate computations may appear to be inconsistent with those that would result from using decimal form. Regardless, the resulting standard deviations are correct and identical to those that would result from using decimal rather than percentage form.

4. In practice, analysts rarely know the full range of possible investment outcomes and their probabilities. In these cases, analysts use historical data to estimate the standard deviation. The formula that applies in this situation is

$$\sigma_r = \sqrt{\frac{\sum_{j=1}^{n}(r_j - \bar{r})^2}{n - 1}} \tag{8.3a}$$

TABLE 8.5 > Historical Returns and Standard Deviations on Selected Investments (1900–2009)			
Investment	Average nominal return	Standard deviation	Coefficient of variation
Treasury bills	3.9%	4.7%	1.21
Treasury bonds	5.0	10.2	2.04
Common stocks	9.3	20.4	2.19

Source: Elroy Dimson, Paul Marsh, and Mike Staunton, *Triumph of the Optimists: 101 Years of Global Investment Returns* (Princeton, NJ: Princeton University Press, 2002).

Historical Returns and Risk   We can now use the standard deviation as a measure of risk to assess the historical (1900–2009) investment return data in Table 8.1. Table 8.5 repeats the historical nominal average returns in column 1 and shows the standard deviations associated with each of them in column 2. A close relationship can be seen between the investment returns and the standard deviations: Investments with higher returns have higher standard deviations. For example, stocks have the highest average return at 9.3 percent, which is more than double the average return on Treasury bills. At the same time, stocks are much more volatile, with a standard deviation of 20.4 percent, more than four times greater than the standard deviation of Treasury bills. Because higher standard deviations are associated with greater risk, the historical data confirm the existence of a positive relationship between risk and return. That relationship reflects *risk aversion* by market participants, who require higher returns as compensation for greater risk. The historical data in columns 1 and 2 of Table 8.5 clearly show that during the 1900–2009 period, investors were, on average, rewarded with higher returns on higher-risk investments.

Matter of fact

All Stocks Are Not Created Equal

Table 8.5 shows that stocks are riskier than bonds, but are some stocks riskier than others? The answer is emphatically *yes*. A recent study examined the historical returns of large stocks and small stocks and found that the average annual return on large stocks from 1926 through 2009 was 11.8 percent, while small stocks earned 16.7 percent per year on average. The higher returns on small stocks came with a cost, however. The standard deviation of small stock returns was a whopping 32.8 percent, whereas the standard deviation on large stocks was just 20.5 percent.

normal probability distribution
A symmetrical probability distribution whose shape resembles a "bell-shaped" curve.

Normal Distribution   A **normal probability distribution**, depicted in Figure 8.3, resembles a symmetrical "bell-shaped" curve. The symmetry of the curve means that half the probability is associated with the values to the left of the peak and half with the values to the right. As noted on the figure, for normal probability distributions, 68 percent of the possible outcomes will lie between ±1 standard deviation from the expected value, 95 percent of all outcomes will lie between ±2 standard deviations from the expected value, and 99 percent of all outcomes will lie between ±3 standard deviations from the expected value.

FIGURE 8.3 ▶

Bell-Shaped Curve
Normal probability
distribution, with ranges

Example 8.6 ▶

Using the data in Table 8.5 and assuming that the probability distributions of returns for common stocks and bonds are normal, we can surmise that 68% of the possible outcomes would have a return ranging between −11.1% and 29.7% for stocks and between −5.2% and 15.2% for bonds; 95% of the possible return outcomes would range between −31.5% and 50.1% for stocks and between −15.4% and 25.4% for bonds. The greater risk of stocks is clearly reflected in their much wider range of possible returns for each level of confidence (68% or 95%).

Coefficient of Variation—Trading Off Risk and Return

coefficient of variation (CV)
A measure of relative dispersion that is useful in comparing the risks of assets with differing expected returns.

The **coefficient of variation, CV,** is a measure of relative dispersion that is useful in comparing the risks of assets with differing expected returns. Equation 8.4 gives the expression for the coefficient of variation:

$$CV = \frac{\sigma_r}{\bar{r}}$$
(8.4)

A higher coefficient of variation means that an investment has more volatility relative to its expected return. Because investors prefer higher returns and less risk, intuitively one might expect investors to gravitate towards investments with a low coefficient of variation. However, this logic doesn't always apply for reasons that will emerge in the next section. For now, consider the coefficients of variation in column 3 of Table 8.5. That table reveals that Treasury bills have the lowest coefficient of variation and therefore the lowest risk relative to their return. Does this mean that investors should load up on Treasury bills and divest themselves of stocks? Not necessarily.

Example 8.7 ▶

When the standard deviations (from Table 8.4) and the expected returns (from Table 8.3) for assets A and B are substituted into Equation 8.4, the coefficients of variation for A and B are 0.094 (1.41% ÷ 15%) and 0.377 (5.66% ÷ 15%), respectively. Asset B has the higher coefficient of variation and is therefore more risky than asset A—which we already know from the standard deviation. (Because both assets have the same expected return, the coefficient of variation has not provided any new information.)

Personal Finance Example 8.8 ▶ Marilyn Ansbro is reviewing stocks for inclusion in her investment portfolio. The stock she wishes to analyze is Danhaus Industries, Inc. (DII), a diversified manufacturer of pet products. One of her key concerns is risk; as a rule she will invest only in stocks with a coefficient of variation below 0.75. She has gathered price and dividend data (shown in the accompanying table) for DII over the past 3 years, 2010–2012, and assumes that each year's return is equally probable.

	Stock Price		
Year	Beginning	End	Dividend paid
2010	$35.00	$36.50	$3.50
2011	36.50	34.50	3.50
2012	34.50	35.00	4.00

Substituting the price and dividend data for each year into Equation 8.1, we get:

Year	Returns
2010	[$3.50 + ($36.50 − $35.00)] ÷ $35.00 = $5.00 ÷ $35.00 = 14.3%
2011	[$3.50 + ($34.50 − $36.50)] ÷ $36.50 = $1.50 ÷ $36.50 = 4.1%
2012	[$4.00 + ($35.00 − $34.50)] ÷ $34.50 = $4.50 ÷ $34.50 = 13.0%

Substituting into Equation 8.2a, given that the returns are equally probable, we get the average return, $\bar{r}_{2010-2012}$:

$$\bar{r}_{2010-2012} = (14.3\% + 4.1\% + 13.0\%) \div 3 = 10.5\%$$

Substituting the average return and annual returns into Equation 8.3a, we get the standard deviation, $\sigma_{r2010-2012}$:

$$\sigma_{r2010-2012} = \sqrt{[(14.3\% - 10.5\%)^2 + (4.1\% - 10.5\%)^2 + (13.0\% - 10.5\%)^2] \div (3-1)}$$
$$= \sqrt{(14.44\% + 40.96\% + 6.25\%) \div 2} = \sqrt{30.825\%} = 5.6\%$$

Finally, substituting the standard deviation of returns and the average return into Equation 8.4, we get the coefficient of variation, CV:

$$CV = 5.6\% \div 10.5\% = 0.53$$

Because the coefficient of variation of returns on the DII stock over the 2010–2012 period of 0.53 is well below Marilyn's maximum coefficient of variation of 0.75, she concludes that the DII stock would be an acceptable investment.

→ **REVIEW QUESTIONS**

8–4 Explain how the *range* is used in scenario analysis.

8–5 What does a plot of the *probability distribution* of outcomes show a decision maker about an asset's risk?

8–6 What relationship exists between the size of the *standard deviation* and the degree of asset risk?

8–7 What does the *coefficient of variation* reveal about an investment's risk that the standard deviation does not?

LG 3   LG 4   ## 8.3 Risk of a Portfolio

In real-world situations, the risk of any single investment would not be viewed independently of other assets. New investments must be considered in light of their impact on the risk and return of an investor's *portfolio* of assets. The financial manager's goal is to create an **efficient portfolio,** one that provides the maximum return for a given level of risk. We therefore need a way to measure the return and the standard deviation of a portfolio of assets. As part of that analysis, we will look at the statistical concept of *correlation,* which underlies the process of diversification that is used to develop an efficient portfolio.

efficient portfolio
A portfolio that maximizes return for a given level of risk.

PORTFOLIO RETURN AND STANDARD DEVIATION

The *return on a portfolio* is a weighted average of the returns on the individual assets from which it is formed. We can use Equation 8.5 to find the portfolio return, r_p:

$$r_p = (w_1 \times r_1) + (w_2 \times r_2) + \cdots + (w_n \times r_n) = \sum_{j=1}^{n} w_j \times r_j \qquad (8.5)$$

where

w_j = proportion of the portfolio's total dollar value represented by asset j

r_j = return on asset j

Of course, $\sum_{j=1}^{n} w_j = 1$, which means that 100 percent of the portfolio's assets must be included in this computation.

Example 8.9 ▶   James purchases 100 shares of Wal-Mart at a price of $55 per share, so his total investment in Wal-Mart is $5,500. He also buys 100 shares of Cisco Systems at $25 per share, so the total investment in Cisco stock is $2,500. Combining these two holdings, James's total portfolio is worth $8,000. Of the total, 68.75% is invested in Wal-Mart ($5,500 ÷ $8,000) and 31.25% is invested in Cisco Systems ($2,500 ÷ $8,000). Thus, $w_1 = 0.6875$, $w_2 = 0.3125$, and $w_1 + w_2 = 1.0$.

The *standard deviation of a portfolio's returns* is found by applying the formula for the standard deviation of a single asset. Specifically, Equation 8.3 is used when the probabilities of the returns are known, and Equation 8.3a (from footnote 4) is applied when analysts use historical data to estimate the standard deviation.

Example 8.10 ▶ Assume that we wish to determine the expected value and standard deviation of returns for portfolio XY, created by combining equal portions (50% each) of assets X and Y. The forecasted returns of assets X and Y for each of the next 5 years (2013–2017) are given in columns 1 and 2, respectively, in part A of Table 8.6. In column 3, the weights of 50% for both assets X and Y along with their respective returns from columns 1 and 2 are substituted into Equation 8.5. Column 4 shows the results of the calculation—an expected portfolio return of 12% for each year, 2013 to 2017.

Furthermore, as shown in part B of Table 8.6, the expected value of these portfolio returns over the 5-year period is also 12% (calculated by using Equation 8.2a, in footnote 3). In part C of Table 8.6, portfolio XY's standard deviation is calculated to be 0% (using Equation 8.3a, in footnote 4). This value should not be surprising because the portfolio return each year is the same—12%. Portfolio returns do not vary through time.

TABLE 8.6 ▷ Expected Return, Expected Value, and Standard Deviation of Returns for Portfolio XY

A. Expected Portfolio Returns

Year	Forecasted return Asset X (1)	Forecasted return Asset Y (2)	Portfolio return calculation[a] (3)	Expected portfolio return, r_p (4)
2013	8%	16%	$(0.50 \times 8\%) + (0.50 \times 16\%) =$	12%
2014	10	14	$(0.50 \times 10\%) + (0.50 \times 14\%) =$	12
2015	12	12	$(0.50 \times 12\%) + (0.50 \times 12\%) =$	12
2016	14	10	$(0.50 \times 14\%) + (0.50 \times 10\%) =$	12
2017	16	8	$(0.50 \times 16\%) + (0.50 \times 8\%) =$	12

B. Expected Value of Portfolio Returns, 2013–2017[b]

$$\bar{r}_p = \frac{12\% + 12\% + 12\% + 12\% + 12\%}{5} = \frac{60\%}{5} = \underline{\underline{12}}\%$$

C. Standard Deviation of Expected Portfolio Returns[c]

$$\sigma_{r_p} = \sqrt{\frac{(12\% - 12\%)^2 + (12\% - 12\%)^2 + (12\% - 12\%)^2 + (12\% - 12\%)^2 + (12\% - 12\%)^2}{5 - 1}}$$

$$= \sqrt{\frac{0\% + 0\% + 0\% + 0\% + 0\%}{4}}$$

$$= \sqrt{\frac{0\%}{4}} = \underline{\underline{0}}\%$$

---

[a]Using Equation 8.5.
[b]Using Equation 8.2a found in footnote 3.
[c]Using Equation 8.3a found in footnote 4.

correlation
A statistical measure of the relationship between any two series of numbers.

positively correlated
Describes two series that move in the same direction.

negatively correlated
Describes two series that move in opposite directions.

correlation coefficient
A measure of the degree of correlation between two series.

perfectly positively correlated
Describes two *positively correlated* series that have a *correlation coefficient* of +1.

perfectly negatively correlated
Describes two *negatively correlated* series that have a *correlation coefficient* of −1.

CORRELATION

Correlation is a statistical measure of the relationship between any two series of numbers. The numbers may represent data of any kind, from returns to test scores. If two series tend to vary in the same direction, they are **positively correlated.** If the series vary in opposite directions, they are **negatively correlated.** For example, suppose we gathered data on the retail price and weight of new cars. It is likely that we would find that larger cars cost more than smaller ones, so we would say that among new cars weight and price are positively correlated. If we also measured the fuel efficiency of these vehicles (as measured by the number of miles they can travel per gallon of gasoline), we would find that lighter cars are more fuel efficient than heavier cars. In that case, we would say that fuel economy and vehicle weight are negatively correlated.[5]

The degree of correlation is measured by the **correlation coefficient,** which ranges from +1 for **perfectly positively correlated** series to −1 for **perfectly negatively correlated** series. These two extremes are depicted for series M and N in Figure 8.4. The perfectly positively correlated series move exactly together without exception; the perfectly negatively correlated series move in exactly opposite directions.

DIVERSIFICATION

The concept of correlation is essential to developing an efficient portfolio. To reduce overall risk, it is best to *diversify* by combining, or adding to the portfolio, assets that have the lowest possible correlation. Combining assets that have a low correlation with each other can reduce the overall variability of a portfolio's returns. Figure 8.5 (see page 324) shows the returns that two assets, F and G, earn over time. Both assets earn the same average or expected return, $\bar{r}$, but note that when F's return is above average, the return on G is below average and vice versa. In other words, returns on F and G are negatively correlated, and when these two assets are combined in a portfolio, the risk of that portfolio falls without reducing the average return (that is, the portfolio's average return is also $\bar{r}$).

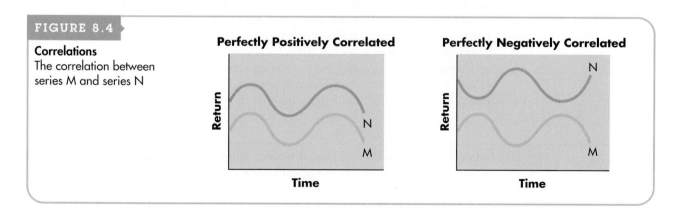

FIGURE 8.4

Correlations
The correlation between series M and series N

5. Note here that we are talking about general tendencies. For instance, a large hybrid SUV might have better fuel economy than a smaller sedan powered by a conventional gas engine. This does not change the fact that the general tendency is for lighter cars to achieve better fuel economy.

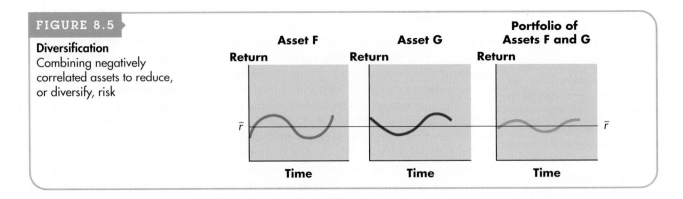

FIGURE 8.5

Diversification
Combining negatively correlated assets to reduce, or diversify, risk

For risk-averse investors, this is very good news. They get rid of something that they don't like (risk) without having to sacrifice what they do like (return). Even if assets are positively correlated, the lower the correlation between them, the greater the risk reduction that can be achieved through diversification.

Some assets are **uncorrelated**—that is, there is no interaction between their returns. Combining uncorrelated assets can reduce risk, not as effectively as combining negatively correlated assets but more effectively than combining positively correlated assets. The *correlation coefficient for uncorrelated assets is close to zero* and acts as the midpoint between perfectly positive and perfectly negative correlation.

The creation of a portfolio that combines two assets with perfectly positively correlated returns results in overall portfolio risk that at minimum equals that of the least risky asset and at maximum equals that of the most risky asset. However, a portfolio combining two assets with less than perfectly positive correlation *can* reduce total risk to a level below that of either of the components. For example, assume that you buy stock in a company that manufactures machine tools. The business is very *cyclical*, so the stock will do well when the economy is expanding, and it will do poorly during a recession. If you bought shares in another machine-tool company, with sales positively correlated with those of your firm, the combined portfolio would still be cyclical and risk would not be reduced a great deal. Alternatively, however, you could buy stock in a discount retailer, whose sales are *countercyclical*. It typically performs worse during economic expansions than it does during recessions (when consumers are trying to save money on every purchase). A portfolio that contained both of these stocks might be less volatile than either stock on its own.

uncorrelated
Describes two series that lack any interaction and therefore have a *correlation coefficient* close to zero.

Example 8.11 ▶ Table 8.7 presents the forecasted returns from three different assets—X, Y, and Z—over the next 5 years, along with their expected values and standard deviations. Each of the assets has an expected return of 12% and a standard deviation of 3.16%. The assets therefore have equal return and equal risk. The return patterns of assets X and Y are perfectly negatively correlated. When X enjoys its highest return, Y experiences its lowest return, and vice versa. The returns of assets X and Z are perfectly positively correlated. They move in precisely the same direction, so when the return on X is high, so is the return on Z. (*Note:* The

| TABLE 8.7 | Forecasted Returns, Expected Values, and Standard Deviations for Assets X, Y, and Z and Portfolios XY and XZ |

	Assets			Portfolios	
Year	X	Y	Z	XY[a] (50% X + 50% Y)	XZ[b] (50% X + 50% Z)
2013	8%	16%	8%	12%	8%
2014	10	14	10	12	10
2015	12	12	12	12	12
2016	14	10	14	12	14
2017	16	8	16	12	16
Statistics:[c]					
Expected value	12%	12%	12%	12%	12%
Standard deviation[d]	3.16%	3.16%	3.16%	0%	3.16%

[a]Portfolio XY, which consists of 50 percent of asset X and 50 percent of asset Y, illustrates *perfect negative correlation* because these two return streams behave in completely opposite fashion over the 5-year period. Its return values shown here were calculated in part A of Table 8.6.

[b]Portfolio XZ, which consists of 50 percent of asset X and 50 percent of asset Z, illustrates *perfect positive correlation* because these two return streams behave identically over the 5-year period. Its return values were calculated by using the same method demonstrated for portfolio XY in part A of Table 8.6.

[c]Because the probabilities associated with the returns are not given, the general equations, Equation 8.2a in footnote 3 and Equation 8.3a in footnote 4, were used to calculate expected values and standard deviations, respectively. Calculation of the expected value and standard deviation for portfolio XY is demonstrated in parts B and C, respectively, of Table 8.6.

[d]The portfolio standard deviations can be directly calculated from the standard deviations of the component assets with the following formula:

$$\sigma_{r_p} = \sqrt{w_1^2\sigma_1^2 + w_2^2\sigma_2^2 + 2w_1w_2c_{1,2}\sigma_1\sigma_2}$$

where w_1 and w_2 are the proportions of component assets 1 and 2, σ_1 and σ_2 are the standard deviations of component assets 1 and 2, and $c_{1,2}$ is the correlation coefficient between the returns of component assets 1 and 2.

returns for X and Z are identical.)[6] Now let's consider what happens when we combine these assets in different ways to form portfolios.

Portfolio XY   Portfolio XY (shown in Table 8.7) is created by combining equal portions of assets X and Y, the perfectly negatively correlated assets. (Calculation of portfolio XY's annual returns, the expected portfolio return, and the standard deviation of returns was demonstrated in Table 8.6 on page 322.) The risk in this portfolio, as reflected by its standard deviation, is reduced to 0%, whereas the expected return remains at 12%. Thus, the combination results in the complete elimination of risk because in each and every year the portfolio earns a 12% return.[7] *Whenever assets are perfectly negatively correlated, some combination of the two assets exists such that the resulting portfolio's returns are risk free.*

Portfolio XZ   Portfolio XZ (shown in Table 8.7) is created by combining equal portions of assets X and Z, the perfectly positively correlated assets. Individually, assets X and Z have the same standard deviation, 3.16%, and because they

---

6. Identical return streams are used in this example to permit clear illustration of the concepts, but it is *not* necessary for return streams to be identical for them to be perfectly positively correlated. Any return streams that move exactly together—regardless of the relative magnitude of the returns—are perfectly positively correlated.

7. Perfect negative correlation means that the ups and downs experienced by one asset are exactly offset by movements in the other asset. Therefore, the portfolio return does not vary over time.

always move together, combining them in a portfolio does nothing to reduce risk—the portfolio standard deviation is also 3.16%. As was the case with portfolio XY, the expected return of portfolio XZ is 12%. Because both of these portfolios provide the same expected return, but portfolio XY achieves that expected return with no risk, portfolio XY is clearly preferred by risk-averse investors over portfolio XZ.

CORRELATION, DIVERSIFICATION, RISK, AND RETURN

In general, the lower the correlation between asset returns, the greater the risk reduction that investors can achieve by diversifying. The following example illustrates how correlation influences the risk of a portfolio but not the portfolio's expected return.

Example 8.12 ▶   Consider two assets—Lo and Hi—with the characteristics described in the table below:

Asset	Expected return, $\bar{r}$	Risk (standard deviation), σ
Lo	6%	3%
Hi	8	8

Clearly, asset Lo offers a lower return than Hi does, but Lo is also less risky than Hi. It is natural to think that a portfolio combining Lo and Hi would offer a return that is between 6% and 8% and that the portfolio's risk would also fall between the risk of Lo and Hi (between 3% and 8%). That intuition is only partly correct.

The performance of a portfolio consisting of assets Lo and Hi depends not only on the expected return and standard deviation of each asset (given above), but also on how the returns on the two assets are correlated. We will illustrate the results of three specific scenarios: (1) returns on Lo and Hi are perfectly positively correlated, (2) returns on Lo and Hi are uncorrelated, and (3) returns on Lo and Hi are perfectly negatively correlated.

The results of the analysis appear in Figure 8.6. Whether the correlation between Lo and Hi is +1, 0, or −1, a portfolio of those two assets must have an expected return between 6% and 8%. That is why the line segments at left in Figure 8.6 all range between 6% and 8%. However, the standard deviation of a portfolio depends critically on the correlation between Lo and Hi. Only when Lo and Hi are perfectly positively correlated can it be said that the portfolio standard deviation must fall between 3% (Lo's standard deviation) and 8% (Hi's standard deviation). As the correlation between Lo and Hi becomes weaker (that is, as the correlation coefficient falls), investors may find that they can form portfolios of Lo and Hi with standard deviations that are even less than 3% (that is, portfolios that are less risky than holding asset Lo by itself). That is why the line segments at right in Figure 8.6 vary. In the special case when Lo and Hi are perfectly negatively correlated, it is possible to diversify away all of the risk and form a portfolio that is risk free.

FIGURE 8.6

Possible Correlations
Range of portfolio return ($\bar{r}_p$) and risk (σ_{r_p}) for combinations of assets Lo and Hi for various correlation coefficients

INTERNATIONAL DIVERSIFICATION

One excellent practical example of portfolio diversification involves including foreign assets in a portfolio. The inclusion of assets from countries with business cycles that are not highly correlated with the U.S. business cycle reduces the portfolio's responsiveness to market movements. The ups and the downs of different markets around the world offset each other, at least to some extent, and the result is a portfolio that is less risky than one invested entirely in the U.S. market.

Returns from International Diversification

Over long periods, internationally diversified portfolios tend to perform better (meaning that they earn higher returns relative to the risks taken) than purely domestic portfolios. However, over shorter periods such as a year or two, internationally diversified portfolios may perform better or worse than domestic portfolios. For example, consider what happens when the U.S. economy is performing relatively poorly and the dollar is depreciating in value against most foreign currencies. At such times, the dollar returns to U.S. investors on a portfolio of foreign assets can be very attractive. However, international diversification can yield subpar returns, particularly when the dollar is appreciating in value relative to other currencies. When the U.S. currency appreciates, the dollar value of a foreign-currency-denominated portfolio of assets declines. Even if this portfolio yields a satisfactory return in foreign currency, the return to U.S. investors will be reduced when foreign profits are translated into dollars. Subpar local currency portfolio returns, coupled with an appreciating dollar, can yield truly dismal dollar returns to U.S. investors.

Overall, though, the logic of international portfolio diversification assumes that these fluctuations in currency values and relative performance will average out over long periods. Compared to similar, purely domestic portfolios, an internationally diversified portfolio will tend to yield a comparable return at a lower level of risk.

political risk
Risk that arises from the possibility that a host government will take actions harmful to foreign investors or that political turmoil will endanger investments.

Risks of International Diversification

In addition to the risk induced by currency fluctuations, several other financial risks are unique to international investing. Most important is **political risk,** which

GLOBAL focus

An International Flavor to Risk Reduction

in practice Earlier in this chapter (see Table 8.5 on page 318), we learned that from 1900 through 2009 the U.S. stock market produced an average annual nominal return of 9.3 percent, but that return was associated with a relatively high standard deviation: 20.4 percent per year. Could U.S. investors have done better by diversifying globally? The answer is a qualified yes. Elroy Dimson, Paul Marsh, and Mike Staunton calculated the historical returns on a portfolio that included U.S. stocks as well as stocks from 18 other countries. This diversified portfolio produced returns that were not quite as high as the U.S. average, just 8.6 percent per year. However, the globally diversified portfolio was also less volatile, with an annual standard deviation of 17.8 percent. Dividing the standard deviation by the annual return produces a coefficient of variation for the globally diversified portfolio of 2.07, slightly lower than the 2.10 coefficient of variation reported for U.S. stocks in Table 8.5.

▶ *International mutual funds do not include any domestic assets whereas global mutual funds include both foreign and domestic assets. How might this difference affect their correlation with U.S. equity mutual funds?*

Source: Elroy Dimson, Paul Marsh, and Mike Staunton, Triumph of the Optimists: 101 Years of Global Investment Returns (Princeton University Press, 2002).

arises from the possibility that a host government will take actions harmful to foreign investors or that political turmoil will endanger investments. Political risks are particularly acute in developing countries, where unstable or ideologically motivated governments may attempt to block return of profits by foreign investors or even seize (nationalize) their assets in the host country. For example, reflecting President Chavez's desire to broaden the country's socialist revolution, Venezuela issued a list of priority goods for import that excluded a large percentage of the necessary inputs to the automobile production process. As a result, Toyota halted auto production in Venezuela, and three other auto manufacturers temporarily closed or deeply cut their production there. Chavez also has forced most foreign energy firms to reduce their stakes and give up control of oil projects in Venezuela.

For more discussion of reducing risk through international diversification, see the *Global Focus* box above.

→ **REVIEW QUESTIONS**

8–8 What is an *efficient portfolio?* How can the return and standard deviation of a portfolio be determined?

8–9 Why is the *correlation* between asset returns important? How does diversification allow risky assets to be combined so that the risk of the portfolio is less than the risk of the individual assets in it?

8–10 How does international diversification enhance risk reduction? When might international diversification result in subpar returns? What are *political risks*, and how do they affect international diversification?

8.4 Risk and Return: The Capital Asset Pricing Model (CAPM)

Thus far we have observed a tendency for riskier investments to earn higher returns, and we have learned that investors can reduce risk through diversification. Now we want to quantify the relationship between risk and return. In other words, we want to measure how much additional return an investor should expect from taking a little extra risk. The classic theory that links risk and return for all assets is the **capital asset pricing model (CAPM)**. We will use the CAPM to understand the basic risk–return tradeoffs involved in all types of financial decisions.

TYPES OF RISK

In the last section we saw that the standard deviation of a portfolio is often less than the standard deviation of the individual assets in the portfolio. That's the power of diversification. To see this more clearly, consider what happens to the risk of a portfolio consisting of a single security (asset), to which we add securities randomly selected from, say, the population of all actively traded securities. Using the standard deviation of return, $\sigma_r p$, to measure the total portfolio risk, Figure 8.7 depicts the behavior of the total portfolio risk (y axis) as more securities are added (x axis). With the addition of securities, the total portfolio risk declines, as a result of diversification, and tends to approach a lower limit.

The **total risk** of a security can be viewed as consisting of two parts:

$$\text{Total security risk} = \text{Nondiversifiable risk} + \text{Diversifiable risk} \qquad (8.6)$$

Diversifiable risk (sometimes called *unsystematic risk*) represents the portion of an asset's risk that is associated with random causes that can be eliminated through diversification. It is attributable to firm-specific events, such as strikes, lawsuits, regulatory actions, or the loss of a key account. Figure 8.7 shows that diversifiable risk gradually disappears as the number of stocks in the portfolio increases. **Nondiversifiable risk** (also called *systematic risk*) is attributable to

capital asset pricing model (CAPM)
The basic theory that links risk and return for all assets.

total risk
The combination of a security's *nondiversifiable risk* and *diversifiable risk*.

diversifiable risk
The portion of an asset's risk that is attributable to firm-specific, random causes; can be eliminated through diversification. Also called *unsystematic risk*.

nondiversifiable risk
The relevant portion of an asset's risk attributable to market factors that affect all firms; cannot be eliminated through diversification. Also called *systematic risk*.

FIGURE 8.7

Risk Reduction
Portfolio risk and diversification

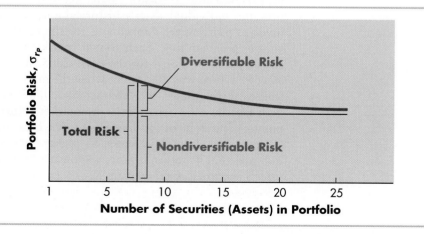

market factors that affect all firms; it cannot be eliminated through diversification. Factors such as war, inflation, the overall state of the economy, international incidents, and political events account for nondiversifiable risk. In Figure 8.7, nondiversifiable risk is represented by the horizontal black line below which the blue curve can never go, no matter how diversified the portfolio becomes.

Because any investor can easily create a portfolio of assets that will eliminate virtually all diversifiable risk, *the only relevant risk is nondiversifiable risk.* Any investor or firm therefore must be concerned solely with nondiversifiable risk. The measurement of nondiversifiable risk is thus of primary importance in selecting assets with the most desired risk–return characteristics.

THE MODEL: CAPM

The capital asset pricing model (CAPM) links nondiversifiable risk to expected returns. We will discuss the model in five sections. The first section deals with the beta coefficient, which is a measure of nondiversifiable risk. The second section presents an equation of the model itself, and the third section graphically describes the relationship between risk and return. The fourth section discusses the effects of changes in inflationary expectations and risk aversion on the relationship between risk and return. The fifth section offers some comments on the CAPM.

Beta Coefficient

beta coefficient (b)
A relative measure of nondiversifiable risk. An *index* of the degree of movement of an asset's return in response to a change in the *market return.*

market return
The return on the market portfolio of all traded securities.

The **beta coefficient,** *b,* is a relative measure of nondiversifiable risk. It is an *index* of the degree of movement of an asset's return in response to a change in the *market return.* An asset's historical returns are used in finding the asset's beta coefficient. The **market return** is the return on the market portfolio of all traded securities. The *Standard & Poor's 500 Stock Composite Index* or some similar stock index is commonly used as the market return. Betas for actively traded stocks can be obtained from a variety of sources, but you should understand how they are derived and interpreted and how they are applied to portfolios.

Deriving Beta from Return Data An asset's historical returns are used in finding the asset's beta coefficient. Figure 8.8 plots the relationship between the returns of two assets—R and S—and the market return. Note that the horizontal (x) axis measures the historical market returns and that the vertical (y) axis measures the individual asset's historical returns. The first step in deriving beta involves plotting the coordinates for the market return and asset returns from various points in time. Such annual "market return–asset return" coordinates are shown *for asset S only* for the years 2005 through 2012. For example, in 2012, asset S's return was 20 percent when the market return was 10 percent. By use of statistical techniques, the "characteristic line" that best explains the relationship between the asset return and the market return coordinates is fit to the data points.[8] The slope of this line is *beta.* The beta for asset R is about 0.80, and that for asset S is about 1.30. Asset S's higher beta (steeper characteristic line slope) indicates that its return is more responsive to changing market returns. *Therefore asset S is more risky than asset R.*

---

8. The empirical measurement of beta is approached by using *least-squares regression analysis.*

FIGURE 8.8

Beta Derivation[a]
Graphical derivation of beta for assets R and S

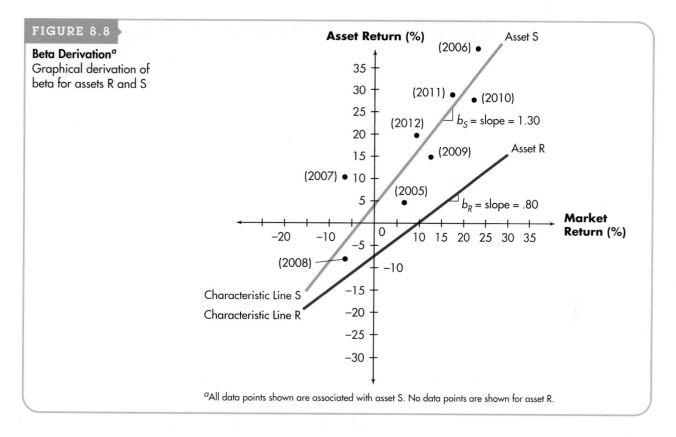

[a]All data points shown are associated with asset S. No data points are shown for asset R.

Interpreting Betas   The beta coefficient for the entire market equals 1.0. All other betas are viewed in relation to this value. Asset betas may be positive or negative, but positive betas are the norm. The majority of beta coefficients fall between 0.5 and 2.0. The return of a stock that is half as responsive as the market ($b = 0.5$) should change by 0.5 percent for each 1 percent change in the return of the market portfolio. A stock that is twice as responsive as the market ($b = 2.0$) should experience a 2 percent change in its return for each 1 percent change in the return of the market portfolio. Table 8.8 provides various beta values and their interpretations. Beta coefficients for actively traded stocks can be obtained from published sources such as *Value Line Investment Survey,* via the Internet, or through brokerage firms. Betas for some selected stocks are given in Table 8.9.

TABLE 8.8   Selected Beta Coefficients and Their Interpretations

Beta	Comment	Interpretation
2.0	Move in same	Twice as responsive as the market
1.0	direction as	Same response as the market
0.5	market	Only half as responsive as the market
0		Unaffected by market movement
−0.5	Move in opposite	Only half as responsive as the market
−1.0	direction to	Same response as the market
−2.0	market	Twice as responsive as the market

TABLE 8.9	Beta Coefficients for Selected Stocks (June 7, 2010)		
Stock	**Beta**	**Stock**	**Beta**
Amazon.com	0.99	JP Morgan Chase & Co.	1.16
Anheuser-Busch	1.00	Bank of America	2.58
Ford Motor	2.72	Microsoft	0.99
Disney	1.25	Nike, Inc.	0.92
eBay	1.75	PepsiCo, Inc.	0.57
ExxonMobil Corp.	0.37	Qualcomm	0.89
Gap (The), Inc.	1.31	Sempra Energy	0.60
General Electric	1.68	Wal-Mart Stores	0.29
Intel	1.12	Xerox	1.50
Int'l Business Machines	0.68	Yahoo! Inc.	0.92

Source: www.finance.yahoo.com

Portfolio Betas The beta of a portfolio can be easily estimated by using the betas of the individual assets it includes. Letting w_j represent the proportion of the portfolio's total dollar value represented by asset j, and letting b_j equal the beta of asset j, we can use Equation 8.7 to find the portfolio beta, b_p:

$$b_p = (w_1 \times b_1) + (w_2 \times b_2) + \cdots + (w_n \times b_n) = \sum_{j=1}^{n} w_j \times b_j \qquad (8.7)$$

Of course, $\sum_{j=1}^{n} w_j = 1$, which means that 100 percent of the portfolio's assets must be included in this computation.

Portfolio betas are interpreted in the same way as the betas of individual assets. They indicate the degree of responsiveness of the *portfolio's* return to changes in the market return. For example, when the market return increases by 10 percent, a portfolio with a beta of 0.75 will experience a 7.5 percent increase in its return ($0.75 \times 10\%$); a portfolio with a beta of 1.25 will experience a 12.5 percent increase in its return ($1.25 \times 10\%$). Clearly, a portfolio containing mostly low-beta assets will have a low beta, and one containing mostly high-beta assets will have a high beta.

Personal Finance Example 8.13 ▶ Mario Austino, an individual investor, wishes to assess the risk of two small portfolios he is considering—V and W. Both portfolios contain five assets, with the proportions and betas shown in Table 8.10. The betas for the two portfolios, b_V and b_W, can be calculated by substituting data from the table into Equation 8.7:

$b_V = (0.10 \times 1.65) + (0.30 \times 1.00) + (0.20 \times 1.30) + (0.20 \times 1.10) + (0.20 \times 1.25)$
$\quad = 0.165 + 0.300 + 0.260 + 0.220 + 0.250 = 1.195 \approx \underline{1.20}$

$b_W = (0.10 \times .80) + (0.10 \times 1.00) + (0.20 \times .65) + (0.10 \times .75) + (0.50 \times 1.05)$
$\quad = 0.080 + 0.100 + 0.130 + 0.075 + 0.525 = \underline{0.91}$

TABLE 8.10	Mario Austino's Portfolios V and W			
	Portfolio V		Portfolio W	
Asset	Proportion	Beta	Proportion	Beta
1	0.10	1.65	0.10	0.80
2	0.30	1.00	0.10	1.00
3	0.20	1.30	0.20	0.65
4	0.20	1.10	0.10	0.75
5	0.20	1.25	0.50	1.05
Totals	1.00		1.00	

Portfolio V's beta is about 1.20, and portfolio W's is 0.91. These values make sense because portfolio V contains relatively high-beta assets, and portfolio W contains relatively low-beta assets. Mario's calculations show that portfolio V's returns are more responsive to changes in market returns and are therefore more risky than portfolio W's. He must now decide which, if either, portfolio he feels comfortable adding to his existing investments.

The Equation

Using the beta coefficient to measure nondiversifiable risk, the *capital asset pricing model (CAPM)* is given in Equation 8.8:

$$r_j = R_F + [b_j \times (r_m - R_F)] \qquad (8.8)$$

where

$$r_j = \text{required return on asset } j$$

R_F = risk-free rate of return, commonly measured by the return on a U.S. Treasury bill

b_j = beta coefficient or index of nondiversifiable risk for asset j

r_m = market return; return on the market portfolio of assets

risk-free rate of return, (R_F) The required return on a *risk-free asset,* typically a 3-month U.S. Treasury bill.

U.S. Treasury bills (T-bills) Short-term IOUs issued by the U.S. Treasury; considered the *risk-free asset.*

The CAPM can be divided into two parts: (1) the **risk-free rate of return, R_F,** which is the required return on a *risk-free asset,* typically a 3-month **U.S. Treasury bill (T-bill),** a short-term IOU issued by the U.S. Treasury, and (2) the *risk premium.* These are, respectively, the two elements on either side of the plus sign in Equation 8.8. The $(r_m - R_F)$ portion of the risk premium is called the *market risk premium* because it represents the premium the investor must receive for taking the average amount of risk associated with holding the market portfolio of assets.

Historical Risk Premiums Using the historical return data for stocks, bonds, and Treasury bills for the 1900–2009 period shown in Table 8.1, we can calculate the risk premiums for each investment category. The calculation (consistent with Equation 8.8) involves merely subtracting the historical

U.S. Treasury bill's average return from the historical average return for a given investment:

Investment	Risk premium[a]
Stocks	9.3% − 3.9% = 5.4%
Treasury bonds	5.0 − 3.9 = 1.1

[a]Return values obtained from Table 8.1.

Reviewing the risk premiums calculated above, we can see that the risk premium is higher for stocks than for bonds. This outcome makes sense intuitively because stocks are riskier than bonds (equity is riskier than debt).

Example 8.14 ▶   Benjamin Corporation, a growing computer software developer, wishes to determine the required return on an asset Z, which has a beta of 1.5. The risk-free rate of return is 7%; the return on the market portfolio of assets is 11%. Substituting $b_Z = 1.5$, $R_F = 7\%$, and $r_m = 11\%$ into the capital asset pricing model given in Equation 8.8 yields a required return of

$$r_Z = 7\% + [1.5 \times (11\% - 7\%)] = 7\% + 6\% = \underline{13\%}$$

The market risk premium of 4% (11% − 7%), when adjusted for the asset's index of risk (beta) of 1.5, results in a risk premium of 6% (1.5 × 4%). That risk premium, when added to the 7% risk-free rate, results in a 13% required return.

Other things being equal, *the higher the beta, the higher the required return, and the lower the beta, the lower the required return.*

The Graph: The Security Market Line (SML)

security market line (SML)
The depiction of the *capital asset pricing model* (CAPM) as a graph that reflects the required return in the marketplace for each level of nondiversifiable risk (beta).

When the capital asset pricing model (Equation 8.8) is depicted graphically, it is called the **security market line (SML)**. The SML will, in fact, be a straight line. It reflects the required return in the marketplace for each level of nondiversifiable risk (beta). In the graph, risk as measured by beta, b, is plotted on the x axis, and required returns, r, are plotted on the y axis. The risk–return trade-off is clearly represented by the SML.

Example 8.15 ▶   In the preceding example for Benjamin Corporation, the risk-free rate, R_F, was 7%, and the market return, r_m, was 11%. The SML can be plotted by using the two sets of coordinates for the betas associated with R_F and r_m, b_{R_F} and b_m (that is, $b_{R_F} = 0$,[9] $R_F = 7\%$; and $b_m = 1.0$, $r_m = 11\%$). Figure 8.9 presents the resulting security market line. As traditionally shown, the security market line in

---

9. Because R_F is the rate of return on a risk-free asset, the beta associated with the risk-free asset, b_{R_F}, would equal 0. The zero beta on the risk-free asset reflects not only its absence of risk but also that the asset's return is unaffected by movements in the market return.

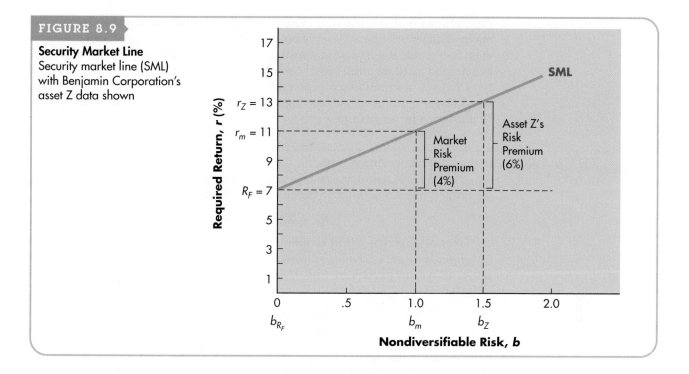

FIGURE 8.9

Security Market Line
Security market line (SML) with Benjamin Corporation's asset Z data shown

Figure 8.9 presents the required return associated with all positive betas. The market risk premium of 4% (r_m of 11% − R_F of 7%) has been highlighted. For a beta for asset Z, b_Z, of 1.5, its corresponding required return, r_Z, is 13%. Also shown in the figure is asset Z's risk premium of 6% (r_Z of 13% − R_F of 7%). It should be clear that for assets with betas greater than 1, the risk premium is greater than that for the market; for assets with betas less than 1, the risk premium is less than that for the market.

Shifts in the Security Market Line

The security market line is not stable over time, and shifts in the security market line can result in a change in required return. The position and slope of the SML are affected by two major forces—inflationary expectations and risk aversion—which are analyzed next.[10]

Changes in Inflationary Expectations Changes in inflationary expectations affect the risk-free rate of return, R_F. The equation for the risk-free rate of return is

$$R_F = r^* + IP \qquad (8.9)$$

This equation shows that, assuming a constant real rate of interest, r^*, changes in inflationary expectations, reflected in an inflation premium, IP, will result in corresponding changes in the risk-free rate. Therefore, a change in inflationary

---

10. A firm's beta can change over time as a result of changes in the firm's asset mix, in its financing mix, or in external factors not within management's control, such as earthquakes, toxic spills, and so on.

expectations that results from events such as international trade embargoes or major changes in Federal Reserve policy will result in a shift in the SML. Because the risk-free rate is a basic component of all rates of return, any change in R_F will be reflected in *all* required rates of return.

Changes in inflationary expectations result in parallel shifts in the SML in direct response to the magnitude and direction of the change. This effect can best be illustrated by an example.

Example 8.16 ▶   In the preceding example, using the CAPM, the required return for asset Z, r_Z, was found to be 13%. Assuming that the risk-free rate of 7% includes a 2% real rate of interest, r^*, and a 5% inflation premium, *IP*, then Equation 8.9 confirms that

$$R_F = 2\% + 5\% = 7\%$$

Now assume that recent economic events have resulted in an *increase of 3% in inflationary expectations, raising the inflation premium* to 8% (IP_1). As a result, all returns likewise rise by 3%. In this case, the new returns (noted by subscript 1) are

$$R_{F_1} = 10\% \text{ (rises from 7\% to 10\%)}$$
$$r_{m_1} = 14\% \text{ (rises from 11\% to 14\%)}$$

Substituting these values, along with asset Z's beta (b_Z) of 1.5, into the CAPM (Equation 8.8), we find that asset Z's new required return (r_{Z_1}) can be calculated:

$$r_{Z_1} = 10\% + [1.5 \times (14\% - 10\%)] = 10\% + 6\% = \underline{16\%}$$

Comparing r_{Z_1} of 16% to r_Z of 13%, we see that the change of 3% in asset Z's required return exactly equals the change in the inflation premium. The same 3% increase results for all assets.

Figure 8.10 depicts the situation just described. It shows that the 3% increase in inflationary expectations results in a parallel shift upward of 3% in the SML. Clearly, the required returns on all assets rise by 3%. Note that the rise in the inflation premium from 5% to 8% (*IP* to IP_1) causes the risk-free rate to rise from 7% to 10% (R_F to R_{F_1}) and the market return to increase from 11% to 14% (r_m to r_{m_1}). The security market line therefore shifts upward by 3% (SML to SML_1), causing the required return on all risky assets, such as asset Z, to rise by 3%. The important lesson here is that *a given change in inflationary expectations will be fully reflected in a corresponding change in the returns of all assets, as reflected graphically in a parallel shift of the SML.*

Changes in Risk Aversion   The slope of the security market line reflects the general risk preferences of investors in the marketplace. As discussed earlier, most investors are *risk averse*—they require increased returns for increased risk. This positive relationship between risk and return is graphically represented by the SML, which depicts the relationship between nondiversifiable risk as measured by beta (*x* axis) and the required return (*y* axis). The slope of the SML reflects the degree of risk aversion: *the steeper its slope, the greater the degree of risk aversion* because a higher level of return will be required for each level of risk as measured by beta. In other words, *risk premiums increase with increasing risk avoidance.*

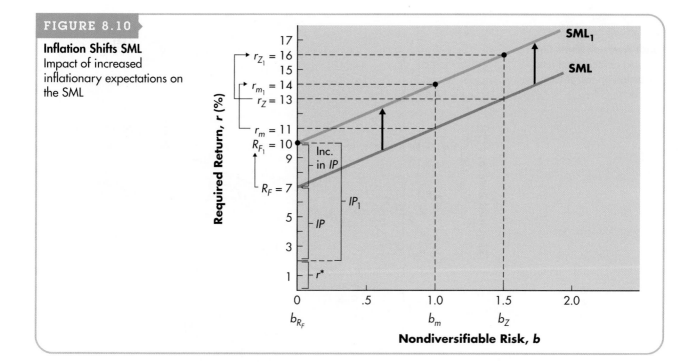

FIGURE 8.10

Inflation Shifts SML
Impact of increased inflationary expectations on the SML

Changes in risk aversion, and therefore shifts in the SML, result from changing preferences of investors, which generally result from economic, political, and social events. Examples of events that *increase* risk aversion include a stock market crash, assassination of a key political leader, and the outbreak of war. In general, widely shared expectations of hard times ahead tend to cause investors to become more risk averse, requiring higher returns as compensation for accepting a given level of risk. The impact of increased risk aversion on the SML can best be demonstrated by an example.

Example 8.17 ▶

In the preceding examples, the SML in Figure 8.9 reflected a risk-free rate (R_F) of 7%, a market return (r_m) of 11%, a market risk premium ($r_m - R_F$) of 4%, and a required return on asset Z (r_Z) of 13% with a beta (b_Z) of 1.5. Assume that recent economic events have made investors more risk averse, causing a new higher market return (r_{m_1}) of 14%. Graphically, this change would cause the SML to pivot upward as shown in Figure 8.11, causing a new market risk premium ($r_{m_1} - R_F$) of 7%. As a result, the required return on all risky assets will increase. For asset Z, with a beta of 1.5, the new required return (r_{Z_1}) can be calculated by using the CAPM (Equation 8.8):

$$r_{Z_1} = 7\% + [1.5 \times (14\% - 7\%)] = 7\% + 10.5\% = \underline{17.5\%}$$

This value can be seen on the new security market line (SML_1) in Figure 8.11. Note that although asset Z's risk, as measured by beta, did not change, its required return has increased because of the increased risk aversion reflected in the market risk premium. To summarize, *greater risk aversion results in higher required returns for each level of risk. Similarly, a reduction in risk aversion causes the required return for each level of risk to decline.*

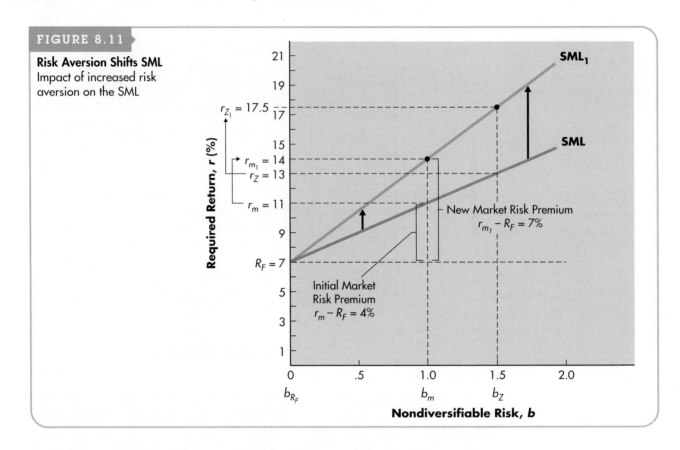

FIGURE 8.11

Risk Aversion Shifts SML
Impact of increased risk
aversion on the SML

Some Comments on the CAPM

The capital asset pricing model generally relies on historical data. The betas may or may not actually reflect the *future* variability of returns. Therefore, the required returns specified by the model can be viewed only as rough approximations. Users of betas commonly make subjective adjustments to the historically determined betas to reflect their expectations of the future.

The CAPM was developed to explain the behavior of security prices and provide a mechanism whereby investors could assess the impact of a proposed security investment on their portfolio's overall risk and return. It is based on an assumed efficient market with the following characteristics: many small investors, all having the same information and expectations with respect to securities; no restrictions on investment, no taxes, and no transaction costs; and rational investors, who view securities similarly and are risk averse, preferring higher returns and lower risk.

Although the perfect world described in the preceding paragraph appears to be unrealistic, studies have provided support for the existence of the expectational relationship described by the CAPM in active markets such as the New York Stock Exchange. The CAPM also sees widespread use in corporations that use the model to assess the required returns that their shareholders demand (and therefore, the returns that the firm's managers need to achieve when they invest shareholders' money).

In more depth

To read about *CAPM Survives Criticism*, go to
www.myfinancelab.com

→ REVIEW QUESTIONS

8–11 How are total risk, nondiversifiable risk, and diversifiable risk related? Why is nondiversifiable risk the *only relevant risk?*

8–12 What risk does *beta* measure? How can you find the beta of a portfolio?

8–13 Explain the meaning of each variable in the *capital asset pricing model (CAPM)* equation. What is the *security market line (SML)?*

8–14 What impact would the following changes have on the security market line and therefore on the required return for a given level of risk? (**a**) An *increase* in inflationary expectations. (**b**) Investors become *less* risk-averse.

Summary

FOCUS ON VALUE

A firm's risk and expected return directly affect its share price. Risk and return are the two key determinants of the firm's value. It is therefore the financial manager's responsibility to assess carefully the risk and return of all major decisions to ensure that the expected returns justify the level of risk being introduced.

The financial manager can expect to achieve **the firm's goal of increasing its share price** (and thereby benefiting its owners) by taking only those actions that earn returns at least commensurate with their risk. Clearly, financial managers need to recognize, measure, and evaluate risk–return trade-offs to ensure that their decisions contribute to the creation of value for owners.

REVIEW OF LEARNING GOALS

LG 1   Understand the meaning and fundamentals of risk, return, and risk preferences. Risk is a measure of the uncertainty surrounding the return that an investment will produce. The total rate of return is the sum of cash distributions, such as interest or dividends, plus the change in the asset's value over a given period, divided by the investment's beginning-of-period value. Investment returns vary both over time and between different types of investments. Investors may be risk averse, risk neutral, or risk seeking. Most financial decision makers are risk averse. A risk averse decision maker requires a higher expected return on a more risky investment alternative.

LG 2   Describe procedures for assessing and measuring the risk of a single asset. The risk of a single asset is measured in much the same way as the risk of a portfolio of assets. Scenario analysis and probability distributions can be used to assess risk. The range, the standard deviation, and the coefficient of variation can be used to measure risk quantitatively.

LG 3   Discuss the measurement of return and standard deviation for a portfolio and the concept of correlation. The return of a portfolio is calculated as the weighted average of returns on the individual assets from which it is formed. The portfolio standard deviation is found by using the formula for the standard deviation of a single asset.

Correlation—the statistical relationship between any two series of numbers—can be positively correlated, negatively correlated, or uncorrelated. At the extremes, the series can be perfectly positively correlated or perfectly negatively correlated.

LG 4 **Understand the risk and return characteristics of a portfolio in terms of correlation and diversification and the impact of international assets on a portfolio.** Diversification involves combining assets with low correlation to reduce the risk of the portfolio. The range of risk in a two-asset portfolio depends on the correlation between the two assets. If they are perfectly positively correlated, the portfolio's risk will be between the individual assets' risks. If they are perfectly negatively correlated, the portfolio's risk will be between the risk of the more risky asset and zero.

International diversification can further reduce a portfolio's risk. Foreign assets have the risk of currency fluctuation and political risks.

LG 5 **Review the two types of risk and the derivation and role of beta in measuring the relevant risk of both a security and a portfolio.** The total risk of a security consists of nondiversifiable and diversifiable risk. Diversifiable risk can be eliminated through diversification. Nondiversifiable risk is the only relevant risk. Nondiversifiable risk is measured by the beta coefficient, which is a relative measure of the relationship between an asset's return and the market return. Beta is derived by finding the slope of the "characteristic line" that best explains the historical relationship between the asset's return and the market return. The beta of a portfolio is a weighted average of the betas of the individual assets that it includes.

LG 6 **Explain the capital asset pricing model (CAPM), its relationship to the security market line (SML), and the major forces causing shifts in the SML.** The CAPM uses beta to relate an asset's risk relative to the market to the asset's required return. The graphical depiction of the CAPM is SML, which shifts over time in response to changing inflationary expectations and/or changes in investor risk aversion. Changes in inflationary expectations result in parallel shifts in the SML. Increasing risk aversion results in a steepening in the slope of the SML. Decreasing risk aversion reduces the slope of the SML. Although it has some shortcomings, the CAPM provides a useful conceptual framework for evaluating and linking risk and return.

Opener-in-Review

The table below shows the annual returns in each year from 2007 through 2009 of the Close Special Situations Fund (a British fund specializing in small stocks), and the Financial Times Stock Index (FTSE), an index that tracks the performance of the 100 largest companies on the U.K. stock market:

Year	Close Fund	FTSE
2007	−4.8%	2.1%
2008	−57.3%	−30.9%
2009	246.9%	22.1%

For both the Close Fund and the FTSE, calculate the average annual return and its standard deviation. What are the general patterns that you see? Provide one reason that the performance of the FTSE differs from that of the Close Fund.

Self-Test Problems   (Solutions in Appendix)

LG 3 **LG 4** **ST8–1** **Portfolio analysis**   You have been asked for your advice in selecting a portfolio of assets and have been given the following data:

	Expected return		
Year	Asset A	Asset B	Asset C
2013	12%	16%	12%
2014	14	14	14
2015	16	12	16

You have been told that you can create two portfolios—one consisting of assets A and B and the other consisting of assets A and C—by investing equal proportions (50%) in each of the two component assets.

a. What is the expected return for each asset over the 3-year period?
b. What is the standard deviation for each asset's return?
c. What is the expected return for each of the two portfolios?
d. How would you characterize the correlations of returns of the two assets making up each of the two portfolios identified in part **c**?
e. What is the standard deviation for each portfolio?
f. Which portfolio do you recommend? Why?

LG 5 **LG 6** **ST8–2** **Beta and CAPM**   Currently under consideration is an investment with a beta, b, of 1.50. At this time, the risk-free rate of return, R_F, is 7%, and the return on the market portfolio of assets, r_m, is 10%. You believe that this investment will earn an annual rate of return of 11%.

a. If the return on the market portfolio were to increase by 10%, what would you expect to happen to the investment's return? What if the market return were to decline by 10%?
b. Use the capital asset pricing model (CAPM) to find the *required return* on this investment.
c. On the basis of your calculation in part **b**, would you recommend this investment? Why or why not?
d. Assume that as a result of investors becoming less risk-averse, the market return drops by 1% to 9%. What impact would this change have on your responses in parts **b** and **c**?

Warm-Up Exercises   All problems are available in 🔷myfinancelab .

LG 1   **E8–1**   An analyst predicted last year that the stock of Logistics, Inc., would offer a total return of at least 10% in the coming year. At the beginning of the year, the firm had a stock market value of $10 million. At the end of the year, it had a market value of $12 million even though it experienced a loss, or negative net income, of $2.5 million. Did the analyst's prediction prove correct? Explain using the values for total annual return.

LG 2   **E8–2**   Four analysts cover the stock of Fluorine Chemical. One forecasts a 5% return for the coming year. A second expects the return to be negative 5%. A third predicts a 10% return. A fourth expects a 3% return in the coming year. You are relatively confident that the return will be positive but not large, so you arbitrarily assign probabilities of being correct of 35%, 5%, 20%, and 40%, respectively, to the analysts' forecasts. Given these probabilities, what is Fluorine Chemical's *expected return* for the coming year?

LG 2   **E8–3**   The expected annual returns are 15% for investment 1 and 12% for investment 2. The standard deviation of the first investment's return is 10%; the second investment's return has a standard deviation of 5%. Which investment is less risky based solely on *standard deviation*? Which investment is less risky based on *coefficient of variation*? Which is a better measure given that the expected returns of the two investments are not the same?

LG 3   **E8–4**   Your portfolio has three asset classes. U.S. government T-bills account for 45% of the portfolio, large-company stocks constitute another 40%, and small-company stocks make up the remaining 15%. If the expected returns are 3.8% for the T-bills, 12.3% for the large-company stocks, and 17.4% for the small-company stocks, what is the expected return of the portfolio?

LG 5   **E8–5**   You wish to calculate the risk level of your portfolio based on its beta. The five stocks in the portfolio with their respective weights and betas are shown in the accompanying table. Calculate the beta of your portfolio.

Stock	Portfolio weight	Beta
Alpha	20%	1.15
Centauri	10	0.85
Zen	15	1.60
Wren	20	1.35
Yukos	35	1.85

LG 6   **E8–6**   a. Calculate the required rate of return for an asset that has a beta of 1.8, given a risk-free rate of 5% and a market return of 10%.

b. If investors have become more risk-averse due to recent geopolitical events, and the market return rises to 13%, what is the required rate of return for the same asset?

c. Use your findings in part **a** to graph the initial *security market line (SML),* and then use your findings in part **b** to graph (on the same set of axes) the shift in the SML.

Problems

All problems are available in 🔷 myfinancelab .

LG 1 **P8–1** **Rate of return** Douglas Keel, a financial analyst for Orange Industries, wishes to estimate the rate of return for two similar-risk investments, X and Y. Douglas's research indicates that the immediate past returns will serve as reasonable estimates of future returns. A year earlier, investment X had a market value of $20,000; investment Y had a market value of $55,000. During the year, investment X generated cash flow of $1,500 and investment Y generated cash flow of $6,800. The current market values of investments X and Y are $21,000 and $55,000, respectively.

a. Calculate the expected rate of return on investments X and Y using the most recent year's data.

b. Assuming that the two investments are equally risky, which one should Douglas recommend? Why?

LG 1 **P8–2** **Return calculations** For each of the investments shown in the following table, calculate the rate of return earned over the unspecified time period.

Investment	Cash flow during period	Beginning-of-period value	End-of-period value
A	−$ 800	$ 1,100	$ 100
B	15,000	120,000	118,000
C	7,000	45,000	48,000
D	80	600	500
E	1,500	12,500	12,400

LG 1 **P8–3** **Risk preferences** Sharon Smith, the financial manager for Barnett Corporation, wishes to evaluate three prospective investments: X, Y, and Z. Sharon will evaluate each of these investments to decide whether they are superior to investments that her company already has in place, which have an expected return of 12% and a standard deviation of 6%. The expected returns and standard deviations of the investments are as follows:

Investment	Expected return	Standard deviation
X	14%	7%
Y	12	8
Z	10	9

a. If Sharon were *risk neutral*, which investments would she select? Explain why.

b. If she were *risk averse*, which investments would she select? Why?

c. If she were *risk seeking*, which investments would she select? Why?

d. Given the traditional risk preference behavior exhibited by financial managers, which investment would be preferred? Why?

LG 2 **P8–4** **Risk analysis** Solar Designs is considering an investment in an expanded product line. Two possible types of expansion are being considered. After investigating the possible outcomes, the company made the estimates shown in the following table.

	Expansion A	Expansion B
Initial investment	$12,000	$12,000
Annual rate of return		
Pessimistic	16%	10%
Most likely	20%	20%
Optimistic	24%	30%

a. Determine the *range* of the rates of return for each of the two projects.
b. Which project is less risky? Why?
c. If you were making the investment decision, which one would you choose? Why? What does this imply about your feelings toward risk?
d. Assume that expansion B's most likely outcome is 21% per year and that all other facts remain the same. Does this change your answer to part **c**? Why?

LG 2   P8–5   Risk and probability   Micro-Pub, Inc., is considering the purchase of one of two microfilm cameras, R and S. Both should provide benefits over a 10-year period, and each requires an initial investment of $4,000. Management has constructed the accompanying table of estimates of rates of return and probabilities for pessimistic, most likely, and optimistic results.

a. Determine the *range* for the rate of return for each of the two cameras.
b. Determine the *expected value* of return for each camera.
c. Purchase of which camera is riskier? Why?

	Camera R		Camera S	
	Amount	Probability	Amount	Probability
Initial investment	$4,000	1.00	$4,000	1.00
Annual rate of return				
Pessimistic	20%	0.25	15%	0.20
Most likely	25%	0.50	25%	0.55
Optimistic	30%	0.25	35%	0.25

LG 2   P8–6   Bar charts and risk   Swan's Sportswear is considering bringing out a line of designer jeans. Currently, it is negotiating with two different well-known designers. Because of the highly competitive nature of the industry, the two lines of jeans have been given code names. After market research, the firm has established the expectations shown in the following table about the annual rates of return:

		Annual rate of return	
Market acceptance	Probability	Line J	Line K
Very poor	0.05	0.0075	0.010
Poor	0.15	0.0125	0.025
Average	0.60	0.0850	0.080
Good	0.15	0.1475	0.135
Excellent	0.05	0.1625	0.150

Use the table to:

a. Construct a bar chart for each line's annual rate of return.

b. Calculate the *expected value* of return for each line.

c. Evaluate the relative riskiness for each jean line's rate of return using the bar charts.

LG 2   **P8–7**   **Coefficient of variation**   Metal Manufacturing has isolated four alternatives for meeting its need for increased production capacity. The following table summarizes data gathered relative to each of these alternatives.

Alternative	Expected return	Standard deviation of return
A	20%	7.0%
B	22	9.5
C	19	6.0
D	16	5.5

a. Calculate the *coefficient of variation* for each alternative.

b. If the firm wishes to minimize risk, which alternative do you recommend? Why?

LG 2   **P8–8**   **Standard deviation versus coefficient of variation as measures of risk**   Greengage, Inc., a successful nursery, is considering several expansion projects. All of the alternatives promise to produce an acceptable return. Data on four possible projects follow.

Project	Expected return	Range	Standard deviation
A	12.0%	4.0%	2.9%
B	12.5	5.0	3.2
C	13.0	6.0	3.5
D	12.8	4.5	3.0

a. Which project is least risky, judging on the basis of *range?*

b. Which project has the lowest *standard deviation?* Explain why standard deviation may not be an entirely appropriate measure of risk for purposes of this comparison.

c. Calculate the *coefficient of variation* for each project. Which project do you think Greengage's owners should choose? Explain why.

Personal Finance Problem

LG 1   **LG 2**   **P8–9**   **Rate of return, standard deviation, coefficient of variation**   Mike is searching for a stock to include in his current stock portfolio. He is interested in Hi-Tech Inc.; he has been impressed with the company's computer products and believes Hi-Tech is an innovative market player. However, Mike realizes that any time you consider a technology stock, risk is a major concern. The rule he follows is to include only securities with a coefficient of variation of returns below 0.90.

Mike has obtained the following price information for the period 2009 through 2012. Hi-Tech stock, being growth-oriented, did not pay any dividends during these 4 years.

	Stock price	
Year	Beginning	End
2009	$14.36	$21.55
2010	21.55	64.78
2011	64.78	72.38
2012	72.38	91.80

a. Calculate the *rate of return* for each year, 2009 through 2012, for Hi-Tech stock.
b. Assume that each year's return is equally probable, and calculate the *average return* over this time period.
c. Calculate the *standard deviation* of returns over the past 4 years. (*Hint:* Treat these data as a sample.)
d. Based on **b** and **c** determine the *coefficient of variation* of returns for the security.
e. Given the calculation in **d** what should be Mike's decision regarding the inclusion of Hi-Tech stock in his portfolio?

LG 2 **P8–10** **Assessing return and risk** Swift Manufacturing must choose between two asset purchases. The annual rate of return and the related probabilities given in the following table summarize the firm's analysis to this point.

Project 257		Project 432	
Rate of return	Probability	Rate of return	Probability
−10%	0.01	10%	0.05
10	0.04	15	0.10
20	0.05	20	0.10
30	0.10	25	0.15
40	0.15	30	0.20
45	0.30	35	0.15
50	0.15	40	0.10
60	0.10	45	0.10
70	0.05	50	0.05
80	0.04		
100	0.01		

a. For each project, compute:
   (1) The range of possible rates of return.
   (2) The expected return.
   (3) The standard deviation of the returns.
   (4) The coefficient of variation of the returns.
b. Construct a bar chart of each distribution of rates of return.
c. Which project would you consider less risky? Why?

LG 2 **P8–11** **Integrative—Expected return, standard deviation, and coefficient of variation** Three assets—F, G, and H—are currently being considered by Perth Industries. The probability distributions of expected returns for these assets are shown in the following table.

	Asset F		Asset G		Asset H	
j	Pr_j	Return, r_j	Pr_j	Return, r_j	Pr_j	Return, r_j
1	0.10	40%	0.40	35%	0.10	40%
2	0.20	10	0.30	10	0.20	20
3	0.40	0	0.30	−20	0.40	10
4	0.20	−5			0.20	0
5	0.10	−10			0.10	−20

a. Calculate the expected value of return, $\bar{r}$, for each of the three assets. Which provides the largest expected return?
b. Calculate the standard deviation, σ_r, for each of the three assets' returns. Which appears to have the greatest risk?
c. Calculate the coefficient of variation, CV, for each of the three assets' returns. Which appears to have the greatest *relative* risk?

LG 2 **P8–12** **Normal probability distribution** Assuming that the rates of return associated with a given asset investment are normally distributed; that the expected return, $\bar{r}$, is 18.9%; and that the coefficient of variation, CV, is 0.75; answer the following questions:
a. Find the standard deviation of returns, σ_r.
b. Calculate the range of expected return outcomes associated with the following probabilities of occurrence: (1) 68%, (2) 95%, (3) 99%.
c. Draw the probability distribution associated with your findings in parts **a** and **b**.

Personal Finance Problem

LG 3 **P8–13** **Portfolio return and standard deviation** Jamie Wong is considering building an investment portfolio containing two stocks, L and M. Stock L will represent 40% of the dollar value of the portfolio, and stock M will account for the other 60%. The expected returns over the next 6 years, 2013–2018, for each of these stocks are shown in the following table.

	Expected return	
Year	Stock L	Stock M
2013	14%	20%
2014	14	18
2015	16	16
2016	17	14
2017	17	12
2018	19	10

a. Calculate the expected portfolio return, r_p, for *each* of the 6 years.
b. Calculate the expected value of portfolio returns, $\bar{r}_p$, over the 6-year period.
c. Calculate the standard deviation of expected portfolio returns, σ_{r_p}, over the 6-year period.
d. How would you characterize the correlation of returns of the two stocks L and M?
e. Discuss any benefits of diversification achieved by Jamie through creation of the portfolio.

LG 3   **P8–14** **Portfolio analysis**   You have been given the expected return data shown in the first table on three assets—F, G, and H—over the period 2013–2016.

	Expected return		
Year	Asset F	Asset G	Asset H
2013	16%	17%	14%
2014	17	16	15
2015	18	15	16
2016	19	14	17

Using these assets, you have isolated the three investment alternatives shown in the following table.

Alternative	Investment
1	100% of asset F
2	50% of asset F and 50% of asset G
3	50% of asset F and 50% of asset H

a. Calculate the expected return over the 4-year period for each of the three alternatives.
b. Calculate the standard deviation of returns over the 4-year period for each of the three alternatives.
c. Use your findings in parts **a** and **b** to calculate the coefficient of variation for each of the three alternatives.
d. On the basis of your findings, which of the three investment alternatives do you recommend? Why?

LG 4   **P8–15** **Correlation, risk, and return**   Matt Peters wishes to evaluate the risk and return behaviors associated with various combinations of assets V and W under three assumed degrees of correlation: perfectly positive, uncorrelated, and perfectly negative. The expected returns and standard deviations calculated for each of the assets are shown in the following table.

Asset	Expected return, $\bar{r}$	Risk (standard deviation), σ_r
V	8%	5%
W	13	10

a. If the returns of assets V and W are *perfectly positively correlated* (correlation coefficient = +1), describe the *range* of (1) expected return and (2) risk associated with all possible portfolio combinations.

b. If the returns of assets V and W are *uncorrelated* (correlation coefficient = 0), describe the *approximate range* of (1) expected return and (2) risk associated with all possible portfolio combinations.

c. If the returns of assets V and W are *perfectly negatively correlated* (correlation coefficient = −1), describe the *range* of (1) expected return and (2) risk associated with all possible portfolio combinations.

Personal Finance Problem

LG 1   LG 4   **P8–16 International investment returns**   Joe Martinez, a U.S. citizen living in Brownsville, Texas, invested in the common stock of Telmex, a Mexican corporation. He purchased 1,000 shares at 20.50 pesos per share. Twelve months later, he sold them at 24.75 pesos per share. He received no dividends during that time.

a. What was Joe's investment return (in percentage terms) for the year, on the basis of the peso value of the shares?

b. The exchange rate for pesos was 9.21 pesos per US$1.00 at the time of the purchase. At the time of the sale, the exchange rate was 9.85 pesos per US$1.00. Translate the purchase and sale prices into US$.

c. Calculate Joe's investment return on the basis of the US$ value of the shares.

d. Explain why the two returns are different. Which one is more important to Joe? Why?

LG 5   **P8–17 Total, nondiversifiable, and diversifiable risk**   David Talbot randomly selected securities from all those listed on the New York Stock Exchange for his portfolio. He began with a single security and added securities one by one until a total of 20 securities were held in the portfolio. After each security was added, David calculated the portfolio standard deviation, σ_{r_p}. The calculated values are shown in the following table.

Number of securities	Portfolio risk, σ_{r_p}	Number of securities	Portfolio risk, σ_{r_p}
1	14.50%	11	7.00%
2	13.30	12	6.80
3	12.20	13	6.70
4	11.20	14	6.65
5	10.30	15	6.60
6	9.50	16	6.56
7	8.80	17	6.52
8	8.20	18	6.50
9	7.70	19	6.48
10	7.30	20	6.47

a. Plot the data from the table above on a graph that has the number of securities on the *x*-axis and the portfolio standard deviation on the *y*-axis.

b. Divide the total portfolio risk in the graph into its *nondiversifiable* and *diversifiable* risk components, and label each of these on the graph.

c. Describe which of the two risk components is the *relevant risk,* and explain why it is relevant. How much of this risk exists in David Talbot's portfolio?

LG 5   **P8–18**   **Graphical derivation of beta**   A firm wishes to estimate graphically the betas for two assets, A and B. It has gathered the return data shown in the following table for the market portfolio and for both assets over the last 10 years, 2003–2012.

| | Actual return | | |
Year	Market portfolio	Asset A	Asset B
2003	6%	11%	16%
2004	2	8	11
2005	−13	−4	−10
2006	−4	3	3
2007	−8	0	−3
2008	16	19	30
2009	10	14	22
2010	15	18	29
2011	8	12	19
2012	13	17	26

a. On a set of "market return (x axis)–asset return (y axis)" axes, use the data given to draw the characteristic line for asset A and for asset B.
b. Use the characteristic lines from part **a** to estimate the betas for assets A and B.
c. Use the betas found in part **b** to comment on the relative risks of assets A and B.

LG 5   **P8–19**   **Graphical derivation and interpreting beta**   You are analyzing the performance of two stocks. The first, shown in Panel A, is Cyclical Industries Incorporated. Cyclical

Panel A   **Panel B**

Industries makes machine tools and other heavy equipment, the demand for which rises and falls closely with the overall state of the economy. The second stock, shown in Panel B, is Biotech Cures Corporation. Biotech Cures uses biotechnology to develop new pharmaceutical compounds to treat incurable diseases. Biotech's fortunes are driven largely by the success or failure of its scientists to discover new and effective drugs. Each data point on the graph shows the monthly return on the stock of interest and the monthly return on the overall stock market. The lines drawn through the data points represent the characteristic lines for each security.

a. Which stock do you think has a higher standard deviation? Why?
b. Which stock do you think has a higher beta? Why?
c. Which stock do you think is riskier? What does the answer to this question depend on?

LG 5 **P8–20** **Interpreting beta** A firm wishes to assess the impact of changes in the market return on an asset that has a beta of 1.20.

a. If the market return increased by 15%, what impact would this change be expected to have on the asset's return?
b. If the market return decreased by 8%, what impact would this change be expected to have on the asset's return?
c. If the market return did not change, what impact, if any, would be expected on the asset's return?
d. Would this asset be considered more or less risky than the market? Explain.

LG 5 **P8–21** **Betas** Answer the questions below for assets A to D shown in the table.

Asset	Beta
A	0.50
B	1.60
C	−0.20
D	0.90

a. What impact would a *10% increase* in the market return be expected to have on each asset's return?
b. What impact would a *10% decrease* in the market return be expected to have on each asset's return?
c. If you believed that the market return would *increase* in the near future, which asset would you prefer? Why?
d. If you believed that the market return would *decrease* in the near future, which asset would you prefer? Why?

Personal Finance Problem

LG 5 **P8–22** **Betas and risk rankings** You are considering three stocks—A, B, and C—for possible inclusion in your investment portfolio. Stock A has a beta of 0.80, stock B has a beta of 1.40, and stock C has a beta of −0.30.

a. Rank these stocks from the most risky to the least risky.
b. If the return on the market portfolio increased by 12%, what change would you expect in the return for each of the stocks?
c. If the return on the market portfolio decreased by 5%, what change would you expect in the return for each of the stocks?

    d. If you felt that the stock market was getting ready to experience a significant decline, which stock would you probably add to your portfolio? Why?

    e. If you anticipated a major stock market rally, which stock would you add to your portfolio? Why?

Personal Finance Problem

LG 5   **P8–23   Portfolio betas**   Rose Berry is attempting to evaluate two possible portfolios, which consist of the same five assets held in different proportions. She is particularly interested in using beta to compare the risks of the portfolios, so she has gathered the data shown in the following table.

		Portfolio weights	
Asset	Asset beta	Portfolio A	Portfolio B
1	1.30	10%	30%
2	0.70	30	10
3	1.25	10	20
4	1.10	10	20
5	0.90	40	20
Totals		100%	100%

    a. Calculate the betas for portfolios A and B.

    b. Compare the risks of these portfolios to the market as well as to each other. Which portfolio is more risky?

LG 6   **P8–24   Capital asset pricing model (CAPM)**   For each of the cases shown in the following table, use the capital asset pricing model to find the required return.

Case	Risk-free rate, R_F	Market return, r_m	Beta, b
A	5%	8%	1.30
B	8	13	0.90
C	9	12	−0.20
D	10	15	1.00
E	6	10	0.60

Personal Finance Problem

LG 5   LG 6   P8–25   Beta coefficients and the capital asset pricing model   Katherine Wilson is wondering how much risk she must undertake to generate an acceptable return on her portfolio. The risk-free return currently is 5%. The return on the overall stock market is 16%. Use the CAPM to calculate how high the beta coefficient of Katherine's portfolio would have to be to achieve each of the following expected portfolio returns.

    a. 10%

    b. 15%

    c. 18%

    d. 20%

    e. Katherine is risk averse. What is the highest return she can expect if she is unwilling to take more than an average risk?

LG 6 **P8–26** **Manipulating CAPM** Use the basic equation for the capital asset pricing model (CAPM) to work each of the following problems.

a. Find the *required return* for an asset with a beta of 0.90 when the risk-free rate and market return are 8% and 12%, respectively.

b. Find the *risk-free rate* for a firm with a required return of 15% and a beta of 1.25 when the market return is 14%.

c. Find the *market return* for an asset with a required return of 16% and a beta of 1.10 when the risk-free rate is 9%.

d. Find the *beta* for an asset with a required return of 15% when the risk-free rate and market return are 10% and 12.5%, respectively.

Personal Finance Problem

LG 1 **LG 3** **P8–27** **Portfolio return and beta** Jamie Peters invested $100,000 to set up the following
LG 5 **LG 6** portfolio one year ago:

Asset	Cost	Beta at purchase	Yearly income	Value today
A	$20,000	0.80	$1,600	$20,000
B	35,000	0.95	1,400	36,000
C	30,000	1.50	—	34,500
D	15,000	1.25	375	16,500

a. Calculate the portfolio beta on the basis of the original cost figures.

b. Calculate the percentage return of each asset in the portfolio for the year.

c. Calculate the percentage return of the portfolio on the basis of original cost, using income and gains during the year.

d. At the time Jamie made his investments, investors were estimating that the market return for the coming year would be 10%. The estimate of the risk-free rate of return averaged 4% for the coming year. Calculate an expected rate of return for each stock on the basis of its beta and the expectations of market and risk-free returns.

e. On the basis of the actual results, explain how each stock in the portfolio performed relative to those CAPM-generated expectations of performance. What factors could explain these differences?

LG 6 **P8–28** **Security market line (SML)** Assume that the risk-free rate, R_F, is currently 9% and that the market return, r_m, is currently 13%.

a. Draw the security market line (SML) on a set of "nondiversifiable risk (*x* axis)–required return (*y* axis)" axes.

b. Calculate and label the *market risk premium* on the axes in part **a**.

c. Given the previous data, calculate the required return on asset A having a beta of 0.80 and asset B having a beta of 1.30.

d. Draw in the betas and required returns from part **c** for assets A and B on the axes in part **a**. Label the *risk premium* associated with each of these assets, and discuss them.

LG 6 **P8–29** **Shifts in the security market line** Assume that the risk-free rate, R_F, is currently 8%, the market return, r_m, is 12%, and asset A has a beta, b_A, of 1.10.

a. Draw the security market line (SML) on a set of "nondiversifiable risk (*x* axis)– required return (*y* axis)" axes.

b. Use the CAPM to calculate the required return, r_A, on asset A, and depict asset A's beta and required return on the SML drawn in part **a**.

c. Assume that as a result of recent economic events, inflationary expectations have declined by 2%, lowering R_F and r_m to 6% and 10%, respectively. Draw the new SML on the axes in part **a,** and calculate and show the new required return for asset A.

d. Assume that as a result of recent events, investors have become more risk averse, causing the market return to rise by 1%, to 13%. Ignoring the shift in part **c,** draw the new SML on the same set of axes that you used before, and calculate and show the new required return for asset A.

e. From the previous changes, what conclusions can be drawn about the impact of (1) decreased inflationary expectations and (2) increased risk aversion on the required returns of risky assets?

LG 6 **P8–30** **Integrative—Risk, return, and CAPM** Wolff Enterprises must consider several investment projects, A through E, using the capital asset pricing model (CAPM) and its graphical representation, the security market line (SML). Relevant information is presented in the following table.

Item	Rate of return	Beta, b
Risk-free asset	9%	0.00
Market portfolio	14	1.00
Project A	—	1.50
Project B	—	0.75
Project C	—	2.00
Project D	—	0.00
Project E	—	−0.50

a. Calculate (1) the required rate of return and (2) the risk premium for each project, given its level of nondiversifiable risk.

b. Use your findings in part **a** to draw the security market line (required return relative to nondiversifiable risk).

c. Discuss the relative nondiversifiable risk of projects A through E.

d. Assume that recent economic events have caused investors to become less risk-averse, causing the market return to decline by 2%, to 12%. Calculate the new required returns for assets A through E, and draw the new security market line on the same set of axes that you used in part **b.**

e. Compare your findings in parts **a** and **b** with those in part **d.** What conclusion can you draw about the impact of a decline in investor risk aversion on the required returns of risky assets?

LG 1 **P8–31** **ETHICS PROBLEM** Risk is a major concern of almost all investors. When shareholders invest their money in a firm, they expect managers to take risks with those funds. What do you think are the ethical limits that managers should observe when taking risks with other people's money?

Spreadsheet Exercise

Jane is considering investing in three different stocks or creating three distinct two-stock portfolios. Jane considers herself to be a rather conservative investor. She is able to obtain forecasted returns for the three securities for the years 2013 through 2019. The data are as follows:

Year	Stock A	Stock B	Stock C
2013	10%	10%	12%
2014	13	11	14
2015	15	8	10
2016	14	12	11
2017	16	10	9
2018	14	15	9
2019	12	15	10

In any of the possible two-stock portfolios, the weight of each stock in the portfolio will be 50%. The three possible portfolio combinations are AB, AC, and BC.

TO DO

Create a spreadsheet similar to Tables 8.6 and 8.7 to answer the following:

a. Calculate the expected return for each individual stock.
b. Calculate the standard deviation for each individual stock.
c. Calculate the expected returns for portfolio AB, AC, and BC.
d. Calculate the standard deviations for portfolios AB, AC, and BC.
e. Would you recommend that Jane invest in the single stock A or the portfolio consisting of stocks A and B? Explain your answer from a risk–return viewpoint.
f. Would you recommend that Jane invest in the single stock B or the portfolio consisting of stocks B and C? Explain your answer from a risk–return viewpoint.

 Visit **www.myfinancelab.com** for **Chapter Case: *Analyzing Risk and Return on Chargers Products'***
Investments, Group Exercises, and numerous online resources.

9 The Cost of Capital

Learning Goals

LG 1 Understand the basic concept and sources of capital associated with the cost of capital.

LG 2 Explain what is meant by the marginal cost of capital.

LG 3 Determine the cost of long-term debt, and explain why the after-tax cost of debt is the relevant cost of debt.

LG 4 Determine the cost of preferred stock.

LG 5 Calculate the cost of common stock equity, and convert it into the cost of retained earnings and the cost of new issues of common stock.

LG 6 Calculate the weighted average cost of capital (WACC), and discuss alternative weighting schemes.

Why This Chapter Matters to You

In your *professional* life

ACCOUNTING You need to understand the various sources of capital and how their costs are calculated to provide the data necessary to determine the firm's overall cost of capital.

INFORMATION SYSTEMS You need to understand the various sources of capital and how their costs are calculated to develop systems that will estimate the costs of those sources of capital, as well as the overall cost of capital.

MANAGEMENT You need to understand the cost of capital to select long-term investments after assessing their acceptability and relative rankings.

MARKETING You need to understand the firm's cost of capital because proposed projects must earn returns in excess of it to be acceptable.

OPERATIONS You need to understand the firm's cost of capital to assess the economic viability of investments in plant and equipment needed to improve or grow the firm's capacity.

In your *personal* life

Knowing your *personal cost of capital* will allow you to make informed decisions about your personal consuming, borrowing, and investing. Managing your personal wealth is a lot like managing the wealth of a business—you need to understand the trade-offs between consuming wealth and growing wealth and how growing wealth can be accomplished by investing your own monies or borrowed monies. Understanding the cost of capital concepts will allow you to make better long-term decisions and maximize the value of your personal wealth.

Falling Short of Expectations

For years, General Electric was perhaps the most admired company in the world. From 1990 through 2000, its stock rose more than 800 percent, making it one of the world's most valuable companies and earning its long-time CEO, Jack Welch, the title of "Manager of the Century" from *Fortune* magazine. GE's stock price peaked in August 2000 at $60.50. Since then, however, GE stock has lost its luster, falling by roughly 50 percent and trailing far behind benchmarks such as the Standard & Poor's 500 Stock Index. In 2009, GE cut its dividend for the first time since the Great Depression and lost its coveted AAA credit rating.

Why did GE perform so poorly? A simple answer is that GE's business investments failed to earn a return sufficient to meet the expectations of investors. When a firm's operating results disappoint investors, its stock price will fall as investors sell their shares and move to a more attractive investment. As one expert explained, "GE has been destroying shareholder capital for years. Their cost of capital is about 5 percent, and their return on assets is about 1 percent. That mathematic equation can't remain too much longer."[1]

For companies to succeed, their investments have to earn a rate of return that exceeds investors' expectations. But how do companies know what investors expect? The answer is that companies have to measure their cost of capital. Read on to learn how firms do that.

1. *Pros Say*, December 15, 2009, cnbc.com, www.cnbc.com/id/34440926.

LG 1   LG 2 **9.1** **Overview of the Cost of Capital**

cost of capital
Represents the firm's cost of financing and is the minimum rate of return that a project must earn to increase firm value.

Chapter 1 established that the goal of the firm is to maximize shareholder wealth, and it told us that financial managers achieve this goal by investing in risky projects that add value to the firm. In this chapter, you will learn about the cost of capital, which is the rate of return that financial managers use to evaluate all possible investment opportunities to determine which ones to invest in on behalf of the firm's shareholders. The **cost of capital** represents the firm's cost of financing and is the minimum rate of return that a project must earn to increase firm value. In particular, the cost of capital refers to the cost of the next dollar of financing necessary to finance a new investment opportunity. Investments with a rate of return above the cost of capital will increase the value of the firm, and projects with a rate of return below the cost of capital will decrease firm value.

The cost of capital is an extremely important financial concept. It acts as a major link between the firm's long-term investment decisions and the wealth of the firm's owners as determined by the market value of their shares. Financial managers are ethically bound to invest only in projects that they expect to exceed the cost of capital; see the *Focus on Ethics* box for more discussion of this responsibility.

THE BASIC CONCEPT

A firm's cost of capital is estimated at a given point in time and reflects the *expected average future cost of funds over the long run*. Although firms typically raise

---

focus on ETHICS

The Ethics of Profit

in practice *Business Week* once referred to Peter Drucker as "The Man Who Invented Management." In his role as writer and management consultant, Drucker stressed the importance of ethics to business leaders. He believed that it was the ethical responsibility of a business to earn a profit. In his mind, profitable businesses create opportunities, while unprofitable ones waste society's resources. Drucker once said, "Profit is not the explanation, cause, or rationale of business behavior and business decisions, but rather the test of their validity. If archangels instead of businessmen sat in directors' chairs, they would still have to be concerned with profitability, despite their total lack of personal interest in making profits."[a]

But what happens when businesses abandon ethics for profits? Consider

Merck's experience with the drug, Vioxx. Introduced in 1999, Vioxx was an immediate success, quickly reaching $2.5 billion in annual sales. However, a Merck study launched in 1999 eventually found that patients who took Vioxx suffered from an increased risk of heart attacks and strokes. Despite the risks, Merck continued to market and sell Vioxx. By the time Vioxx was withdrawn from the market, an estimated 20 million Americans had taken the drug, 88,000 had suffered Vioxx-related heart attacks, and 38,000 had died.

News of the 2004 Vioxx withdrawal hit Merck's stock hard. The company's shares fell 27 percent on the day of the announcement, slashing $27 billion off the firm's market capitalization. Moody's, Standard & Poor's, and Fitch cut Merck's credit ratings,

costing the firm its coveted AAA rating. The company's bottom line also suffered, as net income fell 21 percent in the final three months of 2004.

The recall dealt a major blow to Merck's reputation. The company was criticized for aggressively marketing Vioxx despite its serious side effects. Questions were also raised about the research reports Merck had submitted in support of the drug. Lawsuits followed. In 2008, Merck agreed to fund a $4.85 billion settlement to resolve approximately 50,000 Vioxx-related lawsuits. The company had also incurred $1.53 billion in legal costs by the time of the settlement.

▶ *The Vioxx recall increased Merck's cost of capital. What effect would an increased cost of capital have on a firm's future investments?*

[a]Peter F. Drucker, *The Essential Drucker* (New York: Collins Business Essentials, 2001).

money in lumps, the cost of capital reflects the entirety of the firm's financing activities. For example, if a firm raises funds with debt (borrowing) today and at some future point sells common stock to raise additional financing, then the respective costs of both forms of capital should be reflected in the firm's cost of capital. Most firms attempt to maintain an optimal mix of debt and equity financing. In practice, this mix is commonly a range, such as 40 percent to 50 percent debt, rather than a point, such as 55 percent debt. This range is called a *target capital structure*—a topic that will be addressed in Chapter 13. Here, it is sufficient to say that although firms raise money in lumps, they tend toward some desired *mix of financing*.

To capture all of the relevant financing costs, assuming some desired mix of financing, we need to look at the *overall cost of capital* rather than just the cost of any single source of financing.

Example 9.1 ▶ A firm is *currently* faced with an investment opportunity. Assume the following:

Best project available today

$$\text{Cost} = \$100,000$$
$$\text{Life} = 20 \text{ years}$$
$$\text{Expected Return} = 7\%$$

Least costly financing source available

$$\text{Debt} = 6\%$$

Because it can earn 7% on the investment of funds costing only 6%, the firm undertakes the opportunity. Imagine that *1 week later* a new investment opportunity is available:

Best project available 1 week later

$$\text{Cost} = \$100,000$$
$$\text{Life} = 20 \text{ years}$$
$$\text{Expected Return} = 12\%$$

Least costly financing source available

$$\text{Equity} = 14\%$$

In this instance, the firm rejects the opportunity because the 14% financing cost is greater than the 12% expected return.

What if instead the firm used a *combined* cost of financing? By weighting the cost of each source of financing by its relative *proportion* in the firm's target capital structure, the firm can obtain a *weighted average cost of capital*. Assuming that a 50–50 mix of debt and equity is targeted, the weighted average cost here would be 10% [(0.50 × 6% debt) + (0.50 × 14% equity)]. With this average cost of financing, the first opportunity would have been rejected (7% expected return < 10% weighted average cost), and the second would have been accepted (12% expected return > 10% weighted average cost).

SOURCES OF LONG-TERM CAPITAL

In this chapter, our concern is only with the *long-term* sources of capital available to a firm because these are the sources that supply the financing necessary to support the firm's *capital budgeting* activities. Capital budgeting is the process of evaluating and selecting long-term investments. This process is intended to achieve the firm's goal of maximizing shareholders' wealth. Although the entire capital budgeting process is discussed throughout Part 5, at this point it is sufficient to say that capital budgeting activities are chief among the responsibilities of financial managers and that they cannot be carried out without knowing the appropriate cost of capital with which to judge the firm's investment opportunities.

There are four basic sources of long-term capital for firms: long-term debt, preferred stock, common stock, and retained earnings. All entries on the right-hand side of the balance sheet, other than current liabilities, represent these sources:

Not every firm will use all of these sources of financing, but most firms will have some mix of funds from these sources in their capital structures. Although a firm's existing mix of financing sources may reflect its target capital structure, it is ultimately the marginal cost of capital necessary to raise the next marginal dollar of financing that is relevant for evaluating the firm's future investment opportunities.

→ REVIEW QUESTIONS

9–1 What is the *cost of capital?*

9–2 What role does the cost of capital play in the firm's long-term investment decisions? How does it relate to the firm's ability to maximize shareholder wealth?

9–3 What does the firm's capital structure represent?

9–4 What are the typical sources of long-term capital available to the firm?

LG 3   9.2 Cost of Long-Term Debt

cost of long-term debt
The financing cost associated with new funds raised through long-term borrowing.

The **cost of long-term debt** is the financing cost associated with new funds raised through long-term borrowing. Typically, the funds are raised through the sale of corporate bonds.

NET PROCEEDS

net proceeds
Funds actually received by the firm from the sale of a security.

The **net proceeds** from the sale of a bond, or any security, are the funds that the firm receives from the sale. The total proceeds are reduced by the **flotation costs,**

flotation costs
The total costs of issuing and selling a security.

which represent the total costs of issuing and selling securities. These costs apply to all public offerings of securities—debt, preferred stock, and common stock. They include two components: (1) *underwriting costs*—compensation earned by investment bankers for selling the security—and (2) *administrative costs*—issuer expenses such as legal, accounting, and printing.

Example 9.2 ▶ Duchess Corporation, a major hardware manufacturer, is contemplating selling $10 million worth of 20-year, 9% coupon (stated *annual* interest rate) bonds, each with a par value of $1,000. Because bonds with similar risk earn returns greater than 9%, the firm must sell the bonds for $980 to compensate for the lower coupon interest rate. The flotation costs are 2% of the par value of the bond (0.02 × $1,000), or $20. The *net proceeds* to the firm from the sale of each bond are therefore $960 ($980 minus $20).

BEFORE-TAX COST OF DEBT

The before-tax cost of debt, r_d, is simply the rate of return the firm must pay on new borrowing. A firm's before-tax cost of debt for bonds can be found in any of three ways: quotation, calculation, or approximation.

Using Market Quotations

A relatively quick method for finding the before-tax cost of debt is to observe the *yield to maturity (YTM)* on the firm's existing bonds or bonds of similar risk issued by other companies. The market price of existing bonds reflects the rate of return required by the market. For example, if the market requires a YTM of 9.7 percent for a similar-risk bond, then this value can be used as the before-tax cost of debt, r_d, for new bonds. Bond yields are widely reported by sources such as *The Wall Street Journal*.

Calculating the Cost

This approach finds the before-tax cost of debt by calculating the YTM generated by the bond cash flows. From the issuer's point of view, this value is the *cost to maturity* of the cash flows associated with the debt. The yield to maturity can be calculated by using a financial calculator or an electronic spreadsheet. It represents the annual before-tax percentage cost of the debt.

Example 9.3 ▶ In the preceding example, $960 were the net proceeds of a 20-year bond with a $1,000 par value and 9% coupon interest rate. The calculation of the annual cost is quite simple. The cash flow pattern associated with this bond's sales consists of an initial inflow (the net proceeds) followed by a series of annual outlays (the interest payments). In the final year, when the debt is retired, an outlay representing the repayment of the principal also occurs. The cash flows associated with Duchess Corporation's bond issue are as follows:

End of year(s)	Cash flow
0	$ 960
1–20	−$ 90
20	−$1,000

The initial $960 inflow is followed by annual interest outflows of $90 (9% coupon interest rate × $1,000 par value) over the 20-year life of the bond. In year 20, an outflow of $1,000 (the repayment of the principal) occurs. We can determine the cost of debt by finding the YTM, which is the discount rate that equates the present value of the bond outflows to the initial inflow.

Calculator Use   (*Note:* Most calculators require either the present value [net proceeds] or the future value [annual interest payments and repayment of principal] to be input as negative numbers when we calculate yield to maturity. That approach is used here.) Using the calculator and the inputs shown at the left, you should find the before-tax cost of debt (yield to maturity) to be 9.452%.

Input	Function
20	N
960	PV
−90	PMT
−1000	FV
	CPT
	I

Solution
9.452

Spreadsheet Use   The before-tax cost of debt on the Duchess Corporation bond can be calculated using an Excel spreadsheet. The following Excel spreadsheet shows that by referencing the cells containing the bond's net proceeds, coupon payment, years to maturity, and par value as part of Excel's RATE function you can quickly determine that the appropriate before-tax cost of debt for Duchess Corporation's bond is 9.452%.

	A	B
1	FINDING THE YTM ON A 20-YEAR BOND	
2	Net proceeds from sale of bond	$960
3	Coupon payment	$90
4	Years to maturity	20
5	Par value (principal)	$1,000
6	Before-tax cost of debt	9.452%
	Entry in Cell B6 is =RATE(B4,−B3,B2,−B5). A minus sign appears before B3 and B5 because coupon payment and par value are treated as cash outflows.	

Although you may not recognize it, both the calculator and the Excel function are using trial-and-error to find the bond's YTM—they just do it faster than you can.

Approximating the Cost

Although not as precise as using a calculator, there is a method for quickly approximating the before-tax cost of debt. The before-tax cost of debt, r_d, for a bond with a $1,000 par value can be approximated by using the following equation:

$$r_d = \frac{I + \dfrac{\$1,000 - N_d}{n}}{\dfrac{N_d + \$1,000}{2}} \tag{9.1}$$

where

$$I = \text{annual interest in dollars}$$
$$N_d = \text{net proceeds from the sale of debt (bond)}$$
$$n = \text{number of years to the bond's maturity}$$

Example 9.4 ▶ Substituting the appropriate values from the Duchess Corporation example into the approximation formula given in Equation 9.1, we get:

$$r_d = \frac{\$90 + \dfrac{\$1,000 - \$960}{20}}{\dfrac{\$960 + \$1,000}{2}} = \frac{\$90 + \$2}{\$980}$$

$$= \frac{\$92}{\$980} = 0.09388 \text{ or } \underline{9.388\%}$$

This approximate value of before-tax cost of debt is close to the 9.452%, but it lacks the precision of the value derived using the calculator or spreadsheet.

AFTER-TAX COST OF DEBT

Unlike the dividends paid to equityholders, the interest payments paid to bondholders are tax deductible for the firm, so the interest expense on debt reduces the firm's taxable income and, therefore, the firm's tax liability. To find the firm's *net* cost of debt, we must account for the tax savings created by debt and solve for the cost of long-term debt on an after-tax basis. The after-tax cost of debt, r_i, can be found by multiplying the before-tax cost, r_d, by 1 minus the tax rate, T, as stated in the following equation:

$$r_i = r_d \times (1 - T) \tag{9.2}$$

Example 9.5 ▶ Duchess Corporation has a 40% tax rate. Using the 9.452% before-tax debt cost calculated above, and applying Equation 9.2, we find an after-tax cost of debt of 5.67% [9.452% × (1 − 0.40)]. Typically, the cost of long-term debt for a given firm is less than the cost of preferred or common stock, partly because of the tax deductibility of interest.

Personal Finance Example 9.6 ▶ Kait and Kasim Sullivan, a married couple in the 28% federal income-tax bracket, wish to borrow $60,000 to pay for a new luxury car. To finance the purchase, they can either borrow the $60,000 through the auto dealer at an annual interest rate of 6.0%, or they can take a $60,000 second mortgage on their home. The best annual rate they can get on the second mortgage is 7.2%. They already have qualified for both of the loans being considered.

  If they borrow from the auto dealer, the interest on this "consumer loan" will not be deductible for federal tax purposes. However, the interest on the second mortgage would be tax deductible because the tax law allows individuals to deduct interest paid on a home mortgage. To choose the least-cost financing, the Sullivans calculated the after-tax cost of both sources of long-term debt. Because interest on the auto loan is *not* tax deductible, its after-tax cost equals its stated cost of 6.0%. Because the interest on the second mortgage *is* tax deductible, its after-tax cost can be found using Equation 9.2:

$$\text{After-tax cost of debt} = \text{Before-tax cost of debt} \times (1 - \text{Tax rate})$$

$$7.2\% \times (1 - 0.28) = 7.2\% \times 0.72 = \underline{5.2\%}$$

Because the 5.2% after-tax cost of the second mortgage is less than the 6.0% cost of the auto loan, the Sullivans should use the second mortgage to finance the auto purchase.

→ **REVIEW QUESTIONS**

9–5 What are the *net proceeds* from the sale of a bond? What are *flotation costs,* and how do they affect a bond's net proceeds?

9–6 What methods can be used to find the before-tax cost of debt?

9–7 How is the before-tax cost of debt converted into the after-tax cost?

LG 4   **9.3 Cost of Preferred Stock**

Preferred stock represents a special type of ownership interest in the firm. It gives preferred stockholders the right to receive their *stated* dividends before the firm can distribute any earnings to common stockholders. The key characteristics of preferred stock were described in Chapter 7. However, the one aspect of preferred stock that requires review is dividends.

PREFERRED STOCK DIVIDENDS

Most preferred stock dividends are stated as a *dollar amount:* "*x* dollars per year." When dividends are stated this way, the stock is often referred to as "*x*-dollar preferred stock." Thus a "$4 preferred stock" is expected to pay preferred stockholders $4 in dividends each year on each share of preferred stock owned.

Sometimes preferred stock dividends are stated as an *annual percentage rate.* This rate represents the percentage of the stock's par, or face, value that equals the annual dividend. For instance, an 8 percent preferred stock with a $50 par value would be expected to pay an annual dividend of $4 per share (0.08 × $50 par = $4). Before the cost of preferred stock is calculated, any dividends stated as percentages should be converted to annual dollar dividends.

CALCULATING THE COST OF PREFERRED STOCK

cost of preferred stock, r_p
The ratio of the preferred stock dividend to the firm's net proceeds from the sale of preferred stock.

The **cost of preferred stock, r_p,** is the ratio of the preferred stock dividend to the firm's net proceeds from the sale of the preferred stock. The net proceeds represent the amount of money to be received minus any flotation costs. Equation 9.3 gives the cost of preferred stock, r_p, in terms of the annual dollar dividend, D_p, and the net proceeds from the sale of the stock, N_p:

$$r_p = \frac{D_p}{N_p} \tag{9.3}$$

Example 9.7 ▶   Duchess Corporation is contemplating issuance of a 10% preferred stock that they expect to sell for $87 per share. The cost of issuing and selling the stock will be $5 per share. The first step in finding the cost of the stock is to calculate the dollar amount of the annual preferred dividend, which is $8.70 (0.10 × $87). The net proceeds per share from the proposed sale of stock equals the sale price minus the flotation costs ($87 − $5 = $82). Substituting the annual dividend, D_p, of $8.70 and the net proceeds, N_p, of $82 into Equation 9.3 gives the cost of preferred stock, 10.6% ($8.70 ÷ $82).

The cost of Duchess's preferred stock (10.6%) is much greater than the cost of its long-term debt (5.67%). This difference exists both because the cost of long-term debt (the interest) is tax deductible and because preferred stock is riskier than long-term debt.

→ REVIEW QUESTION

9–8 How would you calculate the cost of preferred stock?

LG 5   9.4 Cost of Common Stock

In more depth

To read about *Subjective Techniques*, go to www.myfinancelab.com

 myfinancelab®

cost of common stock equity, r_s
The rate at which investors discount the expected dividends of the firm to determine its share value.

constant-growth valuation (Gordon growth) model
Assumes that the value of a share of stock equals the present value of all future dividends (assumed to grow at a constant rate) that it is expected to provide over an infinite time horizon.

The *cost of common stock* is the return required on the stock by investors in the marketplace. There are two forms of common stock financing: (1) retained earnings and (2) new issues of common stock. As a first step in finding each of these costs, we must estimate the cost of common stock equity.

FINDING THE COST OF COMMON STOCK EQUITY

The **cost of common stock equity**, r_s, is the rate at which investors discount the expected common stock dividends of the firm to determine its share value. Two techniques are used to measure the cost of common stock equity. One relies on the constant-growth valuation model, the other on the capital asset pricing model (CAPM).

Using the Constant-Growth Valuation (Gordon Growth) Model

In Chapter 7 we found the value of a share of stock to be equal to the present value of all future dividends, which in one model were assumed to grow at a constant annual rate over an infinite time horizon. This is the **constant-growth valuation model**, also known as the **Gordon growth model**. The key expression derived for this model was presented as Equation 7.4 and is restated here:

$$P_0 = \frac{D_1}{r_s - g} \tag{9.4}$$

where

P_0 = value of common stock
D_1 = per-share dividend *expected* at the end of year 1
r_s = required return on common stock
g = constant rate of growth in dividends

Solving Equation 9.4 for r_s results in the following expression for the *cost of common stock equity:*

$$r_s = \frac{D_1}{P_0} + g \qquad (9.5)$$

Equation 9.5 indicates that the cost of common stock equity can be found by dividing the dividend expected at the end of year 1 by the current market price of the stock (the "dividend yield") and adding the expected growth rate (the "capital gains yield").

Example 9.8 ▶ Duchess Corporation wishes to determine its cost of common stock equity, r_s. The market price, P_0, of its common stock is $50 per share. The firm expects to pay a dividend, D_1, of $4 at the end of the coming year, 2013. The dividends paid on the outstanding stock over the past 6 years (2007 through 2012) were as follows:

Year	Dividend
2012	$3.80
2011	3.62
2010	3.47
2009	3.33
2008	3.12
2007	2.97

Using a financial calculator or electronic spreadsheet, in conjunction with the technique described for finding growth rates in Chapter 5, we can calculate the annual rate at which dividends have grown, g, from 2007 to 2012. It turns out to be approximately 5% (more precisely, it is 5.05%). Substituting $D_1 = \$4$, $P_0 = \$50$, and $g = 5\%$ into Equation 9.5 yields the cost of common stock equity:

$$r_s = \frac{\$4}{\$50} + 0.05 = 0.08 + 0.05 = 0.130 \text{ or } \underline{\underline{13.0\%}}$$

The 13.0% cost of common stock equity represents the return required by *existing* shareholders on their investment. If the actual return is less than that, shareholders are likely to begin selling their stock.

Using the Capital Asset Pricing Model (CAPM)

capital asset pricing model (CAPM)
Describes the relationship between the required return, r_s, and the nondiversifiable risk of the firm as measured by the beta coefficient, b.

Recall from Chapter 8 that the **capital asset pricing model (CAPM)** describes the relationship between the required return, r_s, and the nondiversifiable risk of the firm as measured by the beta coefficient, b. The basic CAPM is:

$$r_s = R_F + [b \times (r_m - R_F)] \qquad (9.6)$$

where

R_F = risk-free rate of return

r_m = market return; return on the market portfolio of assets

Using the CAPM indicates that the cost of common stock equity is the return required by investors as compensation for the firm's nondiversifiable risk, measured by beta.

Example 9.9 ▶	Duchess Corporation now wishes to calculate its cost of common stock equity, r_s, by using the CAPM. The firm's investment advisors and its own analysts indicate that the risk-free rate, R_F, equals 7%; the firm's beta, b, equals 1.5; and the market return, r_m, equals 11%. Substituting these values into Equation 9.6, the company estimates the cost of common stock equity, r_s, to be:

$$r_s = 7.0\% + [1.5 \times (11.0\% - 7.0\%)] = 7.0\% + 6.0\% = \underline{\underline{13.0\%}}$$

The 13.0% cost of common stock equity represents the required return of investors in Duchess Corporation common stock. It is the same as that found by using the constant-growth valuation model.

Comparing Constant-Growth and CAPM Techniques

The CAPM technique differs from the constant-growth valuation model in that it directly considers the firm's risk, as reflected by beta, in determining the *required* return or cost of common stock equity. The constant-growth model does not look at risk; it uses the market price, P_0, as a reflection of the *expected* risk–return preference of investors in the marketplace. The constant-growth valuation and CAPM techniques for finding r_s are theoretically equivalent, though in practice estimates from the two methods do not always agree. The two methods can produce different estimates because they require (as inputs) estimates of other quantities, such as the expected dividend growth rate or the firm's beta.

Another difference is that when the constant-growth valuation model is used to find the cost of common stock equity, it can easily be adjusted for flotation costs to find the cost of new common stock; the CAPM does not provide a simple adjustment mechanism. The difficulty in adjusting the cost of common stock equity calculated by using the CAPM occurs because in its common form the model does not include the market price, P_0, a variable needed to make such an adjustment. Although the CAPM has a stronger theoretical foundation, the computational appeal of the traditional constant-growth valuation model justifies its use throughout this text to measure financing costs of common stock. As a practical matter, analysts might want to estimate the cost of equity using both approaches and then take an average of the results to arrive at a final estimate of the cost of equity.

COST OF RETAINED EARNINGS

cost of retained earnings, r_r
The same as the cost of an *equivalent fully subscribed issue of additional common stock*, which is equal to the cost of common stock equity, r_s.

As you know, dividends are paid out of a firm's earnings. Their payment, made in cash to common stockholders, reduces the firm's retained earnings. Suppose a firm needs common stock equity financing of a certain amount. It has two choices relative to retained earnings: It can issue additional common stock in that amount and still pay dividends to stockholders out of retained earnings, or it can increase common stock equity by retaining the earnings (not paying the cash dividends) in the needed amount. In a strict accounting sense, the retention of earnings increases common stock equity in the same way that the sale of additional shares of common stock does. Thus the **cost of retained earnings, r_r**, to the firm is the same as the cost of an *equivalent fully subscribed issue of additional common stock*.

Stockholders find the firm's retention of earnings acceptable only if they expect that it will earn at least their required return on the reinvested funds.

Viewing retained earnings as a fully subscribed issue of additional common stock, we can set the firm's cost of retained earnings, r_r, equal to the cost of common stock equity as given by Equations 9.5 and 9.6.

$$r_r = r_s \qquad (9.7)$$

It is not necessary to adjust the cost of retained earnings for flotation costs because by retaining earnings the firm "raises" equity capital without incurring these costs.

Example 9.10 ▶ The cost of retained earnings for Duchess Corporation was actually calculated in the preceding examples: It is equal to the cost of common stock equity. Thus r_r equals 13.0%. As we will show in the next section, the cost of retained earnings is always lower than the cost of a new issue of common stock because it entails no flotation costs.

Matter of fact

Retained Earnings, the Preferred Source of Financing

In the United States and most other countries, firms rely more heavily on retained earnings than any other financing source. For example, a 2010 survey of CEOs by the Australian Industry Group and Deloitte reported that the vast majority of Australian firms see retained earnings as their most important source of finance. Almost 65% of CEOs surveyed said that retained earnings was their most preferred source of financing, with bank debt coming in as a distant second choice.[2]

COST OF NEW ISSUES OF COMMON STOCK

cost of a new issue of common stock, r_n
The cost of common stock, net of underpricing and associated flotation costs.

underpriced
Stock sold at a price below its current market price, P_0.

Our purpose in finding the firm's overall cost of capital is to determine the after-tax cost of *new* funds required for financing projects. The **cost of a new issue of common stock, r_n,** is determined by calculating the cost of common stock, net of underpricing and associated flotation costs. Normally, when new shares are issued they are **underpriced**—sold at a discount relative to the current market price, P_0. Underpricing is the difference between the market price and the issue price, which is the price paid by the primary market investors discussed in Chapter 2.

We can use the constant-growth valuation model expression for the cost of existing common stock, r_s, as a starting point. If we let N_n represent the net proceeds from the sale of new common stock after subtracting underpricing and flotation costs, the cost of the new issue, r_n, can be expressed as follows:[3]

$$r_n = \frac{D_1}{N_n} + g \qquad (9.8)$$

---

2. Australian Industry Group and Deloitte, *National CEO Survey: Growth Strategies for Business*, Report, October 2010.

3. An alternative, but computationally less straightforward, form of this equation is

$$r_n = \frac{D_1}{P_0 \times (1 - f)} + g \qquad (9.8a)$$

where f represents the *percentage* reduction in current market price expected as a result of underpricing and flotation costs. Simply stated, N_n in Equation 9.8 is equivalent to $P_0 \times (1 - f)$ in Equation 9.8a. For convenience, Equation 9.8 is used to define the cost of a new issue of common stock, r_n.

The net proceeds from sale of new common stock, N_n, will be less than the current market price, P_0. Therefore, the cost of new issues, r_n, will always be greater than the cost of existing issues, r_s, which is equal to the cost of retained earnings, r_r. *The cost of new common stock is normally greater than any other long-term financing cost.*

Example 9.11 ▶ In the constant-growth valuation example, we found Duchess Corporation's cost of common stock equity, r_s, to be 13%, using the following values: an expected dividend, D_1, of $4; a current market price, P_0, of $50; and an expected growth rate of dividends, g, of 5%.

To determine its cost of *new* common stock, r_n, Duchess Corporation has estimated that on average, new shares can be sold for $47. The $3-per-share underpricing is due to the competitive nature of the market. A second cost associated with a new issue is flotation costs of $2.50 per share that would be paid to issue and sell the new shares. The total underpricing and flotation costs per share are therefore $5.50.

Subtracting the $5.50-per-share underpricing and flotation cost from the current $50 share price results in expected net proceeds of $44.50 per share ($50.00 minus $5.50). Substituting $D_1 = \$4$, $N_n = \$44.50$, and $g = 5\%$ into Equation 9.8 results in a cost of new common stock, r_n, as follows:

$$r_n = \frac{\$4.00}{\$44.50} + 0.05 = 0.09 + 0.05 = 0.140 \text{ or } \underline{14.0\%}$$

Duchess Corporation's cost of new common stock is therefore 14.0%. This is the value to be used in subsequent calculations of the firm's overall cost of capital.

→ REVIEW QUESTIONS

9–9 What premise about share value underlies the constant-growth valuation (Gordon growth) model that is used to measure the cost of common stock equity, r_s?

9–10 How do the constant-growth valuation model and capital asset pricing model methods for finding the cost of common stock differ?

9–11 Why is the cost of financing a project with retained earnings less than the cost of financing it with a new issue of common stock?

LG 6 ## 9.5 Weighted Average Cost of Capital

weighted average cost of capital (WACC), r_a
Reflects the expected average future cost of capital over the long run; found by weighting the cost of each specific type of capital by its proportion in the firm's capital structure.

Now that we have calculated the cost of specific sources of financing, we can determine the overall cost of capital. As noted earlier, the **weighted average cost of capital (WACC)**, r_a, reflects the expected average future cost of capital over the long run. It is found by weighting the cost of each specific type of capital by its proportion in the firm's capital structure.

CALCULATING WEIGHTED AVERAGE COST OF CAPITAL (WACC)

Calculating the weighted average cost of capital (WACC) is straightforward: Multiply the individual cost of each form of financing by its proportion in the firm's capital structure and sum the weighted values. As an equation, the weighted average cost of capital, r_a, can be specified as follows:

$$r_a = (w_i \times r_i) + (w_p \times r_p) + (w_s \times r_{r \text{ or } n}) \qquad (9.9)$$

where

$$w_i = \text{proportion of long-term debt in capital structure}$$
$$w_p = \text{proportion of preferred stock in capital structure}$$
$$w_s = \text{proportion of common stock equity in capital structure}$$
$$w_i + w_p + w_s = 1.0$$

Three important points should be noted in Equation 9.9:

1. For computational convenience, it is best to convert the weights into decimal form and leave the individual costs in percentage terms.
2. *The weights must be nonnegative and sum to 1.0.* Simply stated, WACC must account for all financing costs within the firm's capital structure.
3. The firm's common stock equity weight, w_s, is multiplied by either the cost of retained earnings, r_r, or the cost of new common stock, r_n. Which cost is used depends on whether the firm's common stock equity will be financed using retained earnings, r_r, or new common stock, r_n.

Example 9.12 ▶   In earlier examples, we found the costs of the various types of capital for Duchess Corporation to be as follows:

$$\text{Cost of debt, } r_i = 5.6\%$$
$$\text{Cost of preferred stock, } r_p = 10.6\%$$
$$\text{Cost of retained earnings, } r_r = 13.0\%$$
$$\text{Cost of new common stock, } r_n = 14.0\%$$

The company uses the following weights in calculating its weighted average cost of capital:

Source of capital	Weight
Long-term debt	40%
Preferred stock	10
Common stock equity	50
Total	100%

Because the firm expects to have a sizable amount of retained earnings available ($300,000), it plans to use its cost of retained earnings, r_r, as the cost of common stock equity. Duchess Corporation's weighted average cost of capital is calculated in Table 9.1. The resulting weighted average cost of capital for Duchess is 9.8%. Assuming an unchanged risk level, the firm should accept all projects that will earn a return greater than 9.8%.

TABLE 9.1	Calculation of the Weighted Average Cost of Capital for Duchess Corporation

Source of capital	Weight (1)	Cost (2)	Weighted cost [(1) × (2)] (3)
Long-term debt	0.40	5.6%	2.2%
Preferred stock	0.10	10.6	1.1
Common stock equity	0.50	13.0	6.5
Totals	1.00		WACC = 9.8%

focus on **PRACTICE**

Uncertain Times Make for an Uncertain Weighted Average Cost of Capital

in practice   As U.S. financial markets experienced and recovered from the 2008 financial crisis and 2009 "great recession," firms struggled to keep track of their weighted average cost of capital. The individual component costs were moving rapidly in response to the financial market turmoil. Volatile financial markets can make otherwise manageable cost-of-capital calculations exceedingly complex and inherently error prone—possibly wreaking havoc with investment decisions. If a firm underestimates its cost of capital it risks making investments that are not economically justified, and if a firm overestimates its financing costs it risks foregoing value-maximizing investments.

Although the WACC computation does not change when markets become unstable, the uncertainty surrounding the components that comprise the WACC increases dramatically. The financial crisis pushed credit costs to a point where long-term debt was largely inaccessible, and the great recession saw Treasury bond yields fall to historic lows, making cost of equity projections appear unreasonably low. With these key components in flux, it is exceedingly difficult, if not impossible, for firms to get a handle on a cost of long-term capital.

According to *CFO Magazine*, at least one firm resorted to a two-pronged approach for determining its cost of capital during the uncertain times. Ron Domanico is the chief financial officer (CFO) at Caraustar Industries, Inc., and he reported that his company dealt with the cost-of-capital uncertainty by abandoning the conventional one-size-fits-all approach. "In the past, we had one cost of capital that we applied to all our investment decisions . . . today that's not the case. We have a short-term cost of capital we apply to short-term opportunities, and a longer-term cost of capital we apply to longer-term opportunities . . . and the reality is that the longer-term cost is so high that it has forced us to focus only on those projects that have immediate returns," Mr. Domanico is quoted saying.[a]

Part of Caraustar's motivation for implementing this two-pronged approach was to account for the excessively large spread between short- and long-term debt rates that emerged during the financial market crisis. Mr. Domanico reported that during the crisis Caraustar could borrow short-term funds at the lower of Prime plus 4 percent or LIBOR plus 5 percent—where either rate was reasonable for making short-term investment decisions. Alternatively, long-term investment decisions were being required to clear Caraustar's long-term cost-of-capital calculation accounting for borrowing rates in excess of 12 percent.

▶ *Why don't firms generally use both short- and long-run weighted average costs of capital?*

[a]Randy Myers, "A Losing Formula" (May 2009), www.cfo.com/article.cfm/13522582/c_13526469.

WEIGHTING SCHEMES

Firms can calculate weights on the basis of either *book value* or *market value* using either *historical* or *target* proportions.

book value weights
Weights that use accounting values to measure the proportion of each type of capital in the firm's financial structure.

market value weights
Weights that use market values to measure the proportion of each type of capital in the firm's financial structure.

historical weights
Either book or market value weights based on *actual* capital structure proportions.

target weights
Either book or market value weights based on *desired* capital structure proportions.

Book Value versus Market Value

Book value weights use accounting values to measure the proportion of each type of capital in the firm's financial structure. **Market value weights** measure the proportion of each type of capital at its market value. Market value weights are appealing because the market values of securities closely approximate the actual dollars to be received from their sale. Moreover, because firms calculate the costs of the various types of capital by using prevailing market prices, it seems reasonable to use market value weights. In addition, the long-term investment cash flows to which the cost of capital is applied are estimated in terms of current as well as future market values. *Market value weights are clearly preferred over book value weights.*

Historical versus Target

Historical weights can be either book or market value weights based on *actual* capital structure proportions. For example, past or current book value proportions would constitute a form of historical weighting, as would past or current market value proportions. Such a weighting scheme would therefore be based on real—rather than desired—proportions.

Target weights, which can also be based on either book or market values, reflect the firm's *desired* capital structure proportions. Firms using target weights establish such proportions on the basis of the "optimal" capital structure they wish to achieve. (The development of these proportions and the optimal structure are discussed in detail in Chapter 13.)

When one considers the somewhat approximate nature of the calculation of weighted average cost of capital, the choice of weights may not be critical. However, from a strictly theoretical point of view, the *preferred weighting scheme is target market value proportions,* and we assume these throughout this chapter.

In more depth

To read about *Changes in the Weighted Average Cost of Capital,* go to www.myfinancelab.com

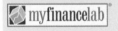

▶ **Personal Finance Example 9.13** ▶ Chuck Solis currently has three loans outstanding, all of which mature in exactly 6 years and can be repaid without penalty any time prior to maturity. The outstanding balances and annual interest rates on these loans are noted in the following table.

Loan	Outstanding balance	Annual interest rate
1	$26,000	9.6%
2	9,000	10.6
3	45,000	7.4

After a thorough search, Chuck found a lender who would loan him $80,000 for 6 years at an annual interest rate of 9.2% on the condition that the loan proceeds be used to fully repay the three outstanding loans, which combined have an outstanding balance of $80,000 ($26,000 + $9,000 + $45,000).

Chuck wishes to choose the least costly alternative: (1) to do nothing or (2) to borrow the $80,000 and pay off all three loans. He calculates the weighted average cost of his current debt by weighting each debt's annual interest cost by the proportion of the $80,000 total it represents and then summing the three weighted values as follows:

Weighted average
cost of current debt $= [(\$26{,}000 \div \$80{,}000) \times 9.6\%] + [(\$9{,}000 \div \$80{,}000)$
$\times 10.6\%] + [(\$45{,}000 \div \$80{,}000) \times 7.4\%]$
$= (.3250 \times 9.6\%) + (.1125 \times 10.6\%) + (.5625 \times 7.4\%)$
$= 3.12\% + 1.19\% + 4.16\% = 8.47\% \approx \underline{\underline{8.5\%}}$

Given that the weighted average cost of the $80,000 of current debt of 8.5% is below the 9.2% cost of the new $80,000 loan, Chuck should do nothing, and just continue to pay off the three loans as originally scheduled.

→ REVIEW QUESTIONS

9–12 What is the *weighted average cost of capital (WACC),* and how is it calculated?

9–13 What is the relationship between the firm's target capital structure and the *weighted average cost of capital (WACC)?*

9–14 Describe the logic underlying the use of *target weights* to calculate the WACC, and compare and contrast this approach with the use of *historical weights.* What is the preferred weighting scheme?

Summary

FOCUS ON VALUE

The cost of capital is an extremely important rate of return, particularly in capital budgeting decisions. It is the expected average future cost to the firm of funds over the long run. Because the cost of capital is the pivotal rate of return used in the investment decision process, its accuracy can significantly affect the quality of these decisions.

Underestimation of the cost of capital can make poor projects look attractive; overestimation can make good projects look unattractive. By applying the techniques presented in this chapter to estimate the firm's cost of capital, the financial manager will improve the likelihood that the firm's long-term decisions will be consistent with the firm's overall goal of **maximizing stock price (owner wealth).**

REVIEW OF LEARNING GOALS

LG 1   **Understand the basic concept and sources of capital associated with the cost of capital.** The cost of capital is the minimum rate of return that a firm must earn on its investments to grow firm value. A weighted average cost of capital should be used to find the expected average future cost of funds over the long run. The individual costs of the basic sources of capital (long-term debt, preferred stock, retained earnings, and common stock) can be calculated separately.

LG 2   **Explain what is meant by the marginal cost of capital.** The relevant cost of capital for a firm is the marginal cost of capital necessary to raise the next marginal dollar of financing to fund the firm's future investment opportunities. A firm's future investment opportunities in expectation will be required to exceed the firm's cost of capital.

LG 3 **Determine the cost of long-term debt, and explain why the after-tax cost of debt is the relevant cost of debt.** The before-tax cost of long-term debt can be found by using cost quotations, calculations (either by calculator or spreadsheet), or an approximation. The after-tax cost of debt is calculated by multiplying the before-tax cost of debt by 1 minus the tax rate. The after-tax cost of debt is the relevant cost of debt because it is the lowest possible cost of debt for the firm due to the deductibility of interest expenses.

LG 4 **Determine the cost of preferred stock.** The cost of preferred stock is the ratio of the preferred stock dividend to the firm's net proceeds from the sale of preferred stock.

LG 5 **Calculate the cost of common stock equity, and convert it into the cost of retained earnings and the cost of new issues of common stock.** The cost of common stock equity can be calculated by using the constant-growth valuation (Gordon growth) model or the CAPM. The cost of retained earnings is equal to the cost of common stock equity. An adjustment in the cost of common stock equity to reflect underpricing and flotation costs is necessary to find the cost of new issues of common stock.

LG 6 **Calculate the weighted average cost of capital (WACC), and discuss alternative weighting schemes.** The firm's WACC reflects the expected average future cost of funds over the long run. It combines the costs of specific types of capital after weighting each of them by its proportion. The theoretically preferred approach uses target weights based on market values.

Opener-in-Review

The chapter opener claimed that GE's cost of capital in late 2009 was about 5%. Suppose that GE could use $1 billion to make an investment that would generate positive cash flow of $60 million every year in perpetuity. At a 5 percent discount rate, what would be the value of this cash flow to investors? How much would such an investment add to GE's market value? Now suppose that the investment actually produces just $10 million per year in perpetuity (or about 1 percent per year relative to the cost of the investment). What is the value of this investment to shareholders, and by how much would GE's market value fall because of this investment?

Self-Test Problem (Solutions in Appendix)

LG 3 **LG** 4
LG 5 **LG** 6

ST9–1 Individual costs and WACC Humble Manufacturing is interested in measuring its overall cost of capital. The firm is in the 40% tax bracket. Current investigation has gathered the following data:

Debt The firm can raise debt by selling $1,000-par-value, 10% coupon interest rate, 10-year bonds on which *annual interest* payments will be made. To sell the issue, an average discount of $30 per bond must be given. The firm must also pay flotation costs of $20 per bond.

Preferred stock The firm can sell 11% (annual dividend) preferred stock at its $100-per-share par value. The cost of issuing and selling the preferred stock is expected to be $4 per share.

Common stock The firm's common stock is currently selling for $80 per share. The firm expects to pay cash dividends of $6 per share next year. The firm's dividends have been growing at an annual rate of 6%, and this rate is expected to continue in the future. The stock will have to be underpriced by $4 per share, and flotation costs are expected to amount to $4 per share.

Retained earnings The firm expects to have $225,000 of retained earnings available in the coming year. Once these retained earnings are exhausted, the firm will use new common stock as the form of common stock equity financing.

a. Calculate the individual cost of each source of financing. (Round to the nearest 0.1%.)
b. Calculate the firm's weighted average cost of capital using the weights shown in the following table, which are based on the firm's target capital structure proportions. (Round to the nearest 0.1%.)

Source of capital	Weight
Long-term debt	40%
Preferred stock	15
Common stock equity	45
Total	100%

c. In which, if any, of the investments shown in the following table do you recommend that the firm invest? Explain your answer. How much new financing is required?

Investment opportunity	Expected rate of return	Initial investment
A	11.2%	$100,000
B	9.7	500,000
C	12.9	150,000
D	16.5	200,000
E	11.8	450,000
F	10.1	600,000
G	10.5	300,000

Warm-Up Exercises

All problems are available in myfinancelab.

LG 3 **E9–1** A firm raises capital by selling $20,000 worth of debt with flotation costs equal to 2% of its par value. If the debt matures in 10 years and has a coupon interest rate of 8%, what is the bond's YTM?

LG 4   E9–2   Your firm, People's Consulting Group, has been asked to consult on a potential preferred stock offering by Brave New World. This 15% preferred stock issue would be sold at its par value of $35 per share. Flotation costs would total $3 per share. Calculate the cost of this preferred stock.

LG 5   E9–3   Duke Energy has been paying dividends steadily for 20 years. During that time, dividends have grown at a compound annual rate of 7%. If Duke Energy's current stock price is $78 and the firm plans to pay a dividend of $6.50 next year, what is Duke's *cost of common stock equity*?

LG 6   E9–4   Weekend Warriors, Inc., has 35% debt and 65% equity in its capital structure. The firm's estimated after-tax cost of debt is 8% and its estimated cost of equity is 13%. Determine the firm's *weighted average cost of capital (WACC)*.

LG 6   E9–5   Oxy Corporation uses debt, preferred stock, and common stock to raise capital. The firm's capital structure targets the following proportions: debt, 55%; preferred stock, 10%; and common stock, 35%. If the cost of debt is 6.7%, preferred stock costs 9.2%, and common stock costs 10.6%, what is Oxy's *weighted average cost of capital (WACC)*?

Problems

All problems are available in 🌐myfinancelab .

LG 1   P9–1   Concept of cost of capital   Wren Manufacturing is in the process of analyzing its investment decision-making procedures. The two projects evaluated by the firm during the past month were projects 263 and 264. The basic variables surrounding each project analysis and the resulting decision actions are summarized in the following table.

Basic variables	Project 263	Project 264
Cost	$64,000	$58,000
Life	15 years	15 years
Expected return	8%	15%
Least-cost financing		
Source	Debt	Equity
Cost (after-tax)	7%	16%
Decision		
Action	Invest	Don't invest
Reason	8% > 7% cost	15% < 16% cost

a. Evaluate the firm's decision-making procedures, and explain why the acceptance of project 263 and rejection of project 264 may not be in the owners' best interest.
b. If the firm maintains a capital structure containing 40% debt and 60% equity, find its *weighted average cost* using the data in the table.
c. If the firm had used the weighted average cost calculated in part **b**, what actions would have been indicated relative to projects 263 and 264?
d. Compare and contrast the firm's actions with your findings in part **c**. Which decision method seems more appropriate? Explain why.

LG 3 **P9–2** **Cost of debt using both methods** Currently, Warren Industries can sell 15-year, $1,000-par-value bonds paying *annual interest* at a 12% coupon rate. As a result of current interest rates, the bonds can be sold for $1,010 each; flotation costs of $30 per bond will be incurred in this process. The firm is in the 40% tax bracket.
  a. Find the net proceeds from sale of the bond, N_d.
  b. Show the cash flows from the firm's point of view over the maturity of the bond.
  c. Calculate the before-tax and after-tax costs of debt.
  d. Use the *approximation formula* to estimate the before-tax and after-tax costs of debt.
  e. Compare and contrast the costs of debt calculated in parts **c** and **d**. Which approach do you prefer? Why?

Personal Finance Problem

LG 3 **P9–3** **Before-tax cost of debt and after-tax cost of debt** David Abbot is interested in purchasing a bond issued by Sony. He has obtained the following information on the security:

Sony bond		
Par value $1,000	Coupon interest rate 6%	Tax bracket 20%
Cost $ 930	Years to maturity 10	

Answer the following questions.
  a. Calculate the *before-tax cost* of the Sony bond.
  b. Calculate the *after-tax cost* of the Sony bond given David's tax bracket.

LG 3 **P9–4** **Cost of debt using the approximation formula** For each of the following $1,000-par-value bonds, assuming *annual interest* payment and a 40% tax rate, calculate the *after-tax* cost to maturity using the *approximation formula*.

Bond	Life (years)	Underwriting fee	Discount (−) or premium (+)	Coupon interest rate
A	20	$25	−$20	9%
B	16	40	+10	10
C	15	30	−15	12
D	25	15	Par	9
E	22	20	−60	11

LG 3 **P9–5** **The cost of debt** Gronseth Drywall Systems, Inc., is in discussions with its investment bankers regarding the issuance of new bonds. The investment banker has informed the firm that different maturities will carry different coupon rates and sell at different prices. The firm must choose among several alternatives. In each case, the bonds will have a $1,000 par value and flotation costs will be $30 per bond. The company is taxed at a rate of 40%. Calculate the *after-tax cost of financing* with each of the following alternatives.

Alternative	Coupon rate	Time to maturity (years)	Premium or discount
A	9%	16	$250
B	7	5	50
C	6	7	par
D	5	10	− 75

Personal Finance Problem

LG 3   **P9–6**   **After-tax cost of debt**   Rick and Stacy Stark, a married couple, are interested in purchasing their first boat. They have decided to borrow the boat's purchase price of $100,000. The family is in the 28% federal income tax bracket. There are two choices for the Stark family: They can borrow the money from the boat dealer at an annual interest rate of 8%, or they could take out a $100,000 second mortgage on their home. Currently, home equity loans are at rates of 9.2%. There is no problem securing either of these two alternative financing choices.

Rick and Stacy learn that if they borrow from the boat dealership, the interest will not be tax deductible. However, the interest on the second mortgage will qualify as being tax deductible on their federal income tax return.

a. Calculate the *after-tax cost* of borrowing from the boat dealership.
b. Calculate the *after-tax cost* of borrowing through a second mortgage on their home.
c. Which source of borrowing is less costly for the Stark family?

LG 4   **P9–7**   **Cost of preferred stock**   Taylor Systems has just issued preferred stock. The stock has a 12% annual dividend and a $100 par value and was sold at $97.50 per share. In addition, flotation costs of $2.50 per share must be paid.

a. Calculate the *cost of the preferred stock*.
b. If the firm sells the preferred stock with a 10% annual dividend and nets $90.00 after flotation costs, what is its cost?

LG 4   **P9–8**   **Cost of preferred stock**   Determine the cost for each of the following preferred stocks.

Preferred stock	Par value	Sale price	Flotation cost	Annual dividend
A	$100	$101	$9.00	11%
B	40	38	$3.50	8%
C	35	37	$4.00	$5.00
D	30	26	5% of par	$3.00
E	20	20	$2.50	9%

LG 5   **P9–9**   **Cost of common stock equity—CAPM**   J&M Corporation common stock has a beta, *b*, of 1.2. The risk-free rate is 6%, and the market return is 11%.

a. Determine the risk premium on J&M common stock.
b. Determine the required return that J&M common stock should provide.
c. Determine J&M's *cost of common stock equity* using the CAPM.

LG 5 **P9–10** **Cost of common stock equity** Ross Textiles wishes to measure its cost of common stock equity. The firm's stock is currently selling for $57.50. The firm expects to pay a $3.40 dividend at the end of the year (2013). The dividends for the past 5 years are shown in the following table.

Year	Dividend
2012	$3.10
2011	2.92
2010	2.60
2009	2.30
2008	2.12

After underpricing and flotation costs, the firm expects to net $52 per share on a new issue.

a. Determine the growth rate of dividends from 2008 to 2012.

b. Determine the net proceeds, N_n, that the firm will actually receive.

c. Using the constant-growth valuation model, determine the *cost of retained earnings, r_r.*

d. Using the constant-growth valuation model, determine the *cost of new common stock, r_n.*

LG 5 **P9–11** **Retained earnings versus new common stock** Using the data for each firm shown in the following table, calculate the *cost of retained earnings* and the *cost of new common stock* using the constant-growth valuation model.

Firm	Current market price per share	Dividend growth rate	Projected dividend per share next year	Underpricing per share	Flotation cost per share
A	$50.00	8%	$2.25	$2.00	$1.00
B	20.00	4	1.00	0.50	1.50
C	42.50	6	2.00	1.00	2.00
D	19.00	2	2.10	1.30	1.70

LG 3 LG 4
LG 5 LG 6 **P9–12** **The effect of tax rate on WACC** Equity Lighting Corp. wishes to explore the effect on its cost of capital of the rate at which the company pays taxes. The firm wishes to maintain a capital structure of 30% debt, 10% preferred stock, and 60% common stock. The cost of financing with retained earnings is 14%, the cost of preferred stock financing is 9%, and the before-tax cost of debt financing is 11%. Calculate the weighted average cost of capital (WACC) given the tax rate assumptions in parts **a** to **c.**

a. Tax rate = 40%

b. Tax rate = 35%

c. Tax rate = 25%

d. Describe the relationship between changes in the rate of taxation and the weighted average cost of capital.

LG 6   **P9–13**   **WACC—Book weights**   Ridge Tool has on its books the amounts and specific (after-tax) costs shown in the following table for each source of capital.

Source of capital	Book value	Individual cost
Long-term debt	$700,000	5.3%
Preferred stock	50,000	12.0
Common stock equity	650,000	16.0

a. Calculate the firm's *weighted average cost of capital using book value weights*.
b. Explain how the firm can use this cost in the investment decision-making process.

LG 6   **P9–14**   **WACC—Book weights and market weights**   Webster Company has compiled the information shown in the following table.

Source of capital	Book value	Market value	After-tax cost
Long-term debt	$4,000,000	$3,840,000	6.0%
Preferred stock	40,000	60,000	13.0
Common stock equity	1,060,000	3,000,000	17.0
Totals	$5,100,000	$6,900,000	

a. Calculate the weighted average cost of capital using *book value weights*.
b. Calculate the weighted average cost of capital using *market value weights*.
c. Compare the answers obtained in parts **a** and **b**. Explain the differences.

LG 6   **P9–15**   **WACC and target weights**   After careful analysis, Dexter Brothers has determined that its optimal capital structure is composed of the sources and target market value weights shown in the following table.

Source of capital	Target market value weight
Long-term debt	30%
Preferred stock	15
Common stock equity	55
Total	100%

The cost of debt is estimated to be 7.2%; the cost of preferred stock is estimated to be 13.5%; the cost of retained earnings is estimated to be 16.0%; and the cost of new common stock is estimated to be 18.0%. All of these are after-tax rates. The company's debt represents 25%, the preferred stock represents 10%, and the common stock equity represents 65% of total capital on the basis of the market values of the three components. The company expects to have a significant amount of retained earnings available and does not expect to sell any new common stock.

a. Calculate the weighted average cost of capital on the basis of *historical market value weights*.
b. Calculate the weighted average cost of capital on the basis of *target market value weights*.
c. Compare the answers obtained in parts **a** and **b**. Explain the differences.

LG 3 **LG 4** **P9–16** **Cost of capital** Edna Recording Studios, Inc., reported earnings available to
LG 5 **LG 6** common stock of $4,200,000 last year. From those earnings, the company paid a dividend of $1.26 on each of its 1,000,000 common shares outstanding. The capital structure of the company includes 40% debt, 10% preferred stock, and 50% common stock. It is taxed at a rate of 40%.
a. If the market price of the common stock is $40 and dividends are expected to grow at a rate of 6% per year for the foreseeable future, what is the company's *cost of retained earnings* financing?
b. If underpricing and flotation costs on new shares of common stock amount to $7.00 per share, what is the company's *cost of new common stock* financing?
c. The company can issue $2.00 dividend preferred stock for a market price of $25.00 per share. Flotation costs would amount to $3.00 per share. What is the *cost of preferred stock* financing?
d. The company can issue $1,000-par-value, 10% coupon, 5-year bonds that can be sold for $1,200 each. Flotation costs would amount to $25.00 per bond. Use the estimation formula to figure the approximate *cost of debt* financing.
e. What is the *WACC?*

LG 3 **LG 4** **P9–17** **Calculation of individual costs and WACC** Dillon Labs has asked its financial
LG 5 **LG 6** manager to measure the cost of each specific type of capital as well as the weighted average cost of capital. The weighted average cost is to be measured by using the following weights: 40% long-term debt, 10% preferred stock, and 50% common stock equity (retained earnings, new common stock, or both). The firm's tax rate is 40%.

Debt The firm can sell for $980 a 10-year, $1,000-par-value bond paying *annual interest* at a 10% coupon rate. A flotation cost of 3% of the par value is required in addition to the discount of $20 per bond.

Preferred stock Eight percent (annual dividend) preferred stock having a par value of $100 can be sold for $65. An additional fee of $2 per share must be paid to the underwriters.

Common stock The firm's common stock is currently selling for $50 per share. The dividend expected to be paid at the end of the coming year (2013) is $4. Its dividend payments, which have been approximately 60% of earnings per share in each of the past 5 years, were as shown in the following table.

Year	Dividend
2012	$3.75
2011	3.50
2010	3.30
2009	3.15
2008	2.85

It is expected that to attract buyers, new common stock must be underpriced $5 per share, and the firm must also pay $3 per share in flotation costs. Dividend payments are expected to continue at 60% of earnings. (Assume that $r_r = r_s$.)

a. Calculate the after-tax cost of debt.

b. Calculate the cost of preferred stock.

c. Calculate the cost of common stock.

d. Calculate the WACC for Dillon Labs.

Personal Finance Problem

LG 6 **P9–18** **Weighted average cost of capital** John Dough has just been awarded his degree in business. He has three education loans outstanding. They all mature in 5 years and can be repaid without penalty any time before maturity. The amounts owed on each loan and the annual interest rate associated with each loan are given in the following table.

Loan	Balance due	Annual interest rate
1	$20,000	6%
2	12,000	9
3	32,000	5

John can also combine the total of his three debts (that is, $64,000) and create a consolidated loan from his bank. His bank will charge a 7.2% annual interest rate for a period of 5 years.

Should John do nothing (leave the three individual loans as is) or create a consolidated loan (the $64,000 question)?

LG 3 LG 4
LG 5 LG 6

P9–19 **Calculation of individual costs and WACC** Lang Enterprises is interested in measuring its overall cost of capital. Current investigation has gathered the following data. The firm is in the 40% tax bracket.

Debt The firm can raise debt by selling $1,000-par-value, 8% coupon interest rate, 20-year bonds on which *annual interest* payments will be made. To sell the issue, an average discount of $30 per bond would have to be given. The firm also must pay flotation costs of $30 per bond.

Preferred stock The firm can sell 8% preferred stock at its $95-per-share par value. The cost of issuing and selling the preferred stock is expected to be $5 per share. Preferred stock can be sold under these terms.

Common stock The firm's common stock is currently selling for $90 per share. The firm expects to pay cash dividends of $7 per share next year. The firm's dividends have been growing at an annual rate of 6%, and this growth is expected to continue into the future. The stock must be underpriced by $7 per share, and flotation costs are expected to amount to $5 per share. The firm can sell new common stock under these terms.

Retained earnings When measuring this cost, the firm does not concern itself with the tax bracket or brokerage fees of owners. It expects to have available $100,000 of retained earnings in the coming year; once these retained earnings are exhausted, the firm will use new common stock as the form of common stock equity financing.

a. Calculate the after-tax cost of debt.
b. Calculate the cost of preferred stock.
c. Calculate the cost of common stock.
d. Calculate the firm's weighted average cost of capital using the capital structure weights shown in the following table. (Round answer to the nearest 0.1%.)

Source of capital	Weight
Long-term debt	30%
Preferred stock	20
Common stock equity	50
Total	100%

LG 6   **P9–20**   **Weighted average cost of capital**   American Exploration, Inc., a natural gas producer, is trying to decide whether to revise its target capital structure. Currently it targets a 50–50 mix of debt and equity, but it is considering a target capital structure with 70% debt. American Exploration currently has 6% after-tax cost of debt and a 12% cost of common stock. The company does not have any preferred stock outstanding.

a. What is American Exploration's current WACC?
b. Assuming that its cost of debt and equity remain unchanged, what will be American Exploration's WACC under the revised target capital structure?
c. Do you think shareholders are affected by the increase in debt to 70%? If so, how are they affected? Are their common stock claims riskier now?
d. Suppose that in response to the increase in debt, American Exploration's shareholders increase their required return so that cost of common equity is 16%. What will its new WACC be in this case?
e. What does your answer in part **b** suggest about the tradeoff between financing with debt versus equity?

LG 1   **P9–21**   **ETHICS PROBLEM**   During the 1990s, General Electric put together a long string of consecutive quarters in which the firm managed to meet or beat the earnings forecasts of Wall Street stock analysts. Some skeptics wondered if GE "managed" earnings to meet Wall Street's expectations, meaning that GE used accounting gimmicks to conceal the true volatility in its business. How do you think GE's long run of meeting or beating earnings forecasts affected its cost of capital? If investors learn that GE's performance was achieved largely through accounting gimmicks, how do you think they would respond?

Spreadsheet Exercise

Nova Corporation is interested in measuring the cost of each specific type of capital as well as the weighted average cost of capital. Historically, the firm has raised capital in the following manner:

Source of capital	Weight
Long-term debt	35%
Preferred stock	12
Common stock equity	53

The tax rate of the firm is currently 40%. The needed financial information and data are as follows:

Debt   Nova can raise debt by selling $1,000-par-value, 6.5% coupon interest rate, 10-year bonds on which *annual interest payments* will be made. To sell the issue, an average discount of $20 per bond needs to be given. There is an associated flotation cost of 2% of par value.

Preferred stock   Preferred stock can be sold under the following terms: The security has a par value of $100 per share, the annual dividend rate is 6% of the par value, and the flotation cost is expected to be $4 per share. The preferred stock is expected to sell for $102 before cost considerations.

Common stock   The current price of Nova's common stock is $35 per share. The cash dividend is expected to be $3.25 per share next year. The firm's dividends have grown at an annual rate of 5%, and it is expected that the dividend will continue at this rate for the foreseeable future. The flotation costs are expected to be approximately $2 per share. Nova can sell new common stock under these terms.

Retained earnings   The firm expects to have available $100,000 of retained earnings in the coming year. Once these retained earnings are exhausted, the firm will use new common stock as the form of common stock equity financing. (*Note:* When measuring this cost, the firm does not concern itself with the tax bracket or brokerage fees of owners.)

TO DO

Create a spreadsheet to answer the following questions:

a. Calculate the after-tax cost of debt.
b. Calculate the cost of preferred stock.
c. Calculate the cost of retained earnings.
d. Calculate the cost of new common stock.
e. Calculate the firm's weighted average cost of capital using retained earnings and the capital structure weights shown in the table above.
f. Calculate the firm's weighted average cost of capital using new common stock and the capital structure weights shown in the table above.

 Visit **www.myfinancelab.com** for **Chapter Case: *Making Star Products' Financing/Investment Decision,*** Group Exercises, and numerous online resources.

Integrative Case 4

Eco Plastics Company

Since its inception, Eco Plastics Company has been revolutionizing plastic and trying to do its part to save the environment. Eco's founder, Marion Cosby, developed a biodegradable plastic that her company is marketing to manufacturing companies throughout the southeastern United States. After operating as a private company for six years, Eco went public in 2009 and is listed on the Nasdaq stock exchange.

As the chief financial officer of a young company with lots of investment opportunities, Eco's CFO closely monitors the firm's cost of capital. The CFO keeps tabs on each of the individual costs of Eco's three main financing sources: long-term debt, preferred stock, and common stock. The target capital structure for ECO is given by the weights in the following table:

Source of capital	Weight
Long-term debt	30%
Preferred stock	20
Common stock equity	50
Total	100%

At the present time, Eco can raise debt by selling 20-year bonds with a $1,000 par value and a 10.5% annual coupon interest rate. Eco's corporate tax rate is 40%, and its bonds generally require an average discount of $45 per bond and flotation costs of $32 per bond when being sold. Eco's outstanding preferred stock pays a 9% dividend and has a $95-per-share par value. The cost of issuing and selling additional preferred stock is expected to be $7 per share. Because Eco is a young firm that requires lots of cash to grow it does not currently pay a dividend to common stock holders. To track the cost of common stock the CFO uses the capital asset pricing model (CAPM). The CFO and the firm's investment advisors believe that the appropriate risk-free rate is 4% and that the market's expected return equals 13%. Using data from 2009 through 2012, Eco's CFO estimates the firm's beta to be 1.3.

Although Eco's current target capital structure includes 20% preferred stock, the company is considering using debt financing to retire the outstanding preferred stock, thus shifting their target capital structure to 50% long-term debt and 50% common stock. If Eco shifts its capital mix from preferred stock to debt, its financial advisors expect its beta to increase to 1.5.

TO DO

a. Calculate Eco's current after-tax cost of long-term debt.
b. Calculate Eco's current cost of preferred stock.
c. Calculate Eco's current cost of common stock.
d. Calculate Eco's current weighted average cost capital.
e. (1) Assuming that the debt financing costs do not change, what effect would a shift to a more highly leveraged *capital structure* consisting of 50% long-term debt, 0% preferred stock, and 50% common stock have on the risk premium for Eco's common stock? What would be Eco's new cost of common equity?
   (2) What would be Eco's new weighted average cost of capital?
   (3) Which capital structure—the original one or this one—seems better? Why?

385

Part 5 — Long-Term Investment Decisions

Chapters in This Part

Probably nothing that financial managers do is more important to the long-term success of a company than making good investment decisions. The term *capital budgeting* describes the process for evaluating and selecting investment projects. Often, capital expenditures can be very large, such as building a new plant or launching a new product line. These endeavors can create enormous value for shareholders, but they can also bankrupt the company. In this section, you'll learn how financial managers decide which investment opportunities to pursue.

Chapter 10 covers the capital budgeting tools that financial managers and analysts use to evaluate the merits of an investment. Some of these techniques are quite intuitive and simple to use, such as payback analysis. Other techniques are a little more complex, such as the NPV and IRR approaches. In general, the more complex techniques provide more comprehensive evaluations, however, the simpler approaches often lead to the same value-maximizing decisions.

Chapter 11 illustrates how to develop the capital budgeting cash flows that the techniques covered in Chapter 10 require. After studying this chapter, you will understand the inputs that are necessary to build the relevant cash flows that are required to determine whether a particular investment is likely to create or destroy value for shareholders.

Chapter 12 introduces additional techniques for evaluating the risks inherent with capital investment projects. Because of the often huge scale of capital investments and their importance to the firm's financial well-being, managers invest a tremendous amount of time and energy trying to understand the risks associated with these projects.

10 Capital Budgeting Techniques

Learning Goals

Why This Chapter Matters to You

In your *professional* life

ACCOUNTING You need to understand capital budgeting techniques to help determine the relevant cash flows associated with proposed capital expenditures.

INFORMATION SYSTEMS You need to understand capital budgeting techniques to design decision modules that help reduce the amount of work required to analyze proposed capital expenditures.

MANAGEMENT You need to understand capital budgeting techniques to correctly analyze the relevant cash flows of proposed projects and decide whether to accept or reject them.

MARKETING You need to understand capital budgeting techniques to grasp how proposals for new marketing programs, for new products, and for the expansion of existing product lines will be evaluated by the firm's decision makers.

OPERATIONS You need to understand capital budgeting techniques to know how proposals for the acquisition of new equipment and plants will be evaluated by the firm's decision makers.

In your *personal* life

You can use the capital budgeting techniques used by financial managers to measure either the value of a given asset purchase or its compound rate of return. The IRR technique is widely applied in personal finance to measure both actual and forecast rate of returns on investment securities, real estate, credit card debt, consumer loans, and leases.

Treats—Waffles and More, Cairo

Capital Budgeting Techniques Work a Treat

"Come to Treats for Waffles and More" is the attractive slogan of a small dessert shop in Cairo, Egypt. With waffles and pancakes being their favorite desserts, Shamel El-Sherei and Shehab El-Sherei always dreamed of having their own business that would sell them to others so they could enjoy them as well. As they were still at university, Shamel and Shehab thought this plan would have to be postponed until they had enough experience and knowledge to open their own business without the risk of losing all their savings. However, after an introductory course in managerial finance the pair learned how their idea could be realized and thereafter they started applying the theories of capital budgeting to their project. Having learned that the first step for any project assessment is to look at the cash flow, they studied the costs of buying the necessary equipment and renting a location, and considered other expenses of starting the business. They estimated that they would need 100,000 EGP of initial investment and 12,500 EGP each month to cover expenses. They then added these costs to the expected profit from selling the waffles and pancakes to derive the expected cash flow for their project. The expected revenues from selling the desserts were estimated to be 25 EGP on average per item, with a total of 100 sold per day. This equalled a net cash inflow of 30,000 EGP in the first year which they estimated would rise by 15 percent per year for the next 3 years.

Using these data they calculated the profitability of their idea using net present value and internal rate of return; both figures turned out to be quite promising. The net present value of the cash flow was 16,757 EGP at a cost of capital of 10 percent. This reflected an internal rate of return of 17 percent. In addition to the profitability indicators, Shamel and Shehab wanted to know how long it would take them to regain the savings they would invest in the business. To get the additional insight into the riskiness of their project, they calculated the payback period. This delivered a number lower than they expected and was therefore a positive indicator. Based on all these results, Shamel and Shehab were convinced their idea was not merely a dream but a realistic, profitable business model, and they decided to start their project without further delay.

With the help of the capital budgeting techniques introduced in this chapter, Shamel and Shehab were able to turn their dream plan into reality. A year after its opening, Treats—Waffles and More is considered one of the top dessert places in Cairo, and is ranked fourth in the well-known local magazine, *G-mag*.

LG 1 | **10.1** Overview of Capital Budgeting

capital budgeting
The process of evaluating and selecting long-term investments that are consistent with the firm's goal of maximizing owners' wealth.

Long-term investments represent sizable outlays of funds that commit a firm to some course of action. Consequently, the firm needs procedures to analyze and select its long-term investments. **Capital budgeting** is the process of evaluating and selecting long-term investments that are consistent with the firm's goal of maximizing owners' wealth. Firms typically make a variety of long-term investments, but the most common is in *fixed assets*, which include property (land), plant, and equipment. These assets, often referred to as *earning assets*, generally provide the basis for the firm's earning power and value.

Because firms treat capital budgeting (investment) and financing decisions *separately*, Chapters 10 through 12 concentrate on fixed-asset acquisition without regard to the specific method of financing used. We begin by discussing the motives for capital expenditure.

MOTIVES FOR CAPITAL EXPENDITURE

capital expenditure
An outlay of funds by the firm that is expected to produce benefits over a period of time *greater than* 1 year.

operating expenditure
An outlay of funds by the firm resulting in benefits received *within* 1 year.

A **capital expenditure** is an outlay of funds by the firm that is expected to produce benefits over a period of time *greater than* 1 year. An **operating expenditure** is an outlay resulting in benefits received *within* 1 year. Fixed-asset outlays are capital expenditures, but not all capital expenditures are classified as fixed assets. A $60,000 outlay for a new machine with a usable life of 15 years is a capital expenditure that would appear as a fixed asset on the firm's balance sheet. A $60,000 outlay for an advertising campaign that is expected to produce benefits over a long period is also a capital expenditure but would rarely be shown as a fixed asset.

Companies make capital expenditures for many reasons. The basic motives for capital expenditures are to expand operations, to replace or renew fixed assets, or to obtain some other, less tangible benefit over a long period.

STEPS IN THE PROCESS

capital budgeting process
Five distinct but interrelated steps: *proposal generation, review and analysis, decision making, implementation,* and *follow-up.*

The **capital budgeting process** consists of five distinct but interrelated steps:

1. *Proposal generation.* Proposals for new investment projects are made at all levels within a business organization and are reviewed by finance personnel. Proposals that require large outlays are more carefully scrutinized than less costly ones.
2. *Review and analysis.* Financial managers perform formal review and analysis to assess the merits of investment proposals.
3. *Decision making.* Firms typically delegate capital expenditure decision making on the basis of dollar limits. Generally, the board of directors must authorize expenditures beyond a certain amount. Often plant managers are given authority to make decisions necessary to keep the production line moving.
4. *Implementation.* Following approval, expenditures are made and projects implemented. Expenditures for a large project often occur in phases.
5. *Follow-up.* Results are monitored, and actual costs and benefits are compared with those that were expected. Action may be required if actual outcomes differ from projected ones.

Each step in the process is important. Review and analysis and decision making (Steps 2 and 3) consume the majority of time and effort, however. Follow-up (Step 5) is an important but often ignored step aimed at allowing the firm to improve the accuracy of its cash flow estimates continuously. Because of their fundamental importance, this and the following chapters give primary consideration to review and analysis and to decision making.

BASIC TERMINOLOGY

Before we develop the concepts, techniques, and practices related to the capital budgeting process, we need to explain some basic terminology. In addition, we will present some key assumptions that are used to simplify the discussion in the remainder of this chapter and in Chapters 11 and 12.

Independent versus Mutually Exclusive Projects

independent projects
Projects whose cash flows are unrelated to (or independent of) one another; the acceptance of one *does not eliminate* the others from further consideration.

Most investments can be placed into one of two categories: (1) independent projects or (2) mutually exclusive projects. **Independent projects** are those whose cash flows are unrelated to (or independent of) one another; the acceptance of one project *does not eliminate* the others from further consideration. **Mutually exclusive projects** are those that have the same function and therefore compete with one another. The acceptance of one *eliminates* from further consideration all other projects that serve a similar function. For example, a firm in need of increased production capacity could obtain it by (1) expanding its plant, (2) acquiring another company, or (3) contracting with another company for production. Clearly, accepting any one option eliminates the immediate need for either of the others.

mutually exclusive projects
Projects that compete with one another, so that the acceptance of one *eliminates* from further consideration all other projects that serve a similar function.

Unlimited Funds versus Capital Rationing

unlimited funds
The financial situation in which a firm is able to accept all independent projects that provide an acceptable return.

The availability of funds for capital expenditures affects the firm's decisions. If a firm has **unlimited funds** for investment (or if it can raise as much money as it needs by borrowing or issuing stock), making capital budgeting decisions is quite simple: All independent projects that will provide an acceptable return can be accepted. Typically, though, firms operate under **capital rationing** instead. This means that they have only a fixed number of dollars available for capital expenditures and that numerous projects will compete for these dollars. Procedures for dealing with capital rationing are presented in Chapter 12. The discussions here and in the following chapter assume unlimited funds.

capital rationing
The financial situation in which a firm has only a fixed number of dollars available for capital expenditures, and numerous projects compete for these dollars.

Accept–Reject versus Ranking Approaches

accept–reject approach
The evaluation of capital expenditure proposals to determine whether they meet the firm's minimum acceptance criterion.

Two basic approaches to capital budgeting decisions are available. The **accept–reject approach** involves evaluating capital expenditure proposals to determine whether they meet the firm's minimum acceptance criterion. This approach can be used when the firm has unlimited funds, as a preliminary step when evaluating mutually exclusive projects, or in a situation in which capital must be rationed. In these cases, only acceptable projects should be considered.

ranking approach
The ranking of capital expenditure projects on the basis of some predetermined measure, such as the rate of return.

The second method, the **ranking approach,** involves ranking projects on the basis of some predetermined measure, such as the rate of return. The project with the highest return is ranked first, and the project with the lowest return is ranked last. Only acceptable projects should be ranked. Ranking is useful in selecting the "best" of a group of mutually exclusive projects and in evaluating projects with a view of capital rationing.

TABLE 10.1	Capital Expenditure Data for Bennett Company	
	Project A	Project B
Initial investment	$42,000	$45,000
Year	Operating cash inflows	
1	$14,000	$28,000
2	14,000	12,000
3	14,000	10,000
4	14,000	10,000
5	14,000	10,000

CAPITAL BUDGETING TECHNIQUES

Large firms evaluate dozens, perhaps even hundreds, of different ideas for new investments each year. To ensure that the investment projects selected have the best chance of increasing the value of the firm, financial managers need tools to help them evaluate the merits of individual projects and to rank competing investments. A number of techniques are available for performing such analyses. The preferred approaches integrate time value procedures, risk and return considerations, and valuation concepts to select capital expenditures that are consistent with the firm's goal of maximizing owners' wealth. This chapter focuses on the use of these techniques in an environment of certainty.

In more depth

To read about *The Accounting Rate of Return,* go to www.myfinancelab.com

 myfinancelab

Bennett Company's Relevant Cash Flows

We will use one basic problem to illustrate all the techniques described in this chapter. The problem concerns Bennett Company, a medium-sized metal fabricator that is currently contemplating two projects: Project A requires an initial investment of $42,000; project B requires an initial investment of $45,000. The projected relevant cash flows for the two projects are presented in Table 10.1 and depicted on the time lines in Figure 10.1. Both projects involve one initial cash

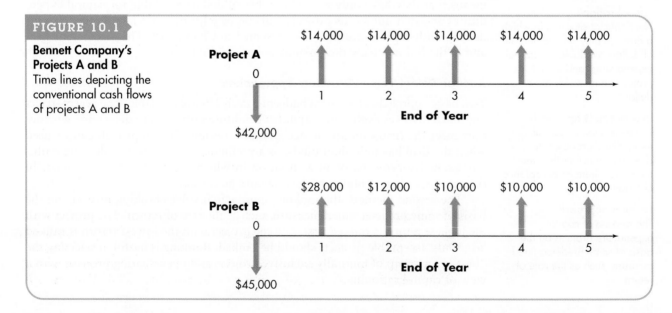

FIGURE 10.1

Bennett Company's Projects A and B
Time lines depicting the conventional cash flows of projects A and B

outlay followed by annual cash inflows, a fairly typical pattern for new investments. We begin with a look at the three most popular capital budgeting techniques: payback period, net present value, and internal rate of return.

→ REVIEW QUESTION

10–1 What is the financial manager's goal in selecting investment projects for the firm? Define the capital budgeting process and explain how it helps managers achieve their goal.

LG 2 ## 10.2 Payback Period

payback period
The amount of time required for a firm to recover its initial investment in a project, as calculated from *cash inflows*.

Payback periods are commonly used to evaluate proposed investments. The **payback period** is the amount of time required for the firm to recover its initial investment in a project, as calculated from *cash inflows*. In the case of an *annuity* (such as the Bennett Company's project A), the payback period can be found by dividing the initial investment by the annual cash inflow. For a *mixed stream* of cash inflows (such as project B), the yearly cash inflows must be accumulated until the initial investment is recovered. Although popular, the payback period is generally viewed as an *unsophisticated capital budgeting technique*, because it does not *explicitly* consider the time value of money.

DECISION CRITERIA

When the payback period is used to make accept–reject decisions, the following decision criteria apply:

- If the payback period is *less than* the maximum acceptable payback period, *accept* the project.
- If the payback period is *greater than* the maximum acceptable payback period, *reject* the project.

The length of the maximum acceptable payback period is determined by management. This value is set *subjectively* on the basis of a number of factors, including the type of project (expansion, replacement or renewal, other), the perceived risk of the project, and the perceived relationship between the payback period and the share value. It is simply a value that management feels, on average, will result in value-creating investment decisions.

Example 10.1 ▶

We can calculate the payback period for Bennett Company's projects A and B using the data in Table 10.1. *For project A, which is an annuity, the payback period is 3.0 years ($42,000 initial investment ÷ $14,000 annual cash inflow).* Because project B generates a mixed stream of cash inflows, the calculation of its payback period is not as clear-cut. In year 1, the firm will recover $28,000 of its $45,000 initial investment. By the end of year 2, $40,000 ($28,000 from year 1 + $12,000 from year 2) will have been recovered. At the end of year 3, $50,000 will have been recovered. Only 50% of the year-3 cash inflow of $10,000 is needed to complete the payback of the initial $45,000. *The payback period for project B is therefore 2.5 years (2 years + 50% of year 3).*

If Bennett's maximum acceptable payback period were 2.75 years, project A would be rejected and project B would be accepted. If the maximum acceptable payback period were 2.25 years, both projects would be rejected. If the projects were being ranked, B would be preferred over A because it has a shorter payback period.

PROS AND CONS OF PAYBACK ANALYSIS

Large firms sometimes use the payback approach to evaluate small projects, and small firms use it to evaluate most projects. Its popularity results from its computational simplicity and intuitive appeal. By measuring how quickly the firm recovers its initial investment, the payback period also gives *implicit* consideration to the timing of cash flows and therefore to the time value of money. Because it can be viewed as a measure of *risk exposure,* many firms use the payback period as a decision criterion or as a supplement to other decision techniques. The longer the firm must wait to recover its invested funds, the greater the possibility of a calamity. Hence, the shorter the payback period the lower the firm's risk exposure.

The major weakness of the payback period is that the appropriate payback period is merely a subjectively determined number. It cannot be specified in light of the wealth maximization goal because it is not based on discounting cash flows to determine whether they add to the firm's value. Instead, the appropriate payback period is simply the maximum acceptable period of time over which management decides that a project's cash flows must break even (that is, just equal to the initial investment). The *Focus on Practice* box offers more information about these time limits in actual practice.

Personal Finance Example 10.2 ▶ Seema Mehdi is considering investing $20,000 to obtain a 5% interest in a rental property. Her good friend and real estate agent, Akbar Ahmed, put the deal together and he conservatively estimates that Seema should receive between $4,000 and $6,000 per year in cash from her 5% interest in the property. The deal is structured in a way that forces all investors to maintain their investment in the property for at least 10 years. Seema expects to remain in the 25% income-tax bracket for quite a while. To be acceptable, Seema requires the investment to pay itself back in terms of after-tax cash flows in less than 7 years.

Seema's calculation of the payback period on this deal begins with calculation of the range of annual after-tax cash flow:

$$\text{After-tax cash flow} = (1 - \text{tax rate}) \times \text{Pre-tax cash flow}$$
$$= (1 - 0.25) \times \$4,000 = \$3,000$$
$$= (1 - 0.25) \times \$6,000 = \$4,500$$

The after-tax cash flow ranges from $3,000 to $4,500. Dividing the $20,000 initial investment by each of the estimated after-tax cash flows, we get the payback period:

$$\text{Payback period} = \text{Initial investment} \div \text{After-tax cash flow}$$
$$= \$20,000 \div \$3,000 = 6.67 \text{ years}$$
$$= \$20,000 \div \$4,500 = 4.44 \text{ years}$$

Because Seema's proposed rental property investment will pay itself back between 4.44 and 6.67 years, which is a range below her maximum payback of 7 years, the investment is acceptable.

focus on PRACTICE

Limits on Payback Analysis

in practice   In tough economic times, the standard for a payback period is often reduced. Chief information officers (CIOs) are apt to reject projects with payback periods of more than 2 years. "We start with payback period," says Ron Fijalkowski, CIO at Strategic Distribution, Inc., in Bensalem, Pennsylvania. "For sure, if the payback period is over 36 months, it's not going to get approved. But our rule of thumb is we'd like to see 24 months. And if it's close to 12, it's probably a no-brainer."

While easy to compute and easy to understand, the payback period's simplicity brings with it some drawbacks. "Payback gives you an answer that tells you a bit about the beginning stage of a project, but it doesn't tell you much about the full lifetime of the project," says Chris Gardner, a cofounder of iValue LLC, an IT valuation consultancy

in Barrington, Illinois. "The simplicity of computing payback may encourage sloppiness, especially the failure to include all costs associated with an investment, such as training, maintenance, and hardware upgrade costs," says Douglas Emond, senior vice president and chief technology officer at Eastern Bank in Lynn, Massachusetts. For example, he says, "you may be bringing in a hot new technology, but uh-oh, after implementation you realize that you need a .Net guru in-house, and you don't have one."

But the payback method's emphasis on the short term has a special appeal for IT managers. "That's because the history of IT projects that take longer than 3 years is disastrous," says Gardner. Indeed, Ian Campbell, chief research officer at Nucleus Research, Inc., in Wellesley, Massachusetts, says payback period is an absolutely essential metric for evaluating IT projects—

even more important than discounted cash flow (NPV and IRR)—because it spotlights the risks inherent in lengthy IT projects. "It should be a hard and fast rule to never take an IT project with a payback period greater than 3 years, unless it's an infrastructure project you can't do without," Campbell says.

Whatever the weaknesses of the payback period method of evaluating capital projects, the simplicity of the method does allow it to be used in conjunction with other, more sophisticated measures. It can be used to screen potential projects and winnow them down to the few that merit more careful scrutiny with, for example, net present value (NPV).

▶ *In your view, if the payback period method is used in conjunction with the NPV method, should it be used before or after the NPV evaluation?*

Source: Gary Anthes, "ROI Guide: Payback Period," Computerworld.com (February 17, 2003), www.computerworld.com/ s/article/78529/ROI_Guide_Payback_Period?taxono.

A second weakness is that this approach fails to take *fully* into account the time factor in the value of money.[1] This weakness can be illustrated by an example.

Example 10.3 ▶   DeYarman Enterprises, a small medical appliance manufacturer, is considering two mutually exclusive projects named Gold and Silver. The firm uses only the payback period to choose projects. The cash flows and payback period for each project are given in Table 10.2. Both projects have 3-year payback periods, which would suggest that they are equally desirable. But comparison of the pattern of cash inflows over the first 3 years shows that more of the $50,000 initial investment in project Silver is recovered sooner than is recovered for project Gold. For example, in year 1, $40,000 of the $50,000 invested in project Silver is recovered, whereas only $5,000 of the $50,000 investment in project Gold is recovered. Given the time value of money, project Silver would clearly be preferred over

---

1. To consider differences in timing explicitly in applying the payback method, the *discounted payback period* is sometimes used. It is found by first calculating the present value of the cash inflows at the appropriate discount rate and then finding the payback period by using the present value of the cash inflows.

TABLE 10.2	Relevant Cash Flows and Payback Periods for DeYarman Enterprises' Projects	
	Project gold	Project silver
Initial investment	$50,000	$50,000
Year	Operating cash inflows	
1	$ 5,000	$40,000
2	5,000	2,000
3	40,000	8,000
4	10,000	10,000
5	10,000	10,000
Payback period	3 years	3 years

project Gold, in spite of the fact that both have identical 3-year payback periods. The payback approach does not fully account for the time value of money, which, if recognized, would cause project Silver to be preferred over project Gold.

A third weakness of payback is its failure to recognize cash flows that occur *after* the payback period.

Example 10.4 ▶   Rashid Company, a software developer, has two investment opportunities, X and Y. Data for X and Y are given in Table 10.3. The payback period for project X is 2 years; for project Y it is 3 years. Strict adherence to the payback approach suggests that project X is preferable to project Y. However, if we look beyond the payback period, we see that project X returns only an additional $1,200 ($1,000 in year 3 + $100 in year 4 + $100 in year 5), whereas project Y returns an additional $7,000 ($4,000 in year 4 + $3,000 in year 5). On the basis of this information, project Y appears preferable to X. The payback approach ignored the cash inflows occurring after the end of the payback period.

TABLE 10.3	Calculation of the Payback Period for Rashid Company's Two Alternative Investment Projects	
	Project X	Project Y
Initial investment	$10,000	$10,000
Year	Operating cash inflows	
1	$5,000	$3,000
2	5,000	4,000
3	1,000	3,000
4	100	4,000
5	100	3,000
Payback period	2 years	3 years

→ **REVIEW QUESTIONS**

10–2 What is the *payback period?* How is it calculated?

10–3 What weaknesses are commonly associated with the use of the payback period to evaluate a proposed investment?

LG 3   **10.3** Net Present Value (NPV)

The method used by most large companies to evaluate investment projects is called *net present value (NPV)*. The intuition behind the NPV method is simple. When firms make investments, they are spending money that they obtained, in one form or another, from investors. Investors expect a return on the money that they give to firms, so a firm should undertake an investment only if the present value of the cash flow that the investment generates is greater than the cost of making the investment in the first place. Because the *NPV* method takes into account the time value of investors' money, it is a more *sophisticated capital budgeting technique* than the payback rule. The NPV method discounts the firm's cash flows at the firm's cost of capital. This rate—as discussed in Chapter 9—is the minimum return that must be earned on a project to satisfy the firm's investors. Projects with lower returns fail to meet investors' expectations and therefore decrease firm value, and projects with higher returns increase firm value.

net present value (NPV)
A sophisticated capital budgeting technique; found by subtracting a project's initial investment from the present value of its cash inflows discounted at a rate equal to the firm's cost of capital.

The **net present value** (**NPV**) is found by subtracting a project's initial investment (CF_0) from the present value of its cash inflows (CF_t) discounted at a rate equal to the firm's cost of capital (r).

NPV = Present value of cash inflows − Initial investment

$$NPV = \sum_{t=1}^{n} \frac{CF_t}{(1 + r)^t} - CF_0 \qquad (10.1)$$

When NPV is used, both inflows and outflows are measured in terms of present dollars. For a project that has cash outflows beyond the initial investment, the net present value of a project would be found by subtracting the present value of outflows from the present value of inflows.

DECISION CRITERIA

When NPV is used to make accept–reject decisions, the decision criteria are as follows:

• If the NPV is *greater than* $0, *accept* the project.

• If the NPV is *less than* $0, *reject* the project.

If the NPV is greater than $0, the firm will earn a return greater than its cost of capital. Such action should increase the market value of the firm, and therefore the wealth of its owners by an amount equal to the NPV.

Example 10.5 ▶   We can illustrate the net present value (NPV) approach by using the Bennett Company data presented in Table 10.1. If the firm has a 10% cost of capital, the net present values for projects A (an annuity) and B (a mixed stream) can be

FIGURE 10.2

Calculation of NPVs for Bennett Company's Capital Expenditure Alternatives
Time lines depicting the cash flows and NPV calculations for projects A and B

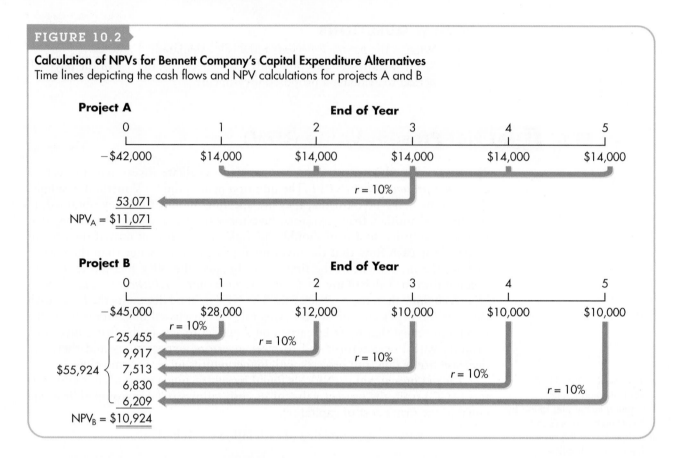

calculated as shown on the time lines in Figure 10.2. These calculations result in net present values for projects A and B of $11,071 and $10,924, respectively. Both projects are acceptable, because the net present value of each is greater than $0. If the projects were being ranked, however, project A would be considered superior to B, because it has a higher net present value than that of B ($11,071 versus $10,924).

Calculator Use   The preprogrammed NPV function in a financial calculator can be used to simplify the NPV calculation. The keystrokes for project A—the annuity—typically are as shown at left. Note that because project A is an annuity, only its first cash inflow, $CF_1 = 14000$, is input, followed by its frequency, $N = 5$.

The keystrokes for project B—the mixed stream—are as shown on page 399. Because the last three cash inflows for project B are the same ($CF_3 = CF_4 = CF_5 = 10,000$), after inputting the first of these cash inflows, CF_3, we merely input its frequency, $N = 3$.

The calculated NPVs for projects A and B of $11,071 and $10,924, respectively, agree with the NPVs already cited.

Spreadsheet Use   The NPVs can be calculated as shown on the following Excel spreadsheet.

Project B

Input	Function
−45000	CF₀
28000	CF₁
12000	CF₂
10000	CF₃
3	N
10	I
	NPV

Solution

10,924.40

	A	B	C
1		DETERMINING THE NET PRESENT VALUE	
2	Firm's cost of capital		10%
3		Year-End Cash Flow	
4	Year	Project A	Project B
5	0	$ (42,000)	$ (45,000)
6	1	$ 14,000	$ 28,000
7	2	$ 14,000	$ 12,000
8	3	$ 14,000	$ 10,000
9	4	$ 14,000	$ 10,000
10	5	$ 14,000	$ 10,000
11	NPV	$ 11,071	$ 10,924
12	Choice of project		Project A

Entry in Cell B11 is
=NPV(C2,B6:B10)+B5
Copy the entry in Cell B11 to Cell C11.
Entry in Cell C12 is =IF(B11>C11,B4,C4).

NPV AND THE PROFITABILITY INDEX

A variation of the NPV rule is called the profitability index (PI). For a project that has an initial cash outflow followed by cash inflows, the profitability index (PI) is simply equal to the present value of cash inflows divided by the initial cash outflow:[2]

$$PI = \frac{\sum_{t=1}^{n} \dfrac{CF_t}{(1+r)^t}}{CF_0} \qquad (10.2)$$

When companies evaluate investment opportunities using the PI, the decision rule they follow is to invest in the project when the index is greater than 1.0. When the PI is greater than one, that implies that the present value of cash inflows is greater than the (absolute value of the) initial cash outflow, so a profitability index greater than one corresponds to a net present value greater than zero. In other words, the NPV and PI methods will always come to the same conclusion regarding whether a particular investment is worth doing or not.

Example 10.6 ▶   We can refer back to Figure 10.2, which shows the present value of cash inflows for projects A and B, to calculate the PI for each of Bennett's investment options:

$$PI_A = \$53,071 \div \$42,000 = 1.26$$
$$PI_B = \$55,924 \div \$45,000 = 1.24$$

According to the profitability index, both projects are acceptable (because PI > 1.0 for both), which shouldn't be surprising because we already know that both projects

2. To be a bit more precise, the denominator in Equation 10.2 should be a positive number, so we are taking the absolute value of the initial cash outflow.

have positive NPVs. Furthermore, in this particular case, the NPV rule and the PI both indicate that project A is preferred over project B. It is not always true that the NPV and PI methods will rank projects in exactly the same order. Different rankings can occur when alternative projects require initial outlays that have very different magnitudes.

NPV AND ECONOMIC VALUE ADDED

Economic Value Added (or EVA), a registered trademark of the consulting firm Stern Stewart & Co., is another close cousin of the NPV method. Whereas the NPV approach calculates the value of an investment over its entire life, the EVA approach is typically used to measure an investment's performance on a year-by-year basis. The EVA method begins the same way that NPV does—by calculating a project's net cash flows. However, the EVA approach subtracts from those cash flows a charge that is designed to capture the return that the firm's investors demand on the project. That is, the EVA calculation asks whether a project generates positive cash flows *above and beyond what investors demand*. If so, then the project is worth undertaking.

pure economic profit
A profit above and beyond the normal competitive rate of return in a line of business.

The EVA method determines whether a project earns a *pure economic profit*. When accountants say that a firm has earned a profit, they mean that revenues are greater than expenses. But the term **pure economic profit** refers to a profit that is higher than expected given the competitive rate of return on a particular line of business. A firm that shows a positive profit on its income statement may or may not earn a pure economic profit, depending on how large the profit is relative to the capital invested in the business. For instance, in the first quarter of 2010, TomTom, the European maker of portable GPS devices, reported a net profit of €3 million. Does that seem like a large profit? Perhaps not when you consider that TomTom's balance sheet showed total assets of over €2.5 billion. In other words, TomTom's profit represented a return of just 0.0012 percent on the firm's assets. That return was below the rate offered on risk-free government securities in 2010, so it clearly fell below the expectations of TomTom's investors (who would have expected a higher return as compensation for the risks they were taking), so the company earned a *pure economic loss* that quarter. Stated differently, TomTom's EVA in the first quarter of 2010 was negative.

Example 10.7 ▶   Suppose a certain project costs $1,000,000 up front, but after that it will generate net cash inflows each year (in perpetuity) of $120,000. To calculate the NPV of this project, we would simply discount the cash flows and add them up. If the firm's cost of capital is 10%, then the project's NPV is:[3]

$$NPV = -\$1,000,000 + (\$120,000 \div 0.10) = \$200,000$$

To calculate the investment's economic value added in any particular year, we start with the annual $120,000 cash flow. Next, we assign a charge that accounts for the return that investors demand on the capital that the firm has invested in the project. In this case, the firm invested $1,000,000, and investors

---

3. We are using Equation 5.14 to calculate the present value of the perpetual stream of $120,000 cash flows.

expect a 10% return. That means that the project's annual capital charge is $100,000 ($1,000,000 × 10%), and its EVA is $20,000 per year:

$$\text{EVA} = \text{project cash flow} - [(\text{cost of capital}) \times (\text{invested capital})]$$
$$= \$120,000 - \$100,000 = \$20,000$$

In other words, this project earns more than its cost of capital each year, so the project is clearly worth doing. To calculate the EVA for the project over its entire life, we would simply discount the annual EVA figures using the firm's cost of capital. In this case, the project produces an annual EVA of $20,000 in perpetuity. Discounting this at 10% gives a project EVA of $200,000 ($20,000 ÷ 0.10), identical to the NPV. In this example, both the NPV and EVA methods reach the same conclusion, namely that the project creates $200,000 in value for shareholders. If the cash flows in our example had fluctuated through time rather than remaining fixed at $120,000 per year, an analyst would calculate the investment's EVA every year, then discount those figures to the present using the firm's cost of capital. If the resulting figure is positive, then the project generates a positive EVA and is worth doing.

→ REVIEW QUESTIONS

10–4 How is the *net present value (NPV)* calculated for a project with a *conventional cash flow pattern?*

10–5 What are the acceptance criteria for NPV? How are they related to the firm's market value?

10–6 Explain the similarities and differences between NPV, PI, and EVA.

LG 4 ## 10.4 Internal Rate of Return (IRR)

internal rate of return (IRR)
The discount rate that equates the NPV of an investment opportunity with $0 (because the present value of cash inflows equals the initial investment); it is the rate of return that the firm will earn if it invests in the project and receives the given cash inflows.

The *internal rate of return (IRR)* is one of the most widely used *capital budgeting techniques*. The **internal rate of return (IRR)** is the discount rate that equates the NPV of an investment opportunity with $0 (because the present value of cash inflows equals the initial investment). It is the rate of return that the firm will earn if it invests in the project and receives the given cash inflows. Mathematically, the IRR is the value of r in Equation 10.1 that causes NPV to equal $0.

$$\$0 = \sum_{t=1}^{n} \frac{CF_t}{(1 + IRR)^t} - CF_0 \tag{10.3}$$

$$\sum_{t=1}^{n} \frac{CF_t}{(1 + IRR)^t} = CF_0 \tag{10.3a}$$

DECISION CRITERIA

When IRR is used to make accept–reject decisions, the decision criteria are as follows:

- If the IRR is *greater than* the cost of capital, *accept* the project.
- If the IRR is *less than* the cost of capital, *reject* the project.

These criteria guarantee that the firm will earn at least its required return. Such an outcome should increase the market value of the firm and, therefore, the wealth of its owners.

CALCULATING THE IRR

Most financial calculators have a preprogrammed IRR function that can be used to simplify the IRR calculation. With these calculators, you merely punch in all cash flows just as if to calculate NPV and then depress IRR to find the internal rate of return. Computer software, including spreadsheets, is also available for simplifying these calculations. All NPV and IRR values presented in this and subsequent chapters are obtained by using these functions on a popular financial calculator.

Example 10.8 ▶   We can demonstrate the internal rate of return (IRR) approach by using the Bennett Company data presented in Table 10.1. Figure 10.3 uses time lines to depict the framework for finding the IRRs for Bennett's projects A and B. We can see in the figure that the IRR is the unknown discount rate that causes the NPV to equal $0.

Calculator Use   To find the IRR using the preprogrammed function in a financial calculator, the keystrokes for each project are the same as those shown on pages 398 and 399 for the NPV calculation, except that the last two NPV keystrokes (punching **I** and then **NPV**) are replaced by a single **IRR** keystroke.

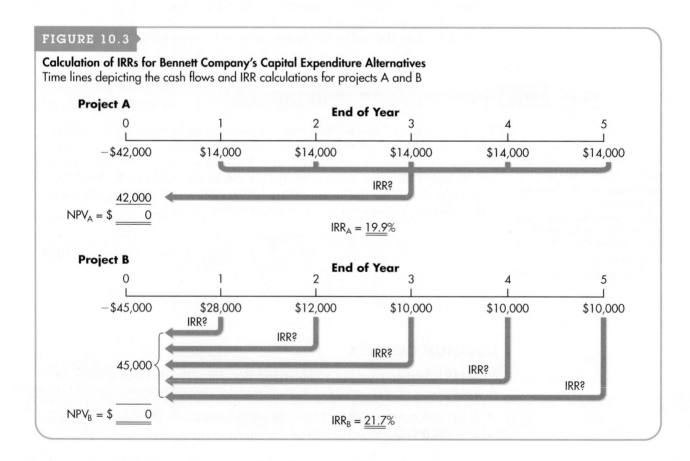

FIGURE 10.3

Calculation of IRRs for Bennett Company's Capital Expenditure Alternatives
Time lines depicting the cash flows and IRR calculations for projects A and B

Comparing the IRRs of projects A and B given in Figure 10.3 to Bennett Company's 10% cost of capital, we can see that both projects are acceptable because

$$IRR_A = 19.9\% > 10.0\% \text{ cost of capital}$$
$$IRR_B = 21.7\% > 10.0\% \text{ cost of capital}$$

Comparing the two projects' IRRs, we would prefer project B over project A because $IRR_B = 21.7\% > IRR_A = 19.9\%$. If these projects are mutually exclusive, meaning that we can choose one project or the other but not both, the IRR decision technique would recommend project B.

Spreadsheet Use   The internal rate of return also can be calculated as shown on the following Excel spreadsheet.

	A	B	C
1	DETERMINING THE INTERNAL RATE OF RETURN		
2		Year-End Cash Flow	
3	Year	Project A	Project B
4	0	$ (42,000)	$ (45,000)
5	1	$ 14,000	$ 28,000
6	2	$ 14,000	$ 12,000
7	3	$ 14,000	$ 10,000
8	4	$ 14,000	$ 10,000
9	5	$ 14,000	$ 10,000
10	IRR	19.9%	21.7%
11	Choice of project		Project B

Entry in Cell B10 is =IRR(B4:B9).
Copy the entry in Cell B10 to Cell C10.
Entry in Cell C11 is =IF(B10>C10,B3,C3).

It is interesting to note in the preceding Example 10.8 that the IRR suggests that project B, which has an IRR of 21.7%, is preferable to project A, which has an IRR of 19.9%. This conflicts with the NPV rankings obtained in an earlier example. Such conflicts are not unusual. *There is no guarantee that NPV and IRR will rank projects in the same order. However, both methods should reach the same conclusion about the acceptability or nonacceptability of projects.*

Personal Finance Example 10.9 ▶ Tony DiLorenzo is evaluating an investment opportunity. He is comfortable with the investment's level of risk. Based on competing investment opportunities, he feels that this investment must earn a minimum compound annual after-tax return of 9% to be acceptable. Tony's initial investment would be $7,500, and he expects to receive annual after-tax cash flows of $500 per year in each of the first 4 years, followed by $700 per year at the end of years 5 through 8. He plans to sell the investment at the end of year 8 and net $9,000, after taxes.

To calculate the investment's IRR (compound annual return), Tony first summarizes the after-tax cash flows as shown in the following table:

Year	Cash flow (− or +)
0	−$7,500 (Initial investment)
1	500
2	500
3	500
4	500
5	700
6	700
7	700
8	9,700 ($700 + $9,000)

Substituting the after-tax cash flows for years 0 through 8 into a financial calculator or spreadsheet, he finds the investment's IRR of 9.54%. Given that the expected IRR of 9.54% exceeds Tony's required minimum IRR of 9%, the investment is acceptable.

→ REVIEW QUESTIONS

10–7 What is the *internal rate of return (IRR)* on an investment? How is it determined?

10–8 What are the acceptance criteria for IRR? How are they related to the firm's market value?

10–9 Do the net present value (NPV) and internal rate of return (IRR) always agree with respect to accept–reject decisions? With respect to ranking decisions? Explain.

LG 5   LG 6   **10.5** Comparing NPV and IRR Techniques

To understand the differences between the NPV and IRR techniques and decision makers' preferences in their use, we need to look at net present value profiles, conflicting rankings, and the question of which approach is better.

NET PRESENT VALUE PROFILES

net present value profile
Graph that depicts a project's NPVs for various discount rates.

Projects can be compared graphically by constructing **net present value profiles** that depict the project's NPVs for various discount rates. These profiles are useful in evaluating and comparing projects, especially when conflicting rankings exist. They are best demonstrated via an example.

Example 10.10 ▶   To prepare net present value profiles for Bennett Company's two projects, A and B, the first step is to develop a number of "discount rate–net present value" coordinates. Three coordinates can be easily obtained for each project; they are at discount

TABLE 10.4	Discount Rate–NPV Coordinates for Projects A and B	
	Net present value	
Discount rate	Project A	Project B
0%	$28,000	$25,000
10	11,071	10,924
19.9	0	—
21.7	—	0

rates of 0%, 10% (the cost of capital, r), and the IRR. The net present value at a 0% discount rate is found by merely adding all the cash inflows and subtracting the initial investment. Using the data in Table 10.1 and Figure 10.1, we get

For project A:

$$(\$14{,}000 + \$14{,}000 + \$14{,}000 + \$14{,}000 + \$14{,}000) - \$42{,}000 = \$28{,}000$$

For project B:

$$(\$28{,}000 + \$12{,}000 + \$10{,}000 + \$10{,}000 + \$10{,}000) - \$45{,}000 = \$25{,}000$$

The net present values for projects A and B at the 10% cost of capital are $11,071 and $10,924, respectively (from Figure 10.2). Because the IRR is the discount rate for which net present value equals zero, the IRRs (from Figure 10.3) of 19.9% for project A and 21.7% for project B result in $0 NPVs. The three sets of coordinates for each of the projects are summarized in Table 10.4.

Plotting the data from Table 10.4 results in the net present value profiles for projects A and B shown in Figure 10.4. The figure reveals three important facts:

1. The IRR of project B is greater than the IRR of project A, so managers using the IRR method to rank projects will always choose B over A if both projects are acceptable.

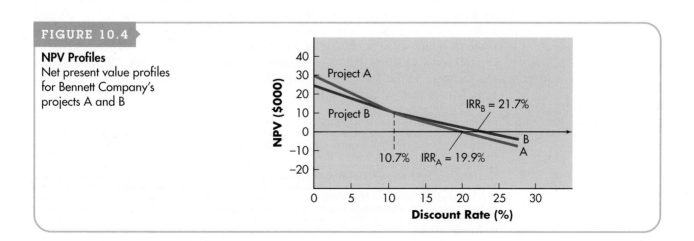

FIGURE 10.4

NPV Profiles
Net present value profiles for Bennett Company's projects A and B

2. The NPV of project A is sometimes higher and sometimes lower than the NPV of project B; thus, the NPV method will not consistently rank A above B or vice versa. The NPV ranking will depend on the firm's cost of capital.

3. When the cost of capital is approximately 10.7%, projects A and B have identical NPVs.

The cost of capital for Bennett Company is 10%, and at that rate project A has a higher NPV than project B (the red line is above the blue line in Figure 10.4 when the discount rate is 10%). Therefore, the NPV and IRR methods rank the two projects differently. If Bennett's cost of capital were a little higher, say 12%, the NPV method would rank project B over project A and there would be no conflict in the rankings provided by the NPV and IRR approaches.

CONFLICTING RANKINGS

conflicting rankings
Conflicts in the ranking given a project by NPV and IRR, resulting from *differences in the magnitude and timing of cash flows.*

intermediate cash inflows
Cash inflows received prior to the termination of a project.

Ranking different investment opportunities is an important consideration when projects are mutually exclusive or when capital rationing is necessary. When projects are mutually exclusive, ranking enables the firm to determine which project is best from a financial standpoint. When capital rationing is necessary, ranking projects will provide a logical starting point for determining which group of projects to accept. As we'll see, **conflicting rankings** using NPV and IRR result from *differences in the reinvestment rate assumption, the timing of each project's cash flows, and the magnitude of the initial investment.*

Reinvestment Assumption

One underlying cause of conflicting rankings is different implicit assumptions about the *reinvestment* of **intermediate cash inflows**—cash inflows received prior to the termination of a project. NPV assumes that intermediate cash inflows are reinvested at the cost of capital, whereas IRR assumes that intermediate cash inflows are reinvested at a rate equal to the project's IRR.[4] These differing assumptions can be demonstrated with an example.

Example 10.11 ▶
A project requiring a $170,000 initial investment is expected to provide operating cash inflows of $52,000, $78,000, and $100,000 at the end of each of the next 3 years. The NPV of the project (at the firm's 10% cost of capital) is $16,867 and its IRR is 15%. Clearly, the project is acceptable (NPV = $16,867 > $0 and IRR = 15% > 10% cost of capital). Table 10.5 demonstrates calculation of the project's future value at the end of its 3-year life, assuming both a 10% (its cost of capital) and a 15% (its IRR) rate of return. A future value of $248,720 results from reinvestment at the 10% cost of capital, and a future value of $258,470 results from reinvestment at the 15% IRR.

---

4. To eliminate the reinvestment rate assumption of the IRR, some practitioners calculate the *modified internal rate of return (MIRR)*. The MIRR is found by converting each operating cash inflow to its future value measured at the end of the project's life and then summing the future values of all inflows to get the project's *terminal value*. Each future value is found by using the cost of capital, thereby eliminating the reinvestment rate criticism of the traditional IRR. The MIRR represents the discount rate that causes the terminal value just to equal the initial investment. Because it uses the cost of capital as the reinvestment rate the MIRR is generally viewed as a better measure of a project's true profitability than the IRR. Although this technique is frequently used in commercial real estate valuation and is a preprogrammed function on some financial calculators, its failure to resolve the issue of conflicting rankings and its theoretical inferiority to NPV have resulted in the MIRR receiving only limited attention and acceptance in the financial literature.

TABLE 10.5	Reinvestment Rate Comparisons for a Project[a]			
			Reinvestment rate	
	Operating cash inflows	Number of years earnings interest (t)	10% Future value	15% Future value
Year				
1	$ 52,000	2	$ 62,920	$ 68,770
2	78,000	1	85,800	89,700
3	100,000	0	100,000	100,000
		Future value end of year 3	$248,720	$258,470

NPV @ 10% = $16,867

IRR = 15%

[a]Initial investment in this project is $170,000.

If the future value in each case in Table 10.5 were viewed as the return received 3 years from today from the $170,000 initial investment, the cash flows would be those given in Table 10.6. The NPVs and IRRs in each case are shown below the cash flows in Table 10.6. You can see that at the 10% reinvestment rate, the NPV remains at $16,867; reinvestment at the 15% IRR produces an NPV of $24,418.

From this result, it should be clear that the NPV technique assumes reinvestment at the cost of capital (10% in this example). (Note that with reinvestment at 10%, the IRR would be 13.5%.) On the other hand, the IRR technique assumes an ability to reinvest intermediate cash inflows at the IRR. If reinvestment does not occur at this rate, the IRR will differ from 15%. Reinvestment at a rate lower than the IRR would result in an IRR lower than that calculated (at 13.5%, for example, if the reinvestment rate were only 10%). Reinvestment at a rate higher than the IRR would result in an IRR higher than that calculated.

In more depth

To read about *Modified Internal Rate of Return,* go to www.myfinancelab.com

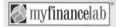 myfinancelab

TABLE 10.6	Project Cash Flows after Reinvestment	
	Reinvestment rate	
	10%	15%
Initial investment	$170,000	
Year	Operating cash inflows	
1	$ 0	$ 0
2	0	0
3	248,720	258,470
NPV @ 10%	$ 16,867	$ 24,418
IRR	13.5%	15.0%

Timing of the Cash Flow

Another reason why the IRR and NPV methods may provide different rankings for investment options has to do with differences in the timing of cash flows. Go back to the timelines for investments A and B in Figure 10.1 on page 392. The up-front investment required by each investment is similar, but after that the timing of each project's cash flows is quite different. Project B has a large cash inflow almost immediately (in Year 1), whereas Project A provides cash flows that are distributed evenly across time. Because so much of Project B's cash flows arrive early in its life (especially compared to the timing for Project A), the NPV of Project B will not be particularly sensitive to changes in the discount rate. Project A's NPV, on the other hand, will fluctuate more as the discount rate changes. In essence, Project B is somewhat akin to a short-term bond, whose price doesn't change much when interest rates move, and Project A is more like a long-term bond whose price fluctuates a great deal when rates change.

You can see this pattern if you review the NPV profiles for projects A and B in Figure 10.4 on page 405. The red line representing project A is considerably steeper than the blue line representing project B. At very low discount rates, project A has a higher NPV, but as the discount rate increases, the NPV of project A declines rapidly. When the discount rate is high enough, the NPV of project B overtakes that of project A.

We can summarize this discussion as follows. Because project A's cash flows arrive later than project B's cash flows do, when the firm's cost of capital is relatively low (to be specific, below about 10.7 percent), the NPV method will rank project A ahead of project B. At a higher cost of capital, the early arrival of project B's cash flows becomes more advantageous, and the NPV method will rank project B over project A. The differences in the timing of cash flows between the two projects does not affect the ranking provided by the IRR method, which always puts project B ahead of project A. Table 10.7 illustrates how the conflict in rankings between the NPV and IRR approaches depends on the firm's cost of capital.

Magnitude of the Initial Investment

Suppose someone offered you the following two investment options. You could invest $2 today and receive $3 tomorrow, or you could invest $1,000 today and receive $1,100 tomorrow. The first investment provides a return (an IRR) of 50 percent in just one day, a return that surely would surpass any reasonable hurdle rate. But after making this investment, you're only better off by $1. On the

TABLE 10.7	Ranking Projects A and B Using IRR and NPV Methods	
Method	Project A	Project B
IRR		✓
NPV		
if $r < 10.7\%$	✓	
if $r > 10.7\%$		✓

other hand, the second choice offers a return of 10 percent in a single day. That's far less than the first opportunity, but earning 10 percent in a single day is still a very high return. In addition, if you accept this investment, you will be $100 better off tomorrow than you were today.

Most people would choose the second option presented above, even though the rate of return on that option (10 percent) is far less than the rate offered by the first option (50 percent). They reason (correctly) that it is sometimes better to accept a lower return on a larger investment than to accept a very high return on a small investment. Said differently, most people know that they are better off taking the investment that pays them a $100 profit in just one day rather than the investment that generates just a $1 profit.[5]

The preceding example illustrates what is known as the scale (or magnitude) problem. The scale problem occurs when two projects are very different in terms of how much money is required to invest in each project. In these cases, the IRR and NPV methods may rank projects differently. The IRR approach (and the PI method) may favor small projects with high returns (like the $2 loan that turns into $3), whereas the NPV approach favors the investment that makes the investor the most money (like the $1,000 investment that yields $1,100 in one day). In the case of the Bennett Company's projects, the scale problem is not likely to be the cause of the conflict in project rankings because the initial investment required to fund each project is quite similar.

To summarize, it is important for financial managers to keep an eye out for conflicts in project rankings provided by the NPV and IRR methods, but differences in the magnitude and timing of cash inflows do not guarantee conflicts in ranking. In general, the greater the difference between the magnitude and timing of cash inflows, the greater the likelihood of conflicting rankings. Conflicts based on NPV and IRR can be reconciled computationally; to do so, one creates and analyzes an incremental project reflecting the difference in cash flows between the two mutually exclusive projects.

WHICH APPROACH IS BETTER?

Many companies use both the NPV and IRR techniques because current technology makes them easy to calculate. But it is difficult to choose one approach over the other because the theoretical and practical strengths of the approaches differ. Clearly, it is wise to evaluate NPV and IRR techniques from both theoretical and practical points of view.

Theoretical View

On a purely theoretical basis, NPV is the better approach to capital budgeting as a result of several factors. Most important, the NPV measures how much wealth a project creates (or destroys if the NPV is negative) for shareholders. Given that the financial manager's objective is to maximize shareholder wealth, the NPV approach has the clearest link to this objective and, therefore, is the "gold standard" for evaluating investment opportunities.

---

5. Note that the profitability index also provides an incorrect ranking in this example. The first option has a PI of 1.5 ($3 ÷ $2), and the second option's PI equals 1.1 ($1,100 ÷ $1,000). Just like the IRR, the PI suggests that the first option is better, but we know that the second option makes more money.

multiple IRRs
More than one IRR resulting from a capital budgeting project with a *nonconventional cash flow pattern;* the maximum number of IRRs for a project is equal to the number of sign changes in its cash flows.

In addition, certain mathematical properties may cause a project with a *nonconventional cash flow pattern* to have **multiple IRRs**—more than one IRR.[6] Mathematically, the maximum number of *real* roots to an equation is equal to its number of sign changes. Take an equation like $x^2 - 5x + 6 = 0$, which has two sign changes in its coefficients—from positive $(+x^2)$ to negative $(-5x)$ and then from negative $(-5x)$ to positive $(+6)$. If we factor the equation (remember factoring from high school math?), we get $(x - 2) \times (x - 3)$, which means that x can equal either 2 or 3—there are two correct values for x. Substitute them back into the equation, and you'll see that both values work.

This same outcome can occur when finding the IRR for projects with nonconventional cash flows, because they have more than one sign change. Clearly, when multiple IRRs occur for nonconventional cash flows, the analyst faces the time-consuming need to interpret their meanings so as to evaluate the project. The fact that such a challenge does not exist when using NPV enhances its theoretical superiority.

Practical View

Evidence suggests that in spite of the theoretical superiority of NPV, *financial managers use the IRR approach just as often as the NPV method.* The appeal of the IRR technique is due to the general disposition of business people to think in terms of *rates of return* rather than actual *dollar returns.* Because interest rates, profitability, and so on are most often expressed as annual rates of return, the use of IRR makes sense to financial decision makers. They tend to find NPV less intuitive because it does not measure benefits *relative to the amount invested.* Because a variety of techniques are available for avoiding the pitfalls of the IRR, its widespread use does not imply a lack of sophistication on the part of financial decision makers. Clearly, corporate financial analysts are responsible for identifying and resolving problems with the IRR before the decision makers use it as a decision technique.

> ## Matter of fact
>
> ### Which Methods Do Companies Actually Use?
> A recent survey asked chief financial officers (CFOs) what methods they used to evaluate capital investment projects. One interesting finding was that many companies use more than one of the approaches we've covered in this chapter. The most popular approaches by far were IRR and NPV, used by 76 percent and 75 percent (respectively) of the CFOs responding to the survey. These techniques enjoy wider use in larger firms, with the payback approach being more common in smaller firms.[7]

---

6. A conventional cash flow pattern is one in which the up-front cash flow is negative and all subsequent cash flows are positive. A nonconventional pattern occurs if the up-front cash flow is positive and subsequent cash flows are negative (for example, when a firm sells extended warranties and pays benefits later) or when the cash flows oscillate between positive and negative (as might occur when firms have to reinvest in a project to extend its life).

7. John R. Graham and Campball R. Harvey, "The Theory and Practice of Corporate Finance: Evidence from the Field," *Journal of Financial Economics* 60 (2001), pp. 187–243.

focus on ETHICS

Nonfinancial Considerations in Project Selection

in practice   The Kuwait Fund[a] for Economic Development, also known as the Kuwait Fund, was established in December 1961 with paid-up capital of $500 million as the first institution in the Middle East that took an active role in the international development efforts. The Kuwait Fund finances development projects and their feasibility studies in developing countries. In addition, the fund subscribes to the capital of international and regional development institutions. The fund's operations are focused primarily on the sectors of agriculture and irrigation, transport and communications, energy, industry, and water and sewage. One of the major objectives of the Kuwait Fund is to build a solid bridge of friendship and solidarity between the state of Kuwait and the developing nations. The success of the Kuwait Fund in achieving this objective helped the state of Kuwait to get the necessary votes in the United Nations and the U.N. Security Council for the war against Iraq to liberate Kuwait in 1991.

The fund extends its assistance to different types of entities, which include:

- Central and provincial governments, public utilities, and other public corporations.
- Development institutions, whether international, regional or national and, in particular, development finance institutions.
- Corporate entities that undertake projects that are jointly owned by a number of developing countries, as well as mixed or private enterprises with corporate personality, and not oriented toward profit making.

The Kuwait Fund offers the following forms of assistance:

- Direct loans or the provision of guarantees.
- Providing grants-in-aid to finance technical, economic, and financial studies whether in relation to projects financed by the Kuwait Fund or otherwise.
- Subscription to the capital or contribution to the resources of development finance institutions.
- Subscription to the capital of eligible developmental enterprises.

During the fiscal year 2008–2009, the Kuwait Fund financed up to 754 projects with a total value of about $15 billion. All these projects were financed at a required rate of return or internal rate of return lower than the cost of capital. The fund's total losses for the fiscal year 2008–2009 amounted to about $904 million, resulting mainly from unrealized loss on investments held for trading. The value of the fund's total assets decreased by about $952 million by the end of the current fiscal period, equivalent to 6.2 percent of total assets for that year, amounting to about $15.4 billion.

▶ *What are the potential benefits to the state of Kuwait of the ethical behavior of the Kuwait Fund?*

▶ *What are the risks and costs associated with the objectives of the Kuwait Fund?*

▶ *After the liberation of Kuwait and the end of Saddam Hussein's leadership, do you think that the Kuwait Fund should continue to follow the same capital budgeting principles?*

[a]The Kuwait Fund, **www.kuwait-fund.org**

In addition, decision makers should keep in mind that nonfinancial considerations may be important elements in project selection, as discussed in the *Focus on Ethics* box.

→ REVIEW QUESTIONS

10–10 How is a *net present value profile* used to compare projects? What causes conflicts in the ranking of projects via net present value and internal rate of return?

10–11 Does the assumption concerning the reinvestment of intermediate cash inflow tend to favor NPV or IRR? In practice, which technique is preferred and why?

Summary

FOCUS ON VALUE

The financial manager must apply appropriate decision techniques to assess whether proposed investment projects create value. Net present value (NPV) and internal rate of return (IRR) are the generally preferred capital budgeting techniques. Both use the cost of capital as the required return. The appeal of NPV and IRR stems from the fact that both indicate whether a proposed investment creates or destroys shareholder value.

NPV clearly indicates the expected dollar amount of wealth creation from a proposed project, whereas IRR only provides the same accept-or-reject decision as NPV. As a consequence of some fundamental differences, NPV and IRR do not necessarily rank projects in the same way. NPV is the theoretically preferred approach. In practice, however, IRR enjoys widespread use because of its intuitive appeal. Regardless, the application of NPV and IRR to good estimates of relevant cash flows should enable the financial manager to recommend projects that are consistent with the firm's goal of **maximizing shareholder wealth.**

REVIEW OF LEARNING GOALS

LG 1 **Understand the key elements of the capital budgeting process.** Capital budgeting techniques are the tools used to assess project acceptability and ranking. Applied to each project's relevant cash flows, they indicate which capital expenditures are consistent with the firm's goal of maximizing owners' wealth.

LG 2 **Calculate, interpret, and evaluate the payback period.** The payback period is the amount of time required for the firm to recover its initial investment, as calculated from cash inflows. Shorter payback periods are preferred. The payback period is relatively easy to calculate, has simple intuitive appeal, considers cash flows, and measures risk exposure. Its weaknesses include lack of linkage to the wealth maximization goal, failure to consider time value explicitly, and the fact that it ignores cash flows that occur after the payback period.

LG 3 **Calculate, interpret, and evaluate the net present value (NPV) and economic value added (EVA).** Because it gives explicit consideration to the time value of money, NPV is considered a sophisticated capital budgeting technique. NPV measures the amount of value created by a given project; only positive NPV projects are acceptable. The rate at which cash flows are discounted in calculating NPV is called the discount rate, required return, cost of capital, or opportunity cost. By whatever name, this rate represents the minimum return that must be earned on a project to leave the firm's market value unchanged. The EVA method begins the same way that NPV does—by calculating a project's net cash flows. However, the EVA approach subtracts from those cash flows a charge that is designed to capture the return that the firm's investors demand on the project. That is, the EVA calculation asks whether a project generates positive cash flows above and beyond what investors demand. If so, then the project is worth undertaking.

LG 4   **Calculate, interpret, and evaluate the internal rate of return (IRR).** Like NPV, IRR is a sophisticated capital budgeting technique. IRR is the compound annual rate of return that the firm will earn by investing in a project and receiving the given cash inflows. By accepting only those projects with IRRs in excess of the firm's cost of capital, the firm should enhance its market value and the wealth of its owners. Both NPV and IRR yield the same accept–reject decisions, but they often provide conflicting rankings.

LG 5   **Use net present value profiles to compare NPV and IRR techniques.** A net present value profile is a graph that depicts projects' NPVs for various discount rates. The NPV profile is prepared by developing a number of "discount rate–net present value" coordinates (including discount rates of 0 percent, the cost of capital, and the IRR for each project) and then plotting them on the same set of discount rate–NPV axes.

LG 6   **Discuss NPV and IRR in terms of conflicting rankings and the theoretical and practical strengths of each approach.** Conflicting rankings of projects frequently emerge from NPV and IRR as a result of differences in the reinvestment rate assumption, as well as the magnitude and timing of cash flows. NPV assumes reinvestment of intermediate cash inflows at the more conservative cost of capital; IRR assumes reinvestment at the project's IRR. On a purely theoretical basis, NPV is preferred over IRR because NPV assumes the more conservative reinvestment rate and does not exhibit the mathematical problem of multiple IRRs that often occurs when IRRs are calculated for nonconventional cash flows. In practice, the IRR is more commonly used because it is consistent with the general preference of business professionals for rates of return, and corporate financial analysts can identify and resolve problems with the IRR before decision makers use it.

Opener-in-Review

The chapter opener described the establishment of a dessert shop in Cairo, Egypt. The owners did some capital budgeting calculations to assess the profitability of their idea.

a. Based on the given numbers, what is the monthly revenue needed to reach the 30,000 EGP cash inflow in the first year? If the shop manages to sell 100 items per day on 30 working days per month, how much profit is needed per item to reach the 30,000 EGP net cash inflow?

b. The chapter opener lists other figures the two owners have calculated to assess the profitability of their project. Using these figures and the techniques introduced in this chapter, calculate NPV, IRR, and payback period. Are the figures calculated by the owners correct?

Self-Test Problem   (Solutions in Appendix)

LG 2 **LG 3** **ST10–1** **All techniques with NPV profile—Mutually exclusive projects**   Fitch Industries
LG 4 **LG 5** **LG 6**   is in the process of choosing the better of two equal-risk, mutually exclusive capital
expenditure projects—M and N. The relevant cash flows for each project are shown
in the following table. The firm's cost of capital is 14%.

	Project M	Project N
Initial investment (CF_0)	$28,500	$27,000
Year (t)	Cash inflows (CF_t)	
1	$10,000	$11,000
2	10,000	10,000
3	10,000	9,000
4	10,000	8,000

a. Calculate each project's *payback period*.
b. Calculate the *net present value (NPV)* for each project.
c. Calculate the *internal rate of return (IRR)* for each project.
d. Summarize the preferences dictated by each measure you calculated, and
    indicate which project you would recommend. Explain why.
e. Draw the *net present value profiles* for these projects on the same set of
    axes, and explain the circumstances under which a conflict in rankings
    might exist.

Warm-Up Exercises   All problems are available in myfinancelab.

LG 2 **E10–1**   Elysian Fields, Inc., uses a maximum payback period of 6 years and currently must
choose between two mutually exclusive projects. Project Hydrogen requires an initial outlay of $25,000; project Helium requires an initial outlay of $35,000. Using
the expected cash inflows given for each project in the following table, calculate
each project's *payback period*. Which project meets Elysian's standards?

	Expected cash inflows	
Year	Hydrogen	Helium
1	$6,000	$7,000
2	6,000	7,000
3	8,000	8,000
4	4,000	5,000
5	3,500	5,000
6	2,000	4,000

LG 3   **E10–2**   Herky Foods is considering acquisition of a new wrapping machine. The initial investment is estimated at $1.25 million, and the machine will have a 5-year life with no salvage value. Using a 6% discount rate, determine the *net present value (NPV)* of the machine given its expected operating cash inflows shown in the following table. Based on the project's NPV, should Herky make this investment?

Year	Cash inflow
1	$400,000
2	375,000
3	300,000
4	350,000
5	200,000

LG 3   **E10–3**   Axis Corp. is considering investment in the best of two mutually exclusive projects. Project Kelvin involves an overhaul of the existing system; it will cost $45,000 and generate cash inflows of $20,000 per year for the next 3 years. Project Thompson involves replacement of the existing system; it will cost $275,000 and generate cash inflows of $60,000 per year for 6 years. Using an 8% cost of capital, calculate each project's NPV, and make a recommendation based on your findings.

LG 4   **E10–4**   Billabong Tech uses the *internal rate of return (IRR)* to select projects. Calculate the IRR for each of the following projects and recommend the best project based on this measure. Project T-Shirt requires an initial investment of $15,000 and generates cash inflows of $8,000 per year for 4 years. Project Board Shorts requires an initial investment of $25,000 and produces cash inflows of $12,000 per year for 5 years.

LG 4   LG 5   **E10–5**   Cooper Electronics uses *NPV profiles* to visually evaluate competing projects. Key data for the two projects under consideration are given in the following table. Using these data, graph, on the same set of axes, the NPV profiles for each project using discount rates of 0%, 8%, and the IRR.

	Terra	Firma
Initial investment	$30,000	$25,000
Year	Operating cash inflows	
1	$ 7,000	$6,000
2	10,000	9,000
3	12,000	9,000
4	10,000	8,000

Problems   All problems are available in [myfinancelab].

LG 2   **P10–1**   **Payback period**   Jordan Enterprises is considering a capital expenditure that requires an initial investment of $42,000 and returns after-tax cash inflows of $7,000 per year for 10 years. The firm has a maximum acceptable payback period of 8 years.
  a. Determine the *payback period* for this project.
  b. Should the company accept the project? Why or why not?

LG 2   **P10–2**   **Payback comparisons**   Nova Products has a 5-year maximum acceptable payback period. The firm is considering the purchase of a new machine and must choose between two alternative ones. The first machine requires an initial investment of $14,000 and generates annual after-tax cash inflows of $3,000 for each of the next 7 years. The second machine requires an initial investment of $21,000 and provides an annual cash inflow after taxes of $4,000 for 20 years.

   a. Determine the *payback period* for each machine.
   b. Comment on the acceptability of the machines, assuming that they are independent projects.
   c. Which machine should the firm accept? Why?
   d. Do the machines in this problem illustrate any of the weaknesses of using payback? Discuss.

LG 2   **P10–3**   **Choosing between two projects with acceptable payback periods**   Shell Camping Gear, Inc., is considering two mutually exclusive projects. Each requires an initial investment of $100,000. John Shell, president of the company, has set a maximum payback period of 4 years. The after-tax cash inflows associated with each project are shown in the following table:

	Cash inflows (CF_t)	
Year	Project A	Project B
1	$10,000	$40,000
2	20,000	30,000
3	30,000	20,000
4	40,000	10,000
5	20,000	20,000

   a. Determine the *payback period* of each project.
   b. Because they are mutually exclusive, Shell must choose one. Which should the company invest in?
   c. Explain why one of the projects is a better choice than the other.

Personal Finance Problem

LG 2   **P10–4**   **Long-term investment decision, payback method**   Bill Williams has the opportunity to invest in project A that costs $9,000 today and promises to pay annual end-of-year payments of $2,200, $2,500, $2,500, $2,000, and $1,800 over the next 5 years. Or, Bill can invest $9,000 in project B that promises to pay annual end-of-year payments of $1,500, $1,500, $1,500, $3,500, and $4,000 over the next 5 years.

   a. How long will it take for Bill to recoup his initial investment in project A?
   b. How long will it take for Bill to recoup his initial investment in project B?
   c. Using the *payback period,* which project should Bill choose?
   d. Do you see any problems with his choice?

LG 3   **P10–5**   **NPV**   Calculate the *net present value (NPV)* for the following 20-year projects. Comment on the acceptability of each. Assume that the firm has an opportunity cost of 14%.

   a. Initial investment is $10,000; cash inflows are $2,000 per year.
   b. Initial investment is $25,000; cash inflows are $3,000 per year.
   c. Initial investment is $30,000; cash inflows are $5,000 per year.

LG 3   **P10–6**   **NPV for varying costs of capital**   Dane Cosmetics is evaluating a new fragrance-mixing machine. The machine requires an initial investment of $24,000 and will generate after-tax cash inflows of $5,000 per year for 8 years. For each of the costs of capital listed, (1) calculate the *net present value (NPV)*, (2) indicate whether to accept or reject the machine, and (3) explain your decision.
   a.   The cost of capital is 10%.
   b.   The cost of capital is 12%.
   c.   The cost of capital is 14%.

LG 3   **P10–7**   **Net present value—Independent projects**   Using a 14% cost of capital, calculate the *net present value* for each of the independent projects shown in the following table, and indicate whether each is acceptable.

	Project A	Project B	Project C	Project D	Project E
Initial investment (CF_0)	$26,000	$500,000	$170,000	$950,000	$80,000
Year (t)			Cash inflows (CF_t)		
1	$4,000	$100,000	$20,000	$230,000	$ 0
2	4,000	120,000	19,000	230,000	0
3	4,000	140,000	18,000	230,000	0
4	4,000	160,000	17,000	230,000	20,000
5	4,000	180,000	16,000	230,000	30,000
6	4,000	200,000	15,000	230,000	0
7	4,000		14,000	230,000	50,000
8	4,000		13,000	230,000	60,000
9	4,000		12,000		70,000
10	4,000		11,000		

LG 3   **P10–8**   **NPV**   Simes Innovations, Inc., is negotiating to purchase exclusive rights to manufacture and market a solar-powered toy car. The car's inventor has offered Simes the choice of either a one-time payment of $1,500,000 today or a series of five year-end payments of $385,000.
   a.   If Simes has a cost of capital of 9%, which form of payment should it choose?
   b.   What yearly payment would make the two offers identical in value at a cost of capital of 9%?
   c.   Would your answer to part **a** of this problem be different if the yearly payments were made at the beginning of each year? Show what difference, if any, that change in timing would make to the present value calculation.
   d.   The after-tax cash inflows associated with this purchase are projected to amount to $250,000 per year for 15 years. Will this factor change the firm's decision about how to fund the initial investment?

LG 3   **P10–9**   **NPV and maximum return**   A firm can purchase a fixed asset for a $13,000 initial investment. The asset generates an annual after-tax cash inflow of $4,000 for 4 years.
   a.   Determine the *net present value (NPV)* of the asset, assuming that the firm has a 10% cost of capital. Is the project acceptable?
   b.   Determine the maximum required rate of return (closest whole-percentage rate) that the firm can have and still accept the asset. Discuss this finding in light of your response in part **a**.

LG 3   **P10–10**   **NPV—Mutually exclusive projects**   Hook Industries is considering the replacement of one of its old drill presses. Three alternative replacement presses are under consideration. The relevant cash flows associated with each are shown in the following table. The firm's cost of capital is 15%.

	Press A	Press B	Press C
Initial investment (CF_0)	$85,000	$60,000	$130,000
Year (t)		Cash inflows (CF_t)	
1	$18,000	$12,000	$50,000
2	18,000	14,000	30,000
3	18,000	16,000	20,000
4	18,000	18,000	20,000
5	18,000	20,000	20,000
6	18,000	25,000	30,000
7	18,000	—	40,000
8	18,000	—	50,000

a. Calculate the *net present value (NPV)* of each press.
b. Using NPV, evaluate the acceptability of each press.
c. Rank the presses from best to worst using NPV.
d. Calculate the *profitability index (PI)* for each press.
e. Rank the presses from best to worst using *PI*.

Personal Finance Problem

LG 3   **P10–11**   **Long-term investment decision, NPV method**   Jenny Jenks has researched the financial pros and cons of entering into an elite MBA program at her state university. The tuition and needed books for a master's program will have an upfront cost of $100,000. On average, a person with an MBA degree earns an extra $20,000 per year over a business career of 40 years. Jenny feels that her opportunity cost of capital is 6%. Given her estimates, find the *net present value (NPV)* of entering this MBA program. Are the benefits of further education worth the associated costs?

LG 2   **LG 3**   **P10–12**   **Payback and NPV**   Neil Corporation has three projects under consideration. The cash flows for each project are shown in the following table. The firm has a 16% cost of capital.

	Project A	Project B	Project C
Initial investment (CF_0)	$40,000	$40,000	$40,000
Year (t)		Cash inflows (CF_t)	
1	$13,000	$ 7,000	$19,000
2	13,000	10,000	16,000
3	13,000	13,000	13,000
4	13,000	16,000	10,000
5	13,000	19,000	7,000

a. Calculate each project's *payback period*. Which project is preferred according to this method?
b. Calculate each project's *net present value (NPV)*. Which project is preferred according to this method?
c. Comment on your findings in parts **a** and **b**, and recommend the best project. Explain your recommendation.

LG 3   **P10–13**   **NPV and EVA**   A project costs $2.5 million up front and will generate cash flows in perpetuity of $240,000. The firm's cost of capital is 9%.
a. Calculate the project's NPV.
b. Calculate the annual EVA in a typical year.
c. Calculate the overall project EVA and compare to your answer in part **a**.

LG 4   **P10–14**   **Internal rate of return**   For each of the projects shown in the following table, calculate the *internal rate of return (IRR)*. Then indicate, for each project, the maximum cost of capital that the firm could have and still find the IRR acceptable.

	Project A	Project B	Project C	Project D
Initial investment (CF_0)	$90,000	$490,000	$20,000	$240,000
Year (t)		Cash inflows (CF_t)		
1	$20,000	$150,000	$7,500	$120,000
2	25,000	150,000	7,500	100,000
3	30,000	150,000	7,500	80,000
4	35,000	150,000	7,500	60,000
5	40,000	—	7,500	—

LG 4   **P10–15**   **IRR—Mutually exclusive projects**   Bell Manufacturing is attempting to choose the better of two mutually exclusive projects for expanding the firm's warehouse capacity. The relevant cash flows for the projects are shown in the following table. The firm's cost of capital is 15%.

	Project X	Project Y
Initial investment (CF_0)	$500,000	$325,000
Year (t)	Cash inflows (CF_t)	
1	$100,000	$140,000
2	120,000	120,000
3	150,000	95,000
4	190,000	70,000
5	250,000	50,000

a. Calculate the *IRR* to the nearest whole percent for each of the projects.
b. Assess the acceptability of each project on the basis of the IRRs found in part **a**.
c. Which project, on this basis, is preferred?

Personal Finance Problem

LG 4   **P10–16**   **Long-term investment decision, IRR method**   Billy and Mandy Jones have $25,000 to invest. On average, they do not make any investment that will not return at least 7.5% per year. They have been approached with an investment opportunity that requires $25,000 upfront and has a payout of $6,000 at the end of each of the next 5 years. Using the *internal rate of return (IRR)* method and their requirements, determine whether Billy and Mandy should undertake the investment.

LG 4   **P10–17**   **IRR, investment life, and cash inflows**   Oak Enterprises accepts projects earning more than the firm's 15% cost of capital. Oak is currently considering a 10-year project that provides annual cash inflows of $10,000 and requires an initial investment of $61,450. (*Note:* All amounts are after taxes.)

   a. Determine the *IRR* of this project. Is it acceptable?

   b. Assuming that the cash inflows continue to be $10,000 per year, how many *additional years* would the flows have to continue to make the project acceptable (that is, to make it have an IRR of 15%)?

   c. With the given life, initial investment, and cost of capital, what is the minimum annual cash inflow that the firm should accept?

LG 3   **LG** 4   **P10–18**   **NPV and IRR**   Benson Designs has prepared the following estimates for a long-term project it is considering. The initial investment is $18,250, and the project is expected to yield after-tax cash inflows of $4,000 per year for 7 years. The firm has a 10% cost of capital.

   a. Determine the *net present value (NPV)* for the project.

   b. Determine the *internal rate of return (IRR)* for the project.

   c. Would you recommend that the firm accept or reject the project? Explain your answer.

LG 3   **LG** 4   **P10–19**   **NPV, with rankings**   Botany Bay, Inc., a maker of casual clothing, is considering four projects. Because of past financial difficulties, the company has a high cost of capital at 15%. Which of these projects would be acceptable under those cost circumstances?

	Project A	Project B	Project C	Project D
Initial investment (CF_0)	$50,000	$100,000	$80,000	$180,000
Year (t)		Cash inflows (CF_t)		
1	$20,000	$35,000	$20,000	$100,000
2	20,000	50,000	40,000	80,000
3	20,000	50,000	60,000	60,000

   a. Calculate the *NPV* of each project, using a cost of capital of 15%.

   b. Rank acceptable projects by NPV.

   c. Calculate the *IRR* of each project, and use it to determine the highest cost of capital at which all of the projects would be acceptable.

LG 2   LG 3   **P10–20** **All techniques, conflicting rankings** Nicholson Roofing Materials, Inc., is consid-
LG 4   ering two mutually exclusive projects, each with an initial investment of $150,000.
          The company's board of directors has set a maximum 4-year payback requirement
          and has set its cost of capital at 9%. The cash inflows associated with the two
          projects are shown in the following table.

	Cash inflows (CF_t)	
Year	Project A	Project B
1	$45,000	$75,000
2	45,000	60,000
3	45,000	30,000
4	45,000	30,000
5	45,000	30,000
6	45,000	30,000

a. Calculate the *payback period* for each project.
b. Calculate the *NPV* of each project at 0%.
c. Calculate the *NPV* of each project at 9%.
d. Derive the *IRR* of each project.
e. Rank the projects by each of the techniques used. Make and justify a recommendation.

LG 2   LG 3   **P10–21** **Payback, NPV, and IRR** Rieger International is attempting to evaluate the feasi-
LG 4   bility of investing $95,000 in a piece of equipment that has a 5-year life. The firm
          has estimated the *cash inflows* associated with the proposal as shown in the
          following table. The firm has a 12% cost of capital.

Year (t)	Cash inflows (CF_t)
1	$20,000
2	25,000
3	30,000
4	35,000
5	40,000

a. Calculate the *payback period* for the proposed investment.
b. Calculate the *net present value (NPV)* for the proposed investment.
c. Calculate the *internal rate of return (IRR)*, rounded to the nearest whole percent,
   for the proposed investment.
d. Evaluate the acceptability of the proposed investment using NPV and IRR. What
   recommendation would you make relative to implementation of the project?
   Why?

LG 3   LG 4   **P10–22** **NPV, IRR, and NPV profiles** Thomas Company is considering two mutually exclu-
LG 5   sive projects. The firm, which has a 12% cost of capital, has estimated its cash flows
          as shown in the following table.

	Project A	Project B
Initial investment (CF_0)	$130,000	$85,000
Year (t)	Cash inflows (CF_t)	
1	$25,000	$40,000
2	35,000	35,000
3	45,000	30,000
4	50,000	10,000
5	55,000	5,000

a. Calculate the *NPV* of each project, and assess its acceptability.
b. Calculate the *IRR* for each project, and assess its acceptability.
c. Draw the *NPV profiles* for both projects on the same set of axes.
d. Evaluate and discuss the rankings of the two projects on the basis of your findings in parts **a, b,** and **c.**
e. Explain your findings in part **d** in light of the pattern of cash inflows associated with each project.

P10–23   All techniques—Decision among mutually exclusive investments   Pound Industries is attempting to select the best of three mutually exclusive projects. The initial investment and after-tax cash inflows associated with these projects are shown in the following table.

Cash flows	Project A	Project B	Project C
Initial investment (CF_0)	$60,000	$100,000	$110,000
Cash inflows (CF_t), $t = 1$ to 5	$20,000	$ 31,500	$ 32,500

a. Calculate the *payback period* for each project.
b. Calculate the *net present value (NPV)* of each project, assuming that the firm has a cost of capital equal to 13%.
c. Calculate the *internal rate of return (IRR)* for each project.
d. Draw the *net present value profiles* for both projects on the same set of axes, and discuss any conflict in ranking that may exist between NPV and IRR.
e. Summarize the preferences dictated by each measure, and indicate which project you would recommend. Explain why.

P10–24   All techniques with NPV profile—Mutually exclusive projects   Projects A and B, of equal risk, are alternatives for expanding Rosa Company's capacity. The firm's cost of capital is 13%. The cash flows for each project are shown in the following table.
a. Calculate each project's *payback period*.
b. Calculate the *net present value (NPV)* for each project.
c. Calculate the *internal rate of return (IRR)* for each project.
d. Draw the *net present value profiles* for both projects on the same set of axes, and discuss any conflict in ranking that may exist between NPV and IRR.
e. Summarize the preferences dictated by each measure, and indicate which project you would recommend. Explain why.

	Project A	Project B
Initial investment (CF_0)	$80,000	$50,000
Year (t)	Cash inflows (CF_t)	
1	$15,000	$15,000
2	20,000	15,000
3	25,000	15,000
4	30,000	15,000
5	35,000	15,000

LG 6   **P10–25**   **Integrative—Multiple IRRs**   Froogle Enterprises is evaluating an unusual investment project. What makes the project unusual is the stream of cash inflows and outflows shown in the following table:

Year	Cash flow
0	$ 200,000
1	−920,000
2	1,582,000
3	−1,205,200
4	343,200

a. Why is it difficult to calculate the *payback period* for this project?

b. Calculate the investment's net present value at each of the following discount rates: 0%, 5%, 10%, 15%, 20%, 25%, 30%, 35%.

c. What does your answer to part **b** tell you about this project's *IRR?*

d. Should Froogle invest in this project if its cost of capital is 5%? What if the cost of capital is 15%?

e. In general, when faced with a project like this, how should a firm decide whether to invest in the project or reject it?

LG 3   LG 4   **P10–26**   **Integrative—Conflicting Rankings**   The High-Flying Growth Company (HFGC) has
LG 5   been growing very rapidly in recent years, making its shareholders rich in the process. The average annual rate of return on the stock in the last few years has been 20%, and HFGC managers believe that 20% is a reasonable figure for the firm's cost of capital. To sustain a high growth rate, the HFGC CEO argues that the company must continue to invest in projects that offer the highest rate of return possible. Two projects are currently under review. The first is an expansion of the firm's production capacity, and the second project involves introducing one of the firm's existing products into a new market. Cash flows from each project appear in the following table.

a. Calculate the NPV, IRR, and PI for both projects.

b. Rank the projects based on their NPVs, IRRs, and PIs.

c. Do the rankings in part **b** agree or not? If not, why not?

d. The firm can only afford to undertake one of these investments, and the CEO favors the product introduction because it offers a higher rate of return (that is, a higher IRR) than the plant expansion. What do you think the firm should do? Why?

Year	Plant expansion	Product introduction
0	−$3,500,000	−$500,000
1	1,500,000	250,000
2	2,000,000	350,000
3	2,500,000	375,000
4	2,750,000	425,000

LG 1   LG 6   P10–27   ETHICS PROBLEM Gap, Inc., is trying to incorporate human resource and supplier considerations into its management decision making. Here is Gap's report of findings from a recent Social Responsibility Report:

> Because factory owners sometimes try to hide violations, Gap emphasizes training for factory managers. However, due to regional differences, the training varies from one site to another. The report notes that 10 to 25 percent of workers in China, Taiwan, and Saipan have been harassed and humiliated. Less than half of the factories in sub-Saharan Africa have adequate worker safety regulations and infrastructure. In Mexico, Latin America, and the Caribbean, 25 to 50 percent of the suppliers fail to pay even the minimum wage.

Calvert Group, Ltd., a mutual fund family that focuses on "socially responsible investing," had this to say about the impact of Gap's report:

> With revenues of $15.9 billion and over 300,000 employees worldwide, Gap leads the U.S. apparel sector and has contracts with over 3,000 factories globally. Calvert has been in dialogue with Gap for about five years, the last two as part of the Working Group.
>
> Gap's supplier monitoring program focuses on remediation, because its suppliers produce for multiple apparel companies and would likely move their capacity to different clients rather than adopt conditions deemed too demanding. About one-third of the factories Gap examined comfortably met Gap's criteria, another third had barely acceptable conditions, and the final third missed the minimum standards. Gap terminated contracts with 136 factories where it found conditions to be beyond remediation.
>
> Increased transparency and disclosure are crucial in measuring a company's commitment to raising human rights standards and improving the lives of workers. Gap's report is an important first step in the direction of a model format that other companies can adapt.[8]

If Gap were to aggressively pursue renegotiations with suppliers, based on this report, what is the likely effect on Gap's expenses in the next 5 years? In your opinion, what would be the impact on its stock price in the immediate future? After 10 years?

---

8. www.calvert.com/news_newsArticle.asp?article=4612&image=cn.gif&keepleftnav=Calvert+News

Spreadsheet Exercise

The Drillago Company is involved in searching for locations in which to drill for oil. The firm's current project requires an initial investment of $15 million and has an estimated life of 10 years. The expected future cash inflows for the project are as shown in the following table:

Year	Cash inflows
1	$ 600,000
2	1,000,000
3	1,000,000
4	2,000,000
5	3,000,000
6	3,500,000
7	4,000,000
8	6,000,000
9	8,000,000
10	12,000,000

The firm's current cost of capital is 13%.

TO DO

Create a spreadsheet to answer the following:

a. Calculate the project's *net present value (NPV)*. Is the project acceptable under the NPV technique? Explain.
b. Calculate the project's *internal rate of return (IRR)*. Is the project acceptable under the IRR technique? Explain.
c. In this case, did the two methods produce the same results? Generally, is there a preference between the NPV and IRR techniques? Explain.
d. Calculate the *payback period* for the project. If the firm usually accepts projects that have payback periods between 1 and 7 years, is this project acceptable?

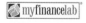 Visit **www.myfinancelab.com** for **Chapter Case: *Making Norwich Tool's Lathe Investment Decision,*** Group Exercises, and numerous online resources.

11 Capital Budgeting Cash Flows

Learning Goals

LG 1 Discuss the three major cash flow components.

LG 2 Discuss relevant cash flows, expansion versus replacement decisions, sunk costs and opportunity costs, and international capital budgeting.

LG 3 Calculate the initial investment associated with a proposed capital expenditure.

LG 4 Discuss the tax implications associated with the sale of an old asset.

LG 5 Find the relevant operating cash inflows associated with a proposed capital expenditure.

LG 6 Determine the terminal cash flow associated with a proposed capital expenditure.

Why This Chapter Matters to You

In your *professional* life

ACCOUNTING You need to understand capital budgeting cash flows to provide revenue, cost, depreciation, and tax data for use both in monitoring existing projects and in developing cash flows for proposed projects.

INFORMATION SYSTEMS You need to understand capital budgeting cash flows to maintain and facilitate the retrieval of cash flow data for both completed and existing projects.

MANAGEMENT You need to understand capital budgeting cash flows so that you will understand which cash flows are relevant in making decisions about proposals for acquiring additional production facilities, for new marketing programs, for new products, and for the expansion of existing product lines.

MARKETING You need to understand capital budgeting cash flows so that you can make revenue and cost estimates for proposals for new marketing programs, for new products, and for the expansion of existing product lines.

OPERATIONS You need to understand capital budgeting cash flows so that you can make revenue and cost estimates for proposals for the acquisition of new equipment and production facilities.

In your *personal* life

You are not mandated to provide financial statements prepared using GAAP, so you naturally focus on cash flows. When considering a major outflow of funds (for example, purchase of a house, funding of a college education), you can project the associated cash flows and use these estimates to assess the value and affordability of the assets and any associated future outlays.

Maintaining Its Project Inventory

As the largest publicly traded oil company in the world, ExxonMobil's long-term investments are at the heart of its ability to generate shareholder wealth. Its 2009 earnings of more than $19 billion resulted in a 16 percent return on capital invested. Through dividends and share repurchases, ExxonMobil returned $26 billion to its shareholders in 2009 and more than $150 billion over the previous five years.

To maintain its petroleum reserves, ExxonMobil must continually add to its inventory of discovered oil and gas resources. It holds exploration rights to 109 million undeveloped acres in 37 countries. Each year, the company initiates a number of megaprojects that add to its exploration rights, locate and "prove" additional reserves, or increase the productivity of currently producing wells.

Total capital and exploration expenditures in 2009 amounted to a record $27 billion. Within the next 5 years, ExxonMobil anticipates investing more than $125 billion. ExxonMobil has partnered with Qatar Petroleum to develop a global-scale petrochemical complex in Ras Laffan Industrial City, Qatar. The plant is expected to start up in late 2015, and it will include two 650,000 ton-per-year polyethylene plants, a 1.6 million-ton-per-year steam cracker, and a 700,000 ton-per-year ethylene glycol facility.

While Exxon is often able to bring in projects on or under budget, increasing costs could cause some future development projects to go over budget. Drilling and exploration costs are expected to rise. Recent high oil prices have led to a surge in demand for exploration, and the cost of drilling equipment and workers has jumped at least 15 percent a year during the last several years. Further complicating oil production efforts in the future will be an increase in the use of less-than-suitable oil sources, such as shale oil and tar sands.

Like ExxonMobil, every firm must evaluate the costs and returns of projects for expansion, asset replacement or renewal, research and development, advertising, and other areas that require a long-term commitment of funds in expectation of future returns. Chapter 11 explains how to identify the relevant cash outflows and inflows that must be considered in making major investment decisions.

LG 1   LG 2   ## 11.1 Relevant Cash Flows

relevant cash flows
The *incremental cash outflow (investment) and resulting subsequent inflows* associated with a proposed capital expenditure.

incremental cash flows
The *additional* cash flows—outflows or inflows—expected to result from a proposed capital expenditure.

Chapter 10 introduced the capital budgeting process and the techniques financial managers use for evaluating and selecting long-term investments. To evaluate investment opportunities, financial managers must determine the **relevant cash flows** associated with the project. These are the *incremental cash outflows (investment) and inflows (return)*. The **incremental cash flows** represent the *additional* cash flows—outflows or inflows—expected to result from a proposed capital expenditure. As noted in Chapter 4, cash flows rather than accounting figures are used because cash flows directly affect the firm's ability to pay bills and purchase assets. The nearby *Focus on Ethics* box discusses the accuracy of cash flow estimates and cites one reason that even well-estimated deals may not work out as planned.

The remainder of this chapter is devoted to the procedures for measuring the relevant cash flows associated with proposed capital expenditures.

MAJOR CASH FLOW COMPONENTS

The cash flows of any project may include three basic components: (1) an initial investment, (2) operating cash inflows, and (3) terminal cash flow. All projects—whether for expansion, replacement or renewal, or some other purpose—have the first two components. Some, however, lack the final component, terminal cash flow.

---

focus on ETHICS

A Question of Accuracy

in practice The process of capital budgeting based on projected cash flows has been a part of the investment decision process for more than 40 years. This procedure for evaluating investment opportunities works well when cash flows can be estimated with certainty, but in real-world corporate practice, many investment decisions involve a high degree of uncertainty. The decision is even more complicated when the project under consideration is the acquisition of another company or part of another company.

Because estimates of the cash flows from an investment project involve making assumptions about the future, they may be subject to considerable error. The problem becomes more complicated as the period of time under consideration becomes longer and when the project is unique in nature with no comparables. Other complications may arise involving accounting for additional

(extraordinary) cash flows—for example, the cost of litigation, compliance with tougher environmental standards, or the costs of disposal or recycling of an asset at the completion of the project.

All too often, the initial champagne celebration gives way once the final cost of a deal is tallied. In fact, taken as a whole, mergers and acquisitions in recent years have produced a disheartening *negative* 12 percent return on investment. While the financial data necessary to generate discounted cash flow estimates are ever more readily available, these days more attention is being paid to the accuracy of the numbers. Inspired in part by post-Enron focus on governance and the threat of shareholder lawsuits, board members have been pushing corporate managers to make a stronger case for the deals they propose. Says Glenn Gurtcheff, managing director and co-head of middle market M&A for Piper Jaffray & Co.,

"They're not just taking the company's audited and unaudited financial statements at face value; they are really diving into the numbers and trying to understand not just their accuracy, but what they mean in terms of trends."

If valuation has improved so much, why do analyses show that companies often overpay? The answer lies in the imperial CEO. Improvements in valuation techniques can be negated when the process deteriorates into a game of tweaking the numbers to justify a deal the CEO wants to do, regardless of price. This "make it work" form of capital budgeting often results in building the empire under the CEO's control at the expense of the firm's shareholders.

▶ *What would your options be when faced with the demands of an imperial CEO who expects you to "make it work"? Brainstorm several options.*

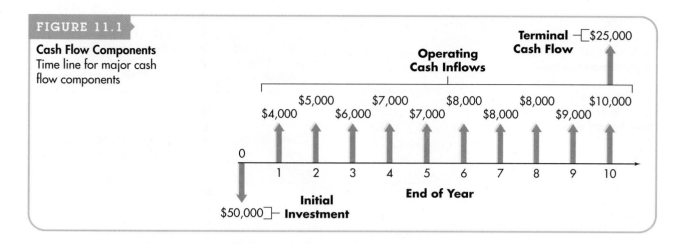

FIGURE 11.1

Cash Flow Components
Time line for major cash flow components

initial investment
The relevant cash outflow for a proposed project at time zero.

operating cash inflows
The incremental after-tax cash inflows resulting from implementation of a project during its life.

terminal cash flow
The after-tax nonoperating cash flow occurring in the final year of a project. It is usually attributable to liquidation of the project.

Figure 11.1 depicts on a time line the cash flows for a project. The **initial investment** for the proposed project is $50,000. This is the relevant cash outflow at time zero. The **operating cash inflows,** which are the incremental after-tax cash inflows resulting from implementation of the project during its life, gradually increase from $4,000 in its first year to $10,000 in its tenth and final year. The **terminal cash flow** is the after-tax nonoperating cash flow occurring in the final year of the project. It is usually attributable to liquidation of the project. In this case it is $25,000, received at the end of the project's 10-year life. Note that the terminal cash flow does *not* include the $10,000 operating cash inflow for year 10.

EXPANSION VERSUS REPLACEMENT DECISIONS

Developing relevant cash flow estimates is most straightforward in the case of *expansion decisions.* In this case, the initial investment, operating cash inflows, and terminal cash flow are merely the after-tax cash outflow and inflows associated with the proposed capital expenditure.

Identifying relevant cash flows for *replacement decisions* is more complicated, because the firm must identify the *incremental* cash outflow and inflows that would result from the proposed replacement. The initial investment in the case of replacement is the difference between the initial investment needed to acquire the new asset and any after-tax cash inflows expected from liquidation of the old asset. The operating cash inflows are the difference between the operating cash inflows from the new asset and those from the old asset. The terminal cash flow is the difference between the after-tax cash flows expected upon termination of the new and the old assets. These relationships are shown in Figure 11.2.

Actually, all capital budgeting decisions can be viewed as replacement decisions. *Expansion decisions are merely replacement decisions in which all cash flows from the old asset are zero.* In light of this fact, this chapter focuses primarily on replacement decisions.

SUNK COSTS AND OPPORTUNITY COSTS

When estimating the relevant cash flows associated with a proposed capital expenditure, the firm must recognize any sunk costs and opportunity costs. These costs are easy to mishandle or ignore, particularly when determining a project's

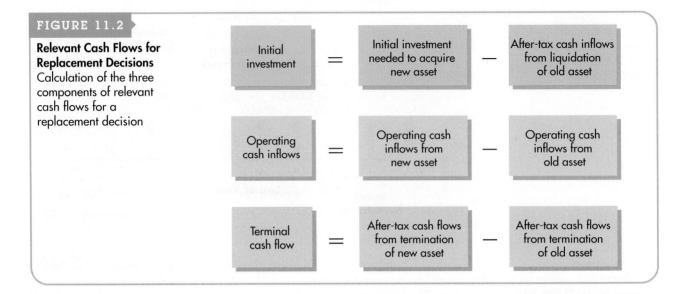

FIGURE 11.2

Relevant Cash Flows for Replacement Decisions
Calculation of the three components of relevant cash flows for a replacement decision

sunk costs
Cash outlays that have already been made (past outlays) and therefore have no effect on the cash flows relevant to a current decision.

opportunity costs
Cash flows that could be realized from the best alternative use of an owned asset.

incremental cash flows. **Sunk costs** are cash outlays that have already been made (past outlays) and therefore have no effect on the cash flows relevant to the current decision. As a result, *sunk costs should not be included in a project's incremental cash flows.*

Opportunity costs are cash flows that could be realized from the best alternative use of an owned asset. They therefore represent cash flows that *will not be realized* as a result of employing that asset in the proposed project. Because of this, any *opportunity costs should be included as cash outflows when one is determining a project's incremental cash flows.*

Example 11.1 ▶   Jankow Equipment is considering renewing its drill press X12, which it purchased 3 years earlier for $237,000, by retrofitting it with the computerized control system from an obsolete piece of equipment it owns. The obsolete equipment could be sold today for a high bid of $42,000, but without its computerized control system, it would be worth nothing. Jankow is in the process of estimating the labor and materials costs of retrofitting the system to drill press X12 and the benefits expected from the retrofit. The $237,000 cost of drill press X12 is a *sunk cost* because it represents an earlier cash outlay. It *would not be included* as a cash outflow when determining the cash flows relevant to the retrofit decision. Although Jankow owns the obsolete piece of equipment, the proposed use of its computerized control system represents an *opportunity cost* of $42,000—the highest price at which it could be sold today. This opportunity cost *would be included* as a cash outflow associated with using the computerized control system.

INTERNATIONAL CAPITAL BUDGETING AND LONG-TERM INVESTMENTS

Although the same basic capital budgeting principles are used for domestic and international projects, several additional factors must be addressed in evaluating foreign investment opportunities. International capital budgeting differs from the domestic version because (1) cash outflows and inflows occur in a foreign currency, and (2) foreign investments entail potentially significant political risk. Both of these risks can be minimized through careful planning.

Companies face both long-term and short-term *currency risks* related to both the invested capital and the cash flows resulting from it. Long-term currency risk can be minimized by financing the foreign investment at least partly in the local capital markets. This step ensures that the project's revenues, operating costs, and financing costs will be in the local currency. Likewise, the dollar value of short-term, local-currency cash flows can be protected by using special securities and strategies such as futures, forwards, and options market instruments.

Political risks can be minimized by using both operating and financial strategies. For example, by structuring the investment as a joint venture and selecting a well-connected local partner, the U.S. company can minimize the risk of its operations being seized or harassed. Companies also can protect themselves from having their investment returns blocked by local governments by structuring the financing of such investments as debt rather than as equity. Debt-service payments are legally enforceable claims, whereas equity returns (such as dividends) are not. Even if local courts do not support the claims of the U.S. company, the company can threaten to pursue its case in U.S. courts.

foreign direct investment
The transfer of capital, managerial, and technical assets to a foreign country.

In spite of the preceding difficulties, **foreign direct investment (FDI)**, which involves the transfer of capital, managerial, and technical assets to a foreign country, has surged in recent years. This is evident in the growing market values of foreign assets owned by U.S.–based companies and of foreign direct investment in the United States, particularly by British, Canadian, Dutch, German, and Japanese companies. Furthermore, foreign direct investment by U.S. companies seems to be accelerating. See the *Global Focus* box on page 432 for a discussion of recent foreign direct investment in China.

Matter of fact

FDI in the Middle East

According to the U.N. World Investment 2009 Report, foreign direct investment (FDI) in the Middle East fell by 24 percent to $68 billion in 2009. The report stated that cross-border mergers and acquisitions and Greenfield investments in the region involving large FDI were badly hit. Greenfield investments occur when corporations enter new markets to develop or expand production facilities. The FDI reductions have occurred in most of the region's countries, except Qatar, which showed an increase of 112 percent in 2009. Dubai was hit hard, showing a 71 percent decline of FDI. Saudi Arabia remained the largest recipient of FDI, with inflows reaching $36 billion. Also, the FDI outflows fell by 39 percent to $23 billion, $13 billion of the decrease coming from the United Arab Emirates.

→ REVIEW QUESTIONS

11–1 Why is it important to evaluate capital budgeting projects on the basis of *incremental cash flows*?

11–2 What three components of cash flow may exist for a given project? How can expansion decisions be treated as replacement decisions? Explain.

GLOBAL focus

Changes May Influence Future Investments in China

in practice Foreign direct investment in China soared in 2009. Not including banks, insurance, and securities, foreign direct investment amounted to $90 billion. China's economy has surged more than tenfold since 1980, the first year it allowed foreign investments, when money began pouring into factories on China's east coast.

China's trade surplus in 2009 was $196 billion. With a strong foreign exchange surplus, China is no longer desperate for capital from overseas but is now primarily interested in foreign skills and technologies. Prime Minister Wen Jiabao wants to steer investments toward the manufacturing of higher-value products and toward less-developed regions. Wen is giving tax breaks and promising speedy approvals for investments away from areas in the east, such as Shanghai and the Pearl River Delta.

Typical of foreign investors in China is Intel Capital, a subsidiary of **Intel Corporation.** As of the middle of 2010, Intel Capital's portfolio had $200 million invested in 25 Chinese companies. Intel Capital is no beginner at foreign investment; it has invested more than $4 billion in more than 1,000 companies around the world.

China allows three types of foreign investments: a *wholly foreign-owned enterprise* (WFOE) in which the firm is entirely funded with foreign capital; a *joint venture* in which the foreign partner must provide at least 25 percent of initial capital; and a *representative office* (RO), the most common and easily established entity, which cannot perform business activities that directly result in profits. Generally an RO is the first step in establishing a China presence and includes mechanisms for upgrading to a WFOE or joint venture.

As with any foreign investment, investing in China is not without risk. One potential risk facing foreign investors in China is that the communist government could decide to nationalize private companies. Many public companies in China are firms that were once owned by the communist government, such as China Life Insurance Company, and it is always possible that the communist government may decide that it wishes to own and control these companies again. The list of governments similar to China's that have nationalized private companies is fairly long. While there is no evidence that this will happen in China, it should be considered one of the risks.

▶ *Although China has been actively campaigning for foreign investment, how do you think having a communist government affects its foreign investment?*

11–3 What effect do *sunk costs* and *opportunity costs* have on a project's incremental cash flows?

11–4 How can *currency risk* and *political risk* be minimized when one is making *foreign direct investment?*

LG 3   **LG** 4   **11.2** Finding the Initial Investment

The term *initial investment* as used here refers to the relevant cash outflows to be considered when evaluating a prospective capital expenditure. Our discussion of capital budgeting will focus on projects with initial investments that occur at *time zero*—the time at which the expenditure is made. The initial investment is calculated by subtracting all cash inflows occurring at time zero from all cash outflows occurring at time zero.

The basic format for determining the initial investment is given in Table 11.1. The cash flows that must be considered when determining the initial investment associated with a capital expenditure are the installed cost of the new asset, the after-tax proceeds (if any) from the sale of an old asset, and the change (if any) in

TABLE 11.1	The Basic Format for Determining Initial Investment

Installed cost of new asset =
    Cost of new asset
    + Installation costs
− After-tax proceeds from sale of old asset =
    Proceeds from sale of old asset
    ∓ Tax on sale of old asset
± Change in net working capital
────────────────────────────────
Initial investment

cost of new asset
The net outflow necessary to acquire a new asset.

installation costs
Any added costs that are necessary to place an asset into operation.

installed cost of new asset
The *cost of new asset* plus its *installation costs;* equals the asset's depreciable value.

after-tax proceeds from sale of old asset
The difference between the old asset's sale proceeds and any applicable taxes or tax refunds related to its sale.

proceeds from sale of old asset
The cash inflows, net of any *removal* or *cleanup costs,* resulting from the sale of an existing asset.

tax on sale of old asset
Tax that depends on the relationship between the old asset's sale price and *book value* and on existing government tax rules.

net working capital. Note that if there are no installation costs and the firm is not replacing an existing asset, then the cost (purchase price) of the new asset, adjusted for any change in net working capital, is equal to the initial investment.

INSTALLED COST OF NEW ASSET

As shown in Table 11.1, the installed cost of the new asset is found by adding the cost of the new asset to its installation costs. The **cost of new asset** is the net out-flow that its acquisition requires. Usually, we are concerned with the acquisition of a fixed asset for which a definite purchase price is paid. **Installation costs** are any added costs that are necessary to place an asset into operation. The Internal Revenue Service (IRS) requires the firm to add installation costs to the purchase price of an asset to determine its depreciable value, which is expensed over a period of years. The **installed cost of new asset,** calculated by adding the *cost of new asset* to its *installation costs,* equals its depreciable value.

AFTER-TAX PROCEEDS FROM SALE OF OLD ASSET

Table 11.1 shows that the **after-tax proceeds from sale of old asset** decrease the firm's initial investment in the new asset. These proceeds are the difference between the old asset's sale proceeds and any applicable taxes or tax refunds related to its sale. The **proceeds from sale of old asset** are the net cash inflows it provides. This amount is net of any costs incurred in the process of removing the asset. Included in these *removal costs* are *cleanup costs,* such as those related to removal and disposal of chemical and nuclear wastes. These costs may not be trivial.

The proceeds from the sale of an old asset are normally subject to some type of tax.[1] This **tax on sale of old asset** depends on the relationship between its sale price and *book value* and on existing government tax rules.

---

1. A brief discussion of the tax treatment of ordinary and capital gains income was presented in Chapter 2. Because corporate capital gains and ordinary income are taxed at the same rate, for convenience, we do not differentiate between them in the following discussions.

book value
The strict accounting value of an asset, calculated by subtracting its accumulated depreciation from its installed cost.

Book Value

The **book value** of an asset is its strict accounting value. It can be calculated by using the following equation:

$$\text{Book value} = \text{Installed cost of asset} - \text{Accumulated depreciation} \quad (11.1)$$

Example 11.2 ▶

Hudson Industries, a small electronics company, 2 years ago acquired a machine tool with an installed cost of $100,000. The asset was being depreciated under MACRS using a 5-year recovery period. Table 4.2 (on page 117) shows that under MACRS for a 5-year recovery period, 20% and 32% of the installed cost would be depreciated in years 1 and 2, respectively. In other words, 52% (20% + 32%) of the $100,000 cost, or $52,000 (0.52 × $100,000), would represent the accumulated depreciation at the end of year 2. Substituting into Equation 11.1, we get

$$\text{Book value} = \$100,000 - \$52,000 = \underline{\$48,000}$$

The book value of Hudson's asset at the end of year 2 is therefore $48,000.

Basic Tax Rules

Three potential tax situations can occur when a firm sells an asset. These situations depend on the relationship between the asset's sale price and its book value. The two key forms of taxable income and their associated tax treatments are defined and summarized in Table 11.2. The assumed tax rates used throughout this text are noted in the final column. There are three possible tax situations. The asset may be sold (1) for more than its book value, (2) for its book value, or (3) for less than its book value. An example will illustrate.

Example 11.3 ▶

The old asset purchased 2 years ago for $100,000 by Hudson Industries has a current book value of $48,000. What will happen if the firm now decides to sell the asset and replace it? The tax consequences depend on the sale price. Figure 11.3 depicts the taxable income resulting from four possible sale prices in light of the asset's initial purchase price of $100,000 and its current book value of

---

TABLE 11.2 ▷ **Tax Treatment on Sales of Assets**

Form of taxable income	Definition	Tax treatment	Assumed tax rate
Gain on sale of asset	Portion of the sale price that is *greater than* book value.	All gains above book value are taxed as ordinary income.	40%
Loss on sale of asset	Amount by which sale price is *less than* book value.	If the asset is depreciable and used in business, loss is deducted from ordinary income.	40% of loss is a tax savings
		If the asset is *not* depreciable or is *not* used in business, loss is deductible only against capital gains.	40% of loss is a tax savings

---

FIGURE 11.3

Taxable Income from Sale of Asset
Taxable income from sale of asset at various sale prices for Hudson Industries

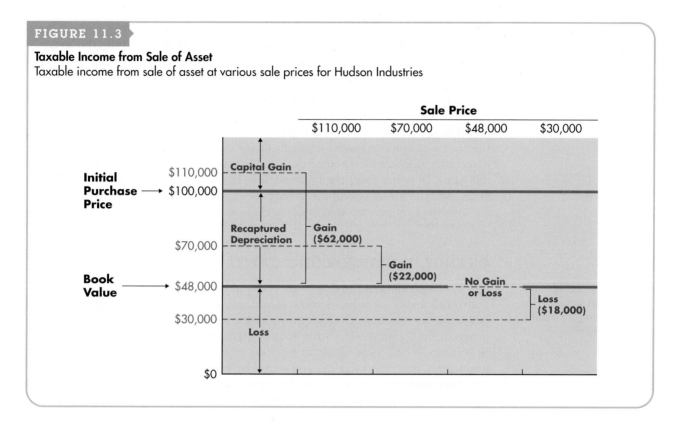

$48,000. The taxable consequences of each of these sale prices are described in the following paragraphs.

The sale of the asset for more than its book value   If Hudson sells the old asset for $110,000, it realizes a gain of $62,000 ($110,000 − $48,000). Technically this gain is made up of two parts—a capital gain and **recaptured depreciation,** which is the portion of the sale price that is above book value and below the initial purchase price. For Hudson, the capital gain is $10,000 ($110,000 sale price − $100,000 initial purchase price); recaptured depreciation is $52,000 (the $100,000 initial purchase price − $48,000 book value).

recaptured depreciation
The portion of an asset's sale price that is above its book value and below its initial purchase price.

Both the $10,000 capital gain and the $52,000 recaptured depreciation are shown under the $110,000 sale price in Figure 11.3. The total gain above book value of $62,000 is taxed as ordinary income at the 40% rate, resulting in taxes of $24,800 (0.40 × $62,000). These taxes should be used in calculating the initial investment in the new asset, using the format in Table 11.1. In effect, the taxes raise the amount of the firm's initial investment in the new asset by reducing the proceeds from the sale of the old asset.

If Hudson instead sells the old asset for $70,000, it experiences a gain above book value (in the form of *recaptured depreciation*) of $22,000 ($70,000 − $48,000), as shown under the $70,000 sale price in Figure 11.3. This gain is taxed as ordinary income. Because the firm is assumed to be in the 40% tax bracket, the taxes on the $22,000 gain are $8,800 (0.40 × $22,000). This amount in taxes should be used in calculating the initial investment in the new asset.

The sale of the asset for its book value   If the asset is sold for $48,000, its book value, the firm breaks even. There is no gain or loss, as shown under the $48,000 sale price in Figure 11.3. Because *no tax results from selling an asset for its book value,* there is no tax effect on the initial investment in the new asset.

The sale of the asset for less than its book value   If Hudson sells the asset for $30,000, it experiences a loss of $18,000 ($48,000 − $30,000), as shown under the $30,000 sale price in Figure 11.3. If this is a depreciable asset used in the business, the firm may use the loss to offset ordinary operating income. If the asset is *not* depreciable or is *not* used in the business, the firm can use the loss only to offset capital gains. In either case, the loss will save the firm $7,200 (0.40 × $18,000) in taxes. And, if current operating earnings or capital gains are not sufficient to offset the loss, the firm may be able to apply these losses to prior or future years' taxes.

CHANGE IN NET WORKING CAPITAL

net working capital
The difference between the firm's current assets and its current liabilities.

Net working capital is the difference between the firm's current assets and its current liabilities. This topic is treated in depth in Chapter 15; at this point it is important to note that changes in net working capital often accompany capital expenditure decisions. If a firm acquires new machinery to expand its level of operations, it will experience an increase in levels of cash, accounts receivable, inventories, accounts payable, and accruals. These increases result from the need for more cash to support expanded operations, more accounts receivable and inventories to support increased sales, and more accounts payable and accruals to support increased outlays made to meet expanded product demand. As noted in Chapter 4, increases in cash, accounts receivable, and inventories are *outflows of cash,* whereas increases in accounts payable and accruals are *inflows of cash.*

change in net working capital
The difference between a change in current assets and a change in current liabilities.

The difference between the change in current assets and the change in current liabilities is the **change in net working capital.** Generally, current assets increase by more than current liabilities, resulting in an increased investment in net working capital. This increased investment is treated as an initial outflow.[2] If the change in net working capital were negative, it would be shown as an initial inflow. The change in net working capital—regardless of whether it is an increase or a decrease—*is not taxable* because it merely involves a net buildup or net reduction of current accounts.

Example 11.4 ▶   Danson Company, a metal products manufacturer, is contemplating expanding its operations. Financial analysts expect that the changes in current accounts summarized in Table 11.3 will occur and will be maintained over the life of the expansion. Current assets are expected to increase by $22,000, and current liabilities are expected to increase by $9,000, resulting in a $13,000 increase in net working capital. In this case, the change will represent an increased net working capital investment and will be treated as a cash outflow in calculating the initial investment.

---

2. When changes in net working capital apply to the initial investment associated with a proposed capital expenditure, they are for convenience assumed to be instantaneous and thereby occurring at time zero. In practice, the change in net working capital will frequently occur over a period of months as the capital expenditure is implemented.

TABLE 11.3	Calculation of Change in Net Working Capital for Danson Company

Current account	Change in balance	
Cash	+ $ 4,000	
Accounts receivable	+ 10,000	
Inventories	+ 8,000	
(1) Current assets		+$22,000
Accounts payable	+ $ 7,000	
Accruals	+ 2,000	
(2) Current liabilities		+ 9,000
Change in net working capital [(1) − (2)]		+$13,000

CALCULATING THE INITIAL INVESTMENT

A variety of tax and other considerations enter into the initial investment calculation. The following example illustrates calculation of the initial investment according to the format in Table 11.1.[3]

Example 11.5 ▶ Powell Corporation, a large, diversified manufacturer of aircraft components, is trying to determine the initial investment required to replace an old machine with a new, more sophisticated model. The proposed machine's purchase price is $380,000, and an additional $20,000 will be necessary to install it. It will be depreciated under MACRS using a 5-year recovery period. The present (old) machine was purchased 3 years ago at a cost of $240,000 and was being depreciated under MACRS using a 5-year recovery period. The firm has found a buyer willing to pay $280,000 for the present machine and to remove it at the buyer's expense. The firm expects that a $35,000 increase in current assets and an $18,000 increase in current liabilities will accompany the replacement; these changes will result in a $17,000 ($35,000 − $18,000) *increase* in net working capital. The firm pays taxes at a rate of 40%.

The only component of the initial investment calculation that is difficult to obtain is taxes. The book value of the present machine can be found by using the depreciation percentages from Table 4.2 (on page 117) of 20%, 32%, and 19% for years 1, 2, and 3, respectively. The resulting *book value* is $69,600 ($240,000 − [(0.20 + 0.32 + 0.19) × $240,000]). A *gain* of $210,400 ($280,000 − $69,600) is realized on the sale. The total taxes on the gain are $84,160 (0.40 × $210,400). These taxes must be subtracted from the $280,000 sale price of the present machine to calculate the after-tax proceeds from its sale.

---

3. Throughout the discussions of capital budgeting, all assets evaluated as candidates for replacement are assumed to be depreciable assets that are directly used in the business, so any losses on the sale of these assets can be applied against ordinary operating income. The decisions are also structured to ensure that the usable life remaining on the old asset is just equal to the life of the new asset; this assumption enables us to avoid the problem of unequal lives, which is discussed in Chapter 12.

Substituting the relevant amounts into the format in Table 11.1 results in an initial investment of $221,160, which represents the net cash outflow required at time zero.

Installed cost of proposed machine

Cost of proposed machine	$380,000	
+ Installation costs	20,000	
Total installed cost—proposed (depreciable value)		$400,000
− After-tax proceeds from sale of present machine		
Proceeds from sale of present machine	$280,000	
− Tax on sale of present machine	84,160	
Total after-tax proceeds—present		195,840
+ Change in net working capital		17,000
Initial investment		$221,160

→ **REVIEW QUESTIONS**

11–5 Explain how each of the following inputs is used to calculate the *initial investment*: (**a**) cost of new asset, (**b**) installation costs, (**c**) proceeds from sale of old asset, (**d**) tax on sale of old asset, and (**e**) change in net working capital.

11–6 How is the *book value* of an asset calculated? What are the two key forms of taxable income?

11–7 What three tax situations may result from the sale of an asset that is being replaced?

11–8 Referring to the basic format for calculating initial investment, explain how a firm would determine the *depreciable value* of the new asset.

_{LG 5}   **11.3** **Finding the Operating Cash Inflows**

The benefits expected from a capital expenditure or "project" are embodied in its *operating cash inflows*, which are *incremental after-tax cash inflows*. In this section, we use the income statement format to develop clear definitions of the terms *after-tax, cash inflows,* and *incremental*.

INTERPRETING THE TERM *AFTER-TAX*

Benefits expected to result from proposed capital expenditures must be measured on an *after-tax basis* because the firm will not have the use of any benefits until it has satisfied the government's tax claims. These claims depend on the firm's taxable income, so deducting taxes *before* making comparisons between proposed investments is necessary for consistency when evaluating capital expenditure alternatives.

INTERPRETING THE TERM *CASH INFLOWS*

All benefits expected from a proposed project must be measured on a *cash flow basis*. Cash inflows represent dollars that can be spent, not merely "accounting profits." There is a simple technique for converting after-tax net profits into operating cash inflows. The basic calculation requires adding depreciation and any other *noncash charges* (amortization and depletion) deducted as expenses on the firm's income statement back to net profits after taxes. Because depreciation is commonly found on income statements, it is the only noncash charge we consider.

Example 11.6 ▶   Powell Corporation's estimates of its revenue and expenses (excluding depreciation and interest), with and without the proposed new machine described in Example 11.5, are given in Table 11.4. Note that both the expected usable life of the proposed machine and the remaining usable life of the present machine are 5 years. The amount to be depreciated with the proposed machine is calculated by summing the purchase price of $380,000 and the installation costs of $20,000. The proposed machine is to be depreciated under MACRS using a 5-year recovery period.[4] The resulting depreciation on this machine for each of the 6 years, as well as the remaining 3 years of depreciation (years 4, 5, and 6) on the present machine, are calculated in Table 11.5 (see page 440).[5]

The *operating cash inflows* each year can be calculated by using the income statement format shown in Table 11.6 (see page 440). Note that we exclude interest because we are focusing purely on the "investment decision." The interest is relevant to the "financing decision," which is separately considered. Because we exclude interest expense, "earnings before interest and taxes" (EBIT) is equivalent to "net profits before taxes," and the calculation of "operating cash inflow" in

TABLE 11.4	Powell Corporation's Revenue and Expenses (Excluding Depreciation and Interest) for Proposed and Present Machines					
	With proposed machine			**With present machine**		
Year	Revenue (1)	Expenses (excl. depr. and int.) (2)		Year	Revenue (1)	Expenses (excl. depr. and int.) (2)
1	$2,520,000	$2,300,000		1	$2,200,000	$1,990,000
2	2,520,000	2,300,000		2	2,300,000	2,110,000
3	2,520,000	2,300,000		3	2,400,000	2,230,000
4	2,520,000	2,300,000		4	2,400,000	2,250,000
5	2,520,000	2,300,000		5	2,250,000	2,120,000

---

4. As noted in Chapter 4, it takes $n + 1$ years to depreciate an n-year class asset under current tax law. Therefore, MACRS percentages are given for each of 6 years for use in depreciating an asset with a 5-year recovery period.

5. It is important to recognize that, although both machines will provide 5 years of use, the proposed new machine will be depreciated over the 6-year period, whereas the present machine, as noted in the preceding example, has been depreciated over 3 years and therefore has remaining only its final 3 years (years 4, 5, and 6) of depreciation (12%, 12%, and 5%, respectively, under MACRS).

TABLE 11.5	Depreciation Expense for Proposed and Present Machines for Powell Corporation

Year	Cost (1)	Applicable MACRS depreciation percentages (from Table 4.2) (2)	Depreciation [(1) × (2)] (3)
With proposed machine			
1	$400,000	20%	$ 80,000
2	400,000	32	128,000
3	400,000	19	76,000
4	400,000	12	48,000
5	400,000	12	48,000
6	400,000	5	20,000
Totals		100%	$400,000
With present machine			
1	$240,000	12% (year-4 depreciation)	$28,800
2	240,000	12 (year-5 depreciation)	28,800
3	240,000	5 (year-6 depreciation)	12,000
4		Because the present machine is at the end of the third year of its cost recovery at the time the analysis is performed, it has only the final 3 years of depreciation (as noted above) still applicable.	0
5			0
6			0
Total			$69,600[a]

[a]The total $69,600 represents the book value of the present machine at the end of the third year, as calculated in Example 11.5.

Table 11.6 is equivalent to "operating cash flow (OCF)" (defined in Equation 4.3, on page 122). Simply stated, the income statement format calculates OCF.

Substituting the data from Tables 11.4 and 11.5 into this format and assuming a 40% tax rate, we get Table 11.7. It demonstrates the calculation of operating cash inflows for each year for both the proposed and the present machine. Because the proposed machine is depreciated over 6 years, the analysis must be performed

TABLE 11.6	Calculation of Operating Cash Inflows Using the Income Statement Format

Revenue
− Expenses (excluding depreciation and interest)
Earnings before depreciation, interest, and taxes (EBDIT)
− Depreciation
Earnings before interest and taxes (EBIT)
− Taxes (rate = T)
Net operating profit after taxes [NOPAT = EBIT × $(1 - T)$]
+ Depreciation
Operating cash inflows (same as OCF in Equation 4.3)

TABLE 11.7	Calculation of Operating Cash Inflows for Powell Corporation's Proposed and Present Machines					
	Year 1	Year 2	Year 3	Year 4	Year 5	Year 6
With proposed machine						
Revenue[a]	$2,520,000	$2,520,000	$2,520,000	$2,520,000	$2,520,000	$ 0
− Expenses (excluding depreciation and interest)[b]	2,300,000	2,300,000	2,300,000	2,300,000	2,300,000	0
Earnings before depreciation, interest, and taxes	$ 220,000	$ 220,000	$ 220,000	$ 220,000	$ 220,000	$ 0
− Depreciation[c]	80,000	128,000	76,000	48,000	48,000	20,000
Earnings before interest and taxes	$ 140,000	$ 92,000	$ 144,000	$ 172,000	$ 172,000	−$20,000
− Taxes (rate, T = 40%)	56,000	36,800	57,600	68,800	68,800	− 8,000
Net operating profit after taxes	$ 84,000	$ 55,200	$ 86,400	$ 103,200	$ 103,200	−$12,000
+ Depreciation[c]	80,000	128,000	76,000	48,000	48,000	20,000
Operating cash inflows	$ 164,000	$ 183,200	$ 162,400	$ 151,200	$ 151,200	$ 8,000
With present machine						
Revenue[a]	$2,200,000	$2,300,000	$2,400,000	$2,400,000	$2,250,000	$ 0
− Expenses (excluding depreciation and interest)[b]	1,990,000	2,110,000	2,230,000	2,250,000	2,120,000	0
Earnings before depreciation, interest, and taxes	$ 210,000	$ 190,000	$ 170,000	$ 150,000	$ 130,000	$ 0
− Depreciation[c]	28,800	28,800	12,000	0	0	0
Earnings before interest and taxes	$ 181,200	$ 161,200	$ 158,000	$ 150,000	$ 130,000	$ 0
− Taxes (rate, T = 40%)	72,480	64,480	63,200	60,000	52,000	0
Net operating profit after taxes	$ 108,720	$ 96,720	$ 94,800	$ 90,000	$ 78,000	$ 0
+ Depreciation[c]	28,800	28,800	12,000	0	0	0
Operating cash inflows	$ 137,520	$ 125,520	$ 106,800	$ 90,000	$ 78,000	$ 0

[a]From column 1 of Table 11.4.
[b]From column 2 of Table 11.4.
[c]From column 3 of Table 11.5.

over the 6-year period to capture fully the tax effect of its year-6 depreciation. The resulting operating cash inflows are shown in the final row of Table 11.7 for each machine. The $8,000 year-6 operating cash inflow for the proposed machine results solely from the tax benefit of its year-6 depreciation deduction.[6]

INTERPRETING THE TERM *INCREMENTAL*

The final step in estimating the operating cash inflows for a proposed replacement project is to calculate the *incremental (relevant)* cash inflows. Incremental operating cash inflows are needed because our concern is *only* with the change in operating cash inflows that result from the proposed project. Clearly, if this were an expansion project, the project's cash flows would be the incremental cash flows.

---

6. Although here we have calculated the year-6 operating cash inflow for the proposed machine, this cash flow will later be eliminated as a result of the assumed sale of the machine at the end of year 5.

TABLE 11.8	Incremental (Relevant) Operating Cash Inflows for Powell Corporation		

	Operating cash inflows		
Year	Proposed machine[a] (1)	Present machine[a] (2)	Incremental (relevant) [(1) − (2)] (3)
1	$164,000	$137,520	$26,480
2	183,200	125,520	57,680
3	162,400	106,800	55,600
4	151,200	90,000	61,200
5	151,200	78,000	73,200
6	8,000	0	8,000

[a]From final row for respective machine in Table 11.7.

Example 11.7 ▶

Table 11.8 demonstrates the calculation of Powell Corporation's *incremental (relevant) operating cash inflows* for each year. The estimates of operating cash inflows developed in Table 11.7 appear in columns 1 and 2. Column 2 values represent the amount of operating cash inflows that Powell Corporation will receive if it does not replace the present machine. If the proposed machine replaces the present machine, the firm's operating cash inflows for each year will be those shown in column 1. Subtracting the present machine's operating cash inflows from the proposed machine's operating cash inflows, we get the incremental operating cash inflows for each year, shown in column 3. These cash flows represent the amounts by which each respective year's cash inflows will increase as a result of the replacement. For example, in year 1, Powell Corporation's cash inflows would increase by $26,480 if the proposed project were undertaken. Clearly, these are the relevant inflows to be considered when evaluating the benefits of making a capital expenditure for the proposed machine.[7]

7. The following equation can be used to calculate more directly the incremental cash inflow in year t, ICI_t.

$$ICI_t = [\Delta EBDIT_t \times (1 - T)] + (\Delta D_t \times T)$$

where

$\Delta EBDIT_t$ = change in earnings before depreciation, interest, and taxes [revenues−expenses (excl. depr. and int.)] in year t
ΔD_t = change in depreciation expense in year t
T = firm's marginal tax rate

Applying this formula to the Powell Corporation data given in Tables 11.4 and 11.5 for year 3, we get the following values of variables:

$$\Delta EBDIT_3 = (\$2,520,000 - \$2,300,000) - (\$2,400,000 - \$2,230,000)$$
$$= \$220,000 - \$170,000 = \$50,000$$
$$\Delta D_3 = \$76,000 - \$12,000 = \$64,000$$
$$T = 0.40$$

Substituting into the equation yields

$$ICI_3 = [\$50,000 \times (1 - 0.40)] + (\$64,000 \times 0.40)$$
$$= \$30,000 + \$25,600 = \underline{\$55,600}$$

The $55,600 of incremental cash inflow for year 3 is the same value as that calculated for year 3 in column 3 of Table 11.8.

→ **REVIEW QUESTIONS**

11–9 How does depreciation enter into the calculation of operating cash inflows? How does the income statement format in Table 11.6 relate to Equation 4.3 (on page 122) for finding operating cash flow (OCF)?

11–10 How are the *incremental (relevant) operating cash inflows* that are associated with a replacement decision calculated?

LG 6 ## 11.4 Finding the Terminal Cash Flow

Terminal cash flow is the cash flow resulting from termination and liquidation of a project at the end of its economic life. It represents the after-tax cash flow, exclusive of operating cash inflows, that occurs in the final year of the project. When it applies, this flow can significantly affect the capital expenditure decision. Terminal cash flow can be calculated for replacement projects by using the basic format presented in Table 11.9.

PROCEEDS FROM SALE OF ASSETS

The proceeds from sale of the new and the old asset, often called "salvage value," represent the amount *net of any removal or cleanup costs* expected on termination of the project. For replacement projects, proceeds from both the new asset and the old asset must be considered. For expansion and renewal types of capital expenditures, the proceeds from the old asset are zero. Of course, it is not unusual for the value of an asset to be zero at the termination of a project.

TAXES ON SALE OF ASSETS

When the investment being analyzed involves replacing an old asset with a new one, there are two key elements in finding the terminal cash flow. First, at the end of the project's life, the firm will dispose of the new asset, so the after-tax proceeds from selling the new asset represent a cash inflow. However, remember that if the firm had not replaced the old asset, the firm would have received proceeds from disposal of the old asset at the end of the project (rather than counting those proceeds up front as part of the initial investment). Therefore, we must count as a cash outflow the after-tax proceeds that the firm would have received from disposal of the old asset. Taxes come into play whenever an asset is sold for a value different from its book value. If the net proceeds from the sale are expected to exceed

TABLE 11.9	The Basic Format for Determining Terminal Cash Flow

After-tax proceeds from sale of new asset =
    Proceeds from sale of new asset
   ∓ Tax on sale of new asset
− After-tax proceeds from sale of old asset =
    Proceeds from sale of old asset
   ∓ Tax on sale of old asset
± Change in net working capital
Terminal cash flow

book value, a tax payment shown as an *outflow* (deduction from sale proceeds) will occur. When the net proceeds from the sale are less than book value, a tax benefit shown as a cash *inflow* (addition to sale proceeds) will result. For assets sold to net exactly book value, no taxes will be due.

CHANGE IN NET WORKING CAPITAL

When we calculated the initial investment, we took into account any change in net working capital that is attributable to the new asset. Now, when we calculate the terminal cash flow, the change in net working capital represents the reversion of any initial net working capital investment. Most often, this will show up as a cash inflow due to the reduction in net working capital; with termination of the project, the need for the increased net working capital investment is assumed to end.[8] Because the net working capital investment is in no way consumed, the amount recovered at termination will equal the amount shown in the calculation of the initial investment. Tax considerations are not involved.

Calculating the terminal cash flow involves the same procedures as those used to find the initial investment. In the following example, the terminal cash flow is calculated for a replacement decision.

Example 11.8 ▶   Continuing with the Powell Corporation example, assume that the firm expects to be able to liquidate the new machine at the end of its 5-year usable life to net $50,000 after paying removal and cleanup costs. Had it not been replaced by the new machine, the old machine would have been liquidated at the end of the 5 years to net $10,000. The firm expects to recover its $17,000 net working capital investment upon termination of the project. The firm pays taxes at a rate of 40%.

From the analysis of the operating cash inflows presented earlier, we can see that the proposed (new) machine will have a book value of $20,000 (equal to the year-6 depreciation) at the end of 5 years. The present (old) machine would have been fully depreciated and therefore would have a book value of zero at the end of the 5 years. Because the sale price of $50,000 for the proposed (new) machine is below its initial installed cost of $400,000 but greater than its book value of $20,000, taxes will have to be paid only on the recaptured depreciation of $30,000 ($50,000 sale proceeds − $20,000 book value). Applying the ordinary tax rate of 40% to this $30,000 results in a tax of $12,000 (0.40 × $30,000) on the sale of the proposed machine. Its after-tax sale proceeds would therefore equal $38,000 ($50,000 sale proceeds − $12,000 taxes). Because the old machine would have been sold for $10,000 at termination, which is less than its original purchase price of $240,000 and above its book value of zero, it would have experienced a taxable gain of $10,000 ($10,000 sale price − $0 book value). Applying the 40% tax rate to the $10,000 gain, the firm would have owed a tax of $4,000 (0.40 × $10,000) on the sale of the old machine at the end of year 5. Its after-tax sale proceeds from the old machine would have equalled $6,000 ($10,000 sale price − $4,000 taxes). Substituting the appropriate values into the format in Table 11.9 results in the terminal cash inflow of $49,000.

---

8. As noted earlier, the change in net working capital is for convenience assumed to occur instantaneously—in this case, on termination of the project.

After-tax proceeds from sale of proposed machine

Proceeds from sale of proposed machine	$50,000	
− Tax on sale of proposed machine	12,000	
Total after-tax proceeds—proposed		$38,000
− **After-tax proceeds from sale of present machine**		
Proceeds from sale of present machine	$10,000	
− Tax on sale of present machine	4,000	
Total after-tax proceeds—present		6,000
+ **Change in net working capital**		17,000
Terminal cash flow		$49,000

→ **REVIEW QUESTION**

11–11 Explain how the *terminal cash flow* is calculated for replacement projects.

11.5 **Summarizing the Relevant Cash Flows**

The initial investment, operating cash inflows, and terminal cash flow together represent a project's *relevant cash flows*. These cash flows can be viewed as the incremental after-tax cash flows attributable to the proposed project. They represent, in a cash flow sense, how much better or worse off the firm will be if it chooses to implement the proposal.

Example 11.9 ▶   The relevant cash flows for Powell Corporation's proposed replacement expenditure can be shown graphically, on a time line. *Note that because the new asset is assumed to be sold at the end of its 5-year usable life, the year-6 incremental operating cash inflow calculated in Table 11.8 has no relevance; the terminal cash flow effectively replaces this value in the analysis.*

Time line for Powell Corporation's relevant cash flows with the proposed machine

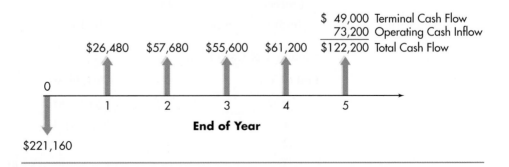

With these cash flow estimates in hand, a financial manager could then calculate the investment's NPV or IRR using the techniques covered in Chapter 10.

Personal Finance Example 11.10 ▶ After receiving a sizable bonus from her employer, Tina Talor is contemplating the purchase of a new car. She feels that by estimating and analyzing its cash flows she could make a more rational decision about whether to make this large purchase. Tina's cash flow estimates for the car purchase are as follows:

Negotiated price of new car	$23,500
Taxes and fees on new car purchase	$ 1,650
Proceeds from sale of old car	$ 9,750
Estimated value of new car in 3 years	$10,500
Estimated value of old car in 3 years	$ 5,700
Estimated annual repair costs on new car	0 (in warranty)
Estimated annual repair costs on old car	$ 400

Using the cash flow estimates, Tina calculates the initial investment, operating cash inflows, terminal cash flow, and a summary of all cash flows for the car purchase.

Initial Investment

Total cost of new car		
Cost of car	$23,500	
+ Taxes and fees	1,650	$25,150
− Proceeds from sale of old car		9,750
Initial investment		$15,400

Operating Cash Inflows	**Year 1**	**Year 2**	**Year 3**
Cost of repairs on new car	$ 0	$ 0	$ 0
− Cost of repairs on old car	400	400	400
Operating cash inflows (savings)	$400	$400	$400

Terminal Cash Flow—End of Year 3

Proceeds from sale of new car	$10,500
− Proceeds from sale of old car	5,700
Terminal cash flow	$ 4,800

Summary of Cash Flows

End of Year	**Cash Flow**	
0	−$15,400	
1	+ 400	
2	+ 400	
3	+ 5,200	($400 + $4,800)

The cash flows associated with Tina's car purchase decision reflect her net costs of the new car over the assumed 3-year ownership period, but they ignore the many intangible benefits of owning a car. Whereas the fuel cost and basic transportation service provided are assumed to be the same with the new car as with the old car, Tina will have to decide if the cost of moving up to a new car can be justified in terms of intangibles, such as luxury and prestige.

→ REVIEW QUESTION

11–12 Diagram and describe the three components of the relevant cash flows for a capital budgeting project.

Summary

FOCUS ON VALUE

A key responsibility of financial managers is to review and analyze proposed investment decisions to make sure that the firm undertakes only those that contribute positively to the value of the firm. Utilizing a variety of tools and techniques, financial managers estimate the cash flows that a proposed investment will generate and then apply decision techniques to assess the investment's impact on the firm's value. The most difficult and important aspect of this capital budgeting process is developing good estimates of the relevant cash flows.

The relevant cash flows are the incremental after-tax cash flows resulting from a proposed investment. These estimates represent the cash flow benefits that are likely to accrue to the firm as a result of implementing the investment. By applying to the cash flows decision techniques that capture the time value of money and risk factors, the financial manager can estimate how the investment will affect the firm's share price. Consistent application of capital budgeting procedures to proposed long-term investments should therefore allow the firm to **maximize its stock price.**

REVIEW OF LEARNING GOALS

LG 1 **Discuss the three major cash flow components.** The three major cash flow components of any project can include: (1) an initial investment, (2) operating cash inflows, and (3) terminal cash flow. The initial investment occurs at *time zero,* the operating cash inflows occur during the project life, and the terminal cash flow occurs at the end of the project.

LG 2 **Discuss relevant cash flows, expansion versus replacement decisions, sunk costs and opportunity costs, and international capital budgeting.** The relevant cash flows for capital budgeting decisions are the initial investment, the operating cash inflows, and the terminal cash flow. For replacement decisions, these flows are the difference between the cash flows of the new asset and the old asset. Expansion decisions are viewed as replacement decisions in which all cash flows from the old asset are zero. When estimating relevant cash flows, ignore sunk costs and include opportunity costs as cash outflows. In international capital budgeting, currency risks and political risks can be minimized through careful planning.

LG 3   **Calculate the initial investment associated with a proposed capital expenditure.** The initial investment is the initial outflow required, taking into account the installed cost of the new asset, the after-tax proceeds from the sale of the old asset, and any change in net working capital. The initial investment is reduced by finding the after-tax proceeds from sale of the old asset. The book value of an asset is used to determine the taxes owed as a result of its sale. Either of two forms of taxable income—a gain or a loss—can result from sale of an asset, depending on whether the asset is sold for (1) more than book value, (2) book value, or (3) less than book value. The change in net working capital is the difference between the change in current assets and the change in current liabilities expected to accompany a given capital expenditure.

LG 4   **Discuss the tax implications associated with the sale of an old asset.** There is typically a tax implication from the sale of an old asset. The tax implication depends on the relationship between its sale price and book value and on existing government tax rules. Generally, if the old asset is sold for an amount greater than its book value, then the difference is subject to a capital gains tax, and if the old asset is sold for an amount less than its book value, then the company is entitled to tax deduction equal to the difference.

LG 5   **Find the relevant operating cash inflows associated with a proposed capital expenditure.** The operating cash inflows are the incremental after-tax cash inflows expected to result from a project. The income statement format involves adding depreciation back to net operating profit after taxes and gives the operating cash inflows, which are the same as operating cash flows (OCF), associated with the proposed and present projects. The relevant (incremental) cash inflows for a replacement project are the difference between the operating cash inflows of the proposed project and those of the present project.

LG 6   **Determine the terminal cash flow associated with a proposed capital expenditure.** The terminal cash flow represents the after-tax cash flow (exclusive of operating cash inflows) that is expected from liquidation of a project. It is calculated for replacement projects by finding the difference between the after-tax proceeds from sale of the new and the old asset at termination and then adjusting this difference for any change in net working capital. Sale price and depreciation data are used to find the taxes and the after-tax sale proceeds on the new and old assets. The change in net working capital typically represents the reversion of any initial net working capital investment.

Opener-in-Review

The chapter opener talked about ExxonMobil's considerable investment in long-term projects and the sometimes difficult task of having projects come in on budget. How are project cash flows affected by budget overruns? In the capital budgeting process, how should financial managers account for the potential of budget overruns?

Self-Test Problems   (Solutions in Appendix)

LG 3 **LG 4** **ST11–1** **Book value, taxes, and initial investment**   Irvin Enterprises is considering the purchase of a new piece of equipment to replace the current equipment. The new equipment costs $75,000 and requires $5,000 in installation costs. It will be depreciated under MACRS using a 5-year recovery period. The old piece of equipment was purchased 4 years ago for an installed cost of $50,000; it was being depreciated under MACRS using a 5-year recovery period. The old equipment can be sold today for $55,000 net of any removal or cleanup costs. As a result of the proposed replacement, the firm's investment in net working capital is expected to increase by $15,000. The firm pays taxes at a rate of 40%. (Table 4.2 on page 117 contains the applicable MACRS depreciation percentages.)

a. Calculate the book value of the old piece of equipment.
b. Determine the taxes, if any, attributable to the sale of the old equipment.
c. Find the *initial investment* associated with the proposed equipment replacement.

LG 3 **LG 4** **ST11–2** **Determining relevant cash flows**   A machine currently in use was originally purchased 2 years ago for $40,000. The machine is being depreciated under MACRS using a 5-year recovery period; it has 3 years of usable life remaining. The current machine can be sold today to net $42,000 after removal and cleanup costs. A new machine, using a 3-year MACRS recovery period, can be purchased at a price of $140,000. It requires $10,000 to install and has a 3-year usable life. If the new machine is acquired, the investment in accounts receivable will be expected to rise by $10,000, the inventory investment will increase by $25,000, and accounts payable will increase by $15,000. *Earnings before depreciation, interest, and taxes* are expected to be $70,000 for each of the next 3 years with the old machine and to be $120,000 in the first year and $130,000 in the second and third years with the new machine. At the end of 3 years, the market value of the old machine will equal zero, but the new machine could be sold to net $35,000 before taxes. The firm is subject to a 40% tax rate. (Table 4.2 on page 117 contains the applicable MACRS depreciation percentages.)

a. Determine the *initial investment* associated with the proposed replacement decision.
b. Calculate the *incremental operating cash inflows* for years 1 to 4 associated with the proposed replacement. (*Note:* Only depreciation cash flows must be considered in year 4.)
c. Calculate the *terminal cash flow* associated with the proposed replacement decision. (*Note:* This is at the end of year 3.)
d. Depict on a time line the relevant cash flows found in parts **a, b,** and **c** that are associated with the proposed replacement decision, assuming that it is terminated at the end of year 3.

Warm-Up Exercises   All problems are available in ⬛myfinancelab.

LG 2 **E11–1** If Halley Industries reimburses employees who earn master's degrees and who agree to remain with the firm for an additional 3 years, should the expense of the tuition reimbursement be categorized as a *capital expenditure* or an *operating expenditure*?

LG 2   **E11–2**   Iridium Corp. has spent $3.5 billion over the past decade developing a satellite-based telecommunication system. It is currently trying to decide whether to spend an additional $350 million on the project. The firm expects that this outlay will finish the project and will generate cash flow of $15 million per year over the next 5 years. A competitor has offered $450 million for the satellites already in orbit. Classify the firm's outlays as *sunk costs* or *opportunity costs,* and specify the *relevant cash flows.*

LG 3   **LG** 4   **E11–3**   Canvas Reproductions, Inc., has spent $4,500 dollars researching a new project. The project requires $20,000 worth of new machinery, which would cost $3,000 to install. The company would realize $4,500 in after-tax proceeds from the sale of old machinery. If Canvas's working capital is unaffected by this project, what is the initial investment amount for this project?

LG 3   **LG** 4   **E11–4**   A few years ago, Largo Industries implemented an inventory auditing system at an installed cost of $175,000. Since then, it has taken depreciation deductions totaling $124,250. What is the system's current *book value?* If Largo sold the system for $110,000, how much *recaptured depreciation* would result?

LG 5   **E11–5**   Bryson Sciences is planning to purchase a high-powered microscopy machine for $55,000 and incur an additional $7,500 in installation expenses. It is replacing similar microscopy equipment that can be sold to net $35,000, resulting in taxes from a gain on the sale of $11,250. Because of this transaction, current assets will increase by $6,000 and current liabilities will increase by $4,000. Calculate the *initial investment* in the high-powered microscopy machine.

Problems   All problems are available in ⬛myfinancelab .

LG 2   **P11–1**   **Classification of expenditures**   Given the following list of outlays, indicate whether each is normally considered a *capital expenditure* or an *operating expenditure.* Explain your answers.
a. An initial lease payment of $5,000 for electronic point-of-sale cash register systems.
b. An outlay of $20,000 to purchase patent rights from an inventor.
c. An outlay of $80,000 for a major research and development program.
d. An $80,000 investment in a portfolio of marketable securities.
e. A $300 outlay for an office machine.
f. An outlay of $2,000 for a new machine tool.
g. An outlay of $240,000 for a new building.
h. An outlay of $1,000 for a marketing research report.

LG 1   **LG** 2   **P11–2**   **Relevant cash flow and timeline depiction**   For each of the following projects, determine the *relevant cash flows,* and depict the cash flows on a time line.
a. A project that requires an initial investment of $120,000 and will generate annual operating cash inflows of $25,000 for the next 18 years. In each of the 18 years, maintenance of the project will require a $5,000 cash outflow.
b. A new machine with an installed cost of $85,000. Sale of the old machine will yield $30,000 after taxes. Operating cash inflows generated by the replacement will exceed the operating cash inflows of the old machine by $20,000 in each

year of a 6-year period. At the end of year 6, liquidation of the new machine will yield $20,000 after taxes, which is $10,000 greater than the after-tax proceeds expected from the old machine had it been retained and liquidated at the end of year 6.

c. An asset that requires an initial investment of $2 million and will yield annual operating cash inflows of $300,000 for each of the next 10 years. Operating cash outlays will be $20,000 for each year except year 6, when an overhaul requiring an additional cash outlay of $500,000 will be required. The asset's liquidation value at the end of year 10 is expected to be zero.

LG 3 **P11–3** **Expansion versus replacement cash flows** Edison Systems has estimated the cash flows over the 5-year lives for two projects, A and B. These cash flows are summarized in the table below.

a. If project A were actually a *replacement* for project B and if the $12,000 initial investment shown for project B were the after-tax cash inflow expected from liquidating it, what would be the *relevant cash flows* for this replacement decision?

b. How can an *expansion decision* such as project A be viewed as a special form of a replacement decision? Explain.

	Project A	Project B
Initial investment	$40,000	$12,000[a]
Year	Operating cash inflows	
1	$10,000	$ 6,000
2	12,000	6,000
3	14,000	6,000
4	16,000	6,000
5	10,000	6,000

[a]After-tax cash inflow expected from liquidation.

LG 2 **P11–4** **Sunk costs and opportunity costs** Masters Golf Products, Inc., spent 3 years and $1,000,000 to develop its new line of club heads to replace a line that is becoming obsolete. To begin manufacturing them, the company will have to invest $1,800,000 in new equipment. The new clubs are expected to generate an increase in operating cash inflows of $750,000 per year for the next 10 years. The company has determined that the existing line could be sold to a competitor for $250,000.

a. How should the $1,000,000 in development costs be classified?

b. How should the $250,000 sale price for the existing line be classified?

c. Depict all of the known relevant cash flows on a time line.

LG 2 **P11–5** **Sunk costs and opportunity costs** Covol Industries is developing the relevant cash flows associated with the proposed replacement of an existing machine tool with a new, technologically advanced one. Given the following costs related to the proposed project, explain whether each would be treated as a *sunk cost* or an *opportunity cost* in developing the relevant cash flows associated with the proposed replacement decision.

a. Covol would be able to use the same tooling, which had a book value of $40,000, on the new machine tool as it had used on the old one.

b. Covol would be able to use its existing computer system to develop programs for operating the new machine tool. The old machine tool did not require these programs. Although the firm's computer has excess capacity available, the capacity could be leased to another firm for an annual fee of $17,000.

c. Covol would have to obtain additional floor space to accommodate the larger new machine tool. The space that would be used is currently being leased to another company for $10,000 per year.

d. Covol would use a small storage facility to store the increased output of the new machine tool. The storage facility was built by Covol 3 years earlier at a cost of $120,000. Because of its unique configuration and location, it is currently of no use to either Covol or any other firm.

e. Covol would retain an existing overhead crane, which it had planned to sell for its $180,000 market value. Although the crane was not needed with the old machine tool, it would be used to position raw materials on the new machine tool.

Personal Finance Problem

LG 2 **P11–6 Sunk and opportunity cash flows** Dave and Ann Stone have been living at their present home for the past 6 years. During that time, they have replaced the water heater for $375, have replaced the dishwasher for $599, and have had to make miscellaneous repair and maintenance expenditures of approximately $1,500. They have decided to move out and rent the house for $975 per month. Newspaper advertising will cost $75. Dave and Ann intend to paint the interior of the home and power-wash the exterior. They estimate that that will run about $900.

The house should be ready to rent after that. In reviewing the financial situation, Dave views all the expenditures as being relevant, and so he plans to net out the estimated expenditures discussed above from the rental income.

a. Do Dave and Ann understand the difference between *sunk costs* and *opportunity costs*? Explain the two concepts to them.

b. Which of the expenditures should be classified as sunk cash flows and which should be viewed as opportunity cash flows?

LG 3 **P11–7 Book value** Find the book value for each of the assets shown in the accompanying table, assuming that MACRS depreciation is being used. (*Note:* See Table 4.2 on page 117 for the applicable depreciation percentages.)

Asset	Installed cost	Recovery period (years)	Elapsed time since purchase (years)
A	$ 950,000	5	3
B	40,000	3	1
C	96,000	5	4
D	350,000	5	1
E	1,500,000	7	5

LG 3 LG 4 **P11–8 Book value and taxes on sale of assets** Troy Industries purchased a new machine 3 years ago for $80,000. It is being depreciated under MACRS with a 5-year recovery period using the percentages given in Table 4.2 on page 117. Assume a 40% tax rate.

a. What is the *book value* of the machine?

b. Calculate the firm's tax liability if it sold the machine for each of the following amounts: $100,000; $56,000; $23,200; and $15,000.

LG 3   LG 4   **P11–9**   **Tax calculations**   For each of the following cases, determine the total taxes resulting from the transaction. Assume a 40% tax rate. The asset was purchased 2 years ago for $200,000 and is being depreciated under MACRS using a 5-year recovery period. (See Table 4.2 on page 117 for the applicable depreciation percentages.)
  a. The asset is sold for $220,000.
  b. The asset is sold for $150,000.
  c. The asset is sold for $96,000.
  d. The asset is sold for $80,000.

LG 3   **P11–10**   **Change in net working capital calculation**   Samuels Manufacturing is considering the purchase of a new machine to replace one it believes is obsolete. The firm has total current assets of $920,000 and total current liabilities of $640,000. As a result of the proposed replacement, the following *changes* are anticipated in the levels of the current asset and current liability accounts noted.

Account	Change
Accruals	+$ 40,000
Marketable securities	0
Inventories	− 10,000
Accounts payable	+ 90,000
Notes payable	0
Accounts receivable	+ 150,000
Cash	+ 15,000

  a. Using the information given, calculate any *change in net working capital* that is expected to result from the proposed replacement action.
  b. Explain why a change in these current accounts would be relevant in determining the *initial investment* for the proposed capital expenditure.
  c. Would the change in net working capital enter into any of the other cash flow components that make up the relevant cash flows? Explain.

LG 3   LG 4   **P11–11**   **Calculating initial investment**   Vastine Medical, Inc., is considering replacing its existing computer system, which was purchased 2 years ago at a cost of $325,000. The system can be sold today for $200,000. It is being depreciated using MACRS and a 5-year recovery period (see Table 4.2, page 117). A new computer system will cost $500,000 to purchase and install. Replacement of the computer system would not involve any change in net working capital. Assume a 40% tax rate.
  a. Calculate the *book value* of the existing computer system.
  b. Calculate the after-tax proceeds of its sale for $200,000.
  c. Calculate the *initial investment* associated with the replacement project.

LG 3   LG 4   **P11–12**   **Initial investment—Basic calculation**   Cushing Corporation is considering the purchase of a new grading machine to replace the existing one. The existing machine was purchased 3 years ago at an installed cost of $20,000; it was being depreciated under MACRS using a 5-year recovery period. (See Table 4.2 on page 117 for the applicable depreciation percentages.) The existing machine is expected to have a usable life of at least 5 more years. The new machine costs $35,000 and requires $5,000 in installation costs; it will be depreciated using a 5-year recovery period under MACRS. The existing machine can currently be sold for $25,000 without incurring any removal or cleanup costs. The firm is subject to a 40% tax rate. Calculate the *initial investment* associated with the proposed purchase of a new grading machine.

LG 3 **LG 4** **P11–13** **Initial investment at various sale prices** Edwards Manufacturing Company (EMC) is considering replacing one machine with another. The old machine was purchased 3 years ago for an installed cost of $10,000. The firm is depreciating the machine under MACRS, using a 5-year recovery period. (See Table 4.2 on page 117 for the applicable depreciation percentages.) The new machine costs $24,000 and requires $2,000 in installation costs. The firm is subject to a 40% tax rate. In each of the following cases, calculate the *initial investment* for the replacement.

a. EMC sells the old machine for $11,000.
b. EMC sells the old machine for $7,000.
c. EMC sells the old machine for $2,900.
d. EMC sells the old machine for $1,500.

LG 3 **LG 4** **P11–14** **Calculating initial investment** DuPree Coffee Roasters, Inc., wishes to expand and modernize its facilities. The installed cost of a proposed computer-controlled automatic-feed roaster will be $130,000. The firm has a chance to sell its 4-year-old roaster for $35,000. The existing roaster originally cost $60,000 and was being depreciated using MACRS and a 7-year recovery period (see Table 4.2 on page 117). DuPree is subject to a 40% tax rate.

a. What is the *book value* of the existing roaster?
b. Calculate the after-tax proceeds of the sale of the existing roaster.
c. Calculate the *change in net working capital* using the following figures:

Anticipated Changes in Current Assets and Current Liabilities	
Accruals	−$20,000
Inventory	+ 50,000
Accounts payable	+ 40,000
Accounts receivable	+ 70,000
Cash	0
Notes payable	+ 15,000

d. Calculate the *initial investment* associated with the proposed new roaster.

LG 5 **P11–15** **Depreciation** A firm is evaluating the acquisition of an asset that costs $64,000 and requires $4,000 in installation costs. If the firm depreciates the asset under MACRS, using a 5-year recovery period (see Table 4.2 on page 117 for the applicable depreciation percentages), determine the depreciation charge for each year.

LG 5 **P11–16** **Incremental operating cash inflows** A firm is considering renewing its equipment to meet increased demand for its product. The cost of equipment modifications is $1.9 million plus $100,000 in installation costs. The firm will depreciate the equipment modifications under MACRS, using a 5-year recovery period. (See Table 4.2 on page 117 for the applicable depreciation percentages.) Additional sales revenue from the renewal should amount to $1.2 million per year, and additional operating expenses and other costs (excluding depreciation and interest) will amount to 40% of the additional sales. The firm is subject to a tax rate of 40%. (*Note:* Answer the following questions for each of the next 6 *years.*)

a. What incremental earnings before depreciation, interest, and taxes will result from the renewal?
b. What incremental net operating profits after taxes will result from the renewal?
c. What *incremental operating cash inflows* will result from the renewal?

Personal Finance Problem

LG 5   **P11–17**   **Incremental operating cash flows**   Richard and Linda Thomson operate a local lawn maintenance service for commercial and residential property. They have been using a John Deere riding mower for the past several years and feel it is time to buy a new one. They would like to know the incremental (relevant) cash flows associated with the replacement of the old riding mower. The following data are available.

There are 5 years of remaining useful life on the old mower.

The old mower has a zero book value.

The new mower is expected to last 5 years.

The Thomsons will follow a 5-year MACRS recovery period for the new mower.

Depreciable value of the new mower is $1,800.

They are subject to a 40% tax rate.

The new mower is expected to be more fuel efficient, maneuverable, and durable than previous models and can result in reduced operating expenses of $500 per year.

The Thomsons will buy a maintenance contract that calls for annual payments of $120.

Create an *incremental operating cash flow* statement for the replacement of Richard and Linda's John Deere riding mower. Show the incremental operating cash flow for the next 6 years.

LG 5   **P11–18**   **Incremental operating cash inflows—Expense reduction**   Miller Corporation is considering replacing a machine. The replacement will reduce operating expenses (that is, increase earnings before depreciation, interest, and taxes) by $16,000 per year for each of the 5 years the new machine is expected to last. Although the old machine has zero book value, it can be used for 5 more years. The depreciable value of the new machine is $48,000. The firm will depreciate the machine under MACRS using a 5-year recovery period (see Table 4.2 on page 117 for the applicable depreciation percentages) and is subject to a 40% tax rate. Estimate the *incremental operating cash inflows* generated by the replacement. (*Note:* Be sure to consider the depreciation in year 6.)

LG 5   **P11–19**   **Incremental operating cash inflows**   Strong Tool Company has been considering purchasing a new lathe to replace a fully depreciated lathe that will last 5 more years. The new lathe is expected to have a 5-year life and depreciation charges of $2,000 in year 1; $3,200 in year 2; $1,900 in year 3; $1,200 in both year 4 and year 5; and $500 in year 6. The firm estimates the revenues and expenses (excluding depreciation and interest) for the new and the old lathes to be as shown in the table at the top of page 456. The firm is subject to a 40% tax rate.

	New lathe		Old lathe	
Year	Revenue	Expenses (excluding depreciation and interest)	Revenue	Expenses (excluding depreciation and interest)
1	$40,000	$30,000	$35,000	$25,000
2	41,000	30,000	35,000	25,000
3	42,000	30,000	35,000	25,000
4	43,000	30,000	35,000	25,000
5	44,000	30,000	35,000	25,000

a. Calculate the *operating cash inflows* associated with each lathe. (*Note:* Be sure to consider the depreciation in year 6.)

b. Calculate the *incremental (relevant) operating cash inflows* resulting from the proposed lathe replacement.

c. Depict on a time line the incremental operating cash inflows calculated in part **b.**

LG 5   **P11–20**   **Determining incremental operating cash inflows**   Scenic Tours, Inc., is a provider of bus tours throughout the New England area. The corporation is considering the replacement of 10 of its older buses. The existing buses were purchased 4 years ago at a total cost of $2,700,000 and are being depreciated using MACRS and a 5-year recovery period (see Table 4.2, page 117). The new buses would have larger passenger capacity and better fuel efficiency as well as lower maintenance costs. The total cost for 10 new buses is $3,000,000. Like the older buses, the new ones would be depreciated using MACRS and a 5-year recovery period. Scenic is subject to a tax rate of 40%. The accompanying table presents revenues and cash expenses (excluding depreciation and interest) for the proposed purchase as well as the present fleet. Use all of the information given to calculate *incremental (relevant) operating cash inflows* for the proposed bus replacement.

	Year					
	1	2	3	4	5	6
With the proposed new buses						
Revenue	$1,850,000	$1,850,000	$1,830,000	$1,825,000	$1,815,000	$1,800,000
Expenses (excluding depreciation and interest)	460,000	460,000	468,000	472,000	485,000	500,000
With the present buses						
Revenue	$1,800,000	$1,800,000	$1,790,000	$1,785,000	$1,775,000	$1,750,000
Expenses (excluding depreciation and interest)	500,000	510,000	520,000	520,000	530,000	535,000

LG 6   **P11–21**   **Terminal cash flow—Various lives and sale prices**   Looner Industries is currently analyzing the purchase of a new machine that costs $160,000 and requires $20,000 in installation costs. Purchase of this machine is expected to result in an increase in net working capital of $30,000 to support the expanded level of operations. The firm plans to depreciate the machine under MACRS using a 5-year recovery period

(see Table 4.2 on page 117 for the applicable depreciation percentages) and expects to sell the machine to net $10,000 before taxes at the end of its usable life. The firm is subject to a 40% tax rate.

a. Calculate the *terminal cash flow* for a usable life of (1) 3 years, (2) 5 years, and (3) 7 years.

b. Discuss the effect of usable life on terminal cash flows using your findings in part **a**.

c. Assuming a 5-year usable life, calculate the terminal cash flow if the machine were sold to net (1) $9,000 or (2) $170,000 (before taxes) at the end of 5 years.

d. Discuss the effect of sale price on terminal cash flow using your findings in part **c**.

LG 6 **P11–22** **Terminal cash flow—Replacement decision** Russell Industries is considering replacing a fully depreciated machine that has a remaining useful life of 10 years with a newer, more sophisticated machine. The new machine will cost $200,000 and will require $30,000 in installation costs. It will be depreciated under MACRS using a 5-year recovery period (see Table 4.2 on page 117 for the applicable depreciation percentages). A $25,000 increase in net working capital will be required to support the new machine. The firm's managers plan to evaluate the potential replacement over a 4-year period. They estimate that the old machine could be sold at the end of 4 years to net $15,000 before taxes; the new machine at the end of 4 years will be worth $75,000 before taxes. Calculate the *terminal cash flow* at the end of year 4 that is relevant to the proposed purchase of the new machine. The firm is subject to a 40% tax rate.

LG 3 **LG 4** **LG 5** **LG 6** **P11–23** **Relevant cash flows for a marketing campaign** Marcus Tube, a manufacturer of high-quality aluminum tubing, has maintained stable sales and profits over the past 10 years. Although the market for aluminum tubing has been expanding by 3% per year, Marcus has been unsuccessful in sharing this growth. To increase its sales, the firm is considering an aggressive marketing campaign that centers on regularly running ads in all relevant trade journals and exhibiting products at all major regional and national trade shows. The campaign is expected to require an *annual* tax-deductible expenditure of $150,000 over the next 5 years. Sales revenue, as shown in the accompanying income statement for 2012, totaled $20,000,000. If the proposed marketing campaign is not initiated, sales are expected to remain at this level in each of the next 5 years, 2013 through 2017. With the marketing campaign, sales

Marcus Tube Income Statement for the Year Ended December 31, 2012	
Sales revenue	$20,000,000
Less: Cost of goods sold (80%)	16,000,000
Gross profits	$ 4,000,000
Less: Operating expenses	
General and administrative expense (10%)	$2,000,000
Depreciation expense	500,000
Total operating expense	$ 2,500,000
Earnings before interest and taxes	$ 1,500,000
Less: Taxes (rate = 40%)	600,000
Net operating profit after taxes	$ 900,000

Marcus Tube Sales Forecast	
Year	Sales revenue
2013	$20,500,000
2014	21,000,000
2015	21,500,000
2016	22,500,000
2017	23,500,000

are expected to rise to the levels shown in the accompanying table for each of the next 5 years; cost of goods sold is expected to remain at 80% of sales; general and administrative expense (exclusive of any marketing campaign outlays) is expected to remain at 10% of sales; and annual depreciation expense is expected to remain at $500,000. Assuming a 40% tax rate, find the *relevant cash flows* over the next 5 years associated with the proposed marketing campaign.

LG 3 **LG 4** **P11–24** **Relevant cash flows—No terminal value**   Central Laundry and Cleaners is consid-
LG 5 ering replacing an existing piece of machinery with a more sophisticated machine. The old machine was purchased 3 years ago at a cost of $50,000, and this amount was being depreciated under MACRS using a 5-year recovery period. The machine has 5 years of usable life remaining. The new machine that is being considered costs $76,000 and requires $4,000 in installation costs. The new machine would be depreciated under MACRS using a 5-year recovery period. The firm can currently sell the old machine for $55,000 without incurring any removal or cleanup costs. The firm is subject to a tax rate of 40%. The revenues and expenses (excluding depreciation and interest) associated with the new and the old machines for the next 5 years are given in the table below. (Table 4.2 on page 117 contains the applicable MACRS depreciation percentages.)

	New machine		Old machine	
Year	Revenue	Expenses (excl. depr. and int.)	Revenue	Expenses (excl. depr. and int.)
1	$750,000	$720,000	$674,000	$660,000
2	750,000	720,000	676,000	660,000
3	750,000	720,000	680,000	660,000
4	750,000	720,000	678,000	660,000
5	750,000	720,000	674,000	660,000

a. Calculate the *initial investment* associated with replacement of the old machine by the new one.
b. Determine the *incremental operating cash inflows* associated with the proposed replacement. (*Note:* Be sure to consider the depreciation in year 6.)
c. Depict on a time line the *relevant cash flows* found in parts **a** and **b** associated with the proposed replacement decision.

LG 3 **LG 4** **P11–25** **Integrative—Determining relevant cash flows**   Lombard Company is contemplating
LG 5 **LG 6** the purchase of a new high-speed widget grinder to replace the existing grinder. The existing grinder was purchased 2 years ago at an installed cost of $60,000; it was being depreciated under MACRS using a 5-year recovery period. The existing grinder is expected to have a usable life of 5 more years. The new grinder costs $105,000 and requires $5,000 in installation costs; it has a 5-year usable life and would be depreciated under MACRS using a 5-year recovery period. Lombard can currently sell the existing grinder for $70,000 without incurring any removal or cleanup costs. To support the increased business resulting from purchase of the new grinder, accounts receivable would increase by $40,000, inventories by $30,000, and accounts payable by $58,000. At the end of 5 years, the existing grinder would have a market value of zero; the new grinder would be sold to net $29,000 after removal

and cleanup costs and before taxes. The firm is subject to a 40% tax rate. The estimated *earnings before depreciation, interest, and taxes* over the 5 years for both the new and the existing grinder are shown in the following table. (Table 4.2 on page 117 contains the applicable MACRS depreciation percentages.)

	Earnings before depreciation, interest, and taxes	
Year	New grinder	Existing grinder
1	$43,000	$26,000
2	43,000	24,000
3	43,000	22,000
4	43,000	20,000
5	43,000	18,000

a. Calculate the *initial investment* associated with the replacement of the existing grinder by the new one.
b. Determine the *incremental operating cash inflows* associated with the proposed grinder replacement. (*Note:* Be sure to consider the depreciation in year 6.)
c. Determine the *terminal cash flow* expected at the end of year 5 from the proposed grinder replacement.
d. Depict on a time line the *relevant cash flows* associated with the proposed grinder replacement decision.

Personal Finance Problem

LG 3 LG 4 LG 5 LG 6 **P11–26** **Determining relevant cash flows for a new boat** Jan and Deana have been dreaming about owning a boat for some time and have decided that estimating its cash flows will help them in their decision process. They expect to have a disposable annual income of $24,000. Their cash flow estimates for the boat purchase are as follows:

Negotiated price of the new boat	$70,000
Sales tax rate (applicable to purchase price)	6.5%
Boat trade-in	0
Estimated value of new boat in 4 years	$40,000
Estimated monthly repair and maintenance	$800
Estimated monthly docking fee	$500

Using these cash flow estimates, calculate the following:
a. The initial investment
b. Operating cash flow
c. Terminal cash flow
d. Summary of annual cash flow
e. Based on their disposable annual income, what advice would you give Jan and Deana regarding the proposed boat purchase?

LG 3 LG 4
LG 5 LG 6

P11–27 **Integrative—Determining relevant cash flows** Atlantic Drydock is considering replacing an existing hoist with one of two newer, more efficient pieces of equipment. The existing hoist is 3 years old, cost $32,000, and is being depreciated under MACRS using a 5-year recovery period. Although the existing hoist has only 3 years (years 4, 5, and 6) of depreciation remaining under MACRS, it has a remaining usable life of 5 years. Hoist A, one of the two possible replacement hoists, costs $40,000 to purchase and $8,000 to install. It has a 5-year usable life and will be depreciated under MACRS using a 5-year recovery period. Hoist B costs $54,000 to purchase and $6,000 to install. It also has a 5-year usable life and will be depreciated under MACRS using a 5-year recovery period.

Increased investments in net working capital will accompany the decision to acquire hoist A or hoist B. Purchase of hoist A would result in a $4,000 increase in net working capital; hoist B would result in a $6,000 increase in net working capital. The projected *earnings before depreciation, interest, and taxes* with each alternative hoist and the existing hoist are given in the following table.

Year	Earnings before depreciation, interest, and taxes		
	With hoist A	With hoist B	With existing hoist
1	$21,000	$22,000	$14,000
2	21,000	24,000	14,000
3	21,000	26,000	14,000
4	21,000	26,000	14,000
5	21,000	26,000	14,000

The existing hoist can currently be sold for $18,000 and will not incur any removal or cleanup costs. At the end of 5 years, the existing hoist can be sold to net $1,000 before taxes. Hoists A and B can be sold to net $12,000 and $20,000 before taxes, respectively, at the end of the 5-year period. The firm is subject to a 40% tax rate. (Table 4.2 on page 117 contains the applicable MACRS depreciation percentages.)

a. Calculate the *initial investment* associated with each alternative.
b. Calculate the *incremental operating cash inflows* associated with each alternative. (*Note:* Be sure to consider the depreciation in year 6.)
c. Calculate the *terminal cash flow* at the end of year 5 associated with each alternative.
d. Depict on a time line the *relevant cash flows* associated with each alternative.

LG 1 LG 2
LG 3 LG 4
LG 5 LG 6

P11–28 **Integrative—Complete investment decision** Wells Printing is considering the purchase of a new printing press. The total installed cost of the press is $2.2 million. This outlay would be partially offset by the sale of an existing press. The old press has zero book value, cost $1 million 10 years ago, and can be sold currently for $1.2 million before taxes. As a result of acquisition of the new press, sales in each of the next 5 years are expected to be $1.6 million higher than with the existing press, but product costs (excluding depreciation) will represent 50% of sales. The new press will not affect the firm's net working capital requirements. The new press will be depreciated under MACRS using a 5-year recovery period. The firm is subject to a

40% tax rate. Wells Printing's cost of capital is 11%. (*Note:* Assume that the old and the new presses will each have a terminal value of $0 at the end of year 6.)

a. Determine the *initial investment* required by the new press.

b. Determine the *operating cash inflows* attributable to the new press. (*Note:* Be sure to consider the depreciation in year 6.)

c. Determine the *payback period.*

d. Determine the *net present value (NPV)* and the *internal rate of return (IRR)* related to the proposed new press.

e. Make a recommendation to accept or reject the new press, and justify your answer.

LG 1 LG 2 P11–29 Integrative—Investment decision Holliday Manufacturing is considering the
LG 3 LG 4 replacement of an existing machine. The new machine costs $1.2 million and
LG 5 LG 6 requires installation costs of $150,000. The existing machine can be sold currently for $185,000 before taxes. It is 2 years old, cost $800,000 new, and has a $384,000 book value and a remaining useful life of 5 years. It was being depreciated under MACRS using a 5-year recovery period (see Table 4.2 on page 117) and therefore has the final 4 years of depreciation remaining. If it is held for 5 more years, the machine's market value at the end of year 5 will be $0. Over its 5-year life, the new machine should reduce operating costs by $350,000 per year. The new machine will be depreciated under MACRS using a 5-year recovery period. The new machine can be sold for $200,000 net of removal and cleanup costs at the end of 5 years. An increased investment in net working capital of $25,000 will be needed to support operations if the new machine is acquired. Assume that the firm has adequate operating income against which to deduct any loss experienced on the sale of the existing machine. The firm has a 9% cost of capital and is subject to a 40% tax rate.

a. Develop the *relevant cash flows* needed to analyze the proposed replacement.

b. Determine the *net present value (NPV)* of the proposal.

c. Determine the *internal rate of return (IRR)* of the proposal.

d. Make a recommendation to accept or reject the replacement proposal, and justify your answer.

e. What is the highest cost of capital that the firm could have and still accept the proposal? Explain.

LG 2 P11–30 ETHICS PROBLEM Cash flow projections are a central component to the analysis of new investment ideas. In most firms, the person responsible for making these projections is not the same person who generated the investment idea in the first place. Why?

Spreadsheet Exercise

Damon Corporation, a sports equipment manufacturer, has a machine currently in use that was originally purchased 3 years ago for $120,000. The firm depreciates the machine under MACRS using a 5-year recovery period. Once removal and cleanup costs are taken into consideration, the expected net selling price for the present machine will be $70,000.

Damon can buy a new machine for a net price of $160,000 (including installation costs of $15,000). The proposed machine will be depreciated under MACRS using a 5-year recovery period. If the firm acquires the new machine, its working capital needs will change—accounts receivable will increase $15,000, inventory will increase $19,000, and accounts payable will increase $16,000.

Earnings before depreciation, interest, and taxes (EBDIT) for the present machine are expected to be $95,000 for each of the successive 5 years. For the proposed machine, the expected EBDIT for each of the next 5 years are $105,000, $110,000, $120,000, $120,000, and $120,000, respectively. The corporate tax rate (*T*) for the firm is 40%. (Table 4.2 on page 117 contains the applicable MACRS depreciation percentages.)

Damon expects to be able to liquidate the proposed machine at the end of its 5-year usable life for $24,000 (after paying removal and cleanup costs). The present machine is expected to net $8,000 upon liquidation at the end of the same period. Damon expects to recover its net working capital investment upon termination of the project. The firm is subject to a tax rate of 40%.

TO DO

Create a spreadsheet similar to Tables 11.1, 11.5, 11.7, and 11.9 to answer the following:

a. Create a spreadsheet to calculate the *initial investment.*
b. Create a spreadsheet to prepare a *depreciation schedule* for both the proposed and the present machine. Both machines are depreciated under MACRS using a 5-year recovery period. Remember, the present machine has only 3 years of depreciation remaining.
c. Create a spreadsheet to calculate the *operating cash inflows* for Damon Corporation for both the proposed and the present machine.
d. Create a spreadsheet to calculate the *terminal cash flow* associated with the project.

 Visit **www.myfinancelab.com** for **Chapter Case: *Developing Relevant Cash Flows for Clark Upholstery Company's Machine Renewal or Replacement Decision,*** Group Exercises, and numerous online resources.

12 Risk and Refinements in Capital Budgeting

Learning Goals

LG 1 Understand the importance of recognizing risk in the analysis of capital budgeting projects.

LG 2 Discuss risk and cash inflows, scenario analysis, and simulation as behavioral approaches for dealing with risk.

LG 3 Review the unique risks that multinational companies face.

LG 4 Describe the determination and use of risk-adjusted discount rates (RADRs), portfolio effects, and the practical aspects of RADRs.

LG 5 Select the best of a group of unequal-lived, mutually exclusive projects using annualized net present values (ANPVs).

LG 6 Explain the role of real options and the objective and procedures for selecting projects under capital rationing.

Why This Chapter Matters to You

In your *professional* life

ACCOUNTING You need to understand the risk caused by the variability of cash flows, how to compare projects with unequal lives, and how to measure project returns when capital is being rationed.

INFORMATION SYSTEMS You need to understand how risk is incorporated into capital budgeting techniques and how those techniques may be refined in the face of special circumstances, so as to design decision modules for use in analyzing proposed capital projects.

MANAGEMENT You need to understand behavioral approaches for dealing with risk, including international risk, in capital budgeting decisions; how to risk-adjust discount rates; how to refine capital budgeting techniques when projects have unequal lives or when capital must be rationed; and how to recognize real options embedded in capital projects.

MARKETING You need to understand how the risk of proposed projects is measured in capital budgeting, how projects with unequal lives will be evaluated, how to recognize and treat real options embedded in proposed projects, and how projects will be evaluated when capital must be rationed.

OPERATIONS You need to understand how proposals for the acquisition of new equipment and plants will be evaluated by the firm's decision makers, especially projects that are risky, have unequal lives, or may need to be abandoned or slowed, or when capital is limited.

In your *personal* life
Risk is present in all long-term decisions. When making personal financial decisions, you should consider risk in the decision-making process. Simply put, you should demand higher returns for greater risk. Failing to incorporate risk into your financial decision-making process will likely result in poor decisions and reduced wealth.

Worst Case Scenario

On April 20, 2010, an explosion destroyed BP's Deepwater Horizon offshore oil rig, resulting in the largest oil spill in U.S. history. As much as 2.5 million gallons of oil spewed into the Gulf of Mexico each day, eventually reaching the shoreline in several states and causing serious harm to the environment. Under pressure from the Obama administration, BP agreed to establish a $20 billion fund to pay for spill-related expenses such as clean-up costs and compensation for lost income for individuals and businesses directly harmed by the accident.

When managers undertake large investments, they often invest a tremendous amount of time and money trying to understand the risks associated with these investments. In the case of BP, an accident at a rig that cost $500 million to build cost the company more than $20 billion. As news of the accident and subsequent spill evolved, BP's stock price plunged, falling from $60 to less than $30 in just 7 weeks, wiping out more than $90 billion of the firm's market capitalization.

This chapter focuses on the tools available to managers that help them better understand the risks of major investments.

LG 1   **12.1 Introduction to Risk in Capital Budgeting**

In our discussion of capital budgeting thus far, we have assumed that all investment projects have the same level of risk for the firm. In other words, we assumed that all projects are equally risky, and the acceptance of any project would not change the firm's overall risk. In actuality, these situations are rare—projects are not equally risky, and the acceptance of a project can affect the firm's overall risk. We begin this chapter by relaxing these assumptions and focusing on how managers evaluate the risks of different projects. Naturally, we will utilize many of the risk concepts developed in Chapter 8.

We continue the Bennett Company example from Chapter 10. The relevant cash flows and NPVs for Bennett Company's two mutually exclusive projects—A and B—appear in Table 12.1.

In the following three sections, we use the basic risk concepts presented in Chapter 8 to demonstrate behavioral approaches for dealing with risk, international risk considerations, and the use of risk-adjusted discount rates to explicitly recognize risk in the analysis of capital budgeting projects.

→ **REVIEW QUESTION**

12–1 Are most mutually exclusive capital budgeting projects equally risky? If you think about a firm as a portfolio of many different kinds of investments, how can the acceptance of a project change a firm's overall risk?

TABLE 12.1	Relevant Cash Flows and NPVs for Bennett Company's Projects	
	Project A	Project B
A. Relevant cash flows		
Initial investment	$42,000	$45,000
Year	Operating cash inflows	
1	$14,000	$28,000
2	14,000	12,000
3	14,000	10,000
4	14,000	10,000
5	14,000	10,000
B. Decision technique		
NPV @ 10% cost of capital[a]	$11,071	$10,924

[a]From Figure 10.2 on page 398; calculated using a financial calculator.

LG 2 | 12.2 Behavioral Approaches for Dealing with Risk

Behavioral approaches can be used to get a "feel" for the level of project risk, whereas other approaches try to quantify and measure project risk. Here we present a few behavioral approaches for dealing with risk in capital budgeting: risk and cash inflows, scenario analysis, and simulation.

RISK AND CASH INFLOWS

risk (in capital budgeting)
The uncertainty surrounding the cash flows that a project will generate or, more formally, the degree of variability of cash flows.

In the context of capital budgeting, the term **risk** refers to the uncertainty surrounding the cash flows that a project will generate. More formally, risk in capital budgeting is the degree of variability of cash flows. Projects with a broad range of possible cash flows are more risky than projects that have a narrow range of possible cash flows.

In many projects, risk stems almost entirely from the *cash flows* that a project will generate several years in the future because the initial investment is generally known with relative certainty. These cash flows, of course, derive from a number of variables related to revenues, expenditures, and taxes. Examples include the level of sales, the cost of raw materials, labor rates, utility costs, and tax rates. We will concentrate on the risk in the cash flows, but remember that this risk actually results from the interaction of these underlying variables. Therefore, to assess the risk of a proposed capital expenditure, the analyst needs to evaluate the probability that the cash inflows will be large enough to produce a positive NPV.

Example 12.1 ▶

Treadwell Tire Company, a tire retailer with a 10% cost of capital, is considering investing in either of two mutually exclusive projects, A and B. Each requires a $10,000 initial investment, and both are expected to provide constant annual cash inflows over their 15-year lives. For either project to be acceptable, its NPV must be greater than zero. Another way to say this is that the present value of the annuity (that is, the project's cash inflows) must be greater than the initial cash outflow. If we let *CF* equal the annual cash inflow and let CF_0 equal the initial investment, the following condition must be met for projects with annuity cash inflows, such as A and B, to be acceptable:[1]

breakeven cash inflow
The minimum level of cash inflow necessary for a project to be acceptable, that is, NPV > $0.

$$\text{NPV} = \left(\frac{CF}{i}\right) \times \left[1 - \frac{1}{(1 + i)^n}\right] - CF_0 > \$0 \qquad (12.1)$$

By substituting $i = 10\%$, $n = 15$ years, and $CF_0 = \$10,000$, we can find the **breakeven cash inflow**—the minimum level of cash inflow necessary for Treadwell's projects to be acceptable.

Calculator Use Recognizing that the initial investment (CF_0) is the present value (PV), we can use the calculator inputs shown at the left to find the breakeven cash inflow (CF), which is an ordinary annuity (PMT).

Input	Function
10000	PV
15	N
10	I
	CPT
	PMT

Solution
1,314.74

---

1. This equation makes use of the algebraic shortcut for the present value of an annuity, introduced as Equation 5.11 on page 173.

Spreadsheet Use   The breakeven cash inflow also can be calculated as shown on the following Excel spreadsheet.

	A	B
1	BREAKEVEN CASH INFLOW	
2	Cost of capital	10%
3	Number of years	15
4	Initial investment	$10,000
5	Breakeven cash inflow	$1,314.74
Entry in Cell B5 is =PMT(B2,B3,−B4). The minus sign appears before B4 because the initial investment is a cash outflow.		

The calculator and spreadsheet values indicate that, for the projects to be acceptable, they must have annual cash inflows of at least $1,315. Given this breakeven level of cash inflows, the risk of each project can be assessed by determining the probability that the project's cash inflows will equal or exceed this breakeven level. The various statistical techniques that would determine that probability are covered in more advanced courses.[2] For now, we can simply assume that such a statistical analysis results in the following:

Probability of $CF_A > \$1,315 \rightarrow 100\%$

Probability of $CF_B > \$1,315 \rightarrow 65\%$

Because project A is certain (100% probability) to have a positive net present value, whereas there is only a 65% chance that project B will have a positive NPV, project A seems less risky than project B. Of course, the expected level of annual cash inflow and NPV associated with each project must be evaluated in view of the firm's risk preference before the preferred project is selected.

The example clearly identifies risk as it is related to the chance that a project is acceptable, but it does not address the issue of cash flow variability. Even though project B has a greater chance of loss than project A, it might result in higher potential NPVs. Recall that it is the *combination* of risk and return that determines value. Similarly, the worth of a capital expenditure and its impact on the firm's value must be viewed in light of both risk and return. The analyst must therefore consider the *variability* of cash inflows and NPVs to assess project risk and return fully.

SCENARIO ANALYSIS

Scenario analysis can be used to deal with project risk to capture the variability of cash inflows and NPVs. *Scenario analysis* is a behavioral approach that uses several possible alternative outcomes (scenarios), to obtain a sense of the variability of returns, measured here by NPV. This technique is often useful in getting a feel for the variability of return in response to changes in a key outcome. In capital

---

2. Normal distributions are commonly used to develop the concept of the *probability of success*—that is, of a project having a positive NPV. The reader interested in learning more about this technique should see any second- or MBA-level managerial finance text.

TABLE 12.2	Scenario Analysis of Treadwell's Projects A and B	
	Project A	Project B
Initial investment	$10,000	$10,000
	Annual cash inflows	
Outcome		
Pessimistic	$1,500	$ 0
Most likely	2,000	2,000
Optimistic	2,500	4,000
Range	1,000	4,000
	Net present values[a]	
Outcome		
Pessimistic	$1,409	−$10,000
Most likely	5,212	5,212
Optimistic	9,015	20,424
Range	7,606	30,424

[a]These values were calculated by using the corresponding annual cash inflows. A 10% cost of capital and a 15-year life for the annual cash inflows were used.

budgeting, one of the most common scenario approaches is to estimate the NPVs associated with pessimistic (worst), most likely (expected), and optimistic (best) estimates of cash inflow. The *range* can be determined by subtracting the pessimistic-outcome NPV from the optimistic-outcome NPV.

Example 12.2 ▶ Continuing with Treadwell Tire Company, assume that the financial manager created three scenarios for each project: pessimistic, most likely, and optimistic. The cash inflows and resulting NPVs in each case are summarized in Table 12.2. Comparing the ranges of cash inflows ($1,000 for project A and $4,000 for B) and, more important, the ranges of NPVs ($7,606 for project A and $30,424 for B) makes it clear that project A is less risky than project B. Given that both projects have the same most likely NPV of $5,212, the assumed risk-averse decision maker will take project A because it has less risk (smaller NPV range) and no possibility of loss (all NPVs > $0).

The widespread availability of computers and spreadsheets has greatly enhanced the use of scenario analysis because technology allows analysts to quickly create a wide range of different scenarios.

SIMULATION

simulation
A statistics-based behavioral approach that applies predetermined probability distributions and random numbers to estimate risky outcomes.

Simulation is a statistics-based behavioral approach that applies predetermined probability distributions and random numbers to estimate risky outcomes. By tying the various cash flow components together in a mathematical model and

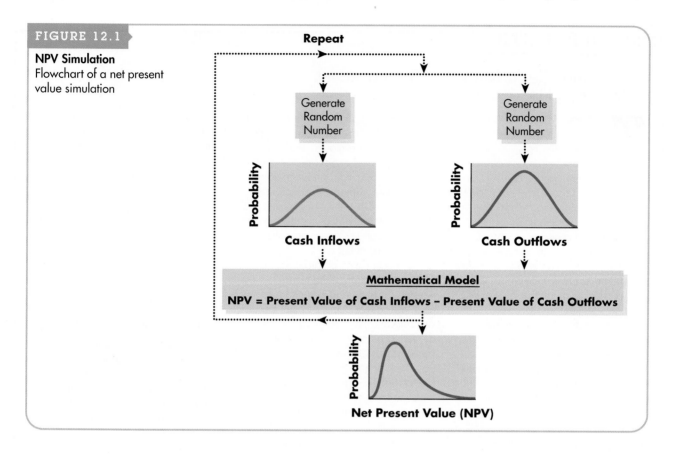

FIGURE 12.1

NPV Simulation
Flowchart of a net present
value simulation

Repeat

Generate
Random
Number

Generate
Random
Number

Probability

Cash Inflows

Probability

Cash Outflows

Mathematical Model

NPV = Present Value of Cash Inflows – Present Value of Cash Outflows

Probability

Net Present Value (NPV)

repeating the process numerous times, the financial manager can develop a probability distribution of project returns.

Figure 12.1 presents a flowchart of the simulation of the net present value of a project. The process of generating random numbers and using the probability distributions for cash inflows and cash outflows enables the financial manager to determine values for each of these variables. Substituting these values into the mathematical model results in an NPV. By repeating this process perhaps a thousand times, managers can create a probability distribution of net present values.

Although Figure 12.1 simulates only gross cash inflows and cash outflows, more sophisticated simulations using individual inflow and outflow components, such as sales volume, sale price, raw material cost, labor cost, or maintenance expense, are quite common. From the distribution of returns, the decision maker can determine not only the expected value of the return but also the probability of achieving or surpassing a given return. The use of computers has made the simulation approach feasible. Monte Carlo simulation programs, made popular by widespread use of personal computers, are described in the nearby *Focus on Practice* box.

The output of simulation provides an excellent basis for decision making, because it enables the decision maker to view a continuum of risk–return trade-offs rather than a single-point estimate.

In more depth

To read about *Monte Carlo Simulations,* go to www .myfinancelab.com

| focus on **PRACTICE** |

The Monte Carlo Method: The Forecast Is for Less Uncertainty

in practice Most capital budgeting decisions involve some degree of uncertainty. For example, a company faces some degree of uncertainty associated with the demand for a new product. One method of accounting for this uncertainty is to average the highest and the lowest prediction of sales. However, such a method is flawed. Producing the average of the expected possible demand can lead to gross overproduction or gross underproduction, neither of which is as profitable as having the right volume of production.

To combat uncertainty in the decision-making process, some companies use a Monte Carlo simulation program to model possible outcomes. Developed by mathematicians in World War II while working on the atomic bomb, the *Monte Carlo method* was not widely used until the advent of the personal computer. A Monte Carlo

simulation program randomly generates values for uncertain variables over and over to simulate a model. The simulation then requires project practitioners to develop low, high, and most likely cost estimates along with correlation coefficients. Once these inputs are derived, the Monte Carlo program can be run through just a few simulations, or thousands, in just a few seconds.

A Monte Carlo program usually builds a histogram of the results, referred to as a *frequency chart,* for each forecast or output cell that the user wants to analyze. The program then delivers a percentage *certainty* that a particular forecast will fall within a specified range, much like a weather forecast. The program also has an optimization feature that allows a project manager with budget constraints to figure out which combination of possible projects will result in the highest profit.

One of the problems with using a Monte Carlo program is the difficulty of establishing the correct input ranges for the variables and determining the correlation coefficients for those variables. However, the work put into developing the input for the program can often clarify some uncertainty in a proposed project. Although Monte Carlo simulation is not the perfect answer to capital budgeting problems, it is another tool that corporations, including ALCOA, Motorola, RJR Nabisco, and Walt Disney, use to manage risk and make more informed business and strategic decisions.

▶ *A Monte Carlo simulation program requires the user to first build an Excel spreadsheet model that captures the input variables for the proposed project. What issues and what benefits can the user derive from this process?*

→ **REVIEW QUESTIONS**

12–2 Define *risk* in terms of the cash flows from a capital budgeting project. How can determination of the *breakeven cash inflow* be used to gauge project risk?

12–3 Describe how each of the following behavioral approaches can be used to deal with project risk: (**a**) scenario analysis and (**b**) simulation.

LG 3 | **12.3** International Risk Considerations

exchange rate risk
The danger that an unexpected change in the exchange rate between the dollar and the currency in which a project's cash flows are denominated will reduce the market value of that project's cash flow.

Although the basic techniques of capital budgeting are the same for multinational companies (MNCs) as for purely domestic firms, firms that operate in several countries face risks that are unique to the international arena. Two types of risk are particularly important, exchange rate risk and political risk.

Exchange rate risk reflects the danger that an unexpected change in the exchange rate between the dollar and the currency in which a project's cash flows are denominated will reduce the market value of that project's cash flow. The dollar value of future cash inflows can be dramatically altered if the local currency depreciates against the dollar. In the short term, specific cash flows can be hedged

Matter of fact

Adjusting for Currency Risk

A survey of chief financial officers (CFOs) found that more than 40 percent of the CFOs felt that it was important to adjust an investment project's cash flows or discount rates to account for foreign exchange risk.

transfer prices
Prices that subsidiaries charge each other for the goods and services traded between them.

by using financial instruments such as currency futures and options. Long-term exchange rate risk can best be minimized by financing the project, in whole or in part, in local currency.

Political risk is much harder to protect against. Firms that make investments abroad may find that the host-country government can limit the firm's ability to return profits back home. Governments can seize the firm's assets or otherwise interfere with a project's operation. The difficulties of managing political risk after the fact make it even more important that managers account for political risks *before* making an investment. They can do so either by adjusting a project's expected cash inflows to account for the probability of political interference or by using *risk-adjusted discount rates* (discussed later in this chapter) in capital budgeting formulas. In general, it is much better to adjust individual project cash flows for political risk subjectively than to use a blanket adjustment for all projects.

In addition to unique risks that MNCs must face, several other special issues are relevant only for international capital budgeting. One of these special issues is *taxes*. Because only after-tax cash flows are relevant for capital budgeting, financial managers must carefully account for taxes paid to foreign governments on profits earned within their borders. They must also assess the impact of these tax payments on the parent company's U.S. tax liability.

Another special issue in international capital budgeting is *transfer pricing*. Much of the international trade involving MNCs is, in reality, simply the shipment of goods and services from one of a parent company's subsidiaries to another subsidiary located abroad. The parent company therefore has great discretion in setting **transfer prices,** the prices that subsidiaries charge each other for the goods and services traded between them. The widespread use of transfer pricing in international trade makes capital budgeting in MNCs very difficult unless the transfer prices that are used accurately reflect actual costs and incremental cash flows.

Finally, MNCs often must approach international capital projects from a *strategic point of view,* rather than from a strictly financial perspective. For example, an MNC may feel compelled to invest in a country to ensure continued access, even if the project itself may not have a positive net present value. This motivation was important for Japanese automakers that set up assembly plants in the United States in the early 1980s. For much the same reason, U.S. investment in Europe surged during the years before the market integration of the European Community in 1992. MNCs often invest in production facilities in the home country of major rivals to deny these competitors an uncontested home market. MNCs also may feel compelled to invest in certain industries or countries to achieve a broad corporate objective such as completing a product line or diversifying raw material sources, even when the project's cash flows may not be sufficiently profitable.

→ REVIEW QUESTION

12–4 Briefly explain how the following items affect the capital budgeting decisions of multinational companies: (**a**) exchange rate risk; (**b**) political risk; (**c**) tax law differences; (**d**) transfer pricing; and (**e**) a strategic, rather than a strict, financial viewpoint.

LG 4 12.4 Risk-Adjusted Discount Rates

The approaches for dealing with risk that have been presented so far enable the financial manager to get a "feel" for project risk. Unfortunately, they do not explicitly recognize project risk. We will now illustrate the most popular risk-adjustment technique that employs the net present value (NPV) decision method. The NPV decision rule of accepting only those projects with NPVs > $0 will continue to hold. Close examination of the basic equation for NPV, Equation 10.1, should make it clear that because the initial investment (CF_0) is known with certainty, a project's risk is embodied in the present value of its cash inflows:

$$NPV = \sum_{t=1}^{n} \frac{CF_t}{(1 + r)^t} - CF_0$$

Two opportunities to adjust the present value of cash inflows for risk exist: (1) The cash inflows (CF_t) can be adjusted, or (2) the discount rate (r) can be adjusted. Adjusting the cash inflows is highly subjective, so here we describe the more popular process of adjusting the discount rate. In addition, we consider the portfolio effects of project analysis as well as the practical aspects of the risk-adjusted discount rate.

DETERMINING RISK-ADJUSTED DISCOUNT RATES (RADRS)

A popular approach for risk adjustment involves the use of risk-adjusted discount rates (RADRs). This approach uses Equation 10.1 but employs a risk-adjusted discount rate, as noted in the following expression:[3]

$$NPV = \sum_{t=1}^{n} \frac{CF_t}{(1 + RADR)^t} - CF_0 \tag{12.2}$$

risk-adjusted discount rate (RADR)
The rate of return that must be earned on a given project to compensate the firm's owners adequately—that is, to maintain or improve the firm's share price.

The **risk-adjusted discount rate (RADR)** is the rate of return that must be earned on a given project to compensate the firm's owners adequately—that is, to maintain or improve the firm's share price. The higher the risk of a project, the higher the RADR, and therefore the lower the net present value for a given stream of cash inflows.

Personal Finance Example 12.3 ▶ Talor Namtig is considering investing $1,000 in either of two stocks—A or B. She plans to hold the stock for exactly 5 years and expects both stocks to pay $80 in annual end-of-year cash dividends. At the end of year 5 she estimates that stock A can be sold to net $1,200 and stock B can be sold to net $1,500. Talor has carefully researched the two stocks and feels that although stock A has average risk, stock B is considerably riskier. Her research indicates that she should earn an annual return on an average-risk stock of 11%. Because stock B is considerably riskier, she will require a 14% return from it.

---

3. The risk-adjusted discount rate approach can be applied in using the internal rate of return as well as the net present value. When the IRR is used, the risk-adjusted discount rate becomes the cutoff rate that must be exceeded by the IRR for the project to be accepted. When NPV is used, the projected cash inflows are merely discounted at the risk-adjusted discount rate.

Talor makes the following calculations to find the risk-adjusted net present values (NPVs) for the two stocks:

$$NPV_A = \frac{\$80}{(1\,+\,0.11)^1} + \frac{\$80}{(1\,+\,0.11)^2} + \frac{\$80}{(1\,+\,0.11)^3} + \frac{\$80}{(1\,+\,0.11)^4}$$
$$+ \frac{\$80}{(1\,+\,0.11)^5} + \frac{\$1{,}200}{(1\,+\,0.11)^5} - \$1{,}000 = \$7.81$$

$$NPV_B = \frac{\$80}{(1\,+\,0.14)^1} + \frac{\$80}{(1\,+\,0.14)^2} + \frac{\$80}{(1\,+\,0.14)^3} + \frac{\$80}{(1\,+\,0.14)^4}$$
$$+ \frac{\$80}{(1\,+\,0.14)^5} + \frac{\$1{,}500}{(1\,+\,0.14)^5} - \$1{,}000 = \$53.70$$

Although Talor's calculations indicate that both stock investments are acceptable (NPVs > $0), on a risk-adjusted basis, she should invest in Stock B because it has a higher NPV.

Because the logic underlying the use of RADRs is closely linked to the capital asset pricing model (CAPM) developed in Chapter 8, here we review CAPM and discuss its use in finding RADRs.

Review of CAPM

In Chapter 8, we used the *capital asset pricing model (CAPM)* to link the *relevant* risk and return for all assets traded in *efficient markets*. In the development of the CAPM, the *total risk* of an asset was defined as

$$\text{Total risk} = \text{Nondiversifiable risk} + \text{Diversifiable risk} \qquad (12.3)$$

For assets traded in an efficient market, the *diversifiable risk*, which results from uncontrollable or random events, can be eliminated through diversification. The relevant risk is therefore the *nondiversifiable risk*—the risk for which owners of these assets are rewarded. Nondiversifiable risk for securities is commonly measured by using *beta*, which is an index of the degree of movement of an asset's return in response to a change in the market return.

Using beta, b_j, to measure the relevant risk of any asset j, the CAPM is

$$r_j = R_F + [b_j \times (r_m - R_F)] \qquad (12.4)$$

where

$$r_j = \text{required return on asset } j$$
$$R_F = \text{risk-free rate of return}$$
$$b_j = \text{beta coefficient for asset } j$$
$$r_m = \text{return on the market portfolio of assets}$$

In Chapter 8, we demonstrated that the required return on any asset could be determined by substituting values of R_F, b_j, and r_m into the CAPM—Equation 12.4. Any security that is expected to earn in excess of its required return would be acceptable, and those that are expected to earn an inferior return would be rejected.

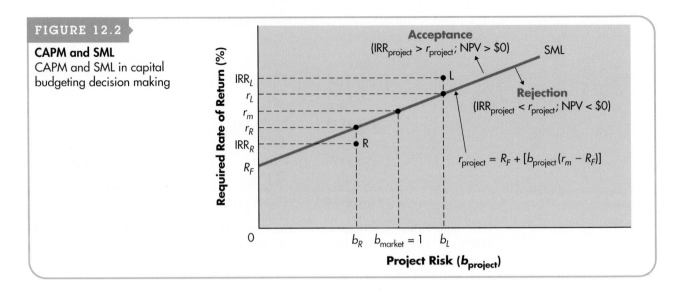

FIGURE 12.2

CAPM and SML
CAPM and SML in capital budgeting decision making

Using CAPM to Find RADRs

If we assume for a moment that real corporate assets such as computers, machine tools, and special-purpose machinery are traded in efficient markets, the CAPM can be redefined as noted in Equation 12.5:

$$r_{\text{project } j} = R_F + [b_{\text{project } j} \times (r_m - R_F)] \tag{12.5}$$

The *security market line* (SML)—the graphical depiction of the CAPM—is shown for Equation 12.5 in Figure 12.2. Any project having an IRR above the SML would be acceptable, because its IRR would exceed the required return, r_{project}; any project with an IRR below r_{project} would be rejected. In terms of NPV, any project falling above the SML would have a positive NPV, and any project falling below the SML would have a negative NPV.[4]

Example 12.4 ▶

Figure 12.2 shows two projects, L and R. Project L has a beta, b_L, and generates an internal rate of return, IRR_L. The required return for a project with risk b_L is r_L. Because project L generates a return greater than that required ($IRR_L > r_L$), project L is acceptable. Project L will have a positive NPV when its cash inflows are discounted at its required return, r_L. Project R, on the other hand, generates an IRR below that required for its risk, b_R ($IRR_R < r_R$). This project will have a negative NPV when its cash inflows are discounted at its required return, r_R. Project R should be rejected.

---

4. As noted earlier, whenever the IRR is above the cost of capital or required return (IRR > r), the NPV is positive, and whenever the IRR is below the cost of capital or required return (IRR < r), the NPV is negative. Because by definition the IRR is the discount rate that causes NPV to equal zero and the IRR and NPV always agree on accept–reject decisions, the relationship noted in Figure 12.2 logically follows.

---

focus on ETHICS

Ethics and the Cost of Capital

in practice At the dawn of the new millennium, the company formerly known as British Petroleum was trying to reinvent itself. BP introduced a new corporate logo, a green, yellow, and white sunburst, which "symbolized energy in all its dynamic forms." In their 2009 sustainability review, BP defined sustainability as "the capacity to endure as a group: by renewing assets; creating and delivering better products and services that meet the evolving needs of society; attracting successive generations of employees; contributing to a sustainable environment; and retaining the trust and support of our customers, shareholders and the communities in which we operate."[a]

However, BP's environmental track record didn't always support the image the company was trying to portray. In 2005, a fire at BP's Texas City Refinery killed fifteen workers and injured many more. The following year, BP shut down their Prudhoe Bay oil field due to corrosion in an oil transit line that resulted in an oil spill. BP was widely criticized for these events, but that did not stop BP from causing the largest oil spill in U.S. history.

The Deepwater Horizon accident and subsequent oil spill had a significant impact on BP's cost of capital. By June 2010, BP's stock price was 50 percent below precrisis levels, and the company's bonds traded at levels comparable to junk-rated companies. Over the course of a single week, when BP's "top kill" attempt to stop the leak proved unsuccessful, the yield on the company's main 5-year dollar bond jumped by 2 percent. The bond rating agencies downgraded BP, although the firm continued to possess one of the highest investment grade credit ratings. However, the rating agencies warned that further downgrades could follow if the crisis, and the expected costs, continued to escalate.

▶ *Is the ultimate goal of the firm, to maximize the wealth of the owners for whom the firm is being operated, ethical?*

▶ *Why might ethical companies benefit from a lower cost of capital than less ethical companies?*

[a]www.bp.com/liveassets/bp_internet/globalbp/STAGING/global_assets/e_s_assets/e_s_assets_2009/downloads_pdfs/bp_sustainability_review_2009.pdf

---

APPLYING RADRS

Because the CAPM is based on an assumed efficient market, which does *not* always exist for real corporate (nonfinancial) assets such as plant and equipment, managers sometimes argue that the CAPM is not directly applicable in calculating RADRs. Instead, financial managers sometimes assess the *total risk* of a project and use it to determine the risk-adjusted discount rate (RADR), which can be used in Equation 12.2 to find the NPV.

To avoid damaging its market value, the firm must use the correct discount rate to evaluate a project. The nearby *Focus on Ethics* box describes a real example of a company that failed to recognize (or that ignored) certain risks associated with their business operations. As a result, the firm experienced monetary sanctions. If a firm fails to incorporate all relevant risks in its decision-making process, it may discount a risky project's cash inflows at too low a rate and accept the project. The firm's market price may drop later as investors recognize that the firm itself has become more risky. Conversely, if the firm discounts a project's cash inflows at too high a rate, it will reject acceptable projects. Eventually the firm's market price may drop because investors who believe that the firm is being overly conservative will sell their stock, putting downward pressure on the firm's market value.

Unfortunately, there is no formal mechanism for linking *total project risk* to the level of required return. As a result, most firms subjectively determine the RADR by adjusting their existing required return. They adjust it up or down depending on whether the proposed project is more or less risky, respectively, than the average risk of the firm. This CAPM-type of approach provides a "rough estimate" of the project risk and required return because both the project risk measure and the linkage between risk and required return are estimates.

Example 12.5 ▶

Bennett Company wishes to use the risk-adjusted discount rate approach to determine, according to NPV, whether to implement project A or project B. In addition to the data presented in part A of Table 12.1, Bennett's management after much analysis subjectively assigned "risk indexes" of 1.6 to project A and 1.0 to project B. The risk index is merely a numerical scale used to classify project risk: Higher index values are assigned to higher-risk projects, and vice versa. The CAPM-type relationship used by the firm to link risk (measured by the risk index) and the required return (RADR) is shown in the following table. Management developed this relationship after analyzing CAPM and the risk–return relationships of the projects that they considered and implemented during the past few years.

	Risk index	Required return (RADR)
	0.0	6% (risk-free rate, R_F)
	0.2	7
	0.4	8
	0.6	9
	0.8	10
Project B →	1.0	11
	1.2	12
	1.4	13
Project A →	1.6	14
	1.8	16
	2.0	18

Project A

Input	Function
−42000	CF$_0$
14000	CF$_1$
5	N
14	I
	NPV

Solution
6,063.13

Project B

Input	Function
−45000	CF$_0$
28000	CF$_1$
12000	CF$_2$
10000	CF$_3$
3	N
11	I
	NPV

Solution
9,798.43

Because project A is riskier than project B, its RADR of 14% is greater than project B's 11%. The net present value of each project, calculated using its RADR, is found as shown on the time lines in Figure 12.3. The results clearly show that project B is preferable, because its risk-adjusted NPV of $9,798 is greater than the $6,063 risk-adjusted NPV for project A. As reflected by the NPVs in part B of Table 12.1, if the discount rates were not adjusted for risk, project A would be preferred to project B.

Calculator Use We can again use the preprogrammed NPV function in a financial calculator to simplify the NPV calculation. The keystrokes for project A—the annuity—typically are as shown at the left. The keystrokes for project B—the mixed stream—are also shown at the left. The calculated NPVs for projects A and B of $6,063 and $9,798, respectively, agree with those shown in Figure 12.3.

Spreadsheet Use Analysis of projects using risk-adjusted discount rates (RADRs) also can be performed as shown on the following Excel spreadsheet.

	A	B	C	D
1	ANALYSIS OF PROJECTS USING RISK-ADJUSTED DISCOUNT RATES			
2	Year	Cash Inflow	Present Value	Formulas for Calculated Values in Column C
3	Project A			
4	1-5	$ 14,000	$48,063	–PV(C7,5,B4,0)
5	Initial Investment		$42,000	
6	Net Present Value		$ 6,063	C4–C5
7	Required Return (RADAR)		14%	
8	Project B			
9	1	$ 28,000	$25,225	–PV(C17,A9,0,B9,0)
10	2	12,000	9,739	–PV(C17,A10,0,B10,0)
11	3	10,000	7,312	–PV(C17,A11,0,B11,0)
12	4	10,000	6,587	–PV(C17,A12,0,B12,0)
13	5	10,000	5,935	–PV(C17,A13,0,B13,0)
14	Present value		$54,798	SUM(C9:C13) or NPV(C17,B9:B13)
15	Initial Investment		$45,000	
16	Net Present Value		$ 9,798	C14–C15
17	Required Return (RADAR)		11%	
18	Choice of project		B	IF(C6>=C16,"A","B")

The minus signs appear before the entries in Cells D4 and D9:D13 to convert the results to positive values.

FIGURE 12.3

Calculation of NPVS for Bennett Company's Capital Expenditure Alternatives Using RADRs

Time lines depicting the cash flows and NPV calculations using RADRs for projects A and B

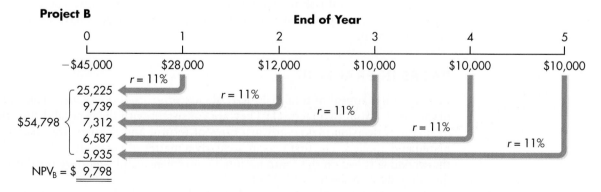

Note: When we use the risk indexes of 1.6 and 1.0 for projects A and B, respectively, along with the table above, a risk-adjusted discount rate (RADR) of 14% results for project A and an RADR of 11% results for project B.

The usefulness of risk-adjusted discount rates should now be clear. The real difficulty lies in estimating project risk and linking it to the required return (RADR).

PORTFOLIO EFFECTS

As noted in Chapter 8, because investors are not rewarded for taking diversifiable risk, they should hold a diversified portfolio of securities. Because a business firm can be viewed as a portfolio of assets, is it similarly important that the firm maintain a diversified portfolio of assets?

It seems logical that by holding a diversified portfolio the firm could reduce the variability of its cash flows. By combining two projects with negatively correlated cash inflows, the firm could reduce the combined cash inflow variability—and therefore the risk.

Are firms rewarded for diversifying risk in this fashion? If they are, the value of the firm could be enhanced through diversification into other lines of business. Surprisingly, the value of the stock of firms whose shares are traded publicly in an efficient marketplace is generally *not* affected by diversification. In other words, diversification is not normally rewarded and therefore is generally not necessary.

Why are firms not rewarded for diversification? Because investors themselves can diversify by holding securities in a variety of firms; they do not need the firm to do it for them. And investors can diversify more readily—they can make transactions more easily and at a lower cost because of the greater availability of information and trading mechanisms.

Of course, if a firm acquires a new line of business and its cash flows tend to respond more to changing economic conditions (that is, greater nondiversifiable risk), greater returns would be expected. If, for the additional risk, the firm earned a return in excess of that required (IRR $>$ r), the value of the firm could be enhanced. Also, other benefits, such as increased cash, greater borrowing capacity, guaranteed availability of raw materials, and so forth, could result from and therefore justify diversification, in spite of any immediate impact on cash flow.

Although a strict theoretical view supports the use of a technique that relies on the CAPM framework, the presence of market imperfections causes the market for real corporate assets to be inefficient at least some of the time. The relative inefficiency of this market, coupled with difficulties associated with measurement of nondiversifiable project risk and its relationship to return, tend to favor the use of total risk to evaluate capital budgeting projects. Therefore, the use of *total risk* as an approximation for the relevant risk does have widespread practical appeal.

RADRS IN PRACTICE

In spite of the appeal of total risk, *RADRs are often used in practice*. Their popularity stems from two facts: (1) They are consistent with the general disposition of financial decision makers toward rates of return, and (2) they are easily estimated and applied. The first reason is clearly a matter of personal preference, but the second is based on the computational convenience and well-developed procedures involved in the use of RADRs.

In practice, firms often establish a number of *risk classes,* with an RADR assigned to each. Like the CAPM-type risk–return relationship described earlier,

TABLE 12.3	Bennett Company's Risk Classes and RADRs	
Risk class	Description	Risk-adjusted discount rate, RADR
I	*Below-average risk:* Projects with low risk. Typically involve routine replacement without renewal of existing activities.	8%
II	*Average risk:* Projects similar to those currently implemented. Typically involve replacement or renewal of existing activities.	10% [a]
III	*Above-average risk:* Projects with higher than normal, but not excessive, risk. Typically involve expansion of existing or similar activities.	14%
IV	*Highest risk:* Projects with very high risk. Typically involve expansion into new or unfamiliar activities.	20%

[a]This RADR is actually the firm's cost of capital, which is discussed in detail in Chapter 9. It represents the firm's required return on its existing portfolio of projects, which is assumed to be unchanged with acceptance of the "average-risk" project.

management develops the risk classes and RADRs based on both CAPM and the risk–return behaviors of past projects. Each new project is then subjectively placed in the appropriate risk class, and the corresponding RADR is used to evaluate it. This is sometimes done on a division-by-division basis, in which case each division has its own set of risk classes and associated RADRs, similar to those for Bennett Company in Table 12.3. The use of *divisional costs of capital* and associated risk classes enables a large multidivisional firm to incorporate differing levels of divisional risk into the capital budgeting process and still recognize differences in the levels of individual project risk.

Example 12.6 ▶ Assume that the management of Bennett Company decided to use risk classes to analyze projects and so placed each project in one of four risk classes according to its perceived risk. The classes ranged from I for the lowest-risk projects to IV for the highest-risk projects. Associated with each class was an RADR appropriate to the level of risk of projects in the class, as given in Table 12.3. Bennett classified as lower-risk those projects that tend to involve routine replacement or renewal activities; higher-risk projects involve expansion, often into new or unfamiliar activities.

The financial manager of Bennett has assigned project A to class III and project B to class II. The cash flows for project A would be evaluated using a 14% RADR, and project B's would be evaluated using a 10% RADR.[5] The NPV of project A at 14% was calculated in Figure 12.3 to be $6,063, and the NPV for project B at a 10% RADR was shown in Table 12.1 to be $10,924. Clearly, with RADRs based on the use of risk classes, project B is preferred over project A.

---

5. Note that the 10 percent RADR for project B using the risk classes in Table 12.3 differs from the 11 percent RADR used in the preceding example for project B. This difference is attributable to the less precise nature of the use of risk classes.

As noted earlier, this result is contrary to the preferences shown in Table 12.1, where differing risks of projects A and B were not taken into account.

→ REVIEW QUESTIONS

12–5 Describe the basic procedures involved in using *risk-adjusted discount rates (RADRs)*. How is this approach related to the *capital asset pricing model (CAPM)?*

12–6 Explain why a firm whose stock is actively traded in the securities markets need not concern itself with diversification. In spite of this, how is the risk of capital budgeting projects frequently measured? Why?

12–7 How are *risk classes* often used to apply RADRs?

LG 5   LG 6   ## 12.5 Capital Budgeting Refinements

Refinements must often be made in the analysis of capital budgeting projects to accommodate special circumstances. These adjustments permit the relaxation of certain simplifying assumptions presented earlier. Three areas in which special forms of analysis are frequently needed are (1) comparison of mutually exclusive projects having unequal lives, (2) recognition of real options, and (3) capital rationing caused by a binding budget constraint.

COMPARING PROJECTS WITH UNEQUAL LIVES

The financial manager must often select the best of a group of unequal-lived projects. If the projects are independent, the length of the project lives is not critical. But when unequal-lived projects are mutually exclusive, the impact of differing lives must be considered because the projects do not provide service over comparable time periods. This is especially important when continuing service is needed from the project under consideration. The discussions that follow assume that the unequal-lived, mutually exclusive projects being compared *are ongoing.* If they were not, the project with the highest NPV would be selected.

The Problem

A simple example will demonstrate the basic problem of noncomparability caused by the need to select the best of a group of mutually exclusive projects with differing usable lives.

Example 12.7 ▶   The AT Company, a regional cable television company, is evaluating two projects, X and Y. The relevant cash flows for each project are given in the following table. The applicable cost of capital for use in evaluating these equally risky projects is 10%.

	Project X	Project Y
Initial investment	$70,000	$85,000
Year	Annual cash inflows	
1	$28,000	$35,000
2	33,000	30,000
3	38,000	25,000
4	—	20,000
5	—	15,000
6	—	10,000

Project X

Project Y

Calculator Use   Employing the preprogrammed NPV function in a financial calculator, we use the keystrokes shown at the left for project X and for project Y to find their respective NPVs of $11,277.24 and $19,013.27.

Spreadsheet Use   The net present values of two projects with unequal lives also can be compared as shown on the following Excel spreadsheet.

	A	B	C
1	COMPARISON OF NET PRESENT VALUES OF TWO PROJECTS WITH UNEQUAL LIVES		
2		Cost of Capital	10%
3		Year-End Cash Flows	
4	Year	Project X	Project Y
5	0	$ (70,000)	$ (85,000)
6	1	$ 28,000	$ 35,000
7	2	$ 33,000	$ 30,000
8	3	$ 38,000	$ 25,000
9	4		$ 20,000
10	5		$ 15,000
11	6		$ 10,000
12	NPV	$ 11,277.24	$ 19,013.27
13	Choice of project		Project Y

Entry in Cell B12 is
=NPV(C2,B6:B11)+B5.
Copy the entry in Cell B12 to Cell C12.
Entry in Cell C13 is =IF(B12>=C12,B4,C4).

Ignoring the differences in project lives, we can see that both projects are acceptable (both NPVs are greater than zero) and that project Y is preferred over project X. If the projects were independent and only one could be accepted, project Y—with the larger NPV—would be preferred. If the projects were mutually exclusive, their differing lives would have to be considered. Project Y provides 3 more years of service than project X.

The analysis in the preceding example is incomplete if the projects are mutually exclusive (which will be our assumption throughout the remaining discussions). To compare these unequal-lived, mutually exclusive projects correctly, we must consider the differing lives in the analysis; an incorrect decision could result from simply using NPV to select the better project. Although a number of approaches are available for dealing with unequal lives, here we present the most efficient technique—the *annualized net present value (ANPV) approach*.

Annualized Net Present Value (ANPV) Approach

annualized net present value (ANPV) approach
An approach to evaluating unequal-lived projects that converts the net present value of unequal-lived, mutually exclusive projects into an equivalent annual amount (in NPV terms).

The **annualized net present value (ANPV) approach**[6] converts the net present value of unequal-lived, mutually exclusive projects into an equivalent annual amount (in NPV terms) that can be used to select the best project.[7] This net present value based approach can be applied to unequal-lived, mutually exclusive projects by using the following steps:

Step 1   Calculate the net present value of each project j, NPV_j, over its life, n_j, using the appropriate cost of capital, r.

Step 2   Convert the NPV_j into an annuity having life n_j. That is, find an annuity that has the same life and the same NPV as the project.

Step 3   Select the project that has the highest ANPV.

Example 12.8 ▶

Project X

Project Y

By using the AT Company data presented earlier for projects X and Y, we can apply the three-step ANPV approach as follows:

Step 1   The net present values of projects X and Y discounted at 10%—as calculated in the preceding example for a single purchase of each asset—are

$$NPV_X = \$11,277.24$$
$$NPV_Y = \$19,013.27$$

Step 2   In this step, we want to convert the NPVs from Step 1 into annuities. For project X, we are trying to find the answer to the question, what 3-year annuity (equal to the life of project X) has a present value of $11,277.24 (the NPV of project X)? Likewise, for project Y we want to know what 6-year annuity has a present value of $19,013.27. Once we have these values, we can determine which project, X or Y, delivers a higher annual cash flow on a present value basis.

Calculator Use   The keystrokes required to find the ANPV on a financial calculator are identical to those demonstrated in Chapter 5 for finding the annual payments on an installment loan. These keystrokes are shown at the left for project X and for project Y. The resulting ANPVs for projects X and Y are $4,534.74 and $4,365.59, respectively.

Spreadsheet Use   The annualized net present values of two projects with unequal lives also can be compared as shown on the following Excel spreadsheet.

---

6. This approach is also called the "equivalent annual annuity (EAA)" or the "equivalent annual cost." The term *annualized net present value (ANPV)* is used here due to its descriptive clarity.

7. The theory underlying this as well as other approaches for comparing projects with unequal lives assumes that each project can be replaced in the future for the same initial investment and that each will provide the same expected future cash inflows. Although changing technology and inflation will affect the initial investment and expected cash inflows, the lack of specific attention to them does not detract from the usefulness of this technique.

	A	B	C
1	COMPARISON OF ANNUALIZED NET PRESENT VALUES OF TWO PROJECTS WITH UNEQUAL LIVES		
2		Cost of Capital	10%
3		Year-End Cash Flows	
4	Year	Project X	Project Y
5	0	$ (70,000)	$ (85,000)
6	1	$ 28,000	$ 35,000
7	2	$ 33,000	$ 30,000
8	3	$ 38,000	$ 25,000
9	4		$ 20,000
10	5		$ 15,000
11	6		$ 10,000
12	NPV	$ 11,277.24	$ 19,013.27
13	ANPV	$ 4,534.74	$ 4,365.59
14	Choice of project		Project X

Entry in Cell B12 is
=NPV(C2,B6:B11)+B5.
Copy the entry in Cell B12 to Cell C12.
Entry in Cell B13 is =B12/PV(C2,3,−1).
Entry in Cell C13 is =C12/PV(C2,6,−1).
Entry in Cell C14 is =IF(B13>=C13,B4,C4).

Step 3 Reviewing the ANPVs calculated in Step 2, we can see that project X would be preferred over project Y. Given that projects X and Y are mutually exclusive, project X would be the recommended project because it provides the higher annualized net present value.

RECOGNIZING REAL OPTIONS

The procedures described in Chapters 10 and 11 and thus far in this chapter suggest that to make capital budgeting decisions, we must (1) estimate relevant cash flows, (2) apply an appropriate decision technique such as NPV or IRR to those cash flows, and (3) recognize and adjust the decision technique for project risk. Although this traditional procedure is believed to yield good decisions, a more *strategic approach* to these decisions has emerged in recent years. This more modern view considers any **real options**—opportunities that are embedded in capital projects ("real," rather than financial, asset investments) that enable managers to alter their cash flows and risk in a way that affects project acceptability (NPV). Because these opportunities are more likely to exist in, and be more important to, large "strategic" capital budgeting projects, they are sometimes called *strategic options*.

Table 12.4 briefly describes some of the more common types of real options—abandonment, flexibility, growth, and timing. It should be clear from their descriptions that each of these types of options could be embedded in a capital budgeting decision and that explicit recognition of them would probably alter the cash flow and risk of a project and change its NPV.

By explicitly recognizing these options when making capital budgeting decisions, managers can make improved, more strategic decisions that consider in advance the economic impact of certain contingent actions on project cash flow

real options
Opportunities that are embedded in capital projects that enable managers to alter their cash flows and risk in a way that affects project acceptability (NPV). Also called *strategic options*.

TABLE 12.4	Major Types of Real Options

Option type	Description
Abandonment option	The option to abandon or terminate a project prior to the end of its planned life. This option allows management to avoid or minimize losses on projects that turn bad. Explicitly recognizing the abandonment option when evaluating a project often increases its NPV.
Flexibility option	The option to incorporate flexibility into the firm's operations, particularly production. It generally includes the opportunity to design the production process to accept multiple inputs, use flexible production technology to create a variety of outputs by reconfiguring the same plant and equipment, and to purchase and retain excess capacity in capital-intensive industries subject to wide swings in output demand and long lead time in building new capacity from scratch. Recognition of this option embedded in a capital expenditure should increase the NPV of the project.
Growth option	The option to develop follow-on projects, expand markets, expand or retool plants, and so on, that would not be possible without implementation of the project that is being evaluated. If a project being considered has the measurable potential to open new doors if successful, then recognition of the cash flows from such opportunities should be included in the initial decision process. Growth opportunities embedded in a project often increase the NPV of the project in which they are embedded.
Timing option	The option to determine when various actions with respect to a given project are taken. This option recognizes the firm's opportunity to delay acceptance of a project for one or more periods, to accelerate or slow the process of implementing a project in response to new information, or to shut down a project temporarily in response to changing product market conditions or competition. As in the case of the other types of options, the explicit recognition of timing opportunities can improve the NPV of a project that fails to recognize this option in an investment decision.

and risk. The explicit recognition of real options embedded in capital budgeting projects will cause the project's *strategic NPV* to differ from its *traditional NPV*, as indicated by Equation 12.7.

$$NPV_{strategic} = NPV_{traditional} + \text{Value of real options} \qquad (12.7)$$

Application of this relationship is illustrated in the following example.

Example 12.9 ▶ Assume that a strategic analysis of Bennett Company's projects A and B (see cash flows and NPVs in Table 12.1) finds no real options embedded in project A and two real options embedded in project B. The two real options in project B are as follows: (1) The project would have, during the first two years, some downtime that would result in unused production capacity that could be used to perform contract manufacturing for another firm, and (2) the project's computerized control system could, with some modification, control two other machines, thereby reducing labor cost, without affecting operation of the new project.

Bennett's management estimated the NPV of the contract manufacturing over the two years following implementation of project B to be $1,500 and the NPV of the computer control sharing to be $2,000. Management felt there was a 60% chance that the contract manufacturing option would be exercised and only a 30% chance that the computer control sharing option would be exercised. The combined value of these two real options would be the sum of their expected values:

Value of real options for project B $= (0.60 \times \$1,500) + (0.30 \times \$2,000)$
$$= \$900 + \$600 = \$1,500$$

Substituting the $1,500 real options value along with the traditional NPV of $10,924 for project B (from Table 12.1) into Equation 12.7, we get the strategic NPV for project B:

$$\text{NPV}_{\text{strategic}} = \$10,924 + \$1,500 = \underline{\$12,424}$$

Bennett Company's project B therefore has a strategic NPV of $12,424, which is above its traditional NPV and now exceeds project A's NPV of $11,071. Clearly, recognition of project B's real options improved its NPV (from $10,924 to $12,424) and causes it to be preferred over project A (NPV of $12,424 for B > NPV of $11,071 for A), which has no real options embedded in it.

It is important to realize that the recognition of attractive real options when determining NPV could cause an otherwise unacceptable project ($\text{NPV}_{\text{traditional}} < \$0$) to become acceptable ($\text{NPV}_{\text{strategic}} > \$0$). The failure to recognize the value of real options could therefore cause management to reject projects that are acceptable. Although doing so requires more strategic thinking and analysis, it is important for the financial manager to identify and incorporate real options in the NPV process. The procedures for doing this efficiently are emerging, and the use of the strategic NPV that incorporates real options is expected to become more commonplace in the future.

CAPITAL RATIONING

Firms commonly operate under *capital rationing*—they have more acceptable independent projects than they can fund. In theory, capital rationing should not exist. Firms should accept all projects that have positive NPVs (or IRRs > the cost of capital). However, in practice, most firms operate under capital rationing. Generally, firms attempt to isolate and select the best acceptable projects subject to a capital expenditure budget set by management. Research has found that management internally imposes capital expenditure constraints to avoid what it deems to be "excessive" levels of new financing, particularly debt. Although failing to fund all acceptable independent projects is theoretically inconsistent with the goal of maximizing owner wealth, here we will discuss capital rationing procedures because they are widely used in practice.

The objective of *capital rationing* is to select the group of projects that provides the *highest overall net present value* and does not require more dollars than are budgeted. As a prerequisite to capital rationing, the best of any mutually exclusive projects must be chosen and placed in the group of independent projects. Two basic approaches to project selection under capital rationing are discussed here.

Internal Rate of Return Approach

internal rate of return approach
An approach to capital rationing that involves graphing project IRRs in descending order against the total dollar investment to determine the group of acceptable projects.

investment opportunities schedule (IOS)
The graph that plots project IRRs in descending order against the total dollar investment.

The **internal rate of return approach** involves graphing project IRRs in descending order against the total dollar investment. This graph is called the **investment opportunities schedule (IOS).** By drawing the cost-of-capital line and then imposing a budget constraint, the financial manager can determine the group of acceptable projects. The problem with this technique is that it does not guarantee the maximum dollar return to the firm. It merely provides a satisfactory solution to capital-rationing problems.

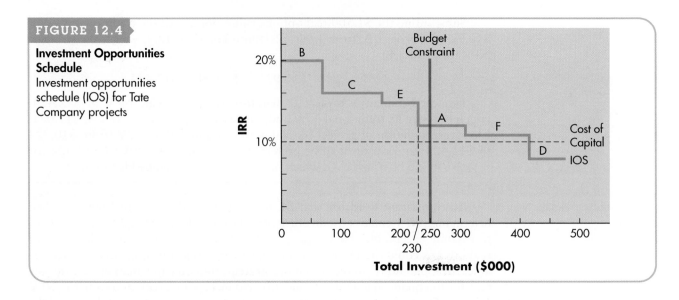

FIGURE 12.4

Investment Opportunities Schedule

Investment opportunities schedule (IOS) for Tate Company projects

---

Example 12.10 ▶   Tate Company, a fast-growing plastics company, is confronted with six projects competing for its fixed budget of $250,000. The initial investment and IRR for each project are shown in the following table:

Project	Initial investment	IRR
A	$ 80,000	12%
B	70,000	20
C	100,000	16
D	40,000	8
E	60,000	15
F	110,000	11

The firm has a cost of capital of 10%. Figure 12.4 presents the IOS that results from ranking the six projects in descending order on the basis of their IRRs. According to the schedule, only projects B, C, and E should be accepted. Together they will absorb $230,000 of the $250,000 budget. Projects A and F are acceptable but cannot be chosen because of the budget constraint. Project D is not worthy of consideration; its IRR is less than the firm's 10% cost of capital.

The drawback of this approach is that there is no guarantee that the acceptance of projects B, C, and E will maximize *total dollar returns* and therefore owners' wealth.

---

net present value approach
An approach to capital rationing that is based on the use of present values to determine the group of projects that will maximize owners' wealth.

Net Present Value Approach

The **net present value approach** is based on the use of present values to determine the group of projects that will maximize owners' wealth. It is implemented by ranking projects on the basis of IRRs and then evaluating the present value of the benefits from each potential project to determine *the combination of projects*

TABLE 12.5	Rankings for Tate Company Projects		
Project	Initial investment	IRR	Present value of inflows at 10%
B	$ 70,000	20%	$112,000
C	100,000	16	145,000
E	60,000	15	79,000
A	80,000	12	100,000
F	110,000	11	126,500
D	40,000	8	36,000

Cutoff point (IRR < 10%)

with the highest overall present value. This is the same as maximizing net present value because the entire budget is viewed as the total initial investment. Any portion of the firm's budget that is not used does not increase the firm's value. At best, the unused money can be invested in marketable securities or returned to the owners in the form of cash dividends. In either case, the wealth of the owners is not likely to be enhanced.

Example 12.11 ▶ The projects described in the preceding example are ranked in Table 12.5 on the basis of IRRs. The present value of the cash inflows associated with the projects is also included in the table. Projects B, C, and E, which together require $230,000, yield a present value of $336,000. However, if projects B, C, and A were implemented, the total budget of $250,000 would be used, and the present value of the cash inflows would be $357,000. This is greater than the return expected from selecting the projects on the basis of the highest IRRs. Implementing B, C, and A is preferable because they maximize the present value for the given budget. *The firm's objective is to use its budget to generate the highest present value of inflows.* Assuming that any unused portion of the budget does not gain or lose money, the total NPV for projects B, C, and E would be $106,000 ($336,000 − $230,000), whereas the total NPV for projects B, C, and A would be $107,000 ($357,000 − $250,000). Selection of projects B, C, and A will therefore maximize NPV.

→ REVIEW QUESTIONS

12–8 Explain why a mere comparison of the NPVs of unequal-lived, ongoing, mutually exclusive projects is inappropriate. Describe the *annualized net present value (ANPV) approach* for comparing unequal-lived, mutually exclusive projects.

12–9 What are *real options?* What are some major types of real options?

12–10 What is the difference between the *strategic NPV* and the *traditional NPV?* Do they always result in the same accept–reject decisions?

12–11 What is *capital rationing?* In theory, should capital rationing exist? Why does it frequently occur in practice?

12–12 Compare and contrast the *internal rate of return approach* and the *net present value approach* to capital rationing. Which is better? Why?

Summary

FOCUS ON VALUE

Not all capital budgeting projects have the same level of risk as the firm's existing portfolio of projects. The financial manager must adjust projects for differences in risk when evaluating their acceptability. Without such an adjustment, management could mistakenly accept projects that destroy shareholder value or could reject projects that create shareholder value. To ensure that neither of these outcomes occurs, the financial manager must make sure that only those projects that create shareholder value are recommended.

Risk-adjusted discount rates (RADRs) provide a mechanism for adjusting the discount rate so that it is consistent with the risk–return preferences of market participants. Procedures for comparing projects with unequal lives, for explicitly recognizing real options embedded in capital projects, and for selecting projects under capital rationing enable the financial manager to refine the capital budgeting process further. These procedures, along with risk-adjustment techniques, should enable the financial manager to make capital budgeting decisions that are consistent with the firm's goal of **maximizing stock price.**

REVIEW OF LEARNING GOALS

LG 1 **Understand the importance of recognizing risk in the analysis of capital budgeting projects.** The cash flows associated with capital budgeting projects typically have different levels of risk, and the acceptance of a project generally affects the firm's overall risk. Thus it is important to incorporate risk considerations in capital budgeting. Various behavioral approaches can be used to get a "feel" for the level of project risk. Other approaches explicitly recognize project risk in the analysis of capital budgeting projects.

LG 2 **Discuss risk and cash inflows, scenario analysis, and simulation as behavioral approaches for dealing with risk.** Risk in capital budgeting is the degree of variability of cash flows, which for conventional capital budgeting projects stems almost entirely from net *cash flows*. Finding the breakeven cash inflow and estimating the probability that it will be realized make up one behavioral approach for assessing capital budgeting risk. Scenario analysis is another behavioral approach for capturing the variability of cash inflows and NPVs. Simulation is a statistically based approach that results in a probability distribution of project returns.

LG 3 **Review the unique risks that multinational companies face.** Although the basic capital budgeting techniques are the same for multinational and purely domestic companies, firms that operate in several countries must also deal with exchange rate and political risks, tax law differences, transfer pricing, and strategic issues.

LG 4 **Describe the determination and use of risk-adjusted discount rates (RADRs), portfolio effects, and the practical aspects of RADRs.** The risk of a project whose initial investment is known with certainty is embodied in the present value of its cash inflows, using NPV. Two opportunities to adjust the present value of cash inflows for risk exist—adjust the cash inflows or adjust the discount rate.

Because adjusting the cash inflows is highly subjective, adjusting discount rates is more popular. RADRs use a market-based adjustment of the discount rate to calculate NPV. The RADR is closely linked to CAPM, but because real corporate assets are generally not traded in an efficient market the CAPM cannot be applied directly to capital budgeting. Instead, firms develop some CAPM-type relationship to link a project's risk to its required return, which is used as the discount rate. Often, for convenience, firms will rely on total risk as an approximation for relevant risk when estimating required project returns. RADRs are commonly used in practice because decision makers find rates of return easy to estimate and apply.

LG 5 **Select the best of a group of unequal-lived, mutually exclusive projects using annualized net present values (ANPVs).** The ANPV approach is the most efficient method of comparing ongoing, mutually exclusive projects that have unequal usable lives. It converts the NPV of each unequal-lived project into an equivalent annual amount—its ANPV. The ANPV can be calculated using equations, a financial calculator, or a spreadsheet. The project with the highest ANPV is best.

LG 6 **Explain the role of real options and the objective and procedures for selecting projects under capital rationing.** Real options are opportunities that are embedded in capital projects and that allow managers to alter their cash flow and risk in a way that affects project acceptability (NPV). By explicitly recognizing real options, the financial manager can find a project's strategic NPV. Some of the more common types of real options are abandonment, flexibility, growth, and timing options. The strategic NPV improves the quality of the capital budgeting decision.

Capital rationing exists when firms have more acceptable independent projects than they can fund. Capital rationing commonly occurs in practice. Its objective is to select from all acceptable projects the group that provides the highest overall net present value and does not require more dollars than are budgeted. The two basic approaches for choosing projects under capital rationing are the internal rate of return approach and the net present value approach. The NPV approach better achieves the objective of using the budget to generate the highest present value of inflows.

Opener-in-Review

The chapter opener and the *Focus on Ethics* box on page 475 described some of the consequences of the accident at BP's Deepwater Horizon oil rig. The company put up $20 billion to help pay for damages related to the oil spill, yet BP's market value declined by more than $90 billion. That means that the market assessed BP an additional penalty of roughly $70 billion, above and beyond the direct costs associated with the spill. Describe the effects that an increase in BP's cost of capital could have on the market value of BP. Oil spills have happened before, so it is plausible that engineers and analysts at BP could have imagined a worst-case scenario in which a major spill occurred at one of the firm's offshore rigs. How might a thorough scenario analysis have influenced BP's offshore drilling activities?

Self-Test Problems   (Solutions in Appendix)

LG 4   **ST12–1**   **Risk-adjusted discount rates**   CBA Company is considering two mutually exclusive projects, A and B. The following table shows the CAPM-type relationship between a risk index and the required return (RADR) applicable to CBA Company.

Risk index	Required return (RADR)
0.0	7.0% (risk-free rate, R_F)
0.2	8.0
0.4	9.0
0.6	10.0
0.8	11.0
1.0	12.0
1.2	13.0
1.4	14.0
1.6	15.0
1.8	16.0
2.0	17.0

Project data are shown as follows:

	Project A	Project B
Initial investment (CF_0)	$15,000	$20,000
Project life	3 years	3 years
Annual cash inflow (CF)	$7,000	$10,000
Risk index	0.4	1.8

a. Ignoring any differences in risk and assuming that the firm's cost of capital is 10%, calculate the *net present value (NPV)* of each project.
b. Use NPV to evaluate the projects, using *risk-adjusted discount rates (RADRs)* to account for risk.
c. Compare, contrast, and explain your findings in parts **a** and **b**.

Warm-Up Exercises   All problems are available in ⬛myfinancelab.

LG 2   **E12–1**   Birkenstock is considering an investment in a nylon-knitting machine. The machine requires an initial investment of $25,000, has a 5-year life, and has no residual value at the end of the 5 years. The company's cost of capital is 12%. Known with less certainty are the actual after-tax cash inflows for each of the 5 years. The company has estimated expected cash inflows for three scenarios: pessimistic, most likely, and optimistic. These expected cash inflows are listed in the following table. Calculate the range for the NPV given in each scenario.

	Expected cash inflows		
Year	Pessimistic	Most likely	Optimistic
1	$5,500	$ 8,000	$10,500
2	6,000	9,000	12,000
3	7,500	10,500	14,500
4	6,500	9,500	11,500
5	4,500	6,500	7,500

LG 2 **E12–2** You wish to evaluate a project requiring an initial investment of $45,000 and having a useful life of 5 years. What minimum amount of annual cash inflow do you need if your firm has an 8% cost of capital? If the project is forecast to earn $12,500 per year over the 5 years, what is its IRR? Is the project acceptable?

LG 4 **E12–3** Like most firms in its industry, Yeastime Bakeries uses a subjective risk assessment tool of its own design. The tool is a simple index by which projects are ranked by level of perceived risk on a scale of 0–10. The scale is recreated in the following table.

Risk index	Required return
0	4.0% (current risk-free rate)
1	4.5
2	5.0
3	5.5
4	6.0
5	6.5 (current IRR)
6	7.0
7	7.5
8	8.0
9	8.5
10	9.0

The firm is analyzing two projects based on their RADRs. Project Sourdough requires an initial investment of $12,500 and is assigned a risk index of 6. Project Greek Salad requires an initial investment of $7,500 and is assigned a risk index of 8. The two projects have 7-year lives. Sourdough is projected to generate cash inflows of $5,500 per year. Greek Salad is projected to generate cash inflows of $4,000 per year. Use each project's RADR to select the better project.

LG 5 **E12–4** Outcast, Inc., has hired you to advise the firm on a capital budgeting issue involving two unequal-lived, mutually exclusive projects, M and N. The cash flows for each project are presented in the following table. Calculate the NPV and the *annualized net present value (ANPV)* for each project using the firm's cost of capital of 8%. Which project would you recommend?

	Project M	Project N
Initial investment	$35,000	$55,000
Year	Cash inflows	
1	$12,000	$18,000
2	25,000	15,000
3	30,000	25,000
4	—	10,000
5	—	8,000
6	—	5,000
7	—	5,000

LG 6   **E12–5**   Longchamps Electric is faced with a capital budget of $150,000 for the coming year. It is considering six investment projects and has a cost of capital of 7%. The six projects are listed in the following table, along with their initial investments and their IRRs. Using the data given, prepare an *investment opportunities schedule (IOS)*. Which projects does the IOS suggest should be funded? Does this group of projects maximize NPV? Explain.

Project	Initial investment	IRR
1	$75,000	8%
2	40,000	10
3	35,000	7
4	50,000	11
5	45,000	9
6	20,000	6

Problems

All problems are available in 🔷 myfinancelab .

LG 1   **P12–1**   **Recognizing risk**   Caradine Corp., a media services firm with net earnings of $3,200,000 in the last year, is considering the following projects.

Project	Initial investment	Details
A	$ 35,000	Replace existing office furnishings.
B	500,000	Purchase digital film-editing equipment for use with several existing accounts.
C	450,000	Develop proposal to bid for a $2,000,000-per-year 10-year contract with the U.S. Navy, not now an account.
D	685,000	Purchase the exclusive rights to market a quality educational television program in syndication to local markets in the European Union, a part of the firm's existing business activities.

The media services business is cyclical and highly competitive. The board of directors has asked you, as chief financial officer, to do the following:
   a. Evaluate the risk of each proposed project and rank it "low," "medium," or "high."
   b. Comment on why you chose each ranking.

LG 2 **P12–2** **Breakeven cash inflows** Etsitty Arts, Inc., a leading producer of fine cast silver jewelry, is considering the purchase of new casting equipment that will allow it to expand the product line into award plaques. The proposed initial investment is $35,000. The company expects that the equipment will produce steady income throughout its 12-year life.
   a. If Etsitty requires a 14% return on its investment, what minimum yearly cash inflow will be necessary for the company to go forward with this project?
   b. How would the minimum yearly cash inflow change if the company required a 10% return on its investment?

LG 2 **P12–3** **Breakeven cash inflows and risk** Pueblo Enterprises is considering investing in either of two mutually exclusive projects, X and Y. Project X requires an initial investment of $30,000; project Y requires $40,000. Each project's cash inflows are 5-year annuities: Project X's inflows are $10,000 per year; project Y's are $15,000. The firm has unlimited funds and, in the absence of risk differences, accepts the project with the highest NPV. The cost of capital is 15%.
   a. Find the NPV for each project. Are the projects acceptable?
   b. Find the *breakeven cash inflow* for each project.
   c. The firm has estimated the probabilities of achieving various ranges of cash inflows for the two projects, as shown in the following table. What is the probability that each project will achieve the breakeven cash inflow found in part **b**?

Range of cash inflow	Probability of achieving cash inflow in given range	
	Project X	Project Y
$0 to $5,000	0%	5%
$5,000 to $7,500	10	10
$7,500 to $10,000	60	15
$10,000 to $12,500	25	25
$12,500 to $15,000	5	20
$15,000 to $20,000	0	15
Above $20,000	0	10

   d. Which project is more risky? Which project has the potentially higher NPV? Discuss the risk–return tradeoffs of the two projects.
   e. If the firm wished to minimize losses (that is, NPV < $0), which project would you recommend? Which would you recommend if the goal was achieving a higher NPV?

LG 2 **P12–4** **Basic scenario analysis** Murdock Paints is in the process of evaluating two mutually exclusive additions to its processing capacity. The firm's financial analysts have developed pessimistic, most likely, and optimistic estimates of the annual cash inflows associated with each project. These estimates are shown in the following table.

	Project A	Project B
Initial investment (CF_0)	$8,000	$8,000
Outcome	Annual cash inflows (CF)	
Pessimistic	$ 200	$ 900
Most likely	1,000	1,000
Optimistic	1,800	1,100

   a. Determine the *range* of annual cash inflows for each of the two projects.
   b. Assume that the firm's cost of capital is 10% and that both projects have 20-year lives. Construct a table similar to this for the NPVs for each project. Include the *range* of NPVs for each project.
   c. Do parts **a** and **b** provide consistent views of the two projects? Explain.
   d. Which project do you recommend? Why?

LG 2   **P12–5**   **Scenario analysis**   James Secretarial Services is considering the purchase of one of two new personal computers, P and Q. The company expects both to provide benefits over a 10-year period, and each has a required investment of $3,000. The firm uses a 10% cost of capital. Management has constructed the following table of estimates of annual cash inflows for pessimistic, most likely, and optimistic results.

	Computer P	Computer Q
Initial investment (CF_0)	$3,000	$3,000
Outcome	Annual cash inflows (CF)	
Pessimistic	$ 500	$ 400
Most likely	750	750
Optimistic	1,000	1,200

   a. Determine the *range* of annual cash inflows for each of the two computers.
   b. Construct a table similar to this for the NPVs associated with each outcome for both computers.
   c. Find the *range* of NPVs, and subjectively compare the risks associated with purchasing these computers.

Personal Finance Problem

LG 2   **P12–6**   **Impact of inflation on investments**   You are interested in an investment project that costs $7,500 initially. The investment has a 5-year horizon and promises future end-of-year cash inflows of $2,000, $2,000, $2,000, $1,500, and $1,500, respectively. Your current opportunity cost is 6.5% per year. However, the Fed has stated that inflation may rise by 1% or may fall by the same amount over the next 5 years.

Assume a direct positive impact of inflation on the prevailing rates (Fisher effect) and answer the following questions.

a. What is the *net present value (NPV)* of the investment under the current required rate of return?

b. What is the *net present value (NPV)* of the investment under a period of rising inflation?

c. What is the *net present value (NPV)* of the investment under a period of falling inflation?

d. From your answers in **a, b,** and **c,** what relationship do you see emerge between changes in inflation and asset valuation?

LG 2   **P12–7**   **Simulation**   Ogden Corporation has compiled the following information on a capital expenditure proposal:

(1) The projected cash *inflows* are normally distributed with a mean of $36,000 and a standard deviation of $9,000.

(2) The projected cash *outflows* are normally distributed with a mean of $30,000 and a standard deviation of $6,000.

(3) The firm has an 11% cost of capital.

(4) The probability distributions of cash inflows and cash outflows are not expected to change over the project's 10-year life.

a. Describe how the foregoing data can be used to develop a simulation model for finding the net present value of the project.

b. Discuss the advantages of using a simulation to evaluate the proposed project.

LG 4   **P12–8**   **Risk-adjusted discount rates—Basic**   Country Wallpapers is considering investing in one of three mutually exclusive projects, E, F, and G. The firm's cost of capital, r, is 15%, and the risk-free rate, R_F, is 10%. The firm has gathered the basic cash flow and risk index data for each project, as shown in the following table.

	Project (j)		
	E	F	G
Initial investment (CF_0)	$15,000	$11,000	$19,000
Year (t)	Cash inflows (CF_t)		
1	$6,000	$6,000	$ 4,000
2	6,000	4,000	6,000
3	6,000	5,000	8,000
4	6,000	2,000	12,000
Risk index (RI_j)	1.80	1.00	0.60

a. Find the *net present value (NPV)* of each project using the firm's cost of capital. Which project is preferred in this situation?

b. The firm uses the following equation to determine the risk-adjusted discount rate, $RADR_j$, for each project j:

$$RADR_j = R_F + [RI_j \times (r - R_F)]$$

where

$$R_F = \text{risk-free rate of return}$$
$$RI_j = \text{risk index for project } j$$
$$r = \text{cost of capital}$$

Substitute each project's risk index into this equation to determine its RADR.

c. Use the RADR for each project to determine its *risk-adjusted NPV*. Which project is preferable in this situation?

d. Compare and discuss your findings in parts **a** and **c.** Which project do you recommend that the firm accept?

LG 4   **P12–9**   **Risk-adjusted discount rates—Tabular**   After a careful evaluation of investment alternatives and opportunities, Masters School Supplies has developed a CAPM-type relationship linking a risk index to the required return (RADR), as shown in the following table.

Risk index	Required return (RADR)
0.0	7.0% (risk-free rate, R_F)
0.2	8.0
0.4	9.0
0.6	10.0
0.8	11.0
1.0	12.0
1.2	13.0
1.4	14.0
1.6	15.0
1.8	16.0
2.0	17.0

The firm is considering two mutually exclusive projects, A and B. Following are the data the firm has been able to gather about the projects.

	Project A	Project B
Initial investment (CF_0)	$20,000	$30,000
Project life	5 years	5 years
Annual cash inflow (CF)	$7,000	$10,000
Risk index	0.2	1.4

All the firm's cash inflows have already been adjusted for taxes.

a. Evaluate the projects using *risk-adjusted discount rates.*

b. Discuss your findings in part **a,** and recommend the preferred project.

Personal Finance Problem

LG 4   **P12–10**   **Mutually exclusive investments and risk**   Lara Fredericks is interested in two mutually exclusive investments. Both investments cover the same time horizon of 6 years. The cost of the first investment is $10,000, and Lara expects equal and consecutive year-end payments of $3,000. The second investment promises equal and consecutive payments of $3,800 with an initial outlay of $12,000 required. The current required return on the first investment is 8.5%, and the second carries a required return of 10.5%.

a. What is the *net present value* of the first investment?

b. What is the *net present value* of the second investment?

c. Being mutually exclusive, which investment should Lara choose? Explain.

d. Which investment was relatively more risky? Explain.

LG 4 **P12–11** **Risk-adjusted rates of return using CAPM** Centennial Catering, Inc., is considering two mutually exclusive investments. The company wishes to use a CAPM-type risk-adjusted discount rate (RADR) in its analysis. Centennial's managers believe that the appropriate market rate of return is 12%, and they observe that the current risk-free rate of return is 7%. Cash flows associated with the two projects are shown in the following table.

	Project X	Project Y
Initial investment (CF_0)	$70,000	$78,000
Year (t)	Cash inflows (CF_t)	
1	$30,000	$22,000
2	30,000	32,000
3	30,000	38,000
4	30,000	46,000

a. Use a *risk-adjusted discount rate* approach to calculate the net present value of each project, given that project X has an RADR factor of 1.20 and project Y has an RADR factor of 1.40. The RADR factors are similar to project betas. (Use Equation 12.5 to calculate the required project return for each.)

b. Discuss your findings in part **a**, and recommend the preferred project.

LG 4 **P12–12** **Risk classes and RADR** Moses Manufacturing is attempting to select the best of three mutually exclusive projects, X, Y, and Z. Although all the projects have 5-year lives, they possess differing degrees of risk. Project X is in class V, the highest-risk class; project Y is in class II, the below-average-risk class; and project Z is in class III, the average-risk class. The basic cash flow data for each project and the risk classes and risk-adjusted discount rates (RADRs) used by the firm are shown in the following tables.

	Project X	Project Y	Project Z
Initial investment (CF_0)	$180,000	$235,000	$310,000
Year (t)	Cash inflows (CF_t)		
1	$80,000	$50,000	$90,000
2	70,000	60,000	90,000
3	60,000	70,000	90,000
4	60,000	80,000	90,000
5	60,000	90,000	90,000

Risk Classes and RADRs		
Risk class	Description	Risk-adjusted discount rate (RADR)
I	Lowest risk	10%
II	Below-average risk	13
III	Average risk	15
IV	Above-average risk	19
V	Highest risk	22

a. Find the *risk-adjusted NPV* for each project.
b. Which project, if any, would you recommend that the firm undertake?

LG 5 **P12–13**   **Unequal lives—ANPV approach**   Evans Industries wishes to select the best of three possible machines, each of which is expected to satisfy the firm's ongoing need for additional aluminum-extrusion capacity. The three machines—A, B, and C—are equally risky. The firm plans to use a 12% cost of capital to evaluate each of them. The initial investment and annual cash inflows over the life of each machine are shown in the following table.

	Machine A	Machine B	Machine C
Initial investment (CF_0)	$92,000	$65,000	$100,500
Year (*t*)	Cash inflows (CF_t)		
1	$12,000	$10,000	$30,000
2	12,000	20,000	30,000
3	12,000	30,000	30,000
4	12,000	40,000	30,000
5	12,000	—	30,000
6	12,000	—	—

a. Calculate the *NPV* for each machine over its life. Rank the machines in descending order on the basis of NPV.
b. Use the *annualized net present value (ANPV)* approach to evaluate and rank the machines in descending order on the basis of ANPV.
c. Compare and contrast your findings in parts **a** and **b**. Which machine would you recommend that the firm acquire? Why?

LG 5 **P12–14**   **Unequal lives—ANPV approach**   Portland Products is considering the purchase of one of three mutually exclusive projects for increasing production efficiency. The firm plans to use a 14% cost of capital to evaluate these equal-risk projects. The initial investment and annual cash inflows over the life of each project are shown in the following table.

	Project X	Project Y	Project Z
Initial investment (CF_0)	$78,000	$52,000	$66,000
Year (t)	Cash inflows (CF_t)		
1	$17,000	$28,000	$15,000
2	25,000	38,000	15,000
3	33,000	—	15,000
4	41,000	—	15,000
5	—	—	15,000
6	—	—	15,000
7	—	—	15,000
8	—	—	15,000

a. Calculate the *NPV* for each project over its life. Rank the projects in descending order on the basis of NPV.

b. Use the *annualized net present value (ANPV)* approach to evaluate and rank the projects in descending order on the basis of ANPV.

c. Compare and contrast your findings in parts **a** and **b**. Which project would you recommend that the firm purchase? Why?

LG 5 **P12–15** **Unequal lives—ANPV approach** JBL Co. has designed a new conveyor system. Management must choose among three alternative courses of action: (1) The firm can sell the design outright to another corporation with payment over 2 years. (2) It can license the design to another manufacturer for a period of 5 years, its likely product life. (3) It can manufacture and market the system itself; this alternative will result in 6 years of cash inflows. The company has a cost of capital of 12%. Cash flows associated with each alternative are as shown in the following table.

Alternative	Sell	License	Manufacture
Initial investment (CF_0)	$200,000	$200,000	$450,000
Year (t)	Cash inflows (CF_t)		
1	$200,000	$250,000	$200,000
2	250,000	100,000	250,000
3	—	80,000	200,000
4	—	60,000	200,000
5	—	40,000	200,000
6	—	—	200,000

a. Calculate the *net present value* of each alternative and rank the alternatives on the basis of NPV.

b. Calculate the *annualized net present value (ANPV)* of each alternative and rank them accordingly.

c. Why is ANPV preferred over NPV when ranking projects with unequal lives?

Personal Finance Problem

LG 5   **P12–16**   **NPV and ANPV decisions**   Richard and Linda Butler decide that it is time to purchase a high-definition (HD) television because the technology has improved and prices have fallen over the past 3 years. From their research, they narrow their choices to two sets, the Samsung 42-inch LCD with 1080p capability and the Sony 42-inch LCD with 1080p features. The price of the Samsung is $2,350 and the Sony will cost $2,700. They expect to keep the Samsung for 3 years; if they buy the more expensive Sony unit, they will keep the Sony for 4 years. They expect to be able to sell the Samsung for $400 by the end of 3 years; they expect they could sell the Sony for $350 at the end of year 4. Richard and Linda estimate the end-of-year entertainment benefits (that is, not going to movies or events and watching at home) from the Samsung to be $900 and for the Sony to be $1,000. Both sets can be viewed as quality units and are equally risky purchases. They estimate their opportunity cost to be 9%.

The Butlers wish to choose the better alternative from a purely financial perspective. To perform this analysis they wish to do the following:

a. Determine the *NPV* of the Samsung HD LCD.
b. Determine the *ANPV* of the Samsung HD LCD.
c. Determine the *NPV* of the Sony HD LCD.
d. Determine the *ANPV* of the Sony HD LCD.
e. Which set should the Butlers purchase and why?

LG 6   **P12–17**   **Real options and the strategic NPV**   Jenny Rene, the CFO of Asor Products, Inc., has just completed an evaluation of a proposed capital expenditure for equipment that would expand the firm's manufacturing capacity. Using the traditional NPV methodology, she found the project unacceptable because

$$\text{NPV}_{\text{traditional}} = -\$1,700 < \$0$$

Before recommending rejection of the proposed project, she has decided to assess whether there might be real options embedded in the firm's cash flows. Her evaluation uncovered three options:

Option 1: Abandonment—The project could be abandoned at the end of 3 years, resulting in an addition to NPV of $1,200.

Option 2: Growth—If the projected outcomes occurred, an opportunity to expand the firm's product offerings further would become available at the end of 4 years. Exercise of this option is estimated to add $3,000 to the project's NPV.

Option 3: Timing—Certain phases of the proposed project could be delayed if market and competitive conditions caused the firm's forecast revenues to develop more slowly than planned. Such a delay in implementation at that point has an NPV of $10,000.

Jenny estimated that there was a 25% chance that the abandonment option would need to be exercised, a 30% chance that the growth option would be exercised, and only a 10% chance that the implementation of certain phases of the project would affect timing.

a. Use the information provided to calculate the *strategic NPV*, NPV$_{\text{strategic}}$, for Asor Products' proposed equipment expenditure.
b. Judging on the basis of your findings in part **a**, what action should Jenny recommend to management with regard to the proposed equipment expenditure?
c. In general, how does this problem demonstrate the importance of considering real options when making capital budgeting decisions?

LG 6   **P12–18**   **Capital rationing—IRR and NPV approaches**   Valley Corporation is attempting to select the best of a group of independent projects competing for the firm's fixed capital budget of $4.5 million. The firm recognizes that any unused portion of this budget will earn less than its 15% cost of capital, thereby resulting in a present value of inflows that is less than the initial investment. The firm has summarized, in the following table, the key data to be used in selecting the best group of projects.

Project	Initial investment	IRR	Present value of inflows at 15%
A	$5,000,000	17%	$5,400,000
B	800,000	18	1,100,000
C	2,000,000	19	2,300,000
D	1,500,000	16	1,600,000
E	800,000	22	900,000
F	2,500,000	23	3,000,000
G	1,200,000	20	1,300,000

a. Use the *internal rate of return (IRR) approach* to select the best group of projects.
b. Use the *net present value (NPV) approach* to select the best group of projects.
c. Compare, contrast, and discuss your findings in parts **a** and **b**.
d. Which projects should the firm implement? Why?

LG 6   **P12–19**   **Capital rationing—NPV approach**   A firm with a 13% cost of capital must select the optimal group of projects from those shown in the following table, given its capital budget of $1 million.

Project	Initial investment	NPV at 13% cost of capital
A	$300,000	$ 84,000
B	200,000	10,000
C	100,000	25,000
D	900,000	90,000
E	500,000	70,000
F	100,000	50,000
G	800,000	160,000

a. Calculate the *present value of cash inflows* associated with each project.
b. Select the optimal group of projects, keeping in mind that unused funds are costly.

LG 4   **P12–20**   **ETHICS PROBLEM**   The Environmental Protection Agency sometimes imposes penalties on firms that pollute the environment (see the *Focus on Ethics* box on page 475). But did you know that there is a legal market for pollution? A mechanism that has been developed to limit excessive air pollution is to use carbon credits. Carbon credits are a tradable permit scheme that allows businesses that cannot meet their greenhouse-gas-emissions limits to purchase carbon credits from businesses that are below their quota. By allowing credits to be bought and sold, a business for which reducing its emissions would be expensive or prohibitive can pay another business to make the reduction for it. Do you agree with this arrangement? How would you feel as an investor in a company that utilizes carbon credits to legally exceed its pollution limits?

Spreadsheet Exercise

Isis Corporation has two projects that it would like to undertake. However, due to capital restraints, the two projects—Alpha and Beta—must be treated as mutually exclusive. Both projects are equally risky, and the firm plans to use a 10% cost of capital to evaluate each. Project Alpha has an estimated life of 12 years, and project Beta has an estimated life of 9 years. The cash flow data have been prepared as shown in the following table.

	Cash flows	
	Project Alpha	**Project Beta**
CF_0	−$5,500,000	−$6,500,000
CF_1	300,000	400,000
CF_2	500,000	600,000
CF_3	500,000	800,000
CF_4	550,000	1,100,000
CF_5	700,000	1,400,000
CF_6	800,000	2,000,000
CF_7	950,000	2,500,000
CF_8	1,000,000	2,000,000
CF_9	1,250,000	1,000,000
CF_{10}	1,500,000	
CF_{11}	2,000,000	
CF_{12}	2,500,000	

TO DO

Create a spreadsheet to answer the following questions.

a. Calculate the *NPV* for each project over its respective life. Rank the projects in descending order on the basis of NPV. Which one would you choose?
b. Use the *annualized net present value (ANPV) approach* to evaluate and rank the projects in descending order on the basis of ANPV. Which one would you choose?
c. Compare and contrast your findings in parts **a** and **b.** Which project would you recommend that the firm choose? Explain.

 Visit **www.myfinancelab.com** for **Chapter Case:** *Evaluating Cherone Equipment's Risky Plans for Increasing Its Production Capacity,* Group Exercises, and numerous online resources.

Integrative Case 5

Lasting Impressions Company

Lasting Impressions (LI) Company is a medium-sized commercial printer of promotional advertising brochures, booklets, and other direct-mail pieces. The firm's major clients are ad agencies based in New York and Chicago. The typical job is characterized by high quality and production runs of more than 50,000 units. LI has not been able to compete effectively with larger printers because of its existing older, inefficient presses. The firm is currently having problems cost-effectively meeting run length requirements as well as meeting quality standards.

The general manager has proposed the purchase of one of two large, six-color presses designed for long, high-quality runs. The purchase of a new press would enable LI to reduce its cost of labor and therefore the price to the client, putting the firm in a more competitive position. The key financial characteristics of the old press and of the two proposed presses are summarized in what follows.

Old press Originally purchased 3 years ago at an installed cost of $400,000, it is being depreciated under MACRS using a 5-year recovery period. The old press has a remaining economic life of 5 years. It can be sold today to net $420,000 before taxes; if it is retained, it can be sold to net $150,000 before taxes at the end of 5 years.

Press A This highly automated press can be purchased for $830,000 and will require $40,000 in installation costs. It will be depreciated under MACRS using a 5-year recovery period. At the end of the 5 years, the machine could be sold to net $400,000 before taxes. If this machine is acquired, it is anticipated that the current account changes shown in the following table would result.

Cash	+	$ 25,400
Accounts receivable	+	120,000
Inventories	−	20,000
Accounts payable	+	35,000

Press B This press is not as sophisticated as press A. It costs $640,000 and requires $20,000 in installation costs. It will be depreciated under MACRS using a 5-year recovery period. At the end of 5 years, it can be sold to net $330,000 before taxes. Acquisition of this press will have no effect on the firm's net working capital investment.

The firm estimates that its earnings before depreciation, interest, and taxes with the old press and with press A or press B for each of the 5 years would be as shown in Table 1 (see page 504). The firm is subject to a 40% tax rate. The firm's cost of capital, r, applicable to the proposed replacement is 14%.

TABLE 1

	Earnings before Depreciation, Interest, and Taxes for Lasting Impressions Company's Presses		
Year	Old press	Press A	Press B
1	$120,000	$250,000	$210,000
2	120,000	270,000	210,000
3	120,000	300,000	210,000
4	120,000	330,000	210,000
5	120,000	370,000	210,000

TO DO

a. For each of the two proposed replacement presses, determine:
   (1) Initial investment.
   (2) Operating cash inflows. (*Note:* Be sure to consider the depreciation in year 6.)
   (3) Terminal cash flow. (*Note:* This is at the end of year 5.)
b. Using the data developed in part **a,** find and depict on a time line the relevant cash flow stream associated with each of the two proposed replacement presses, assuming that each is terminated at the end of 5 years.
c. Using the data developed in part **b,** apply each of the following decision techniques:
   (1) Payback period. (*Note:* For year 5, use only the operating cash inflows—that is, exclude terminal cash flow—when making this calculation.)
   (2) Net present value (NPV).
   (3) Internal rate of return (IRR).
d. Draw *net present value profiles* for the two replacement presses on the same set of axes, and discuss conflicting rankings of the two presses, if any, resulting from use of NPV and IRR decision techniques.
e. Recommend which, if either, of the presses the firm should acquire if the firm has (1) unlimited funds or (2) capital rationing.
f. What is the impact on your recommendation of the fact that the operating cash inflows associated with press A are characterized as very risky in contrast to the low-risk operating cash inflows of press B?

Part 6 Long-Term Financial Decisions

Chapters in This Part

The last three chapters focused on how firms should invest money, but those chapters were silent on where firms obtained the money to invest in the first place. In the next two chapters, we examine firms' long-term financial decisions. Broadly speaking, these chapters focus on the trade-offs associated with different sources of investment capital.

Chapter 13 looks at the firm's most basic long-term financial decision—whether to raise money by selling stock (equity) or by borrowing money (debt). A firm's mix of debt and equity financing is called its capital structure. Some firms choose a capital structure that contains no debt at all, while other firms rely more heavily on debt financing than on equity. The capital structure choice is extremely important because how much debt a firm uses influences the returns that a firm can provide to its investors as well as the risks associated with those returns. More debt generally means higher returns but also higher risks. Chapter 13 illustrates how firms balance that trade-off.

Chapter 14 focuses on payout policy. Payout policy refers to the decisions that firms make about whether and how to distribute cash to shareholders via dividends and share repurchases. We can make a similar observation about payout policy that we made about capital structure. Some firms choose to distribute no cash at all, while other firms pay billions in dividends and stock buybacks each year. Paying out cash is tangible proof that a company is generating cash flow for its investors, but once firms start paying dividends, any move to reduce dividends or to stop paying them altogether will likely lead to a sharp reduction in the firm's stock price. Chapter 14 explains the factors that firms consider when forming their payout policies.

13 Leverage and Capital Structure

Learning Goals

LG 1 Discuss leverage, capital structure, breakeven analysis, the operating breakeven point, and the effect of changing costs on the breakeven point.

LG 2 Understand operating, financial, and total leverage and the relationships among them.

LG 3 Describe the types of capital, external assessment of capital structure, the capital structure of non–U.S. firms, and capital structure theory.

LG 4 Explain the optimal capital structure using a graphical view of the firm's cost-of-capital functions and a zero-growth valuation model.

LG 5 Discuss the EBIT–EPS approach to capital structure.

LG 6 Review the return and risk of alternative capital structures, their linkage to market value, and other important considerations related to capital structure.

Why This Chapter Matters to You

In your *professional* life

ACCOUNTING You need to understand how to calculate and analyze operating and financial leverage and to be familiar with the tax and earnings effects of various capital structures.

INFORMATION SYSTEMS You need to understand the types of capital and what capital structure is because you will provide much of the information needed in management's determination of the best capital structure for the firm.

MANAGEMENT You need to understand leverage so that you can control risk and magnify returns for the firm's owners and to understand capital structure theory so that you can make decisions about the firm's optimal capital structure.

MARKETING You need to understand breakeven analysis, which you will use in pricing and product feasibility decisions.

OPERATIONS You need to understand the impact of fixed and variable operating costs on the firm's breakeven point and its operating leverage because these costs will have a major impact on the firm's risk and return.

In your *personal* life

Like corporations, you routinely incur debt, using both credit cards for short-term needs and negotiated long-term loans. When you borrow over the long term, you experience the benefits and consequences of leverage. Also, the level of your outstanding debt relative to net worth is conceptually the same as a firm's capital structure. It reflects your financial risk and affects the availability and cost of borrowing.

Genzyme Corp.

Trading Equity for Debt

As the broader U.S. stock market roared back to life in 2009, shares in the biotechnology firm, Genzyme, dropped 28 percent. Contamination problems at Genzyme's main manufacturing facility prompted the firm to stop production during the cleanup, and that in turn led to production shortages of some of the firms best-selling drugs. That performance irked one of Genzyme's largest shareholders, Carl Icahn, who promptly launched a proxy fight to gain four seats on the company's board of directors. In June 2010, Genzyme reached an agreement with Icahn giving his representatives two seats on their board.

Just eight days later, Genzyme's stock rose 3.7 percent on the announcement that the company would issue $1 billion in debt. Genzyme planned to use the proceeds from the issue, along with $1 billion in cash reserves, to repurchase approximately 40 million shares of common stock. That move represented a significant shift in the firm's capital structure (that is, its mix of debt and equity financing), a move that would put more cash in the hands of shareholders and apply more pressure on Genzyme management to generate positive cash flow from the business. With more of its financing coming from debt, Genzyme was adding financial leverage to its business, meaning that if the firm succeeds in selling its products, the returns to shareholders will be magnified. However, if Genzyme instead experiences further declines in its business, paying back the debt may prove to be difficult, and returns to shareholders will suffer as a result.

13.1 Leverage

leverage
Refers to the effects that fixed costs have on the returns that shareholders earn; higher leverage generally results in higher but more volatile returns.

Leverage refers to the effects that fixed costs have on the returns that shareholders earn. By "fixed costs" we mean costs that do not rise and fall with changes in a firm's sales. Firms have to pay these fixed costs whether business conditions are good or bad. These fixed costs may be operating costs, such as the costs incurred by purchasing and operating plant and equipment, or they may be financial costs, such as the fixed costs of making debt payments. Generally, leverage magnifies both returns and risks. A firm with more leverage may earn higher returns on average than a firm with less leverage, but the returns on the more leveraged firm will also be more volatile.

Many business risks are out of the control of managers, but not the risks associated with leverage. Managers can limit the impact of leverage by adopting strategies that rely more heavily on variable costs than on fixed costs. For example, a basic choice that many firms confront is whether to make their own products or to outsource manufacturing to another firm. A company that does its own manufacturing may invest billions in factories around the world. These factories generate costs whether they are running or not. In contrast, a company that outsources production can completely eliminate its manufacturing costs simply by not placing orders. Costs for a firm like this are more variable and will generally rise and fall as demand warrants.

In the same way, managers can influence leverage in their decisions about how the company raises money to operate. The amount of leverage in the firm's **capital structure**—the mix of long-term debt and equity maintained by the firm—can significantly affect its value by affecting return and risk. The more debt a firm issues, the higher are its debt repayment costs, and those costs must be paid regardless of how the firm's products are selling. Because leverage can have such a large impact on a firm, the financial manager must understand how to measure and evaluate leverage, particularly when making capital structure decisions.

Table 13.1 uses an income statement to highlight where different sources of leverage come from.

capital structure
The mix of long-term debt and equity maintained by the firm.

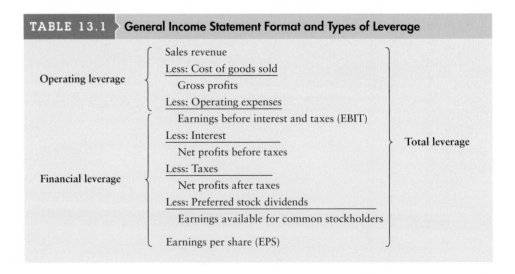

TABLE 13.1 **General Income Statement Format and Types of Leverage**

Operating leverage {	Sales revenue	} **Total leverage**
	Less: Cost of goods sold	
	Gross profits	
	Less: Operating expenses	
Financial leverage {	Earnings before interest and taxes (EBIT)	
	Less: Interest	
	Net profits before taxes	
	Less: Taxes	
	Net profits after taxes	
	Less: Preferred stock dividends	
	Earnings available for common stockholders	
	Earnings per share (EPS)	

- *Operating leverage* is concerned with the relationship between the firm's sales revenue and its earnings before interest and taxes (EBIT) or *operating profits*. When costs of operations (such as cost of goods sold and operating expenses) are largely fixed, small changes in revenue will lead to much larger changes in EBIT.

- *Financial leverage* is concerned with the relationship between the firm's EBIT and its common stock earnings per share (EPS). On the income statement, you can see that the deductions taken from EBIT to get to EPS include interest, taxes, and preferred dividends. Taxes are clearly variable, rising and falling with the firm's profits, but interest expense and preferred dividends are usually fixed. When these fixed items are large (that is, when the firm has a lot of financial leverage), small changes in EBIT produce larger changes in EPS.

- *Total leverage* is the combined effect of operating and financial leverage. It is concerned with the relationship between the firm's sales revenue and EPS.

We will examine the three types of leverage concepts in detail. First, though, we will look at breakeven analysis, which lays the foundation for leverage concepts by demonstrating the effects of fixed costs on the firm's operations.

BREAKEVEN ANALYSIS

breakeven analysis
Used to indicate the level of operations necessary to cover all costs and to evaluate the profitability associated with various levels of sales; also called *cost-volume-profit analysis*.

operating breakeven point
The level of sales necessary to cover all *operating costs*; the point at which EBIT = $0.

Firms use **breakeven analysis**, also called *cost-volume-profit analysis*, (1) to determine the level of operations necessary to cover all costs and (2) to evaluate the profitability associated with various levels of sales. The firm's **operating breakeven point** is the level of sales necessary to cover all *operating costs*. At that point, earnings before interest and taxes (EBIT) equals $0.[1]

The first step in finding the operating breakeven point is to divide the cost of goods sold and operating expenses into fixed and variable operating costs. *Fixed costs* are costs that the firm must pay in a given period regardless of the sales volume achieved during that period. These costs are typically contractual; rent, for example, is a fixed cost. Because fixed costs do not vary with sales, we typically measure them relative to time. For example, we would typically measure rent as the amount due *per month*. *Variable costs* vary directly with sales volume. Shipping costs, for example, are a variable cost.[2] We typically measure variable costs in dollars per unit sold.

Algebraic Approach

Using the following variables, we can recast the operating portion of the firm's income statement given in Table 13.1 into the algebraic representation shown in Table 13.2.

$$P = \text{sale price per unit}$$
$$Q = \text{sales quantity in units}$$
$$FC = \text{fixed } \textit{operating} \text{ cost per period}$$
$$VC = \text{variable } \textit{operating} \text{ cost per unit}$$

---

1. Quite often, the breakeven point is calculated so that it represents the point at which *all costs—both operating and financial*—are covered. For now, we focus on the operating breakeven point as a way to introduce the concept of operating leverage. We will discuss financial leverage later.

2. Some costs, commonly called *semifixed* or *semivariable*, are partly fixed and partly variable. An example is sales commissions that are fixed for a certain volume of sales and then increase to higher levels for higher volumes. For convenience and clarity, we assume that all costs can be classified as either fixed or variable.

	Item	Algebraic representation
TABLE 13.2	**Operating Leverage, Costs, and Breakeven Analysis**	
Operating leverage	Sales revenue	$(P \times Q)$
	Less: Fixed operating costs	$- \quad FC$
	Less: Variable operating costs	$-(VC \times Q)$
	Earnings before interest and taxes	EBIT

Rewriting the algebraic calculations in Table 13.2 as a formula for earnings before interest and taxes yields Equation 13.1:

$$\text{EBIT} = (P \times Q) - FC - (VC \times Q) \qquad (13.1)$$

Simplifying Equation 13.1 yields:

$$\text{EBIT} = Q \times (P - VC) - FC \qquad (13.2)$$

As noted above, the operating breakeven point is the level of sales at which all fixed and variable *operating costs* are covered—the level at which EBIT equals $0. Setting EBIT equal to $0 and solving Equation 13.2 for Q yields:

$$Q = \frac{FC}{P - VC} \qquad (13.3)$$

Q is the firm's operating breakeven point.[3]

Example 13.1 ▶   Assume that Cheryl's Posters, a small poster retailer, has fixed operating costs of $2,500. Its sale price is $10 per poster, and its variable operating cost is $5 per poster. Applying Equation 13.3 to these data yields:

$$Q = \frac{\$2,500}{\$10 - \$5} = \frac{\$2,500}{\$5} = 500 \text{ units}$$

At sales of 500 units, the firm's EBIT should just equal $0. The firm will have positive EBIT for sales greater than 500 units and negative EBIT, or a loss, for sales less than 500 units. We can confirm this by substituting values above and below 500 units, along with the other values given, into Equation 13.1.

---

3. Because the firm is assumed to be a single-product firm, its operating breakeven point is found in terms of unit sales, Q. For multiproduct firms, the operating breakeven point is generally found in terms of dollar sales, S. This is done by substituting the contribution margin, which is 100 percent minus total variable operating costs as a percentage of total sales, denoted $VC\%$, into the denominator of Equation 13.3. The result is Equation 13.3a:

$$S = \frac{FC}{1 - VC\%} \qquad (13.3a)$$

This multiproduct-firm breakeven point assumes that the firm's product mix remains the same at all levels of sales.

FIGURE 13.1

Breakeven Analysis
Graphical operating
breakeven analysis

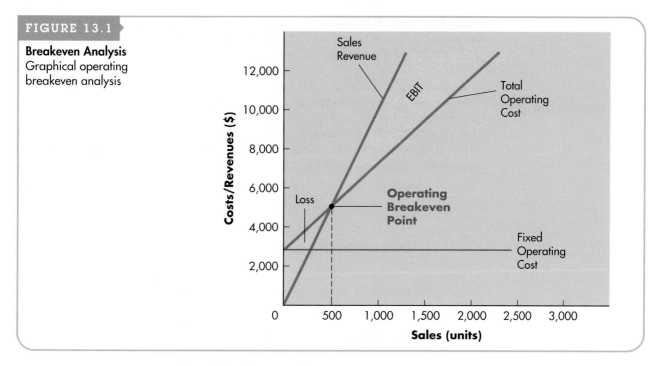

Graphical Approach

Figure 13.1 presents in graphical form the breakeven analysis of the data in the preceding example. The firm's operating breakeven point is the point at which its *total operating cost*—the sum of its fixed and variable operating costs—equals sales revenue. At this point, EBIT equals $0. The figure shows that for sales *below* 500 units, total operating cost exceeds sales revenue, and EBIT is less than $0 (a loss). For sales *above* the breakeven point of 500 units, sales revenue exceeds total operating cost, and EBIT is greater than $0.

Changing Costs and the Operating Breakeven Point

A firm's operating breakeven point is sensitive to a number of variables: fixed operating cost (FC), the sale price per unit (P), and the variable operating cost per unit (VC). Refer to Equation 13.3 to see how increases or decreases in these variables affect the breakeven point. The sensitivity of the breakeven sales volume (Q) to an *increase* in each of these variables is summarized in Table 13.3. As

TABLE 13.3	Sensitivity of Operating Breakeven Point to Increases in Key Breakeven Variables

Increase in variable	Effect on operating breakeven point
Fixed operating cost (FC)	Increase
Sale price per unit (P)	Decrease
Variable operating cost per unit (VC)	Increase

Note: Decreases in each of the variables shown would have the opposite effect on the operating breakeven point.

might be expected, an increase in cost (*FC* or *VC*) tends to increase the operating breakeven point, whereas an increase in the sale price per unit (*P*) decreases the operating breakeven point.

Example 13.2 ▶   Assume that Cheryl's Posters wishes to evaluate the impact of several options: (1) increasing fixed operating costs to $3,000, (2) increasing the sale price per unit to $12.50, (3) increasing the variable operating cost per unit to $7.50, and (4) simultaneously implementing all three of these changes. Substituting the appropriate data into Equation 13.3 yields the following results:

$$(1) \text{ Operating breakeven point} = \frac{\$3,000}{\$10 - \$5} = 600 \text{ units}$$

$$(2) \text{ Operating breakeven point} = \frac{\$2,500}{\$12.50 - \$5} = 333\frac{1}{3} \text{ units}$$

$$(3) \text{ Operating breakeven point} = \frac{\$2,500}{\$10 - \$7.50} = 1,000 \text{ units}$$

$$(4) \text{ Operating breakeven point} = \frac{\$3,000}{\$12.50 - \$7.50} = 600 \text{ units}$$

Comparing the resulting operating breakeven points to the initial value of 500 units, we can see that the cost increases (actions 1 and 3) raise the breakeven point, whereas the revenue increase (action 2) lowers the breakeven point. The combined effect of increasing all three variables (action 4) also results in an increased operating breakeven point.

Personal Finance Example 13.3 ▶   Rick Polo is considering having a new fuel-saving device installed in his car. The installed cost of the device is $240 paid up front, plus a monthly fee of $15. He can terminate use of the device any time without penalty. Rick estimates that the device will reduce his average monthly gas consumption by 20%, which, assuming no change in his monthly mileage, translates into a savings of about $28 per month. He is planning to keep the car for 2 more years and wishes to determine whether he should have the device installed in his car.

To assess the financial feasibility of purchasing the device, Rick calculates the number of months it will take for him to break even. Letting the installed cost of $240 represent the fixed cost (*FC*), the monthly savings of $28 represent the benefit (*P*), and the monthly fee of $15 represent the variable cost (*VC*), and substituting these values into the breakeven point equation, Equation 13.3, we get:

$$\text{Breakeven point (in months)} = \$240 \div (\$28 - \$15) = \$240 \div \$13$$
$$= \underline{18.5 \text{ months}}$$

Because the fuel-saving device pays itself back in 18.5 months, which is less than the 24 months that Rick is planning to continue owning the car, he should have the fuel-saving device installed in his car.

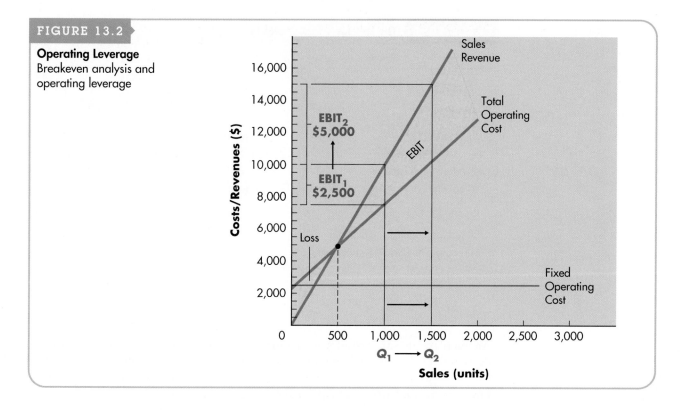

FIGURE 13.2

Operating Leverage
Breakeven analysis and operating leverage

OPERATING LEVERAGE

operating leverage
The use of *fixed operating costs* to magnify the effects of changes in sales on the firm's earnings before interest and taxes.

Operating leverage results from the existence of *fixed costs* that the firm must pay to operate. Using the structure presented in Table 13.2, we can define **operating leverage** as the use of *fixed operating costs* to magnify the effects of changes in sales on the firm's earnings before interest and taxes.

Example 13.4 ▶

Using the data for Cheryl's Posters (sale price, $P = \$10$ per unit; variable operating cost, $VC = \$5$ per unit; fixed operating cost, $FC = \$2,500$), Figure 13.2 presents the operating breakeven graph originally shown in Figure 13.1. The additional notations on the graph indicate that as the firm's sales increase from 1,000 to 1,500 units (Q_1 to Q_2), its EBIT increases from $2,500 to $5,000 (EBIT$_1$ to EBIT$_2$). In other words, a 50% increase in sales (1,000 to 1,500 units) results in a 100% increase in EBIT ($2,500 to $5,000). Table 13.4 includes the data for Figure 13.2 as well as relevant data for a 500-unit sales level. We can illustrate two cases using the 1,000-unit sales level as a reference point.

Case 1 A 50% *increase* in sales (from 1,000 to 1,500 units) results in a 100% *increase* in earnings before interest and taxes (from $2,500 to $5,000).

Case 2 A 50% *decrease* in sales (from 1,000 to 500 units) results in a 100% *decrease* in earnings before interest and taxes (from $2,500 to $0).

From the preceding example, we see that operating leverage works in *both directions*. When a firm has fixed operating costs, operating leverage is present.

TABLE 13.4 > **The EBIT for Various Sales Levels**

	Case 2		Case 1
	−50%		+50%
Sales (in units)	500	1,000	1,500
Sales revenue[a]	$5,000	$10,000	$15,000
Less: Variable operating costs[b]	2,500	5,000	7,500
Less: Fixed operating costs	2,500	2,500	2,500
Earnings before interest and taxes (EBIT)	$ 0	$ 2,500	$ 5,000
	−100%		+100%

[a]Sales revenue = $10/unit × sales in units.
[b]Variable operating costs = $5/unit × sales in units.

An increase in sales results in a more-than-proportional increase in EBIT; a decrease in sales results in a more-than-proportional decrease in EBIT.

Measuring the Degree of Operating Leverage (DOL)

degree of operating leverage (DOL)
The numerical measure of the firm's operating leverage.

The **degree of operating leverage (DOL)** is a numerical measure of the firm's operating leverage. It can be derived using the following equation:[4]

$$DOL = \frac{\text{Percentage change in EBIT}}{\text{Percentage change in sales}} \qquad (13.4)$$

Whenever the percentage change in EBIT resulting from a given percentage change in sales is greater than the percentage change in sales, operating leverage exists. This means that as long as DOL is greater than 1, there is operating leverage.

Example 13.5 ▶

Applying Equation 13.4 to cases 1 and 2 in Table 13.4 yields the following results:

Case 1: $\dfrac{+100\%}{+50\%} = 2.0$

Case 2: $\dfrac{-100\%}{-50\%} = 2.0$

Because the result is greater than 1, operating leverage exists. For a given base level of sales, the higher the value resulting from applying Equation 13.4, the greater the degree of operating leverage.

---

4. The degree of operating leverage also depends on the base level of sales used as a point of reference. The closer the base sales level used is to the operating breakeven point, the greater the operating leverage. *Comparison of the degree of operating leverage of two firms is valid only when the same base level of sales is used for both firms.*

A more direct formula for calculating the degree of operating leverage at a base sales level, Q, is shown in Equation 13.5.[5]

$$\text{DOL at base sales level } Q = \frac{Q \times (P - VC)}{Q \times (P - VC) - FC} \quad (13.5)$$

Example 13.6 ▶

Substituting $Q = 1,000$, $P = \$10$, $VC = \$5$, and $FC = \$2,500$ into Equation 13.5 yields the following result:

$$\text{DOL at 1,000 units} = \frac{1,000 \times (\$10 - \$5)}{1,000 \times (\$10 - \$5) - \$2,500} = \frac{\$5,000}{\$2,500} = 2.0$$

The use of the formula results in the same value for DOL (2.0) as that found by using Table 13.4 and Equation 13.4.[6]

See the *Focus on Practice* box for a discussion of operating leverage at software maker Adobe.

focus on PRACTICE

Adobe's Leverage

in practice Adobe Systems, the second largest PC software company in the United States, dominates the graphic design, imaging, dynamic media, and authoring-tool software markets. Website designers favor its Photoshop and Illustrator software applications, and Adobe's Acrobat software has become a standard for sharing documents online.

Adobe's ability to manage discretionary expenses helps keep its bottom line strong. Adobe has an additional advantage: *operating leverage*, the use of fixed operating costs to magnify the effect of changes in sales on earnings before interest and taxes (EBIT). Adobe and its peers in the software industry incur the bulk of their costs early in a product's life cycle, in the research and development and initial marketing stages. The up-front development costs are fixed, and subsequent production costs are practically zero. The economies of scale are huge: Once a company sells enough copies to cover its fixed costs, incremental dollars go primarily to profit.

As demonstrated in the following table, operating leverage magnified Adobe's *increase* in EBIT in 2007 while magnifying the *decrease* in EBIT in 2009. A 22.6 percent increase in 2007 sales resulted in EBIT growth of 39.7 percent. In 2008, EBIT increased just a little faster than sales did, but in 2009 as the economy endured a severe recession, Adobe revenues plunged 17.7 percent. The effect of operating leverage was that EBIT declined even faster, posting a 35.3 percent drop.

▶ *Summarize the pros and cons of operating leverage.*

Item	FY2007	FY2008	FY2009
Sales revenue (millions)	$3,158	$3,580	$2,946
EBIT (millions)	$947	$1,089	$705
(1) Percent change in sales	22.6%	13.4%	−17.7%
(2) Percent change in EBIT	39.7%	15.0%	−35.3%
DOL [(2) ÷ (1)]	1.8	1.1	2.0

Source: Adobe Systems Inc., "2009 Annual Report," http://www.adobe.com/aboutadobe/invrelations/pdfs/fy09_10k.pdf.

5. Technically, the formula for DOL given in Equation 13.5 should include absolute value signs because it is possible to get a negative DOL when the EBIT for the base sales level is negative. Because we assume that the EBIT for the base level of sales is positive, we do not use the absolute value signs.

6. When total revenue in dollars from sales—instead of unit sales—is available, the following equation, in which TR = total revenue in dollars at a base level of sales and TVC = total variable operating costs in dollars, can be used:

$$\text{DOL at base dollar sales } TR = \frac{TR - TVC}{TR - TVC - FC}$$

This formula is especially useful for finding the DOL for multiproduct firms. It should be clear that because in the case of a single-product firm, $TR = Q \times P$ and $TVC = Q \times VC$, substitution of these values into Equation 13.5 results in the equation given here.

Fixed Costs and Operating Leverage

Changes in fixed operating costs affect operating leverage significantly. Firms sometimes can alter the mix of fixed and variable costs in their operations. For example, a firm could make fixed-dollar lease payments rather than payments equal to a specified percentage of sales. Or it could compensate sales representatives with a fixed salary and bonus rather than on a pure percent-of-sales commission basis. The effects of changes in fixed operating costs on operating leverage can best be illustrated by continuing our example.

Example 13.7 ▶

Assume that Cheryl's Posters exchanges a portion of its variable operating costs for fixed operating costs by eliminating sales commissions and increasing sales salaries. This exchange results in a reduction in the variable operating cost per unit from $5 to $4.50 and an increase in the fixed operating costs from $2,500 to $3,000. Table 13.5 presents an analysis like that in Table 13.4, but using the new costs. Although the EBIT of $2,500 at the 1,000-unit sales level is the same as before the shift in operating cost structure, Table 13.5 shows that the firm has increased its operating leverage by shifting to greater fixed operating costs.

With the substitution of the appropriate values into Equation 13.5, the degree of operating leverage at the 1,000-unit base level of sales becomes

$$\text{DOL at 1,000 units} = \frac{1,000 \times (\$10 - \$4.50)}{1,000 \times (\$10 - \$4.50) - \$3,000} = \frac{\$5,500}{\$2,500} = 2.2$$

Comparing this value to the DOL of 2.0 before the shift to more fixed costs makes it clear that the higher the firm's fixed operating costs relative to variable operating costs, the greater the degree of operating leverage.

FINANCIAL LEVERAGE

financial leverage
The use of *fixed financial costs* to magnify the effects of changes in earnings before interest and taxes on the firm's earnings per share.

Financial leverage results from the presence of *fixed financial costs* that the firm must pay. Using the framework in Table 13.1, we can define **financial leverage** as

TABLE 13.5 **Operating Leverage and Increased Fixed Costs**

		Case 2		Case 1
		−50%		+50%
Sales (in units)		500	1,000	1,500
Sales revenue[a]		$5,000	$10,000	$15,000
Less: Variable operating costs[b]		2,250	4,500	6,750
Less: Fixed operating costs		3,000	3,000	3,000
Earnings before interest and taxes (EBIT)		−$ 250	$ 2,500	$ 5,250
		−110%		+110%

[a]Sales revenue was calculated as indicated in Table 13.4.
[b]Variable operating costs = $4.50/unit × sales in units.

the use of *fixed financial costs* to magnify the effects of changes in earnings before interest and taxes on the firm's earnings per share. The two most common fixed financial costs are (1) interest on debt and (2) preferred stock dividends. These charges must be paid regardless of the amount of EBIT available to pay them.[7]

Example 13.8 ▶

Chen Foods, a small Asian food company, expects EBIT of $10,000 in the current year. It has a $20,000 bond with a 10% (annual) coupon rate of interest and an issue of 600 shares of $4 (annual dividend per share) preferred stock outstanding. It also has 1,000 shares of common stock outstanding. The annual interest on the bond issue is $2,000 (0.10 × $20,000). The annual dividends on the preferred stock are $2,400 ($4.00/share × 600 shares). Table 13.6 presents the earnings per share (EPS) corresponding to levels of EBIT of $6,000, $10,000, and $14,000, assuming that the firm is in the 40% tax bracket. The table illustrates two situations:

Case 1 A 40% *increase* in EBIT (from $10,000 to $14,000) results in a 100% *increase* in earnings per share (from $2.40 to $4.80).

Case 2 A 40% *decrease* in EBIT (from $10,000 to $6,000) results in a 100% *decrease* in earnings per share (from $2.40 to $0).

TABLE 13.6 ▷ The EPS for Various EBIT Levels[a]

	Case 2 −40%		Case 1 +40%
EBIT	$6,000	$10,000	$14,000
Less: Interest (I)	2,000	2,000	2,000
Net profits before taxes	$4,000	$8,000	$12,000
Less: Taxes ($T = 0.40$)	1,600	3,200	4,800
Net profits after taxes	$2,400	$4,800	$7,200
Less: Preferred stock dividends (PD)	2,400	2,400	2,400
Earnings available for common (EAC)	$0	$2,400	$4,800
Earnings per share (EPS)	$\frac{\$0}{1{,}000} = \$0$	$\frac{\$2{,}400}{1{,}000} = \$2.40$	$\frac{\$4{,}800}{1{,}000} = \$4.80$

−100% +100%

[a]As noted in Chapter 2, for accounting and tax purposes, interest is a *tax-deductible expense*, whereas dividends must be paid from after-tax cash flows.

7. Although a firm's board of directors can elect to stop paying preferred stock dividends, the firm typically cannot pay dividends on common stock until the preferred shareholders receive all of the dividends that they are owed. Although failure to pay preferred dividends cannot force the firm into bankruptcy, it increases the common stockholders' risk because they cannot receive dividends until the claims of preferred stockholders are satisfied.

The effect of financial leverage is such that an increase in the firm's EBIT results in a more-than-proportional increase in the firm's earnings per share, whereas a decrease in the firm's EBIT results in a more-than-proportional decrease in EPS.

Measuring the Degree of Financial Leverage (DFL)

degree of financial leverage (DFL)
The numerical measure of the firm's financial leverage.

The **degree of financial leverage (DFL)** is a numerical measure of the firm's financial leverage. Computing it is much like computing the degree of operating leverage. The following equation presents one approach for obtaining the DFL.[8]

$$DFL = \frac{\text{Percentage change in EPS}}{\text{Percentage change in EBIT}} \tag{13.6}$$

Whenever the percentage change in EPS resulting from a given percentage change in EBIT is greater than the percentage change in EBIT, financial leverage exists. This means that whenever DFL is greater than 1, there is financial leverage.

Example 13.9 ▶ Applying Equation 13.6 to cases 1 and 2 in Table 13.6 yields

Case 1: $\dfrac{+100\%}{+40\%} = 2.5$

Case 2: $\dfrac{-100\%}{-40\%} = 2.5$

In both cases, the quotient is greater than 1, so financial leverage exists. The higher this value is, the greater the degree of financial leverage.

Personal Finance Example 13.10 ▶ Shanta and Ravi Shandra, a married couple with no children, wish to assess the impact of additional long-term borrowing on their degree of financial leverage (DFL). The Shandras currently have $4,200 available after meeting all of their monthly living (operating) expenses, *before* making monthly loan payments. They currently have monthly loan payment obligations of $1,700 and are considering the purchase of a new car, which would result in a $500 per month increase (to $2,200) in their total monthly loan payments. Because a large portion of Ravi's monthly income represents commissions, the Shandras feel that the $4,200 per month currently available for making loan payments could vary by 20% above or below that amount.

To assess the potential impact of the additional borrowing on their financial leverage, the Shandras calculate their DFL for both their current ($1,700) and proposed ($2,200) loan payments as follows, using the currently available $4,200 as a base and a 20% change.

---

8. This approach is valid only when the same base level of EBIT is used to calculate and compare these values. In other words, *the base level of EBIT must be held constant to compare the financial leverage associated with different levels of fixed financial costs.*

	Current DFL			Proposed DFL		
Available for making loan payments	$4,200	(+20%)	$5,040	$4,200	(+20%)	$5,040
Less: Loan payments	1,700		1,700	2,200		2,200
Available after loan payments	$2,500	(+33.6%)	$3,340	$2,000	(+42%)	$2,840

$$\text{DFL} = \frac{+33.6\%}{+20\%} = \underline{\underline{1.68}} \qquad\qquad \text{DFL} = \frac{+42\%}{+20\%} = \underline{\underline{2.10}}$$

Based on their calculations, the amount the Shandras will have available after loan payments with their current debt changes by 1.68% for every 1% change in the amount they will have available for making the loan payments. This is considerably less responsive—and therefore less risky—than the 2.10% change in the amount available after loan payments for each 1% change in the amount available for making loan payments with the proposed additional $500 in monthly debt payments. Although it appears that the Shandras can afford the additional loan payments, they must decide if, given the variability of Ravi's income, they feel comfortable with the increased financial leverage and risk.

A more direct formula for calculating the degree of financial leverage at a base level of EBIT is given by Equation 13.7, where the notation from Table 13.6 is used.[9] Note that in the denominator the term $1/(1 - T)$ converts the after-tax preferred stock dividend to a before-tax amount for consistency with the other terms in the equation.

$$\text{DFL at base level EBIT} = \frac{\text{EBIT}}{\text{EBIT} - I - \left(PD \times \dfrac{1}{1 - T}\right)} \qquad (13.7)$$

Example 13.11 ▶ Substituting EBIT = $10,000, I = $2,000, PD = $2,400, and the tax rate (T = 0.40) into Equation 13.7 yields the following result:

$$\text{DFL at \$10,000 EBIT} = \frac{\$10,000}{\$10,000 - \$2,000 - \left(\$2,400 \times \dfrac{1}{1 - 0.40}\right)}$$

$$= \frac{\$10,000}{\$4,000} = 2.5$$

Note that the formula given in Equation 13.7 provides a more direct method for calculating the degree of financial leverage than the approach illustrated using Table 13.6 and Equation 13.6.

---

9. By using the formula for DFL in Equation 13.7, it is possible to get a negative value for the DFL if the EPS for the base level of EBIT is negative. Rather than show absolute value signs in the equation, we instead assume that the base-level EPS is positive.

TOTAL LEVERAGE

total leverage
The use of *fixed costs, both operating and financial,* to magnify the effects of changes in sales on the firm's earnings per share.

We also can assess the combined effect of operating and financial leverage on the firm's risk by using a framework similar to that used to develop the individual concepts of leverage. This combined effect, or **total leverage,** can be defined as the use of *fixed costs, both operating and financial,* to magnify the effects of changes in sales on the firm's earnings per share. Total leverage can therefore be viewed as the *total impact of the fixed costs* in the firm's operating and financial structure.

> **Example 13.12 ▶**   Cables Inc., a computer cable manufacturer, expects sales of 20,000 units at $5 per unit in the coming year and must meet the following obligations: variable operating costs of $2 per unit, fixed operating costs of $10,000, interest of $20,000, and preferred stock dividends of $12,000. The firm is in the 40% tax bracket and has 5,000 shares of common stock outstanding. Table 13.7 presents the levels of earnings per share associated with the expected sales of 20,000 units and with sales of 30,000 units.
>
> The table illustrates that as a result of a 50% increase in sales (from 20,000 to 30,000 units), the firm would experience a 300% increase in earnings per share (from $1.20 to $4.80). Although it is not shown in the table, a 50% decrease in sales would, conversely, result in a 300% decrease in earnings per share. The linear nature of the leverage relationship accounts for the fact that sales changes of equal magnitude in opposite directions result in EPS changes of equal magnitude in the corresponding direction. At this point, it should be clear that whenever a

TABLE 13.7 ▶ The Total Leverage Effect

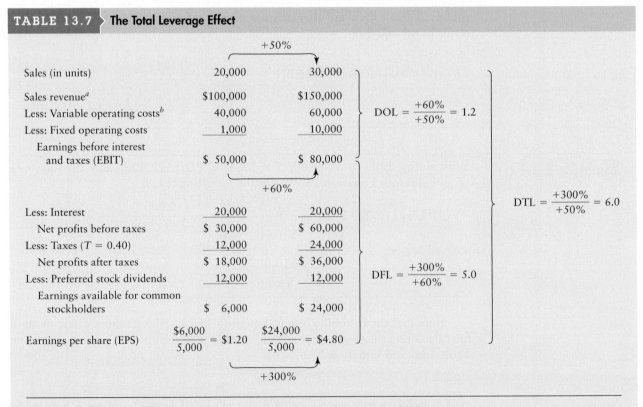

	20,000	30,000	
Sales (in units)	20,000	30,000	
Sales revenue[a]	$100,000	$150,000	
Less: Variable operating costs[b]	40,000	60,000	$DOL = \dfrac{+60\%}{+50\%} = 1.2$
Less: Fixed operating costs	1,000	10,000	
Earnings before interest and taxes (EBIT)	$ 50,000	$ 80,000	
Less: Interest	20,000	20,000	
Net profits before taxes	$ 30,000	$ 60,000	
Less: Taxes (T = 0.40)	12,000	24,000	
Net profits after taxes	$ 18,000	$ 36,000	$DFL = \dfrac{+300\%}{+60\%} = 5.0$
Less: Preferred stock dividends	12,000	12,000	
Earnings available for common stockholders	$ 6,000	$ 24,000	
Earnings per share (EPS)	$\dfrac{\$6,000}{5,000} = \$1.20$	$\dfrac{\$24,000}{5,000} = \$4.80$	

+50% (from 20,000 to 30,000)
+60% (EBIT)
+300% (EPS)

$DTL = \dfrac{+300\%}{+50\%} = 6.0$

[a]Sales revenue = $5/unit × sales in units.
[b]Variable operating costs = $2/unit × sales in units.

firm has fixed costs—operating or financial—in its structure, total leverage will exist.

Measuring the Degree of Total Leverage (DTL)

degree of total leverage (DTL)
The numerical measure of the firm's total leverage.

The **degree of total leverage (DTL)** is a numerical measure of the firm's total leverage. It can be computed much like operating and financial leverage are computed. The following equation presents one approach for measuring DTL:[10]

$$DTL = \frac{\text{Percentage change in EPS}}{\text{Percentage change in sales}} \qquad (13.8)$$

Whenever the percentage change in EPS resulting from a given percentage change in sales is greater than the percentage change in sales, total leverage exists. This means that as long as the DTL is greater than 1, there is total leverage.

Example 13.13 ▶

Applying Equation 13.8 to the data in Table 13.7 yields

$$DTL = \frac{+300\%}{+50\%} = 6.0$$

Because this result is greater than 1, total leverage exists. The higher the value is, the greater the degree of total leverage.

A more direct formula for calculating the degree of total leverage at a given base level of sales, Q, is given by Equation 13.9,[11] which uses the same notation that was presented earlier:

$$DTL \text{ at base sales level } Q = \frac{Q \times (P - VC)}{Q \times (P - VC) - FC - I - \left(PD \times \dfrac{1}{1 - T}\right)} \qquad (13.9)$$

Example 13.14 ▶

Substituting $Q = 20{,}000$, $P = \$5$, $VC = \$2$, $FC = \$10{,}000$, $I = \$20{,}000$, $PD = \$12{,}000$, and the tax rate ($T = 0.40$) into Equation 13.9 yields

DTL at 20,000 units

$$= \frac{20{,}000 \times (\$5 - \$2)}{20{,}000 \times (\$5 - \$2) - \$10{,}000 - \$20{,}000 - \left(\$12{,}000 \times \dfrac{1}{1 - 0.40}\right)}$$

$$= \frac{\$60{,}000}{\$10{,}000} = 6.0$$

Clearly, the formula used in Equation 13.9 provides a more direct method for calculating the degree of total leverage than the approach illustrated using Table 13.7 and Equation 13.8.

---

10. This approach is valid only when the same base level of sales is used to calculate and compare these values. In other words, *the base level of sales must be held constant if we are to compare the total leverage associated with different levels of fixed costs.*

11. By using the formula for DTL in Equation 13.9, it is possible to get a negative value for the DTL if the EPS for the base level of sales is negative. For our purposes, rather than show absolute value signs in the equation, we instead assume that the base-level EPS is positive.

Relationship of Operating, Financial, and Total Leverage

Total leverage reflects the *combined impact* of operating and financial leverage on the firm. High operating leverage and high financial leverage will cause total leverage to be high. The opposite will also be true. The relationship between operating leverage and financial leverage is *multiplicative* rather than *additive*. The relationship between the degree of total leverage (DTL) and the degrees of operating leverage (DOL) and financial leverage (DFL) is given by Equation 13.10:

$$DTL = DOL \times DFL \tag{13.10}$$

Example 13.15 ▶ Substituting the values calculated for DOL and DFL, shown on the right-hand side of Table 13.7, into Equation 13.10 yields

$$DTL = 1.2 \times 5.0 = 6.0$$

The resulting degree of total leverage is the same value that we calculated directly in the preceding examples.

The *Focus on Ethics* box considers some ethical issues relating to the topic of leverage.

focus on ETHICS

Repo 105

(in practice) Lehman Brothers' fall was perhaps the most stunning development of the financial crisis. Dating back to the mid-1800s, the firm had survived the Great Depression and numerous recessions to become a major player on Wall Street and around the world. Lehman's business included investment banking, sales, research and trading, investment management, private equity, and private banking. Lehman was also a major player in the subprime mortgage industry, which would ultimately lead to the firm's undoing.

In the years before the subprime mortgage crisis, financial firms borrowed heavily. Lehman was no exception. By early 2008, Lehman had $32 in debt for each $1 in equity. That much leverage implied that a small drop in the value of Lehman's assets could wipe out the firm.

Lehman's exposure to the subprime mortgage industry left it vulnerable during the crisis. As its financial health deteriorated, Lehman used off–balance sheet transactions to hide the extent of its indebtedness. The transactions, known within Lehman as Repo 105s, were executed near the end of each quarter, just before Lehman filed its quarterly financial reports. In these repos, Lehman sold some of its assets with an agreement to buy them back (with interest) a few days later. Lehman used the cash from the asset sale to pay down other liabilities. The Repo 105 transactions enabled Lehman to reduce both total liabilities and total assets and allowed the firm to report lower leverage ratios. With the start of a new quarter, Lehman would unwind the transactions and restore the liabilities to their balance sheet.

The effects of Lehman's Repo 105 transactions were sizeable, allowing the firm to briefly remove as much as $50 billion in debt from its balance sheet. Because Lehman did not detail the Repo 105 transactions in their financial statements, outsiders were unaware of the transactions. Within Lehman, concerns were raised over the Repo 105 program. The firm's Global Financial Controller, Martin Kelly, warned of the "reputational risk" to Lehman if the public became aware of the firm's reliance on such transactions.[a]

▶ Assume that Lehman's Repo 105 transactions fall within the limits allowed by Generally Accepted Accounting Principles as Lehman's management has argued. What are the ethical implications of undertaking transactions expressly to temporarily hide how much money a firm has borrowed?

[a]M. Spector and M. Corkery, "What Lehman's Central Players Knew," *Wall Street Journal*, March 20, 2010, http://online.wsj.com.

→ REVIEW QUESTIONS

13–1 What is meant by the term *leverage?* How are operating leverage, financial leverage, and total leverage related to the income statement?

13–2 What is the *operating breakeven point?* How do changes in fixed operating costs, the sale price per unit, and the variable operating cost per unit affect it?

13–3 What is *operating leverage?* What causes it? How is the *degree of operating leverage (DOL)* measured?

13–4 What is *financial leverage?* What causes it? How is the *degree of financial leverage (DFL)* measured?

13–5 What is the general relationship among operating leverage, financial leverage, and the total leverage of the firm? Do these types of leverage complement one another? Why or why not?

LG 3 LG 4 13.2 The Firm's Capital Structure

Capital structure is one of the most complex areas of financial decision making because of its interrelationship with other financial decision variables. Poor capital structure decisions can result in a high cost of capital, thereby lowering the NPVs of projects and making more of them unacceptable. Effective capital structure decisions can lower the cost of capital, resulting in higher NPVs and more acceptable projects—and thereby increasing the value of the firm.

TYPES OF CAPITAL

All of the items on the right-hand side of the firm's balance sheet, excluding current liabilities, are sources of capital. The following simplified balance sheet illustrates the basic breakdown of total capital into its two components, *debt capital* and *equity capital:*

The cost of debt is lower than the cost of other forms of financing. Lenders demand relatively lower returns because they take the least risk of any contributors of long-term capital. Lenders have a higher priority of claim against any earnings or assets available for payment, and they can exert far greater legal pressure against the company to make payment than can owners of preferred or common stock.

The tax deductibility of interest payments also lowers the debt cost to the firm substantially.

Unlike debt capital, which the firm must eventually repay, *equity capital* remains invested in the firm indefinitely—it has no maturity date. The two basic sources of equity capital are (1) preferred stock and (2) common stock equity, which includes common stock and retained earnings. Common stock is typically the most expensive form of equity, followed by retained earnings and then preferred stock. Our concern here is the relationship between debt and equity capital. In general, the more debt a firm uses, the greater will be the firm's financial leverage. That leverage makes the claims of common stockholders even more risky. In addition, a firm that increases its use of leverage significantly can see its cost of debt rise as lenders begin to worry about the firm's ability to repay its debts. Whether the firm borrows very little or a great deal, it is always true that the claims of common stockholders are riskier than those of lenders, so the cost of equity always exceeds the cost of debt.

EXTERNAL ASSESSMENT OF CAPITAL STRUCTURE

We saw earlier that *financial leverage* results from the use of fixed-cost financing, such as debt and preferred stock, to magnify return and risk. The amount of leverage in the firm's capital structure can affect its value by affecting return and risk. Those outside the firm can make a rough assessment of capital structure by using measures found in the firm's financial statements. Some of these important debt ratios were presented in Chapter 3. For example, a direct measure of the degree of indebtedness is the *debt ratio* (total liabilities ÷ total assets). The higher this ratio is, the greater the relative amount of debt (or financial leverage) in the firm's capital structure. Measures of the firm's ability to meet contractual payments associated with debt include the *times interest earned ratio* (EBIT ÷ interest) and the *fixed-payment coverage ratio* (see page 78). These ratios provide indirect information on financial leverage. Generally, the smaller these ratios, the greater the firm's financial leverage and the less able it is to meet payments as they come due.

The level of debt (financial leverage) that is acceptable for one industry or line of business can be highly risky in another, because different industries and lines of business have different operating characteristics. Table 13.8 presents the debt and times interest earned ratios for selected industries and lines of business. Significant industry differences can be seen in these data. Differences in debt positions are also likely to exist *within* an industry or line of business.

Personal Finance Example 13.16 ▶ Those who lend to individuals, like lenders to corporations, typically use ratios to assess the applicant's ability to meet the contractual payments associated with the requested debt. The lender, after obtaining information from a loan application and other sources, calculates ratios and compares them to predetermined allowable values. Typically, if the applicant's ratio values are within the acceptable range, the lender will make the requested loan.

The best example of this process is a real estate mortgage loan application. The mortgage lender usually invokes the following two requirements:

1. Monthly mortgage payments < 25% to 30% of monthly gross (before-tax) income
2. Total monthly installment payments (including the mortgage payment) < 33% to 38% of monthly gross (before-tax) income

TABLE 13.8	Debt Ratios for Selected Industries and Lines of Business (Fiscal Year April 1, 2008 through March 31, 2009)					

Industry or line of business	Debt ratio	Times interest earned ratio	Industry or line of business	Debt ratio	Times interest earned ratio
Manufacturing industries			**Retailing industries**		
Book printing	57.8%	1.5	Department stores	61.7	1.9
Dairy products	71.6	4.9	New car dealers	82.0	1.2
Electronic computers	59.0	2.2	Supermarkets and grocery stores	69.8	3.6
Iron and steel forgings	58.6	5.5	**Service industries**		
Machine tools, metal cutting types	65.9	3.1	Advertising agencies	87.5	5.9
Women's and girls' dresses	57.8	1.5	General automotive repair	99.2	2.9
Wholesaling industries			Insurance agencies and brokerages	82.2	5.0
Furniture	65.5	3.9	Offices of Certified Public Accountants	69.7	8.5
General groceries	68.6	3.6			
Men's and boys' clothing	57.6	4.0			
Wines and distilled alcoholic beverages	66.8	3.7			

Source: RMA Annual Statement Studies, 2009–2010 (Philadelphia: Risk Management Association, 2009). Copyright © 2009 by Risk Management Association.

Assume that the Loo family is applying for a mortgage loan. The family's monthly gross (before-tax) income is $5,380, and they currently have monthly installment loan obligations that total $560. The $200,000 mortgage loan they are applying for will require monthly payments of $1,400. The lender requires (1) the monthly mortgage payment to be less than 28% of monthly gross income and (2) total monthly installment payments (including the mortgage payment) to be less than 37% of monthly gross income. The lender calculates and evaluates these ratios for the Loos, as shown below.

1. Mort. pay. ÷ Gross income = $1,400 ÷ $5,380

    = 26% < 28% maximum, therefore **OK**

2. Tot. instal.pay. ÷ Gross income = ($560 + $1,400) ÷ $5,380

    = $1,960 ÷ $5,380

    = 36.4% < 37% maximum, therefore **OK**

Because the Loos' ratios meet the lender's standards, assuming they have adequate funds for the down payment and meet other lender requirements, the Loos will be granted the loan.

CAPITAL STRUCTURE OF NON–U.S. FIRMS

In general, non–U.S. companies have much higher degrees of indebtedness than their U.S. counterparts. Most of the reasons relate to the fact that U.S. capital markets are more developed than those elsewhere and have played a greater role in corporate financing than has been the case in other countries. In most European countries and especially in Japan and other Pacific Rim nations, large commercial banks are more actively involved in the financing of corporate activity than has been true in the United States. Furthermore, in many of these countries, banks are allowed to make large equity investments in nonfinancial corporations—a practice prohibited for U.S. banks. Finally, share ownership tends to be more tightly controlled among founding-family, institutional, and even public investors in Europe and Asia than it is for most large U.S. corporations. Tight ownership enables owners to understand the firm's financial condition better, resulting in their willingness to tolerate a higher degree of indebtedness.

Matter of fact

Leverage around the World

A recent study of the use of long-term debt in 42 countries found that firms in Argentina used more long-term debt than firms in any other country. Relative to their assets, firms in Argentina used almost 60 percent more long-term debt than did U.S. companies. Indian firms were heavy users of long-term debt as well. At the other end of the spectrum, companies from Italy, Greece, and Poland used very little long-term debt. In those countries, firms used only about 40 percent as much long-term debt as did their U.S. counterparts.

On the other hand, similarities do exist between U.S. corporations and corporations in other countries. First, the same industry patterns of capital structure tend to be found all around the world. For example, in nearly all countries, pharmaceutical and other high-growth industrial firms tend to have lower debt ratios than do steel companies, airlines, and electric utility companies. In part, this has to do with the nature of assets held by these firms. High-growth firms whose main assets are intangibles (such as patents and rights to intellectual property) tend to borrow less than firms that have tangible assets that can be pledged as collateral for loans. Second, the capital structures of the largest U.S.–based multinational companies, which have access to capital markets around the world, typically resemble the capital structures of multinational companies from other countries more than they resemble those of smaller U.S. companies. In other words, in most countries there is a tendency for larger firms to borrow more than smaller firms do. Third, companies that are riskier and have more volatile income streams tend to borrow less, as do firms that are highly profitable. Finally, the worldwide trend is away from reliance on banks for financing and toward greater reliance on security issuance. Over time, the differences in the capital structures of U.S. and non–U.S. firms will probably lessen.

CAPITAL STRUCTURE THEORY

Research suggests that there is an optimal capital structure range. *It is not yet possible to provide financial managers with a precise methodology for determining a firm's optimal capital structure.* Nevertheless, financial theory does offer help in understanding how a firm's capital structure affects the firm's value. In 1958, Franco Modigliani and Merton H. Miller[12] (commonly known as "M and M") demonstrated algebraically that, assuming perfect markets,[13] the

---

12. Franco Modigliani and Merton H. Miller, "The Cost of Capital, Corporation Finance, and the Theory of Investment," *American Economic Review* (June 1958), pp. 261–297.

13. Perfect-market assumptions include (1) no taxes, (2) no brokerage or flotation costs for securities, (3) symmetrical information—investors and managers have the same information about the firm's investment prospects, and (4) investor ability to borrow at the same rate as corporations.

In more depth

To read about *Capital Structure Irrelevance,* go to www.myfinancelab.com

 myfinance**lab**®

capital structure that a firm chooses does not affect its value. Many researchers, including M and M, have examined the effects of less restrictive assumptions on the relationship between capital structure and the firm's value. The result is a theoretical *optimal* capital structure based on balancing the benefits and costs of debt financing. The major benefit of debt financing is the *tax shield,* which allows interest payments to be deducted in calculating taxable income. The cost of debt financing results from (1) the increased probability of bankruptcy caused by debt obligations, (2) the *agency costs* of the lender's constraining the firm's actions, and (3) the costs associated with managers having more information about the firm's prospects than do investors.

Tax Benefits

Allowing firms to deduct interest payments on debt when calculating taxable income reduces the amount of the firm's earnings paid in taxes, thereby making more earnings available for bondholders and stockholders. The deductibility of interest means the cost of debt, r_i, to the firm is subsidized by the government. Letting r_d equal the before-tax cost of debt and letting T equal the tax rate, from Chapter 9 (Equation 9.2), we have $r_i = r_d \times (1 - T)$.

Probability of Bankruptcy

The chance that a firm will become bankrupt because of an inability to meet its obligations as they come due depends largely on its levels of both business risk and financial risk.

Business Risk   We define *business risk* as the risk to the firm of being unable to cover its operating costs. In general, the greater the firm's *operating leverage*—the use of fixed operating costs—the higher its business risk. Although operating leverage is an important factor affecting business risk, two other factors—revenue stability and cost stability—also affect it. *Revenue stability* reflects the relative variability of the firm's sales revenues. Firms with stable levels of demand and product prices tend to have stable revenues. The result is low levels of business risk. Firms with highly volatile product demand and prices have unstable revenues that result in high levels of business risk. *Cost stability* reflects the relative predictability of input prices such as those for labor and materials. The more predictable and stable these input prices are, the lower the business risk; the less predictable and stable they are, the higher the business risk.

Business risk varies among firms, regardless of their lines of business, and is not affected by capital structure decisions. The level of business risk must be taken as a "given." The higher a firm's business risk, the more cautious the firm must be in establishing its capital structure. Firms with high business risk therefore tend toward less highly leveraged capital structures, and firms with low business risk tend toward more highly leveraged capital structures. We will hold business risk constant throughout the discussions that follow.

Example 13.17 ▶   Cooke Company, a soft drink manufacturer, is preparing to make a capital structure decision. It has obtained estimates of sales and the associated levels of earnings before interest and taxes (EBIT) from its forecasting group: There is a 25% chance that sales will total $400,000, a 50% chance that sales will total $600,000, and a 25% chance that sales will total $800,000. Fixed operating

| TABLE 13.9 | Sales and Associated EBIT Calculations for Cooke Company ($000) |

Probability of sales	0.25	0.50	0.25
Sales revenue	$400	$600	$800
Less: Fixed operating costs	200	200	200
Less: Variable operating costs (50% of sales)	200	300	400
Earnings before interest and taxes (EBIT)	$ 0	$100	$200

costs total $200,000, and variable operating costs equal 50% of sales. These data are summarized, and the resulting EBIT calculated, in Table 13.9.

The table shows that there is a 25% chance that the EBIT will be $0, a 50% chance that it will be $100,000, and a 25% chance that it will be $200,000. When developing the firm's capital structure, the financial manager must accept as given these levels of EBIT and their associated probabilities. These EBIT data effectively reflect a certain level of business risk that captures the firm's operating leverage, sales revenue variability, and cost predictability.

Financial Risk   The firm's capital structure directly affects its *financial risk*, which is the risk to the firm of being unable to cover required financial obligations. The penalty for not meeting financial obligations is bankruptcy. The more fixed-cost financing—debt (including financial leases) and preferred stock—a firm has in its capital structure, the greater its financial leverage and risk. Financial risk depends on the capital structure decision made by the management, and that decision is affected by the business risk the firm faces.

Total Risk   The *total risk* of a firm—business and financial risk combined—determines its probability of bankruptcy. Financial risk, its relationship to business risk, and their combined impact can be demonstrated by continuing the Cooke Company example.

Example 13.18 ▶   Cooke Company's current capital structure is as follows:

Current capital structure	
Long-term debt	$ 0
Common stock equity (25,000 shares at $20)	500,000
Total capital (assets)	$500,000

Let us assume that the firm is considering seven alternative capital structures. If we measure these structures using the debt ratio, they are associated with ratios of 0%, 10%, 20%, 30%, 40%, 50%, and 60%. Assuming that (1) the firm has no current liabilities, (2) its capital structure currently contains all equity as shown, and (3) the total amount of capital remains constant[14] at $500,000, the

---

14. This assumption is needed so that we can assess alternative capital structures without having to consider the returns associated with the investment of additional funds raised. Attention here is given only to the *mix* of capital, not to its investment.

TABLE 13.10	Capital Structures Associated with Alternative Debt Ratios for Cooke Company

	Capital structure ($000)			Shares of common stock outstanding (000)
Debt ratio (1)	Total assets[a] (2)	Debt [(1) × (2)] (3)	Equity [(2) − (3)] (4)	[(4) ÷ $20][b] (5)
0%	$500	$ 0	$500	25.00
10	500	50	450	22.50
20	500	100	400	20.00
30	500	150	350	17.50
40	500	200	300	15.00
50	500	250	250	12.50
60	500	300	200	10.00

[a]Because the firm, for convenience, is assumed to have no current liabilities, its total assets equal its total capital of $500,000.

[b]The $20 value represents the book value per share of common stock equity noted earlier.

mix of debt and equity associated with the seven debt ratios would be as shown in Table 13.10. Also shown in the table is the number of shares of common stock outstanding under each alternative.

Associated with each of the debt levels in column 3 of Table 13.10 would be an interest rate that would be expected to increase with increases in financial leverage. The level of debt, the associated interest rate (assumed to apply to *all* debt), and the dollar amount of annual interest associated with each of the alternative capital structures are summarized in Table 13.11. Because both the level of debt and the interest rate increase with increasing financial leverage (debt ratios), the annual interest increases as well.

Table 13.12 on page 530 uses the levels of EBIT and associated probabilities developed in Table 13.9, the number of shares of common stock found in column 5 of Table 13.10, and the annual interest values calculated in column 3 of Table 13.11 to calculate the earnings per share (EPS) for debt ratios of 0%, 30%, and 60%.

TABLE 13.11	Level of Debt, Interest Rate, and Dollar Amount of Annual Interest Associated with Cooke Company's Alternative Capital Structures

Capital structure debt ratio	Debt ($000) (1)	Interest rate on *all* debt (2)	Interest ($000) [(1) × (2)] (3)
0%	$ 0	0.0%	$ 0.00
10	50	9.0	4.50
20	100	9.5	9.50
30	150	10.0	15.00
40	200	11.0	22.00
50	250	13.5	33.75
60	300	16.5	49.50

TABLE 13.12	Calculation of EPS for Selected Debt Ratios ($000) for Cooke Company		
Probability of EBIT	0.25	0.50	0.25
Debt ratio = 0%			
EBIT (Table 13.9)	$ 0.00	$100.00	$200.00
Less: Interest (Table 13.11)	0.00	0.00	.00
Net profits before taxes	$ 0.00	$100.00	$200.00
Less: Taxes ($T = 0.40$)	0.00	40.00	80.00
Net profits after taxes	$ 0.00	$ 60.00	$120.00
EPS (25.0 shares, Table 13.10)	$ 0.00	$ 2.40	$ 4.80
Expected EPS[a]	$2.40		
Standard deviation of EPS[a]	$1.70		
Coefficient of variation of EPS[a]	0.71		
Debt ratio = 30%			
EBIT (Table 13.9)	$ 0.00	$100.00	$200.00
Less: Interest (Table 13.11)	15.00	15.00	15.00
Net profits before taxes	($15.00)	$ 85.00	$185.00
Less: Taxes ($T = 0.40$)	(6.00)[b]	34.00	74.00
Net profits after taxes	($ 9.00)	$ 51.00	$111.00
EPS (17.50 shares, Table 13.10)	(0.51)	$ 2.91	$ 6.34
Expected EPS[a]	$2.91		
Standard deviation of EPS[a]	$2.42		
Coefficient of variation of EPS[a]	0.83		
Debt ratio = 60%			
EBIT (Table 13.9)	$ 0.00	$100.00	$200.00
Less: Interest (Table 13.11)	49.50	49.50	49.50
Net profits before taxes	($49.50)	$ 50.50	$150.50
Less: Taxes ($T = 0.40$)	(19.80)[b]	0.20	60.20
Net profits after taxes	($29.70)	$ 30.30	$ 90.30
EPS (10.00 shares, Table 13.10)	($ 2.97)	$ 3.03	$ 9.03
Expected EPS[a]	$3.03		
Standard deviation of EPS[a]	$4.24		
Coefficient of variation of EPS[a]	1.40		

[a]The procedures used to calculate the expected value, standard deviation, and coefficient of variation were presented in Chapter 8.

[b]It is assumed that the firm receives the tax benefit from its loss in the current period as a result of applying the *tax loss carryback* procedures specified in the tax law but not discussed in this text.

A 40% tax rate is assumed. Also shown are the resulting expected EPS, the standard deviation of EPS, and the coefficient of variation of EPS associated with each debt ratio.[15]

---

15. For explanatory convenience, the *coefficient of variation of EPS,* which measures total (nondiversifiable and diversifiable) risk, is used throughout this chapter as a proxy for beta, which measures the relevant nondiversifiable risk.

TABLE 13.13	Expected EPS, Standard Deviation, and Coefficient of Variation for Alternative Capital Structures for Cooke Company		
Capital structure debt ratio	Expected EPS (1)	Standard deviation of EPS (2)	Coefficient of variation of EPS [(2) ÷ (1)] (3)
0%	$2.40	$1.70	0.71
10	2.55	1.88	0.74
20	2.72	2.13	0.78
30	2.91	2.42	0.83
40	3.12	2.83	0.91
50	3.18	3.39	1.07
60	3.03	4.24	1.40

Table 13.13 summarizes the pertinent data for the seven alternative capital structures. The values shown for 0%, 30%, and 60% debt ratios were developed in Table 13.12, whereas calculations of similar values for the other debt ratios (10%, 20%, 40%, and 50%) are not shown. Because the coefficient of variation measures the risk relative to the expected EPS, it is the preferred risk measure for use in comparing capital structures. As the firm's financial leverage increases, so does its coefficient of variation of EPS. As expected, an increasing level of risk is associated with increased levels of financial leverage.

The relative risks of the two extremes of the capital structures evaluated in Table 13.12 (debt ratios = 0% and 60%) can be illustrated by showing the probability distribution of EPS associated with each of them. Figure 13.3 shows these

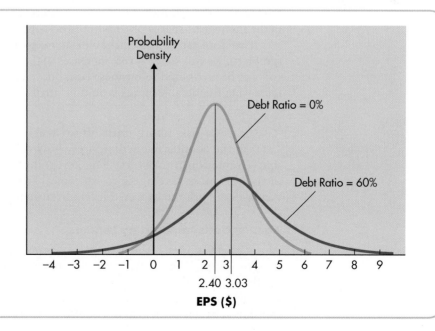

FIGURE 13.3

Probability Distributions
Probability distributions of EPS for debt ratios of 0 percent and 60 percent for Cooke Company

FIGURE 13.4

Expected EPS and Coefficient of Variation of EPS
Expected EPS and coefficient of variation of EPS for alternative capital structures for Cooke Company

two distributions. The expected level of EPS increases with increasing financial leverage, and so does risk as reflected by the difference in dispersion between the distributions. Clearly, the uncertainty of the expected EPS, as well as the chance of experiencing negative EPS, is greater when higher degrees of financial leverage are employed.

Further, the nature of the risk–return trade-off associated with the seven capital structures under consideration can be clearly observed by plotting the expected EPS and coefficient of variation relative to the debt ratio. Plotting the data from Table 13.13 results in Figure 13.4. The figure shows that as debt is substituted for equity (as the debt ratio increases), the level of EPS rises and then begins to fall (graph **a**). The graph demonstrates that the peak of earnings per share occurs at a debt ratio of 50%. The decline in earnings per share beyond that ratio results from the fact that the significant increases in interest are not fully offset by the reduction in the number of shares of common stock outstanding.

If we look at the risk behavior as measured by the coefficient of variation (graph **b**), we can see that risk increases with increasing leverage. A portion of the risk can be attributed to business risk, but the portion that changes in response to increasing financial leverage would be attributed to financial risk.

Clearly, a risk–return trade-off exists relative to the use of financial leverage. Later in the chapter, we will address how to combine these risk–return factors into a valuation framework. The key point to recognize here is that as a firm introduces more leverage into its capital structure, it will typically experience increases in both the expected level of return and the associated risk.

Agency Costs Imposed by Lenders

As noted in Chapter 1, the managers of firms typically act as *agents* of the owners (stockholders). The owners give the managers the authority to manage the firm for the owners' benefit. The *agency problem* created by this relationship extends not only to the relationship between owners and managers but also to the relationship between owners and lenders.

When a lender provides funds to a firm, the interest rate charged is based on the lender's assessment of the firm's risk. The lender–borrower relationship, therefore, depends on the lender's expectations for the firm's subsequent behavior. The borrowing rates are, in effect, locked in when the loans are negotiated. After obtaining a loan at a certain rate, the firm could increase its risk by investing in risky projects or by incurring additional debt. Such action could weaken the lender's position in terms of its claim on the cash flow of the firm. From another point of view, if these risky investment strategies paid off, the stockholders would benefit. Because payment obligations to the lender remain unchanged, the excess cash flows generated by a positive outcome from the riskier action would enhance the value of the firm to its owners. In other words, if the risky investments pay off, the owners receive all the benefits; if the risky investments do not pay off, the lenders share in the costs.

Clearly, an incentive exists for the managers acting on behalf of the stockholders to "take advantage" of lenders. To avoid this situation, lenders impose certain monitoring techniques on borrowers, who as a result incur *agency costs*. The most obvious strategy is to deny subsequent loan requests or to increase the cost of future loans to the firm. But this strategy is an after-the-fact approach. Therefore, lenders typically protect themselves by including in the loan agreement provisions that limit the firm's ability to alter its business and financial risk. These loan provisions tend to center on issues such as the minimum level of liquidity, asset acquisitions, executive salaries, and dividend payments.

By including appropriate provisions in the loan agreement, the lender can control the firm's risk and thus protect itself against the adverse consequences of this agency problem. Of course, in exchange for incurring agency costs by agreeing to the operating and financial constraints placed on it by the loan provisions, the firm should benefit by obtaining funds at a lower cost.

Asymmetric Information

The Pecking Order Theory   When two parties in an economic transaction have different information, we say that there is **asymmetric information.** In the context of capital structure decisions, asymmetric information simply means that managers of the firm have more information about the firm's operations and future prospects than investors have. To understand how asymmetric information between managers and investors could have implications for a firm's capital structure, consider the following situation.

asymmetric information
The situation in which managers of a firm have more information about operations and future prospects than do investors.

Suppose that managers of a firm have a highly profitable investment opportunity that requires financing. Managers would like to tell investors about this great investment opportunity, but investors are skeptical. After all, managers always have incentives to claim that their investment decisions will lead to fabulous profits, but investors have no way to verify these claims. If managers try to sell stock to finance the investments, investors are only willing to pay a price that reflects the verifiable information that they have, which means that managers have to sell stock at a discount (relative to the price that they could get if there were no asymmetric information). This makes raising new equity very costly, and sometimes managers may decide to pass up positive NPV investments to avoid having to sell equity to investors at a discount.

One solution to this problem is for managers to maintain financial slack, cash reserves from retained earnings that they can use to finance new investments.

When firms do not have enough financial slack to finance their profitable investment opportunities, managers will prefer to raise external financing by issuing debt rather than equity. Providers of debt financing receive a fixed return, so when the new investment begins to generate high returns for the firm, those cash flows will largely go to the firm's existing stockholders.

pecking order
A hierarchy of financing that begins with retained earnings, which is followed by debt financing and finally external equity financing.

All of this suggests that there is a financial **pecking order**, meaning a hierarchy of financing that begins with retained earnings, followed by debt, and finally new stock issues. When managers want to finance a new project, they will first do so using retained earnings. If internally generated cash is insufficient to fund new investments, then managers will raise external financing through the debt markets. Issuing new equity is their last resort.

This pecking order theory is consistent with several facts about firms' financing decisions. First, the vast majority of new investments are funded through retained earnings—firms raise external financing infrequently. Second, firms do raise debt with greater frequency than equity as the pecking order theory predicts. Third, as we have already noted, there is a general tendency for profitable companies (who have plenty of financial slack) to borrow less than unprofitable firms.

Signaling   There is an old saying that goes, "put your money where your mouth is." The idea is that anyone can brag, but only those who are willing to put real dollars at stake behind their claims ought to be believed. How does this aphorism relate to capital structure decisions? Suppose, for example, that management has information that the prospects for the firm's future are very good. Managers could issue a press release trying to convince investors that the firm's future is bright, but investors will want tangible evidence for the claims. Furthermore, providing that evidence has to be costly to the firm; otherwise, other firms with less rosy prospects will just mimic the actions of the firm with truly excellent prospects. One thing that managers might do is to borrow a lot of money by issuing debt. In so doing, they are demonstrating to the market that they have faith that the firm will generate sufficient cash flows in the future to retire the outstanding debt. Firms whose prospects are not as good will hesitate to issue a lot of debt because they may have difficulty repaying the debt and may even go bankrupt. In other words, issuing debt is a credible **signal** that managers believe the firm's performance will be very good in the future. Debt financing is a *positive signal* suggesting that management believes that the stock is "undervalued" and therefore a bargain.

signal
A financing action by management that is believed to reflect its view of the firm's stock value; generally, debt financing is viewed as a *positive signal* that management believes the stock is "undervalued," and a stock issue is viewed as a *negative signal* that management believes the stock is "overvalued."

By the same token, when firms decide to issue stock, investors worry that this could be a *negative signal*, indicating that managers believe the firm's future profitability may be rather poor and that the stock price is currently overvalued. Therefore, investors often interpret the announcement of a stock issue as bad news, and the stock price declines.

Most research casts doubt on the importance of signaling as a primary determinant of firms' capital structure choices. For instance, we have already seen that the most profitable firms tend to borrow less, whereas the signaling theory says that profitable firms should borrow more as a way to convince investors of just how high the firm's future profits will be. Furthermore, in surveys that ask managers to describe how they choose between debt and equity financing, they rarely say that they choose debt as a way to convey information to investors. Still, the signaling theory predicts that a firm's stock price should rise when it issues debt and fall when it issues equity, and that is exactly what happens in the real world much of the time.

OPTIMAL CAPITAL STRUCTURE

What, then, *is* the optimal capital structure, even if it exists (so far) only in theory? To provide some insight into an answer, we will examine some basic financial relationships. Because the value of a firm equals the present value of its future cash flows, it follows that *the value of the firm is maximized when the cost of capital is minimized.* In other words, the present value of future cash flows is at its highest when the discount rate (the cost of capital) is at its lowest. By using a modification of the simple zero-growth valuation model (see Equation 7.2 in Chapter 7), we can define the value of the firm, *V*, by Equation 13.11:

$$V = \frac{\text{EBIT} \times (1 - T)}{r_a} = \frac{\text{NOPAT}}{r_a} \qquad (13.11)$$

where

$$\text{EBIT} = \text{earnings before interest and taxes}$$
$$T = \text{tax rate}$$
$$\text{NOPAT} = \text{net operating profits after taxes, which is the after-tax operating earnings available to the debt and equity holders, EBIT} \times (1 - T)$$
$$r_a = \text{weighted average cost of capital}$$

Clearly, if we assume that NOPAT (and therefore EBIT) is constant, the value of the firm, *V*, is maximized by minimizing the weighted average cost of capital, r_a.

Cost Functions

Figure 13.5(*a*) plots three cost functions—the cost of debt, the cost of equity, and the weighted average cost of capital (WACC)—as a function of financial leverage measured by the debt ratio (debt to total assets). The *cost of debt, r_i,* remains low because of the tax shield, but it slowly increases as leverage increases, to compensate lenders for increasing risk. The *cost of equity, r_s,* is above the cost of debt. It increases as financial leverage increases, but it generally increases more rapidly than the cost of debt. The cost of equity rises because the stockholders require a higher return as leverage increases, to compensate for the higher degree of financial risk.

The *weighted average cost of capital, r_a,* results from a weighted average of the firm's debt and equity capital costs. At a debt ratio of zero, the firm is 100 percent equity financed. As debt is substituted for equity and as the debt ratio increases, the WACC declines because the after-tax debt cost is less than the equity cost ($r_i < r_s$). In this range, the tax benefits of additional debt outweigh the costs of borrowing more. However, as the debt ratio continues to increase, the increased debt and equity costs eventually cause the WACC to rise (after point *M* in Figure 13.5(*a*)). In other words, the bankruptcy costs, agency costs, and other costs associated with higher debt levels eventually outweigh the additional tax benefits that the firm could generate by borrowing even more. This behavior results in a U-shaped, or saucer-shaped, weighted average cost-of-capital function, r_a.

optimal capital structure
The capital structure at which the weighted average cost of capital is minimized, thereby maximizing the firm's value.

Graphical View of Optimal Structure

Because the maximization of value, *V*, is achieved when the overall cost of capital, r_a, is at a minimum (see Equation 13.11), the **optimal capital structure** is that

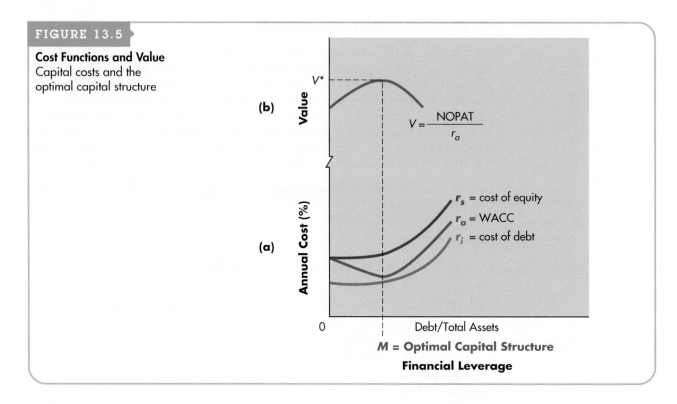

FIGURE 13.5

Cost Functions and Value
Capital costs and the optimal capital structure

(b)

Value

V^*

$V = \dfrac{NOPAT}{r_a}$

(a)

Annual Cost (%)

r_s = cost of equity
r_a = WACC
r_i = cost of debt

0

Debt/Total Assets

M = Optimal Capital Structure

Financial Leverage

at which the weighted average cost of capital, r_a, is minimized. In Figure 13.5(a), point M represents the *minimum weighted average cost of capital*—the point of optimal financial leverage and hence of optimal capital structure for the firm. Figure 13.5(b) plots the value of the firm that results from substitution of r_a in Figure 13.5(a) for various levels of financial leverage into the zero-growth valuation model in Equation 13.11. As shown in Figure 13.5(b), at the optimal capital structure, point M, the value of the firm is maximized at V^*.

Simply stated, minimizing the weighted average cost of capital allows management to undertake a larger number of profitable projects, thereby further increasing the value of the firm. However, as a practical matter, there is no way to calculate the optimal capital structure implied by Figure 13.5. Because it is impossible either to know or to remain at the precise optimal capital structure, firms generally try to operate in a *range* that places them near what they believe to be the optimal capital structure. In other words, firms usually manage toward a *target capital structure*.

→ **REVIEW QUESTIONS**

13–6 What is a firm's *capital structure?* What ratios assess the degree of financial leverage in a firm's capital structure?

13–7 In what ways are the capital structures of U.S. and non–U.S. firms different? How are they similar?

13–8 What is the major benefit of debt financing? How does it affect the firm's cost of debt?

13–9 What are *business risk* and *financial risk?* How does each of them influence the firm's capital structure decisions?

13–10 Briefly describe the *agency problem* that exists between owners and lenders. How do lenders cause firms to incur *agency costs* to resolve this problem?

13–11 How does *asymmetric information* affect the firm's capital structure decisions? How do the firm's financing actions give investors *signals* that reflect management's view of stock value?

13–12 How do the cost of debt, the cost of equity, and the weighted average cost of capital (WACC) behave as the firm's financial leverage increases from zero? Where is the *optimal capital structure?* What is its relationship to the firm's value at that point?

LG 5 13.3 EBIT–EPS Approach to Capital Structure

EBIT–EPS approach
An approach for selecting the capital structure that maximizes earnings per share (EPS) over the expected range of earnings before interest and taxes (EBIT).

It should be clear from earlier chapters that the goal of the financial manager is to maximize owner wealth—that is, the firm's stock price. One of the widely followed variables affecting the firm's stock price is its earnings, which represents the returns earned on behalf of owners. In spite of the fact that focusing on earnings ignores risk (the other key variable affecting the firm's stock price), earnings per share (EPS) can be conveniently used to analyze alternative capital structures. The **EBIT–EPS approach** to capital structure involves selecting the capital structure that maximizes EPS over the expected range of earnings before interest and taxes (EBIT).

PRESENTING A FINANCING PLAN GRAPHICALLY

To analyze the effects of a firm's capital structure on the owners' returns, we consider the relationship between earnings before interest and taxes (EBIT) and earnings per share (EPS). In other words, we want to see how changes in EBIT lead to changes in EPS under different capital structures. In all of our examples we will assume that business risk remains constant. That is, the firm's basic operational risks remain constant, and only financial risk varies as capital structures change. EPS is used to measure the owners' returns, which are expected to be closely related to share price.[16]

Data Required

To draw a graph illustrating how changes in EBIT lead to changes in EPS, we simply need to find two coordinates and plot a straight line between them. On our graph, we will plot EBIT on the horizontal axis and EPS on the vertical axis. The following example illustrates the approach for constructing the graph.

---

16. The relationship that is expected to exist between EPS and owner wealth is not one of cause and effect. As indicated in Chapter 1, the maximization of profits does not necessarily ensure that owners' wealth is also maximized. Nevertheless, it is expected that the movement of earnings per share will have some effect on owners' wealth, because EPS data constitute one of the few pieces of information investors receive, and they often bid the firm's share price up or down in response to the level of these earnings.

FIGURE 13.6

EBIT–EPS Approach
A comparison of selected capital structures for Cooke Company (data from Table 13.12)

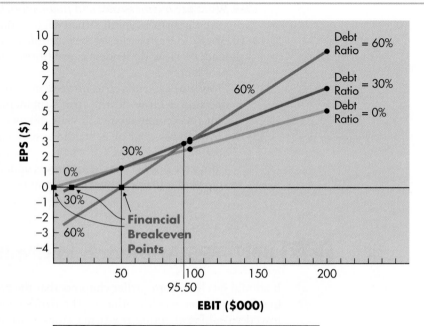

Capital structure debt ratio	EBIT	
	$100,000	**$200,000**
	Earnings per share (EPS)	
0%	$2.40	$4.80
30	2.91	6.34
60	3.03	9.03

Example 13.19 ▶   We can plot coordinates on the EBIT–EPS graph by assuming specific EBIT values and calculating the EPS associated with them.[17] Such calculations for three capital structures—debt ratios of 0%, 30%, and 60%—for Cooke Company were presented in Table 13.12. For EBIT values of $100,000 and $200,000, the associated EPS values calculated there are summarized in the table below the graph in Figure 13.6.

Plotting the Data

The Cooke Company data can be plotted on a set of EBIT–EPS axes, as shown in Figure 13.6. The figure shows the level of EPS expected for each level of EBIT. For levels of EBIT below the x-axis intercept, a loss (negative EPS) results. Each

---

17. A convenient method for finding one EBIT—EPS coordinate is to calculate the *financial breakeven point,* the level of EBIT for which the firm's EPS just equals $0. It is the level of EBIT needed just to cover all fixed financial costs—annual interest (I) and preferred stock dividends (PD). The equation for the financial breakeven point is

$$\text{Financial breakeven point} = I + \frac{PD}{1 - T}$$

where T is the tax rate. It can be seen that when $PD = \$0$, the financial breakeven point is equal to I, the annual interest payment.

financial breakeven point
The level of EBIT necessary to just cover all *fixed financial costs;* the level of EBIT for which EPS = $0.

of the *x*-axis intercepts is a **financial breakeven point,** the level of EBIT necessary to just cover all *fixed financial costs* (EPS = $0).

COMPARING ALTERNATIVE CAPITAL STRUCTURES

We can compare alternative capital structures by graphing financing plans as shown in Figure 13.6.

Example 13.20 ▶ Cooke Company's capital structure alternatives were plotted on the EBIT–EPS axes in Figure 13.6. This figure shows that each capital structure is superior to the others in terms of maximizing EPS over certain ranges of EBIT. Having no debt at all (debt ratio = 0%) is best for levels of EBIT between $0 and $50,000. That makes sense because when business conditions are relatively weak, Cooke would have difficulty meeting its financial obligations if it had any debt. Between $50,000 and $95,500 of EBIT, the capital structure associated with a debt ratio of 30% produces higher EPS than either of the other two capital structures. And when EBIT exceeds $95,500, the 60% debt ratio capital structure provides the highest earnings per share.[18] Again, the intuition behind this result is fairly straightforward. When business is booming, the best thing for shareholders is for the firm to use a great deal of debt. The firm pays lenders a relatively low rate of return, and the shareholders keep the rest.

CONSIDERING RISK IN EBIT–EPS ANALYSIS

When interpreting EBIT–EPS analysis, it is important to consider the risk of each capital structure alternative. Graphically, the risk of each capital structure can be viewed in light of two measures: (1) the *financial breakeven point* (EBIT-axis intercept) and (2) the *degree of financial leverage* reflected in the slope of the capital structure line: *The higher the financial breakeven point and the steeper the slope of the capital structure line, the greater the financial risk.*[19]

---

18. An algebraic technique can be used to find the *indifference points* between the capital structure alternatives. This technique involves expressing each capital structure as an equation stated in terms of earnings per share, setting the equations for two capital structures equal to each other, and solving for the level of EBIT that causes the equations to be equal. When we use the notation from footnote 17 and let *n* equal the number of shares of common stock outstanding, the general equation for the earnings per share from a financing plan is

$$\text{EPS} = \frac{(1 - T) \times (\text{EBIT} - I) - PD}{n}$$

Comparing Cooke Company's 0% and 30% capital structures, we get

$$\frac{(1 - 0.40) \times (\text{EBIT} - \$0) - \$0}{25.00} = \frac{(1 - 0.40) \times (\text{EBIT} - \$15.00) - \$0}{17.50}$$

$$\frac{0.60 \times \text{EBIT}}{25.00} = \frac{0.60 \times \text{EBIT} - \$9.00}{17.50}$$

$$10.50 \times \text{EBIT} = 15.00 \times \text{EBIT} - \$225.00$$

$$\$225.00 = 4.50 \times \text{EBIT}$$

$$\text{EBIT} = \$50$$

The calculated value of the indifference point between the 0% and 30% capital structures is therefore $50,000, as can be seen in Figure 13.6.

19. The degree of financial leverage (DFL) is reflected in the slope of the EBIT–EPS function. The steeper the slope, the greater the degree of financial leverage, because the change in EPS (*y* axis) that results from a given change in EBIT (*x* axis) increases with increasing slope and decreases with decreasing slope.

Further assessment of risk can be performed by using ratios. As financial leverage (measured by the debt ratio) increases, we expect a corresponding decline in the firm's ability to make scheduled interest payments (measured by the times interest earned ratio).

Example 13.21 ▶

Reviewing the three capital structures plotted for Cooke Company in Figure 13.6, we can see that as the debt ratio increases, so does the financial risk of each alternative. Both the financial breakeven point and the slope of the capital structure lines increase with increasing debt ratios. If we use the $100,000 EBIT value, for example, the times interest earned ratio (EBIT ÷ interest) for the zero-leverage capital structure is infinity ($100,000 ÷ $0); for the 30% debt case, it is 6.67 ($100,000 ÷ $15,000); and for the 60% debt case, it is 2.02 ($100,000 ÷ $49,500). Because lower times interest earned ratios reflect higher risk, these ratios support the conclusion that the risk of the capital structures increases with increasing financial leverage. The capital structure for a debt ratio of 60% is riskier than that for a debt ratio of 30%, which in turn is riskier than the capital structure for a debt ratio of 0%.

BASIC SHORTCOMING OF EBIT–EPS ANALYSIS

The most important point to recognize when using EBIT–EPS analysis is that this technique tends to concentrate on *maximizing earnings* rather than maximizing owner wealth as reflected in the firm's stock price. The use of an EPS-maximizing approach generally ignores risk. If investors did not require risk premiums (additional returns) as the firm increased the proportion of debt in its capital structure, a strategy involving maximizing EPS would also maximize stock price. But because risk premiums increase with increases in financial leverage, the maximization of EPS *does not* ensure owner wealth maximization. To select the best capital structure, firms must integrate both return (EPS) and risk (via the required return, r_s) into a valuation framework consistent with the capital structure theory presented earlier.

→ REVIEW QUESTION

13–13 Explain the *EBIT–EPS approach* to capital structure. Include in your explanation a graph indicating the *financial breakeven point*; label the axes. Is this approach consistent with maximization of the owners' wealth?

LG 6 **13.4** Choosing the Optimal Capital Structure

A wealth maximization framework for use in making capital structure decisions should include the two key factors of return and risk. This section describes the procedures for linking to market value the return and risk associated with alternative capital structures.

LINKAGE

To determine the firm's value under alternative capital structures, the firm must find the level of return that it must earn to compensate owners for the risk being incurred. This approach is consistent with the overall valuation framework developed in Chapters 6 and 7 and applied to capital budgeting decisions in Chapters 10 through 12.

The required return associated with a given level of financial risk can be estimated in a number of ways. Theoretically, the preferred approach would be first to estimate the beta associated with each alternative capital structure and then to use the CAPM framework presented in Equation 8.8 to calculate the required return, r_s. A more operational approach involves linking the financial risk associated with each capital structure alternative directly to the required return. Such an approach is similar to the CAPM-type approach demonstrated in Chapter 12 for linking project risk and required return (RADR). Here it involves estimating the required return associated with each level of financial risk, as measured by a statistic such as the coefficient of variation of EPS. Regardless of the approach used, one would expect the required return to increase as the financial risk increases.

Example 13.22 ▶ Cooke Company, using as risk measures the coefficients of variation of EPS associated with each of the seven alternative capital structures, estimated the associated required returns. These are shown in Table 13.14. As expected, the estimated required return of owners, r_s, increases with increasing risk, as measured by the coefficient of variation of EPS.

ESTIMATING VALUE

The value of the firm associated with alternative capital structures can be estimated by using one of the standard valuation models. If, for simplicity, we assume that all earnings are paid out as dividends, we can use a zero-growth valuation model such as that developed in Chapter 7. The model, originally stated in Equation 7.2, is restated here with EPS substituted for dividends (because in each year the dividends would equal EPS):

$$P_0 = \frac{\text{EPS}}{r_s} \tag{13.12}$$

By substituting the expected level of EPS and the associated required return, r_s, into Equation 13.12, we can estimate the per-share value of the firm, P_0.

TABLE 13.14 ⟩	Required Returns for Cooke Company's Alternative Capital Structures	
Capital structure debt ratio	Coefficient of variation of EPS (from column 3 of Table 13.13) (1)	Estimated required return, r_s (2)
0%	0.71	11.5%
10	0.74	11.7
20	0.78	12.1
30	0.83	12.5
40	0.91	14.0
50	1.07	16.5
60	1.40	19.0

TABLE 13.15	Calculation of Share Value Estimates Associated with Alternative Capital Structures for Cooke Company		
Capital structure debt ratio	Expected EPS (from column 1 of Table 13.13) (1)	Estimated required return, r_s (from column 2 of Table 13.14) (2)	Estimated share value [(1) ÷ (2)] (3)
0%	$2.40	0.115	$20.87
10	2.55	0.117	21.79
20	2.72	0.121	22.48
30	2.91	0.125	23.28
40	3.12	0.140	22.29
50	3.18	0.165	19.27
60	3.03	0.190	15.95

Example 13.23 ▶ We can now estimate the value of Cooke Company's stock under each of the alternative capital structures. Substituting the expected EPS (column 1 of Table 13.13) and the required returns, r_s (column 2 of Table 13.14 in decimal form), into Equation 13.12 for each of the capital structures, we obtain the share values given in column 3 of Table 13.15. Plotting the resulting share values against the associated debt ratios, as shown in Figure 13.7, clearly illustrates that the maximum share value occurs at the capital structure associated with a debt ratio of 30%.

FIGURE 13.7 ▶

Estimating Value
Estimated share value and EPS for alternative capital structures for Cooke Company

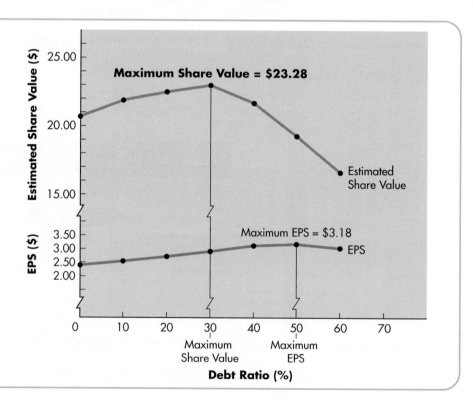

MAXIMIZING VALUE VERSUS MAXIMIZING EPS

Throughout this text, we have specified the goal of the financial manager as maximizing owner wealth, not profit. Although some relationship exists between expected profit and value, there is no reason to believe that profit-maximizing strategies necessarily result in wealth maximization. It is therefore the wealth of the owners as reflected in the estimated share value that should serve as the criterion for selecting the best capital structure. A final look at Cooke Company will highlight this point.

Example 13.24 ▶   Further analysis of Figure 13.7 clearly shows that although the firm's profits (EPS) are maximized at a debt ratio of 50%, share value is maximized at a 30% debt ratio. Therefore, the preferred capital structure would be the 30% debt ratio. The two approaches provide different conclusions because EPS maximization does not consider risk.

SOME OTHER IMPORTANT CONSIDERATIONS

Because there is really no practical way to calculate the optimal capital structure, any quantitative analysis of capital structure must be tempered with other important considerations. Table 13.16 summarizes some of the more important additional factors involved in capital structure decisions.

TABLE 13.16	Important Factors to Consider in Making Capital Structure Decisions	
Concern	Factor	Description
Business risk	Revenue stability	Firms that have stable and predictable revenues can more safely undertake highly leveraged capital structures than can firms with volatile patterns of sales revenue. Firms with growing sales tend to benefit from added debt; they can reap the positive benefits of financial leverage, which magnifies the effect of these increases.
	Cash flow	When considering a new capital structure, the firm must focus on its ability to generate the cash flows necessary to meet obligations. Cash forecasts reflecting an ability to service debts (and preferred stock) must support any shift in capital structure.
Agency costs	Contractual obligations	A firm may be contractually constrained with respect to the type of funds that it can raise. For example, a firm might be prohibited from selling additional debt except when the claims of holders of such debt are made subordinate to the existing debt. Contractual constraints on the sale of additional stock, as well as on the ability to distribute dividends on stock, might also exist.
	Management preferences	Occasionally, a firm will impose an internal constraint on the use of debt to limit its risk exposure to a level deemed acceptable to management. In other words, because of risk aversion, the firm's management constrains the firm's capital structure at a level that may or may not be the true optimum.

(continued)

TABLE 13.16	Important Factors to Consider in Making Capital Structure Decisions (*continued*)

Concern	Factor	Description
	Control	A management group concerned about control may prefer to issue debt rather than (voting) common stock. Under favorable market conditions, a firm that wanted to sell equity could make a *preemptive offering* or issue *nonvoting shares*, allowing each shareholder to maintain proportionate ownership. Generally, only in closely held firms or firms threatened by takeover does control become a major concern in the capital structure decision.
Asymmetric information	External risk assessment	The firm's ability to raise funds quickly and at favorable rates depends on the external risk assessments of lenders and bond raters. The firm must consider the impact of capital structure decisions both on share value and on published financial statements from which lenders and raters assess the firm's risk.
	Timing	At times when interest rates are low, debt financing might be more attractive; when interest rates are high, the sale of stock may be more appealing. Sometimes both debt and equity capital become unavailable at reasonable terms. General economic conditions— especially those of the capital market—can thus significantly affect capital structure decisions.

→ **REVIEW QUESTIONS**

13–14 Why do *maximizing EPS* and *maximizing value* not necessarily lead to the same conclusion about the optimal capital structure?

13–15 What important factors in addition to quantitative factors should a firm consider when it is making a capital structure decision?

Summary

FOCUS ON VALUE

The amount of leverage (fixed-cost assets or funds) employed by a firm directly affects its risk, return, and share value. Generally, higher leverage raises risk and return, and lower leverage reduces risk and return. Operating leverage concerns the level of fixed operating costs; financial leverage focuses on fixed financial costs, particularly interest on debt and any preferred stock dividends. The firm's capital structure determines its financial leverage. Because of its fixed interest payments, the more debt a firm employs relative to its equity, the greater its financial leverage.

The value of the firm is clearly affected by its degree of operating leverage and by the composition of its capital structure. The financial manager must therefore carefully consider the types of operating and financial costs the firm will incur, recognizing that higher risk comes with greater fixed costs. Major decisions with regard to both operating cost structure and capital structure must therefore focus on their impact on the firm's value. The firm should implement only those leverage and capital structure decisions that are consistent with its goal of **maximizing its stock price**.

REVIEW OF LEARNING GOALS

LG 1 **Discuss leverage, capital structure, breakeven analysis, the operating breakeven point, and the effect of changing costs on it.** Leverage results from the use of fixed costs to magnify returns to a firm's owners. Capital structure, the firm's mix of long-term debt and equity, affects leverage and therefore the firm's value. Breakeven analysis measures the level of sales necessary to cover total operating costs. The operating breakeven point may be calculated algebraically, by dividing fixed operating costs by the difference between the sale price per unit and variable operating cost per unit, or it may be determined graphically. The operating breakeven point increases with increased fixed and variable operating costs and decreases with an increase in sale price, and vice versa.

LG 2 **Understand operating, financial, and total leverage and the relationships among them.** Operating leverage is the use of fixed operating costs by the firm to magnify the effects of changes in sales on EBIT. The higher the fixed operating costs, the greater the operating leverage. Financial leverage is the use of fixed financial costs by the firm to magnify the effects of changes in EBIT on EPS. The higher the fixed financial costs, the greater the financial leverage. The total leverage of the firm is the use of fixed costs—both operating and financial—to magnify the effects of changes in sales on EPS.

LG 3 **Describe the types of capital, external assessment of capital structure, the capital structure of non–U.S. firms, and capital structure theory.** Debt capital and equity capital make up a firm's capital structure. Capital structure can be externally assessed by using financial ratios—debt ratio, times interest earned ratio, and fixed-payment coverage ratio. Non–U.S. companies tend to have much higher degrees of indebtedness than do their U.S. counterparts, primarily because U.S. capital markets are more developed.

Research suggests that there is an optimal capital structure that balances the firm's benefits and costs of debt financing. The major benefit of debt financing is the tax shield. The costs of debt financing include the probability of bankruptcy, agency costs imposed by lenders, and asymmetric information, which typically causes firms to raise funds in a pecking order so as to send positive signals to the market and thereby enhance shareholder wealth.

LG 4 **Explain the optimal capital structure using a graphical view of the firm's cost-of-capital functions and a zero-growth valuation model.** The zero-growth valuation model defines the firm's value as its net operating profits after taxes (NOPAT), or after-tax EBIT, divided by its weighted average cost of capital. Assuming that NOPAT is constant, the value of the firm is maximized by minimizing its weighted average cost of capital (WACC). The optimal capital structure minimizes the WACC. Graphically, the firm's WACC exhibits a U-shape, whose minimum value defines the optimal capital structure that maximizes owner wealth.

LG 5 **Discuss the EBIT–EPS approach to capital structure.** The EBIT–EPS approach evaluates capital structures in light of the returns they provide the firm's owners and their degree of financial risk. Under the EBIT–EPS approach, the preferred capital structure is the one that is expected to provide maximum EPS over the firm's expected range of EBIT. Graphically, this approach reflects risk in terms of the financial breakeven point and the slope of the capital structure line. The major shortcoming of EBIT–EPS analysis is that it concentrates on maximizing earnings (returns) rather than owners' wealth, which considers risk as well as return.

LG 6   **Review the return and risk of alternative capital structures, their linkage to market value, and other important considerations related to capital structure.** The best capital structure can be selected by using a valuation model to link return and risk factors. The preferred capital structure is the one that results in the highest estimated share value, not the highest EPS. Other important nonquantitative factors must also be considered when making capital structure decisions.

Opener-in-Review

Prior to its June 2010 debt issue, Genzyme showed about $1.1 billion in long-term debt (including other long-term liabilities) and $7.5 billion in stockholder equity on its balance sheet. What was the ratio of long-term debt to stockholder equity? What was the value of this ratio after the debt-for-equity transaction described at the beginning of this chapter?

Self-Test Problems   (Solutions in Appendix)

LG 1 **LG 2**   **ST13–1**   **Breakeven point and all forms of leverage**   TOR most recently sold 100,000 units at $7.50 each; its variable operating costs are $3.00 per unit, and its fixed operating costs are $250,000. Annual interest charges total $80,000, and the firm has 8,000 shares of $5 (annual dividend) preferred stock outstanding. It currently has 20,000 shares of common stock outstanding. Assume that the firm is subject to a 40% tax rate.

   a. At what level of sales (in units) would the firm break even on operations (that is, EBIT = $0)?

   b. Calculate the firm's *earnings per share (EPS)* in tabular form at (1) the current level of sales and (2) a 120,000-unit sales level.

   c. Using the current *$750,000 level of sales as a base*, calculate the firm's degree of operating leverage (DOL).

   d. Using the EBIT *associated with the $750,000 level of sales as a base*, calculate the firm's degree of financial leverage (DFL).

   e. Use the degree of total leverage (DTL) concept to determine the effect (in percentage terms) of a 50% increase in TOR's sales *from the $750,000 base level* on its earnings per share.

LG 5   **ST13–2**   **EBIT–EPS analysis**   Newlin Electronics is considering additional financing of $10,000. It currently has $50,000 of 12% (annual interest) bonds and 10,000 shares of common stock outstanding. The firm can obtain the financing through a 12% (annual interest) bond issue or through the sale of 1,000 shares of common stock. The firm has a 40% tax rate.

   a. Calculate two EBIT–EPS coordinates for each plan by selecting any two EBIT values and finding their associated EPS values.

 b. Plot the two financing plans on a set of EBIT–EPS axes.
 c. On the basis of your graph in part **b,** at what level of EBIT does the bond plan become superior to the stock plan?

LG 3 **LG 6** **ST13–3** **Optimal capital structure** Hawaiian Macadamia Nut Company has collected the data in the following table with respect to its capital structure, expected earnings per share, and required return.

Capital structure debt ratio	Expected earnings per share	Required return, r_s
0%	$3.12	13%
10	3.90	15
20	4.80	16
30	5.44	17
40	5.51	19
50	5.00	20
60	4.40	22

 a. Compute the *estimated share value* associated with each of the capital structures, using the simplified method described in this chapter (see Equation 13.12).
 b. Determine the optimal capital structure on the basis of (1) maximization of expected earnings per share and (2) maximization of share value.
 c. Which capital structure do you recommend? Why?

Warm-Up Exercises All problems are available in ⟐myfinancelab.

LG 1 **E13–1** Canvas Reproductions has fixed operating costs of $12,500 and variable operating costs of $10 per unit and sells its paintings for $25 each. At what level of unit sales will the company break even in terms of EBIT?

LG 1 **E13–2** The Great Fish Taco Corporation currently has fixed operating costs of $15,000, sells its premade tacos for $6 per box, and incurs variable operating costs of $2.50 per box. If the firm has a potential investment that would simultaneously raise its fixed costs to $16,500 and allow it to charge a per-box sale price of $6.50 due to better-textured tacos, what will the impact be on its operating breakeven point in boxes?

LG 2 **E13–3** Chico's has sales of 15,000 units at a price of $20 per unit. The firm incurs fixed operating costs of $30,000 and variable operating costs of $12 per unit. What is Chico's *degree of operating leverage (DOL)* at a base level of sales of 15,000 units?

LG 2 **E13–4** Parker Investments has EBIT of $20,000, interest expense of $3,000, and preferred dividends of $4,000. If it pays taxes at a rate of 38%, what is Parker's *degree of financial leverage (DFL)* at a base level of EBIT of $20,000?

LG 4 **E13–5** Cobalt Industries had sales of 150,000 units at a price of $10 per unit. It faced fixed operating costs of $250,000 and variable operating costs of $5 per unit. The company is subject to a tax rate of 38% and has a weighted average cost of capital of 8.5%. Calculate Cobalt's *net operating profits after taxes (NOPAT),* and use it to estimate the value of the firm.

Problems

All problems are available in 🔷myfinancelab .

LG 1   **P13–1**   **Breakeven point—Algebraic**   Kate Rowland wishes to estimate the number of flower arrangements she must sell at $24.95 to break even. She has estimated fixed operating costs of $12,350 per year and variable operating costs of $15.45 per arrangement. How many flower arrangements must Kate sell to break even on operating costs?

LG 1   **P13–2**   **Breakeven comparisons—Algebraic**   Given the price and cost data shown in the accompanying table for each of the three firms, F, G, and H, answer the questions that follow.

Firm	F	G	H
Sale price per unit	$ 18.00	$ 21.00	$ 30.00
Variable operating cost per unit	6.75	13.50	12.00
Fixed operating cost	45,000	30,000	90,000

a. What is the *operating breakeven point* in units for each firm?
b. How would you rank these firms in terms of their risk?

LG 1   **P13–3**   **Breakeven point—Algebraic and graphical**   Fine Leather Enterprises sells its single product for $129.00 per unit. The firm's fixed operating costs are $473,000 annually, and its variable operating costs are $86.00 per unit.
a. Find the firm's *operating breakeven point* in units.
b. Label the *x* axis "Sales (units)" and the *y* axis "Costs/Revenues ($)," and then graph the firm's sales revenue, total operating cost, and fixed operating cost functions on these axes. In addition, label the operating breakeven point and the areas of loss and profit (EBIT).

LG 1   **P13–4**   **Breakeven analysis**   Barry Carter is considering opening a music store. He wants to estimate the number of CDs he must sell to break even. The CDs will be sold for $13.98 each, variable operating costs are $10.48 per CD, and annual fixed operating costs are $73,500.
a. Find the *operating breakeven point* in number of CDs.
b. Calculate the total operating costs at the breakeven volume found in part **a**.
c. If Barry estimates that at a minimum he can sell 2,000 CDs *per month*, should he go into the music business?
d. How much EBIT will Barry realize if he sells the minimum 2,000 CDs per month noted in part **c**?

Personal Finance Problem

LG 1   **P13–5**   **Breakeven analysis**   Paul Scott has a 2008 Cadillac that he wants to update with a geo-tracker device so he will have access to road maps and directions. After-market equipment can be fitted for a flat fee of $500, and the service provider requires monthly charges of $20. In his line of work as a traveling salesman, he estimates that this device can save him time and money—about $35 per month (as the price of gas keeps increasing).

In order to determine the financial feasibility of purchasing the geo-tracker, Paul wants to determine the number of months it will take to break even. He plans to keep the car for another 3 years.

a. Calculate the *breakeven point* for the device in months.

b. Based on **a**, should Paul have the tracker installed in his car?

LG 1 **P13–6** **Breakeven point—Changing costs/revenues** JWG Company publishes *Creative Crosswords*. Last year the book of puzzles sold for $10 with variable operating cost per book of $8 and fixed operating costs of $40,000. How many books must JWG sell this year to achieve the *breakeven point* for the stated operating costs, given the following different circumstances?

a. All figures remain the same as for last year.

b. Fixed operating costs increase to $44,000; all other figures remain the same.

c. The selling price increases to $10.50; all costs remain the same as for last year.

d. Variable operating cost per book increases to $8.50; all other figures remain the same.

e. What conclusions about the operating breakeven point can be drawn from your answers?

LG 1 **P13–7** **Breakeven analysis** Molly Jasper and her sister, Caitlin Peters, got into the novelties business almost by accident. Molly, a talented sculptor, often made little figurines as gifts for friends. Occasionally, she and Caitlin would set up a booth at a crafts fair and sell a few of the figurines along with jewelry that Caitlin made. Little by little, demand for the figurines, now called Mollycaits, grew, and the sisters began to reproduce some of the favorites in resin, using molds of the originals. The day came when a buyer for a major department store offered them a contract to produce 1,500 figurines of various designs for $10,000. Molly and Caitlin realized that it was time to get down to business. To make bookkeeping simpler, Molly had priced all of the figurines at $8.00. Variable operating costs amounted to an average of $6.00 per unit. To produce the order, Molly and Caitlin would have to rent industrial facilities for a month, which would cost them $4,000.

a. Calculate Mollycaits' *operating breakeven point*.

b. Calculate Mollycaits' EBIT on the department store order.

c. If Molly renegotiates the contract at a price of $10.00 per figurine, what will the EBIT be?

d. If the store refuses to pay more than $8.00 per unit but is willing to negotiate quantity, what quantity of figurines will result in an EBIT of $4,000?

e. At this time, Mollycaits come in 15 different varieties. Whereas the average variable cost per unit is $6.00, the actual cost varies from unit to unit. What recommendation would you have for Molly and Caitlin with regard to pricing and/or the numbers and types of units that they offer for sale?

LG 2 **P13–8** **EBIT sensitivity** Stewart Industries sells its finished product for $9 per unit. Its fixed operating costs are $20,000, and the variable operating cost per unit is $5.

a. Calculate the firm's earnings before interest and taxes (EBIT) for sales of 10,000 units.

b. Calculate the firm's EBIT for sales of 8,000 and 12,000 units, respectively.

c. Calculate the percentage changes in sales (from the 10,000-unit base level) and associated percentage changes in EBIT for the shifts in sales indicated in part **b**.

d. On the basis of your findings in part **c**, comment on the sensitivity of changes in EBIT in response to changes in sales.

LG 2   **P13–9**   **Degree of operating leverage**   Grey Products has fixed operating costs of $380,000, variable operating costs of $16 per unit, and a selling price of $63.50 per unit.

    a. Calculate the *operating breakeven point* in units.

    b. Calculate the firm's EBIT at 9,000, 10,000, and 11,000 units, respectively.

    c. With 10,000 units as a base, what are the percentage changes in units sold and EBIT as sales move from the base to the other sales levels used in part **b**?

    d. Use the percentages computed in part **c** to determine the *degree of operating leverage (DOL)*.

    e. Use the formula for degree of operating leverage to determine the DOL at 10,000 units.

LG 2   **P13–10**   **Degree of operating leverage—Graphical**   Levin Corporation has fixed operating costs of $72,000, variable operating costs of $6.75 per unit, and a selling price of $9.75 per unit.

    a. Calculate the *operating breakeven point* in units.

    b. Compute the *degree of operating leverage (DOL)* using the following unit sales levels as a base: 25,000, 30,000, 40,000. Use the formula given in the chapter.

    c. Graph the DOL figures that you computed in part **b** (on the *y* axis) against base sales levels (on the *x* axis).

    d. Compute the degree of operating leverage at 24,000 units; add this point to your graph.

    e. What principle do your graph and figures illustrate?

LG 2   **P13–11**   **EPS calculations**   Southland Industries has $60,000 of 16% (annual interest) bonds outstanding, 1,500 shares of preferred stock paying an annual dividend of $5 per share, and 4,000 shares of common stock outstanding. Assuming that the firm has a 40% tax rate, compute *earnings per share (EPS)* for the following levels of EBIT:

    a. $24,600

    b. $30,600

    c. $35,000

LG 2   **P13–12**   **Degree of financial leverage**   Northwestern Savings and Loan has a current capital structure consisting of $250,000 of 16% (annual interest) debt and 2,000 shares of common stock. The firm pays taxes at the rate of 40%.

    a. Using EBIT values of $80,000 and $120,000, determine the associated *earnings per share (EPS)*.

    b. Using $80,000 of EBIT as a base, calculate the *degree of financial leverage (DFL)*.

    c. Rework parts **a** and **b** assuming that the firm has $100,000 of 16% (annual interest) debt and 3,000 shares of common stock.

Personal Finance Problem

LG 2   **P13–13**   **Financial leverage**   Max Small has outstanding school loans that require a monthly payment of $1,000. He needs to purchase a new car for work and estimates that this will add $350 per month to his existing monthly obligations. Max will have $3,000 available after meeting all of his monthly living (operating) expenses. This amount could vary by plus or minus 10%.

    a. To assess the potential impact of the additional borrowing on his financial leverage, calculate the *DFL* in tabular form for both the current and proposed loan payments using Max's available $3,000 as a base and a 10% change.

    b. Can Max afford the additional loan payment?

    c. Should Max take on the additional loan payment?

LG 2 **LG 5** **P13–14** **DFL and graphical display of financing plans**   Wells and Associates has EBIT of $67,500. Interest costs are $22,500, and the firm has 15,000 shares of common stock outstanding. Assume a 40% tax rate.

a. Use the degree of financial leverage (DFL) formula to calculate the *DFL* for the firm.

b. Using a set of EBIT–EPS axes, plot Wells and Associates' financing plan.

c. If the firm also has 1,000 shares of preferred stock paying a $6.00 annual dividend per share, what is the DFL?

d. Plot the financing plan, including the 1,000 shares of $6.00 preferred stock, on the axes used in part **b.**

e. Briefly discuss the graph of the two financing plans.

LG 1 **LG 2** **P13–15** **Integrative—Multiple leverage measures**   Play-More Toys produces inflatable beach balls, selling 400,000 balls per year. Each ball produced has a variable operating cost of $0.84 and sells for $1.00. Fixed operating costs are $28,000. The firm has annual interest charges of $6,000, preferred dividends of $2,000, and a 40% tax rate.

a. Calculate the *operating breakeven point* in units.

b. Use the degree of operating leverage (DOL) formula to calculate *DOL.*

c. Use the degree of financial leverage (DFL) formula to calculate *DFL.*

d. Use the degree of total leverage (DTL) formula to calculate *DTL.* Compare this to the product of DOL and DFL calculated in parts **b** and **c.**

LG 2 **P13–16** **Integrative—Leverage and risk**   Firm R has sales of 100,000 units at $2.00 per unit, variable operating costs of $1.70 per unit, and fixed operating costs of $6,000. Interest is $10,000 per year. Firm W has sales of 100,000 units at $2.50 per unit, variable operating costs of $1.00 per unit, and fixed operating costs of $62,500. Interest is $17,500 per year. Assume that both firms are in the 40% tax bracket.

a. Compute the degree of operating, financial, and total leverage for firm R.

b. Compute the degree of operating, financial, and total leverage for firm W.

c. Compare the relative risks of the two firms.

d. Discuss the principles of leverage that your answers illustrate.

LG 1 **LG 2** **P13–17** **Integrative—Multiple leverage measures and prediction**   Carolina Fastener, Inc., makes a patented marine bulkhead latch that wholesales for $6.00. Each latch has variable operating costs of $3.50. Fixed operating costs are $50,000 per year. The firm pays $13,000 interest and preferred dividends of $7,000 per year. At this point, the firm is selling 30,000 latches per year and is taxed at a rate of 40%.

a. Calculate Carolina Fastener's *operating breakeven point.*

b. On the basis of the firm's current sales of 30,000 units per year and its interest and preferred dividend costs, calculate its EBIT and earnings available for common.

c. Calculate the firm's *degree of operating leverage (DOL).*

d. Calculate the firm's *degree of financial leverage (DFL).*

e. Calculate the firm's *degree of total leverage (DTL).*

f. Carolina Fastener has entered into a contract to produce and sell an additional 15,000 latches in the coming year. Use the DOL, DFL, and DTL to predict and calculate the changes in EBIT and earnings available for common. Check your work by a simple calculation of Carolina Fastener's EBIT and earnings available for common, using the basic information given.

Personal Finance Problem

LG 3 **P13–18** **Capital structure**   Kirsten Neal is interested in purchasing a new house given that mortgage rates are at a historical low. Her bank has specific rules regarding an applicant's ability to meet the contractual payments associated with the requested debt. Kirsten must submit personal financial data for her income, expenses, and existing installment loan payments. The bank then calculates and compares certain ratios to predetermined allowable values to determine if it will make the requested loan. The requirements are as follows:

(1) Monthly mortgage payments < 28% of monthly gross (before-tax) income.

(2) Total monthly installment payments (including the mortgage payments) < 37% of monthly gross (before-tax) income.

Kirsten submits the following personal financial data:

Monthly gross (before-tax) income	$ 4,500
Monthly installment loan obligations	375
Requested mortgage	150,000
Monthly mortgage payments	1,100

a. Calculate the ratio for requirement 1.

b. Calculate the ratio for requirement 2.

c. Assuming that Kirsten has adequate funds for the down payment and meets other lender requirements, will Kirsten be granted the loan?

LG 3   **P13–19**   **Various capital structures**   Charter Enterprises currently has $1 million in total assets and is totally equity financed. It is contemplating a change in its capital structure. Compute the amount of debt and equity that would be outstanding if the firm were to shift to each of the following debt ratios: 10%, 20%, 30%, 40%, 50%, 60%, and 90%. (*Note:* The amount of total assets would not change.) Is there a limit to the debt ratio's value?

LG 3   **P13–20**   **Debt and financial risk**   Tower Interiors has made the forecast of sales shown in the following table. Also given is the probability of each level of sales.

Sales	Probability
$200,000	0.20
300,000	0.60
400,000	0.20

The firm has fixed operating costs of $75,000 and variable operating costs equal to 70% of the sales level. The company pays $12,000 in interest per period. The tax rate is 40%.

a. Compute the earnings before interest and taxes (EBIT) for each level of sales.

b. Compute the earnings per share (EPS) for each level of sales, the expected EPS, the standard deviation of the EPS, and the coefficient of variation of EPS, assuming that there are 10,000 shares of common stock outstanding.

c. Tower has the opportunity to reduce its leverage to zero and pay no interest. This will require that the number of shares outstanding be increased to 15,000. Repeat part **b** under this assumption.

d. Compare your findings in parts **b** and **c**, and comment on the effect of the reduction of debt to zero on the firm's financial risk.

LG 4 **P13–21** **EPS and optimal debt ratio**   Williams Glassware has estimated, at various debt ratios, the expected earnings per share and the standard deviation of the earnings per share as shown in the following table.

Debt ratio	Earnings per share (EPS)	Standard deviation of EPS
0%	$2.30	$1.15
20	3.00	1.80
40	3.50	2.80
60	3.95	3.95
80	3.80	5.53

a. Estimate the *optimal debt ratio* on the basis of the relationship between earnings per share and the debt ratio. You will probably find it helpful to graph the relationship.
b. Graph the relationship between the *coefficient of variation* and the debt ratio. Label the areas associated with business risk and financial risk.

LG 5 **P13–22** **EBIT–EPS and capital structure**   Data-Check is considering two capital structures. The key information is shown in the following table. Assume a 40% tax rate.

Source of capital	Structure A	Structure B
Long-term debt	$100,000 at 16% coupon rate	$200,000 at 17% coupon rate
Common stock	4,000 shares	2,000 shares

a. Calculate two *EBIT–EPS coordinates* for each of the structures by selecting any two EBIT values and finding their associated EPS values.
b. Plot the two capital structures on a set of EBIT–EPS axes.
c. Indicate over what EBIT range, if any, each structure is preferred.
d. Discuss the leverage and risk aspects of each structure.
e. If the firm is fairly certain that its EBIT will exceed $75,000, which structure would you recommend? Why?

LG 5 **P13–23** **EBIT–EPS and preferred stock**   Litho-Print is considering two possible capital structures, A and B, shown in the following table. Assume a 40% tax rate.

Source of capital	Structure A	Structure B
Long-term debt	$75,000 at 16% coupon rate	$50,000 at 15% coupon rate
Preferred stock	$10,000 with an 18% annual dividend	$15,000 with an 18% annual dividend
Common stock	8,000 shares	10,000 shares

a. Calculate two *EBIT–EPS coordinates* for each of the structures by selecting any two EBIT values and finding their associated EPS values.
b. Graph the two capital structures on the same set of EBIT–EPS axes.

c. Discuss the leverage and risk associated with each of the structures.

d. Over what range of EBIT is each structure preferred?

e. Which structure do you recommend if the firm expects its EBIT to be $35,000? Explain.

LG 3 LG 4 LG 6 P13–24 Integrative—Optimal capital structure Medallion Cooling Systems, Inc., has total assets of $10,000,000, EBIT of $2,000,000, and preferred dividends of $200,000 and is taxed at a rate of 40%. In an effort to determine the optimal capital structure, the firm has assembled data on the cost of debt, the number of shares of common stock for various levels of indebtedness, and the overall required return on investment:

Capital structure debt ratio	Cost of debt, r_d	Number of common stock shares	Required return, r_s
0%	0%	200,000	12%
15	8	170,000	13
30	9	140,000	14
45	12	110,000	16
60	15	80,000	20

a. Calculate *earnings per share* for each level of indebtedness.

b. Use Equation 13.12 and the earnings per share calculated in part **a** to calculate a *price per share* for each level of indebtedness.

c. Choose the optimal capital structure. Justify your choice.

LG 3 LG 4 LG 6 P13–25 Integrative—Optimal capital structure Nelson Corporation has made the following forecast of sales, with the associated probabilities of occurrence noted.

Sales	Probability
$200,000	0.20
300,000	0.60
400,000	0.20

The company has fixed operating costs of $100,000 per year, and variable operating costs represent 40% of sales. The existing capital structure consists of 25,000 shares of common stock that have a $10 per share book value. No other capital items are outstanding. The marketplace has assigned the following required returns to risky earnings per share.

Coefficient of variation of EPS	Estimated required return, r_s
0.43	15%
0.47	16
0.51	17
0.56	18
0.60	22
0.64	24

The company is contemplating *shifting its capital structure* by substituting debt in the capital structure for common stock. The three different debt ratios under consideration are shown in the following table, along with an estimate, for each ratio, of the corresponding required interest rate on *all* debt.

Debt ratio	Interest rate on *all* debt
20%	10%
40	12
60	14

The tax rate is 40%. The market value of the equity for a leveraged firm can be found by using the simplified method (see Equation 13.12).

a. Calculate the expected earnings per share (EPS), the standard deviation of EPS, and the coefficient of variation of EPS for the three proposed capital structures.

b. Determine the *optimal capital structure*, assuming (1) maximization of earnings per share and (2) maximization of share value.

c. Construct a graph (similar to Figure 13.7) showing the relationships in part **b**. (*Note:* You will probably have to sketch the lines, because you have only three data points.)

LG 3   LG 4

LG 5   LG 6

P13–26 **Integrative—Optimal capital structure** The board of directors of Morales Publishing, Inc., has commissioned a capital structure study. The company has total assets of $40,000,000. It has earnings before interest and taxes of $8,000,000 and is taxed at a rate of 40%.

a. Create a spreadsheet like the one in Table 13.10 showing values of debt and equity as well as the total number of shares, assuming a book value of $25 per share.

% Debt	Total assets	$ Debt	$ Equity	Number of shares @ $25
0%	$40,000,000	$_____	$_____	_____
10	40,000,000	_____	_____	_____
20	40,000,000	_____	_____	_____
30	40,000,000	_____	_____	_____
40	40,000,000	_____	_____	_____
50	40,000,000	_____	_____	_____
60	40,000,000	_____	_____	_____

b. Given the before-tax cost of debt at various levels of indebtedness, calculate the yearly interest expenses.

% Debt	$ Total debt	Before-tax cost of debt, r_d	$ Interest expense
0%	$_____	0.0%	$_____
10	_____	7.5	_____
20	_____	8.0	_____
30	_____	9.0	_____
40	_____	11.0	_____
50	_____	12.5	_____
60	_____	15.5	_____

c. Using EBIT of $8,000,000, a 40% tax rate, and the information developed in parts **a** and **b,** calculate the most likely earnings per share for the firm at various levels of indebtedness. Mark the level of indebtedness that maximizes EPS.

% Debt	EBIT	Interest expense	EBT	Taxes	Net income	Number of shares	EPS
0%	$8,000,000	$_____	$_____	$_____	$_____	_____	$_____
10	8,000,000	_____	_____	_____	_____	_____	_____
20	8,000,000	_____	_____	_____	_____	_____	_____
30	8,000,000	_____	_____	_____	_____	_____	_____
40	8,000,000	_____	_____	_____	_____	_____	_____
50	8,000,000	_____	_____	_____	_____	_____	_____
60	8,000,000	_____	_____	_____	_____	_____	_____

d. Using the EPS developed in part **c,** the estimates of required return, r_s, and Equation 13.12, estimate the value per share at various levels of indebtedness. Mark the level of indebtedness in the following table that results in the maximum price per share, P_0.

Debt	EPS	r_s	P_0
0%	$_____	10.0%	$_____
10	_____	10.3	_____
20	_____	10.9	_____
30	_____	11.4	_____
40	_____	12.6	_____
50	_____	14.8	_____
60	_____	17.5	_____

e. Prepare a recommendation to the board of directors of Morales Publishing that specifies the degree of indebtedness that will accomplish the firm's goal of optimizing shareholder wealth. Use your findings in parts **a** through **d** to justify your recommendation.

LG 3   LG 4

LG 5   LG 6
P13–27 **Integrative—Optimal capital structure** Country Textiles, which has fixed operating costs of $300,000 and variable operating costs equal to 40% of sales, has made the following three sales estimates, with their probabilities noted.

Sales	Probability
$ 600,000	0.30
900,000	0.40
1,200,000	0.30

The firm wishes to analyze five possible capital structures—0%, 15%, 30%, 45%, and 60% debt ratios. The firm's total assets of $1 million are assumed to be constant. Its common stock has a book value of $25 per share, and the firm is in the 40% tax bracket. The following additional data have been gathered for use in analyzing the five capital structures under consideration.

Capital structure debt ratio	Before-tax cost of debt, r_d	Required return, r_s
0%	0.0%	10.0%
15	8.0	10.5
30	10.0	11.6
45	13.0	14.0
60	17.0	20.0

a. Calculate the level of EBIT associated with each of the three levels of sales.
b. Calculate the amount of debt, the amount of equity, and the number of shares of common stock outstanding for each of the five capital structures being considered.
c. Calculate the annual interest on the debt under each of the five capital structures being considered. (*Note:* The before-tax cost of debt, r_d, is the interest rate applicable to *all* debt associated with the corresponding debt ratio.)
d. Calculate the EPS associated with each of the three levels of EBIT calculated in part **a** for each of the five capital structures being considered.
e. Calculate (1) the expected EPS, (2) the standard deviation of EPS, and (3) the coefficient of variation of EPS for each of the five capital structures, using your findings in part **d**.
f. Plot the expected EPS and coefficient of variation of EPS against the capital structures (*x* axis) on separate sets of axes, and comment on the return and risk relative to capital structure.
g. Using the EBIT–EPS data developed in part **d**, plot the 0%, 30%, and 60% capital structures on the same set of EBIT–EPS axes, and discuss the ranges over which each is preferred. What is the major problem with the use of this approach?
h. Using the valuation model given in Equation 13.12 and your findings in part **e**, estimate the share value for each of the capital structures being considered.
i. Compare and contrast your findings in parts **f** and **h**. Which structure is preferred if the goal is to *maximize EPS?* Which structure is preferred if the goal is to *maximize share value?* Which capital structure do you recommend? Explain.

LG 3   **P13–28**   **ETHICS PROBLEM**   "Information asymmetry lies at the heart of the ethical dilemma that managers, stockholders, and bondholders confront when companies initiate management buyouts or swap debt for equity." Comment on this statement. What steps might a board of directors take to ensure that the company's actions are ethical with regard to all parties?

Spreadsheet Exercise

Starstruck Company would like to determine its optimal capital structure. Several of its managers believe that the best method is to rely on the estimated earnings per share (EPS) of the firm because they feel that profits and stock price are closely related. The financial managers have suggested another method that uses estimated required returns to estimate the share value of the firm. The following financial data are available.

Capital structure debt ratio	Estimated EPS	Estimated required return
0%	$1.75	11.40%
10	1.90	11.80
20	2.25	12.50
30	2.55	13.25
40	3.18	18.00
50	3.06	19.00
60	3.10	25.00

TO DO

a. Based on the given financial data, create a spreadsheet to calculate the estimated share values associated with the seven alternative capital structures. Refer to Table 13.15.

b. Use Excel to graph the relationship between capital structure and the estimated EPS of the firm. What is the optimal debt ratio? Refer to Figure 13.7.

c. Use Excel to graph the relationship between capital structure and the estimated share value of the firm. What is the optimal debt ratio? Refer to Figure 13.7.

d. Do both methods lead to the same *optimal capital structure?* Which method do you favor? Explain.

e. What is the major difference between the EPS and share value methods?

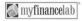 Visit **www.myfinancelab.com** for **Chapter Case:** *Evaluating Tampa Manufacturing's Capital Structure,* Group Exercises, and numerous online resources.

14 Payout Policy

Learning Goals

LG 1 Understand cash payout procedures, their tax treatment, and the role of dividend reinvestment plans.

LG 2 Describe the residual theory of dividends and the key arguments with regard to dividend irrelevance and relevance.

LG 3 Discuss the key factors involved in establishing a dividend policy.

LG 4 Review and evaluate the three basic types of dividend policies.

LG 5 Evaluate stock dividends from accounting, shareholder, and company points of view.

LG 6 Explain stock splits and the firm's motivation for undertaking them.

Why This Chapter Matters to You

In your *professional* life

ACCOUNTING You need to understand the types of dividends and payment procedures for them because you will need to record and report the declaration and payment of dividends; you also will provide the financial data that management must have to make dividend decisions.

INFORMATION SYSTEMS You need to understand types of dividends, payment procedures, and the financial data that the firm must have to make and implement dividend decisions.

MANAGEMENT To make appropriate dividend decisions for the firm, you need to understand types of dividends, arguments about the relevance of dividends, the factors that affect dividend policy, and types of dividend policies.

MARKETING You need to understand factors affecting dividend policy because you may want to argue that the firm would be better off retaining funds for use in new marketing programs or products, rather than paying them out as dividends.

OPERATIONS You need to understand factors affecting dividend policy because you may find that the firm's dividend policy imposes limitations on planned expansion, replacement, or renewal projects.

In your *personal* life

Many individual investors buy common stock for the anticipated cash dividends. From a personal finance perspective, you should understand why and how firms pay dividends and the informational and financial implications of receiving them. Such understanding will help you select common stocks that have dividend-paying patterns consistent with your long-term financial goals.

Global Investment House

The Payback Time

Global Investment House is a Kuwaiti investment company established in 1998 to meet the high expectations of local and international clients. During the initial years of its operations, Global focused primarily on investment products in Kuwait. After establishing its position in Kuwait, Global launched a strategy of geographical expansion into GCC countries, the Middle East and North Africa, and emerging markets. In 2003, Global was listed on the Kuwait Stock Exchange followed by listings in Bahrain and Dubai. In May 2008, Global became the first Kuwaiti company to be listed on the London Stock Exchange. In 2008, Global had one of the largest principle investments and proprietary trading operations in the region with an asset size of $12,000 million and was the second-largest investment company in the region.

Global, like many companies and banks in the region and worldwide, was affected by the global financial crisis. In December 2008, the company defaulted on a syndicated debt. Immediately, Global appointed HSBC as its international financial advisor to assist in restructuring its debt in default with its 53 lending banks across the world, from China to New York. In 2009, however, Global found itself in the limelight after it partially defaulted on loans. But "the bomb could be diffused," said chairperson Maha Al-Ghunaim.[1] Global rescheduled its $1.7 billion debt with its creditors, becoming the first Kuwait investment firm that wished to pay back its defaulted loans. If it fails to repay $700 million of debt in two years, the creditors can convert the amount into shares.

Global has since worked very hard with its creditors and continues to service all coupon and interest payments on a timely basis. By the end of 2010, Global paid an extra 25 percent of its scheduled payback payments. The company's full cooperation and transparency with its lenders has been recognized by the banks. It has also set Global apart from other borrowers in default and has set precedents for other restructurings in the region.

---

1. "Kuwait Banking: Recovery of Kuwait Banking Sector," http://www.marcopolis.net/kuwait-banking-recovery-of-kuwait-banking-sector.htm.

LG 1 **14.1** **The Basics of Payout Policy**

ELEMENTS OF PAYOUT POLICY

payout policy
Decisions that a firm makes regarding whether to distribute cash to shareholders, how much cash to distribute, and the means by which cash should be distributed.

The term **payout policy** refers to the decisions that firms make about whether to distribute cash to shareholders, how much cash to distribute, and by what means the cash should be distributed. While these decisions are probably less important than the investment decisions covered in Chapters 10 through 12 and the financing choices discussed in Chapter 13, they are nonetheless decisions that managers and boards of directors face routinely. Investors monitor firms' payout policies carefully, and unexpected changes in those policies can have significant effects on firms' stock prices. The recent history of Best Buy demonstrates many of the important dimensions of payout policy.

Like most rapidly growing firms, Best Buy decided not to pay any cash to shareholders for many years, preferring instead to reinvest the cash that the business generated to build and operate new stores. As the firm matured, managers decided that cash flow from operations was sufficient to continue to reinvest in growth *and* return some cash to shareholders. However, in Best Buy's case, the decision to begin distributing cash to shareholders in 2003 was not driven *entirely* by the slowdown in the company's growth rate. In addition, a significant change to the tax code that year made dividends much more attractive to investors on an after-tax basis. Best Buy's largest shareholder at the time was its founder, Richard Schulze, who stood to receive about $20 million in dividends annually. Mr. Schulze would pay much less tax on these dividends after the 2003 tax law changes.

But dividends are not the only means by which firms can distribute cash to shareholders. Firms can also conduct share repurchases, in which they typically buy back some of their outstanding common stock through purchases in the open market. Best Buy, like many other companies, uses both methods to put cash in the hands of their stockholders. In its first year of paying out cash to shareholders, Best Buy paid $130 million in dividends and bought back $100 million worth of common stock. From 2005 through 2008, Best Buy actually distributed more cash via share repurchases than through dividends, but, when the financial crisis hit, the company temporarily eliminated all share repurchases while maintaining its quarterly dividend payments.

If we generalize the lessons about payout policy from Best Buy's recent financial history, we may expect that:

1. Rapidly growing firms generally do not pay out cash to shareholders.
2. Slowing growth, positive cash flow generation, and favorable tax conditions can prompt firms to initiate cash payouts to investors. The ownership base of the company can also be an important factor in the decision to distribute cash.
3. Cash payouts can be made through dividends or share repurchases. Many companies use both methods. In some years, more cash is paid out via dividends, but sometimes share repurchases are larger than dividend payments.
4. When business conditions are weak, firms are more willing to reduce share buybacks than to cut dividends.

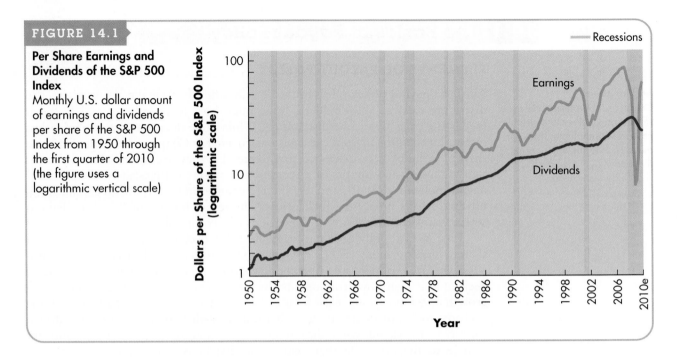

FIGURE 14.1

Per Share Earnings and Dividends of the S&P 500 Index
Monthly U.S. dollar amount of earnings and dividends per share of the S&P 500 Index from 1950 through the first quarter of 2010 (the figure uses a logarithmic vertical scale)

TRENDS IN EARNINGS AND DIVIDENDS

Figure 14.1 illustrates both long-term trends and cyclical movements in earnings and dividends paid by large U.S. firms that are part of the S&P 500 stock index. The figure plots monthly earnings and dividend payments from 1950 through the first quarter of 2010. The top line represents the earnings per share of the S&P500 index, and the lower line represents dividends per share. The vertical bars highlight 10 periods during which the U.S. economy was in recession. Several important lessons can be gleaned from the figure. First, observe that over the long term the earnings and dividends lines tend to move together. Figure 14.1 uses a logarithmic scale, so that the slope of each line represents the growth rate of earnings or dividends. Over the 60 years shown in the figure, the two lines tend to have about the same slope, meaning that earnings and dividends grow at about the same rate when you take a long-term perspective. This makes perfect sense—firms pay dividends out of earnings, so for dividends to grow over the long-term, earnings must grow too.

Second, the earnings series is much more volatile than the dividends series. That is, the line plotting earnings per share is quite bumpy, but the dividend line is much smoother. This suggests that firms do not adjust their dividend payments each time earnings move up or down. Instead, firms tend to smooth dividends, increasing them slowly when earnings are growing rapidly and maintaining dividend payments, rather than cutting them, when earnings decline.

To see this second point more clearly, look closely at the vertical bars in Figure 14.1. It is apparent that during recessions corporate earnings usually decline, but dividends either do not decline at all or do not decline as sharply as earnings. In six of the last ten recessions, dividends were actually higher when the recession ended than just before it began, although the last two recessions are notable exceptions to this pattern. Notice also that, just after the end of a recession, earnings typically increase quite rapidly. Dividends increase, too, but not as fast.

Matter of fact

P&G's Dividend History

Few companies have replicated the dividend achievements of the consumer products giant Procter & Gamble (P&G). P&G has paid dividends every year for more than a century, and it increased its dividend in every year from 1956 through 2009.

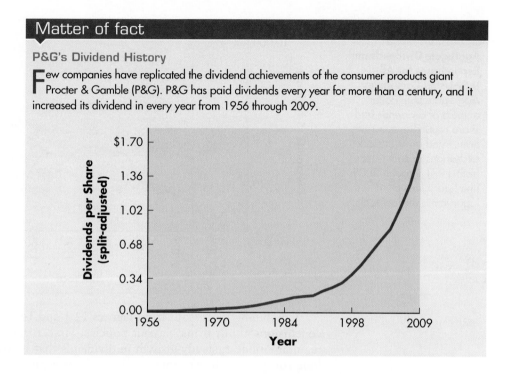

A third lesson from Figure 14.1 is that the effect of the recent recession on both corporate earnings and dividends was large by historical standards. An enormous earnings decline occurred from 2007 to 2009. That forced firms to cut dividends more drastically than they had in years, but even so the drop in dividends was slight compared to the earnings decrease.

TRENDS IN DIVIDENDS AND SHARE REPURCHASES

When firms want to distribute cash to shareholders, they can either pay dividends or repurchase outstanding shares. Figure 14.2 plots aggregate dividends and share repurchases from 1971 through 2009 for all firms listed on U.S. stock exchanges (again, the figure uses a logarithmic vertical scale). A quick glance at the figure reveals that share repurchases played a relatively minor role in firms' payout practices in the 1970s. In 1971, for example, aggregate dividends totaled $14.6 billion, but share repurchases that year were just $1.3 billion. Since 1975, share repurchases have been growing rapidly, first eclipsing total dividend payments in 2005. That year, firms paid $522 billion in dividends, but they repurchased almost $590 billion worth of stock. Share repurchases continued to outpace dividends for the next four years, peaking at more than $1 trillion in 2007.

Whereas total dividends rise smoothly over time, Figure 14.2 shows that share repurchases display much more volatility. The largest drops in repurchase activity occurred in 1974–1975, 1981, 1986, 1990–1991, 2001–2002, and 2008–2009. All of these correspond to periods when the U.S. economy was mired in or just emerging from a recession. During most of these periods, dividends continued to grow modestly. Only during the recent, severe recession did both share repurchases and dividends fall.

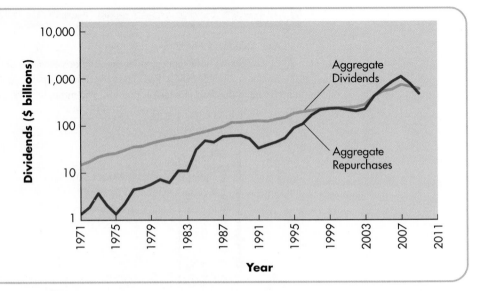

FIGURE 14.2

Aggregate Dividends and Repurchases for All U.S.–Listed Companies
Aggregate U.S. dollar amount of dividends and share repurchases for all firms listed on U.S. stock exchanges in each year from 1971 through 2009 (the figure uses a logarithmic vertical scale)

Combining the lessons from Figures 14.1 and 14.2, we can draw three broad conclusions about firms' payout policies. First, firms exhibit a strong desire to maintain modest, steady growth in dividends that is roughly consistent with the long-run growth in earnings. Second, share repurchases have accounted for a growing fraction of total cash payouts over time. Third, when earnings fluctuate,

---

focus on ETHICS

Are Buybacks Really a Bargain?

in practice   When CBS announced in March 2007 that it would buy back $1.4 billion worth of stock, its sagging share price saw the biggest spike since the media giant parted ways with Viacom in 2005. The 4.5 percent jump may have been an omen of good fortune—at the very least it showed how much shareholders like buybacks.

Companies have been gobbling up their own shares faster than ever in a world of inexpensive capital and swollen balance sheets. Since 2003, the market for buybacks has boomed, with repurchases nearly on a par with capital expenditures. Some, however, have questioned the moves and motives that lead to a big buyback.

In addition to simply returning cash to shareholders, many companies also repurchase stock because they believe

their stock is undervalued. Yet new research shows that companies often use creative financial reporting to push earnings downward before buybacks, making the stock seem undervalued and causing its price to bounce higher after the buyback. That pleases investors who then amplify the effect by pushing the price even higher.

"Managers who are acting opportunistically can use their reporting discretion to reduce the repurchase price by temporarily deflating earnings," argue Guojin Gong, Henock Louis, and Amy Sun at Penn State University's Smeal College of Business. Observing data from 1,720 companies, the authors say companies can easily create an apparent slump by speeding up or slowing down expense recognition, changing inventory accounting, or revising estimates of bad debt—all

classic methods of making the numbers look worse without actually breaking accounting rules.

The penalty for being caught deliberately managing earnings in advance of a buyback could be severe. With the variety of accounting scandals that popped up regularly in the early 2000s, executives would no doubt be wary of deflating earnings just to get a boost from a buyback. Still, that's what Louis believes some are doing. "I don't think what they're doing is illegal," he says. "But it's misleading their investors."

▶ *Do you agree that corporate managers would manipulate their stock's value prior to a buyback, or do you believe that corporations are more likely to initiate a buyback to enhance shareholder value?*

firms adjust their short-term payouts primarily by adjusting share repurchases (rather than dividends), cutting buybacks during recessions, and increasing them rapidly during economic expansions.

Matter of fact

Share Repurchases Gain Worldwide Popularity

The growing importance of share repurchases in corporate payout policy is not confined to the United States. In most of the world's largest economies, repurchases have been on the rise in recent years, eclipsing dividend payments at least some of the time in countries as diverse as Belgium, Denmark, Finland, Hungary, Ireland, Japan, Netherlands, South Korea, and Switzerland. A recent study of payout policy at firms from 25 different countries found that share repurchases rose at an annual rate of 19 percent from 1999 through 2008.

→ REVIEW QUESTIONS

14–1 What are the two ways that firms can distribute cash to shareholders?

14–2 Why do rapidly growing firms generally pay no dividends?

14–3 The dividend payout ratio equals dividends paid divided by earnings. How would you expect this ratio to behave during a recession? What about during an economic boom?

 ## 14.2 The Mechanics of Payout Policy

CASH DIVIDEND PAYMENT PROCEDURES

At quarterly or semiannual meetings, a firm's board of directors decides whether and in what amount to pay cash dividends. If the firm has already established a precedent of paying dividends, the decision facing the board is usually whether to maintain or increase the dividend, and that decision is based primarily on the firm's recent performance and its ability to generate cash flow in the future. Boards rarely cut dividends unless they believe that the firm's ability to generate cash is in serious jeopardy. Figure 14.3 plots the number of U.S. firms that increased or decreased their dividend payment in each year from 1999 through 2009. Clearly, the number of firms increasing their dividends is far greater than the number of companies cutting dividends in most years. When the economy is strong, as it was from 2003 to 2006, the ratio of firms increasing dividends to those cutting dividends may be 30 to 1 or higher. However, a sign of the severity of the most recent recession was that in 2009 this ratio was just 1.5 to 1. That year, 1,191 firms increased their dividend, while 804 firms cut dividends.

When a firm's directors declare a dividend, they issue a statement indicating the dividend amount and setting three important dates—the *date of record*, the *ex-dividend date*, and the *payment date*. All persons whose names are recorded as stockholders on the **date of record** receive the dividend. These stockholders are often referred to as *holders of record*.

Because of the time needed to make bookkeeping entries when a stock is traded, the stock begins selling **ex dividend** 2 *business days* prior to the date of record. Purchasers of a stock selling ex dividend do not receive the current dividend. A simple

date of record (dividends)
Set by the firm's directors, the date on which all persons whose names are recorded as stockholders receive a declared dividend at a specified future time.

ex dividend
A period beginning 2 *business days* prior to the date of record, during which a stock is sold without the right to receive the current dividend.

U.S. Firms Increasing or Decreasing Dividends
Number of U.S. firms that increased or decreased their dividend payment in each year from 1999 through 2009

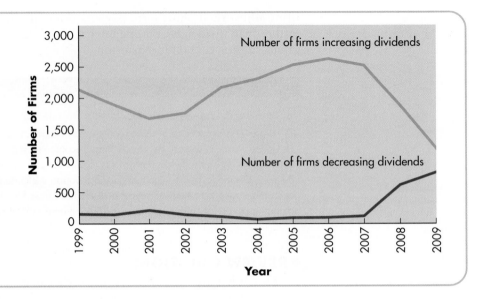

payment date
Set by the firm's directors, the actual date on which the firm mails the dividend payment to the holders of record.

way to determine the first day on which the stock sells ex dividend is to subtract 2 business days from the date of record.

The **payment date** is the actual date on which the firm mails the dividend payment to the holders of record. It is generally a few weeks after the record date. An example will clarify the various dates and the accounting effects.

Example 14.1 ▶ On June 24, 2010, the board of directors of Best Buy announced that the firm's next quarterly cash dividend would be $0.15 per share, payable on October 26, 2010 to shareholders of record on Tuesday, October 5, 2010. Best Buy shares would begin trading ex dividend on the previous Friday, October 1. At the time of the announcement, Best Buy had 420,061,666 shares of common stock outstanding, so the total dividend payment would be $63,009,250. Figure 14.4 shows a time line depicting the key dates relative to the Best Buy dividend. Before the dividend was declared, the key accounts of the firm were as follows (dollar values quoted in thousands):[2]

Cash	$1,826,000	Dividends payable	$ 0
		Retained earnings	5,797,000

When the dividend was announced by the directors, $63 million of the retained earnings ($0.15 per share × 420 million shares) was transferred to the dividends payable account. The key accounts thus became

Cash	$1,826,000	Dividends payable	$ 63,009
		Retained earnings	5,733,991

2. The accounting transactions described here reflect only the effects of the dividend. Best Buy's actual financial statements during this period obviously reflect many other transactions.

FIGURE 14.4

Dividend Payment Time Line
Time line for the announcement and payment of a cash dividend for Best Buy

Declaration Date
Thursday, June 24

Board of directors declares $0.15 per share dividend, payable to holders of record on Tuesday, October 5, payable on Tuesday, October 26.

Ex Dividend Date
Friday, October 1

Date of Record
Tuesday, October 5

Stock begins to sell ex dividend on Friday, October 1, which is 2 business days before the Tuesday, October 5, date of record.

Payment Date
Tuesday, October 26

Checks of $0.15 per share are mailed on Tuesday, October 26, to all holders of record on Tuesday, October 5.

Time ⟶

When Best Buy actually paid the dividend on October 26, this produced the following balances in the key accounts of the firm:

Cash	$1,763,000	Dividends payable	$	0
		Retained earnings		5,734,000

The net effect of declaring and paying the dividend was to reduce the firm's total assets (and stockholders' equity) by $63 million.

SHARE REPURCHASE PROCEDURES

The mechanics of cash dividend payments are virtually the same for every dividend paid by every public company. With share repurchases, firms can use at least two different methods to get cash into the hands of shareholders. The most common method of executing a share repurchase program is called an open-market share repurchase. In an **open-market share repurchase,** as the name suggests, firms simply buy back some of their outstanding shares on the open market. Firms have a great deal of latitude regarding when and how they execute these open-market purchases. Some firms make purchases in fixed amounts at regular intervals, while other firms try to behave more opportunistically, buying back more shares when they think the share price is relatively low and fewer shares when the price is high.

In contrast, firms sometimes repurchase shares through a *self-tender offer* or simply a *tender offer*. In a **tender offer,** a firm announces the price it is willing to pay to buy back shares and the quantity of shares it wishes to repurchase. The tender offer price is usually set at a significant premium above the current market price. Shareholders who want to participate let the firm know how many shares they would like to sell back to the firm at the stated price. If shareholders do not offer to sell back as many shares as the firm wants to repurchase, the firm may either cancel or extend the offer. If the offer is oversubscribed, meaning that shareholders want to sell more shares than the firms wants to repurchase, then

open-market share repurchase
A share repurchase program in which firms simply buy back some of their outstanding shares on the open market.

tender offer repurchase
A repurchase program in which a firm offers to repurchase a fixed number of shares, usually at a premium relative to the market value, and shareholders decide whether or not they want to sell back their shares at that price.

Dutch auction repurchase
A repurchase method in which the firm specifies how many shares it wants to buy back and a range of prices at which it is willing to repurchase shares. Investors specify how many shares they will sell at each price in the range, and the firm determines the minimum price required to repurchase its target number of shares. All investors who tender receive the same price.

the firm typically repurchases shares on a pro rata basis. For example, if the firm wants to buy back 10 million shares, but 20 million shares are tendered by investors, then the firm would repurchase exactly half of the shares tendered by each shareholder.

A third method of buying back shares is called a **Dutch auction.** In a Dutch auction, the firm specifies a range of prices at which it is willing to repurchase shares and the quantity of shares that it desires. Investors can tender their shares to the firm at any price in the specified range, and this allows the firm to trace out a demand curve for their stock. That is, the demand curve specifies how many shares investors will sell back to the firm at each price in the offer range. This allows the firm to determine the minimum price required to repurchase the desired quantity of shares, and every shareholder receives that price.

Example 14.2 ▶

In July 2010, Fidelity National Information Services announced a Dutch auction repurchase for 86 million common shares at prices ranging from $29 to $31.50 per share. Fidelity shareholders were instructed to contact the company to indicate how many shares they would be willing to sell at different prices in this range. Suppose that after accumulating this information from investors, Fidelity constructed the following demand schedule:

Offer price	Shares tendered	Cumulative total
$29	5,000,000	5,000,000
29.25	10,000,000	15,000,000
29.50	15,000,000	30,000,000
29.75	18,000,000	48,000,000
30	18,500,000	66,500,000
31.25	19,500,000	86,000,000
31.50	20,000,000	106,000,000

At a price of $31.25, shareholders are willing to tender a total of 86 million shares, exactly the amount that Fidelity wants to repurchase. Each shareholder who expressed a willingness to tender their shares at a price of $31.25 *or less* receives $31.25, and Fidelity repurchases all 86 million shares at a cost of roughly $2.7 billion.

TAX TREATMENT OF DIVIDENDS AND REPURCHASES

For many years, dividends and share repurchases had very different tax consequences. The dividends that investors received were generally taxed at ordinary income tax rates. Therefore, if a firm paid $10 million in dividends, that payout would trigger significant tax liabilities for the firm's shareholders (at least those subject to personal income taxes). On the other hand, when firms repurchased shares, the taxes triggered by that type of payout were generally much lower. There were several reasons for this. Only those shareholders who sold their shares as part of the repurchase program had any potential tax liability. Shareholders who did not participate did not owe any taxes. Furthermore, some shareholders who did participate in the repurchase program might not owe any taxes on the funds they received if they were tax-exempt institutions or if they sold their shares at a loss. Finally, even those shareholders who participated in the repurchase program and sold their shares for a profit paid taxes only at the (usually lower) capital gains tax rate, and even that tax only applied to the gain, not to the entire value of the shares repurchased. Consequently, investors could generally expect to pay far less in taxes on money that a firm distributed through a share repurchase compared to money paid out as dividends. That differential tax treatment in part explains the growing popularity of share repurchase programs in the 1980s and 1990s.

The *Jobs and Growth Tax Relief Reconciliation Act of 2003* significantly changed the tax treatment of corporate dividends for most taxpayers. Prior to passage of the 2003 law, dividends received by investors were taxed as ordinary income at rates as high as 35 percent. The 2003 act reduced the tax rate on corporate dividends for most taxpayers to the tax rate applicable to capital gains, which is a maximum rate of 5 percent to 15 percent, depending on the taxpayer's tax bracket. This change significantly diminishes the degree of "double taxation" of dividends, which results when the corporation is first taxed on its income and then shareholders pay taxes on the dividends that they receive. After-tax cash flow to dividend recipients is much greater at the lower applicable tax rate; the result is noticeably higher dividend payouts by corporations today than prior to passage of the 2003 legislation. (For more details on the impact of the 2003 act, see the *Focus on Practice* box.)

focus on PRACTICE

Capital Gains and Dividend Tax Treatment Extended to 2010

in practice In 1980, the percentage of firms paying monthly, quarterly, semiannual, or annual dividends stood at 60 percent. By the end of 2002, this had declined to 20 percent. In May 2003, President George W. Bush signed into law the *Jobs and Growth Tax Relief Reconciliation Act of 2003* (JGTRRA). Prior to that new law, dividends were taxed once as part of corporate earnings and again as the personal income of the investor, in both cases with a potential top rate of 35 percent. The result was an effective tax rate of 57.75 percent on some dividends. Though the 2003 tax law did not completely eliminate the double taxation of dividends, it reduced the maximum possible effect of the double taxation of dividends to 44.75 percent. For taxpayers in the lower tax brackets, the combined effect was a maximum of 38.25 percent.

Both the number of companies paying dividends and the amount of dividends spiked following the lowering of tax rates on dividends. For example, total dividends paid rose almost 14 percent in the first quarter after the new tax law was enacted, and the percentage of firms initiating dividends rose by nearly 40 percent the same quarter.

The tax rates under JGTRRA were originally programmed to expire at the end of 2008. However, in May 2006, Congress passed the *Tax Increase Prevention and Reconciliation Act of 2005* (TIPRA), extending the beneficial tax rates for 2 more years. Taxpayers in tax brackets above 15 percent paid a 15 percent rate on dividends paid before December 31, 2008. For taxpayers with a marginal tax rate of 15 percent or lower, the dividend tax rate was 5 percent until December 31, 2007, and 0 percent from 2008 to 2010.

Long-term capital gains tax rates were reduced to the same rates as the new dividend tax rates through 2010. Pre-JGTRRA taxation of dividends reappears in 2011 unless further legislation makes the law permanent. As this book went to press in 2010, it was unclear whether legislators would extend the dividend tax break beyond 2010. Those arguing for an extension pointed toward the weak economy and suggested that taxes needed to remain low to stimulate business investment and job creation. Others noted that the U.S. budget deficit was at an all-time high, so some combination of higher taxes and reduced spending was necessary to avoid economic problems associated with too much debt.

▶ *How might the expected future reappearance of higher tax rates on individuals receiving dividends affect corporate dividend payout policies?*

Personal Finance Example 14.3 ▶ The board of directors of Espinoza Industries, Inc., on October 4 of the current year, declared a quarterly dividend of $0.46 per share payable to all holders of record on Friday, October 30, with a payment date of November 19. Rob and Kate Heckman, who purchased 500 shares of Espinoza's common stock on Thursday, October 15, wish to determine whether they will receive the recently declared dividend and, if so, when and how much they would net after taxes from the dividend given that the dividends would be subject to a 15% federal income tax.

Given the Friday, October 30, date of record, the stock would begin selling *ex dividend* 2 business days earlier on Wednesday, October 28. Purchasers of the stock on or before Tuesday, October 27, would receive the right to the dividend. Because the Heckmans purchased the stock on October 15, they would be eligible to receive the dividend of $0.46 per share. Thus, the Heckmans will receive $230 in dividends ($0.46 per share × 500 shares), which will be mailed to them on the November 19 payment date. Because they are subject to a 15% federal income tax on the dividends, the Heckmans will net $195.50 [(1 − 0.15) × $230] after taxes from the Espinoza Industries dividend.

DIVIDEND REINVESTMENT PLANS

dividend reinvestment plans (DRIPs)
Plans that enable stockholders to use dividends received on the firm's stock to acquire additional shares—even fractional shares—at little or no transaction cost.

Today many firms offer **dividend reinvestment plans (DRIPs)**, which enable stockholders to use dividends received on the firm's stock to acquire additional shares—even fractional shares—at little or no transaction cost. Some companies even allow investors to make their *initial purchases* of the firm's stock directly from the company without going through a broker. With DRIPs, plan participants typically can acquire shares at about 5 percent below the prevailing market price. From its point of view, the firm can issue new shares to participants more economically, avoiding the underpricing and flotation costs that would accompany the public sale of new shares. Clearly, the existence of a DRIP may enhance the market appeal of a firm's shares.

STOCK PRICE REACTIONS TO CORPORATE PAYOUTS

What happens to the stock price when a firm pays a dividend or repurchases shares? In theory, the answers to those questions are straightforward. Take a dividend payment for example. Suppose a firm has $1 billion in assets, financed entirely by 10 million shares of common stock. Each share should be worth $100 ($1 billion ÷ 10,000,000 shares). Now suppose that the firm pays a $1 per share cash dividend, for a total dividend payout of $10 million. The assets of the firm fall to $990 million. Because shares outstanding remain at 10 million, each share should be worth $99. In other words, the stock price should fall by $1, exactly the amount of the dividend. The reduced share price simply reflects that cash formerly held by the firm is now in the hands of investors. To be precise, this reduction in share price should occur not when the dividend checks are mailed but rather when the stock begins trading ex dividend.

For share repurchases, the intuition is "you get what you pay for." In other words, if the firm buys back shares at the going market price, the reduction in cash is exactly offset by the reduction in the number of shares outstanding, so the market price of the stock should remain the same. Once again, consider the firm with

$1 billion in assets and 10 million shares outstanding worth $100 each. Let's say the firm decides to distribute $10 million in cash by repurchasing 100,000 shares of stock. After the repurchase is completed, the firm's assets will fall by $10 million to $990 million, but the shares outstanding will fall by 100,000 to 9,900,000. The new share price is therefore $990,000,000 ÷ 9,900,000, or $100, as before.

In practice, taxes and a variety of other market imperfections may cause the actual change in share price in response to a dividend payment or share repurchase to deviate from what we expect in theory. Furthermore, the stock price reaction to a cash payout may be different than the reaction to an announcement about an upcoming payout. For example, when a firm announces that it will increase its dividend, the share price usually rises on that news, even though the share price will fall when the dividend is actually paid. The next section discusses the impact of payout policy on the value of the firm in greater depth.

→ REVIEW QUESTIONS

14–4 Who are *holders of record?* When does a stock sell *ex dividend?*

14–5 What effect did the *Jobs and Growth Tax Relief Reconciliation Act of 2003* have on the taxation of corporate dividends? On corporate dividend payouts?

14–6 What benefit is available to participants in a *dividend reinvestment plan?* How might the firm benefit?

LG 2   ## 14.3 Relevance of Payout Policy

The financial literature has reported numerous theories and empirical findings concerning payout policy. Although this research provides some interesting insights about payout policy, capital budgeting and capital structure decisions are generally considered far more important than payout decisions. In other words, firms should not sacrifice good investment and financing decisions for a payout policy of questionable importance.

The most important question about payout policy is this: Does payout policy have a significant effect on the value of a firm? A number of theoretical and empirical answers to this question have been proposed, but as yet there is no widely accepted rule to help a firm find its "optimal" payout policy. Most of the theories that have been proposed to explain the consequences of payout policy have focused on dividends. From here on, we will use the terms *dividend policy* and *payout policy* interchangeably, meaning that we make no distinction between dividend payouts and share repurchases in terms of the theories that try to explain whether these policies have an effect on firm value.

RESIDUAL THEORY OF DIVIDENDS

residual theory of dividends
A school of thought that suggests that the dividend paid by a firm should be viewed as a *residual*—the amount left over after all acceptable investment opportunities have been undertaken.

The **residual theory of dividends** is a school of thought that suggests that the dividend paid by a firm should be viewed as a *residual*—the amount left over after all acceptable investment opportunities have been undertaken. Using this approach, the firm would treat the dividend decision in three steps, as follows:

Step 1 Determine its optimal level of capital expenditures, which would be the level that exploits all of a firm's positive NPV projects.

Step 2 Using the optimal capital structure proportions (see Chapter 13), estimate the total amount of equity financing needed to support the expenditures generated in Step 1.

Step 3 Because the cost of retained earnings, r_r, is less than the cost of new common stock, r_n, use retained earnings to meet the equity requirement determined in Step 2. If retained earnings are inadequate to meet this need, sell new common stock. If the available retained earnings are in excess of this need, distribute the surplus amount—the residual—as dividends.

According to this approach, as long as the firm's equity need exceeds the amount of retained earnings, no cash dividend is paid. The argument for this approach is that it is sound management to be certain that the company has the money it needs to compete effectively. This view of dividends suggests that the required return of investors, r_s, is *not* influenced by the firm's dividend policy—a premise that in turn implies that dividend policy is irrelevant in the sense that it does not affect firm value.

THE DIVIDEND IRRELEVANCE THEORY

dividend irrelevance theory
Miller and Modigliani's theory that in a perfect world, the firm's value is determined solely by the earning power and risk of its assets (investments) and that the manner in which it splits its earnings stream between dividends and internally retained (and reinvested) funds does not affect this value.

The residual theory of dividends implies that if the firm cannot invest its earnings to earn a return that exceeds the cost of capital it should distribute the earnings by paying dividends to stockholders. This approach suggests that dividends represent an earnings residual rather than an active decision variable that affects the firm's value. Such a view is consistent with the **dividend irrelevance theory** put forth by Merton H. Miller and Franco Modigliani (M and M).[3] They argue that the firm's value is determined solely by the earning power and risk of its assets (investments) and that the manner in which it splits its earnings stream between dividends and internally retained (and reinvested) funds does not affect this value. M and M's theory suggests that in a perfect world (certainty, no taxes, no transactions costs, and no other market imperfections), the value of the firm is unaffected by the distribution of dividends.

Of course, real markets do not satisfy the "perfect markets" assumptions of Modigliani and Miller's original theory. One market imperfection that may be important is taxation. Historically, dividends have usually been taxed at higher rates than capital gains. A firm that pays out its earnings as dividends may trigger higher tax liabilities for its investors than a firm that retains earnings. As a firm retains earnings, its share price should rise, and investors enjoy capital gains. Investors can defer paying taxes on these gains indefinitely simply by not selling their shares. Even if they do sell their shares, they may pay a relatively low tax rate on the capital gains. In contrast, when a firm pays dividends, investors receive cash immediately and pay taxes at the rates dictated by then-current tax laws.

Even though this discussion makes it seem that retaining profits rather than paying them out as dividends may be better for shareholders on an after-tax basis, Modigliani and Miller argue that this may not be the case. They observe that not all investors are subject to income taxation. Some institutional investors, such as pension funds, do not pay taxes on the dividends and capital gains that

In more depth

To read about *Why Dividends Might Not Matter*, go to www.myfinancelab.com

---

3. Merton H. Miller and Franco Modigliani, "Dividend Policy, Growth and the Valuation of Shares," *Journal of Business* 34 (October 1961), pp. 411–433.

they earn. For these investors, the payout policies of different firms have no impact on the taxes that investors have to pay. Therefore, Modigliani and Miller argue, there can be a **clientele effect** in which different types of investors are attracted to firms with different payout policies due to tax effects. Tax-exempt investors may invest more heavily in firms that pay dividends because they are not affected by the typically higher tax rates on dividends. Investors who would have to pay higher taxes on dividends may prefer to invest in firms that retain more earnings rather than paying dividends. If a firm changes its payout policy, the value of the firm will not change—what will change is the type of investor who holds the firm's shares. According to this argument, tax clienteles mean that payout policies cannot affect firm value, but they can affect the ownership base of the company.

In summary, M and M and other proponents of dividend irrelevance argue that, all else being equal, an investor's required return—and therefore the value of the firm—is unaffected by dividend policy. In other words, there is no "optimal" dividend policy for a particular firm.

ARGUMENTS FOR DIVIDEND RELEVANCE

Modigliani and Miller's assertion that dividend policy was irrelevant was a radical idea when it was first proposed. The prevailing wisdom at the time was that payout policy could improve the value of the firm and therefore was relevant. The key argument in support of **dividend relevance theory** is attributed to Myron J. Gordon and John Lintner,[4] who suggest that there is, in fact, a direct relationship between the firm's dividend policy and its market value. Fundamental to this proposition is their **bird-in-the-hand argument,** which suggests that investors see current dividends as less risky than future dividends or capital gains: "A bird in the hand is worth two in the bush." Gordon and Lintner argue that current dividend payments reduce investor uncertainty, causing investors to discount the firm's earnings at a lower rate and, all else being equal, to place a higher value on the firm's stock. Conversely, if dividends are reduced or are not paid, investor uncertainty will increase, raising the required return and lowering the stock's value.

Modigliani and Miller argued that the bird-in-the-hand theory was a fallacy. They said that investors who want immediate cash flow from a firm that did not pay dividends could simply sell off a portion of their shares. Remember, the stock price of a firm that retains earnings should rise over time as cash builds up inside the firm. By selling a few shares every quarter or every year, investors could, according to Modigliani and Miller, replicate the same cash flow stream that they would have received if the firm had paid dividends rather than retaining earnings.

Studies have shown that large changes in dividends do affect share price. Increases in dividends result in increased share price, and decreases in dividends result in decreased share price. One interpretation of this evidence is that it is not the dividends per se that matter but rather the **informational content** of dividends with respect to future earnings. In other words, investors view a change in dividends, up or down, as a *signal* that management expects future earnings to change in the same direction. Investors view an increase in dividends as a *positive*

clientele effect
The argument that different payout policies attract different types of investors but still do not change the value of the firm.

dividend relevance theory
The theory, advanced by Gordon and Lintner, that there is a direct relationship between a firm's dividend policy and its market value.

bird-in-the-hand argument
The belief, in support of *dividend relevance theory,* that investors see current dividends as less risky than future dividends or capital gains.

informational content
The information provided by the dividends of a firm with respect to future earnings, which causes owners to bid up or down the price of the firm's stock.

---

4. Myron J. Gordon, "Optimal Investment and Financing Policy," *Journal of Finance* 18 (May 1963), pp. 264–272; and John Lintner, "Dividends, Earnings, Leverage, Stock Prices, and the Supply of Capital to Corporations," *Review of Economics and Statistics* 44 (August 1962), pp. 243–269.

signal, and they bid up the share price. They view a decrease in dividends as a *negative signal* that causes investors to sell their shares, resulting in the share price decreasing.

Another argument in support of the idea that dividends can affect the value of the firm is the *agency cost theory*. Recall that agency costs are costs that arise due to the separation between the firm's owners and its managers. Managers sometimes have different interests than owners. Managers may want to retain earnings simply to increase the size of the firm's asset base. There is greater prestige and perhaps higher compensation associated with running a larger firm. Shareholders are aware of the temptations that managers face, and they worry that retained earnings may not be invested wisely. The *agency cost theory* says that a firm that commits to paying dividends is reassuring shareholders that managers will not waste their money. Given this reassurance, investors will pay higher prices for firms that promise regular dividend payments.

Although many other arguments related to dividend relevance have been put forward, *empirical studies have not provided evidence that conclusively settles the debate about whether and how payout policy affects firm value.* As we have already said, even if dividend policy really matters, it is almost certainly less important than other decisions that financial mangers make, such as the decision to invest in a large new project or the decision about what combination of debt and equity the firm should use to finance its operations. Still, most financial managers today, especially those running large corporations, believe that payout policy can affect the value of the firm.

→ REVIEW QUESTIONS

14–7 Does following the *residual theory of dividends* lead to a stable dividend? Is this approach consistent with dividend relevance?

14–8 Contrast the basic arguments about dividend policy advanced by Miller and Modigliani (M and M) and by Gordon and Lintner.

LG 3   ## 14.4 Factors Affecting Dividend Policy

dividend policy
The firm's plan of action to be followed whenever it makes a dividend decision.

The firm's **dividend policy** represents a plan of action to be followed whenever it makes a dividend decision. Firms develop policies consistent with their goals. Before we review some of the popular types of dividend policies, we discuss six factors that firms consider in establishing a dividend policy. They are legal constraints, contractual constraints, the firm's growth prospects, owner considerations, and market considerations.

LEGAL CONSTRAINTS

Most states prohibit corporations from paying out as cash dividends any portion of the firm's "legal capital," which is typically measured by the par value of common stock. Other states define legal capital to include not only the par value of the common stock but also any paid-in capital in excess of par. These *capital impairment restrictions* are generally established to provide a sufficient equity base to protect creditors' claims. An example will clarify the differing definitions of capital.

> **Example 14.4 ▶**

The stockholders' equity account of Miller Flour Company, a large grain processor, is presented in the following table.

Miller Flour Company Stockholders' Equity	
Common stock at par	$100,000
Paid-in capital in excess of par	200,000
Retained earnings	140,000
Total stockholders' equity	$440,000

In states where the firm's legal capital is defined as the par value of its common stock, the firm could pay out $340,000 ($200,000 + $140,000) in cash dividends without impairing its capital. In states where the firm's legal capital includes all paid-in capital, the firm could pay out only $140,000 in cash dividends.

Firms sometimes impose an earnings requirement limiting the amount of dividends. With this restriction, the firm cannot pay more in cash dividends than the sum of its most recent and past retained earnings. However, *the firm is not prohibited from paying more in dividends than its current earnings.*[5]

> **Example 14.5 ▶**

Assume that Miller Flour Company, from the preceding example, in the year just ended has $30,000 in earnings available for common stock dividends. As the table in Example 14.4 indicates, the firm has past retained earnings of $140,000. Thus it can legally pay dividends of up to $170,000.

If a firm has overdue liabilities or is legally insolvent or bankrupt, most states prohibit its payment of cash dividends. In addition, the Internal Revenue Service prohibits firms from accumulating earnings to reduce the owners' taxes. If the IRS can determine that a firm has accumulated an excess of earnings to allow owners to delay paying ordinary income taxes on dividends received, it may levy an **excess earnings accumulation tax** on any retained earnings above $250,000 for most businesses.

excess earnings accumulation tax
The tax the IRS levies on retained earnings above $250,000 for most businesses when it determines that the firm has accumulated an excess of earnings to allow owners to delay paying ordinary income taxes on dividends received.

During the recent financial crisis, a number of financial institutions received federal financial assistance. Those firms had to agree to restrictions on dividend payments to shareholders until they repaid the money that they received from the government. Bank of America, for example, had more than 30 years of consecutive dividend increases before accepting federal bailout money. As part of their bailout, Bank of America had to cut dividends to $0.01 per share.

_____

5. A firm that has an operating loss in the current period can still pay cash dividends as long as sufficient retained earnings against which to charge the dividend are available and, of course, as long as it has the cash with which to make the payments.

CONTRACTUAL CONSTRAINTS

Often the firm's ability to pay cash dividends is constrained by restrictive provisions in a loan agreement. Generally, these constraints prohibit the payment of cash dividends until the firm achieves a certain level of earnings, or they may limit dividends to a certain dollar amount or percentage of earnings. Constraints on dividends help to protect creditors from losses due to the firm's insolvency.

GROWTH PROSPECTS

The firm's financial requirements are directly related to how much it expects to grow and what assets it will need to acquire. It must evaluate its profitability and risk to develop insight into its ability to raise capital externally. In addition, the firm must determine the cost and speed with which it can obtain financing. Generally, a large, mature firm has adequate access to new capital, whereas a rapidly growing firm may not have sufficient funds available to support its acceptable projects. A growth firm is likely to have to depend heavily on internal financing through retained earnings, so it is likely to pay out only a very small percentage of its earnings as dividends. A more established firm is in a better position to pay out a large proportion of its earnings, particularly if it has ready sources of financing.

OWNER CONSIDERATIONS

The firm must establish a policy that has a favorable effect on the wealth of the *majority* of owners. One consideration is the *tax status of a firm's owners*. If a firm has a large percentage of wealthy stockholders who have sizable incomes, it may decide to pay out a *lower* percentage of its earnings to allow the owners to delay the payment of taxes until they sell the stock. Because cash dividends are taxed at the same rate as capital gains (as a result of the 2003 Tax Act), this strategy benefits owners through the tax deferral rather than as a result of a lower tax rate. Lower-income shareholders, however, who need dividend income, will prefer a *higher* payout of earnings.

A second consideration is the *owners' investment opportunities*. A firm should not retain funds for investment in projects yielding lower returns than the owners could obtain from external investments of equal risk. If it appears that the owners have better opportunities externally, the firm should pay out a higher percentage of its earnings. If the firm's investment opportunities are at least as good as similar-risk external investments, a lower payout is justifiable.

A final consideration is the *potential dilution of ownership*. If a firm pays out a high percentage of earnings, new equity capital will have to be raised with common stock. The result of a new stock issue may be dilution of both control and earnings for the existing owners. By paying out a low percentage of its earnings, the firm can minimize the possibility of such dilution.

catering theory
A theory that says firms cater to the preferences of investors, initiating or increasing dividend payments during periods in which high-dividend stocks are particularly appealing to investors.

MARKET CONSIDERATIONS

One of the more recent theories proposed to explain firms' payout decisions is called the *catering theory*. According to the **catering theory**, investors' demands for dividends fluctuate over time. For example, during an economic boom accompanied by a rising stock market, investors may be more attracted to stocks that offer prospects of large capital gains. When the economy is in recession and the stock market is falling, investors may prefer the security of a dividend. The catering theory suggests that firms are more likely to initiate dividend payments or to increase existing payouts when investors exhibit a strong preference for dividends. Firms *cater to* the preferences of investors.

→ REVIEW QUESTION

14–9 What five factors do firms consider in establishing *dividend policy?* Briefly describe each of them.

LG 4 14.5 Types of Dividend Policies

The firm's dividend policy must be formulated with two basic objectives in mind: providing for sufficient financing and maximizing the wealth of the firm's owners. Three different dividend policies are described in the following sections. A particular firm's cash dividend policy may incorporate elements of each.

dividend payout ratio
Indicates the percentage of each dollar earned that a firm distributes to the owners in the form of cash. It is calculated by dividing the firm's cash dividend per share by its earnings per share.

constant-payout-ratio dividend policy
A dividend policy based on the payment of a certain percentage of earnings to owners in each dividend period.

CONSTANT-PAYOUT-RATIO DIVIDEND POLICY

One type of dividend policy involves use of a constant payout ratio. The **dividend payout ratio** indicates the percentage of each dollar earned that the firm distributes to the owners in the form of cash. It is calculated by dividing the firm's cash dividend per share by its earnings per share. With a **constant-payout-ratio dividend policy,** the firm establishes that a certain percentage of earnings is paid to owners in each dividend period.

The problem with this policy is that if the firm's earnings drop or if a loss occurs in a given period, the dividends may be low or even nonexistent. Because dividends are often considered an indicator of the firm's future condition and status, the firm's stock price may be adversely affected.

Example 14.6 ► Peachtree Industries, a miner of potassium, has a policy of paying out 40% of earnings in cash dividends. In periods when a loss occurs, the firm's policy is to pay no cash dividends. Data on Peachtree's earnings, dividends, and average stock prices for the past 6 years follow.

Year	Earnings/share	Dividends/share	Average price/share
2012	−$0.50	$0.00	$42.00
2011	3.00	1.20	52.00
2010	1.75	0.70	48.00
2009	−1.50	0.00	38.00
2008	2.00	0.80	46.00
2007	4.50	1.80	50.00

Dividends increased in 2010 and in 2011 but decreased in the other years. In years of decreasing dividends, the firm's stock price dropped; when dividends increased, the price of the stock increased. Peachtree's sporadic dividend payments appear to make its owners uncertain about the returns they can expect.

REGULAR DIVIDEND POLICY

regular dividend policy
A dividend policy based on the payment of a fixed-dollar dividend in each period.

The **regular dividend policy** is based on the payment of a fixed-dollar dividend in each period. Often, firms that use this policy increase the regular dividend once a *sustainable* increase in earnings has occurred. Under this policy, dividends are almost never decreased.

Example 14.7 ▶ The dividend policy of Woodward Laboratories, a producer of a popular artificial sweetener, is to pay annual dividends of $1.00 per share until per-share earnings have exceeded $4.00 for 3 consecutive years. At that point, the annual dividend is raised to $1.50 per share, and a new earnings plateau is established. The firm does not anticipate decreasing its dividend unless its liquidity is in jeopardy. Data for Woodward's earnings, dividends, and average stock prices for the past 12 years follow.

Year	Earnings/share	Dividends/share	Average price/share
2012	$4.50	$1.50	$47.50
2011	3.90	1.50	46.50
2010	4.60	1.50	45.00
2009	4.20	1.00	43.00
2008	5.00	1.00	42.00
2007	2.00	1.00	38.50
2006	6.00	1.00	38.00
2005	3.00	1.00	36.00
2004	0.75	1.00	33.00
2003	0.50	1.00	33.00
2002	2.70	1.00	33.50
2001	2.85	1.00	35.00

Whatever the level of earnings, Woodward Laboratories paid dividends of $1.00 per share through 2009. In 2010, the dividend increased to $1.50 per share because earnings in excess of $4.00 per share had been achieved for 3 years. In 2010, the firm also had to establish a new earnings plateau for further dividend increases. Woodward Laboratories' average price per share exhibited a stable, increasing behavior in spite of a somewhat volatile pattern of earnings.

target dividend-payout ratio
A dividend policy under which the firm attempts to pay out a certain *percentage* of earnings as a stated dollar dividend and adjusts that dividend toward a target payout as proven earnings increases occur.

Often a regular dividend policy is built around a **target dividend-payout ratio.** Under this policy, the firm attempts to pay out a certain *percentage* of earnings, but rather than let dividends fluctuate it pays a stated dollar dividend and adjusts that dividend toward the target payout as proven earnings increases occur. For instance, Woodward Laboratories appears to have a target payout ratio of around 35 percent. The payout was about 35 percent ($1.00 ÷ $2.85) when the dividend policy was set in 2001, and, when the dividend was raised to $1.50 in 2010, the payout ratio was about 33 percent ($1.50 ÷ $4.60).

LOW-REGULAR-AND-EXTRA DIVIDEND POLICY

low-regular-and-extra dividend policy
A dividend policy based on paying a low regular dividend, supplemented by an additional ("extra") dividend when earnings are higher than normal in a given period.

extra dividend
An additional dividend optionally paid by the firm when earnings are higher than normal in a given period.

Some firms establish a **low-regular-and-extra dividend policy,** paying a low regular dividend, supplemented by an additional ("extra") dividend when earnings are higher than normal in a given period. By calling the additional dividend an **extra dividend,** the firm avoids setting expectations that the dividend increase will be permanent. This policy is especially common among companies that experience cyclical shifts in earnings.

By establishing a low regular dividend that is paid each period, the firm gives investors the stable income necessary to build confidence in the firm, and the extra dividend permits them to share in the earnings from an especially good period. Firms using this policy must raise the level of the regular dividend once proven increases in earnings have been achieved. The extra dividend should not be a regular event; otherwise, it becomes meaningless. The use of a target dividend-payout ratio in establishing the regular dividend level is advisable.

→ REVIEW QUESTION

14–10 Describe a constant-payout-ratio dividend policy, a regular dividend policy, and a low-regular-and-extra dividend policy. What are the effects of these policies?

LG 5 LG 6 **14.6** Other Forms of Dividends

Two common transactions that bear some resemblance to cash dividends are stock dividends and stock splits. Although the stock dividends and stock splits are closely related to each other, their economic effects are quite different than those of cash dividends or share repurchases.

STOCK DIVIDENDS

stock dividend
The payment, to existing owners, of a dividend in the form of stock.

A **stock dividend** is the payment, to existing owners, of a dividend in the form of stock. Often firms pay stock dividends as a replacement for or a supplement to cash dividends. In a stock dividend, investors simply receive additional shares in proportion to the shares they already own. No cash is distributed, and no real value is transferred from the firm to investors. Instead, because the number of outstanding shares increases, the stock price declines roughly in line with the amount of the stock dividend.

Accounting Aspects

In an accounting sense, the payment of a stock dividend is a shifting of funds between stockholders' equity accounts rather than an outflow of funds. When a firm declares a stock dividend, the procedures for announcement and distribution

small (ordinary) stock dividend
A stock dividend representing less than 20 percent to 25 percent of the common stock outstanding when the dividend is declared.

are the same as those described earlier for a cash dividend. The accounting entries associated with the payment of a stock dividend vary depending on its size. A **small (ordinary) stock dividend** is a stock dividend that represents less than 20 percent to 25 percent of the common stock outstanding when the dividend is declared. Small stock dividends are most common.

Example 14.8 ▶ The current stockholders' equity on the balance sheet of Garrison Corporation, a distributor of prefabricated cabinets, is as shown in the following accounts.

Preferred stock	$ 300,000
Common stock (100,000 shares at $4 par)	400,000
Paid-in capital in excess of par	600,000
Retained earnings	700,000
Total stockholders' equity	$2,000,000

Garrison, which has 100,000 shares of common stock outstanding, declares a 10% stock dividend when the market price of its stock is $15 per share. Because 10,000 new shares (10% of 100,000) are issued at the prevailing market price of $15 per share, $150,000 ($15 per share × 10,000 shares) is shifted from retained earnings to the common stock and paid-in capital accounts. A total of $40,000 ($4 par × 10,000 shares) is added to common stock, and the remaining $110,000 [($15 − $4) × 10,000 shares] is added to the paid-in capital in excess of par. The resulting account balances are as follows:

Preferred stock	$ 300,000
Common stock (110,000 shares at $4 par)	440,000
Paid-in capital in excess of par	710,000
Retained earnings	550,000
Total stockholders' equity	$2,000,000

The firm's total stockholders' equity has not changed; funds have merely been *shifted* among stockholders' equity accounts.

Shareholder's Viewpoint

The shareholder receiving a stock dividend typically receives nothing of value. After the dividend is paid, the per-share value of the shareholder's stock decreases in proportion to the dividend in such a way that the market value of his or her total holdings in the firm remains unchanged. Therefore stock dividends are usually nontaxable. The shareholder's proportion of ownership in the firm also remains the same, and *as long as the firm's earnings remain unchanged,* so does his or her share of total earnings. (However, if the firm's earnings and cash dividends increase when the stock dividend is issued, an increase in share value is likely to result.)

Example 14.9 ▶ Ms. X owned 10,000 shares of Garrison Corporation's stock. The company's most recent earnings were $220,000, and earnings are not expected to change in the near future. Before the stock dividend, Ms. X owned 10% (10,000 shares ÷ 100,000 shares) of the firm's stock, which was selling for $15 per share. Earnings per share were $2.20 ($220,000 ÷ 100,000 shares). Because Ms. X owned 10,000 shares, her earnings were $22,000 ($2.20 per share × 10,000 shares). After receiving the 10% stock dividend, Ms. X has 11,000 shares, which again is 10% of the ownership (11,000 shares ÷ 110,000 shares). The market price of the stock can be expected to drop to $13.64 per share [$15 × (1.00 ÷ 1.10)], which means that the market value of Ms. X's holdings is $150,000 (11,000 shares × $13.64 per share). This is the same as the initial value of her holdings (10,000 shares × $15 per share). The future earnings per share drops to $2 ($220,000 ÷ 110,000 shares) because the same $220,000 in earnings must now be divided among 110,000 shares. Because Ms. X still owns 10% of the stock, her share of total earnings is still $22,000 ($2 per share × 11,000 shares).

In summary, if the firm's earnings remain constant and total cash dividends do not increase, a stock dividend results in a lower per-share market value for the firm's stock.

The Company's Viewpoint

Stock dividends are more costly to issue than cash dividends, but certain advantages may outweigh these costs. Firms find the stock dividend to be a way to give owners something without having to use cash. Generally, when a firm needs to preserve cash to finance rapid growth, it uses a stock dividend. When the stockholders recognize that the firm is reinvesting the cash flow so as to maximize future earnings, the market value of the firm should at least remain unchanged. However, if the stock dividend is paid so as to retain cash to satisfy past-due bills, a decline in market value may result.

STOCK SPLITS

stock split
A method commonly used to lower the market price of a firm's stock by increasing the number of shares belonging to each shareholder.

Although not a type of dividend, *stock splits* have an effect on a firm's share price similar to that of stock dividends. A **stock split** is a method commonly used to lower the market price of a firm's stock by increasing the number of shares belonging to each shareholder. In a 2-for-1 split, for example, two new shares are exchanged for each old share, with each new share being worth half the value of each old share. A stock split has no effect on the firm's capital structure and is usually nontaxable.

Quite often, a firm believes that its stock is priced too high and that lowering the market price will enhance trading activity. Stock splits are often made prior to issuing additional stock to enhance that stock's marketability and stimulate market activity. It is not unusual for a stock split to cause a slight increase in the market value of the stock, attributable to its informational content and to the fact that *total* dividends paid commonly increase slightly after a split.[6]

---

6. Eugene F. Fama, Lawrence Fisher, Michael C. Jensen, and Richard Roll, "The Adjustment of Stock Prices to New Information," *International Economic Review* 10 (February 1969), pp. 1–21, found that the stock price increases before the split announcement and that the increase in stock price is maintained if dividends per share are increased but is lost if dividends per share are *not* increased, following the split.

Example 14.10 ▶ Delphi Company, a forest products concern, had 200,000 shares of $2-par-value common stock and no preferred stock outstanding. Because the stock is selling at a high market price, the firm has declared a 2-for-1 stock split. The total before- and after-split stockholders' equity is shown in the following table.

Before split		After 2-for-1 split	
Common stock		Common stock	
(200,000 shares at $2 par)	$ 400,000	(400,000 shares at $1 par)	$ 400,000
Paid-in capital in excess		Paid-in-capital in excess	
of par	4,000,000	of par	4,000,000
Retained earnings	2,000,000	Retained earnings	2,000,000
Total stockholders' equity	$6,400,000	Total stockholders' equity	$6,400,000

The insignificant effect of the stock split on the firm's books is obvious.

reverse stock split
A method used to raise the market price of a firm's stock by exchanging a certain number of outstanding shares for one new share.

Stock can be split in any way desired. Sometimes a **reverse stock split** is made: The firm exchanges a certain number of outstanding shares for one new share. For example, in a 1-for-3 split, one new share is exchanged for three old shares. In a reverse stock split, the firm's stock price rises due to the reduction in shares outstanding. Firms may conduct a reverse split if their stock price is getting so low that the exchange where the stock trades threatens to delist the stock. For example, the New York Stock Exchange requires that the average closing price of a listed security must be no less than $1 over any consecutive 30-day trading period. In June of 2010, the video chain Blockbuster asked shareholders to approve a reverse stock split to prevent the NYSE from delisting Blockbuster's stock. Shareholders didn't approve the measure, and the NYSE delisted Blockbuster stock the following month.

Personal Finance Example 14.11 ▶ Shakira Washington, a single investor in the 25% federal income tax bracket, owns 260 shares of Advanced Technology, Inc., common stock. She originally bought the stock 2 years ago at its initial public offering (IPO) price of $9 per share. The stock of this fast-growing technology company is currently trading for $60 per share, so the current value of her Advanced Technology stock is $15,600 (260 shares × $60 per share). Because the firm's board believes that the stock would trade more actively in the $20 to $30 price range, it just announced a 3-for-1 stock split. Shakira wishes to determine the impact of the stock split on her holdings and taxes.

Because the stock will split 3 for 1, after the split Shakira will own 780 shares (3 × 260 shares). She should expect the market price of the stock to drop to $20 (1/3 × $60) immediately after the split; the value of her after-split holding will be $15,600 (780 shares × $20 per share). Because the $15,600 value of her after-split holdings in Advanced Technology stock exactly equals the before-split value of $15,600, Shakira has experienced neither a gain nor a loss on the stock as a result of the 3-for-1 split. Even if there were a gain or loss attributable to the split, Shakira would not have any tax liability unless she actually sold the stock and realized that (or any other) gain or loss.

→ **REVIEW QUESTIONS**

14–11 Why do firms issue *stock dividends?* Comment on the following statement: "I have a stock that promises to pay a 20 percent stock dividend every year, and therefore it guarantees that I will break even in 5 years."

14–12 Compare a *stock split* with a *stock dividend.*

Summary

FOCUS ON VALUE

Payout policy refers to the cash flows that a firm distributes to its common stockholders. A share of common stock gives its owner the right to receive all future dividends. The present value of all those future dividends expected over a firm's assumed infinite life determines the firm's stock value.

Corporate payouts not only represent cash flows to shareholders but also contain useful information about the firm's current and future performance. Such information affects the shareholders' perception of the firm's risk. A firm can also pay stock dividends, initiate stock splits, or repurchase stock. All of these dividend-related actions can affect the firm's risk, return, and value as a result of their cash flows and informational content.

Although the theory of relevance of dividends is still evolving, the behavior of most firms and stockholders suggests that dividend policy affects share prices. Therefore financial managers try to develop and implement dividend policy that is consistent with the firm's goal of **maximizing stock price.**

REVIEW OF LEARNING GOALS

LG 1 **Understand cash payout procedures, their tax treatment, and the role of dividend reinvestment plans.** The board of directors makes the cash payout decision and, for dividends, establishes the record and payment dates. As a result of a tax-law change in 2003, most taxpayers pay taxes on corporate dividends at a maximum rate of 5 percent to 15 percent, depending on the taxpayer's tax bracket. Some firms offer dividend reinvestment plans that allow stockholders to acquire shares in lieu of cash dividends.

LG 2 **Describe the residual theory of dividends and the key arguments with regard to dividend irrelevance and relevance.** The residual theory suggests that dividends should be viewed as the earnings left after all acceptable investment opportunities have been undertaken. Miller and Modigliani argue in favor of dividend irrelevance, using a perfect world in which market imperfections such as transaction costs and taxes do not exist. Gordon and Lintner advance the theory of dividend relevance, basing their argument on the uncertainty-reducing effect of dividends, supported by their bird-in-the-hand argument. Empirical studies fail to provide clear support of dividend relevance. Even so, the actions of financial managers and stockholders tend to support the belief that dividend policy does affect stock value.

LG 3 **Discuss the key factors involved in establishing a dividend policy.** A firm's dividend policy should provide for sufficient financing and maximize stockholders' wealth. Dividend policy is affected by legal and contractual constraints, by growth prospects, and by owner and market considerations. Legal constraints prohibit corporations from paying out as cash dividends any portion of the firm's "legal capital." Nor can firms with overdue liabilities and legally insolvent or bankrupt firms pay cash dividends. Contractual constraints result from restrictive provisions in the firm's loan agreements. Growth prospects affect the relative importance of retaining earnings rather than paying them out in dividends. The tax status of owners, the owners' investment opportunities, and the potential dilution of ownership are important owner considerations. Finally, market considerations are related to the stockholders' preference for the continuous payment of fixed or increasing streams of dividends.

LG 4   **Review and evaluate the three basic types of dividend policies.** With a constant-payout-ratio dividend policy, the firm pays a fixed percentage of earnings to the owners each period; dividends move up and down with earnings, and no dividend is paid when a loss occurs. Under a regular dividend policy, the firm pays a fixed-dollar dividend each period; it increases the amount of dividends only after a proven increase in earnings. The low-regular-and-extra dividend policy is similar to the regular dividend policy, except that it pays an extra dividend when the firm's earnings are higher than normal.

LG 5   **Evaluate stock dividends from accounting, shareholder, and company points of view.** Firms may pay stock dividends as a replacement for or supplement to cash dividends. The payment of stock dividends involves a shifting of funds between capital accounts rather than an outflow of funds. Stock dividends do not change the market value of stockholders' holdings, proportion of ownership, or share of total earnings. Therefore, stock dividends are usually nontaxable. However, stock dividends may satisfy owners and enable the firm to preserve its market value without having to use cash.

LG 6   **Explain stock splits and the firm's motivation for undertaking them.** Stock splits are used to enhance trading activity of a firm's shares by lowering or raising their market price. A stock split merely involves accounting adjustments; it has no effect on the firm's cash or on its capital structure and is usually nontaxable.

Firms can repurchase stock in lieu of paying a cash dividend, to retire outstanding shares. Reducing the number of outstanding shares increases earnings per share and the market price per share. Stock repurchases also defer the tax payments of stockholders.

Opener-in-Review

Over the period of September 2009 to September 2010, Global's liabilities and equity dropped. At the end of September 2009, Global's liabilities dropped by $885.5 million from $2.478 million, and as of September 30, 2009, equity dropped by $491 million from $977 million. Over this period, which decline was faster, debt or equity? What does that mean? Do these figures send a good or bad signal to the market? Why?

Self-Test Problem   (Solutions in Appendix)

LG 6   **ST14–1**   **Stock repurchase**   The Off-Shore Steel Company has earnings available for common stockholders of $2 million and has 500,000 shares of common stock outstanding at $60 per share. The firm is currently contemplating the payment of $2 per share in cash dividends.

a. Calculate the firm's current *earnings per share (EPS)* and *price/earnings (P/E) ratio*.

b. If the firm can repurchase stock at $62 per share, how many shares can be purchased in lieu of making the proposed cash dividend payment?

c. How much will the EPS be after the proposed repurchase? Why?

d. If the stock sells at the old P/E ratio, what will the market price be after repurchase?

e. Compare and contrast the earnings per share before and after the proposed repurchase.

f. Compare and contrast the stockholders' position under the dividend and repurchase alternatives.

Warm-Up Exercises   All problems are available in [myfinancelab].

LG 1   **E14–1**   Stephanie's Cafes, Inc., has declared a dividend of $1.30 per share for shareholders of record on Tuesday, May 2. The firm has 200,000 shares outstanding and will pay the dividend on May 24. How much cash will be needed to pay the dividend? When will the stock begin selling *ex dividend?*

LG 2   **E14–2**   Chancellor Industries has retained earnings available of $1.2 million. The firm plans to make two investments that require financing of $950,000 and $1.75 million, respectively. Chancellor uses a target capital structure with 60% debt and 40% equity. Apply the *residual theory* to determine what dividends, if any, can be paid out, and calculate the resulting *dividend payout ratio*.

LG 3   **E14–3**   Ashkenazi Companies has the following stockholders' equity account:

Common stock (350,000 shares at $3 par)	$1,050,000
Paid-in capital in excess of par	2,500,000
Retained earnings	750,000
Total stockholders' equity	$4,300,000

Assuming that state laws define legal capital solely as the par value of common stock, how much of a *per-share dividend* can Ashkenazi pay? If legal capital were more broadly defined to include all paid-in capital, how much of a *per-share dividend* could Ashkenazi pay?

LG 4   **E14–4**   The board of Kopi Industries is considering a new dividend policy that would set dividends at 60% of earnings. The recent past has witnessed earnings per share (EPS) and dividends paid per share as follows:

Year	EPS	Dividend/share
2009	$1.75	$0.95
2010	1.95	1.20
2011	2.05	1.25
2012	2.25	1.30

Based on Kopi's historical dividend payout ratio, discuss whether a *constant payout ratio* of 60% would benefit shareholders.

LG 5 **E14–5** The current stockholders' equity account for Hilo Farms is as follows:

Common stock (50,000 shares at $3 par)	$150,000
Paid-in capital in excess of par	250,000
Retained earnings	450,000
Total stockholders' equity	$850,000

Hilo has announced plans to issue an additional 5,000 shares of common stock as part of its stock dividend plan. The current market price of Hilo's common stock is $20 per share. Show how the proposed *stock dividend* would affect the stockholder's equity account.

Problems

All problems are available in myfinancelab .

LG 1 **P14–1** **Dividend payment procedures** At the quarterly dividend meeting, Wood Shoes declared a cash dividend of $1.10 per share for holders of record on Monday, July 10. The firm has 300,000 shares of common stock outstanding and has set a payment date of July 31. Prior to the dividend declaration, the firm's key accounts were as follows:

Cash	$500,000	Dividends payable	$	0
		Retained earnings	2,500,000	

a. Show the entries after the meeting adjourned.
b. When is the *ex dividend* date?
c. What values would the key accounts have after the July 31 payment date?
d. What effect, if any, will the dividend have on the firm's total assets?
e. Ignoring general market fluctuations, what effect, if any, will the dividend have on the firm's stock price on the ex dividend date?

Personal Finance Problem

LG 1 **P14–2** **Dividend payment** Kathy Snow wishes to purchase shares of Countdown Computing, Inc. The company's board of directors has declared a cash dividend of $0.80 to be paid to holders of record on Wednesday, May 12.
a. What is the last day that Kathy can purchase the stock (trade date) and still receive the dividend?
b. What day does this stock begin trading ex dividend?

c. What change, if any, would you expect in the price per share when the stock begins trading on the ex dividend day?

d. If Kathy held the stock for less than one quarter and then sold it for $39 per share, would she achieve a higher investment return by (1) buying the stock *prior to* the ex dividend date at $35 per share and collecting the $0.80 dividend, or (2) buying it *on* the ex dividend date at $34.20 per share but not receiving the dividend?

LG 2 **P14–3** **Residual dividend policy** As president of Young's of California, a large clothing chain, you have just received a letter from a major stockholder. The stockholder asks about the company's dividend policy. In fact, the stockholder has asked you to estimate the amount of the dividend that you are likely to pay next year. You have not yet collected all the information about the expected dividend payment, but you do know the following:

(1) The company follows a residual dividend policy.

(2) The total capital budget for next year is likely to be one of three amounts, depending on the results of capital budgeting studies that are currently under way. The capital expenditure amounts are $2 million, $3 million, and $4 million.

(3) The forecasted level of potential retained earnings next year is $2 million.

(4) The target or optimal capital structure is a debt ratio of 40%.

You have decided to respond by sending the stockholder the best information available to you.

a. Describe a *residual dividend policy.*

b. Compute the amount of the dividend (or the amount of new common stock needed) and the dividend payout ratio for each of the three capital expenditure amounts.

c. Compare, contrast, and discuss the amount of dividends (calculated in part **b**) associated with each of the three capital expenditure amounts.

LG 3 **P14–4** **Dividend constraints** The Howe Company's stockholders' equity account follows:

Common stock (400,000 shares at $4 par)	$1,600,000
Paid-in capital in excess of par	1,000,000
Retained earnings	1,900,000
Total stockholders' equity	$4,500,000

The earnings available for common stockholders from this period's operations are $100,000, which have been included as part of the $1.9 million retained earnings.

a. What is the *maximum dividend per share* that the firm can pay? (Assume that legal capital includes *all* paid-in capital.)

b. If the firm has $160,000 in cash, what is the largest per-share dividend it can pay without borrowing?

c. Indicate the accounts and changes, if any, that will result if the firm pays the dividends indicated in parts **a** and **b**.

d. Indicate the effects of an $80,000 cash dividend on stockholders' equity.

LG 3 **P14–5** **Dividend constraints** A firm has $800,000 in paid-in capital, retained earnings of $40,000 (including the current year's earnings), and 25,000 shares of common stock outstanding. In the current year, it has $29,000 of earnings available for the common stockholders.

a. What is the most the firm can pay in cash dividends to each common stock-holder? (Assume that legal capital includes *all* paid-in capital.)

b. What effect would a cash dividend of $0.80 per share have on the firm's balance sheet entries?

c. If the firm cannot raise any new funds from external sources, what do you consider the key constraint with respect to the magnitude of the firm's dividend payments? Why?

LG 4   **P14–6**   **Low-regular-and-extra dividend policy**   Bennett Farm Equipment Sales, Inc., is in a highly cyclic business. Although the firm has a target payout ratio of 25%, its board realizes that strict adherence to that ratio would result in a fluctuating dividend and create uncertainty for the firm's stockholders. Therefore, the firm has declared a regular dividend of $0.50 per share per year with extra cash dividends to be paid when earnings justify them. Earnings per share for the last several years are as follows:

Year	EPS	Year	EPS
2012	$3.00	2009	$2.80
2011	2.40	2008	2.15
2010	2.20	2007	1.97

a. Calculate the *payout ratio* for each year on the basis of the regular $0.50 dividend and the cited EPS.

b. Calculate the difference between the regular $0.50 dividend and a 25% payout for each year.

c. Bennett has established a policy of paying an extra dividend of $0.25 only when the difference between the regular dividend and a 25% payout amounts to $1.00 or more. Show the regular and extra dividends in those years when an extra dividend would be paid. What would be done with the "extra" earnings that are not paid out?

d. The firm expects that future earnings per share will continue to cycle but will remain above $2.20 per share in most years. What factors should be considered in making a revision to the amount paid as a regular dividend? If the firm revises the regular dividend, what new amount should it pay?

LG 4   **P14–7**   **Alternative dividend policies**   Over the last 10 years, a firm has had the earnings per share shown in the following table.

Year	Earnings per share	Year	Earnings per share
2012	$4.00	2007	$2.40
2011	3.80	2006	1.20
2010	3.20	2005	1.80
2009	2.80	2004	−0.50
2008	3.20	2003	0.25

a. If the firm's dividend policy were based on a *constant payout ratio* of 40% for all years with positive earnings and 0% otherwise, what would be the annual dividend for each year?

b. If the firm had a dividend payout of $1.00 per share, increasing by $0.10 per share whenever the dividend payout fell below 50% for two consecutive years, what annual dividend would the firm pay each year?

c. If the firm's policy were to pay $0.50 per share each period except when earnings per share exceed $3.00, when an extra dividend equal to 80% of earnings beyond $3.00 would be paid, what annual dividend would the firm pay each year?

d. Discuss the pros and cons of each dividend policy described in parts **a** through **c**.

LG 4 **P14–8** **Alternative dividend policies**   Given the earnings per share over the period 2005–2012 shown in the following table, determine the annual dividend per share under each of the policies set forth in parts **a** through **d**.

Year	Earnings per share
2012	$1.40
2011	1.56
2010	1.20
2009	−0.85
2008	1.05
2007	0.60
2006	1.00
2005	0.44

a. Pay out 50% of earnings in all years with positive earnings.

b. Pay $0.50 per share and increase to $0.60 per share whenever earnings per share rise above $0.90 per share for two consecutive years.

c. Pay $0.50 per share except when earnings exceed $1.00 per share, in which case pay an extra dividend of 60% of earnings above $1.00 per share.

d. Combine the policies described in parts **b** and **c**. When the dividend is raised (in part **b**), raise the excess dividend base (in part **c**) from $1.00 to $1.10 per share.

e. Compare and contrast each of the dividend policies described in parts **a** through **d**.

LG 5 **P14–9** **Stock dividend—Firm**   Columbia Paper has the following stockholders' equity account. The firm's common stock has a current market price of $30 per share.

Preferred stock	$100,000
Common stock (10,000 shares at $2 par)	20,000
Paid-in capital in excess of par	280,000
Retained earnings	100,000
Total stockholders' equity	$500,000

a. Show the effects on Columbia of a 5% stock dividend.

b. Show the effects of (1) a 10% and (2) a 20% stock dividend.

c. In light of your answers to parts **a** and **b**, discuss the effects of stock dividends on stockholders' equity.

LG 5   **P14–10**   **Cash versus stock dividend**   Milwaukee Tool has the following stockholders' equity account. The firm's common stock currently sells for $4 per share.

Preferred stock	$ 100,000
Common stock (400,000 shares at $1 par)	400,000
Paid-in capital in excess of par	200,000
Retained earnings	320,000
Total stockholders' equity	$1,020,000

a. Show the effects on the firm of a *cash* dividend of $0.01, $0.05, $0.10, and $0.20 per share.
b. Show the effects on the firm of a 1%, 5%, 10%, and 20% *stock* dividend.
c. Compare the effects in parts **a** and **b**. What are the significant differences between the two methods of paying dividends?

Personal Finance Problem

LG 5   **P14–11**   **Stock dividend—Investor**   Sarah Warren currently holds 400 shares of Nutri-Foods. The firm has 40,000 shares outstanding. The firm most recently had earnings available for common stockholders of $80,000, and its stock has been selling for $22 per share. The firm intends to retain its earnings and pay a 10% stock dividend.
a. How much does the firm currently earn per share?
b. What proportion of the firm does Warren currently own?
c. What proportion of the firm will Warren own after the stock dividend? Explain your answer.
d. At what market price would you expect the stock to sell after the stock dividend?
e. Discuss what effect, if any, the payment of stock dividends will have on Warren's share of the ownership and earnings of Nutri-Foods.

Personal Finance Problem

LG 5   **P14–12**   **Stock dividend—Investor**   Security Data Company has outstanding 50,000 shares of common stock currently selling at $40 per share. The firm most recently had earnings available for common stockholders of $120,000, but it has decided to retain these funds and is considering either a 5% or a 10% stock dividend in lieu of a cash dividend.
a. Determine the firm's current *earnings per share*.
b. If Sam Waller currently owns 500 shares of the firm's stock, determine his proportion of ownership currently and under each of the proposed stock dividend plans. Explain your findings.
c. Calculate and explain the market price per share under each of the stock dividend plans.
d. For each of the proposed stock dividends, calculate the earnings per share after payment of the stock dividend.
e. What is the value of Waller's holdings under each of the plans? Explain.
f. Should Waller have any preference with respect to the proposed stock dividends? Why or why not?

LG 6   **P14–13**   **Stock split—Firm**   Growth Industries' current stockholders' equity account is as follows:

Preferred stock	$ 400,000
Common stock (600,000 shares at $3 par)	1,800,000
Paid-in capital in excess of par	200,000
Retained earnings	800,000
Total stockholders' equity	$3,200,000

a. Indicate the change, if any, expected if the firm declares a 2-for-1 stock split.
b. Indicate the change, if any, expected if the firm declares a 1-for-1$\frac{1}{2}$ *reverse* stock split.
c. Indicate the change, if any, expected if the firm declares a 3-for-1 stock split.
d. Indicate the change, if any, expected if the firm declares a 6-for-1 stock split.
e. Indicate the change, if any, expected if the firm declares a 1-for-4 *reverse* stock split.

Personal Finance Problem

LG 6   **P14–14**   **Stock splits**   Nathan Detroit owns 400 shares of the food company General Mills, Inc., which he purchased during the recession in January 2009 for $35 per share. General Mills is regarded as a relatively safe company because it provides a basic product that consumers need in good and bad economic times. Nathan read in the *Wall Street Journal* that the company's board of directors had voted to split the stock 2-for-1. In June 2010, just before the stock split, General Mills shares were trading for $75.14.

  Answer the following questions about the impact of the stock split on his holdings and taxes. Nathan is in the 28% federal income tax bracket.

a. How many shares of General Mills will Nathan own after the stock split?
b. Immediately after the split, what do you expect the value of General Mills to be?
c. Compare the total value of Nathan's stock holdings before and after the split, given that the price of General Mills stock immediately after the split was $37.50. What do you find?
d. Does Nathan experience a gain or loss on the stock as a result of the 2-for-1 split?
e. What is Nathan's tax liability from the event?

LG 5   **LG 6**   **P14–15**   **Stock split versus stock dividend—Firm**   Mammoth Corporation is considering a 3-for-2 stock split. It currently has the stockholders' equity position shown. The current stock price is $120 per share. The most recent period's earnings available for common stock are included in retained earnings.

Preferred stock	$ 1,000,000
Common stock (100,000 shares at $3 par)	300,000
Paid-in capital in excess of par	1,700,000
Retained earnings	10,000,000
Total stockholders' equity	$13,000,000

a. What effects on Mammoth would result from the *stock split?*
b. What change in stock price would you expect to result from the stock split?
c. What is the maximum cash dividend per share that the firm could pay on common stock before and after the stock split? (Assume that legal capital includes *all* paid-in capital.)

    d. Contrast your answers to parts **a** through **c** with the circumstances surrounding a 50% *stock dividend*.

    e. Explain the differences between stock splits and stock dividends.

LG 5 **LG 6** **P14–16** **Stock dividend versus stock split—Firm**   The board of Wicker Home Health Care, Inc., is exploring ways to expand the number of shares outstanding in an effort to reduce the market price per share to a level that the firm considers more appealing to investors. The options under consideration are a 20% stock dividend and, alternatively, a 5-for-4 stock split. At the present time, the firm's equity account and other per-share information are as follows:

Preferred stock	$ 0
Common stock (100,000 shares at $1 par)	100,000
Paid-in capital in excess of par	900,000
Retained earnings	700,000
Total stockholders' equity	$1,700,000
Price per share	$30.00
Earnings per share	$3.60
Dividend per share	$1.08

    a. Show the effect on the equity accounts and per-share data of a 20% *stock dividend*.

    b. Show the effect on the equity accounts and per-share data of a 5-for-4 *stock split*.

    c. Which option will accomplish Wicker's goal of reducing the current stock price while maintaining a stable level of retained earnings?

    d. What legal constraints might encourage the firm to choose a stock split over a stock dividend?

LG 6 **P14–17** **Stock repurchase**   The following financial data on the Bond Recording Company are available:

Earnings available for common stockholders	$800,000
Number of shares of common stock outstanding	400,000
Earnings per share ($800,000 ÷ 400,000)	$2
Market price per share	$20
Price/earnings (P/E) ratio ($20 ÷ $2)	10

The firm is currently considering whether it should use $400,000 of its earnings to pay cash dividends of $1 per share or to repurchase stock at $21 per share.

    a. Approximately how many shares of stock can the firm repurchase at the $21-per-share price, using the funds that would have gone to pay the cash dividend?

    b. Calculate the *EPS* after the repurchase. Explain your calculations.

    c. If the stock still sells at 10 times earnings, what will the *market price* be after the repurchase?

    d. Compare the pre- and postrepurchase earnings per share.

    e. Compare and contrast the stockholders' positions under the dividend and repurchase alternatives. What are the tax implications under each alternative?

LG 6   **P14–18**   **Stock repurchase**   Harte Textiles, Inc., a maker of custom upholstery fabrics, is concerned about preserving the wealth of its stockholders during a cyclic downturn in the home furnishings business. The company has maintained a constant dividend payout of $2.00 tied to a target payout ratio of 40%. Management is preparing a share repurchase recommendation to present to the firm's board of directors. The following data have been gathered from the last two years:

	2011	2012
Earnings available for common stockholders	$1,260,000	$1,200,000
Number of shares outstanding	300,000	300,000
Earnings per share	$4.20	$4.00
Market price per share	$23.50	$20.00
Price/earnings ratio	5.6	5.0

  a. How many shares should the company have outstanding in 2012 if its earnings available for common stockholders in that year are $1,200,000 and it pays a dividend of $2.00, given that its desired payout ratio is 40%?

  b. How many shares would Harte have to repurchase to have the level of shares outstanding calculated in part **a**?

LG 6   **P14–19**   **ETHICS PROBLEM**   Assume that you are the CFO of a company contemplating a stock repurchase next quarter. You know that there are several methods of reducing the current quarterly earnings, which may cause the stock price to fall prior to the announcement of the proposed stock repurchase. What course of action would you recommend to your CEO? If your CEO came to you first and recommended reducing the current quarter's earnings, what would be your response?

Spreadsheet Exercise

One way to lower the market price of a firm's stock is via a stock split. Rock-O Corporation finds itself in a different situation: Its stock has been selling at relatively low prices. To increase the market price of the stock, the company chooses to use a *reverse stock split* of 2-for-3.

  The company currently has 700,000 common shares outstanding and no preferred stock. The common stock carries a par value of $1. At this time, the paid-in capital in excess of par is $7,000,000, and the firm's retained earnings are $3,500,000.

TO DO

Create a spreadsheet to determine the following:

  a. The stockholders' equity section of the balance sheet *before* the reverse stock split.
  b. The stockholders' equity section of the balance sheet *after* the reverse stock split.

 Visit **www.myfinancelab.com** for **Chapter Case:** *Establishing General Access Company's Dividend Policy and Initial Dividend,* Group Exercises, and numerous online resources.

O'Grady Apparel Company

O'Grady Apparel Company was founded nearly 160 years ago when an Irish merchant named Garrett O'Grady landed in Los Angeles with an inventory of heavy canvas, which he hoped to sell for tents and wagon covers to miners headed for the California goldfields. Instead, he turned to the sale of harder-wearing clothing.

Today, O'Grady Apparel Company is a small manufacturer of fabrics and clothing whose stock is traded in the OTC market. In 2012, the Los Angeles–based company experienced sharp increases in both domestic and European markets resulting in record earnings. Sales rose from $15.9 million in 2008 to $18.3 million in 2012 with earnings per share of $3.28 and $3.84, respectively.

European sales represented 29% of total sales in 2012, up from 24% the year before and only 3% in 2007, 1 year after foreign operations were launched. Although foreign sales represent nearly one-third of total sales, the growth in the domestic market is expected to affect the company most markedly. Management expects sales to surpass $21 million in 2013, and earnings per share are expected to rise to $4.40. (Selected income statement items are presented in Table 1.)

Because of the recent growth, Margaret Jennings, the corporate treasurer, is concerned that available funds are not being used to their fullest potential. The projected $1,300,000 of internally generated 2013 funds is expected to be insufficient to meet the company's expansion needs. Management has set a policy of maintaining the current capital structure proportions of 25% long-term debt, 10% preferred stock, and 65% common stock equity for at least the next 3 years. In addition, it plans to continue paying out 40% of its earnings as dividends. Total capital expenditures are yet to be determined.

Jennings has been presented with several competing investment opportunities by division and product managers. However, because funds are limited, choices of which projects to accept must be made. A list of investment opportunities is shown in Table 2. To analyze the effect of the increased financing requirements on the weighted average cost of capital (WACC), Jennings contacted a leading investment banking firm that provided the financing cost data given in Table 3. O'Grady is in the 40% tax bracket.

TABLE 1

Selected Income Statement Items				
	2010	2011	2012	Projected 2013
Net sales	$13,860,000	$15,940,000	$18,330,000	$21,080,000
Net profits after taxes	$1,520,000	$1,750,000	$2,020,000	$2,323,000
Earnings per share (EPS)	2.88	3.28	3.84	4.40
Dividends per share	1.15	1.31	1.54	1.76

TABLE 2

	Investment Opportunities	
Investment opportunity	Internal rate of return (IRR)	Initial investment
A	21%	$400,000
B	19	200,000
C	24	700,000
D	27	500,000
E	18	300,000
F	22	600,000
G	17	500,000

TABLE 3

Financing Cost Data

Long-term debt: The firm can raise $700,000 of additional debt by selling 10-year, $1,000, 12% annual interest rate bonds to net $970 after flotation costs. Any debt in excess of $700,000 will have a before-tax cost, r_d, of 18%.

Preferred stock: Preferred stock, regardless of the amount sold, can be issued with a $60 par value and a 17% annual dividend rate. It will net $57 per share after flotation costs.

Common stock equity: The firm expects its dividends and earnings to continue to grow at a constant rate of 15% per year. The firm's stock is currently selling for $20 per share. The firm expects to have $1,300,000 of available retained earnings. Once the retained earnings have been exhausted, the firm can raise additional funds by selling new common stock, netting $16 per share after underpricing and flotation costs.

TO DO

a. Over the relevant ranges noted in the following table, calculate the after-tax cost of each source of financing needed to complete the table.

Source of capital	Range of new financing	After-tax cost (%)
Long-term debt	$0–$700,000	_____
	$700,000 and above	_____
Preferred stock	$0 and above	_____
Common stock equity	$0–$1,300,000	_____
	$1,300,000 and above	_____

b. (1) Determine the *break point* associated with common equity. A break point represents the total amount of financing that the firm can raise before it triggers an increase in the cost of a particular financing source. For example, O'Grady plans to use 25% long-term debt in its capital structure. That means that for every $1 in debt that the firm uses, it will use $3 from other financing sources (total financing is then $4, and because $1 comes from long-term debt, it's share in the total is the desired 25%). From Table 3, we see that after the firm raises $700,000 in long-term debt, the cost of this financing source begins to rise. Therefore, the firm can raise total capital of $2.8 million before the cost of debt will rise ($700,000 in debt plus $2.1 million in other sources to maintain the 25% proportion for debt). Therefore, $2.8 million is the break point for debt. If the firms wants to maintain a capital structure with 25% long-term debt and it also wants to raise more than $2.8 million in total financing, then it will require more than $700,000 in long-term debt, and it will trigger the higher cost of the additional debt it issues beyond $700,000.

  (2) Using the break points developed in part (1), determine each of the ranges of *total* new financing over which the firm's weighted average cost of capital (WACC) remains constant.

  (3) Calculate the weighted average cost of capital for each range of total new financing. Draw a graph with the WACC on the vertical axis and total money raised on the horizontal axis, and show how the firm's WACC increases in "steps" as the amount of money raised increases.

c. (1) Sort the investment opportunities described in Table 2 from highest to lowest return, and plot a line on the graph you drew in part (3) above showing how much money is required to fund the investments, starting with the highest return and going to the lowest. In other words, this line will plot the relationship between the IRR on the firm's investments and the total financing required to undertake those investments.

  (2) Which, if any, of the available investments would you recommend that the firm accept? Explain your answer.

d. (1) Assuming that the specific financing costs do not change, what effect would a shift to a more highly leveraged *capital structure* consisting of 50% long-term debt, 10% preferred stock, and 40% common stock have on your previous findings? (*Note:* Rework parts **b** and **c** using these capital structure weights.)

  (2) Which capital structure—the original one or this one—seems better? Why?

e. (1) What type of *dividend policy* does the firm appear to employ? Does it seem appropriate given the firm's recent growth in sales and profits and given its current investment opportunities?

  (2) Would you recommend an alternative dividend policy? Explain. How would this policy affect the investments recommended in part **c**(2)?

Part 7

Short-term financial decisions are guided by the same financial management principles as long-term financial decisions, but the time frame is different: days, weeks, and months rather than years. Working capital management focuses on the management of short-term cash flows by evaluating their timing, risk, and impact on firm value. While long-term financial decisions ultimately determine the firm's ability to maximize shareholder wealth, there may not be a long term if financial managers fail to make effective short-term financial decisions.

Chapter 15 discusses the techniques and strategies for managing working capital and current assets. The fundamentals of net working capital and the importance of the cash conversion cycle are introduced. Chapter 16 discusses the importance of controlling accounts payable expenses and managing other current liabilities. You will learn how some companies use current liabilities, including accounts payable, accruals, lines of credit, commercial paper, and short-term loans, to finance current assets. Successful adherence to the fundamentals of working capital management will help ensure that the firm can meet its operating obligations and maximize its long-term investments.

15 Working Capital and Current Assets Management

Learning Goals

LG 1 Understand working capital management, net working capital, and the related trade-off between profitability and risk.

LG 2 Describe the cash conversion cycle, its funding requirements, and the key strategies for managing it.

LG 3 Discuss inventory management: differing views, common techniques, and international concerns.

LG 4 Explain the credit selection process and the quantitative procedure for evaluating changes in credit standards.

LG 5 Review the procedures for quantitatively considering cash discount changes, other aspects of credit terms, and credit monitoring.

LG 6 Understand the management of receipts and disbursements, including float, speeding up collections, slowing down payments, cash concentration, zero-balance accounts, and investing in marketable securities.

Why This Chapter Matters to You

In your *professional* life

ACCOUNTING You need to understand the cash conversion cycle and the management of inventory, accounts receivable, and receipts and disbursements of cash.

INFORMATION SYSTEMS You need to understand the cash conversion cycle, inventory, accounts receivable, and receipts and disbursements of cash to design financial information systems that facilitate effective working capital management.

MANAGEMENT You need to understand the management of working capital so that you can efficiently manage current assets and decide whether to finance the firm's funds requirements aggressively or conservatively.

MARKETING You need to understand credit selection and monitoring because sales will be affected by the availability of credit to purchasers; sales will also be affected by inventory management.

OPERATIONS You need to understand the cash conversion cycle because you will be responsible for reducing the cycle through the efficient management of production, inventory, and costs.

In your *personal* life
You often will be faced with short-term purchasing decisions, which tend to focus on consumable items. Many involve trade-offs between quantity and price: Should you buy large quantities in order to pay a lower unit price, hold the items, and use them over time? Or should you buy smaller quantities more frequently and pay a slightly higher unit price? Analyzing these types of short-term purchasing decisions will help you make the most of your money.

Hing Yiap

Focusing on Working Capital

The leading garment seller Hing Yiap has come a long way from its meek beginning as a producer of a limited range of plain singlets and T-shirts in rented shop-houses to become a successful listed company, selling its own sports-inspired fashion and casual wear brands and American brand "B.U.M. Equipment." The company operates in three business segments: manufacturing, which includes textile knitting and the manufacture of garments; trading, which includes wholesale and retail sales; and distribution of ready-made sports and casual wear. Hing Yiap came to realize the importance of sound working capital in 2005, in particular inventory and receivables management. The current ratio dropped from 2.12 in 2003 to 1.74 in 2005, and the proportion of inventory in total current assets increased from 62 percent to 71 percent over the same period. The inventory management was poor, as reflected in number of days of inventory reaching its peak of 685.15 days in 2003.

Higher sublicense fees and operating expenses and competitors' low-priced merchandise preordained loss of Hing Yiap's market share. This was compounded by the failure of four department stores and initiatives such as B.U.M. City, a special lifestyle chain store targeting teenagers and young adults. The proportion of inventory in total current assets increased due to lethargic designs, and the likelihood of receivables turning into doubtful debt became inevitable with retailers' inability to sell merchandise. Hing Yiap realized that it had poor working capital management, admitting that change needed to come from within to recapture its market share.

Starting in 2006, management decided on a new work flow, design, and stock management, resulting in cost control, improved gross profit margins, and an increase in cash flow from operations. The gross profit rose from RM 9.82 million in 2003 to RM 35.08 million in 2007, and the current ratio increased to 2.43 in 2007, mainly driven by the decrease in the inventories proportion in the total current assets. Khoo Henn Kuan, CEO of Hing Yiap, said, "We changed the work flow, where designers, merchandisers, and sales teams worked together to come up with designs. As a result, we are a lot sharper. We used to have 60 to 70 percent of our stock to mark down after every six months. Today, every three to four months, we have already sold off 60 to 70 percent of our stock at normal prices, so we're a lot more profitable."

By the end of 2009, Hing Yiap was able to turn working capital into cash boosted by new products at a high profit margin, with a quick inventory turnover and reduction in operating expenses.

LG 1 **15.1** **Net Working Capital Fundamentals**

The firm's balance sheet provides information about the structure of the firm's investments on the one hand and the structure of its financing sources on the other hand. The structures chosen should consistently lead to the maximization of the value of the owners' investment in the firm.

WORKING CAPITAL MANAGEMENT

working capital (or short-term financial) management
Management of current assets and current liabilities.

The importance of efficient working capital management is indisputable given that a firm's viability relies on the financial manager's ability to effectively manage receivables, inventory, and payables. The goal of **working capital (or short-term financial) management** is to manage each of the firm's current assets (inventory, accounts receivable, marketable securities, and cash) and current liabilities (notes payable, accruals, and accounts payable) to achieve a balance between profitability and risk that contributes positively to the firm's value.

Firms are able to reduce financing costs or increase the funds available for expansion by minimizing the amount of funds tied up in working capital. Therefore, it should not be surprising to learn that working capital is one of the financial manager's most important and time-consuming activities. A study of *Fortune* 1000 firms found that more than one-third of financial managers' time is spent managing current assets and about one-fourth of their time is spent managing current liabilities.[1]

Matter of fact

CFOs Value Working Capital Management

A survey of CFOs from firms around the world suggests that working capital management is atop the list of most valued finance functions. Among 19 different finance functions, CFOs viewed working capital management as equally important as capital structure, debt issuance and management, bank relationships, and tax management. Their satisfaction with the performance of working capital management was quite the opposite, however. CFOs viewed the performance of working capital management as being better only than the performance of pension management. Consistent with their view that working capital management is a high-value but low-satisfaction activity, it was identified as the finance function second most in need of additional resources.[2]

Next, we use *net working capital* to consider the basic relationship between current assets and current liabilities and then use the *cash conversion cycle* to consider the key aspects of current asset management. In the following chapter, we consider current liability management.

---

1. Lawrence J. Gitman and Charles E. Maxwell, "Financial Activities of Major U.S. Firms: Survey and Analysis of Fortune's 1000," *Financial Management* (Winter 1985), pp. 57–65.

2. Henri Servaes and Peter Tufano, "CFO Views on the Importance and Execution of the Finance Function," *CFO Views* (January 2006), pp. 1–104.

NET WORKING CAPITAL

working capital
Current assets, which represent the portion of investment that circulates from one form to another in the ordinary conduct of business.

Current assets, commonly called **working capital,** represent the portion of investment that circulates from one form to another in the ordinary conduct of business. This idea embraces the recurring transition from cash to inventories to accounts receivable and back to cash. As cash substitutes, *marketable securities* are considered part of working capital.

Current liabilities represent the firm's short-term financing, because they include all debts of the firm that come due (must be paid) in 1 year or less. These debts usually include amounts owed to suppliers (accounts payable), employees and governments (accruals), and banks (notes payable), among others. (You can refer to Chapter 3 for a full discussion of balance sheet items.)

net working capital
The difference between the firm's current assets and its current liabilities.

As noted in Chapter 11, **net working capital** is defined as the difference between the firm's current assets and its current liabilities. When current assets exceed current liabilities, the firm has *positive net working capital*. When current assets are less than current liabilities, the firm has *negative net working capital*.

The conversion of current assets from inventory to accounts receivable to cash provides the cash used to pay current liabilities. The cash outlays for current liabilities are relatively predictable. When an obligation is incurred, the firm generally knows when the corresponding payment will be due. What is difficult to predict are the cash inflows—the conversion of the current assets to more liquid forms. The more predictable its cash inflows, the less net working capital a firm needs. Because most firms are unable to match cash inflows to cash outflows with certainty, they usually need current assets that more than cover outflows for current liabilities. In general, the greater the margin by which a firm's current assets cover its current liabilities, the better able it will be to pay its bills as they come due.

TRADE-OFF BETWEEN PROFITABILITY AND RISK

profitability
The relationship between revenues and costs generated by using the firm's assets—both current and fixed—in productive activities.

A trade-off exists between a firm's profitability and its risk. **Profitability,** in this context, is the relationship between revenues and costs generated by using the firm's assets—both current and fixed—in productive activities. A firm can increase its profits by (1) increasing revenues or (2) decreasing costs. **Risk,** in the context of working capital management, is the probability that a firm will be unable to pay its bills as they come due. A firm that cannot pay its bills as they come due is said to be **insolvent.** It is generally assumed that the greater the firm's net working capital, the lower its risk. In other words, the more net working capital, the more liquid the firm and therefore the lower its risk of becoming insolvent. Using these definitions of profitability and risk, we can demonstrate the trade-off between them by considering changes in current assets and current liabilities separately.

risk (of insolvency)
The probability that a firm will be unable to pay its bills as they come due.

insolvent
Describes a firm that is unable to pay its bills as they come due.

Changes in Current Assets

We can demonstrate how changing the level of the firm's current assets affects its profitability–risk trade-off by using the ratio of current assets to total assets. This ratio indicates the *percentage of total assets* that is current. For purposes of illustration, we will assume that the level of total assets remains unchanged. The effects on both profitability and risk of an increase or decrease in this ratio are summarized in the upper portion of Table 15.1 (on page 602). When the ratio

TABLE 15.1	Effects of Changing Ratios on Profits and Risk		
Ratio	Change in ratio	Effect on profit	Effect on risk
Current assets / Total assets	Increase	Decrease	Decrease
	Decrease	Increase	Increase
Current liabilities / Total assets	Increase	Increase	Increase
	Decrease	Decrease	Decrease

increases—that is, when current assets increase—profitability decreases. Why? Because current assets are less profitable than fixed assets. Fixed assets are more profitable because they add more value to the product than that provided by current assets. Without fixed assets, the firm could not produce the product.

The risk effect, however, decreases as the ratio of current assets to total assets increases. The increase in current assets increases net working capital, thereby reducing the risk of insolvency. In addition, as you go down the asset side of the balance sheet, the risk associated with the assets increases: Investment in cash and marketable securities is less risky than investment in accounts receivable, inventories, and fixed assets. Accounts receivable investment is less risky than investment in inventories and fixed assets. Investment in inventories is less risky than investment in fixed assets. The nearer an asset is to cash, the less risky it is. The opposite effects on profit and risk result from a decrease in the ratio of current assets to total assets.

In an effort to manage the risk effect, firms have been steadily moving away from riskier current asset components, such as inventory. Figure 15.1 shows that over time current assets consistently account for about 60 percent of total assets in U.S. manufacturing firms, but inventory levels are dropping dramatically.

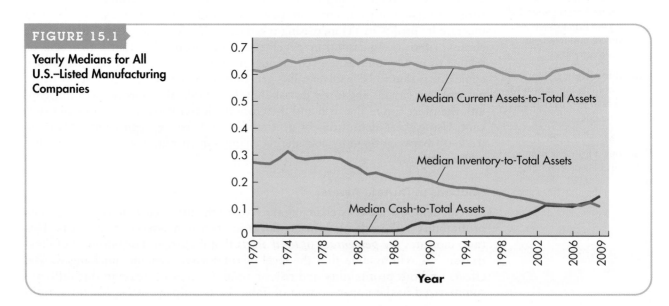

FIGURE 15.1

Yearly Medians for All U.S.–Listed Manufacturing Companies

The fact that current assets relative to total assets remains fairly constant while inventory investment is shrinking indicates that U.S. manufacturing firms are substituting less risky current assets for inventory, the riskiest current asset. Indeed, Figure 15.1 shows that cash levels are increasing relative to total assets.

Changes in Current Liabilities

We also can demonstrate how changing the level of the firm's current liabilities affects its profitability–risk trade-off by using the ratio of current liabilities to total assets. This ratio indicates the percentage of total assets that has been financed with current liabilities. Again, assuming that total assets remain unchanged, the effects on both profitability and risk of an increase or decrease in the ratio are summarized in the lower portion of Table 15.1. When the ratio increases, profitability increases. Why? Because the firm uses more of the less-expensive current liabilities financing and less long-term financing. Current liabilities are less expensive because only notes payable, which represent about 20 percent of the typical manufacturer's current liabilities, have a cost. The other current liabilities are basically debts on which the firm pays no charge or interest. However, when the ratio of current liabilities to total assets increases, the risk of insolvency also increases because the increase in current liabilities in turn decreases net working capital. The opposite effects on profit and risk result from a decrease in the ratio of current liabilities to total assets.

→ REVIEW QUESTIONS

15–1 Why is *working capital management* one of the most important and time-consuming activities of the financial manager? What is *net working capital?*

15–2 What is the relationship between the predictability of a firm's cash inflows and its required level of net working capital? How are net working capital, liquidity, and *risk of insolvency* related?

15–3 Why does an increase in the ratio of current assets to total assets decrease both profits and risk as measured by net working capital? How do changes in the ratio of current liabilities to total assets affect profitability and risk?

LG 2 ## 15.2 Cash Conversion Cycle

cash conversion cycle (CCC)
The length of time required for a company to convert cash invested in its operations to cash received as a result of its operations.

Central to working capital management is an understanding of the firm's *cash conversion cycle.*[3] The **cash conversion cycle (CCC)** measures the length of time required for a company to convert cash invested in its operations to cash received as a result of its operations. This cycle frames discussion of the management of the firm's current assets in this chapter and that of the management of current

3. The conceptual model that is used in this section to demonstrate basic short-term financial management strategies was developed by Lawrence J. Gitman in "Estimating Corporate Liquidity Requirements: A Simplified Approach," *The Financial Review* (1974), pp. 79–88, and refined and operationalized by Lawrence J. Gitman and Kanwal S. Sachdeva in "A Framework for Estimating and Analyzing the Required Working Capital Investment," *Review of Business and Economic Research* (Spring 1982), pp. 35–44.

liabilities in Chapter 16. Here, we begin by demonstrating the calculation and application of the cash conversion cycle.

CALCULATING THE CASH CONVERSION CYCLE

operating cycle (OC)
The time from the beginning of the production process to collection of cash from the sale of the finished product.

A firm's **operating cycle (OC)** is the time from the beginning of the production process to collection of cash from the sale of the finished product. The operating cycle encompasses two major short-term asset categories, inventory and accounts receivable. It is measured in elapsed time by summing the *average age of inventory (AAI)* and the *average collection period (ACP):*

$$OC = AAI + ACP \tag{15.1}$$

Matter of fact

**Increasing Speed
Lowers Working Capital**

A firm can lower its working capital if it can speed up its operating cycle. For example, if a firm accepts bank credit (like a Visa card), it will receive cash sooner after the sale is transacted than if it has to wait until the customer pays its accounts receivable.

However, the process of producing and selling a product also includes the purchase of production inputs (raw materials) on account, which results in accounts payable. Accounts payable reduce the number of days a firm's resources are tied up in the operating cycle. The time it takes to pay the accounts payable, measured in days, is the *average payment period (APP)*. The operating cycle less the average payment period yields the cash conversion cycle. The formula for the cash conversion cycle is

$$CCC = OC - APP \tag{15.2}$$

Substituting the relationship in Equation 15.1 into Equation 15.2, we can see that the cash conversion cycle has three main components, as shown in Equation 15.3: (1) average age of the inventory, (2) average collection period, and (3) average payment period:

$$CCC = AAI + ACP - APP \tag{15.3}$$

Clearly, if a firm changes any of these time periods, it changes the amount of resources tied up in the day-to-day operation of the firm.

Example 15.1 ▶

In 2007, International Business Machines Corp. (IBM) had annual revenues of $98,786 million, cost of revenue of $57,057 million, and accounts payable of $8,054 million. IBM had an average age of inventory (AAI) of 17.5 days, an average collection period (ACP) of 44.8 days, and an average payment period (APP) of 51.2 days (IBM's purchases were $57,416 million). Thus the cash conversion cycle for IBM was 11.1 days (17.5 + 44.8 − 51.2). Figure 15.2 presents IBM's cash conversion cycle as a time line.

The resources IBM had invested in this cash conversion cycle (assuming a 365-day year) were

Inventory	= $57,057 million × (17.5 ÷ 365) =	$ 2,735,609,589
+ Accounts receivable	= 98,786 million × (44.8 ÷ 365) =	12,124,966,575
− Accounts payable	= 57,416 million × (51.2 ÷ 365) =	8,053,970,411
	= Resources invested	= $ 6,806,605,753

With more than $6.8 billion committed to working capital, IBM was surely motivated to make improvements. Changes in any of the component cycles will change the resources tied up in IBM's operations.

FIGURE 15.2

Time Line for IBM's Cash Conversion Cycle
IBM's operating cycle in 2007 was 62.3 days, and its cash conversion cycle is 11.1 days.

As of the end of 2009, IBM had lowered its average collection period to 24.9 days. This dramatic increase in working capital efficiency reduced IBM's operating cycle nearly 20 days and caused IBM's cash conversion cycle to plummet to −7.6 days. The negative cash conversion cycle implies that IBM does not have to pay its suppliers until nearly 8 days after it has collected its receivables. Most importantly, IBM's aggressive working capital management allowed it to recover billions in working capital.

FUNDING REQUIREMENTS OF THE CASH CONVERSION CYCLE

We can use the cash conversion cycle as a basis for discussing how the firm funds its required investment in operating assets. We first differentiate between permanent and seasonal funding needs and then describe aggressive and conservative seasonal funding strategies.

permanent funding requirement
A constant investment in operating assets resulting from constant sales over time.

Permanent versus Seasonal Funding Needs

If the firm's sales are constant, then its investment in operating assets should also be constant, and the firm will have only a **permanent funding requirement**. If the firm's sales are cyclic, then its investment in operating assets will vary over time with its sales cycles, and the firm will have **seasonal funding requirements** in addition to the permanent funding required for its minimum investment in operating assets.

seasonal funding requirement
An investment in operating assets that varies over time as a result of cyclic sales.

Example 15.2 ▶ Nicholson Company holds, on average, $50,000 in cash and marketable securities, $1,250,000 in inventory, and $750,000 in accounts receivable. Nicholson's business is very stable over time, so its operating assets can be viewed as permanent. In addition, Nicholson's accounts payable of $425,000 are stable over time. Thus Nicholson has a permanent investment in operating assets of $1,625,000 ($50,000 + $1,250,0000 + $750,000 − $425,000). That amount would also equal its permanent funding requirement.

In contrast, Semper Pump Company, which produces bicycle pumps, has seasonal funding needs. Semper has seasonal sales, with its peak sales being driven by the summertime purchases of bicycle pumps. Semper holds, at minimum, $25,000 in cash and marketable securities, $100,000 in inventory, and $60,000 in accounts receivable. At peak times, Semper's inventory increases to $750,000, and its accounts receivable increase to $400,000. To capture production efficiencies, Semper produces pumps at a constant rate throughout the year. Thus accounts payable remain at $50,000 throughout the year. Accordingly, Semper has a permanent funding requirement for its minimum level of operating assets of $135,000 ($25,000 + $100,000 + $60,000 − $50,000) and peak seasonal funding requirements (in excess of its permanent need) of $990,000 [($25,000 + $750,000 + $400,000 − $50,000) − $135,000]. Semper's total funding requirements for operating assets vary from a minimum of $135,000 (permanent) to a seasonal peak of $1,125,000 ($135,000 + $990,000). Figure 15.3 depicts these needs over time.

aggressive funding strategy
A funding strategy under which the firm funds its seasonal requirements with short-term debt and its permanent requirements with long-term debt.

conservative funding strategy
A funding strategy under which the firm funds both its seasonal and its permanent requirements with long-term debt.

Aggressive versus Conservative Seasonal Funding Strategies

Short-term funds are typically less expensive than long-term funds. (The yield curve is typically upward sloping.) However, long-term funds allow the firm to lock in its cost of funds over a period of time and thus avoid the risk of increases in short-term interest rates. Also, long-term funding ensures that the required funds are available to the firm when needed. Short-term funding exposes the firm to the risk that it may not be able to obtain the funds needed to cover its seasonal peaks. Under an **aggressive funding strategy**, the firm funds its seasonal requirements with short-term debt and its permanent requirements with long-term debt. Under a **conservative funding strategy**, the firm funds both its seasonal and its permanent requirements with long-term debt.

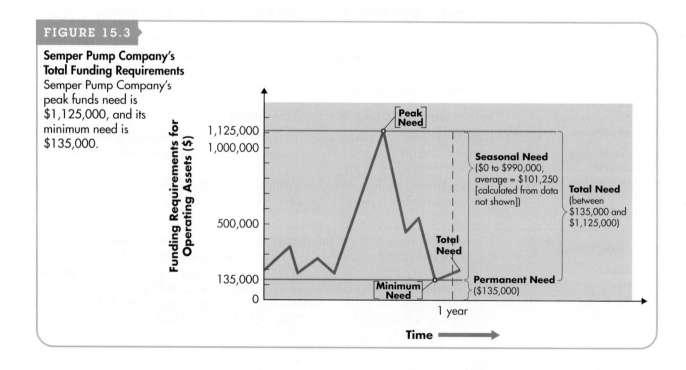

FIGURE 15.3

Semper Pump Company's Total Funding Requirements
Semper Pump Company's peak funds need is $1,125,000, and its minimum need is $135,000.

Example 15.3 ▸ Semper Pump Company has a permanent funding requirement of $135,000 in operating assets and seasonal funding requirements that vary between $0 and $990,000 and average $101,250 (calculated from data not shown). If Semper can borrow short-term funds at 6.25% and long-term funds at 8%, and if it can earn 5% on the investment of any surplus balances, then the annual cost of an aggressive strategy for seasonal funding will be

$$
\begin{aligned}
\text{Cost of short-term financing} &= 0.0625 \times \$101{,}250 = \$\ 6{,}328.13 \\
+\ \text{Cost of long-term financing} &= 0.0800 \times\ \ 135{,}000 = \ \ 10{,}800.00 \\
-\ \text{Earnings on surplus balances} &= 0.0500 \times\ \ \ \ \ \ \ \ \ \ 0 = \underline{\ \ \ \ \ \ \ \ \ \ \ \ 0} \\
\text{Total cost of aggressive strategy} & \hspace{4cm} \underline{\$17{,}128.13}
\end{aligned}
$$

Because under this strategy the amount of financing exactly equals the estimated funding need, no surplus balances exist.

Alternatively, Semper can choose a conservative strategy, under which surplus cash balances are fully invested. (In Figure 15.3, this surplus will be the difference between the peak need of $1,125,000 and the total need, which varies between $135,000 and $1,125,000 during the year.) The cost of the conservative strategy will be

$$
\begin{aligned}
\text{Cost of short-term financing} &= 0.0625 \times \$\ \ \ \ \ \ \ \ 0 = \$\ \ \ \ \ \ \ \ \ 0 \\
+\ \text{Cost of long-term financing} &= 0.0800 \times\ \ 1{,}125{,}000 = \ \ 90{,}000.00 \\
-\ \text{Earnings on surplus balances} &= 0.0500 \times\ \ \ \ 888{,}750 = \underline{\ \ 44{,}437.50} \\
\text{Total cost of conservative strategy} & \hspace{4cm} \underline{\$45{,}562.50}
\end{aligned}
$$

The average surplus balance would be calculated by subtracting the sum of the permanent need ($135,000) and the average seasonal need ($101,250) from the seasonal peak need ($1,125,000) to get $888,750 ($1,125,000 − $135,000 − $101,250). This represents the surplus amount of financing that on average could be invested in short-term assets that earn a 5% annual return.

It is clear from these calculations that for Semper, the aggressive strategy is far less expensive than the conservative strategy. However, it is equally clear that Semper has substantial peak-season operating-asset needs and that it must have adequate funding available to meet the peak needs and ensure ongoing operations.

Clearly, the aggressive strategy's heavy reliance on short-term financing makes it riskier than the conservative strategy because of interest rate swings and possible difficulties in obtaining needed short-term financing quickly when seasonal peaks occur. The conservative strategy avoids these risks through the locked-in interest rate and long-term financing, but it is more costly because of the negative spread between the earnings rate on surplus funds (5 percent in the example) and the cost of the long-term funds that create the surplus (8 percent in the example). Where the firm operates, between the extremes of the aggressive and conservative seasonal funding strategies, depends on management's disposition toward risk and the strength of its banking relationships.

STRATEGIES FOR MANAGING THE CASH CONVERSION CYCLE

Some firms establish a *target* cash conversion cycle and then monitor and manage the *actual* cash conversion cycle toward the targeted value. A positive cash conversion cycle, as was the case for IBM in 2008, means the firm must use negotiated liabilities (such as bank loans) to support its operating assets. Negotiated liabilities carry an explicit cost, so the firm benefits by minimizing their use in supporting operating assets. Simply stated, the goal is to *minimize the length of the cash conversion cycle,* which minimizes negotiated liabilities. This goal can be realized through use of the following strategies:

1. *Turn over inventory as quickly as possible* without stockouts that result in lost sales.
2. *Collect accounts receivable as quickly as possible* without losing sales from high-pressure collection techniques.
3. *Manage mail, processing, and clearing time* to reduce them when collecting from customers and to increase them when paying suppliers.
4. *Pay accounts payable as slowly as possible* without damaging the firm's credit rating.

Techniques for implementing these four strategies are the focus of the remainder of this chapter and the following chapter.

→ **REVIEW QUESTIONS**

15–4 What is the difference between the firm's *operating cycle* and its *cash conversion cycle?*

15–5 Why is it helpful to divide the funding needs of a seasonal business into its permanent and seasonal funding requirements when developing a funding strategy?

15–6 What are the benefits, costs, and risks of an *aggressive funding strategy* and of a *conservative funding strategy?* Under which strategy is the borrowing often in excess of the actual need?

15–7 Why is it important for a firm to minimize the length of its cash conversion cycle?

LG 3   **15.3** Inventory Management

The first component of the cash conversion cycle is the average age of inventory. The objective for managing inventory, as noted earlier, is to turn over inventory as quickly as possible without losing sales from stockouts. The financial manager tends to act as an advisor or "watchdog" in matters concerning inventory. He or she does not have direct control over inventory but does provide input to the inventory management process.

DIFFERING VIEWPOINTS ABOUT INVENTORY LEVEL

Differing viewpoints about appropriate inventory levels commonly exist among a firm's finance, marketing, manufacturing, and purchasing managers. Each views inventory levels in light of his or her own objectives. The *financial manager's* general disposition toward inventory levels is to keep them low, to ensure that the firm's money is not being unwisely invested in excess resources. The *marketing manager,* on the other hand, would like to have large inventories of the firm's finished products. This would ensure that all orders could be filled quickly, eliminating the need for backorders due to stockouts.

The *manufacturing manager's* major responsibility is to implement the production plan so that it results in the desired amount of finished goods of acceptable quality available on time at a low cost. In fulfilling this role, the manufacturing manager would keep raw materials inventories high to avoid production delays. He or she also would favor large production runs for the sake of lower unit production costs, which would result in high finished goods inventories.

The *purchasing manager* is concerned solely with the raw materials inventories. He or she must have on hand, in the correct quantities at the desired times and at a favorable price, whatever raw materials are required by production. Without proper control, in an effort to get quantity discounts or in anticipation of rising prices or a shortage of certain materials, the purchasing manager may purchase larger quantities of resources than are actually needed at the time.

COMMON TECHNIQUES FOR MANAGING INVENTORY

Numerous techniques are available for effectively managing the firm's inventory. Here we briefly consider four commonly used techniques.

ABC System

ABC inventory system
Inventory management technique that divides inventory into three groups—A, B, and C, in descending order of importance and level of monitoring, on the basis of the dollar investment in each.

A firm using the **ABC inventory system** divides its inventory into three groups: A, B, and C. The A group includes those items with the largest dollar investment. Typically, this group consists of 20 percent of the firm's inventory items but 80 percent of its investment in inventory. The B group consists of items that account for the next largest investment in inventory. The C group consists of a large number of items that require a relatively small investment.

The inventory group of each item determines the item's level of monitoring. The A group items receive the most intense monitoring because of the high dollar investment. Typically, A group items are tracked on a perpetual inventory system that allows daily verification of each item's inventory level. B group items are frequently controlled through periodic, perhaps weekly, checking of their levels. C group items are monitored with unsophisticated techniques, such as the two-bin method. With the **two-bin method,** the item is stored in two bins. As an item is needed, inventory is removed from the first bin. When that bin is empty, an order is placed to refill the first bin while inventory is drawn from the second bin. The second bin is used until empty, and so on.

two-bin method
Unsophisticated inventory-monitoring technique that is typically applied to C group items and involves reordering inventory when one of two bins is empty.

The large dollar investment in A and B group items suggests the need for a better method of inventory management than the ABC system. The EOQ model, discussed next, is an appropriate model for the management of A and B group items.

economic order quantity (EOQ) model
Inventory management technique for determining an item's optimal order size, which is the size that minimizes the total of its *order costs* and *carrying costs.*

Economic Order Quantity (EOQ) Model

One of the most common techniques for determining the optimal order size for inventory items is the **economic order quantity (EOQ) model.** The EOQ model considers various costs of inventory and then determines what order size minimizes total inventory cost.

EOQ assumes that the relevant costs of inventory can be divided into *order costs* and *carrying costs.* (The model excludes the actual cost of the inventory item.) Each of them has certain key components and characteristics. **Order costs** include the fixed clerical costs of placing and receiving orders: the cost of writing a purchase

order costs
The fixed clerical costs of placing and receiving an inventory order.

carrying costs
The variable costs per unit of holding an item in inventory for a specific period of time.

order, of processing the resulting paperwork, and of receiving an order and checking it against the invoice. Order costs are stated in dollars per order. **Carrying costs** are the variable costs per unit of holding an item of inventory for a specific period of time. Carrying costs include storage costs, insurance costs, the costs of deterioration and obsolescence, and the opportunity or financial cost of having funds invested in inventory. These costs are stated in dollars per unit per period.

Order costs decrease as the size of the order increases. Carrying costs, however, increase with increases in the order size. The EOQ model analyzes the trade-off between order costs and carrying costs to determine the *order quantity that minimizes the total inventory cost.*

Mathematical Development of EOQ   A formula can be developed for determining the firm's EOQ for a given inventory item, where

$$S = \text{usage in units per period}$$
$$O = \text{order cost per order}$$
$$C = \text{carrying cost per unit per period}$$
$$Q = \text{order quantity in units}$$

The first step is to derive the cost functions for order cost and carrying cost. The order cost can be expressed as the product of the cost per order and the number of orders. Because the number of orders equals the usage during the period divided by the order quantity (S/Q), the order cost can be expressed as follows:

$$\text{Order cost} = O \times (S \div Q) \tag{15.4}$$

The carrying cost is defined as the cost of carrying a unit of inventory per period multiplied by the firm's average inventory. The average inventory is the order quantity divided by 2 ($Q/2$), because inventory is assumed to be depleted at a constant rate. Thus carrying cost can be expressed as follows:

$$\text{Carrying cost} = C \times (Q \div 2) \tag{15.5}$$

total cost of inventory
The sum of order costs and carrying costs of inventory.

The firm's **total cost of inventory** is found by summing the order cost and the carrying cost. Thus the total cost function is

$$\text{Total cost} = [O \times (S \div Q)] + [C \times (Q \div 2)] \tag{15.6}$$

Because the EOQ is defined as the order quantity that minimizes the total cost function, we must solve the total cost function for the EOQ.[4] The resulting equation is

$$\text{EOQ} = \sqrt{\frac{2 \times S \times O}{C}} \tag{15.7}$$

---

4. In this simple model the EOQ occurs at the point where the order cost $[O \times (S \div Q)]$ just equals the carrying cost $[C \times (Q \div 2)]$. To demonstrate, we set the two costs equal and solve for Q:

$$[O \times (S \div Q)] = [C \times (Q \div 2)]$$

Then cross-multiplying, we get:

$$2 \times O \times S = C \times Q^2$$

Dividing both sides by C, we get:

$$Q^2 = (2 \times O \times S) \div C, \text{ so } Q = \sqrt{(2 \times O \times S) \div C}$$

Although the EOQ model has weaknesses, it is certainly better than subjective decision making. Despite the fact that the use of the EOQ model is outside the control of the financial manager, the financial manager must be aware of its utility and must provide certain inputs, specifically with respect to inventory carrying costs.

Personal Finance Example 15.4 ▶ Individuals sometimes are confronted with personal finance decisions involving cost trade-offs similar to the trade-off between the fixed order costs and variable carrying costs of inventory that corporations face. Take the case of the von Dammes, who are trying to decide whether a conventional car (uses gas) or a hybrid car (uses gas and electric battery) would be more cost effective.

The von Dammes plan to keep whichever car they choose for 3 years and expect to drive it 12,000 miles in each of those years. They will use the same dollar amount of financing repaid under the same terms for either car, and they expect the cars to have identical repair costs over the 3-year ownership period. They also assume that the trade-in value of the two cars at the end of 3 years will be identical. Both cars use regular unleaded gas, which they estimate will cost, on average, $3.20 per gallon over the 3 years. The key data for each car follows:

	Conventional	Hybrid
Total cost	$24,500	$27,300
Average miles per gallon	27	42

We can begin by calculating the total fuel cost for each car over the 3-year ownership period:

Conventional: [(3 years × 12,000 miles per year) ÷ 27 miles per gallon]
× $3.20 per gallon
= 1,333.33 gallons × $3.20 per gallon = $4,267

Hybrid: [(3 years × 12,000 miles per year) ÷ 42 miles per gallon]
× $3.20 per gallon
= 857.14 gallons × $3.20 per gallon = $2,743

To buy the hybrid car, the von Dammes will have to pay $2,800 more ($27,300 − $24,500) than the cost of the conventional car, but they will save about $1,524 ($4,267 − $2,743) in fuel costs over the 3-year ownership period. Ignoring differences in timing, on a strict economic basis *they should buy the conventional car because the $2,800 marginal cost of the hybrid results in a marginal fuel cost savings of only $1,524.* Clearly, other factors such as environmental concerns and the reasonableness of the assumptions could affect their decision.

---

reorder point
The point at which to reorder inventory, expressed as days of lead time × daily usage.

Reorder Point Once the firm has determined its economic order quantity, it must determine when to place an order. The **reorder point** reflects the number of days of lead time the firm needs to place and receive an order and the firm's daily usage of the inventory item. Assuming that inventory is used at a constant rate, the formula for the reorder point is

$$\text{Reorder point} = \text{Days of lead time} \times \text{Daily usage} \quad (15.8)$$

For example, if a firm knows it takes 3 days to place and receive an order, and if it uses 15 units per day of the inventory item, then the reorder point is 45 units of inventory (3 days × 15 units/day). Thus, as soon as the item's inventory level falls to the reorder point (45 units, in this case) an order will be placed at the item's EOQ. If the estimates of lead time and usage are correct, then the order will arrive exactly as the inventory level reaches zero. However, lead times and usage rates are not precise, so most firms hold **safety stock** (extra inventory) to prevent stockouts of important items.

safety stock
Extra inventory that is held to prevent stockouts of important items.

Example 15.5 ▶ MAX Company, a producer of dinnerware, has an A group inventory item that is vital to the production process. This item costs $1,500, and MAX uses 1,100 units of the item per year. MAX wants to determine its optimal order strategy for the item. To calculate the EOQ, we need the following inputs:

$$\text{Order cost per order} = \$150$$
$$\text{Carrying cost per unit per year} = \$200$$

Substituting into Equation 15.7, we get

$$\text{EOQ} = \sqrt{\frac{2 \times 1,100 \times \$150}{\$200}} \approx \underline{\underline{41}} \text{ units}$$

The reorder point for MAX depends on the number of days MAX operates per year. Assuming that MAX operates 250 days per year and uses 1,100 units of this item, its daily usage is 4.4 units (1,100 ÷ 250). If its lead time is 2 days and MAX wants to maintain a safety stock of 4 units, the reorder point for this item is 12.8 units [(2 × 4.4) + 4]. However, orders are made only in whole units, so the order is placed when the inventory falls to 13 units.

The firm's goal for inventory is to turn it over as quickly as possible without stockouts. Inventory turnover is best calculated by dividing cost of goods sold by average inventory. The EOQ model determines the optimal order size and, indirectly, through the assumption of constant usage, the average inventory. Thus the EOQ model determines the firm's optimal inventory turnover rate, given the firm's specific costs of inventory.

Just-in-Time (JIT) System

just-in-time (JIT) system
Inventory management technique that minimizes inventory investment by having materials arrive at exactly the time they are needed for production.

The **just-in-time (JIT) system** is used to minimize inventory investment. The philosophy is that materials should arrive at exactly the time they are needed for production. Ideally, the firm would have only work-in-process inventory. Because its objective is to minimize inventory investment, a JIT system uses no (or very little) safety stock. Extensive coordination among the firm's employees, its suppliers, and shipping companies must exist to ensure that material inputs arrive on time. Failure of materials to arrive on time results in a shutdown of the production line until the materials arrive. Likewise, a JIT system requires high-quality parts from

focus on PRACTICE

RFID: The Wave of the Future

in practice Wal-Mart Stores, Inc., the world's number one retailer, operates more than 8,400 retail units under 55 different banners in 15 countries and employs more than two million people around the world. What's more, Wal-Mart came in first place among retailers in *Fortune* magazine's 2010 Most Admired Companies survey. With fiscal 2010 sales of $405 billion, Wal-Mart is able to exert tremendous pressure on its suppliers. When Wal-Mart announced in April 2004 that it was beginning a pilot program to test *radio frequency identification* (RFID) technology to improve its inventory and supply chain management, suppliers and competitors took notice.

One of the first companies to introduce bar codes in the early 1980s, Wal-Mart required its top 100 suppliers to put RFID tags on shipping crates and pallets by January 2005, with the next 200 largest suppliers using the technology by January 2006. As of February 2007, Wal-Mart officials said that 600 of its suppliers were RFID-enabled. Although Wal-Mart's ultimate goal is to have all of its 100,000-plus suppliers on board using electronic product codes (EPC) with RFID technology, progress has slowed as Wal-Mart's suppliers remain unconvinced of RFID's cost savings.

The major issue with RFID tags is per-chip cost. In 2004, when Wal-Mart announced its intent to use RFID tags, they sold for 30 to 50 cents each. Wal-Mart requested a price of 5 cents per tag, expecting increased demand and economies of scale to push the price down to make them more competitive with inexpensive barcodes. Increased demand has brought the price of current-generation RFID tags to about 15 cents apiece, but barcodes cost only a fraction of a cent. Barcodes help track inventory and can match a product to a price, but they lack the electronic tags' ability to store more detailed information, such as the serial number of a product, the location of the factory that made it, when it was made, and when it was sold.

Wal-Mart expects the RFID technology to improve its inventory management, and it remains committed to advancing its use of RFID. During the 2010 National Retail Federation's Big Show convention, Wal-Mart's CIO, Rollin Ford, said, "We're still bullish on RFID." He also indicated that Wal-Mart ran some apparel pilots last year that showed good results and that the retailer plans to "eat what we cook." Wal-Mart manufactures some apparel items and controls its own supply chain, and Ford indicated that Wal-Mart plans to use RFID technology in its apparel supply chain. Wal-Mart will then share the benefits and best practices with its suppliers, which might want to achieve the same benefits from the technology.

▶ *What problem might occur with the full implementation of RFID technology in retail industries? Specifically, consider the amount of data that might be collected.*

Source: "2010 Most Admired Companies," *Fortune* (March 22, 2010); Wal-Mart, *Wal-Mart 2010 Financial Report,* http://cdn.walmartstores.com/sites/AnnualReport/2010/PDF/01_WMT%202010_Financials.pdf; Mark Roberti, "Wal-Mart CIO Still 'Bullish' on RFID." *RFID Journal* retail blog, http://www.rfidjournal.com/article/view/ 7315.

suppliers. When quality problems arise, production must be stopped until the problems are resolved.

The goal of the JIT system is manufacturing efficiency. It uses inventory as a tool for attaining efficiency by emphasizing quality of the materials used and their timely delivery. When JIT is working properly, it forces process inefficiencies to surface.

Knowing the level of inventory is, of course, an important part of any inventory management system. As described in the *Focus on Practice* box, radio frequency identification technology may be the "next new thing" in improving inventory and supply chain management.

Computerized Systems for Resource Control

materials requirement planning (MRP) system Inventory management technique that applies EOQ concepts and a computer to compare production needs to available inventory balances and determine when orders should be placed for various items on a product's *bill of materials.*

Today a number of systems are available for controlling inventory and other resources. One of the most basic is the **materials requirement planning (MRP) system.** It is used to determine what materials to order and when to order them. MRP applies EOQ concepts to determine how much to order. Using a computer,

manufacturing resource planning II (MRP II)
A sophisticated computerized system that integrates data from numerous areas such as finance, accounting, marketing, engineering, and manufacturing and generates production plans as well as numerous financial and management reports.

enterprise resource planning (ERP)
A computerized system that electronically integrates external information about the firm's suppliers and customers with the firm's departmental data so that information on all available resources—human and material—can be instantly obtained in a fashion that eliminates production delays and controls costs.

MRP simulates each product's bill of materials, inventory status, and manufacturing process. The *bill of materials* is simply a list of all parts and materials that go into making the finished product. For a given production plan, the computer simulates material requirements by comparing production needs to available inventory balances. On the basis of the time it takes for a product that is in process to move through the various production stages and the lead time to get materials, the MRP system determines when orders should be placed for various items on the bill of materials. The objective of this system is to lower the firm's inventory investment without impairing production. If the firm's pretax opportunity cost of capital for investments of equal risk is 20 percent, every dollar of investment released from inventory will increase before-tax profits by $0.20.

A popular extension of MRP is **manufacturing resource planning II (MRP II)**, which integrates data from numerous areas such as finance, accounting, marketing, engineering, and manufacturing using a sophisticated computer system. This system generates production plans as well as numerous financial and management reports. In essence, it models the firm's processes so that the effects of changes in one area of operations on other areas can be assessed and monitored. For example, the MRP II system would allow the firm to assess the effect of an increase in labor costs on sales and profits.

Whereas MRP and MRP II tend to focus on internal operations, **enterprise resource planning (ERP)** systems expand the focus to the external environment by including information about suppliers and customers. ERP electronically integrates all of a firm's departments so that, for example, production can call up sales information and immediately know how much must be produced to fill customer orders. Because all available resources—human and material—are known, the system can eliminate production delays and control costs. ERP systems automatically note changes, such as a supplier's inability to meet a scheduled delivery date, so that necessary adjustments can be made.

INTERNATIONAL INVENTORY MANAGEMENT

International inventory management is typically much more complicated for exporters in general, and for multinational companies in particular, than for purely domestic firms. The production and manufacturing economies of scale that might be expected from selling products globally may prove elusive if products must be tailored for individual local markets, as frequently happens, or if actual production takes place in factories around the world. When raw materials, intermediate goods, or finished products must be transported over long distances—particularly by ocean shipping—there will be more delays, confusion, damage, and theft than occur in a one-country operation. The international inventory manager, therefore, puts a premium on flexibility. He or she is usually less concerned about ordering the economically optimal quantity of inventory than about making sure that sufficient quantities of inventory are delivered where they are needed, when they are needed, and in a condition to be used as planned.

→ REVIEW QUESTIONS

15–8 What are likely to be the viewpoints of each of the following managers about the levels of the various types of inventory: finance, marketing, manufacturing, and purchasing? Why is inventory an investment?

15–9 Briefly describe the following techniques for managing inventory: ABC system, economic order quantity (EOQ) model, just-in-time (JIT) system, and computerized systems for resource control—MRP, MRP II, and ERP.

15–10 What factors make managing inventory more difficult for exporters and multinational companies?

_{LG 4} _{LG 5}   **15.4 Accounts Receivable Management**

The second component of the cash conversion cycle is the average collection period. This period is the average length of time from a sale on credit until the payment becomes usable funds for the firm. The average collection period has two parts. The first part is the time from the sale until the customer mails the payment. The second part is the time from when the payment is mailed until the firm has the collected funds in its bank account. The first part of the average collection period involves managing the credit available to the firm's customers, and the second part involves collecting and processing payments. This section of the chapter discusses the firm's accounts receivable credit management.

The objective for managing accounts receivable is to collect accounts receivable as quickly as possible without losing sales from high-pressure collection techniques. Accomplishing this goal encompasses three topics: (1) credit selection and standards, (2) credit terms, and (3) credit monitoring.

CREDIT SELECTION AND STANDARDS

Credit selection involves application of techniques for determining which customers should receive credit. This process involves evaluating the customer's creditworthiness and comparing it to the firm's **credit standards**, its minimum requirements for extending credit to a customer.

credit standards
The firm's minimum requirements for extending credit to a customer.

five C's of credit
The five key dimensions—character, capacity, capital, collateral, and conditions—used by credit analysts to provide a framework for in-depth credit analysis.

Five C's of Credit

One popular credit selection technique is the **five C's of credit,** which provides a framework for in-depth credit analysis. Because of the time and expense involved, this credit selection method is used for large-dollar credit requests. The five C's are

1. *Character:* The applicant's record of meeting past obligations.
2. *Capacity:* The applicant's ability to repay the requested credit, as judged in terms of financial statement analysis focused on cash flows available to repay debt obligations.
3. *Capital:* The applicant's debt relative to equity.
4. *Collateral:* The amount of assets the applicant has available for use in securing the credit. The larger the amount of available assets, the greater the chance that a firm will recover funds if the applicant defaults.
5. *Conditions:* Current general and industry-specific economic conditions, and any unique conditions surrounding a specific transaction.

Analysis via the five C's of credit does not yield a specific accept/reject decision, so its use requires an analyst experienced in reviewing and granting credit requests. Application of this framework tends to ensure that the firm's credit customers will pay, without being pressured, within the stated credit terms.

Credit Scoring

credit scoring
A credit selection method
commonly used with high-
volume/small-dollar credit
requests; relies on a credit
score determined by applying
statistically derived weights to
a credit applicant's scores on
key financial and credit
characteristics.

Credit scoring is a method of credit selection that firms commonly use with high-volume/small-dollar credit requests. **Credit scoring** applies statistically derived weights to a credit applicant's scores on key financial and credit characteristics to predict whether he or she will pay the requested credit in a timely fashion. Simply stated, the procedure results in a score that measures the applicant's overall credit strength, and the score is used to make the accept/reject decision for granting the applicant credit. Credit scoring is most commonly used by large credit card operations, such as those of banks, oil companies, and department stores. The purpose of credit scoring is to make a relatively informed credit decision quickly and inexpensively, recognizing that the cost of a single bad scoring decision is small. However, if bad debts from scoring decisions increase, then the scoring system must be reevaluated.

Changing Credit Standards

The firm sometimes will contemplate changing its credit standards in an effort to improve its returns and create greater value for its owners. To demonstrate, consider the following changes and effects on profits expected to result from the *relaxation* of credit standards.

Effects of Relaxation of Credit Standards		
Variable	Direction of change	Effect on profits
Sales volume	Increase	Positive
Investment in accounts receivable	Increase	Negative
Bad-debt expenses	Increase	Negative

If credit standards were tightened, the opposite effects would be expected.

Example 15.6 ▶ Dodd Tool, a manufacturer of lathe tools, is currently selling a product for $10 per unit. Sales (all on credit) for last year were 60,000 units. The variable cost per unit is $6. The firm's total fixed costs are $120,000.

The firm is currently contemplating a *relaxation of credit standards* that is expected to result in the following: a 5% increase in unit sales to 63,000 units; an increase in the average collection period from 30 days (the current level) to 45 days; an increase in bad-debt expenses from 1% of sales (the current level) to 2%. The firm determines that its cost of tying up funds in receivables is 15% before taxes.

To determine whether to relax its credit standards, Dodd Tool must calculate its effect on the firm's additional profit contribution from sales, the cost of the marginal investment in accounts receivable, and the cost of marginal bad debts.

Additional Profit Contribution from Sales   Because fixed costs are "sunk" and therefore are unaffected by a change in the sales level, the only cost relevant to a change in sales is variable costs. Sales are expected to increase by 5%, or 3,000 units. The profit contribution per unit will equal the difference between the sale price per unit ($10) and the variable cost per unit ($6). The profit contribution per unit therefore will be $4. The total additional profit contribution from sales will be $12,000 (3,000 units × $4 per unit).

Cost of the Marginal Investment in Accounts Receivable   To determine the cost of the marginal investment in accounts receivable, Dodd must find the difference between the cost of carrying receivables under the two credit standards. Because its concern is only with the out-of-pocket costs, *the relevant cost is the variable cost.* The average investment in accounts receivable can be calculated by using the following formula:

$$\text{Average investment in accounts receivable} = \frac{\text{Total variable cost of annual sales}}{\text{Turnover of accounts receivable}} \qquad (15.9)$$

where

$$\text{Turnover of accounts receivable} = \frac{365}{\text{Average collection period}}$$

The total variable cost of annual sales under the present and proposed plans can be found as follows, using the variable cost per unit of $6.

Total variable cost of annual sales

Under present plan: ($6 × 60,000 units) = $360,000

Under proposed plan: ($6 × 63,000 units) = $378,000

The turnover of accounts receivable is the number of times each year that the firm's accounts receivable are actually turned into cash. It is found by dividing the average collection period into 365 (the number of days assumed in a year).

Turnover of accounts receivable

Under present plan: $\dfrac{365}{30} = 12.2$

Under proposed plan: $\dfrac{365}{45} = 8.1$

By substituting the cost and turnover data just calculated into Equation 15.9 for each case, we get the following average investments in accounts receivable:

Average investment in accounts receivable

Under present plan: $\dfrac{\$360,000}{12.2} = \$29,508$

Under proposed plan: $\dfrac{\$378,000}{8.1} = \$46,667$

We calculate the marginal investment in accounts receivable and its cost as follows:

Cost of marginal investment in accounts receivable

Average investment under proposed plan	$46,667
− Average investment under present plan	29,508
Marginal investment in accounts receivable	$17,159
× Cost of funds tied up in receivables	0.15
Cost of marginal investment in A/R	$ 2,574

The resulting value of $2,574 is considered a cost because it represents the maximum amount that could have been earned before taxes on the $17,159 had it been placed in an equally risky investment earning 15% before taxes.

Cost of Marginal Bad Debts   We find the cost of marginal bad debts by taking the difference between the levels of bad debts before and after the proposed relaxation of credit standards.

> *Cost of marginal bad debts*
>
>   Under proposed plan: $(0.02 \times \$10/\text{unit} \times 63{,}000 \text{ units}) = \$12{,}600$
>
> $-$ Under present plan: $(0.01 \times \$10/\text{unit} \times 60{,}000 \text{ units}) = \underline{\hphantom{xxx}6{,}000}$
>
>   Cost of marginal bad debts $\underline{\underline{\$\hphantom{x}6{,}600}}$

Note that the bad-debt costs are calculated by using the sale price per unit ($10) to deduct not just the true loss of variable cost ($6) that results when a customer fails to pay its account but also the profit contribution per unit (in this case $4) that is included in the "additional profit contribution from sales." Thus the resulting cost of marginal bad debts is $6,600.

Making the Credit Standard Decision   To decide whether to relax its credit standards, the firm must compare the additional profit contribution from sales to the added costs of the marginal investment in accounts receivable and marginal bad debts. If the additional profit contribution is greater than marginal costs, credit standards should be relaxed.

Example 15.7 ▶

The results and key calculations related to Dodd Tool's decision whether to relax its credit standards are summarized in Table 15.2. The net addition to total profits resulting from such an action will be $2,826 per year. Therefore, the firm *should* relax its credit standards as proposed.

The procedure described here for evaluating a proposed change in credit standards is also commonly used to evaluate other changes in the management of accounts receivable. If Dodd Tool had been contemplating tightening its credit standards, for example, the cost would have been a reduction in the profit contribution from sales, and the return would have been from reductions in the cost of the investment in accounts receivable and in the cost of bad debts. Another application of this procedure is demonstrated later in the chapter.

Managing International Credit

Credit management is difficult enough for managers of purely domestic companies, and these tasks become much more complex for companies that operate internationally. This is partly because (as we have seen before) international operations typically expose a firm to *exchange rate risk*. It is also due to the dangers and delays involved in shipping goods long distances and in having to cross international borders.

Exports of finished goods are usually priced in the currency of the importer's local market; most commodities, on the other hand, are priced in dollars. Therefore, a U.S. company that sells a product in Japan, for example, would have

TABLE 15.2	Effects on Dodd Tool of a Relaxation of Credit Standards

Additional profit contribution from sales		
$\quad$ [3,000 units $\times$ ($10 − $6)]		$12,000
Cost of marginal investment in A/R^a		
$\quad$ Average investment under proposed plan:		
$\quad\dfrac{\$6 \times 63{,}000}{8.1} = \dfrac{\$378{,}000}{8.1}$	$46,667	
$-$ Average investment under present plan:		
$\quad\dfrac{\$6 \times 60{,}000}{12.2} = \dfrac{\$360{,}000}{12.2}$	$\underline{29{,}508}$	
$\quad$ Marginal investment in A/R	$17,159	
$\quad\quad$ Cost of marginal investment in A/R (0.15 $\times$ $17,159)		($ 2,574)
Cost of marginal bad debts		
$\quad$ Bad debts under proposed plan (0.02 $\times$ $10 $\times$ 63,000)	$12,600	
$-$ Bad debts under present plan (0.01 $\times$ $10 $\times$ 60,000)	$\underline{6{,}000}$	
$\quad\quad$ Cost of marginal bad debts		($ 6,600)
Net profit from implementation of proposed plan		$\underline{\$\ 2{,}826}$

^{a}The denominators 8.1 and 12.2 in the calculation of the average investment in accounts receivable under the proposed and present plans are the accounts receivable turnovers for each of these plans (365 ÷ 45 = 8.1 and 365 ÷ 30 = 12.2).

to price that product in Japanese yen and extend credit to a Japanese wholesaler in the local currency (yen). If the yen *depreciates* against the dollar before the U.S. exporter collects on its account receivable, the U.S. company experiences an exchange rate loss; the yen collected are worth fewer dollars than expected at the time the sale was made. Of course, the dollar could just as easily depreciate against the yen, yielding an exchange rate gain to the U.S. exporter. Most companies fear the loss more than they welcome the gain.

For a major currency such as the Japanese yen, the exporter can *hedge* against this risk by using the currency futures, forward, or options markets, but it is costly to do so, particularly for relatively small amounts. If the exporter is selling to a customer in a developing country—where 40 percent of U.S. exports are now sold—there will probably be no effective instrument available for protecting against exchange rate risk at any price. This risk may be further magnified because credit standards may be much lower (and acceptable collection techniques much different) in developing countries than in the United States. Although it may seem tempting to just "not bother" with exporting, U.S. companies no longer can concede foreign markets to international rivals. These export sales, if carefully monitored and (where possible) effectively hedged against exchange rate risk, often prove to be very profitable.

CREDIT TERMS

credit terms
The terms of sale for customers who have been extended credit by the firm.

Credit terms are the terms of sale for customers who have been extended credit by the firm. Terms of *net 30* mean the customer has 30 days from the beginning of the credit period (typically *end of month* or *date of invoice)* to pay the full

cash discount
A percentage deduction from the purchase price; available to the credit customer who pays its account within a specified time.

invoice amount. Some firms offer **cash discounts,** percentage deductions from the purchase price for paying within a specified time. For example, terms of *2/10 net 30* mean the customer can take a 2 percent discount from the invoice amount if the payment is made within 10 days of the beginning of the credit period or can pay the full amount of the invoice within 30 days.

A firm's business strongly influences its regular credit terms. For example, a firm selling perishable items will have very short credit terms because its items have little long-term collateral value; a firm in a seasonal business may tailor its terms to fit the industry cycles. A firm wants its regular credit terms to conform to its industry's standards. If its terms are more restrictive than its competitors', it will lose business; if its terms are less restrictive than its competitors', it will attract poor-quality customers that probably could not pay under the standard industry terms. The bottom line is that a firm should compete on the basis of quality and price of its product and service offerings, not its credit terms. Accordingly, the firm's regular credit terms should match the industry standards, but individual customer terms should reflect the riskiness of the customer.

Cash Discount

Including a cash discount in the credit terms is a popular way to speed up collections without putting pressure on customers. The cash discount provides an incentive for customers to pay sooner. By speeding collections, the discount decreases the firm's investment in accounts receivable, but it also decreases the per-unit profit. Additionally, initiating a cash discount should reduce bad debts because customers will pay sooner, and it should increase sales volume because customers who take the discount pay a lower price for the product. Accordingly, firms that consider offering a cash discount must perform a benefit–cost analysis to determine whether extending a cash discount is profitable.

Example 15.8 ▶

MAX Company has annual sales of $10 million and an average collection period of 40 days (turnover = 365 ÷ 40 = 9.1). In accordance with the firm's credit terms of net 30, this period is divided into 32 days until the customers place their payments in the mail (not everyone pays within 30 days) and 8 days to receive, process, and collect payments once they are mailed. MAX is considering initiating a cash discount by changing its credit terms from net 30 to 2/10 net 30. The firm expects this change to reduce the amount of time until the payments are placed in the mail, resulting in an average collection period of 25 days (turnover = 365 ÷ 25 = 14.6).

As noted earlier in Example 15.5, MAX has a raw material with current annual usage of 1,100 units. Each finished product produced requires one unit of this raw material at a variable cost of $1,500 per unit, incurs another $800 of variable cost in the production process, and sells for $3,000 on terms of net 30. Variable costs therefore total $2,300 ($1,500 + $800). MAX estimates that 80% of its customers will take the 2% discount and that offering the discount will increase sales of the finished product by 50 units (from 1,100 to 1,150 units) per year but will not alter its bad-debt percentage. MAX's opportunity cost of funds invested in accounts receivable is 14%. Should MAX offer the proposed cash discount? An analysis similar to that demonstrated earlier for the credit standard decision, presented in Table 15.3, shows a net loss from the cash discount of $6,640. Thus *MAX should not initiate the proposed cash discount.* However, other discounts may be advantageous.

TABLE 15.3	Analysis of Initiating a Cash Discount for MAX Company	
Additional profit contribution from sales		
$[50 \text{ units} \times (\$3,000 - \$2,300)]$		$35,000
Cost of marginal investment in A/R[a]		
Average investment presently (without discount):		
$\dfrac{\$2,300 \times 1,100 \text{ units}}{9.1} = \dfrac{\$2,530,000}{9.1}$	$278,022	
$-$ Average investment with proposed cash discount:[b]		
$\dfrac{\$2,300 \times 1,150 \text{ units}}{14.6} = \dfrac{\$2,645,000}{14.6}$	181,164	
Reduction in accounts receivable investment	$ 96,858	
Cost savings from reduced investment in accounts receivable $(0.14 \times \$96,858)$[c]		$13,560
Cost of cash discount $(0.02 \times 0.80 \times 1,150 \times \$3,000)$		($55,200)
Net profit from initiation of proposed cash discount		($ 6,640)

[a]In analyzing the investment in accounts receivable, we use the variable cost of the product sold ($1,500 raw materials cost + $800 production cost = $2,300 per unit variable cost) instead of the sale price, because the variable cost is a better indicator of the firm's investment.

[b]The average investment in accounts receivable with the proposed cash discount is estimated to be tied up for an average of 25 days instead of the 40 days under the original terms.

[c]MAX's opportunity cost of funds is 14%.

Cash Discount Period

cash discount period
The number of days after the beginning of the credit period during which the cash discount is available.

The financial manager can change the **cash discount period,** the number of days after the beginning of the credit period during which the cash discount is available. The net effect of changes in this period is difficult to analyze because of the nature of the forces involved. For example, if a firm were to increase its cash discount period by 10 days (for example, changing its credit terms from 2/10 net 30 to 2/20 net 30), the following changes would be expected to occur: (1) Sales would increase, positively affecting profit. (2) Bad-debt expenses would decrease, positively affecting profit. (3) The profit per unit would decrease as a result of more people taking the discount, negatively affecting profit.

The difficulty for the financial manager lies in assessing what impact an increase in the cash discount period would have on the firm's investment in accounts receivable. This investment will decrease because of non–discount takers now paying earlier. However, the investment in accounts receivable will increase for two reasons: (1) Discount takers will still get the discount but will pay later, and (2) new customers attracted by the new policy will result in new accounts receivable. If the firm were to decrease the cash discount period, the effects would be the opposite of those just described.

Credit Period

credit period
The number of days after the beginning of the credit period until full payment of the account is due.

Changes in the **credit period,** the number of days after the beginning of the credit period until full payment of the account is due, also affect a firm's profitability. For example, increasing a firm's credit period from net 30 days to net 45 days should increase sales, positively affecting profit. But both the investment in accounts receivable and bad-debt expenses would also increase, negatively affecting profit. The increased investment in accounts receivable would result from both more sales and generally slower pay, on average, as a result of the longer credit period. The increase in bad-debt expenses results from the fact that the longer the credit period, the more time available for a firm to fail, making it unable to pay its accounts payable. A decrease in the length of the credit period is likely to have the opposite effects. Note that the variables affected by an increase in the credit period behave in the same way they would have if the credit standards had been relaxed, as demonstrated earlier in Table 15.2.

CREDIT MONITORING

credit monitoring
The ongoing review of a firm's accounts receivable to determine whether customers are paying according to the stated credit terms.

The final issue a firm should consider in its accounts receivable management is credit monitoring. **Credit monitoring** is an ongoing review of the firm's accounts receivable to determine whether customers are paying according to the stated credit terms. If they are not paying in a timely manner, credit monitoring will alert the firm to the problem. Slow payments are costly to a firm because they lengthen the average collection period and thus increase the firm's investment in accounts receivable. Two frequently used techniques for credit monitoring are average collection period and aging of accounts receivable. In addition, a number of popular collection techniques are used by firms.

Average Collection Period

The *average collection period* is the second component of the cash conversion cycle. As noted in Chapter 3, it is the average number of days that credit sales are outstanding. The average collection period has two components: (1) the time from sale until the customer places the payment in the mail and (2) the time to receive, process, and collect the payment once it has been mailed by the customer. The formula for finding the average collection period is

$$\text{Average collection period} = \frac{\text{Accounts receivable}}{\text{Average sales per day}} \qquad (15.10)$$

Assuming receipt, processing, and collection time is constant, the average collection period tells the firm, on average, when its customers pay their accounts.

Knowing its average collection period enables the firm to determine whether there is a general problem with accounts receivable. For example, a firm that has credit terms of net 30 would expect its average collection period (minus receipt, processing, and collection time) to equal about 30 days. If the actual collection period is significantly greater than 30 days, the firm has reason to review its credit operations. If the firm's average collection period is increasing over time, it has cause for concern about its accounts receivable management. A first step in analyzing an accounts receivable problem is to "age" the accounts receivable. By this process the firm can determine whether the problem exists in its accounts receivable in general or is attributable to a few specific accounts.

Aging of Accounts Receivable

aging schedule
A credit-monitoring technique that breaks down accounts receivable into groups on the basis of their time of origin; it indicates the percentages of the total accounts receivable balance that have been outstanding for specified periods of time.

An **aging schedule** breaks down accounts receivable into groups on the basis of their time of origin. The breakdown is typically made on a month-by-month basis, going back 3 or 4 months. The resulting schedule indicates the percentages of the total accounts receivable balance that have been outstanding for specified periods of time. The purpose of the aging schedule is to enable the firm to pinpoint problems. A simple example will illustrate the form and evaluation of an aging schedule.

Example 15.9 ▶   The accounts receivable balance on the books of Dodd Tool on December 31, 2012, was $200,000. The firm extends net 30-day credit terms to its customers. To gain insight into the firm's relatively lengthy—51.3-day—average collection period, Dodd prepared the following aging schedule.

Age of account	Balance outstanding	Percentage of total balance outstanding
0–30 days	$ 80,000	40%
31–60 days	36,000	18
61–90 days	52,000	26
91–120 days	26,000	13
Over 120 days	6,000	3
Totals at 12/31/12	$200,000	100%

Because Dodd extends 30-day credit terms to its customers, they have 30 days after the end of the month of sale to remit payment. Therefore, the 40% of the balance outstanding with an age of 0–30 days is *current*. The balances outstanding for 31–60 days, 61–90 days, 91–120 days, and over 120 days are *overdue*.

Reviewing the aging schedule, we see that 40% of the accounts are current (age < 30 days) and the remaining 60% are overdue (age > 30 days). Eighteen percent of the balance outstanding is 1–30 days overdue, 26% is 31–60 days overdue, 13% is 61–90 days overdue, and 3% is more than 90 days overdue. Although the collections seem generally slow, a noticeable irregularity in these data is the high percentage of the balance outstanding that is 31–60 days overdue (ages of 61–90 days). Clearly, a problem must have occurred 61–90 days ago. Investigation may find that the problem can be attributed to the hiring of a new credit manager, the acceptance of a new account that made a large credit purchase but has not yet paid for it, or ineffective collection policy. When this type of discrepancy is found in the aging schedule, the analyst should determine, evaluate, and remedy its cause.

In more depth

To read about *Accounts Receivable Financing*, go to www.myfinancelab.com

 myfinancelab®

Popular Collection Techniques

A number of collection techniques, ranging from letters to legal action, are employed. As an account becomes more and more overdue, the collection effort becomes more personal and more intense. In Table 15.4 the popular collection techniques are listed, and briefly described, in the order typically followed in the collection process.

→ REVIEW QUESTIONS

   15–11 What is the role of the *five C's of credit* in the credit selection activity?
   15–12 Explain why *credit scoring* is typically applied to consumer credit decisions rather than to mercantile credit decisions.

TABLE 15.4	Popular Collection Techniques
Technique[a]	Brief description
Letters	After a certain number of days, the firm sends a polite letter reminding the customer of the overdue account. If the account is not paid within a certain period after this letter has been sent, a second, more demanding letter is sent.
Telephone calls	If letters prove unsuccessful, a telephone call may be made to the customer to request immediate payment. If the customer has a reasonable excuse, arrangements may be made to extend the payment period. A call from the seller's attorney may be used.
Personal visits	This technique is much more common at the consumer credit level, but it may also be effectively employed by industrial suppliers. Sending a local salesperson or a collection person to confront the customer can be very effective. Payment may be made on the spot.
Collection agencies	A firm can turn uncollectible accounts over to a collection agency or an attorney for collection. The fees for this service are typically quite high; the firm may receive less than 50 cents on the dollar from accounts collected in this way.
Legal action	Legal action is the most stringent step, an alternative to the use of a collection agency. Not only is direct legal action expensive, but it may force the debtor into bankruptcy without guaranteeing the ultimate receipt of the overdue amount.

[a]The techniques are listed in the order in which they are typically followed in the collection process.

15–13 What are the basic trade-offs in a *tightening* of credit standards?

15–14 Why are the risks involved in international credit management more complex than those associated with purely domestic credit sales?

15–15 Why do a firm's regular credit terms typically conform to those of its industry?

15–16 Why should a firm actively monitor the accounts receivable of its credit customers? How are the *average collection period* and an *aging schedule* used for credit monitoring?

LG 6 | 15.5 Management of Receipts and Disbursements

As discussed in the previous section, the average collection period (the second component of the cash conversion cycle) has two parts: (1) the time from sale until the customer mails the payment and (2) the receipt, processing, and collection time. The third component of the cash conversion cycle, the average payment period, also has two parts: (1) the time from purchase of goods on account until the firm mails its payment and (2) the receipt, processing, and collection time required by the firm's suppliers. The receipt, processing, and collection time for the firm, both from its customers and to its suppliers, is the focus of receipts and disbursements management.

FLOAT

float
Funds that have been sent by the payer but are not yet usable funds to the payee.

Float refers to funds that have been sent by the payer but are not yet usable funds to the payee. Float is important in the cash conversion cycle because its presence lengthens both the firm's average collection period and its average payment period. However, the goal of the firm should be to shorten its average collection

mail float
The time delay between when payment is placed in the mail and when it is received.

processing float
The time between receipt of a payment and its deposit into the firm's account.

clearing float
The time between deposit of a payment and when spendable funds become available to the firm.

period and lengthen its average payment period. Both can be accomplished by managing float.

Float has three component parts:
1. **Mail float** is the time delay between when payment is placed in the mail and when it is received.
2. **Processing float** is the time between receipt of the payment and its deposit into the firm's account.
3. **Clearing float** is the time between deposit of the payment and when spendable funds become available to the firm. This component of float is attributable to the time required for a check to clear the banking system.

Some popular techniques for managing the component parts of float to speed up collections and slow down payments are described here.

SPEEDING UP COLLECTIONS

Speeding up collections reduces customer *collection float* time and thus reduces the firm's average collection period, which reduces the investment the firm must make in its cash conversion cycle. In our earlier examples, MAX Company had annual sales of $10 million and 8 days of total collection float (receipt, processing, and collection time). If MAX can reduce its float time by 3 days, it will reduce its investment in the cash conversion cycle by $82,192 [$10,000,000 × (3 ÷ 365)].

lockbox system
A collection procedure in which customers mail payments to a post office box that is emptied regularly by the firm's bank, which processes the payments and deposits them in the firm's account. This system speeds up collection time by reducing processing time as well as mail and clearing time.

A popular technique for speeding up collections is a lockbox system. A **lockbox system** works as follows: Instead of mailing payments to the company, customers mail payments to a post office box. The firm's bank empties the post office box regularly, processes each payment, and deposits the payments in the firm's account. Deposit slips, along with payment enclosures, are sent (or transmitted electronically) to the firm by the bank so that the firm can properly credit customers' accounts. Lockboxes are geographically dispersed to match the locations of the firm's customers. A lockbox system affects all three components of float. Lockboxes reduce mail time and often clearing time by being near the firm's customers. Lockboxes reduce processing time to nearly zero because the bank deposits payments before the firm processes them. Obviously a lockbox system reduces collection float time, but not without a cost; therefore, a firm must perform an economic analysis to determine whether to implement a lockbox system.

Lockbox systems are commonly used by large firms whose customers are geographically dispersed. However, a firm does not have to be large to benefit from a lockbox. Smaller firms can also benefit from a lockbox system. The benefit to small firms often comes primarily from transferring the processing of payments to the bank.

SLOWING DOWN PAYMENTS

controlled disbursing
The strategic use of mailing points and bank accounts to lengthen mail float and clearing float, respectively.

Float is also a component of the firm's average payment period. In this case, the float is in the favor of the firm. The firm may benefit by increasing all three of the components of its *payment float*. One popular technique for increasing payment float is **controlled disbursing**, which involves the strategic use of mailing points and bank accounts to lengthen mail float and clearing float, respectively. Firms must use this approach carefully, though, because longer payment periods may strain supplier relations.

The nearby *Focus on Ethics* box takes a closer look at the ethical issues involved in slowing down payments through controlled disbursing and other

focus on ETHICS

Stretching Accounts Payable—Is It a Good Policy?

in practice   Stretching payables has often been considered good cash management. By delaying bill payments as long as possible without damaging the firm's credit, companies get interest-free loans from suppliers. Some businesses deliberately increase their accounts payable lag to cover temporary cash shortages.

There are two negative ramifications of stretching accounts payables (A/P). First, the stretching out of payables can be pushed too far, and a business can get tagged as a slow payer. Vendors will eventually put increasing pressure on the company to make more timely payments.

Stretching accounts payables also raises ethical issues. First, it may cause the firm to violate the agreement it entered with its supplier when it purchased the merchandise. More important to investors, the firm may stretch A/P to artificially boost reported operating cash flow during a reporting period. In other words, firms can improve reported operating cash flows due solely to a decision to slow the payment rate to vendors. Unfortunately for investors, the improvement in operating cash flows may be unsustainable if vendors force the company to improve its payment record; at a minimum, any year-over-year improvement in operating cash flow may be unsustainable.

The extension of payables can be identified by monitoring *days sales payables* (DSP), calculated as the end-of-period accounts payable balance divided by the cost of goods sold and multiplied by the number of days in the period. As DSP grows, operating cash flows are boosted.

A more complicated version of stretching payables is the financing of payables. This occurs when a company uses a third-party financial institution to pay the vendor in the current period and pays back the bank in a subsequent period. This approach reclassifies the amount from accounts payable to short-term loans. The reclassification results in a decrease to operating cash flow in that quarter and an increase in financing cash flow. Normally, cash expenditures for accounts payable are included in operating activities. Because the timing and extent of vendor financing is at the discretion of company management, the temptation to manipulate operating cash flows may prove too great for some.

Setting aside the ethical ramifications of stretching accounts payable, there may be financial incentives for avoiding the practice. Companies that can move to an automated A/P system may be able to take advantage of beneficial early payment discounts that provide a far better risk-free rate of return than stretching out accounts payable. For example, a 2/10 net 30 discount equates to about a 36 percent annualized return. Viewed this way, an A/P balance may be the most expensive debt on the balance sheet.

▶ *While vendor discounts for early payment are very rewarding, what are some of the difficulties that may arise to keep a firm from taking advantage of those discounts?*

methods—a technique known collectively as *stretching accounts payable*. This is a topic we will come back to in Chapter 16.

In summary, a reasonable overall policy for float management is (1) to collect payments as quickly as possible because, once the payment is in the mail, the funds belong to the firm; and (2) to delay making payment to suppliers because, once the payment is mailed, the funds belong to the supplier.

CASH CONCENTRATION

cash concentration
The process used by the firm to bring lockbox and other deposits together into one bank, often called the *concentration bank*.

Cash concentration is the process used by the firm to bring lockbox and other deposits together into one bank, often called the *concentration bank*. Cash concentration has three main advantages. First, it creates a large pool of funds for use in making short-term cash investments. Because there is a fixed-cost component in the transaction cost associated with such investments, investing a single pool of funds reduces the firm's transaction costs. The larger investment pool also allows the firm to choose from a greater variety of short-term investment vehicles.

Second, concentrating the firm's cash in one account improves the tracking and internal control of the firm's cash. Third, having one concentration bank enables the firm to implement payment strategies that reduce idle cash balances.

There are a variety of mechanisms for transferring cash from the lockbox bank and other collecting banks to the concentration bank. One mechanism is a **depository transfer check (DTC)**, which is an unsigned check drawn on one of the firm's bank accounts and deposited in another. For cash concentration, a DTC is drawn on each lockbox or other collecting bank account and deposited in the concentration bank account. Once the DTC has cleared the bank on which it is drawn (which may take several days), the transfer of funds is completed. Most firms currently provide deposit information by telephone to the concentration bank, which then prepares and deposits into its account the DTC drawn on the lockbox or other collecting bank account.

A second mechanism is an **ACH (automated clearinghouse) transfer,** which is a preauthorized electronic withdrawal from the payer's account. A computerized clearing facility (called the *automated clearinghouse,* or *ACH*) makes a paperless transfer of funds between the payer and payee banks. An ACH settles accounts among participating banks. Individual accounts are settled by respective bank balance adjustments. ACH transfers clear in one day. For cash concentration, an ACH transfer is made from each lockbox bank or other collecting bank to the concentration bank. An ACH transfer can be thought of as an electronic DTC, but because the ACH transfer clears in one day, it provides benefits over a DTC; however, both banks in the ACH transfer must be members of the clearinghouse.

A third cash concentration mechanism is a **wire transfer.** A wire transfer is an electronic communication that, via bookkeeping entries, removes funds from the payer's bank and deposits them in the payee's bank. Wire transfers can eliminate mail and clearing float and may reduce processing float as well. For cash concentration, the firm moves funds using a wire transfer from each lockbox or other collecting account to its concentration account. Wire transfers are a substitute for DTC and ACH transfers, but they are more expensive.

It is clear that the firm must balance the costs and benefits of concentrating cash to determine the type and timing of transfers from its lockbox and other collecting accounts to its concentration account. The transfer mechanism selected should be the one that is most profitable. (The profit per period of any transfer mechanism equals earnings on the increased availability of funds minus the cost of the transfer system.)

ZERO-BALANCE ACCOUNTS

Zero-balance accounts (ZBAs) are disbursement accounts that always have an end-of-day balance of zero. The purpose is to eliminate nonearning cash balances in corporate checking accounts. A ZBA works well as a disbursement account under a cash concentration system.

ZBAs work as follows: Once all of a given day's checks are presented for payment from the firm's ZBA, the bank notifies the firm of the total amount of checks, and the firm transfers funds into the account to cover the amount of that day's checks. This leaves an end-of-day balance of $0 (zero dollars). The ZBA enables the firm to keep all of its operating cash in an interest-earning account, thereby eliminating idle cash balances. Thus a firm that used a ZBA in conjunction with a cash concentration system would need two accounts. The firm would concentrate its

depository transfer check (DTC)
An unsigned check drawn on one of a firm's bank accounts and deposited in another.

ACH (automated clearinghouse) transfer
Preauthorized electronic withdrawal from the payer's account and deposit into the payee's account via a settlement among banks by the *automated clearinghouse,* or *ACH.*

wire transfer
An electronic communication that, via bookkeeping entries, removes funds from the payer's bank and deposits them in the payee's bank.

zero-balance account (ZBA)
A disbursement account that always has an end-of-day balance of zero because the firm deposits money to cover checks drawn on the account only as they are presented for payment each day.

cash from the lockboxes and other collecting banks into an interest-earning account and would write checks against its ZBA. The firm would cover the exact dollar amount of checks presented against the ZBA with transfers from the interest-earning account, leaving the end-of-day balance in the ZBA at $0.

A ZBA is a disbursement-management tool. As we discussed earlier, the firm would prefer to maximize its payment float. However, some cash managers feel that actively attempting to increase float time on payments is unethical. A ZBA enables the firm to maximize the use of float on each check without altering the float time of payments to its suppliers. Keeping all the firm's cash in an interest-earning account enables the firm to maximize earnings on its cash balances by capturing the full float time on each check it writes.

Personal Finance Example 15.10 ▶ Megan Laurie, a 25-year-old nurse, works at a hospital that pays her every 2 weeks by direct deposit into her checking account, which pays no interest and has no minimum balance requirement. She takes home about $1,800 every 2 weeks—or about $3,600 per month. She maintains a checking account balance of around $1,500. Whenever it exceeds that amount she transfers the excess into her savings account, which currently pays 1.5% annual interest. She currently has a savings account balance of $17,000 and estimates that she transfers about $600 per month from her checking account into her savings account.

Megan pays her bills immediately when she receives them. Her monthly bills average about $1,900, and her monthly cash outlays for food and gas total about $900. An analysis of Megan's bill payments indicates that on average she pays her bills 8 days early. Most marketable securities are currently yielding about 4.2% annual interest. Megan is interested in learning how she might better manage her cash balances.

Megan talks with her sister, who has had a finance course, and they come up with three ways for Megan to better manage her cash balance:

1. **Invest current balances.** Megan can transfer her current savings account balances into a liquid marketable security, thereby increasing the rate of interest earned from 1.5% to about 4.2%. On her current $17,000 balance, she will immediately increase her annual interest earnings by about $460 [(0.042 − 0.015) × $17,000].
2. **Invest monthly surpluses.** Megan can transfer monthly the $600 from her checking account to the liquid marketable security, thereby increasing the annual earnings on each monthly transfer by about $16 [(0.042 − 0.015) × $600], which for the 12 transfers would generate additional annual earnings of about $192 (12 months × $16).
3. **Slow down payments.** Rather than paying her bills immediately on receipt, Megan can pay her bills nearer their due date. By doing this she can gain 8 days of disbursement float each month, or 96 days per year (8 days per month × 12 months), on an average of $1,900 of bills. Assuming she can earn 4.2% annual interest on the $1,900, slowing down her payments would save about $21 annually [(96 ÷ 365) × 0.042 × $1,900].

Based on these three recommendations, Megan would increase her annual earnings by a total of about $673 ($460 + $192 + $21). Clearly, Megan can grow her earnings by better managing her cash balances.

INVESTING IN MARKETABLE SECURITIES

Marketable securities are short-term, interest-earning, money market instruments that can easily be converted into cash. Marketable securities are classified as part of the firm's liquid assets. The firm uses them to earn a return on temporarily idle funds. To be truly marketable, a security must have (1) a ready market so as to minimize the amount of time required to convert it into cash, and (2) safety of principal, which means that it experiences little or no loss in value over time.

The securities that are most commonly held as part of the firm's marketable-securities portfolio are divided into two groups: (1) government issues, which have relatively low yields as a consequence of their low risk; and (2) nongovernment issues, which have slightly higher yields than government issues with similar maturities because of the slightly higher risk associated with them. Table 15.5 summarizes the key features for popular marketable securities.

TABLE 15.5 ▶ **Features of Popular Marketable Securities**

Security	Issuer	Description	Initial maturity	Risk and return
Government Issues				
Treasury bills	U.S. Treasury	Issued weekly at auction; sold at a discount; strong secondary market	4, 13, and 26 weeks	Lowest, virtually risk-free
Treasury notes	U.S. Treasury	Stated interest rate; interest paid semiannually; strong secondary market	1 to 10 years	Low, but higher than U.S. Treasury bills
Treasury bonds	U.S. Treasury	Stated interest rate; interest paid semiannually; strong secondary market	11 to 30 years	Less than corporate bonds, but higher than U.S. Treasury bills and notes
Federal agency issues	Agencies of federal goverment	Not an obligation of U.S. Treasury; strong secondary market	9 months to 30 years	Slightly higher than U.S. Treasury issues
Nongovernment Issues				
Negotiable certificates of deposit (CDs)	Commercial banks	Represent specific cash deposits in commercial banks; amounts and maturities tailored to investor needs; large denominations; good secondary market	1 month to 3 years	Higher than U.S. Treasury issues and comparable to commercial paper
Commercial paper	Corporation with a high credit standing	Unsecured note of issuer; large denominations	3 to 270 days	Higher than U.S. Treasury issues and comparable to negotiable CDs
Banker's acceptances	Banks	Results from a bank guarantee of a business transaction; sold at discount from maturity value	30 to 180 days	About the same as negotiable CDs and commercial paper but higher than U.S. Treasury issues

(continued)

TABLE 15.5	Features of Popular Marketable Securities (*continued*)			
Security	Issuer	Description	Initial maturity	Risk and return
Nongovernment Issues				
Eurodollar deposits	Foreign banks	Deposits of currency not native to the country in which the bank is located; large denominations; active secondary market	1 day to 3 years	High, due to less regulation of despository banks and some foreign exchange risk
Money market mutual funds	Professional portfolio management companies	Professionally managed portfolios of marketable securities; provide instant liquidity	None—depends on wishes of investor	Vary, but generally higher than U.S. Treasury issues and comparable to negotiable CDs and commercial paper
Repurchase agreements	Bank or securities dealer	Bank or securities dealer sells specific securities to firm and agrees to repurchase them at a specific price and time	Customized to purchaser's needs	Generally slightly below that associated with the outright purchase of the security

→ **REVIEW QUESTIONS**

15–17 What is *float*, and what are its three components?

15–18 What are the firm's objectives with regard to *collection float* and to *payment float?*

15–19 What are the three main advantages of *cash concentration?*

15–20 What are three mechanisms of cash concentration? What is the objective of using a *zero-balance account (ZBA)* in a cash concentration system?

15–21 What two characteristics make a security marketable? Why are the yields on nongovernment marketable securities generally higher than the yields on government issues with similar maturities?

Summary

FOCUS ON VALUE

It is important for a firm to maintain a reasonable level of net working capital. To do so, it must balance the high profit and high risk associated with low levels of current assets and high levels of current liabilities against the low profit and low risk that result from high levels of current assets and low levels of current liabilities. A strategy that achieves a reasonable balance between profits and risk should positively contribute to the firm's value.

Similarly, the firm should manage its cash conversion cycle by turning inventory quickly; collecting accounts receivable quickly; managing mail, processing, and clearing time; and paying accounts payable slowly. These strategies should enable the firm to manage its current accounts efficiently and to minimize the amount of resources invested in operating assets.

The financial manager can manage inventory, accounts receivable, and cash receipts to minimize the firm's operating cycle investment, thereby reducing the amount of resources needed to support its business. Employing these strategies, and managing accounts payable and cash disbursements so as to shorten the cash conversion cycle, should minimize the negotiated liabilities needed to support the firm's resource requirements. Active management of the firm's net working capital and current assets should positively contribute to the firm's goal of **maximizing its stock price**.

REVIEW OF LEARNING GOALS

LG 1 Understand working capital management, net working capital, and the related trade-off between profitability and risk. Working capital (or short-term financial) management focuses on managing each of the firm's current assets (inventory, accounts receivable, cash, and marketable securities) and current liabilities (accounts payable, accruals, and notes payable) in a manner that positively contributes to the firm's value. Net working capital is the difference between current assets and current liabilities. Risk, in the context of short-term financial decisions, is the probability that a firm will be unable to pay its bills as they come due. Assuming a constant level of total assets, the higher a firm's ratio of current assets to total assets, the less profitable the firm and the less risky it is. The converse is also true. With constant total assets, the higher a firm's ratio of current liabilities to total assets, the more profitable and the more risky the firm is. The converse of this statement is also true.

LG 2 Describe the cash conversion cycle, its funding requirements, and the key strategies for managing it. The cash conversion cycle has three components: (1) average age of inventory, (2) average collection period, and (3) average payment period. The length of the cash conversion cycle determines the amount of time resources are tied up in the firm's day-to-day operations. The firm's investment in short-term assets often consists of both permanent and seasonal funding requirements. The seasonal requirements can be financed using either an aggressive (low-cost, high-risk) financing strategy or a conservative (high-cost, low-risk) financing strategy. The firm's funding decision for its cash conversion cycle ultimately depends on management's disposition toward risk and the strength of the firm's banking relationships. To minimize its reliance on negotiated liabilities, the financial manager seeks to (1) turn over inventory as quickly as possible, (2) collect accounts receivable as quickly as possible, (3) manage mail, processing, and clearing time, and (4) pay accounts payable as slowly as possible. Use of these strategies should minimize the length of the cash conversion cycle.

LG 3 Discuss inventory management: differing views, common techniques, and international concerns. The viewpoints of marketing, manufacturing, and purchasing managers about the appropriate levels of inventory tend to cause higher inventories than those deemed appropriate by the financial manager. Four commonly used techniques for effectively managing inventory to keep its level low are (1) the ABC system, (2) the economic order quantity (EOQ) model, (3) the just-in-time (JIT) system, and (4) computerized systems for resource control—MRP, MRP II, and ERP. International inventory managers place greater emphasis on making sure that sufficient quantities of inventory are delivered where and when needed, and in the right condition, than on ordering the economically optimal quantities.

LG 4   **Explain the credit selection process and the quantitative procedure for evaluating changes in credit standards.** Credit selection techniques determine which customers' creditworthiness is consistent with the firm's credit standards. Two popular credit selection techniques are the five C's of credit and credit scoring. Changes in credit standards can be evaluated mathematically by assessing the effects of a proposed change on profits from sales, the cost of accounts receivable investment, and bad-debt costs.

LG 5   **Review the procedures for quantitatively considering cash discount changes, other aspects of credit terms, and credit monitoring.** Changes in credit terms—the cash discount, the cash discount period, and the credit period—can be quantified similarly to changes in credit standards. Credit monitoring, the ongoing review of accounts receivable, frequently involves use of the average collection period and an aging schedule. Firms use a number of popular collection techniques.

LG 6   **Understand the management of receipts and disbursements, including float, speeding up collections, slowing down payments, cash concentration, zero-balance accounts, and investing in marketable securities.** Float refers to funds that have been sent by the payer but are not yet usable funds to the payee. The components of float are mail time, processing time, and clearing time. Float occurs in both the average collection period and the average payment period. One technique for speeding up collections is a lockbox system. A popular technique for slowing payments is controlled disbursing.

The goal for managing operating cash is to balance the opportunity cost of nonearning balances against the transaction cost of temporary investments. Firms commonly use depository transfer checks (DTCs), ACH transfers, and wire transfers to transfer lockbox receipts to their concentration banks quickly. Zero-balance accounts (ZBAs) can be used to eliminate nonearning cash balances in corporate checking accounts. Marketable securities are short-term, interest-earning, money market instruments used by the firm to earn a return on temporarily idle funds. They may be government or nongovernment issues.

Opener-in-Review

Hing Yiap has been able to recuperate its lost market share by reducing its working capital. How can a company turn around using a more focused working capital management approach?

Self-Test Problems   (Solutions in Appendix)

LG 2   **ST15–1   Cash conversion cycle**   Hurkin Manufacturing Company pays accounts payable on the tenth day after purchase. The average collection period is 30 days, and the average age of inventory is 40 days. The firm currently has annual sales of about

$18 million and purchases of $14 million. The firm is considering a plan that would stretch its accounts payable by 20 days. If the firm pays 12% per year for its resource investment, what annual savings can it realize by this plan? Assume a 360-day year.

LG 3 **ST15–2** **EOQ analysis** Thompson Paint Company uses 60,000 gallons of pigment per year. The cost of ordering pigment is $200 per order, and the cost of carrying the pigment in inventory is $1 per gallon per year. The firm uses pigment at a constant rate every day throughout the year.
   a. Calculate the EOQ.
   b. Assuming that it takes 20 days to receive an order once it has been placed, determine the reorder point in terms of gallons of pigment. (*Note:* Use a 365-day year.)

LG 4 **ST15–3** **Relaxing credit standards** Regency Rug Repair Company is trying to decide whether it should relax its credit standards. The firm repairs 72,000 rugs per year at an average price of $32 each. Bad-debt expenses are 1% of sales, the average collection period is 40 days, and the variable cost per unit is $28. Regency expects that if it does relax its credit standards, the average collection period will increase to 48 days and that bad debts will increase to $1^1/_2$% of sales. Sales will increase by 4,000 repairs per year. If the firm has a required rate of return on equal-risk investments of 14%, what recommendation would you give the firm? Use your analysis to justify your answer. (*Note:* Use a 365-day year.)

Warm-Up Exercises

All problems are available in 🌐 myfinancelab .

LG 2 **E15–1** Sharam Industries has a 120-day *operating cycle*. If its average age of inventory is 50 days, how long is its average collection period? If its average payment period is 30 days, what is its *cash conversion cycle*? Place all of this information on a time line similar to Figure 15.2 on page 605.

LG 2 **E15–2** Icy Treats, Inc., is a seasonal business that sells frozen desserts. At the peak of its summer selling season the firm has $35,000 in cash, $125,000 in inventory, $70,000 in accounts receivable, and $65,000 in accounts payable. During the slow winter period the firm holds $10,000 in cash, $55,000 in inventory, $40,000 in accounts receivable, and $35,000 in accounts payable. Calculate Icy Treats' minimum and peak funding requirements.

LG 3 **E15–3** Mama Leone's Frozen Pizzas uses 50,000 units of cheese per year. Each unit costs $2.50. The ordering cost for the cheese is $250 per order, and its carrying cost is $0.50 per unit per year. Calculate the firm's *economic order quantity (EOQ)* for the cheese. Mama Leone's operates 250 days per year and maintains a minimum inventory level of 2 days' worth of cheese as a safety stock. If the lead time to receive orders of cheese is 3 days, calculate the *reorder point*.

LG 4 **E15–4** Forrester Fashions has annual credit sales of 250,000 units with an average collection period of 70 days. The company has a per-unit variable cost of $20 and a per-unit sale price of $30. Bad debts currently are 5% of sales. The firm estimates that a proposed relaxation of credit standards would not affect its 70-day average collection period but would increase bad debts to 7.5% of sales, which would increase to 300,000 units per year. Forrester requires a 12% return on investments. Show all necessary calculations required to evaluate Forrester's proposed relaxation of credit standards.

LG 5   E15–5   Klein's Tools is considering offering a cash discount to speed up the collection of accounts receivable. Currently the firm has an average collection period of 65 days, annual sales are 35,000 units, the per-unit price is $40, and the per-unit variable cost is $29. A 2% cash discount is being considered. Klein's Tools estimates that 80% of its customers will take the 2% discount. If sales are expected to rise to 37,000 units per year and the firm has a 15% required rate of return, what minimum average collection period is required to approve the cash discount plan?

Problems

All problems are available in ⬢myfinancelab .

LG 2   P15–1   Cash conversion cycle   American Products is concerned about managing cash efficiently. On the average, inventories have an age of 90 days, and accounts receivable are collected in 60 days. Accounts payable are paid approximately 30 days after they arise. The firm has annual sales of about $30 million. Assume there is no difference in the investment per dollar of sales in inventory, receivables, and payables and that there is a 365-day year.
a. Calculate the firm's *operating cycle*.
b. Calculate the firm's *cash conversion cycle*.
c. Calculate the amount of resources needed to support the firm's cash conversion cycle.
d. Discuss how management might be able to reduce the cash conversion cycle.

LG 2   P15–2   Changing cash conversion cycle   Camp Manufacturing turns over its inventory eight times each year, has an average payment period of 35 days, and has an average collection period of 60 days. The firm's annual sales are $3.5 million. Assume there is no difference in the investment per dollar of sales in inventory, receivables, and payables and that there is a 365-day year.
a. Calculate the firm's *operating cycle* and *cash conversion cycle*.
b. Calculate the firm's daily cash operating expenditure. How much in resources must be invested to support its cash conversion cycle?
c. If the firm pays 14% for these resources, by how much would it increase its annual profits by *favorably* changing its current cash conversion cycle by 20 days?

LG 2   P15–3   Multiple changes in cash conversion cycle   Garrett Industries turns over its inventory six times each year; it has an average collection period of 45 days and an average payment period of 30 days. The firm's annual sales are $3 million. Assume there is no difference in the investment per dollar of sales in inventory, receivables, and payables; and assume a 365-day year.
a. Calculate the firm's *cash conversion cycle*, its daily cash operating expenditure, and the amount of resources needed to support its cash conversion cycle.

b. Find the firm's cash conversion cycle and resource investment requirement if it makes the following changes simultaneously.
   (1) Shortens the average age of inventory by 5 days.
   (2) Speeds the collection of accounts receivable by an average of 10 days.
   (3) Extends the average payment period by 10 days.
c. If the firm pays 13% for its resource investment, by how much, if anything, could it increase its annual profit as a result of the changes in part **b?**
d. If the annual cost of achieving the profit in part **c** is $35,000, what action would you recommend to the firm? Why?

LG 2 **P15–4** **Aggressive versus conservative seasonal funding strategy** Dynabase Tool has forecast its total funds requirements for the coming year as shown in the following table.

Month	Amount	Month	Amount
January	$2,000,000	July	$12,000,000
February	2,000,000	August	14,000,000
March	2,000,000	September	9,000,000
April	4,000,000	October	5,000,000
May	6,000,000	November	4,000,000
June	9,000,000	December	3,000,000

a. Divide the firm's monthly funds requirement into (1) a *permanent* component and (2) a *seasonal* component, and find the monthly average for each of these components.
b. Describe the amount of long-term and short-term financing used to meet the total funds requirement under (1) an *aggressive funding strategy* and (2) a *conservative funding strategy.* Assume that, under the aggressive strategy, long-term funds finance permanent needs and short-term funds are used to finance seasonal needs.
c. Assuming that short-term funds cost 12% annually and that the cost of long-term funds is 17% annually, use the averages found in part **a** to calculate the total cost of each of the strategies described in part **b.**
d. Discuss the profitability–risk trade-offs associated with the aggressive strategy and those associated with the conservative strategy.

LG 3 **P15–5** **EOQ analysis** Tiger Corporation purchases 1,200,000 units per year of one component. The fixed cost per order is $25. The annual carrying cost of the item is 27% of its $2 cost.
a. Determine the EOQ under each of the following conditions: (1) no changes, (2) order cost of zero, and (3) carrying cost of zero.
b. What do your answers illustrate about the EOQ model? Explain.

LG 3 **P15–6** **EOQ, reorder point, and safety stock** Alexis Company uses 800 units of a product per year on a continuous basis. The product has a fixed cost of $50 per order, and its carrying cost is $2 per unit per year. It takes 5 days to receive a shipment after an order is placed, and the firm wishes to hold 10 days' usage in inventory as a safety stock.
a. Calculate the EOQ.
b. Determine the average level of inventory. (*Note:* Use a 365-day year to calculate daily usage.)

c. Determine the *reorder point*.

d. Indicate which of the following variables change if the firm does not hold the safety stock: (1) order cost, (2) carrying cost, (3) total inventory cost, (4) reorder point, (5) economic order quantity. Explain.

Personal Finance Problem

LG 3 **P15–7** **Marginal costs** Jimmy Johnson is interested in buying a new Jeep SUV. There are two options available, a V-6 model and a V-8 model. Whichever model he chooses, he plans to drive it for a period of 5 years and then sell it. Assume that the trade-in value of the two vehicles at the end of the 5-year ownership period will be identical.

There are definite differences between the two models, and Jimmy needs to make a financial comparison. The manufacturer's suggested retail price (MSRP) of the V-6 and V-8 are $30,260 and $44,320, respectively. Jimmy believes the difference of $14,060 to be the marginal cost difference between the two vehicles. However, there is much more data available, and you suggest to Jimmy that his analysis may be too simple and will lead him to a poor financial decision. Assume that the prevailing discount rate for both vehicles is 5.5% annually. Other pertinent information on this purchase is shown in the following table:

	V-6	V-8
MSRP	$30,260	$44,320
Engine (liters)	3.7	5.7
Cylinders	6	8
Depreciation over 5 years	$17,337	$25,531
Finance charges* over entire 5-year period	$5,171	$7,573
Insurance over 5 years	$7,546	$8,081
Taxes and fees over 5 years	$2,179	$2,937
Maintenance/repairs over 5 years	$5,600	$5,600
Average miles per gallon	19	14
Ownership period in years	5	5
Miles driven per year over 5 years	15,000	15,000
Cost per gallon of gas over 5-year ownership	$3.15	$3.15

*The finance charges are the difference between the total principal and interest paid over the entire 5-year period less the actual cost of the SUV. Assuming an annual 5.5% discount rate over each of the 5 years and the respective present values of $30,260 for the V-6 and $44,320 for the V-8, the annual annuity payments are $7,086.20 and $10,379.70, respectively. [V-6: (5 × $7,086.20) − $30,260 = $5,171, and V-8: (5 × $10,379.70) − $44,320 = $7,573]

a. Calculate the total "true" cost for each vehicle over the 5-year ownership period.

b. Calculate the total fuel cost for each vehicle over the 5-year ownership period.

c. What is the marginal fuel cost from purchasing the larger V-8 SUV?

d. What is the marginal cost of purchasing the larger and more expensive V-8 SUV?

e. What is the total marginal cost associated with purchasing the V-8 SUV? How does this figure compare with the $14,060 that Jimmy calculated?

LG 4 **P15–8** **Accounts receivable changes without bad debts** Tara's Textiles currently has credit sales of $360 million per year and an average collection period of 60 days. Assume that the price of Tara's products is $60 per unit and that the variable costs are $55 per unit. The firm is considering an accounts receivable change that will result in a 20% increase in sales and a 20% increase in the average collection period. No change in bad debts is expected. The firm's equal-risk opportunity cost on its investment in accounts receivable is 14%. (*Note:* Use a 365-day year.)

a. Calculate the *additional profit contribution from sales* that the firm will realize if it makes the proposed change.

b. What *marginal investment in accounts receivable* will result?

c. Calculate the *cost of the marginal investment in accounts receivable*.

d. Should the firm implement the proposed change? What other information would be helpful in your analysis?

LG 4 **P15–9** **Accounts receivable changes with bad debts** A firm is evaluating an accounts receivable change that would increase bad debts from 2% to 4% of sales. Sales are currently 50,000 units, the selling price is $20 per unit, and the variable cost per unit is $15. As a result of the proposed change, sales are forecast to increase to 60,000 units.

a. What are bad debts in dollars currently and under the proposed change?

b. Calculate the *cost of the marginal bad debts* to the firm.

c. Ignoring the additional profit contribution from increased sales, if the proposed change saves $3,500 and causes no change in the average investment in accounts receivable, would you recommend it? Explain.

d. Considering *all* changes in costs and benefits, would you recommend the proposed change? Explain.

e. Compare and discuss your answers in parts **c** and **d**.

LG 4 **P15–10** **Relaxation of credit standards** Lewis Enterprises is considering relaxing its credit standards to increase its currently sagging sales. As a result of the proposed relaxation, sales are expected to increase by 10% from 10,000 to 11,000 units during the coming year; the average collection period is expected to increase from 45 to 60 days; and bad debts are expected to increase from 1% to 3% of sales. The sale price per unit is $40, and the variable cost per unit is $31. The firm's required return on equal-risk investments is 25%. Evaluate the proposed relaxation, and make a recommendation to the firm. (*Note:* Assume a 365-day year.)

LG 5 **P15–11** **Initiating a cash discount** Gardner Company currently makes all sales on credit and offers no cash discount. The firm is considering offering a 2% cash discount for payment within 15 days. The firm's current average collection period is 60 days, sales are 40,000 units, selling price is $45 per unit, and variable cost per unit is $36. The firm expects that the change in credit terms will result in an increase in sales to 42,000 units, that 70% of the sales will take the discount, and that the average collection period will fall to 30 days. If the firm's required rate of return on equal-risk investments is 25%, should the proposed discount be offered? (*Note:* Assume a 365-day year.)

LG 5 **P15–12** **Shortening the credit period** A firm is contemplating *shortening* its credit period from 40 to 30 days and believes that, as a result of this change, its average collection period will decline from 45 to 36 days. Bad-debt expenses are expected to decrease from 1.5% to 1% of sales. The firm is currently selling 12,000 units but believes that as a result of the proposed change, sales will decline to 10,000 units. The sale price per unit is $56, and the variable cost per unit is $45. The firm has a required return on equal-risk investments of 25%. Evaluate this decision, and make a recommendation to the firm. (*Note:* Assume a 365-day year.)

LG 5 **P15–13** **Lengthening the credit period** Parker Tool is considering lengthening its credit period from 30 to 60 days. All customers will continue to pay on the net date. The firm currently bills $450,000 for sales and has $345,000 in variable costs. The change in credit terms is expected to increase sales to $510,000. Bad-debt expenses will increase from 1% to 1.5% of sales. The firm has a required rate of return on equal-risk investments of 20%. (*Note:* Assume a 365-day year.)

a. What *additional profit contribution from sales* will be realized from the proposed change?

b. What is the *cost of the marginal investment in accounts receivable?*

c. What is the *cost of the marginal bad debts?*

d. Do you recommend this change in credit terms? Why or why not?

LG 6   **P15–14**   **Float**   Simon Corporation has daily cash receipts of $65,000. A recent analysis of its collections indicated that customers' payments were in the mail an average of 2.5 days. Once received, the payments are processed in 1.5 days. After payments are deposited, it takes an average of 3 days for these receipts to clear the banking system.

a. How much *collection float (in days)* does the firm currently have?

b. If the firm's opportunity cost is 11%, would it be economically advisable for the firm to pay an annual fee of $16,500 to reduce collection float by 3 days? Explain why or why not.

LG 6   **P15–15**   **Lockbox system**   Eagle Industries feels that a lockbox system can shorten its accounts receivable collection period by 3 days. Credit sales are $3,240,000 per year, billed on a continuous basis. The firm has other equally risky investments that earn a return of 15%. The cost of the lockbox system is $9,000 per year. (*Note:* Assume a 365-day year.)

a. What amount of cash will be made available for other uses under the lockbox system?

b. What net benefit (cost) will the firm realize if it adopts the lockbox system? Should it adopt the proposed lockbox system?

LG 6   **P15–16**   **Zero-balance account**   Union Company is considering establishment of a zero-balance account. The firm currently maintains an average balance of $420,000 in its disbursement account. As compensation to the bank for maintaining the zero-balance account, the firm will have to pay a monthly fee of $1,000 and maintain a $300,000 non–interest-earning deposit in the bank. The firm currently has no other deposits in the bank. Evaluate the proposed zero-balance account, and make a recommendation to the firm, assuming that it has a 12% opportunity cost.

Personal Finance Problem

LG 6   **P15–17**   **Management of cash balance**   Alexis Morris, an assistant manager at a local department store, gets paid every 2 weeks by direct deposit into her checking account. This account pays no interest and has no minimum balance requirement. Her monthly income is $4,200. Alexis has a "target" cash balance of around $1,200, and whenever it exceeds that amount she transfers the excess into her savings account, which currently pays 2.0% annual interest. Her current savings balance is $15,000, and Alexis estimates she transfers about $500 per month from her checking account into her savings account. Alexis doesn't waste any time in paying her bills, and her monthly bills average about $2,000. Her monthly cash outlay for food, gas, and other sundry items totals about $850. Reviewing her payment habits indicates that on average she pays her bills 9 days early. At this time, most marketable securities are yielding about 4.75% annual interest.

Show how Alexis can better manage her cash balance.

a. What can Alexis do regarding the handling of her current balances?

b. What do you suggest that she do with her monthly surpluses?

c. What do you suggest Alexis do about the manner in which she pays her bills?
d. Can Alexis grow her earnings by better managing her cash balances? Show your work.

 P15–18 **ETHICS PROBLEM** A group of angry shareholders has placed a corporate resolution before all shareholders at a company's annual stockholders' meeting. The resolution demands that the company *stretch its accounts payable,* because these shareholders have determined that all of the company's competitors do so, and the firm operates in a highly competitive industry. How could management at the annual stockholders' meeting defend the firm's practice of paying suppliers on time?

Spreadsheet Exercise

The current balance in accounts receivable for Eboy Corporation is $443,000. This level was achieved with annual (365 days) credit sales of $3,544,000. The firm offers its customers credit terms of *net 30*. However, in an effort to help its cash flow position and to follow the actions of its rivals, the firm is considering changing its credit terms from net 30 to *2/10 net 30*. The objective is to speed up the receivable collections and thereby improve the firm's cash flows. Eboy would like to increase its accounts receivable turnover to 12.0.

The firm works with a raw material whose current annual usage is 1,450 units. Each finished product requires one unit of this raw material at a variable cost of $2,600 per unit and sells for $4,200 on terms of net 30. It is estimated that 70% of the firm's customers will take the 2% cash discount and that, with the discount, sales of the finished product will increase by 50 units per year. The firm's opportunity cost of funds invested in accounts receivable is 12.5%

In analyzing the investment in accounts receivable, use the variable cost of the product sold instead of the sale price, because the variable cost is a better indicator of the firm's investment.

TO DO

Create a spreadsheet similar to Table 15.3 to analyze whether the firm should initiate the proposed cash discount. What is your advice? Make sure you calculate the following:

a. Additional profit contribution from sales.
b. Average investment in accounts receivable at present (without cash discount).
c. Average investment in accounts receivable with the proposed cash discount.
d. Reduction in investment in accounts receivable.
e. Cost savings from reduced investment in accounts receivable.
f. Cost of the cash discount.
g. Net profit (loss) from initiation of proposed cash discount.

16 Current Liabilities Management

Learning Goals

LG 1 Review accounts payable, the key components of credit terms, and the procedures for analyzing those terms.

LG 2 Understand the effects of stretching accounts payable on their cost and the use of accruals.

LG 3 Describe interest rates and the basic types of unsecured bank sources of short-term loans.

LG 4 Discuss the basic features of commercial paper and the key aspects of international short-term loans.

LG 5 Explain the characteristics of secured short-term loans and the use of accounts receivable as short-term-loan collateral.

LG 6 Describe the various ways in which inventory can be used as short-term-loan collateral.

Why This Chapter Matters to You

In your *professional* life

ACCOUNTING You need to understand how to analyze supplier credit terms to decide whether the firm should take or give up cash discounts; you also need to understand the various types of short-term loans, both unsecured and secured, that you will be required to record and report.

INFORMATION SYSTEMS You need to understand what data the firm will need to process accounts payable, track accruals, and meet bank loans and other short-term debt obligations in a timely manner.

MANAGEMENT You need to know the sources of short-term loans so that, if short-term financing is needed, you will understand its availability and cost.

MARKETING You need to understand how accounts receivable and inventory can be used as loan collateral; the procedures used by the firm to secure short-term loans with such collateral could affect customer relationships.

OPERATIONS You need to understand the use of accounts payable as a form of short-term financing and the effect on one's suppliers of stretching payables; you also need to understand the process by which a firm uses inventory as collateral.

In your *personal* life
Management of current liabilities is an important part of your financial strategy. It takes discipline to avoid viewing cash and credit purchases equally. You need to borrow for a purpose, not convenience. You need to repay credit purchases in a timely fashion. Excessive use of short-term credit, particularly with credit cards, can create personal liquidity problems and, at the extreme, personal bankruptcy.

Memorial Sloan-Kettering Cancer Center

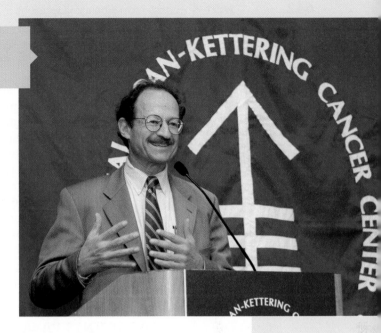

Reducing Accounts Payable Expenses

Automating accounts payables can save both time and expense. Much of the savings comes from eliminating the processing of paper invoices—a time-consuming process of matching purchase orders with invoices, checking that shipments or services were received, and then writing and mailing a check. For decades, nearly every large company employed staffs of dozens of accounts payable clerks to do the work.

Memorial Sloan-Kettering Cancer Center, the New York–based nonprofit medical research and health care institution, was looking for a better way to process the nearly half-million invoices it receives annually from suppliers. It turned to JPMorgan Business Settlement Network, which provides a network that enables companies to issue purchase orders, receive invoices, and make electronic payments to suppliers.

Sloan-Kettering's goal was to speed up the payment process while eliminating paper invoicing and most of the labor-intensive work of matching invoices and purchase orders. Sloan-Kettering was determined to convince hundreds of major suppliers to change the way they billed the organization for some $413 million worth of goods and services. "People don't realize that what you save on printing a check is nowhere near the costs associated with entering an invoice into an ERP system, ensuring that the data on the invoice is valid, and handling a dispute. Simply placing the burden of resolving an invoice discrepancy onto the supplier is a tremendous cost savings," said Barbara Cassera, manager of financial systems at Sloan-Kettering.

By moving to JPMorgan Order-to-Pay Processing, the percentage of electronic invoices went from 50 percent to 75 percent in the first year. The cash conversion cycle dropped from 80 to just 20 days on average. On-time payment jumped to 95 percent of all invoices, and discounts are generated on more than 50 percent of all invoices. With the ability to validate invoices in real time, Sloan-Kettering has eliminated exceptions on 16 percent of invoices that contained them. When errors are detected, the electronic processing service automatically sends all problem invoices back to suppliers for correction and resubmission.

By making these strategic changes, Sloan-Kettering is receiving more than $500,000 annually in supplier discounts. In addition, Sloan-Kettering has found that the time saved on the sheer volume of invoices processed electronically has enabled the accounts payable department to reduce its full-time staff, saving more than $120,000 annually.

16.1 Spontaneous Liabilities

spontaneous liabilities
Financing that arises from the normal course of business; the two major short-term sources of such liabilities are accounts payable and accruals.

unsecured short-term financing
Short-term financing obtained without pledging specific assets as collateral.

Spontaneous liabilities arise from the normal course of business. For example, when a retailer orders goods for inventory, the manufacturer of those goods usually does not demand immediate payment but instead extends a short-term loan to the retailer that appears on the retailer's balance sheet under accounts payable. The more goods the retailer orders, the greater will be the accounts payable balance. Also in response to increasing sales, the firm's accruals increase as wages and taxes rise because of greater labor requirements and the increased taxes on the firm's increased earnings. There is normally no explicit cost attached to either of these current liabilities, although they do have certain implicit costs. In addition, both are forms of **unsecured short-term financing**—short-term financing obtained without pledging specific assets as collateral. The firm should take advantage of these "interest-free" sources of unsecured short-term financing whenever possible.

ACCOUNTS PAYABLE MANAGEMENT

Accounts payable are the major source of unsecured short-term financing for business firms. They result from transactions in which merchandise is purchased but no formal note is signed to show the purchaser's liability to the seller. The purchaser in effect agrees to pay the supplier the amount required in accordance with credit terms normally stated on the supplier's invoice. The discussion of accounts payable here is presented from the viewpoint of the purchaser.

Role in the Cash Conversion Cycle

accounts payable management
Management by the firm of the time that elapses between its purchase of raw materials and its mailing payment to the supplier.

The average payment period is the final component of the *cash conversion cycle* introduced in Chapter 15. The average payment period has two parts: (1) the time from the purchase of raw materials until the firm mails the payment and (2) payment float time (the time it takes after the firm mails its payment until the supplier has withdrawn spendable funds from the firm's account). In the preceding chapter, we discussed issues related to payment float time. Here we discuss the firm's management of the time that elapses between its purchase of raw materials and its mailing payment to the supplier. This activity is **accounts payable management**.

When the seller of goods charges no interest and offers no discount to the buyer for early payment, the buyer's goal is to pay as slowly as possible without damaging its credit rating. This means that accounts should be paid on the last day possible, given the supplier's stated credit terms. For example, if the terms are net 30, then the account should be paid 30 days from the *beginning of the credit period*, which is typically either the *date of invoice* or the *end of the month (EOM)* in which the purchase was made. This allows for the maximum use of an interest-free loan from the supplier and will not damage the firm's credit rating (because the account is paid within the stated credit terms). In addition, some firms offer an explicit or implicit "grace period" that extends a few days beyond the stated payment date; if taking advantage of that grace period does no harm to the buyer's relationship with the seller, the buyer will typically take advantage of the grace period.

| Example 16.1 ► | In 2009, Hewlett-Packard Company (HPQ), the world's largest technology company, had annual revenue of $114,552 million, cost of revenue of $87,524 million, and accounts payable of $14,809 million. HPQ had an average age of inventory (AAI) of 29.2 days, an average collection period (ACP) of 53.3 days, and an average payment period (APP) of 60.4 days (HPQ's purchases were $89,492 million). Thus, the cash conversion cycle for HPQ was 22.1 days (29.2 + 53.3 − 60.4). |

The resources HPQ had invested in this cash conversion cycle (assuming a 365-day year) were

Inventory	=	$ 87,524 million × (29.2 ÷ 365) =	$ 7,001,920,000
+ Accounts receivable =		114,552 million × (53.3 ÷ 365) =	16,727,730,411
− Accounts payable	=	89,492 million × (60.4 ÷ 365) =	14,809,087,123
		= Resources invested	= $ 8,920,563,288

Based on HPQ's APP and average accounts payable, the daily accounts payable generated by HPQ is $245,183,562 ($14,809,087,123 ÷ 60.4). If HPQ were to increase its average payment period by 5 days, its accounts payable would increase by about $1,226 million (5 × $245,183,562). As a result, HPQ's cash conversion cycle would decrease by 5 days, and the firm would reduce its investment in operations by $1,226 million. Clearly, if this action did not damage HPQ's credit rating, it would be in the company's best interest.

Analyzing Credit Terms

The credit terms that a firm is offered by its suppliers enable it to delay payments for its purchases. Because the supplier's cost of having its money tied up in merchandise after it is sold is probably reflected in the purchase price, the purchaser is already indirectly paying for this benefit. Sometimes a supplier will offer a cash discount for early payment. In that case, the purchaser should carefully analyze credit terms to determine the best time to repay the supplier. The purchaser must weigh the benefits of paying the supplier as late as possible against the costs of passing up the discount for early payment.

Taking the Cash Discount If a firm intends to take a cash discount, it should pay on the last day of the discount period. There is no added benefit from paying earlier than that date.

| Example 16.2 ► | Lawrence Industries, operator of a small chain of video stores, purchased $1,000 worth of merchandise on February 27 from a supplier extending terms of 2/10 net 30 EOM. If the firm takes the cash discount, it must pay $980 [$1,000 − (0.02 × $1,000)] by March 10, thereby saving $20. |

cost of giving up a cash discount
The implied rate of interest paid to delay payment of an account payable for an additional number of days.

Giving Up the Cash Discount If the firm chooses to give up the cash discount, it should pay on the final day of the credit period. There is an implicit cost associated with giving up a cash discount. The **cost of giving up a cash discount** is the implied rate of interest paid to delay payment of an account payable for an additional number of days. In other words, when a firm gives up a discount, it pays a higher cost for the goods that it orders. The higher cost that the firm pays is like interest on a loan, and the length of this loan is the number of additional

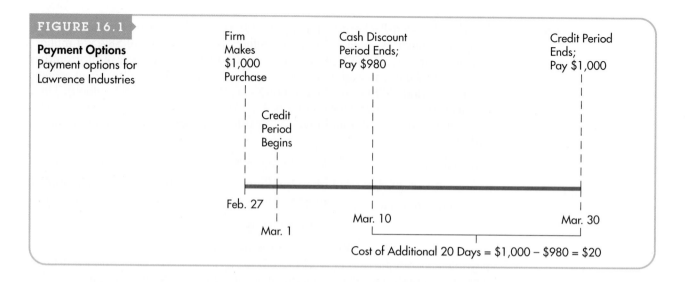

FIGURE 16.1

Payment Options
Payment options for Lawrence Industries

Firm Makes $1,000 Purchase

Credit Period Begins

Cash Discount Period Ends; Pay $980

Credit Period Ends; Pay $1,000

Feb. 27

Mar. 1

Mar. 10

Mar. 30

Cost of Additional 20 Days = $1,000 − $980 = $20

days that the purchaser can delay payment to the seller. This cost can be illustrated by a simple example. The example assumes that payment will be made on the last possible day (either the final day of the cash discount period or the final day of the credit period).

Example 16.3 ▶

In Example 16.2, we saw that Lawrence Industries could take the cash discount on its February 27 purchase by paying $980 on March 10. If Lawrence gives up the cash discount, it can pay on March 30. To keep its money for an extra 20 days, the firm must give up an opportunity to pay $980 for its $1,000 purchase. In other words, it will cost the firm $20 to delay payment for 20 days. Figure 16.1 shows the payment options that are open to the company.

To calculate the cost of giving up the cash discount, the *true purchase price* must be viewed as the *discounted cost of the merchandise,* which is $980 for Lawrence Industries. Another way to say this is that Lawrence Industries' supplier charges $980 for the goods as long as the bill is paid in 10 days. If Lawrence takes 20 additional days to pay (by paying on day 30 rather than on day 10), they have to pay the supplier an additional $20 in "interest." Therefore, the interest rate on this transaction is 2.04% ($20 ÷ $980). Keep in mind that the 2.04% interest rate applies to a 20-day loan. To calculate an annualized interest rate, we multiply the interest rate on this transaction times the number of 20-day periods during a year. Equation 16.1 provides the general expression for calculating the annual percentage cost of giving up a cash discount:[1]

$$\text{Cost of giving up cash discount} = \frac{CD}{100\% - CD} \times \frac{365}{N} \qquad (16.1)$$

---

1. Equation 16.1 and the related discussions are based on the assumption that only one discount is offered. In the event that multiple discounts are offered, calculation of the cost of giving up the discount must be made for each alternative.

where

$$CD = \text{stated cash discount in percentage terms}$$
$$N = \text{number of days that payment can be}$$
$$\text{delayed by giving up the cash discount}$$

Substituting the values for CD (2%) and N (20 days) into Equation 16.1 results in an annualized cost of giving up the cash discount of 37.24% $[(2\% \div 98\%) \times (365 \div 20)]$.

A simple way to *approximate* the cost of giving up a cash discount is to use the stated cash discount percentage, CD, in place of the first term of Equation 16.1:

$$\text{Approximate cost of giving up cash discount} = CD \times \frac{365}{N} \qquad (16.2)$$

The smaller the cash discount, the closer the approximation to the actual cost of giving it up. Using this approximation, the cost of giving up the cash discount for Lawrence Industries is 36.5% $[2\% \times (365 \div 20)]$.

Using the Cost of Giving Up a Cash Discount in Decision Making   The financial manager must determine whether it is advisable to take a cash discount. A primary consideration influencing this decision is the cost of other short-term sources of funding. When a firm can obtain financing from a bank or other institution at a lower cost than the implicit interest rate offered by its suppliers, the firm is better off borrowing from the bank and taking the discount offered by the supplier.

Example 16.4 ▶   Mason Products, a large building-supply company, has four possible suppliers, each offering different credit terms. Otherwise, their products and services are identical. Table 16.1 presents the credit terms offered by suppliers A, B, C, and D and the cost of giving up the cash discounts in each transaction. The approximation method of calculating the cost of giving up a cash discount (Equation 16.2) has been used. The cost of giving up the cash discount from supplier A is 36.5%; from supplier B, 8.1%; from supplier C, 21.9%; and from supplier D, 29.2%.

If the firm needs short-term funds, which it can borrow from its bank at an interest rate of 13%, and if each of the suppliers is viewed *separately,* which (if any) of the suppliers' cash discounts will the firm give up? In dealing with supplier A, the firm takes the cash discount, because the cost of giving it up is 36.5%, and

TABLE 16.1	Cash Discounts and Associated Costs for Mason Products	

Supplier	Credit terms	Approximate cost of giving up a cash discount
A	2/10 net 30 EOM	36.5%
B	1/10 net 55 EOM	8.1
C	3/20 net 70 EOM	21.9
D	4/10 net 60 EOM	29.2

then borrows the funds it requires from its bank at 13% interest. With supplier B, the firm would do better to give up the cash discount, because the cost of this action is less than the cost of borrowing money from the bank (8.1% versus 13%). With either supplier C or supplier D, the firm should take the cash discount, because in both cases the cost of giving up the discount is greater than the 13% cost of borrowing from the bank.

The example shows that the cost of giving up a cash discount is relevant when one is evaluating a single supplier's credit terms in light of certain *bank borrowing costs*. However, other factors relative to payment strategies may also need to be considered. For example, some firms, particularly small firms and poorly managed firms, routinely give up *all* discounts because they either lack alternative sources of unsecured short-term financing or fail to recognize the implicit costs of their actions.

stretching accounts payable
Paying bills as late as possible without damaging the firm's credit rating.

Effects of Stretching Accounts Payable

A strategy that is often employed by a firm is **stretching accounts payable**—that is, paying bills as late as possible without damaging its credit rating. Such a strategy can reduce the cost of giving up a cash discount.

Example 16.5 ▶   Lawrence Industries was extended credit terms of 2/10 net 30 EOM. The cost of giving up the cash discount, assuming payment on the last day of the credit period, was approximately 36.5% [2% × (365 ÷ 20)]. If the firm were able to stretch its account payable to 70 days without damaging its credit rating, the cost of giving up the cash discount would be only 12.2% [2% × (365 ÷ 60)]. Stretching accounts payable reduces the implicit cost of giving up a cash discount.

Although stretching accounts payable may be financially attractive, it raises an important ethical issue: It may cause the firm to violate the agreement it entered into with its supplier when it purchased merchandise. Clearly, a supplier would not look kindly on a customer who regularly and purposely postponed paying for purchases.

Personal Finance Example 16.6 ▶   Jack and Mary Nobel, a young married couple, are in the process of purchasing a 50-inch HD TV at a cost of $1,900. The electronics dealer currently has a special financing plan that would allow them to either (1) put $200 down and finance the balance of $1,700 at 3% annual interest over 24 months, resulting in payments of $73 per month; or (2) receive an immediate $150 cash rebate, thereby paying only $1,750 cash. The Nobels, who have saved enough to pay cash for the TV, can currently earn 5% annual interest on their savings. They wish to determine whether to borrow or to pay cash to purchase the TV.

The upfront outlay for the financing alternative is the $200 down payment, whereas the Nobels will pay out $1,750 up front under the cash purchase alternative. So the cash purchase will require an initial outlay that is $1,550 ($1,750 − $200) greater than under the financing alternative. Assuming that they can earn a simple interest rate of 5% on savings, the cash purchase will cause the Nobels to give up an opportunity to earn $155 (2 years × 0.05 × $1,550) over the 2 years.

If they choose the financing alternative, the $1,550 would grow to $1,705 ($1,550 + $155) at the end of 2 years. But under the financing alternative, the Nobels will pay out a total of $1,752 (24 months $\times$ $73 per month) over the 2-year loan term. The cost of the financing alternative can be viewed as $1,752, and the cost of the cash payment (including forgone interest earnings) would be $1,705. Because it is less expensive, *the Nobels should pay cash for the TV*. The lower cost of the cash alternative is largely the result of the $150 cash rebate.

ACCRUALS

accruals
Liabilities for services received for which payment has yet to be made.

The second spontaneous source of short-term business financing is accruals. **Accruals** are liabilities for services received for which payment has yet to be made. The most common items accrued by a firm are wages and taxes. Because taxes are payments to the government, their accrual cannot be manipulated by the firm. However, the accrual of wages can be manipulated to some extent. This is accomplished by delaying payment of wages, thereby receiving an interest-free loan from employees who are paid sometime after they have performed the work. The pay period for employees who earn an hourly rate is often governed by union regulations or by state or federal law. However, in other cases, the frequency of payment is at the discretion of the company's management.

focus on ETHICS

Accruals Management

in practice On June 2, 2010, Diebold, Inc., agreed to pay a $25 million fine to settle accounting fraud charges brought by the U.S. Securities and Exchange Commission (SEC). According to the SEC, the management of the Ohio-based manufacturer of ATMs, bank security systems, and electronic voting machines regularly received reports comparing the company's earnings to analyst forecasts. When earnings were below forecasts, management identified opportunities, some of which amounted to accounting fraud, to close the gap.

"Diebold's financial executives borrowed from many different chapters of the deceptive accounting playbook to fraudulently boost the company's bottom line," SEC Enforcement Director Robert Khuzami said in a statement. "When executives disregard their professional obligations to investors, both they and their companies face significant legal consequences."[a]

A number of the SEC's claims focused on premature revenue recognition. For example, Diebold was charged with improper use of "bill and hold" transactions. Under generally accepted accounting principles, revenue is typically recognized after a product is shipped. However, in some cases, sellers can recognize revenue before shipment for certain bill and hold transactions. The SEC claimed that Diebold improperly used bill and hold accounting to record revenue prematurely.

The SEC also claimed that Diebold manipulated various accounting accruals. Diebold was accused of understating liabilities tied to its Long Term Incentive Plan, commissions to be paid to sales personnel, and incentives to be paid to service personnel. Diebold temporarily reduced a liability account set up for payment of customer rebates. The company was also accused of overstating the value of inventory and improper inventory write-ups.

Each of these activities allowed Diebold to inflate the company's financial performance. According to the SEC's complaint, Diebold's fraudulent activities misstated reported pretax earnings by at least $127 million between 2002 and 2007. Two years prior to the settlement, Diebold restated earnings for the period covered by the charges.

The clawback provision of the 2002 Sarbanes-Oxley antifraud law requires executives to repay compensation they receive while their company misled shareholders. Diebold's former CEO, Walden O'Dell, agreed to return $470,000 in cash, plus stock and options. The SEC is currently pursuing a lawsuit against three other former Diebold executives for their part in the matter.

▶ *Why might financial managers still be tempted to manage earnings when a clawback is a legitimate possibility?*

[a]U.S. Securities and Exchange Commission, "SEC Charges Diebold and Former Executives with Accounting Fraud," press release, June 2, 2010, **www.sec.gov/news/press/2010/2010-93.htm**.

Example 16.7 ▶

Tenney Company, a large janitorial service company, currently pays its employees at the end of each work week. The weekly payroll totals $400,000. If the firm were to extend the pay period so as to pay its employees 1 week later throughout an entire year, the employees would in effect be lending the firm $400,000 for a year. If the firm could earn 10% annually on invested funds, such a strategy would be worth $40,000 per year (0.10 × $400,000).

→ REVIEW QUESTIONS

16–1 What are the two major sources of spontaneous short-term financing for a firm? How do their balances behave relative to the firm's sales?

16–2 Is there a cost associated with *taking a cash discount*? Is there any cost associated with *giving up a cash discount*? How do short-term borrowing costs affect the cash discount decision?

16–3 What is "stretching accounts payable"? What effect does this action have on the cost of giving up a cash discount?

LG 3 LG 4 **16.2 Unsecured Sources of Short-Term Loans**

Businesses obtain unsecured short-term loans from two major sources, banks and sales of commercial paper. Unlike the spontaneous sources of unsecured short-term financing, bank loans and commercial paper are negotiated and result from actions taken by the firm's financial manager. Bank loans are more popular because they are available to firms of all sizes; commercial paper tends to be available only to large firms. In addition, firms can use international loans to finance international transactions.

BANK LOANS

short-term, self-liquidating loan
An unsecured short-term loan in which the use to which the borrowed money is put provides the mechanism through which the loan is repaid.

Banks are a major source of unsecured short-term loans to businesses. The major type of loan made by banks to businesses is the **short-term, self-liquidating loan**. These loans are intended merely to carry the firm through seasonal peaks in financing needs that are due primarily to buildups of inventory and accounts receivable. As the firm converts inventories and receivables into cash, the funds needed to retire these loans are generated. In other words, the use to which the borrowed money is put provides the mechanism through which the loan is repaid—hence the term *self-liquidating*.

Banks lend unsecured, short-term funds in three basic ways: through single-payment notes, lines of credit, and revolving credit agreements. Before we look at these types of loans, we consider loan interest rates.

prime rate of interest (prime rate)
The lowest rate of interest charged by leading banks on business loans to their most important business borrowers.

Loan Interest Rates

The interest rate on a bank loan can be a fixed or a floating rate, typically based on the prime rate of interest. The **prime rate of interest (prime rate)** is the lowest rate of interest charged by leading banks on business loans to their most important business borrowers. The prime rate fluctuates with changing supply-and-demand relationships for short-term funds. Banks generally determine the rate to be charged to various borrowers by adding a premium to the prime rate to adjust it for the borrower's "riskiness." The premium may amount to 4 percent or more, although most unsecured short-term loans carry premiums of less than 2 percent.

fixed-rate loan
A loan with a rate of interest that is determined at a set increment above the prime rate and remains unvarying until maturity.

floating-rate loan
A loan with a rate of interest initially set at an increment above the prime rate and allowed to "float," or vary, above prime *as the prime rate varies* until maturity.

Fixed- and Floating-Rate Loans   Loans can have either fixed or floating interest rates. On a **fixed-rate loan,** the rate of interest is determined at a set increment above the prime rate on the date of the loan and remains unvarying at that fixed rate until maturity. On a **floating-rate loan,** the increment above the prime rate is initially established, and the rate of interest is allowed to "float," or vary, above prime *as the prime rate varies* until maturity. Generally, the increment above the prime rate will be *lower* on a floating-rate loan than on a fixed-rate loan of equivalent risk because the lender bears less risk with a floating-rate loan. As a result of the volatile nature of the prime rate during recent years, today *most short-term business loans are floating-rate loans.*

Method of Computing Interest   Once the *nominal (or stated) annual rate* is established, the method of computing interest is determined. Interest can be paid either when a loan matures or in advance. If interest is paid *at maturity*, the *effective (or true) annual rate*—the actual rate of interest paid—for an assumed 1-year period is equal to

$$\frac{\text{Interest}}{\text{Amount borrowed}} \qquad (16.3)$$

Most bank loans to businesses require the interest payment at maturity.

When interest is paid *in advance,* it is deducted from the loan so that the borrower actually receives less money than is requested (and less than they must repay). Loans on which interest is paid in advance are called **discount loans.** The *effective annual rate for a discount loan,* assuming a 1-year period, is calculated as

discount loan
Loan on which interest is paid in advance by being deducted from the amount borrowed.

$$\frac{\text{Interest}}{\text{Amount borrowed} - \text{Interest}} \qquad (16.4)$$

Paying interest in advance raises the effective annual rate above the stated annual rate.

Example 16.8 ▶   Wooster Company, a manufacturer of athletic apparel, wants to borrow $10,000 at a stated annual rate of 10% interest for 1 year. If the interest on the loan is paid at maturity, the firm will pay $1,000 (0.10 × $10,000) for the use of the $10,000 for the year. At the end of the year, Wooster will write a check to the lender for $11,000, consisting of the $1,000 interest as well as the return of the $10,000 principal. Substituting into Equation 16.3 reveals that the effective annual rate is therefore

$$\frac{\$1,000}{\$10,000} = 10.0\%$$

If the money is borrowed at the same *stated* annual rate for 1 year but interest is paid in advance, the firm still pays $1,000 in interest, but it receives only $9,000 ($10,000 − $1,000). The effective annual rate in this case is

$$\frac{\$1,000}{\$10,000 - \$1,000} = \frac{\$1,000}{\$9,000} = 11.1\%$$

In this case, at the end of the year Wooster writes a check to the lender for $10,000, having "paid" the $1,000 in interest up front by borrowing just $9,000. Paying interest in advance thus makes the effective annual rate (11.1%) greater than the stated annual rate (10.0%).

Single-Payment Notes

single-payment note
A short-term, one-time loan made to a borrower who needs funds for a specific purpose for a short period.

A **single-payment note** can be obtained from a commercial bank by a credit-worthy business borrower. This type of loan is usually a one-time loan made to a borrower who needs funds for a specific purpose for a short period. The resulting instrument is a *note,* signed by the borrower, that states the terms of the loan, including the length of the loan and the interest rate. This type of short-term note generally has a maturity of 30 days to 9 months or more. The interest charged is usually tied in some way to the prime rate of interest.

Example 16.9 ▶   Gordon Manufacturing, a producer of rotary mower blades, recently borrowed $100,000 from each of two banks—bank A and bank B. The loans were incurred on the same day, when the prime rate of interest was 6%. Each loan involved a 90-day note with interest to be paid at the end of 90 days. The interest rate was set at $1\frac{1}{2}\%$ above the prime rate on bank A's *fixed-rate note.* Over the 90-day period, the rate of interest on this note will remain at $7\frac{1}{2}\%$ (6% prime rate + $1\frac{1}{2}\%$ increment) regardless of fluctuations in the prime rate. The total interest cost on this loan is $1,849 [$100,000 × ($7\frac{1}{2}\%$ × 90 ÷ 365)], which means that the 90-day rate on this loan is 1.85% ($1,849 ÷ $100,000).

Assuming that the loan from bank A is rolled over each 90 days throughout the year under the same terms and circumstances, we can find its effective *annual* interest rate by using Equation 5.17. Because the loan costs 1.85% for 90 days, it is necessary to compound (1 + 0.0185) for 4.06 periods in the year (that is, 365 ÷ 90) and then subtract 1:

$$\text{Effective annual rate} = (1 + 0.0185)^{4.06} - 1$$
$$= 1.0773 - 1 = 0.0773 = \underline{7.73\%}$$

The effective annual rate of interest on the fixed-rate, 90-day note is 7.73%.

Bank B set the interest rate at 1% above the prime rate on its *floating-rate note.* The rate charged over the 90 days will vary directly with the prime rate. Initially, the rate will be 7% (6% + 1%), but when the prime rate changes, so will the rate of interest on the note. For instance, if after 30 days the prime rate rises to 6.5%, and after another 30 days it drops to 6.25%, the firm will be paying 0.575% for the first 30 days (7% × 30 ÷ 365), 0.616% for the next 30 days (7.5% × 30 ÷ 365), and 0.596% for the last 30 days (7.25% × 30 ÷ 365). Its total interest cost will be $1,787 [$100,000 × (0.575% + 0.616% + 0.596%)], resulting in a 90-day rate of 1.79% ($1,787 ÷ $100,000).

Again, assuming the loan is rolled over each 90 days throughout the year under the same terms and circumstances, its effective *annual* rate is 7.46%:

$$\text{Effective annual rate} = (1 + 0.01787)^{4.06} - 1$$
$$= 1.0746 - 1 = 0.0746 = \underline{7.46\%}$$

Clearly, in this case the floating-rate loan would have been less expensive than the fixed-rate loan because of its generally lower effective annual rate.

Personal Finance Example 16.10 ▶ Megan Schwartz has been approved by Clinton National Bank for a 180-day loan of $30,000 that will allow her to make the down payment and close the loan on her new condo. She needs the funds to bridge the time until the sale of her current condo, from which she expects to receive $42,000.

Clinton National offered Megan the following two financing options for the $30,000 loan: (1) a *fixed-rate loan* at 2% above the prime rate or (2) a *variable-rate loan* at 1% above the prime rate. Currently, the prime rate of interest is 8%, and the consensus forecast of a group of mortgage economists for changes in the prime rate over the next 180 days is as follows:

60 days from today the prime rate will rise by 1%

90 days from today the prime rate will rise another $\frac{1}{2}$%

150 days from today the prime rate will drop by 1%

Using the forecast prime rate changes, Megan wishes to determine the lowest interest-cost loan for the next 6 months.

Fixed-Rate Loan: Total interest cost over 180 days
$$= \$30,000 \times (0.08 + 0.02) \times (180 \div 365)$$
$$= \$30,000 \times 0.04932 \approx \underline{\$1,480}$$

Variable-Rate Loan: The applicable interest rate would begin at 9% (8% + 1%) and remain there for 60 days. Then the applicable rate would rise to 10% (9% + 1%) for the next 30 days, and then to 10.50% (10% + 0.50%) for the next 60 days. Finally the applicable rate would drop to 9.50% (10.50% − 1%) for the final 30 days.

Total interest cost over 180 days
$$= \$30,000 \times [(0.09 \times 60 \div 365) + (0.10 \times 30 \div 365)$$
$$+ (0.105 \times 60 \div 365) + (0.095 \times 30 \div 365)]$$
$$= \$30,000 \times (0.01479 + 0.00822 + 0.01726 + 0.00781)$$
$$= \$30,000 \times 0.04808 \approx \underline{\$1,442}$$

Because the estimated total interest cost on the variable-rate loan of $1,442 is less than the total interest cost of $1,480 on the fixed-rate loan, *Megan should take the variable-rate loan.* By doing this she will save about $38 ($1,480 − $1,442) in interest cost over the 180 days.

---

line of credit
An agreement between a commercial bank and a business specifying the amount of unsecured short-term borrowing the bank will make available to the firm over a given period of time.

Lines of Credit

A **line of credit** is an agreement between a commercial bank and a business, specifying the amount of unsecured short-term borrowing the bank will make available to the firm over a given period of time. It is similar to the agreement under which issuers of bank credit cards, such as MasterCard, Visa, and Discover, extend preapproved credit to cardholders. A line-of-credit agreement is typically made for a period of 1 year and often places certain constraints on the borrower. It is *not a guaranteed loan* but indicates that if the bank has sufficient funds available, it will allow the borrower to owe it *up to* a certain amount of money. The amount of a line of credit is the *maximum amount the firm can owe the bank* at any point in time.

When applying for a line of credit, the borrower may be required to submit such documents as its cash budget, pro forma income statement, pro forma balance sheet, and recent financial statements. If the bank finds the customer acceptable, the line of credit will be extended. The major attraction of a line of credit from the bank's point of view is that it eliminates the need to examine the creditworthiness of a customer each time it borrows money within the year.

Interest Rates   The interest rate on a line of credit is normally stated as a floating rate—the *prime rate plus a premium*. If the prime rate changes, the interest rate charged on new *as well as outstanding* borrowing automatically changes. The amount a borrower is charged in excess of the prime rate depends on its creditworthiness. The more creditworthy the borrower, the lower the premium (interest increment) above prime, and vice versa.

operating-change restrictions
Contractual restrictions that a bank may impose on a firm's financial condition or operations as part of a line-of-credit agreement.

Operating-Change Restrictions   In a line-of-credit agreement, a bank may impose **operating-change restrictions,** which give it the right to revoke the line if any major changes occur in the firm's financial condition or operations. The firm is usually required to submit up-to-date, and preferably audited, financial statements for periodic review. In addition, the bank typically needs to be informed of shifts in key managerial personnel or in the firm's operations before changes take place. Such changes may affect the future success and debt-paying ability of the firm and thus could alter its credit status. If the bank does not agree with the proposed changes and the firm makes them anyway, the bank has the right to revoke the line of credit.

compensating balance
A required checking account balance equal to a certain percentage of the amount borrowed from a bank under a line-of-credit or revolving credit agreement.

Compensating Balances   To ensure that the borrower will be a "good customer," many short-term unsecured bank loans—single-payment notes and lines of credit—require the borrower to maintain, in a checking account, a **compensating balance** equal to a certain percentage of the amount borrowed. Banks frequently require compensating balances of 10 to 20 percent. A compensating balance not only forces the borrower to be a good customer of the bank but may also raise the interest cost to the borrower.

Example 16.11 ▶

Estrada Graphics, a graphic design firm, has borrowed $1 million under a line-of-credit agreement. It must pay a stated interest rate of 10% and maintain, in its checking account, a compensating balance equal to 20% of the amount borrowed, or $200,000. Thus it actually receives the use of only $800,000. To use that amount for a year, the firm pays interest of $100,000 (0.10 × $1,000,000). The effective annual rate on the funds is therefore 12.5% ($100,000 ÷ $800,000), 2.5% more than the stated rate of 10%.

If the firm normally maintains a balance of $200,000 or more in its checking account, the effective annual rate equals the stated annual rate of 10% because none of the $1 million borrowed is needed to satisfy the compensating-balance requirement. If the firm normally maintains a $100,000 balance in its checking account, only an additional $100,000 will have to be tied up, leaving it with $900,000 of usable funds. The effective annual rate in this case would be 11.1% ($100,000 ÷ $900,000). Thus a compensating balance raises the cost of borrowing *only if* it is larger than the firm's normal cash balance.

---

annual cleanup
The requirement that for a certain number of days during the year borrowers under a line of credit carry a zero loan balance (that is, owe the bank nothing).

Annual Cleanups   To ensure that money lent under a line-of-credit agreement is actually being used to finance seasonal needs, many banks require an **annual cleanup**. This means that the borrower must have a loan balance of zero—that is, owe the bank nothing—for a certain number of days during the year. Insisting that the borrower carry a zero loan balance for a certain period ensures that short-term loans do not turn into long-term loans.

All the characteristics of a line-of-credit agreement are negotiable to some extent. Today, banks bid competitively to attract large, well-known firms. A prospective borrower should attempt to negotiate a line of credit with the most favorable interest rate, for an optimal amount of funds, and with a minimum of restrictions. Borrowers today frequently pay fees to lenders instead of maintaining deposit balances as compensation for loans and other services. The lender attempts to get a good return with maximum safety. Negotiations should produce a line of credit that is suitable to both borrower and lender.

revolving credit agreement
A line of credit *guaranteed* to a borrower by a commercial bank regardless of the scarcity of money.

commitment fee
The fee that is normally charged on a *revolving credit agreement;* it often applies to the *average unused portion* of the borrower's credit line.

Revolving Credit Agreements

A **revolving credit agreement** is nothing more than a *guaranteed line of credit*. It is guaranteed in the sense that the commercial bank assures the borrower that a specified amount of funds will be made available regardless of the scarcity of money. The interest rate and other requirements are similar to those for a line of credit. It is not uncommon for a revolving credit agreement to be for a period greater than 1 year.[2] Because the bank guarantees the availability of funds, a **commitment fee** is normally charged on a revolving credit agreement. This fee often applies to the average unused balance of the borrower's credit line. It is normally about 0.5 percent of the *average unused portion* of the line.

Example 16.12 ▶   REH Company, a major real estate developer, has a $2 million revolving credit agreement with its bank. Its average borrowing under the agreement for the past year was $1.5 million. The bank charges a commitment fee of 0.5% on the average unused balance. Because the average unused portion of the committed funds was $500,000 ($2 million − $1.5 million), the commitment fee for the year was $2,500 (0.005 × $500,000). Of course, REH also had to pay interest on the actual $1.5 million borrowed under the agreement. Assuming that $112,500 interest was paid on the $1.5 million borrowed, the effective cost of the agreement was 7.67% [($112,500 + $2,500) ÷ $1,500,000]. Although more expensive than a line of credit, a revolving credit agreement can be less risky from the borrower's viewpoint, because the availability of funds is guaranteed.

---

2. Many authors classify the revolving credit agreement as a form of *intermediate-term financing*, defined as having a maturity of 1 to 7 years. In this text, we do not use the intermediate-term financing classification; only short-term and long-term classifications are made. Because many revolving credit agreements are for more than 1 year, they can be classified as a form of long-term financing; however, they are discussed here because of their similarity to line-of-credit agreements.

COMMERCIAL PAPER

commercial paper
A form of financing consisting of short-term, unsecured promissory notes issued by firms with a high credit standing.

Commercial paper is a form of financing that consists of short-term, unsecured promissory notes issued by firms with a high credit standing. Generally, only large firms of unquestionable financial soundness are able to issue commercial paper. Most commercial paper issues have maturities ranging from 3 to 270 days. Although there is no set denomination, such financing is generally issued in multiples of $100,000 or more. A large portion of the commercial paper today is issued by finance companies; manufacturing firms account for a smaller portion of this type of financing. Businesses often purchase commercial paper, which they hold as marketable securities, to provide an interest-earning reserve of liquidity. For further information on recent use of commercial paper, see the *Focus on Practice* box.

Interest on Commercial Paper

Commercial paper is sold at a discount from its *par*, or *face, value*. The size of the discount and the length of time to maturity determine the interest paid by the

---

focus on PRACTICE

The Ebb and Flow of Commercial Paper

in practice The difficult economic and credit environment in the post–September 11 era, combined with historically low interest rates and a deep desire by corporate issuers to reduce exposure to refinancing risk, had a depressing effect on commercial paper volumes from 2001 through 2003. According to the Federal Reserve, U.S. nonfinancial commercial paper, for example, declined 68 percent over the 3-year period, from $315.8 billion outstanding at the beginning of 2001 to $101.4 billion by December 2003. In addition to lower volume, credit quality of commercial paper declined over the same period, with the ratio of downgrades outpacing upgrades 17 to 1 in 2002.

In 2004, signs emerged that the volume and rating contraction in commercial paper was finally coming to an end. The most encouraging of these was the pickup in economic growth, which spurs the need for short-term debt to finance corporate working capital. Although commercial paper is typically used to fund working capital, it is often boosted by a sudden surge of borrowing activity

for other strategic activities—mergers and acquisitions and long-term capital investments, among others. According to Federal Reserve Board data, at the end of July 2004, total U.S. commercial paper outstanding was $1.33 trillion.

By 2006, commercial paper surged to $1.98 trillion—an increase of 21.5 percent over 2005 levels. However, after peaking at $2.22 trillion, the tide changed in response to the credit crisis that began in August 2007. According to Federal Reserve data, as of October 1, 2008, the commercial paper market had contracted to $1.6 trillion, a reduction of nearly 28 percent, and new issues virtually dried up for several weeks. With much of the commercial paper outstanding at the start of the credit crisis coming up for renewal, the Federal Reserve began operating the Commercial Paper Funding Facility (CPFF) on October 27, 2008. The CPFF was intended to provide a liquidity backstop to U.S. issuers of commercial paper and, thereby, increase the availability of credit in short-term capital markets. CPFF allowed for the Federal Reserve Bank of New York to finance

the purchase of highly rated unsecured and asset-backed commercial paper from eligible issuers.

Even with the CPFF up and running, companies that were worried about their ability to roll over their outstanding commercial paper every few weeks turned to long-term debt to meet their liquidity needs. Merrill Lynch & Co. and Bloomberg data showed that, to manage short-term liability risk, companies were paying as much as $75 million in additional annual interest to swap long-term debt for $1 billion of 30-day commercial paper.

With the recession in the rearview mirror and short-term credit markets working again, the CPFF was closed on February 1, 2010. As of mid-2010, the U.S. commercial paper market appeared to be hitting bottom at around $1.06 trillion and showing signs of recovering.

▶ *What factors contribute to an expansion of the commercial paper market? What factors cause a contraction in the commercial paper market?*

issuer of commercial paper. The actual interest earned by the purchaser is determined by certain calculations, illustrated by the following example.

Example 16.13 ▶ Bertram Corporation, a large shipbuilder, has just issued $1 million worth of commercial paper that has a 90-day maturity and sells for $990,000. At the end of 90 days, the purchaser of this paper will receive $1 million for its $990,000 investment. The interest paid on the financing is therefore $10,000 on a principal of $990,000. The effective 90-day rate on the paper is 1.01% ($10,000 ÷ $990,000). Assuming that the paper is rolled over each 90 days throughout the year (that is, 365 ÷ 90 = 4.06 times per year), the effective annual rate for Bertram's commercial paper, found by using Equation 4.24, is 4.16% $[(1 + 0.0101)^{4.06} - 1]$.

An interesting characteristic of commercial paper is that its interest cost is *normally* 2 percent to 4 percent below the prime rate. In other words, firms are able to raise funds more cheaply by selling commercial paper than by borrowing from a commercial bank. The reason is that many suppliers of short-term funds do not have the option, as banks do, of making low-risk business loans at the prime rate. They can invest safely only in marketable securities such as Treasury bills and commercial paper.

Although the stated interest cost of borrowing through the sale of commercial paper is normally lower than the prime rate, the *overall cost* of commercial paper may not be less than that of a bank loan. Additional costs include various fees and flotation costs. In addition, even if it is slightly more expensive to borrow from a commercial bank, it may at times be advisable to do so to establish a good working relationship with a bank. This strategy ensures that when money is tight, funds can be obtained promptly and at a reasonable interest rate.

Matter of fact

Lending Limits

Commercial banks are legally prohibited from lending amounts in excess of 15 percent (plus an additional 10 percent for loans secured by readily marketable collateral) of the bank's unimpaired capital and surplus to any one borrower. This restriction is intended to protect depositors by forcing the commercial bank to spread its risk across a number of borrowers. In addition, smaller commercial banks do not have many opportunities to lend to large, high-quality business borrowers.

INTERNATIONAL LOANS

In some ways, arranging short-term financing for international trade is no different from financing purely domestic operations. In both cases, producers must finance production and inventory and then continue to finance accounts receivable before collecting any cash payments from sales. In other ways, however, the short-term financing of international sales and purchases is fundamentally different from that of strictly domestic trade.

International Transactions

The important difference between international and domestic transactions is that payments are often made or received in a foreign currency. Not only must a U.S. company pay the costs of doing business in the foreign exchange market, but it also is exposed to *exchange rate risk*. A U.S.-based company that exports goods and has accounts receivable denominated in a foreign currency faces the risk that the U.S. dollar will appreciate in value relative to the foreign currency. The risk to a U.S. importer with foreign-currency-denominated accounts payable is that the dollar will depreciate. Although *exchange rate risk* can often be *hedged* by using currency forward, futures, or options markets, doing so is costly and is not possible for all foreign currencies.

Typical international transactions are large in size and have long maturity dates. Therefore, companies that are involved in international trade generally have to finance larger dollar amounts for longer time periods than companies that operate domestically. Furthermore, because foreign companies are rarely well known in the United States, some financial institutions are reluctant to lend to U.S. exporters or importers, particularly smaller firms.

Financing International Trade

letter of credit
A letter written by a company's bank to the company's foreign supplier, stating that the bank guarantees payment of an invoiced amount if all the underlying agreements are met.

Several specialized techniques have evolved for financing international trade. Perhaps the most important financing vehicle is the **letter of credit,** a letter written by a company's bank to the company's foreign supplier, stating that the bank guarantees payment of an invoiced amount if all the underlying agreements are met. The letter of credit essentially substitutes the bank's reputation and creditworthiness for that of its commercial customer. A U.S. exporter is more willing to sell goods to a foreign buyer if the transaction is covered by a letter of credit issued by a well-known bank in the buyer's home country.

Firms that do business in foreign countries on an ongoing basis often finance their operations, at least in part, in the local market. A company that has an assembly plant in Mexico, for example, might choose to finance its purchases of Mexican goods and services with peso funds borrowed from a Mexican bank. This not only minimizes exchange rate risk but also improves the company's business ties to the host community. Multinational companies, however, sometimes finance their international transactions through dollar-denominated loans from international banks. The *Eurocurrency loan markets* allow creditworthy borrowers to obtain financing on attractive terms.

Transactions between Subsidiaries

Much international trade involves transactions between corporate subsidiaries. A U.S. company might, for example, manufacture one part in an Asian plant and another part in the United States, assemble the product in Brazil, and sell it in Europe. The shipment of goods back and forth between subsidiaries creates accounts receivable and accounts payable, but the parent company has considerable discretion about how and when payments are made. In particular, the parent can minimize foreign exchange fees and other transaction costs by "netting" what affiliates owe each other and paying only the net amount due, rather than having both subsidiaries pay each other the gross amounts due.

→ REVIEW QUESTIONS

16–4 How is the *prime rate of interest* relevant to the cost of short-term bank borrowing? What is a *floating-rate loan?*

16–5 How does the *effective annual rate* differ between a loan requiring interest payments *at maturity* and another, similar loan requiring interest *in advance?*

16–6 What are the basic terms and characteristics of a *single-payment note?* How is the *effective annual rate* on such a note found?

16–7 What is a *line of credit?* Describe each of the following features that are often included in these agreements: (**a**) operating-change restrictions; (**b**) compensating balance; and (**c**) annual cleanup.

16–8 What is a *revolving credit agreement?* How does this arrangement differ from the line-of-credit agreement? What is a *commitment fee?*

16–9 How do firms use *commercial paper* to raise short-term funds? Who can issue commercial paper? Who buys commercial paper?

16–10 What is the important difference between international and domestic transactions? How is a *letter of credit* used in financing international trade transactions? How is "netting" used in transactions between subsidiaries?

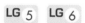 **16.3 Secured Sources of Short-Term Loans**

secured short-term financing
Short-term financing (loan) that has specific assets pledged as collateral.

security agreement
The agreement between the borrower and the lender that specifies the collateral held against a secured loan.

When a firm has exhausted its sources of unsecured short-term financing, it may be able to obtain additional short-term loans on a secured basis. **Secured short-term financing** has specific assets pledged as collateral. The *collateral* commonly takes the form of an asset, such as accounts receivable or inventory. The lender obtains a security interest in the collateral through the execution of a **security agreement** with the borrower that specifies the collateral held against the loan. In addition, the terms of the loan against which the security is held form part of the security agreement. A copy of the security agreement is filed in a public office within the state—typically, a county or state court. Filing provides subsequent lenders with information about which assets of a prospective borrower are unavailable for use as collateral. The filing requirement protects the lender by legally establishing the lender's security interest.

CHARACTERISTICS OF SECURED SHORT-TERM LOANS

Although many people believe that holding collateral as security reduces the risk that a loan will default, lenders do not usually view loans in this way. Lenders recognize that holding collateral can reduce losses if the borrower defaults, but *the presence of collateral has no impact on the risk of default.* A lender requires collateral to ensure recovery of some portion of the loan in the event of default. What the lender wants above all, however, is to be repaid as scheduled. In general, lenders prefer to make less risky loans at lower rates of interest than to be in a position in which they must liquidate collateral.

Collateral and Terms

Lenders of secured short-term funds prefer collateral that has a duration closely matched to the term of the loan. Current assets are the most desirable short-term-loan collateral because they can normally be converted into cash much sooner than fixed assets. Thus, the short-term lender of secured funds generally accepts only liquid current assets as collateral.

percentage advance
The percentage of the book value of the collateral that constitutes the principal of a secured loan.

Typically, the lender determines the desirable **percentage advance** to make against the collateral. This percentage advance constitutes the principal of the secured loan and is normally between 30 and 100 percent of the book value of the collateral. It varies according to the type and liquidity of collateral.

The interest rate that is charged on secured short-term loans is typically *higher* than the rate on unsecured short-term loans. Lenders do not normally consider secured loans less risky than unsecured loans. In addition, negotiating and administering secured loans is more troublesome for the lender than negotiating and administering unsecured loans. The lender therefore normally requires added compensation in the form of a service charge, a higher interest rate, or both.

Institutions Extending Secured Short-Term Loans

The primary sources of secured short-term loans to businesses are commercial banks and commercial finance companies. Both institutions deal in short-term loans secured primarily by accounts receivable and inventory. We have already described the operations of commercial banks. **Commercial finance companies** are lending institutions that make *only* secured loans—both short-term and long-term—to businesses. Unlike banks, finance companies are not permitted to hold deposits.

commercial finance companies
Lending institutions that make *only* secured loans—both short-term and long-term—to businesses.

Only when its unsecured and secured short-term borrowing power from the commercial bank is exhausted will a borrower turn to the commercial finance company for additional secured borrowing. Because the finance company generally ends up with higher-risk borrowers, its interest charges on secured short-term loans are usually higher than those of commercial banks. The leading U.S. commercial finance companies include The CIT Group and GE Corporate Financial Services.

USE OF ACCOUNTS RECEIVABLE AS COLLATERAL

Two commonly used means of obtaining short-term financing with accounts receivable are *pledging accounts receivable* and *factoring accounts receivable*. Actually, only a pledge of accounts receivable creates a secured short-term loan; factoring really entails the *sale* of accounts receivable at a discount. Although factoring is not actually a form of secured short-term borrowing, it does involve the use of accounts receivable to obtain needed short-term funds.

Pledging Accounts Receivable

pledge of accounts receivable
The use of a firm's accounts receivable as security, or collateral, to obtain a short-term loan.

A **pledge of accounts receivable** is often used to secure a short-term loan. Because accounts receivable are normally quite liquid, they are an attractive form of short-term-loan collateral.

The Pledging Process   When a firm requests a loan against accounts receivable, the lender first evaluates the firm's accounts receivable to determine their desirability as collateral. The lender makes a list of the acceptable accounts, along with the billing dates and amounts. If the borrowing firm requests a loan for a fixed amount, the lender needs to select only enough accounts to secure the funds requested. If the borrower wants the maximum loan available, the lender evaluates all the accounts to select the maximum amount of acceptable collateral.

After selecting the acceptable accounts, the lender normally adjusts the dollar value of these accounts for expected returns on sales and other allowances. If a customer whose account has been pledged returns merchandise or receives some type of allowance, such as a cash discount for early payment, the amount of the collateral is

In more depth

To read about *Pledging Accounts Receivable: The Pledging Process*, go to www.myfinancelab.com

lien
A publicly disclosed legal claim on loan collateral.

nonnotification basis
The basis on which a borrower, having pledged an account receivable, continues to collect the account payments without notifying the account customer.

notification basis
The basis on which an account customer whose account has been pledged (or factored) is notified to remit payment directly to the lender (or factor).

factoring accounts receivable
The outright sale of accounts receivable at a discount to a *factor* or other financial institution.

factor
A financial institution that specializes in purchasing accounts receivable from businesses.

nonrecourse basis
The basis on which accounts receivable are sold to a factor with the understanding that the factor accepts all credit risks on the purchased accounts.

automatically reduced. For protection from such occurrences, the lender normally reduces the value of the acceptable collateral by a fixed percentage.

Next, the percentage to be advanced against the collateral must be determined. The lender evaluates the quality of the acceptable receivables and the expected cost of their liquidation. This percentage represents the principal of the loan and typically ranges between 50 and 90 percent of the face value of acceptable accounts receivable. To protect its interest in the collateral, the lender files a **lien,** which is a publicly disclosed legal claim on the collateral.

Notification   Pledges of accounts receivable are normally made on a **nonnotification basis,** meaning that a customer whose account has been pledged as collateral is not notified. Under the nonnotification arrangement, the borrower still collects the pledged account receivable, and the lender trusts the borrower to remit these payments as they are received. If a pledge of accounts receivable is made on a **notification basis,** the customer is notified to remit payment directly to the lender.

Pledging Cost   The stated cost of a pledge of accounts receivable is normally 2 to 5 percent above the prime rate. In addition to the stated interest rate, a service charge of up to 3 percent may be levied by the lender to cover its administrative costs. Clearly, pledges of accounts receivable are a high-cost source of short-term financing.

Factoring Accounts Receivable

Factoring accounts receivable involves selling them outright, at a discount, to a financial institution. A **factor** is a financial institution that specializes in purchasing accounts receivable from businesses. Although it is not the same as obtaining a short-term loan, factoring accounts receivable is similar to borrowing with accounts receivable as collateral.

Factoring Agreement   A factoring agreement normally states the exact conditions and procedures for the purchase of an account. The factor, like a lender against a pledge of accounts receivable, chooses accounts for purchase, selecting only those that appear to be acceptable credit risks. Where factoring is to be on a continuing basis, the factor will actually make the firm's credit decisions because this will guarantee the acceptability of accounts. Factoring is normally done on a *notification basis,* and the factor receives payment of the account directly from the customer. In addition, most sales of accounts receivable to a factor are made on a **nonrecourse basis,** meaning that the factor agrees to accept all credit risks. Thus, if a purchased account turns out to be uncollectible, the factor must absorb the loss.

Matter of fact

Quasi Factoring

The use of credit cards such as MasterCard, Visa, and Discover by consumers has some similarity to factoring because the vendor that accepts the card is reimbursed at a discount for purchases made with the card. The difference between factoring and credit cards is that cards are nothing more than a line of credit extended by the issuer, which charges the vendors a fee for accepting the cards. In factoring, the factor does not analyze credit until after the sale has been made; in many cases (except when factoring is done on a continuing basis), the initial credit decision is the responsibility of the vendor, not the factor that purchases the account.

Typically, the factor is not required to pay the firm until the account is collected or until the last day of the credit period, whichever occurs first. The factor sets up an account similar to a bank deposit account for each customer. As payment is received or as due dates arrive, the factor deposits money into the seller's account, from which the seller is free to make withdrawals as needed.

In many cases, if the firm leaves the money in the account, a *surplus* will exist on which the factor will pay interest. In other instances, the factor may make *advances* to the firm against uncollected accounts that are not yet due. These advances represent a negative balance in the firm's account, on which interest is charged.

Factoring Cost   Factoring costs include commissions, interest levied on advances, and interest earned on surpluses. The factor deposits in the firm's account the book value of the collected or due accounts purchased by the factor, less the commissions. The commissions are typically stated as a 1 to 3 percent discount from the book value of factored accounts receivable. The *interest levied on advances* is generally 2 to 4 percent above the prime rate. It is levied on the actual amount advanced. The *interest paid on surpluses* is generally between 0.2 percent and 0.5 percent per month.

Although its costs may seem high, factoring has certain advantages that make it attractive to many firms. One is the ability it gives the firm to *turn accounts receivable immediately into cash* without having to worry about repayment. Another advantage is that it ensures a *known pattern of cash flows*. In addition, if factoring is undertaken on a continuing basis, the firm *can eliminate its credit and collection departments*.

In more depth

To read about *Factoring: Use of Factoring Accounts*, go to www.myfinancelab.com

 myfinancelab

USE OF INVENTORY AS COLLATERAL

Inventory is generally second to accounts receivable in desirability as short-term loan collateral. Inventory normally has a market value that is greater than its book value, which is used to establish its value as collateral. A lender whose loan is secured with inventory will probably be able to sell that inventory for at least book value if the borrower defaults on its obligations.

The most important characteristic of inventory being evaluated as loan collateral is *marketability*. A warehouse of *perishable* items, such as fresh peaches, may be quite marketable, but if the cost of storing and selling the peaches is high, they may not be desirable collateral. *Specialized items,* such as moon-roving vehicles, are not desirable collateral either, because finding a buyer for them could be difficult. When evaluating inventory as possible loan collateral, the lender looks for items with very stable market prices that have ready markets and that lack undesirable physical properties.

Floating Inventory Liens

floating inventory lien
A secured short-term loan against inventory under which the lender's claim is on the borrower's inventory in general.

A lender may be willing to secure a loan under a **floating inventory lien,** which is a claim on inventory in general. This arrangement is most attractive when the firm has a stable level of inventory that consists of a diversified group of relatively inexpensive merchandise. Inventories of items such as auto tires, screws and bolts, and shoes are candidates for floating-lien loans. Because it is difficult for a lender to verify the presence of the inventory, the lender generally advances less than 50 percent of the book value of the average inventory. The interest charge

In more depth

To read about *Floating Inventory Liens,* go to www.myfinancelab.com

 myfinancelab

trust receipt inventory loan
A secured short-term loan against inventory under which the lender advances 80 to 100 percent of the cost of the borrower's relatively expensive inventory items in exchange for the borrower's promise to repay the lender, with accrued interest, immediately after the sale of each item of collateral.

on a floating lien is 3 to 5 percent above the prime rate. Commercial banks often require floating liens as extra security on what would otherwise be an unsecured loan. Floating-lien inventory loans may also be available from commercial finance companies.

Trust Receipt Inventory Loans

A **trust receipt inventory loan** often can be made against relatively expensive automotive, consumer durable, and industrial goods that can be identified by serial number. Under this agreement, the borrower keeps the inventory, and the lender may advance 80 to 100 percent of its cost. The lender files a *lien* on all the items financed. The borrower is free to sell the merchandise but is *trusted* to remit the amount lent, along with accrued interest, to the lender immediately after the sale. The lender then releases the lien on the item. The lender makes periodic checks of the borrower's inventory to make sure that the required collateral remains in the hands of the borrower. The interest charge to the borrower is normally 2 percent or more above the prime rate.

Trust receipt loans are often made by manufacturers' wholly owned financing subsidiaries, known as *captive finance companies,* to their customers. Captive finance companies are especially popular in industries that manufacture consumer durable goods because they provide the manufacturer with a useful sales tool. For example, General Motors Acceptance Corporation (GMAC), the financing subsidiary of General Motors, grants these types of loans to its dealers. Trust receipt loans are also available through commercial banks and commercial finance companies.

Warehouse Receipt Loans

warehouse receipt loan
A secured short-term loan against inventory under which the lender receives control of the pledged inventory collateral, which is stored by a designated warehousing company on the lender's behalf.

A **warehouse receipt loan** is an arrangement whereby the lender, which may be a commercial bank or finance company, receives control of the pledged inventory collateral, which is stored by a designated agent on the lender's behalf. After selecting acceptable collateral, the lender hires a warehousing company to act as its agent and take possession of the inventory.

Two types of warehousing arrangements are possible. A *terminal warehouse* is a central warehouse that is used to store the merchandise of various customers. The lender normally uses such a warehouse when the inventory is easily transported and can be delivered to the warehouse relatively inexpensively. Under a *field warehouse* arrangement, the lender hires a field-warehousing company to set up a warehouse on the borrower's premises or to lease part of the borrower's warehouse to store the pledged collateral. Regardless of the type of warehouse, the warehousing company places a guard over the inventory. Only on written approval of the lender can any portion of the secured inventory be released by the warehousing company.

The actual lending agreement specifically states the requirements for the release of inventory. As with other secured loans, the lender accepts only collateral that it believes to be readily marketable and advances only a portion—generally 75 to 90 percent—of the collateral's value. The specific costs of warehouse receipt loans are generally higher than those of any other secured lending arrangements because of the need to hire and pay a warehousing company to guard and supervise the collateral. The basic interest charged on warehouse receipt loans is higher than that charged on unsecured loans, generally ranging

In more depth

To read about *Warehouse Receipt Loans,* go to www .myfinancelab.com

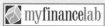

from 3 to 5 percent above the prime rate. In addition to the interest charge, the borrower must absorb the costs of warehousing by paying the warehouse fee, which is generally between 1 and 3 percent of the amount of the loan. The borrower is normally also required to pay the insurance costs on the warehoused merchandise.

→ REVIEW QUESTIONS

16–11 Are secured short-term loans viewed as more risky or less risky than unsecured short-term loans? Why?

16–12 In general, what interest rates and fees are levied on secured short-term loans? Why are these rates generally *higher* than the rates on unsecured short-term loans?

16–13 Describe and compare the basic features of the following methods of using *accounts receivable* to obtain short-term financing: (a) pledging accounts receivable, and (b) factoring accounts receivable. Be sure to mention the institutions that offer each of them.

16–14 For the following methods of using *inventory* as short-term loan collateral, describe the basic features of each, and compare their use: (a) floating lien, (b) trust receipt loan, and (c) warehouse receipt loan.

Summary

FOCUS ON VALUE

Current liabilities represent an important and generally inexpensive source of financing for a firm. The level of short-term (current liabilities) financing employed by a firm affects its profitability and risk. Accounts payable and accruals are spontaneous liabilities that should be carefully managed because they represent free financing. Notes payable, which represent negotiated short-term financing, should be obtained at the lowest cost under the best possible terms. Large, well-known firms can obtain unsecured short-term financing through the sale of commercial paper. On a secured basis, the firm can obtain loans from banks or commercial finance companies, using either accounts receivable or inventory as collateral.

The financial manager must obtain the right quantity and form of current liabilities financing to provide the lowest-cost funds with the least risk. Such a strategy should positively contribute to the firm's goal of **maximizing the stock price.**

REVIEW OF LEARNING GOALS

LG 1 Review accounts payable, the key components of credit terms, and the procedures for analyzing those terms. The major spontaneous source of short-term financing is accounts payable. They are the primary source of short-funds. Credit terms may differ with respect to the credit period, cash discount, cash discount period, and beginning of the credit period. Cash discounts should be given up only when a firm in need of short-term funds must pay an interest rate on borrowing that is greater than the cost of giving up the cash discount.

LG 2 **Understand the effects of stretching accounts payable on their cost and the use of accruals.** Stretching accounts payable can lower the cost of giving up a cash discount. Accruals, which result primarily from wage and tax obligations, are virtually free.

LG 3 **Describe interest rates and the basic types of unsecured bank sources of short-term loans.** Banks are the major source of unsecured short-term loans to businesses. The interest rate on these loans is tied to the prime rate of interest by a risk premium and may be fixed or floating. It should be evaluated by using the effective annual rate. Whether interest is paid when the loan matures or in advance affects the rate. Bank loans may take the form of a single-payment note, a line of credit, or a revolving credit agreement.

LG 4 **Discuss the basic features of commercial paper and the key aspects of international short-term loans.** Commercial paper is an unsecured IOU issued by firms with a high credit standing. International sales and purchases expose firms to exchange rate risk. Such transactions are larger and of longer maturity than domestic transactions, and they can be financed by using a letter of credit, by borrowing in the local market, or through dollar-denominated loans from international banks. On transactions between subsidiaries, "netting" can be used to minimize foreign exchange fees and other transaction costs.

LG 5 **Explain the characteristics of secured short-term loans and the use of accounts receivable as short-term-loan collateral.** Secured short-term loans are those for which the lender requires collateral—typically, current assets such as accounts receivable or inventory. Only a percentage of the book value of acceptable collateral is advanced by the lender. These loans are more expensive than unsecured loans. Commercial banks and commercial finance companies make secured short-term loans. Both pledging and factoring involve the use of accounts receivable to obtain needed short-term funds.

LG 6 **Describe the various ways in which inventory can be used as short-term-loan collateral.** Inventory can be used as short-term-loan collateral under a floating lien, a trust receipt arrangement, or a warehouse receipt loan.

Opener-in-Review

In the chapter opener you learned that Memorial Sloan-Kettering Cancer Center had created significant cash flow by using electronic invoicing and taking advantage of discounts on accounts payable. Do these gains in working capital efficiency affect Sloan-Kettering's operating risk, and if so how?

Self-Test Problem   (Solution in Appendix)

LG 1   **LG 2**   **ST16–1**   **Cash discount decisions**   The credit terms for each of three suppliers are shown in the following table. (*Note:* Assume a 365-day year.)

Supplier	Credit terms
X	1/10 net 55 EOM
Y	2/10 net 30 EOM
Z	2/20 net 60 EOM

a. Determine the *approximate* cost of giving up the cash discount from each supplier.

b. Assuming that the firm needs short-term financing, indicate whether it would be better to give up the cash discount or take the discount and borrow from a bank at 15% annual interest. Evaluate each supplier *separately* using your findings in part **a**.

c. What impact, if any, would the fact that the firm could stretch its accounts payable (net period only) by 20 days from supplier Z have on your answer in part **b** relative to this supplier?

Warm-Up Exercises   All problems are available in 🔷myfinancelab .

LG 1   **E16–1**   Lyman Nurseries purchased seeds costing $25,000 with terms of 3/15 net 30 EOM on January 12. How much will the firm pay if it takes the cash discount? What is the *approximate cost of giving up the cash discount*, using the simplified formula?

LG 2   **E16–2**   Cleaner's, Inc., is switching to paying employees every 2 weeks rather than weekly and will therefore "skip" 1 week's pay. The firm has 25 employees who work a 60-hour week and earn an average wage of $12.50 per hour. Using a 10% rate of interest, how much will this change save the firm annually?

LG 3   **E16–3**   Jasmine Scents has been given two competing offers for short-term financing. Both offers are for borrowing $15,000 for 1 year. The first offer is a *discount loan* at 8%; the second offer is for interest to be paid *at maturity* at a stated interest rate of 9%. Calculate the *effective annual rates* for each loan and indicate which loan offers the better terms.

LG 3   **E16–4**   Jackson Industries has borrowed $125,000 under a line-of-credit agreement. While the company normally maintains a checking account balance of $15,000 in the lending bank, this credit line requires a 20% compensating balance. The stated interest rate on the borrowed funds is 10%. What is the *effective annual rate of interest* on the line of credit?

LG 4   **E16–5**   Horizon Telecom sold $300,000 worth of 120-day commercial paper for $298,000. What is the dollar amount of interest paid on the commercial paper? What is the *effective 120-day rate* on the paper?

Problems

All problems are available in ◆myfinancelab .

LG 1   P16–1   Payment dates   Determine when a firm must pay for purchases made and invoices dated on November 25 under each of the following credit terms:
  a. net 30 date of invoice
  b. net 30 EOM
  c. net 45 date of invoice
  d. net 60 EOM

LG 1   P16–2   Cost of giving up cash discounts   Determine the *cost of giving up the cash discount* under each of the following terms of sale. (*Note:* Assume a 365-day year.)
  a. 2/10 net 30
  b. 1/10 net 30
  c. 2/10 net 45
  d. 3/10 net 45
  e. 1/10 net 60
  f. 3/10 net 30
  g. 4/10 net 180

LG 1   P16–3   Credit terms   Purchases made on credit are due in full by the end of the billing period. Many firms extend a discount for payment made in the first part of the billing period. The original invoice contains a type of shorthand notation that explains the credit terms that apply. (*Note:* Assume a 365-day year.)
  a. Write the shorthand expression of credit terms for each of the following:

Cash discount	Cash discount period	Credit period	Beginning of credit period
1%	15 days	45 days	date of invoice
2	10	30	end of month
2	7	28	date of invoice
1	10	60	end of month

  b. For each of the sets of credit terms in part **a**, calculate the number of days until full payment is due for invoices dated March 12.
  c. For each of the sets of credit terms, calculate the *cost of giving up the cash discount.*
  d. If the firm's cost of short-term financing is 8%, what would you recommend in regard to taking the discount or giving it up in each case?

LG 1   P16–4   Cash discount versus loan   Erica Stone works in an accounts payable department. She has attempted to convince her boss to take the discount on the 3/10 net 45 credit terms most suppliers offer, but her boss argues that giving up the 3% discount is less costly than a short-term loan at 14%. Prove to whoever is wrong that the other is correct. (*Note:* Assume a 365-day year.)

Personal Finance Problem

LG 2   P16–5   Borrow or pay cash for an asset   Bob and Carol Gibbs are set to move into their first apartment. They visited Furniture R'Us, looking for a dining room table and buffet. Dining room sets are typically one of the more expensive home furnishing items, and the store offers financing arrangements to customers. Bob and Carol have the cash to pay for the furniture, but it would definitely deplete their savings, so they want to look at all their options.

The dining room set costs $3,000 and Furniture R'Us offers a financing plan that would allow them to either (1) put 10% down and finance the balance at 4% annual interest over 24 months or (2) receive an immediate $200 cash rebate, thereby paying only $2,800 cash to buy the furniture.

Bob and Carol currently earn 5.2% annual interest on their savings.

a. Calculate the cash down payment for the loan.
b. Calculate the monthly payment on the available loan. (*Hint:* Treat the current loan as an annuity and solve for the monthly payment.)
c. Calculate the initial cash outlay under the cash purchase option.
d. Assuming that they can earn a simple interest rate of 5.2% on savings, what will Bob and Carol give up (opportunity cost) over the 2 years if they pay cash?
e. What is the cost of the cash alternative at the end of 2 years?
f. Should Bob and Carol choose the financing or the cash alternative?

LG 1 **LG 2** **P16–6** **Cash discount decisions**   Prairie Manufacturing has four possible suppliers, all of which offer different credit terms. Except for the differences in credit terms, their products and services are virtually identical. The credit terms offered by these suppliers are shown in the following table. (*Note:* Assume a 365-day year.)

Supplier	Credit terms
J	1/10 net 30 EOM
K	2/20 net 80 EOM
L	1/20 net 60 EOM
M	3/10 net 55 EOM

a. Calculate the *approximate cost of giving up the cash discount* from each supplier.
b. If the firm needs short-term funds, which are currently available from its commercial bank at 16%, and if each of the suppliers is viewed *separately,* which, if any, of the suppliers' cash discounts should the firm give up? Explain why.
c. What impact, if any, would the fact that the firm could stretch by 30 days its accounts payable (net period only) from supplier M have on your answer in part **b** relative to this supplier?

LG 2 **P16–7** **Changing payment cycle**   On accepting the position of chief executive officer and chairman of Reeves Machinery, Frank Cheney changed the firm's weekly payday from Monday afternoon to the following Friday afternoon. The firm's weekly payroll was $10 million, and the cost of short-term funds was 13%. If the effect of this change was to delay check clearing by 1 week, what *annual* savings, if any, were realized?

LG 2 **P16–8** **Spontaneous sources of funds, accruals**   When Tallman Haberdashery, Inc., merged with Meyers Men's Suits, Inc., Tallman's employees were switched from a weekly to a biweekly pay period. Tallman's weekly payroll amounted to $750,000. The cost of funds for the combined firms is 11%. What annual savings, if any, are realized by this change of pay period?

LG 3   **P16–9**   **Cost of bank loan**   Data Back-Up Systems has obtained a $10,000, 90-day bank loan at an annual interest rate of 15%, payable at maturity. (*Note:* Assume a 365-day year.)

a. How much interest (in dollars) will the firm pay on the 90-day loan?

b. Find the *90-day rate* on the loan.

c. Annualize your result in part **b** to find the *effective annual rate* for this loan, assuming that it is rolled over every 90 days throughout the year under the same terms and circumstances.

Personal Finance Problem

LG 3   **P16–10**   **Unsecured sources of short-term loans**   John Savage has obtained a short-term loan from First Carolina Bank. The loan matures in 180 days and is in the amount of $45,000. John needs the money to cover start-up costs in a new business. He hopes to have sufficient backing from other investors by the end of the next 6 months. First Carolina Bank offers John two financing options for the $45,000 loan: a *fixed-rate loan* at 2.5% above prime rate, or a *variable-rate loan* at 1.5% above prime.

Currently, the prime rate of interest is 6.5%, and the consensus forecasts of a group of mortgage economists for changes in the prime rate over the next 180 days are as follows: Sixty days from today the prime rate will rise by 0.5%; 90 days from today the prime rate will rise another 1%; 180 days from today the prime rate will drop by 0.5%.

Using the forecast prime rate changes, answer the following questions.

a. Calculate the total interest cost over 180 days for a *fixed-rate loan.*

b. Calculate the total interest cost over 180 days for a *variable-rate loan.*

c. Which is the lower-interest-cost loan for the next 180 days?

LG 3   **P16–11**   **Effective annual rate**   A financial institution made a $10,000, 1-year discount loan at 10% interest, requiring a compensating balance equal to 20% of the face value of the loan. Determine the *effective annual rate* associated with this loan. (*Note:* Assume that the firm currently maintains $0 on deposit in the financial institution.)

LG 3   **P16–12**   **Compensating balances and effective annual rates**   Lincoln Industries has a line of credit at Bank Two that requires it to pay 11% interest on its borrowing and to maintain a compensating balance equal to 15% of the amount borrowed. The firm has borrowed $800,000 during the year under the agreement. Calculate the *effective annual rate* on the firm's borrowing in each of the following circumstances:

a. The firm normally maintains no deposit balances at Bank Two.

b. The firm normally maintains $70,000 in deposit balances at Bank Two.

c. The firm normally maintains $150,000 in deposit balances at Bank Two.

d. Compare, contrast, and discuss your findings in parts **a**, **b**, and **c**.

LG 3   **P16–13**   **Compensating balance versus discount loan**   Weathers Catering Supply, Inc., needs to borrow $150,000 for 6 months. State Bank has offered to lend the funds at a 9% annual rate subject to a 10% compensating balance. (*Note:* Weathers currently maintains $0 on deposit in State Bank.) Frost Finance Co. has offered to lend the funds at a 9% annual rate with discount-loan terms. The principal of both loans would be payable at maturity as a single sum.

a. Calculate the *effective annual rate of interest* on each loan.

b. What could Weathers do that would reduce the effective annual rate on the State Bank loan?

LG 3   P16–14   Integrative—Comparison of loan terms   Cumberland Furniture wishes to establish a prearranged borrowing agreement with a local commercial bank. The bank's terms for a line of credit are 3.30% over the prime rate, and each year the borrowing must be reduced to zero for a 30-day period. For an equivalent revolving credit agreement, the rate is 2.80% over prime with a commitment fee of 0.50% on the average unused balance. With both loans, the required compensating balance is equal to 20% of the amount borrowed. (*Note:* Cumberland currently maintains $0 on deposit at the bank.) The prime rate is currently 8%. Both agreements have $4 million borrowing limits. The firm expects on average to borrow $2 million during the year no matter which loan agreement it decides to use.

a. What is the *effective annual rate* under the line of credit?

b. What is the *effective annual rate* under the revolving credit agreement? (*Hint:* Compute the ratio of the dollars that the firm will pay in interest and commitment fees to the dollars that the firm will effectively have use of.)

c. If the firm does expect to borrow an average of half the amount available, which arrangement would you recommend for the borrower? Explain why.

LG 4   P16–15   Cost of commercial paper   Commercial paper is usually sold at a discount. Fan Corporation has just sold an issue of 90-day commercial paper with a face value of $1 million. The firm has received initial proceeds of $978,000. (*Note:* Assume a 365-day year.)

a. What *effective annual rate* will the firm pay for financing with commercial paper, assuming that it is rolled over every 90 days throughout the year?

b. If a brokerage fee of $9,612 was paid from the initial proceeds to an investment banker for selling the issue, what *effective annual rate* will the firm pay, assuming that the paper is rolled over every 90 days throughout the year?

LG 5   P16–16   Accounts receivable as collateral   Kansas City Castings (KCC) is attempting to obtain the maximum loan possible using accounts receivable as collateral. The firm extends net-30-day credit. The amounts that are owed KCC by its 12 credit customers, the average age of each account, and the customer's average payment period are as shown in the following table:

Customer	Account receivable	Average age of account	Average payment period of customer
A	$37,000	40 days	30 days
B	42,000	25	50
C	15,000	40	60
D	8,000	30	35
E	50,000	31	40
F	12,000	28	30
G	24,000	30	70
H	46,000	29	40
I	3,000	30	65
J	22,000	25	35
K	62,000	35	40
L	80,000	60	70

a. If the bank will accept all accounts that can be collected in 45 days or less as long as the customer has a history of paying within 45 days, which accounts will be acceptable? What is the total dollar amount of accounts receivable collateral? (*Note:* Accounts receivable that have an average age greater than the customer's average payment period are also excluded.)

b. In addition to the conditions in part **a**, the bank recognizes that 5% of credit sales will be lost to returns and allowances. Also, the bank will lend only 80% of the acceptable collateral (after adjusting for returns and allowances). What level of funds would be made available through this lending source?

LG 5 **P16–17** **Accounts receivable as collateral** Springer Products wishes to borrow $80,000 from a local bank using its accounts receivable to secure the loan. The bank's policy is to accept as collateral any accounts that are normally paid within 30 days of the end of the credit period, as long as the average age of the account is not greater than the customer's average payment period. Springer's accounts receivable, their average ages, and the average payment period for each customer are shown in the following table. The company extends terms of net 30 days.

Customer	Account receivable	Average age of account	Average payment period of customer
A	$20,000	10 days	40 days
B	6,000	40	35
C	22,000	62	50
D	11,000	68	65
E	2,000	14	30
F	12,000	38	50
G	27,000	55	60
H	19,000	20	35

a. Calculate the dollar amount of acceptable accounts receivable collateral held by Springer Products.

b. The bank reduces collateral by 10% for returns and allowances. What is the level of acceptable collateral under this condition?

c. The bank will advance 75% against the firm's acceptable collateral (after adjusting for returns and allowances). What amount can Springer borrow against these accounts?

LG 3 **LG 5** **P16–18** **Accounts receivable as collateral, cost of borrowing** Maximum Bank has analyzed the accounts receivable of Scientific Software, Inc. The bank has chosen eight accounts totaling $134,000 that it will accept as collateral. The bank's terms include a lending rate set at prime + 3% and a 2% commission charge. The prime rate currently is 8.5%.

a. The bank will adjust the accounts by 10% for returns and allowances. It then will lend up to 85% of the adjusted acceptable collateral. What is the maximum amount that the bank will lend to Scientific Software?

b. What is Scientific Software's *effective annual rate of interest* if it borrows $100,000 for 12 months? For 6 months? For 3 months? (*Note:* Assume a 365-day year and a prime rate that remains at 8.5% during the life of the loan.)

LG 5   **P16–19**   **Factoring**   Blair Finance factors the accounts of the Holder Company. All eight factored accounts are shown in the following table, with the amount factored, the date due, and the status on May 30. Indicate the amounts that Blair should have remitted to Holder as of May 30 and the dates of those remittances. Assume that the factor's commission of 2% is deducted as part of determining the amount of the remittance.

Account	Amount	Date due	Status on May 30
A	$200,000	May 30	Collected May 15
B	90,000	May 30	Uncollected
C	110,000	May 30	Uncollected
D	85,000	June 15	Collected May 30
E	120,000	May 30	Collected May 27
F	180,000	June 15	Collected May 30
G	90,000	May 15	Uncollected
H	30,000	June 30	Collected May 30

LG 1   **LG 6**   **P16–20**   **Inventory financing**   Raymond Manufacturing faces a liquidity crisis—it needs a loan of $100,000 for 1 month. Having no source of additional unsecured borrowing, the firm must find a secured short-term lender. The firm's accounts receivable are quite low, but its inventory is considered liquid and reasonably good collateral. The book value of the inventory is $300,000, of which $120,000 is finished goods. (*Note:* Assume a 365-day year.)

(1) City-Wide Bank will make a $100,000 *trust receipt* loan against the finished goods inventory. The annual interest rate on the loan is 12% on the outstanding loan balance plus a 0.25% administration fee levied against the $100,000 initial loan amount. Because it will be liquidated as inventory is sold, the average amount owed over the month is expected to be $75,000.

(2) Sun State Bank will lend $100,000 against a *floating lien* on the book value of inventory for the 1-month period at an annual interest rate of 13%.

(3) Citizens' Bank and Trust will lend $100,000 against a *warehouse receipt* on the finished goods inventory and charge 15% annual interest on the outstanding loan balance. A 0.5% warehousing fee will be levied against the average amount borrowed. Because the loan will be liquidated as inventory is sold, the average loan balance is expected to be $60,000.

a. Calculate the dollar cost of each of the proposed plans for obtaining an initial loan amount of $100,000.

b. Which plan do you recommend? Why?

c. If the firm had made a purchase of $100,000 for which it had been given terms of 2/10 net 30, would it increase the firm's profitability to give up the discount and not borrow as recommended in part **b**? Why or why not?

LG 2   **P16–21**   **ETHICS PROBLEM**   Rancco Inc. reported total sales of $73 million last year, including $13 million in revenue (labor, sales to tax-exempt entities) exempt from sales tax. The company collects sales tax at a rate of 5%. In reviewing its information as part of its loan application, you notice that Rancco's sales tax payments show a total of $2 million in payments over the same time period. What are your conclusions regarding the financial statements that you are reviewing? How might you verify any discrepancies?

Spreadsheet Exercise

Your company is considering manufacturing carrying cases for the portable video game machines that are currently popular. Management decides to borrow $200,000 from each of two banks—First American and First Citizen. On the day that you visit both banks, the quoted prime interest rate is 7%. Each loan is similar in that each involves a 60-day note, with interest to be paid at the end of 60 days.

The interest rate was set at 2% above the prime rate on First American's *fixed-rate note*. Over the 60-day period, the rate of interest on this note will remain at the 2% premium over the prime rate regardless of fluctuations in the prime rate.

First Citizen sets its interest rate at 1.5% above the prime rate on its *floating-rate note*. The rate charged over the 60 days will vary directly with the prime rate.

TO DO

First, create a spreadsheet to calculate the following for the First American loan:

a. Calculate the total dollar interest cost on the loan. Assume a 365-day year.
b. Calculate the *60-day rate* on the loan.
c. Assume that the loan is rolled over each 60 days throughout the year under identical conditions and terms. Calculate the *effective annual rate of interest* on the fixed-rate, 60-day First American note.

Next, create a spreadsheet to calculate the following for the First Citizen loan:

d. Calculate the initial interest rate.
e. If the prime rate immediately jumps to 7.5%, and after 30 days it drops to 7.25%, calculate the interest rate for the first 30 days and the second 30 days of the loan.
f. Calculate the total dollar interest cost.
g. Calculate the *60-day rate of interest*.
h. Assume the loan is rolled over each 60 days throughout the year under the same conditions and terms. Calculate the *effective annual rate of interest*.
i. Which loan would you choose, and why?

 Visit www.myfinancelab.com for **Chapter Case: *Selecting Kanton Company's Financing Strategy and Unsecured Short-Term Borrowing Arrangement,*** Group Exercises, and numerous online resources.

Casa de Diseño

In January 2012, Teresa Leal was named treasurer of Casa de Diseño. She decided that she could best orient herself by systematically examining each area of the company's financial operations. She began by studying the firm's short-term financial activities.

Casa de Diseño is located in Southern California and specializes in a furniture line called "Ligne Moderna." Of high quality and contemporary design, the furniture appeals to the customer who wants something unique for his or her home or apartment. Most Ligne Moderna furniture is built by special order because a wide variety of upholstery, accent trimming, and colors is available. The product line is distributed through exclusive dealership arrangements with well-established retail stores. Casa de Diseño's manufacturing process virtually eliminates the use of wood. Plastic and metal provide the basic framework, and wood is used only for decorative purposes.

Casa de Diseño entered the plastic-furniture market in late 2004. The company markets its plastic-furniture products as indoor–outdoor items under the brand name "Futuro." Futuro plastic furniture emphasizes comfort, durability, and practicality and is distributed through wholesalers. The Futuro line has been very successful, accounting for nearly 40 percent of the firm's sales and profits in 2011. Casa de Diseño anticipates some additions to the Futuro line and also some limited change of direction in its promotion in an effort to expand the applications of the plastic furniture.

Leal has decided to study the firm's cash management practices. To determine the effects of these practices, she must first determine the current operating and cash conversion cycles. In her investigations, she found that Casa de Diseño purchases all of its raw materials and production supplies on open account. The company is operating at production levels that preclude volume discounts. Most suppliers do not offer cash discounts, and Casa de Diseño usually receives credit terms of net 30. An analysis of Casa de Diseño's accounts payable showed that its average payment period is 30 days. Leal consulted industry data and found that the industry average payment period was 39 days. Investigation of six California furniture manufacturers revealed that their average payment period was also 39 days.

Next, Leal studied the production cycle and inventory policies. Casa de Diseño tries not to hold any more inventory than necessary in either raw materials or finished goods. The average inventory age was 110 days. Leal determined that the industry standard, as reported in a survey done by *Furniture Age,* the trade association journal, was 83 days.

Casa de Diseño sells to all of its customers on a net-60 basis, in line with the industry trend to grant such credit terms on specialty furniture. Leal discovered, by aging the accounts receivable, that the average collection period for the firm was 75 days. Investigation of the trade association's and California manufacturers' averages showed that the same collection period existed where net-60 credit terms were given. Where cash discounts were offered, the collection period was significantly shortened. Leal believed that if Casa de Diseño were to offer credit terms of 3/10 net 60, the average collection period could be reduced by 40 percent.

Casa de Diseño was spending an estimated $26,500,000 per year on operating-cycle investments. Leal considered this expenditure level to be the minimum she could expect the firm to disburse during 2012. Her concern was whether the firm's cash management was as efficient as it could be. She knew that the company paid 15 percent annual interest for its resource investment. For this reason, she was concerned about the financing cost resulting from any inefficiencies in the management of Casa de Diseño's cash conversion cycle. (*Note:* Assume a 365-day year and that the operating-cycle investment per dollar of payables, inventory, and receivables is the same.)

TO DO

a. Assuming a constant rate for purchases, production, and sales throughout the year, what are Casa de Diseño's existing operating cycle (OC), cash conversion cycle (CCC), and resource investment need?
b. If Leal can optimize Casa de Diseño's operations according to industry standards, what will Casa de Diseño's operating cycle (OC), cash conversion cycle (CCC), and resource investment need to be under these more efficient conditions?
c. In terms of resource investment requirements, what is the cost of Casa de Diseño's operational inefficiency?
d. (1) If in addition to achieving industry standards for payables and inventory, the firm can reduce the average collection period by offering credit terms of 3/10 net 60, what additional savings in resource investment costs will result from the shortened cash conversion cycle, assuming that the level of sales remains constant?
   (2) If the firm's sales (all on credit) are $40,000,000 and 45% of the customers are expected to take the cash discount, by how much will the firm's annual revenues be reduced as a result of the discount?
   (3) If the firm's variable cost of the $40,000,000 in sales is 80%, determine the reduction in the average investment in accounts receivable and the annual savings that will result from this reduced investment, assuming that sales remain constant.
   (4) If the firm's bad-debts expenses decline from 2% to 1.5% of sales, what annual savings will result, assuming that sales remain constant?
   (5) Use your findings in parts (2) through (4) to assess whether offering the cash discount can be justified financially. Explain why or why not.
e. On the basis of your analysis in parts **a** through **d**, what recommendations would you offer Teresa Leal?
f. Review for Teresa Leal the key sources of short-term financing, other than accounts payable, that she may consider for financing Casa de Diseño's resource investment need calculated in part **b**. Be sure to mention both unsecured and secured sources.

Special Topics in Managerial Finance

It has become a cliché to say that business is becoming more complex and more global over time, but, like all clichés, there is a ring of truth in that statement. In this final part, we examine three special topics that are among the most challenging and exciting topics in all of finance.

Chapter 17 introduces hybrid and derivative securities. A hybrid is a security that has characteristics similar to other securities. For example, preferred stock is a hybrid because it has some debt-like and some equity-like features. Just as many bonds pay a fixed interest rate, preferred stock pays a fixed dividend. However, preferred stock is more like equity in that investors who hold preferred shares cannot force a firm into bankruptcy if it stops paying preferred dividends. A derivative is a security that derives its value from some other security. For example, a call option is a derivative because its value increases (decreases) if the stock price increases (decreases). Perhaps surprisingly, investors can use derivatives to either speculate on price changes in the stock market or to protect themselves against such movements.

Chapter 18 focuses on mergers, leveraged buyouts, and bankruptcy. These are three of the biggest "events" that can happen in the life of a corporation, and certainly most large companies acquire other companies from time to time. Chapter 18 explains the techniques that firms use to execute various types of mergers and acquisitions and highlights the motivations behind those transactions. The chapter also discusses a significant event that firms generally want to avoid—business failure. We discuss the different types and causes of business failures as well as several mechanisms that are used to resolve these failures.

Chapter 19 emphasizes global dimensions of financial management, starting with an overview of trading blocs and other international institutions that have a significant impact on multinational businesses. The chapter offers in-depth coverage of the financial risks associated with doing business internationally, especially risks related to movements in exchange rates, and the techniques that firms use to manage those risks. Finally, Chapter 19 provides a glimpse into the wide range of options available to multinational firms for raising money in markets around the world.

17 Hybrid and Derivative Securities

Learning Goals

LG 1 Differentiate between hybrid and derivative securities and their roles in the corporation.

LG 2 Review the types of leases, leasing arrangements, the lease-versus-purchase decision, the effects of leasing on future financing, and the advantages and disadvantages of leasing.

LG 3 Describe the types of convertible securities, their general features, and financing with convertibles.

LG 4 Demonstrate the procedures for determining the straight bond value, the conversion (or stock) value, and the market value of a convertible bond.

LG 5 Explain the key characteristics of stock purchase warrants, the implied price of an attached warrant, and the values of warrants.

LG 6 Define options and discuss calls and puts, options markets, options trading, the role of call and put options in fund raising, and hedging foreign-currency exposures with options.

Why This Chapter Matters to You

In your *professional* life

ACCOUNTING You need to understand the types of leasing arrangements and the general features of convertible securities, stock purchase warrants, and options, which you will be required to record and report.

INFORMATION SYSTEMS You need to understand types of leasing arrangements and of convertible securities to design systems that will track data used to make lease-or-purchase and conversion decisions.

MANAGEMENT You need to understand when and why it may make better sense to lease assets rather than to purchase them. You need to understand how convertible securities and stock purchase warrants work to decide when the firm would benefit from their use. You also need to understand the impact of call and put options on the firm.

MARKETING You need to understand leasing as a way to finance a new project proposal. You also should understand how hybrid securities can be used to raise funds for new projects.

OPERATIONS You need to understand the role of leasing in financing new equipment. You also need to understand the maintenance obligations associated with leased equipment.

In your *personal* life

Understanding hybrid and derivative securities will benefit you in your investment activities. Even more useful is an understanding of leasing, which you may use to finance certain long-lived assets such as housing or cars. Knowing how to analyze and compare leasing to the alternative of purchasing should help you to better manage your personal finances.

Boeing

"We'll Buy It, You Fly It"

On July 21, 2010, the Irish aircraft leasing company, Avolon, announced that it had signed a deal to purchase 12 next-generation Boeing 737-800 airplanes. The 737-800 aircraft was designed to be more fuel efficient than its predecessors and had a list price of $80 million. Avolon CEO, Dómhnal Slattery, said his company would be seeking more than $1 billion in new equity capital to fund its ongoing growth.

Avolon's business model did not call for it to fly airplanes but rather to lease them to airlines in transactions known as sale-leasebacks. In a sale-leaseback, the airline agrees to lease an airplane from Avolon for 8 to 10 years. At the end of that period, the airline may have the option to purchase the airplane, or ownership may revert to the leasing company.

Aircraft are just one example of equipment that is leased. Other commonly leased equipment includes computers, oil-drilling equipment, railway cars, cable television, medical equipment, pollution-control devices, and solar energy devices. Most leased equipment is expensive and would require large cash outlays if purchased outright. Leasing provides an easier method of obtaining an up-to-date piece of equipment with a much smaller cash outlay.

Leasing is a tool that 80 percent of U.S. businesses have used at some time to acquire equipment. By leasing a large piece of equipment, the lessee can improve cash flow, keep pace with technology by leasing the latest models, and sometimes improve the company's financial ratios by excluding some leased assets (operating leases) from the balance sheet.

In this chapter, we'll demonstrate how to analyze lease financing, a hybrid financing technique that incorporates elements of debt and equity. You will also learn about other hybrids including convertible securities, stock purchase warrants, and derivative securities such as stock options.

17.1 Overview of Hybrids and Derivatives

hybrid security
A form of debt or equity financing that possesses characteristics of *both* debt and equity financing.

derivative security
A security that is neither debt nor equity but derives its value from an underlying asset that is often another security; called "derivatives," for short.

Chapters 6 and 7 described the characteristics of the key securities—corporate bonds, common stock, and preferred stock—used by corporations to raise long-term funds. In their simplest form, bonds are pure debt and common stock is pure equity. Preferred stock, on the other hand, is a form of equity that promises to pay fixed periodic dividends that are similar to the fixed contractual interest payments on bonds. Because it blends the characteristics of *both* debt (a fixed dividend payment) and equity (ownership), preferred stock is considered a **hybrid security**. Other popular hybrid securities include financial leases, convertible securities, and stock purchase warrants. Each of these hybrid securities is described in the following pages.

The final section of this chapter focuses on *options*, a popular **derivative security**—a security that is neither debt nor equity but derives its value from an underlying asset that is often another security. As you'll learn, *derivatives* are not used by corporations to raise funds but rather serve as a useful tool for managing certain aspects of the firm's risk.

→ REVIEW QUESTION

17–1 Differentiate between a *hybrid security* and a *derivative security*.

17.2 Leasing

leasing
The process by which a firm can obtain the use of certain fixed assets for which it must make a series of contractual, periodic, tax-deductible payments.

lessee
The receiver of the services of the assets under a lease contract.

lessor
The owner of assets that are being leased.

operating lease
A *cancelable* contractual arrangement whereby the lessee agrees to make periodic payments to the lessor, often for 5 or fewer years, to obtain an asset's services; generally, the total payments over the term of the lease are *less* than the lessor's initial cost of the leased asset.

Leasing enables the firm to obtain the use of certain fixed assets for which it must make a series of contractual, periodic, tax-deductible payments. The **lessee** is the receiver of the services of the assets under the lease contract; the **lessor** is the owner of the assets. Leasing can take a number of forms.

TYPES OF LEASES

The two basic types of leases that are available to a business are *operating leases* and *financial leases* (often called *capital leases* by accountants).

Operating Leases

An **operating lease** is normally a contractual arrangement whereby the lessee agrees to make periodic payments to the lessor, often for 5 or fewer years, to obtain an asset's services. Such leases are generally *cancelable* at the option of the lessee, who may be required to pay a penalty for cancellation. Assets that are leased under operating leases have a usable life that is *longer* than the term of the lease. Usually, however, they would become less efficient and technologically obsolete if leased for a longer period. Computer systems are prime examples of assets whose relative efficiency is expected to diminish as the technology changes. The operating lease is therefore a common arrangement for obtaining such systems, as well as for other relatively short-lived assets such as automobiles.

If an operating lease is held to maturity, the lessee at that time returns the leased asset to the lessor, who may lease it again or sell the asset. Normally, the asset still has a positive market value at the termination of the lease. In some instances, the lease contract gives the lessee the opportunity to purchase the leased asset. Generally, the total payments made by the lessee to the lessor are *less* than the lessor's initial cost of the leased asset.

Financial (or Capital) Leases

financial (or capital) lease
A *longer-term* lease than an operating lease that is *noncancelable* and obligates the lessee to make payments for the use of an asset over a predefined period of time; the total payments over the term of the lease are *greater* than the lessor's initial cost of the leased asset.

A **financial (or capital) lease** is a *longer-term* lease than an operating lease. Financial leases are *noncancelable* and obligate the lessee to make payments for the use of an asset over a predefined period of time. Financial leases are commonly used for leasing land, buildings, and large pieces of equipment. The noncancelable feature of the financial lease makes it similar to certain types of long-term debt. The lease payment becomes a fixed, tax-deductible expenditure that must be paid at predefined dates. As with debt, failure to make the contractual lease payments can result in bankruptcy for the lessee.

With a financial lease, the total payments over the term of the lease are *greater* than the lessor's initial cost of the leased asset. In other words, the lessor must receive more than the asset's purchase price to earn its required return on the investment. Technically, under *FASB (Financial Accounting Standards Board) Statement No. 13,* "Accounting for Leases," a financial (or capital) lease is defined as one that has *any* of the following elements:

1. The lease transfers ownership of the property to the lessee by the end of the lease term.
2. The lease contains an option to purchase the property at a "bargain price." Such an option must be exercisable at a "fair market value."
3. The lease term is equal to 75 percent or more of the estimated economic life of the property (exceptions exist for property leased toward the end of its usable economic life).
4. At the beginning of the lease, the present value of the lease payments is equal to 90 percent or more of the fair market value of the leased property.

The emphasis in this chapter is on financial leases, because they result in inescapable long-term financial commitments by the firm.

The *Focus on Practice* box on page 680 discusses leasing by Disney that did not have a happy ending.

LEASING ARRANGEMENTS

direct lease
A lease under which a lessor owns or acquires the assets that are leased to a given lessee.

sale-leaseback arrangement
A lease under which the lessee sells an asset to a prospective lessor and then *leases back* the same asset, making fixed periodic payments for its use.

leveraged lease
A lease under which the lessor acts as an equity participant, supplying only about 20 percent of the cost of the asset, while a lender supplies the balance.

Lessors use three primary techniques for obtaining assets to be leased. The method depends largely on the desires of the prospective lessee.

1. A **direct lease** results when a lessor owns or acquires the assets that are leased to a given lessee. In other words, the lessee did not previously own the assets that it is leasing.
2. In a **sale-leaseback arrangement,** lessors acquire leased assets by purchasing assets already owned by the lessee and leasing them back. This technique is normally initiated by a firm that needs funds for operations. By selling an existing asset to a lessor and then *leasing it back,* the lessee receives cash for the asset immediately, while obligating itself to make fixed periodic payments for use of the leased asset.
3. Leasing arrangements that include one or more third-party lenders are **leveraged leases.** Under a leveraged lease, the lessor acts as an equity participant,

focus on PRACTICE

Leases to Airlines End on a Sour Note

in practice The Walt Disney Company is in the business of providing entertainment experiences based on its rich legacy of creative content and exceptional story-telling. From theme parks and resorts to motion pictures and cartoons, the Walt Disney Company presents tales in which many Disney characters live happily ever after. However, one Disney tale that did not have a happy ending was Disney's investment in leveraged aircraft leases.

Using a structure known as a *leveraged lease*, cash-rich Disney purchased airplanes in the early 1990s and leased them out to air carriers. The deals, with ironclad terms, were seen as safe and offered tax advantages. Since the 1980s, large corporations have been leasing out planes to take advantage of tax rules that allow for accelerated depreciation of large

equipment. Under a typical leveraged lease, Disney put up 20 percent of the purchase price. The rest was borrowed under a loan using the plane as collateral. None of Disney's other assets were put at risk.

During the 1990s, leveraged leases were attractive investments that boosted a company's return on investment. However, the destruction of the World Trade Center on September 11, 2001, and the ensuing reaction to potential terrorist threats crippled air travel and put U.S. air carriers under tremendous financial pressure. The result for United Airlines was bankruptcy. Under bankruptcy protection, United was able to break any lease it didn't want, giving the airline powerful leverage to renegotiate lower lease payments, at lower market rates. When no deal was reached, United Airlines was able to walk away from the

leases. Disney had to write off entirely the $114 million book value assigned to its investment in two Boeing 747s and two 767s leased to United. Pursuing the matter in the courts, Disney was able to recoup $50 million from United for its lost tax benefits.

With additional aircraft leased out to Delta Air Lines (five aircraft, $119 million), the Disney tale of leveraged leases had not reached its final reel. Delta Air Lines announced 7,000 jobs cut in September 2004 as part of a $5 billion cost-saving program and entered bankruptcy in late 2005. At that time Disney was forced to declare a write-off of $68 million for its Delta leases, and the company eventually left the aircraft-leasing business entirely.

▶ *Were the Disney leases of aircraft to United Airlines operating leases or financial leases?*

---

maintenance clauses
Provisions normally included in an operating lease that require the lessor to maintain the assets and to make insurance and tax payments.

renewal options
Provisions especially common in operating leases that grant the lessee the right to re-lease assets at the expiration of the lease.

purchase options
Provisions frequently included in both operating and financial leases that allow the lessee to purchase the leased asset at maturity, typically for a prespecified price.

supplying only about 20 percent of the cost of the asset, and a lender supplies the balance. Leveraged leases are especially popular in structuring leases of very expensive assets.

A lease agreement typically specifies whether the lessee is responsible for maintenance of the leased assets. Operating leases normally include **maintenance clauses** requiring the lessor to maintain the assets and to make insurance and tax payments. Financial leases nearly always require the lessee to pay maintenance and other costs.

The lessee is usually given the option to renew a lease at its expiration. **Renewal options,** which grant lessees the right to re-lease assets at expiration, are especially common in operating leases because their term is generally shorter than the usable life of the leased assets. **Purchase options** allowing the lessee to purchase the leased asset at maturity, typically for a prespecified price, are frequently included in both operating and financial leases.

The lessor can be one of a number of parties. In operating leases, the lessor is likely to be the manufacturer's leasing subsidiary or an independent leasing company. Financial leases are frequently handled by independent leasing companies or by the leasing subsidiaries of large financial institutions such as commercial banks and life insurance companies. Life insurance companies are especially active in real estate leasing. Pension funds, like commercial banks, have also been increasing their leasing activities.

LEASE-VERSUS-PURCHASE DECISION

**lease-versus-purchase (or
lease-versus-buy) decision**
The decision facing firms
needing to acquire new fixed
assets: whether to lease the
assets or to purchase them,
using borrowed funds or
available liquid resources.

Firms that are contemplating the acquisition of new fixed assets commonly confront the **lease-versus-purchase (or lease-versus-buy) decision.** The alternatives available are (1) lease the assets, (2) borrow funds to purchase the assets, or (3) purchase the assets using available liquid resources. Alternatives 2 and 3, although they differ, are analyzed in a similar fashion; even if the firm has the liquid resources with which to purchase the assets, the use of these funds is viewed as equivalent to borrowing. Therefore, we need to compare only the leasing and purchasing alternatives.

The lease-versus-purchase decision involves application of the capital budgeting methods presented in Chapters 10 through 12. First, we determine the relevant cash flows and then apply present value techniques. The following steps are involved in the analysis:

Step 1 Find the *after-tax cash outflows for each year under the lease alternative.* This step generally involves a fairly simple tax adjustment of the annual lease payments. In addition, the cost of exercising a purchase option in the final year of the lease term must frequently be included.[1]

Step 2 Find the *after-tax cash outflows for each year under the purchase alternative.* This step involves adjusting the sum of the scheduled loan payment and maintenance cost outlay for the tax shields resulting from the tax deductions attributable to maintenance, depreciation, and interest.

Step 3 Calculate the *present value of the cash outflows* associated with the lease (from Step 1) and purchase (from Step 2) alternatives using the *after-tax cost of debt* as the discount rate. The after-tax cost of debt is used to evaluate the lease-versus-purchase decision because the decision itself involves the choice between two *financing* techniques—leasing and borrowing—that have very low risk.

Step 4 Choose the alternative with the *lower present value* of cash outflows from Step 3. It will be the *least-cost* financing alternative.

The application of each of these steps is demonstrated in the following example.

Example 17.1 ▶ Roberts Company, a small machine shop, is contemplating acquiring a new machine that costs $24,000. Arrangements can be made to lease or purchase the machine. The firm is in the 40% tax bracket.

Lease The firm would obtain a 5-year lease requiring annual end-of-year lease payments of $6,000. All maintenance costs would be paid by the lessor, and insurance and other costs would be borne by the lessee. The lessee would exercise its option to purchase the machine for $1,200 at termination of the lease.[2]

---

1. Including the cost of exercising a purchase option in the cash flows for the lease alternative ensures that under both lease and purchase alternatives the firm owns the asset at the end of the relevant time horizon. The other approach would be to include the cash flows from sale of the asset in the cash flows for the purchase alternative at the end of the lease term. These strategies guarantee avoidance of unequal lives, which were discussed in Chapter 12. In addition, they make any subsequent cash flows irrelevant because these would be either identical or nonexistent, respectively, under each alternative.

2. Lease payments are generally made at the beginning of the year. To simplify the following discussions, *end-of-year lease payments are assumed.* We are assuming that the machine's market value and book value are both $1,200 at the end of 5 years.

Purchase   The firm would finance the purchase of the machine with a 9%, 5-year loan requiring end-of-year installment payments of $6,170.[3] The machine would be depreciated under MACRS using a 5-year recovery period. The firm would pay $1,500 per year for a service contract that covers all maintenance costs; insurance and other costs would be borne by the firm. The firm plans to keep the machine and use it beyond its 5-year recovery period.

Using these data, we can apply the steps presented earlier:

Step 1   The after-tax cash outflow from the lease payments can be found by multiplying the before-tax payment of $6,000 by 1 minus the tax rate, T, of 40%.

$$\text{After-tax cash outflow from lease} = \$6,000 \times (1 - T)$$
$$= \$6,000 \times (1 - 0.40) = \$3,600$$

Therefore, the lease alternative results in annual cash outflows over the 5-year lease of $3,600. In the final year, the $1,200 cost of the purchase option would be added to the $3,600 lease outflow to get a total cash outflow in year 5 of $4,800 ($3,600 + $1,200).

Step 2   The after-tax cash outflow from the purchase alternative is a bit more difficult to find. First, the interest component of each annual loan payment must be determined because the Internal Revenue Service allows the deduction of interest only—not principal—from income for tax purposes.[4] Table 17.1 presents the calculations necessary to split the loan payments

TABLE 17.1   **Determining the Interest and Principal Components of the Roberts Company Loan Payments**

| End of year | Loan payments (1) | Beginning-of-year principal (2) | Payments | | End-of-year principal $[(2) - (4)]$ (5) |
			Interest $[0.09 \times (2)]$ (3)	Principal $[(1) - (3)]$ (4)	
1	$6,170	$24,000	$2,160	$4,010	$19,990
2	6,170	19,990	1,799	4,371	15,619
3	6,170	15,619	1,406	4,764	10,855
4	6,170	10,855	977	5,193	5,662
5	6,170	5,662	510	5,660	—[a]

[a]The values in this table have been rounded to the nearest dollar, which results in a slight difference ($2) between the beginning-of-year-5 principal (in column 2) and the year-5 principal payment (in column 4).

3. The annual loan payment on the 9 percent, 5-year loan of $24,000 is calculated by using the loan amortization technique described in Chapter 5. To calculate the loan payment in Excel, you would use the "pmt" function, entering into any blank cell, =pmt(0.09,5,24000,0,0). In the terms inside the parenthesis, 0.09 is the interest rate, 5 is the term of the lease in years, and 24,000 is the amount being borrowed (or equivalently, the cost of the new machine). The final two zeros inside the parenthesis tell Excel that after 5 years the loan is totally paid off (zero remaining balance) and that payments are made at the end of each year. The exact loan payment is $6,170.22, but in the example we round down to the nearest dollar.

4. When the rate of interest on the loan used to finance the purchase just equals the cost of debt, the present value of the after-tax loan payments (annual loan payments − interest tax shields) discounted at the after-tax cost of debt just equals the initial loan principal. In such a case, it is unnecessary to amortize the loan to determine the payment amount and the amounts of interest when finding after-tax cash outflows. The loan payments and interest payments (columns 1 and 4 in Table 17.2) can be ignored, and, in their place, the initial loan principal ($24,000) is shown as an outflow occurring at time zero. To allow for a loan interest rate that is different from the firm's cost of debt and for easier understanding, here we isolate the loan payments and interest payments rather than use this computationally more efficient approach.

TABLE 17.2	After-Tax Cash Outflows Associated with Purchasing for Roberts Company						
End of year	Loan payments (1)	Maintenance costs (2)	Depreciation (3)	Interest^a (4)	Total deductions [(2) + (3) + (4)] (5)	Tax shields [(0.40 × (5)] (6)	After-tax cash outflows [(1) + (2) − (6)] (7)
1	$6,170	$1,500	$4,800	$2,160	$ 8,460	$3,384	$4,286
2	6,170	1,500	7,680	1,799	10,979	4,392	3,278
3	6,170	1,500	4,560	1,406	7,466	2,986	4,684
4	6,170	1,500	2,880	977	5,357	2,143	5,527
5	6,170	1,500	2,880	510	4,890	1,956	5,714

^{a}From Table 17.1, column 3.

into their interest and principal components. Columns 3 and 4 show the annual interest and principal paid.

In Table 17.2, the annual loan payment is shown in column 1, and the annual maintenance cost, which is a tax-deductible expense, is shown in column 2. Next, we find the annual depreciation write-off resulting from the $24,000 machine. Using the applicable MACRS 5-year recovery period depreciation percentages—20% in year 1, 32% in year 2, 19% in year 3, and 12% in years 4 and 5—given in Table 4.2 on page 117 results in the annual depreciation for years 1 through 5 given in column 3 of Table 17.2.[5]

Table 17.2 presents the calculations required to determine the cash outflows[6] associated with borrowing to purchase the new machine. Column 7 of the table presents the after-tax cash outflows associated with the purchase alternative. A few points should be clarified with respect to the calculations in Table 17.2. The major cash outflows are the total loan payment for each year given in column 1 and the annual maintenance cost in column 2. The sum of these two outflows is reduced by the tax savings from writing off the maintenance, depreciation, and interest expenses associated with the new machine and its financing. The resulting cash outflows are the after-tax cash outflows associated with the purchase alternative.

Step 3   The present values of the cash outflows associated with the lease (from Step 1) and purchase (from Step 2) alternatives are calculated in Table 17.3 using the firm's 6% after-tax cost of debt.[7] The sum of the present values of the cash outflows for the leasing alternative is given in column 2 of Table 17.3, and the sum of those for the purchasing alternative is given in column 4.

---

5. We are ignoring depreciation in year 6 because regardless of which option the company selects there will be $1,200 worth of depreciation remaining.

6. Although other cash outflows such as insurance and operating expenses may be relevant here, they would be the same under the lease and purchase alternatives and therefore would cancel out in the final analysis.

7. If we ignore any flotation costs, the firm's after-tax cost of debt would be 5.4% [9% debt cost × (1 − 0.40 tax rate)]. To reflect both the flotation costs associated with selling new debt and the possible need to sell the debt at a discount, we use an after-tax debt cost of 6% as the applicable discount rate. A more detailed discussion of techniques for calculating the after-tax cost of debt is found in Chapter 9.

TABLE 17.3	Comparison of Cash Outflows Associated with Leasing versus Purchasing for Roberts Company			
	Leasing		Purchasing	
End of year	After-tax cash outflows (1)	Present value of outflows (2)	After-tax cash outflows[a] (3)	Present value of outflows (4)
1	$3,600	$ 3,396	$4,286	$ 4,043
2	3,600	3,204	3,278	2,917
3	3,600	3,023	4,684	3,933
4	3,600	2,852	5,527	4,378
5	4,800[b]	3,587	5,714	4,270
	PV of cash outflows	$16,062	PV of cash outflows	$19,541

[a]From column 7 of Table 17.2.
[b]After-tax lease payment outflow of $3,600 plus the $1,200 cost of exercising the purchase option.

Step 4   Because the present value of cash outflows for leasing ($16,062) is lower than that for purchasing ($19,541), *the leasing alternative is preferred.* Leasing results in an incremental savings of $3,479 ($19,541 − $16,062) and is therefore the less costly alternative.

The techniques described here for comparing lease and purchase alternatives may be applied in different ways. The approach illustrated by the Roberts Company data is one of the most straightforward. It is important to recognize that the lower cost of one alternative over the other results from factors such as the differing tax brackets of the lessor and lessee, different tax treatments of leases versus purchases, and differing risks and borrowing costs for lessor and lessee. Therefore, when making a lease-versus-purchase decision, the firm will find that inexpensive borrowing opportunities, high required lessor returns, and a low risk of obsolescence increase the attractiveness of purchasing. Subjective factors must also be included in the decision-making process. Like most financial decisions, the lease-versus-purchase decision requires some judgment or intuition.

Personal Finance Example 17.2 ▶   Jake Jiminez is considering either leasing or purchasing a new Honda Fit that will cost $15,000. The 3-year lease requires an initial payment of $1,800 and monthly payments of $300. Purchasing requires a $2,500 down payment, sales tax of 5% ($750), and 36 monthly payments of $392. He estimates the trade-in value of the new car will be $8,000 at the end of 3 years. Assuming Jake can earn 4% annual interest on his savings and is subject to a 5% sales tax on purchases, we can make a reasonable recommendation to Jake using the following analysis (for simplicity, ignoring the time value of money).

Lease Cost

Down payment	$ 1,800
Total lease payments (36 months × $300/month)	10,800
Opportunity cost of initial payment (3 years × 0.04 × $1,800)	216
Total cost of leasing	$12,816

Purchase Cost

Down payment	$ 2,500
Sales tax (0.05 × $15,000)	750
Total loan payments (36 months × $392/month)	14,112
Opportunity cost of down payment (3 years × 0.04 × $2,500)	300
Less: Estimated trade-in value of car at end of loan	(8,000)
Total cost of purchasing	$ 9,662

Because the total cost of leasing of $12,816 is greater than the $9,662 total cost of purchasing, Jake should purchase rather than lease the car.

EFFECTS OF LEASING ON FUTURE FINANCING

Because leasing is considered a type of financing, it affects the firm's future financing, just as having existing debt has an impact on a firm's ability to borrow even more. Lease payments are shown as a tax-deductible expense on the firm's income statement. Anyone analyzing the firm's income statement would probably recognize that an asset is being leased, although the amount and term of the lease would be unclear.

capitalized lease
A *financial (capital) lease* that has the present value of all its payments included as an asset and corresponding liability on the firm's balance sheet, as required by the Financial Accounting Standards Board (FASB) in *FASB Statement No. 13.*

The Financial Accounting Standards Board (FASB), in *FASB Statement No. 13,* "Accounting for Leases," requires explicit disclosure of *financial (capital) lease* obligations on the firm's balance sheet. Such a lease must be shown as a **capitalized lease,** meaning that the present value of all its payments is included as an asset and corresponding liability on the firm's balance sheet. An *operating lease,* on the other hand, need not be capitalized, but its basic features must be disclosed in a footnote to the financial statements. *FASB Statement No. 13,* of course, establishes detailed guidelines to be used in capitalizing leases. Subsequent standards have further refined lease capitalization and disclosure procedures.

Example 17.3 ▶

Jeffrey Company, a manufacturer of water purifiers, is leasing an asset under a 10-year lease requiring annual end-of-year payments of $15,000. The lease can be capitalized merely by calculating the present value of the lease payments over the life of the lease. However, the rate at which the payments should be discounted is difficult to determine.[8] If 10% were used, the present, or capitalized, value of the lease would be $92,169. This value would be shown as an asset and

---

8. The Financial Accounting Standards Board in *Statement No. 13* established certain guidelines for the appropriate discount rate to use when capitalizing leases. Most commonly, the rate that the lessee would have incurred to borrow the funds to buy the asset with a secured loan under terms similar to the lease repayment schedule is used. This simply represents the *before-tax cost of a secured debt.*

corresponding liability on the firm's balance sheet, which should result in an accurate reflection of the firm's true financial position.

Because the consequences of missing a financial lease payment are the same as those of missing an interest or principal payment on debt, a financial analyst must view the lease as a long-term financial commitment of the lessee. With FASB *Statement No. 13*, the inclusion of each financial (capital) lease as an asset and corresponding liability (that is, long-term debt) provides for a balance sheet that more accurately reflects the firm's financial status. It thereby permits various types of financial ratio analyses to be performed directly on the statement by any interested party.

ADVANTAGES AND DISADVANTAGES OF LEASING

Leasing has a number of commonly cited advantages and disadvantages that managers should consider when making a lease-versus-purchase decision. It is not unusual for a number of them to apply in a given situation. Table 17.4 describes the commonly cited advantages and disadvantages of leasing.

TABLE 17.4 ▷ **Advantages and Disadvantages of Leasing**

Advantages

- The firm may *avoid the cost of obsolescence*. This is especially true in the case of operating leases, which generally have relatively short lives.
- A lessee *avoids many of the restrictive covenants* (such as minimum liquidity, subsequent borrowing, and cash dividend payments) that are normally included as part of a long-term loan but are *not* normally found in a lease agreement.
- In the case of low-cost assets that are infrequently acquired, leasing—especially operating leases—may provide the firm with needed *financing flexibility*. The firm does not have to arrange other financing for these assets.
- Sale-leaseback arrangements may permit the firm to *increase its liquidity* by converting an *existing* asset into cash. This can benefit a firm that is short of working capital or in a liquidity bind.
- Leasing allows the lessee, in effect, to *depreciate land,* which would be prohibited if the land were purchased. Because the lessee who leases land is permitted to deduct the *total lease payment* as an expense for tax purposes, the effect is the

same as if the firm had purchased the land and then depreciated it.

- Because leasing may not increase the assets or liabilities on the firm's balance sheet, leasing may result in misleading *financial ratios*. Understating assets and liabilities can cause certain ratios, such as the total asset turnover, to look better than they might be. With the adoption of *FASB Statement No. 13,* this advantage no longer applies to financial leases, although it remains a potential advantage for operating leases.
- Leasing provides *100 percent financing*. Most loan agreements for the purchase of fixed assets require a down payment; thus the borrower is able to borrow only 90 to 95 percent of the purchase price of the asset.
- In the case of *bankruptcy* or *reorganization,* the maximum claim of lessors against the corporation is 3 years of lease payments. If debt is used to purchase an asset, the creditors have a claim that is equal to the total outstanding loan balance.

Disadvantages

- In many leases the *return to the lessor is quite high;* the firm might be better off borrowing to purchase the asset.
- The *terminal value* of an asset, if any, is realized by the lessor. If the lessee had purchased the asset, it could have claimed its terminal value. Of course, an expected terminal value when recognized by the lessor results in lower lease payments.

- The lessee is generally *prohibited from making improvements* on the leased property or asset without the lessor's approval. However, lessors generally encourage leasehold improvements when these are expected to enhance the asset's salvage value.
- If a lessee leases an *asset that subsequently becomes obsolete,* it still must make lease payments over the remaining term of the lease. This is true even if the asset is unusable.

→ **REVIEW QUESTIONS**

17–2 What is *leasing?* Define, compare, and contrast *operating leases* and *financial (or capital) leases.* How does the Financial Accounting Standards Board's *Statement No. 13* define a financial (or capital) lease? Describe three methods used by lessors to acquire assets to be leased.

17–3 Describe the four basic steps involved in the *lease-versus-purchase decision* process. How are capital budgeting methods applied in this process?

17–4 What type of lease must be treated as a *capitalized lease* on the balance sheet? How does the financial manager capitalize a lease?

17–5 List and discuss the commonly cited advantages and disadvantages that should be considered when deciding whether to lease or purchase.

 ## 17.3 Convertible Securities

conversion feature
An option that is included as part of a bond or a preferred stock issue and allows its holder to change the security into a stated number of shares of common stock.

A **conversion feature** is an option that is included as part of a bond or a preferred stock issue and allows its holder to change the security into a stated number of shares of common stock. The conversion feature typically enhances the marketability of an issue.

TYPES OF CONVERTIBLE SECURITIES

Corporate bonds and preferred stocks may be convertible into common stock. The most common type of convertible security is the bond. Convertibles normally have an accompanying *call feature,* which permits the issuer to retire or encourage conversion of outstanding convertibles when appropriate.

Convertible Bonds

convertible bond
A bond that can be changed into a specified number of shares of common stock.

straight bond
A bond that is nonconvertible, having no conversion feature.

A **convertible bond** can be changed into a specified number of shares of common stock. It is nearly always a *debenture*—an unsecured bond—with a call feature. Because the conversion feature provides the purchaser with the possibility of becoming a stockholder on favorable terms, convertible bonds are generally a less expensive form of financing than similar-risk nonconvertible or **straight bonds.** The conversion feature adds a degree of speculation to a bond issue, although the issue still maintains its value as a bond.

Convertible Preferred Stock

convertible preferred stock
Preferred stock that can be changed into a specified number of shares of common stock.

straight preferred stock
Preferred stock that is nonconvertible, having no conversion feature.

Convertible preferred stock is preferred stock that can be changed into a specified number of shares of common stock. It can normally be sold with a lower stated dividend than a similar-risk nonconvertible or **straight preferred stock.** The reason is that the convertible preferred holder is assured of the fixed dividend payment associated with a preferred stock and also may receive the appreciation resulting from increases in the market price of the underlying common stock. Convertible preferred stock behaves much like convertible bonds. The following discussions will concentrate on the more widespread convertible bonds.

> **Matter of fact**
>
> **Convertibles Market Active in 2010**
>
> In the first quarter of 2010, firms issued roughly $6 billion in convertible securities in the United States. However, with the historically low interest rates prevailing at that time, many companies decided to refinance some of their outstanding debts, so more convertibles were retired than issued, resulting in a net decline in the size of the overall market for convertibles.

GENERAL FEATURES OF CONVERTIBLES

Convertible securities are nearly always convertible at any time during the life of the security. Occasionally, conversion is permitted only for a limited number of years—say, for 5 or 10 years after issuance of the convertible.

conversion ratio
The ratio at which a convertible security can be exchanged for common stock.

conversion price
The per-share price that is effectively paid for common stock as the result of conversion of a convertible security.

Conversion Ratio

The **conversion ratio** is the ratio at which a convertible security can be exchanged for common stock. The conversion ratio can be stated in two ways:

1. Sometimes the conversion ratio is stated in terms of a given number of shares of common stock. To find the **conversion price**, which is the per-share price that is effectively paid for common stock as the result of conversion, divide the *par value* (not the market value) of the convertible security by the conversion ratio.

| Example 17.4 ▶ | Western Wear Company, a manufacturer of denim products, has outstanding a bond that has a $1,000 par value and is convertible into 25 shares of common stock. The bond's conversion ratio is 25. The conversion price for the bond is $40 per share ($1,000 ÷ 25). |

2. Sometimes, instead of the conversion ratio, the conversion price is given. The conversion ratio can be obtained by dividing the *par value* of the convertible by the conversion price.

| Example 17.5 ▶ | Mosher Company, a franchiser of seafood restaurants, has outstanding a convertible 20-year bond with a par value of $1,000. The bond is convertible at $50 per share into common stock. The conversion ratio is 20 ($1,000 ÷ $50). |

The issuer of a convertible security normally establishes a conversion ratio or conversion price that *sets the conversion price per share at the time of issuance above the current market price of the firm's stock*. If the prospective purchasers do not expect conversion ever to be feasible, they will purchase a straight security or some other convertible issue.

conversion (or stock) value
The value of a convertible security measured in terms of the market price of the common stock into which it can be converted.

Conversion (or Stock) Value

The **conversion (or stock) value** is the value of the convertible measured in terms of the market price of the common stock into which it can be converted. The conversion value can be found simply by multiplying the conversion ratio by the current market price of the firm's common stock.

Example 17.6 ▶ McNamara Industries, a petroleum processor, has outstanding a $1,000 bond that is convertible into common stock at $62.50 per share. The conversion ratio is therefore 16 ($1,000 ÷ $62.50). Because the current market price of the common stock is $65 per share, the conversion value is $1,040 (16 × $65). Because the conversion value is above the bond value of $1,000, conversion is a viable option for the owner of the convertible security.

Effect on Earnings per Share

The presence of **contingent securities**, which include convertibles as well as warrants and stock options (described later in this chapter), affects the reporting of the firm's earnings per share (EPS). Firms with contingent securities, which if converted or exercised would dilute (that is, lower) earnings per share, are required to report earnings in two ways—*basic EPS* and *diluted EPS*.

Basic EPS are calculated without regard to any contingent securities. They are found by dividing earnings available for common stockholders by the number of shares of common stock outstanding. We use this standard method of calculating EPS throughout this textbook.

Diluted EPS are calculated under the assumption that *all* contingent securities that would have dilutive effects are converted and exercised and are therefore common stock. They are found by adjusting basic EPS for the impact of converting all convertibles and exercising all warrants and options that would have dilutive effects on the firm's earnings. This approach treats as common stock *all* contingent securities. It is calculated by dividing earnings available for common stockholders (adjusted for interest and preferred stock dividends that would *not* be paid, given assumed conversion of *all* outstanding contingent securities that would have dilutive effects) by the number of shares of common stock that would be outstanding if *all* contingent securities that would have dilutive effects were converted and exercised. Rather than demonstrate these accounting calculations,[9] suffice it to say that firms with outstanding convertibles, warrants, and/or stock options must report basic and diluted EPS on their income statements.

FINANCING WITH CONVERTIBLES

Using convertible securities to raise long-term funds can help the firm achieve its cost-of-capital and capital structure goals. There also are a number of more specific motives and considerations involved in evaluating convertible financing.

Motives for Convertible Financing

Convertibles can be used for a variety of reasons. One popular motive is their use as a form of *deferred common stock financing*. When a convertible security is issued, both issuer and purchaser expect the security to be converted into common stock at some future point. Because the security is first sold with a conversion price above the current market price of the firm's stock, conversion is initially not attractive. The issuer of a convertible could alternatively sell common

contingent securities
Convertibles, warrants, and stock options. Their presence affects the reporting of a firm's earnings per share (EPS).

basic EPS
Earnings per share (EPS) calculated without regard to any contingent securities.

diluted EPS
Earnings per share (EPS) calculated under the assumption that *all* contingent securities that would have dilutive effects are converted and exercised and are therefore common stock.

9. For excellent discussions and demonstrations of the two methods of reporting EPS, see Donald A. Kieso, Jerry J. Weygandt, and Terry D. Warfield, *Intermediate Accounting*, 12th ed. (New York: John Wiley, 2007), pp. 792–805, 812–816.

stock, but only at or below its current market price. By selling the convertible, the issuer in effect makes a *deferred sale* of common stock. As the market price of the firm's common stock rises to a higher level, conversion may occur. Deferring the issuance of new common stock until the market price of the stock has increased means that fewer shares will have to be issued, thereby decreasing the dilution of both ownership and earnings.

Another motive for convertible financing is its *use as a "sweetener" for financing*. Because the purchaser of the convertible is given the opportunity to become a common stockholder and share in the firm's future success, *convertibles can be normally sold with lower interest rates than nonconvertibles*. Therefore, from the firm's viewpoint, including a conversion feature reduces the interest cost of debt. The purchaser of the issue sacrifices a portion of interest return for the potential opportunity to become a common stockholder. Another important motive for issuing convertibles is that, generally speaking, *convertible securities can be issued with far fewer restrictive covenants than nonconvertibles*. Because many investors view convertibles as equity, the covenant issue is not as important to them.

A final motive for using convertibles is to *raise cheap funds temporarily*. By using convertible bonds, the firm can temporarily raise debt, which is typically less expensive than common stock, to finance projects. Once such projects are under way, the firm may wish to shift its capital structure to a less highly lever-aged position. A conversion feature gives the issuer the opportunity, through actions of convertible holders, to shift its capital structure at a future time.

Other Considerations

When the price of the firm's common stock rises above the conversion price, the market price of the convertible security will normally rise to a level close to its conversion value. When this happens, many convertible holders will not convert because they already have the market price benefit obtainable from conversion and can still receive fixed periodic interest payments. Because of this behavior, virtually all convertible securities have a *call feature* that enables the issuer to encourage or *"force"* conversion. The call price of the security generally exceeds the security's par value by an amount equal to 1 year's stated interest on the security. Although the issuer must pay a premium for calling a security, the call privilege is generally not exercised until the conversion value of the security is 10 to 15 percent *above the call price*. This type of premium above the call price helps to assure the issuer that the holders of the convertible will convert it when the call is made, instead of accepting the call price.

overhanging issue
A convertible security that cannot be forced into conversion by using the call feature.

Unfortunately, there are instances when the market price of a security does not reach a level sufficient to stimulate the conversion of associated convertibles. A convertible security that cannot be forced into conversion by using the call feature is called an **overhanging issue**. An overhanging issue can be quite detrimental to a firm. If the firm were to call the issue, the bondholders would accept the call price rather than convert the bonds. In this case, the firm not only would have to pay the call premium but would also require additional financing to pay off the bonds at their par value. If the firm raised these funds through the sale of equity, a large number of shares would have to be issued because of their low market price. This, in turn, could result in the dilution of existing ownership. Another means of financing the call would be the use of debt or preferred stock, but this use would leave the firm's capital structure no less leveraged than before the call.

DETERMINING THE VALUE OF A CONVERTIBLE BOND

The key characteristic of convertible securities that enhances their marketability is their ability to minimize the possibility of a loss while providing a possibility of capital gains. Here we discuss the three values of a convertible bond: (1) the straight bond value, (2) the conversion value, and (3) the market value.

Straight Bond Value

straight bond value
The price at which a convertible bond would sell in the market without the conversion feature.

The **straight bond value** of a convertible bond is the price at which it would sell in the market without the conversion feature. This value is found by determining the value of a nonconvertible bond with similar payments issued by a firm with the same risk. The straight bond value is typically the *floor*, or minimum, price at which the convertible bond would be traded. The straight bond value equals the present value of the bond's interest and principal payments discounted at the interest rate the firm would have to pay on a nonconvertible bond.

Example 17.7 ▶

Duncan Company, a Southeastern discount store chain, has just sold a $1,000-par-value, 20-year convertible bond with a 12% coupon interest rate. The bond interest will be paid at the end of each year, and the principal will be repaid at maturity.[10] A straight bond could have been sold with a 14% coupon interest rate, so that is the discount rate that we use to calculate the straight bond value of Duncan's convertible. The straight bond value of the convertible is calculated as shown:

Year(s)	Payments	Present value
1–20	$ 120[a]	$794.78
20	1,000	72.76
	Straight bond value	$867.54

[a]$1,000 at 12% = $120 interest per year.

This value, $867.54, is the minimum price at which the convertible bond is expected to sell. Generally, only in certain instances in which the stock's market price is below the conversion price will the bond be expected to sell at this level.

Conversion (or Stock) Value

Recall that the *conversion (or stock) value* of a convertible security is the value of the convertible measured in terms of the market price of the common stock into which the security can be converted. When the market price of the common stock exceeds the conversion price, the conversion (or stock) value exceeds the par value. An example will clarify the point.

Example 17.8 ▶

Duncan Company's convertible bond, described in Example 17.7, is convertible at $50 per share. Each bond can be converted into 20 shares because each bond has

---

10. Just as we did in Chapter 6, we continue to assume the payment of annual rather than semiannual bond interest. This assumption simplifies the calculations involved, while maintaining the conceptual accuracy of the procedures presented.

a $1,000 par value. The conversion values of the bond when the stock is selling at $30, $40, $50, $60, $70, and $80 per share are shown in the following table:

Market price of stock	Conversion value
$30	$ 600
40	800
50 (conversion price)	1,000 (par value)
60	1,200
70	1,400
80	1,600

When the market price of the common stock exceeds the $50 conversion price, the conversion value exceeds the $1,000 par value. Because the straight bond value (calculated in Example 17.7) is $867.54, the bond will, in a stable environment, never sell for less than this amount, regardless of how low its conversion value is. If the market price per share were $30, the bond would still sell for $867.54—not $600—because its value as a bond would dominate.

Market Value

market premium
The amount by which the market value exceeds the straight or conversion value of a convertible security.

The market value of a convertible is likely to be greater than its straight value or its conversion value. The amount by which the market value exceeds its straight or conversion value is called the **market premium.** The general relationships among the straight bond value, conversion value, market value, and market premium for Duncan Company's convertible bond are shown in Figure 17.1. The straight bond value acts as a floor for the security's value up to the point X, where the stock

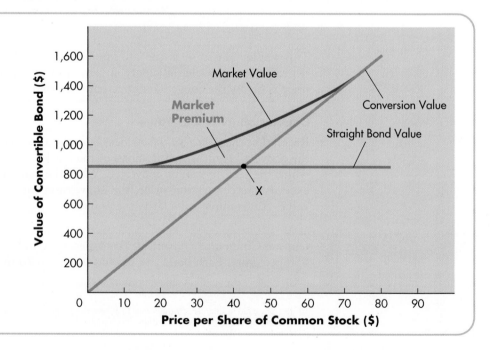

FIGURE 17.1

Values and Market Premium
The values and market premium for Duncan Company's convertible bond

price is high enough to cause the conversion value to exceed the straight bond value. The market premium is attributed to the fact that the convertible gives investors a chance to experience attractive capital gains from increases in the stock price, while taking less risk. The floor (straight bond value) provides protection against losses resulting from a decline in the stock price caused by falling profits or other factors. The market premium tends to be greatest when the straight bond value and conversion (or stock) value are nearly equal. Investors perceive the benefits of these two sources of value to be greatest at this point.

→ REVIEW QUESTIONS

17–6 What is the *conversion feature?* What is a *conversion ratio?* How do convertibles and other *contingent securities* affect EPS? Briefly describe the motives for convertible financing.

17–7 When the market price of the stock rises above the conversion price, why may a convertible security *not* be converted? How can the *call feature* be used to force conversion in this situation? What is an *overhanging issue?*

17–8 Define the *straight bond value, conversion (or stock) value, market value,* and *market premium* associated with a convertible bond, and describe the general relationships among them.

LG 5 | 17.4 Stock Purchase Warrants

stock purchase warrants
Instruments that give their holders the right to purchase a certain number of shares of the issuer's common stock at a specified price over a certain period of time.

Stock purchase warrants are similar to stock *rights,* which were briefly described in Chapter 7. **Stock purchase warrants** give their holders the right to purchase a certain number of shares of the issuer's common stock at a specified price over a certain period of time. (Of course, holders of warrants earn no income until the warrants are exercised or sold.) Warrants also bear some similarity to convertibles in that they provide for the injection of additional equity capital into the firm at some future date.

KEY CHARACTERISTICS

Warrants are often attached to debt issues as "sweeteners." When a firm makes a large bond issue, the attachment of stock purchase warrants may add to the marketability of the issue and lower the required interest rate. As sweeteners, warrants are similar to conversion features. Often, when a new firm is raising its initial capital, suppliers of debt will require warrants to permit them to share in whatever success the firm achieves. In addition, established companies sometimes offer warrants with debt to compensate for risk and thereby lower the interest rate and/or provide for fewer *restrictive covenants.*

exercise (or option) price
The price at which holders of warrants can purchase a specified number of shares of common stock.

Exercise Prices

The price at which holders of warrants can purchase a specified number of shares of common stock is normally referred to as the **exercise (or option) price.** This price is usually set at 10 to 20 percent above the market price of the firm's stock at the time of issuance. Until the market price of the stock exceeds the exercise price, holders of warrants will not exercise them because they can purchase the stock more inexpensively in the marketplace.

Warrants normally have a life of no more than 10 years, although some have infinite lives. Unlike convertible securities, warrants cannot be called, but their limited life stimulates holders to exercise their warrants when the exercise price is below the market price of the firm's stock.

Warrant Trading

A warrant is usually *detachable,* which means that the bondholder may sell the warrant without selling the security to which it is attached. Many detachable warrants are actively traded in both broker and dealer markets. Many actively traded warrants are listed on the American Stock Exchange. Warrants often provide investors with better opportunities for gain (with increased risk) than the underlying common stock.

Comparison of Warrants to Rights and Convertibles

The similarity between a warrant and a right should be clear. Both result in new equity capital, although the warrant provides for *deferred* equity financing. The life of a right is typically not more than a few months; a warrant is generally exercisable for a period of years. Rights are issued at a subscription price *below* the prevailing market price of the stock; warrants are generally issued at an exercise price 10 to 20 percent *above* the prevailing market price.

Warrants and convertibles also have similarities. The exercise of a warrant shifts the firm's capital structure to a less highly leveraged position because new common stock is issued without any change in debt. If a convertible bond were converted, the reduction in leverage would be even more pronounced because common stock would be issued in exchange for a reduction in debt. In addition, the exercise of a warrant provides an influx of new capital; with convertibles, the new capital is raised when the securities are originally issued rather than when they are converted. The influx of new equity capital resulting from the exercise of a warrant does not occur until the firm has achieved a certain degree of success that is reflected in an increased price for its stock. In this case, the firm conveniently obtains needed funds.

IMPLIED PRICE OF AN ATTACHED WARRANT

implied price of a warrant
The price effectively paid for each warrant attached to a bond.

When warrants are attached to a bond, the **implied price of a warrant**—the price that is effectively paid for each attached warrant—can be found by first using Equation 17.1:

$$\text{Implied price of } all \text{ warrants} = \frac{\text{Price of bond with}}{\text{warrants attached}} - \text{Straight bond value} \qquad (17.1)$$

The straight bond value is found in a fashion similar to that used in valuing convertible bonds. Dividing the implied price of *all* warrants by the number of warrants attached to each bond results in the implied price of *each* warrant.

Example 17.9 ▶ Martin Marine Products, a manufacturer of marine drive shafts and propellers, just issued a 10.5%-coupon-interest-rate, $1,000-par, 20-year bond paying annual interest and having 20 warrants attached for the purchase of the firm's stock. The bonds were initially sold for their $1,000 par value. When issued, similar-risk straight bonds were selling to yield a 12% rate of return. The straight value of the bond would be the present value of its payments discounted at the 12% yield on similar-risk straight bonds:

Year(s)	Payments	Present value
1–20	$ 105[a]	$784.29
20	1,000	103.67
	Straight bond value	$887.96

[a]$1,000 at 10.5% = $105 interest per year.

Substituting the $1,000 price of the bond with warrants attached and the $887.96 straight bond value into Equation 17.1, we get an implied price of *all* warrants of $112.04:

Implied price of *all* warrants = $1,000 − $887.96 = $112.04

Dividing the implied price of *all* warrants by the number of warrants attached to each bond—20 in this case—we find the implied price of *each* warrant:

Implied price of *each* warrant = $112.04 ÷ 20 = $5.60

Therefore, by purchasing Martin Marine Products' bond with warrants attached for $1,000, one is effectively paying $5.60 for each warrant.

The implied price of each warrant is meaningful only when compared to the specific features of the warrant—the number of shares that can be purchased and the specified exercise price. These features can be analyzed in light of the prevailing common stock price to estimate the true *market value* of each warrant. Clearly, if the implied price is above the estimated market value, the price of the bond with warrants attached may be too high. If the implied price is below the estimated market value, the bond may be quite attractive. Firms must therefore price their bonds with warrants attached in a way that causes the implied price of its warrants to fall slightly below their estimated market value. Such an approach allows the firm to sell the bonds more easily at a lower coupon interest rate than would apply to straight debt, thereby reducing its debt service costs.

VALUES OF WARRANTS

warrant premium
The difference between the market value and the theoretical value of a warrant.

Like a convertible security, a warrant has both a market value and a theoretical value. The difference between these values, or the **warrant premium**, depends largely on investor expectations and on the ability of investors to get more leverage from the warrants than from the underlying stock.

Theoretical Value of a Warrant

The *theoretical value* of a stock purchase warrant is the amount one would expect the warrant to sell for in the marketplace. Equation 17.2 gives the theoretical value of a warrant:

$$TVW = (P_0 - E) \times N \tag{17.2}$$

where

TVW = theoretical value of a warrant
P_0 = current market price of a share of common stock
E = exercise price of the warrant
N = number of shares of common stock obtainable with one warrant

The use of Equation 17.2 can be illustrated by the following example.

Example 17.10 ▶ Dustin Electronics, a major producer of transistors, has outstanding warrants that are exercisable at $40 per share and entitle holders to purchase three shares of common stock. The warrants were initially attached to a bond issue to sweeten the bond. The common stock of the firm is currently selling for $45 per share. Substituting $P_0 = \$45$, $E = \$40$ and $N = 3$ into Equation 17.2 yields a theoretical warrant value of $15 [($45 − $40) × 3].

Market Value of a Warrant

The market value of a stock purchase warrant is generally above the theoretical value of the warrant. Only when the theoretical value of the warrant is very high or the warrant is near its expiration date are the market and theoretical values close. The general relationship between the theoretical and market values of Dustin Electronics' warrants is presented graphically in Figure 17.2. The market value of warrants generally exceeds the theoretical value by the greatest amount when the stock's market price is close to the warrant exercise price per share. The amount of time until expiration also affects the market value of the warrant. Generally speaking, the closer the warrant is to its expiration date, the more likely that its market value will equal its theoretical value.

Warrant Premium

The *warrant premium,* or the amount by which the market value of Dustin Electronics' warrants exceeds the theoretical value of these warrants, is also shown in Figure 17.2. This premium results from a combination of positive investor expectations and the ability of the investor with a fixed sum to invest to obtain much larger potential returns (and risk) by trading in warrants rather than the underlying stock.

Personal Finance Example 17.11 ▶ Stan Buyer has $2,430, which he is interested in investing in Dustin Electronics. The firm's stock is currently selling for $45 per share, and its warrants are selling for $18 per warrant. Each warrant entitles the holder to purchase three shares of Dustin's common stock at $40 per share. Because the stock is selling for $45 per share, the theoretical warrant value, calculated in the preceding example, is $15 [($45 − $40) × 3].

FIGURE 17.2

Values and Warrant Premium
The values and warrant premium for Dustin Electronics' stock purchase warrants

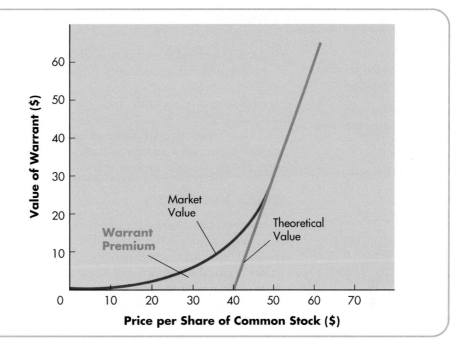

The warrant premium results from positive investor expectations and leverage opportunities. Stan Buyer could spend his $2,430 in either of two ways: He could purchase 54 shares of common stock at $45 per share or 135 warrants at $18 per warrant, ignoring brokerage fees. If Mr. Buyer purchases the stock and its price rises to $48, he will gain $162 ($3 per share × 54 shares) by selling the stock. If instead he purchases the 135 warrants and the stock price increases by $3 per share, Mr. Buyer will gain approximately $1,215. Because the price of a share of stock rises by $3, the price of each warrant can be expected to rise by $9 (because each warrant can be used to purchase three shares of common stock). A gain of $9 per warrant on 135 warrants means a total gain of $1,215 on the warrants.

The greater leverage associated with trading warrants should be clear from the example. Of course, because leverage works both ways, it results in greater risk. If the market price fell by $3, the loss on the stock would be $162, whereas the loss on the warrants would be close to $1,215. Clearly, investing in warrants is more risky than investing in the underlying stock.

→ **REVIEW QUESTIONS**

17–9 What are *stock purchase warrants?* What are the similarities and key differences between the effects of warrants and those of convertibles on the firm's capital structure and its ability to raise new capital?

17–10 What is the *implied price of a warrant?* How is it estimated? To be effective, how should it be related to the estimated *market value* of a warrant?

17–11 What is the general relationship between the theoretical and market values of a warrant? In what circumstances are these values quite close? What is a *warrant premium?*

option
An instrument that provides its holder with an opportunity to purchase or sell a specified asset at a stated price on or before a set *expiration date.*

In the most general sense, an **option** can be viewed as an instrument that provides its holder with an opportunity to purchase or sell a specified asset at a stated price on or before a set *expiration date.* Options are probably the most popular type of *derivative security.* Today, the interest in options centers on options on common stock.[11] The development of organized options exchanges has created markets in which to trade these securities. Three basic forms of options are rights, warrants, and calls and puts. Rights are discussed in Chapter 7, and warrants were described in the preceding section.

CALLS AND PUTS

call option
An option to *purchase* a specified number of shares of a stock (typically 100) on or before a specified future date at a stated price.

strike price
The price at which the holder of a call option can buy (or the holder of a put option can sell) a specified amount of stock at any time prior to the option's expiration date.

The two most common types of options are calls and puts. A **call option** is an option to *purchase* a specified number of shares of a stock (typically 100) on or before a specified future date at a stated price. The stock that the option holder has the right to buy is called the *underlying asset,* and the call option derives its value from the value of the underlying stock (hence the term derivative security). Call options usually expire in a few months, although some call options have much longer lives. The **strike price** is the price at which the holder of the option can buy a specified amount of stock at any time prior to the option's expiration date. A call option is most valuable when its strike price is well below the market price of the underlying stock (hence, the option gives the holder the right to buy the stock at a bargain price). When the strike price of a call option is less than the market price of the stock, the option is said to be *in the money.* The exchange where the option trades generally sets option strike prices at or near the prevailing market price of the stock at the time the option is listed for trading. For example, if a firm's stock is currently selling for $50 per share, an option exchange might list option contracts for trading with strike prices of $45, $50, and $55. Like other securities, the value of a call option is determined by the interactions of buyers and sellers trading options in the market. A call option's market price is called the *option premium,* and it represents the price one must pay to acquire the right to buy the stock at the strike price.

put option
An option to *sell* a specified number of shares of a stock (typically 100) on or before a specified future date at a stated price.

A **put option** is an option to *sell* a specified number of shares of a stock (typically 100) on or before a specified future date at a stated strike price. Like the call option, the strike price of the put is set close to the market price of the underlying stock at the time of issuance. The lives and costs of puts are similar to those of calls. A put option is *in the money* when the market price of the underlying stock is below the strike price. In that case, the option holder can sell the stock at an above-market price.

OPTIONS MARKETS

There are two ways of making options transactions. The first involves making a transaction through one of 20 or so call and put options dealers with the help of

---

11. *Real* options—opportunities embedded in capital projects that enable management to alter their cash flows and risk—were discussed in Chapter 12. The *options* described here differ from real options; they are a type of derivative security that derives its value from an underlying financial asset, typically common stock. Although some of the analytical tools used to value both types of options are similar, the focus here is merely on the definitional aspects of options. The models used to value these options are typically discussed in more advanced financial management textbooks.

a stockbroker. The other, more popular mechanism is the organized options exchanges. The dominant exchange is the *Chicago Board Options Exchange (CBOE),* which was established in 1973. Other exchanges on which options are traded include the International Securities Exchange (ISE), the American Stock Exchange, and the Philadelphia Stock Exchange. The options traded on these exchanges are standardized and thus are considered registered securities. Each option is for 100 shares of the underlying stock. The price at which options transactions can be made is determined by the forces of supply and demand.

Matter of fact

Recession Cools Option Trading

Like most other companies, the Chicago Board Options Exchange saw a decline in its business in 2009 due to the recession. The CBOE reported total options trading volume that year of 1.135 billion option contracts, down from 1.193 billion in 2008. The steepest decline came in an area that had been the CBOE's fastest growing line of business—options on exchange traded funds. ETF option trading fell in 2009 to 277 million contracts, down 16 percent from the prior year.

OPTIONS TRADING

The most obvious motive for purchasing call options is the expectation that the market price of the underlying stock will *rise* by more than enough to cover the cost of the option, thereby allowing the purchaser of the call to profit.

Personal Finance Example 17.12 ▶ Assume that Cindy Peters pays $250 for a 3-month *call option* on Wing Enterprises, a maker of aircraft components, at a strike price of $50. This means that by paying $250, Cindy is guaranteed that she can purchase 100 shares of Wing at $50 per share at any time during the next 3 months. If Wing's stock price rises above $50, then Cindi could exercise her option to buy the stock at $50 and then immediately sell it in the open market at the higher market price. The stock price must climb $2.50 per share ($250 ÷ 100 shares) to $52.50 per share to cover the cost of the option (ignoring any brokerage fees). If the stock price rises more than that, then Cindi earns a net profit from buying and exercising the option. For example, if the stock price were to rise to $60 per share during the period, Cindy's net profit would be $750. She could make a $10 profit per share by exercising her right to buy shares at $50 and then immediately selling them in the open market for $60 each. Because she has the right to buy 100 shares, Cindy's gross profit on this transaction would be $1,000, but because she spent $250 to acquire the option in the first place, her net profit would be $750.

Because this $750 profit would be earned on a $250 initial investment, it illustrates the high potential return on investment that options offer (a 200 percent gain in this example). Of course, had the stock price not risen above $50 per share, Cindy would have lost the $250 she invested because there would have been no reason to exercise the option, and her return on that investment would have been negative 100%. Had the stock price risen to between $50 and $52.50 per share, Cindy would have exercised the option, though the gain from exercising would not have been large enough to completely offset the original $250 purchase price of the option.

Put options are often purchased in the expectation that the share price of a given security will *decline* over the life of the option. Investors gain from put options when the price of the underlying stock declines by more than the per-share cost of the option. The logic underlying the purchase of a put is exactly the opposite of that underlying the use of call options.

Personal Finance Example 17.13 ▶   Assume that Don Kelly pays $325 for a 6-month *put option* on Dante United, a baked goods manufacturer, at a strike price of $40. Don purchased the put option in expectation that the stock price would drop because of the introduction of a new product line by Dante's chief competitor. By paying $325, Don is assured that he can sell 100 shares of Dante at $40 per share at any time during the next 6 months. If the stock price drops below $40, Don can purchase 100 shares at the prevailing market price and then exercise his option to sell them for $40 each. The stock price must drop by $3.25 per share ($325 ÷ 100 shares) to $36.75 per share to cover the cost of the option (ignoring any brokerage fees). If the stock price falls more than that, then Don can make a profit from buying and exercising the option. For example, if the stock price were to drop to $30 per share during the period, Don could buy 100 shares on the open market for $3,000 and then exercise his right to sell those shares for $40 each (or $4,000 total). Don's net profit would be $675 [(100 shares × $40/share) − (100 shares × $30/share) − $325].

Because that $675 return would be earned on only a $325 investment, it illustrates the high potential return on investment that options offer. Of course, had the stock price risen above $40 per share, Don would have lost the $325 he invested because there would have been no reason to exercise the option. Had the stock price fallen to between $36.75 and $40.00 per share, Don would have exercised the option to reduce his loss to an amount less than $325.

In more depth

To read about *Exotic Option Trading Strategies*, go to www.myfinancelab.com

 myfinancelab®

Some investors buy puts not to speculate on a potential price decline but to protect themselves from that event. Purchasers of puts commonly own the underlying shares, and buying puts provides a way to protect the value of the shares that the investor already owns. For example, an investor who owns 100 shares of Intel Corp. stock, currently selling for $22 per share, could buy put options on Intel stock with a $20 strike price. This guarantees that even if the price of Intel stock plummets, the investor will be able to sell her shares for $20 each.

ROLE OF CALL AND PUT OPTIONS IN FUND RAISING

Although call and put options are extremely popular investment vehicles, they play *no* direct role in the fund-raising activities of the firm. These options are issued by investors and option exchanges, not businesses. *They are not a source of financing to the firm because the firm does not receive the proceeds when investors buy options, nor do firms receive funds when investors exercise options to buy shares.* Buyers of options have no say in the firm's management, and they do not have voting rights; only stockholders are given these privileges. Despite the popularity of options as investments, the financial manager has very little need to deal with them, especially as part of fund-raising activities.

However, financial managers do work with stock options when they are part of employee compensation packages. Employee stock options are a form of call

focus on ETHICS

Options Backdating

in practice Granting stock options to executives as well as rank-and-file employees was a popular practice in the technology sector for many years. Start-up companies who couldn't afford to pay high salaries could offer stock options to employees who were willing to take the risk that the options would be worth a great deal if the company took off. Even technology giants such as Microsoft and Intel routinely granted options to nearly all of their employees, many of whom became wealthy as tech stocks boomed through the 1990s.

Typically, an employee stock option has a strike price equal to the market price of the company's stock at the time the option is granted. That practice ensures that employees make a profit on their options only when the stock price rises after the options are awarded. One way that firms could make their stock option grants even more valuable to employees is through a practice known as *backdating*. Backdating occurs when a firm uses hindsight to establish an option grant date at a time when the firm's stock price was at a temporary low point. For example, on April 1, managers might look back and determine that the lowest stock price in the prior

quarter occurred on February 20. Managers announce that options were granted on February 20 with a strike price equal to the stock price at that time. Of course, with the benefit of hindsight, managers know that the stock price on April 1 is much higher than it was on February 20, so these "backdated" options already have a built-in profit. Finance professors Erik Lie of the University of Iowa and Randall Heron of Indiana University published several studies showing that the timing of employee stock option grants at market low points was too widespread to be coincidental, so they concluded that many option grants had been backdated. The SEC subsequently conducted a yearlong investigation and began to crack down on companies with questionable policies governing stock-option grants. At least 257 companies have announced internal reviews or have been subject to SEC or Justice Department inquiries related to options backdating. Firms that were investigated saw significant drops in the market prices of their shares. As a result of the increased scrutiny, a number of top-level executives at a variety of companies either resigned or were fired. A number of companies announced that they would have to issue a restatement

of prior results to record charges against earnings that should have been recorded when the options were granted.

While backdating of options is not necessarily illegal, the issues relating to backdating of options involve failure to provide full disclosure to shareholders, failure to pay extra applicable taxes, and earnings statements that should have reflected the modified grant dates. Any of these three issues could yield civil (and perhaps criminal) legal action.

Fortunately, accelerated reporting requirements have made unreported backdating more difficult. Section 403 of the Sarbanes-Oxley Act of 2002 now requires that directors and officers report options grants to the SEC within 2 business days, instead of within weeks and months as allowed under the prior law.

▶ *If firms wanted to grant stock options with strike prices below the current market price of their stock, they could do so. Why do you think instead some firms chose to backdate options, making it appear as though the options had been granted with strike prices equal to the current stock market price when in fact the options were in the money at the time of the grant?*

options. As the *Focus on Ethics* box discusses, a number of companies and company executives have skated close to, or over, the ethical edge with regard to backdating of options.

HEDGING FOREIGN-CURRENCY EXPOSURES WITH OPTIONS

hedging
Offsetting or protecting against the risk of adverse price movements.

The Chicago Mercantile Exchange (CME) and the Philadelphia Stock Exchange (PHLX) offer exchange-traded options contracts on the Canadian dollar, the euro, the Japanese yen, the Swiss franc, and several other important currencies. *Currency options* are used by a wide range of traders, from the largest multinational companies to small exporters and importers, as well as by individual investors and speculators. Options allow companies to **hedge,** which involves offsetting or protecting against the risk of adverse price movements, while simultaneously preserving the possibility of profiting from favorable price movements. Using options to hedge risk is similar to purchasing insurance. The firm pays a premium (the cost of the option), and in exchange it receives a cash inflow if the event that the firm is hedging against actually occurs. If the event does not occur, then the option expires as worthless and the money spent to acquire the option is lost, just as would be the case if you purchased auto insurance and never had an accident.

Example 17.14 ▶ Assume that a U.S. exporter just booked a sale denominated in Swiss francs with payment due upon delivery in 3 months. The exporter is exposed to currency risk because when it receives francs in payment it will sell those francs in exchange for dollars, but the exchange rate at which that transaction will occur is unknown. If the Swiss franc declines in value, then the dollar value of the payment that the exporter will receive in 3 months is reduced (because each franc buys fewer dollars on the foreign exchange market). The company could hedge the risk of depreciation in the franc by purchasing a Swiss franc put option. This would give the company the right to sell Swiss francs at a fixed price (say, one franc in exchange for $1.04). This option would become valuable if the value of the Swiss franc was less than $1.04 when the payment in francs arrives in 3 months. On the other hand, if one Swiss franc was worth more than $1.04 when the exporter received payment, the firm would allow the put option to expire unexercised and would instead convert the Swiss francs received in payment into dollars at the new, higher dollar price. The exporter would be protected from adverse price risk but would still be able to profit from favorable price movements.

→ REVIEW QUESTIONS

17–12 What is an *option?* Define *calls* and *puts*. What role, if any, do call and put options play in the fund-raising activities of the firm?

17–13 How can the firm use currency options to *hedge* foreign-currency exposures resulting from international transactions?

Summary

FOCUS ON VALUE

In addition to basic corporate securities like stocks and bonds, the firm can use hybrid securities in its fund-raising activities. These securities, which possess characteristics of both debt and equity, enable the firm to raise funds at less cost or to provide for desired future changes in the firm's capital structure.

Leasing, particularly financial (capital) leases, may enable the firm to use the lease as a substitute for the debt-financed purchase of an asset, with more attractive risk–return trade-offs. Similarly, by issuing convertible rather than straight debt or by attaching stock purchase warrants to a bond issue or debt financing, the firm may provide lenders with the potential to benefit from stock price movements in exchange for a lower interest rate or less restrictive covenants in the bond or debt agreement. Although options are not a source of financing to the firm, this derivative security can help provide incentives to employees. Currency options can be used to hedge adverse currency movements in international transactions.

Clearly, the financial manager should use hybrid and derivative securities to increase return (often by lowering financing costs) and reduce risk. By taking only those actions believed to result in attractive risk–return trade-offs, the financial manager can positively contribute to the firm's goal of **maximizing the stock price.**

REVIEW OF LEARNING GOALS

LG 1   **Differentiate between hybrid and derivative securities and their roles in the corporation.** Hybrid securities are forms of debt or equity financing that possess characteristics of both debt and equity. Common hybrid securities include preferred stock, financial leases, convertible securities, and stock purchase warrants. Derivative securities are neither debt nor equity and derive their value from an underlying asset that is often another security. Options are a popular derivative security.

LG 2   **Review the types of leases, leasing arrangements, the lease-versus-purchase decision, the effects of leasing on future financing, and the advantages and disadvantages of leasing.** A lease enables the firm to make contractual, tax-deductible payments to obtain the use of fixed assets. Operating leases are generally 5 or fewer years in term, cancelable, and renewable, and they provide for maintenance by the lessor. Financial leases are longer-term, noncancelable, and not renewable, and they nearly always require the lessee to maintain the asset. *FASB Statement No. 13* provides specific guidelines for defining a financial (capital) lease. A lessor can obtain assets to be leased through a direct lease, a sale-leaseback arrangement, or a leveraged lease. The lease-versus-purchase decision can be evaluated by calculating the after-tax cash outflows associated with the leasing and purchasing alternatives. The more desirable alternative is the one that has the lower present value of after-tax cash outflows. *FASB Statement No. 13* requires firms to show financial leases as assets and corresponding liabilities on their balance sheets; operating leases must be shown in footnotes to the financial statements. Advantages and disadvantages should be considered when making lease-versus-purchase decisions.

LG 3   **Describe the types of convertible securities, their general features, and financing with convertibles.** Corporate bonds and preferred stock may both be convertible into common stock. The conversion ratio indicates the number of shares for which a convertible can be exchanged and determines the conversion price. A conversion privilege is nearly always available at any time in the life of the security. The conversion value is the value of the convertible measured in terms of the market price of the common stock into which it can be converted. The presence of convertibles and other contingent securities (warrants and stock options) often requires the firm to report both basic and diluted earnings per share (EPS). Convertibles are used to obtain deferred common stock financing, to "sweeten" bond issues, to minimize restrictive covenants, and to raise cheap funds temporarily. The call feature is sometimes used to encourage or "force" conversion; occasionally, an overhanging issue results.

LG 4 **Demonstrate the procedures for determining the straight bond value, the conversion (or stock) value, and the market value of a convertible bond.** The straight bond value of a convertible is the price at which it would sell in the market without the conversion feature. It typically represents the minimum value at which a convertible bond trades. The conversion value is found by multiplying the conversion ratio by the current market price of the underlying common stock. The market value of a convertible generally exceeds both its straight and conversion values, resulting in a market premium. The premium is largest when the straight and conversion values are nearly equal.

LG 5 **Explain the key characteristics of stock purchase warrants, the implied price of an attached warrant, and the values of warrants.** Stock purchase warrants enable their holders to purchase a certain number of shares of common stock at the specified exercise price. Warrants are often attached to debt issues as "sweeteners," generally have limited lives, are detachable, and may be traded in broker and dealer markets. Warrants are similar to stock rights, except that the exercise price of a warrant is initially set above the underlying stock's current market price. Warrants are similar to convertibles, but exercising them has a less pronounced effect on the firm's leverage and brings in new funds. The implied price of an attached warrant can be found by dividing the difference between the bond price with warrants attached and the straight bond value by the number of warrants attached to each bond. The market value of a warrant usually exceeds its theoretical value, creating a warrant premium. Investors generally get more leverage from trading warrants than from trading the underlying stock.

LG 6 **Define options and discuss calls and puts, options markets, options trading, the role of call and put options in fund raising, and hedging foreign-currency exposures with options.** An option provides its holder with an opportunity to purchase or sell a specified asset at a stated price on or before a set expiration date. Rights, warrants, and calls and puts are all options. Calls are options to purchase common stock, and puts are options to sell common stock. Options exchanges provide organized marketplaces in which purchases and sales of call and put options can be made. The options traded on the exchanges are standardized, and the prices at which they trade are determined by the forces of supply and demand. Call and put options do not play a direct role in the fund-raising activities of the financial manager. Currency options can be used to hedge the firm's foreign-currency exposures resulting from international transactions.

Opener-in-Review

When you think of airlines, you probably expect that their primary asset is airplanes, yet many airlines primarily lease the aircraft that they fly. In what other industries might you expect to find that the main asset required to operate is leased rather than owned by firms in the industry?

Self-Test Problems (Solutions in Appendix)

LG 2 **ST17–1** **Lease versus purchase** The Hot Bagel Shop wishes to evaluate two plans for financing an oven: leasing and borrowing to purchase. The firm is in the 40% tax bracket.

> **Lease** The shop can lease the oven under a 5-year lease requiring annual end-of-year payments of $5,000. All maintenance costs will be paid by the lessor, and insurance and other costs will be borne by the lessee. The lessee will exercise its option to purchase the asset for $4,000 at termination of the lease.

> **Purchase** The oven costs $20,000 and will have a 5-year life. It will be depreciated under MACRS using a 5-year recovery period. (See Table 4.2 on page 117 for the applicable depreciation percentages.) The total purchase price will be financed by a 5-year, 15% loan requiring equal annual end-of-year payments of $5,967. The firm will pay $1,000 per year for a service contract that covers all maintenance costs; insurance and other costs will be borne by the firm. The firm plans to keep the equipment and use it beyond its 5-year recovery period.

> **a.** For the leasing plan, calculate the following:
> (1) The after-tax cash outflow each year.
> (2) The present value of the cash outflows, using a 9% *discount rate.*
> **b.** For the purchasing plan, calculate the following:
> (1) The annual interest expense deductible for tax purposes for each of the 5 years.
> (2) The after-tax cash outflow resulting from the purchase for each of the 5 years.
> (3) The present value of the cash outflows, using a 9% *discount rate.*
> **c.** Compare the present values of the cash outflow streams for these two plans, and determine which plan would be preferable. Explain your answer.

LG 4 **ST17–2** **Finding convertible bond values** Mountain Mining Company has an outstanding issue of convertible bonds with a $1,000 par value. These bonds are convertible into 40 shares of common stock. They have an 11% annual coupon interest rate and a 25-year maturity. The interest rate on a straight bond of similar risk is currently 13%.

a. Calculate the *straight bond value* of the bond.
b. Calculate the *conversion (or stock) value* of the bond when the market price of the common stock is $20, $25, $28, $35, and $50 per share.
c. For each of the stock prices given in part **b,** at what price would you expect the bond to sell? Why?
d. What is the least you would expect the bond to sell for, regardless of the common stock price behavior?

Warm-Up Exercises All problems are available in [myfinancelab].

LG 2 **E17–1** N and M Corp. is considering leasing a new machine for $25,000 per year. The lease arrangement calls for a 5-year lease with an option to purchase the machine at the end of the lease for $3,500. The firm is in the 34% tax bracket. What is the present value of the lease outflows, including the purchase option, if lease payments are made at the end of each year and if the after-tax cost of debt is 7%?

LG 3   **E17–2**   During the past 2 years Meacham Industries issued three separate convertible bonds. For each of them, calculate the *conversion price:*
a. A $1,000-par-value bond that is convertible into 10 shares of common stock.
b. A $2,000-par-value bond that is convertible into 20 shares of common stock.
c. A $1,500-par-value bond that is convertible into 30 shares of common stock.

LG 3   **E17–3**   Newcomb Company has a bond outstanding with a $1,500 par value and convertible at $30 per share. What is the bond's *conversion ratio?* If the underlying stock currently trades at $25 per share, what is the bond's *conversion value?* Would it be advisable for a bondholder to exercise the conversion option?

LG 4   **E17–4**   Crystal Cafes recently sold a $2,000-par-value, 10-year convertible bond with an 8% coupon interest rate. The interest payments will be paid annually at the end of each year and the principal will be repaid at maturity. A similar bond without a conversion feature would have sold with a 9% coupon interest rate. What is the minimum price that the Crystal Cafes' convertible bond should sell for?

LG 6   **E17–5**   A 6-month call option on 100 shares of SRS Corp. stock is selling for $300. The strike price for the option is $40. The stock is currently selling at $38 per share. Ignoring brokerage fees, what price must the stock achieve to just cover the expense of the option? If the stock price rises to $45, what will the net profit on the option contract be?

Problems   All problems are available in 🔲myfinancelab.

LG 2   **P17–1**   **Lease cash flows**   Given the lease payments and terms shown in the following table, determine the *yearly after-tax cash outflows* for each firm, assuming that lease payments are made at the end of each year and that the firm is in the 40% tax bracket. Assume that no purchase option exists.

Firm	Annual lease payment	Term of lease
A	$100,000	4 years
B	80,000	14
C	150,000	8
D	60,000	25
E	20,000	10

LG 2   **P17–2**   **Loan interest**   For each of the loan amounts, interest rates, annual payments, and loan terms shown in the following table, calculate the *annual interest paid* each year over the term of the loan, assuming that the payments are made at the end of each year.

Loan	Amount	Interest rate	Annual payment	Term
A	$14,000	10%	$ 4,416	4 years
B	17,500	12	10,355	2
C	2,400	13	1,017	3
D	49,000	14	14,273	5
E	26,500	16	7,191	6

LG 2 **P17–3** **Loan payments and interest** Schuyler Company wishes to purchase an asset costing $117,000. The full amount needed to finance the asset can be borrowed at 14% interest. The terms of the loan require equal end-of-year payments for the next 6 years. Determine the total annual loan payment, and break it into the amount of interest and the amount of principal paid for each year. (*Hint:* Use the techniques presented in Chapter 5 to find the loan payment.)

LG 2 **P17–4** **Lease versus purchase** JLB Corporation is attempting to determine whether to lease or purchase research equipment. The firm is in the 40% tax bracket, and its after-tax cost of debt is currently 8%. The terms of the lease and of the purchase are as follows:

> **Lease** Annual end-of-year lease payments of $25,200 are required over the 3-year life of the lease. All maintenance costs will be paid by the lessor; insurance and other costs will be borne by the lessee. The lessee will exercise its option to purchase the asset for $5,000 at termination of the lease.
>
> **Purchase** The research equipment, costing $60,000, can be financed entirely with a 14% loan requiring annual end-of-year payments of $25,844 for 3 years. The firm in this case will depreciate the equipment under MACRS using a 3-year recovery period. (See Table 4.2 on page 117 for the applicable depreciation percentages.) The firm will pay $1,800 per year for a service contract that covers all maintenance costs; insurance and other costs will be borne by the firm. The firm plans to keep the equipment and use it beyond its 3-year recovery period.

a. Calculate the *after-tax cash outflows* associated with each alternative.
b. Calculate the present value of each cash outflow stream, using the after-tax cost of debt.
c. Which alternative—lease or purchase—would you recommend? Why?

LG 2 **P17–5** **Lease versus purchase** Northwest Lumber Company needs to expand its facilities. To do so, the firm must acquire a machine costing $80,000. The machine can be leased or purchased. The firm is in the 40% tax bracket, and its after-tax cost of debt is 9%. The terms of the lease and purchase plans are as follows:

> **Lease** The leasing arrangement requires end-of-year payments of $19,800 over 5 years. All maintenance costs will be paid by the lessor; insurance and other costs will be borne by the lessee. The lessee will exercise its option to purchase the asset for $24,000 at termination of the lease.
>
> **Purchase** If the firm purchases the machine, its cost of $80,000 will be financed with a 5-year, 14% loan requiring equal end-of-year payments of $23,302. The machine will be depreciated under MACRS using a 5-year recovery period. (See Table 4.2 on page 117 for the applicable depreciation percentages.) The firm will pay $2,000 per year for a service contract that covers all maintenance costs; insurance and other costs will be borne by the firm. The firm plans to keep the equipment and use it beyond its 5-year recovery period.

a. Determine the *after-tax cash outflows* of Northwest Lumber under each alternative.
b. Find the present value of each after-tax cash outflow stream, using the after-tax cost of debt.
c. Which alternative—lease or purchase—would you recommend? Why?

LG 2   **P17–6**   **Lease-versus-purchase decision**   Joanna Browne is considering either leasing or purchasing a new Chrysler Sebring convertible that has a manufacturer's suggested retail price (MSRP) of $33,000. The dealership offers a 3-year lease that requires a capital payment of $3,300 ($3,000 down payment + $300 security deposit) and monthly payments of $494. Purchasing requires a $2,640 down payment, sales tax of 6.5% ($2,145), and 36 monthly payments of $784. Joanna estimates the value of the car will be $17,000 at the end of 3 years. She can earn 5% annual interest on her savings and is subject to a 6.5% sales tax on purchases.

Make a reasonable recommendation to Joanna using a lease-versus-purchase analysis that, for simplicity, ignores the time value of money.

a. Calculate the total cost of leasing.
b. Calculate the total cost of purchasing.
c. Which should Joanna do?

LG 2   **P17–7**   **Capitalized lease values**   Given the lease payments, terms remaining until the leases expire, and discount rates shown in the following table, calculate the *capitalized value* of each lease, assuming that lease payments are made annually at the end of each year.

Lease	Lease payment	Remaining term	Discount rate
A	$ 40,000	12 years	10%
B	120,000	8	12
C	9,000	18	14
D	16,000	3	9
E	47,000	20	11

LG 3   **P17–8**   **Conversion price**   Calculate the *conversion price* for each of the following convertible bonds:

a. A $1,000-par-value bond that is convertible into 20 shares of common stock.
b. A $500-par-value bond that is convertible into 25 shares of common stock.
c. A $1,000-par-value bond that is convertible into 50 shares of common stock.

LG 3   **P17–9**   **Conversion ratio**   What is the *conversion ratio* for each of the following bonds?

a. A $1,000-par-value bond that is convertible into common stock at $43.75 per share.
b. A $1,000-par-value bond that is convertible into common stock at $25 per share.
c. A $600-par-value bond that is convertible into common stock at $30 per share.

LG 3   **P17–10**   **Conversion (or stock) value**   What is the *conversion (or stock) value* of each of the following convertible bonds?

a. A $1,000-par-value bond that is convertible into 25 shares of common stock. The common stock is currently selling for $50 per share.
b. A $1,000-par-value bond that is convertible into 12.5 shares of common stock. The common stock is currently selling for $42 per share.
c. A $1,000-par-value bond that is convertible into 100 shares of common stock. The common stock is currently selling for $10.50 per share.

LG 3   **P17–11**   **Conversion (or stock) value**   Find the *conversion (or stock) value* for each of the $1,000-par-value convertible bonds described in the following table.

Convertible	Conversion ratio	Current market price of stock
A	25	$42.25
B	16	50.00
C	20	44.00
D	5	19.50

LG 4   **P17–12**   **Straight bond value**   Calculate the *straight bond value* for each of the bonds shown in the table below.

Bond	Par value	Coupon interest rate (paid annually)	Interest rate on equal-risk straight bond	Years to maturity
A	$1,000	10%	14%	20
B	800	12	15	14
C	1,000	13	16	30
D	1,000	14	17	25

LG 4   **P17–13**   **Determining values—Convertible bond**   Eastern Clock Company has an outstanding issue of convertible bonds with a $1,000 par value. These bonds are convertible into 50 shares of common stock. They have a 10% annual coupon interest rate and a 20-year maturity. The interest rate on a straight bond of similar risk is currently 12%.
a. Calculate the *straight bond value* of the bond.
b. Calculate the *conversion (or stock) value* of the bond when the market price of the common stock is $15, $20, $23, $30, and $45 per share.
c. For each of the stock prices given in part **b,** at what price would you expect the bond to sell? Why?
d. What is the least you would expect the bond to sell for, regardless of the common stock price behavior?

LG 4   **P17–14**   **Determining values—Convertible bond**   Craig's Cake Company has an outstanding issue of 15-year convertible bonds with a $1,000 par value. These bonds are convertible into 80 shares of common stock. They have a 13% annual coupon interest rate, whereas the interest rate on straight bonds of similar risk is 16%.
a. Calculate the *straight bond value* of this bond.
b. Calculate the *conversion (or stock) value* of the bond when the market price is $9, $12, $13, $15, and $20 per share of common stock.
c. For each of the common stock prices given in part **b,** at what price would you expect the bond to sell? Why?
d. Graph the straight value and conversion value of the bond for each common stock price given. Plot the per-share common stock prices on the *x* axis and the bond values on the *y* axis. Use this graph to indicate the minimum market value of the bond associated with each common stock price.

LG 5   **P17–15**   **Implied prices of attached warrants**   Calculate the implied price of *each* warrant for each of the bonds shown in the following table.

Bond	Price of bond with warrants attached	Par value	Coupon interest rate (paid annually)	Interest rate on equal-risk straight bond	Years to maturity	Number of warrants attached to bond
A	$1,000	$1,000	12 %	13%	15	10
B	1,100	1,000	9.5	12	10	30
C	500	500	10	11	20	5
D	1,000	1,000	11	12	20	20

LG 5   **P17–16**   **Evaluation of the implied price of an attached warrant**   Dinoo Mathur wishes to determine whether the $1,000 price asked for Stanco Manufacturing's bond is fair in light of the theoretical value of the attached warrants. The $1,000-par-value, 30-year, 11.5%-coupon-interest-rate bond pays annual interest and has 10 warrants attached for purchase of common stock. The theoretical value of each warrant is $12.50. The interest rate on an equal-risk straight bond is currently 13%.

a. Find the *straight value* of Stanco Manufacturing's bond.
b. Calculate the implied price of *all* warrants attached to Stanco's bond.
c. Calculate the implied price of *each* warrant attached to Stanco's bond.
d. Compare the implied price for each warrant calculated in part **c** to its theoretical value. On the basis of this comparison, what assessment would you give Dinoo with respect to the fairness of Stanco's bond price? Explain.

LG 5   **P17–17**   **Warrant values**   Kent Hotels has warrants that allow the purchase of three shares of its outstanding common stock at $50 per share. The common stock price per share and the market value of the warrant associated with that stock price are shown in the table.

Common stock price per share	Market value of warrant
$42	$ 2
46	8
48	9
54	18
58	28
62	38
66	48

a. For each of the common stock prices given, calculate the *theoretical warrant value*.
b. Graph the theoretical and market values of the warrant on a set of axes with per-share common stock price on the *x* axis and warrant value on the *y* axis.
c. If the warrant value is $12 when the market price of common stock is $50, does this contradict or support the graph you have constructed? Explain.
d. Specify the area of *warrant premium*. Why does this premium exist?
e. If the expiration date of the warrants is quite close, would you expect your graph to look different? Explain.

Personal Finance Problem

LG 5 **P17–18 Common stock versus warrant investment** Susan Michaels is evaluating the Burton Tool Company's common stock and warrants to choose the better investment. The firm's stock is currently selling for $50 per share; its warrants to purchase three shares of common stock at $45 per share are selling for $20. Ignoring transaction costs, Ms. Michaels has $8,000 to invest. She is quite optimistic with respect to Burton because she has certain "inside information" about the firm's prospects with respect to a large government contract.

a. How many shares of stock and how many warrants can Ms. Michaels purchase?
b. Suppose Ms. Michaels purchased the stock, held it 1 year, and then sold it for $60 per share. What total gain would she realize, ignoring brokerage fees and taxes?
c. Suppose Ms. Michaels purchased warrants and held them for 1 year and the market price of the stock increased to $60 per share. Ignoring brokerage fees and taxes, what would be her total gain if the market value of the warrants increased to $45 and she sold out?
d. What benefit, if any, would the warrants provide? Are there any differences in the risk of these two alternative investments? Explain.

Personal Finance Problem

LG 5 **P17–19 Common stock versus warrant investment** Tom Baldwin can invest $6,300 in the common stock or the warrants of Lexington Life Insurance. The common stock is currently selling for $30 per share. Its warrants, which provide for the purchase of two shares of common stock at $28 per share, are currently selling for $7. The stock is expected to rise to a market price of $32 within the next year, so the expected theoretical value of a warrant over the next year is $8. The expiration date of the warrant is 1 year from the present.

a. If Mr. Baldwin purchases the stock, holds it for 1 year, and then sells it for $32, what is his total gain? (Ignore brokerage fees and taxes.)
b. If Mr. Baldwin purchases the warrants and converts them to common stock in 1 year, what is his total gain if the market price of common shares is actually $32? (Ignore brokerage fees and taxes.)
c. Repeat parts a and b, assuming that the market price of the stock in 1 year is (1) $30 and (2) $28.
d. Discuss the two alternatives and the tradeoffs associated with them.

LG 6 **P17–20 Options profits and losses** For each of the *100-share options* shown in the following table, use the underlying stock price at expiration and other information to determine the amount of profit or loss an investor would have had, ignoring brokerage fees.

Option	Type of option	Cost of option	Strike price per share	Underlying stock price per share at expiration
A	Call	$200	$50	$55
B	Call	350	42	45
C	Put	500	60	50
D	Put	300	35	40
E	Call	450	28	26

Personal Finance Problem

LG 6   **P17–21**   **Call option**   Carol Krebs is considering buying 100 shares of Sooner Products, Inc., at $62 per share. Because she has read that the firm will probably soon receive certain large orders from abroad, she expects the price of Sooner to increase to $70 per share. As an alternative, Carol is considering purchase of a call option for 100 shares of Sooner at a strike price of $60. The 90-day option will cost $600. Ignore any brokerage fees or dividends.

a. What will Carol's profit be on the stock transaction if its price does rise to $70 and she sells?

b. How much will Carol earn on the option transaction if the underlying stock price rises to $70?

c. How high must the stock price rise for Carol to break even on the option transaction?

d. Compare, contrast, and discuss the relative profit and risk associated with the stock and the option transactions.

Personal Finance Problem

LG 6   **P17–22**   **Put option**   Ed Martin, the pension fund manager for Stark Corporation, is considering purchase of a put option in anticipation of a price decline in the stock of Carlisle, Inc. The option to sell 100 shares of Carlisle, Inc., at any time during the next 90 days at a strike price of $45 can be purchased for $380. The stock of Carlisle is currently selling for $46 per share.

a. Ignoring any brokerage fees or dividends, what profit or loss will Ed make if he buys the option and the lowest price of Carlisle stock during the 90 days is $46, $44, $40, and $35?

b. What effect would the fact that the price of Carlisle's stock slowly rose from its initial $46 level to $55 at the end of 90 days have on Ed's purchase?

c. In light of your findings, discuss the potential risks and returns from using put options to attempt to profit from an anticipated decline in share price.

LG 6   **P17–23**   **ETHICS PROBLEM**   A hedge fund charged with managing part of Harvard University's endowment purchased more than 1 million put options on Enron stock not long before the company went bankrupt, making tens of millions of dollars in the process. Some members of the university argued that profiting on the collapse of Enron was unethical. What do you say?

Spreadsheet Exercise

Morris Company, a small manufacturing firm, wants to acquire a new machine that costs $30,000. Arrangements can be made to lease or purchase the machine. The firm is in the 40% tax bracket. The firm has gathered the following information about the two alternatives:

Lease   Morris would obtain a 5-year lease requiring annual end-of-year lease payments of $10,000. The lessor would pay all maintenance costs; insurance and other costs would be borne by the lessee. Morris would be given the right to exercise its option to purchase the machine for $3,000 at the end of the lease term.

Purchase   Morris can finance the purchase of the machine with an 8.5%, 5-year loan requiring annual end-of-year installment payments. The machine would be depreciated under MACRS using a 5-year recovery period. The exact depreciation rates over the next six periods would be 20%, 32%, 19%, 12%, 12%, and 5%, respectively. Morris would pay $1,200 per year for a service contract that covers all maintenance costs. The firm plans to keep the machine and use it beyond its 5-year recovery period.

TO DO

Create a spreadsheet similar to Tables 17.1, 17.2, and 17.3 to answer the following:

a. Calculate the after-tax cash outflow from the lease for Morris Company.
b. Calculate the annual loan payment.
c. Determine the interest and principal components of the loan payments.
d. Calculate the after-tax cash outflows associated with the purchasing option.
e. Calculate and compare the present values of the cash outflows associated with both the leasing and purchasing options.
f. Which alternative is preferable? Explain.

 Visit www.myfinancelab.com for **Chapter Case:** *Financing L. Rashid Company's Chemical Waste Disposal System,* Group Exercises, and numerous online resources.

18 Mergers, LBOs, Divestitures, and Business Failure

Learning Goals

LG 1 Understand merger fundamentals, including terminology, motives for merging, and types of mergers.

LG 2 Describe the objectives and procedures used in leveraged buyouts (LBOs) and divestitures.

LG 3 Demonstrate the procedures used to value the target company, and discuss the effect of stock swap transactions on earnings per share.

LG 4 Discuss the merger negotiation process, holding companies, and international mergers.

LG 5 Understand the types and major causes of business failure and the use of voluntary settlements to sustain or liquidate the failed firm.

LG 6 Explain bankruptcy legislation and the procedures involved in reorganizing or liquidating a bankrupt firm.

Why This Chapter Matters to You

In your *professional* life

ACCOUNTING You need to understand mergers, leveraged buyouts, and divestitures of assets to record and report these organizational changes; you also need to understand bankruptcy procedures because you will play a large part in any reorganization or liquidation.

INFORMATION SYSTEMS You need to understand what data must be tracked in the case of mergers, leveraged buyouts, divestitures of assets, or bankruptcy, to devise the systems needed to effect these organizational changes.

MANAGEMENT You need to understand the motives for mergers so that you will know when and why a merger is a good idea. Also, you may need to know how to fend off an unwelcome takeover attempt, when to divest the firm of assets for strategic reasons, and what options are available in the case of business failure.

MARKETING You need to understand mergers and divestitures, which may enable the firm to grow, diversify, or achieve synergy and therefore require changes in the firm's marketing organization, plans, and goals.

OPERATIONS You need to understand mergers and divestitures because ongoing operations will be significantly affected by these organizational changes. Also, you should know that business failure may result in reorganization of the firm to provide adequate financing for ongoing operations.

In your *personal* life
As an investor, you should understand corporate mergers, leveraged buyouts, and divestitures. More important, though, is an understanding of the causes and remedies associated with corporate bankruptcy. Clearly, an unstated personal financial goal is to avoid bankruptcy, an outcome that those who develop and implement reasonable personal financial plans are not likely to experience.

Creating Value by Going Private

Although we commonly think about private firms going public to create value (as in the opening story in Chapter 1), quite often firms are taken private to create value. In February 2010, IMS Health, Inc. became a private company when it was acquired through a leveraged buyout (LBO) by investment funds managed by TPG Capital and the CPP Investment Board in a transaction valued at $5.8 billion. Operating in more than 100 countries, IMS is the world's leading provider of market intelligence to the pharmaceutical and health care industries. The LBO of IMS marked the first buyout to exceed $5 billion since the 2008 financial crisis.

When private investors believe that a company is not well-positioned to create value as a public company, the company may become the target of an LBO. Prior to completing the buyout of IMS, Mark Wiseman, a senior vice president at CPP, said, "We look forward to working together and in partnership with [IMS] management to help grow the business." By taking IMS private, TPG and CPP expect to capitalize on growth potential that did not exist or was not accessible while IMS was a public company. There can be several reasons for this, such as the company's current business plan, current analyst and trading practices, the increasing cost of regulatory compliance, and other public company obligations.

Most LBOs have the support of management and shareholders because both parties stand to gain from any expected value creation. In support of the deal, the IMS Chairman remarked "this transaction enables our shareholders to realize substantial value from their investment in IMS with an immediate cash premium, while at the same time strengthening our position to capture long-term growth opportunities." Expressing a prominent shareholder view, Charles Bobrinskoy, vice chairman at Ariel Investments, which owned 7 percent of IMS, stated, "While we believe that IMS is a very valuable company, it is clear to us that this value will not be recognized in the public markets. It may be better for IMS to be a private company."

LG 1 ## 18.1 Merger Fundamentals

Firms sometimes use mergers to expand externally by acquiring control of another firm. Whereas the overriding objective for a merger should be to improve the firm's share value, a number of more immediate motivations such as diversification, tax considerations, and increasing owner liquidity frequently exist. Sometimes mergers are pursued to acquire specific assets owned by the target rather than by a desire to run the target as a going concern. Here we discuss merger fundamentals—terminology, motives, and types. In the following sections, we will describe the related topics of leveraged buyouts (LBOs) and divestitures and will review the procedures used to analyze and negotiate mergers.

TERMINOLOGY

corporate restructuring
The activities involving expansion or contraction of a firm's operations or changes in its asset or financial (ownership) structure.

In the broadest sense, activities involving expansion or contraction of a firm's operations or changes in its asset or financial (ownership) structure are called **corporate restructuring.** The topics addressed in this chapter—mergers, LBOs, and divestitures—are some of the most common forms of corporate restructuring. Here, we define some basic merger terminology; other terms are introduced and defined as needed in subsequent discussions.

Mergers, Consolidations, and Holding Companies

merger
The combination of two or more firms, in which the resulting firm maintains the identity of one of the firms, usually the larger.

consolidation
The combination of two or more firms to form a completely new corporation.

holding company
A corporation that has voting control of one or more other corporations.

subsidiaries
The companies controlled by a holding company.

A **merger** occurs when two or more firms are combined and the resulting firm maintains the identity of one of the firms. Usually, the assets and liabilities of the smaller firm are merged into those of the larger firm. **Consolidation,** by contrast, involves the combination of two or more firms to form a completely new corporation. The new corporation normally absorbs the assets and liabilities of the companies from which it is formed. Because of the similarity of mergers and consolidations, we use the term *merger* throughout this chapter to refer to both.

A **holding company** is a corporation that has voting control of one or more other corporations. Having control in large, widely held companies generally requires ownership of between 10 and 20 percent of the outstanding stock. The companies controlled by a holding company are normally referred to as its **subsidiaries.** Control of a subsidiary is typically obtained by purchasing a sufficient number of shares of its stock.

Acquiring versus Target Companies

acquiring company
The firm in a merger transaction that attempts to acquire another firm.

target company
The firm in a merger transaction that the acquiring company is pursuing.

The firm in a merger transaction that attempts to acquire another firm is commonly called the **acquiring company.** The firm that the acquiring company is pursuing is referred to as the **target company.** Generally, the acquiring company identifies, evaluates, and negotiates with the management and/or shareholders of the target company. Occasionally, the management of a target company initiates its acquisition by seeking out potential acquirers.

Friendly versus Hostile Takeovers

Mergers can occur on either a friendly or a hostile basis. Typically, after identifying the target company, the acquirer initiates discussions. If the target management is receptive to the acquirer's proposal, it may endorse the merger and recommend shareholder approval. If the stockholders approve the merger, the transaction is typically consummated either through a cash purchase of shares by the acquirer or through an exchange of the acquirer's stock, or some combination of stock and cash for the target firm's shares. This type of negotiated transaction is known as a **friendly merger.**

If the takeover target's management does not support the proposed takeover, it can fight the acquirer's actions. In this case, the acquirer can attempt to gain control of the firm by buying sufficient shares of the target firm in the marketplace. This is typically accomplished by using a *tender offer,* which, as noted in Chapter 14, is a formal offer to purchase a given number of shares at a specified price. This type of unfriendly transaction is commonly referred to as a **hostile merger.** Clearly, hostile mergers are more difficult to consummate because the target firm's management acts to deter rather than facilitate the acquisition. Regardless, hostile takeovers are sometimes successful.

Strategic versus Financial Mergers

Mergers are undertaken for either strategic or financial reasons. **Strategic mergers** seek to achieve various economies of scale by eliminating redundant functions, increasing market share, improving raw material sourcing and finished product distribution, and so on.[1] In these mergers, the operations of the acquiring and target firms are combined to achieve synergies, thereby causing the performance of the merged firm to exceed that of the premerged firms. The mergers of Intel and McAfee (both high-tech firms) and Norwest and Wells Fargo (both banks) are examples of strategic mergers. An interesting variation of the strategic merger involves the purchase of specific product lines (rather than the whole company) for strategic reasons. The acquisition of HarperCollins's college publishing division by Addison-Wesley is an example of such a merger.

Financial mergers are based on the acquisition of companies that can be restructured to improve their cash flow. These mergers involve the acquisition of the target firm by an acquirer, which may be another company or a group of investors that may even include the target firm's existing management. The objective of the acquirer is to cut costs drastically and sell off certain unproductive or noncompatible assets in an effort to increase the target firm's cash flow. The increased cash flow is used to service the sizable debt that is typically incurred to finance these transactions. Financial mergers are based not on the firm's ability to achieve economies of scale but rather on the acquirer's belief that through restructuring, the firm's unrealized value can be unlocked.

The ready availability of *junk bond* financing throughout the 1980s fueled the financial merger mania during that period. With the collapse of the junk bond market in the early 1990s, the bankruptcy filings of a number of prominent financial mergers of the 1980s, and the rising stock market of the later 1990s, financial mergers lost their luster. As a result, the strategic merger, which does not rely so heavily on debt, continues to dominate today.

friendly merger
A merger transaction endorsed by the target firm's management, approved by its stockholders, and easily consummated.

hostile merger
A merger transaction that the target firm's management does not support, forcing the acquiring company to try to gain control of the firm by buying shares in the marketplace.

strategic merger
A merger transaction undertaken to achieve economies of scale.

financial merger
A merger transaction undertaken with the goal of restructuring the acquired company to improve its cash flow and unlock its unrealized value.

---

1. A somewhat similar nonmerger arrangement is the *strategic alliance,* an agreement typically between a large company with established products and channels of distribution and an emerging technology company with a promising research and development program in areas of interest to the larger company. In exchange for its financial support, the larger, established company obtains a stake in the technology being developed by the emerging company. Today, strategic alliances are commonplace in the biotechnology, information technology, and software industries.

Matter of fact

Limits on Growth

Certain legal constraints on mergers and acquisitions exist—especially when a proposed acquisition will lead to reduced competition. The various antitrust laws, which are enforced by the Federal Trade Commission (FTC) and the Justice Department, prohibit business combinations that eliminate competition.

MOTIVES FOR MERGING

Firms merge to fulfill certain objectives. The overriding goal for merging is maximization of the owners' wealth as reflected in the acquirer's share price. More specific motives include growth or diversification, synergy, fund raising, increased managerial skill or technology, tax considerations, increased ownership liquidity, and defense against takeover. These motives should be pursued when they lead to owner wealth maximization.

Growth or Diversification

Companies that desire rapid growth in *size* or *market share* or diversification in *the range of their products* may find that a merger can fulfill this objective. Instead of relying entirely on internal or "organic" growth, the firm may achieve its growth or diversification objectives much faster by merging with an existing firm. Such a strategy is often less costly than the alternative of developing the necessary production capacity. If a firm that wants to expand operations can find a suitable going concern, it may avoid many of the risks associated with the design, manufacture, and sale of additional or new products. Moreover, when a firm expands or extends its product line by acquiring another firm, it may remove a potential competitor.

Synergy

The *synergy* of mergers is the economies of scale resulting from the merged firms' lower overhead. These economies of scale from lowering the combined overhead increase earnings to a level greater than the sum of the earnings of each of the independent firms. Synergy is most obvious when firms merge with other firms in the same line of business because many redundant functions and employees can be eliminated. Staff functions, such as purchasing and sales, are probably most greatly affected by this type of combination.

Fund Raising

Often, firms combine to enhance their fund-raising ability. A firm may be unable to obtain funds for its own internal expansion but able to obtain funds for external business combinations. Quite often, one firm may combine with another that has high liquid assets and low levels of liabilities. The acquisition of this type of "cash-rich" company immediately increases the firm's borrowing power by decreasing its financial leverage. This should allow funds to be raised externally at lower cost.

Increased Managerial Skill or Technology

Occasionally, a firm will have good potential that it finds itself unable to develop fully because of deficiencies in certain areas of management or an absence of needed product or production technology. If the firm cannot hire the management or develop the technology it needs, it might combine with a compatible firm that has the needed managerial personnel or technical expertise. Of course, any merger should contribute to maximizing the owners' wealth.

Tax Considerations

Quite often, tax considerations are a key motive for merging. In such a case, the tax benefit generally stems from the fact that one of the firms has a **tax loss carryforward**. This means that the company's tax loss can be applied against a limited

tax loss carryforward
In a merger, the tax loss of one of the firms that can be applied against a limited amount of future income of the merged firm over 20 years or until the total tax loss has been fully recovered, whichever comes first.

amount of future income of the merged firm over 20 years or until the total tax loss has been fully recovered, whichever comes first.[2] Two situations could actually exist. A company with a tax loss could acquire a profitable company to use the tax loss. In this case, the acquiring firm would boost the combination's after-tax earnings by reducing the taxable income of the acquired firm. A tax loss may also be useful when a profitable firm acquires a firm that has such a loss. In either situation, however, the merger must be justified not only on the basis of the tax benefits but also on grounds consistent with the goal of owner wealth maximization. Moreover, the tax benefits described can be used only in mergers—not in the formation of holding companies—because only in the case of mergers are operating results reported on a consolidated basis. An example will clarify the use of the tax loss carryforward.

Example 18.1 ▶ Bergen Company, a wheel bearing manufacturer, has a total of $450,000 in tax loss carryforwards resulting from operating tax losses of $150,000 per year in each of the past 3 years. To use these losses and to diversify its operations, Hudson Company, a molder of plastics, has acquired Bergen through a merger. Hudson expects to have *earnings before taxes* of $300,000 per year. We assume that these earnings are realized, that they fall within the annual limit that is legally allowed for application of the tax loss carryforward resulting from the merger (see footnote 2), that the Bergen portion of the merged firm just breaks even, and that Hudson is in the 40% tax bracket. The total taxes paid by the two firms and their after-tax earnings without and with the merger are as shown in Table 18.1.

TABLE 18.1 ▷ **Total Taxes and After-Tax Earnings for Hudson Company without and with Merger**				
		Year		Total for
	1	2	3	3 years
Total taxes and after-tax earnings without merger				
(1) Earnings before taxes	$300,000	$300,000	$300,000	$900,000
(2) Taxes [0.40 × (1)]	120,000	120,000	120,000	360,000
(3) Earnings after taxes [(1) − (2)]	$180,000	$180,000	$180,000	$540,000
Total taxes and after-tax earnings with merger				
(4) Earnings before losses	$300,000	$300,000	$300,000	$900,000
(5) Tax loss carryforward	300,000	150,000	0	450,000
(6) Earnings before taxes [(4) − (5)]	$ 0	$150,000	$300,000	$450,000
(7) Taxes [0.40 × (6)]	0	60,000	120,000	180,000
(8) Earnings after taxes [(4) − (7)]	$300,000	$240,000	$180,000	$720,000

---

2. To deter firms from combining solely to take advantage of tax loss carryforwards, the *Tax Reform Act of 1986* imposed an annual limit on the amount of taxable income against which such losses can be applied. The annual limit is determined by formula and is tied to the value of the loss corporation before the combination. Although not fully eliminating this motive for combination, the act makes it more difficult for firms to justify combinations solely on the basis of tax loss carryforwards.

With the merger the total tax payments are less—$180,000 (total of line 7) versus $360,000 (total of line 2). With the merger the total after-tax earnings are more—$720,000 (total of line 8) versus $540,000 (total of line 3). The merged firm is able to deduct the tax loss over 20 years or until the total tax loss is fully recovered, whichever comes first. In this example, the total tax loss is fully deducted by the end of year 2.

Increased Ownership Liquidity

The merger of two small firms or of a small and a larger firm may provide the owners of the small firm(s) with greater liquidity. This is due to the higher marketability associated with the shares of larger firms. Instead of holding shares in a small firm that has a very "thin" market, the owners will receive shares that are traded in a broader market and can thus be liquidated more readily. Also, owning shares for which market price quotations are readily available provides owners with a better sense of the value of their holdings. Especially in the case of small, closely held firms, the improved liquidity of ownership obtainable through merger with an acceptable firm may have considerable appeal.

Defense against Takeover

Occasionally, when a firm becomes the target of an unfriendly takeover, it will acquire another company as a defensive tactic. Such a strategy typically works like this: The original target firm takes on additional debt to finance its defensive acquisition; because of the debt load, the target firm becomes too highly leveraged financially to be of any further interest to its suitor. To be effective, a defensive takeover must create greater value for shareholders than they would have realized had the firm been merged with its suitor.

TYPES OF MERGERS

horizontal merger
A merger of two firms *in the same line of business.*

vertical merger
A merger in which a firm acquires *a supplier or a customer.*

congeneric merger
A merger in which one firm acquires another firm that is *in the same general industry* but is neither in the same line of business nor a supplier or customer.

conglomerate merger
A merger combining firms in *unrelated businesses.*

The four types of mergers are the (1) horizontal merger, (2) vertical merger, (3) congeneric merger, and (4) conglomerate merger. A **horizontal merger** results when two firms *in the same line of business* are merged. An example is the merger of two machine tool manufacturers. This form of merger results in the expansion of a firm's operations in a given product line and at the same time eliminates a competitor. A **vertical merger** occurs when a firm acquires *a supplier or a customer.* For example, the merger of a machine tool manufacturer with its supplier of castings is a vertical merger. The economic benefit of a vertical merger stems from the firm's increased control over the acquisition of raw materials or the distribution of finished goods.

A **congeneric merger** is achieved by acquiring a firm that is *in the same general industry* but is neither in the same line of business nor a supplier or customer. An example is the merger of a machine tool manufacturer with the manufacturer of industrial conveyor systems. The benefit of a congeneric merger is the resulting ability to use the same sales and distribution channels to reach customers of both businesses. A **conglomerate merger** involves the combination of firms in *unrelated businesses.* The merger of a machine tool manufacturer with a chain of fast-food restaurants is an example of this kind of merger. The key benefit of the conglomerate merger is its ability to *reduce risk* by merging firms that have different seasonal or cyclic patterns of sales and earnings.

→ REVIEW QUESTIONS

18–1 Define and differentiate among the members of each of the following sets of terms: (**a**) mergers, consolidations, and holding companies; (**b**) acquiring company and target company; (**c**) friendly merger and hostile merger; and (**d**) strategic merger and financial merger.

18–2 Briefly describe each of the following motives for merging: (**a**) growth or diversification, (**b**) synergy, (**c**) fund raising, (**d**) increased managerial skill or technology, (**e**) tax considerations, (**f**) increased ownership liquidity, and (**g**) defense against takeover.

18–3 Briefly describe each of the following types of mergers: (**a**) horizontal, (**b**) vertical, (**c**) congeneric, and (**d**) conglomerate.

LG 2   ## 18.2 LBOs and Divestitures

Before we address the mechanics of merger analysis and negotiation, you need to understand two topics that are closely related to mergers—leveraged buyouts (LBOs) and divestitures. An LBO is a method of structuring an acquisition, and divestitures involve the sale of a firm's assets.

LEVERAGED BUYOUTS (LBOS)

leveraged buyout (LBO)
An acquisition technique involving the use of a large amount of debt to purchase a firm; an example of a *financial merger.*

A popular technique that was widely used during the 1980s to make acquisitions is the **leveraged buyout (LBO),** which involves the use of a large amount of debt to purchase a firm. LBOs are a clear-cut example of a *financial merger* undertaken to create a high-debt private corporation with improved cash flow and value. Typically, in an LBO, 90 percent or more of the purchase price is financed with debt. A large part of the borrowing is secured by the acquired firm's assets, and the lenders, because of the high risk, take a portion of the firm's equity. *Junk bonds* have been routinely used to raise the large amounts of debt needed to finance LBO transactions. Of course, the purchasers in an LBO expect to use the improved cash flow to service the large amount of junk bond and other debt incurred in the buyout.

An attractive candidate for acquisition via a leveraged buyout should possess three key attributes:

1. It must have a good position in its industry, with a solid profit history and reasonable expectations of growth.
2. The firm should have a relatively low level of debt and a high level of "bankable" assets that can be used as loan collateral.
3. It must have stable and predictable cash flows that are adequate to meet interest and principal payments on the debt and provide adequate working capital.

Of course, a willingness on the part of existing ownership and management to sell the company on a leveraged basis is also needed.

Many LBOs did not live up to original expectations. One of the largest ever was the late 1988, $24.5 billion buyout of RJR Nabisco by KKR. RJR was taken public in 1991, and the firm continued to struggle under the heavy debt of the LBO for a few years before improving its debt position and credit rating. Campeau

Corporation's buyouts of Allied Stores and Federated Department Stores resulted in its later filing for bankruptcy protection, from which reorganized companies later emerged. In earlier years, other highly publicized LBOs have defaulted on the high-yield debt incurred to finance the buyout. Although the LBO remains a viable financing technique under the right circumstances, its use is greatly diminished from the frenzied pace of the 1980s. Whereas the LBOs of the 1980s were used, often indiscriminately, for hostile takeovers, today LBOs are most often used to finance management buyouts.

DIVESTITURES

operating unit
A part of a business, such as a plant, division, product line, or subsidiary, that contributes to the actual operations of the firm.

divestiture
The selling of some of a firm's assets for various strategic reasons.

Companies often achieve external expansion by acquiring an **operating unit**—plant, division, product line, subsidiary, and so on—of another company. In such a case, the seller generally believes that the value of the firm will be enhanced by converting the unit into cash or some other more productive asset. The selling of some of a firm's assets is called **divestiture**. Unlike business failure, divestiture is often undertaken for positive motives: to generate cash for expansion of other product lines, to get rid of a poorly performing operation, to streamline the corporation, or to restructure the corporation's business in a manner consistent with its strategic goals.

Personal Finance Example 18.2 ▶ A personal finance decision that young families with children frequently face is whether a stay-at-home parent should "divest" his or her child-care duties, hire child care, and return to work. Whereas the emotional aspects of such a decision are nonquantifiable, the economics of such a decision are measurable.

Take the case of Elena and Gino Deluca, who have two children, ages 2 and 4. They are in the process of analyzing whether it makes economic sense to hire child care and have Elena return to work as a credit analyst. They estimate that Elena will earn $5,800 per month gross, including her employer's 401(k) contributions. In addition, she expects to receive monthly employer-paid benefits that include health insurance, life insurance, and pension contributions totaling $1,800. She expects her federal and state income taxes to total about $1,900 per month. The Delucas estimate total additional expenses (child care, clothing and personal expenses, meals away from home, and transportation) related to Elana's job to total $1,500 per month. They summarized these monthly estimates as follows:

Additional gross income	$5,800	
+ Employer-paid benefits	1,800	
(1) Additional income and benefits		$7,600
Additional taxes	1,900	
+ Additional expenses	1,500	
(2) Additional taxes and expenses		3,400
Net income (loss) [(1) − (2)]		$4,200

Because the Delucas will increase their net income by $4,200 per month, having Elena divest her child-care responsibilities and hire child care is economically justifiable.

Firms divest themselves of operating units by a variety of methods. One involves the *sale of a product line to another firm.* An example is Paramount's sale of Simon and Schuster to Pearson PLC to free up cash and allow Paramount to focus its business better on global mass consumer markets. Outright sales of operating units can be accomplished on a cash or stock swap basis via the procedures described later in this chapter. A second method that has become popular involves the *sale of the unit to existing management.* This sale is often achieved through the use of a *leveraged buyout (LBO).*

spin-off
A form of divestiture in which an operating unit becomes an independent company through the issuance of shares in it, on a pro rata basis, to the parent company's shareholders.

Sometimes divestiture is achieved through a **spin-off,** which results in an operating unit becoming an independent company. A spin-off is accomplished by issuing shares in the divested operating unit on a pro rata basis to the parent company's shareholders. Such an action allows the unit to be separated from the corporation and to trade as a separate entity. An example was the decision by AT&T to spin off its Global Information Solutions unit (formerly and now NCR, which produces electronic terminals and computers), to allow AT&T to focus better on its core communications business. Like outright sale, this approach achieves the divestiture objective, although it does not bring additional cash or stock to the parent company. The final and least popular approach to divestiture involves *liquidation of the operating unit's individual assets.*

breakup value
The value of a firm measured as the sum of the values of its operating units if each were sold separately.

Regardless of the method used to divest a firm of an unwanted operating unit, the goal typically is to create a more lean and focused operation that will enhance the efficiency as well as the profitability of the enterprise and create maximum value for shareholders. Recent divestitures seem to suggest that many operating units are worth much more to others than to the firm itself. Comparisons of postdivestiture and predivestiture market values have shown that the **breakup value**—the sum of the values of a firm's operating units if each were sold separately—of many firms is significantly greater than their combined value. As a result of market valuations, divestiture often creates value in excess of the cash or stock received in the transaction. Although these outcomes frequently occur, financial theory has been unable to explain them fully and satisfactorily.

→ REVIEW QUESTIONS

18–4 What is a *leveraged buyout (LBO)?* What are the three key attributes of an attractive candidate for acquisition via an LBO?

18–5 What is an *operating unit?* What is a *divestiture?* What are four common methods used by firms to divest themselves of operating units? What is *breakup value?*

LG 3 LG 4 18.3 Analyzing and Negotiating Mergers

We now turn to the procedures that are used to analyze and negotiate mergers. Initially, we will consider how to value the target company and how to use stock swap transactions to acquire companies. Next, we will look at the merger negotiation process. We will then review the major advantages and disadvantages of holding companies. Finally, we will discuss international mergers.

VALUING THE TARGET COMPANY

Once the acquiring company isolates a target company that it wishes to acquire, it must estimate the target's value. The value is then used, along with a proposed financing scheme, to negotiate the transaction—on a friendly or hostile basis. The value of the target is estimated by using the valuation techniques presented in Chapter 7 and applied to long-term investment decisions in Chapters 10, 11, and 12. Similar capital budgeting techniques are applied whether the target firm is being acquired for its assets or as a going concern.

Acquisitions of Assets

Occasionally, a firm is acquired not for its income-earning potential but as a collection of assets (generally fixed assets) that the acquiring company needs. The price paid for this type of acquisition depends largely on which assets are being acquired; consideration must also be given to the value of any tax losses. To determine whether the purchase of assets is financially justified, the acquirer must estimate both the costs and the benefits of the target assets. This is a capital budgeting problem (see Chapters 10, 11, and 12), because an initial cash outlay is made to acquire assets, and as a result, future cash inflows are expected.

Example 18.3 ▶ Clark Company, a major manufacturer of electrical transformers, is interested in acquiring certain fixed assets of Noble Company, an industrial electronics company. Noble, which has tax loss carryforwards from losses over the past 5 years, is interested in selling out, but it wishes to sell out entirely, not just to get rid of certain fixed assets. A condensed balance sheet for Noble Company follows.

Noble Company Balance Sheet			
Assets		**Liabilities and Stockholders' Equity**	
Cash	$ 2,000	Total liabilities	$ 80,000
Marketable securities	0	Stockholders' equity	120,000
Accounts receivable	8,000	Total liabilities and	
Inventories	10,000	stockholders' equity	$200,000
Machine A	10,000		
Machine B	30,000		
Machine C	25,000		
Land and buildings	115,000		
Total assets	$200,000		

Clark Company needs only machines B and C and the land and buildings. However, it has made some inquiries and has arranged to sell the accounts receivable, inventories, and machine A for $23,000. Because there is also $2,000 in cash, Clark will get $25,000 for the excess assets. Noble wants $100,000 for the entire company, which means that Clark will have to pay the firm's creditors $80,000 and its owners $20,000. The actual outlay required of Clark after liquidating the unneeded assets will be $75,000 [($80,000 + $20,000) − $25,000].

TABLE 18.2	Net Present Value of Noble Company's Assets	
Year(s)	Cash inflows	Present value
1–5	$14,000	$51,743
6	12,000	6,416
7	12,000	5,780
8	12,000	5,207
9	12,000	4,691
10	12,000	4,226
	Present value of inflows	$78,063
	Less: Cash outlay required	75,000
	Net present value	$ 3,063

In other words, to obtain the use of the desired assets (machines B and C and the land and buildings) and the benefits of Noble's tax losses, Clark must pay $75,000. The *after-tax cash inflows* that are expected to result from the new assets and applicable tax losses are $14,000 per year for the next 5 years and $12,000 per year for the following 5 years. The desirability of this asset acquisition can be determined by calculating the net present value of this outlay using Clark Company's 11% cost of capital, as shown in Table 18.2. *Because the net present value of $3,063 is greater than zero, Clark's value should be increased by acquiring Noble Company's assets.*

Acquisitions of Going Concerns

Acquisitions of target companies that are going concerns are best analyzed by using capital budgeting techniques similar to those described for asset acquisitions. The methods of estimating expected cash flows from an acquisition are similar to those used in estimating capital budgeting cash flows. Typically, *pro forma income statements* reflecting the postmerger revenues and costs attributable to the target company are prepared (see Chapter 4). They are then adjusted to reflect the expected cash flows over the relevant time period. Whenever a firm considers acquiring a target company that has different risk behaviors, it should risk-adjust the cost of capital before applying the appropriate capital budgeting techniques (see Chapter 12).

Example 18.4 ▶   Square Company, a major media company, is contemplating the acquisition of Circle Company, a small independent film producer that can be purchased for $60,000. Square currently has a high degree of financial leverage, which is reflected in its 13% cost of capital. Because of the low financial leverage of Circle Company, Square estimates that its overall cost of capital will drop to 10% after the acquisition. Because the effect of the less risky capital structure cannot be reflected in the expected cash flows, the postmerger cost of capital (10%) must be used to evaluate

TABLE 18.3	Net Present Value of the Circle Company Acquisition	
Year(s)	Cash inflows	Present value
1–10	$ 5,000	$30,723
11–18	13,000	26,739
19–30	4,000	4,902
	Present value of inflows	$62,364
	Less: Cash purchase price	60,000
	Net present value	$ 2,364

the cash flows that are expected from the acquisition. The postmerger cash flows attributable to the target company are forecast over a 30-year time horizon. These estimated cash flows (all inflows) and the resulting net present value of the target company, Circle Company, are shown in Table 18.3.

Because the $2,364 net present value of the target company is greater than zero, the merger is acceptable. Note that if the effect of the changed capital structure on the cost of capital had not been considered, the acquisition would have been found unacceptable, because the net present value *at a 13% cost of capital* is negative $11,868.

STOCK SWAP TRANSACTIONS

Once the value of the target company is determined, the acquirer must develop a proposed financing package. The simplest (but probably the least common) case is a pure cash purchase. Beyond this extreme case, there are virtually an infinite number of financing packages that use various combinations of cash, debt, preferred stock, and common stock.

stock swap transaction
An acquisition method in which the acquiring firm exchanges its shares for shares of the target company according to a predetermined ratio.

Here we look at the other extreme—**stock swap transactions,** in which the acquisition is paid for using an exchange of common stock. The acquiring firm exchanges its shares for shares of the target company according to a predetermined ratio. The *ratio of exchange* of shares is determined in the merger negotiations. This ratio affects the various financial yardsticks that are used by existing and prospective shareholders to value the merged firm's shares. The use of stock swaps to finance mergers is a popular approach.

Ratio of Exchange

ratio of exchange
The ratio of the amount *paid* per share of the target company to the market price per share of the acquiring firm.

When one firm swaps its stock for the shares of another firm, the firms must determine the number of shares of the acquiring firm to be exchanged for each share of the target firm. The first requirement, of course, is that the acquiring company have sufficient shares available to complete the transaction. Often, a firm's repurchase of shares (discussed in Chapter 14) is necessary to obtain sufficient shares for such a transaction. The acquiring firm generally offers enough of its own shares that the value of the shares given up exceeds the value of one target share. The actual **ratio of exchange** is merely the ratio of the amount *paid* per share of the target company to the market price per share of the acquiring firm. It is calculated in this manner because the acquiring firm pays the target firm in stock, which has a value equal to its market price.

Example 18.5 ▶   Grand Company, a leather products concern whose stock is currently selling for $80 per share, is interested in acquiring Small Company, a producer of belts. To prepare for the acquisition, Grand has been repurchasing its own shares over the past 3 years. Small's stock is currently selling for $75 per share, but in the merger negotiations Grand has found it necessary to offer Small $110 per share. Because Grand does not have sufficient financial resources to purchase the firm for cash and does not wish to raise these funds, Small has agreed to accept Grand's stock in exchange for its shares. As stated, Grand's stock currently sells for $80 per share, and it must pay $110 per share for Small's stock. Therefore, the ratio of exchange is 1.375 ($110 ÷ $80). This means that Grand Company must exchange 1.375 shares of its stock for each share of Small's stock.

Effect on Earnings per Share

Although cash flows and value are the primary focus of merger analysis, it is useful to consider the effects of a proposed merger on earnings per share—the accounting returns that are related to cash flows and value (see Chapter 7). Ordinarily, the resulting earnings per share differ from the premerger earnings per share for both the acquiring firm and the target firm. They depend largely on the ratio of exchange and the premerger earnings per share of each firm. It is best to view the initial and long-run effects of the ratio of exchange on earnings per share separately.

Initial Effect   When the ratio of exchange is equal to 1 and both the acquiring firm and the target firm have the *same* premerger earnings per share, the merged firm's earnings per share will initially remain constant. In this rare instance, both the acquiring firm and the target firm would also have equal price/earnings (P/E) ratios. In actuality, the earnings per share of the merged firm are generally above the premerger earnings per share of one firm and below the premerger earnings per share of the other, after the necessary adjustment has been made for the ratio of exchange.

Example 18.6 ▶   As we saw in the preceding example, Grand Company is contemplating acquiring Small Company by swapping 1.375 shares of its stock for each share of Small's stock. The current financial data related to the earnings and market price for each of these companies are given in Table 18.4.

TABLE 18.4 ▷ Grand Company's and Small Company's Financial Data

Item	Grand Company	Small Company
(1) Earnings available for common stock	$500,000	$100,000
(2) Number of shares of common stock outstanding	125,000	20,000
(3) Earnings per share [(1) ÷ (2)]	$4	$5
(4) Market price per share	$80	$75
(5) Price/earnings (P/E) ratio [(4) ÷ (3)]	20	15

TABLE 18.5	Summary of the Effects on Earnings per Share of a Merger between Grand Company and Small Company at $110 per Share

	Earnings per share	
Stockholders	Before merger	After merger
Grand Company	$4.00	$3.93[a]
Small Company	5.00	5.40[b]

[a] $\dfrac{\$500,000 + \$100,000}{125,000 + (1.375 \times 20,000)} = \$3.93$

[b] $\$3.93 \times 1.375 = \$5.40$

To complete the merger and retire the 20,000 shares of Small Company stock outstanding, Grand will have to issue and (or) use treasury stock totaling 27,500 shares (1.375 × 20,000 shares). Once the merger is completed, Grand will have 152,500 shares of common stock (125,000 + 27,500) outstanding. If the earnings of each of the firms remain constant, the merged company will be expected to have earnings available for the common stockholders of $600,000 ($500,000 + $100,000). The earnings per share of the merged company therefore should equal approximately $3.93 ($600,000 ÷ 152,500 shares).

It would appear at first that Small Company's shareholders have sustained a decrease in per-share earnings from $5 to $3.93, but because each share of Small Company's original stock is equivalent to 1.375 shares of the merged company's stock the equivalent earnings per share are actually $5.40 ($3.93 × 1.375). In other words, as a result of the merger, Grand Company's original shareholders experience a decrease in earnings per share from $4 to $3.93 to the benefit of Small Company's shareholders, whose earnings per share increase from $5 to $5.40. These results are summarized in Table 18.5.

The postmerger earnings per share for owners of the acquiring and target companies can be explained by comparing the price/earnings ratio paid by the acquiring company with its initial P/E ratio. Table 18.6 summarizes this relationship. By paying more than its current value per dollar of earnings to acquire each dollar of earnings (P/E paid > P/E of acquiring company), the acquiring firm transfers the claim on a portion of its premerger earnings to the owners of the

TABLE 18.6	Effect of Price/Earnings (P/E) Ratios on Earnings per Share (EPS)

	Effect on EPS	
Relationship between P/E paid and P/E of acquiring company	Acquiring company	Target company
P/E paid > P/E of acquiring company	Decrease	Increase
P/E paid = P/E of acquiring company	Constant	Constant
P/E paid < P/E of acquiring company	Increase	Decrease

target firm. Therefore, on a postmerger basis *the target firm's EPS increases, and the acquiring firm's EPS decreases.* Note that this outcome is *nearly always* the case because the acquirer typically pays, on average, a 50 percent premium above the target firm's market price, which results in the P/E paid being much above its own P/E. The P/E ratios associated with the Grand–Small merger demonstrate the effect of the merger on EPS.

Example 18.7 ▶

Grand Company's P/E ratio is 20, and the P/E ratio paid for Small Company's earnings was 22 ($110 ÷ $5). Because the P/E paid for Small Company was greater than the P/E for Grand Company (22 versus 20), the effect of the merger was to decrease the EPS for original holders of shares in Grand Company (from $4.00 to $3.93) and to increase the effective EPS of original holders of shares in Small Company (from $5.00 to $5.40).

Long-Run Effect   The long-run effect of a merger on the earnings per share of the merged company depends largely on whether the earnings of the merged firm grow. Often, although an initial decrease in the per-share earnings of the stock held by the original owners of the acquiring firm is expected, the long-run effects of the merger on earnings per share are quite favorable. Because firms generally expect growth in earnings, the key factor enabling the acquiring company to experience higher future EPS than it would have without the merger is that the earnings attributable to the target company's assets grow more rapidly than those resulting from the acquiring company's premerger assets. An example will clarify this point.

Example 18.8 ▶

In 2012, Grand Company acquired Small Company by swapping 1.375 shares of its common stock for each share of Small Company. Other key financial data and the effects of this exchange ratio were discussed in preceding examples. The total earnings of Grand Company were expected to grow at an annual rate of 3% without the merger; Small Company's earnings were expected to grow at a 7% annual rate without the merger. The same growth rates are expected to apply to the component earnings streams with the merger. The table in Figure 18.1 shows the future effects on EPS for Grand Company without and with the proposed Small Company merger, on the basis of these growth rates.

The table indicates that the earnings per share without the merger will be greater than the EPS with the merger for the years 2012 through 2014. After 2014, however, the EPS will be higher than they would have been without the merger as a result of the faster earnings growth rate of Small Company (7% versus 3%). Although a few years are required for this difference in the growth rate of earnings to pay off, in the future Grand Company will receive an earnings benefit as a result of merging with Small Company at a 1.375 ratio of exchange. The long-run earnings advantage of the merger is clearly depicted in Figure 18.1.[3]

---

3. To discover properly whether the merger is beneficial, the earnings estimates under each alternative would have to be made over a long period of time—say, 50 years—and then converted to cash flows and discounted at the appropriate rate. The alternative with the higher present value would be preferred. For simplicity, only the basic intuitive view of the long-run effect is presented here.

FIGURE 18.1

Future EPS
Future EPS without and with the Grand–Small merger

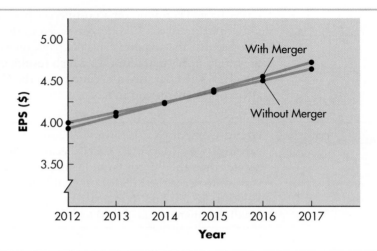

| | Without merger | | With merger | |
Year	Total earnings[a]	Earnings per share[b]	Total earnings[c]	Earnings per share[d]
2012	$500,000	$4.00	$600,000	$3.93
2013	515,000	4.12	622,000	4.08
2014	530,450	4.24	644,940	4.23
2015	546,364	4.37	668,868	4.39
2016	562,755	4.50	693,835	4.55
2017	579,638	4.64	719,893	4.72

[a]Based on a 3% annual growth rate.
[b]Based on 125,000 shares outstanding.
[c]Based on a 3% annual growth in the Grand Company's earnings and a 7% annual growth in the Small Company's earnings.
[d]Based on 152,500 shares outstanding [125,000 shares + (1.375 × 20,000 shares)].

Effect on Market Price per Share

The market price per share does not necessarily remain constant after the acquisition of one firm by another. Adjustments occur in the marketplace in response to changes in expected earnings, the dilution of ownership, changes in risk, and certain other operating and financial changes. By using the ratio of exchange, we can calculate a **ratio of exchange in market price.** It indicates the market price per share of the acquiring firm *paid* for each dollar of market price per share of the target firm. This ratio, the *MPR*, is defined by Equation 18.1:

ratio of exchange in market price
Indicates the market price per share of the acquiring firm *paid* for each dollar of market price per share of the target firm.

$$MPR = \frac{MP_{\text{acquiring}} \times RE}{MP_{\text{target}}} \tag{18.1}$$

where

$$
\begin{aligned}
MPR &= \text{market price ratio of exchange} \\
MP_{\text{acquiring}} &= \text{market price per share of the acquiring firm} \\
MP_{\text{target}} &= \text{market price per share of the target firm} \\
RE &= \text{ratio of exchange}
\end{aligned}
$$

> **Example 18.9** ▶

The market price of Grand Company's stock was $80, and that of Small Company's was $75. The ratio of exchange was 1.375. Substituting these values into Equation 18.1 yields a ratio of exchange in market price of 1.47 [($80 × 1.375) ÷ $75]. This means that $1.47 of the market price of Grand Company is given in exchange for every $1.00 of the market price of Small Company.

The ratio of exchange in market price is normally greater than 1, which indicates that to acquire a firm, the acquirer must pay a premium above the target's market price. Even so, the original owners of the acquiring firm may still gain, because the merged firm's stock may sell at a price/earnings ratio above the individual premerger ratios. This results from the improved risk and return relationship perceived by shareholders and other investors.

> **Example 18.10** ▶

The financial data developed earlier for the Grand–Small merger can be used to explain the market price effects of a merger. If the earnings of the merged company remain at the premerger levels, and if the stock of the merged company sells at an assumed multiple of 21 times earnings, the values in Table 18.7 can be expected. Although Grand Company's earnings per share decline from $4.00 to $3.93 (see Table 18.5), the market price of its shares will increase from $80.00 to $82.53 as a result of the merger.

Although the behavior exhibited in the preceding example is not unusual, the financial manager must recognize that only with proper management of the merged enterprise can its market value be improved. If the merged firm cannot achieve sufficiently high earnings in view of its risk, there is no guarantee that its market price will reach the forecast value. Nevertheless, a policy of acquiring firms with low P/Es can produce favorable results for the owners of the acquiring firm. Acquisitions are especially attractive when the acquiring firm's stock price is high, because fewer shares must be exchanged to acquire a given firm.

MERGER NEGOTIATION PROCESS

investment bankers
Financial intermediaries who, in addition to their role in selling new security issues, can be hired by acquirers in mergers to find suitable target companies and assist in negotiations.

Mergers are often handled by **investment bankers**—financial intermediaries who, in addition to their role in selling new security issues (described in Chapter 7), can be hired by acquirers to find suitable target companies and assist in negotiations. Once a target company is selected, the investment banker negotiates with its management or investment banker. Likewise, when management wishes to sell the firm or an operating unit of the firm, it will hire an investment banker to seek out potential buyers.

TABLE 18.7	Postmerger Market Price of Grand Company Using a P/E Ratio of 21
Item	Merged company
(1) Earnings available for common stock	$600,000
(2) Number of shares of common stock outstanding	152,500
(3) Earnings per share [(1) ÷ (2)]	$3.93
(4) Price/earnings (P/E) ratio	21
(5) Expected market price per share [(3) × (4)]	$82.53

If attempts to negotiate with the management of the target company break down, the acquiring firm, often with the aid of its investment banker, can make a direct appeal to shareholders by using *tender offers* (as explained in the following discussion). The investment banker is typically compensated with a fixed fee, a commission tied to the transaction price, or a combination of fees and commissions.

Management Negotiations

To initiate negotiations, the acquiring firm must make an offer either in cash or based on a stock swap with a specified ratio of exchange. The target company then reviews the offer and, in light of alternative offers, accepts or rejects the terms presented. A desirable merger candidate may receive more than a single offer. Normally, it is necessary to resolve certain nonfinancial issues related to the existing management, product line policies, financing policies, and the independence of the target firm. The key factor, of course, is the per-share price offered in cash or reflected in the ratio of exchange. Sometimes negotiations break down.

Tender Offers

When negotiations for an acquisition fail, tender offers may be used to negotiate a "hostile merger" directly with the firm's stockholders. As noted in Chapter 14, a *tender offer* is a formal offer to purchase a given number of shares of a firm's stock at a specified price. The offer is made to all the stockholders at a premium above the market price. Occasionally, the acquirer will make a **two-tier offer,** in which the terms offered are more attractive to those who tender shares early. For example, the acquirer offers to pay $25 per share for the first 60 percent of the outstanding shares tendered and only $23 per share for the remaining shares. The stockholders are advised of a tender offer through announcements in financial newspapers or through direct communications from the offering firm. Sometimes a tender offer is made to add pressure to existing merger negotiations. In other cases, the tender offer may be made without warning as an attempt at an abrupt corporate takeover.

Fighting Hostile Takeovers

If the management of a target firm does not favor a merger or considers the price offered in a proposed merger too low, it is likely to take defensive actions to ward off the *hostile takeover.* Such actions are generally taken with the assistance of investment bankers and lawyers who help the firm develop and employ effective **takeover defenses.** There are obvious strategies, such as informing stockholders of the alleged damaging effects of a takeover, acquiring another company (discussed earlier in the chapter), or attempting to sue the acquiring firm on antitrust or other grounds. In addition, many other defenses exist (some with colorful names)—white knight, poison pills, greenmail, leveraged recapitalization, golden parachutes, and shark repellents.

The **white knight** strategy involves the target firm finding a more suitable acquirer (the "white knight") and prompting it to compete with the initial hostile acquirer to take over the firm. If being taken over is nearly certain, the target firm attempts to be taken over by a firm deemed most acceptable to its management. **Poison pills** typically involve the creation of securities that give their holders certain rights that become effective when a takeover is attempted. The "pill" allows the shareholders to receive special voting rights or securities that make the firm

two-tier offer
A *tender offer* in which the terms offered are more attractive to those who tender shares early.

takeover defenses
Strategies for fighting hostile takeovers.

white knight
A takeover defense in which the target firm finds an acquirer more to its liking than the initial hostile acquirer and prompts the two to compete to take over the firm.

poison pill
A takeover defense in which a firm issues securities that give their holders certain rights that become effective when a takeover is attempted; these rights make the target firm less desirable to a hostile acquirer.

greenmail
A takeover defense under which a target firm repurchases, through private negotiation, a large block of stock at a premium from one or more shareholders to end a hostile takeover attempt by those shareholders.

leveraged recapitalization
A takeover defense in which the target firm pays a large debt-financed cash dividend, increasing the firm's financial leverage and thereby deterring the takeover attempt.

golden parachutes
Provisions in the employment contracts of key executives that provide them with sizable compensation if the firm is taken over; deters hostile takeovers to the extent that the cash outflows required are large enough to make the takeover unattractive.

shark repellents
Antitakeover amendments to a corporate charter that constrain the firm's ability to transfer managerial control of the firm as a result of a merger.

less desirable to the hostile acquirer. **Greenmail** is a strategy by which the firm repurchases, through private negotiation, a large block of stock at a premium from one or more shareholders to end a hostile takeover attempt by those shareholders. Clearly, greenmail is a form of corporate blackmail by the holders of a large block of shares.

Another defense against hostile takeover involves the use of a **leveraged recapitalization,** which is a strategy involving the payment of a large debt-financed cash dividend. This strategy significantly increases the firm's financial leverage, thereby deterring the takeover attempt. In addition, as a further deterrent, the recapitalization is often structured to increase the equity and control of the existing management. **Golden parachutes** are provisions in the employment contracts of key executives that provide them with sizable compensation if the firm is taken over. Golden parachutes deter hostile takeovers to the extent that the cash outflows required by these contracts are large enough to make the takeover unattractive to the acquirer. Another defense is use of **shark repellents,** which are antitakeover amendments to the corporate charter that constrain the firm's ability to transfer managerial control of the firm as a result of a merger. Although this defense could entrench existing management, many firms have had these amendments ratified by shareholders.

Because takeover defenses tend to insulate management from shareholders, the potential for litigation is great when these strategies are employed. Lawsuits are sometimes filed against management by dissident shareholders. In addition, federal and state governments frequently intervene when a proposed takeover is deemed to be in violation of federal or state law. A number of states have legislation on their books limiting or restricting hostile takeovers of companies domiciled within their boundaries.

HOLDING COMPANIES

A *holding company* is a corporation that has voting control of one or more other corporations. The holding company may need to own only a small percentage of the outstanding shares to have this voting control. In the case of companies with a relatively small number of shareholders, as much as 30 to 40 percent of the stock may be required. In the case of firms with a widely dispersed ownership, 10 to 20 percent of the shares may be sufficient to gain voting control. A holding company that wants to obtain voting control of a firm may use direct market purchases or tender offers to acquire needed shares. Although there are relatively few holding companies and they are far less important than mergers, it is helpful to understand their key advantages and disadvantages.

Advantages of Holding Companies

The primary advantage of holding companies is the *leverage effect* that permits the firm to control a large amount of assets with a relatively small dollar investment. In other words, the owners of a holding company can *control* significantly larger amounts of assets than they could *acquire* through mergers.

Example 18.11 ▶ Carr Company, a holding company, currently holds voting control of two subsidiaries—company X and company Y. Table 18.8 presents the balance sheets for Carr and its two subsidiaries. Carr owns approximately 17% ($10 ÷ $60) of

TABLE 18.8	Balance Sheets for Carr Company and Its Subsidiaries

Assets		Liabilities and Stockholders' Equity	
Carr Company			
Common stock holdings		Long-term debt	$ 6
Company X	$ 10	Preferred stock	6
Company Y	14	Common stock equity	12
Total	$ 24	Total	$ 24
Company X			
Current assets	$ 30	Current liabilities	$ 15
Fixed assets	70	Long-term debt	25
Total	$100	Common stock equity	60
		Total	$100
Company Y			
Current assets	$ 20	Current liabilities	$ 10
Fixed assets	140	Long-term debt	60
Total	$160	Preferred stock	20
		Common stock equity	70
		Total	$160

company X and 20% ($14 ÷ $70) of company Y. These holdings are sufficient for voting control.

The owners of Carr Company's $12 worth of equity have control over $260 worth of assets (company X's $100 worth and company Y's $160 worth). Thus the owners' equity represents only about 4.6% ($12 ÷ $260) of the total assets controlled. From the discussions of ratio analysis, leverage, and capital structure in Chapters 3 and 13, you should recognize that this is quite a high degree of leverage. If an individual stockholder or even another holding company owns $3 of Carr Company's stock, which is assumed to be sufficient for its control, it will in actuality control the whole $260 of assets. The investment itself in this case would represent only 1.15% ($3 ÷ $260) of the assets controlled.

The high leverage obtained through a holding company arrangement greatly magnifies earnings and losses for the holding company. Quite often, a **pyramiding** of holding companies occurs when one holding company controls other holding companies, thereby causing an even greater magnification of earnings and losses. The greater the leverage, the greater the risk involved. The risk–return trade-off is a key consideration in the holding company decision.

Another commonly cited advantage of holding companies is the *risk protection* resulting from the fact that the failure of one of the companies (such as Y in the preceding example) does not result in the failure of the entire holding company. Because each subsidiary is a separate corporation, the failure of one company should cost the holding company, at maximum, no more than its investment in that subsidiary. Other advantages include the following: (1) Certain state *tax*

pyramiding
An arrangement among holding companies wherein one holding company controls other holding companies, thereby causing an even greater magnification of earnings and losses.

benefits may be realized by each subsidiary in its state of incorporation. (2) *Lawsuits or legal actions* against a subsidiary do not threaten the remaining companies. (3) It is *generally easy to gain control* of a firm, because stockholder or management approval is not generally necessary.

Disadvantages of Holding Companies

A major disadvantage of holding companies is the *increased risk* resulting from the leverage effect. When general economic conditions are unfavorable, a loss by one subsidiary may be magnified. For example, if subsidiary company X in Table 18.8 experiences a loss, its inability to pay dividends to Carr Company could result in Carr Company's inability to meet its scheduled payments.

Another disadvantage is *double taxation*. Before paying dividends, a subsidiary must pay federal and state taxes on its earnings. Although a 70 percent tax exclusion is allowed on dividends received by one corporation from another, the remaining 30 percent received is taxable. (In the event that the holding company owns between 20 and 80 percent of the stock in a subsidiary, the exclusion is 80 percent; if it owns more than 80 percent of the stock in the subsidiary, 100 percent of the dividends are excluded.) If a subsidiary were part of a merged company, double taxation would *not* exist.

The fact that holding companies are *difficult to analyze* is another disadvantage. Security analysts and investors typically have difficulty understanding holding companies because of their complexity. As a result, these firms tend to sell at low multiples of earnings (P/Es), and the shareholder value of holding companies may suffer.

A final disadvantage of holding companies is the generally *high cost of administration* that results from maintaining each subsidiary company as a separate entity. A merger, on the other hand, is likely to result in certain administrative economies of scale. The need for coordination and communication between the holding company and its subsidiaries may further elevate these costs.

INTERNATIONAL MERGERS

Perhaps in no other area does U.S. financial practice differ more fundamentally from practices in other countries than in the field of mergers. Outside of the United States (and, to a lesser degree, Great Britain), hostile takeovers are virtually nonexistent, and in some countries (such as Japan), takeovers of any kind are uncommon. The emphasis in the United States and Great Britain on shareholder value and reliance on public capital markets for financing is generally not shared by companies in continental Europe. This is because companies there are generally smaller and because other stakeholders, such as employees, bankers, and governments, are accorded greater consideration. The U.S. approach is also not the norm in Japan and other Asian nations.

Changes in Western Europe

Today, there are signs that Western Europe is moving toward a U.S.-style approach to shareholder value and public capital market financing. Since the European Union's (EU's) economic and monetary union (EMU) integration involving the introduction of a single European currency, the euro, on January 1, 2002, the number, size, and importance of cross-border European mergers has continued to grow rapidly. Nationally focused companies want to achieve economies of scale in manufacturing, encourage international product development strategies, and develop distribution networks across the continent. They are also driven by the need to compete with U.S. companies, which have been operating on a continent-wide basis in Europe for decades.

These larger Europe-based companies are expected to become even more formidable competitors as more national barriers are removed. Although the vast majority of these cross-border mergers are friendly in nature, a few have been actively resisted by target firm managements. It seems clear that as European companies come to rely more on public capital markets for financing, and as the market for common stock becomes more truly European in character, rather than French or British or German, active markets for European corporate equity will continue to evolve.

Foreign Takeovers of U.S. Companies

Both European and Japanese companies have been active as acquirers of U.S. companies in recent years. Foreign companies purchased U.S. firms for two major reasons: to gain access to the world's single largest, richest, and least regulated market and to acquire world-class technology. British companies have been historically the most active acquirers of U.S. firms. In the late 1980s, Japanese corporations surged to prominence with a series of very large acquisitions, including two in the entertainment industry: Sony's purchase of Columbia Pictures and Matsushita's acquisition of MCA. More recently, German firms have become especially active acquirers of U.S. companies as producing export goods in Germany has become prohibitively expensive. (German workers have some of the world's highest wages and one of the shortest workweeks.) The *Global Focus* box describes recent mergers by Australian media giant News Corp. It seems inevitable that, in the years ahead, foreign companies will continue to acquire U.S. firms even as U.S. companies continue to seek attractive acquisitions abroad.

↱ REVIEW QUESTIONS

18–6 Describe the procedures that are typically used by an acquirer to value a target company, whether it is being acquired for its assets or as a going concern.

18–7 What is the *ratio of exchange?* Is it based on the current market prices of the shares of the acquiring and target firms? Why may a long-run view of the merged firm's earnings per share change a merger decision?

18–8 What role do *investment bankers* often play in the merger negotiation process? What is a *tender offer?* When and how is it used?

18–9 Briefly describe each of the following *takeover defenses* against a hostile merger: (**a**) white knight, (**b**) poison pill, (**c**) greenmail, (**d**) leveraged recapitalization, (**e**) golden parachutes, and (**f**) shark repellents.

18–10 What key advantages and disadvantages are associated with holding companies? What is *pyramiding* and what are its consequences?

18–11 Discuss the differences in merger practices between U.S. companies and companies in other countries. What changes are occurring in international merger activity, particularly in Western Europe and Japan?

GLOBAL focus

International Mergers

in practice In July 2005, Australian-based media giant News Corp launched a series of acquisitions involving U.S. assets. The first was a $580 million buyout of Intermix Media, owner of Myspace.com, the fifth most viewed Internet domain in the United States at the time. Rupert Murdoch, the media mogul running News Corp, calculated that the Myspace networking site would drive traffic to his Fox TV sites.

Murdoch's next purchase came in September 2006, when News Corp acquired, from Verisign, a majority stake in Jamba, which runs Jamster, a download service for such commodities as ring tones and screen "wallpapers." News Corp's intent was to hardwire Fox's presence in the entire content lifecycle, from creation, through production, to delivery on your cell phone screen. It already had a mobile content provider, Mobizzo, launched in June 2005 under the Fox Mobile Entertainment division. Among the things Mobizzo was designed to offer were 1-minute episodes derived from Fox properties such as its *American Idol* franchise.

In May 2007, News Corp set its sight on a new target, Dow Jones, publisher of *The Wall Street Journal* and *Barron's* and the owner of other financial news and content assets including the Dow Jones Newswires, the financial website MarketWatch, and several stock market indicators (for example, the Dow Jones Industrial Average). Murdoch's News Corp bid $5 billion for Dow Jones but faced resistance from members of the Bancroft family—descendents of Clarence Barron, the "father of financial journalism"—which controls more than 50 percent of the voting power in the company. The News Corp bid was remarkable for its premium, which would value Dow Jones at more than double its trading value prior to the bid.

International mergers, such as the ones pursued by News Corp, are not as easy to execute as domestic mergers. Complicating matters are multiple legal and regulatory regimes, cultural differences, and complex timing requirements involving simultaneously closing the deal in multiple jurisdictions. Further complications may arise from a potential distrust of employees or owners from another country. In the Dow Jones case, the Dow Jones board and the Bancroft family sought to negotiate some level of independence for the *Journal* so that it may remain free of corporate interference.

Ultimately, Rupert Murdoch would have his way. On December 13, 2007, News Corp announced the completion of its acquisition of Dow Jones. The terms of the merger agreement provided that each share of Dow Jones common stock was entitled to receive, at the election of the holder, either $60.00 in cash or 2.8681 share of Class B common units of Ruby Newco LLC, a wholly owned subsidiary of News Corp. Ruby Newco Class B common units are convertible after a period of time into a share of News Corp Class A common stock. On completion of the merger, Dow Jones became a wholly owned subsidiary of Ruby Newco and Natalie Bancroft was appointed to the Company's Board of Directors.

▶ *If you had been a shareholder of Dow Jones, what trade-offs would you have considered when deciding whether to take the $60.00 per share or the shares in Ruby Newco?*

LG 5 ## 18.4 Business Failure Fundamentals

A business failure is an unfortunate circumstance. Although the majority of firms that fail do so within the first year or two of life, other firms grow, mature, and fail much later. The failure of a business can be viewed in a number of ways and can result from one or more causes.

TYPES OF BUSINESS FAILURE

A firm may fail because its *returns are negative or low*. A firm that consistently reports operating losses will probably experience a decline in market value. If the firm fails to earn a return that is greater than its cost of capital, it can be viewed as having failed. Negative or low returns, unless remedied, are likely to result eventually in one of the following more serious types of failure.

insolvency
Business failure that occurs when a firm is unable to pay its liabilities as they come due.

A second type of failure, **insolvency,** occurs when a firm is unable to pay its liabilities as they come due. When a firm is insolvent, its assets are still greater than its liabilities, but it is confronted with a *liquidity crisis.* If some of its assets can be converted into cash within a reasonable period, the company may be able to escape complete failure. If not, the result is the third and most serious type of failure, bankruptcy.

bankruptcy
Business failure that occurs when the stated value of a firm's liabilities exceeds the fair market value of its assets.

Bankruptcy occurs when the stated value of a firm's liabilities exceeds the fair market value of its assets. A bankrupt firm has a *negative* stockholders' equity.[4] This means that the claims of creditors cannot be satisfied unless the firm's assets can be liquidated for more than their book value. Although bankruptcy is an obvious form of failure, *the courts treat insolvency and bankruptcy in the same way.* They are both considered to indicate the financial failure of the firm.

MAJOR CAUSES OF BUSINESS FAILURE

The primary cause of business failure is *mismanagement,* which accounts for more than 50 percent of all cases. Numerous specific managerial faults can cause the firm to fail. Overexpansion, poor financial actions, an ineffective sales force, and high production costs can all singly or in combination cause failure. For example, *poor financial actions* include bad capital budgeting decisions (based on unrealistic sales and cost forecasts, failure to identify all relevant cash flows, or failure to assess risk properly), poor financial evaluation of the firm's strategic plans prior to making financial commitments, inadequate or nonexistent cash flow planning, and failure to control receivables and inventories. Because all major corporate decisions are eventually measured in terms of dollars, the financial manager may play a key role in avoiding or causing a business failure. It is his or her duty to monitor the firm's financial pulse. For example, Enron Corporation's early 2002 bankruptcy (the largest ever) was attributed mainly to questionable partnerships set up by Enron's CFO, Andrew Fastow. Those partnerships were intended to hide Enron's debt, inflate its profits, and enrich its top management. In late 2001, these transactions lost large amounts of money, causing the corporation to file bankruptcy and resulting in criminal charges against Enron's key executives as well as its auditor, Arthur Andersen, which failed to accurately disclose Enron's financial condition.

Economic activity—especially economic downturns—can contribute to the failure of a firm.[5] If the economy goes into a recession, sales may decrease abruptly, leaving the firm with high fixed costs and insufficient revenues to cover them. Rapid rises in interest rates just prior to a recession can further contribute to cash flow problems and make it more difficult for the firm to obtain and maintain needed financing.

A final cause of business failure is *corporate maturity.* Firms, like individuals, do not have infinite lives. Like a product, a firm goes through the stages of birth,

---

4. Because on a balance sheet the firm's assets equal the sum of its liabilities and stockholders' equity, the only way a firm that has more liabilities than assets can balance its balance sheet is to have a *negative* stockholders' equity.

5. The success of some firms runs countercyclical to economic activity, and other firms are unaffected by economic activity. For example, the auto repair business is likely to grow during a recession because people are less likely to buy new cars and therefore need more repairs on their unwarrantied older cars. The sales of boats and other luxury items may decline during a recession, whereas sales of staple items such as electricity are likely to be unaffected. In terms of beta—the measure of nondiversifiable risk developed in Chapter 8—a negative-beta stock would be associated with a firm whose behavior is generally countercyclical to economic activity.

---

focus on **ETHICS**

Too Big to Fail?

in practice Some see proof of the global financial crisis in the fact that even the surplus economies were not immune from its impact. This argument does not hold in the case of Kuwait, where only seven local conventional banks, three Islamic banks, and ten branches of foreign banks operate in the country. According to the Kuwait Institute of Banking Studies, the banking sector was the only profitable business sector in Kuwait during the financial year of 2009.

The Kuwaiti banking sector extended credit policy beyond the repayment ability of the borrower. Consumer loans backed by the borrower's income exceeded the credit limits, while the majority of corporate loans were backed by collaterals of real estate properties or portfolios of securities. This caused 10.96 percent

of all conventional bank loans to become nonperforming loans in 2009. The off balance sheet items counted for 42 percent of conventional banks' total assets over the 2006 to 2009 period, reaching $48,568 million at the end of 2007. The nature of Kuwaiti banks and the global financial crisis, which began in 2007, forced Gulf Bank, Kuwait's second-largest conventional bank, to suffer falling profits due to bad debt and the impact of weak risk management.

In October 2008, Gulf Bank experienced substantial losses on currency derivative contracts, entered on behalf of certain clients, due to sharp adverse movements in the exchange rates of certain foreign currencies and interest rates. Gulf Bank closed all its open derivative positions with counterparties carrying all the loss. To settle its obligations, Gulf

Bank received financial support from the Central Bank of Kuwait (CBK) of approximately $1,500 million at a nominal interest rate of 0.5 percent. This left the bank with $746 million of total loss. Most Gulf Bank depositors panicked and demanded their money, which forced the CBK to guarantee all deposits. The following day, the CBK suspended Gulf Bank's shares from being traded in the stock exchange. Later, CBK proposed a bill to parliament to guarantee all deposits in Kuwaiti banks.

▶ *Who benefited and who lost when the Gulf Bank became "too big to fail"?*

▶ *Explain the responsibilities and rules of each party: clients, banks, central bank, or/and the capital market regulators of this case.*

---

growth, maturity, and eventual decline. The firm's management should attempt to prolong the growth stage through research, new products, and mergers. Once the firm has matured and has begun to decline, it should seek to be acquired by another firm or liquidate before it fails. Effective management planning should help the firm to postpone decline and ultimate failure.

VOLUNTARY SETTLEMENTS

voluntary settlement

An arrangement between an insolvent or bankrupt firm and its creditors enabling it to bypass many of the costs involved in legal bankruptcy proceedings.

When a firm becomes insolvent or bankrupt, it may arrange with its creditors a **voluntary settlement,** which enables it to bypass many of the costs involved in legal bankruptcy proceedings. The settlement is normally initiated by the debtor firm, because such an arrangement may enable it to continue to exist or to be liquidated in a manner that gives the owners the greatest chance of recovering part of their investment. The debtor arranges a meeting between itself and all its creditors. At the meeting, a committee of creditors is selected to analyze the debtor's situation and recommend a plan of action. The recommendations of the committee are discussed with both the debtor and the creditors, and a plan for sustaining or liquidating the firm is drawn up.

Voluntary Settlement to Sustain the Firm

Normally, the rationale for sustaining a firm depends on whether the firm's recovery is feasible. By sustaining the firm, the creditor can continue to receive

extension
An arrangement whereby the firm's creditors receive payment in full, although not immediately.

composition
A pro rata cash settlement of creditor claims by the debtor firm; a uniform percentage of each dollar owed is paid.

creditor control
An arrangement in which the creditor committee replaces the firm's operating management and operates the firm until all claims have been settled.

business from it. A number of strategies are commonly used. An **extension** is an arrangement whereby the firm's creditors receive payment in full, although not immediately. Normally, when creditors grant an extension, they require the firm to make cash payments for purchases until all past debts have been paid. A second arrangement, called **composition,** is a pro rata cash settlement of creditor claims. Instead of receiving full payment of their claims, creditors receive only a partial payment. A uniform percentage of each dollar owed is paid in satisfaction of each creditor's claim.

A third arrangement is **creditor control.** In this case, the creditor committee may decide that maintaining the firm is feasible only if the operating management is replaced. The committee may then take control of the firm and operate it until all claims have been settled. Sometimes, a plan involving some combination of extension, composition, and creditor control will result. An example of this is a settlement whereby the debtor agrees to pay a total of 75 cents on the dollar in three annual installments of 25 cents on the dollar, and the creditors agree to sell additional merchandise to the firm on 30-day terms if the existing management is replaced by new management that is acceptable to them.

Voluntary Settlement Resulting in Liquidation

After the situation of the firm has been investigated by the creditor committee, the only acceptable course of action may be liquidation of the firm. Liquidation can be carried out in two ways—privately or through the legal procedures provided by bankruptcy law. If the debtor firm is willing to accept liquidation, legal procedures may not be required. Generally, the avoidance of litigation enables the creditors to obtain *quicker* and *higher* settlements. However, all the creditors must agree to a private liquidation for it to be feasible.

The objective of the voluntary liquidation process is to recover as much per dollar owed as possible. Under voluntary liquidation, common stockholders (the firm's true owners) cannot receive any funds until the claims of all other parties have been satisfied. A common procedure is to have a meeting of the creditors at which they make an **assignment** by passing the power to liquidate the firm's assets to an adjustment bureau, a trade association, or a third party, which is designated the *assignee.* The assignee's job is to liquidate the assets, obtaining the best price possible. The assignee is sometimes referred to as the *trustee* because it is entrusted with the title to the company's assets and the responsibility to liquidate them efficiently. Once the trustee has liquidated the assets, it distributes the recovered funds to the creditors and owners (if any funds remain for the owners). The final action in a private liquidation is for the creditors to sign a release attesting to the satisfactory settlement of their claims.

assignment
A voluntary liquidation procedure by which a firm's creditors pass the power to liquidate the firm's assets to an adjustment bureau, a trade association, or a third party, which is designated the *assignee.*

→ REVIEW QUESTIONS

18–12 What are the three types of business failure? What is the difference between *insolvency* and *bankruptcy?* What are the major causes of business failure?

18–13 Define an *extension* and a *composition,* and explain how they might be combined to form a voluntary settlement plan to sustain the firm. How is a voluntary settlement resulting in liquidation handled?

LG 6 **18.5** Reorganization and Liquidation in Bankruptcy

If a voluntary settlement for a failed firm cannot be agreed on, the firm can be forced into bankruptcy by its creditors. As a result of bankruptcy proceedings, the firm may be either reorganized or liquidated. Although firms of all sizes go bankrupt, it is usually the larger firms that are most recognizable. The following *Matter of Fact* box lists ten of the largest U.S. bankruptcies.

Matter of fact

Ten Largest U.S. Bankruptcies

Company	Bankruptcy date	Total assets pre-bankruptcy ($ billions)
Lehman Brothers Holdings, Inc.	Sept. 15, 2008	$691.0
Washington Mutual	Sept. 26, 2008	327.9
Worldcom, Inc.	July 21, 2002	103.9
General Motors	June 1, 2009	91.0
CIT Group	Nov. 1, 2009	71.0
Enron Corp.	Dec. 2, 2001	65.5
Conseco, Inc.	Dec. 17, 2002	61.0
Chrysler	April 30, 2009	39.0
Thornburg Mortgage	May 1, 2009	36.5
Pacific Gas and Electric Co.	April 6, 2001	36.0

BANKRUPTCY LEGISLATION

Bankruptcy Reform Act of 1978
The governing bankruptcy legislation in the United States today.

Chapter 7
The portion of the *Bankruptcy Reform Act of 1978* that details the procedures to be followed when liquidating a failed firm.

Chapter 11
The portion of the *Bankruptcy Reform Act of 1978* that outlines the procedures for reorganizing a failed (or failing) firm, whether its petition is filed voluntarily or involuntarily.

Bankruptcy in the legal sense occurs when the firm cannot pay its bills or when its liabilities exceed the fair market value of its assets. In either case, a firm may be declared legally bankrupt. However, creditors generally attempt to avoid forcing a firm into bankruptcy if it appears to have opportunities for future success.

The governing bankruptcy legislation in the United States today is the **Bankruptcy Reform Act of 1978,** which significantly modified earlier bankruptcy legislation. This law contains eight odd-numbered chapters (1 through 15) and one even-numbered chapter (12). A number of these chapters would apply in the instance of failure; the two key ones are Chapters 7 and 11. **Chapter 7** of the Bankruptcy Reform Act of 1978 details the procedures to be followed when liquidating a failed firm. Chapter 7 typically comes into play once it has been determined that a fair, equitable, and feasible basis for the reorganization of a failed firm does not exist (although a firm may of its own accord choose not to reorganize and may instead go directly into liquidation). **Chapter 11** outlines the procedures for reorganizing a failed (or failing) firm, whether its petition is filed voluntarily or involuntarily. If a workable plan for reorganization cannot be developed, the firm will be liquidated under Chapter 7.

REORGANIZATION IN BANKRUPTCY (CHAPTER 11)

voluntary reorganization
A petition filed by a failed firm on its own behalf for reorganizing its structure and paying its creditors.

involuntary reorganization
A petition initiated by an outside party, usually a creditor, for the reorganization and payment of creditors of a failed firm.

There are two basic types of reorganization petitions—voluntary and involuntary. Any firm that is not a municipal or financial institution can file a petition for **voluntary reorganization** on its own behalf.[6] **Involuntary reorganization** is initiated by an outside party, usually a creditor. An involuntary petition against a firm can be filed if one of three conditions is met:

1. The firm has past-due debts of $5,000 or more.
2. Three or more creditors can prove that they have aggregate unpaid claims of $5,000 against the firm. If the firm has fewer than 12 creditors, any creditor that is owed more than $5,000 can file the petition.
3. The firm is *insolvent,* which means that (a) it is not paying its debts as they come due, (b) within the preceding 120 days a custodian (a third party) was appointed or took possession of the debtor's property, or (c) the fair market value of the firm's assets is less than the stated value of its liabilities.

Procedures

debtor in possession (DIP)
The term for a firm that files a reorganization petition under Chapter 11 and then develops, if feasible, a reorganization plan.

A reorganization petition under Chapter 11 must be filed in a federal bankruptcy court. On the filing of this petition, the filing firm becomes the **debtor in possession** (**DIP**) of the assets. If creditors object to the filing firm being the debtor in possession, they can ask the judge to appoint a trustee. After reviewing the firm's situation, the debtor in possession submits a plan of reorganization and a disclosure statement summarizing the plan to the court. A hearing is held to determine whether the plan is *fair, equitable,* and *feasible* and whether the disclosure statement contains adequate information. The court's approval or disapproval is based on its evaluation of the plan in light of these standards. A plan is considered *fair and equitable* if it *maintains the priorities* of the contractual claims of the creditors, preferred stockholders, and common stockholders. The court must also find the reorganization plan *feasible,* which means that it must be *workable.* The reorganized corporation must have sufficient working capital, enough funds to cover fixed charges, adequate credit prospects, and the ability to retire or refund debts as proposed by the plan.

Once approved, the plan and the disclosure statement are given to the firm's creditors and shareholders for their acceptance. Under the Bankruptcy Reform Act, creditors and owners are separated into groups with similar types of claims. In the case of creditor groups, approval of the plan is required by holders of at least two-thirds of the dollar amount of claims, as well as by a numerical majority of creditors. In the case of ownership groups (preferred and common stockholders), two-thirds of the shares in each group must approve the reorganization plan for it to be accepted. Once accepted and confirmed by the court, the plan is put into effect as soon as possible.

Personal Finance Example 18.12 ▶   Individuals, like corporations, sometimes fail financially. Typically, a lack of financial planning, a heavy debt load, or an economic recession are factors that cause debtors to start missing payments and

---

6. Firms sometimes file a voluntary petition to obtain temporary legal protection from creditors or from prolonged litigation. Once they have straightened out their financial or legal affairs—prior to further reorganization or liquidation actions—they will have the petition dismissed. Although such actions are not the intent of the bankruptcy law, difficulty in enforcing the law has allowed this abuse to occur.

experiencing deterioration in their credit ratings. Unless they take corrective action, repossession of debt-financed property and eventually personal bankruptcy will follow. Individuals in dire financial straits have two legal options: a wage earner plan or straight bankruptcy.

A *wage earner plan,* defined under *Chapter 13* of the U.S. Bankruptcy Code, is a "work-out" procedure that involves some type of debt restructuring— typically establishing a debt-repayment schedule that is workable in light of the individual's personal income. This is similar to *reorganization* in a corporate bankruptcy. A majority of creditors must agree to this plan, under which interest payments and late fees are waived during the repayment period. If approved, the individual, who retains the use of and title to all assets, makes payments to the court, which then pays off all creditors.

Straight bankruptcy is allowed under *Chapter 7* of the bankruptcy code. It is a legal procedure, similar to *liquidation* in corporate bankruptcy, that effectively allows the debtor to "wipe the slate clean and start anew." However straight bankruptcy does not eliminate all of a debtor's obligations, nor does the debtor lose all of his or her assets. For example, the debtor must make certain tax payments and keep up alimony and child-support payments but can retain certain payments from Social Security, retirement, and disability benefits. Depending on state law, the debtor can retain a certain amount of equity in a home, a car, and other assets.

Role of the Debtor in Possession (DIP)

Because reorganization activities are largely in the hands of the debtor in possession (DIP), it is useful to understand the DIP's responsibilities. The DIP's first responsibility is the valuation of the firm to determine whether reorganization is appropriate. To do this, the DIP must estimate both the *liquidation value* of the business and its value as a *going concern.* If the firm's value as a going concern is less than its liquidation value, the DIP will recommend liquidation. If the opposite is found to be true, the DIP will recommend reorganization, and a plan of reorganization must be drawn up.

The key portion of the reorganization plan generally concerns the firm's capital structure. Because most firms' financial difficulties result from high fixed charges, the company's capital structure is generally *recapitalized* to reduce these charges. Under **recapitalization,** debts are generally exchanged for equity or the maturities of existing debts are extended. When recapitalizing the firm, the DIP seeks to build a mix of debt and equity that will allow the firm to meet its debts and provide a reasonable level of earnings for its owners.

recapitalization
The reorganization procedure under which a failed firm's debts are generally exchanged for equity or the maturities of existing debts are extended.

Once the revised capital structure has been determined, the DIP must establish a plan for exchanging outstanding obligations for new securities. The guiding principle is to observe priorities. Senior claims (those with higher legal priority) must be satisfied before junior claims (those with lower legal priority). To comply with this principle, senior suppliers of capital must receive a claim on new capital equal to their previous claim. The common stockholders are the last to receive any new securities. (It is not unusual for them to receive nothing.) Security holders do not necessarily have to receive the same type of security they held before; often they receive a combination of securities. Once the debtor in possession has determined the new capital structure and distribution of capital, it will submit the reorganization plan and disclosure statement to the court as described.

LIQUIDATION IN BANKRUPTCY (CHAPTER 7)

The liquidation of a bankrupt firm usually occurs once the bankruptcy court has determined that reorganization is not feasible. A petition for reorganization must normally be filed by the managers or creditors of the bankrupt firm. If no petition is filed, if a petition is filed and denied, or if the reorganization plan is denied, the firm must be liquidated.

Procedures

When a firm is adjudged bankrupt, the judge may appoint a *trustee* to perform the many routine duties required in administering the bankruptcy. The trustee takes charge of the property of the bankrupt firm and protects the interest of its creditors. A meeting of creditors must be held between 20 and 40 days after the bankruptcy judgment. At this meeting, the creditors are made aware of the prospects for the liquidation. The trustee is given the responsibility to liquidate the firm, keep records, examine creditors' claims, disburse money, furnish information as required, and make final reports on the liquidation. In essence, the trustee is responsible for the liquidation of the firm. Occasionally, the court will call subsequent creditor meetings, but only a final meeting for closing the bankruptcy is required.

Priority of Claims

secured creditors
Creditors who have specific assets pledged as collateral and, in liquidation of the failed firm, receive proceeds from the sale of those assets.

unsecured, or general, creditors
Creditors who have a general claim against all the firm's assets other than those specifically pledged as collateral.

It is the trustee's responsibility to liquidate all the firm's assets and to distribute the proceeds to the holders of *provable claims*. The courts have established certain procedures for determining the provability of claims. The priority of claims, which is specified in Chapter 7 of the Bankruptcy Reform Act, must be maintained by the trustee when distributing the funds from liquidation. Any **secured creditors** have specific assets pledged as collateral and, in liquidation, receive proceeds from the sale of those assets. If these proceeds are inadequate to fully satisfy their claims, the secured creditors become **unsecured**, or **general, creditors** for the unrecovered amount, because specific collateral no longer exists. These and all other unsecured creditors will divide up, on a pro rata basis, any funds remaining after all prior claims have been satisfied. If the proceeds from the sale of secured assets are in excess of the claims against them, the excess funds become available to meet claims of unsecured creditors.

The complete order of priority of claims is given in Table 18.9. In spite of the priorities listed in items 1 through 7, secured creditors have first claim on proceeds from the sale of their collateral. The claims of unsecured creditors, including the unpaid claims of secured creditors, are satisfied next, and then, finally, the claims of preferred and common stockholders.

Final Accounting

After the trustee has liquidated all the bankrupt firm's assets and distributed the proceeds to satisfy all provable claims in the appropriate order of priority, he or she makes a final accounting to the bankruptcy court and creditors. Once the court approves the final accounting, the liquidation is complete.

In more depth

To read about *Prioritizing Claims: Order of Priority of Claims in Liquidation,* go to www.myfinancelab.com

myfinancelab

→ **REVIEW QUESTIONS**

18–14 What is the concern of Chapter 11 of the Bankruptcy Reform Act of 1978? How is the *debtor in possession (DIP)* involved in (1) the valuation of the firm, (2) the recapitalization of the firm, and (3) the exchange of obligations using the priority rule?

TABLE 18.9	**Order of Priority of Claims in Liquidation of a Failed Firm**

1. The expenses of administering the bankruptcy proceedings.
2. Any unpaid interim expenses incurred in the ordinary course of business between filing the bankruptcy petition and formal action by the court in an involuntary proceeding. (This step is *not* applicable in a voluntary bankruptcy.)
3. Wages of not more than $4,650 per worker that have been earned by workers in the 90-day period immediately preceding the commencement of bankruptcy proceedings.
4. Unpaid employee benefit plan contributions that were to be paid in the 180-day period preceding the filing of bankruptcy or the termination of business, whichever occurred first. For any employee, the sum of this claim plus eligible unpaid wages (item 3) cannot exceed $4,650.
5. Claims of farmers or fishermen in a grain-storage or fish-storage facility, not to exceed $4,650 for each producer.
6. Unsecured customer deposits, not to exceed $2,100 each, resulting from purchasing or leasing a good or service from the failed firm.
7. Taxes legally due and owed by the bankrupt firm to the federal government, state government, or any other governmental subdivision.
8. Claims of secured creditors, who receive the proceeds from the sale of collateral held, regardless of the preceding priorities. If the proceeds from the liquidation of the collateral are insufficient to satisfy the secured creditors' claims, the secured creditors become unsecured creditors for the unpaid amount.
9. Claims of unsecured creditors. The claims of unsecured, or general, creditors and unsatisfied portions of secured creditors' claims (item 8) are all treated equally.
10. Preferred stockholders, who receive an amount up to the par, or stated, value of their preferred stock.
11. Common stockholders, who receive any remaining funds, which are distributed on an equal per-share basis. If different classes of common stock are outstanding, priorities may exist.

18–15 What is the concern of Chapter 7 of the Bankruptcy Reform Act of 1978? Under which conditions is a firm liquidated in bankruptcy? Describe the procedures (including the role of the *trustee*) involved in liquidating the bankrupt firm.

18–16 Indicate in which order the following claims would be settled when distributing the proceeds from liquidating a bankrupt firm: (**a**) claims of preferred stockholders; (**b**) claims of secured creditors; (**c**) expenses of administering the bankruptcy; (**d**) claims of common stockholders; (**e**) claims of unsecured, or general, creditors; (**f**) taxes legally due; (**g**) unsecured deposits of customers; (**h**) certain eligible wages; (**i**) unpaid employee benefit plan contributions; (**j**) unpaid interim expenses incurred between the time of filing and formal action by the court; and (**k**) claims of farmers or fishermen in a grain-storage or fish-storage facility.

Summary

FOCUS ON VALUE

The financial manager is sometimes involved in corporate restructuring activities, which involve the expansion and contraction of the firm's operations or changes in its asset or ownership structure. A variety of motives could drive a firm toward a merger, but the overriding goal should be maximization of the owners' wealth. Occasionally, merger transactions are heavily debt-financed leveraged buyouts (LBOs). In other cases, firms attempt to improve value by divesting themselves of certain operating units that they believe constrain the firm's value, particularly when the breakup value is believed to be greater than the firm's current value.

Whether the firm makes a cash purchase or uses a stock swap to acquire another firm, the risk-adjusted net present value of the transaction should be positive. In stock swap transactions, the long-run impact on the firm's earnings and risk can be evaluated to estimate the acquiring firm's postacquisition value. Only in cases where additional value is created should the transaction be undertaken.

Business failure, though unpleasant, must be treated similarly; a failing firm should be reorganized only when such an act will maximize the owners' wealth. Otherwise, liquidation should be pursued in a fashion that allows the owners the greatest amount of recovery. Regardless of whether the firm is growing, contracting, or being reorganized or liquidated in bankruptcy, the firm should take action only when that action is believed to result in a positive contribution to the **maximization of the owners' wealth.**

REVIEW OF LEARNING GOALS

LG 1   **Understand merger fundamentals, including terminology, motives for merging, and types of mergers.** Mergers result from the combining of firms. Typically, the acquiring company pursues and attempts to merge with the target company, on either a friendly or a hostile basis. Mergers are undertaken either for strategic reasons to achieve economies of scale or for financial reasons to restructure the firm to improve its cash flow. The overriding goal of merging is maximization of share price. Other specific merger motives include growth or diversification, synergy, fund raising, increased managerial skill or technology, tax considerations, increased ownership liquidity, and defense against takeover. The four basic types of mergers are horizontal, vertical, congeneric, and conglomerate.

LG 2   **Describe the objectives and procedures used in leveraged buyouts (LBOs) and divestitures.** LBOs involve use of a large amount of debt to purchase a firm. Divestiture involves the sale of a firm's assets, typically an operating unit; the spin-off of assets into an independent company; or the liquidation of assets. Motives for divestiture include cash generation and corporate restructuring.

LG 3   **Demonstrate the procedures used to value the target company, and discuss the effect of stock swap transactions on earnings per share.** The value of a target company can be estimated by applying capital budgeting techniques to the relevant cash flows. All proposed mergers with positive net present values are considered acceptable. In a stock swap transaction, a ratio of exchange must be established to measure the amount paid per share of the target company relative to the per-share market price of the acquiring firm. The resulting relationship between the price/earnings (P/E) ratio paid by the acquiring firm and its initial P/E affects the merged firm's earnings per share (EPS) and market price. If the P/E paid is greater than the P/E of the acquiring company, the EPS of the acquiring company decrease and the EPS of the target company increase.

LG 4   **Discuss the merger negotiation process, holding companies, and international mergers.** Acquirers commonly hire investment bankers to find a suitable target company and assist in negotiations. A merger can be negotiated with the target firm's management or, in the case of a hostile merger, directly with the firm's shareholders by using tender offers. Management of the target firm can employ various takeover defenses—a white knight, poison pill, greenmail, leveraged recapitalization, golden parachutes, and shark repellents. A holding company can be created by one firm gaining control of other companies, often by owning as little as 10 to 20 percent of their stock. The chief advantages of holding companies are the leverage effect, risk protection, tax benefits, protection against lawsuits, and the ease of gaining control of a subsidiary. Disadvantages include increased risk due to the magnification of losses, double taxation, difficulty of analysis, and the high cost of administration. Today, mergers of companies in Western Europe have moved toward the U.S.-style approach to shareholder value and public capital market financing. Both European and Japanese companies have become active acquirers of U.S. firms.

LG 5   **Understand the types and major causes of business failure and the use of voluntary settlements to sustain or liquidate the failed firm.** A firm may fail because it has negative or low returns, is insolvent, or is bankrupt. The major causes of business failure are mismanagement, downturns in economic activity, and corporate maturity. Voluntary settlements are initiated by the debtor and can result in sustaining the firm via an extension, a composition, creditor control of the firm, or a combination of these strategies. If creditors do not agree to a plan to sustain a firm, they may recommend voluntary liquidation, which bypasses many of the legal requirements and costs of bankruptcy proceedings.

LG 6   **Explain bankruptcy legislation and the procedures involved in reorganizing or liquidating a bankrupt firm.** A failed firm can voluntarily or involuntarily file in federal bankruptcy court for reorganization under Chapter 11 or for liquidation under Chapter 7 of the Bankruptcy Reform Act of 1978. Under Chapter 11, the judge will appoint the debtor in possession, which develops a reorganization plan. A firm that cannot be reorganized under Chapter 11 or does not petition for reorganization is liquidated under Chapter 7. The responsibility for liquidation is placed in the hands of a court-appointed trustee, whose duties include liquidating assets, distributing the proceeds, and making a final accounting. Liquidation procedures follow a priority of claims for distribution of the proceeds from the sale of assets.

Opener-in-Review

In the chapter opener you learned about the leveraged buyout of IMS Health, Inc. Although the private investors conducting the leveraged buyout, the management of IMS, and the shareholders of IMS were all in support of the deal, what significant risk is associated with an LBO transaction?

Self-Test Problems   (Solutions in Appendix)

LG 3   ST18–1   Cash acquisition decision   Luxe Foods is contemplating acquisition of Valley Canning Company for a cash price of $180,000. Luxe currently has high financial leverage and therefore has a cost of capital of 14%. As a result of acquiring Valley Canning, which is financed entirely with equity, the firm expects its financial leverage to be reduced and its cost of capital to drop to 11%. The acquisition of Valley Canning is expected to increase Luxe's cash inflows by $20,000 per year for the first 3 years and by $30,000 per year for the following 12 years.

  a. Determine whether the proposed cash acquisition is desirable. Explain your answer.

  b. If the firm's financial leverage would actually remain unchanged as a result of the proposed acquisition, would this alter your recommendation in part **a?** Support your answer with numerical data.

LG 3   ST18–2   Expected EPS—Merger decision   At the end of 2012, Lake Industries had 80,000 shares of common stock outstanding and had earnings available for common of $160,000. Butler Company, at the end of 2012, had 10,000 shares of common stock outstanding and had earned $20,000 for common shareholders. Lake's earnings are expected to grow at an annual rate of 5%, and Butler's growth rate in earnings should be 10% per year.

  a. Calculate *earnings per share (EPS)* for Lake Industries for each of the next 5 years (2013–2017), assuming that there is no merger.

  b. Calculate the next 5 years' (2013–2017) *earnings per share (EPS)* for Lake if it acquires Butler at a *ratio of exchange* of 1.1.

  c. Compare your findings in parts **a** and **b,** and explain why the merger looks attractive when viewed over the long run.

Warm-Up Exercises   All problems are available in 🔷myfinancelab.

LG 1   E18–1   Toni's Typesetters is analyzing a possible merger with Pete's Print Shop. Toni's has a tax loss carryforward of $200,000, which it could apply to Pete's expected earnings before taxes of $100,000 per year for the next 5 years. Using a 34% tax rate, compare the *earnings after taxes* for Pete's over the next 5 years both *without* and *with* the merger.

LG 3   E18–2   Cautionary Tales, Inc., is considering the acquisition of Danger Corp. at its asking price of $150,000. Cautionary would immediately sell some of Danger's assets for $15,000 if it makes the acquisition. Danger has a cash balance of $1,500 at the time of the acquisition. If Cautionary believes it can generate after-tax cash inflows of $25,000 per year for the next 7 years from the Danger acquisition, should the firm make the acquisition? Base your recommendation on the net present value of the outlay using Cautionary's 10% cost of capital.

LG 3   E18–3   Willow Enterprises is considering the acquisition of Steadfast Corp. in a stock swap transaction. Currently, Willow's stock is selling for $45 per share. Although

Steadfast's shares are currently trading at $30 per share, the firm's asking price is $60 per share.

a. If Willow accepts Steadfast's terms, what is the *ratio of exchange?*

b. If Steadfast has 15,000 shares outstanding, how many new shares must Willow issue to consummate the transaction?

c. If Willow has 110,000 shares outstanding before the acquisition, and earnings for the merged company are estimated to be $450,000, what is the *EPS* for the merged company?

LG 3   **E18–4**   Phylum Plants' stock is currently trading at a price of $55 per share. The company is considering the acquisition of Taxonomy Central, whose stock is currently trading at $20 per share. The transaction would require Phylum to swap its shares for those of Taxonomy, which would be paid $60 per share. Calculate the *ratio of exchange* and the *ratio of exchange in market price* for this transaction.

LG 4   **E18–5**   All-Stores, Inc., is a holding company that has voting control over both General Stores and Star Stores. All-Stores owns General Stores and Star Stores common stock valued at $15,000 and $12,000, respectively. General's balance sheet lists $130,000 of total assets; Star has total assets of $110,000. All-Stores has total common stock equity of $20,000.

a. What *percentage of the total assets controlled* by All-Stores does its common stock equity represent?

b. If a stockholder holds $5,000 worth of All-Stores common stock equity, and this amount gives this stockholder voting control, what *percentage of the total assets controlled* does this stockholder's equity investment represent?

Problems   All problems are available in ⓐmyfinancelab .

LG 1   LG 3   **P18–1**   **Tax effects of acquisition**   Connors Shoe Company is contemplating the acquisition of Salinas Boots, a firm that has shown large operating tax losses over the past few years. As a result of the acquisition, Connors believes that the total pretax profits of the merger will not change from their present level for 15 years. The tax loss carryforward of Salinas is $800,000, and Connors projects that its annual earnings before taxes will be $280,000 per year for each of the next 15 years. These earnings are assumed to fall within the annual limit legally allowed for application of the tax loss carryforward resulting from the proposed merger (see footnote 2 on page 719). The firm is in the 40% tax bracket.

a. If Connors does not make the acquisition, what will be the company's tax liability and earnings after taxes each year over the next 15 years?

b. If the acquisition is made, what will be the company's tax liability and earnings after taxes each year over the next 15 years?

c. If Salinas can be acquired for $350,000 in cash, should Connors make the acquisition, judging on the basis of tax considerations? (Ignore present value.)

LG 1   LG 3   **P18–2**   **Tax effects of acquisition**   Trapani Tool Company is evaluating the acquisition of Sussman Casting. Sussman has a tax loss carryforward of $1.8 million. Trapani can purchase Sussman for $2.1 million. It can sell the assets for $1.6 million—their book value. Trapani expects its earnings before taxes in the 5 years after the merger to be as shown in the following table.

Year	Earnings before taxes
1	$150,000
2	400,000
3	450,000
4	600,000
5	600,000

The expected earnings given are assumed to fall within the annual limit that is legally allowed for application of the tax loss carryforward resulting from the proposed merger (see footnote 2 on page 719). Trapani is in the 40% tax bracket.

a. Calculate the firm's tax payments and earnings after taxes for each of the next 5 years *without* the merger.

b. Calculate the firm's tax payments and earnings after taxes for each of the next 5 years *with* the merger.

c. What are the total benefits associated with the tax losses from the merger? (Ignore present value.)

d. Discuss whether you would recommend the proposed merger. Support your decision with figures.

LG 1   LG 3   P18–3   Tax benefits and price   Hahn Textiles has a tax loss carryforward of $800,000. Two firms are interested in acquiring Hahn for the tax loss advantage. Reilly Investment Group has expected earnings before taxes of $200,000 per year for each of the next 7 years and a cost of capital of 15%. Webster Industries has expected earnings before taxes for the next 7 years as shown in the following table.

	Webster Industries
Year	Earnings before taxes
1	$ 80,000
2	120,000
3	200,000
4	300,000
5	400,000
6	400,000
7	500,000

Both Reilly's and Webster's expected earnings are assumed to fall within the annual limit legally allowed for application of the tax loss carryforward resulting from the proposed merger (see footnote 2 on page 719). Webster has a cost of capital of 15%. Both firms are subject to a 40% tax rate on ordinary income.

a. What is the tax advantage of the merger each year for Reilly?

b. What is the tax advantage of the merger each year for Webster?

c. What is the maximum cash price each interested firm would be willing to pay for Hahn Textiles? (*Hint:* Calculate the present value of the tax advantages.)

d. Use your answers in parts **a** through **c** to explain why a target company can have different values to different potential acquiring firms.

LG 3 **P18–4** **Asset acquisition decision** Zarin Printing Company is considering the acquisition of Freiman Press at a cash price of $60,000. Freiman Press has liabilities of $90,000. Freiman has a large press that Zarin needs; the remaining assets would be sold to net $65,000. As a result of acquiring the press, Zarin would experience an increase in cash inflow of $20,000 per year over the next 10 years. The firm has a 14% cost of capital.

a. What is the *effective or net cost* of the large press?

b. If this is the only way Zarin can obtain the large press, should the firm go ahead with the merger? Explain your answer.

c. If the firm could purchase a press that would provide slightly better quality and $26,000 annual cash inflow for 10 years for a price of $120,000, which alternative would you recommend? Explain your answer.

LG 3 **P18–5** **Cash acquisition decision** Benson Oil is being considered for acquisition by Dodd Oil. The combination, Dodd believes, would increase its cash inflows by $25,000 for each of the next 5 years and by $50,000 for each of the following 5 years. Benson has high financial leverage, and Dodd can expect its cost of capital to increase from 12% to 15% if the merger is undertaken. The cash price of Benson is $125,000.

a. Would you recommend the merger?

b. Would you recommend the merger if Dodd could use the $125,000 to purchase equipment that will return cash inflows of $40,000 per year for each of the next 10 years?

c. If the cost of capital did not change with the merger, would your decision in part **b** be different? Explain.

Personal Finance Problem

LG 3 **P18–6** **Divestitures** In corporate settings, it is not unusual for firms to assess the financial viability of a business unit and decide whether to retain it within the corporation or divest it. The selling of units that do not seem to "fit" should bring about greater synergy for the firm. This same logic can be applied in a personal finance situation as well. An important question that comes up for families with two working parents and young children is whether one of the working adults should stay at home or whether the family should use day-care services.

Assume that Ted and Maggie Smith have two young children who need child-care services. Currently, Maggie is a stay-at-home mother but could go back to her former job as a marketing analyst. She estimates that she could earn $3,800 per month gross, including her employer's 401(k) contributions. She will receive monthly employer-paid benefits that include health insurance, life insurance, and pension contributions totaling $1,200.

Maggie expects her federal and state income taxes to total about $1,300 per month. The Smiths have calculated that total additional expenses such as child care, clothing, personal expenses, meals away from home, and transportation related to Maggie's job could total $1,400 per month.

Does it make economic sense for the Smiths to hire child care and have Maggie return to work? To answer this question, calculate the net income or loss from her possible return to work.

LG 3 **P18–7** **Ratio of exchange and EPS** Marla's Cafe is attempting to acquire the Victory Club. Certain financial data on these corporations are summarized in the following table.

Item	Marla's Cafe	Victory Club
Earnings available for common stock	$20,000	$8,000
Number of shares of common stock outstanding	20,000	4,000
Market price per share	$12	$24

Marla's Cafe has sufficient authorized but unissued shares to carry out the proposed merger.

a. If the *ratio of exchange* is 1.8, what will be the earnings per share (EPS) based on the original shares of each firm?
b. Repeat part **a** if the *ratio of exchange* is 2.0.
c. Repeat part **a** if the *ratio of exchange* is 2.2.
d. Discuss the principle illustrated by your answers to parts **a** through **c**.

LG 3 **P18–8** **EPS and merger terms** Cleveland Corporation is interested in acquiring Lewis Tool Company by swapping 0.4 share of its stock for each share of Lewis stock. Certain financial data on these companies are given in the following table.

Item	Cleveland Corporation	Lewis Tool
Earnings available for common stock	$200,000	$50,000
Number of shares of common stock outstanding	50,000	20,000
Earnings per share (EPS)	$4.00	$2.50
Market price per share	$50.00	$15.00
Price/earnings (P/E) ratio	12.5	6

Cleveland has sufficient authorized but unissued shares to carry out the proposed merger.

a. How many new shares of stock will Cleveland have to issue to make the proposed merger?
b. If the earnings for each firm remain unchanged, what will the *postmerger earnings per share* be?
c. How much, effectively, has been earned on behalf of each of the original shares of Lewis stock?
d. How much, effectively, has been earned on behalf of each of the original shares of Cleveland Corporation's stock?

LG 3 **P18–9** **Ratio of exchange** Calculate the *ratio of exchange* (1) of shares and (2) in market price for each of the cases shown in the following table. What does each ratio signify? Explain.

	Current market price per share		
Case	Acquiring company	Target company	Price per share offered
A	$50	$25	$ 30.00
B	80	80	100.00
C	40	60	70.00
D	50	10	12.50
E	25	20	25.00

LG 3 **P18–10** **Expected EPS—Merger decision** Graham & Sons wishes to evaluate a proposed merger into the RCN Group. Graham had 2012 earnings of $200,000, has 100,000 shares of common stock outstanding, and expects earnings to grow at an annual rate of 7%. RCN had 2012 earnings of $800,000, has 200,000 shares of common stock outstanding, and expects its earnings to grow at 3% per year.

a. Calculate the *expected earnings per share (EPS)* for Graham & Sons for each of the next 5 years (2013–2017) *without* the merger.

b. What would Graham's stockholders earn in each of the next 5 years (2013–2017) on each of their Graham shares swapped for RCN shares at a ratio of (1) 0.6 and (2) 0.8 share of RCN for 1 share of Graham?

c. Graph the premerger and postmerger EPS figures developed in parts **a** and **b** with the year on the x axis and the EPS on the y axis.

d. If you were the financial manager for Graham & Sons, which would you recommend from part **b,** (1) or (2)? Explain your answer.

LG 3 **P18–11** **EPS and postmerger price** Data for Henry Company and Mayer Services are given in the following table. Henry Company is considering merging with Mayer by swapping 1.25 shares of its stock for each share of Mayer stock. Henry Company expects its stock to sell at the same price/earnings (P/E) multiple after the merger as before merging.

Item	Henry Company	Mayer Services
Earnings available for common stock	$225,000	$50,000
Number of shares of common stock outstanding	90,000	15,000
Market price per share	$45	$50

a. Calculate the *ratio of exchange* in market price.

b. Calculate the earnings per share (EPS) and price/earnings (P/E) ratio for each company.

c. Calculate the price/earnings (P/E) ratio used to purchase Mayer Services.

d. Calculate the *postmerger earnings per share (EPS)* for Henry Company.

e. Calculate the expected market price per share of the merged firm. Discuss this result in light of your findings in part **a.**

LG 4 **P18–12** **Holding company** Scully Corporation holds enough stock in company A and company B to give it voting control of both firms. Consider the accompanying simplified balance sheets for these companies.

Assets		Liabilities and Stockholders' Equity	
Scully Corporation			
Common stock holdings		Long-term debt	$ 40,000
Company A	$ 40,000	Preferred stock	25,000
Company B	60,000	Common stock equity	35,000
Total	$100,000	Total	$100,000
Company A			
Current assets	$100,000	Current liabilities	$100,000
Fixed assets	400,000	Long-term debt	200,000
Total	$500,000	Common stock equity	200,000
		Total	$500,000
Company B			
Current assets	$180,000	Current liabilities	$100,000
Fixed assets	720,000	Long-term debt	500,000
Total	$900,000	Common stock equity	300,000
		Total	$900,000

a. What *percentage of the total assets controlled* by Scully Corporation does its common stock equity represent?

b. If another company owns 15% of the common stock of Scully Corporation and, by virtue of this fact, has voting control, what *percentage of the total assets controlled* does the outside company's equity represent?

c. How does a holding company effectively provide a great deal of control for a small dollar investment?

d. Answer parts **a** and **b** in light of the following additional facts.
   (1) Company A's fixed assets consist of $20,000 of common stock in Company C. This level of ownership provides voting control.
   (2) Company C's total assets of $400,000 include $15,000 of stock in Company D, which gives Company C voting control over Company D's $50,000 of total assets.
   (3) Company B's fixed assets consist of $60,000 of stock in both Company E and Company F. In both cases, this level of ownership gives it voting control. Companies E and F have total assets of $300,000 and $400,000, respectively.

LG 5   **P18–13**   **Voluntary settlements**   Classify each of the following voluntary settlements as an extension, a composition, or a combination of the two.

a. Paying all creditors 30 cents on the dollar in exchange for complete discharge of the debt.

b. Paying all creditors in full in three periodic installments.

c. Paying a group of creditors with claims of $10,000 in full over 2 years and immediately paying the remaining creditors 75 cents on the dollar.

LG 5   **P18–14**   **Voluntary settlements**   For a firm with outstanding debt of $125,000, classify each of the following voluntary settlements as an extension, a composition, or a combination of the two.

a. Paying a group of creditors in full in four periodic installments and paying the remaining creditors in full immediately.

b. Paying a group of creditors 90 cents on the dollar immediately and paying the remaining creditors 80 cents on the dollar in two periodic installments.

c. Paying all creditors 15 cents on the dollar.

d. Paying all creditors in full in 180 days.

LG 5   **P18–15**   **Voluntary settlements—Payments**   Jacobi Supply Company recently ran into certain financial difficulties that have resulted in the initiation of voluntary settlement procedures. The firm currently has $150,000 in outstanding debts and approximately $75,000 in liquidatable short-term assets. Indicate, for each of the following plans, whether the plan is an extension, a composition, or a combination of the two. Also indicate the cash payments and timing of the payments required of the firm under each plan.

a. Each creditor will be paid 50 cents on the dollar immediately, and the debts will be considered fully satisfied.

b. Each creditor will be paid 80 cents on the dollar in two quarterly installments of 50 cents and 30 cents. The first installment is to be paid in 90 days.

c. Each creditor will be paid the full amount of its claims in three installments of 50 cents, 25 cents, and 25 cents on the dollar. The installments will be made in 60-day intervals, beginning in 60 days.

d. A group of creditors with claims of $50,000 will be immediately paid in full; the rest will be paid 85 cents on the dollar, payable in 90 days.

Personal Finance Problem

LG 5   **P18–16**   **Bankruptcy legislation—wage-earner plan**   Jon Morgan is in a financial position where he owes more than he earns each month. Due to his lack of financial planning and a heavy debt load, Jon started missing payments and saw his credit rating plunge. Unless corrective action is taken, personal bankruptcy will follow.

Jon recently contacted his lawyer in order to set up a *wage earner plan* with his creditors and establish a debt repayment schedule that is workable in light of his personal income. His creditors have all agreed to a plan under which interest payments and late fees will be waived during the repayment period. The process would have Jon make payments to the court, which then will pay off his creditors.

Jon has outstanding debt of $28,000. His creditors have set a repayment period of 4 years during which monthly principal payments are required. They have waived all interest charges and late fees. Jon's yearly take-home income is $30,600.

a. Calculate the monthly debt repayment amount.

b. Determine how much excess income Jon will have each month after making these payments.

LG 5   **LG 6**   **P18–17**   **ETHICS PROBLEM**   Why might employees and suppliers support management in a Chapter 11 bankruptcy declaration if they will have to wait to be paid, and may never get paid? How can a CEO act ethically toward these two groups of stakeholders in the time before, during, and after the bankruptcy period?

Spreadsheet Exercise

Ram Electric Company is being considered for acquisition by Cavalier Electric. Cavalier expects the combination to increase its cash flows by $100,000 for each of the next 5 years and by $125,000 for each of the following 5 years. Ram Electric has relatively high financial leverage; Cavalier expects its cost of capital to be 12% for the first 5 years and estimates that it will increase to 16% for the following 5 years if the merger is undertaken. The cash price of Ram Electric is $325,000.

TO DO

Create a spreadsheet similar to Table 18.3 to answer the following questions.

  a. Determine the *present value of the expected future cash inflows* over the next 10 years.

  b. Calculate the *net present value (NPV)* for the Ram Electric acquisition.

  c. All else being equal, would you recommend the acquisition of Ram Electric by Cavalier Electric? Explain.

 Visit www.myfinancelab.com for **Chapter Case: *Deciding Whether to Acquire or Liquidate Procras Corporation,*** Group Exercises, and numerous online resources.

19 International Managerial Finance

Learning Goals

LG 1 Understand the major factors that influence the financial operations of multinational companies (MNCs).

LG 2 Describe the key differences between purely domestic and international financial statements—consolidation, translation of individual accounts, and international profits.

LG 3 Discuss exchange rate risk and political risk, and explain how MNCs manage them.

LG 4 Describe foreign direct investment, investment cash flows and decisions, the MNCs' capital structure, and the international debt and equity instruments available to MNCs.

LG 5 Discuss the role of the Eurocurrency market in short-term borrowing and investing (lending) and the basics of international cash, credit, and inventory management.

LG 6 Review recent trends in international mergers and joint ventures.

Why This Chapter Matters to You

In your *professional* life

ACCOUNTING You need to understand the tax rules for multinational companies, how to prepare consolidated financial statements for subsidiary companies, and how to account for international items in financial statements.

INFORMATION SYSTEMS You need to understand that if the firm undertakes foreign operations, it will need systems that track investments and operations in another currency and their fluctuations against the domestic currency.

MANAGEMENT You need to understand both the opportunities and the risks involved in international operations, the possible role of international financial markets in raising capital, and the basic hedging strategies that multinational companies can use to protect themselves against exchange rate risk.

MARKETING You need to understand the potential for expanding into international markets and the ways of doing so (exports, foreign direct investment, mergers, and joint ventures); also, you should know how investment cash flows in foreign projects will be measured.

OPERATIONS You need to understand the costs and benefits of moving operations offshore and/or buying equipment, parts, and inventory in foreign markets. Such an understanding will allow you to participate in the firm's decisions with regard to international operations.

In your *personal* life
Your direct involvement in the global marketplace is most likely to result from expenditures made during foreign travel. In addition, you may invest directly or indirectly (via mutual funds) in the stocks of foreign companies. Probably the greatest personal benefit gained from this chapter is an understanding of exchange rates, which can significantly impact foreign expenditures, purchases, and investment returns.

General Electric

Establishing a Presence in China

General Electric Co., one of the world's largest firms, considers globalization one of its core competencies. In 2009, almost 54 percent, or $84.3 billion, of GE's total revenues was generated outside of the United States. GE believes that global growth requires more than simply shipping products. A global company must be equally committed to developing capabilities and relationships in the markets where it wants to succeed.

One of GE's markets is China, where its revenues totaled $5 billion in 2006. China will invest $400 billion for infrastructure in this decade. The 2008 Olympics in Beijing was one of its massive infrastructure projects, and GE was a major player in helping China prepare for the games. To support its Chinese customers, GE had more than 1,700 sales and service people on the ground in China. It built a Global Research Center in Shanghai to develop the capabilities of its Chinese suppliers. GE has also trained Chinese business leaders in GE management techniques.

GE paid nearly $200 million to become an Olympic sponsor. The hefty sponsorship fee covers four Olympic Games through 2012, but GE was particularly interested in playing a role in Beijing. It targeted about $1 billion in Olympics-related contracts to provide everything from lighting and security at stadiums to electrical equipment at subway stations, treatment systems at wastewater facilities, and ultrasound equipment for diagnosing athletes' ailments. GE's goal was to double its revenue in China to $10 billion by 2010.

GE created a team of 100 engineers and salespeople in Beijing to work on Olympics-related projects. It then broke them up into smaller groups focusing on the Beijing Olympic Committee, Chinese companies developing the stadiums, and the government agencies in charge of transportation. As an Olympic sponsor in several categories, GE provided specific services during the games. Company officials said the company was bidding on 25 to 30 contracts a month.

Like GE, many companies are looking beyond their home country's borders for new market opportunities. Although globalization can bring controversy, companies like GE believe that future growth requires U.S. companies to view the world as their market.

LG ₁ **19.1 The Multinational Company and Its Environment**

multinational companies (MNCs)
Firms that have international assets and operations in foreign markets and draw part of their total revenue and profits from such markets.

Matter of fact

Diversifying Operations

One of the reasons why firms have operations in foreign markets is the portfolio concept discussed in Chapter 8. Just as it is not wise for you to put all of your investment into the stock of one firm, it is not wise for a firm to invest in only one market. By having operations in many markets, firms can smooth out some of the cyclic changes that occur in each market.

North American Free Trade Agreement (NAFTA)
The treaty establishing free trade and open markets among Canada, Mexico, and the United States.

In recent years, as world markets have become more interdependent, international finance has become an increasingly important element in the management of **multinational companies (MNCs)**. Since World War II, an increasing number of firms, including many based in emerging or developing countries, have become MNCs (also referred to as *global firms* or *transnational corporations*) by developing targeted overseas markets, mainly through foreign direct investment (FDI)—that is, by establishing foreign subsidiaries or affiliates—and via mergers and acquisitions. The principles of managerial finance in this text apply to the management of MNCs as well as to purely domestic firms. However, certain factors unique to the international setting tend to complicate the financial management of multinational companies. A simple comparison between a domestic U.S. firm (firm A) and a U.S.-based MNC (firm B), as illustrated in Table 19.1, indicates the influence of some of the international factors on MNCs' operations.

Multinationals face a variety of laws and restrictions when operating in different nation-states. The legal and economic complexities existing in this environment are significantly different from those a domestic firm would face. Here we take a brief look at that environment, starting with key trading blocs.

KEY TRADING BLOCS

In late 1992, the presidents of the United States and Mexico and the prime minister of Canada signed the **North American Free Trade Agreement (NAFTA)**. The U.S. Congress ratified NAFTA in November 1993. This trade pact simply mirrors underlying economic reality—Canada and Mexico are among the largest U.S. trading partners. In 2003–2004, the United States signed a bilateral trade deal

TABLE 19.1	International Factors and Their Influence on MNCs' Operations	
Factor	**Firm A (Domestic)**	**Firm B (MNC)**
Foreign ownership	All assets owned by domestic entities	Portions of equity of foreign investments owned by foreign partners, thus affecting foreign decision making and profits
Multinational capital markets	All debt and equity structures based on the domestic capital market	Opportunities and challenges arise from the different capital markets in which firms can issue debt and equity
Multinational accounting	All consolidation of financial statements based on one currency	Different currencies and specific translation rules influence the consolidation of financial statements into one currency
Foreign exchange risks	All operations in one currency	Fluctuations in foreign exchange markets can affect foreign revenues and profits as well as the overall value of the firm

Central American Free Trade Agreement (CAFTA)
A trade agreement signed in 2003–2004 by the United States, the Dominican Republic, and five Central American countries (Costa Rica, El Salvador, Guatemala, Honduras, and Nicaragua).

European Union (EU)
A significant economic force currently made up of 27 nations that permit free trade within the union.

European Open Market
The transformation of the European Union into a *single* market at year-end 1992.

euro
A single currency adopted on January 1, 1999, by 12 EU nations, which switched to a single set of euro bills and coins on January 1, 2002.

monetary union
The official melding of the national currencies of the EU nations into one currency, the *euro,* on January 1, 2002.

Mercosur
A major South American trading bloc that includes countries that account for more than half of total Latin American GDP.

ASEAN
A large trading bloc that comprises ten member nations, all in Southeast Asia. China is expected to join this bloc in 2010. Also called the *Association of Southeast Asian Nations.*

with Chile and also a regional pact, known as the **Central American Free Trade Agreement (CAFTA),** with the Dominican Republic and five Central American countries (Costa Rica, El Salvador, Guatemala, Honduras, and Nicaragua). Since 1985, the United States has signed bilateral and regional trade agreements with more than 62 other nations.

The **European Union,** or **EU,** has been in existence since 1957. It has a current membership of 27 nations. With a total population estimated at more than 470 million (compared to the U.S. population of about 300 million) and an overall gross national income paralleling that of the United States, the EU is a significant global economic force. The countries of Western Europe opened a new era of free trade within the union when intraregional tariff barriers fell at the end of 1992. This transformation is commonly called the **European Open Market.** Although the EU has managed to reach agreement on most economic, monetary, financial, and legal provisions, debates continue on certain other aspects (some key), including those related to automobile production and imports, monetary union, taxes, and workers' rights.

As a result of the Maastricht Treaty of 1991, 12 EU nations adopted a single currency, the **euro,** as a continent-wide medium of exchange. And beginning January 1, 2002, those 12 EU nations switched to a single set of euro bills and coins, causing the national currencies of all 12 countries participating in **monetary union** to slowly disappear in the following months. As of 2007, 13 members were using the euro as their national currency.

At the same time that the European Union implemented monetary union, (which also involved creating a new European Central Bank), the EU experienced a wave of new applicants, resulting in the May 1, 2004, admission of ten and the January 1, 2007, admission of two new members from Eastern Europe and the Mediterranean region. The rapidly emerging new community of Europe offers both challenges and opportunities to a variety of players, including multinational firms. MNCs today face heightened levels of competition when operating inside the EU. As more of the existing restrictions and regulations are eliminated, for instance, U.S. multinationals will have to face other MNCs, some from within the EU itself.

In addition to NAFTA and the EU, a number of other bilateral or regional trading blocs have emerged. The EU itself has entered into trade accords involving at least 35 countries. Latin America has several such blocs, including its largest, **Mercosur,** which is composed of Argentina, Brazil, Paraguay, Uruguay, and Venezuela. It has a population of more than 250 million and a combined economic size of about US$1.1 trillion. An even larger bloc exists in the form of **ASEAN** (Association of Southeast Asian Nations), with ten members. China has signed a trade deal with ASEAN, to be phased in by 2010. This will create a regional free market encompassing more than 1.8 billion people by 2015. Other trading agreements involving Japan, India, South Korea, Singapore, Australia, New Zealand, and various nations in Africa either have been completed or are under negotiation.

These deals will result in an increasing share of world trade being covered by regional accords. Meanwhile, an unintended consequence is the emergence of contradictions and incompatibilities vis-á-vis the multilateral-based system embedded in WTO (discussed in the next section). All of this will force the multinationals to navigate through a rising number of trade agreements worldwide. Despite the challenges, though, U.S. companies can benefit from the formation of regional and bilateral trade pacts, but only if they are prepared to exploit them. They must offer a desirable mix of products to a collection of varied consumers and be ready to take advantage of a variety of currencies and of financial markets and instruments (such as the Euroequities discussed later in this chapter). They must staff their operations with the appropriate combination of local and foreign personnel and, when necessary, enter into joint ventures and strategic alliances.

GATT AND THE WTO

General Agreement on Tariffs and Trade (GATT)
A treaty that has governed world trade throughout most of the postwar era; it extends free-trading rules to broad areas of economic activity and is policed by the *World Trade Organization (WTO)*.

World Trade Organization (WTO)
International body that polices world trading practices and mediates disputes among member countries.

Although it may seem that the world is splitting into a handful of trading blocs, this is less of a danger than it may appear to be, because many international treaties are in force that guarantee relatively open access to at least the largest economies. The most important such treaty is the **General Agreement on Tariffs and Trade (GATT)**. In 1994, Congress ratified the most recent version of this treaty, which has governed world trade throughout most of the postwar era. The current agreement extends free-trading rules to broad areas of economic activity—such as agriculture, financial services, and intellectual property rights—that had not previously been covered by international treaty and were thus effectively off-limits to foreign competition.

The 1994 GATT treaty also established a new international body, the **World Trade Organization (WTO)**, to police world trading practices and to mediate disputes between member countries. The WTO began operating in January 1995. In 2004, preliminary approvals were granted for an eventual membership of the Russian Federation in the WTO. In December 2001, the People's Republic of China was, after years of controversy, granted membership. As of 2007, the WTO had 151 members. Given the emergence of more bilateral and regional trade accords, however, its long-term prospects and effectiveness are becoming increasingly clouded. Key evidence was the organization's lack of achieving final agreement by 2007 on the global round of trade negotiations, the Doha Round, which began in 2001.

LEGAL FORMS OF BUSINESS ORGANIZATION

In many countries outside the United States, operating a foreign business as a subsidiary or affiliate can take two forms, both similar to the U.S. corporation. In German-speaking nations the two forms are the *Aktiengesellschaft* (A.G.) or the *Gesellschaft mit beschrankter Haftung* (GmbH). In many other countries the similar forms are a *Société Anonyme* (S.A.) or a *Société à Responsibilité Limitée* (S.A.R.L.). The A.G. and the S.A. are the most common forms, but the GmbH and the S.A.R.L. require fewer formalities for formation and operation.

Establishing a business in a form such as the S.A. can involve most of the provisions that govern a U.S.-based corporation. In addition, to operate in many foreign countries it is often essential to enter into joint-venture business agreements with private investors or with government-based agencies of the host country. A

joint venture
A partnership under which the participants have contractually agreed to contribute specified amounts of money and expertise in exchange for stated proportions of ownership and profit.

joint venture is a partnership under which the participants have contractually agreed to contribute specified amounts of money and expertise in exchange for stated proportions of ownership and profit. Joint ventures are common in many emerging and developing nations.

Emerging and developing countries have varying laws and regulations regarding MNCs' subsidiary and joint-venture operations. Whereas many host countries (including Mexico, Brazil, South Korea, and Taiwan) have either completely removed or significantly liberalized their local-ownership requirements, other major economies (including China and India) are just beginning to relax these restrictions. China, for instance, has gradually opened up new economic sectors and industries to partial (and, in a few cases, full) foreign participation. India continues to insist on majority local ownership in wide-ranging segments of its economy. MNCs, especially those based in the United States, the EU, and Japan, will face new challenges and opportunities in the future in terms of ownership requirements, mergers, and acquisitions.

The existence of joint-venture laws and restrictions has implications for the operation of foreign-based subsidiaries. First, majority foreign ownership may result in a substantial degree of management and control by host country participants. This, in turn, can influence day-to-day operations to the detriment of the managerial policies and procedures MNCs normally pursue. Next, foreign ownership may result in disagreements among the partners as to the exact distribution of profits and the portion to be allocated for reinvestment. Moreover, operating in foreign countries, especially on a joint-venture basis, can involve problems regarding the remittance of profits. In the past, the governments of Argentina, Brazil, Venezuela, and Thailand, among others, have imposed ceilings not only on the repatriation (return) of capital by MNCs but also on profit remittances by these firms to the parent companies. These governments usually cite the shortage of foreign exchange as the motivating factor. Finally, from a "positive" point of view, it can be argued that MNCs operating in many of the less developed countries benefit from joint-venture agreements, given the potential risks stemming from political instability in the host countries. This issue will be addressed in detail in subsequent discussions.

TAXES

Multinational companies, unlike domestic firms, have financial obligations in foreign countries. One of their basic responsibilities is international taxation—a complex issue because national governments follow a variety of tax policies. In general, U.S.-based MNCs must take into account several factors.

Tax Rates and Taxable Income

First, MNCs need to examine the *level* of foreign taxes. Among the major industrial countries, corporate tax rates do vary. While the average rates in the United States, Germany, and Japan are close to 40 percent, those in the United Kingdom and Australia are near 30 percent. Ireland has a rate of about 12 percent. Many less industrialized nations maintain relatively moderate rates, partly as an incentive for attracting foreign capital. Certain countries—in particular, the Bahamas, Switzerland, Liechtenstein, the Cayman Islands, and Bermuda—are known for their low tax levels. As discussed in the *Global Focus* box in Chapter 11, China has had a low rate for foreign investors, to encourage investment. These nations typically have no withholding taxes on *intra-MNC dividends*.

Next, there is a question as to the definition of *taxable income*. Some countries tax profits as received on a *cash basis,* whereas others tax profits earned on an *accrual basis.* Differences can also exist in treatments of noncash charges, such as depreciation, amortization, and depletion. Finally, the existence of tax agreements between the United States and other governments can influence not only the total tax bill of the parent MNC but also its international operations and financial activities.

Tax Rules

Different home countries apply varying tax rates and rules to the global earnings of their own multinationals. Moreover, tax rules are subject to frequent modifications. In the United States, for instance, the Tax Reform Act of 1986 resulted in certain changes affecting the taxation of U.S.-based MNCs. Special provisions apply to tax deferrals by MNCs on foreign income; operations set up in U.S. possessions, such as the U.S. Virgin Islands, Guam, and American Samoa; capital gains from the sale of stock in a foreign corporation; and withholding taxes. Furthermore, MNCs (both U.S. and foreign) can be subject to national as well as local taxes. Obviously, these laws can make a big difference in a multinational's tax bill.

As a general practice, the U.S. government claims jurisdiction over *all* the income of an MNC, wherever earned. (Special rules apply to foreign corporations conducting business in the United States.) However, it may be possible for a multinational company to take foreign income taxes as a direct credit against its U.S. tax liabilities. The following example illustrates one way of accomplishing this objective.

Example 19.1 ▶

American Enterprises, a U.S.-based MNC that manufactures heavy machinery, has a foreign subsidiary that earns $100,000 before local taxes. All of the after-tax funds are available to the parent in the form of dividends. The applicable taxes consist of a 35% foreign income tax rate, a foreign dividend withholding tax rate of 10%, and a U.S. tax rate of 34%.

Subsidiary income before local taxes	$100,000
− Foreign income tax at 35%	35,000
Dividend available to be declared	$ 65,000
− Foreign dividend withholding tax at 10%	6,500
MNC's receipt of dividends	$ 58,500

Using the so-called *grossing up procedure,* the MNC will add the full before-tax subsidiary income to its total taxable income. Next, the company calculates the U.S. tax liability on the grossed-up income. Finally, the related taxes paid in the foreign country are applied as a credit against the additional U.S. tax liability:

Additional MNC income		$100,000
U.S. tax liability at 34%	$ 34,000	
− Total foreign taxes paid, to be used as a credit ($35,000 + $6,500)	41,500	41,500
U.S. taxes due		0
Net funds available to the parent MNC		$ 58,500

Because the U.S. tax liability is less than the total taxes paid to the foreign government, *no additional U.S. taxes are due* on the income from the foreign subsidiary. In our example, if tax credits had not been allowed, then "double taxation" by the two authorities, as shown in what follows, would have resulted in a substantial drop in the overall net funds available to the parent MNC:

Subsidiary income before local taxes	$100,000
− Foreign income tax at 35%	35,000
Dividend available to be declared	$ 65,000
− Foreign dividend withholding tax at 10%	6,500
MNC's receipt of dividends	$ 58,500
− U.S. tax liability at 34%	19,890
Net funds available to the parent MNC	$ 38,610

The preceding example clearly demonstrates that the existence of bilateral tax treaties and the subsequent application of tax credits can significantly enhance the overall net funds available to MNCs from their worldwide earnings. Consequently, in an increasingly complex and competitive international financial environment, international taxation is one of the variables that multinational corporations should fully utilize to their advantage.

FINANCIAL MARKETS

Euromarket
The international financial market that provides for borrowing and lending currencies outside their country of origin.

During the last two decades the **Euromarket**—which provides for borrowing and lending currencies outside their country of origin—has grown rapidly. The Euromarket provides multinational companies with an "external" opportunity to borrow or lend funds and to do so with less government regulation.

Growth of the Euromarket

The Euromarket has grown large for several reasons. First, beginning in the early 1960s, the Russians wanted to maintain their dollar earnings outside the legal jurisdiction of the United States, mainly because of the Cold War. Second, the consistently large U.S. balance-of-payments deficits helped to "scatter" dollars around the world. Third, the existence of specific regulations and controls on dollar deposits in the United States, including interest rate ceilings imposed by the government, helped to send such deposits to places outside the United States.

These and other factors have combined and contributed to the creation of an "external" capital market. Its size cannot be accurately determined, mainly because of its lack of regulation and control. Several sources that periodically estimate its size are the Bank for International Settlements (BIS), Morgan Guaranty Trust, the World Bank, and the Organization for Economic Cooperation and Development (OECD). By 2007, the overall size of the Euromarket was well above $4.0 trillion *net* international lending.

offshore centers
Certain cities or states (including London, Singapore, Bahrain, Nassau, Hong Kong, and Luxembourg) that have achieved prominence as major centers for Euromarket business.

One aspect of the Euromarket is the so-called **offshore centers**. Certain cities or states around the world—including London, Singapore, Bahrain, Nassau, Hong Kong, and Luxembourg—are considered major offshore centers for Euromarket business. The availability of communication and transportation facilities, along with language, costs, time zones, taxes, and local banking regulations, are among the main reasons for the prominence of these centers.

In recent decades, various new financial instruments have appeared in the international financial markets. One is interest rate and currency swaps. Another is various combinations of forward and options contracts on different currencies.

A third is new types of bonds and notes—along with an international version of U.S. commercial paper—with flexible characteristics in terms of currency, maturity, and interest rate. More details will be provided in subsequent discussions.

Major Participants

The U.S. dollar continues to dominate various segments of the global financial markets. For example, central banks worldwide maintain the major portion of their reserves in the dollar. Yet, in other activities—including currency in circulation and the international bond market—the euro has surpassed the dollar, with more challenges coming from other, potential contenders such as the Chinese yuan. Similarly, although U.S. banks and other financial institutions continue to play a significant role in the global markets, financial giants from Japan and Europe have become major participants in the Euromarket.

In the three decades leading up to the new millennium, many countries in Latin America, Asia, and Africa borrowed in the global financial markets. They accumulated huge international debts, resulting in many financial and currency crises. Clearly, as the 1997 financial/currency crises of Asia, the 1998 currency collapse of Russia, and the 2001–2002 default of Argentina showed, too much international debt, along with unstable economies and currencies, can cause massive financial losses and problems for the world's MNCs. The latest IMF data, however, confirm that, beginning in 2000, nonindustrialized countries' external debt (as a percentage of exports of goods and services) has been declining and is expected to continue to do so. Many of these nations have replaced their foreign-currency debts with local-currency instruments. Also, they have further liberalized their respective economies by allowing long-term capital inflows of foreign direct investments, thus reducing their exposure to foreign exchange risk.

Although nation-states may have slowed down their official borrowings in this decade, private enterprises, including multinational companies, continue to obtain funds (and invest) in international markets. Both Eurocurrency and Eurobond markets are extensively used by MNCs.

→ REVIEW QUESTIONS

19–1 What are the important international trading blocs? What is the *European Union* and what is its single unit of currency? What is *GATT?* What is the *WTO?*

19–2 What is a *joint venture?* Why is it often essential to use this arrangement? What effect do joint-venture laws and restrictions have on the operation of foreign-based subsidiaries?

19–3 From the point of view of a U.S.-based MNC, what key tax factors need to be considered?

19–4 Discuss the major reasons for the growth of the *Euromarket.* What is an *offshore center?* Name the major participants in the Euromarket.

LG 2   19.2 Financial Statements

Several features differentiate internationally based reports from domestically oriented financial statements. Among these are the issues of foreign subsidiary characterization, the functional currency approach of U.S. MNCs, and the translation of individual accounts.

TABLE 19.2	Subsidiary/Currency Operations and Translation Method

Type of operation	Translation method
Integrated foreign entity (international practice)	Operates as an extension of the parent MNC; temporal method is the primary translation tool
Self-sustaining foreign entity (international practice)	Operates independent of the parent multinational; the current-rate method is the primary approach
Functional currency approach (used by U.S. MNCs)	The dominant currency in which the foreign subsidiary conducts its activities; it may be the same as the parent's (in which case, the temporal method is applied), the subsidiary's (the current-rate method), or a third currency (temporal, then current)

Source: David K. Eiteman, Arthur I. Stonehill, and Michael H. Moffett, *Multinational Business Finance,* 11th ed. (Boston, MA: Addison-Wesley, 2007), pp. 336–342.

SUBSIDIARY CHARACTERIZATION AND FUNCTIONAL CURRENCY

For a multinational company based outside the United States, its foreign subsidiaries' type of operations will determine the translation method the firm will use. For U.S.-based MNCs, the determining factor is the functional currency of each subsidiary. Table 19.2 provides further details on these points.

TRANSLATION OF INDIVIDUAL ACCOUNTS

Unlike domestic items in financial statements, international items require translation back into U.S. dollars. Since December 1982, all financial statements of U.S. multinationals (with the exceptions noted below) have had to conform to *Statement No. 52* issued by the Financial Accounting Standards Board (FASB). The basic rules of *FASB No. 52* are given in Figure 19.1.

FASB No. 52
Statement issued by the FASB requiring U.S. multinationals first to convert the financial statement accounts of foreign subsidiaries into the *functional currency* and then to translate the accounts into the parent firm's currency using the *all-current-rate method.*

functional currency
The currency in which a subsidiary primarily generates and expends cash and in which its accounts are maintained.

all-current-rate method
The method by which the *functional-currency-denominated* financial statements of an MNC's subsidiary are translated into the parent company's currency.

FASB No. 52

Under **FASB No. 52,** the *current-rate method* is implemented in a two-step process. First, each subsidiary's balance sheet and income statement are *measured* in terms of the functional currency by using generally accepted accounting principles (GAAP). That is, each subsidiary translates foreign-currency elements into the **functional currency**—the currency in which a subsidiary primarily generates and expends cash and in which its accounts are maintained before financial statements are submitted to the parent for consolidation.

In the second step, the functional-currency-denominated financial statements of the foreign subsidiary are translated into the parent's currency. This is done using the **all-current-rate method,** which requires the translation of all balance sheet items at the closing rate and all income statement items at average rates.

Each of these steps can result in certain gains or losses. The first step can lead to transaction (cash) gains or losses. Whether realized or not, these gains or losses are charged directly to current income. The completion of the second step can result in translation (accounting) adjustments, which are excluded from current income. Instead, the MNC discloses and charges these amounts to a separate component of stockholders' equity.

FIGURE 19.1

Procedure Flow Chart for U.S. Translation Practices
Purpose: Foreign currency financial statements must be translated into U.S. dollars

Source: David K. Eiteman, Arthur I. Stonehill, and Michael H. Moffett, *Multinational Business Finance,* 11th ed. (Boston, MA: Addison-Wesley, 2007), p. 341.

Temporal Method

temporal method
A method that requires specific assets and liabilities to be translated at so-called historical exchange rates and foreign-exchange translation gains or losses to be reflected in the current year's income.

The temporal method, along with a variation called *monetary/non-monetary method,* is an alternative translation approach used throughout the world. For U.S.-based multinationals, as highlighted in both Table 19.2 and Figure 19.1, when the functional currency is the U.S. dollar or a third currency, the **temporal method** is used. This method requires that specific assets and liabilities be translated at so-called historical exchange rates and that foreign-exchange translation gains or losses be reflected in current year's income. Also, if a U.S. MNC has a subsidiary in a *hyperinflation* country—defined as a host nation experiencing a cumulative inflation of more than 100 percent over a 3-year period—then the temporal method is used. (In some countries, the inflation rates can be significantly higher. In Zimbabwe, for example, in early 2007 the *monthly* inflation rate exceeded 1,500 percent.)

→ REVIEW QUESTION

19–5 Under *FASB No. 52,* what are the translation rules for financial statement accounts? How does the *temporal method* differ from these rules?

LG 3 19.3 Risk

The concept of risk clearly applies to international investments as well as to purely domestic ones. However, MNCs must take into account additional factors, including both exchange rate and political risks.

EXCHANGE RATE RISKS

exchange rate risk
The risk caused by varying exchange rates between two currencies.

Because multinational companies operate in many different foreign markets, portions of these firms' revenues and costs are based on foreign currencies. To understand the **exchange rate risk** caused by varying exchange rates between two currencies, we examine the relationships that exist among various currencies, the causes of exchange rate changes, and the impact of currency fluctuations.

Relationships among Currencies

Since the mid-1970s, the major currencies of the world have had a *floating*—as opposed to a *fixed*—relationship with respect to the U.S. dollar and to one another. Among the currencies regarded as being major (or "hard") currencies are the British pound sterling (£), the European Union euro (€), the Japanese yen (¥), the Canadian dollar (C$), and, of course, the U.S. dollar (US$). As previously pointed out, by 2007, 13 members of the EU had adopted the euro, in circulation since 2002. It has gained wide acceptance and usage in international transactions—particularly debt securities issues.

foreign exchange rate
The value of two currencies with respect to each other.

The value of two currencies with respect to each other, or their **foreign exchange rate**, is expressed as follows:

$$US\$1.00 = ¥119.77$$
$$¥1.00 = US\$0.008349$$

Because the U.S. dollar has served as the principal currency of international finance for more than 60 years, the usual exchange rate quotation in international markets is given as ¥119.77/US$, where the unit of account is the Japanese yen and the unit of currency being priced is one U.S. dollar. In this case, the dollar is the currency that is actually being priced. Expressing the exchange rate as US$0.008349/¥ would indicate a dollar price for the Japanese yen.

floating relationship
The fluctuating relationship of the values of two currencies with respect to each other.

fixed (or semifixed) relationship
The constant (or relatively constant) relationship of a currency to one of the major currencies, a combination (basket) of major currencies, or some type of international foreign exchange standard.

For the major currencies, the existence of a **floating relationship** means that the value of any two currencies with respect to each other is allowed to fluctuate on a daily basis. Conversely, some of the nonmajor currencies of the world try to maintain a **fixed (or semifixed) relationship** with respect to one of the major currencies, a combination (basket) of major currencies, or some type of international foreign exchange standard.

spot exchange rate
The rate of exchange between two currencies on any given day.

forward exchange rate
The rate of exchange between two currencies at some specified future date.

Every day, foreign exchange markets establish two key prices that govern trade in the world's major currencies. One price is the **spot exchange rate**—the rate on that day. The other price is the **forward exchange rate**—the rate at some specified future date. The foreign exchange rates given in Figure 19.2 illustrate these concepts. For instance, the figure shows that at the close on Friday, July 30, 2010, the spot rate for the Japanese yen was US$0.011574 (or ¥86.40/US$, as usually stated), and the forward (future) rate was US$0.011577/¥ (or ¥86.38/US$) for 1-month delivery. In other words, on July 30, 2010, one could execute a contract to take delivery of Japanese yen in 1 month at a dollar price of US$0.011577/¥. Forward rates are also quoted for 3-month and 6-month contracts (with other, tailor-made contracts of desired maturities available to clients through the interbank market). For all such contracts, the agreements and signatures are completed on, say, July 30, 2010, but the actual exchange of dollars and Japanese yen between buyers and sellers will take place on the future date (say, 1 month later).

Figure 19.2 also illustrates the differences between floating currencies and those that are either fixed or exhibit less movement over time. The middle data columns in Figure 19.2 show the 1-day and year-to-date (YTD) percentage change in each currency's movement vis-à-vis the U.S. dollar. All the major currencies previously mentioned, along with minor (or "soft") currencies such as the Indian rupee and the Thai baht, have experienced some changes since the beginning of

FIGURE 19.2

Exchange Rates (Friday, July 30, 2010)
Spot and forward exchange rate quotations (partial listing)

Exchange Rates: New York Closing Snapshot						
Friday, July 30, 2010			Find Historical Data	WHAT'S THIS?		
US-dollar foreign-exchange rates in late New York trading				VIEW AS SPREADSHEET		
	IN US$		US$ VS. % CHG		PER US$	
Country/currency	Fri	Thurs	1-Day	YTD	Fri	Thurs
Americas						
Argentina peso*	0.2537	0.2540	0.12	3.7	3.9417	3.9370
Brazil real	0.5687	0.5679	−0.14	0.9	1.7584	1.7609
⋮						
Mexico peso*	0.0790	0.0788	−0.32	−3.2	12.6566	12.6968
Peru new sol	0.3545	0.3543	−0.06	−2.4	2.8209	2.8225
Uruguay peso†	0.04770	0.04770	unch	7.3	20.96	20.96
Venezuela b. fuerte	0.23285056	0.23285056	unch	100.0	4.2946	4.2946
Asia-Pacific						
Australian dollar	0.9047	0.9004	−0.40	−0.7	1.1053	1.1106
China yuan	0.1476	0.1476	unch	−0.8	6.7740	6.7762
Hong Kong dollar	0.1287	0.1288	unch	0.2	7.7675	7.7663
India rupee	0.02156	0.02151	−0.23	unch	46.3822	46.49
Indonesia rupiah	0.0001119	0.0001114	−0.45	−5.2	8937	8977
Japan yen	0.011574	0.011515	−0.51	−7.2	86.40	86.84
1-mos forward	0.011577	0.01152	−0.52	−7.2	86.38	86.83
3-mos forward	0.011584	0.01153	−0.51	−7.2	86.33	86.77
6-mos forward	0.011597	0.01154	−0.51	−7.2	86.23	86.67
Malaysia ringgit§	0.3141	0.3142	unch	−7.0	3.1837	3.1827
New Zealand dollar	0.7253	0.7239	−0.20	unch	1.3787	1.3814
⋮						
Taiwan dollar	0.03126	0.03127	unch	unch	31.990	31.980
Thailand baht	0.03100	0.03103	0.10	−3.3	32.258	32.227
Vietnam dong	0.00005	0.00005	unch	3.3	19075	19075
Europe						
Czech Rep. koruna**	0.05255	0.05272	0.32	3.2	19.030	18.968
Denmark krone	0.1749	0.1755	0.34	10.0	5.7176	5.6980
Euro area eruo	1.3033	1.3078	0.35	9.8	0.7673	0.7646
Hungary forint	0.004591	0.004599	0.17	15.2	217.82	217.44
Norway krone	0.1646	0.1641	−0.30	4.8	6.0753	6.0938
⋮						
Turkey lira**	0.6634	0.6616	−0.28	0.7	1.5074	1.5116
UK pound	1.5690	1.5611	−0.52	3.0	0.6373	0.6406
1-mos forward	1.5688	1.5608	−0.52	3.0	0.6374	0.6407
3-mos forward	1.5683	1.5604	−0.51	3.0	0.6376	0.6409
6-mos forward	1.5674	1.5596	−0.50	3.0	0.6380	0.6412
Middle East/Africa						
Bahrain dinar	2.6526	2.6526	unch	unch	0.3770	0.3770
Egypt pound*	0.1754	0.1754	unch	3.9	5.7009	5.7009
Israel shekel	0.2654	0.2643	−0.41	−0.6	3.7679	3.7836
Jordan dinar	1.4129	1.4129	unch	unch	0.7078	0.7078
Kenya shilling	0.01247	0.01248	0.06	5.7	80.200	80.150
Kuwait dinar	3.4771	3.4778	unch	0.2	0.2876	0.2875
Lebanon pound	0.0006662	0.0006664	unch	−0.1	1501.05	1500.60
Saudi Arabia riyal	0.2666	0.2667	unch	unch	3.7509	3.7495
South Africa rand	0.1371	0.1367	−0.29	−1.5	7.2939	7.3153
UAE dirham	0.2723	0.2723	unch	unch	3.6724	3.6724
SDR††	1.5185	1.5217	0.20	3.2	0.6585	0.6572

*Floating rate; †Financial; §Government rate; **Commercial rate; ††Special Drawing Rights (SDR); from the International Monetary Fund; based on exchange rates for U.S., British and Japanese currencies.
Note: Based on trading among banks of $1 million and more, as quoted at 4 p.m. ET by Thomson Reuters.
Source: Thomson Reuters

Source: The Wall Street Journal, http://online.wsj.com/mdc/public/page/2_3021-forex.html?mod=mdc_curr_pglnk, July 30, 2010.

the year. On the other hand, the Kuwaiti dinar and the Saudi Arabian riyal have undergone no change over this period.

For the floating currencies, changes in the value of foreign exchange rates are called appreciation or depreciation. For any currency that is fixed in value (with respect to the U.S. dollar or another major currency), changes in values are called official *revaluation* or *devaluation*, but these terms have the same meanings as *appreciation* and *depreciation*, respectively.

Personal Finance Example 19.2 ▶ Floyd Armstrong, an avid cyclist, is considering a bicycling tour that for 1 week during the Tour de France will ride ahead of the actual race. The cost of the tour, which includes ground transportation, hotels, and route support in France, is 3,675 euros (€). He estimates that his round-trip airfare (including shipment of his bike) from his home in Iowa will be $1,100; in addition he will incur another $100 in incidental U.S. travel expenses. Floyd estimates the cost of meals in France to be about €400, and he plans to take an additional $1,000 to buy gifts and other merchandise while in France. From Figure 19.2, the current exchange rate is US$1.3033/€1.00 (or €0.7673/US$1.00). Given this information, Floyd wishes to determine (1) the total dollar cost of the trip and (2) the amount in euros he will need to cover the cost of meals, gifts, and other merchandise while in France.

(1) Total cost of trip in U.S. dollars

Cost of tour (€3,675 × US$1.3033/€)	$4,790
Round-trip airfare	1,100
Incidental U.S. travel expenses	100
Cost of meals in France (€400 × US$1.3033/€)	521
Gifts and other merchandise	1,000
Total cost of trip in $	$7,511

(2) Amount of euros needed in France

Cost of meals in France	€ 400
Gifts and other merchandice ($US1,000 × €0.7673)	767
Amount of €s needed in France	€1,167

The total cost of Floyd's trip would be $7,511, and he would need 1,167 euros to cover his cost of meals, gifts, and other merchandise while in France.

What Causes Exchange Rates to Change?

Although several economic and political factors influence foreign exchange rate movements, by far the most important explanation for long-term changes in exchange rates is a differing inflation rate between two countries. Countries that experience high inflation rates will see their currencies decline in value (depreciate) relative to the currencies of countries with lower inflation rates.

Example 19.3 ▶ Assume that the current exchange rate between the United States and the new nation of Farland is 2 Farland guineas (FG) per U.S. dollar, FG 2.00/US$, which is also equal to $0.50/FG. This exchange rate means that a basket of goods worth $100 in the United States sells for $100 × FG 2/US$ = FG 200 in Farland, and vice versa (goods worth FG 200 in Farland sell for $100 in the United States).

Now assume that inflation is running at a 25% annual rate in Farland but at only a 2% annual rate in the United States. In one year, the same basket of goods will sell for 1.25 × FG 200 = FG 250 in Farland, and for 1.02 × $100 = $102 in the United States. These relative prices imply that in 1 year, FG 250 will be worth $102, so the exchange rate in 1 year should change to FG 250/$102 = FG 2.45/US$, or $0.41/FG. In other words, the Farland guinea will depreciate from FG 2/US$ to FG 2.45/US$, while the dollar will appreciate from $0.50/FG to $0.41/FG.

This simple example can also predict the level of interest rates in the two countries. To be enticed to save money, an investor must be offered a return that exceeds the country's inflation rate—otherwise, there would be no reason to forgo the pleasure of spending money (consuming) today because inflation would make that money less valuable 1 year from now. Let's assume that this *real rate of interest* is 3 percent per year in both Farland and the United States. Using Equation 6.1 (page 224), we can now reason that the *nominal rate of interest*— the quoted market rate, not adjusted for risk—will be approximately equal to the real rate plus the inflation rate in each country, or 3 + 25 = 28 percent in Farland and 3 + 2 = 5 percent in the United States.[1]

Impact of Currency Fluctuations

Multinational companies face exchange rate risks under both floating and fixed arrangements. Floating currencies can be used to illustrate these risks. Consider the U.S. dollar–U.K. British pound relationship; note that the forces of international supply and demand, as well as economic and political elements, help to shape both the spot and the forward rates between these two currencies. Because the MNC cannot control much (or most) of these "outside" elements, the company faces potential changes in exchange rates. These changes can, in turn, affect the MNC's revenues, costs, and profits as measured in U.S. dollars. For fixed-rate currencies, official revaluation or devaluation, like the changes brought about by the market in the case of floating currencies, can affect the MNC's operations and its dollar-based financial position.

Example 19.4 ▶ MNC, Inc., a multinational manufacturer of dental drills, has a subsidiary in Great Britain that at the end of 2012 had the financial statements shown in Table 19.3 on page 772. The figures for the balance sheet and income statement are given in the local currency, British pounds (£). Using an assumed foreign exchange rate of £0.70/US$ for December 31, 2012, MNC has translated the statements into U.S. dollars. For simplicity, it is assumed that all the local figures are expected to remain the same during 2113. As a result, as of January 1, 2013, the subsidiary expects to show the same British pound figures on 12/31/13 as on 12/31/12. However, because of the *appreciation* in the assumed value of the British pound

---

1. This is an approximation of the true relationship, which is actually multiplicative. The correct formula says that 1 plus the nominal rate of interest, r, is equal to the product of 1 plus the real rate of interest, r^*, and 1 plus the inflation rate, IP; that is, $(1 + r) = (1 + r^*) \times (1 + IP)$. This means that the nominal interest rates for Farland and the United States should be 28.75 percent and 5.06 percent, respectively.

TABLE 19.3	Financial Statements for MNC, Inc.'s, British Subsidiary

Translation of Balance Sheet

	12/31/12		12/31/13
Assets	£	US$^a	US$^b
Cash	8.00	11.43	13.33
Inventory	60.00	85.72	100.00
Plant and equipment (net)	32.00	45.71	53.34
Total	100.00	142.86	166.67
Liabilities and Stockholders' Equity			
Debt	48.00	68.57	80.00
Paid-in capital	40.00	57.15	66.67
Retained earnings	12.00	17.14	20.00
Total	100.00	142.86	166.67

Translation of Income Statement

Sales	600.00	857.14	1,000.00
Cost of goods sold	550.00	785.71	916.67
Operating profits	50.00	71.43	83.33

^{a}Foreign exchange rate assumed: US$1.00 = £0.70

^{b}Foreign exchange rate assumed: US$1.00 = £0.60

Note: This example is simplified to show how the balance sheet and income statement are subject to foreign exchange rate fluctuations. For the applicable rules on the translation of foreign accounts, review Section 19.2 on international financial statements.

relative to the dollar, from £0.70/US$ to £0.60/US$, the translated dollar values of the items on the balance sheet, along with the dollar profit value on 12/31/13, are higher than those of the previous year. The changes are due only to fluctuations in the foreign exchange rate. In this case, the British pound *appreciated* relative to the U.S. dollar, which means that the U.S. dollar *depreciated* relative to the British pound.

There are additional complexities attached to each individual account in the financial statements. For instance, it matters whether a subsidiary's debt is all in the local currency, all in U.S. dollars, or in several currencies. Moreover, it is important which currency (or currencies) the revenues and costs are denominated in. The risks shown so far relate to what is called the **accounting exposure.** In other words, foreign exchange rate fluctuations affect individual accounts in the financial statements.

A different, and perhaps more important, risk element concerns **economic exposure,** which is the potential impact of foreign exchange rate fluctuations on the firm's value. Given that all future revenues and thus net profits can be subject to foreign exchange rate changes, it is obvious that the *present value* of the net profits derived from foreign operations will have, as a part of its total diversifiable risk, an element reflecting appreciation (revaluation) or depreciation (devaluation) of various currencies with respect to the U.S. dollar.

accounting exposure
The risk resulting from the effects of changes in foreign exchange rates on the translated value of a firm's financial statement accounts denominated in a given foreign currency.

economic exposure
The risk resulting from the effects of changes in foreign exchange rates on the firm's value.

What can the management of MNCs do about these risks? The actions will depend on the attitude of the management toward risk. This attitude, in turn, translates into how aggressively management wants to hedge (that is, protect against) the company's undesirable positions and exposures. The firm can use the money markets, the forward (futures) markets, and the foreign-currency options markets—either individually or in combination—to hedge foreign exchange exposures. Further details on certain hedging strategies are described later.

POLITICAL RISKS

political risk
The potential discontinuity or seizure of an MNC's operations in a host country via the host's implementation of specific rules and regulations.

Another important risk facing MNCs is political risk. **Political risk** refers to a host government's implementation of specific rules and regulations that can result in the discontinuity or seizure of the operations of a foreign company. Political risk is usually manifested in the form of nationalization, expropriation, or confiscation. In general, the host government takes over the assets and operations of a foreign firm, usually without proper (or any) compensation.

macro political risk
The subjection of *all* foreign firms to *political risk* (takeover) by a host country because of political change, revolution, or the adoption of new policies.

micro political risk
The subjection of an individual firm, a specific industry, or companies from a particular foreign country to *political risk* (takeover) by a host country.

Political risk has two basic paths, *macro* and *micro*. **Macro political risk** refers to political change, revolution, or the adoption of new policies by a host government, which subject *all* foreign firms in the country to political risk. In other words, no individual country or firm is treated differently; all assets and operations of foreign firms are taken over wholesale. An example of macro political risk occurred after communist regimes came to power in China in 1949 and Cuba in 1959–1960. **Micro political risk,** on the other hand, refers to the case in which an individual firm, a specific industry, or companies from a particular foreign country are subjected to takeover. In the first decade of the twenty-first century—especially in the second half—Russia, Venezuela, and Bolivia were among those countries that had either nationalized the operations or suspended the long-term contractual agreements held by foreign multinationals in their respective nations. Recent years have also seen the emergence of a *third* path to political risk that encompasses "global" events such as terrorism, antiglobalization movements and protests, Internet-based risks, and concerns over poverty, AIDS, and the environment, all of which affect various MNCs' operations worldwide.

Although political risk can take place in any country—even in the United States—the political instability of many developing nations generally makes the positions of multinational companies most vulnerable there. At the same time, some of these countries have the most promising markets for the goods and services MNCs offer. The main question, therefore, is how to engage in operations and foreign investment in such countries and yet avoid or minimize the potential political risk.

Table 19.4 shows some of the approaches that MNCs may be able to adopt to cope with political risk. The *negative approaches* are generally used by firms in extractive industries such as oil and gas and mining. The *external approaches* are also of limited use. The best policies MNCs can follow are the *positive approaches*, which have both economic and political aspects.

In recent years, MNCs have been relying on a variety of complex forecasting techniques whereby international experts, using available historical data, predict the chances for political instability in a host country and the potential effects on MNC operations. Events in Afghanistan, Pakistan, India, and Russia, among

TABLE 19.4	Approaches for Coping with Political Risks	

Positive approaches		Negative approaches
Prior negotiation of controls and operating contracts		License or patent restrictions under international agreements
Prior agreement for sale	Direct	Control of external raw materials
Joint venture with government or local private sector		Control of transportation to (external) markets
Use of locals in management		Control of downstream processing
Joint venture with local banks		Control of external markets
Equity participation by middle class	Indirect	
Local sourcing		
Local retail outlets		

External approaches to minimize loss

International insurance or investment guarantees

Thinly capitalized firms:

    Local financing

    External financing secured only by the local operation

Source: Rita M. Rodriguez and E. Eugene Carter, *International Financial Management,* 3rd ed. (Englewood Cliffs, NJ: Prentice-Hall, 1984), p. 512.

others, however, point to the limited use of such techniques and tend to reinforce the usefulness of the positive approaches.

A final point relates to the introduction by most host governments in the last two decades of comprehensive sets of rules, regulations, and incentives. Known as **national entry control systems,** they are aimed at regulating inflows of *foreign direct investments* involving MNCs. They are designed to extract more benefits from MNCs' presence by regulating flows of a variety of factors—local ownership, level of exportation, use of local inputs, number of local managers, internal geographic location, level of local borrowing, and the percentages of profits to be remitted and of capital to be repatriated to parent firms. Host countries expect that as MNCs comply with these regulations, the potential for acts of political risk will decline, thus benefiting the MNCs as well.

national entry control systems
Comprehensive rules, regulations, and incentives introduced by host governments to regulate inflows of *foreign direct investments* from MNCs and at the same time extract more benefits from their presence.

→ **REVIEW QUESTIONS**

19–6 Define *spot exchange rate* and *forward exchange rate.* Define and compare *accounting exposures* and *economic exposures* to exchange rate fluctuations.

19–7 Explain how differing inflation rates between two countries affect their exchange rate over the long term.

focus on ETHICS

Chiquita's Slippery Situation

in practice For many people, the little blue "Chiquita" sticker is as familiar as a banana's yellow peel. One of the world's two largest banana companies (along with Dole Food Co.), Cincinnati-based Chiquita is a global business with operations on six continents. Chiquita sources its bananas from Latin America, operating banana farms stretching from Mexico to Ecuador. Chiquita is so heavily invested in the region that, for a time, it was the largest employer in Latin America.

Bananas are not the only item in Chiquita's product line, but they are by far the most important, representing over 50 percent of the company's sales. Because the banana industry is highly competitive, Chiquita's relationships in Latin America are vital to its success. This is reflected in the following statement from the company's 2009 Annual Report: "To compete successfully, we must be able to source bananas of uniformly high quality at a competitive cost, maintain strong customer relationships, and quickly and reliably transport and distribute products to worldwide markets."

Unfortunately, some of the countries where Chiquita operates are unsafe and unstable. A prime example is Colombia, where militant organizations, such as the United Self-Defense Forces of Colombia (AUC), wield a considerable amount of power.

In 1997, Chiquita received threats to its facilities and employees and, through its Colombian subsidiary, began making payments to the AUC in exchange for protection. Although the extortion payments were not technically illegal when Chiquita first started making them, they posed an ethical challenge. The legality of the payments changed in 2001 when the U.S. State Department identified the AUC as a specially designated foreign terrorist organization, making it illegal for Chiquita to do business with them.

In 2003, Chiquita sought guidance from the U.S. Justice Department and admitted to paying millions of dollars to the AUC. The payments finally stopped in 2004 when Chiquita sold its Colombian banana operations to a local company. Chiquita settled its case with the U.S. Justice Department in 2007 by pleading guilty to a single felony count and agreeing to pay a $25 million fine. This gave Chiquita the dubious distinction of becoming the first U.S. corporation ever convicted of financial dealings with terrorists.

▶ *Chiquita saw their options in Colombia as (a) pay extortion to a terrorist organization or (b) put their employees' safety at risk. Is it ethical to break the law in an effort to save lives?*

▶ *What, if anything, do you think Chiquita should have done differently?*

19–8 Discuss *macro* and *micro political risk*. What is the emerging *third* path to political risk? Describe some techniques for dealing with political risk.

LG 4   19.4 Long-Term Investment and Financing Decisions

Important long-term aspects of international managerial finance include foreign direct investment, investment cash flows and decisions, capital structure, long-term debt, and equity capital. Here we consider the international dimensions of these topics.

foreign direct investment (FDI)
The transfer of capital, managerial, and technical assets to a foreign country, by a multinational firm.

FOREIGN DIRECT INVESTMENT

Foreign direct investment (FDI) is the transfer of capital, managerial, and technical assets to a foreign country, by a multinational firm. FDI can be explained on the basis of two main approaches, the *OLI paradigm* and *strategic motives* by MNCs. The first encompasses "O" (owner-specific) advantages in an MNC's home market, "L" (location-specific) characteristics abroad, and "I" (internalization) through which the multinational controls the value chain in its industry. The second refers to companies that invest abroad as they seek markets, raw materials, production efficiency, knowledge, and/or political safety.

The equity participation on the part of an MNC can be 100 percent (resulting in a wholly owned foreign subsidiary) or less (leading to a joint-venture project with foreign participants). In contrast to short-term foreign portfolio investments undertaken by individuals and companies (such as internationally diversified mutual funds), FDI involves equity participation, managerial control, and day-to-day operational activities on the part of MNCs. Therefore, FDI projects will be subjected not only to business, financial, inflation, and exchange rate risks (as would foreign portfolio investments) but also to the additional element of political risk.

For several decades, U.S.-based MNCs dominated the international scene in terms of both the *flow* and the *stock* of FDI. The total FDI stock of U.S.-based MNCs, for instance, increased from $7.7 billion in 1929 to more than $2,050 billion at the end of 2005. Since the 1970s, though, their global presence is being challenged by MNCs based in Western Europe, Japan, and other developed and developing nations. In fact, even the "home" market of U.S. multinationals is being challenged by foreign firms. For instance, in 1960, FDI *into* the United States amounted to only 11.5 percent of U.S. investment overseas. According to figures released by the U.S. Department of Commerce's Bureau of Economic Analysis, at the end of 2005, the U.S. direct investment position abroad on a historical-cost basis was about $2,070 billion, while the foreign direct investment position in the United States on a historical-cost basis stood at about $1,635 billion. The latter figure is close to 80 percent of the former.

Matter of fact

Adjusting Discount Rates

The discount rates used by the parent and subsidiary to calculate the NPV will be different. The parent company has to add in a risk premium based on the possibility of exchange rates changing and the risk of not being able to get the cash out of the foreign country.

INVESTMENT CASH FLOWS AND DECISIONS

Measuring the amount invested in a foreign project, its resulting cash flows, and the associated risk is difficult. The returns and NPVs of such investments can significantly vary from the subsidiary's and parent's points of view. Therefore, several factors that are unique to the international setting need to be examined when one is making long-term investment decisions.

First, firms need to consider elements related to a parent company's *investment* in a subsidiary and the concept of taxes. For example, in the case of manufacturing investments, questions may arise as to the value of the equipment a parent may contribute to the subsidiary. Is the value based on market conditions in the parent country or in the local host economy? In general, the market value in the host country is the relevant "price."

The existence of different taxes—as pointed out earlier—can complicate measurement of the *cash flows* to be received by the parent because different definitions of taxable income can arise. There are still other complications when it comes to measuring the actual cash flows. From a parent firm's viewpoint, the cash flows are those that are repatriated from the subsidiary. In some countries, however, such cash flows may be totally or partially blocked. Obviously, depending on the life of the project in the host country, the returns and NPVs associated with such projects can vary significantly from the subsidiary's and the parent's points of view. For instance, for a project of only 5 years' duration, if all yearly cash flows are blocked by the host government, the subsidiary may show a "normal" or even superior return and NPV, although the parent may show no return at all. For a project of longer life, even if cash flows are blocked for the first few years, the remaining years' cash flows can contribute to the parent's returns and NPV.

Finally, there is the issue of *risk* attached to international cash flows. The three basic types of risks are (1) business and financial risks, (2) inflation and exchange rate risks, and (3) political risks. The first category reflects the type of industry the subsidiary is in as well as its financial structure. We will present more details on financial risks later. As for the other two categories, we have already discussed the risks of having investments, profits, and assets/liabilities in different currencies and the potential impacts of political risks.

The presence of the three types of risks will influence the discount rate to be used when evaluating international cash flows. The basic rule is this: The local cost of equity capital (applicable to the local business and financial environments within which a subsidiary operates) is the starting discount rate. To this rate, the MNC would add the risks stemming from exchange rate and political factors, and from it, would subtract the benefits reflecting the parent's lower capital costs.

CAPITAL STRUCTURE

Both theory and empirical evidence indicate that the capital structures of multinational companies differ from those of purely domestic firms. Furthermore, differences are observed among the capital structures of MNCs domiciled in various countries. Several factors tend to influence the capital structures of MNCs.

International Capital Markets

MNCs, unlike smaller, domestic firms, have access to the Euromarket (discussed earlier) and the variety of financial instruments available there. Because of their access to the international bond and equity markets, MNCs may have lower long-term financing costs, which result in differences between the capital structures of MNCs and those of purely domestic companies. Similarly, MNCs based in different countries and regions may have access to different currencies and markets, resulting in variances in capital structures for these multinationals.

International Diversification

It is well established that MNCs, in contrast to domestic firms, can achieve further risk reduction in their cash flows by diversifying internationally. International diversification may lead to varying degrees of debt versus equity. Empirically, the evidence on debt ratios is mixed. Some studies have found MNCs' debt proportions to be higher than those of domestic firms. Other studies have concluded the opposite, citing imperfections in certain foreign markets, political risk factors, and complexities in the international financial environment that cause higher agency costs of debt for MNCs.

> **Personal Finance Example 19.5 ▶** An important aspect of personal financial planning involves channeling savings into investments that can grow and fund long-term financial goals. Investors can invest in both domestic and foreign-based companies. Investing internationally offers greater diversification than investing only domestically. A number of academic studies overwhelmingly support the argument that well-structured international diversification does indeed reduce

GLOBAL focus

Take an Overseas Assignment to Take a Step Up the Corporate Ladder

in practice There is nothing like an extended stay in a foreign country to get a different perspective on world events, and there are sound career-enhancing reasons to work abroad. International experience can give you a competitive edge and may be vital to career advancement. Such experience goes far beyond mastering country-specific tax and accounting codes.

The demand for employees interested in an overseas assignment was on an upward trend from 2005 to 2008. Driven by a booming global economy, more than two-thirds of multinational corporations reported an increase in the number of international assignments in 2006, according to the Global Relocation Trends Survey, published annually by GMAC Global Relocation Services. A similar percentage of employers sent even more employees on overseas assignments in 2007 as compared to 2006.

As a result of the global recession, a record number of companies cut overseas assignments of employees in 2009. Forty-six percent of multinational companies reported a decrease in the number of international assignments, but with the economy stabilizing 44 percent of multinational firms expected the number of international assignments to increase in 2010.

On arrival in a foreign city, the tendency for expatriates is to live in a section of the city favored by other visitors from home. For security reasons, some executives also travel everywhere by chauffeured limo with an English-speaking driver. It is possible for U.S. executives to live abroad for an extended period of time without soaking up much of the local culture. Doing so may increase one's comfort level but at the loss of some of the valuable lessons to be learned from living abroad.

Oversees assignments do not come without some sacrifices. Long overseas postings can put stress on a family. The most common reason for turning down an international assignment involved family concerns such as children's education, family adjustment, partner resistance, and language. The second most common reason for refusing an assignment was concern for a spouse's career, not unlike the same concern some employees have about a job that requires a cross-country transfer.

Yet as globalization has pushed companies across more borders, CFOs with international experience have found themselves in greater demand. Some chief executives value international experience in their CFOs more highly than either mergers and acquisitions or capital-raising experience.

▶ *If going abroad for a full-immersion assignment is not possible, what are some substitutes for a global assignment that may provide some—albeit limited—global experience?*

---

the risk of a portfolio and increase the return of portfolios of comparable risk. One study found that over the 10 years ended in 1994, a diversified portfolio consisting of 70% domestic and 30% foreign stocks reduced risk by about 5% and increased return by about 7%.

To capture these higher returns and lower risks, most individual investors buy *international mutual funds*. These funds take advantage of international economic developments by (1) capitalizing on changing foreign market conditions and (2) positioning their investments to benefit from devaluation of the dollar. Clearly, individuals should consider including some international investments— probably international mutual funds—in their investment portfolios.

Country Factors

A number of studies conclude that certain factors unique to each host country can cause differences in capital structures. These factors include legal, tax, political, social, and financial aspects, as well as the overall relationship between the public and private sectors. Owing to these factors, differences have been found not only among MNCs based in various countries but also among the foreign subsidiaries of an MNC. However, because no one capital structure is ideal for all MNCs, each multinational has to consider a set of global and domestic factors when deciding on the appropriate capital structure for both the overall corporation and its subsidiaries. Understanding country factors can help financial managers make better-informed decisions. As the *Global Focus* box discusses, one way to improve one's ability to understand how business is conducted in other countries is to take an overseas assignment.

LONG-TERM DEBT

As noted earlier, multinational companies have access to a variety of international financial instruments. Here we will discuss international bonds, the role of international financial institutions in underwriting such instruments, and the use of various techniques by MNCs to change the structure of their long-term debt.

International Bonds

international bond
A bond that is initially sold outside the country of the borrower and is often distributed in several countries.

In general, an **international bond** is one that is initially sold outside the country of the borrower and is often distributed in several countries. When a bond is issued by a foreign corporation or government and is denominated in the investor's home currency and sold in the investor's home market, it is called a foreign bond. For example, an MNC based in Germany might float a foreign bond issue in the British capital market underwritten by a British syndicate and denominated in British pounds. When an international bond is sold to investors in countries with currencies other than the currency in which the bond is denominated, it is called a **Eurobond.** Thus, an MNC based in the United States might float a Eurobond in several European capital markets, underwritten by an international syndicate and denominated in U.S. dollars.

foreign bond
A bond that is issued by a foreign corporation or government and is denominated in the investor's home currency and sold in the investor's home market.

The U.S. dollar and the euro are the most frequently used currencies for Eurobond issues, with the euro rapidly increasing in popularity relative to the U.S. dollar. In the foreign bond category, the U.S. dollar and the euro are major choices. Low interest rates, the general stability of the currency, and the overall efficiency of the European Union's capital markets are among the primary reasons for the growing popularity of the euro.

Eurobond
A bond issued by an international borrower and sold to investors in countries with currencies other than the currency in which the bond is denominated.

Eurobonds are much more popular than foreign bonds. These instruments are heavily used, especially in relation to Eurocurrency loans in recent years, by major market participants, including U.S. corporations. The so-called *equity-linked Eurobonds* (that is, Eurobonds convertible to equity), especially those offered by a number of U.S. firms, have found strong demand among Euromarket participants. It is expected that more of these innovative types of instruments will emerge on the international scene in the coming years.

A final point concerns the levels of interest rates in international markets. In the case of foreign bonds, interest rates are usually directly correlated with the domestic rates prevailing in the respective countries. For Eurobonds, several interest rates may be influential. For instance, for a Eurodollar bond, the interest rate will reflect several different rates, most notably the U.S. long-term rate, the Eurodollar rate, and long-term rates in other countries.

The Role of International Financial Institutions

For *foreign bonds,* the underwriting institutions are those that handle bond issues in the respective countries in which such bonds are issued. For *Eurobonds,* a number of financial institutions in the United States, Western Europe, and Japan form international underwriting syndicates. The underwriting costs for Eurobonds are comparable to those for bond flotation in the U.S. domestic market. Although

U.S. institutions once dominated the Eurobond scene, economic and financial strengths exhibited by some Western European (especially German) financial firms have led to an erosion in that dominance. Since 1986, a number of European firms have shared with U.S. firms the top positions in terms of acting as lead underwriters of Eurobond issues. However, U.S. investment banks continue to dominate most other international security issuance markets—such as international equity, medium-term note, syndicated loan, and commercial paper markets. U.S. corporations account for well over half of the worldwide securities issues made each year.

To raise funds through international bond issues, many MNCs establish their own financial subsidiaries. Many U.S.-based MNCs, for example, have created subsidiaries in the United States and Western Europe, especially in Luxembourg. Such subsidiaries can be used to raise large amounts of funds in "one move," the funds being redistributed wherever MNCs need them. (Special tax rules applicable to such subsidiaries also make them desirable to MNCs.)

Changing the Structure of Debt

As will be more fully explained later, MNCs can use *hedging strategies* to change the structure/characteristics of their long-term assets and liabilities. For instance, multinationals can use *interest rate swaps* to obtain a desired stream of interest payments (for example, fixed rate) in exchange for another (for example, floating rate). With *currency swaps,* they can exchange an asset/liability denominated in one currency (for example, the U.S. dollar) for another (for example, the British pound). The use of these tools allows MNCs to gain access to a broader set of markets, currencies, and maturities, thus leading to both cost savings and a means of restructuring the existing assets/liabilities. There has been significant growth in such use during the last few years, and this trend is expected to continue.

EQUITY CAPITAL

Here we look at how multinational companies can raise equity capital abroad. They can sell their shares in international capital markets, or they can use joint ventures, which the host country sometimes requires.

Equity Issues and Markets

One means of raising equity funds for MNCs is to have the parent's stock distributed internationally and owned by stockholders of different nationalities. Despite some advancements made in recent years that have allowed numerous MNCs to simultaneously list their respective stocks on a number of exchanges, the world's equity markets continue to be dominated by distinct *national* stock exchanges (such as the New York, London, and Tokyo exchanges). At the end of 2006, for example, a rather small portion of each of the world's major stock exchanges consisted of "foreign company" listings. Many commentators agree that most MNCs would benefit enormously from an **international stock market** that had uniform rules and regulations governing the major stock exchanges. Unfortunately, it will likely be many years before such a market becomes a reality.

Even with the full financial integration of the European Union, some European stock exchanges continue to compete with each other. Others have called for more cooperation in forming a single market capable of competing with the New

international stock market
A market with uniform rules and regulations governing major stock exchanges. MNCs would benefit greatly from such a market, which has yet to evolve.

York and Tokyo exchanges. As noted above, from the multinationals' perspective, the most desirable outcome would be to have uniform international rules and regulations with respect to all the major national stock exchanges. Such uniformity would allow MNCs unrestricted access to an international equity market paralleling the international currency and bond markets.

Joint Ventures

Earlier, we discussed the basic aspects of foreign ownership of international operations. Worth emphasizing here is that certain laws and regulations enacted by a number of host countries require MNCs to maintain less than 50 percent ownership in their subsidiaries in those countries. For a U.S.-based MNC, for example, establishing foreign subsidiaries in the form of joint ventures means that a certain portion of the firm's total international equity stock is (indirectly) held by foreign owners.

In establishing a foreign subsidiary, an MNC may wish to use as little equity and as much debt as possible, with the debt coming from local sources in the host country or the MNC itself. Each of these actions can be supported: The use of local debt can be a good protective measure to lessen the potential impacts of political risk. Because local sources are involved in the capital structure of a subsidiary, there may be fewer threats from local authorities in the event of changes in government or the imposing of new regulations on foreign business.

In support of the other action—having *more MNC-based debt* in a subsidiary's capital structure—many host governments are less restrictive toward intra-MNC interest payments than toward intra-MNC dividend remittances. The parent firm, therefore, may be in a better position if it has more MNC-based debt than equity in the capital structure of its subsidiaries.

→ REVIEW QUESTIONS

19–9 Indicate how NPV can differ depending on whether it is measured from the parent MNC's point of view or from that of the foreign subsidiary, when cash flows may be blocked by local authorities.

19–10 Briefly discuss some of the international factors that cause the capital structures of MNCs to differ from those of purely domestic firms.

19–11 Describe the difference between *foreign bonds* and *Eurobonds*. Explain how each is sold, and discuss the determinant(s) of their interest rates.

19–12 What are the long-run advantages of having more *local* debt and less MNC-based equity in the capital structure of a foreign subsidiary?

LG 5   19.5 Short-Term Financial Decisions

In international operations, the usual domestic sources of short-term financing, along with other sources, are available to MNCs. Included are accounts payable, accruals, bank and nonbank sources in each subsidiary's local environment, and the Euromarket. Our emphasis here is on the "foreign" sources.

The local economic market is a basic source of both short- and long-term financing for a subsidiary of a multinational company. Moreover, the subsidiary's borrowing and lending status, relative to a local firm in the same economy, can be

Eurocurrency markets
The portion of the Euromarket that provides short-term, foreign-currency financing to subsidiaries of MNCs.

nominal interest rate
In the international context, the stated interest rate charged on financing when only the MNC parent's currency is involved.

effective interest rate
In the international context, the rate equal to the nominal rate plus (or minus) any forecast appreciation (or depreciation) of a foreign currency relative to the currency of the MNC parent.

superior because the subsidiary can rely on the potential backing and guarantee of its parent MNC. One drawback, however, is that most local markets and local currencies are regulated by local authorities. A subsidiary may ultimately choose to turn to the Euromarket and take advantage of borrowing and investing in an unregulated financial forum.

The Euromarket offers nondomestic long-term financing opportunities through Eurobonds, which were discussed in Chapter 6. Short-term financing opportunities are available in **Eurocurrency markets.** The forces of supply and demand are among the main factors determining exchange rates in Eurocurrency markets. Each currency's normal interest rate is influenced by economic policies pursued by the respective "home" government. For example, the interest rates offered in the Euromarket on the U.S. dollar are greatly affected by the prime rate inside the United States, and the dollar's exchange rates with other major currencies are influenced by the supply and demand forces in such markets (and in response to interest rates).

Unlike borrowing in the domestic markets, where only one currency and a **nominal interest rate** are involved, financing activities in the Euromarket can involve several currencies and both nominal and effective interest rates. **Effective interest rates** are equal to nominal rates plus (or minus) any forecast appreciation (or depreciation) of a foreign currency relative to the currency of the MNC parent. Stated differently, the figures for effective rates are derived by adjusting the nominal interest rates for the impact of foreign-currency movements on both the principal and interest amounts. Equation 19.1 can be used to calculate the effective interest rate for a specific currency (E), given the nominal interest rate for the currency (N) and its forecast percentage change (F):

$$E = N + F + (N \times F) \qquad (19.1)$$

An example will illustrate the application and interpretation of this relationship.

Example 19.6 ▶ A multinational plastics company, International Molding, has subsidiaries in Switzerland (local currency, Swiss franc, Sf) and Japan (local currency, Japanese yen, ¥). On the basis of each subsidiary's forecast operations, the short-term financial needs (in equivalent U.S. dollars) are as follows:

Switzerland: $80 million excess cash to be invested (lent)

Japan: $60 million funds to be raised (borrowed)

On the basis of all the available information, the parent firm has provided each subsidiary with the figures given in the table on page 783 for exchange rates and interest rates. (The figures for the effective rates shown are derived using Equation 19.1.)

From the MNC's point of view, the effective rates of interest, which take into account each currency's forecast percentage change (appreciation or depreciation) relative to the U.S. dollar, are the main considerations in investment and borrowing decisions. (It is assumed here that because of local regulations, a subsidiary is *not* permitted to use the domestic market of *any other* subsidiary.) The relevant question is where funds should be invested and borrowed.

For investment purposes, the highest available effective rate of interest is 3.30% in the US$ Euromarket. Therefore, the Swiss subsidiary should invest the

	Currency		
Item	US$	Sf	¥
Spot exchange rates		Sf 1.27/US$	¥108.37/US$
Forecast percent change		−2.0%	+1.0%
Interest rates			
Nominal			
Euromarket	3.30%	4.10%	1.50%
Domestic	3.00%	3.80%	1.70%
Effective			
Euromarket	3.30%	2.01%	2.51%
Domestic	3.00%	1.72%	2.71%

$80 million in Swiss francs in U.S. dollars. To raise funds, the cheapest source *open* to the Japanese subsidiary is the 2.01% effective rate for the Swiss franc in the Euromarket. The subsidiary should therefore raise the $60 million in Swiss francs in the Euromarket. These two transactions will result in the most revenues and least costs, respectively.

Several points should be made with respect to the preceding example. First, this is a simplified case of the actual workings of the Eurocurrency markets. The example ignores taxes, intersubsidiary investing and borrowing, and periods longer or shorter than a year. Nevertheless, it shows how the existence of many currencies can provide both challenges and opportunities for MNCs. Next, the focus has been solely on accounting values; of greater importance would be the impact of these actions on market value. Finally, it is important to note the following details about the figures presented. The forecast percentage change data are those normally supplied by the MNC's international financial managers. Management may instead want a *range of forecasts,* from the most likely to the least likely. In addition, the company's management is likely to take a specific position in terms of its response to any remaining exchange rate exposures. If any action is to be taken, certain amounts of one or more currencies will be borrowed and then invested in other currencies in the hope of realizing potential gains to offset potential losses associated with the exposures.

CASH MANAGEMENT

In its international cash management, a multinational firm can respond to exchange rate risks by protecting (hedging) its undesirable cash and marketable securities exposures or by making certain adjustments in its operations. The former approach is more applicable in responding to *accounting exposures,* the latter to *economic exposures.* Here, we examine each of these two approaches.

Hedging Strategies

hedging strategies
Techniques used to offset or protect against risk; in the international context, these include borrowing or lending in different currencies; undertaking contracts in the forward, futures, and/or options markets; and swapping assets/liabilities with other parties.

Hedging strategies are techniques used to offset or protect against risk. In international cash management, these strategies include actions such as borrowing or lending in different currencies; undertaking contracts in the forward, futures, and/or options markets; and swapping assets/liabilities with other parties. Table 19.5

TABLE 19.5	Exchange Rate Risk-Hedging Tools	
Tool	Description	Impact on risk
Borrowing or lending	Borrowing or lending in different currencies to take advantage of interest rate differentials and foreign exchange appreciation/depreciation; can be either on a certainty basis with "up-front" costs or speculative.	Can be used to offset exposures in existing assets/liabilities and in expected revenues/expenses.
Forward contract	"Tailor-made" contracts representing an *obligation* to buy/sell, with the amount, rate, and maturity agreed upon between the two parties; has little up-front cost.	Can eliminate downside risk but locks out any upside potential.
Futures contract	Standardized contracts offered on organized exchanges; same basic tool as a forward contract but less flexible because of standardization; more flexibility because of secondary-market access; has some up-front cost.	Can eliminate downside risk, plus position can be nullified, creating possible upside potential.
Options	Tailor-made or standardized contracts providing the *right* to buy or to sell an amount of the currency, at a particular price, during a specified time period; has up-front cost (premium).	Can eliminate downside risk and retain unlimited upside potential.
Interest rate swap	Allows the trading of one interest rate stream (e.g., on a fixed-rate U.S. dollar instrument) for another (e.g., on a floating-rate U.S. dollar instrument); fee to be paid to the intermediary.	Permits firms to change the interest rate structure of their assets/liabilities and achieves cost savings via broader market access.
Currency swap	Two parties exchange principal amounts of two different currencies initially; they pay each other's interest payments and then reverse principal amounts at a preagreed exchange rate at maturity; more complex than interest rate swaps.	Has all the features of interest rate swaps, plus allows firms to change the currency structure of their assets/liabilities.
Hybrids	A variety of combinations of some of the preceding tools; may be quite costly and/or speculative.	Can create, with the right combination, a perfect hedge against certain exchange rate exposures.

Note: The participants in these activities include MNCs, financial institutions, and brokers. The organized exchanges include Amsterdam, Chicago, London, New York, Philadelphia, and Zurich, among others. Although most of these tools can be used for short-term exposure management, some, such as swaps, are more appropriate for long-term hedging strategies.

briefly outlines some of the major hedging tools available to MNCs. By far, the most commonly used technique is hedging with a forward contract.

To demonstrate how you can use a forward contract to hedge exchange rate risk, assume you are a financial manager for Boeing Company, which has just booked a sale of three airplanes worth $360 million to Japan's All Nippon Airways. The sale is denominated in Japanese yen, and the current spot exchange rate is ¥108.37/US$. Therefore, you have priced this airplane sale at ¥39.0132 billion. If delivery were to occur today, there would be no foreign exchange risk. However, delivery and payment will not occur for 90 days. If this transaction is not hedged, Boeing will be exposed to a significant risk of loss if the Japanese yen depreciates over the next 3 months.

Suppose that between now and the delivery date, the dollar appreciates against the yen from ¥108.37/US$ to ¥110.25/US$. On delivery of the airplanes, the agreed-upon ¥39.0132 billion will then be worth only US$353.861 million

[(¥39.0132 billion) ÷ (¥110.25/US$)], rather than the US$360 million you originally planned for—a foreign exchange *loss* of more than US$6.1 million. If, instead of remaining unhedged, you had sold the ¥39.0132 billion forward 3 months earlier at the 90-day forward rate of ¥107.92/US$ offered by your bank, you could have locked in a net dollar sale price of US$361.501 million [(¥39.0132 billion/US$) ÷ (¥107.92/US$)], realizing a foreign exchange *gain* of more than $1.5 million. Clearly, this is a better alternative. Of course, if you had remained unhedged, and the Japanese yen had appreciated beyond ¥107.92/US$, your firm would have experienced an even larger foreign exchange profit—but most MNCs prefer to make profits through sales of goods and services rather than by speculating on the direction of exchange rates.

Adjustments in Operations

In responding to exchange rate fluctuations, MNCs can give their international cash flows some protection through appropriate adjustments in assets and liabilities. Two routes are available to a multinational company. The first centers on the operating relationships that a subsidiary of an MNC maintains with *other* firms—*third parties*. Depending on management's expectation of a local currency's position, adjustments in operations would involve the reduction of liabilities if the currency is appreciating or the reduction of financial assets if it is depreciating. For example, if a U.S.-based MNC with a subsidiary in Mexico expects the peso to *appreciate* in value relative to the U.S. dollar, local customers' accounts receivable would be *increased* and accounts payable would be reduced if at all possible. Because the dollar is the currency in which the MNC parent will have to prepare consolidated financial statements, the net result in this case would be favorably to increase the Mexican subsidiary's resources in local currency. If the peso were instead expected to *depreciate*, the local customers' accounts receivable would be *reduced* and accounts payable would be increased, thereby reducing the Mexican subsidiary's resources in the local currency.

The second route focuses on the operating relationship a subsidiary has with its parent or with other subsidiaries within the same MNC. In dealing with exchange rate risks, a subsidiary can rely on *intra-MNC accounts*. Specifically, undesirable exchange rate exposures can be corrected to the extent that the subsidiary can take the following steps:

1. In appreciation-prone countries, collect intra-MNC accounts receivable as soon as possible, and delay payment of intra-MNC accounts payable as long as possible.
2. In depreciation-prone countries, collect intra-MNC accounts receivable as late as possible, and pay intra-MNC accounts payable as soon as possible.

This technique is known as "leading and lagging" or simply as "leads and lags."

Example 19.7 ▶ Assume that a U.S.-based parent company, American Computer Corporation (ACC), both buys parts from and sells parts to its wholly owned Mexican subsidiary, Tijuana Computer Company (TCC). Assume further that ACC has accounts payable of $10,000,000 that it is scheduled to pay TCC in 30 days and, in turn, has accounts receivable of (Mexican peso) MP 115.00 million due from TCC within 30 days. Because today's exchange rate is MP 11.50/US$, the accounts receivable are also worth $10,000,000. Therefore, parent and subsidiary owe each other equal amounts (though in different currencies), and both are payable in 30 days, but because TCC is a wholly owned subsidiary of ACC the parent has complete discretion over the timing of these payments.

If ACC believes that the Mexican peso will depreciate from MP 11.50/US$ to, say, MP 12.75/US$ during the next 30 days, the combined companies can profit by collecting the weak currency (MP) debt immediately but delaying payment of the strong currency (US$) debt for the full 30 days allowed. If parent and subsidiary do this, and the peso depreciates as predicted, the net result is that the MP 115.00 million payment from TCC to ACC is made immediately and is safely converted into $10,000,000 at today's exchange rate. In comparison, the delayed $10,000,000 payment from ACC to TCC will be worth MP 127.50 million [($10 million) × (MP 12.75/US$)]. Thus the Mexican subsidiary will experience a foreign exchange trading profit of MP 12.50 million (MP 127.50 million − MP 115.00 million), whereas the U.S. parent receives the full amount ($10 million) due from TCC and therefore is unharmed.

As this example suggests, the manipulation of an MNC's consolidated intracompany accounts by one subsidiary generally benefits one subsidiary (or the parent) while leaving the other subsidiary (or the parent) unharmed. The exact degree and direction of the actual manipulations, however, may depend on the tax status of each country. The MNC obviously would want to have the exchange rate losses in the country with the higher tax rate. Finally, changes in intra-MNC accounts can also be subject to restrictions and regulations put forward by the respective host countries of various subsidiaries.

CREDIT AND INVENTORY MANAGEMENT

Multinational firms based in different countries compete for the same global export markets. Therefore, it is essential that they offer attractive credit terms to potential customers. Increasingly, however, the maturity of developed markets is forcing MNCs to maintain and increase revenues by exporting and selling a higher percentage of their output to developing countries. Given the risks associated with these buyers, as partly evidenced by their lack of a major (hard) currency, the MNC must use a variety of tools to protect such revenues. In addition to the use of hedging and various asset and liability adjustments (described earlier), MNCs should seek the backing of their respective governments in both identifying target markets and extending credit. Multinationals based in a number of Western European nations and those based in Japan benefit from extensive involvement of government agencies that provide them with the needed service and financial support. For U.S.-based MNCs, government agencies such as the Export-Import Bank do not provide a comparable level of support.

In terms of inventory management, MNCs must consider a number of factors related to both economics and politics. In addition to maintaining the appropriate level of inventory in various locations around the world, a multinational firm must deal with exchange rate fluctuations, tariffs, nontariff barriers, integration schemes such as the EU, and other rules and regulations. Politically, inventories could be subjected to wars, expropriations, blockages, and other forms of government intervention.

→ **REVIEW QUESTIONS**

19–13 What is the *Eurocurrency market?* What are the main factors determining foreign exchange rates in that market? Differentiate between the *nominal interest rate* and the *effective interest rate* in this market.

19–14 Discuss the steps to be followed in adjusting a subsidiary's accounts relative to *third parties* when that subsidiary's local currency is expected to *appreciate* in value in relation to the currency of the parent MNC.

19–15 Outline the changes to be undertaken in *intra-MNC accounts* if a subsidiary's currency is expected to *depreciate* in value relative to the currency of the parent MNC.

LG 6   # 19.6 Mergers and Joint Ventures

The motives for domestic mergers—growth or diversification, synergy, fund raising, increased managerial skill or technology, tax considerations, increased ownership liquidity, and defense against takeover—are all applicable to MNCs' international mergers and joint ventures. And we should consider several additional points.

First, international mergers and joint ventures, especially those involving European firms acquiring assets in the United States, increased significantly beginning in the 1980s. MNCs based in Western Europe, Japan, and North America are numerous. Moreover, a fast-growing group of MNCs has emerged in the past two decades, some based in the so-called newly industrialized countries (including Singapore, South Korea, Taiwan, and China's Hong Kong), and others operating from emerging nations (such as Brazil, Argentina, Mexico, Israel, China, Malaysia, Thailand, and India). Even though many of these companies were hit hard by economic and currency crises (Asia in 1997, Russia in 1998, and Latin America in 2001–2003), top firms from these and other countries have been able to survive and even prosper. Additionally, many Western companies have taken advantage of these economies' weakness to buy into companies that were previously off-limits to foreign investors. This has added further to the number and value of international mergers.

The U.S. economy is among the largest recipients of FDI inflows. Most of the foreign direct investors in the United States come from seven countries: the United Kingdom, Canada, France, the Netherlands, Japan, Switzerland, and Germany. The available data indicate that in terms of the method of entry— namely mergers and acquisitions (M&A) versus "establishments"—an overwhelming share of outlays committed by foreign multinationals in the United States between 1980 and 2006 has consisted of M&A. These firms prefer M&A through which they can target U.S. companies for their advanced technology (for example, biotechnology firms), worldwide brands (restaurant chains and food products), entertainment/media (theme parks), and financial institutions (investment banks). In contrast, in most emerging/developing nations (including China), FDI inflows take place primarily via establishments.

Although the United States remains one of the most "open" countries to FDI inflows, some of its actions in recent years have been viewed as less than welcoming. In 2005, for example, the U.S. governnment opposed a bid by a Chinese state-owned oil company (CNOOC) to purchase an American one (UNOCAL), which led to the ultimate withdrawal of the offer. Then, in 2005 and 2006, similar opposition, along with an identical outcome, took place in relation to a bid by a firm owned by the government of Dubai (in the United Arab Emirates) to acquire port operations in the United States.

Another trend is the current increase in the number of joint ventures between companies based in Japan and firms domiciled elsewhere in the industrialized world, especially U.S.-based MNCs. In the eyes of some U.S. corporate executives, such business ventures are viewed as a "ticket into the Japanese market" as well as a way to curb a potentially tough competitor.

Developing countries, too, have been attracting foreign direct investments in many industries. Meanwhile, during the last two decades, a number of these nations have adopted specific policies and regulations aimed at controlling the inflows of foreign investments, a major provision being the 49 percent ownership limitation applied to MNCs. Of course, international competition among MNCs has benefited some developing countries in their attempts to extract concessions from the multinationals. However, an increasing number of such nations have shown greater flexibility in their recent dealings with MNCs, as MNCs have become more reluctant to form joint ventures under the stated conditions. Furthermore, it is likely that as more developing countries recognize the need for foreign capital and technology, they will show even greater flexibility in their agreements with MNCs.

A final point relates to the existence of international holding companies. Places such as Liechtenstein and Panama have long been considered promising spots for forming holding companies because of their favorable legal, corporate, and tax environments. International holding companies control many business entities in the form of subsidiaries, branches, joint ventures, and other agreements. For international legal (especially tax-related) reasons, as well as anonymity, such holding companies have become increasingly popular in recent years.

→ REVIEW QUESTION

19–16 What are some of the major reasons for the rapid expansion in international mergers and joint ventures of firms?

Summary

FOCUS ON VALUE

The growing interdependence of world markets has increased the importance of international finance in managing the multinational company (MNC). As a result, the financial manager must deal with international issues related to taxes, financial markets, accounting and profit measurement and repatriation, exchange rate risks caused by doing business in more than one currency, political risks, financing (both debt and equity) and capital structure, short-term financing, cash management issues related to hedging and adjustments in operations, and merger and joint-venture opportunities.

The complexity of each of these issues is significantly greater for the multinational firm than for a purely domestic firm. Consequently, the financial manager must approach actions and decisions in the multinational firm using both standard financial tools and techniques and additional procedures that recognize the legal, institutional, and operating differences that exist in the multinational environment. Just as in a purely domestic firm, action should be undertaken only after the financial manager has determined that it will contribute to the parent company's overall goal of **maximizing the owners' wealth** as reflected in its share price.

REVIEW OF LEARNING GOALS

LG 1   **Understand the major factors that influence the financial operations of multinational companies (MNCs).** Important international trading blocs emerged in the 1990s: one in the Americas as a result of NAFTA; the European Union (EU); and Mercosur in South America. The EU is becoming even more competitive as it achieves monetary union and many of its members use the euro as a single currency. Free trade among the largest economic powers is governed by the General Agreement on Tariffs and Trade (GATT) and is policed by the World Trade Organization (WTO).

Setting up operations in foreign countries can entail special problems related to the legal form of business organization chosen, the degree of ownership allowed by the host country, and possible restrictions and regulations on the return of capital and profits. Taxation of multinational companies is a complex issue because of the existence of varying tax rates, differing definitions of taxable income, measurement differences, and tax treaties.

The existence and expansion of dollars held outside the United States have contributed to the development of a major international financial market, the Euromarket. The large international banks, developing and industrialized nations, and multinational companies participate as borrowers and lenders in this market.

LG 2   **Describe the key differences between purely domestic and international financial statements—consolidation, translation of individual accounts, and international profits.** Regulations that apply to international operations complicate the preparation of foreign-based financial statements. Rulings in the United States require the determination for translation purposes of the functional currency used in the operations of a foreign subsidiary. Individual accounts of subsidiaries must be translated back into U.S. dollars using the procedures outlined in *FASB No. 52* and/or the temporal method. This standard also requires that only certain transactional gains or losses from international operations be included in the U.S. parent's income statement.

LG 3   **Discuss exchange rate risk and political risk, and explain how MNCs manage them.** Economic exposure from exchange rate risk results from the existence of different currencies and their impact on the value of foreign operations. Long-term changes in foreign exchange rates result primarily from differing inflation rates in the two countries. The money markets, the forward (futures) markets, and the foreign-currency options markets can be used to hedge foreign exchange exposure. Political risks stem mainly from the implications of political instability for the assets and operations of MNCs. MNCs can employ negative, external, and positive approaches to cope with political risk.

LG 4   **Describe foreign direct investment, investment cash flows and decisions, the MNCs' capital structure, and the international debt and equity instruments available to MNCs.** Foreign direct investment (FDI) involves an MNC's transfer of capital, managerial, and technical assets from its home country to the host country. The investment cash flows of FDIs are subject to a variety of factors, including taxes in host countries, regulations that may block the repatriation of MNCs' cash flow, various business and financial risks, and the application of a local cost of capital.

The capital structures of MNCs differ from those of purely domestic firms because of the MNCs' access to the Euromarket and the financial instruments it offers, their ability to reduce risk in their cash flows through international diversification, and the impact of factors unique to each host country. MNCs can raise long-term debt by issuing international bonds in various currencies. Foreign bonds are sold primarily in the country of the currency of issue; Eurobonds are sold primarily in countries other than the country of the issue's currency. MNCs can raise equity through sale of shares in international capital markets or through joint ventures. In establishing foreign subsidiaries, it may be more advantageous to issue debt than MNC-owned equity.

LG 5 **Discuss the role of the Eurocurrency market in short-term borrowing and investing (lending) and the basics of international cash, credit, and inventory management.** Eurocurrency markets allow multinationals to invest (lend) and raise (borrow) short-term funds in a variety of currencies and to protect themselves against exchange rate risk. MNCs consider effective interest rates, which take into account currency fluctuations, in making investment and borrowing decisions. MNCs invest in the currency with the highest effective rate and borrow in the currency with the lowest effective rate. MNCs must offer competitive credit terms and maintain adequate inventories to provide timely delivery to foreign buyers. Obtaining the backing of foreign governments is helpful to MNCs in effectively managing credit and inventory.

LG 6 **Review recent trends in international mergers and joint ventures.** International mergers and joint ventures, including international holding companies, increased significantly beginning in the 1980s. Special factors affecting these mergers include economic and trade conditions and various regulations imposed on MNCs by host countries.

Opener-in-Review

In the chapter opener you read about General Electric's commitment to a global focus. What makes entering an international marketplace attractive for companies like GE, and what are some common risks associated with operating internationally?

Self-Test Problem (Solution in Appendix)

LG 1 **ST19–1** **Tax credits** A U.S.-based MNC has a foreign subsidiary that earns $150,000 before local taxes, with all the after-tax funds to be available to the parent in the form of dividends. The applicable taxes consist of a 32% foreign income tax rate, a foreign dividend withholding tax rate of 8%, and a U.S. tax rate of 34%. Calculate the net funds available to the parent MNC if:
a. Foreign taxes can be applied as a credit against the MNC's U.S. tax liability.
b. No tax credits are allowed.

Warm-Up Exercises

All problems are available in myfinancelab.

LG 1 **E19–1** Santana Music is a U.S.-based MNC whose foreign subsidiary had pretax income of $55,000; all after-tax income is available in the form of dividends to the parent company. The local tax rate is 40%, the foreign dividend withholding tax rate is 5%, and the U.S. tax rate is 34%. Compare the net funds available to the parent corporation (a) if foreign taxes can be applied against the U.S. tax liability and (b) if they cannot.

LG 3 **E19–2** Assume that the Mexican peso currently trades at 12 pesos to the U.S. dollar. During the year U.S. inflation is expected to average 3%, while Mexican inflation is expected to average 5%. What is the current value of one peso in terms of U.S. dollars? Given the relative inflation rates, what will the exchange rates be 1 year from now? Which currency is expected to *appreciate* and which currency is expected to *depreciate* over the next year?

LG 5 **E19–3** If Like A Lot Corp. borrows yen at a nominal annual interest rate of 2% and during the year the yen appreciates by 10%, what will the *effective annual interest rate* be for the loan?

LG 3 **LG 5** **E19–4** Carry Trade, Inc., borrows yen when the yen is trading at ¥110/US$. If the nominal annual interest rate of the loan is 3% and at the end of the year the yen trades at ¥120/US$, what is the *effective annual interest rate* of the loan?

LG 5 **E19–5** Denim Industries can borrow its needed financing for expansion using one of two foreign lending facilities. It can borrow at a nominal annual interest rate of 8% in Mexican pesos or at 3% in Canadian dollars. If the peso is expected to depreciate by 10% and the Canadian dollar is expected to appreciate by 3%, which loan has the lower *effective annual interest rate*?

Problems

All problems are available in myfinancelab.

LG 1 **P19–1** **Tax credits** A U.S.-based MNC has a foreign subsidiary that earns $250,000 before local taxes, with all the after-tax funds to be available to the parent in the form of dividends. The applicable taxes consist of a 33% foreign income tax rate, a foreign dividend withholding tax rate of 9%, and a U.S. tax rate of 34%. Calculate the net funds available to the parent MNC if:
a. Foreign taxes can be applied as a credit against the MNC's U.S. tax liability.
b. No tax credits are allowed.

LG 3 **P19–2** **Translation of financial statements** A U.S.-based MNC has a subsidiary in France (local currency, euro, €). The balance sheet and income statement of the subsidiary follow. On December 31, 2112, the exchange rate is US$1.20/€. Assume that the local (euro) figures for the statements remain the same on December 21, 2113. Calculate the U.S. dollar-translated figures for the two ending time periods, assuming that between December 31, 2112, and December 31, 2113, the euro has appreciated against the U.S. dollar by 6%.

Translation of Income Statement			
	December 31, 2112		December 31, 2113
	Euro	US$	US$
Sales	30,000.00		
Cost of goods sold	29,750.00	_____	_____
Operating profits	250.00	══════	══════

Translation of Balance Sheet			
	December 31, 2112		December 31, 2113
Assets	Euro	US$	US$
Cash	40.00		
Inventory	300.00		
Plant and equipment (net)	160.00	_____	_____
Total	500.00	══════	══════
Liabilities and Stockholders' Equity			
Debt	240.00		
Paid-in capital	200.00		
Retained earnings	60.00	_____	_____
Total	500.00	══════	══════

Personal Finance Problem

LG 3   **P19–3**   **Exchange rates**   Fred Nappa is planning to take a wine-tasting tour through Italy this summer. The tour will cost 2,750 euros (€) and includes transportation, hotels, and a guide. Fred estimates that round-trip airfare from his home in North Carolina to Rome, Italy, will be $1,490; he also will incur another $300 (U.S.) in incidental travel expenses. Fred estimates the cost of meals in Italy to be about €500, and he will take an additional $1,000 to cover miscellaneous expenditures. Currently the exchange rate is US$1.3411/€1.00 (or €.7456/US$1.00).

a. Determine the total dollar cost of the trip to Italy.

b. Determine the amount of euros (€) Fred will need to cover meals and miscellaneous expenditures.

Personal Finance Problem

LG 4   **P19–4**   **International investment diversification**   The economies of the world tend to rise and fall in cycles that offset each other. International stocks can provide possible diversification for a portfolio heavy on U.S. equities. Because research on foreign companies is usually difficult for individual investors to track on their own, a foreign equity mutual fund offers the investor the expertise of a global fund manager.

Foreign-stock funds provide exposure to overseas markets at varying levels of risk. Economic and currency risk can swing in a positive or negative direction.

Hence, diversification is the key to managing risk. Funds that invest overseas fall into four basic categories: global, international, emerging-market, and country-specific. The wider the reach of the fund, the less risky it is likely to be.

a. Go to http://finance.yahoo.com. Click on the "Investing" tab and then click on "Mutual Funds." On the left, under "Education" click on "Types of Mutual Funds." In the middle of the page, click on "Foreign Stock Funds Explained."

b. Briefly explain the differences between the following funds:
(1) Global fund
(2) International fund
(3) Emerging-market fund
(4) Country-specific fund

LG 5   **P19–5**   **Euromarket investment and fund raising**   A U.S.-based multinational company has two subsidiaries, one in Mexico (local currency, Mexican peso, MP) and one in Japan (local currency, yen, ¥). Forecasts of business operations indicate the following short-term financing position for each subsidiary (in equivalent U.S. dollars):

Mexico: $80 million excess cash to be invested (lent)

Japan: $60 million funds to be raised (borrowed)

The management gathered the following data:

Item	US $	Currency MP	¥
Spot exchange rates		MP 11.60/US$	¥108.25/US$
Forecast percent change		−3.0%	+1.5%
Interest rates			
Nominal			
Euromarket	4.00%	6.20%	2.00%
Domestic	3.75%	5.90%	2.15%
Effective			
Euromarket	_____	_____	_____
Domestic	_____	_____	_____

Determine the *effective interest rates* for all three currencies in both the Euromarket and the domestic market; then indicate where the funds should be invested and raised. (*Note:* Assume that because of local regulations, a subsidiary is *not* permitted to use the domestic market of *any other* subsidiary.)

LG 1   **P19–6**   **ETHICS PROBLEM**   Is there a conflict between maximizing shareholder wealth and never paying bribes when doing business abroad? If so, how might you explain the firm's position to shareholders asking why the company does not pay bribes when its foreign competitors in various nations clearly do so?

Spreadsheet Exercise

As the financial manager for a large multinational corporation (MNC), you have been asked to assess the firm's *economic exposure*. The two major currencies, other than the U.S. dollar, that affect the company are the Mexican peso (MP) and the British pound (£). You have been given the projected future cash flows for next year:

Currency	Total inflow	Total outflow
British pounds	£17,000,000	£11,000,000
Mexican pesos	MP 100,000,000	MP 25,000,000

The current expected exchange rate in U.S. dollars with respect to the two currencies is as follows:

Currency	Exchange rate
British pounds	$1.66
Mexican pesos	$0.10

TO DO

Assume that the movements in the Mexican peso and the British pound are highly correlated. Create a spreadsheet to answer the following questions.

a. Determine the net cash flows for both the Mexican peso and the British pound.
b. Determine the net cash flow as measured in U.S. dollars. It will represent the value of the *economic exposure*.
c. Provide your assessment as to the company's degree of economic exposure. In other words, is it high or low based on your findings in part **b**?

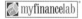 Visit www.myfinancelab.com for **Chapter Case: *Assessing a Direct Investment in Chile by U.S. Computer Corporation,*** Group Exercises, and numerous online resources.

Organic Solutions

Organic Solutions (OS), one of the nation's largest plant wholesalers in the southeastern United States, was poised for expansion. Through strong profitability, a conservative dividend policy, and some recent realized gains in real estate, OS had a strong cash position and was searching for a target company to acquire. The executive members on the acquisition search committee had agreed that they preferred to find a firm in a similar line of business rather than one that would provide broad diversification. This would be their first acquisition, and they preferred to stay in a familiar line of business. Jennifer Morgan, director of marketing, had identified the targeted lines of business through exhaustive market research.

Ms. Morgan had determined that the servicing of plants in large commercial offices, hotels, zoos, and theme parks would complement the existing wholesale distribution business. Frequently, OS was requested by its large clients to bid on a service contract. However, the company was neither staffed nor equipped to enter this market. Ms. Morgan was familiar with the major plant service companies in the Southeast and had suggested Green Thumbs, Inc. (GTI), as an acquisition target because of its significant market share and excellent reputation.

GTI had successfully commercialized a market that had been dominated by small local contractors and in-house landscaping departments. Beginning with a contract from one of the largest theme parks in the United States, GTI's growth in sales had compounded remarkably over its 8-year history. GTI had also been selected because of its large portfolio of long-term service contracts with several major *Fortune* 500 companies. These contracted clients would provide a captive customer base for the wholesale distribution of OS's plant products.

At the National Horticultural meeting in Los Angeles this past March, Ms. Morgan and OS's chief financial officer, Jack Levine, had approached the owner of GTI (a closely held corporation) to determine whether a merger offer would be welcomed. GTI's majority owner and president, Herb Merrell, had reacted favorably and subsequently provided financial data, including GTI's earnings record and current balance sheet. This data is presented in Tables 1 (below) and 2 (on the next page).

Jack Levine had estimated that the incremental cash inflow after taxes from the acquisition would be $18,750,000 for years 1 and 2; $20,500,000 for year 3; $21,750,000 for year 4; $24,000,000 for year 5; and $25,000,000 for years 6 through 30. He also estimated that the company should earn a rate of return of at least 16% on an investment of this type. Additional financial data for 2012 are given in Table 3.

TABLE 1

Green Thumbs, Inc. Earning Record			
Year	EPS	Year	EPS
2005	$2.20	2006	$2.85
2006	2.35	2007	3.00
2007	2.45	2008	3.10
2008	2.60	2009	3.30

TABLE 2

Green Thumbs, Inc. Balance Sheet (December 31, 2012)

Assets		Liabilities and Equity	
Cash	$ 2,500,000	Current liabilities	$ 5,250,000
Accounts receivable	1,500,000	Mortgage payable	3,125,000
Inventories	7,625,000	Common stock	15,625,000
Land	7,475,000	Retained earnings	9,000,000
Fixed assets (net)	13,900,000	Total liabilities and equity	$33,000,000
Total assets	$33,000,000		

TABLE 3

OS and GTI Financial Data (December 31, 2012)

Item	OS	GTI
Earnings available for common stock	$35,000,000	$15,246,000
Number of shares of common stock	10,000,000	4,620,000
Market price per share	$50	$30[a]

[a]Estimated by Organic Solutions.

TO DO

a. What is the maximum price that Organic Solutions should offer GTI for a cash acquisition? (*Note:* Assume the relevant time horizon for analysis is 30 years.)

b. If OS planned to sell bonds to finance 80% of the cash acquisition price found in part **a,** how might issuance of each of the following bonds affect the firm? Describe the characteristics and pros and cons of each bond:
   (1) Straight bonds.
   (2) Convertible bonds.
   (3) Bonds with stock purchase warrants attached.

c. (1) What is the *ratio of exchange* in a stock swap acquisition if OS pays $30 per share for GTI? Explain why.
   (2) What effect will this swap of stock have on the EPS of the original shareholders of (i) Organic Solutions and (ii) Green Thumbs, Inc.? Explain why.
   (3) If the earnings attributed to GTI's assets grow at a much slower rate than those attributed to OS's premerger assets, what effect might this have on the EPS of the merged firm over the long run?

d. What other merger proposals could OS make to GTI's owners?

e. What impact would the fact that GTI is actually a foreign-based company have on the foregoing analysis? Describe the added regulations, costs, benefits, and risks that are likely to be associated with such an international merger.

Solutions to Self-Test Problems

Chapter 1

ST1–1

Accounting view (accrual basis)		Financial view (cash basis)	
Worldwide Rugs income statement for the year ended 12/31		**Worldwide Rugs cash flow statement for the year ended 12/31**	
Sales revenue	$3,000,000	Cash inflow	$2,550,000
Less: Costs	2,500,000	Less: Cash outflow	2,500,000
Net profit	$ 500,000	Net cash flow	$ 50,000

a. $3,000,000 − $2,500,000 = $500,000

b. Yes, from an accounting perspective Worldwide Rug was profitable. It generated a 20% profit ($500,000/$2,500,000 = 0.20) on its investment.

c. $2,550,000 − $2,500,000 = $50,000

d. It generated a positive cash flow, but it only represents a 2% return on investment ($50,000/$2,500,000 = 0.02), and it may not be enough to cover operating costs.

e. Given the risk associated with importing and Worldwide Rug's ability to collect on its accounts receivables, a 2% return on investment seems unlikely to lead to long-term success. Without adequate cash inflows to meet its obligations, the firm will not survive, regardless of its level of profits.

Chapter 2

ST2–1 a. Capital gains = $180,000 sale price − $150,000 original purchase price = $30,000

b. Total taxable income = $280,000 operating earnings + $30,000 capital gain = $310,000

c. Firm's tax liability:

Using Table 2.1:

Total taxes due = $22,250 + [0.39 × ($310,000 − $100,000)]

$$= \$22,250 + (0.39 \times \$210,000) = \$22,250 + \$81,900$$

$$= \underline{\underline{\$104,150}}$$

d. Average tax rate $= \dfrac{\$104,150}{\$310,000} = \underline{\underline{33.6\%}}$

Marginal tax rate $= \underline{\underline{39\%}}$

Chapter 3

ST3–1

Ratio	Too high	Too low
Current ratio = current assets/ current liabilities	May indicate that the firm is holding excessive cash, accounts receivable, or inventory.	May indicate poor ability to satisfy short-term obligations.
Inventory turnover = CGS/inventory	May indicate lower level of inventory, which may cause stockouts and lost sales.	May indicate poor inventory management, excessive inventory, or obsolete inventory.
Times interest earned = earnings before interest and taxes/interest		May indicate poor ability to pay contractual interest payments.
Gross profit margin = gross profits/sales	Indicates the low cost of merchandise sold relative to the sales price; may indicate non-competitive pricing and potential lost sales.	Indicates the high cost of the merchandise sold relative to the sales price; may indicate either a low sales price or a high cost of goods sold.
Return on total assets = net profits after taxes/ total assets		Indicates ineffective management in generating profits with the available assets.
Price/earnings (P/E) ratio = market price per share of common stock/earnings per share	Investors may have an excessive degree of confidence in the firm's future and underestimate its risk.	Investors lack confidence in the firm's future outcomes and feel that the firm has an excessive level of risk.

ST3–2

O'Keefe Industries
Balance Sheet
December 31, 2012

Assets		Liabilities and Stockholders' Equity	
Cash	$ 32,720	Accounts payable	$ 120,000
Marketable securities	25,000	Notes payable	160,000[e]
Accounts receivable	197,280[a]	Accruals	20,000
Inventories	225,000[b]	Total current liabilities	$ 300,000[d]
Total current assets	$ 480,000	Long-term debt	$ 600,000[f]
Net fixed assets	$1,020,000[c]	Stockholders' equity	$ 600,000
Total assets	$1,500,000	Total liabilities and stockholders' equity	$1,500,000

[a]Average collection period (ACP) = 40 days
ACP = Accounts receivable/Average sales per day
40 = Accounts receivable/($1,800,000/365)
40 = Accounts receivable/$4,932
$197,280 = Accounts receivable

[b]Inventory turnover = 6.0
Inventory turnover = Cost of goods sold/Inventory
6.0 = [Sales × (1 − Gross profit margin)]/Inventory
6.0 = [$1,800,000 × (1 − 0.25)]/Inventory
$225,000 = Inventory

[c]Total asset turnover = 1.20
Total asset turnover = Sales/Total assets
1.20 = $1,800,000/Total assets
$1,500,000 = Total assets
Total assets = Current assets + Net fixed assets
$1,500,000 = $480,000 + Net fixed assets
$1,020,000 = Net fixed assets

[d]Current ratio = 1.60
Current ratio = Current assets/Current liabilities
1.60 = $480,000/Current liabilities
$300,000 = Current liabilities

[e] $\text{Notes payable} = \text{Total current liabilities} - \text{Accounts payable} - \text{Accruals}$
$= \$300,000 - \$120,000 - \$20,000$
$= \$160,000$

[f]Debt ratio = 0.60
Debt ratio = Total liabilities/Total assets
0.60 = Total liabilities/$1,500,000
$900,000 = Total liabilities

$\text{Total liabilities} = \text{Current liabilities} + \text{Long-term debt}$
$900,000 = $300,000 + Long-term debt
$600,000 = Long-term debt

Chapter 4

ST4–1   a.   Depreciation Schedule

Year	Cost[a] (1)	Percentages (from Table 4.2) (2)	Depreciation [(1) × (2)] (3)
1	$150,000	20%	$ 30,000
2	150,000	32	48,000
3	150,000	19	28,500
4	150,000	12	18,000
5	150,000	12	18,000
6	150,000	5	7,500
	Totals	100%	$150,000

[a]$140,000 asset cost + $10,000 installation cost.

b. Operating cash flow:

Year	EBIT (1)	NOPAT [(1) × (1 − 0.40)] (2)	Depreciation (3)	Operating cash flows [(2) + (3)] (4)
1	$160,000	$96,000	$30,000	$126,000
2	160,000	96,000	48,000	144,000
3	160,000	96,000	28,500	124,500
4	160,000	96,000	18,000	114,000
5	160,000	96,000	18,000	114,000
6	160,000	96,000	7,500	103,500

c. Change in net fixed assets in year 6 = $0 − $7,500 = −$7,500

NFAI in year 6 = −$7,500 + $7,500 = $0

Change in current assets in year 6 = $110,000 − $90,000 = $20,000

Change in (Accounts payable + Accruals) in year 6 = ($45,000 + $7,000) − ($40,000 + $8,000) = $52,000 − $48,000 = $4,000

NCAI in year 6 = $20,000 − $4,000 = $16,000

For year 6

FCF = OCF − NFAI − NCAI

    = $103,500* − $0 − $16,000 = $87,500

*From part **b**, column 4 value for year 6.

d. In part **b** we can see that, in each of the six years, the operating cash flow is positive, which means that the firm is generating cash that it could use to invest in fixed assets or working capital, or it could distribute some of the cash flow to investors by paying interest or dividends. The free cash flow (FCF) calculated in part **c** for year 6 represents the cash flow available to investors—providers of debt and equity—after covering all operating needs and paying for net fixed asset investment (NFAI) and net current asset investment (NCAI) that occurred during the year.

ST4–2   a.

	Carroll Company Cash Budget April–June					Accounts receivable at end of June	
	February	March	April	May	June	July	August
Forecast sales	$500	$600	$400	$200	$200		
Cash sales (0.30)	$150	$180	$120	$ 60	$ 60		
Collections of A/R							
Lagged 1 month [(0.7 × 0.7) = 0.49]		245	294	196	98	$ 98	
Lagged 2 months [(0.3 × 0.7) = 0.21]			105	126	84	42	$42
						$140 + $42 = $182	
Total cash receipts			$519	$382	$242		
Less: Total cash disbursements			600	500	200		
Net cash flow			($ 81)	($118)	$ 42		
Add: Beginning cash			115	34	(84)		
Ending cash			$ 34	($ 84)	($ 42)		
Less: Minimum cash balance			25	25	25		
Required total financing (notes payable)			—	$109	$ 67		
Excess cash balance (marketable securities)			$ 9	—	—		

b. Carroll Company would need a maximum of $109 in financing over the 3-month period.

c.

Account	Amount	Source of amount
Cash	$ 25	Minimum cash balance—June
Notes payable	67	Required total financing—June
Marketable securities	0	Excess cash balance—June
Accounts receivable	182	Calculation at right of cash budget statement

ST4–3   a.

Euro Designs, Inc., Pro Forma Income Statement for the Year Ended December 31, 2013	
Sales revenue (given)	$3,900,000
Less: Cost of goods sold (0.55)[a]	2,145,000
Gross profits	$1,755,000
Less: Operating expenses (0.12)[b]	468,000
Operating profits	$1,287,000
Less: Interest expense (given)	325,000
Net profits before taxes	$ 962,000
Less: Taxes (0.40 × $962,000)	384,800
Net profits after taxes	$ 577,200
Less: Cash dividends (given)	320,000
To retained earnings	$ 257,200

[a]From 2009: CGS/Sales = $1,925,000/$3,500,000 = 0.55.
[b]From 2009: Oper. Exp./Sales = $420,000/$3,500,000 = 0.12.

    b. The percent-of-sales method may underestimate actual 2013 pro forma income by assuming that all costs are variable. If the firm has fixed costs, which by definition would not increase with increasing sales, the 2013 pro forma income would probably be underestimated.

Chapter 5

ST5–1   **a.** *Bank A:*

$FV_3 = \$10,000 \times (1 + 0.04)^3 = \$10,000 \times 1.125 = \underline{\$11,250}$

(Calculator solution = $11,248.64)

Bank B:

$FV_3 = \$10,000 \times (1 + 0.04/2)^6 = \$10,000 \times 1.126 = \underline{\$11,260}$

(Calculator solution = $11,261.62)

Bank C:

$FV_3 = \$10,000 \times (1 + 0.04/4)^{12} = \$10,000 \times 1.127 = \underline{\$11,270}$

(Calculator solution = $11,268.25)

  b. *Bank A:*

$EAR = (1 + 0.04/1)^1 - 1 = (1 + 0.04)^1 - 1 = 1.04 - 1 = 0.04 = \underline{\underline{4\%}}$

Bank B:

$EAR = (1 + 0.04/2)^2 - 1 = (1 + 0.02)^2 - 1$
$\qquad = 1.0404 - 1 = 0.0404 = \underline{4.04\%}$

Bank C:

$EAR = (1 + 0.04/4)^4 - 1 = (1 + 0.01)^4 - 1 = 1.0406 - 1$
$\qquad = 0.0406 = \underline{4.06\%}$

  c. Ms. Martin should deal with Bank C: The quarterly compounding of interest at the given 4% rate results in the highest future value as a result of the corresponding highest effective annual rate.

  d. *Bank D:*

$FV_3 = \$10,000 \times e^{0.04 \times 3} = \$10,000 \times e^{0.12}$
$\qquad = \$10,000 \times 1.127497 = \underline{\$11,274.97}$

This alternative is better than Bank C; it results in a higher future value because of the use of continuous compounding, which with otherwise identical cash flows always results in the highest future value of any compounding period.

ST5–2   **a.** On the surface, annuity Y looks more attractive than annuity X because it provides $1,000 more each year than does annuity X. Of course, the fact that X is an annuity due means that the $9,000 would be received at the beginning each year, unlike the $10,000 at the end of each year, and this makes annuity X more appealing than it otherwise would be.

  b. *Annuity X:*

$FV_6 = \$9,000 \times \{[(1 + 0.15)^6 - 1]/0.15\} \times (1 + 0.15)$
$\qquad = \$9,000 \times 8.754 \times 1.15 = \underline{\$90,603.90}$

(Calculator solution = $90,601.19)

Annuity Y:

$FV_6 = \$10,000 \times \{[(1 + 0.15)^6 - 1]/0.15\}$

$= \$10,000 \times 8.754 = \underline{\$87,540.00}$

(Calculator solution = $87,537.38)

c. Annuity X is more attractive because its future value at the end of year 6, FV_6, of $90,603.90 is greater than annuity Y's end-of-year-6 future value, FV_6, of $87,540.00. The subjective assessment in part **a** was incorrect. The benefit of receiving annuity X's cash inflows at the beginning of each year appears to have outweighed the fact that annuity Y's annual cash inflow, which occurs at the end of each year, is $1,000 larger ($10,000 vs. $9,000) than annuity X's.

ST5–3 *Alternative A:*

Cash flow stream:

$PV_5 = \$700/0.09 \times [1 - 1/(1 + 0.09)^5]$

$= \$700/0.09 \times 0.350 = \underline{\$2,723}$

(Calculator solution = $2,722.76)

Single amount: $\underline{\$2,825}$

Alternative B:

Cash flow stream:

Year (n)	Present value calculation	Present value
1	$1,100/(1 + 0.09) =	$1,009.17
2	900/(1 + 0.09)² =	757.51
3	700/(1 + 0.09)³ =	540.53
4	500/(1 + 0.09)⁴ =	354.21
5	300/(1 + 0.09)⁵ =	194.98
	Present value	$2,856.40

(Calculator solution = $2,856.41)

Single amount: $\underline{\$2,800}$

Conclusion: Alternative B in the form of a cash flow stream is preferred because its present value of $2,856.40 is greater than the other three values.

ST5–4 $CF = \$8,000/\{[(1 + 0.07)^5 - 1]/0.07\}$

$CF = \$8,000/5.751$

$CF = \$1,391.06$

(Calculator solution = $1,391.13)

Judi should deposit $1,391.06 at the end of each of the 5 years to meet her goal of accumulating $8,000 at the end of the fifth year.

ST6–1   **a.** $B_0 = I/r_d \times [1 - 1/(1 + r_d)^n] + M \times 1/(1 + r_d)^n$

$I = 0.08 \times \$1,000 = \$80$

$M = \$1,000$

$n = 12$ yrs

   1. $r_d = 7\%$

$B_0 = \$80/0.07 \times [1 - 1/(1 + 0.07)^{12}] + \$1,000 \times 1/(1 + 0.07)^{12}$

$= (\$1,142.86 \times 0.556) + (\$1,000 \times 0.444)$

$= \$635.43 + \$444.00 = \underline{\$1,079.43}$

(Calculator solution = \$1,079.43)

   2. $r_d = 8\%$

$B_0 = \$80/0.08 \times [1 - 1/(1 + 0.08)^{12}] + \$1,000 \times 1/(1 + 0.08)^{12}$

$= (\$1,000 \times 0.603) + (\$1,000 \times 0.397)$

$= \$603.00 + \$397.00 = \underline{\$1,000.00}$

(Calculator solution = \$1,000.00)

   3. $r_d = 10\%$

$B_0 = \$80/0.10 \times [1 - 1/(1 + 0.10)^{12}] + \$1,000 \times 1/(1 + 0.10)^{12}$

$= (\$800 \times 0.681) + (\$1,000 \times 0.319)$

$= \$544.80 + \$319.00 = \underline{\$863.80}$

(Calculator solution = \$863.73)

   b. **1.** $r_d = 7\%$, $B_0 = \$1,079.43$; sells at a *premium*

   2. $r_d = 8\%$, $B_0 = \$1,000.00$; sells at its *par value*

   3. $r_d = 10\%$, $B_0 = \$863.80$; sells at a *discount*

   c. $B_0 = (I/2)/r_d \times [1 - 1/(1 + r_d/2)^{2n}] + M \times 1/(1 + r_d/2)^{2n}$

$= (\$80/2)/(0.10/2) \times [1 - 1/(1 + 0.10/2)^{24}]$

$\quad + \$1,000 \times 1/(1 + 0.10/2)^{24}$

$= \$800 \times 0.690 + \$1,000 \times 0.310$

$= \$552.00 + \$310.00 = \underline{\$862.00}$

(Calculator solution = \$862.01)

ST6–2   **a.** $B_0 = \$1,150$

$I = 0.11 \times \$1,000 = \$110$ Current yield $= \dfrac{\text{annual interest}}{\text{current price}}$

$M = \$1,000$

$n = 18$ yrs $= \dfrac{\$110}{\$1,150} = 9.57\%$

b. $1,150 = \$110/r_d \times [1 - 1/(1 + r_d)^{18}] + \$1,000 \times 1/(1 + r_d)^{18}$

Because if $r_d = 11\%$, $B_0 = \$1,000 = M$, try $r_d = 10\%$.

$B_0 = \$110/0.10 \times [1 - 1/(1 + 0.10)^{18}] + \$1,000 \times 1/(1 + 0.10)^{18}$
$\quad = (\$1,100 \times 0.820) + (\$1,000 \times 0.180)$
$\quad = \$902.00 + \$180.00 = \$1,082.00$

Because $\$1,082.00 < \$1,150$, try $r_d = 9\%$.

$B_0 = \$110/0.09 \times [1 - 1/(1 + 0.09)^{18}] + \$1,000 \times 1/(1 + 0.09)^{18}$
$\quad = (\$1,222.22 \times 0.788) + (\$1,000 \times 0.212)$
$\quad = \$963.11 + \$212.00 = \$1,175.11$

Because the $1,175.11 value at 9% is higher than $1,150, and the $1,082.00 value at 10% rate is lower than $1,150, the bond's yield to maturity must be between 9% and 10%. Because the $1,175.11 value is closer to $1,150, rounding to the nearest whole percent, the YTM is 9%. (By using interpolation, the more precise YTM value is 9.27%.)

(Calculator solution = 9.26%)

c. The YTM of 9.27% is below both the bond's 11% coupon interest rate and its current yield of 9.57% calculated in part **a**, because the bond's market value of $1,150 is above its $1,000 par value. Whenever a bond's market value is above its par value (it sells at a *premium*), its YTM and current yield will be below its coupon interest rate; when a bond sells at *par*, the YTM and current yield will equal its coupon interest rate; and when the bond sells for less than par (at a *discount*), its YTM and current yield will be greater than its coupon interest rate. Observe also that the current yield measures the bond's coupon payment relative to its current price. When the bond sells at a premium, its YTM will be below its current yield because the YTM also takes into account that the bondholder will receive just $1,000 back at maturity, which represents a loss relative to the bond's current market price. In other words, the YTM is measuring both the value of the coupon payment that the investor receives (just like the current yield does) and the "loss" that the bondholder endures when the bond matures.

Chapter 7

ST7–1 $D_0 = \$1.80/\text{share}$

$\quad r_s = 12\%$

a. *Zero growth:*

$$P_0 = \frac{D_1}{r_s} = \frac{D_1 = D_0 = \$1.80}{0.12} = \underline{\$15/\text{share}}$$

b. *Constant growth, g = 5%:*

$D_1 = D_0 \times (1 + g) = \$1.80 = (1 + 0.05) = \$1.89/\text{share}$

$$P_0 = \frac{D_1}{r_s - g} = \frac{\$1.89}{0.12 - 0.05} = \frac{\$1.89}{0.07} = \underline{\$27/\text{share}}$$

c. *Variable growth, $N = 3$, $g_1 = 5\%$ for years 1 to 3 and $g_2 = 4\%$ for years 4 to ∞:*

$$D_1 = D_0 \times (1 + g_1)^1 = \$1.80 \times (1 + 0.05)^1 = \$1.89/\text{share}$$
$$D_2 = D_0 \times (1 + g_1)^2 = \$1.80 \times (1 + 0.05)^2 = \$1.98/\text{share}$$
$$D_3 = D_0 \times (1 + g_1)^3 = \$1.80 \times (1 + 0.05)^3 = \$2.08/\text{share}$$
$$D_4 = D_3 \times (1 + g_2) = \$2.08 \times (1 + 0.04) = \$2.16/\text{share}$$

$$P_0 = \sum_{t=1}^{N} \frac{D_0 \times (1 + g_1)^t}{(1 + r_s)^t} + \left(\frac{1}{(1 + r_s)^N} \times \frac{D_{N+1}}{r_s - g_2} \right)$$

$$\sum_{t=1}^{N} \frac{D_0 \times (1 + g_1)^t}{(1 + r_s)^t} = \frac{1.89}{(1 + 0.12)^1} + \frac{1.98}{(1 + 0.12)^2} + \frac{2.08}{(1 + 0.12)^3}$$

$$= \$1.69 + \$1.58 + \$1.48 = \$4.75$$

$$\left[\frac{1}{(1 + r_s)^N} \times \frac{D_{N+1}}{r_s - g_2} \right] = \frac{1}{(1 + 0.12)^3} \times \frac{D_4 = \$2.16}{0.12 - 0.04}$$

$$= 0.712 \times \$27.00 = \$19.22$$

$$P_0 = \sum_{t=1}^{N} \frac{D_0 \times (1 + g_1)^t}{(1 + r_s)^t} + \left[\frac{1}{(1 + r_s)^N} \times \frac{D_{N+1}}{r_s - g_2} \right] = \$4.75 + \$19.22$$

$$= \underline{\$23.97/\text{share}}$$

ST7–2 a. **Step 1:** Present value of free cash flow from end of 2017 to infinity measured at the end of 2016:

$$FCF_{2017} = \$1,500,000 \times (1 + 0.04) = \$1,560,000$$

$$\text{Value of } FCF_{2017 \to \infty} = \frac{\$1,560,000}{0.10 - 0.04} = \frac{\$1,560,000}{0.06} = \underline{\$26,000,000}$$

Step 2: Add the value found in Step 1 to the 2016 FCF.

Total $FCF_{2016} = \$1,500,000 + \$26,000,000 = \underline{\$27,500,000}$

Step 3: Find the sum of the present values of the FCFs for 2013 through 2016 to determine company value, V_C.

Year (t)	Present value calculation	Present value of FCF_t
2013	$\$ \quad 800,000/(1 + 0.10) \ =$	$ 727,272.73
2014	$1,200,000/(1 + 0.10)^2 =$	991,735.54
2015	$1,400,000/(1 + 0.10)^3 =$	1,051,840.72
2016	$27,500,000/(1 + 0.10)^4 =$	18,782,870.02
	Value of entire company, $V_C =$	$21,553,719.01

(Calculator solution = $21,553,719.01)

b. Common Stock value, $V_S = V_C - V_D - V_P$

$V_C = \$21,553,719.01$ (calculated in part **a**)

$V_D = \$12,500,000$ (given)

$V_P = \$0$ (given)

$V_S = \$21,553,719.01 - \$12,500,000 - \$0 = \underline{\$9,053,719.01}$

(Calculator solution = $9,053,719.01)

    c. Price per share $= \dfrac{\$9,053,719.01}{500,000} = \underline{\underline{\$18.11/\text{share}}}$

(Calculator solution $= \$18.11/\text{share}$)

Chapter 8

ST8–1   **a.** Expected return, $\bar{r} = \dfrac{\Sigma \text{ Returns}}{3}$

$$\bar{r}_A = \frac{12\% + 14\% + 16\%}{3} = \frac{42\%}{3} = \underline{\underline{14\%}}$$

$$\bar{r}_B = \frac{16\% + 14\% + 12\%}{3} = \frac{42\%}{3} = \underline{\underline{14\%}}$$

$$\bar{r}_C = \frac{12\% + 14\% + 16\%}{3} = \frac{42\%}{3} = \underline{\underline{14\%}}$$

  b. Standard deviation, $\sigma_r = \sqrt{\dfrac{\displaystyle\sum_{j=1}^{n}(r_i - \bar{r})^2}{n - 1}}$

$$\sigma_{r_A} = \sqrt{\frac{(12\% - 14\%)^2 + (14\% - 14\%)^2 + (16\% - 14\%)^2}{3 - 1}}$$

$$= \sqrt{\frac{4\% + 0\% + 4\%}{2}} = \sqrt{\frac{8\%}{2}} = \underline{\underline{2\%}}$$

$$\sigma_{r_B} = \sqrt{\frac{(16\% - 14\%)^2 + (14\% - 14\%)^2 + (12\% - 14\%)^2}{3 - 1}}$$

$$= \sqrt{\frac{4\% + 0\% + 4\%}{2}} = \sqrt{\frac{8\%}{2}} = \underline{\underline{2\%}}$$

$$\sigma_{r_C} = \sqrt{\frac{(12\% - 14\%)^2 + (14\% - 14\%)^2 + (16\% - 14\%)^2}{3 - 1}}$$

$$= \sqrt{\frac{4\% + 0\% + 4\%}{2}} = \sqrt{\frac{8\%}{2}} = \underline{\underline{2\%}}$$

  c.

	Annual expected returns	
Year	**Portfolio AB**	**Portfolio AC**
2010	$(0.50 \times 12\%) + (0.50 \times 16\%) = 14\%$	$(0.50 \times 12\%) + (0.50 \times 12\%) = 12\%$
2011	$(0.50 \times 14\%) + (0.50 \times 14\%) = 14\%$	$(0.50 \times 14\%) + (0.50 \times 14\%) = 14\%$
2012	$(0.50 \times 16\%) + (0.50 \times 12\%) = 14\%$	$(0.50 \times 16\%) + (0.50 \times 16\%) = 16\%$

Over the 3-year period:

$$\bar{r}_{AB} = \frac{14\% + 14\% + 14\%}{3} = \frac{42\%}{3} = \underline{\underline{14\%}}$$

$$\bar{r}_{AC} = \frac{12\% + 14\% + 16\%}{3} = \frac{42\%}{3} = \underline{\underline{14\%}}$$

   d. AB is perfectly negatively correlated.

   AC is perfectly positively correlated.

   e. Standard deviation of the portfolios

$$\sigma_{r_{AB}} = \sqrt{\frac{(14\% - 14\%)^2 + (14\% - 14\%)^2 + (14\% - 14\%)^2}{3 - 1}}$$

$$= \sqrt{\frac{(0\% + 0\% + 0\%)}{2}} = \sqrt{\frac{0\%}{2}} = \underline{\underline{0\%}}$$

$$\sigma_{r_{AC}} = \sqrt{\frac{(12\% - 14\%)^2 + (14\% - 14\%)^2 + (16\% - 14\%)^2}{3 - 1}}$$

$$= \sqrt{\frac{4\% + 0\% + 4\%}{2}} = \sqrt{\frac{8\%}{2}} = \underline{\underline{2\%}}$$

   f. Portfolio AB is preferred because it provides the same return (14%) as AC but with less risk $[(\sigma_{r_{AB}} = 0\%) < (\sigma_{r_{AC}} = 2\%)]$.

ST8–2 a. When the market return increases by 10%, the investment's return would be expected to increase by 15% ($1.50 \times 10\%$). When the market return decreases by 10%, the investment's return would be expected to decrease by 15% $[1.50 \times (-10\%)]$.

   b. $r_j = R_F + [b_j \times (r_m - R_F)]$
   $= 7\% + [1.50 \times (10\% - 7\%)]$
   $= 7\% + 4.5\% = \underline{\underline{11.5\%}}$

   c. No, the investment should be rejected because its *expected* return of 11% is less than the 11.5% return *required* from the investment.

   d. $r_j = 7\% + [1.50 \times (9\% - 7\%)]$
   $= 7\% + 3\% = \underline{\underline{10\%}}$

   The investment would now be acceptable because its *expected* return of 11% is now in excess of the *required* return, which has declined to 10% as a result of investors in the marketplace becoming less risk averse.

Chapter 9

ST9–1 a. Cost of debt, r_i (using approximation formula)

$$r_d = \frac{I + \dfrac{\$1,000 - N_d}{n}}{\dfrac{N_d + \$1,000}{2}}$$

$I = 0.10 \times \$1,000 = \$100$

$N_d = \$1,000 - \$30 \text{ discount} - \$20 \text{ flotation cost} = \$950$

$n = 10 \text{ years}$

$$r_d = \frac{\$100 + \dfrac{\$1,000 - \$950}{10}}{\dfrac{\$950 + \$1,000}{2}} = \frac{\$100 + \$5}{\$975} = 10.8\%$$

(Calculator solution = 10.8%)

$r_i = r_d \times (1 - T)$

$T = 0.40$

$r_i = 10.8\% \times (1 - 0.40) = \underline{6.5\%}$

Cost of preferred stock, r_p

$$r_p = \frac{D_p}{N_p}$$

$D_p = 0.11 \times \$100 = \$11$

$N_p = \$100 - \$4 \text{ flotation cost} = \$96$

$$r_p = \frac{\$11}{\$96} = \underline{11.5\%}$$

Cost of retained earnings, r_r

$$r_r = r_s = \frac{D_1}{P_0} + g$$

$$= \frac{\$6}{\$80} + 6.0\% = 7.5\% + 6.0\% = \underline{13.5\%}$$

Cost of new common stock, r_n

$$r_n = \frac{D_1}{N_n} + g$$

$D_1 = \$6$

$N_n = \$80 - \$4 \text{ underpricing} - \$4 \text{ flotation cost} = \$72$

$g = 6.0\%$

$$r_n = \frac{\$6}{\$72} + 6.0\% = 8.3\% + 6.0\% = \underline{14.3\%}$$

b. WACC for total new financing < $500,000. This level of new financing is obtained by using retained earning so the cost of common equity is equal to the cost of retained earnings.

Source of capital	Weight (1)	Cost (2)	Weighted cost [(1) × (2)] (3)
Long-term debt	.40	6.5%	2.6%
Preferred stock	.15	11.5	1.7
Common stock equity	.45	13.5	6.1
Totals	1.00		10.4%
Weighted average cost of capital = 10.4%			

WACC for total new financing > $500,000. This level of new financing requires the use of new common stock so the cost of common equity is equal to the cost of new common stock.

	Weight (1)	Cost (2)	Weighted cost [(1) × (2)] (3)
Source of capital			
Long-term debt	.40	6.5%	2.6%
Preferred stock	.15	11.5	1.7
Common stock equity	.45	14.3	6.4
Totals	1.00		10.7%

Weighted average cost of capital = 10.7%

c.

Investment opportunity	Internal rate of return (IRR)	Initial investment	Cumulative investment
D	16.5%	$200,000	$ 200,000
C	12.9	150,000	350,000
E	11.8	450,000	800,000
A	11.2	100,000	900,000
G	10.5	300,000	1,200,000
F	10.1	600,000	1,800,000
B	9.7	500,000	2,300,000

Projects D, C, E, and A should be accepted because their respective IRRs exceed the WMCC. They will require $900,000 of total new financing.

Chapter 10

ST10–1 a. Payback period:

Project M: $= \dfrac{\$28,500}{\$10,000} = \underline{\underline{2.85}}$ years

Project N:

Year (t)	Cash inflows (CF_t)	Cumulative cash inflows
1	$11,000	$11,000
2	10,000	21,000 ←
3	9,000	30,000
4	8,000	38,000

$$2 + \frac{\$27,000 - \$21,000}{\$9,000} \text{ years}$$

$$2 + \frac{\$6,000}{\$9,000} \text{ years} = \underline{\underline{2.67}} \text{ years}$$

b. Net present value (NPV):

Project M: NPV = $10,000/0.14 × [1 − 1/(1 + 0.14)^4] − $28,500

$$= (\$71,428.57 \times 0.408) - \$28,500$$

$$= \$29,142.86 - \$28,500 = \underline{\$642.86}$$

(Calculator solution = $637.12)

Project N:

Year (t)	Present value	Present values
1	$11,000/(1 + 0.14) =	$ 9,649.12
2	10,000/(1 + 0.14)^2 =	7,694.68
3	9,000/(1 + 0.14)^3 =	6,074.74
4	8,000/(1 + 0.14)^4 =	4,736.64
	Present value of cash inflows	28,155.18
	− Initial investment	27,000.00
	Net present value (NPV)	$ 1,155.18

(Calculator solution = $1,155.18)

c. Internal rate of return (IRR):

Project M: NPV = 0 = $10,000/IRR × [1 − 1/(1 + IRR)^4] − $28,500

Since a 14% discount rate results in a positive NPV of $637.12 the IRR must be greater than 14%, but not a lot greater. Guess 15%.

Project M: NPV = $10,000/0.15 × [1 − 1/(1 + 0.15)^4] − $28,500

$$= (\$66,666.67 \times 0.428) - \$28,500$$

$$= \$8,533.34 - \$28,500 = \underline{\$33.34}$$

$$IRR \approx \underline{\underline{15\%}}$$

(Calculator solution = 15.09%)

Project N:

NPV = 0 = 11,000/(1 + IRR) + 10,000/(1 + IRR)^2 + 9,000/(1 + IRR)^3 + 8,000/(1 + IRR)^4 − 27,000

Because a 14% discount rate results in a positive NPV of $1,155.18 the IRR must be greater than 14%. Guess 15%.

Project N:

NPV = 11,000/(1 + 0.15) + 10,000/(1 + 0.15)^2

$$+ \ 9,000/(1 + 0.15)^3 + 8,000/(1 + 0.15)^4 - 27,000$$

$$= 9,565.22 + 7,561.44 + 5,917.65 + 4,574.03 - 27,000$$

$$= \$618.34$$

Because a 15% discount rate results in a positive NPV of $618.34 the IRR must be greater than 15%. Guess 16%

Project N:

$$NPV = 11,000/(1 + 0.16) + 10,000/(1 + 0.16)^2$$
$$+ 9,000/(1 + 0.16)^3 + 8,000/(1 + 0.16)^4 - 27,000$$
$$= 9,482.76 + 7,431.63 + 5,765.92 + 4,418.33 - 27,000$$
$$= \$98.64$$

So IRR $\approx$ <u>16%</u>

(Calculator solution = 16.19%)

d.

	Project	
	M	N
Payback period	2.85 years	2.67 years[a]
NPV	$642.86	$1,155.18[a]
IRR	15%	16%[a]

[a]Preferred project.

Project N is recommended because it has the shorter payback period and the higher NPV, which is greater than zero, and the larger IRR, which is greater than the 14% cost of capital.

e. Net present value profiles:

	Data	
	NPV	
Discount rate	Project M	Project N
0%	$11,500[a]	$11,000[b]
14	642.86	1,155.18
15	0	—
16	—	0

[a]($10,000 + $10,000 + $10,000 + $10,000) − $28,500
    = $40,000 − $28,500
    = $11,500
[b]($11,000 + $10,000 + $9,000 + $8,000) − $27,000
    = $38,000 − $27,000
    = $11,000

From the NPV profile that follows, it can be seen that if the firm has a cost of capital below approximately 6% (exact value is 5.75%), conflicting rankings of the projects would exist using the NPV and IRR decision techniques. Because the firm's cost of capital is 14%, it can be seen in part **d** that no conflict exists.

Chapter 11

ST11–1 **a.**   Book value = Installed cost − Accumulated depreciation

Installed cost = $50,000

Accumulated depreciation = $50,000 × (0.20 + 0.32 + 0.19 + 0.12)

= $50,000 × 0.83 = $41,500

Book value = $50,000 − $41,500 = $8,500

b. Taxes on sale of old equipment:

Gain on sale = Sale price − Book value

= $55,000 − $8,500 = $46,500

Taxes = 0.40 × $46,500 = $18,600

c. Initial investment:

Installed cost of new equipment	
Cost of new equipment	$75,000
+ Installation costs	5,000
Total installed cost—new	$80,000
− After-tax proceeds from sale of old equipment	
Proceeds from sale of old equipment	55,000
− Taxes on sale of old equipment	18,600
Total after-tax proceeds—old	$36,400
+ Change in net working capital	15,000
Initial investment	$58,600

ST11–2 a. Initial investment:

Installed cost of new machine

Cost of new machine	$140,000
+ Installation costs	10,000
Total installed cost—new (depreciable value)	$150,000
− After-tax proceeds from sale of old machine	
Proceeds from sale of old machine	42,000
− Taxes on sale of old machine[1]	9,120
Total after-tax proceeds—old	$ 32,880
+ Change in net working capital[2]	20,000
Initial investment	$137,120

---

[1]Book value of old machine $= \$40,000 - [(0.20 + 0.32) \times \$40,000]$
$= \$40,000 - (0.52 \times \$40,000)$
$= \$40,000 - \$20,800 = \$19,200$
Gain on sale $= \$42,000 - \$19,200 = \$22,800$
Taxes $= 0.40 \times \$22,800 = \underline{\$9,120}$

[2]Change in net working capital $= +\$10,000 + \$25,000 - \$15,000$
$= \$35,000 - \$15,000 = \underline{\$20,000}$

b. Incremental operating cash inflows:

Calculation of Depreciation Expense

Year	Cost (1)	Applicable MACRS depreciation percentages (from Table 4.2) (2)	Depreciation [(1) × (2)] (3)
With new machine			
1	$150,000	33%	$ 49,500
2	150,000	45	67,500
3	150,000	15	22,500
4	150,000	7	10,500
		Totals 100%	$150,000
With old machine			
1	$ 40,000	19% (year-3 depreciation)	$ 7,600
2	40,000	12 (year-4 depreciation)	4,800
3	40,000	12 (year-5 depreciation)	4,800
4	40,000	5 (year-6 depreciation)	2,000
		Total	$19,200[a]

[a]The total of $19,200 represents the book value of the old machine at the end of the second year, which was calculated in part a.

Calculation of Operating Cash Inflows

	Year			
	1	**2**	**3**	**4**
With new machine				
Earnings before depr., int., and taxes[a]	$120,000	$130,000	$130,000	$ 0
− Depreciation[b]	49,500	67,500	22,500	10,500
Earnings before int. and taxes	$ 70,500	$ 62,500	$107,500	−$10,500
− Taxes (rate, $T = 40\%$)	28,200	25,000	43,000	− 4,200
Net operating profit after taxes	$ 42,300	$ 37,500	$ 64,500	−$ 6,300
+ Depreciation[b]	49,500	67,500	22,500	10,500
Operating cash inflows	91,800	$105,000	$ 87,000	$ 4,200
With old machine				
Earnings before depr., int., and taxes[a]	$ 70,000	$ 70,000	$ 70,000	$ 0
− Depreciation[c]	7,600	4,800	4,800	2,000
Earnings before int. and taxes	$ 62,400	$ 65,200	$ 65,200	−$ 2,000
− Taxes (rate, $T = 40\%$)	24,960	26,080	26,080	− 800
Net operating profit after taxes	$ 37,440	$ 39,120	$ 39,120	−$ 1,200
+ Depreciation	7,600	4,800	4,800	2,000
Operating cash inflows	$ 45,040	$ 43,920	$ 43,920	$ 800

[a]Given in the problem.
[b]From column 3 of the preceding table, top.
[c]From column 3 of the preceding table, bottom.

Calculation of Incremental Operating Cash Inflows

Operating cash inflows

Year	New machine[a] (1)	Old machine[a] (2)	Incremental (relevant) [(1) − (2)] (3)
1	$ 91,800	$45,040	$46,760
2	105,000	43,920	61,080
3	87,000	43,920	43,080
4	4,200	800	3,400

[a]From the final row for the respective machine in the preceding table.

c. Terminal cash flow (end of year 3):

After-tax proceeds from sale of new machine

Proceeds from sale of new machine	$35,000
Taxes on sale of new machine[3]	9,800
Total after-tax proceeds—new	$25,200
− After-tax proceeds from sale of old machine	
Proceeds from sale of old machine	0
− Tax on sale of old machine[4]	−800
Total after-tax proceeds—old	$ 800
+ Change in net working capital	20,000
Terminal cash flow	$44,400

---

[3]Book value of new machine at end of year 3
= $150,000 − [(0.33 + 0.45 + 0.15) × $150,000] = $150,000 − (0.93 × $150,000)
= $15,000 − $139,500 = $10,500
Tax on sale = 0.40 × ($35,000 sale price − $10,500 book value)
= 0.40 × $24,500 = $9,800

[4]Book value of old machine at end of year 3
= $40,000 − [(0.20 + 0.32 + 0.19 + 0.12 + 0.12) × $40,000] = $40,000 − (0.95 × $40,000)
= $40,000 − $38,000 = $2,000
Tax on sale = 0.40 × ($0 sale price − $2,000 book value)
= 0.40 × −$2,000 = −$800 (i.e., $800 tax saving)

d.

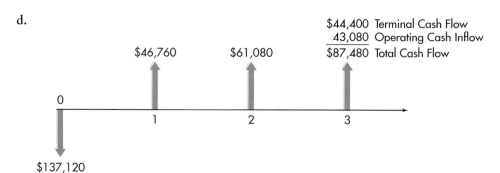

$44,400 Terminal Cash Flow
43,080 Operating Cash Inflow
$87,480 Total Cash Flow

$46,760 $61,080

0

1   2   3

$137,120

End of Year

Note: The year-4 incremental operating cash inflow of $3,400 is not directly included; it is instead reflected in the book values used to calculate the taxes on sale of the machines at the end of year 3 and is therefore part of the terminal cash flow.

Chapter 12

ST12–1 a. Net present value (NPV) using a 10% cost of capital:

Project A: NPV = $7,000/0.10 × [1 − 1/(1 + 0.10)^3] − $15,000

= ($70,000.00 × 0.249) − $15,000

= $17,430.00 − $15,000 = $2,430

(Calculator solution = $2,407.96)

Project B:

$$NPV = \$10,000/0.10 \times [1 - 1/(1 + 0.10)^3] - \$20,000$$
$$= (\$100,000.00 \times 0.249) - \$20,000$$
$$= \$24,900.00 - \$20,000 = \underline{\$4,900}^*$$

(Calculator solution = $4,868.52)

---

*Preferred project, because higher NPV.

b. Net present value (NPV) using the risk-adjusted discount rate (*RADR*) for project A of 9% and for project B of 16%.

Project A:

$$NPV = \$7,000/0.09 \times [1 - 1/(1 + 0.09)^3] - \$15,000$$
$$= (\$77,777.78 \times 0.228) - \$15,000$$
$$= \$17,733.33 - \$15,000 = \underline{\$2,733.33}^*$$

(Calculator solution = $2,719.06)

Project B:

$$NPV = \$10,000/0.16 \times [1 - 1/(1 + 0.16)^3] - \$20,000$$
$$= (\$62,500.00 \times 0.359) - \$20,000$$
$$= \$22,437.50 - \$20,000 = \underline{\$2,437.50}$$

(Calculator solution = $2,458.90)

---

*Preferred project, because higher NPV.

c. When the differences in risk were ignored in part **a,** project B was preferred over project A; but when the higher risk of project B is incorporated into the analysis using risk-adjusted discount rates in part **b,** *project A is preferred over project B.* Clearly, project A should be implemented.

Chapter 13

ST13–1 a. $Q = \dfrac{FC}{P - VC}$

$$= \dfrac{\$250,000}{\$7.50 - \$3.00} = \dfrac{\$250,000}{\$4.50} = \underline{55,556} \text{ units}$$

b.

		+20%	
Sales (in units)		100,000	120,000
Sales revenue (units × $7.50/unit)		$750,000	$900,000
Less: Variable operating costs (units × $3.00/unit)		300,000	360,000
Less: Fixed operating costs		250,000	250,000
Earnings before interest and taxes (EBIT)		$200,000	$290,000

+45%

Less: Interest		80,000	80,000
Net profits before taxes		$120,000	$210,000
Less: Taxes ($T = 0.40$)		48,000	84,000
Net profits after taxes		$ 72,000	$126,000
Less: Preferred dividends (8,000 shares × $5.00/share)		40,000	40,000
Earnings available for common		$132,000	$ 86,000
Earnings per share (EPS)	$32,000/20,000 = $1.60/share		$86,000/20,000 = $4.30/share

+169%

c. $\text{DOL} = \dfrac{\text{\% change in EBIT}}{\text{\% change in sales}} = \dfrac{+45\%}{+20\%} = \underline{\underline{2.25}}$

d. $\text{DFL} = \dfrac{\text{\% change in EPS}}{\text{\% change in EBIT}} = \dfrac{+169\%}{+45} = \underline{\underline{3.76}}$

e. $\text{DTL} = \text{DOL} \times \text{DFL}$

$= 2.25 \times 3.76 = \underline{\underline{8.46}}$

Using the other DTL formula:

$\text{DTL} = \dfrac{\text{\% change in EPS}}{\text{\% change in sales}}$

$8.46 = \dfrac{\text{\% change in EPS}}{+50\%}$

$\text{\% change in EPS} = 8.46 \times 0.50 = 4.23 = \underline{\underline{+423\%}}$

ST13–2

Source of capital	Plan A (bond)	Plan B (stock)
Data summary for alternative plans		
Long-term debt	$60,000 at 12% annual interest	$50,000 at 12% annual interest
Annual interest =	0.12 × $60,000 = $7,200	0.12 × $50,000 = $6,000
Common stock	10,000 shares	11,000 shares

a.

	Plan A (bond)		Plan B (stock)	
EBIT[a]	$30,000	$40,000	$30,000	$40,000
Less: Interest	7,200	7,200	6,000	6,000
Net profits before taxes	$22,800	$32,800	$24,000	$34,000
Less: Taxes ($T = 0.40$)	9,120	13,120	9,600	13,600
Net profits after taxes	$13,680	$19,680	$14,400	$20,400
EPS (10,000 shares)	$1.37	$1.97		
(11,000 shares)			$1.31	$1.85

[a]Values were arbitrarily selected; other values could have been used.

	Coordinates	
	EBIT	
	$30,000	$40,000
Financing plan	Earnings per share (EPS)	
A (Bond)	$1.37	$1.97
B (Stock)	1.31	1.85

b.

c. The bond plan (Plan A) becomes superior to the stock plan (Plan B) at *around $20,000* of EBIT, as represented by the dashed vertical line in the figure in part **b.** (*Note:* The actual point is $19,200, which was determined algebraically by using the technique described in footnote 18.)

ST13–3   a.

Capital structure debt ratio	Expected EPS (1)	Required return, r_s (2)	Estimated share value [(1) ÷ (2)] (3)
0%	$3.12	.13	$24.00
10	3.90	.15	26.00
20	4.80	.16	30.00
30	5.44	.17	32.00
40	5.51	.19	29.00
50	5.00	.20	25.00
60	4.40	.22	20.00

b. Using the table in part **a**:

   1. Maximization of EPS: *40% debt ratio*, EPS = $5.51/share (see column 1).

   2. Maximization of share value: *30% debt ratio*, share value = $32.00 (see column 3).

c. Recommend *30% debt ratio* because it results in the maximum share value and is therefore consistent with the firm's goal of owner wealth maximization.

Chapter 14

ST14–1   a.   Earnings per share (EPS) = $\dfrac{\$2{,}000{,}000 \text{ earnings available}}{500{,}000 \text{ shares of common outstanding}}$

   = $\underline{\$4.00/\text{share}}$

   Price/earnings (P/E) ratio = $\dfrac{\$60 \text{ market price}}{\$4.00 \text{ EPS}} = \underline{15}$

b. Proposed dividends = 500,000 shares × $2 per share = $1,000,000

   Shares that can be repurchased = $\dfrac{\$1{,}000{,}000}{\$62} = \underline{16{,}129}$ shares

c. *After proposed repurchase:*

   Shares outstanding = 500,000 − 16,129 = 483,871

   EPS = $\dfrac{\$2{,}000{,}000}{483{,}871} = \underline{\$4.13/\text{share}}$

d. Market price = $4.13/share × 15 = $\underline{\$61.95/\text{share}}$

e. The earnings per share (EPS) are higher after the repurchase because there are fewer shares of stock outstanding (483,871 shares versus 500,000 shares) to divide up the firm's $2,000,000 of available earnings.

f. In both cases, the stockholders would receive $2 per share—a $2 cash dividend in the dividend case or an approximately $2 increase in share price ($60.00 per share to $61.95 per share) in the repurchase case. (*Note:* The difference of $0.05 per share ($2.00 − $1.95) is due to rounding.)

Chapter 15

ST15–1

Basic data		
Time component	Current	Proposed
Average payment period (APP)	10 days	30 days
Average collection period (ACP)	30 days	30 days
Average age of inventory (AAI)	40 days	40 days

Cash conversion cycle (CCC) = AAI + ACP − APP

$CCC_{current}$ = 40 days + 30 days − 10 days = 60 days

$CCC_{proposed}$ = 40 days + 30 days − 30 days = <u>40</u> days

Reduction in CCC   <u>20</u> days

Old accounts payable = 10 days × ($14,000,000 ÷ 360 days) = $388,889

New accounts payable = 30 days × ($14,000,000 ÷ 360 days) = $1,166,667

Change in accounts payable = $1,166,667 − $388,889 = $777,778

Since accounts payable has increased the amount represents a decrease in net working capital.

Reduction in resource investment = $777,778

Annual profit increase = 0.12 × $777,778 = <u>$93,333</u>

ST15–2   **a.** *Data:*

S = 60,000 gallons

O = $200 per order

C = $1 per gallon per year

Calculation:

$$EOQ = \sqrt{\frac{2 \times S \times O}{C}}$$

$$= \sqrt{\frac{2 \times 60,000 \times \$200}{\$1}}$$

$$= \sqrt{24,000,000}$$

$$= \underline{4,899}\ \text{gallons}$$

b. *Data:*

Lead time = 20 days

Daily usage = 60,000 gallons/365 days

= 164.38 gallons/day

Calculation:

Reorder point = lead time in days × daily usage

= 20 days × 164.38 gallons/day

= <u>3,287.6</u> gallons

ST15–3   Tabular Calculation of the Effects of Relaxing Credit Standards on Regency Rug Repair Company:

Additional profit contribution from sales	
[4,000 rugs × ($32 avg. sale price − $28 var. cost)]	$16,000
Cost of marginal investment in accounts receivable	
Average investment under proposed plan:	
$\frac{(\$28 \times 76,000 \text{ rugs})}{365/48} = \frac{\$2,128,000}{7.6}$	$280,000
Average investment under present plan:	
$\frac{(\$28 \times 72,000 \text{ rugs})}{365/40} = \frac{\$2,016,000}{9.1}$	221,538
Marginal investment in A/R	$ 58,462
Cost of marginal investment in A/R (0.14 × $58,462)	($ 8,185)
Cost of marginal bad debts	
Bad debts under proposed plan (0.015 × $32 × 76,000 rugs)	$ 36,480
Bad debts under present plan (0.010 × $32 × 72,000 rugs)	23,040
Cost of marginal bad debts	($13,440)
Net loss from implementation of proposed plan	($ 5,625)

Recommendation: Because a net loss of $5,625 is expected to result from relaxing credit standards, *the proposed plan should not be implemented.*

Chapter 16

ST16–1   a.

Supplier	Approximate cost of giving up cash discount
X	1% × [365/(55 − 10)] = 1% × 365/45 = 1% × 8.1 = 8.1%
Y	2% × [365/(30 − 10)] = 2% × 365/20 = 2% × 18.25 = 36.5%
Z	2% × [365/(60 − 20)] = 2% × 365/40 = 2% × 9.125 = 18.25%

b.

Supplier	Recommendation
X	8.1% cost of giving up discount < 15% interest cost from bank; therefore, *give up discount.*
Y	36.5% cost of giving up discount > 15% interest cost from bank; therefore, *take discount and borrow from bank.*
Z	18.25% cost of giving up discount > 15% interest cost from bank; therefore, *take discount and borrow from bank.*

c. Stretching accounts payable for supplier Z would change the cost of giving up the cash discount to

$2\% \times [365/[(60 + 20) - 20]) = 2\% \times 365/60 = 2\% \times 6.1 = \underline{12.2\%}$

In this case, in light of the 15% interest cost from the bank, the recommended strategy in part **b** would be to *give up the discount* because the 12.2% cost of giving up the discount would be less than the 15% interest cost from the bank.

Chapter 17

ST17–1 a. (1) and (2). In tabular form—after-tax cash outflows in column 3 and present value of the cash outflows in column 5.

End of year	Lease payment (1)	Tax adjustment [(1 − 0.40) = 0.60] (2)	After-tax cash outflows [(1) × (2)] (3)	Present value calculation (4)	Present value of outflows
1	$5,000	0.60	$3,000	$ 3,000/(1 + 0.09) =	$ 2,752.29
2	5,000	0.60	3,000	3,000/(1 + 0.09)² =	2,525.04
3	5,000	0.60	3,000	3,000/(1 + 0.09)³ =	2,316.55
4	5,000	0.60	3,000	3,000/(1 + 0.09)⁴ =	2,125.28
5	5,000	0.60	7,000ᵃ	7,000/(1 + 0.09)⁵ =	4,549.52
				Present value of cash outflows	$14,268.68

ᵃAfter-tax lease payment outflow of $3,000 plus the $4,000 cost of exercising the purchase option.

(Calculator solution = $14,268.68)

b. (1) In tabular form—annual interest expense in column 3.

End of year	Loan payments (1)	Beginning of-year principal (2)	Payments Interest [0.15 × (2)] (3)	Payments principal [(1) − (3)] (4)	End-of-year principal [(2) − (4)] (5)
1	$5,967	$20,000	$3,000	$2,967	$17,033
2	5,967	17,033	2,555	3,412	13,621
3	5,967	13,621	2,043	3,924	9,697
4	5,967	9,697	1,455	4,512	5,185
5	5,967	5,185	778	5,189	—ᵃ

ᵃThe values in this table have been rounded to the nearest dollar, which results in a slight difference ($4) between the beginning-of-year-5 principal (in column 2) and the year-5 principal payment (in column 4).

(2) In tabular form—after-tax cash outflows in column 9.

End of year (1)	Loan payments (1)	Maintenance costs (2)	Cost of oven (3)	Depreciation percentages[a] (4)	Depreciation [(3) × (4)] (5)	Interest[b] (6)	Total deductions [(2) + (5) + (6)] (7)	Tax shields [0.40 × (7)] (8)	After-tax cash outflows [(1) + (2) − (8)] (9)
1	$5,967	$1,000	$20,000	.20	$4,000	$3,000	$8,000	$3,200	$3,767
2	5,967	1,000	20,000	.32	6,400	2,555	9,955	3,982	2,985
3	5,967	1,000	20,000	.19	3,800	2,043	6,843	2,737	4,230
4	5,967	1,000	20,000	.12	2,400	1,455	4,855	1,942	5,025
5	5,967	1,000	20,000	.12	2,400	778	4,178	1,671	5,296

[a]From Table 4.2 on page 117.
[b]From column 3 of table in part b(1).

(3) In tabular form—present value of the cash outflows in column 3.

End of year	After-tax cash outflows[a] (1)	Present value calculation (2)	Present value of outflows (3)
1	$3,767	$3,767/(1 + 0.09) =	$ 3,455.96
2	2,985	2,985/(1 + 0.09)^2 =	2,512.41
3	4,230	4,230/(1 + 0.09)^3 =	3,266.34
4	5,025	5,025/(1 + 0.09)^4 =	3,559.84
5	5,296	5,296/(1 + 0.09)^5 =	3,442.04
		Present value of cash outflows	$16,236.59

[a]From column 9 of table in part b(2).

(Calculator solution = $16,236.59)

c. Because the present value of the lease outflows of $14,268.68 is well below the present value of the purchase outflows of $16,236.59, *the lease is preferred*. Leasing rather than purchasing the oven should result in an incremental savings of $1,967.91 ($16,236.59 purchase cost − $14,268.68 lease cost).

ST17–2   a. Straight bond value:

$B_0 = I/r_d \times [1 - 1/(1 + r_d)^n] + M \times 1/(1 + r_d)^n$

$I = 0.11 \times \$1,000 = \$110$

$M = \$1,000$

$n = 25$ yrs

(1) $r_d = 13\%$

$B_0 = \$110/0.13 \times [1 - 1/(1 + 0.13)^{25}] + \$1,000 \times 1/(1 + 0.13)^{25}$

$= (\$846.15 \times 0.953) + (\$1,000 \times 0.047)$

$= \$806.38 + \$47.00 = \underline{\$853.38}$

(Calculator solution = $853.40)

b. In tabular form:

Market price of stock (1)	Conversion ratio (2)	Conversion value [(1) × (2)] (3)
$20	40	$ 800
25 (conversion price)	40	1,000 (par value)
28	40	1,120
35	40	1,400
50	40	2,000

c. The bond would be expected to sell at the higher of the conversion value and the straight value. In no case would it be expected to sell for less than the straight value of $853.38. Therefore, at a price of $20, the bond would sell for its straight value of $853.38; at prices of $25, $28, $35, and $50, the bond would be expected to sell at the associated conversion values (calculated in part **b**) of $1,000, $1,120, $1,400, and $2,000, respectively.

d. The straight bond value of <u>$853.38</u>.

Chapter 18

ST18–1 **a.** Net present value at 11%:

Year(s)	Cash inflow (1)	Present value calculation at 11% (2)	Present value (3)
1–3	$20,000	$20,000/0.11 × [1 − 1/(1 + 0.11)^3] =	$ 48,874.29
4–15	30,000	30,000/0.11 × [1 − 1/(1 + 0.11)^{12}] × 1/(1 + 0.11)^3 =	142,414.65
		Present value of inflows	$191,288.94
		Less: Cash purchase price	180,000.00
		Net present value (NPV)	$ 11,288.94

(Calculator solution = 11,288.94)

Because the NPV of $11,288.94 is greater than zero, *Luxe Foods should acquire Valley Canning.*

b. In this case, the 14% cost of capital must be used. Net present value at 14%:

Year(s)	Cash inflow (1)	Present value calculation at 14% (2)	Present value (3)
1–3	$20,000	$20,000/0.14 × [1 − 1/(1 + 0.14)^3] =	$ 46,432.64
4–15	30,000	30,000/0.14 × [1 − 1/(1 + 0.14)^{12}] × 1/(1 + 0.14)^3 =	114,616.08
		Present value of inflows	$161,048.72
		Less: Cash purchase price	180,000.00
		Net present value (NPV)	($ 18,951.28)

(Calculator solution = −$18,951.28)

At the higher cost of capital, the *acquisition of Valley by Luxe cannot be justified.*

ST18–2   a.   Lake Industries' EPS without merger:

		Earnings available for common			
Year	Initial value (1)	Future value calculation at 5% (2)	End-of-year value (3)	Number of shares outstanding (4)	EPS [(3) ÷ (4)] (5)
2012	$160,000	$160,000 × (1 + 0.05)^0 =	$160,000	80,000	$2.00
2013	160,000	160,000 × (1 + 0.05)^1 =	168,000	80,000	2.10
2014	160,000	160,000 × (1 + 0.05)^2 =	176,400	80,000	2.21
2015	160,000	160,000 × (1 + 0.05)^3 =	185,220	80,000	2.32
2016	160,000	160,000 × (1 + 0.05)^4 =	194,481	80,000	2.43
2017	160,000	160,000 × (1 + 0.05)^5 =	204,205	80,000	2.55

b.   Number of postmerger shares outstanding for Lake Industries:

$$\text{Number of new shares issued} = \text{Initial number of Butler Company shares} \times \text{Ratio of exchange}$$

$$= 10,000 \times 1.1 = 11,000 \text{ shares}$$

Plus: Lake's premerger shares   80,000

Lake's postmerger shares   91,000 shares

		Earnings available for common					
		Butler Company			Lake Industries		
					Without merger	With merger	
Year	Initial value (1)	Future value calculation at 10% (2)	End-of-year value (3)	End-of-year value[a] (4)	End-of-year value [(3) + (4)] (5)	Number of shares outstanding[b] (6)	EPS [(5) ÷ (6)] (7)
2009	$20,000	$20,000 × (1 + 0.10)^0 =	$20,000	$160,000	$180,000	91,000	$1.98
2010	20,000	20,000 × (1 + 0.10)^1 =	22,000	168,000	190,000	91,000	2.09
2011	20,000	20,000 × (1 + 0.10)^2 =	24,200	176,400	200,600	91,000	2.20
2012	20,000	20,000 × (1 + 0.10)^3 =	26,620	185,220	211,840	91,000	2.33
2013	20,000	20,000 × (1 + 0.10)^4 =	29,280	194,481	223,761	91,000	2.46
2014	20,000	20,000 × (1 + 0.10)^5 =	32,210	204,205	236,415	91,000	2.60

[a] From column 3 of table in part a.

[b] Calculated at beginning of this part.

c. Comparing the EPS without the proposed merger calculated in part **a** (see column 5 of table in part **a**) with the EPS with the proposed merger calculated in part **b** (see column 7 of table in part **b**), we can see that after 2014, the EPS *with* the merger rises above the EPS *without* the merger. Clearly, over the long run, the EPS with the merger will exceed those without the merger. This outcome is attributed to the higher rate of growth associated with Butler's earnings (10% versus 5% for Lake).

Chapter 19

ST19–1 MNC's receipt of dividends can be calculated as follows:

Subsidiary income before local taxes	$150,000
Foreign income tax at 32%	− 48,000
Dividend available to be declared	$102,000
Foreign dividend withholding tax at 8%	− 8,160
MNC's receipt of dividends	$ 93,840

a. If tax credits are allowed, then the so-called grossing up procedure will be applicable:

Additional MNC income		$150,000
U.S. tax liability at 34%	$51,000	
Total foreign taxes paid to be used as a credit ($48,000 + $8,160)	− 56,160	− 56,160
U.S. taxes due		− 0
Net funds available to the MNC		$ 93,840

b. If no tax credits are permitted, then:

MNC's receipt of dividends	$93,840
U.S. tax liability at 34%	− 31,906
Net funds available to the parent MNC	$61,934

Credits

p. 3: Archivo particular/GDA Photo Service/Newscom

p. 31: Richard B. Levine/Levine Roberts Photography/Newscom

p. 57: Kimimasa Mayama/Bloomberg/Getty Images

p. 114: Zuma Press/Newscom

p. 160: John A. Rizzo/PhotoDisc/Getty Images

p. 221: © Norman Chan – Fotolia.com

p. 265: © Mike Stone – Alamy

p. 309: © 2010 Morningstar, Inc. All Rights Reserved. The information contained herein: (1) is proprietary to Morningstar and/or its content providers; (2) may not be copied or distributed; (3) does not constitute investment advice offered by Morningstar; and (4) is not warranted to be accurate, complete or timely. Neither Morningstar nor its content providers are responsible for any damages or losses arising from any use of this information. Past performance is no guarantee of future results. Use of information from Morningstar does not necessarily constitute agreement by Morningstar, Inc. of any investment philosophy or strategy presented in this publication.

p. 357: Bloomberg/Getty Images

p. 389: © Barbara Helgason – Fotolia.com

p. 427: Digital Vision/Getty Images

p. 464: US Coast Guard/Sipa Press/Newscom

p. 507: Blickwinkel/Alamy

p. 560: © Zlatko Guzmic – Fotolia.com

p. 599: © 26kot – Fotolia.com

p. 641: AP Images

p. 677: © Robert Sorbo/Reuters/Corbis

p. 715: Douglas Healey/AP Images

p. 758: Bruce Connolly/Corbis

Glossary

ABC inventory system
Inventory management technique that divides inventory into three groups—A, B, and C, in descending order of importance and level of monitoring, on the basis of the dollar investment in each. (Chapter 15)

ability to service debts
The ability of a firm to make the payments required on a scheduled basis over the life of a debt. (Chapter 3)

accept–reject approach
The evaluation of capital expenditure proposals to determine whether they meet the firm's minimum acceptance criterion. (Chapter 10)

accounting exposure
The risk resulting from the effects of changes in foreign exchange rates on the translated value of a firm's financial statement accounts denominated in a given foreign currency. (Chapter 19)

accounts payable management
Management by the firm of the time that elapses between its purchase of raw materials and its mailing payment to the supplier. (Chapter 16)

accrual basis
In preparation of financial statements, recognizes revenue at the time of sale and recognizes expenses when they are incurred. (Chapter 1)

accruals
Liabilities for services received for which payment has yet to be made. (Chapter 16)

ACH (automated clearinghouse) transfer
Preauthorized electronic withdrawal from the payer's account and deposit into the payee's account via a settlement among banks by the *automated clearinghouse,* or *ACH.* (Chapter 15)

acquiring company
The firm in a merger transaction that attempts to acquire another firm. (Chapter 18)

activity ratios
Measure the speed with which various accounts are converted into sales or cash—inflows or outflows. (Chapter 3)

after-tax proceeds from sale of old asset
The difference between the old asset's sale proceeds and any applicable taxes or tax refunds related to its sale. (Chapter 11)

agency costs
Costs arising from agency problems that are borne by shareholders and represent a loss of shareholder wealth. (Chapter 1)

agency problems
Problems that arise when managers place personal goals ahead of the goals of shareholders. (Chapter 1)

aggressive funding strategy
A funding strategy under which the firm funds its seasonal requirements with short-term debt and its permanent requirements with long-term debt. (Chapter 15)

aging schedule
A credit-monitoring technique that breaks down accounts receivable into groups on the basis of their time of origin; it indicates the percentages of the total accounts receivable balance that have been outstanding for specified periods of time. (Chapter 15)

all-current-rate method
The method by which the *functional-currency-denominated* financial statements of an MNC's subsidiary are translated into the parent company's currency. (Chapter 19)

American depositary receipts (ADRs)
Securities, backed by *American depositary shares (ADSs),* that permit U.S. investors to hold shares of non-U.S. companies and trade them in U.S. markets. (Chapter 7)

American depositary shares (ADSs)
Dollar-denominated receipts for the stocks of foreign companies that are held by a U.S. financial institution overseas. (Chapter 7)

angel capitalists (angels)
Wealthy individual investors who do not operate as a business but invest in promising early-stage companies in exchange for a portion of the firm's equity. (Chapter 7)

annual cleanup
The requirement that for a certain number of days during the year borrowers under a line of credit carry a zero loan balance (that is, owe the bank nothing). (Chapter 16)

annual percentage rate (APR)
The *nominal annual rate* of interest, found by multiplying the periodic rate by the number of periods in one year, that must be disclosed to consumers on credit cards and loans as a result of "truth-in-lending laws." (Chapter 5)

annual percentage yield (APY)
The *effective annual rate* of interest that must be disclosed to consumers by banks on their savings products as a result of "truth-in-savings laws." (Chapter 5)

annualized net present value (ANPV) approach
An approach to evaluating unequal-lived projects that converts the net present value of unequal-lived, mutually exclusive projects into an equivalent annual amount (in NPV terms). (Chapter 12)

annuity
A stream of equal periodic cash flows over a specified time period. These cash flows can be *inflows* of returns earned on investments or *outflows* of funds invested to earn future returns. (Chapter 5)

annuity due
An annuity for which the cash flow occurs at the *beginning* of each period. (Chapter 5)

articles of partnership
The written contract used to formally establish a business partnership. (Chapter 1)

ASEAN
A large trading bloc that comprises ten member nations, all in Southeast Asia. China is expected to join this bloc in 2010. Also called the *Association of Southeast Asian Nations*. (Chapter 19)

ask price
The lowest price at which a security is offered for sale. (Chapter 2)

assignment
A voluntary liquidation procedure by which a firm's creditors pass the power to liquidate the firm's assets to an adjustment bureau, a trade association, or a third party, which is designated the *assignee*. (Chapter 18)

asymmetric information
The situation in which managers of a firm have more information about operations and future prospects than do investors. (Chapter 13)

authorized shares
Shares of common stock that a firm's corporate charter allows it to issue. (Chapter 7)

average age of inventory
Average number of days' sales in inventory. (Chapter 3)

average collection period
The average amount of time needed to collect accounts receivable. (Chapter 3)

average payment period
The average amount of time needed to pay accounts payable. (Chapter 3)

average tax rate
A firm's taxes divided by its taxable income. (Chapter 2)

balance sheet
Summary statement of the firm's financial position at a given point in time. (Chapter 3)

bankruptcy
Business failure that occurs when the stated value of a firm's liabilities exceeds the fair market value of its assets. (Chapter 18)

Bankruptcy Reform Act of 1978
The governing bankruptcy legislation in the United States today. (Chapter 18)

bar chart
The simplest type of probability distribution; shows only a limited number of outcomes and associated probabilities for a given event. (Chapter 8)

basic EPS
Earnings per share (EPS) calculated without regard to any contingent securities. (Chapter 17)

behavioral finance

A growing body of research that focuses on investor behavior and its impact on investment decisions and stock prices. Advocates are commonly referred to as "behaviorists." (Chapter 7)

benchmarking

A type of *cross-sectional analysis* in which the firm's ratio values are compared to those of a key competitor or group of competitors that it wishes to emulate. (Chapter 3)

beta coefficient (*b*)

A relative measure of nondiversifiable risk. An index of the degree of movement of an asset's return in response to a change in the *market return*. (Chapter 8)

bid price

The highest price offered to purchase a security. (Chapter 2)

bird-in-the-hand argument

The belief, in support of *dividend relevance theory,* that investors see current dividends as less risky than future dividends or capital gains. (Chapter 14)

board of directors

Group elected by the firm's stockholders and typically responsible for approving strategic goals and plans, setting general policy, guiding corporate affairs, and approving major expenditures. (Chapter 1)

bond

Long-term debt instrument used by business and government to raise large sums of money, generally from a diverse group of lenders. (Chapter 2)

bond indenture

A legal document that specifies both the rights of the bondholders and the duties of the issuing corporation. (Chapter 6)

book value

The strict accounting value of an asset, calculated by subtracting its accumulated depreciation from its installed cost. (Chapter 11)

book value per share

The amount per share of common stock that would be received if all of the firm's assets were sold for their exact book *(accounting)* value and the proceeds remaining after paying all liabilities (including preferred stock) were divided among the common stockholders. (Chapter 7)

book value weights

Weights that use accounting values to measure the proportion of each type of capital in the firm's financial structure. (Chapter 9)

breakeven analysis

Used to indicate the level of operations necessary to cover all costs and to evaluate the profitability associated with various levels of sales; also called *cost-volume-profit analysis*. (Chapter 13)

breakeven cash inflow

The minimum level of cash inflow necessary for a project to be acceptable, that is, NPV > $0. (Chapter 12)

breakup value

The value of a firm measured as the sum of the values of its operating units if each were sold separately. (Chapter 18)

broker market
The securities exchanges on which the two sides of a transaction, the buyer and seller, are brought together to trade securities. (Chapter 2)

business ethics
Standards of conduct or moral judgment that apply to persons engaged in commerce. (Chapter 1)

call feature
A feature included in nearly all corporate bond issues that gives the issuer the opportunity to repurchase bonds at a stated call price prior to maturity. (Chapter 6)

call option
An option to *purchase* a specified number of shares of a stock (typically 100) on or before a specified future date at a stated price. (Chapter 17)

call premium
The amount by which a bond's *call price* exceeds its par value. (Chapter 6)

call price
The stated price at which a bond may be repurchased, by use of *a call feature*, prior to maturity. (Chapter 6)

callable feature (preferred stock)
A feature of *callable preferred stock* that allows the issuer to retire the shares within a certain period of time and at a specified price. (Chapter 7)

capital asset pricing model (CAPM)
Describes the relationship between the required return, r_s, and the nondiversifiable risk of the firm as measured by the beta coefficient, b. (Chapter 8)

capital asset pricing model (CAPM)
The basic theory that links risk and return for all assets. (Chapter 9)

capital budgeting
The process of evaluating and selecting long-term investments that are consistent with the firm's goal of maximizing owners' wealth. (Chapter 10)

capital budgeting process
Five distinct but interrelated steps: *proposal generation, review and analysis, decision making, implementation,* and *follow-up.* (Chapter 10)

capital expenditure
An outlay of funds by the firm that is expected to produce benefits over a period of time greater than 1 year. (Chapter 10)

capital gain
The amount by which the sale price of an asset exceeds the asset's purchase price. (Chapter 2)

capital market
A market that enables suppliers and demanders of *long-term funds* to make transactions. (Chapter 2)

capital rationing
The financial situation in which a firm has only a fixed number of dollars available for capital expenditures, and numerous projects compete for these dollars. (Chapter 10)

capital structure
The mix of long-term debt and equity maintained by the firm. (Chapter 13)

capitalized lease
A *financial (capital) lease* that has the present value of all its payments included as an asset and corresponding liability on the firm's balance sheet, as required by the Financial Accounting Standards Board (FASB) in *FASB Statement No. 13*. (Chapter 17)

carrying costs
The variable costs per unit of holding an item in inventory for a specific period of time. (Chapter 15)

cash basis
Recognizes revenues and expenses only with respect to actual inflows and out-flows of cash. (Chapter 1)

cash bonuses
Cash paid to management for achieving certain performance goals. (Chapter 1)

cash budget (cash forecast)
A statement of the firm's planned inflows and outflows of cash that is used to estimate its short-term cash requirements. (Chapter 4)

cash concentration
The process used by the firm to bring lockbox and other deposits together into one bank, often called the *concentration bank*. (Chapter 15)

cash conversion cycle (CCC)
The length of time required for a company to convert cash invested in its opera-tions to cash received as a result of its operations. (Chapter 15)

cash disbursements
All outlays of cash by the firm during a given financial period. (Chapter 4)

cash discount
A percentage deduction from the purchase price; available to the credit customer who pays its account within a specified time. (Chapter 15)

cash discount period
The number of days after the beginning of the credit period during which the cash discount is available. (Chapter 15)

cash receipts
All of a firm's inflows of cash during a given financial period. (Chapter 4)

catering theory
A theory that says firms cater to the preferences of investors, initiating or increasing dividend payments during periods in which high-dividend stocks are particularly appealing to investors. (Chapter 14)

Central American Free Trade Agreement (CAFTA)
A trade agreement signed in 2003–2004 by the United States, the Dominican Republic, and five Central American countries (Costa Rica, El Salvador, Guatemala, Honduras, and Nicaragua). (Chapter 19)

change in net working capital
The difference between a change in current assets and a change in current liabili-ties. (Chapter 11)

Chapter 7
The portion of the *Bankruptcy Reform Act of 1978* that details the procedures to be followed when liquidating a failed firm. (Chapter 18)

Chapter 11
The portion of the *Bankruptcy Reform Act of 1978* that outlines the procedures for reorganizing a failed (or failing) firm, whether its petition is filed voluntarily or involuntarily. (Chapter 18)

clearing float
The time between deposit of a payment and when spendable funds become available to the firm. (Chapter 15)

clientele effect
The argument that different payout policies attract different types of investors but still do not change the value of the firm. (Chapter 14)

closely owned (stock)
The common stock of a firm is owned by an individual or a small group of investors (such as a family); these are usually privately owned companies. (Chapter 7)

coefficient of variation (CV)
A measure of relative dispersion that is useful in comparing the risks of assets with differing expected returns. (Chapter 8)

collateral trust bonds
See Table 6.4.

commercial banks
Institutions that provide savers with a secure place to invest their funds and that offer loans to individual and business borrowers. (Chapter 2)

commercial finance companies
Lending institutions that make only secured loans—both short-term and long-term—to businesses. (Chapter 16)

commercial paper
A form of financing consisting of short-term, unsecured promissory notes issued by firms with a high credit standing. (Chapter 16)

commitment fee
The fee that is normally charged on a *revolving credit agreement;* it often applies to the *average unused portion* of the borrower's credit line. (Chapter 16)

common-size income statement
An income statement in which each item is expressed as a percentage of sales. (Chapter 3)

common stock
The purest and most basic form of corporate ownership. (Chapter 1)

compensating balance
A required checking account balance equal to a certain percentage of the amount borrowed from a bank under a line-of-credit or revolving credit agreement. (Chapter 16)

composition
A pro rata cash settlement of creditor claims by the debtor firm; a uniform percentage of each dollar owed is paid. (Chapter 18)

compound interest
Interest that is earned on a given deposit and has become part of the *principal* at the end of a specified period. (Chapter 5)

conflicting rankings
Conflicts in the ranking given a project by NPV and IRR, resulting from *differences in the magnitude and timing of cash flows.* (Chapter 10)

congeneric merger
A merger in which one firm acquires another firm that is *in the same general industry* but is neither in the same line of business nor a supplier or customer. (Chapter 18)

conglomerate merger
A merger combining firms in *unrelated businesses.* (Chapter 18)

conservative funding strategy
A funding strategy under which the firm funds both its seasonal and its permanent requirements with long-term debt. (Chapter 15)

consolidation
The combination of two or more firms to form a completely new corporation. (Chapter 18)

constant-growth model
A widely cited dividend valuation approach that assumes that dividends will grow at a constant rate, but a rate that is less than the required return. (Chapter 7)

constant-growth valuation (Gordon growth) model
Assumes that the value of a share of stock equals the present value of all future dividends (assumed to grow at a constant rate) that it is expected to provide over an infinite time horizon. (Chapter 9)

constant-payout-ratio dividend policy
A dividend policy based on the payment of a certain percentage of earnings to owners in each dividend period. (Chapter 14)

contingent securities
Convertibles, warrants, and stock options. Their presence affects the reporting of a firm's earnings per share (EPS). (Chapter 17)

continuous compounding
Compounding of interest an infinite number of times per year at intervals of microseconds. (Chapter 5)

continuous probability distribution
A probability distribution showing all the possible outcomes and associated probabilities for a given event. (Chapter 8)

controlled disbursing
The strategic use of mailing points and bank accounts to lengthen mail float and clearing float, respectively. (Chapter 15)

controller
The firm's chief accountant, who is responsible for the firm's accounting activities, such as corporate accounting, tax management, financial accounting, and cost accounting. (Chapter 1)

conversion feature
A feature of convertible bonds that allows bondholders to change each bond into a stated number of shares of common stock. (Chapter 6)

conversion feature
An option that is included as part of a bond or a preferred stock issue and allows its holder to change the security into a stated number of shares of common stock. (Chapters 6 and 17)

conversion feature (preferred stock)
A feature of *convertible preferred stock* that allows holders to change each share into a stated number of shares of common stock. (Chapter 7)

conversion (or stock) value
The value of a convertible security measured in terms of the market price of the common stock into which it can be converted. (Chapter 17)

conversion price
The per-share price that is effectively paid for common stock as the result of conversion of a convertible security. (Chapter 17)

conversion ratio
The ratio at which a convertible security can be exchanged for common stock. (Chapter 17)

convertible bond
A bond that can be changed into a specified number of shares of common stock. (Chapter 17)

convertible preferred stock
Preferred stock that can be changed into a specified number of shares of common stock. (Chapter 17)

corporate bond
A long-term debt instrument indicating that a corporation has borrowed a certain amount of money and promises to repay it in the future under clearly defined terms (Chapter 6).

corporate governance
The rules, processes, and laws by which companies are operated, controlled, and regulated. (Chapter 1)

corporate restructuring
The activities involving expansion or contraction of a firm's operations or changes in its asset or financial (ownership) structure. (Chapter 18)

corporation
An entity created by law. (Chapter 1)

correlation
A statistical measure of the relationship between any two series of numbers. (Chapter 8)

correlation coefficient
A measure of the degree of correlation between two series. (Chapter 8)

cost of a new issue of common stock, r_n
The cost of common stock, net of underpricing and associated flotation costs. (Chapter 9)

cost of capital
Represents the firm's cost of financing and is the minimum rate of return that a project must earn to increase firm value. (Chapter 9)

cost of common stock equity, r_s
The rate at which investors discount the expected dividends of the firm to determine its share value. (Chapter 9)

cost of giving up a cash discount
The implied rate of interest paid to delay payment of an account payable for an additional number of days. (Chapter 16)

cost of long-term debt
The financing cost associated with new funds raised through long-term borrowing. (Chapter 9)

cost of new asset
The net outflow necessary to acquire a new asset. (Chapters 9 and 11)

cost of preferred stock, r_p
The ratio of the preferred stock dividend to the firm's net proceeds from the sale of preferred stock. (Chapter 9)

cost of retained earnings, r_r
The same as the cost of an *equivalent fully subscribed issue of additional common stock*, which is equal to the cost of common stock equity, r_s. (Chapter 9)

coupon interest rate
The percentage of a bond's par value that will be paid annually, typically in two equal semiannual payments, as interest. (Chapter 6)

coverage ratios
Ratios that measure the firm's ability to pay certain fixed charges. (Chapter 3)

credit monitoring
The ongoing review of a firm's accounts receivable to determine whether customers are paying according to the stated credit terms. (Chapter 15)

creditor control
An arrangement in which the creditor committee replaces the firm's operating management and operates the firm until all claims have been settled. (Chapter 18)

credit period
The number of days after the beginning of the credit period until full payment of the account is due. (Chapter 15)

credit scoring
A credit selection method commonly used with high-volume/small-dollar credit requests; relies on a credit score determined by applying statistically derived weights to a credit applicant's scores on key financial and credit characteristics. (Chapter 15)

credit standards
The firm's minimum requirements for extending credit to a customer. (Chapter 15)

credit terms
The terms of sale for customers who have been extended credit by the firm. (Chapter 15)

cross-sectional analysis
Comparison of different firms' financial ratios at the same point in time; involves comparing the firm's ratios to those of other firms in its industry or to industry averages. (Chapter 3)

cumulative (preferred stock)
Preferred stock for which all passed (unpaid) dividends in arrears, along with the current dividend, must be paid before dividends can be paid to common stockholders. (Chapter 7)

current assets
Short-term assets, expected to be converted into cash within 1 year or less. (Chapter 3)

current liabilities
Short-term liabilities, expected to be paid within 1 year or less. (Chapter 3)

current rate (translation) method
Technique used by U.S.–based companies to translate their foreign-currency-denominated assets and liabilities into dollars, for consolidation with the parent company's financial statements, using the year-end (current) exchange rate. (Chapter 3)

current ratio
A measure of liquidity calculated by dividing the firm's current assets by its current liabilities. (Chapter 3)

current yield
A measure of a bond's cash return for the year; calculated by dividing the bond's annual interest payment by its current price. (Chapter 6)

date of record (dividends)
Set by the firm's directors, the date on which all persons whose names are recorded as stockholders receive a declared dividend at a specified future time. (Chapter 14)

dealer market
The market in which the buyer and seller are not brought together directly but instead have their orders executed by securities dealers that "make markets" in the given security. (Chapter 2)

debentures
See Table 6.4.

debt
Includes borrowing incurred by a firm, including bonds, and is repaid according to a fixed schedule of payments. (Chapter 7)

debtor in possession (DIP)
The term for a firm that files a reorganization petition under Chapter 11 and then develops, if feasible, a reorganization plan. (Chapter 18)

debt ratio
Measures the proportion of total assets financed by the firm's creditors. (Chapter 3)

deflation
A general trend of falling prices. (Chapter 6)

degree of financial leverage (DFL)
The numerical measure of the firm's financial leverage. (Chapter 13)

degree of indebtedness
Measures the amount of debt relative to other significant balance sheet amounts. (Chapter 3)

degree of operating leverage (DOL)
The numerical measure of the firm's operating leverage. (Chapter 13)

degree of total leverage (DTL)
The numerical measure of the firm's total leverage. (Chapter 13)

depository transfer check (DTC)
An unsigned check drawn on one of a firm's bank accounts and deposited in another. (Chapter 15)

depreciable life
Time period over which an asset is depreciated. (Chapter 4)

depreciation
A portion of the costs of fixed assets charged against annual revenues over time. (Chapter 4)

derivative security
A security that is neither debt nor equity but derives its value from an underlying asset that is often another security; called "derivatives," for short. (Chapter 17)

diluted EPS
Earnings per share (EPS) calculated under the assumption that *all* contingent securities that would have dilutive effects are converted and exercised and are therefore common stock. (Chapter 17)

dilution of earnings
A reduction in each previous shareholder's fractional claim on the firm's earnings resulting from the issuance of additional shares of common stock. (Chapter 7)

dilution of ownership
A reduction in each previous shareholder's fractional ownership resulting from the issuance of additional shares of common stock. (Chapter 7)

direct lease
A lease under which a lessor owns or acquires the assets that are leased to a given lessee. (Chapter 17)

discount
The amount by which a bond sells at a value that is less than its par value. (Chapter 6)

discounting cash flows
The process of finding present values; the inverse of compounding interest. (Chapter 5)

discount loan
Loan on which interest is paid in advance by being deducted from the amount borrowed. (Chapter 16)

diversifiable risk
The portion of an asset's risk that is attributable to firm-specific, random causes; can be eliminated through diversification. Also called *unsystematic risk*. (Chapter 8)

divestiture
The selling of some of a firm's assets for various strategic reasons. (Chapters 8 and 18)

dividend irrelevance theory
Miller and Modigliani's theory that in a perfect world, the firm's value is determined solely by the earning power and risk of its assets (investments) and that the manner in which it splits its earnings stream between dividends and internally retained (and reinvested) funds does not affect this value. (Chapter 14)

dividend payout ratio
Indicates the percentage of each dollar earned that a firm distributes to the owners in the form of cash. It is calculated by dividing the firm's cash dividend per share by its earnings per share. (Chapter 14)

dividend per share (DPS)
The dollar amount of cash distributed during the period on behalf of each outstanding share of common stock. (Chapter 3)

dividend policy
The firm's plan of action to be followed whenever it makes a dividend decision. (Chapter 14)

dividend reinvestment plans (DRIPs)
Plans that enable stockholders to use dividends received on the firm's stock to acquire additional shares—even fractional shares—at little or no transaction cost. (Chapter 14)

dividend relevance theory
The theory, advanced by Gordon and Lintner, that there is a direct relationship between a firm's dividend policy and its market value. (Chapter 14)

dividends
Periodic distributions of cash to the stockholders of a firm. (Chapter 1)

double taxation
Situation that occurs when after-tax corporate earnings are distributed as cash dividends to stockholders, who then must pay personal taxes on the dividend amount. (Chapter 2)

DuPont formula
Multiplies the firm's *net profit margin* by its *total asset turnover* to calculate the firm's *return on total assets (ROA)*. (Chapter 3)

DuPont system of analysis
System used to dissect the firm's financial statements and to assess its financial condition. (Chapter 3)

Dutch auction repurchase
A repurchase method in which the firm specifies how many shares it wants to buy back and a range of prices at which it is willing to repurchase shares. Investors specify how many shares they will sell at each price in the range, and the firm determines the minimum price required to repurchase its target number of shares. All investors who tender receive the same price. (Chapter 14)

earnings per share (EPS)
The amount earned during the period on behalf of each outstanding share of common stock, calculated by dividing the period's total earnings available for

the firm's common stockholders by the number of shares of common stock outstanding. (Chapter 1)

EBIT–EPS approach
An approach for selecting the capital structure that maximizes earnings per share (EPS) over the expected range of earnings before interest and taxes (EBIT). (Chapter 13)

economic exposure
The risk resulting from the effects of changes in foreign exchange rates on the firm's value. (Chapter 19)

economic order quantity (EOQ) model
Inventory management technique for determining an item's optimal order size, which is the size that minimizes the total of its *order costs* and *carrying costs*. (Chapter 15)

effective interest rate
In the international context, the rate equal to the nominal rate plus (or minus) any forecast appreciation (or depreciation) of a foreign currency relative to the currency of the MNC parent. (Chapter 19)

effective (true) annual rate (EAR)
The annual rate of interest actually paid or earned. (Chapter 5)

efficient market
A market that allocates funds to their most productive uses as a result of competition among wealth-maximizing investors and that determines and publicizes prices that are believed to be close to their true value. (Chapter 2)

efficient-market hypothesis (EMH)
Theory describing the behavior of an assumed "perfect" market in which (1) securities are in equilibrium, (2) security prices fully reflect all available information and react swiftly to new information, and (3), because stocks are fully and fairly priced, investors need not waste time looking for mispriced securities. (Chapter 7)

efficient portfolio
A portfolio that maximizes return for a given level of risk. (Chapter 8)

ending cash
The sum of the firm's beginning cash and its net cash flow for the period. (Chapter 4)

enterprise resource planning (ERP)
A computerized system that electronically integrates external information about the firm's suppliers and customers with the firm's departmental data so that information on all available resources—human and material—can be instantly obtained in a fashion that eliminates production delays and controls costs. (Chapter 15)

equipment trust certificates
See Table 6.4.

equity
Funds provided by the firm's owners (investors or stockholders) that are repaid subject to the firm's performance. (Chapter 7)

euro
A single currency adopted on January 1, 1999, by 12 EU nations, which switched to a single set of euro bills and coins on January 1, 2002. (Chapter 19)

Eurobond
A bond issued by an international borrower and sold to investors in countries with currencies other than the currency in which the bond is denominated. (Chapters 6 and 19)

Eurobond market
The market in which corporations and governments typically issue bonds denominated in dollars and sell them to investors located outside the United States. (Chapters 2 and 19)

Eurocurrency market
International equivalent of the domestic money market. (Chapter 2)

Eurocurrency markets
The portion of the Euromarket that provides short-term, foreign-currency financing to subsidiaries of MNCs. (Chapter 19)

Euromarket
The international financial market that provides for borrowing and lending currencies outside their country of origin. (Chapter 19)

European Open Market
The transformation of the European Union into a *single* market at year-end 1992. (Chapter 19)

European Union (EU)
A significant economic force currently made up of 27 nations that permit free trade within the union. (Chapter 19)

ex dividend
A period beginning 2 *business days* prior to the date of record, during which a stock is sold without the right to receive the current dividend. (Chapter 14)

excess cash balance
The (excess) amount available for investment by the firm if the period's ending cash is greater than the desired minimum cash balance; assumed to be invested in marketable securities. (Chapter 4)

excess earnings accumulation tax
The tax the IRS levies on retained earnings above $250,000 for most businesses when it determines that the firm has accumulated an excess of earnings to allow owners to delay paying ordinary income taxes on dividends received. (Chapter 14)

exchange rate risk
The danger that an unexpected change in the exchange rate between the dollar and the currency in which a project's cash flows are denominated will reduce the market value of that project's cash flow. (Chapter 12)

exchange rate risk
The risk caused by varying exchange rates between two currencies. (Chapter 19)

exercise (or option) price
The price at which holders of warrants can purchase a specified number of shares of common stock. (Chapter 17)

expectations theory
The theory that the yield curve reflects investor expectations about future interest rates; an expectation of rising interest rates results in an upward-sloping yield curve, and an expectation of declining rates results in a downward-sloping yield curve. (Chapter 6)

expected value of a return ($\bar{r}$)
The average return that an investment is expected to produce over time. (Chapter 8)

extendible notes
See Table 6.5.

extension
An arrangement whereby the firm's creditors receive payment in full, although not immediately. (Chapter 18)

external financing required ("plug" figure)
Under the judgmental approach for developing a pro forma balance sheet, the amount of external financing needed to bring the statement into balance. It can be either a positive or a negative value. (Chapter 4)

external forecast
A sales forecast based on the relationships observed between the firm's sales and certain key external economic indicators. (Chapter 4)

extra dividend
An additional dividend optionally paid by the firm when earnings are higher than normal in a given period. (Chapter 14)

factor
A financial institution that specializes in purchasing accounts receivable from businesses. (Chapter 16)

factoring accounts receivable
The outright sale of accounts receivable at a discount to a *factor* or other financial institution. (Chapter 16)

FASB No. 52
Statement issued by the FASB requiring U.S. multinationals first to convert the financial statement accounts of foreign subsidiaries into the *functional currency* and then to translate the accounts into the parent firm's currency using the *all-current-rate method*. (Chapter 19)

Federal Deposit Insurance Corporation (FDIC)
An agency created by the Glass-Steagall Act that provides insurance for deposits at banks and monitors banks to ensure their safety and soundness. (Chapter 2)

finance
The science and art of managing money. (Chapter 1)

Financial Accounting Standards Board (FASB)
The accounting profession's rule-setting body, which authorizes *generally accepted accounting principles (GAAP)*. (Chapter 3)

Financial Accounting Standards Board (FASB) Standard No. 52
Mandates that U.S.–based companies translate their foreign-currency-denominated assets and liabilities into dollars, for consolidation with the parent com-

pany's financial statements. This is done by using the *current rate (translation) method*. (Chapters 3 and 19)

financial breakeven point
The level of EBIT necessary to just cover all *fixed financial costs;* the level of EBIT for which EPS = $0. (Chapter 13)

financial institution
An intermediary that channels the savings of individuals, businesses, and governments into loans or investments. (Chapter 2)

financial (or capital) lease
A *longer-term lease* than an operating lease that is noncancelable and obligates the lessee to make payments for the use of an asset over a predefined period of time; the total payments over the term of the lease are *greater* than the lessor's initial cost of the leased asset. (Chapter 17)

financial leverage
The magnification of risk and return through the use of fixed-cost financing, such as debt and preferred stock. (Chapter 3)

financial leverage
The use of *fixed financial costs* to magnify the effects of changes in earnings before interest and taxes on the firm's earnings per share. (Chapter 13)

financial leverage multiplier (FLM)
The ratio of the firm's total assets to its common stock equity. (Chapter 3)

financial manager
Actively manages the financial affairs of all types of businesses, whether private or public, large or small, profit seeking or not for profit. (Chapter 1)

financial markets
Forums in which suppliers of funds and demanders of funds can transact business directly. (Chapter 2)

financial merger
A merger transaction undertaken with the goal of restructuring the acquired company to improve its cash flow and unlock its unrealized value.
(Chapter 18)

financial planning process
Planning that begins with long-term, or *strategic,* financial plans that in turn guide the formulation of short-term, or *operating,* plans and budgets.
(Chapter 4)

financial services
The area of finance concerned with the design and delivery of advice and financial products to individuals, businesses, and governments. (Chapter 1)

financing flows
Cash flows that result from debt and equity financing transactions; include incurrence and repayment of debt, cash inflow from the sale of stock, and cash outflows to repurchase stock or pay cash dividends. (Chapter 4)

five C's of credit
The five key dimensions—character, capacity, capital, collateral, and conditions—used by credit analysts to provide a framework for in-depth credit analysis. (Chapter 15)

fixed (or semifixed) relationship
The constant (or relatively constant) relationship of a currency to one of the major currencies, a combination (basket) of major currencies, or some type of international foreign exchange standard. (Chapter 19)

fixed-payment coverage ratio
Measures the firm's ability to meet all fixed-payment obligations. (Chapter 3)

fixed-rate loan
A loan with a rate of interest that is determined at a set increment above the prime rate and remains unvarying until maturity. (Chapter 16)

flat yield curve
A yield curve that indicates that interest rates do not vary much at different maturities. (Chapter 6)

float
Funds that have been sent by the payer but are not yet usable funds to the payee. (Chapter 15)

floating inventory lien
A secured short-term loan against inventory under which the lender's claim is on the borrower's inventory in general. (Chapter 16)

floating-rate bonds
See Table 6.5.

floating-rate loan
A loan with a rate of interest initially set at an increment above the prime rate and allowed to "float," or vary, above prime *as the prime rate varies* until maturity. (Chapter 16)

floating relationship
The fluctuating relationship of the values of two currencies with respect to each other. (Chapter 19)

flotation costs
The total costs of issuing and selling a security. (Chapter 9)

foreign bond
A bond that is issued by a foreign corporation or government and is denominated in the investor's home currency and sold in the investor's home market. (Chapters 2, 6, and 19)

foreign direct investment
The transfer of capital, managerial, and technical assets to a foreign country. (Chapters 11 and 19)

foreign exchange manager
The manager responsible for managing and monitoring the firm's exposure to loss from currency fluctuations. (Chapter 1)

forward exchange rate
The rate of exchange between two currencies at some specified future date. (Chapter 19)

foreign exchange rate
The value of two currencies with respect to each other. (Chapter 19)

free cash flow (FCF)
The amount of cash flow available to investors (creditors and owners) after the firm has met all operating needs and paid for investments in net fixed assets and net current assets. (Chapter 4)

free cash flow valuation model
A model that determines the value of an entire company as the present value of its expected *free cash flows* discounted at the firm's *weighted average cost of capital,* which is its expected average future cost of funds over the long run. (Chapter 7)

friendly merger
A merger transaction endorsed by the target firm's management, approved by its stockholders, and easily consummated. (Chapter 18)

functional currency
The currency in which a subsidiary primarily generates and expends cash and in which its accounts are maintained. (Chapter 19)

future value
The value at a given future date of an amount placed on deposit today and earning interest at a specified rate. Found by applying *compound interest* over a specified period of time. (Chapter 5)

General Agreement on Tariffs and Trade (GATT)
A treaty that has governed world trade throughout most of the postwar era; it extends free-trading rules to broad areas of economic activity and is policed by the *World Trade Organization (WTO).* (Chapters 3 and 19)

generally accepted accounting principles (GAAP)
The practice and procedure guidelines used to prepare and maintain financial records and reports; authorized by the *Financial Accounting Standards Board (FASB).* (Chapter 3)

Glass-Steagall Act
An act of Congress in 1933 that created the federal deposit insurance program and separated the activities of commercial and investment banks. (Chapter 2)

golden parachutes
Provisions in the employment contracts of key executives that provide them with sizable compensation if the firm is taken over; deters hostile takeovers to the extent that the cash outflows required are large enough to make the takeover unattractive. (Chapter 18)

Gordon growth model
A common name for the *constant-growth model* that is widely cited in dividend valuation. (Chapter 7)

Gramm-Leach-Bliley Act
An act that allows business combinations (that is, mergers) between commercial banks, investment banks, and insurance companies, and thus permits these institutions to compete in markets that prior regulations prohibited them from entering. (Chapter 2)

greenmail
A takeover defense under which a target firm repurchases, through private negotiation, a large block of stock at a premium from one or more shareholders to end a hostile takeover attempt by those shareholders. (Chapter 18)

gross profit margin
Measures the percentage of each sales dollar remaining after the firm has paid for its goods. (Chapter 3)

hedging
Offsetting or protecting against the risk of adverse price movements. (Chapter 17)

hedging strategies
Techniques used to offset or protect against risk; in the international context, these include borrowing or lending in different currencies; undertaking contracts in the forward, futures, and/or options markets; and swapping assets/liabilities with other parties. (Chapter 19)

historical weights
Either book or market value weights based on *actual* capital structure proportions. (Chapter 9)

holding company
A corporation that has voting control of one or more other corporations. (Chapter 18)

horizontal merger
A merger of two firms *in the same line of business*. (Chapter 18)

hostile merger
A merger transaction that the target firm's management does not support, forcing the acquiring company to try to gain control of the firm by buying shares in the marketplace. (Chapter 18)

hybrid security
A form of debt or equity financing that possesses characteristics of *both* debt and equity financing. (Chapter 17)

implied price of a warrant
The price effectively paid for each warrant attached to a bond. (Chapter 17)

incentive plans
Management compensation plans that tie management compensation to share price; one example involves the granting of *stock options*. (Chapter 1)

income bonds
See Table 6.4.

income statement
Provides a financial summary of the firm's operating results during a specified period. (Chapter 3)

incremental cash flows
The *additional* cash flows—outflows or inflows—expected to result from a proposed capital expenditure. (Chapter 11)

independent projects
Projects whose cash flows are unrelated to (or independent of) one another; the acceptance of one does not *eliminate* the others from further consideration. (Chapter 10)

individual investors
Investors who own relatively small quantities of shares so as to meet personal investment goals. (Chapter 1)

inflation
A rising trend in the prices of most goods and services. (Chapter 6)

informational content
The information provided by the dividends of a firm with respect to future earnings, which causes owners to bid up or down the price of the firm's stock. (Chapter 14)

initial investment
The relevant cash outflow for a proposed project at time zero. (Chapter 11)

initial public offering (IPO)
The first public sale of a firm's stock. (Chapter 7)

insolvency
Business failure that occurs when a firm is unable to pay its liabilities as they come due. (Chapter 18)

insolvent
Describes a firm that is unable to pay its bills as they come due. (Chapter 15)

installation costs
Any added costs that are necessary to place an asset into operation. (Chapter 11)

installed cost of new asset
The *cost of new asset* plus its *installation costs;* equals the asset's depreciable value. (Chapter 11)

institutional investors
Investment professionals, such as banks, insurance companies, mutual funds, and pension funds, that are paid to manage and hold large quantities of securities on behalf of others. (Chapter 1)

interest rate
Usually applied to debt instruments such as bank loans or bonds; the compensation paid by the borrower of funds to the lender; from the borrower's point of view, the cost of borrowing funds. (Chapter 6)

interest rate risk
The chance that interest rates will change and thereby change the required return and bond value. Rising rates, which result in decreasing bond values, are of greatest concern. (Chapter 6)

intermediate cash inflows
Cash inflows received prior to the termination of a project. (Chapter 10)

internal forecast
A sales forecast based on a buildup, or consensus, of sales forecasts through the firm's own sales channels. (Chapter 4)

internal rate of return (IRR)
The discount rate that equates the NPV of an investment opportunity with $0 (because the present value of cash inflows equals the initial investment); it is the rate of return that the firm will earn if it invests in the project and receives the given cash inflows. (Chapter 10)

internal rate of return approach
An approach to capital rationing that involves graphing project IRRs in descending order against the total dollar investment to determine the group of acceptable projects. (Chapter 12)

international bond
A bond that is initially sold outside the country of the borrower and is often distributed in several countries. (Chapter 19)

international equity market
A market that allows corporations to sell blocks of shares to investors in a number of different countries simultaneously. (Chapter 2)

international stock market
A market with uniform rules and regulations governing major stock exchanges. MNCs would benefit greatly from such a market, which has yet to evolve. (Chapter 19)

inventory turnover
Measures the activity, or liquidity, of a firm's inventory. (Chapter 3)

inverted yield curve
A *downward-sloping* yield curve indicates that short-term interest rates are generally higher than long-term interest rates. (Chapter 6)

investment banker
Financial intermediary that specializes in selling new security issues and advising firms with regard to major financial transactions. (Chapter 7)

investment bankers
Financial intermediaries who, in addition to their role in selling new security issues, can be hired by acquirers in mergers to find suitable target companies and assist in negotiations. (Chapter 18)

investment banks
Institutions that assist companies in raising capital, advise firms on major transactions such as mergers or financial restructurings, and engage in trading and market making activities. (Chapter 2)

investment flows
Cash flows associated with purchase and sale of both fixed assets and equity investments in other firms. (Chapter 4)

investment opportunities schedule (IOS)
The graph that plots project IRRs in descending order against the total dollar investment. (Chapter 12)

involuntary reorganization
A petition initiated by an outside party, usually a creditor, for the reorganization and payment of creditors of a failed firm. (Chapter 18)

issued shares
Shares of common stock that have been put into circulation; the sum of *outstanding shares* and *treasury stock*. (Chapter 7)

joint venture
A partnership under which the participants have contractually agreed to contribute specified amounts of money and expertise in exchange for stated proportions of ownership and profit. (Chapter 19)

judgmental approach
A simplified approach for preparing the pro forma balance sheet under which the firm estimates the values of certain balance sheet accounts and uses its external financing as a balancing, or "plug," figure. (Chapter 4)

junk bonds
See Table 6.5.

just-in-time (JIT) system
Inventory management technique that minimizes inventory investment by having materials arrive at exactly the time they are needed for production. (Chapter 15)

lease-versus-purchase (or lease-versus-buy) decision
The decision facing firms needing to acquire new fixed assets: whether to lease the assets or to purchase them, using borrowed funds or available liquid resources. (Chapter 17)

leasing
The process by which a firm can obtain the use of certain fixed assets for which it must make a series of contractual, periodic, tax-deductible payments. (Chapter 17)

lessee
The receiver of the services of the assets under a lease contract. (Chapter 17)

lessor
The owner of assets that are being leased. (Chapter 17)

letter of credit
A letter written by a company's bank to the company's foreign supplier, stating that the bank guarantees payment of an invoiced amount if all the underlying agreements are met. (Chapter 16)

letter to stockholders
Typically, the first element of the annual stockholders' report and the primary communication from management. (Chapter 3)

leverage
Refers to the effects that fixed costs have on the returns that shareholders earn; higher leverage generally results in higher but more volatile returns. (Chapter 13)

leveraged buyout (LBO)
An acquisition technique involving the use of a large amount of debt to purchase a firm; an example of a *financial merger*. (Chapter 18)

leveraged lease
A lease under which the lessor acts as an equity participant, supplying only about 20 percent of the cost of the asset, while a lender supplies the balance. (Chapter 17)

leveraged recapitalization
A takeover defense in which the target firm pays a large debt-financed cash dividend, increasing the firm's financial leverage and thereby deterring the takeover attempt. (Chapter 18)

lien
A publicly disclosed legal claim on loan collateral. (Chapter 16)

limited liability
A legal provision that limits stockholders' liability for a corporation's debt to the amount they initially invested in the firm by purchasing stock. (Chapter 1)

limited liability company (LLC)
See Chapter 1 "In More Depth" feature. (Chapter 1)

limited liability partnership (LLP)
See Chapter 1 "In More Depth" feature. (Chapter 1)

limited partnership (LP)
See Chapter 1 "In More Depth" feature. (Chapter 1)

line of credit
An agreement between a commercial bank and a business specifying the amount of unsecured short-term borrowing the bank will make available to the firm over a given period of time. (Chapter 16)

liquidation value per share
The *actual amount* per share of common stock that would be received if all of the firm's assets were sold for their market value, liabilities (including preferred stock) were paid, and any remaining money were divided among the common stockholders. (Chapter 7)

liquidity
A firm's ability to satisfy its short-term obligations *as they come due*. (Chapter 3)

liquidity preference
A general tendency for investors to prefer short-term (that is, more liquid) securities. (Chapter 6)

liquidity preference theory
Theory suggesting that long-term rates are generally higher than short-term rates (hence, the yield curve is upward sloping) because investors perceive short-term investments to be more liquid and less risky than long-term investments. Borrowers must offer higher rates on long-term bonds to entice investors away from their preferred short-term securities. (Chapter 6)

loan amortization
The determination of the equal periodic loan payments necessary to provide a lender with a specified interest return and to repay the loan principal over a specified period. (Chapter 5)

loan amortization schedule
A schedule of equal payments to repay a loan. It shows the allocation of each loan payment to interest and principal. (Chapter 5)

lockbox system
A collection procedure in which customers mail payments to a post office box that is emptied regularly by the firm's bank, which processes the payments and deposits them in the firm's account. This system speeds up collection time by reducing processing time as well as mail and clearing time. (Chapter 15)

long-term debt
Debt for which payment is not due in the current year. (Chapter 3)

long-term (strategic) financial plans
Plans that lay out a company's planned financial actions and the anticipated impact of those actions over periods ranging from 2 to 10 years. (Chapter 4)

low-regular-and-extra dividend policy
A dividend policy based on paying a low regular dividend, supplemented by an additional ("extra") dividend when earnings are higher than normal in a given period. (Chapter 14)

macro political risk
The subjection of all foreign firms to *political risk* (takeover) by a host country because of political change, revolution, or the adoption of new policies. (Chapter 19)

mail float
The time delay between when payment is placed in the mail and when it is received. (Chapter 15)

maintenance clauses
Provisions normally included in an operating lease that require the lessor to maintain the assets and to make insurance and tax payments. (Chapter 17)

managerial finance
Concerns the duties of the *financial manager* in a business. (Chapter 1)

manufacturing resource planning II (MRP II)
A sophisticated computerized system that integrates data from numerous areas such as finance, accounting, marketing, engineering, and manufacturing and generates production plans as well as numerous financial and management reports. (Chapter 15)

marginal cost–benefit analysis
Economic principle that states that financial decisions should be made and actions taken only when the added benefits exceed the added costs. (Chapter 1)

marginal tax rate
The rate at which *additional income* is taxed. (Chapter 2)

marketable securities
Short-term debt instruments, such as U.S. Treasury bills, commercial paper, and negotiable certificates of deposit issued by government, business, and financial institutions, respectively. (Chapter 2)

market/book (M/B) ratio
Provides an assessment of how investors view the firm's performance. Firms expected to earn high returns relative to their risk typically sell at higher M/B multiples. (Chapter 3)

market makers
Securities dealers who "make markets" by offering to buy or sell certain securities at stated prices. (Chapter 2)

market premium
The amount by which the market value exceeds the straight or conversion value of a convertible security. (Chapter 17)

market ratios
Relate a firm's market value, as measured by its current share price, to certain accounting values. (Chapter 3)

market return
The return on the market portfolio of all traded securities. (Chapter 8)

market segmentation theory
Theory suggesting that the market for loans is segmented on the basis of maturity and that the supply of and demand for loans within each segment determine its prevailing interest rate; the slope of the yield curve is determined by the general relationship between the prevailing rates in each market segment. (Chapter 6)

market value weights
Weights that use market values to measure the proportion of each type of capital in the firm's financial structure (Chapter 9).

materials requirement planning (MRP) system
Inventory management technique that applies EOQ concepts and a computer to compare production needs to available inventory balances and determine when orders should be placed for various items on a product's *bill of materials*. (Chapter 15)

Mercosur
A major South American trading bloc that includes countries that account for more than half of total Latin American GDP. (Chapter 19)

merger
The combination of two or more firms, in which the resulting firm maintains the identity of one of the firms, usually the larger. (Chapter 18)

micro political risk
The subjection of an individual firm, a specific industry, or companies from a particular foreign country to *political risk* (takeover) by a host country. (Chapter 19)

mixed stream
A stream of unequal periodic cash flows that reflect no particular pattern. (Chapter 5)

modified accelerated cost recovery system (MACRS)
System used to determine the depreciation of assets for tax purposes. (Chapter 4)

modified DuPont formula
Relates the firm's *return on total assets (ROA)* to its *return on common equity (ROE)* using the *financial leverage multiplier (FLM)*. (Chapter 3)

monetary union
The official melding of the national currencies of the EU nations into one currency, the *euro*, on January 1, 2002. (Chapter 19)

money market
A financial relationship created between suppliers and demanders of *short-term funds*. (Chapter 2)

mortgage-backed securities
Securities that represent claims on the cash flows generated by a pool of mortgages. (Chapter 2)

mortgage bonds
See Table 6.4.

multinational companies (MNCs)
Firms that have international assets and operations in foreign markets and draw part of their total revenue and profits from such markets. (Chapter 19)

multiple IRRs
More than one IRR resulting from a capital budgeting project with a *nonconventional cash flow pattern*; the maximum number of IRRs for a project is equal to the number of sign changes in its cash flows. (Chapter 10)

mutually exclusive projects
Projects that compete with one another, so that the acceptance of one *eliminates* from further consideration all other projects that serve a similar function. (Chapter 10)

Nasdaq market
An all-electronic trading platform used to execute securities trades. (Chapter 2)

national entry control systems
Comprehensive rules, regulations, and incentives introduced by host governments to regulate inflows of *foreign direct investments* from MNCs and at the same time extract more benefits from their presence. (Chapter 19)

negatively correlated
Describes two series that move in opposite directions. (Chapter 8)

net cash flow
The mathematical difference between the firm's cash receipts and its cash disbursements in each period. (Chapter 4)

net operating profits after taxes (NOPAT)
A firm's earnings before interest and after taxes, EBIT $\times$ $(1 - T)$. (Chapter 4)

net present value (NPV)
A sophisticated capital budgeting technique; found by subtracting a project's initial investment from the present value of its cash inflows discounted at a rate equal to the firm's cost of capital. (Chapter 10)

net present value approach
An approach to capital rationing that is based on the use of present values to determine the group of projects that will maximize owners' wealth. (Chapter 12)

net present value profile
Graph that depicts a project's NPVs for various discount rates. (Chapter 10)

net proceeds
Funds actually received by the firm from the sale of a security. (Chapter 9)

net profit margin
Measures the percentage of each sales dollar remaining after all costs and expenses, *including* interest, taxes, and preferred stock dividends, have been deducted. (Chapter 3)

net working capital
The difference between the firm's current assets and its current liabilities. (Chapters 11 and 15)

no-par preferred stock
Preferred stock with no stated face value but with a stated annual dollar dividend. (Chapter 7)

nominal (stated) annual rate
Contractual annual rate of interest charged by a lender or promised by a borrower. (Chapter 5)

nominal interest rate
In the international context, the stated interest rate charged on financing when only the MNC parent's currency is involved. (Chapter 19)

nominal rate of interest
The actual rate of interest charged by the supplier of funds and paid by the demander. (Chapter 6)

noncash charge
An expense that is deducted on the income statement but does not involve the actual outlay of cash during the period; includes depreciation, amortization, and depletion. (Chapter 4)

noncumulative (preferred stock)
Preferred stock for which passed (unpaid) dividends do not accumulate. (Chapter 7)

nondiversifiable risk
The relevant portion of an asset's risk attributable to market factors that affect all firms; cannot be eliminated through diversification. Also called *systematic risk*. (Chapter 8)

nonnotification basis
The basis on which a borrower, having pledged an account receivable, continues to collect the account payments without notifying the account customer. (Chapter 16)

nonrecourse basis
The basis on which accounts receivable are sold to a factor with the understanding that the factor accepts all credit risks on the purchased accounts. (Chapter 16)

nonvoting common stock
Common stock that carries no voting rights; issued when the firm wishes to raise capital through the sale of common stock but does not want to give up its voting control. (Chapter 7)

normal probability distribution
A symmetrical probability distribution whose shape resembles a "bell-shaped" curve. (Chapter 8)

normal yield curve
An *upward-sloping* yield curve indicates that long-term interest rates are generally higher than short-term interest rates. (Chapter 6)

North American Free Trade Agreement (NAFTA)
The treaty establishing free trade and open markets among Canada, Mexico, and the United States. (Chapter 19)

notes to the financial statements
Explanatory notes keyed to relevant accounts in the statements; they provide detailed information on the accounting policies, procedures, calculations, and transactions underlying entries in the financial statements. (Chapter 3)

notification basis
The basis on which an account customer whose account has been pledged (or factored) is notified to remit payment directly to the lender (or factor). (Chapter 16)

offshore centers
Certain cities or states (including London, Singapore, Bahrain, Nassau, Hong Kong, and Luxembourg) that have achieved prominence as major centers for Euromarket business. (Chapter 19)

open-market share repurchase
A share repurchase program in which firms simply buy back some of their outstanding shares on the open market. (Chapter 14)

operating breakeven point
The level of sales necessary to cover all *operating costs*; the point at which EBIT = $0. (Chapter 13)

operating cash flow (OCF)
The cash flow a firm generates from its normal operations; calculated as *net operating profits after taxes (NOPAT)* plus depreciation. (Chapter 4)

operating cash inflows
The incremental after-tax cash inflows resulting from implementation of a project during its life. (Chapter 11)

operating-change restrictions
Contractual restrictions that a bank may impose on a firm's financial condition or operations as part of a line-of-credit agreement. (Chapter 16)

operating cycle (OC)
The time from the beginning of the production process to collection of cash from the sale of the finished product. (Chapter 15)

operating expenditure
An outlay of funds by the firm resulting in benefits received *within* 1 year. (Chapter 10)

operating flows
Cash flows directly related to sale and production of the firm's products and services. (Chapter 4)

operating lease
A cancelable contractual arrangement whereby the lessee agrees to make periodic payments to the lessor, often for 5 or fewer years, to obtain an asset's services; generally, the total payments over the term of the lease are *less* than the lessor's initial cost of the leased asset. (Chapter 17)

operating leverage
The use of *fixed operating costs* to magnify the effects of changes in sales on the firm's earnings before interest and taxes. (Chapter 13)

operating profit margin
Measures the percentage of each sales dollar remaining after all costs and expenses *other than* interest, taxes, and preferred stock dividends are deducted; the "pure profits" earned on each sales dollar. (Chapter 3)

operating unit
A part of a business, such as a plant, division, product line, or subsidiary, that contributes to the actual operations of the firm. (Chapter 18)

opportunity costs
Cash flows that could be realized from the best alternative use of an owned asset. (Chapter 11)

optimal capital structure
The capital structure at which the weighted average cost of capital is minimized, thereby maximizing the firm's value. (Chapter 13)

option
An instrument that provides its holder with an opportunity to purchase or sell a specified asset at a stated price on or before a set *expiration date*. (Chapter 17)

order costs
The fixed clerical costs of placing and receiving an inventory order. (Chapter 15)

ordinary annuity
An annuity for which the cash flow occurs at the *end* of each period. (Chapter 5)

ordinary income
Income earned through the sale of a firm's goods or services. (Chapter 2)

outstanding shares
Issued shares of common stock held by investors, including both private and public investors. (Chapter 7)

overhanging issue
A convertible security that cannot be forced into conversion by using the call feature. (Chapter 17)

over-the-counter (OTC) market
Market where smaller, unlisted securities are traded. (Chapter 2)

paid-in capital in excess of par
The amount of proceeds in excess of the par value received from the original sale of common stock. (Chapter 3)

partnership
A business owned by two or more people and operated for profit. (Chapter 1)

par-value common stock
An arbitrary value established for legal purposes in the firm's corporate charter and which can be used to find the total number of shares outstanding by dividing it into the book value of common stock. (Chapter 7)

par-value preferred stock
Preferred stock with a stated face value that is used with the specified dividend percentage to determine the annual dollar dividend. (Chapter 7)

payback period
The amount of time required for a firm to recover its initial investment in a project, as calculated from cash *inflows*. (Chapter 10)

payment date
Set by the firm's directors, the actual date on which the firm mails the dividend payment to the holders of record. (Chapter 14)

payout policy
Decisions that a firm makes regarding whether to distribute cash to shareholders, how much cash to distribute, and the means by which cash should be distributed. (Chapter 14)

pecking order
A hierarchy of financing that begins with retained earnings, which is followed by debt financing and finally external equity financing. (Chapter 13)

percentage advance
The percentage of the book value of the collateral that constitutes the principal of a secured loan. (Chapter 16)

percent-of-sales method
A simple method for developing the pro forma income statement; it forecasts sales and then expresses the various income statement items as percentages of projected sales. (Chapter 4)

perfectly negatively correlated
Describes two *negatively correlated* series that have a *correlation coefficient* of −1. (Chapter 8)

perfectly positively correlated
Describes two *positively correlated* series that have a *correlation coefficient* of +1. (Chapter 8)

performance plans
Plans that tie management compensation to measures such as EPS or growth in EPS. *Performance shares* and/or *cash bonuses* are used as compensation under these plans. (Chapter 1)

performance shares
Shares of stock given to management for meeting stated performance goals. (Chapter 1)

permanent funding requirement
A constant investment in operating assets resulting from constant sales over time. (Chapter 15)

perpetuity
An annuity with an infinite life, providing continual annual cash flow. (Chapter 5)

pledge of accounts receivable
The use of a firm's accounts receivable as security, or collateral, to obtain a short-term loan. (Chapter 16)

poison pill
A takeover defense in which a firm issues securities that give their holders certain rights that become effective when a takeover is attempted; these rights make the target firm less desirable to a hostile acquirer. (Chapter 18)

political risk
Risk that arises from the possibility that a host government will take actions harmful to foreign investors or that political turmoil will endanger investments. (Chapter 8)

political risk
The potential discontinuity or seizure of an MNC's operations in a host country via the host's implementation of specific rules and regulations. (Chapter 19)

portfolio
A collection, or group, of assets. (Chapter 8)

positively correlated
Describes two series that move in the same direction. (Chapter 8)

preemptive right
Allows common stockholders to maintain their proportionate ownership in the corporation when new shares are issued, thus protecting them from dilution of their ownership. (Chapter 7)

preferred stock
A special form of ownership having a fixed periodic dividend that must be paid prior to payment of any dividends to common stockholders. (Chapter 2)

premium
The amount by which a bond sells at a value that is greater than its par value. (Chapter 6)

present value
The current dollar value of a future amount—the amount of money that would have to be invested today at a given interest rate over a specified period to equal the future amount. (Chapter 5)

president or chief executive officer (CEO)
Corporate official responsible for managing the firm's day-to-day operations and carrying out the policies established by the board of directors. (Chapter 1)

price/earnings multiple approach
A popular technique used to estimate the firm's share value; calculated by multiplying the firm's expected earnings per share (EPS) by the average price/earnings (P/E) ratio for the industry. (Chapter 7)

price/earnings (P/E) ratio
Measures the amount that investors are willing to pay for each dollar of a firm's earnings; the higher the P/E ratio, the greater the investor confidence. (Chapter 3)

primary market
Financial market in which securities are initially issued; the only market in which the issuer is directly involved in the transaction. (Chapter 2)

prime rate of interest (prime rate)
The lowest rate of interest charged by leading banks on business loans to their most important business borrowers. (Chapter 16)

principal
The amount of money on which interest is paid. (Chapter 5)

principal–agent relationship
An arrangement in which an agent acts on the behalf of a principal. For example, shareholders of a company (principals) elect management (agents) to act on their behalf. (Chapter 1)

privately owned (stock)
The common stock of a firm is owned by private investors; this stock is not publicly traded. (Chapter 7)

private placement
The sale of a new security directly to an investor or group of investors. (Chapter 2)

probability
The *chance* that a given outcome will occur. (Chapter 8)

probability distribution
A model that relates probabilities to the associated outcomes. (Chapter 8)

proceeds from sale of old asset
The cash inflows, net of any removal or cleanup costs, resulting from the sale of an existing asset. (Chapter 11)

processing float
The time between receipt of a payment and its deposit into the firm's account. (Chapter 15)

profitability
The relationship between revenues and costs generated by using the firm's assets—both current and fixed—in productive activities. (Chapter 15)

pro forma statements
Projected, or forecast, income statements and balance sheets. (Chapter 4)

prospectus
A portion of a security registration statement that describes the key aspects of the issue, the issuer, and its management and financial position. (Chapter 7)

proxy battle
The attempt by a nonmanagement group to gain control of the management of a firm by soliciting a sufficient number of proxy votes. (Chapter 7)

proxy statement
A statement transferring the votes of a stockholder to another party. (Chapter 7)

Public Company Accounting Oversight Board (PCAOB)
A not-for-profit corporation established by the *Sarbanes-Oxley Act of 2002* to protect the interests of investors and further the public interest in the preparation of informative, fair, and independent audit reports. (Chapter 3)

publicly owned (stock)
The common stock of a firm is owned by public investors; this stock is publicly traded. (Chapter 7)

public offering
The sale of either bonds or stocks to the general public. (Chapter 2)

purchase options
Provisions frequently included in both operating and financial leases that allow the lessee to purchase the leased asset at maturity, typically for a prespecified price. (Chapter 17)

pure economic profit
A profit above and beyond the normal competitive rate of return in a line of business. (Chapter 10)

putable bonds
See Table 6.5.

put option
An option to *sell* a specified number of shares of a stock (typically 100) on or before a specified future date at a stated price. (Chapter 17)

pyramiding
An arrangement among holding companies wherein one holding company controls other holding companies, thereby causing an even greater magnification of earnings and losses. (Chapter 18)

quarterly compounding
Compounding of interest over four periods within the year. (Chapter 5)

quick (acid-test) ratio
A measure of liquidity calculated by dividing the firm's current assets minus inventory by its current liabilities. (Chapter 3)

range
A measure of an asset's risk, which is found by subtracting the return associated with the pessimistic (worst) outcome from the return associated with the optimistic (best) outcome. (Chapter 8)

ranking approach
The ranking of capital expenditure projects on the basis of some predetermined measure, such as the rate of return. (Chapter 10)

ratio analysis
Involves methods of calculating and interpreting financial ratios to analyze and monitor the firm's performance. (Chapter 3)

ratio of exchange
The ratio of the amount *paid* per share of the target company to the market price per share of the acquiring firm. (Chapter 18)

ratio of exchange in market price
Indicates the market price per share of the acquiring firm paid for each dollar of market price per share of the target firm. (Chapter 18)

real options
Opportunities that are embedded in capital projects that enable managers to alter their cash flows and risk in a way that affects project acceptability (NPV). Also called *strategic options*. (Chapter 12)

real rate of interest
The rate that creates equilibrium between the supply of savings and the demand for investment funds in a perfect world, without inflation, where suppliers and demanders of funds have no liquidity preferences and there is no risk. (Chapter 6)

recapitalization
The reorganization procedure under which a failed firm's debts are generally exchanged for equity or the maturities of existing debts are extended. (Chapter 18)

recaptured depreciation
The portion of an asset's sale price that is above its book value and below its initial purchase price. (Chapter 11)

recovery period
The appropriate depreciable life of a particular asset as determined by MACRS. (Chapter 4)

red herring
A preliminary prospectus made available to prospective investors during the waiting period between the registration statement's filing with the SEC and its approval. (Chapter 7)

regular dividend policy
A dividend policy based on the payment of a fixed-dollar dividend in each period. (Chapter 14)

relevant cash flows
The *incremental cash outflow (investment) and resulting subsequent inflows* associated with a proposed capital expenditure. (Chapter 11)

renewal options
Provisions especially common in operating leases that grant the lessee the right to re-lease assets at the expiration of the lease. (Chapter 17)

reorder point
The point at which to reorder inventory, expressed as days of lead time × daily usage. (Chapter 15)

required return
Usually applied to equity instruments such as common stock; the cost of funds obtained by selling an ownership interest. (Chapter 6)

required total financing
Amount of funds needed by the firm if the ending cash for the period is less than the desired minimum cash balance; typically represented by notes payable. (Chapter 4)

residual theory of dividends
A school of thought that suggests that the dividend paid by a firm should be viewed as a *residual*—the amount left over after all acceptable investment opportunities have been undertaken. (Chapter 14)

restrictive covenants
Provisions in a bond indenture that place operating and financial constraints on the borrower. (Chapter 6)

retained earnings
The cumulative total of all earnings, net of dividends, that have been retained and reinvested in the firm since its inception. (Chapter 3)

return on common equity (ROE)
Measures the return earned on the common stockholders' investment in the firm. (Chapter 3)

return on total assets (ROA)
Measures the overall effectiveness of management in generating profits with its available assets; also called the *return on investment (ROI)*. (Chapter 3)

reverse stock split
A method used to raise the market price of a firm's stock by exchanging a certain number of outstanding shares for one new share. (Chapter 14)

revolving credit agreement
A line of credit *guaranteed* to a borrower by a commercial bank regardless of the scarcity of money. (Chapter 16)

rights
Financial instruments that allow stockholders to purchase additional shares at a price below the market price, in direct proportion to their number of owned shares. (Chapter 7)

risk
A measure of the uncertainty surrounding the return that an investment will earn or, more formally, *the variability of returns associated with a given asset*. (Chapter 8)

risk
The chance that actual outcomes may differ from those expected. (Chapter 1)

risk (in capital budgeting)
The uncertainty surrounding the cash flows that a project will generate or, more formally, the degree of variability of cash flows. (Chapter 12)

risk (of insolvency)
The probability that a firm will be unable to pay its bills as they come due. (Chapter 15)

risk-adjusted discount rate (RADR)
The rate of return that must be earned on a given project to compensate the firm's owners adequately—that is, to maintain or improve the firm's share price. (Chapter 12)

risk averse
Requiring compensation to bear risk. (Chapter 1)

risk averse
The attitude toward risk in which investors would require an increased return as compensation for an increase in risk. (Chapter 8)

risk-free rate of return, (R_F)
The required return on a *risk-free asset,* typically a 3-month *U.S. Treasury bill.* (Chapter 8)

risk neutral
The attitude toward risk in which investors choose the investment with the higher return regardless of its risk. (Chapter 8)

risk seeking
The attitude toward risk in which investors prefer investments with greater risk even if they have lower expected returns. (Chapter 8)

S corporation (S corp)
See Chapter 1 "In More Depth" feature.

safety stock
Extra inventory that is held to prevent stockouts of important items. (Chapter 15)

sale-leaseback arrangement
A lease under which the lessee sells an asset to a prospective lessor and then *leases back* the same asset, making fixed periodic payments for its use. (Chapter 17)

sales forecast
The prediction of the firm's sales over a given period, based on external and/or internal data; used as the key input to the short-term financial planning process. (Chapter 4)

Sarbanes-Oxley Act of 2002 (SOX)
An act aimed at eliminating corporate disclosure and conflict of interest problems. Contains provisions about corporate financial disclosures and the relationships among corporations, analysts, auditors, attorneys, directors, officers, and shareholders. (Chapter 1)

scenario analysis
An approach for assessing risk that uses several possible alternative outcomes (scenarios) to obtain a sense of the variability among returns. (Chapter 8)

seasonal funding requirement
An investment in operating assets that varies over time as a result of cyclic sales. (Chapter 15)

secondary market
Financial market in which preowned securities (those that are not new issues) are traded. (Chapter 2)

secured creditors
Creditors who have specific assets pledged as collateral and, in liquidation of the failed firm, receive proceeds from the sale of those assets. (Chapter 18)

secured short-term financing
Short-term financing (loan) that has specific assets pledged as collateral. (Chapter 16)

Securities Act of 1933
An act that regulates the sale of securities to the public via the primary market. (Chapter 2)

Securities and Exchange Commission (SEC)
The primary government agency responsible for enforcing federal securities laws. (Chapter 2)

Securities Exchange Act of 1934
An act that regulates the trading of securities such as stocks and bonds in the secondary market. (Chapter 2)

securities exchanges
Organizations that provide the marketplace in which firms can raise funds through the sale of new securities and purchasers can resell securities. (Chapter 2)

securitization
The process of pooling mortgages or other types of loans and then selling claims or securities against that pool in the secondary market. (Chapter 2)

security agreement
The agreement between the borrower and the lender that specifies the collateral held against a secured loan. (Chapter 16)

security market line (SML)
The depiction of the *capital asset pricing model (CAPM)* as a graph that reflects the required return in the marketplace for each level of nondiversifiable risk (beta). (Chapter 8)

selling group
A large number of brokerage firms that join the originating investment banker(s); each accepts responsibility for selling a certain portion of a new security issue on a commission basis. (Chapter 7)

semiannual compounding
Compounding of interest over two periods within the year. (Chapter 5)

shadow banking system
A group of institutions that engage in lending activities, much like traditional banks, but do not accept deposits and therefore are not subject to the same regulations as traditional banks. (Chapter 2)

shark repellents
Antitakeover amendments to a corporate charter that constrain the firm's ability to transfer managerial control of the firm as a result of a merger. (Chapter 18)

short-term (operating) financial plans
Specify short-term financial actions and the anticipated impact of those actions. (Chapter 4)

short-term, self-liquidating loan
An unsecured short-term loan in which the use to which the borrowed money is put provides the mechanism through which the loan is repaid. (Chapter 16)

signal
A financing action by management that is believed to reflect its view of the firm's stock value; generally, debt financing is viewed as a *positive signal* that management believes the stock is "undervalued," and a stock issue is viewed as a *negative signal* that management believes the stock is "overvalued." (Chapter 13)

simulation
A statistics-based behavioral approach that applies predetermined probability distributions and random numbers to estimate risky outcomes. (Chapter 12)

single-payment note
A short-term, one-time loan made to a borrower who needs funds for a specific purpose for a short period. (Chapter 16)

sinking-fund requirement
A restrictive provision often included in a bond indenture, providing for the systematic retirement of bonds prior to their maturity. (Chapter 6)

small (ordinary) stock dividend
A stock dividend representing less than 20 percent to 25 percent of the common stock outstanding when the dividend is declared. (Chapter 14)

sole proprietorship
A business owned by one person and operated for his or her own profit. (Chapter 1)

spin-off
A form of divestiture in which an operating unit becomes an independent company through the issuance of shares in it, on a pro rata basis, to the parent company's shareholders. (Chapter 18)

spontaneous liabilities
Financing that arises from the normal course of business; the two major short-term sources of such liabilities are accounts payable and accruals. (Chapter 16)

spot exchange rate
The rate of exchange between two currencies on any given day. (Chapter 19)

stakeholders
Groups such as employees, customers, suppliers, creditors, owners, and others who have a direct economic link to the firm. (Chapter 1)

standard debt provisions
Provisions in a *bond indenture* specifying certain record-keeping and general business practices that the bond issuer must follow; normally, they do not place a burden on a financially sound business. (Chapter 6)

standard deviation (σ_r)
The most common statistical indicator of an asset's risk; it measures the dispersion around the expected value. (Chapter 8)

statement of cash flows
Provides a summary of the firm's operating, investment, and financing cash flows and reconciles them with changes in its cash and marketable securities during the period. (Chapter 3)

statement of retained earnings
Reconciles the net income earned during a given year, and any cash dividends paid, with the change in retained earnings between the start and the end of that year. An abbreviated form of the *statement of stockholders' equity*. (Chapter 3)

statement of stockholders' equity
Shows all equity account transactions that occurred during a given year. (Chapter 3)

stock dividend
The payment, to existing owners, of a dividend in the form of stock. (Chapter 14)

stockholders
The owners of a corporation, whose ownership, or equity, takes the form of either common stock or preferred stock. (Chapter 1)

stockholders' report
Annual report that publicly owned corporations must provide to stockholders; it summarizes and documents the firm's financial activities during the past year. (Chapter 3)

stock options
Options extended by the firm that allow management to benefit from increases in stock prices over time. (Chapter 1)

stock purchase warrants
Instruments that give their holders the right to purchase a certain number of shares of the issuer's common stock at a specified price over a certain period of time. (Chapters 6 and 17)

stock split
A method commonly used to lower the market price of a firm's stock by increasing the number of shares belonging to each shareholder. (Chapter 14)

stock swap transaction
An acquisition method in which the acquiring firm exchanges its shares for shares of the target company according to a predetermined ratio. (Chapter 18)

straight bond
A bond that is nonconvertible, having no conversion feature. (Chapter 17)

straight bond value
The price at which a convertible bond would sell in the market without the conversion feature. (Chapter 17)

straight preferred stock
Preferred stock that is nonconvertible, having no conversion feature. (Chapter 17)

strategic merger
A merger transaction undertaken to achieve economies of scale. (Chapter 18)

stretching accounts payable
Paying bills as late as possible without damaging the firm's credit rating. (Chapter 16)

strike price
The price at which the holder of a call option can buy (or the holder of a put option can sell) a specified amount of stock at any time prior to the option's expiration date. (Chapter 17)

subordinated debentures
See Table 6.4.

subordination
In a bond indenture, the stipulation that subsequent creditors agree to wait until all claims of the *senior debt* are satisfied. (Chapter 6)

subsidiaries
The companies controlled by a holding company. (Chapter 18)

sunk costs
Cash outlays that have already been made (past outlays) and therefore have no effect on the cash flows relevant to a current decision. (Chapter 11)

supervoting shares
Stock that carries with it multiple votes per share rather than the single vote per share typically given on regular shares of common stock. (Chapter 7)

takeover defenses
Strategies for fighting hostile takeovers. (Chapter 18)

target company
The firm in a merger transaction that the acquiring company is pursuing. (Chapter 18)

target dividend-payout ratio
A dividend policy under which the firm attempts to pay out a certain percentage of earnings as a stated dollar dividend and adjusts that dividend toward a target payout as proven earnings increases occur. (Chapter 14)

target weights
Either book or market value weights based on *desired* capital structure proportions. (Chapter 9)

tax loss carryforward
In a merger, the tax loss of one of the firms that can be applied against a limited amount of future income of the merged firm over 20 years or until the total tax loss has been fully recovered, whichever comes first. (Chapter 18)

tax on sale of old asset
Tax that depends on the relationship between the old asset's sale price and book value and on existing government tax rules. (Chapter 11)

temporal method
A method that requires specific assets and liabilities to be translated at so-called historical exchange rates and foreign-exchange translation gains or losses to be reflected in the current year's income. (Chapter 19)

tender offer repurchase
A repurchase program in which a firm offers to repurchase a fixed number of shares, usually at a premium relative to the market value, and shareholders decide whether or not they want to sell back their shares at that price. (Chapter 14)

term structure of interest rates
The relationship between the maturity and rate of return for bonds with similar levels of risk. (Chapter 6)

terminal cash flow
The after-tax nonoperating cash flow occurring in the final year of a project. It is usually attributable to liquidation of the project. (Chapter 11)

time line
A horizontal line on which time zero appears at the leftmost end and future periods are marked from left to right; can be used to depict investment cash flows. (Chapter 5)

time-series analysis
Evaluation of the firm's financial performance over time using financial ratio analysis. (Chapter 3)

times interest earned ratio
Measures the firm's ability to make contractual interest payments; sometimes called the *interest coverage ratio*. (Chapter 3)

total asset turnover
Indicates the efficiency with which the firm uses its assets to generate sales. (Chapter 3)

total cost of inventory
The sum of order costs and carrying costs of inventory. (Chapter 15)

total leverage
The use of *fixed costs, both operating and financial,* to magnify the effects of changes in sales on the firm's earnings per share. (Chapter 13)

total rate of return
The total gain or loss experienced on an investment over a given period of time; calculated by dividing the asset's cash distributions during the period, plus change in value, by its beginning-of-period investment value. (Chapter 8)

total risk
The combination of a security's *nondiversifiable risk* and *diversifiable risk*. (Chapter 8)

transfer prices
Prices that subsidiaries charge each other for the goods and services traded between them. (Chapter 12)

treasurer
The firm's chief financial manager, who manages the firm's cash, oversees its pension plans, and manages key risks. (Chapter 1)

treasury stock
Issued shares of common stock held by the firm; often these shares have been repurchased by the firm. (Chapter 7)

trust receipt inventory loan
A secured short-term loan against inventory under which the lender advances 80 to 100 percent of the cost of the borrower's relatively expensive inventory items in exchange for the borrower's promise to repay the lender, with accrued interest, immediately after the sale of each item of collateral. (Chapter 16)

trustee
A paid individual, corporation, or commercial bank trust department that acts as the third party to a *bond indenture* and can take specified actions on behalf of the bondholders if the terms of the indenture are violated. (Chapter 6)

two-bin method
Unsophisticated inventory-monitoring technique that is typically applied to C group items and involves reordering inventory when one of two bins is empty. (Chapter 15)

two-tier offer
A *tender offer* in which the terms offered are more attractive to those who tender shares early. (Chapter 18)

U.S. Treasury bills (T-bills)
Short-term IOUs issued by the U.S. Treasury; considered the *risk-free asset*. (Chapter 8)

uncorrelated
Describes two series that lack any interaction and therefore have a *correlation coefficient* close to zero. (Chapter 8)

underpriced
Stock sold at a price below its current market price, P_0. (Chapter 9)

underwriting
The role of the investment banker in bearing the risk of reselling, at a profit, the securities purchased from an issuing corporation at an agreed-on price. (Chapter 7)

underwriting syndicate
A group of other bankers formed by an *investment banker* to share the financial risk associated with underwriting new securities. (Chapter 7)

unlimited funds
The financial situation in which a firm is able to accept all independent projects that provide an acceptable return. (Chapter 10)

unlimited liability
The condition of a sole proprietorship (or general partnership), giving creditors the right to make claims against the owner's personal assets to recover debts owed by the business. (Chapter 1)

unsecured short-term financing
Short-term financing obtained without pledging specific assets as collateral. (Chapter 16)

unsecured, or general, creditors
Creditors who have a general claim against all the firm's assets other than those specifically pledged as collateral. (Chapter 18)

valuation
The process that links risk and return to determine the worth of an asset. (Chapter 6)

variable-growth model
A dividend valuation approach that allows for a change in the dividend growth rate. (Chapter 7)

venture capital
Privately raised external equity capital used to fund early-stage firms with attractive growth prospects. (Chapter 7)

venture capitalists (VCs)
Providers of venture capital; typically, formal businesses that maintain strong oversight over the firms they invest in and that have clearly defined exit strategies. (Chapter 7)

vertical merger
A merger in which a firm acquires *a supplier or a customer*. (Chapter 18)

voluntary reorganization
A petition filed by a failed firm on its own behalf for reorganizing its structure and paying its creditors. (Chapter 18)

voluntary settlement
An arrangement between an insolvent or bankrupt firm and its creditors enabling it to bypass many of the costs involved in legal bankruptcy proceedings. (Chapter 18)

warehouse receipt loan
A secured short-term loan against inventory under which the lender receives control of the pledged inventory collateral, which is stored by a designated warehousing company on the lender's behalf. (Chapter 16)

warrant premium
The difference between the market value and the theoretical value of a warrant. (Chapter 17)

weighted average cost of capital (WACC), r_a
Reflects the expected average future cost of capital over the long run; found by weighting the cost of each specific type of capital by its proportion in the firm's capital structure. (Chapter 9)

white knight
A takeover defense in which the target firm finds an acquirer more to its liking than the initial hostile acquirer and prompts the two to compete to take over the firm. (Chapter 18)

widely owned (stock)
The common stock of a firm is owned by many unrelated individual or institutional investors. (Chapter 7)

wire transfer
An electronic communication that, via bookkeeping entries, removes funds from the payer's bank and deposits them in the payee's bank. (Chapter 15)

working capital
Current assets, which represent the portion of investment that circulates from one form to another in the ordinary conduct of business. (Chapter 15)

working capital (or short-term financial) management
Management of current assets and current liabilities. (Chapter 15)

World Trade Organization (WTO)
International body that polices world trading practices and mediates disputes among member countries. (Chapter 19)

yield curve
A graphic depiction of the term structure of interest rates. (Chapter 6)

yield to maturity
Compound annual rate of return earned on a debt security purchased on a given day and held to maturity. (Chapter 6)

zero-balance account (ZBA)
A disbursement account that always has an end-of-day balance of zero because the firm deposits money to cover checks drawn on the account only as they are presented for payment each day. (Chapter 15)

zero- (or low-) coupon bonds
See Table 6.5.

zero-growth model
An approach to dividend valuation that assumes a constant, nongrowing dividend stream. (Chapter 7)

Index

Note: Boldface page numbers indicate pages where terms are defined.

Jobs, Steven, 114
Jobs and Growth Tax Relief Reconciliation Act of 2003, 270, 569
Joint ventures, multinational companies, **761**–762, 781, 787–788
JPMorgan Chase, 31, 42
JPMorgan Settlement Network, 641
Judgmental approach, 139–140
Junk bonds, 236–238, 717
Just-in-time (JIT) inventory system, 612–613

K

Kahneman, Daniel, 278
Kelly, Martin, 522
Key Business Ratios, 67
Khoo Henn Kuan, 599
Kuwait
    banking system and financial crisis, 739
    bond securitization process, 225
    Fund for Economic Development, 411
    Global Investment House, 560

L

Leasing, 678–687
    arrangements, types of, 679–680
    capitalized lease, 685–686
    equipment, common types of, 677
    financial (capital) lease, 679
    future financing, impact on, 685–686
    leveraged lease, 679–680
    operating lease, 678–679
    pros/cons of, 686
    versus purchase decision, **681**–684
    renewal and purchase options, 680
Legal action, for collection, 624
Legal capital, 574–575
Lehman Brothers, 33, 42–43, 222, 522
Lessee, 678
Lessor, 678
Letters of credit, 656
Letter to stockholders, 58–59
Leverage, 508–522
    breakeven analysis, 509–513
    financial leverage, 508–509, 516–519
    limiting impact of, 508
    multinational companies, 526
    operating leverage, 513–516
    sources, on income statement, 508–509
    total leverage, 508–509, 520–522
    types of, interrelationships, 522
Leveraged buyouts (LBOs), 721–722
Leveraged lease, 679–680
Leveraged recapitalization, 733
Levitt, Arthur, 288
Liabilities
    accounts payable management, 642–647
    accruals management, 647–648

balance sheet, 62–64
and business forms, 6–7, 9
current, management of, 603
loans, short-term. *See* **Secured short-term financing; Unsecured short-term financing**
spontaneous liabilities, 642–648
Lie, Erik, 701
Lien, 659
Limited liability, 7
Limited liability company (LLC), 9
Limited liability partnership (LLP), 9
Limited partnership (LP), 9
Lines of credit, 651–653
    annual cleanup, 653
    revolving credit agreements, 653
Lintner, John, 573
Liquidation value per share, 287
Liquidity, 71
Liquidity preference, 222
Liquidity preference theory, 228–229
Liquidity ratios, 71–73, 84
Listed exchanges, 38
Loan amortization, 189–190
    schedule for, **189**–190
Loans. *See also* **Secured short-term financing;** Bank loans; Credit; Debt; **Unsecured short-term financing**
    amortizing, 189–190
    discount loans, 649–650
    fixed and floating rate loans, 649
    floating inventory lien, 660–661
    trust receipt inventory loans, 661
    warehouse receipt loans, 661
Lockbox system, 625–627
    cash transfer methods, 627
London Stock Exchange, 38, 270–271
Long-term (strategic) financial plans, 124–125
Long-term debt, 62
    multinational companies, 779–780
Long-term debt, cost of, 360–364
    after-tax costs, 363–364
    before-tax cost, 361–363
Long-term decision-making
    and capital budgeting, 359–360
    capital structure, 523–544
    leverage, 508–522
Long-term funds, 35
Lowe's, 71, 73
Low-regular-and-extra dividend policy, 579

M

Macro political risk, 773
Madoff, Bernard, 310
Mail float, 625
Maintenance clauses, 680
Managerial finance, 4, 15–19
    career opportunities, 10
    function in organization, 15–16

FREQUENTLY USED SYMBOLS AND ABBREVIATIONS

AAI	Average Age of Inventory	EOQ	Economic Order Quantity
ACH	Automated Clearinghouse	EPS	Earnings Per Share
ACP	Average Collection Period	ERP	Enterprise Resource Planning
AF_j	Amount of Funds Available from Financing Source j at a Given Cost	EU	European Union
ANPV	Annualized Net Present Value	EVA	Economic Value Added
A/P	Accounts Payable	FC	Fixed Operating Cost
APP	Average Payment Period	FCF	Free Cash Flow
APR	Annual Percentage Rate	FDI	Foreign Direct Investment
APY	Annual Percentage Yield	FLM	Financial Leverage Multiplier
A/R	Accounts Receivable	FV	Future Value
b_j	Beta Coefficient or Index of Nondiversifiable Risk for Asset j	GAAP	Generally accepted accounting principles
b_p	Portfolio Beta	GATT	General Agreement on Tariffs and Trade
B_0	Value of a Bond	g	Growth Rate
C	Carrying Cost per Unit per Period	I	Interest Payment
CAPM	Capital Asset Pricing Model	IP	Inflation Premium
CCC	Cash Conversion Cycle	IPO	Initial Public Offering
CD	Stated Cash Discount in Percentage Terms	IRR	Internal Rate of Return
CF_0	Initial Investment	JIT	Just-In-Time System
CF_t	Cash Inflow in Period t	LBO	Leveraged Buyout
CV	Coefficient of Variation	m	Number of times per year interest is compounded
D_p	Preferred Stock Dividend	M	Bond's Par Value
D_t	• Per-Share Dividend Expected at the End of Year t	M/B	Market/Book Ratio
	• Depreciation Expense in Year t	MACRS	Modified Accelerated Cost Recovery System
DFL	Degree of Financial Leverage	MNC	Multinational Company
DIP	Debtor in Possession	MP	Market Price per Share
DOL	Degree of Operating Leverage	MPR	Market Price Ratio of Exchange
DPS	Dividends per Share	MRP	Materials Requirement Planning
DTC	Depository Transfer Check	n	• Number of Outcomes Considered
DTL	Degree of Total Leverage		• Number of Periods—Typically, Years
e	Exponential Function = 2.7183		• Years to Maturity
E	Exercise Price of the Warrant	N	• Number of Days Payment Can Be Delayed by Giving up the Cash Discount
EAR	Effective Annual Rate		• Number of Shares of Common Stock Obtainable with One Warrant
EBIT	Earnings Before Interest and Taxes		
EOM	End of the Month	N_d	Net Proceeds from the Sale of Debt (Bond)

continued

FREQUENTLY USED SYMBOLS AND ABBREVIATIONS (CONTINUED)

N_n	Net Proceeds from the Sale of New Common Stock	r_r	Cost of Retained Earnings
N_p	Net Proceeds from the Sale of the Preferred Stock	r_s	• Required Return on Common Stock
			• Cost of Common Stock Equity
NAFTA	North American Free Trade Agreement	R_F	Risk-Free Rate of Interest
NCAI	Net Current Asset Investment	RADR	Risk-Adjusted Discount Rate
NFAI	Net Fixed Asset Investment	RE	Ratio of Exchange
NOPAT	Net operating profits after taxes	ROA	Return on Total Assets
NPV	Net Present Value	ROE	Return on Common Equity
O	Order Cost Per Order	S	• Usage in Units per Period
OC	Operating Cycle		• Sales in Dollars
OCF	Operating Cash Flow	SML	Security Market Line
P	Price (value) of asset	t	Time
P_0	Value of Common Stock	T	Firm's Marginal Tax Rate
$PBDT_t$	Profits Before Depreciation and Taxes in year t	TVW	Theoretical Value of a Warrant
PD	Preferred Stock Dividend	V	• Value of an Asset or Firm
P/E	Price/Earnings Ratio		• Venture Capital
PI	Profitability Index	V_C	Value of Entire Company
PMT	Amount of Payment	V_D	Value of All Debt
Pr	Probability	V_P	Value of Preferred Stock
PV	Present Value	V_S	Value of Common Stock
Q	• Order Quantity in Units	VC	Variable Operating Cost per Unit
	• Sales Quantity in Units	w_j	• Proportion of the Portfolio's Total Dollar Value Represented by Asset j
r	• Actual, Expected ($\bar{r}$), or Required Rate of Return		• Proportion of a Specific Source of Financing j in the Firm's Capital Structure
	• Annual Rate of Interest	WACC	Weighted Average Cost of Capital
	• Cost of Capital	WTO	World Trade Organization
r^*	Real Rate of Interest	YTM	Yield to Maturity
r_a	Weighted Average Cost of Capital	ZBA	Zero Balance Account
r_d	• Required Return on Bond	σ	Standard Deviation
	• Before-Tax Cost of Debt	Σ	Summation Sign
r_i	After-Tax Cost of Debt		
r_j	Required Return on Asset j		
r_m	• Market Return		
	• Return on the Market Portfolio of Assets		
r_p	• Cost of Preferred Stock		
	• Portfolio Return		